The Economics of Transition

The Economics of Transition

Edited by Yegor Gaidar

The MIT Press
Cambridge, Massachusetts
London, England

© 2003 Massachusetts Institute of Technology

All rights reserved. No part of this book may be reproduced in any form by any electronic or mechanical means (including photocopying, recording, or information storage and retrieval) without permission in writing from the publisher.

This book was set in Palatino on 3B2 by Asco Typesetters, Hong Kong, and was printed and bound in the United States of America.

Library of Congress Cataloging-in-Publication Data

The economics of transition / edited by Yegor Gaidar.
    p. cm.
 Includes bibliographical references and index.
 ISBN 0-262-07219-X
  1. Russia (Federation)—Economic policy—1991– 2. Post-communism—Economic aspects—Russia (Federation) I. Gaidar, E. T. (Egor Timurovich)

HC340.12.E275   2003
330.947—dc21
                                                                      2003042130

Contents

Foreword: The Russian Path from Communism Reconsidered   xv
Stanley Fischer
About This Book   xxi
Contributors   xxv

Introduction: Economic Reforms and Revolution   1

Vladimir Mau

1. Exit from Communism   1
2. Revolution and the State   1
3. Revolutionary Economic Crisis   7

I Preconditions for the Postcommunist Transformation   17

1 The Inevitability of Collapse of the Socialist Economy   19

Yegor Gaidar

1.1. Stability of the Socialist Economic System   19
1.2. Characteristics of the Socialist Model of Economic Development   21
1.3. Internal Constraints on Long-Term Development of the Economic System   23
1.4. Several Options for Reforming the Socialist Economy   25
1.5. Signs of Exhaustion of the Growth Model   28

2 The Logic and Nature of the Soviet Economic Crisis   31

Vladimir Mau

2.1. The Reforms of Late Socialism   31
2.2. Ideology and the Reform Program   33

- 2.3. The Practical Problem of Improving the Economic Mechanism   36
- 2.4. Economic Crisis as a Crisis of the State   40

3 The Liberal Market Reform Program   45
Sergei Sinelnikov-Murylev and Alexei Uluykaev
- 3.1. The Range of Opposing Views   45
- 3.2. Debates on How to Achieve Financial Stabilization   46
- 3.3. The Socioeconomic Situation on the Eve of Reforms   50
- 3.4. The Need to Accelerate Reforms   53
- 3.5. Russia's Progress Toward Economic Independence   55
- 3.6. The Essence of Socioeconomic Reforms in Russia's Transition Period   58
- 3.7. Cutting the Budget Deficit   60

II Macroeconomic Processes and Economic Policy of Postcommunist Russia—Main Stages   63

4 General Macroeconomic Problems of the Postsocialist Transition in Russia   65
Sergei Sinelnikov-Murylev and Georgy Trofimov
- 4.1. Financial Relations and Their Place in the Analysis of the Transition Economy   65
- 4.2. Predeterminacy of Economic Reforms in Russia   66
- 4.3. Price Liberalization: A "Shock" in the System of Gradual Reforms   68
- 4.4. Political Restrictions and Delayed Stabilization   72
- 4.5. An Unorthodox Version of Orthodox Stabilization   74
- 4.6. The Fiscal Crisis   79
- 4.7. Conditions and Factors of Economic Growth   85

5 Macroeconomic Stabilization as a Sociopolitical Problem   89
Vladimir Mau
- 5.1. Delayed Stabilization   89
- 5.2. Consolidation of Opposing Factions: Inflationists versus Anti-inflationists   92
- 5.3. The Changing Balance of Forces   94
- 5.4. Constitutional Problems of Macroeconomic Stabilization   98

Contents

6   Problems of Macroeconomic Stabilization at the Stage of
    Economic Liberalization (1992)   105
    Sergei Sinelnikov-Murylev and Georgy Trofimov
    6.1. Tight Budgetary Policy and the Liquidation of Monetary
         Overhang   105
    6.2. The Strengthening of Populism and Weakening of Fiscal
         Policy   107
    6.3. Monetary Policy and Credit Policy in 1992   111
    6.4. The Attempt to Change Fiscal Strategy in the Absence of
         Coordinated Government and Central Bank Actions   116
    6.5. Reconstruction of the State's Revenues and
         Expenditures   118

7   Formation of the Preconditions for Financial Stabilization   127
    Sergei Sinelnikov-Murylev and Georgy Trofimov
    7.1. Influence of Political Factors on State Finances   128
    7.2. Monetary Policy and Credit Policy in 1993   131
    7.3. Reduction of Budget Expenditures After the Constitutional
         Crisis of 1993   135
    7.4. Reconstruction of the 1993 Budget   138
    7.5. Slowing Fiscal Reforms: A "Moderately Tight"
         Policy   139
    7.6. Some Peculiarities of the Budget Process of 1994   145
    7.7. Reconstruction of the 1994 Budget   149
    7.8. Toward a Tight Fiscal Policy   154
    7.9. Monetary Policy and Credit Policy in 1994   155

8   Financial Stabilization in Russia   159
    Vladimir Mau, Sergei Sinelnikov-Murylev, and Georgy
    Trofimov
    8.1. Political Preconditions for Financial Stabilization   159
    8.2. The Monetary Program for 1995   161
    8.3. Budget Policy During Financial Stabilization   163
    8.4. Tightening Monetary Policy and the Inertia of
         Inflation   170
    8.5. The Role of the Exchange Rate in Achieving
         Stabilization   174
    8.6. The Strengthening of the Real Ruble Exchange Rate   177
    8.7. The Crisis on the Interbank Market   179

9 Macroeconomic Stabilization and the Political Process: The Year of the Presidential Elections   183

Vladimir Mau, Sergei Sinelnikov-Murylev, and Georgy Trofimov

9.1. Political Uncertainty and the Economy   183
9.2. Macroeconomic Problems of the 1996 Electoral Contest   185
9.3. Government Economic Policy in Conditions of Electoral Uncertainty   201
9.4. Economic Policy After the Presidential Election   207
9.5. The Phenomenon of Delayed Growth   220

10 Macroeconomic Stabilization and Fiscal Crisis   223

Sergei Arkhipov, Said Batkibekov, Sergei Drobyshevsky, Vladimir Mau, Sergei Sinelnikov-Murylev, and Alexei Uluykaev

10.1. The Political and Economic Situation: A New Window of Opportunity   223
10.2. The Main Areas of Government Activity and the Reaction of the Legislature   226
10.3. Government Finance   228
10.4. A Breakdown of the 1997 Budget   235
10.5. Monetary and Credit Policy   235
10.6. A New Threat to Reforms on the Rise   242
10.7. The Situation on the Currency and Stock Markets   244

11 The Crisis of the Russian Financial System: Key Factors, Economic Policies, and Initial Results   251

Sergei Arkhipov, Said Batkibekov, Sergei Drobyshevsky, Tatiana Drobyshevskaia, Vladimir Mau, Sergei Sinelnikov-Murylev, and Ilya Trounin

11.1. Evolution of the Russian Financial Crisis in 1997–1998   251
11.2. Principal Factors Behind the 1998 Financial Crisis   262
11.3. The Economic and Political Fallout of the Financial Crisis   274

12 Financial Policy in 1999   309

Sergei Arkhipov, Said Batkibekov, Tatiana Drobyshevskaia, Sergei Drobyshevsky, Olga Izryadnova, Sergei Sinelnikov-Murylev, and Ilya Trounin

12.1. Balance of Payments, Monetary Policy, and Real Ruble Exchange Rate   311
12.2. Trends in the Real Sector of the Economy: Revival of Export-Generating and Import-Substituting Industries   330
12.3. The Budget   347
12.4. Social Effects of the Stabilization Policy   363
12.5. Medium-Term Limitations of the Economic Policy   366

13 The Fallout of Russia's Financial Crisis on Its Neighbors   375
Marek Dabrowski
13.1. Overview   375
13.2. Fundamental Flaws of the Transformation Process in CIS Countries   377
13.3. The Shock in Foreign Trade and the Real Sector   380
13.4. Contagion Effect on Financial Markets   383
13.5. The Psychological Factor   385
13.6. Economic Implications of the Crisis   386
13.7. Summary and Conclusions   390

III Institutional Reforms in the Russian Economy   393

14 Privatization, Ownership Redistribution, and Formation of the Institutional Basis for Economic Reforms   395
Alexander Radygin
14.1. Ownership and Privatization: Preliminary Methodological Notes   395
14.2. Privatization Models in Transitional Economies: A Comparative Analysis   404
14.3. The Russian Privatization Model   412
14.4. Major Stages and Results of the Postprivatization Ownership Redistribution   429

15 Main Corporate Governance Mechanisms and Their Specific Features in Russia   461
Alexander Radygin and Natalia Shmeleva
15.1. Corporate Governance in a Transition Economy: Preliminary Methodological Notes   461

15.2. Internal Mechanisms   464
15.3. General Legislative Situation   468
15.4. The Corporate Securities Market   471
15.5. Bankruptcy Procedures   478
15.6. The Market of Corporate Control (Takeovers)   482
15.7. Existing Instruments of Corporate Governance in State-Owned Enterprises and Their Effectiveness   485
15.8. State-Owned Holdings and Financial-Industrial Groups   491
15.9. Conclusion: New Institutional Reform for Long-Term Economic Growth   504

16 Russian Banks in the Transition Period   511
Igor Doronin and Alexander Zakharov
16.1. The Emergence of the Contemporary Banking System in Russia   511
16.2. Concentration of Capital in the Banking Sector   515
16.3. The Functions of Russian Commercial Banks   519
16.4. Commercial Banks and the Real Sector of the Economy   521
16.5. Stability of the Russian Banking System   527
16.6. Monetary and Credit Instruments for Regulating Banks' Liquidity   533
16.7. The Creation of a System for Regulating and Monitoring Bank Activities   537

17 Institutional Reforms in the Agro-Industrial Complex   543
Natalia Karlova, Irina Khramova, Eugenia Serova, and Tatiana Tikhonova
17.1. Reform of the Agricultural Sector and the Fundamental Aims   543
17.2. Institutional Reforms in Agriculture   546
17.3. Institutional Reforms in the Downstream Sector   556
17.4. Formation of an Agricultural Credit System   563
17.5. The System of State Support for Agriculture   574
17.6. Reform of Foreign Trade Regulation of the Agro-Industrial Complex   581
17.7. Conclusions   583

Contents

18 Institutional Reforms in the Sociocultural Sphere   585
   Irina Rozhdestvenskaya and Sergei Shishkin
   18.1. The Need for Reform in Sociocultural Fields   585
   18.2. The State and Special Interest Groups in the Sociocultural Sphere   587
   18.3. The Switch from Free Care to Health Insurance: The Ideology and Aims of Health Reform   589
   18.4. Practical Introduction of the New System to Finance the Health Sector   593
   18.5. Institutional Changes in Education   599
   18.6. Institutional Reforms in Cultural Institutions   602
   18.7. Shadow Privatization in the Social Sphere   605
   18.8. Commercialization of Sociocultural Institutions   607
   18.9. Evolution of the Sociocultural Sectors in the Years of Reform   608

19 Reform in Housing and Public Utilities   617
   Irina Starodubrovskaya
   19.1. General Characteristics of Housing and Public Utilities in the Soviet Period   617
   19.2. The Concept of Reform in Housing and Public Utilities   619
   19.3. Results of the Reform in Housing and Utilities: 1994–1997   622
   19.4. A New Stage of Reform: 1997–1999   628

IV Real Sector of the Economy: Adaptation Problems   635

20 General Trends in the Real Sector in the Reform Period   637
   Evgeni Gavrilenkov and Olga Izryadnova
   20.1. Principal Development Tendencies and Factors of Economic Restructuring   637
   20.2. Production and Use of the GDP   645
   20.3. Restructuring the Real Sector of the Economy   656
   20.4. Investment in the Period of Market Reforms   664

21 Development Specifics of Real Sector Industries   675
   Yuri Bobylev and Eugenia Serova

22 International Business in the Period of Market Reforms   687
   Natalia Leonova, Sergei Prikhodko, and Nadezhda Volovik
   22.1. Liberalization of Foreign Trade: Results and Prospects   687
   22.2. Consequences of the Policy of Foreign Trade Privileges and Preferences   698
   22.3. Commodity Composition of Russia's Foreign Trade   698

V The Social Price of Reforms   715

23 Certain Trends in the Evolution of the Labor Market   717
   Alexander Smirnov
   23.1. Forecasts That Went Wrong   717
   23.2. Part-Time Employment: Objective Data and Subjective Interpretation   720
   23.3. Registered Labor Market Indicators   722
   23.4. Regional Labor Markets   724
   23.5. Workforce Movement: Sectoral Aspects   725
   23.6. Employment Policy Financing   733

24 Household Income in the Period of Economic Reforms   737
   Igor Kolosnytsyn
   24.1. Socioeconomic Differentiation of the Population in Russia, 1992 Through 1999   737
   24.2. Poverty Line Changes   742
   24.3. Impact of Inflation on Nominal Assets of Households; Inflation and Poverty   747
   24.4. Postscript   750

VI Economic Reform and Public Opinion Dynamics   753

25 Key Trends in the Population's Attitudes Toward Market Reforms   755
   Tatiana Koval
   25.1. On the Threshold of Reforms   755

Contents

25.2. The First Stage of Economic Transformation   756
25.3. Privatization and Private Property in Russians' Eyes   761
25.4. Evolution in Attitudes Toward the Economic Reform and Government (1993–1997)   769

26 Some Conclusions   789

Yuri Bobylev, Revold Entov, Olga Izryadnova, Vladimir Mau, Sergei Prikhodko, Alexander Radygin, Eugenia Serova, Sergei Sinelnikov-Murylev, and Sergei Tsukhlo

26.1. Russia's Economic Policy at the Beginning of the New Phase of Economic Reforms   789
26.2. Russia's Economic Development in the Year 2000: Major Outcomes   808

Appendix I   Modeling Inflation Dynamics, 1992 Through 1998   839

Sergei Drobyshevsky

Appendix II   Arrears: A Macroeconomic Analysis   855

Oleg Lugovoy

II.1. Macroeconomic Model of Arrears   855
II.2. Empirical Testing of the Hypotheses   858
II.3. Growth Rates of the Money Supply   863
II.4. Stability of Coefficients and Forecast Qualities of the Model   869
II.5. Elasticities   875
II.6. Money Supply and Arrears: An Analysis Using Distributed Lags   876
II.7. Conclusions   878

Appendix III   Modeling Tax Revenues and the Tax Liabilities of Russian Taxpayers, 1992 Through 1998   881

Pavel Kadotchnikov and Sergei Sinelnikov-Murylev

III.1. Key Factors Determining Tax Liability Dynamics   881
III.2. Modeling Aggregate Tax Revenues, Taking Into Account the Specifics of Major Tax Payments   903
III.3. Conclusions   907

Appendix IV Monetary Policy and the Expectations Hypothesis on the Russian Government Bond Market   911

Sergei Drobyshevsky

IV.1. The Data for the Study   913
IV.2. Analyzing the Properties of GKO Rate Time Series   916
IV.3. Monetary Policy Shocks and the Term Structure of GKO Yields   928
IV.4. Testing Hypotheses About the Term Structure of GKO Rates   943
IV.5. Conclusions   955

Appendix V Leading Indicators of the Russian Currency Crisis in August 1998   959

Sergei Drobyshevsky

Statistical Appendix   973

Name Index   1001
Subject Index   1008

Foreword: The Russian Path from Communism Reconsidered

Stanley Fischer

Understanding postcommunist transformations, especially in the former republics of the Soviet Union, will engage economists for some time to come. Developing a theoretical framework for transition economies is one of the most pressing tasks facing economists today. For Russia, an important part of this task has now been achieved by the authors of this book—the researchers at the Institute for the Economy in Transition (IET), including its director, Yegor Gaidar. Gaidar, the first prime minister of independent Russia, launched the process of transforming this country from a communist system. The IET team enjoys the unique experience of combining economic research with the practical implementation of reforms in more than twenty-five transition economies. After ten years of experience, the evidence is clear: the basic economic reform and growth strategy recommended by mainstream economists and summarized in this book works. With this fact generally acknowledged, analysts have turned their attention to the "crisis" economics emerging in the former republics following the early reforms.

A vital conclusion that is now coming to the fore and that is perfectly presented in this publication is that despite the many disappointments and setbacks in Russia's economic reforms, we should not underestimate what has been achieved so far.

The future path of economic policy in Russia is to achieve sustained and equitable growth. This requires strengthening macroeconomic forces and intensifying sectoral structural reforms, including the social safety net. Although we should not underestimate what has been achieved so far in Russia, the task ahead is daunting.

The global experience illustrates that economic programs are most likely to succeed when they are owned by the country that implements them, and that success is not necessarily dependent on support from international financial institutions and bilateral lenders and providers of technical assistance. Russia's economic policy is more likely to succeed if it is designed by Russians. This was an important lesson of the first postcommunist decade.

The experience of the nations that began the process of economic reform at the end of the cold war is somewhat of an anomaly. In the history of the world, there has never been an occasion when so many countries changed their economic policy at the same time, and all with more or less the same goal. This vast and rich data pool makes it possible to use econometrics to study the growth experience and growth outcomes of the transition.

My colleagues at the International Monetary Fund and I have examined this experience using data from twenty-five countries in order to measure the extent of structural reforms.[1] We conclude that the basic strategy advocated by market-oriented proponents of reform a decade ago is correct, and well understood. Both the stabilization policy and the structural reform, particularly privatization, contribute to growth. And the faster the speed of reforms, the faster is the recovery from the inevitable initial recession and the greater is the future economic potential.

Saying that the basic strategy is well understood is not the same as saying that carrying out a reform policy is easy. The manner in which a strategy is applied varies from country to country, depending on the type of technical and politically difficult choices policymakers face. We therefore salute those policymakers who succeeded, through whatever gifts or insights they possessed, in moving farthest in the transition process.

One question still remains: If the basic growth strategy was so well understood, why have some countries been successful in undertaking the needed reforms, while others have not? For some countries, the answer lies in their inability to implement the reform policies. In Russia's case the problems lie chiefly in the political sphere: in the lack of political or social support for reform, and the consequent problems of governance.

---

1. See S. Fischer, R. Sahay, and C. A. Vegh, "Stabilization and Growth in Transition Economies: The Early Experience," *Journal of Economic Perspectives* 10, no. 2 (1996); S. Fischer and R. Sahay, *The Transition Economies After Ten Years* (Washington, D.C.: International Monetary Fund, 2000).

Foreword

xvii

There is widespread skepticism about the Russian economic reforms of the 1990s. However, one must grant that it was a difficult time, during which Russia achieved important advances. This statement, and the argument of the book, has less to do with the great historical achievements of the past decade—the remarkable extent to which democracy became entrenched in Russia—than with economic achievements. Most fundamentally, there seems to have emerged a consensus that the process of transition is irreversible, and that the establishment of a genuine market-based economy should continue to be an overriding policy objective. This reality, we believe, paves the way to sustained growth and future prosperity for Russia.

Second, a commitment to low inflation and sound fiscal policy is taking hold across a broad spectrum of the populace, as well as among the political elite. That, incidentally, is one of the positive outcomes of the 1998 crisis.

Third, there has been considerable domestic market liberalization, including price and wage liberalization. In addition, most state control over economic activity has been dismantled. Privatization has allowed much of the economy in the private sector to be governed by market incentives.

There has also been a far-reaching liberalization of exchange policies and import-export trade policies. Current account convertibility has been significantly achieved with the unification of the exchange rate. These achievements, unfortunately, are all too often overlooked.

Fourth, the institutional setting for the conduct of macroeconomic policy has improved. There is a modern central bank, the CBR, that employs a modernized payment system. The CBR has liberalized interest rates and eliminated low-interest direct credits. Both steps have strengthened the government's ability to conduct sound monetary policy. Fiscal reforms of the past ten years include a large reduction in subsidies, improvements in the tax system, and the establishment of a vital Treasury.

And fifth, in addition to privatization, other measures required for a well-functioning market economy have been signed into law. These measures include bankruptcy procedures, competition policies, antimonopoly regulations, improved accounting standards, a securities commission, and regulatory agencies overseeing the natural monopolies. Although some success was achieved, these laws were implemented inconsistently and (to this day) incompletely; nevertheless, many of the basic institutions for a market economy have been established. Consequently, the new stage of upcoming reforms starts from a very different place than the reforms that inaugurated the process of transition a decade ago.

Decisive progress was made in achieving macroeconomic stability in Russia in 1996, but fiscal policy and policy implementation in the structural area were poor. The medium-term economic program adopted in 1996 provided a coherent and comprehensive structural agenda, but performance in the structural area during the lifetime of the program was weak. This weakness was a fundamental factor leading to the financial crisis of 1998. Little has been done in the way of deep-rooted structural reform since 1998. Consequently, the good macroeconomic performance post-1998 cannot be sustained without a broad-based acceleration of structural reforms to protect investment activities and to strengthen exports, as well as comprehensive tax and expenditure reforms.

Needed as well is an improved investment climate, primarily for Russian investors but also for foreign ones. A favorable investment climate for foreigners will encourage Russians themselves to invest in Russia. Domestic investment, as is usually the story in every country in the world, makes up by far the greatest proportion of investment capital. The large amount of Russian capital that is now abroad will begin to return only when the investment climate changes.

With these facts in mind, where should the focus of the investment program be? We suggest that the government must radically improve the efficiency of its economic policy and find a way to stimulate entrepreneurial activity. The government needs to enforce deregulation, economic freedom, and the rule of law. It needs to increase transparency in the Russian economy, in both the public and private sectors.

We view six areas as priorities for the next stage of Russian economic reform:

1. Industrial restructuring, including new phases of privatization and other measures needed to improve the business climate. This area includes corporate governance and the rule of law.
2. Measures to eliminate nonpayments and barter trade.

3. Restructuring of the banking system, including reform of Russia's central bank.

4. Tax reform and expenditure reform, including reform of the civil service.

5. Strengthening the social safety net.

6. Agricultural reform and reform of land ownership.

Progress in these areas is crucial for Russia to fuel sustained growth and to allow its people to realize their potential.

About This Book

At the end of the twentieth century, the global community confronted a novel class of problems associated with postcommunist transformation. Although the issue of transition from one socioeconomic system to another is not a new one, it has usually been of marginal interest to economists and political scientists. Perhaps the only strand in world social thought that took a serious interest in the problems of transformation revolving around a change in a sociopolitical system was Marxism. Marxist analysis, however, suffers from two major flaws. First, it treats transformation too simplistically, within the constraints of the hypothesis about socioeconomic systems. In essence, Marxism is limited to an analysis of transition from capitalism to socialism. Second, Marxist analysis is not intellectually persuasive. By and large, the works written under Soviet communism bore the marks of vulgarity and dogmatism characteristic of a totalitarian society.

The collapse of communism dramatically expanded the ranks of "transitologists." One suddenly got the impression that world economic thought had shifted off its axis. And no wonder—twenty-six countries with a combined population of over three hundred million faced a task unparalleled in world economic history: to complete a transition from a system predicated on total statism in economic and political life to one exhibiting the fundamentals of a free market economy and democracy. Moreover, while for a number of countries in Central and Eastern Europe it was a return to a relatively recent past, for the countries of the former Soviet Union such a transition meant resurrecting political and economic principles that had been virtually obliterated from living memory. And since the regime of pre-Bolshevik Russia hardly conformed to the modern criteria of a market-based economy either, the task, unprecedented to start with, was rendered even more difficult. The situation was further complicated by the fact that nobody had time to discuss the problems. Communism imploded between 1988 and 1991, but even as late as 1986–1988 no one was seriously talking about the possibility that the Soviet empire might collapse. Within the Eastern bloc such discussions were understandably out of the question, for political reasons. In the West, the issue was not topical, as sovietologists continued to write about the durability of the system and to speculate whether Gorbachev's reforms would succeed, or whether Gorbachev would follow Khrushchev's path.

Three groups of socioeconomic problems became salient with the collapse of communism and, in one way or another, have fueled the previously missing discussion. They are listed here in their logical order rather than in order of importance. The first set of problems were those associated with liberalization and macroeconomic stabilization. Strictly speaking, these are separate problems, but historically they have always coincided. A systemic crisis in the majority of the former republics coincided with a fiscal crisis (although it varied in severity from country to country), and the freeing of prices turned out to be the flip side of the fight against inflation. This type of problem has been thoroughly studied in the twentieth century by economists both theoretically, at the level of model-building, and empirically, by examining the experience of different countries that were or were not successful in dismantling *dirigisme* and containing inflation.

The second set of problems were institutional problems, primarily those having to do with the construction of a well-developed system of private-property rights. This task was without precedent. To repeat a phrase coined by Lech Walesa, "eggs had to be recreated out of an omelette." Much remained unclear, both theoretically and practically. And questions about which model of development should be followed or what the optimal path to privatization might be could only be answered as the events of the postcommunist transformation played themselves out. The topic had been discussed since the mid-1980s, but there was not, and logically could not be, a well-articulated program. The only point of departure was Coase's well-known theorem: It does not matter how property is distributed, as long as property rights are clearly defined and well-enforced. However, the uniqueness of Soviet society, which rejected private property ownership, raised serious questions about the applicability of standard rules of macroeconomics to the transformation of the former Soviet system.

The third and final set of problems comprised those having to do with the prospect for economic growth. This issue was of particular importance because it brought to the fore the question of how to transform the economic structure of postcommunist societies, what methods should be adopted to transform industrial economies to postindustrial ones, and how well positioned the countries of the Eastern bloc were to catch up to the developed world.

All three groups of questions belong to a new branch of economics—the theory of postcommunist transformation. This branch is still in its formative stage, and it is unclear whether it will develop into a full-fledged scientific discipline. Only future developments can answer this question.

This book addresses mainly the first and second groups of such questions. For the most part, this book examines the practical experience already available. The macroeconomic and institutional problems that were the focus for theoretical economists and politicians throughout the greater part of the 1990s form the core material of the discussions in the book. The book is chiefly concerned with the years 1991–1997, a relatively self-contained period during which liberalization, macroeconomic stabilization (containment of inflation), and mass privatization were largely accomplished.

The book does not attempt to detail the history of Russian economic policy. There is of course a historical context, but it does not determine the nature of the analysis. Rather, the various essays examine a set of economic policy problems faced by a country emerging from communism, various resolutions to these problems, the reasons for the policy options pursued, and finally the consequences of adopting certain policies and not others.

The essays presented here do not attempt to articulate a comprehensive theory of postcommunist transformation. In our view, the time for such a comprehensive theory has not yet come. Instead, we have sought to provide the building blocks for such a theory.

While awaiting the judgment of our readers, we wish to thank our friends and colleagues who helped us selflessly: A. Aganbegyan, A. Aleksashenko, A. Alekseev, D. Vasiliev, S. Vasiliev, L. Gozman, R. Dornbusch, S. Dubinin, O. Vyugin, A. Zakharov, I. Klyamkin,

Yu. Levada, A. Pochinok, A. Sarchev, R. Skidelsky, A. Chubais, S. Shatalov, R. Entov, and E. Yasin.

We are also grateful to our colleagues who provided editorial assistance and helped us prepare this book, particularly V. Stupin, O. Golant, and A. Moiseenkova.

Contributors

Sergei Arkhipov Moskovsky Narodny Bank
Said Batkibekov Institute for the Economy in Transition
Yuri Bobylev Institute for the Economy in Transition
Marek Dabrowski CASE Center, Warsaw, Poland
Igor Doronin Moscow Stock Exchange
Tatiana Drobyshevskaia Institute for the Economy in Transition
Sergei Drobyshevsky Institute for the Economy in Transition
Revold Entov Institute for the Economy in Transition
Stanley Fischer Executive Vice President, Citicorp
Yegor Gaidar Director, Institute for the Economy in Transition, MP
Evgeni Gavrilenkov Chief Economist, Troyka-Dialogue Investment Company
Olga Izryadnova Institute for the Economy in Transition
Pavel Kadotchnikov Institute for the Economy in Transition
Natalia Karlova Institute for the Economy in Transition
Irina Khramova Institute for the Economy in Transition
Igor Kolosnytsyn Institute for the Economy in Transition
Tatiana Koval Institute for the Economy in Transition
Natalia Leonova Institute for the Economy in Transition
Oleg Lugovoy Institute for the Economy in Transition
Vladimir Mau President, Academy of the National Economy, Moscow

Sergei Prikhodko Institute for the Economy in Transition

Alexander Radygin Institute for the Economy in Transition

Irina Rozhdestvenskaya Institute for the Economy in Transition

Eugenia Serova Institute for the Economy in Transition

Sergei Shishkin Institute for the Economy in Transition

Natalia Shmeleva Institute for the Economy in Transition

Sergei Sinelnikov-Murylev Deputy Director, Institute for the Economy in Transition

Alexander Smirnov Higher School of Economics

Irina Starodubrovskaya Institute for the Economy in Transition

Tatiana Tikhonova Institute for the Economy in Transition

Georgy Trofimov Institute of Financial Analysis, Moscow

Ilya Trounin Institute for the Economy in Transition

Sergei Tsukhlo Institute for the Economy in Transition

Alexei Uluykaev First Deputy Minister of Finance of RF, Institute for the Economy in Transition

Nadezhda Volovik Institute for the Economy in Transition

Alexander Zakharov President, Moscow Stock Exchange (MICEX)

Project manager:
Leonid Todorov Institute for the Economy in Transition

Editors:
Nina Glavatskaya Institute for the Economy in Transition
Leonid Lopatnikov Institute for the Economy in Transition

Introduction: Economic Reforms and Revolution

Vladimir Mau

1. Exit from Communism

Russia's exit from the communist system will be the subject of theoretical discussions and political battles for a long time to come. What determined the inevitability of the break with the communist past? What were the mistakes and accomplishments along the way? What dangers were avoided, and conversely, why did many things turn out the way they did?

The fundamental attribute of Russia's development over the transition period is the revolutionary nature of the transformation. In the case of Russia, this observation is of methodological, as opposed to political, significance. The historical experience of revolutions suggests that such shifts have a number of important features. Failure to take them into account makes it impossible to form a true view of the transformation or to assess possible (not just desirable) developmental alternatives.

Russia's emergence from communism can be viewed through the prism of a number of basic characteristics typical of revolutionary transformations. Furthermore, the revolutionary nature of the changes determines not just their depth and radicalism, but also the presence of some transformation-specific regularities, as well as the presence of certain sociopolitical and economic developments during the revolutionary epoch.

2. Revolution and the State

Revolution as a mechanism for transforming the sociopolitical system exhibits a number of characteristics, chief among which are the following.

First is the systemic nature of the changes, their depth, and their radicalism. Revolutionary transformation always entails profound changes in property rights, not to mention a significant revamping of the sociopolitical structure of society. However, as is evident in the history of some countries, not all systemic changes can be correctly viewed as revolutionary. A strong government can implement profound, radical changes that over the long run will undoubtedly have important implications. Such actions, however, are in essence reforms (some refer to it as "revolution from above"). The Meiji Restoration and the reforms of Bismarck in Germany are pertinent examples. Radical, systemic changes can also take place as a result of defeat in war, as happened in Prussia following the Napoleonic wars and in Japan and Germany after World War II.

Nevertheless, the depth of changes induced by revolution should not be overestimated. Normally it is only posterity that comes to judge such changes as revolutionary. In the meantime, the society emerging from revolution seems to most contemporaries a parody of the *ancien régime* rather than a genuinely new developmental alternative. Some scholars emphasize that revolution accomplishes what would in any case be accomplished without it, only at much greater cost.[1] In regard to another criterion, the extent of elite replacement, an in-depth study of past revolutions illustrates that the radicalism of this process has been greatly exaggerated.[2]

The second element that defines a revolution is that a revolutionary transformation must be brought about by internal development factors in any given country and cannot be imposed from outside. This predetermines the political and ideological environment of the revolution, in which, along with the destruction of the state, seemingly unshakable values (be they the "divine powers" of the monarchy, the unity of the nation, or the messianic role of communism) are overturned. That is why national liberation movements as a rule are not revolutions; they always have an ideational-political glue that binds together the atomized forces of the nation. (This is not to deny, however, that national liberation can also be achieved by revolution.)

---

1. Tocqueville was one of the first to analyze this phenomenon. See A. Tocqueville, *Stary poryadok i revolyutsiya* (Moscow: Moskovskiy filosofskiy fond, 1997). For a more in-depth treatment, see A. Hirshman, *The Rhetoric of Reaction: Perversity, Futility, Jeopardy* (Cambridge: Harvard University Press, Belknap Press, 1991).
2. See, for example, J. A. Goldstone, *Revolution and Rebellion in the Early Modern World* (Berkeley: University of California Press, 1991), 296.

The third characteristic is the weakness of the state. Revolution is characterized by the absence of a strong, consolidated political authority able to carry through systemic transformation. Specifically, the weakness of the state fosters a sharp increase in spontaneous socioeconomic processes in society, on the one hand, and, as a result, the emergence of certain transformation-specific regularities on the other.[3]

The last factor is critically important. It is precisely the crisis and the breakdown of state authority following it that make a transformation of a revolutionary (not reformist) type virtually inevitable. Radicalism of the revolutionary rupture gains in force and acquires spontaneity when the state authorities are unable to control and lead the country. We can isolate two reasons for the dramatic weakening of the state before and during the revolutionary period.

One reason is deep fiscal crisis. This occurs when the state loses its traditional sources of budget revenue or when budgetary outlays increase dramatically. The first may have to do with changes in the social structure, for example, as incomes begin to concentrate in new sectors of the economy and the tax system proves unable to adapt to the changing circumstances. The second happens as a consequence of the intensification of external and internal challenges to the incumbent regime and a significant rise in public expenditures. Pertinent examples of such developments include a sharp increase in military expenditure, a rise in the cost of waging war typical for seventeenth-century Europe, or the last stage in the arms race of the cold war. However, a fiscal crisis, which undoubtedly weakens the state, does not make a revolutionary crisis inevitable. If the status quo authorities can cope with it, its manifestations will be limited to reforms of varying intensity.

Another reason for the weakening of the state is transformation of the social structure of a prerevolutionary society in such a way that the powers-to-be prove unable to form and maintain stable

---

3. This interpretation is open to a number of objections because it omits some characteristics considered an integral part of any revolution, chiefly violence, the presence of a spontaneous mass movement, and the radical nature of elite replacement. While these issues deserve special treatment, we point out that whereas violence is undoubtedly present in any revolution, the important question is what degree of violence is sufficient to define transformation as revolution. Thus, violence as a criterion has only limited application. A spontaneous mass movement as a criterion is also a special case: it was relevant for revolutions in predominantly agricultural societies, the potential for which had largely been exhausted by the early twentieth century.

coalitions of social forces in support of their policies. These policies are designed, after all, to resolve the fiscal crisis. One should not dwell on the forces driving the development of such a situation. Suffice it to note that the key issue here is a significant increase in the complexity of the social structure. In particular, the structure that emerges is characterized by new dividing lines that cut across established classes and interest groups. This social phenomenon and process is imposed on the traditional structure of society.

In consequence, state authorities get disoriented and "lose the pillars" upon which their policy rests. What not so long ago strengthened the regime now weakens it. Every attempt of the regime to broaden its social base engenders dissatisfaction on the part of the majority of society, because it does not and cannot adequately take into account the new formation of interests and needs. The consensus on basic values and principles supporting the development of the country is unremittingly eroded.

In essence, the weakening of authority can be traced to the absence of a consensus on basic problems, values, and goals facing society. The absence of a consensus means that the society disintegrates into a multitude of groupings (social, territorial, ethnic) with simultaneously conflicting and overlapping political and economic interests. In such a situation, no government can frame a set of policies that would ensure consolidation of, and thereby support for, a workable majority. The weakness of the state is evident in a number of properties that characterize the development of revolutionary society (properties that are fairly typical of any revolution, regardless of the historical period in which it occurs). Some of the most typical manifestations or properties of the weakness of state power are as follows:

• Instability in economic policy. The revolutionary authorities are searching for new, more effective methods and mechanisms to pursue their objectives, while these objectives are not formulated with sufficient clarity.

• The emergence of multiple poles of power, competing for a position of dominance in society. "Dual power," a term introduced into Russian political discourse by the February revolution of 1917, is in reality a distinguishing mark of any great revolution. Moreover, there can be more than two centers of power. Incidentally, civil war is an extreme form of competition among centers of power.

- The absence of established political institutions, since the old ones are destroyed soon after the beginning of the revolution, while new ones still have to be created. As a result, the most diverse, spontaneously formed organizations and institutions can assume the role of political intermediaries.
- As a consequence of the lack of concretized power, there emerges the absence of sufficiently comprehensible and established "rules of the game." Decision-making procedures used by authorities are not clearly laid down. More often than not, decisions are ignored and, even when implemented, are interpreted in a fairly subjective fashion.

Let us now see how these characteristics of revolutionary society apply to contemporary Russia.

The profound systemic nature of Russian transformation is rarely questioned, as it involves a complex set of features that rarely coalesce in a single country at a given point in time. The socioeconomic transformation of the 1980s to 1990s called for radical changes with respect to property rights, institutional makeup, the constitutional system, the industrial structure, and macroeconomic stabilization.

Each of these elements is in evidence in the contemporary world. Latin America had to tackle stabilization and political reform. Israel dealt with stabilization concurrently with structural transformation. China is implementing profound structural reforms and partial reforms of property rights without political reforms and stabilization. In terms of the complex, manifold nature of these problems, Russia is best compared with the postcommunist countries.

Russia, and in part Ukraine and Belarus, which are of similar transformation type, are significantly different from other postcommunist countries. These countries are in the process of overcoming a socioeconomic system entangled in its own peculiar and contradictory endogenous development, and not imposed from outside. In a sense, the liberation of Central and Eastern Europe (as well as of some republics of the former USSR) from communism can be likened to liberation from external occupation. It is in the nature of being a national liberation movement. Communism had been imposed on those countries and was for them a largely artificial creation.[4]

---

4. One of the arguments supporting the artificial imposition of the communist regime for the countries of Central and Eastern Europe is the relative ease with which they have gone back to their precommunist constitutions, suggesting renewal of a natural process that had been artificially interrupted several decades earlier.

Finally, weakness of the state is of particular importance. It is crucial for understanding the real constraints on the social and economic policies being pursued, comprehending the limits of the possible, and assessing the opportunities grasped and missed. This is all the more important since in the context of contemporary Russia, the argument about the weakness of the state is debatable, for a number of reasons.

For one reason, in the USSR the state showed exceptional stability and strength as well as an ability to impose its will not just on its own people, but also on many foreign countries. As a result, national public opinion was inclined to overestimate the powers of the state. Furthermore, legally and constitutionally, the government in the USSR and in postcommunist Russia alike was and is extremely powerful, remaining in possession of rights considerably exceeding the prerogatives exercised by its democratic (and formally not just democratic) counterparts in other countries.[5]

Nonetheless, the Russian state in the late 1980s and 1990s remained comparatively weak. The following chapters will show how in various areas of economic life the state has constantly equivocated and retreated on encountering more or less tough resistance from other centers of power and competing interest groups. The protracted fiscal crisis (caused primarily but not exclusively by the fall in world oil prices) that gripped the country had considerably communist authorities' ability to maneuver.[6] Against the background of the fiscal crisis, the social structure of Soviet society, in view of its growing complexity, was becoming increasingly removed from the traditional industrial core. A conflict between sectors arising from their divergent interests (typical for a centralized industrial economy) was stressed, with a conflict between profitable and loss-making enterprises within sectors. Divergences in interests between Union republics and regions were similarly exacerbated. A conflict between the strengthened regional elites and the central (Union) elites was

---

5. The strength of the Soviet state and the stability of its political system created an impression of unshakability not just among Soviet students (as might be expected), but also among a large number of Western commentators. Most scholars associated the likelihood of radical changes and revolutionary turbulence with poorly developed and developing countries in Asia and Africa, but not with the USSR. Such was S. P. Huntington's assessment of the situation and prospects in *Political Order in Changing Societies* (New Haven, Conn.: Yale University Press, 1991). This became a methodological tradition of sorts that gained credence by being reproduced in the writings of many political scientists, economists, and sovietologists.
6. See Ye. Gaidar, *Anomalii ekonomicheskogo rosta* (Moscow: Yevraziya, 1996), 161–73.

looming. Splits within the *nomenklatura* began to occur, in contrast to the excessive stability of the 1970s and early 1980s, when cadre mobility was effectively frozen. All of this created an exceptionally conflictual and potentially ungovernable environment.

3. Revolutionary Economic Crisis

The weakness of the state exerts an immediate and varied influence on the state of the economy in revolution. At a general level it causes the emergence and development of a "revolutionary economic crisis"—a lasting, critical condition of the economy that persists for approximately fifteen years and is a natural consequence of the protracted political crisis. This is a crisis attendant upon the transformation of the social system and organically linked to it.

On the one hand, the logic of revolutionary development itself undermines economic decision making. Weak states cannot make effective decisions. The multiplicity of social groupings, their conflicting interests, and their ability to directly influence the state authorities only aggravate the instability of policies; this instability itself becomes a factor in the economic crisis.

On the other hand, the economic crisis feeds the political crisis. No government is able to frame a set of policies that commands a consensus, and therefore no government is able to ensure the consolidation of social forces. This cannot but discredit the authorities, who thus forfeit much of their moral and political leverage. Overcoming the revolutionary economic crisis thus becomes a pressing political problem of considerable complexity.

Historical experience allows us to note a number of common features characterizing revolutionary economic crises. Effectively, all of the problems that currently beset Russia were fully manifest as far back as the English Revolution of the mid-seventeenth century and the French Revolution of the late eighteenth century. Subsequently, different countries under different circumstances (such as Russia, Mexico, China, and Iran) exhibited such essential similarities that they warrant recognition as regularities of revolutionary economic development.

First of all, revolution is accompanied by an acute fiscal crisis. All revolutions started with a crisis of public finances, which in the end ruined the fiscal system. The fiscal crisis led to the collapse of the *ancien régime* and largely predetermined political conflicts, which consequently led to the fall of successive governments as the revolution unfolded.

Historical data suggests two scenarios for the emergence and development of a revolutionary fiscal crisis. The first occurs due to the growing budgetary requirements of the powers-to-be and the shrinking sources of revenue. The fiscal crisis is initially represented as short term, but the capacity for its resolution is circumscribed by the limited legitimacy of the political regime. To resolve the fiscal problems, the government searches for new forms of legitimacy and attempts to tap new sources of authority, which only leads to further erosion of authority and the emergence of competing centers of power. Multipolarity of power only aggravates the economic problems and gives rise to a lasting fiscal and economic crisis.

The second scenario unfolds when the *ancien régime*, as it were, grows into the fiscal crisis, which has already assumed stable and lasting proportions prior to the onset of the revolution. The crisis arising from the ineffectiveness of the existing political and economic system causes paralysis of the government, which, as in the first scenario, is attempting to draw on new sources of legitimacy that are themselves turning into independent and competing centers of power. Events then unfold as in the first scenario.

The crisis of public finances dramatically weakens political authority even further. This affects not just the *ancien régime* but new revolutionary governments—from moderate to radical—which succeed one another in the course of the revolution. The revolutionary government is always a poor government whose most pressing imperative is the search for money to sustain itself.

The loss of the fiscal base stems, as a rule, from two factors. On the one hand, it has to do with the collapse of the state's taxing capacity. The crisis of the state and its delegitimization sooner or later (usually fairly swiftly) undermines the government's ability to collect taxes. As Aftalion has noted, "The refusal to pay taxes is a stable characteristic of the revolutionary period."[7] Such a development can receive an ideological or even "scholarly" blessing. Thus the declaration on the abolition of taxes in France in 1789 was predicted by the teaching of the Physiocrats (which posited land as the only

---

7. F. Aftalion, *The French Revolution: An Economic Interpretation* (Cambridge: Cambridge University Press, 1990), 51.

source of wealth),[8] while the collapse of Russia's public finances in 1918–1920 was interpreted as the natural result of the "extinction of money." Nevertheless, whatever the declared motives, the essential inability of the revolutionary authorities to collect taxes (let alone collect enough to strengthen their power) remains a constant.[9]

On the other hand, the revolutionary shocks are inevitably related to structural shifts in the economic system. Changes in the structure of demand entail changes in the structure of employment. All of this impinges on the overall economic situation in the country; moreover, in the short term the impact is negative, since under such conditions traditional sources of government revenue are destroyed. The old sources are gone, while new ones have not yet arisen. The state weakens further, and the sociopolitical struggle intensifies.

Finding itself in a situation of severe crisis, the revolutionary government first and foremost is concerned with its own survival. After that, if the circumstances are favorable, it concerns itself with the consolidation of its position.

Of the plethora of problems facing the revolutionary government, two are of such key importance that all others are subordinate to them. These two problems are where to get money, and how to build a coalition of socioeconomic forces that will enable the revolutionaries to retain power. These two problems are complementary. Indeed, money can enable the formation of a pro-government coalition, and an already formed and relatively stable bloc of sociopolitical forces contributes to financial stabilization.[10]

---

8. That the existing tax system was already considered extremely unfair in the first months of the French Revolution resulted in the central government's losing control over the flow of budgetary receipts. All the government could do was legitimate the liquidation of taxes as an instrument of the *ancien régime*. Although this accorded well with the theoretical views of the leaders of the National Assembly, in effect it was a forced measure that reflected the weakness of the regime, as evidenced by the fact that the government was compelled to give up its attempts to collect the only tax considered fair—the tax on land.

9. Taxes as a share of the budgetary receipts collected by the revolutionary governments of the great revolutions were minuscule, fluctuating between 2% and 15% of the total volume of income. See S. A. Dalin, *Inflyatsiya v epokhi sotsial'nykh revolyutsiy* (Moscow: Nauka, 1983), 56; S. E. Harris, *The Assignats* (Cambridge: Harvard University Press, 1930), 51.

10. In reality, the interconnection between the fiscal problems and the social problems of the revolution is not so simple. Since the social structure of revolutionary society is extremely mobile and unstable, the social basis of the revolutionary government is also constantly changing. This means that neither financial nor social problems can be properly resolved.

The need to resolve these issues in practice determines the decisions of revolutionary governments. The requirement to retain power takes precedence over ideological schemes and declarations, no matter how the designs and promises of the parties and political groups coming to power are theoretically grounded. This applies also to the so-called radicals who come to power at a certain phase of every "great revolution."

Since the revolutionary authorities are unable to collect taxes, the search for nontraditional sources of revenue becomes the focus of their effort. Such sources can be numerous (such as piracy under state patronage or military operations against neighboring countries with a view to extracting contributions[11]), but two of them have pride of place. The first is the use of the state monopoly to mint (print) money, and consequently represents an inflation tax, and the second is the redistribution of property.

These two mechanisms are closely connected. The first issues of paper money (French assignats) were backed by state-owned land from a nationalized fund. Government bills for confiscated plots were given in England in the 1650s to soldiers of the Revolutionary Army in lieu of payment.

The inflationary mechanism of financing the revolution was first tried on a mass scale in France in the 1790s. At that time, the government's inability to collect taxes meant that the issue of paper money (assignats) was the main source of financing the new regime. Assignats were backed by property, generally land (initially Church lands, then royal lands and property confiscated from the aristocracy), that was to be distributed among the revolutionary masses. Initially, assignats were viewed as debt obligations issued by the state and had to be used to purchase property from the state. However, as the fiscal crisis deepened, revolutionary governments increasingly used assignats as paper money.

The inflationary finance of government spending engendered a classic chain of consequences. An increased supply of paper money caused a rapid rise in prices and a squeezing of coinage from circulation. In response, the government introduced a mandatory rate of exchange, with the result that merchants refused to accept paper money altogether and began to demand metal. Then the government decided to regulate prices by fiat (by setting a ceiling on prices) and to prohibit the use of coins in order to maintain the assignat rate.

---

11. Dalin, *Inflyatsiya v epokhi sotsial'nykh revolyutsiy*, 41–43.

The consequences were predictable: the shops emptied, and the country (at least the cities) faced the threat of starvation. The death penalty for concealment of foodstuffs was backed up by a prohibition on the exportation of consumer goods and the introduction of an effective state monopoly on imports. However, this did not solve the problem either, since price controls caused domestic production to fall catastrophically.

These harsh measures could not ensure economic stability, and not just because of the weakness of the state to implement its own decisions. These decisions went against the multitude of economic interests and put all economic actors, from merchants to the government, in an ambivalent position with regard to compliance.

The Russian events of 1918–1920 followed a similar path. Whereas in France the ideological justification for the destruction of the fiscal system derived from the thesis about the unfairness of taxes, in Bolshevik Russia high inflation was viewed by many as a means to the ultimate end—a nonmonetary communist economy. In all other respects, the situation was very similar to that in France: requisitioning of food, state rationing of foodstuffs, persecution of speculators, and the decisive role of those same speculators in getting supplies to the cities.[12]

The experience of revolutionary France and Russia provides a convincing demonstration that attempts by the authorities to make up for their weakness (and poverty) by a show of toughness and the utilization of additional powers, particularly in the economic realm, leads to mild dysfunction in the best scenario, and to catastrophe in the worst. The state finds itelf in a trap: further centralization of decision making engenders paralysis, while abandonment of rigid regulation may be construed as a sign of weakness. As a result, one is confronted with a "Catch-22" situation, as exemplified in this quotation by one of the deputies of the French Convention: "If we destroy the price ceiling, then, indeed, the price of everything will rise sharply; but if we keep it, there will be nothing to buy."[13]

---

12. This was admitted in 1919 by none other than V. I. Lenin. (*Polnoye sobranie sochineniy*, 39: 375–77). V. A. Bazarov, who was then in opposition, drew the apparently paradoxical conclusion that speculators were the true social basis of the Bolshevik regime, since their business benefited so substantially from the conditions created by the regime. See V. A. Bazarov, "Posledniy syezd bolshevikov i zadachi 'tekushchego momenta'," *Mysl* 10 (1919): 356.

13. Aftalion, *The French Revolution*, 167.

Despite the catastrophic economic consequences of this economic policy, its political consequences were fairly satisfactory: revolutionary regimes could gain in strength and in time abandon inflationary methods of finance. However, to reach this point the political regime had to become sufficiently strong to be able to refrain from making populist decisions geared toward solving the problems of the day, simply in order to ensure its survival.

The second mechanism that may ensure survival of a weak revolutionary government is real estate control. Every revolution has an ideological paradigm oriented toward a certain type of transformation of property rights. However, the guiding model establishes only a general framework, within which the changes are carried out. Specific actions of the revolutionary government are determined by completely different factors—particularly political expediency, coupled with corruption.

In modern history, these mechanisms were first used in England. The governments of the Long Parliament and then of Cromwell, short of cash and hungry for political support, decided to use the land plots owned by the Irish rebels, royalists, the Church, and the Crown to further their interests. This goal was accomplished through direct sales of the land for money and, when the former was impossible, through issuance of securities giving their holders a title to the property in the future.

The first option was used blatantly to buy political allies and further the interests of the business groups that served the revolutionary authorities as a financial and social base. The primary buyers of the confiscated lands were the London merchants who financed the government, the local gentry who filled the ranks of the army, members of Parliament, parliamentary bureaucrats, and generals of the Revolutionary Army.[14] That is, the land sales were in the interests of the London political elite and their financial and political allies.

The events in France in the late eighteenth century were marked by a more pronounced conflict between financial and social objectives informing the sales of land. On the one hand, the acute financial crisis made it necessary to extract a maximum price for the land.

---

14. See J. Thirsk, "The Sales of Royalist Land during the Interregnum," *The Economic History Review* 5, no. 2 (1952); S. I. Archangel'skiy, "Rasprodazha zemel'nych vladeniy storonnikov korolya," *Izvestiya Akademii Nauk SSSR* ser. 7 (Otdeleniye Obshchestvennykh Nauk), no. 5 (1933).

On the other, the need to secure the support of the peasants drove the revolutionary government to speed up sales, which consequently lowered land prices. Land sales had been the subject of debate since the beginning of the revolution. Initially, in an atmosphere of public enthusiasm and the popularity of the new regime, the terms of the property sales were framed with an emphasis on financial results: the land would be sold off in large plots, with a rather short deferral of payment, and largely for cash.

However, the intensification of social conflicts, a series of political crises, the onset of war, and the government's "discovery" of inflationary financing meant that less importance was given to the fiscal side of the land sales. Instead, sociopolitical problems came to the fore: small proprietors were encouraged to acquire the land, the payment period was lengthened (which, given inflation, made the land almost free of charge), and assignats were used on a much wider basis in the transfer of property from the state into private hands.

Nevertheless, as noted by historians of the French Revolution, arguments of social expediency coincided naturally with the personal interests of members of the revolutionary government, and especially those of Parliament. Estates and houses were sold for checks (*mandats territeriaux*) at a price one-tenth of their prerevolutionary value, and the interests of members of Parliament and bureaucrats were frequently discernible behind the deals.[15]

Finally, during the Bolshevik (and Mexican) revolution it was the sociopolitical aspect of property transformation that took on decisive importance. Nationalization was carried out with a view to safeguarding the survival of the revolutionary regime. This was done first by ensuring the support of millions of peasants, then by ensuring the support of industry, in order to concentrate resources for the purpose of waging civil war. Immediate nationalization was not a programmatic demand of the Bolsheviks and was not considered as a short-term economic measure prior to the revolution. However, political circumstances necessitated implementation of measures that conformed to the prevailing ideological sentiments of the time in general and the communist ideology in particular.

The revolutionary transformation of property rights has a number of features and consequences. First, the sale of property always has a smaller fiscal effect than originally expected. This less than expected gain occurs not just because of a conflict between the fiscal and social

---

15. Aftalion, *The French Revolution*, 174–75.

functions of the process, but as a result of the value of the deal in the radical phase of the revolution being sacrificed to speed and the fiscal result being sacrificed to politics. There is also a problem in that the projected revenue from the sale of property is calculated with reference to its prerevolutionary value. Under revolutionary conditions the actual price turns out to be considerably lower.

There are several reasons for this, among which political uncertainty is paramount. As long as the possibility remains that the revolution will fail, there is also a possibility that the fiscal consequences of the deals will be reviewed. Accordingly, a risk premium arises, which the state must carry.

All of this engenders another peculiarity relating to the distribution of property during a revolution. Not only is property sold cheaply, but to a significant extent it falls into the hands of speculators, who intend to resell it in the future. The difference is certainly not pocketed by the state.

The fiscal crisis that besets the revolution at certain stages is accompanied by further deterioration in the plight of the masses. As a rule, this happens in the concluding phase of the revolution, when political consolidation is well-advanced and there are signs of economic revival. This appears to be paradoxical: the revolutionary crisis subsides and the economy stabilizes, but the budgetary problems of the government become more acute. However, such a development is understandable.

Over the greater part of the revolutionary process, revolutionary governments resort to extraordinary measures to strengthen the new regime. These measures, however, are geared toward resolving short-term political difficulties and therefore are inevitably populist and temporary. As the revolutionary potential of the nation is exhausted, step by step the ruling elite becomes consolidated by stengthening its own position and obtaining room to maneuver. Gradually the consolidating elite brings itself to implement oftentimes painful and unpopular but necessary measures to revive the economy.

This means a return to normal economic policymaking without revolutionary excesses and emergencies. This manifests itself in the government's endeavors to live within its means and ensure stability of the country's financial system. In consequence, the final phase of the revolution is characterized by budgetary restrictions and depressed production. The severity of the budgetary crisis is directly related to the scale of inflationary financing.

This can be stated differently. The late-revolutionary deterioration of the economic situation in general and the budgetary crisis in particular are linked to the peculiar position of the consolidating elites and the growing strength of those holding political power. The government becomes strong enough not to have to ingratiate itself with various social forces and not to resort to extravagant populist measures. At the same time, it is still too weak to tackle successfully the whole array of tasks facing it.

These general conclusions, drawn from the historical experience of revolutionary transformations, are clearly applicable to an analysis of Russia's postcommunist development.[16] It is important to stress, however, that the existence of historical parallels is not a warrant for drawing simplistic practical conclusions concerning the problems and prospects of socioeconomic development of other countries. Historical experience serves only to illustrate the problems encountered in different epochs. From such illustrations a better understanding of contemporary problems may emerge. The logic of systemic transformations or the causes of a particular development of events should be considered on a case-by-case basis, without excessive attention to historical analogies. However, the very classification of the epoch as revolutionary gives the scholar a methodological key that is analytically useful.

---

16. For more detail on economic policy under radical social transformation, see V. Mau and I. Starodubrovskaya, *The Challenge of Revolution* (Oxford: Oxford University Press, 2001).

I Preconditions for the Postcommunist Transformation

1 The Inevitability of Collapse of the Socialist Economy

Yegor Gaidar

It became increasingly apparent that the stagnation, crisis, and collapse of socialism that began in Soviet bloc countries in the 1970s was inevitable. The collapse of socialism did not result just from a fatal coincidence of circumstances or from political error. Detailed arguments to support this contention are available in a number of publications, including Gaidar's *Anomalies of Economic Growth*.[1] Below I explain the part of this argument that is necessary in order to understand the central theme of this book: namely, that following the collapse of the USSR in the seventy-fifth year of its existence, market reforms in Russia were simply unavoidable.

1.1. Stability of the Socialist Economic System

After the first decades of its existence, socialism, and above all Soviet socialism, seemed well-entrenched, even unshakable. Moreover, its expansion enabled it to exert increasing influence on the course of world history. During those years the rapid industrial transformation and economic growth were too apparent and difficult to be explained away, as a number of Russian and foreign economists tried to do, as creative accounting. Socialist economic growth is interesting precisely because its rapid pace of industrialization in the 1930s to 1950s, its subsequent crisis, and its ensuing collapse were not statistical inventions but real and interrelated phenomena.

Along with the recognition of the successes that resulted from the strengthening of the communist system, twentieth-century social science literature also developed arguments to show its instability and inefficiency. A few publications making this argument are of

---
1. Ye. Gaidar, *Izbrannye sochineniya,* vol. 2 (Moscow: Yevraziya, 1997).

undeniable merit. These are, first of all, works by von Mises, Bruzkus, and Hayek.[2] They presented a detailed and persuasive case to show that socialism was historically doomed, and that it was impossible to build an efficient system on foundations that presuppose the elimination of private property and competition. However, for a long time these arguments suffered from a considerable flaw: the USSR persisted and, until the early 1970s, continued to develop sufficiently fast enough to alarm the leaders of the Western world. It was likely no accident that Hayek, for example, for all his persuasive arguments against central planning, hardly mentioned the Soviet Union, but rather utilized as examples purportedly socialist countries such as Germany and Italy. The arguments of Mises and Bruzkus, despite their coherence and consistency, are insufficient to explain the systemic causes of the crisis and death of Soviet communism, as well as the general reasons for its failure in competition with Western capitalism. A more painstaking analysis is required, one based on concrete historical experience. Finally, it deserves mention that the vast number of sovietologists who studied the Soviet Union and its satellites carefully (as well as the less numerous dissident analysts who were better acquainted with the internal situation) failed, with rare exceptions, to foresee the rapid developments that led to the demise of communism as a social and economic system.

Of the two chief characteristics of the Soviet socioeconomic system, stability and vulnerability, great importance was attached to the former, while the latter was ignored. Indeed, the system was exceptionally stable, even if its stability consisted in rejecting any innovations that went beyond the limits of the system's own logic. This logic was based on certain types of technology and centralized administration. It did not possess the internal capacity to adapt to the technological and social challenges of the postindustrial world.

Because of its extraordinary stability, the system also turned out to be maladapted to cope with external shocks and destructive internal tensions. Particularly damaging were those problems that could not be solved by mobilizational methods. Such methods had typically, and with some apparent success, been used to address many major economic problems at earlier stages of development.

---

2. Ludwig von Mises, *Sotsializm* (Moscow, 1994); B. Bruzkus, "Problemy narodnogo khozyaystva pri sotsialisticheskom stroe," *Ekonomist* 1, 2, 3 (1922); F. Hayek, *The Road to Serfdom* (New York: Routledge, 1991).

1.2. Characteristics of the Socialist Model of Economic Development

The socialist model of development[3] was created in the USSR in the late 1920s and early 1930s on the basis of the import-substitution model of industrialization.[4] The USSR provided the first experiment in the consistent implementation of import-substituting industrialization. This experience was only later followed by other countries, such as Argentina, India, Brazil, and Mexico. The new socialist model of economic growth (which reflected modifications introduced into the original import-substitution model) was characterized by the following attributes:

• The supremacy of state property and liquidation of legitimate private property independent of the state.

• The dominant role of the state in the mobilization of national savings, their distribution, and their utilization.

• The creation of a management hierarchy encompassing the entire country to coordinate economic activity by direct executive commands, with no role for the marginalized market system.

• Egalitarianism and a lessening of the extreme income inequality characteristic of early capitalism.

• "Catch-up" import-substituting industrialization on the basis of reallocation of resources from agriculture to industry as the cornerstone of structural policy.

• Tight political controls, to exclude any forms of unsanctioned mass activity.

• A messianic ideology promising earthly rewards tomorrow for abstention and hard work today.

---

3. The best-known liberal analyses of the socialist model are Hayek's *Doroga k rabstvu* and von Mises's *Sotsialism*. The most in-depth work assessing the consequences of the socialist experiment in our view is J. Kornai's *The Socialist System: The Political Economy of Communism* (Oxford: Oxford University Press, 1992).

4. For a detailed assessment see Ye. Gaidar, *Anomalii ekonomicheskogo rosta* (Moscow: Yevraziya, 1997), which demonstrates that the model of import-substituting industrialization was, for a limited time, one of the most effective methods of accelerating economic development. However, in the end it caused a considerable technological lag, while attempts to go beyond the possibilities inherent in the model led to falls in production and other undesirable consequences.

This set of institutional innovations temporarily lifts some particular restrictions placed on economic growth by market mechanisms.[5] First, the rate of savings ceases to depend on fluctuating variables such as private savings and investment. Second, high taxes do not suppress economic activity because taxes become independent of the autonomous decisions of private firms. Third, capital flight out of the country is reliably sealed off by pervasive financial controls. Fourth, totalitarian political controls remove restrictions on the amount of financial resources mobilizable by the state. Consequently, the extremely high and stable long-term savings rate that forms allows a sharp increase in economic growth and a spurt in industrialization.

The temporal coincidence of rapid industrialization in the Soviet Union and a deep crisis in the leading capitalist economies from 1929 to 1933 ensured for decades a measure of intellectual respectability for the socialist development formula[6] and made socialism a focus of attention and an object of emulation in many quarters, particularly in countries faced with the challenge of "catch-up" industrialization.

It is well-known that Soviet collectivization, accompanied by the forcible expropriation of a large part of agricultural production, permitted a lowering of incomes in the traditional (agricultural) sector and thus released additional financial resources for industrial development. The fall in living standards in the countryside, moreover, fueled a powerful inflow of labor into the cities.

Consequently, not only did rapid industrialization occur, but a savings rate significantly higher than that possible under market industrialization was also achieved. Importantly, state coercion was the principal instrument for lowering the standard of living in the traditional sector and mobilizing resources for industrialization. This phenomenon assumed a variety of manifestations, including the terror of the gulags.

Thus, the socialist model rapidly and radically resolved the fundamental problem of market-led industrialization: how to overcome

---

5. A comprehensive analysis of the institutional structure of the socialist economy is in Kornai, *The Socialist System*. The author's views on the internal mechanisms of the socialist economy are in Ye. Gaidar, *Ekonomicheskie reformy i ierarkhicheskie struktury* (Moscow: Nauka, 1990).

6. The work of the brilliant economist Joseph Schumpeter, who harbored no sympathies for socialism, is a typical illustration of the deep pessimism obtaining in the 1930–1940s with respect to the ability of capitalism to counter the industrial dynamism exhibited by socialism. See J. Schumpeter, *Capitalism, Socialism, and Democracy*. 3rd edition (New York, 1950.)

inertia in the accumulation of national savings. The accumulation of greater national savings empowered the rapid economic growth in the USSR in the initial phase of industrialization. The strictly military orientation of this growth had as its roots the general conception of Soviet policy as an aggressive idea of world revolution, which was then justified on the basis of the hostile capitalist surroundings.

However, everything has a cost. The removal of market mechanisms, including the related mechanisms of adjustments, incentives for efficient use of resources, and the selection of effective innovations, all allowed a persistently high rate of resource utilization. Additionally, the closed nature of the economy (this also applies to capitalist economies of import-substituting industrialization) allows a lower share of exports, particularly the export share of processing industries in GDP.

It is impossible to know how the Soviet economy would have developed and how it would have affected the well-being of the population if state policy and economic orientation had not been militaristic, and if resources and human capital had not been used to accumulate vast stockpiles of weaponry but rather had been devoted to improving the welfare of ordinary citizens. According to Hayek (on a somewhat different subject concerning the military uses of German motorways), the planning authorities could have deliberately chosen "guns" instead of "butter."[7] Perhaps socialism would have survived another century. Or perhaps a relatively fast rise in the living standards and educational level of the population would have led to an earlier discovery of the fundamental flaws of socialism and consequently a correspondingly earlier collapse. This guessing game, however, is a subject for a different book.

1.3. Internal Constraints on Long-Term Development of the Economic System

Examining the long-term consequences of the socialist model, one can discern internal factors that inhibit the prospects for stable development.

According to Engels's law, the share of foodstuffs in consumption decreases in proportion to the increase in per capita GDP. However, the expenditure on food in absolute terms increases with a rise in the standard of living. Under market-led industrialization the growth of

---

7. See Hayek, *The Road to Serfdom* quoted in *Novy Mir*, no. 7, 1991.

agriculture, while slower than the overall growth of GDP, is stable over the long run and corresponds to the growing level of food consumption. For example, the United States at present is the largest agricultural exporter in the world, while OECD member countries as a whole display a trade balance in agricultural produce close to zero.

In an open economy, where the share of agriculture in the structure of the GDP is limited, the growth of agricultural production need not exceed that of food consumption in order to generate stable economic growth. It is nonetheless important to note that the trend is in this direction.

Socialist industrialization coercively redistributed resources away from agriculture on a massive scale. Such developments resulted in a situation of rapid industrialization, the growth of per capita GDP, and consequently the increased demand for foodstuffs. This very mechanism of socialist resource allocation, which increased the demand for foodstuffs, led to the stagnation of agricultural output and its long-term deformation.

It is these factors that spurred the rapid pace of socialist industrialization (including the lowering of living standards in the countryside and, in the early industrialization phase, the massive redistribution of resources away from the traditional agricultural sector) and engendered the most serious long-term anomaly of socialist growth: *the divergent growth trajectories between industry and agriculture.*

In the early 1960s it became apparent that the ability of the agricultural sector to mobilize financial resources for industrialization was exhausted. This radically changed the economic situation. In the early 1960s the economic advantages of diverting resources from agriculture were confronted by the grim necessity to pay for this diversion. The long-term consequences of the socialist model of industrialization became painfully apparent. In the USSR, however, the discovery of vast reserves of oil and gas in Siberia and the coincidental sharp rise in the prices for these commodities on world markets staved off economic collapse. This new source of revenue in effect delayed the demise of socialism in the USSR.

Oil and gas revenues nonetheless did not address the structural problems of an exhausted agricultural sector. It was this chronic crisis in collectivized agriculture and the shortage of foodstuffs that largely constrained the USSR's further development. The People's Republic of China, which in the 1970s found itself in a similar situation, was forced to abandon the established socialist model of economic development. In one fell swoop (by applying a sort of "shock therapy," in contemporary parlance), agricultural cooperatives were disbanded, and alongside state industry a dynamic, largely export-oriented sector began to develop. The latter became possible only because of the existence of a vast pool of agricultural labor. In the USSR, however, this labor pool had been depleted by the early 1960s. As a result, the socioeconomic structure in the USSR underwent substantial modification, which became officially known as developed or mature socialism. This structure was characterized by declining economic growth with an industrial base that had ossified during the preceding period. However, the maintenance of outdated, inefficient production methods became increasingly expensive. Also, the structural lag vis-à-vis the developed market economies in the key sectors, particularly those that determine the dynamics of technological progress, was widening.

The erosion of the traditional model of socialist growth left the communist elite with two strategic choices: first, to try to restructure the mechanisms of economic regulation (by utilizing market mechanisms in some fashion), or second, to accept the loss of economic growth as a given and to focus on the stable and reliable nature of the system.

1.4. Several Options for Reforming the Socialist Economy

Economic reform had become a pivotal point in the strategic agenda of the USSR and its East European satellites as far back as the late 1960s.[8] That period witnessed attempts to supplement the traditional hierarchical structure with a system of incentives, to give more rights to enterprises, and to restore, on a limited scale, elements of market regulation. Some examples of such reforms include the 1966–1968 period in the USSR, the 1957–1958 and 1965–1968 years in Czechoslovakia, the 1965–1969 and 1973–1979 era in Poland, the 1965–1969 time frame in East Germany, and the reforms initiated in Hungary after 1957.

Any analysis of these attempted reforms leads to the same conclusion: The socialist economy only functions as a well-integrated system that easily repels or formalizes reforms that do not affect its

---

8. P. Sutela, *Economic Thought and Economic Reform in the Soviet Union* (Cambridge: Cambridge University Press, 1991); V. Mau, *V poiskakh planomernosti* (Moscow: Nauka, 1990).

fundamentals. On the other hand, isolated attempts to introduce new indicators, alter the incentive structure, or give wider rights to economic units arouse the interest of the top leadership for a short period but soon thereafter cease to exert tangible influence on the functioning of the hierarchical economy and its deep-rooted mechanisms.[9]

Some analysts even viewed the socialist economy as fundamentally unreformable. They reasoned the following:

1. All lasting changes entail a minimal set of elements designed to alter the nature of the economic system substantially. Among these elements they included a considerably enhanced role for the market in guiding economic activity, significant price liberalization, or the introduction of dual (administrative and market) pricing; a significant expansion in the autonomy of economic units in forming production policy and the system of economic linkages between them; the introduction of various incentives tied to economic performance; and legalization of the private sector in at least some sectors of the economy.

2. As is evident from the few cases of lasting reforms—in Yugoslavia, Hungary, China, and Vietnam, for example—such reforms brought the transformed socialist economies closer to the market economies of import-substituting industrialization. Several characteristics that are common to both transformed socialist economies and market economies include a large role for the state in economic regulation, the bureaucratization of economic activity, high tariff and nontariff barriers to protect the domestic market, well-developed goods markets, and legalization of the private sector.

3. Comprehensive economic reform always tests the stability of the mechanisms utilized for sociopolitical control by the socialist state. Such reforms inevitably result in growing income differentials as well as accelerating, open inflation, both of which undermine the all-important ideological foundations of the socialist regime—egalitarianism and stability. Consequently, the following conditions

---

9. The conclusions are based on Gaidar's *Anomalii ekonomicheskogo rosta*. For difficulties involved in maintaining a reform momentum under socialism see Kornai, *The Socialist System;* L. Balcerowicz, "On the Reformability of Soviet-Type Economic Systems," in *The Evolution of Economic Systems: Essays in Honour of Otta Sick,* (London: 1990), 193–201; idem, "The Soviet-Type Economic System, Reformed System and Innovativeness," *Communist Economics* 2, no. 1 (1990): 3–23; Gaidar, *Ekonomicheskie reformy i ierarkhicheskie struktury.*

are necessary to ensure the success of such reforms: retention of effective political controls by the authoritarian regime; efficient mechanisms of hierarchical management (the system of state orders, rationing, and price controls); and a fairly tight fiscal and monetary policy to contain inflation and prevent a significant disjunction between fixed and free prices.

4. All successful reforms have been undertaken in countries that had not yet completed socialist industrialization and which therefore still possessed additional labor resources in agriculture (as in China in 1978, Vietnam in the mid-1980s, Yugoslavia in 1953, and Hungary in 1957).[10] The USSR, however, in its stage of mature socialism encountered the following manifest difficulties in its reform endeavors. The growth potential of the socialist economy was exhausted, and the anaesthetic of overall growth in income could no longer mask the growing social differentiation. Nor was it possible any longer to create new economic sectors by diverting resources from agriculture. The final problem was the growing conservatism of the political and economic elite, which had grown accustomed to stability and was unreceptive to serious socioeconomic innovations.

The difficulties in reforming the mature industrialized socialist economy, and particularly the experience of Czechoslovakia, where economic reforms paved the way for political destabilization, were daunting. These difficulties, consequently, compelled the leadership of the Communist Party Central Committee to abandon, toward the end of the 1960s, the idea of serious market reforms. At that moment in time, it appeared to some that the rich resource base, the structural rigidities of the economy, and totalitarian political controls guaranteed the USSR and its East European empire long-term stability, regardless of how slowly it economically grew or even stagnated. Even though the potential for socialist industrialization was exhausted and the economy had reached the limits of productivity set by the basic parameters of its model, some Soviet economists reasonably argued that it could operate close to this level for a long time to come.

However, several developments undermined the realization of such a view of the late-socialist world. Specifically, the erosion of the socialist system was intimately tied up with a genuine conflict of interests among the ruling communist elite. (It is consequently no

---

10. Gaidar, *Ekonomicheskie reformy i ierarkhicheskie struktury.*

accident that the privatization processes started under socialism.) Convincing evidence illustrates that the economic development of the USSR, and of the closely integrated economies of the Comecon member countries, was marked by such internal instability. It became crystal-clear at this point of development that a return to a stagnating but stable socialist economy ceased to be feasible. Thus, the decline in production in postsocialist countries in the 1970s and 1980s was rooted not just in difficulties in economic transition but also in the impossibility of maintaining stability within an economic system that had been formed much earlier.

1.5. Signs of Exhaustion of the Growth Model

A second factor determining the quick collapse of the seemingly stable system of the 1970s and 1980s was the nature of socialist growth in these two decades. Oil revenues had replaced the resources released by the traditional sector, which by now were exhausted. The new sources of development finance (which replaced the agricultural turnover tax) included rapidly growing revenues from external economic activity. The external economy, in effect, generated the hard currency required to pay for technology and agricultural imports and permitted further industrial development as well as growth in per capita income. However, instead of channeling these resources into generating a painless exit from socialism and activating market mechanisms, Soviet strategists used these resources to raise per capita GDP to a level thought to be sustainable within the socialist model.

Signs of exhaustion in this growth model, now based on oil revenues, began to appear in the early 1980s. Despite the fast-growing volume of investments in the oil sector—in 1985 they were twice as high as in 1975—and its share in the overall volume of investments, the growth in oil production stalled. From 603 million tonnes in 1980, output dropped to 595 million tonnes in 1985. If over the period of 1970–1980 the physical volume of exports had grown by 62% and the value of exports as a result of the favorable price changes had increased by a factor of 3.7, between 1980 and 1985 the physical volume of exports had grown by only 7.4%, while its value, having peaked in 1983, at $91.4 billion, began to fall, to $86.7 billion in 1985.

Realistically speaking, the launch of the mechanism that led to the collapse of the system, and consequently to a sharp fall in production and the standards of living, dates back to 1983–1985. Attempts to halt the fall in oil production resulted only in modifications to the extraction strategy and an accelerating decline in the rate of oil production. The economy was caught in a vicious circle: lack of funds for capital investment to maintain the level of oil production meant a decline in oil production, which in turn fed a deepening crisis in the energy-intensive sectors of the economy. This process consequently resulted in a further diminution of investment in the oil industry and an accelerated decline in production across all sectors of the economy.

By the early 1980s the USSR had lost the financial room for maneuvering it once had. Also, as a result of the large-scale use of product credits to finance numerous construction projects, in 1984 the principal and interest received by the Soviet Union on loans it had issued to other countries amounted to only 30% of the payments due on its debts. In the meantime, the structure of the Soviet debt was deteriorating as the proportion of medium- and short-term loans grew. This deterioration was reflected in the continuously increasing burden of servicing its debt: $5.9 billion in 1984 rapidly became $15.1 billion in 1986. By the beginning of perestroika, the rate of growth in Soviet foreign-debt obligations had assumed avalanche-like proportions.

In 1985, when Mikhail Gorbachev came to power, the economic situation was only superficially stable (in the sense of Brezhnev-era stability). In reality, the possibilities for maintaining the existing level of production and consumption, let alone raising it, depended on uncontrollable external factors such as world oil and gas prices, discoveries of new oil and gas fields with low extraction costs, and opportunities to issue low-interest debt. However, a fall in world oil prices and the absolute decline in export earnings (from $91.4 billion in 1983 to $86.7 billion in 1985) underscored that there would be no such miracle.

The next chapter discusses the history of economic policy during perestroika.[11] At this point it is worth noting that the impact of decisions made in the economic sphere by Gorbachev and Nikolay Ryzhkov, his prime minister, on the collapse of socialism were not

---

11. See also Ye. Gaidar, *Inflationary Pressure and Economic Reform in the Soviet Union: Economic Transition in Easter Europe* (Oxford: Oxford University Press, 1993); idem, *Russian Reform* (Cambridge: Cambridge University Press, 1995); O. Latsis, *Chto s nami bylo i chto s nami budyet?* (Moscow: Yevraziya, 1995); S. Sinel'nikov, *Byudzhetny krizis v Rossii 1985–1995 gody* (Moscow: Yevraziya, 1995); A. Aslund, *How Russia Became a Market Economy* (Washington, D.C.: Brookings Institution Press, 1995).

as great as is conventionally held. Although much of what they did under the circumstances was indeed erroneous and counterproductive, these mistakes determined only the time frame and the specific mechanisms of the crisis, not the scale and nature of it. The crisis itself was inevitable.

What happened in the USSR was of fundamental importance. The economic growth sustained through oil revenues, although internally unbalanced and unstable, nevertheless brought the country's per capita GDP close to the GDP levels displayed by developed market-based democracies. However, urbanization, progress in education, wider availability of information about the outside world, and the expansion of middle-class patterns of consumption are all factors that undermined the regime. After the first timid liberalization steps taken by Gorbachev in the early period of perestroika, 1985–1987, it was these factors that gave rise to a powerful democratic "wave," which quickly exceeded government control. The coincidental economic crisis, brought about by a fall in oil revenues and the failure of the economic strategy of the past two decades, imparted an added impetus to this wave. In consequence, the communist regimes of Eastern Europe, deprived of the necessary Soviet military support, began to fall.

It is commonplace to blame Gorbachev, who, unlike the Chinese leadership, started with political liberalization, not economic reform. However, given the interconnectedness of the economic and the political spheres, it is much more appropriate to ask whether Gorbachev had any viable alternative. The Soviet leaders of the early 1970s, above all Leonid Brezhnev, gambled on an inherently unreliable oil-based economic growth and chose a strategy that accelerated the historically inevitable and catastrophic collapse of the political and economic institutions of socialism.

2 The Logic and Nature of the Soviet Economic Crisis

Vladimir Mau

In Russia as in other countries, the postcommunist transformation was inextricably linked to the country's passing through a profound economic crisis. Until recently this crisis was discussed chiefly in political terms. Today, however, it is widely recognized that the radical reforms that effectively brought the socialist (communist) epoch to an end were initiated only after Russia had entered a profound economic crisis.

2.1. The Reforms of Late Socialism

The attempts at reforming the Soviet system that were undertaken after Mikhail Gorbachev ascended to power, in 1985, undoubtedly fueled the onset of economic collapse in the USSR. Leaving aside charges of betraying socialism or the fatherland, a number of explanations have been proposed to account for the failure of Gorbachev's economic reforms and the onset of the economic crisis. The positions examined here are typical of those held by both foreign and Russian academics.

First, hard-line sovietologists subscribed to the view that "improved," or market, socialism was completely far-fetched and unrealistic. They believed that the only effective economic system was a "normal," fully capitalist market economy, and they therefore considered that reforms directed toward improving or modernizing Soviet-style socialism were doomed to failure.

Second, a number of experts of the "classical post-Stalinist" school of sovietology held that reform of the Soviet economy was an exceptionally difficult and contradictory undertaking whose realization would require the resolution of a whole series of conflicting problems. The process of reform would therefore inevitably lead to a temporary deterioration in the economic situation. According to this school, a cautious and gradual approach was necessary in order to implement the reforms successfully.[1] Lack of preparedness on the part of the people or the political elite could only intensify the crisis and the upcoming political struggle.

The third approach emphasizes the mistakes made by Gorbachev and his colleagues. According to this approach, perestroika was considerably less successful than might have been expected.[2] This line of argument became particularly popular after the collapse of the Soviet Union and the departure of Gorbachev from power. The majority of Soviet and post-Soviet interpretations to be found in analytical works and the memoirs of key players in the events of 1985–1991 basically present variations on this theory.

Finally, a number of authors consider the initial crisis to have been the result of an unsuccessful attempt by the Soviet leadership to upgrade and adapt the socialist socioeconomic system to the needs of a postindustrial society.[3] However, the economy proved incapable of adapting to the challenges of the time (especially to new technologies), and for the last time the authorities tried to employ the mobilization mechanisms of the Soviet industrial society to break out of the economic and political crisis.

All of these explanations are to some degree correct. The reforms needed were extraordinarily difficult to implement, and likely many mistakes were made in the attempt. Although the goal of achieving "market socialism" by the end of the twentieth century was unrealistic, these arguments still do not explain the speed of the USSR's collapse. The many errors committed cannot be accounted for simply by the difficulty of the problems faced; the *ancien régime* was too stable to collapse purely through the incompetence of its new leaders.

---

1. Alec Nove wrote at the time, "To change everything at once is impossible, but partial change creates contradictions and inconsistencies" (*Pravda International* 12, no. 7 (1987): 36). See also Geoffrey Hosking, *The Awakening of the Soviet Union* (London: Heinemann, 1990), 133–34.
2. Marshall Goldman, *What Went Wrong with Perestroika?* (New York: W. W. Norton, 1991). This line was used largely to justify the mistaken forecasts made by adherents of the "classical" school of sovietology, which were clearly revealed as such by the end of 1991.
3. J. B. Rosser and M. V. Rosser, "Schumpeterian Evolutionary Dynamics and the Collapse of Soviet-Bloc Socialism," *Review of Political Economy* 9, no. 2 (1997).

2.2. Ideology and the Reform Program

By the middle of the 1980s, there was a clear understanding in the USSR that certain reforms had to be made.[4] Economic reforms were openly discussed, and the measures that might be needed to bring about reform were addressed in party documents at various levels. Political reform was also on the agenda, even if it was not openly discussed. The arguments in favor of political reform were suppressed further with each successive Soviet leader's funeral.

There were two possible reform models. Soviet socialism knew two main models of organization of political and economic life: the mobilization pattern and the liberal one. The former was rooted in the period of war communism (1918–1920) and the Stalinist era (1930–1940s)—a period of rigorous centralization of economic life and political repression. The liberal pattern implicitly developed in the 1960s and 1970s and involved some form of decentralization, as well as the introduction of some market elements into the Soviet economic system. The choice between these two approaches was an ideological one and was not fundamentally shaped by the development of the communist system but by the long-term global development of social and economic life.

The success of conservative economic policies in the United States under Ronald Reagan, and in the United Kingdom under Margaret Thatcher, had a tremendous impact on the Soviet elite, the intelligentsia, and the Communist *nomenklatura*. Liberal market doctrines became very attractive and gained wide political support. Despite the bitter confrontation between supporters of the American and Swedish models, as described in M. Albert's popular book, *Capitalism versus Capitalism*,[5] liberal ideology has become a universal imperative of this era, just as the ideas of centralization and *dirigisme* dominated in the first half of the century.[6] No other reform model

---

4. Practically all Western students of Soviet society tied the prospects for implementing certain reforms to Mikhail Gorbachev. Despite the criticism that kremlinology has endured, a number of Western experts pointed this out at the beginning of the 1980s. See Seweryn Bialer and Thane Gustafson, eds., *Russia at the Crossroads: The 26th Party Congress of the CPSU* (London: Allen & Unwin, 1982); Mary McAuley, ed., *The Soviet Union After Brezhnev* (London: Heinemann, 1983); Timothy Colton, *The Dilemmas of Reform in the Soviet Union* (New York: Council for Foreign Relations, 1986).
5. M. Albert, *Capitalism contre Capitalism* (Paris: Editions du Seuil, 1991).
6. Francis Fukuyama's *The End of History and the Last Man* (London: Penguin Books, 1992) will always remain an idiosyncratic credo for this epoch.

was seriously contemplated, since no other model had either social or political roots in the post-Brezhnev Soviet Union.

Liberal ideology per se, however, does not determine the content of a reform program but merely establishes a general foundation for it. The actual program to a large extent depends on the political situation in a given country and on the theoretical and practical experience of that country. The experience of other countries can only be added to the practical experience of the country in question. This theoretical point of view, along with the accumulated experiences of various communist countries, suggest two reform models, the Chinese and the Czech-Hungarian. Both involved market-style reforms, and consequently a move toward market socialism. However, that is just about all the models had in common.

The Chinese model had two distinctive features. First, its goal was the creation of a classic two-sector economy, with a state sector (ineffective as a rule, but strategically important) and a private sector. Second, it was essential that the ruling party maintain strict political control, which essentially meant preserving in full the totalitarian state, whether of communist or of nationalist type.

The Czech-Hungarian model, by contrast, envisaged complete marketization of the national economy (regardless of the type of property in question) and the necessary enactment of political reforms. This rationalization for this model is the structure of a developed industrial economy. In industrial economies the agricultural sector is relatively small, and so, correspondingly, is its role in modernization (especially postindustrial modernization). Also, the role of the service sector in an industrial economy differs radically from its role in a preindustrial or early industrial economy. After the collapse of communism, the service sector was supported by the socio-political maturity of East European countries and the maintenance of macroeconomic order during the commercialization of the economy. These factors made it possible to implement reforms without establishing the relevant political mechanisms for preparing and adopting decisions at all levels of the state apparatus.

Although China's economic reforms yielded impressive results, while the Czech-Hungarian model of market socialism existed more in theory than in actuality, the leadership of the Soviet Union clearly favored the latter reform model.

By the middle of the 1980s the Soviet Union had something resembling a reform program. This program was not in the form of a complete document, but the ideas were clearly articulated in numerous analytical memoranda submitted to the Central Committee (CPSU) and the government, and in various published reports, mostly by economists.[7]

The economic part of this program was already developed in detail. Throughout the 1960s and 1970s, the best Soviet economists worked on a series of problems related to "improving the economic mechanism." At the time, this work was the most dynamic domestically produced scholarship on economic theory. This work was based on the (fairly obvious) thesis that it is impossible to resolve all socioeconomic problems from a "single center," and therefore there must be some means to stimulate local economic agents to renew and develop production. Economists focused on improving production through local means believed that this goal could be achieved by increasing the autonomy of enterprises in making decisions about production and wages, even as the fundamentals of the Soviet economic system—a one-party system, no property rights—were preserved.[8] This implicitly meant preserving Gosplan and other directive organs that governed the economic balance through administrative means.

The program completely failed to address the issue of property-rights reform. The farthest that some academics were willing to go was to formulate questions about the permissibility of "real cooperative property" under socialism.

The program also did not tackle state price-setting. A number of influential reform economists demonstrated that under socialism, a system of balanced prices could be achieved. Such a system, according to the reformers, could be calculated and constantly revised in

---

7. The most important was the report by Tatyana Zaslavskaya, prepared and delivered in a closed seminar at the Novosibirsk Institute of Economics and Organization of Industrial Production under the Academy of Sciences USSR in 1983, which achieved notoriety because of its subsequent publication in Germany and the United States (see *The Washington Post*, 3 August 1983); T. Zaslaskaya, "O sovershenstvovanii proizvodstvennykh otnosheniy sotsializma i zadachakh ekonomicheskoy sotsiologii," in *Rossiskoe obshchestvo na sotsialnom izlome: vzglyad iznutri* (Moscow: VTsIOM, 1997). There was also the preparation of a program for "scientific-technical progress," in which representatives of all generations of reformers took part (N. Fedorenko, S. Shatalin, A. Anchishkin, N. Petrakov, A. Aganbegyan, E. Yasin, Ye. Gaidar, G. Yavlinsky, et al.)

8. For more detail, see Pekka Sutela, *Economic Thought and Economic Reform in the Soviet Union* (Cambridge: Cambridge University Press, 1991); Vladimir Mau, *The Political History of Economic Reform in Russia* (London: CRCE, 1996), 17–32.

accordance with mathematical models. These models would consequently describe the optimal paradigm for the Soviet economy and would in effect form "the optimal national economic plan."

This program had two fundamental flaws. First, it was produced by combining the "best" elements from the two systems, and thus almost by definition could not be consistent, and second, it was too abstract and lacked practical grounding. Thus, realizing reforms through a series of programs was never really a possibility.[9]

2.3. The Practical Problem of Improving the Economic Mechanism

Mikhail Gorbachev's motives for announcing a program to renew the existing system, an announcement he made shortly after coming to power, are not that important. It clearly resulted from a number of factors: the general realization that reforms were necessary and the time was right; the political calculations of Gorbachev (who was patently striving to strengthen his position in power); the imminent economic crisis, symptoms of which were evident in the plummeting growth rates of the Soviet economy; and the strain on the budget resulting from the slump in world oil prices.

Gorbachev's attempts at reforming the Soviet system were not rooted in the realization that an economic or a systemic crisis had begun. Only a narrow circle of experts, generally economists, were more or less aware that a crisis was unfolding. The crisis did not influence everyday life; it did not impinge on the mood of the elite or the public, and it was not a decisive factor in economic decision making. The invisibility of the crisis partly explains the distinctive character of the first phase of Gorbachev's reforms.

It is worth noting that Gorbachev's first attempts at stimulating the Soviet economy were in line with the "mobilization approach." The chief features were (1) a new industrialization drive (with an increased emphasis on the development of the machine-building complex) and, related to that, the raising of growth rates; and (2) a cultural revolution composed of two independent components, both of social significance: a new style of political leadership, and an anti-alcohol campaign. At the same time, a number of organizational

---

9. It is worth noting that the features of the mid-1980s economic reform program identified here are characteristic of all prerevolutionary programs.

changes were made in the bodies responsible for managing the economy. In addition—although this was not publicly announced—a "cadre revolution" was initiated to renew and rejuvenate the cadres.

The cultural scheme for the development of the crisis of late socialism was fairly straightforward, if one considers the revolutionary nature of the events that followed. Having declared at the Twenty-seventh Congress of the CPSU that piecemeal reorganization would not suffice and that the country needed complex economic reforms, Gorbachev turned to a program of cautious market reforms. This program became known as "market socialism," although there was a strict taboo on using this term. The repeated criticisms directed against the program—namely, that it was limited and lacked consistency—do not alter the fact that it was the *only* program available at the time to the new Soviet leadership committed to reform.

The fundamental elements of the series of reforms that were adopted were (1) increasing the autonomy of socialist enterprises by converting them to fully self-financing and self-managing entities; (2) developing individual and cooperative forms of ownership; and (3) attracting foreign capital through joint ventures.[10] The contradictions in this program have been detailed in both the Russian and foreign economic literature,[11] so we will focus only on a few points of particular relevance to this analysis.

First, the macroeconomic limitations of the program became apparent, as increasing enterprises' rights immediately led to an emphasis on consumer priorities, to the detriment of investment. This coincided with the introduction of elections for enterprise directors. This process undermined the position of directors (who by the middle of the 1980s had become de facto owners of the enterprises) and intensified the standard problem encountered in any revolution—how to align formal and real ownership rights.

As a result, a paradoxical situation arose in which enterprise directors were effectively freed from the control of the state bureaucracy (which to a certain extent fulfilled the role of owner vis-à-vis the directors) but were still not subject to the rigors either of a real owner or of the market. The temptation to engage in self-interested

---

10. See *O korennoy perestroyke upravleniya ekonomikoy: sbornik dokumentov* (Moscow: Politizdat, 1987).
11. See, for example, W. Joyce, H. Ticktin, and S. White, eds., *Gorbachev and Gorbachevism* (London: Frank Cass, 1989); Goldman, *What Went Wrong with Perestroika*; P. J. Boettke, *Why Perestroika Failed* (New York: Routledge, 1993).

or criminal activities in this situation was exceptionally strong. The former was prompted by the abnormal dependence on employees, who had an obvious interest in higher wages and a higher level of expenditure on social programs. In fact, the actual degree of dependence was not altogether clear initially. New opportunities for private entrepreneurship encouraged participation in criminal activities, and in fact, certain decisions by the authorities created a particularly favorable environment for using enterprise resources to further the interests of a narrow circle of top managers. All of this was going on years before the issue of reforming property ownership was even put on the agenda, in 1990.[12]

Incomplete reforms of traditional sectors and traditional forms of ownership were combined with the government's resolve to take excessively firm but insufficiently well-thought-out steps in new areas of economic activity. Thus, while real private enterprise was permitted in the form of cooperatives, it was not accompanied by the creation of adequate legal checks on the blatantly criminal collusion between cooperatives and state enterprises that had become "fully self-financing." Moreover, the relevant orders, in traditional Soviet fashion, encouraged the creation of cooperatives under the auspices of state enterprises. A similar situation arose later with commercial banks. In fact, conditions for setting up a bank turned out to be considerably more straightforward in the USSR than in countries with a much more developed market economy. In part this is explained by the government's lack of experience, but to a greater extent it is explained by the pressure of time and circumstances. At the time the economic crisis unfolded, the government was supposed to implement only popular measures and to achieve rapid improvements in living standards.

The initial outcomes of this policy were contradictory. For the last time the mobilization mechanisms for which the Soviet Union was earlier renowned were activated, and gross volume indicators improved somewhat. On closer analysis, however, the improvement

---

12. The overwhelming majority of Western sovietologists were similarly indifferent to this issue. They seemed hypnotized, initially by the fundamental impossibility of privatization in the USSR, and then by the internal logic of the Soviet reformers' program, which gave the appearance of being complete without reform of property rights. In the West, Philip Hanson's publications showed a rare grasp of the ownership issue; see his *Economics, Sovietology, and Mr. Gorbachev's Agenda* (Birmingham, England: University of Birmingham Press, 1988).

in gross volume indicators was accompanied by a profound crisis, evidenced by a rapid drop in the value of the ruble, the rapidly increasing gap between incomes and production (particularly starting in 1988), a deterioration in the trade balance, and a deterioration in the USSR's external debt situation.

Such a turn of events is not particularly unusual in the history of economic policy. Many populist experiments have started in this fashion.[13] Such a sequence of events, known in the literature as the "socialist investment cycle," was characteristic for the USSR. This sequence took the following phases: the realization of an investment program; the slowing of growth rates; the introduction of liberalizing measures; the introduction of measures to boost growth; intensification of the macroeconomic imbalance; and finally a retreat from liberal reforms, which was followed by a new investment program. However, this sequence raises another question of interest: What happens if the government does not retreat from liberal reforms? This is exactly what unfolded at the end of the 1980s.

Some think that in 1980, Gorbachev, while developing democratic principles, had the opportunity to toughen the economic regime. Specifically, there was discussion about implementing a number of unpopular measures, particularly relating to prices and taxes.[14] In reality, the situation was rather different: democratic development at this time obstructed the implementation of a responsible macroeconomic policy. In May 1989 the government came under the control of a democratically elected legislature that was heavily influenced by popular sentiment.[15]

Gorbachev, by virtue of his democratic leanings, did not want to reverse the processes of democratization. In fact, he and his

---

13. The temporally closest example is Chile under the National Front government (1971–1973). Embarking on his peaceful revolution, Salvador Allende implemented a number of measures that led to growth in private consumption. However, the simultaneous rapid depletion of hard currency reserves and the sharp deterioration in the balance of payments signaled an approaching crisis, which struck almost one and a half years after the populist experiment was initiated. The military coup that followed was supposed to solve the problem of restoring macroeconomic stability and economic growth (although in fact this problem was resolved far more immediately). For more on this see Rüdiger Dornbusch and S. Edwards, eds., *The Macroeconomics of Populism in Latin America* (Chicago: University of Chicago Press, 1991).
14. David Kotz with Fred Weir, *Revolution from Above* (New York: Routledge, 1997), 73–86.
15. For more on this see Vladimir Mau, *The Political History of Economic Reform in Russia*, 50–51, 123.

government simply could not embark on such a course and remain in power. The weakening of the state, particularly its totalitarian controls, had begun. The government not only did not want to but, as a result of democratization, could not adopt unpopular but necessary economic decisions. In the second half of the 1980s these necessary actions included price reform, tax reform, and the timely and official commencement of privatization.

2.4. Economic Crisis as a Crisis of the State

Three features characterized the socioeconomic situation in the USSR at the end of the 1980s and the beginning of the 1990s:

1. A gradual deepening of the economic malaise.
2. The rapid restructuring of socioeconomic space through the formation of diverse interest groups.
3. The emergence of a number of centers of political power, and the subsequent mushrooming of competition between different political institutions for control over sociopolitical decision making.

These features are all interconnected. A deepening of the economic crisis accelerates disintegration of the political foundation, which becomes one of the key factors influencing further economic development. The center, however, weakened as a result of its aspirations to represent all interests, gradually cedes power to newly formed or reformed political structures. These newly formed structures cater to the needs of special interest groups.

In this situation a government's policies change considerably, in three particular ways. First, the government becomes reactive; its actions are nothing more than reactions to immediate problems, crises, and clashes. This type of behavior entails the general absence of strategic planning. Second, the predominant factor influencing decisions is the desire to retain power, which allows short-term considerations to take the upper hand. And third, political decisions are made by a weak government, one that is known to be weak by practically all of the other participants in the political struggle. This reality hardens others' bargaining positions vis-à-vis the central authorities.

The USSR leadership recognized the economic crisis. However, this understanding did not lead to a withdrawal of populist policies, although their character changed somewhat. During the period 1986–1989, the central authorities took dangerous, blatantly populist positions, which they were convinced were of social and economic importance and necessity. At the time, the actions of the leadership flowed from a clear and logical program. Later, when the government was steadily losing authority, it took populist positions fully cognizant of the economic risks involved. Moreover, political decisions were strongly influenced by confrontations with other institutions of power. An effective anticrisis program, much less a reform program, was completely lacking.

This became apparent during the confrontation between Union and Russian authorities in 1990–1991. The decisions of both of these groups were politically motivated, with the consequence that economic policy became hostage to a greater political struggle. This struggle was above all exemplified in the loss of control over the state budget. And so a "budget war" began, with the Union republics refusing to transfer tax revenues to the federal treasury. The republics also insisted on switching over to a single-channel system of tax collection, while strengthening their control over the expenditure of the USSR authorities.

Even more acute was the struggle between Union and republic authorities to bring enterprises under tax jurisdiction. Even though the budget deficit was approaching 10% of GDP, the USSR and Russian governments competed with one another to lower the taxes of whichever enterprises recognized their jurisdiction. Consequently, budget revenues continued to decline steadily in real terms. This situation was worsened by the fact that enterprises were granted considerable freedom in setting wholesale prices, while retail prices remained unchanged. This process not only raised budget expenditures, as retail prices had to be subsidized, it also led to a drop in tax receipts, because the turnover tax (one of the main sources of budget revenues) was tied to a fixed sum in the wholesale price. An attempt to strengthen the federal budget by introducing a 5% sales tax in 1991 as a share of retail price foundered from the start, merely providing further proof of the exceptional weakness of the Union's center.[16]

The situation was similar in the agricultural sector. In autumn of 1990, the Council of Ministers of the USSR, in an attempt to

---

16. For more on this see Sergei Sinelnikov, *Byudzhedny krizis v Rossii 1985–1995 gody* (Moscow: Yevraziya, 1995).

overcome the shortage of goods, decided to raise food procurement prices. However, this decision merely undermined the incentives for agricultural producers to sell their own produce, because it now became possible to sell less produce and still meet cash flow requirements and pay taxes. It is worth noting that the Provisional Government of Russia in the summer of 1997 adopted a similar decision. The gloomy fate of that government is well-known.

Another area of conflict between the different centers of power evolved into a protracted debate over who would assume political responsibility for such unavoidable measures as raising retail prices (at this point it was still too early to speak even halfway seriously of price liberalization). The USSR government tried to browbeat leaders of the republics into making decisions jointly. The republics' leaders, not surprisingly, categorically refused to do so. Finally, the central government was forced to do it alone in the spring of 1991, but only after replacing the prime minister.

A battle over economic reform programs also began at this time that later developed into a battle over programs to pull the country out of crisis, and then into a battle over reform programs. Various institutions of power and groups of economists that were connected to influential politicians worked actively on developing these reform programs. Typical of the times was the USSR's official program, prepared under Prime Minister Leonid Abalkin. The authors laid out three possible packages of anticrisis measures and market reforms—radical-liberal, moderate, and conservative. This group declared their commitment to the second course, a moderate reform package. The moderate option not only sought to avoid a swift move to a market economy through liberalization and privatization, it also tried to conserve the existing economic system and to strengthen administrative control over the economy. This option struck the authors as sensible and appropriate. It avoided extremes and, as should be the case with all "scientifically developed plans," promised the smoothest and least painful transition to a market-based economy. There was only one problem: no social forces (economic interest groups) were prepared to support it, and the "government of the moderates" had more or less exhausted its store of political trust. Accordingly, adopting one of the other alternatives, either the conservative or the radical path, would have required a change in the power elite.

Alongside the Abalkin program, two fundamentally different approaches to overcoming the crisis were taking shape. For the most part they do not exist as published documents (although several individual items were presented in programmatic form) because they were more abstract, comprising a series of measures to be discussed in society and whose implementation was considered desirable.

By the beginning of the 1990s a liberal market program had effectively been developed and presented to politicians. The basic feature of this program was the explicit recognition that privatization and some form of price liberalization were necessary. These positions were expressed in the "500 Days" program prepared under Stanislav Shatalin and Gregory Yavlinsky in the autumn of 1990, and in the program of market reforms prepared by Yegor Gaidar and colleagues in the autumn of 1991.

At about the same time, a fundamentally different model emerged that can be called an "administrative stabilization" model. Those social and economic groups that saw rapid transition to the market as a threat to their economic position rallied behind it. Essentially, administrative stabilization programs advocated freezing the processes of democratization (or even rolling them back), increasing control of the economy, and establishing concrete order (including macroeconomic order).

An important feature of these programs was the fundamental willingness of the political groups that stood behind them to take responsibility for their realization. The politicians, of course, were fully aware of the attendant risk to their reputations.

The first attempt at implementing a more or less consistent anti-crisis program of administrative stabilization was undertaken in 1991 with the dismissal of Nikolay Ryzhkov and the formation of a new cabinet of ministers under Valentin Pavlov. Gorbachev, after vacillating between various interest groups, decided to back the conservative wing of the CPSU and the Soviet *nomenklatura*.

The new government immediately set about displaying its strength and readiness to impose order by undertaking a series of senseless but politically clamorous actions, from the dispersion of demonstrators in Vilnius and Riga to the withdrawal of large-denomination ruble notes. The official platform was to support the military-industrial complex and domestic machine-building industry in general. This conservative program also included elements of xenophobic rhetoric, and a number of Western banks were accused of speculating in the Soviet currency. These flourishes were followed by the long-awaited decision on raising prices, which could have been the first step in stabilizing the goods market. A number of relevant draft laws were presented to the legislature that would have committed the country to a "regulated market economy."

This conservative program concluded with an attempt at political consolidation through a coup d'état on 19 August 1991. The coup, which was supported by a fairly broad spectrum of political forces, from the Communists under Ivan Polozkov to Vladimir Zhirinovsky's so-called Liberal Democrats, was carried out under the slogans of consolidation, stability, and patriotism. There was an almost complete absence of socialist or communist rhetoric from the leaders of the coup.

The defeat of the August putsch signaled the demise of "administrative stabilization." The economic situation progressively worsened. The only model that was still untried and that found resonance in the radical mood of the moment was the liberal market model. This model had not been discredited politically, and it enjoyed adequate political support.

Public opinion surveys demonstrated in general that the population was fed up with the authorities' indecisiveness and vacillation and was prepared for radical measures targeted at normalizing the economic situation. In reality, the surveys uncovered a peculiarly ambiguous attitude toward the prospect of reform.[17] However, the personal popularity of Boris Yeltsin added power to the liberal reform mandate. The experience of Poland, which by then had already implemented a similar set of measures for the past two years, also spoke in favor of the program.

Ultimately, at the Fifth Congress of the RSFSR People's Deputies, in November 1991, Yeltsin's program for market reforms was approved by an overwhelming majority. At the time, no one could predict with any precision how the reforms would work out, what forces would obstruct them, and how long it would take to implement them. But the authors of the liberal reforms had no doubt of their eventual success. Yeltsin declared, "Now the issue will be decided as to what kind of country Russia will be in the coming years and decades." This prophecy would be vindicated in full.

---

17. We have in mind the willingness of the majority of those polled to accept a temporary deterioration in their circumstances, and also the combination of support for private property and the market with but hostility toward free prices (see *Zerkalo mneniy* [Moscow: Institut sotsiologii, 1993]).

3   The Liberal Market Reform Program

Sergei Sinelnikov-Murylev
and Alexei Uluykaev

There is a substantial difference between abstract (and exclusively political) analysis targeted toward either enlightening the population or resolving certain political problems and a program that can be realized by implementing practical economic policies.

The 500 Days program mentioned in Chapter 2 represented a set of necessary and salutary reforms, but it completely failed to take into account the fiscal, technical, social, and other such constraints in the implementation of reforms. Who would undertake them? What would the appropriate legal and executive mechanisms be? Were the necessary financial resources available? Would the reforms meet serious opposition, and if so, what would have to be done? None of these questions was even raised, let alone answered.

Program-91—the program of economic reforms developed at the Institute of Economic Policy under Yegor Gaidar with the participation of a number of future members of the reform government—was extremely specific, answering not only the questions what and why, but also how, and how much would it cost. Thus, even in form it was very different from the other programs presented beforehand. It was not a single seamless text, intended as it were for publication as a booklet and for contemplation. Rather, the program was a collection of separate documents (the most important of which was *A Strategy for Russia in the Transition Period*), draft laws, orders, calculations, and appended explanatory notes. The contents of this program remain the subject of bitter dispute even today.

3.1. The Range of Opposing Views

Opinions on market reform can be divided into several categories. Some completely rejected the need for the radical market reform of the Russian economy. This group believed in the need to preserve the fundamentals of the former economic system with some modernization and stimulation. This view can be found in the books of left-wing politicians such as Gennady Zyuganov, Nikolay Ryzhkov, and Yegor Ligachev, and in articles published by socialist economists such as A. Buzgalin and A. Kolganov.

There were also economists and politicians who declared that market reforms were in principle necessary but should be less abrupt and radical. This group asserted that greater state participation in the economy, greater control over state property, and protectionist measures to defend domestic producers were necessary. In general, proponents of this reform path subscribed to the idea of "a special Russian way" of economic modernization. Such a view was promoted in the works of economists Leonid Abalkin, Stanislav Shatalin, Dmitry Lvov, O. Bogomolov, Y. Yaremenko, and Nikolai Shmelev, and was also voiced by so-called "statist politicians," such as Sergei Glazev, Yury Skokov, Arkady Volsky, Sergei Fedorov, and Yury Luzhkov. They believed that mass privatization, liberalization of foreign trade, currency convertibility, and price liberalization measures should not have been implemented. Instead, they supported the creation of powerful financial-industrial groups, selective state assistance to industry, and the provision of additional, mainly state, orders for domestically produced goods.

In a third and final group were those politicians and economists with solid reformist leanings. This group advocated various reform programs but was harshly critical of the reforms actually implemented. In their opinion, the reforms were either not correctly conceived or executed, and the sequence of reforms initiated was simply wrong. This group reasoned that privatization, demonopolization, and the formation of market structures should have been undertaken first, and only then should financial stabilization measures and economic liberalization have been introduced. Very high inflation was not considered a serious danger by this group. Gregory Yavlinsky, Nikolai Petrakov, A. Melnikov, and A. Mikhailov are among those who fall into this category.

3.2. Debates on How to Achieve Financial Stabilization

Beginning in 1992, economists and politicians advanced the most diverse ideas for achieving macroeconomic stabilization in Russia. It

The Liberal Market Reform Program

is worth pointing out that Program-91 in many respects suggested the ideas and recommendations put forward by various academics in upcoming years. Program-91 drew on the accumulated experiences of the previous successes and failures with reforms. Others' views regarding stabilization did change with time. Yavlinsky, for example, abandoned his theory that there was a "natural" level of inflation in Russia—approximately 10%–12% per month—and that this level should be accounted for when determining the size of the budget deficit. As inflation fell in 1995–1996, Yavlinsky, particularly in his campaign speeches as a presidential candidate in 1996, gradually lowered his estimate of the "natural" level of inflation.

A number of economists, including foreign economists, have advanced similar ideas, but generally formulated in stronger arguments. Rüdiger Dornbusch, for example, not convinced that the Russian executive branch possessed the political will to achieve financial stabilization, spoke in favor of indexation in line with inflation. He explained this in terms of the need to reduce economic uncertainty for economic agents, which would lead to increased incentives for saving and investment.[1]

Clearly, protracted high levels of inflation exert a negative influence on economic development and enterprise management. In particular, the management of uncertain macroeconomic variables, such as the relative prices of goods and services, interest rates, the exchange rate, and so on, was impeded. In this regard, the generally positive experience of Brazil, where comprehensive price indexation was introduced in order to stabilize relative prices, is also well-known.[2] However, comprehensive indexation in itself significantly

---

1. See Rüdiger Dornbusch, "Ya investiroval v Rossiyu, chtoby imet' kusok eë budushchego uspekha" (interview), *Kommersant* no. 48 (110), 20 December 1994.
2. See in particular Rüdiger Dornbusch and S. Edwards, eds., *The Macroeconomics of Populism in Latin America* (Chicago: University of Chicago Press, 1991); "Amerique Latine: Vers des sorties de crise Neo-Liberales," *Problemes Economiques* 2 (1990): 169; C. Himmelfarb, *Liberalisme et hyper-inflation en Argentine* (Institute d'Etudes politiques de Grenoble, 1994); *Cahiers des Ameriques Latines* 14 (Paris, 1992); E. Phelps, "Inflation in the Theory of Public Finance," *The Swedish Journal of Economics* 75 (1973); Stanley Fischer and Olivier Blanchard, *Lectures on Macroeconomics* (Cambridge, Mass.: MIT Press, 1990); "Dereglements monetaires et course aux innovations financiers en Amerique Latine," *Problemes Economiques* 2 (1990): 200; P. Salama and J. Valier, "Les Chemins escarpes de la hausse des prix en Amerique Latine," *Revue Tiers Monde* 129 (1992); P. Salama and J. Valier, "Politiques liberales et fin des processus hyperinflationnistes en Amerique Latine," *Problemes d'Amerique Latine* 5 (1992); idem, "The Difficult Road of Rising and Falling Inflation in Latin America," *Canadian Journal of Development Studies* 2 (1993).

complicates the process of financial stabilization, as raising incomes in line with prices tends to directly fuel inflation. In order to avert inflation, measures such as introducing full indexation must be taken reluctantly, and can only be justified when financial stabilization proves impossible due to political constraints.

A number of macroeconomic stabilization policy recommendations have been based on a nonmonetary conception of inflation in Russia. This view can be found in many works by Russian economists[3] and a number of foreign academics.[4] A detailed analysis of nonmonetarist views on the nature of inflation in Russia has been presented in other works.[5]

Among the factors determining inflation, some authors have cited not monetary policy but one or more of the following: (1) an imbalance in the structure of the economy; (2) the difficulty of reallocating resources from one sector to another; (3) the high level of monopoly in the Russian economy; (4) the movement of prices toward world levels after price liberalization; (5) the gradual raising of energy prices

---

3. See, for example, V. Volkonskiy, Ye. Gurevich, and G. Kantorovich, "Evolyutsiya tsen v Rossii: prichiny inflyatsii v ekonomike perekhodnogo perioda," in *Denezhnye i finansovye problemy perekhodnogo perioda v Rossii: rossiysko-frantsuzskiy dialog*, edited by V. Ivanter and Jacques Sapir (Moscow: Nauka, 1995); V. Maevskiy, "Odin iz shansov ozdorovleniya ekonomiki," *Finansy* 1 (1994); N. G. Nozdran' and I. S. Berezin, "Faktory i etapy razvitiya inflyatsii izderzhek v ekonomike Rossii," *Ekonomika i matematicheskie metody* 1 (1994); V. Pugachev and A. Pitelin, "Rossiyskaya inflyatsiya: traktovka, modelirovanie, metody bor'by," *Voprosy ekonomiki* 11 (1994); Barry Ikes, "Inflyatsiya v Rossii: uroki dlya reformatorov," *Voprosy ekonomiki* 3 (1995); A. Afanas'ev and O. Vite, "Inflatsiya izderzhek i finansovaya stabilizatsiya," *Voprosy ekonomiki* 3 (1995); D. Belousov and A. Klepach, "Monetarnye i nemonetarnye faktory inflyatsii v rossiiskoi ekonomike v 1992–1994," *Voprosy ekonomiki* 3 (1995).

4. In the work by M. Aglietta and Jacques Sapir ("Inflyatsiya i defitsit v perekhodnyi period," in *Denezhnye i finansovye problemy perekhodnogo perioda v Rossii: rossiysko-frantsuzkiy dialog*, edited by V. Ivanter and Jacques Sapir [Moscow: Nauka, 1995]), the authors draw conclusions about the nonmonetary character of Russian inflation based on the link between changes in wholesale prices and aggregate money supply. However, these conclusions are highly debatable, for multiple reasons. First, as the authors themselves note, statistical evidence attests to the unreliability of their results. Second, in Russia there is no reliable index of wholesale prices; those published by Goskomstat RF are based not on actual prices but on the prices declared by the enterprises themselves. Third, the argument that the existence of this link attests to the existence of "inflation costs" is itself contentious.

5. See, for example, the work by the Institute of Economic Analysis, "Finansovaya stabilizatsiya v Rossii," 1995. See also B. Granville, "Inflyatsiya: vysokaya tsena i nikakoy otdachi," *Voprosy ekonomiki* 3 (1995); Sergei Sinel'nikov, "Analyse des processus inflationnistes en Russie en 1992–1993," *Hyperinflation et stabilisation en Europe de l'Est et en Amerique Latine: Actes du Seminaire International*, Paris, 4–5 Nov. 1993.

and their liberalization; (6) the inadequacy of enterprises' responses to market conditions, in particular the tendency to set prices according to production costs and not according to supply and demand; (7) enterprises' soft budget constraints; (8) the total absence of responsibility on the part of enterprises for nonfulfillment of their contract obligations, a phenomenon supported by the lack of a functioning bankruptcy mechanism; and (9) the general cronyist mentality prevalent among enterprise managers.

Many conclusions have been reached about the nonmonetary character of Russian inflation and the prevalence of "cost inflation" based on an analysis of these and other factors. (These analyses are generally of a qualitative nature, but occasionally they are also quantitive.) Clearly, these factors do influence inflation. However, in a situation in which inflation exceeds 20%–30% per year, all of these nonmonetary factors fade into insignificance in comparison to factors such as the money supply and changes in economic agents' demand for real cash balances. In the short term, against a background of enterprises' nonmarket responses and shocks such as the liberalization of raw material and energy prices, raising the minimum wage can lead to increased inflation. However, if this increase is not accompanied by an accommodating monetary policy, the general price level will stabilize swiftly.

Nonmonetary views on inflation have served as the basis for criticizing tight fiscal policy as irrational. Members of this school of criticism believe that since inflation is primarily caused by nonmonetary factors, monetary emission should be used (increasing central bank credits to the government and the economy) to raise aggregate demand and stimulate production.

All these views in one way or another argue against the pursuit of financial stabilization as a goal in itself. Discussion of possible alternatives to a tight fiscal policy has been much rarer, although considerably more relevant. For example, Aleksashenko, Kostiukov, and Nikologorsky, among others, raised the important question of the rationality of fixing the exchange rate during the financial stabilization process.[6] In considering this issue, they took into account both the close links between exchange rate policy and control of the

---

6. S. Aleksashenko, Ye. Kostiukov, Nikologorsky, et al., *Upravlyaemy kurs: a pochemu by i net?! (Vozmozhnosti i posledstviya perekhoda k upravlyaemomu kursu rublya)*. (Moscow: Expertniy Institut RSPP, June 1995).

money supply, and the links between the growth of the real ruble exchange rate with the introduction of a fixed exchange rate or currency corridor during periods of inflation. Their analysis showed the desirability of a predictable exchange rate policy in which the exchange rate would lag behind the rate of inflation. Under such a policy, the exchange rate serves as a nominal anchor that restrains inflation, while the growth of the real ruble exchange rate, although having a negative impact on production, stimulates structural reform of the economy.

Russian economic literature has devoted little attention to the problem of choosing between orthodox and heterodox stabilization policies. Orthodox stabilization policy is based on tight control of the money supply and was practiced in the majority of Latin American countries during the 1980s and 1990s. These policies yielded positive results in Chile, Bolivia, and Mexico.[7] Heterodox stabilization, involving an active wage policy aimed at breaking the wage-price spiral, was successfully implemented in Israel.[8] In Russia there was no mechanism for the automatic indexation of wages to consumer prices, and thus there was no need for a specific policy of wage controls.

3.3. The Socioeconomic Situation on the Eve of Reforms

In order to assess the accuracy of the views and recommendations advanced, it is worth examining the actual state of the Russian economy on the eve of reforms, at the end of 1991. At this juncture two questions are relevant: (1) Could radical economic reforms have been delayed? (2) Could the reform program have been altered significantly? To answer these questions it is useful to examine such factors as the gold and hard currency reserves, food and other supplies, goods stocks, and the money supply.

The political and economic situation at the end of 1991 was catastrophic. Over the course of one year, national income had fallen by more than 11%, gross domestic product by 13%, industrial production by 2.8%, agricultural production by 4.5%, extraction of oil and

---

7. M. Bruno, G. di Tella, Rüdiger Dornbusch, and Stanley Fischer, eds., *Inflation Stabilization: The Experiences of Israel, Argentina, Brazil, Bolivia, and Mexico* (Cambridge, Mass.: MIT Press, 1989).
8. M. A. Kiguel and N. Liviatan, "The Old and the New in Heterodox Stabilization Programs," World Bank Working Paper, 1989; idem, "The Business Cycle Associated with Exchange-rate Based Stabilization," *World Bank Economic Review* 6 (1991).

coal by 11%, iron smelting by 17%, and food production by more than 10%. Also, gross grain collection had fallen by 24% and state procurement by 34%. The drop in foreign trade turnover was particularly drastic, falling by 37%, while the volume of exports fell by 35% and the volume of imports fell by 46%.

Moreover, none of the restrictions on demand that were the main factors in the economic recession of the upcoming years were present at the time. Money continued to be pumped into the economy at an ever faster rate than before. A significant part in the development of this crisis was rooted in the struggle between Union and Russian authorities. These two centers of authority were competing to approve all kinds of new social expenditures and to finance ill-thought-out investment programs—both of which increased the budget deficit.

Consequently, all monetary indicators grew significantly. Enterprise profits increased in nominal terms by a factor of 1.9, the income of the population doubled, and the money supply increased by a factor of 4.4. Consumer prices more than doubled (increasing by 101.2%), a phenomenon that was completely uncharacteristic for the socialist economy: a year earlier inflation had been just 5%.

External debt, denominated in convertible currency, increased to $76 billion, while internal hard currency debt rose to $5.6 billion and arrears on clearing operations surpassed $29 billion. Gold and foreign currency reserves decreased sharply, and for the first time in the history of the Soviet Union, gold reserves fell below 300 tonnes (289.6 tonnes on 1 January 1992). The shortfall of hard currency income derived from centralized exports to pay for centralized imports, and clear external debts, reached $10.6 billion in the first ten months of 1991 (prior to the formation of the Yeltsin-Gaidar reform government). In order to cover this deficit, the last USSR government sold part of the country's gold reserves for $3.4 billion and spent hard currency to the tune of $5.5 billion, which it took from the Vneshekonombank USSR accounts of enterprises, organizations, and local governments.

Control over fiscal policy and the money supply quickly unraveled. There was an increase in the dollarization of the economy, money was increasingly replaced by barter, and the administrative restrictions on interregional trade grew. As a consequence, the republics of the former USSR introduced de facto money surrogates (coupons, purchase cards, and so forth) and in a number of cases (Ukraine,

Estonia, Latvia, and Lithuania) prepared to introduce their own national currencies. This led to an increase in the amount of money in circulation, both in the former republics and in Russia, further aggravating the difficult financial situation.

The state budget deficit for 1991 was six times greater than planned and, according to our calculations, reached about 21% of GDP (the sum of the Union and Russian Federation budget deficits). In addition, the former Soviet republics actually stopped transferring money to the Union coffers, which means that the aforementioned estimate of the consolidated state budget deficit for 1991 is on the low side. According to World Bank estimates, based on a calculation of sources available for financing the budget deficit (enterprises' accounts, the population's savings, a current account surplus), the budget deficit totaled 30.9% of GDP.[9]

Combined with this budgetary crisis, there was a goods shortage in almost all categories. The ratio of household money savings to goods stocks sharply deteriorated (by a factor of five compared with 1970 and more than twice compared with 1985). The goods stocks in retail trade fell to a record low.

The situation with the urban food supply most graphically illustrates the prereform socioeconomic situation. (To emphasize the sociopolitical degradation that occurred pre-1991, the Petrograd bread crisis of February 1917, which was of similar magnitude, was the likely cause of the autocracy's overthrow.) Food supplies virtually broke down as a result of the complete paralysis of all levels of the bureaucracy. Thus, in January 1992 food grain reserves were about 3 million tonnes (excluding imports), while the country's requirements were in excess of 5 million tonnes per month. In more than sixty of Russia's eighty-nine regions there were no reserves of food grain at all, and flour could be produced only by the swift processing of imported grain. The minimum required grain import during this period was therefore around 3 million tonnes per month. According to the estimates of Roskhleboprodukt, in the first half of 1992 Russia produced 8.65 million tonnes of grain, where 26 million tonnes were required. Thus the deficit for the first half-year was 17.35 million tonnes, which would have cost over $3 billion to cover.

At the same time, there were a number of instances in which imported grain remained unloaded in Russian ports because there was

---

9. See *Russian Economic Reform: Crossing the Threshold of Structural Change* (World Bank, 1992).

The Liberal Market Reform Program

no foreign currency to pay for its transportation. The prime cause of this was the fact that credit lines were not open because the former USSR's reputation as a first-class debtor had been totally detroyed in the preceding years. In cities throughout the country a strict rationing system was introduced. The sale of all staple foodstuffs was rationed, including meat products, butter, vegetable oil, cereals, pasta, sugar, salt, confectionary, milk products, matches, alcoholic drinks, and tobacco products. Rations of foodstuffs by the end of 1991 were roughly as follows: sugar—1 kg per person per month; meat products—0.5 kg; and butter—0.2 kg. Nonetheless, there were not even sufficient resources to ensure these minimal levels. Supply was simply not guaranteed; food coupons were not exchanged for several months at a time, and people had to stand in long lines to obtain goods.

3.4. The Need to Accelerate Reforms

In light of this economic malaise, the statements of a number of politicians and economists (particularly Gregory Yavlinsky) regarding the need to conduct privatization and demonopolization first, and only then to liberalize prices, seem inappropriate. In 1991 Russia simply did not have such a choice. The destruction of the fundamentals of the economy could have reached catastrophic proportions and become difficult to reverse. In reality there could be no delays in launching market reforms, and without liberalizing prices, this was impossible.

Against the backdrop of deteriorating living standards, the post-August euphoria turned into mass political disappointment over the lack of real reforms. This was the case within the democratic movement as well, which did not know how to utilize the August victory and did not have any serious programs (unless one counts propagandist programs such as the 500 Days plan). It was also true of broad swaths of the population, whose social expectations had been raised after August. These expectations diverged significantly from reality. The country's political leadership quickly used up its stock of goodwill and popular support.

The state bureaucracy did not work, due to expectations of imminent reorganization, retrenchment, and the like. Spontaneous privatization took off like wildfire. State structures, ministries, and departments transformed themselves into concerns, corporations, or associations. Embezzlement of state property took place en masse: civil servants took with them not only the contacts and know-how they had acquired on the job, but also the financial resources they could access. They acquired full control rights over property without being subject to the financial discipline of a real owner. The state proved incapable of exercising any control over the situation.

Negotiations with the leaders of other former republics of the USSR on possible ways of transforming the former Soviet Union, including coordinating reforms and conducting agreed-upon policy in at least the most important areas, reached deadlock. The political and economic policies of the former Soviet republics' governments diverged more and more. Some of the former republics, the Baltics in particular, chose the path of radical socioeconomic reforms. Others tried either to avoid radical reforms completely or to moderate and postpone them as much as possible.

Based on the above, it is clear that the real policy choice at the time was not over the timing of the start of radical reforms or the sequence of reforms, or over whether price liberalization should precede privatization or vice versa. Rather, the real question revolved around two completely different options: (1) whether the reform of the Russian economy should be conducted while keeping the fundamentals of the Soviet state and the integrated economy in place, and therefore also maintaining the rudiments of the corresponding economic policy (as essentially the Gorbachev, Silaev, and Yavlinsky groups proposed), or (2) whether to implement a strategy that would allow Russia to attain economic independence and to conduct independent economic reforms as quickly as possible (as proposed by the authors of Program-91).

Typical apparatchik reactions—fear, failure to comprehend the scale of the challenges, an inability to see the need for systemic transformation behind the concrete problems of monetary overhang, goods shortages, and a disintegrating budget—provided support for the first option. On the other hand, analysis of global experiences, analysis of the developmental alternatives for the Russian economy depending on the selection of this or that scenario, the general political logic of the moment, and the unity of tactical and strategic aims—all of these provided arguments in favor of the second option. In the end, a version of Program-91 was adopted and partially implemented.

3.5. Russia's Progress Toward Economic Independence

The need for realizing this program in particular, out of the many that existed at the time, was determined by a new fundamental understanding of the laws of socioeconomic development in the post-Soviet bloc. This understanding made independent economic reforms—those not coordinated with the other Soviet republics—unavoidable. But these reforms were pursued in close conformity with political and institutional reforms that would promote the consolidation of Russia's sovereign status and establish the institutions of a capitalist socioeconomic system.

Of ultimate political importance was the realization that after August 1991, Russia's relations with the other former Soviet republics and the Union center changed fundamentally. Contrary to the dominant political mythology, which attributes excessive importance to official legal actions, *the Soviet Union effectively collapsed on 19–21 August 1991 and from that moment on existed only nominally, functioning neither as a state machine nor as an organ for conducting economic—or indeed any other—policy.* The issue was not whether the principles on which the Soviet Union had been built were good or bad, but what to do when these principles did not work. The republics declared the federal property located on their territory to be their own, and refused to meet any of their economic obligations to the Union. This was the genesis of uncontrollable mass embezzlement not only of property, but also of rights, obligations, regulations, administrative procedures, and so on.

The Union as a political and economic entity had already ceased to exist, even as speculation about its preservation continued in force. Thus, in the shortest possible time and in the most difficult of circumstances, it was necessary to develop a strategy not only for economic survival, but also for the further development of everything—all spheres of the country and society. All of this had to be developed during the sudden death of one state and the emergence of a new one.

It is important to bear in mind that after the effective collapse of the Union center, the contradictions between Russia's interests and those of the other republics came into play. These contradictions were related to many differences: the size of the economies, their resource endowments, their understanding of the prospects for historical development, and the political weight they had in the eyes of the international community. For the other former Soviet republics, preserving the existing resource flows and fiscal relations—and indeed, discussion of a single economic space and the advantages of economic integration continued—would, however, have opened up the possibility of reconstructing their economies at Russia's expense. This would have entailed a considerable additional burden on the Russian economy, undermining any possibility for socioeconomic revival.

In short, "economic union with immediate political autonomy" was very much in the interests of the other republics because it meant access to Russia's financial and economic resources while freeing the Union's political and legal legacy. Russia's interests lay in "the most rapid achievement of economic independence while preserving political union for a transitional period."

In our opinion, adoption of the first scheme would have led to an aggravation of economic and sociopolitical tensions, including dividing up the fiscal pie, searching out those responsible for underfunding of this or that sphere, latent protectionism, and continuation of the "dual power" of Union and republic institutions. It would also have led to constant vacillations in public expenditure and credit policy shaped by interrepublic compromises, and to an intensification of the inflation crisis. These heightened tensions would therefore have led to chronic political instability, social tension, and the overthrow of democracy on the territory of the former USSR.

In the military sphere, maintaining the Soviet Union would have meant the emergence of new nuclear states with unstable interstate relations and interstate boundaries; the appearance on Russia's borders of new and powerful potential aggressor states; and Russia's joining the international community not as a great power, the legal successor to the former Soviet Union, but as a new subject of the international community, with all the problems that follow.

The only responsible political step was the immediate assertion of full economic autonomy for Russia and the independent implementation of reforms. The other republics could also independently join such reforms (or, more precisely, could not afford to do otherwise).

The political and economic logic of this historical epoch thrust upon Russia the leadership of economic reforms on the territory of the former USSR. The overwhelming majority of the former USSR's export-oriented industries were located in Russia, and therefore only

Russia could take on the Soviet Union's foreign-debt obligations. This action also gave Russia a strong claim to the gold and foreign currency holdings, property abroad, and the debts of other countries to the Soviet Union. Russia, instead of the USSR, became the leading partner of Western states and international financial organizations. Russia held the dominant cards: it had an exceedingly capacious domestic market and exportable natural wealth that could easily be redirected from traditional export markets to developed countries. The foreign economic policy of the other republics, which for the most part were not in this position, was therefore inextricably tied to Russia. Finally, Russia controlled the lion's share of the interrepublic manufacturing infrastructure, and it independently had the material and human capital to run its transportation, communication, and energy systems. Thus, extricating Russia from any kind of long-term, all-encompassing economic union and avoiding any commitment to suprarepublican institutions of economic coordination seemed to be the most sensible course.

Related to this was the insistence that all state property on Russian territory be recognized as Russian property, and also that the Russian state control the money supply in the ruble zone as long as it remained in existence. The only alternative would have been to install mechanisms for conducting an effective and tight monetary policy (and only in this case could a single monetary and banking system have been preserved on the territory of the former Soviet Union). However, as the experience of the following years would show, such mechanisms proved almost impossible to establish even in the monetary union between Russia and Belarus.

As was anticipated by those who developed the Russian program of economic reforms, a considerable balance-of-payments deficit developed in the republics' trade with Russia. This positive balance gave Russia powerful leverage in financial and economic negotiations and interactions with the republics.

It is useful to analyze, both retrospectively and prospectively, the differences between the two fundamental conceptions of economic reform in socialism's legacy: Gaidar's and Yavlinsky's. The program proposed by Yavlinsky essentially entailed holding back economic reform in Russia so that joint reforms could be conducted simultaneously in member republics of the economic union. However, restraining economic reform was clearly impossible, given the dramatic political and economic situation. Gaidar's program, on the other hand, was targeted at implementing economic reform in Russia as quickly as possible, without the restraints of reactionary policies in the other republics. This program permitted the introduction of market mechanisms, guaranteeing the noncatastrophic, systemic transformation of Russia.

3.6. The Essence of Socioeconomic Reforms in Russia's Transition Period

Several points distinguish Program-91 not only from Yavlinsky's program, but also from the other well-known programs of the time (such as those of Saburov, Shatalin, and Abalkin, among others).

First, Program-91 completely rejected the idea of a "special path" for Russian economic development and, in line with the majority of tried and tested stabilization programs throughout the world, concentrated first and foremost on reforming and nursing the monetary sector.

Second, Program-91 was not only an economic reform program but also, perhaps most importantly, a program for the creation of a Russian nation-state. This goal was exemplified by the sovereignty of Russian economic legislation, a national monetary program, a national currency, a Russian tax, a national budget, an independent foreign economic policy, state property, and instruments for state regulation of the economy.

In essence, the philosophy and ideology of the Program-91 reforms are spelled out in two documents, *A Strategy for Russia in the Transition Period* and *Russia's Immediate Economic Prospects*. The other documents—and there were several dozen—represented technical appendices, defining what had to be done and what regulations were needed.

A Strategy for Russia in the Transition Period defined the fundamental course as economic independence within a "soft" political union. This path was approved by President Yeltsin and then put into practice by the Gaidar and Chernomyrdin governments. At the core of this program were not only crucial economic reforms (marketization, liberalization, privatization, and financial stabilization) but also the creation of a sovereign Russian state with all of the necessary instruments, including a stable and convertible national currency, a tax system, a budget, a customs service, an effective monetary system, and a national bank.

The Liberal Market Reform Program

The second most important document produced by the Gaidar group, *Russia's Immediate Economic Prospects*, defined the philosophy of stabilization and reformist policies in the context of creating the institutions of Russian national statehood. It was in this document that the conclusion was first reached (a conclusion that was repeatedly modified in subsequent Russian reform programs) that economic policy in the near future would be defined not by the reformers' ideal plans but by a combination of three critical factors, bequeathed to Russia in the legacy of the Soviet Union's collapsed economy:

- *the inflation crisis* (a massive macroeconomic imbalance manifesting itself in accelerating open inflation and a severe shortage of all goods)
- *the payments crisis* (a severe shortage of gold and foreign currency reserves and the undermining of the country's creditworthiness, which would lead to a sharp drop in imports)
- *the systemic crisis* (the loss of ability of state institutions at all levels to regulate resource flows)

It was not the simple copying of a standard stabilization program, but these specifically Russian political and economic realities that forced Gaidar's group to launch fiscal and monetary policies as the initial objects of their stabilization and reform efforts.

It became clear that in the absence of financial stabilization, with paralyzed nonmarket mechanisms for the distribution of resources, it was impossible to create market mechanisms that could save the country from the very real threat of mass starvation. In particular, it was impossible to channel entrepreneurial activity away from speculation and into production and to attract both domestic and foreign investment.

The initial version of the reform program did not envision full liberalization at the initial stage but streamlining, restructuring, and a substantial increase in the general price level (roughly as the last communist government in Poland under Rakovksy had done). Only after that was it intended that full price liberalization would be implemented, with simultaneous macroeconomic stabilization. The basis this stabilization was to be the introduction of a Russian national currency, which would cut off non-Russian sources of money.

However, by the end of November 1991 this idea had to be abandoned. Working in the government provided access to additional information about the real socioeconomic situation in the country, and this data showed that the country would simply not survive another six months of high inflation (that is, the fast growth of administrative prices with continuing goods shortages). Such a crisis would exhaust the government's stock of trust by the time "real reforms" and "real liberalization" were implemented. Thus, the only option was immediate price liberalization, although this introduced the risk of destabilizing pressures being exerted by rubles emanating from the former Soviet republics.

This was a show of political realism. In reality, separating monetary systems required much more time than was initially thought and, because of complications, had to be implemented in several stages. Russian industrialists, industrialists of the other former Soviet republics, the governments of those republics, and a wide spectrum of political forces from Rutskoy to Yavlinsky all lobbied aggressively for the preservation of the ruble zone. Unfortunately, in the initial phase, such organizations as the International Monetary Fund and the European Commission were also among those advocating maintenance of the ruble zone.

In these conditions the swift introduction of a new currency proved impossible, and for technical reasons as well as political reasons, separating the bank accounts of the former Soviet republics required a good deal of time. This complicated and delayed financial stabilization considerably.

3.7. Cutting the Budget Deficit

A sharp reduction in the budget deficit was a necessary condition for achieving macroeconomic stability. To this end, a significant reduction in expenditures was planned, to be achieved by cutting the military budget, transferring certain expenditures to the former Soviet republics, and implementing price and enterprise subsidies. It was also necessary to find sources of budget revenue that could operate in conditions of high inflation. Above all, this meant a shift to indirect taxation. Along with a turnover and sales tax, a new value-added tax (VAT) and a new excise schedule were introduced. Also, a new export tax on fuel was introduced, while the former system of licenses and quotas was abolished.

The money earmarked for weapons procurement was reduced by a factor of 7.5, centralized capital investments were reduced by a factor of 1.5, price subsidies were cut to a third of previous levels, and the financing of foreign states was almost completely halted (with the exception of CIS countries). In this manner the budget deficit was supposed to be cut overall by at least a factor of three. As it turned out, it was initially reduced even further than expected, and in the first quarter the budget was even in surplus. However, after some time the deficit started to expand again as a result of pressure from sectorial and regional lobbies.

Whereas the introduction of the VAT, a measure that did not directly impinge on significant corporate interests, was possible when the reformers conceived it, the introduction of other measures was more difficult. The abolition of price subsidies had to be carried out gradually over the course of three years owing to powerful opposition, especially in the regions. The cutting of enterprise subsidies was also a rather long-drawn-out process. The government on several occasions announced its intention to abolish licenses and quotas, but not until 1996 did it manage to fully realize this measure.

It was also impossible to start reforms without substantial legislative changes. Several dozen legislative acts underwent amendment, and a number of laws were put forward for re-adoption. The presidential decree on the liberalization of prices and reorganization of trade was the most revolutionary of the acts proposed. First, it permitted enterprises themselves to set the prices on their products. Second, it abolished the centrally planned allocation of resources, granting enterprises the right to buy and sell inputs and products themselves. Third, it allowed trade companies to negotiate prices on all kinds of goods and services. Fourth, it laid the foundations for the commercialization of state supply organizations. Fifth, it introduced control over the prices of monopoly enterprises. Sixth, it laid the foundations for demonopolization of wholesale and retail trade. And seventh, it abolished the ban on nonstate trading firms.

In other words, everything that economists and politicians had discussed for years during the perestroika period was introduced by a single act, and the foundation of the planned economy was completely destroyed. After price liberalization the Russian economy ceased to be socialist. Of course, Russia was far from being a capitalist economy. Although the actual progress of the reforms did not entirely coincide with the reformers' intentions, and a number of the reforms took several years to be fulfilled, Russian capitalism started to revive after a difficult and prolonged interruption.

II Macroeconomic Processes and Economic Policy of Postcommunist Russia— Main Stages

4 General Macroeconomic Problems of the Postsocialist Transition in Russia

Sergei Sinelnikov-Murylev
and Georgy Trofimov

This chapter considers a range of general economic problems that arose in the course of implementing financial stabilization in Russia. All the issues touched on here are comprehensively analyzed in the following chapters. Consequently, we shall not furnish detailed statistical evidence to illustrate the recurring issues of transition under discussion.

4.1. Financial Relations and Their Place in the Analysis of the Transition Economy

In the planned economy, financial relations played a subordinate role to the task of forming (natural-physical) ratios. This was reflected in the priorities of Soviet economics. In accordance, when Russian economic reform pushed the issues of public finance to the fore, it became clear that many of the relationships between economic policy and socioeconomic processes, well established in the context of developed market economies, did not apply naturally to transition economies. This observation applies to two phenomena: (1) the influence of monetary, tax, and budgetary policy on a macroeconomic situation characterized by high rates of inflation, unemployment, interest, and other measures, and (2) the impact of economic policy on the level of relative prices for products and factors of production, on production volumes in various sectors, on the relationships between different factors of production as determined by saving and investment rates, the labor supply, and so on.

A large number of such relationships in transition economies are still underanalyzed. Opportunities for serious research on these topics in Russia and other postcommunist countries are restricted by at least three factors.

First, official statistics do not always accord with reality. Only in the past two to three years have the methods used by Russian statistical agencies begun to be adjusted to international standards. Second, the vast range of theoretical and empirical knowledge accumulated by economic science in the former communist world before the 1990s did not consider the transition from socialism to capitalism as a serious issue. Third, market transformation is characterized by fluctuations in basic macroeconomic indicators of such magnitude that the resulting instability makes it impossible to discover many of these important and traditionally stable relationships.

4.2. Predeterminacy of Economic Reforms in Russia

The sharp budgetary deterioration in 1991 was not unexpected. Fiscal imbalances began to increase in the Soviet Union around the mid-1980s. One of the most important causes of the budget crisis was the degradation of the hierarchical system of economic management. This process was caused by the weakening of the traditionally repressive management mechanism and the removal of inherently socialist production incentives. Attempts to compensate for these changes with partial reforms of the planned economy proved completely ineffective and only accelerated the disintegration of the hierarchical economy. The growth of the share of revenues at the disposal of enterprises caused government revenues to fall. Abandonment of rigid wholesale price controls, while retail prices remained fixed automatically, reduced receipts from the turnover tax[1] and increased government spending on subsidies.

The following factors were also important in inducing budgetary imbalances prior to the disintegration of the socialist system: (1) a fall in oil and energy prices in the second half of the 1980s, (2) errors in economic policy (abortive attempts at new industrialization and the antialcohol campaign, a sharp fall in budgetary income), (3) growth in Afghanistan-related defense expenditures, and (4) technological and natural cataclysms (the Chernobyl disaster, the Spitak earthquake). According to World Bank estimates, in 1991 the budget deficit of the now defunct Soviet Union was around 33% of GDP.[2] This deficit was financed from forced household and enterprise savings.

---

1. This tax was set with reference to the difference between wholesale and retail prices and was one of the main sources of budget revenue.
2. *Russian Economic Reform: Crossing the Threshold of Structural Change* (Washington, D.C.: World Bank, 1992).

This fiscal position unambiguously determined the range of realistic options for reforming the Russian economy by early 1992. It also set the sequence of appropriate measures relating to systemic transformation, financial stabilization, and structural reform. By late 1991 a gradualist transformation of the hierarchical economic system through the simultaneous implementation of institutional and structural changes had ceased to be a viable option. Understandably, the lack of development in the legal system, the absence of market institutions, the dominance of state property, and monopolization of the economy complicated the task of financial stabilization. However, the collapse of the financial system did not allow much time for the institutional transformation required to supplement radical liberalization of the economy.

In the initial phase of economic reforms, the gradual introduction of market elements is typically constrained within the limits of the communist system. The experience of Hungary, Yugoslavia, China, and Vietnam are pertinent examples. In the late 1980s the USSR introduced several measures in accordance with this approach: elements of legalized trade followed the adoption of the Law on Cooperation, the beginnings of banking reform, and a degree of trade liberalization. In principle, further gradual reform would have been possible had it not been for the severe crisis of public finances, the balance of payments, and external debt, as well as the degradation of the system of administrative management and looming hyperinflation. For this reason, the initial strategy of market reforms in postcommunist Russia was framed not in terms of gradualism or "shock therapy" but in reference to economic and physical survival.

Theoretical arguments in favor of gradualism boil down to the following proposition: gradual implementation of reforms entails less social pain and is therefore more likely to be supported by the population at large. Such a series of mutually complementary reforms (price liberalization, privatization, financial stabilization, deregulation of external trade, a set of structural reforms, and so on) is harder to coordinate. Such a reform path carries higher macroeconomic risk in the event of failure, and specific policy mistakes may cause substantial social dislocation. On the other hand, "shock therapy," as distinct from gradual changes, makes reform less prone to reversal.

It is apparent that gradualism is the best strategy when there are serious political obstacles in the way of adopting a comprehensive package of reforms. In Russia, in late 1991, there arose conditions conducive to radical reform, as a result of the August victory of the democratic forces and the emerging economic crisis. However, the window of opportunity turned out to be short-lived: it ended with the beginning of consolidation and the rise in activity of the counterreformist groups as early as spring 1992.

As a rule, reforms do not occur in one fell swoop but as a complex process with a high degree of interdependency. Even in the event of package decision making, of which Russia is a case in point, as the political situation evolves, reforms can be transformed into a sequence of either fairly gradual or delayed measures. Nonetheless, price liberalization in Russia was an exception, since it was implemented within an extremely short span of time and led to effectively irreversible changes not only in the structure of the economy but above all in the behavior of economic agents.

4.3. Price Liberalization: A "Shock" in the System of Gradual Reforms

The price liberalization of early 1992 aimed to solve several problems. The first was to reduce financial imbalances in the economy. This goal was achieved through the reduction of price subsidies and the use of the VAT made possible by free prices. Second, price liberalization for a short period removed the monetary overhang created by the inflationary policies of previous years. Third, changes in relative prices established the preconditions for a more efficient distribution of resources. Fourth, free prices in various forms introduced elements of competition into the behavior of, and interaction between, firms. Finally, the disappearance of product shortages was reflected in household behavior, as it sharply reduced demand and did away with long queues in stores.

The lifting of currency restrictions that followed, in the summer of 1992, entailed a single rate of exchange (internal convertibility of the ruble) and led to reduced import subsidies. Opening up the economy was as important as price liberalization. It became possible, within a short period of time, to generate an inflow of consumer imports and provide a market solution to the problem of chronic product shortages.

The economic reforms of the first months of 1992 were comprehensive in nature. The government stressed putting its fiscal house in order, which was fully consonant with the logic of radical reforms and the macroeconomic requirements of the Russian situation. In particular, defense spending was significantly curtailed, a process that induced a positive structural shift toward demilitarization of the economy.

In 1992 the central bank was not yet an independent institution with the sole responsibility for price stability. Its status in the first two years of reform was quite vague, a reality that made for a poor monetary policy. Monetary targeting, which sharply limits internal financing, was not used. Nevertheless, thanks to the efforts of the reformist government then in charge, during its first months in power the central bank was able to limit the monetary supply. This became possible due to the temporary weakening of the opposition and of the organization of pro-inflationary lobbies in Parliament. The fact that there was no automatic indexing of government spending to inflation was also a positive factor.

As a result of price liberalization, the fall in production accelerated. This effect was observable in all postcommunist countries without exception.[3] The principal reason for the decline in production in postsocialist countries had to do with the "artificiality" of economic growth during the previous decades, a growth based on the exploitation of the USSR's natural resources.[4] The fall in production, then, was triggered by the introduction of market mechanisms, which led to diminishing demand domestically and increased competition from foreign producers. Liberalization of prices revealed not only the true extent of suppressed inflation but also the degree of overproduction that had existed for many years alongside product shortages in the socialist economy.

A reduction in government consumption was one of the factors that determined the depth of the production fall. It may seem that the decline could have been less profound if the state had continued to maintain aggregate demand through artificial means. However, future developments revealed the complete futility of attempts to

---

3. Official statistics most likely overestimated the depth of this fall, as they could not take into account growth in the "gray" sector, nor could they realistically reflect the contribution of services to GDP. Indirectly, this fact can be corroborated by reference to the less dramatic fall in consumption as compared to production. Nonetheless, even adjusted production figures show a considerable decline, by no less than one-third over the years 1989–1994. See E. Gavrilenkov and V. Koen, *How Large Was the Output Collapse in Russia?* (Washington, D.C.: International Monetary Fund, 1995).

4. Ye. Gaidar, *Anomalii ekonomicheskogo rosta* (Moscow: Yevraziya, 1997).

stimulate demand in the context of a transition economy. Any reduction in the decline of production accomplished via injections of credit (against a background of short-term price rigidity) was only temporary.

Therefore, the fall in Russia's GDP in 1992–1996 occurred as a consequence of structural shifts and independently of fiscal and monetary policies. It could not have been prevented by standard techniques of government intervention.

In the first months of reforms, the effect of a contraction in demand was amplified by the disorganization of economic ties. This disorganization led to a sharp fall in supply. The rupture of ties was an inevitable result of the absence of sufficiently developed market mechanisms to guide the behavior of economic agents. Perhaps this is why many enterprise directors from the outset had chosen a conservative strategy meant to preserve the status quo, without expending much effort on searching for new suppliers and buyers. However, in the majority of cases senior management simply proved incapable of assessing the consequences of the unfolding changes and merely hoped for an imminent reversal of reforms.

A sharp rise in prices during 1992 led to a reduction in working capital, from which all enterprises suffered in equal measure. Their reaction to this shock revealed differences in behavior, competence, and managerial incentives. As a result of price liberalization, barter deals and mutual nonpayments began to rise. Barter had been the usual form of exchange in the shortage economy of the 1980s, a phenomenon that supplemented the tenuous production ties imposed from the center. It is not accidental, then, that enterprise directors continued to use these horizontal economic ties in the customary fashion under market conditions. With time, barter became not just a function of a shortage in turnover funds, but also a means for tax evasion.

For many enterprises the growth of mutual arrears in 1992 was to a large extent determined by the drawbacks in the clearing system. In a number of cases, habitual supplies were continued, without any assessment of the financial viability of the counter-party trade. The growth in interenterprise arrears was also driven by high inflation, which encouraged delays in payments by enterprises and financial intermediaries alike. In similar fashion to barter, payment arrears subsequently became useful for tax evasion on a large scale and for the appropriation of a portion of revenues by senior management.[5]

The reaction of economic agents and the state to the inflationary shock in 1992 revealed a fundamental problem inherited from the socialist economy—soft budget constraints. In a situation in which the state wants to prevent the bankruptcy of key enterprises, managers can exploit the situation. Adverse selection applies, giving an advantage to the least efficient enterprises. In particular, the management of such enterprises refrains from restructuring and continues to manufacture outdated products and sell them through nonmonetary exchange.

In the first three reform years such expectations of the managerial elite proved largely justified, since the state itself contributed to the restoration of soft budgetary constraints. For example, the mutual arrears in autumn 1992, which resulted from massive injection of money into the economy, demonstrated the willingness of the state to abandon the principles of financial stabilization and keep nonprofitable enterprises afloat. The inconsistent and gradualist policies

---

5. Appendix I presents a model for the dynamic of nonpayments. The rate of growth in real GDP and real money supply, the real rate of GKOs, and overdue debts with a certain lag are the exogenous variables. Our assessment of the parameters shows that the growth in interfirm arrears was affected by the preceding changes in business activity (negatively), changes in real bond yields in the preceding period (positively), the dynamic of the nominal interest rates of GKOs (positively), nonimplementation of federal government spending (negatively), and preceding changes in overdue debts (positively). Of these factors, nominal and real interest rates have the greatest effect (in terms of elasticity) on payment arrears, in large part because of the liquidity effect relating to the supply of money. Growth in the nominal money supply leads to an inflationary growth of the nominal rate of interest, shrinkage of profits, and growth of payment arrears.

In Appendix II we analyze a set of microeconomic hypotheses explaining the dynamic of interfirm arrears that takes into account the behavior of manufacturers. We evaluate regression equations that link the growth of overdue indebtedness to suppliers to the yield rates and turnover on the GKO market, the price index for manufacturing enterprises, relative electricity prices, the volume of off-loaded products, growth in the share of loss-making enterprises in the economy, budget arrears, the share of money in GDP, the federal budget deficit, and other macroeconomic parameters. The growth in arrears is accompanied by manufacturers' losses, an association that is confirmed by a positive correlation between the size of arrears and the share of loss-making enterprises in the economy. The hypothesis that budget arrears are an important source of arrears in the economy as a whole finds confirmation in the positive correlation between the size of the budget deficit (as an indicator of the state's indebtedness vis-à-vis recipients of budgetary funds) and the dynamic of combined arrears.

pursued in 1993–1994 resulted from essentially the same problem, which was occurring against the background of social exhaustion and the perceivable influence of now consolidated interest groups. The interaction of political and economic motives fueled the inflation of 1992–1994 and subsequently the aggravation of the Russian fiscal crisis.

4.4. Political Restrictions and Delayed Stabilization

Research on Russia's transition economy generally focuses on analyzing the factors that determined economic policy and on the failures in stabilization efforts that ensued until the first success of monetary stabilization in 1995–1996 (a success that was undermined by the financial crisis of August 1998). Particular attention is paid to the balance of forces between reformers and conservatives as expressed in the policies of the government, Parliament, the central bank, and other institutions in some of the Russian regions. An important role in the formation of budgetary policies was played by various lobbies, both traditional (agricultural, military-industrial) and new (banking, export, import, and so on).

Two main reasons account for the instability of budgetary policy after liberalization. First, there was no constitutional framework to regulate the interaction between the legislature, the executive branch, and the judiciary. Given the extent of the opposition to reform, this situation gave rise to incoherent financial policies. Second, the executive branch was essentially coalitional in nature. The coalition included representatives from various interest groups, a reality that led to arbitrary and inconsistent decision making. This state of affairs confirmed the well-known proposition that lobbies exert far greater influence on economic policies in young democracies than in established democracies.[6]

Two other groups of factors were important in determining the state of public finances and budgetary policy. The first group revolves around the level of development of the institutions necessary for effective functioning of a market economy—banking and insurance, bond and stock markets, the judicial system (more broadly, a system for contract enforcement), the Treasury, tax administration,

---

6. A. Alesina and A. Drazen, "Why Are Stabilizations Delayed?" *The American Economic Review* 81 (December 1991); A. Drazen, "The Political Economy of Delayed Reform," *The Journal of Policy Reform* 1, no. 1 (1996).

and so forth. The second group consists of various economic processes that influence the state of public finances and are in turn themselves influenced by budgetary policies. These processes include declines and changes in the structure of the GDP, inflation, changes in nominal and real rates of exchange of the ruble, the dynamic of interfirm arrears, and so on.

Both the level of development of market-economy institutions and the economic processes that affect public finances exert a substantial influence on economic policy as a whole. There are a number of other important factors that interfere with the pursuit of a restrictive monetary policy. First, the weak monetary policy conducted in 1992–1993 was to a significant extent explained by the dependence of the Russian central bank on the country's populist Parliament. This relationship was then being governed by the constitution that was then in effect. Not until 1994 was the practice of preferential central bank credits to enterprises in various sectors brought under control.

Second, until the summer of 1992 there existed numerous centers of ruble printing, one in each of the former Soviet republics, and the definitive disintegration of the ruble zone occurred only around autumn 1993. During this period, beginning with price liberalization, the authorities did not have full control over the money supply. This lack of separation between the monetary systems of the newly independent states was one of the essential factors mitigating the liberalization of Russia's foreign trade. The quantitative restrictions on the export of raw materials, even to other CIS countries, controlled the export of resources in exchange for the rubles issued by the CIS trading partner or the growth in the CIS partner's indebtedness.

Toward the beginning of 1994, Russia saw the formation of the essential institutional conditions necessary to carry out a stabilization program, as well as the political preconditions for its implementation. The adoption of a new constitution in 1993 and the change in the political system were conducive to stabilization, assuming the government had sufficient political will to carry it out. The concentration of authority in the hands of the president ended those days of the government's dependence on the populist Parliament, when the government had to walk a fine line between resigning and continuing reforms. Moreover, the new constitutional-legal environment made budgetary populism in Parliament more difficult. The legislative process became subject to tighter rules, while decisions on the budget could be made by Parliament only with the government's cooperation. All of this made the situation radically different from 1992–1993, when amendments to the budget were numerous and could be easily reviewed at any point. The balance of forces in the Fifth State Duma did not favor the adoption of budgetary amendments of any kind, as left and right factions automatically blocked each other's proposals, and the government was thus forced to maneuver to get its version of the budget approved.

As a result of these changes, the political stability of the democratic regime had increased considerably in comparison to 1992. A factor of great importance in this new stability was a change in the mentality of economic agents, who had learned to read market signals correctly. Meanwhile a financial infrastructure had also arisen that allowed the budget deficit to be financed by borrowing on financial markets rather than by printing money.

Until late 1994, however, Russia did not have the right political conditions to begin implementing the stabilization program. The political will to effect a dramatic change in economic policy was lacking. We should note that in 1995 and the following years, cooperation with the IMF was instrumental in disciplining the government and the central bank in the process of developing economic policy, since the disbursal of loans was accompanied by close monitoring of the economic situation. However, the IMF-Russia story did not end here: in 1994 Russia's monetary program did not meet any sensible criteria, yet it nevertheless was granted IMF approval, and Russia received financing under STF. As a result, the year ended with a rise in inflation, the autumn crisis on the currency market, and a considerable depletion of central bank reserves.

4.5. An Unorthodox Version of Orthodox Stabilization

The 1995 monetary program provided for the abandonment of direct central bank credits to finance the budget deficit. It was envisaged that the deficit would be covered by the sale of government bonds on the securities market. The program did not envisage a fixed exchange rate for the ruble and did not require the ruble to fluctuate within a particular band. Restrictions were imposed on month-by-month growth in the government's assets and liabilities. Thus, the authors of the stabilization program opted for an orthodox policy based on tight control over the money supply as opposed to standard reliance on a nominal anchor (via a fixed rate of exchange). This approach was entirely legitimate, given the situation in the Russian financial markets in 1994. At this time, after a burst of inflation that was followed by a series of speculative attacks on the ruble, the central bank reserves toward the end of January 1995 had plummeted to a critical level.

4.5.1. Confidence and Adjustment of Expectations

A government's wish to put an end to inflation is not enough for stabilization to take place. There is no guarantee that at some time down the road the state (perhaps out of the best of intentions) will not renege on its obligations. The classic solution to such a confidence dilemma is to fix the exchange rate of the national currency. Apart from containing the growth in the price of imports and their substitutes, a commitment to a fixed exchange rate ensures that the declared policy of financial stabilization will be followed through, despite the inevitable sociopolitical excesses.

The length of the stabilization period depends on the speed of adaptation to inflation expectations, an adaptation directly related to the level of confidence. The more time required by economic agents to fathom the actions of the monetary authorities, the more likely it is that unpopular austerity measures will be abandoned and inflation will return. Therefore, a lack of confidence in government policies is a fundamental impediment to the pursuit of stabilization. In Russia this confidence problem was exacerbated by the fact that the stabilization effort of late 1994 to early 1995 was the fourth such attempt since the liberalization of prices.

Adherence to a stabilization program also depends on the length of the time lags inherent in the inflation mechanism. A slowdown in the money supply results in a commensurate slowdown in the growth of prices, with a time lag of several months. However, unlike the price dynamics, the expansion of the money supply is not visible to the general public. This is the main theoretical argument in favor of stabilization with the aid of a fixed exchange rate. Changes in the rate of exchange and inflation are well-known to everyone, but unlike goods prices, they can be directly manipulated by the central bank.

Despite all the advantages of the nominal anchor, fixing the rate in 1995 was not an option, because of the various factors already cited. Consequently, stabilization had to start with a sharp tightening of credit.

4.5.2. Effectiveness of Orthodox Stabilization

The fact that the stabilization policy bore fruit was tied to the monetary nature of inflation during the prestabilization period of 1992–1995. A number of empirical studies were done by the Institute for the Economy in Transition to determine the characteristics of inflation processes in the Russian economy.[7] The econometric models used in these studies indicate that Russian inflation was largely monetary, as shown by a stable statistical correlation between growth in money supply and the consumer price index. An assessment of the parameters of these models enables us to determine the degree to which inflation is inertial as well as the rate at which it slows down as a result of a tightening of the money supply. Such stabilization effects are fully confirmed by the experiences of other countries that have successfully coped with high inflation.[8]

4.5.3. Inertia of Inflation and Budgetary Problems

As no automatic indexation[9] of budgetary expenditure occurred, the "bargaining" in the Russian budgetary process, which resulted from differing inflationary expectations, took on great importance. The lower the rate of inflation built into the budget, the lower the nominal and real government spending. The slower fall in inflation than expected by the monetary program along with the Law on the

---

7. In Appendix III we present a model of inflation that defines the relationship of the growth in prices at point t to its value at point $t-1$ and the growth in money supply during the preceding period. The autoregressionary term reflects the inertia of inflationary processes. This model is good at capturing the price dynamic during the whole time period under study. Importantly, in the first three years of reform, changes in the money supply had a much greater effect on the dynamic of inflation than during the following period, when the growth in prices was stabilized. The lower the rate of inflation, the more susceptible it is to factors relating to price inertia and changes in demand for real retained profits.

The model of money demand presented in Appendix IV traces the demand for real cash balances to the alternative cost of their storage (which is affected by the rate of inflation, changes in the dollar rate of exchange, and yields on government securities) and to the indicator of economic activity—the dynamic of the deflated GDP. Thus, the model is based on the assumption that economic agents change their asset portfolios by reducing the money share.

8. T. Sargent, "The Ends of Four Big Inflations," in his *Rational Expectations and Inflation* (New York: Harper & Row, 1986), 90–109; M. Burda and C. Wyplosz, *Macroeconomics: A European Text* (Oxford: Oxford University Press, 1993).

9. The experience of many countries (see, for example, Rüdiger Dornbusch and S. Edwards, "Macroeconomic Populism," *The Journal of Development Economics* 32 (1991): 247–77) shows that automatic indexation is a serious impediment to stabilization.

Federal Budget for 1995 alleviated the budgetary problems. The growth of prices not envisaged by the budget increased nominal revenues, lowered real expenditure, and lowered the real budget deficit. As a result, the tightening of budgetary policy in 1995 was analogous to the measures taken in the first year of reforms, when the government had been successful in reducing real budgetary outlays.

4.5.4. Interest Rates in the Stabilization Stage

The financial stabilization of 1995 is best described as a steady lowering of inflation accompanied by a lowering of interest rates. A model of such a process is given in Appendix V. The model confirms several things: (1) the highly inertial price dynamics, (2) the presence of liquidity effects in setting interest rates, (3) the "switchover" effect as a result of tight monetary policy, and (4) a shift in the structure of portfolios toward ruble-denominated assets as a result of changes in the expectations of economic agents.[10]

In 1995, due to the fast expansion of internal debt (how this factor influenced the stabilization process is discussed below), it was possible to finance the budget deficit from noninflationary sources. An econometric model has been constructed linking the interest rate of the secondary government short-term bond (GKO) market to the index of inflation and the real volume of government bonds in circulation (which indicates the inertiality of financial portfolios).[11] This

---

10. W. Easterly and H. Wolf, *The Wild Ride of the Ruble* (Washington, D.C.: World Bank, July 1995).

11. An assessment of the relationship between aggregate yields and forward smoothed moving average rates of inflation and real rates of GKO issues gives the following results:

$r_t = 2.02 + 0.61 x_{t,t+12} + 0.4 \pi_{t,t+12}$
   (2.86)   (6.45)   (2.43)

where r_t is the nominal aggregate net yield of GKOs on a monthly basis during week t, $x_{t,t+12}$ is the average real rate of GKO issues on a monthly basis over the following three months, and $\pi_{t,t+12}$ is the monthly rate of growth in the consumer price index over the same period. In parentheses we indicate values for t statistics for relevant parameters of the model; the coefficient of multiple regression equals 0.8 (the regression is based on forty weekly observations over 1995). The yields are calculated on the basis of the data on the aggregate nominal and market value of GKOs in circulation and the average term of their maturity. The model shows a tight link between the budget deficit at the expense of increases in government debt and the dynamic of the interest rate. In the model of the primary GKO market the index of dissatisfied auction demand, reflecting the influence of fiscal surprises on limited liquidity, is used as an explanatory variable.

shows that the inflation rate and the volumes of new GKO issues were statistically important factors determining the dynamic of GKO yields. A 1% increase in the deflated volumes of GKOs in circulation results in the growth of yield ratios by 0.2%–0.3%. A 1% increase in the monthly rate of inflation increases the yield ratios by 0.5%–0.6%. Changes in the rate of inflation turned out to be more important than changes in the real volumes of GKO. Financial stabilization leads to considerable growth of money demand by financial markets, which by 1995 were largely represented by the market for government bonds. At this juncture, the great influence of bond issues on GKO yields should be interpreted as stemming from the limited liquidity on these markets, supplementing Fischer's fundamental factors (inflation and intertemporal preferences). The money drawn by the Ministry of Finance did not disappear from circulation, and to a significant extent was returned to the financial markets. Nevertheless, restrictions on liquidity did not permit banks to accumulate cash quickly in anticipation of changes in the supply of government paper.[12]

Aggravation of the liquidity problem against the background of falling inflation led to a sharp increase in real GKO yields. Moreover, since late 1995, political uncertainty related to the presidential elections of 1996 was playing an increasingly important role. This political uncertainty drove the problem of government debt to the fore at the beginning of the second half of 1995.

The relationship we have established between the rate on the GKO market and the size of internal government debt shows that the state acted as the principal borrower on the internal market during the disinflation period. This could not fail to depress the real sector, contributing to a shrinkage of the tax base. Unfortunately, the excessive growth of government debt turned out to be unavoidable, thanks to the political-economic conditions discussed below.

4.5.5. *The Currency Corridor and Stabilization of Expectations*

In July 1995 the Russian Central Bank introduced a fairly narrow currency corridor (bands of exchange rate fluctuation), which largely

---

12. The hypothesis regarding the inertia of financial portfolios, as developed by monetarists, allows one to describe the effect of limits on liquidity in the model of the representative agent and thus explains the influence of monetary and credit policies on economic variables. See, for example, R. Lucas, "Liquidity and Interest Rates," *The Journal of Economic Theory* 50 (1990): 237–64.

determined the economic situation in the second half of the year. This measure helped to remove uncertainty and increase confidence in the monetary policy. Further dynamics of the exchange rate and the scale of interventions bear witness to the well-known "honeymoon effect,"[13] which helped maintain the exchange rate within the targeted corridor. The central bank no longer needed to sell dollars heavily on the currency market, since the obligation to defend the limits of the corridor removed speculative interest on the fluctuations of the dollar.

The stabilization and strengthening of the ruble's real rate of exchange, which commenced in 1995, stimulated the flow of capital into the country. This process particularly encouraged repatriation of parts of Russia's financial resources. Thus the groundwork was laid for cheaper credit, reduced profitability of speculative financial operations, and increased attention on the part of financial institutions to investment in the manufacturing sector. By the second half of the year a number of major Russian banks had begun to show a steady interest in the establishment of departments specializing in investment procurement, as well as interest in participating in an increasingly heated struggle for shares in privatized enterprises.

Real strengthening of the ruble led to a weaker position for exporters and a stronger competitive position for importers. The government's natural reaction was to raise import duties and to lower export duties and then rescind them altogether. However, this move was manifestly insufficient for exporters not in the raw materials sector and for the few machine-building firms able to break into foreign markets. These economic agents could, in principle, become a reliable sociopolitical base for stabilization. The deterioration in their economic position, however, was unhelpful for the stabilization process.

4.6. The Fiscal Crisis

The replacement in 1992 of the turnover tax by the VAT and excise taxes, as well as implementation of a number of other innovations, gave rise to a situation in which, regardless of low levels of neutrality and insufficient budgetary receipts, the tax system as a whole became

---

13. P. Krugman, "Target Zones and Exchange Rate Dynamics," *Quarterly Journal of Economics* 106 (1991): 669–82.

suitable for a market economy. As a result, in the first year and a half of reforms, tax receipts grew, but this proved to be temporary. In a transition economy with less than perfect legislation, weak tax administration, and no tradition of compliance, the type of tax collection in developed countries (such levels were necessary to finance the spending programs inherited from socialism) could not be ensured. The Russian experience confirms the general tendency of countries with transition economies to lower projected figures for tax collection by approximately 30% for several years after the commencement of economic liberalization. The exceptions are provided by countries with a high degree of sociocultural and national homogeneity and consensus on key aspects of economic policy.

4.6.1. Budgetary Crisis at the Initial Level of Economic Reforms

In essence, the budgetary crisis of 1991–1993 stemmed from the problem of government spending (the level of which was formed under socialism) exceeding revenue on a continuous basis. Under such conditions two options for reforming public finances were available. The first was to achieve adequate revenue through tax reform. The second presupposed a reduction and a change in the structure of government spending. This required a number of systemic changes: military reform, administrative reform, and an overhaul of utilities subventions, with a particular shift from enterprise subsidies to targeted subsidization of needy households. Such an approach could have ensured an enduring budgetary equilibrium, but the attainment of this equilibrium requires time, political will, and social stability. In principle, by late 1994 conditions necessary for the realization of such a strategic option were in place. However, the financial stabilization program being implemented presupposed a continuing budget deficit of significant proportion and a high level of government borrowing.

4.6.2. Factors Influencing the Profile of Tax Receipts

Research on the falling tax receipts during the postreform years shows an absence of a rigid relationship between government revenues and tax policy. The changes to the tax system that were being carried out by Parliament and the government could not explain the changes in real tax receipts flowing into the budget. The main forces behind this dynamic were inflation, a crisis in the system of payments and settlements, erosion of the strict socialist tax discipline, a growing share of the private sector and services in the economy (both of which are characterized by relatively weaker tax compliance), and growth in cash-based economic operations not reflected in company books.[14] In other words, economic agents quickly adjusted to the new style of relations with the state, which had abandoned repressive measures.

The structure of the tax system inherited from socialism also played a negative role in that it was slanted in favor of corporate taxes at the expense of individuals' income tax. The existence of a close and stable link between tax receipts and the dynamic of the GDP testifies to the fact that the sharp fall in economic activity during the postreform years led to the shrinkage of the tax base at the enterprise level and was one of the factors in the deepening budgetary crisis.

Interenterprise arrears under accounting rules based on the cash book method (not with reference to the point when obligations were incurred) led to a further narrowing of the tax base. Incentives appeared for enterprises to use mutual nonpayments for tax evasion. Russia's tax system is biased in its treatment of taxpayers in similar economic circumstances. The fiscal crisis inevitably decreased the number of law-abiding taxpayers who enjoyed no tax benefits and paid tax in full. This situation distorts economic conditions and leads to adverse selection as a result of biased competition. The adverse selection in turn reduces the tax base. It is thus understood why the fiscal crisis in Russia is of a self-reinforcing nature.

---

14. Sergei Sinelnikov et al., *Problemy nalogovoy reformy v Rossii: analiz situatsii i perspectivy razvitiya* (Moscow: Yevraziya, 1998). This work presents the results of an econometric analysis of the relationship between budgetary tax receipts and a number of important macroeconomic parameters. The results show that the general level of tax receipts depends on the same variables as receipts from specific taxes, those which are central to the Russian tax system: the profit tax, VAT, and income tax. This econometric analysis provides a convincing confirmation of the theoretical hypotheses about the nature of relationships between tax receipts and some macroeconomic variables. Tax receipts are determined by the level of economic activity, the dynamic of real GDP, the increasing scale of tax evasion, and the dynamic of the cash share in the money aggregate M2. Sinelnikov and his colleagues show that the statistical relationship between tax receipts and the size of enterprise indebtedness (as well as tax shortages) is significantly negative.

The severity of fiscal problems had already reached extreme proportions: enterprises suffered under a heavy tax burden, while the budgetary system could not ensure tax collection at even base levels. Economists and politicians offered a variety of solutions including (1) reducing the average rate of taxation, which should revive economic activity; (2) increasing the competitiveness of domestic producers, which would lead to an increase in the volume of tax receipts; (3) radically simplifying the tax system; (4) showing necessary toughness in tax collection and force taxpayers to restructure and then repay their debts; (5) decrease opportunities for tax avoidance and reduce the scale of tax evasion; (6) stepping up the fight against the shadow economy, and various other measures.

It must be noted, however, that lowering tax rates in Russia's transition economy did not lead to such positive effects as postulated by proponents of "supply-side" economics (a position that is often invoked by populist politicians in Russia). Such measures as lowering the VAT in 1993 and lowering the profits tax in 1994, revocation of the special tax and the excess wage tax, and the introduction of various tax breaks did not spur investment growth, expansion in economic activity, and a decrease in the incidence of tax evasion. Thus, in Russia, as in the majority of real-world situations, no Laffer effect—an increase in tax receipts with a reduction in tax rates—occurred. This suggests a greater complexity of interrelations between tax policy and economic activity in a transition economy.

An additional explanation for the tax crisis was the growth of barter in the economy and the proliferation of nonmonetary mutual payments between suppliers and their clients. The Ministry of Finance was actively involved in this process in 1995–1997 through the utilization of Treasury obligations, tax exemptions, product credits, various methods of nonmonetary mutual payments, and so on. As a result, many firms operated with minimal working capital. In this environment, lack of funds on firms' current accounts led to budgetary shortfalls. Price distortions evident in nonmonetary settlements between tax payers, the budget, and recipients of budgetary funds led to a narrowing of the tax base. Unfortunately, the statistical methods currently in use do not allow assessment of the scale of such operations and their role in the development of the fiscal crisis.

One of the characteristics of a transition economy is the short-term absence of a direct correlation between privatization of state enterprises and the growth of tax receipts.¹⁵ Even in sectors that did not experience a fall in industrial production, such as the automotive and metallurgy industries, a decrease in tax payments was evident. This trend was due in large measure to the proliferation of tax benefits and tax evasion, as well as to the unfolding payments crisis.

4.6.3. *The Budgetary Crisis at the Time of Stabilization*

Economic policy prior to 1995–1997 had one serious drawback: insufficient attention to tax reform. As inflationary financing of the budget was discontinued, a sharper correlation between government spending and tax receipts emerged. However, facing the choice in 1995–1996 between tax reform and the accumulation of government debt at an ever increasing pace, the government opted for the latter. This decision was taken in view of two things: one, the fiscal problems exacerbated by previous delays in tax reform, and two, the high political risks associated with undertaking such measures in the run-up to the presidential elections. Regardless, abandonment of efforts to boost tax collection by administrative measures during the period of financial stabilization to a certain extent alleviated the austerities pressing upon anti-inflationary policy.¹⁶ The fact that the government, while intent on a major reduction of the budget deficit, did not choose to improve the structure and enhance the efficiency of government spending but rather limited its efforts to its overall reduction was a major determinant of the evolving budgetary crisis.

Thus, Russia confirmed the following general regularity: In conditions of political uncertainty and polarization of popular opinion,

---

15. This idea is developed in, for example, Milton Friedman, *Capitalism and Freedom* (Chicago: University of Chicago Press, 1982); G. Yarrow, "Privatisation in Theory and Practice," in *Economic Policy* (Cambridge: Cambridge University Press, 1986); A. Bizaguet, *Le secteur publique et les privatisations* (Paris: PUF, 1988); J. Vickers and G. Yarrow, *An Economic Analysis* (Cambridge: MIT Press, 1988); S. Kikeri, J. Nellis, and M. Shirley, *Privatization: The Lessons of Experience* (Washington, D.C.: World Bank, 1992); F. Andic, *Privatization Theory and Policy* (Vienna: UNIDO, 1992).
16. As opposed to clear parameters and restrictions contained in the monetary program with respect to the monetary basis, net internal assets, and the maximum budget deficit, tax collection did not play a key role during the period of financial stabilization and could not affect Russia's chances of obtaining IMF credits. Therefore, from the government's point of view it was more important to adhere to the parameters of the monetary program. In general, tax collection was difficult to control, and it was less useful as an indicator to build into agreements between the government and international financial institutions.

the incumbent government does not find it advantageous to undertake fiscal reform.[17] As a rule, under such conditions easier methods of financing are used, such as the inflation tax or expansion of government debt. In 1995–1996 the Russian government opted for the latter, while continuing its fight against inflation.

The growth of government debt could substitute for tax reform and an overhaul of the structure of government spending (as well as reform in the areas financed from the budget) only in the short term. It is no surprise, then, that the stabilization efforts of 1995–1996 proved insufficient to achieve fiscal equilibrium in the long run. The irrationality of the established structure of budgetary expenditure can be explained not only by the government's refusal to carry out the pressing yet politically sensitive budgetary reforms under the influence of interest groups, but also by the haphazard sequestering of effective expenditure relative to its planned levels. The impractical nature of the budgets adopted was a function of populist politics and the lobbying activity of numerous parliamentary factions in the State Duma. The effective amounts and budgetary items subject to sequestration were determined by the political influence of the interest groups involved. The resulting balance of interests arose out of an irrational structure of government spending. Such a state of affairs was characterized by extremely low levels of social expenditure. This led to a fall in the customary standards of social services and confirmed the absence of any real restructuring of the economy, the absence of reform of the armed forces and of the institutions of law and order, and so on. It must be noted that the implementation of these reforms would have led to increased budgetary expenditure in the short to medium term as a factor of the necessary layoffs and the building of the requisite infrastructure.

The strategy of delayed tax and budgetary reform eased the task of macroeconomic stabilization in 1995–1996, although with some serious consequences. The budgetary crisis contributed to growing income inequality, increased social tension, and lowered efficiencies in the delivery of health care, scientific research, and cultural products. The continuing diminution of tax receipts exacerbated the budgetary crisis, while the growing government debt made the economic situation in the country increasingly dependent on international financial markets and the behavior of external creditors.

---

17. A. Cukerman, S. Edwards, and G. Tabellini, "Seigniorage and Political Instability," *The American Economic Review* 82 (1992): 537–55.

In the final analysis, these circumstances led to a deep financial crisis in Russia that interrupted the initially successful stabilization process and pushed the country back by three to four years.

4.7. Conditions and Factors of Economic Growth

4.7.1. Financial Stabilization as the Necessary Condition for Growth

Financial stabilization creates conditions necessary for capital formation. However, macroeconomic stabilization in itself is a necessary but not sufficient condition to stimulate investment in the real sector. The chief problem is indeterminacy in the role of the state, its capabilities, and the limits of permissible intervention in the economy. The abandonment of inflationary financing by state executives during the period in question sharply reduced the role of the federal center in redistribution of the GDP. Apart from a number of positive results, this led to a qualitative shift in the political-economic equilibrium. As the fiscal crisis grew in severity, the government's ability to influence regional-level policies with transfers diminished. This reality affected the stance of regional governments in dealing with bankruptcy, tax discipline, and approaches to structural problems and the problem of wage and pension arrears. A sharp lowering of government revenue and expenditure in the absence of critical reforms in the public sector had a negative impact on social security, education, health care, scientific research, and culture. At this point, it was still too early to speak of at least partial financing of these programs by the private sector, which is why the threat of wasting human capital in the economy remained. As is well-known, investment in human resources plays a key role in generating sustained technology-driven economic growth.[18]

4.7.2. Ownership Rights and Capital Formation

Privatization has been the most significant institutional change of the reform years in Russia. One of the main goals of mass privatization was to do away with state support of enterprises. Another goal was to alter the structure of society in order to create a large class of owners.

---

18. See R. Lucas, "On the Mechanics of Economic Development," *Journal of Monetary Economics* 22 (1988): 3–42.

The first goal was achieved within a fairly short span of time. However, cessation of direct support for enterprises through subsidies and preferential credits does not necessarily mean abandonment of protectionism and does not fully solve the problem of soft budget constraints. This was evident in the growing strength of industrial lobbies as import tariffs and other trade barriers were erected. State protection of strategic industries thus came primarily to reflect group interests that were accordingly manipulated by enterprise management.[19]

The process of bankrupting unviable enterprises was given an added impetus by the tax crisis and the extraordinary measures undertaken by the government in 1996–1997. However, the greater role of the regions in the present political system makes bankruptcy a more difficult endeavor. Protectionism on the part of regional and local authorities is particularly evident with respect to enterprises, which provide a large share of regional or local employment and help maintain the social infrastructure. It is this element, as well as the interlocking relationships between management and regional and local authorities, that impedes any changes in the structure of ownership and control. It matters little if they are geared toward industrial restructuring, changes in specialization, and long-term job creation. Better regulation is not an effective solution to this type of problem.[20]

One of the negative consequences of mass privatization in Russia was the transfer of state property to so-called insiders—managers and employees of the firms. A direct transfer of control over the firms from magnet to outside investors would hardly have been possible

---

19. Proponents of so-called moderate protectionism assert the need to temporarily protect strategic sectors, but fail to take into account the strategic behavior of firm management. The governments put up temporary trade barriers to enable domestic producers to achieve a certain level of competitiveness. However, enterprises consciously forgo investments required for their restructuring. A weak technological level becomes a strategic argument against dismantling barriers and forces governments to continuously extend these protective measures. The temporary trade restrictions become a permanent government policy. This is shown in K. Matsuyama, "Perfect Equilibrium in a Trade Liberalization Game," *The American Economic Review* 80 (1990): 480–92.

20. The new bankruptcy law adopted by the State Duma in effect aims to maximize the probability of survival of insolvent enterprises, not to redistribute ownership and control in an effective manner. In particular, for enterprises of municipal and regional importance, a bankruptcy procedure lasting in excess of ten years is provided for. Evidently this law, like its 1992 predecessor, will retain impediments and high bankruptcy costs for creditors and foreign investors.

without serious social consequences. The explosion of insider control is, in all likelihood, only an intermediate stage in this property transformation process. Chapter 12 discusses Russia's property transformation in great depth. However, considerable time will be required to complete this transformation and to improve management competence and the quality of corporate governance. Here we note only one important political-economic aspect of property transformation: widening social inequality. Income dispersion caused by the redistribution of property distorted returns in comparison to factors of production. This led to distortions in the supply of factors, whereby an increasing share of human resources was diverted away from productive activity. Social inequality, as a rule, is caused by considerable opportunities for rent seeking, which attract the most well-positioned (able) individuals.[21] Additionally, growing income inequalities have an adverse effect on the political preferences of the population. Models of political-economic equilibrium suggest that a high level of inequality makes the median voter more likely to vote for larger redistribution of the GDP, which on average lowers the propensity to invest and save.[22] Such logic greatly simplifies the real link between political and economic mechanisms.[23] In principle, however, it rather accurately reflects the negative effects of dramatic social fragmentation on economic growth. Therefore, this suggests that a socially oriented budgetary policy should mitigate the disparities generated by property distribution.

Finally, social inequality increases the influence of left-wing and populist forces in the legislative and the executive branches of government at all levels. With a stable majority in the State Duma, antireform factions can block the adoption of key market legislation. Thus, the existing constellation of political forces is one of the main obstacles to further development of reforms and the resumption of economic growth.

---

21. See, for example, K. Murphy, A. Shleifer, and R. Vishny, "Income Distribution, Market Size, and Industrialization," *The Quarterly Journal of Economics* 104 (1989): 537–64.
22. A. Alesina and D. Rodrick, "Distributive Politics and Economic Growth," *The Quarterly Journal of Economics* 104 (1994): 465–90; T. Persson and G. Tabellini, "Is Inequality Harmful for Growth?" *The American Economic Review* 84 (1994): 600–21.
23. There are a number of examples contradicting the supposition of a positive correlation between income disparities and the degree of redistribution of GDP. A theoretical and cross-national analysis of this problem is presented in S. Folster and G. Trofimof, "Does Equality Promote Growth?" IET Working Paper Series, no. 2 (1996).

5

Macroeconomic Stabilization as a Sociopolitical Problem

Vladimir Mau

The key objective of macroeconomic stabilization in Russia was to reduce inflation to less than 40% per annum in order to encourage direct investments. This objective was attained only in 1997. However, as the financial crisis of 1998 showed, it was not attained securely, and it took considerably longer to achieve than in the majority of the postcommunist countries of Central and Eastern Europe.

Even a superficial analysis of macroeconomic stabilization in postcommunist Russia allows one to draw two general conclusions about its nature and peculiarities.

First, the fact that stabilization was delayed has been one of the key features of Russia's contemporary transition.[1] Delayed stabilization set the stage for many important trends relating to the development of the country.

Second, inflation in Russia has been distinctly cyclical. This spurred a vigorous debate in Russian economic and policymaking circles regarding the feasibility and admissibility of various anti-inflationary measures. These discussions and the ensuing policy conclusions were more robust and uncompromising than in other postcommunist (and post-Soviet) states.

5.1. Delayed Stabilization

Delayed stabilization is not unique to Russia. It has been comprehensively analyzed in economic literature; however, the analyses

---

[1]. The problem of delayed stabilization has been treated in the literature over the last decade, initially as a reaction to the difficulties encountered by stabilization attempts in Latin America. This problem then became relevant to some postcommunist countries. For a detailed analysis, see A. Alesina and A. Drazen, "Why Are Stabilizations Delayed?" *The American Economic Review* 81 (December 1991): 1170–88; and A. Drazen, "The Political Economy of Delayed Reform," *The Journal of Policy Reform* 1, no. 1 (1996): 25–46.

have largely been confined to Latin American stabilization programs.[2] Research highlights that delayed stabilization is tied to a certain sociopolitical environment, one in which the government is too weak to carry out necessary but unpopular economic measures. This environment is also populated by influential interest groups that do not wish to incur the costs associated with stabilization, and choose to wait until more favorable circumstances permit implementation of the required measures at a lower cost to themselves.

During the period of high inflation in Russia, the belief that inflation was somehow independent of policy and that it was therefore fundamentally impossible to realize a standard stabilization program gained prominence. These conclusions were based on the fairly obvious cyclical nature of macroeconomic variables in 1991–1994, which prompted some commentators to seek unconventional explanations for this phenomenon. Two strands of explanation for the phenomenon of delayed stabilization gained currency. First, Russia was believed to be exceptionally dependent on natural conditions, which required changes in economic policy on a seasonal basis.[3] Second, some "natural" rate of inflation (from 5% to 12% per month) existed that was considered to be a function of the social pain associated with stabilization and that therefore did not allow the government to lower inflation within a reasonably short period of time.[4]

Indeed, seasonality was an important factor in the functioning of the Russian economy. The main channels for its expression were agriculture and the industrial enclaves in the northern and eastern regions, where weak infrastructure did not permit adequate links with the rest of the country throughout the year. Thus, it was concluded that the inevitable slackening of monetary and fiscal policies in spring and summer would lead to inflation in autumn and winter. However, giving undue prominence to the role of seasonality in explanations of economic policy immediately raised key questions.

---

2. See, for example, A. Alesina, *Political Models of Macroeconomic Policy and Fiscal Reform* (Washington, D.C.: IBRD, 1992).
3. In 1992–1995 many Russian economists wrote about the exceptional and naturally negative effect of seasonality on the macroeconomic processes in general and on stabilization efforts in particular. Numerous publications on the subject in *Kommersant*, as well as political statements by Grigori Yavlinsky, fall into this category. See "Ekonomika stanovitsya proshche, dokhodnyye igry slozhnee," *Kommersant-Weekly* 36 (1994): 44; N. Kirichenko and A. Malov, "Oktyabr'skaya revolutsiya svershilas'," *Kommersant-Weekly* 42 (1991): 66; N. Kirichenko, *Kommersant-Weekly* 46 (1994): 59.
4. See, for example, G. Yavlinsky and S. Braguinski, "The Inefficiency of Laissez-Faire in Russia," *Journal of Comparative Economics* 19, no. 1 (1994).

Comparisons of month-by-month inflation rates in 1992–1994 cast some doubt on the seasonality hypothesis. In the second year of Russian reforms (1993), the fall in the inflation rate in July and August that characterized 1992 and 1994 did not occur. On the contrary, the situation in 1993 was completely different. Nonetheless, "seasonality" remained an important argument in economic discourse until 1995, when macroeconomic parameters changed in ways that could not be accommodated within the limits of this hypothesis.

Accordingly, the unremitting if slow suppression of inflation refutes the thesis about a natural rate of inflation. It is no accident that the rate diminished as the "barriers" postulated by the exponents of the natural rate were overcome in the course of stabilization.

Nevertheless, in our view the thesis about a natural rate of inflation is not baseless. This, however, is not a function of social but of political processes. It is not that the suppression of inflation may entail excessive pain. Rather, the weakness of the government hampers its ability to pursue sound economic policy in the presence of strong economic groups with sharply divergent interests. Indeed, monetary and fiscal policy as expressed in the rate of inflation had been at the core of the struggle between these interest groups for a prolonged period.

Inflation in postcommunist Russia between 1992 and 1996 became not just an economic but a key political indicator reflecting the balance of power between various interest groups. This is quite logical, since inflation in social terms represents a redistribution of financial resources, and it is this redistributive conflict that accounts for the politicization of the macroeconomic indicator in question.[5] Postcommunist Russia saw the formation of two opposing groups, and a victory for one from suppression of inflation was a defeat for the other. Interestingly, the power and influence of these respective groups changed as the economic reforms unfolded.

Whereas in late 1991 and early 1992 liberalization and stabilization did not encounter much resistance, by spring of 1992 resistance was virtually absolute. At first the consequences of stabilization were not very well understood and were miscalculated by economic agents. For decades the Soviet economy had operated under conditions of product shortages, and thus firm managers were not acquainted with the workings of supply and demand forces and the nature of

---

5. For more on this, see R. C. K. Burdekin and P. Burkett, *Distributional Conflict and Inflation* (London: Macmillan, 1996).

demand restrictions. Soon, however, with the unexpected contraction of demand and the onset of payment arrears, they came to understand the consequences of liberalization and united in their demand for subsidization. In socioeconomic terms, spring and summer of 1992 were a unique period when the rise of inflation in the country knew no bounds.

This trend could only be counteracted by sowing division among various types of economic agents, a task that was accomplished with the beginning of privatization. From the outset, privatization was intended to strengthen the sociopolitical base for economic liberalization and stabilization. For this reason the Gaidar government in particular thought it possible to ease fiscal and monetary policy in exchange for getting privatization started.

5.2. Consolidation of Opposing Factions: Inflationists versus Anti-inflationists

The political outcome of this development was the consolidation, toward spring of 1993, of two main interest groups, one favoring inflationary policy and the other favoring disinflationary policy. The dividing line between them was defined by their understanding of the role of inflation and the methods for overcoming it. This in effect became the dominant theme in the debate over economic reforms, which replaced the discourse over the administrative and liberal-economic options for stabilization prevalent in 1991.

The inflationist position was clearly defined. The principal elements of this policy included massive fiscal injections into the economy (via credit and budgetary systems) in order to keep weak uncompetitive enterprises afloat, efforts to strengthen the "governability" of the economy by restoration of federal authority vis-à-vis state enterprises, tighter control over export and import operations, and unabashed protectionism. This inflationist group argued that government participation in the structural transformation of the economy was required, including the re-creation of an extensive infrastructure for management of economic agents by state administrative bodies (ministries or industrial committees) or by large monopolistic entities (such as financial-industrial groups) that still remained under government control.

The proponents of this policy included rather diverse groups of economic agents. Some of them benefited directly from inflation, extracting enormous profits during economic instability. For others the policy meant the continuation of government support and averted their otherwise inevitable bankruptcy. It was mostly weak (though often rather large, in employment terms) enterprises that were interested in the "cheap money" policy. These enterprises were unable or unwilling to adapt to competitive conditions and were doomed to fail in the event that a macroeconomic policy based on hard budget constraints took hold.

Banks also benefited from inflation at the time. Their economic well-being, and often their very existence, depended on preferential credits and budgetary subsidies. Finally, inflation provided a source of profit for traders and related intermediaries, which was reflected in their position in the Russian economic-political spectrum.[6] In other words, inflation allowed inefficient enterprises to survive, while commercial banks and trading organizations could make profits far in excess of those in the manufacturing sector.

On the other hand, proponents of an alternative economic policy oriented toward macroeconomic stabilization were also consolidating their interests. The main features of the policy they favored were consistent economic liberalization, tight fiscal and credit policies, and the unswerving pursuit of privatization. This policy can be in essence described as "anti-inflationism." The number of its proponents grew as privatization advanced and an increasing number of enterprises adapted to market conditions, thus affording managers and qualified employees greater opportunities for social and economic advancement. Understandably, anti-inflationary policy commanded the greatest support among agents who already understood their economic strength, who could sell their products on the domestic (or even international) markets, and who were able to implement an active investment strategy, for which macroeconomic stability was the primary precondition.

This regrouping of interests signaled a new and important trend in the reform process. Whereas formerly the dividing line between interests had been the state/private sector boundary, now being part of a given sector now began to lose its significance. An economic agent's position in relation to redistributive flows of "cheap money,"

---

6. Douglass North noted that in a situation of instability, "firms will tend to have short-time horizons," and "the most profitable businesses may be in trade, redistributive activities, or the black market operations" (D. North, *Institutions, Institutional Change and Economic Performance* [Cambridge: Cambridge University Press, 1990], 67).

on the other hand, became a factor of importance. As a result, private as well as state enterprises could be found on both sides of the "economic divide."

5.3. The Changing Balance of Forces

The conflict between these two interest groups, each with fundamentally different claims and expectations regarding government economic policy, predetermined the macroeconomic instability of 1992–1996. However, this general comment does not satisfactorily explain why macroeconomic stabilization briefly became possible. An answer to the last question requires a more comprehensive analysis of social as well as political changes.

A formal, quantitative assessment shows that the initial balance of forces (interest groups) clearly favored the inflationists. This was predicted as early as the late 1980s by a number of commentators who analyzed the performance prospects of various sectors of the Soviet economy under international competition. The results were not encouraging since, as it turned out, only a small number of enterprises—mainly in the oil and gas sector—would be able to compete on the world market should the Soviet economy liberalize and price controls be lifted. Even taking into account the artificiality of such constructions and the possibility of overestimating some factors and underestimating others, it was obvious that the Soviet economy would have severe difficulties adapting to market conditions.

The numerical prevalence of pro-inflationary economic agents, including the flagship enterprises of the national economy, seriously complicated stabilization efforts during the first two to three years of postcommunist economic development. The managers of these enterprises had considerable political weight and access to the upper echelons of power (particularly Parliament and the presidential administration), where Soviet notions about the economic importance of industrial sectors still predominated. The number of employees and the importance of the social functions performed by the enterprise were among the main criteria used to decide which economic agents to support. Such interest group lobbying was especially effective at a time when the executive branch was constitutionally feeble and socially vulnerable.

A large part of the influential and pro-inflationary old managerial elite skillfully manipulated conflicts between the president and Parliament to their advantage. Often they managed to obtain support from one side or the other, or from both, while each branch of government tried to acquire independent sources of financing in order to support its political allies.[7] It is clear from this analysis how constitutional and socioeconomic factors, including the absence of a clear separation of powers, can condition each other.

During a large part of 1992 and 1993, pro-inflationary groups dominated the economic and political landscape of postcommunist Russia, and this was reflected in the main macroeconomic indicators of the country's development. It was at that time that political associations of enterprise directors (particularly the Civic Union, headed by A. Volsky), with pretensions of becoming the leading political force in the country and the main government party, came to prominence.[8]

Moreover, the position of the pro-inflationists tended to strengthen markedly, and their political victory seemed inevitable (which is what happened in Ukraine at the time).[9] The social and economic changes under way at the time were undermining the efforts of the anti-inflationists. This was reflected in the absence (or weakness) of structural transformations in the economy, which enabled pro-inflationists to maintain the existing economic structure through monetary infusions from the center.

As a result, during the first two to three years of reform, the situation of the anti-inflationary forces was in inherent disequilibrium, and their political prospects seemed uncertain. However, the decisive and consistent pursuit of privatization in 1993–1994 was strengthening their ranks and broadening opportunities for true entrepreneurial behavior, as opposed to political rent seeking by state and quasi-private organizations of the traditional Soviet type.

---

7. For more detail see Vladimir Mau, *The Political History of Economic Reform in Russia, 1985–1994* (London: CRCE, 1995), 71–78.

8. From a purely formal point of view, a number of Russian and foreign commentators had the impression that, at certain points in 1992–1993, the Civic Union (and especially its president, Arkady Volsky) were rapidly gaining strength, when many "red" directors sympathetic to the Civic Union entered the government. However, with time it became clear that the appointment of V. Chernomyrdin, V. Shumeyko, G. Khizha, and O. Soskovets as vice-premiers, as well as V. Chernomyrdin's appointment as premier, not only failed to strengthen the influence of the Civic Union on government policy, but also contributed to a sharpening and polarization of the positions of these Soviet managers turned politicians.

9. See M. Dabrowski and R. Antchak, *Ukrainskiy put' k rynochnoy ekonomike 1991–1995* (Warsaw: CASE, 1996).

Regardless, the numerical predominance of the pro-inflationists, combined with an unstable macroeconomic policy, tended to weaken the ranks of potential supporters of an open market economy (aka the anti-inflationists). To clarify, the processes under way at the time should be viewed at two levels.

First, the political activism of enterprises favoring an anti-inflationary policy was waning. This was dictated by the reality of economic life. The hopes for a swift halt to inflation proved unfounded, and therefore those who were interested in a fast and decisive stabilization and who had built their market-survival strategy on the premise that it would occur had to adapt to operating in conditions of long-term hyperinflation. This required the framing of a new strategy and actually dissuaded potentially strong firms from giving support to anti-inflationary political forces—the initiators and implementers of radical market and democratic reforms.

Second, there was an infusion of entrepreneurs into the institutions of the state, as the weak state sought the support of the new, economically strong and influential class of new entrepreneurs. Thus a comfortable environment was created for big business (no matter whether private or quasi-state) in which the struggle for survival was superseded by potential support from institutions of the state. The state itself had to rely on the strongest economic agents, who were actually strong enough to survive on their own, while providing in exchange its only resource—rent seeking. The weak (financially poor) state, while engaged in these survival tactics, channeled the behavior of economic agents in a strategically undesirable direction.[10]

At the same time, social processes, while changing the economic and therefore political influence of various sectors of the economy

---

10. We can refer to various government decisions in support of sectors and enterprises loyal to the executive branch and supportive of market reforms. Support for the automotive industry (above all VAZ) and for a number of banks and financial institutions serve as examples. This is unsurprising: support for car manufacturers for economic (let alone political) reasons seemed a more promising undertaking than support for the agrarians or combine manufacturers. The consequences of such decisions from a strategic point of view were to say the least, controversial. On the one hand, rewarding loyal enterprises seemed to strengthen the position of the reformers in the executive branch, who relied on the support of the most active private businessmen during the most critical moments of political confrontation. On the other hand, rewards often led to the deferral of reforms needed to adapt to genuine market conditions at loyal enterprises, and also encouraged the fusion of the state apparatus with commercial entities, which naturally bred corruption.

and interest groups, gradually transformed the social and political environment. The two most important aspects of this transformation were changed in the financial sector and the transformation and stabilization of constitutional-legal arrangements.

It is not difficult to see that key banks were the main beneficiaries of inflation. Unlike other leading pro-inflationary sectors (such as the Soviet industrial establishment), the banks did not consume resources generated by inflation, but on the contrary in large measure accumulated resources in monetary and material form. Consequently, as the transformation of the banking sector, for a number of reasons,[11] unfolded in a more robust manner than in the majority of other postcommunist countries, private banks in Russia became the strongest participants in the political struggle.

Low inflation and macroeconomic stabilization became attractive to a number of major banks for several reasons. First, such an economic environment created favorable conditions for them to expand their presence in the market for banking services by acquiring smaller banks, which were unable to survive the considerable lowering of the interest rate. Second, the expansion of banking capital into industry that had occurred in the course of privatization made financial institutions more sensitive to the problems of industrial development, at least in the sectors where they had invested, and this required a lowering of inflation to a level conducive to investment.

The strengthening of the banking sector and the rise of an anti-inflationary tilt among banks were conducive to a marked shift in government policy and the strengthening of stabilization and the "reform mergers" (as Albert Hirschman used to say) in government. The numerical prevalence of inefficient enterprises (which still provided the lion's share of employment) remained, but their financial and political prowess was sharply lower. Even the formal changes in the composition of the government in 1994–1997 testified to a dramatic diminution in the influence of the traditional Soviet establishment (the so-called red directors) and a comparable strengthening of the new commercial ventures and the politicians linked to them.[12]

---

11. For details see Chapter 14.
12. For details see Ye. Pappe, "Otraslevye lobbi v pravitel'stve Rossii (1992–1996)," *Pro et Contra* 1 (1996): 61–78.

5.4. Constitutional Problems of Macroeconomic Stabilization

Another area undergoing change was the legal landscape for a market economy. During 1992–1994, important processes were taking place that can be characterized as "constitutional consolidation."[13]

Certain illusions and theoretical constructions in earlier years reflected widespread notions about the "correct" organization of the institutions of the state. The case of the central bank is the most vivid example. One of the key illusions of the eighties was that removing the central bank from executive control and making it accountable to the legislature would follow with the principles of market democracy and be a key factor in stabilizing government economic policy. Yet one principle here was merely substituted for another: independence from the government was mistaken for independence of the monetary authorities. The former is also a possible solution; however, even by the late 1980s it was viewed by experts in the field of constitutional economics as rather old-fashioned. Nevertheless, in Russia in 1990, this was thought of as an idea on the cutting edge of constitutional thought.[14]

The practically unlimited expansion of the budgetary authority of the legislature serves as another example of the substitution of principles. The principle of parliamentary control over public finances

---

13. For a treatment of constitutional problems of macroeconomic stabilization and economic reform see J. S. Hellman, "Constitution and Economic Reform in the Post-Communist Transitions," in *The Rule of Law and Economic Reform in Russia*, edited by J. D. Sachs and K. Pistor (Boulder, Colo.: Westview Press, 1997), 55–78; and V. Mau, *Ekonomicheskaya reforma: skvoz prizmu konstitutsii i politiki* (Moscow: Ad Marginem, 1999).

14. The independence of the central bank from the executive branch is generally considered to favor the conduct of a tight monetary policy. For example, V. Grilli, D. Masciandro, and G. Tabellini ("Institutions and Policies," *Economic Policy* [October 1991]) explain differences in the size of government debt, the budget deficit, and the rate of inflation with reference to political institutions—the constitution, the electoral system, the central bank (and its degree of independence), and so forth. R. Barro and R. Gordon ("Rules, Discretion and Reputation in a Model of Monetary Policy," *Journal of Monetary Economics* 12 [1983]) demonstrate that a pro-inflationary shift can be a consequence of central bank freedom, as well as the general difficulty of pursing a confidence-building monetary policy that allows inflation to be avoided. In Russia over the whole reform period, the government was rather less inclined to pursue a populist inflationary policy than the legislature or the central bank (up until 1995). Accordingly, the independence of the central bank from the government in Russia before the start of stabilization in 1995 made it easier for pro-inflationary forces to push for a loose policy.

was supplanted by infinite parliamentary interference in the budgetary process, including its implementation.

The powers of the branches of government were not clearly delineated (specifically those of the executive and the legislature), nor was their relationship to one another well-defined. Confusion was bred by the overlapping claims of the president, the prime minister, and the Speaker of the Parliament. As the confrontation between the branches of government intensified, local authorities often received contradictory instructions. The reason for such behavior was the apparent desire of each side to mimimize the influence of the others.

The problem lay not so much in branches of government exceeding or not exceeding their authority, but rather in an unclear definition of what their authority was. This confusion, therefore, led to instability and unreliability of decisions. This situation, logically, was not conducive to the stabilization of the country's economy.[15]

As a result, by 1992 a situation of "dual power" had taken hold. This diarchy was brought about by unclear constitutional provisions as well as by a political battle between the president and the parliamentary majority. It is clear that this situation was impinging on the effectiveness of economic policy and in particular on the government's ability to effect macroeconomic stabilization. From the very first steps in realizing its postcommunist (market-oriented) economic policy, the government encountered a number of problems arising from its relative strength vis-à-vis Parliament. These problems hindered the effectiveness of its decision making on key economic and political issues.

At the root of this problem were several factors. First, the legislative process was greatly simplified, and all decisions (including financial ones) could be made without a mandated procedure for preliminary debate and consultation. Laws and amendments could be adopted even without the distribution of written draft legislation to members of Parliament. The procedure for making amendments to the constitution was also fairly simple. As a consequence, in the period of 1991–1992 amendments were frequently made.

Second, mechanisms to counteract populism were weak. In particular, the presidential veto could be overturned by a 50% parliamentary majority.

---

15. For details see Ye. Gaidar, *Dni porazheniy i pobed* (Moscow: Vagrius, 1996), 259–60.

Third, the central bank remained outside the control of the executive branch, while remaining accountable to Parliament. Because of the extremely populist mood of Parliament, this had a negative impact on the consistency of the stabilization policy.

Fourth, poorly regulated intrafederal relations not only weakened the political standing of the federal government, they also undermined its position in such sensitive areas as the budget and taxes.

Fifth, the permeability of borders within the CIS remained a reality, which eroded the integrity of the Russian currency and customs area. Control over monetary flows, given the inadequate regulations then in place, was extremely weak.

The need for a new constitutional framework became clear by mid-1992. By this time the impossibility of conducting a responsible monetary and fiscal policy had expressed itself fully, as had the inclination of Parliament to tinker with the constitution in order to cater to the political requirements of the moment. Interference by the two branches of government with the central bank was pervasive and almost without limits. It was pressure from populist members of Parliament throughout 1992 and part of 1993 that prevented the central bank from raising interest rates to a positive level (in real terms). The interest rate became positive only in the last quarter of 1993, after the dissolution of Parliament on 21 September 1993 and the effective abolition of the Soviet constitution.

It is for these reasons that preferential (reduced even from the official level of the negative real interest rate) credits to selected enterprises were maintained for such a long duration. Finally, the parliamentary leadership interfered even with the day-to-day conduct of monetary policy, including the issuance of banknotes of certain denominations, a process that exacerbated the cash crisis. To this list of parliamentary interferences it is worth adding that the Speaker of the Parliament had an "off-budgetary" stabilization fund of his own that funneled cash to enterprises of his choosing (in short, to the directors who were politically close to him).

The tax system was also beset by problems of a constitutional, legal, and political nature, particularly concerning the distribution of tax receipts between the federal and regional governments. Above all, the distribution of tax receipts was not standardized and became subject to endless bargaining between the center and the regions. Governors used all their power and influence to lower the share they paid into the federal budget, while the federal authorities were too weak to resist this pressure. The consequence was a chain reaction in which concessions to one region led to the "sale" of concessions to others, which happened to be in a similar fiscal position.

The tax issue manifested itself in another phenomenon, which was particularly dangerous in the wake of the breakup of the USSR. The effective dyarchy in the center provoked the regions into not paying taxes to the federal government. Moreover, the leadership of Parliament attempted to use this situation in its confrontation with the president. Thus, in August 1993 the Speaker of the State Duma, R. Khasbulatov, called on members of the federation not to pay taxes to the "government against the people." Such a statement and its possible ramifications could not but affect the government's ability to achieve macroeconomic stabilization.

Thus, by mid-1993 the need for a new constitutional framework was apparent. The issue of changing the constitution was repeatedly raised by the president, who proposed to hold a referendum on the issue. The need for a radical overhaul of the constitution did not elicit objections on the part of the deputies, but they insisted on adoption of the constitution without a referendum, in essence, adopting the draft version supported by the left-wing populist majority of Parliament. The impasse exploded into an open conflict between the president and Parliament that lasted from 21 September until 4 October 1993 and ended in dissolution of the legislature, with new elections held on 12 December. Most importantly, this brought a referendum on the constitution.

The new constitution radically changed the principles governing the political and economic system. It was designed to impart stability to the institutions of the state and minimize the populist influence on economic decision making.

Certainly, there is no sure protection from populism, and even Western democracies with a long history are not immune to it. Therefore, strengthening the power of the executive branch in the constitution of postcommunist Russia (particularly the power of the president) at the expense of the legislature was the only feasible remedy. Experience shows that Parliament is more prone to populist tendencies. A member of Parliament elected by his or her constituency is extremely sensitive and receptive to the demands of the electorate, particularly to various lobbies in his or her district, some of which may have financed the candidate's election campaign. This individual, strictly speaking, does not bear responsibility for the situation in the country, and in fact responsibility for the situation in the member's constituency is also limited. The country's president, on the contrary, while possibly inclined toward populism and receptive to lobbies, is in the final analysis responsible for the results of his actions. The president cannot shift his responsibility to anyone else. The reality of the lack of presidential power became fully evident in Russia and was reflected in the draft of the 1993 constitution approved in the referendum.

The key aspects of the new constitution that were to have an impact on the economy were as follows: The procedure for adoption of legislative acts, particularly those bearing on financial and economic issues, was made considerably more complicated. Three readings were normally mandated, and federal budget acts required four readings. Laws relating to the federal budget, taxes, financial, currency, credit and customs regulations, as well as monetary emissions, had to be vetted by the government. Also, unlike other draft laws, these laws were subject to mandatory deliberation and approval in the Federation Council. Finally, to avoid populism and demagogy, it was forbidden to hold referenda on these issues.

Stabilization of economic policy was aided by the constitutional guarantee of the authority of the central bank, the main function of which was declared to be defending and securing the stability of the currency of the Russian Federation—the ruble. This guarantee was a reaction to the experience of 1992–1993, when the governor of the central bank, partly under pressure from the Supreme Soviet, but in large measure following his own notions about economic policy, concentrated his efforts on keeping industry intact and afloat. These actions resulted in the intensification of the macroeconomic crisis.

The role of the central bank in the system of state institutions was drastically changed from this time. Formally, its independence was not declared, nor was there any mention of its accountability to any branch of government. In effect, according to the 1993 constitution, this meant greater dependence on the executive branch. This dependence was manifested in the participation of the chairman of the central bank in cabinet meetings. However, the constitution declared that "monetary emission is conducted exclusively by the Central Bank of the Russian Federation" and this is done "independently of other organs of the state." Combined with the statute that declared the appointment of the central bank chairman by the State Duma (the lower house of Parliament) upon presidential nomination and his effective five-year tenure, the constitution guaranteed a stable and independent monetary policy, while at the same time requiring coordination of monetary policy with the government. However, as with the strong presidency, the central bank's commitment to monetary and fiscal stability was in large measure dependent on the position of the president and the personal qualities of the central bank chairman.

Nonetheless, one serious problem relating to fiscal policy was not addressed in the new legal framework: the prohibition of a budget deficit. In fact, a constitutional prohibition on adopting a deficit budget is fairly rare in international practice. In postcommunist countries this issue was most comprehensively addressed in Estonia. In Russia, the constitutional prohibition of a budget deficit was never raised in earnest, although the problem was quite real, particularly because there was no social consensus on the basic parameters of the country's future development.

One other factor important from the perspective of macroeconomic stabilization is the sharper delineation of powers between the center and other parts of the federation, including making monetary emission the exclusive power of the central bank. Although later the problem of quasi-money assumed rather severe proportions, the main thrust of the constitution, combined with resolute actions by the government, stopped attempts by some constituents of the federation to engage in monetary emission.

While drafting the constitution in 1993, the federal authorities undertook measures to formalize tax relations in the Russian Federation. This made it possible to get away from the individualized distribution of tax receipts between the federal center and the constituents of the federation. This move also created preconditions for stabilizing the financial system and was also an important step toward modern budgetary federalism.

In a word, despite all the flaws of the 1993 constitution, its main virtue was the creation of clear "rules of the game" in general, and particularly in the financial-economic area. The budgetary process became more manageable, while the central bank was distanced from populist legislators. All of these factors improved the government's ability to carry out a responsible macroeconomic policy.

6

Problems of Macroeconomic Stabilization at the Stage of Economic Liberalization (1992)

Sergei Sinelnikov-Murylev and Georgy Trofimov

Fiscal policy in 1992 can be divided into three distinct phases. The first, from the beginning of the year until late spring, was characterized by a tight budgetary policy; the second, which lasted through the summer, saw the relaxation of budgetary discipline; and the third, from autumn to December, was marked by the adoption of austerity measures and a tightening of budgetary policy.

6.1. Tight Budgetary Policy and the Liquidation of Monetary Overhang

The new government's desire to avoid hyperinflation in the process of price liberalization and liquidation of monetary overhang required fiscal, monetary, and credit policies. The initial draft budget for the first quarter of 1992 envisaged balancing revenue and expenditure through sharp spending cuts (particularly on industry and defense). As data on the actual implementation of the budget show, the government seriously underestimated the difficulties involved in introducing a value-added tax (VAT). In the first months of the year, VAT receipts were extremely low. Only in the second half of 1992 did they become an important source of budget revenue.

Additionally, projected price growth following liberalization was much lower than what actually materialized. In the first budget draft, a roughly twofold price rise was written in for the first quarter, while in reality it turned out to be much higher. The Supreme Soviet's version of the budget projected the republic's budget deficit for the first quarter of Rb 64.7 billion (or 5.8% of projected GDP). This budget provided for cuts in spending by a factor of 1.5 in real terms (from 45% of GDP in 1991 to 31% of GDP in the revised draft of the first-quarter budget). The real budget deficit for January to

March was around 2% of GDP.[1] In April and May 1992 a tight fiscal policy was maintained; in April the national budget deficit was 2.0% of GDP, and in May it was 3.6% of GDP. This deficit was financed by central bank credits.[2] Even though the first-quarter GDP was 20% higher than envisaged in the revised budget, actual nominal revenues and deficit financing by the central bank (2% of GDP) only permitted the fulfillment of expenditures at 74% of planned levels.

This miscalculation is best explained by a greater growth in prices than had been calculated in the budget projections. Consequently, since Russia had no automatic indexation of budget expenditure, high inflation led to the devaluation of budget expenditures (which were fixed in absolute terms).[3] However, the tax system proved flexible in adapting to conditions of high inflation. Thus, by continuously adjusting taxation techniques in 1992, it proved possible to increase the share of tax receipts in GDP.

As the experiences of many countries have shown,[4] the absence of automatic indexation of budget expenditures is an extremely important factor in counteracting hyperinflation. If indexation had been adopted in 1992—and it was on Parliament's agenda—the risk of hyperinflation would have been greatly decreased.[5]

However, nonindexation did not last for long. The degree of de facto indexation of specific budget items was determined by the pressures exerted by various political groups. For example, effective indexation was least pervasive for expenditures in the social sphere.

---

1. Effectively, consolidated budget revenues in the first three months of 1992 were 19.1% of GDP and expenditures were 19.5% of GDP. As a result of serious revenue shortfalls, the expenditure side was fulfilled only as budget receipts permitted. Thus, spending on the economy was only 75% of that planned, spending on the social sphere was 62% of that planned, and spending on maintenance of the state administration was 74% of that planned.
2. In the first quarter of 1992 the volume of central bank credits grew by 70%, of which about 30% were to the government, 60% were to commercial banks, and 10% were to countries in the ruble zone.
3. In January 1992, after price liberalization, consumer prices compared to December 1991 rose by a factor of 3.5, and wholesale prices rose by a factor of 4.8. The following months, up until the end of the summer of 1992, saw a deceleration of price growth to about 10% per month for retail prices and 12%–15% per month for wholesale prices.
4. R. Dornbusch and S. Edwards, eds., *The Macroeconomics of Populism in Latin America* (Chicago: University of Chicago Press, 1991).
5. M. H. Simonsen, "Indexation: Current Theory and the Brazilian Experience," in *Inflation, Debt, and Indexation*, edited by R. Dornbusch and M. Simonsen (Cambridge: MIT Press, 1986).

Changes in price levels after liberalization reflected, with a certain lag, the dynamics of the main monetary aggregates.[6] In the winter and spring of 1992, when a relatively tight monetary policy was in force, M2 grew from 9% to 14% per month. Inflation, however, was much higher because of the sudden drop in money demand following price liberalization. By June 1992 the money supply had basically stabilized, and inflation was chiefly determined by money supply growth, which increased sharply in the summer months.

6.2. The Strengthening of Populism and Weakening of Fiscal Policy

By mid-spring 1992, pressure on the government and the president to increase financial support for both the population and industry was mounting. The need for such support was justified by reference to the "objective difficulties" of the transition period. As a result, from May to August about two dozen laws, presidential decrees, and government resolutions were adopted that allocated additional funds to the social sphere in an amount equivalent to 2.5% of annual GDP.

Domestic industry, the agricultural sector, and other branches of the economy were supported by increasing credits, and the payment arrears problem was solved by the same means. Central bank credits were also extended in order to raise enterprise working capital and for investment purposes.

The seasonality of the Russian economy also had a serious impact on the volume of credits distributed in 1992. The chief recipients of this seasonable credit were the agricultural sector and the industrial enclaves in the northern and eastern regions. Major central bank credits were allocated to the agricultural sector at the end of the spring (4.5% of GDP), and also to firms that shipped goods to the regions of the Far North (1.4% of GDP). Between July and September 1992, such credits, to the tune of about 9% of annual GDP, were allocated to various branches of the economy.[7] Almost all of these credits were issued on preferential terms, and funds for servicing

---

6. See, for example, a series of articles in *Economic International* (1993), *Voprosy ekonomiki* (1995), and the *OECD Economic Survey* (1995).
7. See *Finansy v Rossiyskoy Federatsii v 1992 godu—Goskomstat Rossii* (Moscow: Respublikanskiy informatsionno-izdatel'skiy tsentr, 1994).

them came out of the national budget. Credit policy in 1992 clearly reflected the priorities of the time. Thus, for example, the proportion of credits going to the agro-industrial complex grew considerably (from 7.2% of all credits at the end of May 1992 to 17.6% by the end of the year), while the proportion of credits issued to various branches of industry fell (from 12.4% to 7.5%).

Lobbying by political and economic interest groups was not a new phenomenon in Russia. In the first months after price liberalization, the interests of various pressure groups altered significantly, and focused directly on the redistribution of property and budget revenues.[8] Lobbying groups concentrated their efforts on influencing the budgetary privatization processes. In the financial sphere, lobbying was not limited to the pursuit of budget resources but also included the pursuit of various tax breaks and, in 1992, of central bank credits, a large part of which were effectively budget payments. We should note here the impossibility of successfully implementing "selective" or "precision" budgetary support for specific branches or enterprises by allocating funds or granting tax breaks. Such policies inevitably lead to an imprudent expansion of budget expenditure and a spate of tax breaks.

The rise in activity of various pressure groups in the spring of 1992 played a decisive role in the softening of fiscal and monetary policies.[9] This development consequently led to a sharp increase in budgetary outlays.[10] Thus, the national budget deficit for the first

---

8. As various authors have shown, this is to be expected; in particular, as a result of the activities of lobbying groups representing various interests in the redistribution of GDP, macroeconomic stabilization is delayed. See A. Schleifer and R. Vishny, "Politicians and Firms," *Quarterly Journal of Economics* (November 1994); A. Alesina and A. Drazen, "Why Are Stabilizations Delayed?" NBER Working Paper no. 3053 (August 1989).

9. This confirms the well-known proposition that politics tends to have a stronger effect on economic policy in times of political instability. See S. Haggard and R. R. Kaufman, *The Political Economy of Democratic Transitions* (Princeton, N.J.: Princeton University Press, 1995); A. Alesina, ed., *Macroeconomics and Politics—NBER Macroeconomic Annual* (Cambridge: MIT Press, 1988); A. Alesina and N. Roubini, "Political Cycles in OECD Economies," NBER Working Paper no. 3478 (1990).

10. Compared with the first quarter, government spending on the economy in the first half-year increased from 5.8% to 8.4% of GDP. In the first seven months it was 9.7% of GDP, and in the first eight months it was 10.7% of GDP. Similarly, social expenditure grew by 5% of GDP in the first quarter to 7.9% of GDP over the first eight months of 1992, and expenditure on the state apparatus and law enforcement bodies increased from 0.3% to 0.5% of GDP.

half of 1992 was 6.6% of GDP, and the consolidated budget deficit grew at about the same rate.[11] All in all, the volume of central bank credits in the second half of the year almost tripled[12] (figures for the month-by-month growth of money aggregates are presented in Table 6.1).

In July the federal budget deficit reached 8.2% of GDP, while for the first eight months of the year it was approximately 10.8% of GDP. In July and August, central bank credit growth remained extremely high (about 50% per month), and slowed only somewhat in September.[13]

In response to a May 1992 raising of energy prices and the implementation of additional measures in support of social welfare and the national economy, the 1992 budget had to be revised. In July the law *On the Budgetary System of the Russian Federation for 1992* was adopted. This law set federal budget revenues at 13.1% of GDP, expenditures at 18.4% of GDP, and the deficit at 5.3% of GDP.

This budget, adopted by Parliament, differed substantially from the government's drafts. The parliamentary majority asserted that the government had understated the revenue side of the budget, and therefore proceeded to revise both revenue and expenditure figures upward.[14]

As a result of accelerating inflation, spring and summer spending increases in support of the economy did not produce the desired growth in real incomes and improvement in enterprises' financial situation. Emissionary budget financing meant that additional income was immediately reduced by the inflation tax.

---

11. This was caused by the increase in budgetary expenditures on the economy (from 3.2% to 4.7% of GDP, compared with the first quarter), on the social sphere (from 1.3% to 2.1% of GDP), and on defense (from 3.1% to 4.7% of GDP).
12. Credits to the government were 38% of all central bank credits. Trade surplus with the other states of the ruble zone led to the growth of credits to these countries (to 30% of all central bank credits), while the remaining 32% were to commercial banks.
13. Overall in the third quarter, central bank credits increased by 131%. The government and commercial banks each received roughly a 40% share of these credits, with the remaining 20% going to countries in the ruble zone.
14. In comparison with the government's draft budget, revenues in the adopted law were increased by 4% and spending was increased by 10%. The deficit in the consolidated budget, according to the law, was forecast to be 4.1% of GDP, or 15.5 trillion rubles.

Table 6.1
Monthly Growth of Money Aggregates in 1992

	1992, Month											
	I	II	III	IV	V	VI	VII	VIII	IX	X	XI	XII
M0 (in bill. of rubles)	191	216	255	321	369	458	645	830	950	1,146	1,380	1,678
M2 (in bill. of rubles)	1,054	1,179	1,345	1,482	1,617	2,069	2,644	3,411	4,465	5,671	5,969	7,140
M2 growth rate (%)		12	14	10	9	28	28	29	31	27	5	20
Cash share in M2 (%)	18	18	19	22	23	22	24	24	21	20	23	24
Index of retail prices	245	38	30	22	12	19	11	9	12	23	26	25

M0: Cash.
M1: M0 plus household current accounts, household and enterprise deposits, and Gosstrakh funds.
M2: M1 plus term deposits.
Sources: Central Bank RF, IEPPP.

6.3. Monetary Policy and Credit Policy in 1992

Monetary and credit policies in the first year of reform were characterized by several contradictory trends. First, price liberalization in January 1992 wiped out the monetary overhang, as a result of which economic agents actually determined the real demand for money. Second, a sharp drop in the real demand for money was the unavoidable consequence of price liberalization, as the population bought up goods and hard currency. Third, temporary stabilization in the spring and summer of 1992, following the drop in real demand for money, was a result of effective control over the money supply in the first months of the year. The new burst of inflation in the second half of the year resulted due to a change in the monetary authorities' priorities, chiefly their refusal to control the money supply. We will now examine in more detail the factors influencing monetary policy.

The nominal growth of the money supply was determined by the inflationary regime of the prereform years, a regime that led to a jump in prices in late 1991 and early 1992. Inflationary processes are inertial and, to a certain extent, self-reinforcing. For example, the transaction demand for money in conditions of inflation requires continuous monetary emission. The growth of the nominal money supply more or less accords with the inflationary expectations of economic agents, and thus compensates for the reduction in real cash balances that occurs because of an anticipated increase in the money supply.

A peculiarity of the price liberalization in Russia was that this process occurred during the changeover to a new interenterprise (and interorganization) payments and settlements system. The problems and inadequacies of this system in the first years of reform exacerbated the payment arrears crisis. The easiest way to maintain uninterrupted money circulation in such conditions was to continue to increase the nominal money supply. Thus, even while preserving a financial stabilization course, it was impossible to abandon monetary emissions immediately. In the first four months of 1992, both the central bank and the government tried to adhere to a strategy of moderate containment of inflation.

Starting in the summer of 1992, political factors played an important role in the rapid growth of the money supply, by obstructing consistently tight monetary and credit policies. From a political-economic point of view, the constitution then in force and the balance of political forces then prevalent made abandonment of tight policies unavoidable. As a result, financial stabilization, which is a natural component of the first stage of market reforms, was not launched immediately after price liberalization.

Narrow money, consisting of cash and obligatory reserves in the central bank, increased by a factor of 13 in 1992. The rate of monetary emission started to accelerate in the second quarter, immediately after the change in central bank leadership. This process is demonstrated by the broad money dynamic, including cash, correspondent accounts, and deposits with the central bank (including the accounts of CIS country central banks). The growth rate of this indicator in the first quarter of 1992 was 19% per month, while in the second quarter it was 34% per month. Over the year, broad money grew faster than narrow money, increasing by a factor of 18. This phenomenon can be explained by excess reserves on central bank accounts and by the growth of technical credits to CIS countries, which to a considerable extent subsidized Russian exports to those countries. Russia's net claims on the other states of the ruble zone grew from zero at the beginning of 1992 to about 1 trillion rubles at the end of the year, or 31% of Russia's net domestic assets at the time.

The expansion of the money supply, caused both by a monetization of the budget deficit and by an increase in credits to domestic producers and other states in the ruble zone, accelerated inflation and led to a fall in the ruble exchange rate at the end of the summer. Structural factors also contributed to the acceleration of inflation, among them the deregulation of agricultural prices and the implementation in September of the next phase of fuel price liberalization. The resulting strengthening of economic agents' inflationary expectations could not fail to diminish the demand for money, and thus led to a further acceleration of inflation and a collapse of the ruble exchange rate in September and October.

On 1 August 1992, a unified floating ruble-dollar exchange rate was introduced. At the same time, restrictions on the sale of foreign currency to private persons were lifted, as was the requirement that exporters sell hard currency earnings at a fixed exchange rate. This was a very important step, as multiple rates of exchange distort relative prices and lead to undesirable rent effects.[15]

---

15. In autumn, the monthly growth rate of retail and wholesale prices reached 25%–26%. A fall in the ruble exchange rate in autumn of 1992 that was much more rapid than the rate of inflation reduced the real ruble exchange rate by a factor of 1.5.

As noted earlier, a very important trend in 1992 was the growth of payment arrears. By the middle of the year, the volume of nonpayments had reached 3.2 trillion rubles, exceeding M2 by 62%. Interenterprise arrears grew over the first half of the year by a factor of 67, reaching a total of 2.3 trillion rubles. High inflation was an important factor influencing this development. On the one hand, inflation benefited debtor enterprises by reducing the size of their debts to other enterprises, to the budget, and to extrabudgetary funds. On the other hand, inflation reduced enterprises' working capital. Commercial banks made considerable profits during such inflation through financial intermediaries, taking advantage of imperfections in the payment settlements system.

Attempts by the government and the central bank to resolve this problem were unsuccessful. The changeover from payment orders to a direct debit system proceeded slowly, further disrupting the payments system. Increasing fines against delinquents proved to be largely ineffective. Netting out of debts reduced arrears temporarily, but at the cost of further ruble emission to cover the obligations of net debtors. The settlement of mutual debts started in August 1992 and encompassed interenterprise debts, debts between enterprises and commercial banks, and debts between enterprises and the budget. Repayment of the debts that remained after the netting out of interenterprise debt (335 billion rubles, or 17% of M2, in the middle of 1992) was effected mainly by the central bank.

In general, the chronic nonpayments problem (which began in 1992) should be viewed as a manifestation of the general structural crisis in the economy, a crisis that is unavoidable during the transition to a market economy. Nonpayments allowed enterprises to soften budget constraints and to adapt to market conditions without implementing essential restructuring measures. An important factor in this process was the desire of many enterprise managers to evade taxes and misappropriate enterprise property. The scale of this phenomenon grew dramatically in the early years of reform during a weakening of state controls and the absence of clearly defined property rights. Mutual arrears often served as a cover for illegal deals between enterprise managers and intermediaries.

Sudden changes in monetary and credit policy, which had been occurring since the beginning of the year, ambiguously impacted the behavior of economic agents. On the one hand, a burst of inflation in January (the consumer price index went up by 296%) led to a reduction in real cash balances. This reduction in real demand for money was combined with an increased demand for goods and hard currency. On the other hand, a tight monetary policy in the first four months made it possible to limit inflation and reduce the rate of ruble devaluation, leading to the stabilization of demand for money in the second and third quarters. Whereas average monthly consumer price growth in the first quarter was 80.3%, in the second and third quarters prices grew on average by 13.8% and 10.2%, respectively. The infusion of money into the economy, starting in the summer of 1992, followed a period of tight monetary policy in the early months of the year, and thus did not immediately lead to a reduction in real cash balances. For this reason, the speed of money circulation decreased in October 1992 by more than a factor of two, as a new burst of inflation began. Average price growth in the fourth quarter was 27.8%.

The deceleration of money circulation can also be explained by the fact that many economic agents, from a lack of experience, reacted with delay to signals that economic policy was changing. Thus, the decline in real demand for money lagged behind the growth in the nominal money supply by several months, and as a result, the state benefited from the inflation tax. This benefit did not subside quickly, due to the somewhat irrational behavior of households. Effective devaluation of the inflation tax occurs when budget recipients get significantly less in real terms than the state allocated to them. In Russia, this was linked to deficiencies in the payments system and benefited the commercial banks that serviced the budget.[16]

In 1992, changes in money multipliers that are typical of transition economies occurred. M2 increased tenfold in 1992; that is, it grew more slowly than the monetary base. This was connected to a halving of the money multiplier, expressed as the ratio of M2 to broad money, from 5.5 in December 1991 to 2.1 in December 1992. The principal reason for the halving of the money multiplier was an increase in the share of cash in circulation. High rates of inflation dictated a sharp increase in the nominal demand for cash. However, the changeover to larger denomination banknotes took some time, and the multiplier was higher than normal in the early months of the year. Second, the money of commercial banks and enterprises on

---

16. An analysis of the inflation tax in Russia in 1992–1994 can be found in the survey, *Rossiyskaya ekonomika v pervom polugodii 1994 g.—tendentsii i perspektivy* (Moscow: IEPPP, 1994).

central bank accounts increased at a much faster rate than so-called "inside money" (deposits, correspondent accounts, and the like). Inflation caused a sharp reduction in real interest rates and led to an 18% reduction in real ruble deposits between February 1992 and February 1993. As a result of liberalization in the banking sector, interest rates were better able to adapt to inflation. However, the rise in interest rates during 1992 was not sufficient to compensate for depositors' real losses.

Third, a reduction of the multiplier can be explained by the introduction in 1991 of reserve requirements for commercial banks, which sharply increased in the second quarter of 1992. Reserve requirements on demand deposits were increased tenfold, from 2% to 20%. Sberbank (Russia's main savings bank) accounts were also subjected to reserve requirements, although some deposits, such as those used for housing construction, were exempt. Despite increased reserve requirements, commercial banks increased their excess reserve accounts with the central bank. This apparently paradoxical phenomenon can largely be explained by the underdeveloped interbank settlements system dominant at the time. Banks needed to create additional liquid reserves in order to minimize the quite probable (and often considerable) losses from counter-parties' defaulting on obligations. The cost of holding excess liquid assets was compensated by the relatively low cost of funds attracted by the banks.

Liberalization of the banking sector did not eliminate nonmarket mechanisms for distributing centralized credits. Credits to the government, to enterprises, and to CIS countries were issued at interest rates significantly below market rates. The central bank effectively financed government expenditure and certain sectors of the economy directly. It should be emphasized again that the inflation tax was an effective source of financing the budget deficit, largely because the population adapted fairly slowly to the high inflation regime and therefore was slow to reduce real cash balances.

The central bank's refinancing rate was raised from 20% in January 1992 to 80% in May 1992, where it remained until the end of the year. However, this was not accompanied by a sufficient tightening of credit policy vis-à-vis the government and the economy. Throughout 1992 the refinancing rate was consistently higher than lending rates to the government, and also higher than average interest rates on bank deposits. Although the refinancing rate was thereafter regularly revised in line with inflation, until 1995 it was not really used as an instrument for regulating the money supply. The refinancing rate was mainly used to indicate the market interest-rate ceiling and to calculate fines for breach of contract and tax obligations.

During 1992, credits grew almost tenfold, while M2 grew sevenfold. However, changes in government and central bank policy made the credit dynamic uneven: whereas in the first quarter net domestic credits grew by an average of 13% per month, in the second and third quarters they grew by 20% and 38%, respectively. In the fourth quarter credit expansion slowed down to an average of 11% per month.

In 1992 the consumer price index grew by 2,318% (by 510% between February and December 1992), while wholesale prices for capital and intermediary goods increased by 3,275%. The real decrease in the money supply in 1992 was 75%, while the dollar exchange rate grew 80.4%.

During this period the net volume of central bank credits grew by a factor of 14, with credits to commercial banks increasing by a factor of 20.6 and credits to the federal government increasing by a factor of 10.6. Credits to the government constituted about 37.3% of total central bank credit growth, credits to commercial banks constituted 38.2%, and credits to states in the ruble zone (issued from February 1992) constituted 24%. Credits issued to commercial banks were used to finance the regional expenditures, enterprises, and to settle mutual nonpayments.

6.4. The Attempt to Change Fiscal Strategy in the Absence of Coordinated Government and Central Bank Actions

The acceleration of inflation and the fall in the ruble exchange rate during the second half of 1992 was one of the major macroeconomic problems facing the government at the time. In order to meet the limit set on the size of the federal budget deficit, in the law *On the Budgetary System of the Russian Federation for 1992*, deficit growth in September and December had to be kept within 13.6% of the annual limit. Therefore, in September and November government expenditures were cut sharply. At the same time, in October and November 1992 there was a considerable growth in tax receipts.[17] As a result, in

---

[17]. By December 1992 (over 11 months), expenditure on the national economy was cut to 9.9% of GDP, expenditure on the social sphere was cut to 7.4% of GDP, and expenditure on defense was cut to 4.3% of GDP. Tax receipts increased from 23% of GDP in September to 26.7% in November 1992.

autumn the national budget deficit (excluding quasi-budget operations) fell in absolute terms. As a share of GDP, the budget deficit fell from 10.8% of GDP in August 1992 to 7.5% of GDP in September, and to 4.4% in October. For January to November, the federal budget deficit grew somewhat in absolute terms, but it continued to decline as a share of GDP (to 4.2% of GDP). At the same time, of course, budget arrears in the social sphere and wage arrears grew, and there were delays in paying for weapons deliveries, agricultural produce, and so forth.

In this manner, in autumn of 1992 it proved possible to limit budget expenditures, although this did not create favorable conditions for launching financial stabilization. In December 1992, in connection with the end of the budget year and the need to fulfill the state's expenditure obligations, as well as a result of the weakening in budget policy following the dismissal of Yegor Gaidar as prime minister, there was another sharp increase in budget expenditures (at both the federal and the local level).[18]

The conflict between the government and the Supreme Soviet (and consequently the central bank, which was supported by it) made it impossible to coordinate efforts to implement stabilization measures. Therefore, a peculiar feature of autumn 1992 was an extremely tight budget policy at the same time that considerable growth in the money supply was taking place. For example, in October and November the volume of central bank credits to the government hardly increased, and the considerable growth in central bank credits in the fourth quarter mainly took the form of credits to commercial banks. However, the settlement of interenterprise arrears, conducted by the central bank in autumn 1992, played a significant role. As noted earlier, this process was accompanied by mass monetary emission (Table 6.2). The central bank, which was more subordinate to the Supreme Soviet than to the president at the time, pumped "cheap money" into the economy. The opposition of the central bank to a tightening of fiscal policy in autumn 1992 obstructed the implementation of stabilization in the first half of 1993.[19]

---

18. Central government expenditures increased from 19.7% of GDP over 11 months to 21.8% of GDP for the whole of 1994. Consolidated budget expenditures grew from 29.4% of GDP to 33%.

19. The situation can be considered in terms of game theory as a very simple model of the "coordination game" type (see E. Rasmusen, *Games and Information: An Introduction to Game Theory* (Cambridge: Basil Blackwell, 1987). The government and the central bank are the two players. Each has two strategies: anti-inflationary and pro-inflationary. The choice by one player of the pro-inflationary strategy, regardless of

Table 6.2
Main Accounts of the Russian Monetary and Credit Authorities in 1991–1992 (at End of Period, in Billions of Rubles)

Accounts	December 1991	December 1992
Net foreign assets, including:	246	2,480
Claims on CIS countries	—	1,024
Net domestic assets	69	3,301
Net domestic credits	329	4,600
Net credits to the government	178	1,577
Credits to the economy	7	75
Credits to banks	143	2,947
Other assets	−260	−1,299
Monetary base	314	5,792

Sources: Central Bank RF, IMF.

The contradictory fiscal policy of 1993 could not curb inflation and did not halt the fall in production (which was 19% over the year). The tightening of the budgetary policy (as well as credit and monetary policies) in autumn 1992 led in December to a deceleration in inflation and to a temporary stabilization in the ruble exchange rate. However, the substantial increase in money supply during December in response to credit expansion and growth in the federal budget deficit led to a new inflationary spiral in the middle of December and a sharp drop in the exchange rate at the end of January 1993 (Table 6.3).

6.5. Reconstruction of the State's Revenues and Expenditures

Official Ministry of Finance statistics from 1992–1994 did not include many of the government's financial operations. As a result, as in other countries undergoing the transition to a market economy, budgetary statistics, and particularly the budget deficit, do not adequately reflect the government's fiscal policy. Therefore, here and later on we reconstruct the state's revenues and expenditures (including extrabudgetary funds) by using not only Ministry of Finance statistics,

---

the other player's choice, leads to inflation. The choice by both players of the antiinflationary strategy leads to financial stabilization. If the central bank takes a proinflationary position, the government should also soften its fiscal policy. Such a decision is unlikely to worsen the macroeconomic situation; however, it would have made it possible to avoid the political costs of the tough course, which resulted in the change of government in the middle of December 1992.

Table 6.3
The Ruble Exchange Rate in 1992 (Exchange Rate on 1 January 1992: 159.4 Rb/$1 US)

1992	Rubles per $1 US (at End of Month)
January	180
February	170
March	161
April	155
May	128
June	119
July	136
August	163
September	204
October	338
November	448
December	418

Source: Goskomstat.

but also data from the central bank, Goskomstat, the State Tax Service, the Ministry of Foreign Economic Relations, and the Ministry of Economy. This approach, as far as possible, presents the available data in a generally accepted format.[20]

Table 6.4 is a reconstruction of the consolidated budget for 1992, including extrabudgetary funds. The Ministry of Finance statistics have been adjusted following an analysis of both budget revenues and expenditures.[21]

---

20. See *Manuel de statistiques des finances publiques*, 1987; *Statistiques des finances publiques*, 1992; *Manuel de la balance des paiements*, 1977; *Statistiques des recettes publiques des pays membres de l'OCDE*, 1994; P. Host-Madsen, *Comptes macroeconomiques: Vue d'ensemble* (Washington, D.C.: International Monetary Fund, 1979); M. Blejer and C. Adritnne, *How to Measure the Fiscal Deficit: Analytical and Methodological Issues* (Washington, D.C.: International Monetary Fund, 1993); R. Brid and O. Oldman, *Taxation in Developing Countries* (Washington, D.C.: International Monetary Fund, 1990).
21. Among state revenues are those received in the first half of 1992 as a result of the obligatory conversion of part of export enterprises' hard currency earnings at a higher-than-market ruble exchange rate. In the estimate of 1992 expenditures, import subsidies through the sale of hard currency to import firms, also at a higher-than-market exchange rate, are also factored in. Both the external financing received and the volume of price subsidies are excessively high as a result of application of the current ruble exchange rate to the dollar in the calculations. In 1992 overall the real ruble exchange rate changed by a factor of 11 (26.1/2.32). In 1993, the real ruble exchange rate continued to grow by a factor of 3.1 (9.4/3); in 1994 the nominal dollar exchange rate grew by a factor of 2.8, while inflation grew by a factor of 3.15—thus the real ruble exchange rate grew by a factor of 1.1. In 1995, the real ruble exchange rate grew by 77%. Thus, converting the external credits received in 1992 from dollars to rubles gives a figure several times higher than the estimate.

Table 6.4
Reconstruction of Revenues and Expenditures of the Russian Federation in 1992

	Federal Budget (% of GDP)	Local Budgets (% of GDP)	Extrabudgetary Funds (% of GDP)	Consolidated Budget (% of GDP)	Consolidated Budget (% of Budget)
TAX REVENUES					
1. Income and profit taxes	3.6	7.5		11.1	27
1.1. Income tax		2.4		2.4	6
1.2. Profit tax	3.6	5.1		8.7	21
2. Social Security contributions			8.8	8.8	22
2.1. Employees			0.4	0.4	1
2.2. Employers			8.4	8.4	21
Pension Fund			7.1	7.1	17
Social Security Fund			1.1	1.1	3
Employment Fund			0.2	0.2	0
Social Support Fund			0.1	0.1	0
3. Property taxes	0.1	0.6		0.7	2
3.1. Property tax		0.3		0.3	1
3.2. Land tax	0.1	0.3		0.4	1
4. Domestic taxes on goods and services	9.4	4.0		13.4	33
4.1. VAT	8.3	2.8		11.1	27
4.2. Excise duties	0.6	0.6		1.2	3
4.3. Natural resource royalties		0.6		0.6	2
4.4. Mineral replacement tax	0.4			0.4	1
4.5. Price Control Fund	0.1			0.1	0

5. Foreign trade taxes	3.8	0.0		3.9	10
5.1. Import duties	0.4			0.4	1
5.2. Export duties	1.6	0.0		1.6	4
5.3. Other foreign trade revenues	1.3			1.3	3
5.4. Foreign exchange gain	0.6			0.6	
6. Other taxes	0.5	0.4		1.0	2
7. Extrabudgetary funds			1.0	1.0	2
7.1. Road Fund			0.8	0.8	2
7.2. Fund for financing R&D			0.1	0.1	0
7.3. Fund for regulating energy prices			0.1	0.1	0
Total Tax Revenues	17.4	12.6	9.7	39.7	98
NONTAX REVENUES					
1. Revenues from revaluation of goods		0.1		0.1	0
2. State budget reserves for covering expenditures	0.1	0.2		0.3	1
CAPITAL INCOME	0.1	0.2		0.3	1
1. Income from privatization	0.1	0.2		0.3	
Total Revenues	17.7	13.0	9.7	40.4	100
SUBSIDIES		1.7	0.3	×	
Subsidies to local budgets		1.7		×	
Subsidies to the Pension Fund			0.3	×	
Total Revenues and Subsidies	17.7	14.6	10.0	40.4	100

(continued)

Table 6.4 (continued)

	Federal Budget (% of GDP)	Local Budgets (% of GDP)	Extrabudgetary Funds (% of GDP)	Consolidated Budget	
				(% of GDP)	(% of Budget)
STATE EXPENDITURES AND CREDITS LESS DEBT REPAYMENTS					
State Expenditures	33.3	12.5	7.5	51.3	79
1. State services of general character	0.2	0.4		0.6	1
2. On defense	4.7			4.7	7
3. On law enforcement bodies	1.3	0.0		1.4	2
4. On scientific research	0.6	0.0		0.6	1
5. On social and housing services	2.7	5.4	6.0	13.8	21
5.1. On education	1.3	2.5		3.8	6
5.2. On culture, arts, and the mass media	0.3	0.3		0.6	1
5.3. On public health and sport	0.3	2.3		2.6	4
5.4. On Chernobyl and Semipalatinsk programs	0.4			0.4	1
5.5. On social benefits	0.1	0.3	6.0	6.4	10
5.6. On subsidies to the Pension Fund	0.3			×	
6. State services to the economy	14.0	5.3	1.5	20.9	32
7. On other functions	6.6	1.4		6.3	10
7.1. Other expenditures	1.3	1.4		2.6	4
7.2. On foreign trade	2.3			2.3	4
7.3. On domestic debt servicing	0.7			0.7	1
7.4. On foreign debt servicing	0.7			0.7	1
7.5. Subsidies from the federal budget to other levels of state administration	1.7			×	
8. Other expenditures	3.1			3.1	5

Credits Less Debt Repayments	13.9	0.2	13.8	21
1. To other levels of state administration	0.3		×	8
2. To enterprises	4.9	0.2	5.1	
2.1. From the budget	4.5		4.5	7
2.2. State credits from the central bank	8.7		8.7	13
3. Credits to CIS countries				
Total Expenditures and Credits Less Debt Repayments	47.2	12.7	65.1	100
Revenues and Subsidies Minus Expenditures and Credits Less Debt Repayments	−29.4	2.0	−24.7	
FINANCING				
1. Domestic financing	18.6	0.3		
1.1. By other levels of the state administration				
1.2. By the central bank	18.6	0.3		
1.2.1. Credits to the government for covering the budget deficit	5.5			
1.2.2. Credits to the government	13.1			
	11.0			
2. Foreign financing (net)	−0.1	−2.2	−2.5	
3. Change in monies deposited		−2.0	−2.5	
Total Financing	29.4			

Sources: Ministry of Finance RF, Goskomstat, IET.

The reconstruction of the system of state finances for 1992 shows that budget and extrabudgetary fund revenues were around 40% of GDP.[22] The share of extrabudgetary funds in the revenues of the consolidated budget was 25% (10.0% of GDP), of which the various social funds accounted for 8.8% of GDP. Consolidated budget expenditures in 1992 were 51.3% of GDP, while expenditures and credits (less debt repayments) were 65.1% of GDP; extrabudgetary fund expenditures (7.5% of GDP) are also included in this figure. The overestimate of those revenue and expenditure items that were initially denominated in foreign currency should also be taken into account. Expenditures on the economy reached 20.9% of GDP (including import subsidies—10.5% of GDP, and expenditures from extrabudgetary funds—1.5% of GDP).

Credits (less debt repayments) reached 13.8% of GDP. It is worth noting that credits to CIS countries (8.7% of GDP) were a major item in our adjustment of the budget figures.[23] The large-scale credits extended by Russia in 1992 to the former Soviet republics at first glance appear to be minimal, and not among the expenditure items of the 1991 budget. However, goods deliveries (fuel and energy making up the overwhelming majority) meant that considerable debts to Russia had been accumulating with CIS countries, and thus in effect this item of expenditure was not new. Insofar as Russia before the reforms was a net donor to other Soviet republics, the reduction of these subsidies was a serious political problem that has not been fully resolved even today.

As Table 6.4 shows, federal budget revenues and overall expenditures including credits (less debt repayments) were 29.4% of GDP

---

22. The estimates presented here differ fairly significantly from those published by us in an earlier work (Sergei Sinelnikov, *Byudzhetny krizis v Rossii: 1985–1995* (Moscow: Yevraziya, 1995). This is explained by the fact that payments to extrabudgetary funds were not taxes in the strict sense of the word. Most of the money remained on enterprises' accounts on condition that it be directed to its intended destination. In our previous estimates, these payments which remained on enterprise accounts and which were used to finance the expenditures of the relevant funds (9.1% of GDP) were included among tax receipts. Here we include only extrabudgetary fund revenues that are centralized by the state (9.8% of GDP).

23. The inclusion among Russian government credits of credits extended to former Soviet republics is purely for accounting purposes. In 1992 the government was unable to control these credits, and in the first half-year, because of preservation of a single ruble zone, they were basically automatic. It is necessary to retain these credits in calculations of general government expenditures in order to compare 1992 data with 1993 data.

in 1992. As far as the influence of the fiscal deficit on the monetary situation is concerned, a more informative indicator than the federal budget deficit (as calculated by the Ministry of Finance, 5.3% of GDP) is the balance of federal budget revenues and expenditures, including credits (less repayments), but excluding subsidies to importers that were mainly financed by external credits. This indicator in 1992 was 18.9% of GDP. It is important to note that in this reconstruction, because of the absence of reliable data, sizable central bank credits to the government (among which the most significant credits were to the agricultural sector and for the shipping of goods to regions in the Far North) are not included. Consequently, the reconstruction presented in the table is not fully comparable with its counterparts for the following years.

Financing for the federal budget deficit came from foreign credits (11% of GDP) and central bank credits (18.6% of GDP).[24] This estimate of the volume of foreign financing should not be treated as an absolute figure, because of the distinction between the current exchange rate and the purchasing power parity of the ruble. Tax receipts in the consolidated budget (excluding extrabudgetary funds) in 1992 were 30% of GDP. The total tax revenues of the budget system were 39.7% of GDP, including only the centralized part of money transfers to the extrabudgetary funds. The introduction of VAT and excise duties, thanks to adjustments in the method of collection over the course of the year, compensated for the abolition of the turnover tax. Despite the high level of inflation and the significant time lag between taxes being charged and being transferred to the budget, real profit tax receipts were maintained at 1991 levels. There was also no reduction in the volume of income tax receipts.[25] These four kinds of tax provided 78% of tax revenues to national and local budgets and 48% of revenues to the consolidated budget.

---

24. The difference between official figures for domestic financing and those presented in the table can be explained by the fact that included in central bank domestic financing figures are loans to the government to cover the budget deficit, as well as credits that were not officially included in the 1992 budget, among them credits for the conversion of military-industrial enterprises (0.4% of GDP), for investment (0.6% of GDP), for geological prospecting (0.1% of GDP), for topping up enterprises' working capital (3.3% of GDP), and for CIS countries (8.7% of GDP).

25. The VAT in 1992 was 11.1% of GDP (41.3% of budget revenues), which was 5.4% of GDP more than was collected in turnover tax in 1991. Excise duties in 1992 were 1.2% of GDP (4.2% of budget revenues), and the profit tax was 8.9% of GDP (30.7%). Income tax revenues reached 2.4% of GDP (8.4% of budget revenues).

The aforementioned statistical data demonstrate that the tax reform facilitated the stabilization of tax receipt levels. The introduction of the VAT was necessary to replace the turnover tax, which did not function effectively under market pricing. The effectiveness of this decision can be judged from the statistical data, which demonstrate overall the high level of efficiency of the tax.[26] These data also reveal that the large budget deficit in 1992 was caused not by a fall in revenues but by the difficulties in cutting budget expenditures sharply due to both economic and political forces. Thus, the fundamental macroeconomic result of the tax reform conducted in 1992 was the raising of state revenues to a level at which inflexible budget expenditures could be financed without creating a deficit capable of pushing the economy into a hyperinflationary mode.[27]

---

26. Sinelnikov, *Byudzhetny krizis v Rossii*.
27. Hyperinflation is defined as inflation in excess of 50% per month over three or more months without interruption.

7 Formation of the Preconditions for Financial Stabilization

Sergei Sinelnikov-Murylev
and Georgy Trofimov

The events of 1993–1994 conformed to a fairly precise cyclical pattern. Two clearly defined periods occurred in 1993. The first lasted from January to 21 September, when Boris Yeltsin issued presidential decree No. 1400, "On Gradual Constitutional Reform in the Russian Federation." This period was characterized by confrontation between the executive and legislative branches of government. One consequence of this confrontation was the escalation of expenditures approved by both branches, which were not backed by a commensurate increase in budget revenues. Nevertheless, the Ministry of Finance maintained fairly tight control on actual spending, which led to an increasing gap between approved and realized budget deficits.

The second period was from October to December 1993. The radical change in the balance of political forces in September made it possible to reduce approved expenditures, a reality that brought the possibility of a balanced budget closer.

"Moderately tight" monetary and budget policies were implemented in the first three quarters of 1994. The aim was to combine anti-inflationary policies with centralized support for the national economy and the provision of fairly high levels of social guarantees for the population. In reality, all kinds of expenditures continued to be approved, and although these expenditures were not fully disbursed, they led to double-digit monthly inflation. Finally, in autumn of 1994 the government embarked on a new stabilization course. Despite all the vacillations and retreats, the preconditions for economic stabilization formed slowly but steadily in this period, assisted by various institutional changes, which are discussed in Part III of this book.

7.1. Influence of Political Factors on State Finances

At the beginning of 1993, with no budget approved, budget expenditures for January were already one-third of those provided for in the 1992 budget for the fourth quarter. As a result, in January there was a federal budget surplus of 0.7% of GDP. However, the Supreme Soviet permitted the government to undertake expenditures in the first quarter at levels written into the draft budget for 1993. This decision led to a considerable increase in expenditures in the spring of that year.[1]

Following the approval of a number of laws, the amendment of the tax regime, and also debates in the Supreme Soviet at the beginning of January 1993, consolidated revenues in the draft budget were increased to 28% of GDP while expenditures were increased to 35% of GDP. The budget deficit was set at 6% of GDP. During parliamentary hearings, the draft underwent amendments that led to an overall increase in spending. The growing confrontation between the Supreme Soviet and the government, as well as the intensification of conflicts between different interest groups within the government, meant that the 1993 national budget law was passed only in its second reading at the end of March. The budget deficit in this law was pegged at 18% of GDP. Despite opposition from the Ministry of Finance, President Yeltsin signed the law in mid-May.

The government's stabilization efforts intensified somewhat after Yeltsin's presidential statement of 20 March 1993 and the April referendum, in which support was expressed for the economic reforms. A joint statement on economic policy (approved by the International Monetary Fund) was signed by the central bank and the government, setting quarterly limits on issues of centralized credits. Yeltsin also issued a decree, "On Measures to Control Inflation," placing a moratorium on increasing unbacked budget expenditures. Technical credits to CIS countries were curtailed in May 1993, and instead interstate credits were made available from the Russian budget. The dollar equivalent of these credits was fixed and strict deadlines were set for repayment. In the first two months of the year more than half of central bank credits went to other CIS states. Thereafter the situa-

---

1. In March 1993 there was an abrupt increase in federal budget expenditures. As a result, the federal budget deficit increased to 10.6% of GDP between January and March 1993. The deficit was financed by increasing central bank credits to the government to 11.5% of GDP. The consolidated budget deficit was 7.1% of GDP.

tion changed: beginning in May, the central bank ceased issuing credits to the states within the ruble zone. These credits were channeled through the federal budget and were significantly reduced.

The change in the balance of political forces allowed the Russian Ministry of Finance, headed by Boris Fedorov, to stabilize the budget to a considerable degree, and from May onward to reduce the federal budget deficit to 5%–7% of GDP.[2]

Even as the Russian president was signing the budget law, work was under way to amend it, both because of its unrealistic forecast for 1993 and because the Ministry of Finance took issue with the rather high level of expenditures written into the law. Also, amendment of the budget was necessary because, between May and July, the legislative and executive branches had approved a number of measures raising federal expenditures above the levels allowed in the budget by more than 5% of GDP. These measures included raising state capital investments, increasing social expenditures, and setting grain procurement prices above market levels.[3]

At the end of June 1993, the Supreme Soviet considered a draft budget prepared by the Ministry of Finance that proposed reducing the budget deficit from 18% of GDP to about 10%. However, after parliamentary debate, the draft was altered. On 22 July 1993 the Supreme Soviet passed the law, *On the Elaboration of the Republican Budget Indices for 1993*, in which the budget deficit was set at 22.6% of GDP. President Yeltsin did not sign the law, returning it to Parliament for a second reading. On 27 August 1993, Parliament approved an almost identical version of the budget, adopting the law, *On Amendments and Additions to the Law on the Republican Budget of the Russian Federation for 1993*. This document planned to reduce the deficit to 22.1% of GDP.

The main differences in the positions of the Supreme Soviet and the government, and also in the positions of conservative and reformist wings of the government, were between financial stabilization, on the one hand, and the need to support domestic industry, agriculture, and other sectors of the economy on the other. The

---

2. In May the federal budget deficit was reduced to 5.7% of GDP. In June there was some further reduction in expenditures on the economy and defense, while other expenditures were stabilized. As a result, according to Ministry of Finance data, the deficit for the first half of 1993 was 4.8% of GDP. Federal budget revenues were 13.9% of GDP, and tax receipts were 12.7% of GDP.

3. Moreover, most of these measures were approved after Yeltsin's presidential decree of 3 June 1993, "On Measures to Control Inflation."

Supreme Soviet's rejection of the government's proposals for introducing new taxes in the draft budget led to a fall in the revenues of the consolidated federal budget, in comparison to the draft, of 4% of GDP. At the same time, the Supreme Soviet's amendments raised expenditures by 5% of GDP.

In the summer of 1993, tax receipts started to fall for the first time since 1992. This trend was largely unrelated to the Ministry of Finance's policies but rather to such factors as rising inflation, the growth of debts, and ballooning tax arrears. The erosion of tax discipline played an important part in this trend.[4] The consolidated budget deficit increased from 3.1% of GDP in June to 5.2% of GDP in July and to 6.1% of GDP in August. Throughout autumn of 1993 the situation continued to deteriorate.[5]

Since then, low tax receipts have been the rule. The shortfalls in tax collection, which increased gradually throughout 1993–1995, made it impossible to maintain budget expenditures at socially acceptable levels. This trend marked a new phase in the budget crisis.

The rapidly developing fiscal crisis, rooted in a growing budgetary imbalance and unrealistic budget obligations, was one of the factors exacerbating the political situation in autumn of 1993. In the conflict between the legislative and executive branches, the conservatives' goal was to preserve many elements of socialism and to obstruct reforms by all available means. They chiefly pursued populist policies, a strategy that had serious inflationary consequences. The main battles were waged over economic policy, in particular over the budget, monetary policy, and privatization. Imperfections in the constitution (in force until autumn of 1993) aggravated the confrontation. Had the powers of the different branches of government and the procedures governing the legislative process—especially procedures for resolving critical situations, such as Parliament's repeatedly rejecting draft legislation or the president's refusing to sign the budget into law—been clearly defined, the confrontation would almost certainly

---

4. The fall in tax receipts was as follows: from 28.4% of GDP over the first five months, to 26.8% of GDP in June, 26.3% of GDP in July, 26.3% of GDP in August, and 24.5% of GDP in September.

5. The consolidated budget deficit in September reached 6.9% of GDP, while the national deficit reached 8.7% of GDP. Federal budget expenditure barely increased (21.5% of GDP in August, 21.8% of GDP in September). An additional revenue item was central bank profit, in the sum of 0.5% of GDP. Expenditure was financed by the government's sale of foreign currency (in total, 1.6% of GDP over the first nine months) and of precious metals (0.8% of GDP), and by IMF loans (1.6% of GDP).

not have escalated into armed conflict. However, under the constitution then in force, an intensification of the crisis to such a level was unavoidable.

The executive branch, which generally fought for a tighter fiscal policy, was forced, out of political expediency, to compete with Parliament in adopting populist measures as the conflict heightened. The tremendous growth in budget expenditures at all levels in 1993 was the natural consequence of Russia's flawed constitutional system.

7.2. Monetary Policy and Credit Policy in 1993

Despite the political struggle, the Ministry of Finance managed to introduce a number of measures in the first six months of 1993 as a foundation for future attempts at financial stabilization. These measures included raising the central bank's refinancing rate, abolishing preferential credits to commercial banks for financing agriculture and the northern deliveries, disallowing indexation of enterprises' working capital and refusing further netting out of enterprise arrears, the abolition of easy credits to CIS countries, and the first issue of government securities (GKOs) in May 1993 as a source of financing the budget deficit.

In March 1993, for the first time, a monetary program was adopted that was formulated in a joint declaration of the government and the central bank. The program outlined a number of stabilization measures, such as a clearly stated ceiling on the budget deficit, targets for money supply growth (bringing it down to 7.3% per month by the end of the year), restrictions on the growth of domestic borrowing, and limits on centralized credits to the economy and government. Based on this program, it was predicted that average monthly inflation would be reduced to 5% by the end of 1993.

These efforts, however, were not sufficient to limit the expansion of the money supply. The average monthly growth of the monetary base was around 15% in the first six months of 1993. For the year as a whole, the monetary aggregate M2 grew by 430%, an average of 15% per month.

This expansionary fiscal policy led to a stable although high average monthly inflation rate of around 20% for almost all of 1993. This meant that yearly inflation for 1993 remained at 1992 levels. After the initial leap when prices were first liberalized, the inflation rate from February 1992 to January 1993 inclusive was 860%, and for 1993 it was 840%. The average monthly growth of central bank credits in 1993 of 14.6% was markedly lower than the rate of inflation. This occurred despite the considerable growth in credits issued in March and from July to September, when credits to the government increased sharply.

The new burst of monetary expansion in 1993 was fueled by the economy's adaptation to the high-inflation regime. This adaptation demanded the systematic indexation of wages and pensions, the strengthening of enterprises' working capital, and the steady devaluation of the ruble. At the same time, the mechanism linking the state's finances and monetary policy was strengthened. The percentage of credits issued to the Ministry of Finance out of all central bank credits was 47.6% at the end of 1993, whereas at the end of 1992 it was 37.8%. Consequently, 64% of the overall budget deficit was financed by central bank credits. This degree of financing reflected the considerably greater influence of budgetary policy on the monetary situation in 1993 in comparison to 1992, when credits to the government were only 35%–40% of the total volume of centralized credits. Thus the Russian government failed to avoid the inflationary financing of the state budget that began in mid-1992. High inflation, which enjoyed direct political support from populist forces, gained more and more importance as an element in the functioning of the state's finances.

In the second half of 1992 there was a fairly significant fall in the velocity of money circulation. (The ratio of M2 to average yearly GDP fell from 7.2 in May to 4.5 in October 1992.) This was the result of a delayed public reaction to the increase in the money supply. Thereafter the rising trend of velocity came to dominate, and the ratio of M2 to average yearly GDP increased to 9.5 in December 1995. Changes in the behavior of economic agents, who started to prefer more liquid instruments of transaction, played a part in this process. This was reflected in 1993 in particular by the increase in the share of cash in the monetary base from 40% to 60%, and the decline in the share of money left on banks' correspondent accounts from 47.5% to 25.1%.

What this means is that the real demand for money fell throughout 1993 as enterprises and the population at large adjusted to high inflation. In addition, commercial banks reduced the surplus reserves they held in central bank accounts, an action that attests both to their attempts to minimize losses from inflation and to the emergence of alternative investment opportunities (mainly on the "short" money market). Improvements in the payments system (increased reliability and reductions in the processing time for payments) also accelerated money circulation.

Once one factors in the annual rate of inflation in 1993, the real money supply was practically halved. Such a drop in demand for real cash balances was entirely natural in light of the continued high inflation, the 12% fall in GDP over the year, and the absence of significant transactions on the financial markets. The return at the end of the summer to an exchange rate policy pegged to the actual inflation rate revived commercial banks' interest in short-term foreign exchange speculation. This was also a factor in the drop in real demand for rubles.

Also, in 1993 for the first time there was serious competition among financial intermediaries over setting interest rates on bank loans and deposits. Already in the spring and summer of 1993 real interest rates on deposits covered most inflationary losses, and from the end of 1993 the real refinancing rate became positive. In part this leap in real interest rates was tied to a rise in the refinancing rate in October 1992 to 210% per annum (17.5% per month), and in part it was linked to the lowering of monthly inflation rates to 12.5% in December 1993. The linkage of bank discount rates to interest rates charged on the interbank market signaled the beginning of the period of "expensive" money and high real interest rates. This period continued until the inflationary spiral at the end of 1994.

Credits to commercial banks were tightened at a time when the necessary institutions and instruments for regulating bank liquidity by means of the discount window were absent. Raising the refinancing rate led to a drop in the share of these credits as a percentage of all centralized credits from 38.6% to 35.5% during 1994. This policy entailed a move toward tougher refinancing, although it would be an exaggeration to call it anti-inflationary. The central bank's attempt to limit refinance credits while at the same time maintaining the general inflation regime should be viewed as a kind of palliative measure. This measure was intended to counteract the economy's descent into hyperinflation—a real possibility at a time when the budget deficit was permanently a double-digit percentage of GDP and was financed for the most part through monetary emission.

Table 7.1
The Ruble Exchange Rate in 1993

1993	Rubles per $1 US (at End of Month)
January	572
February	593
March	684
April	823
May	994
June	1,060
July	990
August	993
September	1,169
October	1,186
November	1,231
December	1,247

Source: Goskomstat RF.

Raising real interest rates affected the structure of the financial assets of both the population and enterprises. Ruble deposits became more attractive, leading to a reduction in commercial banks' foreign currency deposits by 35% between January and August 1993. The sudden increase in dollar deposits (by 38%) observed in September 1993 was only temporary and can be explained by the high level of political uncertainty during the constitutional crisis.

The dollar exchange rate in 1993 rose from 572 rubles per US dollar in January to 1,247 rubles in December (Table 7.1). The annual increase in the dollar exchange rate was 182%, while in real terms the exchange rate fell by 70%. However, in the summer of 1993 the nominal exchange rate dropped, caused by the government's refusal to subsidize imports, and a corresponding fall in enterprises' demand for foreign currency. The increase in the trade surplus coincided with success in tightening fiscal policy in the first six months of the year. The interaction of these processes led to a sudden rise in the real ruble exchange rate by a factor of 3.2 in 1993. This phenomenon, common in the course of stabilization, moved domestic prices closer to world levels. The jump in the real ruble exchange rate in 1993 also foreshadowed the hardening of the ruble two years later as a result of the decisive stabilization measures of 1995. In accordance with a higher basic dollar exchange rate, the ruble's fall in 1995 could have been much more painful for the real sector of the economy. This in turn would have provoked a much more profound political backlash from protectionist lobby groups against the 1995 stabilization attempt.

In consequence of the strengthening of the real ruble exchange rate, domestic demand for foreign currency fell. This fall led to the forced accumulation of foreign exchange reserves by the central bank for the first time. In the initial reform years these reserves came mainly from the obligatory sale by exporters of part of their foreign currency earnings as well as from purchases of foreign currency by the central bank. However, the absence of low-risk ruble-denominated financial instruments and a lack of trust in the government's monetary policy stopped any large-scale dedollarization of the economy from occurring in 1993. Gold and foreign currency reserves more than doubled in 1993, from $3 billion to $6.4 billion. Although this increase permitted a normalization in the structure of the central bank's assets, it in no way signified substantial macroeconomic improvements in the foreign exchange structure of economic agents' financial assets. As before, there was a high level of capital flight, and the volume of dollars in circulation was growing. The accumulation of foreign reserves by the central bank led to an expansion of the monetary base. However, direct central bank credits to the government still remained a very important factor in the monetary expansion.

7.3. Reduction of Budget Expenditures After the Constitutional Crisis of 1993

The radical change in the balance of political forces after Yeltsin dissolved of the Supreme Soviet and the Congress of People's Deputies in September 1993 permitted a sharp change in budget policy. The government now had its first real opportunity to bring budget expenditures into line with revenues and to keep within the limits established for central bank credits to the government. A number of decisions were approved that cut excessive state expenditures.[6] The

---

6. These measures included above all the abolition of price indexation on grain and other agricultural products supplied to the state; the abolition of bread subsidies (with the introduction of a bread allowance for needy citizens); the abolition of import subsidies; and the abolition of preferential central bank credits (the only concessionary credits preserved were budget credits). There was a significant cut in state capital investment and a 20% sequester of all expenditure items of the federal budget for the fourth quarter of 1993.

central bank's refinance rate was raised, and the pension fund and other extrabudgetary funds became subordinate to the government.

Despite the tough measures taken in autumn of 1993, previously approved decisions meant that the high level of expenditures and the high budget deficit continued,[7] as did the fall in tax receipts as a share of GDP (Table 7.2).[8] Noteworthy is the fact that budget policy was tightened directly before the Russian State Duma elections. This tightening did not conform to the standard political business cycle, which presupposes a preelection weakening of fiscal policy by those in power in order to try to increase their popularity and chances of reelection.[9] The tightening of budget policy during the election campaign (which began in October) does not fit with standard models and with the experience of dozens of countries around the world. This turn of events, however, can be explained as follows.

First, inflation in August was approaching the dangerous level of 30% per month, threatening the country with hyperinflation and consequently requiring decisive actions. Although fully aware of the political dangers of pursuing a tight macroeconomic course, the government nonetheless could not consider these dangers a valid argument for rejecting fiscal tightening. The political consequences were crystal-clear to Yegor Gaidar from the very beginning.

Second, both President Yeltsin and his economic reformers were heavily influenced by the results of the April referendum, in which

---

7. State expenditures and credits less debt repayments were somewhat higher over twelve months (January–December) than over the first three quarters, rising from 35.3% of GDP to 35.5%. Federal budget spending and credits less debt repayments, in contrast to the situation at the local level, were somewhat reduced. They were 21.2% of GDP over twelve months, compared with 21.8% of GDP over the first nine months of 1993.

8. Tax receipts to the consolidated Russian budget were reduced from 25.4% of GDP between January and September to 24.6% between January and December 1993, and tax receipts to the republican budget were reduced from 11.1% to 10.3%.

9. See W. Nordhaus, "The Political Business Cycle," *Review of Economic Studies* 42 (April 1975): 169–90; A. Lindbeck, "Stabilization Policies in Open Economies with Endogenous Politicians," *The American Economic Review* (1976); D. Hibbs, *The American Political Economy* (Cambridge: Harvard University Press, 1987); N. Roubini and J. Sachs, "Government Spending and Budget Deficits in Industrialized Countries," *Economic Policy* 8 (Spring 1989): 99–132; A. Cukierman, S. Edwards, and G. Tabellini, "Seignorage and Political Instability," NBER Working Paper no. 3199 (1989); K. Rogoff, "Political Budget Cycles," *The American Economic Review* 80 (March 1990): 21–36; G. Tabellini and A. Alesina, "Voting on the Budget Deficit," *The American Economic Review* 80 (March 1990): 37–49; T. Persson and G. Tabellini, "External Debt and Political Instability," NBER Working Paper (1991); A. Alesina, *Political Models of Macroeconomic Policy and Fiscal Reform* (Washington, D.C.: IBRD, 1991); T. Persson and G. Tabellini, *Monetary and Fiscal Policy*, vol. 2 (Cambridge: MIT Press, 1994).

Table 7.2
Monthly Changes in Selected Financial Indicators, 1993 (Percentage Increase or Decrease from Previous Month)

1993	Monetary Base	M2	Total Central Bank Credits	Net Credits to Government	Net Credits to Commercial Banks	Net Credits to Former Soviet Republics	CBR Refinancing Rates	Interbank Interest Rates	Deposit Interest Rates	Monthly Inflation	Real Interbank Interest Rates
I	16	10	44	67	30	14	6.7	9.9	6.4	25.8	-12.8
II	18	10	-22	-59	25	31	6.7	10.8	6.8	24.7	-11.4
III	15	18	17	46	-17	26	6.7	11	7.5	20.1	-7.5
IV	25	23	14	-16	53	19	8.3	11.3	8.3	18.8	-9.5
V	22	24	12	21	20	-1	8.3	11.7	8.7	18.1	-6.1
VI	23	16.8	-8	-61	28	1	11.7	12.1	9.5	19.9	-6.6
VII	19	16	39	349	-13	3	14.2	14.5	10.3	22.4	-6.1
VIII	19	19	30	46	14	23	14.2	15.4	11.1	25.8	-8.4
IX	14	3	31	42	43	1	14.2	15.8	13	23.1	-4.3
X	16	12	17	4	-3	9	17.5	17.1	14.7	19.5	-2.1
XI	13	13	18	-4	-4	8	17.5	17.9	15	16.4	1.7
XII	19	14	39	-17	-2	18	17.5	17.9	15	12.5	4.4

Sources: *Rossiyskaya ekonomika v 1993 g.—tendentsii i perspektivy* (Moscow: IET, 1994); IEPPP; Working Centre for Economic Reforms.

the population expressed support both for the executive branch's political course in general and for its socioeconomic policies in particular.

Third, the existence of a strong and unpopular foe, such as the Supreme Soviet at the time, was assumed, as it were, out of inertia.

The difficult and extremely painful process of cutting state expenditures was immediately reflected in the results of the parliamentary elections of 12 December 1993. In these elections the bloc Russia's Choice, led by Yegor Gaidar and many reformist members of the government, fared poorly, gaining fewer votes than Vladimir Zhirinovsky's Liberal Democratic party. The political sacrifice, however, was felt: the federal budget deficit in 1993 was held at 7.8% of GDP (according to Ministry of Finance statistics), and not only was fiscal catastrophe avoided, but the foundations were laid for the further gradual reduction of inflation.

7.4. Reconstruction of the 1993 Budget

Our data for the 1993 budget differ from the official statistics of the Ministry of Finance.[10] An analysis of the reconstructed budget in Table 7.3 shows that in 1993 tax collection remained at a rather high level. The share of taxes and contributions to off-budget funds was 38% of GDP. The share of state revenues was 40.6% of GDP. Extrabudgetary funds remained at the 1992 level, around 10.6% of GDP. Expenditures from the budget and extrabudgetary funds were 46.3% of GDP, and expenditures together with credits (less debt repayments) were 48.6%. In 1993 the structure of state expenditures changed substantially. Spending on the national economy underwent particularly severe cuts. These cuts were mainly achieved by reducing import subsidies (to 1.2% of GDP).[11]

---

10. In presenting the foreign economic operations of the government, we include in revenues import and export duties and income from the state's monopoly on centralized exports (earnings from the sale of goods less the purchase cost). In expenditures we include the purchase of foreign currency from the national reserves. Thus, according to our estimates, income from foreign economic activity is around 4.1% of GDP.
11. Expenditure on the economy was considerably reduced (to 12.7% of GDP). Capital investments were more than halved. Expenditure on the state administrative apparatus increased by 0.3% of GDP (to 0.9% of GDP); social expenditures increased by 0.7% of GDP to 18% of GDP (including extrabudgetary funds, which were 8.6% of GDP). Defense spending in 1993 was reduced severalfold, to 4.4% of GDP. Expenditure on law enforcement was increased to 1.6% of GDP, while spending on scientific research remained stable at 0.6% of GDP.

The federal budget deficit reached 9.8% of GDP, and the deficit of the state finance system reached 8% of GDP. In 1993 financing of the budget deficit also underwent drastic changes. External financing fell from 37% of all financing to 19%. To a considerable extent this was caused by the growth of the real ruble exchange rate over 1992–1993, which correspondingly lowered the intense demand for foreign debt denominated in dollars. Domestic debt financing was 7.8% of GDP.

7.5. Slowing Fiscal Reforms: A "Moderately Tight" Policy

Following the resolution of the constitutional crisis and the parliamentary elections of December 1993, a real opportunity to achieve financial stabilization came to the fore. The new constitution created a stable balance of power between the executive branch and the legislature by removing the potential for confrontation between branches of government. Such confrontation hitherto had had a deleterious impact on the fiscal system. Although the State Duma elections did not deliver a majority to the reformers, the results allowed the formation of temporary coalitions, which led to the resolution of many vital issues. The adoption of the new constitution put an end to the previous system of dual power, enabling the president and the government to conduct consistent fiscal and monetary policy.

Early 1994 presented two options for economic policy. The first involved taking advantage of the opportunities provided by the new Russian constitution to accelerate the process of reform and to commence financial stabilization. This required fulfilling the budgetary policy established in the fourth quarter of 1993.[12] Methods for fulfilling this policy included passing a tough budget for 1994, sharply limiting expansion of the money supply, and embarking on structural reforms that would permit rationalization of the state's obligations and bring them into line with the financial resources realistically available. This austerity option, advocated at the time by Yegor Gaidar, would have been painful in the short term but would have virtually guaranteed Russia's emergence on a trajectory of stable

---

12. Apart from those decisions noted above, in autumn of 1993 steps were taken to create the basis for cutting government expenditure in 1994. Among them were transformation of the system of state food procurement, a gradual switch to targeted subsidies on housing for needy sectors of the population, the audit of a number of federal investment programs; and the suspension of individual articles of the law *On Grain*.

Table 7.3
Reconstruction of Revenues and Expenditures of the Russian Federation in 1993

	Federal Budget (% of GDP)	Local Budgets (% of GDP)	Extrabudgetary Funds (% of GDP)	Consolidated Budget (% of GDP)	Consolidated Budget (% of Budget)
TAX REVENUES					
1. Income and profit taxes	3.4	9.7		13.0	45.9
1.1. Income tax		2.7		2.7	9.5
1.2. Profit tax	3.4	7.0		10.3	21.6
2. Social Security contributions		0.0	9.1	9.1	19.1
2.1. Employees			0.3	0.3	0.6
2.2. Employers		0.0	8.8	8.8	18.5
Pension Fund			6.5	6.5	13.7
Social Security Fund			1.2	1.2	2.5
Employment Fund			0.4	0.4	0.8
State Medical Insurance Fund			0.6	0.7	1.4
3. Property taxes	0.0	0.0		0.6	1.2
3.1. Property tax		0.5		0.3	0.7
3.2. Land tax	0.0	0.3		0.2	0.4
3.3. Securities tax	0.0	0.2		0.0	0.0
4. Domestic taxes on goods and services	5.5	3.4		8.9	18.6
4.1. VAT	4.5	2.5		6.9	14.5
4.2. Excise duties	0.6	0.5		1.1	2.3
4.3. Natural resource royalties	0.2	0.4		0.5	0.5
4.4. Mineral replacement tax	0.2			0.2	0.4
4.5. Price Control Fund	0.1			0.1	0.3
5. Foreign trade taxes	4.1	0.1		4.2	8.8
5.1. Import duties	0.5			0.5	1.1
5.2. Export duties	1.1			1.1	2.3
5.3. Revenues from state monopoly on centralized exports	2.5			2.5	5.2

Preconditions for Financial Stabilization

6. Other taxes	0.0			0.7	1.4
6.1. State stamp duty	0.0	0.6		0.1	0.2
6.2. Other taxes and duties		0.1		0.6	1.2
7. Extrabudgetary funds:		0.6	1.5	1.5	3.1
Road Fund			1.5	1.5	3.0
Total Tax Revenues	13.1	14.3	10.6	38.0	79.3
NONTAX REVENUES					
1. Central bank profit	1.3			1.3	2.6
2. Other nontax revenues	0.4	0.8		1.1	2.6
CAPITAL INCOME					
1. Income from privatization	0.0	0.2		0.2	0.4
Total Revenues (See continuation)	14.7	15.2	10.6	40.6	84.7
SUBSIDIES		2.6	0.2	×	
1. Subsidies to other levels of state administration		2.6	0.2	×	
1.1. Subsidies to local governments		2.6		×	
1.2. Subsidies to the Pension Fund			0.2	×	
Total Revenues and Subsidies	14.7	17.9	10.8	40.6	84.7
STATE EXPENDITURES AND CREDITS LESS DEBT REPAYMENTS					
1. State expenditures	22.5	16.6	10.1	46.3	91.6
1. State services of general character	0.4	0.5		0.9	1.8
2. On defense	4.4			4.4	8.8
3. On law enforcement bodies		0.1		1.6	3.2
4. On scientific research	0.6	0.0		0.6	1.2

(continued)

Table 7.3 (continued)

	Federal Budget (% of GDP)	Local Budgets (% of GDP)	Extrabudgetary Funds (% of GDP)	Consolidated Budget (% of GDP)	Consolidated Budget (% of Budget)
5. On social and housing services	2.0	7.6	8.6	18.0	35.6
5.1. On education	0.8	3.4		4.3	8.5
5.2. On culture, arts, and the mass media	0.2	0.4		0.6	1.3
5.3. On public health and sport	0.3	3.0		3.3	6.6
5.4. On Youth Policy programs		0.0		0.0	0.0
5.5. On social benefits	0.1	0.4		0.5	1.0
5.6. On subsidies to the Pension Fund	0.2				
5.7. On Chernobyl and Semipalatinsk programs	0.2	0.0		0.2	0.5
5.8. On child benefits		0.4		0.4	0.8
5.9. On social services paid from extrabudgetary funds, including:			8.6	8.6	17.0
Pension Fund			6.4	6.4	12.7
Social Security Fund			1.0	1.0	2.0
Employment Fund			0.2	0.2	0.5
Social Support Fund			0.0	0.0	0.0
Other funds			1.0	1.0	1.9
6. On state services to the economy	4.0	7.3	1.5	12.7	25.2
7. On other functions	9.6	1.1		8.0	15.8
7.1. Other expenditures	2.3	1.0		3.2	6.4
7.2. On foreign trade	3.8	0.0		3.8	7.5
7.3. On domestic debt servicing	0.6			0.6	1.2
7.4. On foreign debt servicing	0.3			0.3	0.5
7.5. Subsidies from the federal budget to other levels of state administration	2.6			×	
7.6. Transfers to the federal budget to finance state programs		0.1		0.1	0.1

CREDITS LESS DEBT REPAYMENTS	2.0	0.4		2.3	4.6
1. To enterprises	1.7	0.4		2.1	4.2
2. Incomplete transfers by the central bank of budget income	0.2			0.2	0.4
3. To foreign governments	−0.3			−0.3	−0.5
4. To CIS states	0.3			0.3	0.6
Total Expenditures and Credits Less Debt Repayments	24.5	17.0	10.1	48.6	100.0
Revenues and Subsidies Minus Expenditures and Credits Less Debt Repayments	−9.8	0.9	0.8	−8.0	−15.9
FINANCING					
1. Domestic financing	7.8	0.0			
1.1. By the central bank (net)	6.1				
1.2. Sale of government securities	0.1				
1.3. IMF credits	0.9				
1.4. Sale of precious metals from the government's reserves	0.7				
1.5. By other levels of state administration		0.0			
2. Foreign financing (net)	1.9				
3. Change in monies deposited	−1.0	−0.8			
Total Financing	9.8	−0.9	−0.8		

Note: In 1993, the GDP was 162,300 billion rubles.

Sources: Ministry of Finance RF, Goskomstat, IEPPP.

economic growth within two years, in time for the next parliamentary and presidential elections.

The second option was less painful in the short term. It constituted the continuation of budgetary support to all interested parties, albeit at the price of high inflation (over 10% per month) and further economic stagnation. Superficially this meant a relaxation of the late 1993 budgetary policy through a more or less generous distribution of "cheap money," but in reality it only prolonged and complicated the processes of economic stabilization. This option could not but fail to have rather dangerous political consequences. It was inevitable that in a matter of months, the "moderately tight" policy (in essence, lax) would result in a further jump in inflation, which would force the government to mount a new attempt at stabilization before long—which is exactly what happened. Nevertheless, the deferred policy of austerity should have been adopted regardless of the run-up to the elections, with all of the ensuing political consequences.

Had the austerity option been chosen, financial stabilization could have begun to bear fruit within a year to eighteen months—that is, by the second half of 1995.[13] Such a turn of events would have created the most favorable conditions for holding the parliamentary elections of December 1995 and the presidential elections of June 1996, and would have further improved the prospects for democracy and economic reform.

In early 1994, however, those in power chose the other option. That year the money supply expanded dramatically, particularly in the spring and summer months. As on previous occasions, the seasonal nature of the Russian economy was used as a justification for monetary emission, although the experience of 1993 had amply shown that the seasonal factor was more of a political phenomenon than a technical one. Indeed, the basic budgetary commitments were literally bludgeoned out of the government during the debates over the state budget for 1994. These debates took place, after considerable delay, in the State Duma in May and June. In other words, the

---

13. This is corroborated by the experience of a number of successful stabilizations; see, for example, G. Calvo, "Temporary Stabilization: Predetermined Exchange Rates," *The Journal of Political Economy* 94 (1986): 1319–29; M. A. Kiguel and N. Liviatan, "Lessons from the Heterodox Stabilization Progress," World Bank Working Papers no. WPS-671 (1991); A. Drazen and E. Helpman, "Inflationary Consequences of Anticipated Macroeconomic Policies," *Review of Economic Studies* 57 (1990): 147–64; S. Rebelo and C. Vegh, "Real Effects of Exchange Rate-Based Stabilization: An Analysis of Competing Theories," NBER Working Paper no. 5197 (1993).

political vulnerability of the government to legislative opposition forced it to increase emissionary financing of the national economy.

In January 1994 a new government crisis occurred. Its fundamental cause is rooted in the disagreements already discussed within the cabinet over economic policy. The trigger, however, was a draft of decisions being prepared by the government. This draft required considerable expenditure and further eroded the foundations for financial stabilization that had been so painstakingly established.

Overall, there was continuity between the government's position in February and March 1994 and its position in the previous year. This continuity is partly explained by the fact that following the departure of Yegor Gaidar and Boris Fedorov from the government in January 1994, Prime Minister Viktor Chernomyrdin's personal responsibility for macroeconomic decision making increased. It became much harder for Chernomyrdin to take populist, financially irresponsible decisions because he could no longer shift blame for failures in the fight against inflation to the monetarists. From then on, while promising and disbursing budgetary outlays, Chernomyrdin had to assume the full burden for their fiscal consequences. This reality served as a check on fiscal policy. Nonetheless, many of the decisions made in the winter and spring raised serious anxieties. These anxieties were subsequently fully justified by the events of autumn 1994 when the ruble exchange rate collapsed and inflation accelerated sharply.

7.6. Some Peculiarities of the Budget Process of 1994

In the period of the so-called "extraordinary legal regime," after the dissolution of the legislature and before the adoption of the new constitution, a number of decrees were issued by the president to ensure the functioning of Russia's fiscal system for 1994. The draft federal budget was presented to the Russian State Duma on 18 March 1994. The draft law effectively proposed no changes to the manner or the structure of state interference in the economy. The government did not suggest any measures to rationalize or reduce state expenditure. The draft law reflected the government's desire to maintain the status quo by not allowing any serious conflicts to arise, and not taking any decisive steps to pull the country out of crisis. Revenues were pegged at 12.2% of GDP, expenditures at 26.8% of GDP, and the deficit at 9.7% of GDP.

This budget draft, however, was described by some economists and politicians as excessively tough.[14] A number of resolutions were presented to increase the state's expenditures. Specifically, these resolutions suggested that the national economy should be supported through the budget deficit, which was to be financed by central bank credits. Consequently, budget revenues were increased to 17.2% of GDP, even though budget implementation in the first quarter had already demonstrated the unrealistic nature in this projection.[15] The federal budget deficit grew from 8.6% to 9.7% of GDP. This draft budget was passed with some small amendments by the State Duma on 24 June 1994 and approved by the Federation Council.

At the beginning of the year, the trend of falling tax receipts continued to intensify, as was the case in the summer of 1993.[16] Under these circumstances the government financed federal budget expenditures in line with revenues received, and with central bank credits issued in accordance with the decision of the government's Commission on Credit Policy on 25 January 1994. As a result, the budget policy in the first quarter of 1994 was even tougher than in 1993.[17]

In the second quarter, the revenue situation improved somewhat[18] (although it is necessary to account for the change in the Ministry of Finance's method for presenting budget revenues in its statistics,

---

14. See, for example, G. Yavlinsky, M. Zadornov, S. Ivanenko, and A. Mikhailov, "Byudzhet 1994," in *Nezavisimaya Gazeta*, 14 April 1994. The following assessment is instructive: "Excessively restrictive issuance of credits and tight restrictions on monetary emission do not slow inflation down, but rather speed it up" (O. T. Bogomolov, "Rynochnye preobrazovaniya v Rossii: analiz i perspektivy," *Predprinimatel'stvo* 1 [1993]).

15. For the first three months of 1994, national budget receipts were 10.7% of GDP and tax receipts were 8.3% of GDP (in 1993 these receipts were 13.3% and 10.3% of GDP, respectively). Tax receipts included the profit tax, for 2.8% of GDP (3.4% in 1993), and the VAT, at 3.7% of GDP (4.5% in 1993). Excise duty revenues were 0.5% of GDP (0.6% in 1993).

16. As a result, consolidated budget revenues in the first quarter were around 23% of GDP (compared with 28% of GDP in 1993) and national budget revenues were 10.7% of GDP (versus 13.3% in 1993).

17. State expenditures were reduced from 19.2% of GDP in 1993 to 16.7% of GDP in the first quarter of 1994. The federal budget deficit for the first three months of 1994 was 6.9% of GDP, compared with 7.8% for 1993. The federal budget deficit was financed mainly by central bank credits.

18. Consolidated budget revenues increased from 22.9% of GDP over the first quarter to 25.4% of GDP over the first six months. Tax revenues increased from 19.1% of GDP to 22.0% of GDP. National budget receipts grew from 10.7% of GDP in the first quarter to 12.6% of GDP in the first half of 1994.

which occurred in May 1994[19]). The implementation of the expenditure side of the budget in the first six months was in accordance with the revenue side. In compliance with the budget law passed on 24 June 1994, the government was permitted to finance expenditures, based on the projections of the approved 1994 federal budget, only as long as tax and other receipts were actually received.[20] Consequently, in similar fashion to 1993, the gap between budget obligations and the actual fulfillment of expenditures grew continually. In the first six months only 72% of planned expenditures were financed by the budget.

In the third quarter of 1994, the tax receipt situation stabilized somewhat.[21] After the adoption of the budget law in the third quarter, the expenditures of the federal government started to increase at a faster rate. The federal budget deficit grew from 7.4% of GDP over the first six months of 1994 to 10.2% of GDP for the first nine months.[22]

An important peculiarity of the budget process further complicated the implementation of a restrictive fiscal policy in 1994. The difficulties were a result of the government's errors in preparing the

---

19. Before May 1994, state income from foreign currency operations was not directly reflected in statistical data. This income accumulated in the national foreign currency reserves, and only the sale of foreign currency from this source was registered in the budget. Starting in May 1994, state income and expenditures connected to foreign currency operations were included in the budget. In our tables, income from the sale of foreign currency reserves by the Ministry of Finance is included in the section on nontax revenues. However, the transfer of this item from the section on income from foreign trade activity led to a change not only in the balance between tax and nontax revenues, but also in the volume of revenues. This is explained by the fact that revenues from the sale of foreign currency only on average reflected earnings from centralized exports and other foreign currency receipts, as there was a lag between the transfer of money to the republic's foreign currency reserves and the receipt of earnings from the sale of those foreign currency reserves.

20. Federal budget expenditures grew from 16.7% of GDP in the second quarter to 17.2% of GDP for the first half-year. Expenditures and credits (less debt repayments) grew from 17.6% of GDP to 20.0%. The federal budget deficit grew from 6.9% of GDP to 7.4%. This deficit was 80% financed by central bank credits (5.1% of GDP), and by the issue of securities (1% of GDP) and foreign loans (1% of GDP), including IMF credits (0.5% of GDP).

21. Consolidated tax receipts were 22.6% of GDP over the period of January to September, while federal tax receipts were maintained at the January to June 1994 level (10.1% of GDP). Overall consolidated budget income over the first three quarters was 25.3% of GDP, while federal income was 11.6% of GDP.

22. This deficit was 80% financed by central bank credits (8.5% of GDP). It was also financed by the issue of securities (1.2% of GDP) and by foreign loans (1.0% of GDP), including IMF loans (0.5% of GDP).

draft budget: the inflation and GDP forecasts (both real and nominal) were exaggerated.[23] Neither the Ministry of Economy nor the Ministry of Finance in their forecasts took into consideration the consequences of the tight fiscal policy at the end of the prior year. While the money aggregate M2 grew at a rate of 14.8% per month on average in 1993, in the last four months of the year growth was about 10%. In the first three months of 1994, M2 grew by 6.8% per month, and inflation fell to 5%–6% over the summer months—much lower than expected. As a result, nominal GDP in the spring of 1994 started to lag behind the forecast. Correspondingly, nominal budget revenues began to lag behind the nominal expenditures fixed in the budget law. In contrast to 1993, the accumulation of unfulfilled budget obligations in 1994 was caused not only by excessive spending promises (which were also a factor) but also by the nominal levels, which were set too high.

Tax receipts were 58% of the figure set by the budget law. However, even factoring in the error in GDP forecasting, there was a 34% shortfall in tax collection. Overall, only 63% of revenues approved in the budget law were collected. This reality accounts for the smaller real GDP of 73%.

Of the budget expenditures set in the law, 75% were met (85% of the adjusted figure). The level of budget sequestrations differed significantly from item to item, and to a large extent was determined by the ability of various forces to lobby successfully for their interests.[24] Thus, irrespective of whether comparatively high expenditures (in real terms) were met, over the year the volume of unfulfilled obligations grew. As in previous years of reform, fulfillment of the expenditure-heavy budget was accomplished by recourse to sequestration. This allowed the government to avoid protracted negotiations with the legislature over the necessary budget cuts and

---

23. A GDP of 725 trillion rubles was written into the budget. This figure turned out to be higher than the actual figure.

24. The only item of expenditure that exceeded its budget target was that on the state administrative apparatus (110% of the level set in the budget). Social expenditures were financed at 75% of planned levels, including expenditures on education, 76%; culture, arts, and the mass media, 67%; health, 61%; and social security, 40%. The economy received only 67% of planned expenditure. Most underfunded, however, were capital investments. Scientific research was in a very difficult situation, receiving only 59% of planned spending, while defense expenditure was 70% of that planned. Somewhat better off were law enforcement bodies, the courts, and the prosecutor's office, which received 82% of planned expenditure.

prevented a catastrophic growth of the budget deficit. However, it is important to point out that these measures increased the discretionary character of budgetary decision making because no clear rules had been established for implementing a sequester. Indeed, the level of financing for any given branch of industry was a function of the influence of special interest groups. Nonetheless, even uniform (nondiscretionary) underfinancing can hardly form a rational way to proceed. It is obvious that in different branches of the economy the return on budget funds varies because of differing priorities.

7.7. Reconstruction of the 1994 Budget

The budget accounting standards used for 1994 were already much closer to international standards than in 1992–1993. In order to calculate state revenues and expenditures, one had to add to the Ministry of Finance's data the extrabudgetary funds, and then add to the expenditure for servicing the internal debt the cost of servicing state short-term bonds (GKOs). The reconstruction of the 1994 budget is shown in Table 7.4.

Federal tax receipts for 1994 were 11.2% of GDP. Together with nontax revenues, total federal budget revenues reached 12.7% of GDP.[25] Total budget revenues combined with off-budget funds made up 36.2% of GDP, well below the figure for 1993 (40.6%). Tax receipts fell from 38% of GDP in 1993 to 33.7% in 1994.[26]

Expenditures and subsidies (excluding debt repayments) were 47.5% of GDP, a figure much less than the corresponding figure for 1993 by 1.1% of GDP.[27] Expenditures were cut most heavily on foreign trade activities (by cutting almost completely advanced payments to enterprises for centralized exports), to 3% of GDP, and expenditures on the national economy were cut to approximately 1% of GDP. There were some increases in social expenditures, the bureaucracy, servicing of domestic debt, and other items.

The federal budget deficit was 11.8% of GDP. This deficit was financed by central bank credits to the tune of 7.6% of GDP, the sale

---

25. Consolidated budget tax receipts over the year were 24.3% of GDP; consolidated budget revenues were 26.9% of GDP.
26. This is explained by the decrease in federal budget tax receipts (by 1.9% of GDP), receipts to local budgets (by 1.2% of GDP), and off-budget funds (by 1.1% of GDP).
27. Expenditures and subsidies excluding debt repayments were 48.6% of GDP in 1993, without including off-budget fund expenditures on enterprises.

Table 7.4
Reconstruction of Revenues and Expenditures of the Russian Federation in 1994

	Federal Budget (% of GDP)	Local Budgets (% of GDP)	Extrabudgetary Funds (% of GDP)	Consolidated Budget (% of GDP)	Consolidated Budget (% of Budget)
TAX REVENUES					
1. Income and profit taxes	2.7	7.8		10.5	29.0
1.1. Income tax	0.0	2.8		2.8	7.6
1.2. Profit tax	2.7	5.0		7.7	21.3
2. Social Security contributions			8.6	8.6	23.7
2.1. Employees			0.2	0.2	0.5
2.2. Employers			8.4	8.4	23.2
Pension Fund			5.8	5.8	15.9
Social Security Fund			1.2	1.2	3.3
Employment Fund			0.5	0.5	1.2
State Medical Insurance Fund			1.0	1.0	2.8
3. Property taxes	0.1	1.0		1.1	3.0
3.1. Property tax		0.8		0.8	2.1
3.2. Land tax	0.0	0.2		0.3	0.7
(See continuation)					
3.3. Securities tax	0.1	0.0		0.1	0.2
4. Domestic taxes on goods and services	5.3	3.2		8.5	23.4
4.1. VAT	3.8	2.2		5.9	16.3
4.2. Excise duties	0.7	0.5		1.2	3.2
4.3. Alcohol production and sales licenses	0.0	0.0		0.0	0.1
4.4. Natural resource royalties	0.1	0.3		0.4	1.1
4.5. Mineral replacement tax	0.1			0.1	0.3
4.6. Special tax	0.7	0.2		0.9	2.5

5. Foreign trade taxes	3.0		8.4
5.1. Import duties	0.4		1.1
5.2. Export duties	0.5		1.4
5.3. Other foreign trade revenues	1.5		4.2
5.4. Revenues from state monopoly on centralized exports	0.6	0.0	1.6
6. Other taxes	0.0	1.0	2.8
6.1. State stamp fee	0.0	0.0	0.2
6.2. Other taxes and duties	0.0	0.9	2.6
7. Extrabudgetary funds		0.8	2.3
7.1. Road Fund		0.8	2.2
7.2. Other extrabudgetary funds		0.0	0.1
Total Tax Revenues	11.2	9.5	33.7	92.7
NONTAX REVENUES			
1. State budget reserves for covering expenditure	0.0		0.1	0.3
2. Central bank profit	0.3		0.3	0.5
3. Foreign exchange gain/loss	0.5		0.5	1.0
4. Other nontax revenues	0.7		1.7	3.5
	0.9			
CAPITAL INCOME			
1. Income from privatization	0.0	0.0	0.1	0.2
Total Revenues	12.7	14.2	36.3	76.5
SUBSIDIES		9.5		
		3.4	×	
		0.1		
Total Revenues and Subsidies	12.7	17.6	36.3	76.5
		9.6		

(continued)

Table 7.4 (continued)

	Federal Budget (% of GDP)	Local Budgets (% of GDP)	Extrabudgetary Funds (% of GDP)	Consolidated Budget (% of GDP)	Consolidated Budget (% of Budget)
STATE EXPENDITURES AND CREDITS LESS DEBT REPAYMENTS					
State Expenditures	21.0	17.1	9.2	43.9	92.3
1. State services of general character	0.6	0.5		1.1	2.4
2. On defense	4.4	0.0		4.4	9.4
3. On law enforcement bodies	1.7	0.1		1.8	3.8
(See continuation)					
4. On scientific research	0.5	0.0		0.5	1.0
5. On social and housing services	1.9	7.8	8.3	18.0	37.8
5.1. On education	0.9	3.5		4.4	9.2
5.2. On culture, arts and the mass media	0.3	0.5		0.7	1.5
5.3. On public health and sport	0.4	2.8		3.1	6.6
5.4. On Social Benefits	0.2	0.4		0.5	1.1
5.5. On Chernobyl and Semipalatinsk programs	0.2	0.0		0.2	0.4
5.6. On child benefits	0.0	0.7		0.7	1.4
5.7. On social services paid from extrabudgetary funds, including:			8.3	8.3	17.5
Pension Fund			5.9	5.9	12.5
Social Security Fund			1.1	1.1	2.2
Employment Fund			0.4	0.4	0.8
Medical Insurance Fund			1.0	1.0	2.0
6. On state services to the economy	2.9	7.2	0.8	10.9	23.0
7. On other functions	9.0	1.5		7.1	15.0
7.1. Other expenditures	1.8	1.5		3.3	6.9
7.2. On foreign trade	0.7	0.0		0.8	1.7

7.3. On domestic debt servicing, including:	2.6		2.6	5.4
7.3.1. On GKO servicing	0.2		0.2	0.5
7.4. On foreign debt servicing	0.5		0.5	1.0
7.5. Subsidies to other levels of state administration	3.4		×	
CREDITS LESS DEBT REPAYMENTS	3.5	0.2	3.6	7.7
1. Budget Loans	2.2	0.2	2.4	5.1
2. State credits to foreign governments	−0.1		−0.1	−0.3
3. Incomplete transfers by the central bank of budget income	0.3		0.3	0.6
4. Foreign credits granted to enterprises	0.8		0.8	1.7
5. Conversion credits	0.1		0.1	0.2
6. Investment credits	0.1		0.1	0.3
7. State credits to CIS countries	0.1		0.1	0.1
Total Expenditures and Credits Less Debt Repayments (See continuation)	24.5	17.3	47.5	100.0
Revenues and Subsidies Minus Expenditures and Credits Less Debt Repayments	−11.8	0.3	−11.2	−23.5
FINANCING				
1. Government securities	2.2			
2. Central bank credits (net)	7.6			
3. Vneshtorgbank credits	0.1			
4. External financing	0.9			
5. Treasury bills	1.1			
6. Other revenues	0.3			
7. Change in monies deposited	−0.5	−0.3	−0.4	
Total Financing	11.8	−0.3	−0.4	

Note: In 1994, the GDP was 630 trillion rubles.
Source: Ministry of Finance RF, Goskomstat, IEPPP.

of government securities (2.2% of GDP), the issue of Treasury bills (1.1%), and foreign borrowing in the sum of 0.9% of GDP.

7.8. Toward a Tight Fiscal Policy

At the beginning of autumn 1994, the government under Viktor Chernomyrdin abruptly changed its macroeconomic policies. Whereas in the summer the government had pursued a moderately tight monetary policy aimed at gradual stabilization with the active support of domestic producers, in August and September it started preparing a fundamentally different policy.[28] This involved substantial tightening of monetary and budgetary policies in order to achieve financial stabilization by the end of 1995. When the budget for 1994 was approved, this change in policy still had little influence on the implementation of the budget (the deficit in the fourth quarter was not reduced). However, between September and December, growth of the money supply was almost halved.

A key factor whose political consequences eased the transition to a tight fiscal policy was the currency crisis of October 1994. As a result of the growth in the money supply between April and June 1994, in October a sudden increase in the rate of inflation occurred, and the ruble exchange rate collapsed. Many articles and speeches have been devoted to the causes of the October currency crisis, attempting to explain it as (1) an intentional act by the Ministry of Finance in order to increase ruble earnings from foreign trade through devaluation; (2) a conspiracy by a number of major commercial banks that were speculating on the devaluation of the ruble; and (3) resulting from the negligence of the Ministry of Finance, the central bank, and other ministerial departments. Of course, the main reason behind the crisis was the monetary and budgetary policy of spring and summer 1994. Holding the budget deficit at 10% of GDP made the currency crisis almost inevitable.

The currency crisis that erupted in September and October 1994 demonstrated once again just how serious Russia's fiscal problems were, a realization that genuinely shocked the political leadership. The chairman of the central bank, Viktor Gerashchenko, and the acting finance minister, Sergei Dubinin, were dismissed. An impor-

---

28. Programmatic statements assumed that the rate of inflation would drop in 1995, and indeed, by the end of the year it was 3%–5% per month.

tant consequence of the crisis was the strengthening of governmental and presidential resolve to pursue a tight fiscal policy.

The tightening of monetary policy in the last quarter of 1994 was in part related to preparations for the 1995 stabilization program and was facilitated in part by political support for a stable, low ruble depreciation against the dollar. This policy cost the central bank a considerable portion of its gold and hard currency reserves. By the beginning of the following year this depletion of reserves had placed the financial system under the threat of a new currency crisis and in principle could have wrecked the 1995 stabilization attempt. Average monthly growth of the money supply fell in the fourth quarter of 1994 to 6%, although in this period the rate of inflation peaked at 16.4% in December. This burst of inflation was purely inertial and occurred as a result of the weakening of central bank policy in the spring and summer of 1994. Inflation was also provoked by a series of speculative attacks on the ruble in August and September, which followed the monetary emission and ended with the exchange rate collapse on 11 October. To add to this situation, military intervention in Chechnya, which began in December 1994, was partly responsible for creating an unfavorable political climate in the country.

7.9. Monetary Policy and Credit Policy in 1994

In accordance with the joint statement of the government and the central bank on economic policy for 1994, the central bank established control over the money supply. To this end, quarterly limits were set on net domestic assets, including limits on net lending to the consolidated government. These restrictions set maximum net domestic assets at 52.5 trillion rubles, and net lending to the consolidated government at 51.6 trillion rubles for the end of 1994. Thus, the lion's share of net domestic assets at the start of financial stabilization in 1995 was made up of central bank credits to the government.

In fact, the net domestic asset level did not exceed the limit set in the monetary program, and on 1 January 1995 was 45.3 trillion rubles. At the same time, credit to the government grew rapidly, reaching 67.3 trillion rubles at the end of the year. This figure was 14 trillion rubles above the limit set in the monetary program. This was due first to the divergence between the budget deficit contained in the monetary program and the one in the 1994 budget (a margin of 16 trillion rubles), and second to the reregistering of some commercial bank debts to the central bank (specifically credits to the agricultural sector and for the northern shipments) as government debt. As a result, nominal credits to the Ministry of Finance almost quintupled, while credits to commercial banks grew by a factor of 2.2. The share of the budget deficit financed by central bank credits grew in 1994 to 90% of the total sum of credits issued, and the share of credits for the refinancing of commercial banks fell to 8%. Starting in 1994, the central bank conducted monthly credit auctions, issuing three-month credits to commercial banks. However, these credits were insignificant in refinancing the banking system.[29]

As a result of the tightening of refinancing policy, commercial banks experienced their first difficulties with liabilities since the beginning of the reforms. This led to greater competition between banks for deposits. The unforeseen fall in inflation in the second and third quarters of 1994 was attended by a significant lowering of interest rates. This lowering attracted large volumes of household savings into the banking sector, and thus mitigated the severity of the liquidity problems caused by the reduction in refinancing credits. Monetary emission, which was particularly intensive in the second and third quarters, effectively solved all of the problems caused by the ineffectiveness of the banking sector. These problems, however, would resurface in the summer of 1995.

The volume of money in circulation (M2) almost tripled over 1994, reaching 97.8 trillion rubles on 1 January 1995. The average monthly growth in the money supply was 9.5%. In 1994 the monetary base almost tripled, and by the end of the year it was 48.2 trillion rubles in absolute terms (Table 7.5). As in the previous year, the money supply in 1994 grew mainly as a result of the centralized crediting of the government and the economy. About 75% of central bank credits issued went to the government. Due to the underdevelopment of the government debt market, domestic financing of the deficit could not be achieved by market borrowing. In addition, the primary deficit remained rather high, at 7%–10% of GDP.

In general, the "moderately tight" fiscal policy conducted in the first three quarters of 1994 was characterized by the absence of any rules and was determined by the shifting balance of political forces and their priorities. The monetary program approved in the spring by a joint declaration of the government and central bank still

---

29. In 1996, Lombard credits replaced credit auctions, and from the end of 1996 they occupied a dominant position in the money supply system.

Table 7.5
Monthly Changes in Selected Financial Indicators, 1994 (Percentage Increase or Decrease from Previous Month)

1994	Monetary Base	M2	Refinancing Rate of the CBR	Interbank Interest Rates on 1–3-Month Credits	Monthly Inflation (CPI)	Real Interbank Interest Rates
I	2	4	17.5	17.9	17.9	0
II	10	7	17.5	17.8	10.8	6.3
III	9	9	17.5	17.5	7.4	9.4
IV	19	17	17.1	16.7	8.5	7.5
V	9	13	16.7	15	6.9	7.6
VI	14	14	12.9	12.6	6	6.2
VII	15	8	12.9	11.3	5.3	5.7
VIII	6	10	10.8	10	4.6	5.2
IX	9	9	10.8	10	7.7	2.2
X	4	4	14.2	12.4	14.7	−2.3
XI	5	5	15	12.9	14.5	−1.9
XII	10	14	15	13.5	16.4	−2.5

Source: The Working Centre for Economic Reform.

failed to impose effective restrictions on the activities of the monetary authorities (just as in 1993). The growth of credit emission was particularly rapid from January to August, displaying an average monthly rate of 12%. As a result, the average monthly rate of inflation rose from 6.4% in the spring and summer to 15.5% in the fourth quarter. The gradual lowering of the dollar exchange rate (about 1% per week), a process maintained throughout the spring and summer, could not avert an outburst of inflationary expectations in the autumn, and, on the contrary, provoked an exchange rate crisis in September and October. This crisis clearly demonstrated that attempts to use a nominal anchor, even a very soft one, while at the same time pursuing a policy of monetary expansion could have deleterious consequences. The Russian experience in 1994 confirmed that regardless of the government's intentions, a purely discretionary macroeconomic policy could not guarantee stability and therefore could not be effective.[30]

---

30. Such government behavior is analyzed in a number of works, including the classic article by F. Kydland and E. Prescott, "Rules Rather than Discretion: The Inconsistency of Optimal Plans," *The Journal of Political Economy* 85 (1977): 473–92. This article analyzes the advantages of stable rules governing tax and monetary policy over a free choice in the selection of policy measures.

8 Financial Stabilization in Russia

Vladimir Mau,
Sergei Sinelnikov-Murylev,
and Georgy Trofimov

The most important phenomenon, both politically and economically, in the period of economic reform was the deferral of stabilization. As the previous chapters demonstrate, the conflict between equal and opposing political forces in what was effectively a system of dual power led to the suspension of financial stabilization (which, together with price liberalization, is the genesis of reform). Stabilization attempts would first yield tangible results only in the second half of 1995.

8.1. Political Preconditions for Financial Stabilization

The success of the macroeconomic stabilization attempt of 1995 was due to the convergence of a number of important and diverse forces at the end of 1994 and the beginning of 1995. The new constitution created conditions propitious for financial stabilization, and, as it turned out, the government had sufficient political will to seize the opportunity. The main changes can be summarized briefly.

First, the 1993 constitution made it very difficult for legislators to approve populist budgets. Strict procedures in the legislative process were instituted. Decisions concerning the budget now can only be approved by the State Duma, backed by a government resolution. Second, the central bank became independent from the legislature. And third, certain changes in attitude facilitated the start of the stabilization process.

By the end of 1994, there was a general understanding among the Russian political elite that a standard set of stabilization measures had to be implemented. For political reasons, the adoption of these measures proved not to be simple. At the end of 1994, Yeltsin faced a choice of paths and mechanisms for consolidating power and stabilizing socioeconomic processes in the country. On the one hand, there was still time (although clearly not enough) before the presidential elections to implement macroeconomic stabilization, with the consequent strengthening of market and democratic institutions. This choice would have set the economy on a trajectory of postcrisis growth. The other option was to toughen the political regime, steal the aggressive nationalist slogans of the opposition (primarily the CPRF and LDPR), and start conducting confrontational domestic and foreign policies while attempting to remove political opponents and purge the political stage of political aspirants on the right and left.

The presidential administration and the government both exhibited a persistent lack of unity. Indeed, sharp and apparently irreconcilable tensions were evident even within the president's entourage. Viktor Chernomyrdin and Anatoly Chubais, with the support of Yeltsin, initiated a program of consistent macroeconomic stabilization. The armed forces, interior and security ministries, and a number of other politicians close to Yeltsin moved, with Yeltsin's support, to resolve the Chechen problem by military means, increasing the risk that the democratic regime would degenerate into an authoritarian one. The prospects of either course revolved around the development of events and the ability of supporters of a "forceful resolution" to achieve their aims and demonstrate their effectiveness.

January 1995 was an unpropitious time for both alternatives. The war in Chechnya did not provide the easy and impressive victory that was supposed to highlight the ability of the Russian authorities to resolve political problems (above all the problems of consolidating their power) by forceful means. The economic situation at this time also remained extremely difficult. The inflationary policy of spring and summer 1994 led to a sharp deterioration in basic macroeconomic indicators. Monthly inflation reached 17% at the beginning of 1995, and there was a sudden drop in living standards. At the end of 1994 and the beginning of 1995, the ruble was subjected to an unprecedented speculative attack by banks. The central bank managed to protect the ruble exchange rate from sharp fluctuations (as happened on Black Tuesday, 11 October 1994), although as a result of interventions, the central bank's reserves fell to a critically low level, comparable with 1992 (at the end of January 1995, central bank gross foreign currency reserves were just $1.5 billion). At this point the government was prepared to carry out a sharp devaluation of the ruble. Such a measure, if the market reaction was favorable (which no one could predict), would have made it possible to rebuild foreign currency reserves, but it also would have aggravated the already high inflation rate. Moreover, in light of the currency crisis of October 1994, it would almost certainly have led to a change of government.

Fixing the ruble exchange rate as an initial stabilization measure was impossible, for a number of reasons. Chief among these reasons was insufficient confidence in the government's 1995 monetary program. At the beginning of the year it was still not clear to what extent the government was committed to its declared policy, and the previous unsuccessful stabilization attempts provided plenty of reason for doubt. Any attempt to return to the practice of inflationary financing of the budget deficit through a fixed ruble exchange rate would have led to the complete collapse of the government's economic program.

Thus, real financial stabilization in Russia could emerge only if a rigorous course, and one that enjoyed IMF support, was pursued in all spheres—budgetary, monetary, and credit. In February 1995, decisive measures on the part of the government and the central bank in February were required to ensure that the IMF extended a series of standby loans. The government's monetary program was achieved as a result of the $6.25 billion granted to cover the 42 trillion ruble budget deficit.

8.2. The Monetary Program for 1995

The traditional monetarist conception of inflation lay at the root of the government's macroeconomic policy plan. In accordance with the program worked out for 1995, the process of monetary stabilization was supposed to be concluded in spring to summer. In the initial version of the program, it was assumed that inflation for 1995 would be around 27%, and that the rate of M2 growth would be about 60% (allowed by the 40% slowdown in the velocity of circulation), with a real GDP contraction of 7%.

In order to fulfill the aims of the program, in 1995 the government proposed:

- Financing the budget deficit (7% of GDP) by issuing domestic debt on market terms, and by external borrowing.

- Ensuring low growth of net central bank credits to commercial banks. Growth of the monetary base in 1995 was to be achieved mainly by increasing foreign currency reserves and by the central bank's purchasing securities on the open market.
- Ensuring a positive real refinancing rate, and using credit auctions as a means for controlling commercial bank liquidity.
- Conducting a policy of controlled nominal devaluation of the ruble while raising its real exchange rate.

The draft budget for 1995, formulated within the parameters of the macroeconomic program, was presented by the government to the State Duma, which rejected it on its first reading. The work of the Conciliation Commission resulted in a partial reassessment of the macroeconomic parameters for 1995 to better take into account the situation that had emerged at the end of 1994: a 10% budget deficit, 16% monthly inflation between November and December, and significantly reduced foreign reserves. The commission consequently increased the average monthly inflation for 1995 to 2.5%–3.0%.

From the end of 1994, the use of direct central bank credits for financing the budget deficit was sharply curtailed. The joint declaration of the government and the central bank on economic policy, of 9 March 1995, rejected the use of direct central bank credits to finance the federal budget deficit. Only short-term credits to cover the shortfall in the first quarter (not exceeding 3.5 trillion rubles) were permitted. The ruble element in the budget deficit was to be covered mainly by the sale of government securities. In accordance with the monetary program, loans to commercial banks were to be provided only on market terms, with interest rates set by auction. Commercial bank refinancing rates could not be lower than the equivalent rate on the interbank market.

In order to control the growth of the money supply, the IMF set limits on net domestic assets, and also set guidelines concerning the size of official foreign currency reserves. Normally, IMF stabilization programs control the money supply by means of net domestic asset targets—in essence, the monetary base is permitted to expand in line with foreign reserves accumulated. The IMF viewed that control of net domestic assets was the key to financial stabilization, insofar as growth in net domestic assets leads directly to inflation.

Financial Stabilization in Russia

Changes were also envisaged in money supply channels. Whereas during 1992–1993 the monetary base was broadened mainly through loans to the government, to economic agents, and to the governments of CIS countries, in 1995 the sources of money supply growth lay in the expansion of the government's securities portfolio and the central bank's increased foreign reserves.

The 1995 financial stabilization program did not envisage fixing the ruble exchange rate and did not impose any restrictions on its movement. This path elected orthodox stabilization, based on control of the money supply, rather than the use of a fixed exchange rate.

8.3. Budget Policy During Financial Stabilization

The budget law for 1995 was approved at its third reading, an item-by-item reading of all revenues and expenditures, on 14 March. Conflicts between State Duma factions obstructed the passing of almost all the amendments, and as a result, the government's version was essentially approved. On the fourth and final reading, on 24 June 1995, the State Duma and the Federation Council adopted the law. The structure of the budget also remained essentially unchanged, with some superficial modifications. Revenues, expenditures, and the budget deficit remained unchanged from the second reading.[1]

In order not to repeat the mistakes of 1994, in which indicators of high inflation were written into the budget, the government based its draft budget forecast on a rapid drop in inflation. It turned out that with the rate of inflation exceeding the rate accounted for in the budget by a factor of 1.44, the nominal expenditures approved in the budget could be financed without increasing the deficit. Federal budget revenues for 1995 exceeded those anticipated in the law of 14 March by a factor of 1.3. The overfulfillment of the revenue side made it possible to finance 15% more spending than was originally

---

1. On 12 August a federal law amending the 1995 federal budget law was approved and signed by Yeltsin. It envisaged some change in the structure of budget expenditures: an increase in spending on a number of items was achieved by cutting expenditures linked to raising the minimal wage, which did not happen as rapidly as was anticipated in the spring (when the budget was approved). On 6 December the 1995 budget law was revised one more time such that budget fulfillment almost coincided with the new figures set in the law.

planned. Overall balancing of the 1995 budget was achieved.[2] Starting in the first quarter, government expenditures were executed not only according to budget revenues received, but also according to proceeds from the financial markets and external loans. Thus, the system of government financing approved in the budget law for 1995, one that practically excluded central bank loans, played a vitally important role in increasing the authorities' responsibility for budget spending.[3] For the whole of 1995, federal budget expenditures and loans (less debt repayment) were 16.9% of GDP. This figure for the consolidated budget was 29.4% of GDP, compared to 37% of GDP in 1994.[4] In real terms, federal budget expenditures were reduced in 1995 compared to the previous year by 34%, and consolidated budget expenditures were reduced by 21%.

The taxation of foreign trade played an important role in achieving the 1995 budget. Individual foreign trade tax breaks were abolished

---

2. Tax payments to the consolidated budget grew from 21.5% of GDP at the beginning of the year to 25% of GDP in April 1995. By the end of the year tax receipts had fallen to 21.7% of GDP. Federal budget tax receipts in 1995 were around 10%–11% of GDP. Nontax revenues to the consolidated budget were 2.2%–3.3% of GDP; the overwhelming majority of these revenues, about 70%–90%, were federal budget revenues, and their dynamics made it possible to eliminate budget expenditure fluctuations. Overall, consolidated budget revenues for 1995 were 26.1% of GDP, while federal budget revenues were around 13.8% of GDP.

3. Compared with 1994, in the first quarter of 1995 federal government expenditures and credits (less debt repayments) were reduced from 24.2% of GDP to 16.3%, and were 83% of that planned for the first quarter. In the second quarter the situation remained roughly the same, and overall for the half-year expenditures and credits (less debt repayments) were reduced to 16.2% of GDP, which was 98% of that planned for the first half-year. Underfulfillment of planned expenditures was greatest for the social and cultural sphere (78%), scientific research (84%), and the economy (84%). Defense expenditures were financed at 87% of planned levels, and law enforcement at 99%.

Expenditures from the consolidated budget for the first half of 1995 were 28.2% of GDP (in 1994, 37.8% of GDP); expenditures and credits less debt repayments were 30.2% of GDP (in 1994, 41.5% of GDP). From January to June 1995 there was a reduction (compared to 1994) in federal budget expenditures in real terms: on the state apparatus, by a factor of two; on defense, by 32%; on law enforcement, by 28%; on scientific research, by 32%; on the social and cultural sphere, by 31%; and on the national economy, by 7%.

In the third quarter, the reduction in real spending on the main items of the federal budget slowed. However, another round of cuts were made toward the end of the year, so that spending over the whole year included 0.27% of GDP on the state administrative apparatus, 2.87% on defense, 1.16% on law enforcement organs, 0.29% on scientific research, 2.18% on the national economy, and 1.12% on the social sphere.

4. Expenditures on state administration were reduced in comparison to 1994 by 48%; on law enforcement bodies, by 15%; on the economy, by 19%; and on the social sphere, by 20%.

Financial Stabilization in Russia

in two stages between 11 March and 15 May.[5] In accordance with the law *On the Issue of Granting Preferential Tax Treatment to Foreign Trade Organizations* of 24 May 1995, all foreign trade tax breaks were abolished except for those covered by the laws: on customs tariffs, on excise duties, on VAT, and in the customs code. As a result of the adoption of this law, additional budget revenues from import duties, according to Ministry of Finance estimates, totaled about $0.5 billion. However, after the enactment of this law, the State Customs Committee allowed various sports funds and other funds for invalids to defer payment of duties.[6] Thus, tax breaks to the largest import organizations were in fact abolished only at the end of the year.[7] Until this time, deferments were extended or losses to the privileged organizations were compensated out of the budget. (According to Ministry of Finance figures, over the year 3 trillion rubles was paid out in compensation.)

Apart from tax privileges, in 1995 new measures were introduced concerning tariff regulation of foreign economic activity. On balance, these measures raised import duties and lowered export duties. However, as Table 8.1 demonstrates, these measures were not reflected in a change in budget revenue figures. This highlights the fact that these revenues in 1995 were determined for the most part not by duty levels but by the size of the import base subject to tariffs, which was determined by the scale of various kinds of preferential tax treatment. Budget revenues from export duties in 1995 were more flexible to change. After some growth in the early months, at the end of the first half-year of 1995, export duties reached 1.1% of GDP (compared with 0.5% of GDP in 1994). Thereafter there was a smooth decline to 0.95% of GDP for the year, which to some extent was compensated for by the growth in excise duty revenues.

In analyzing budget revenue dynamics, it is worth paying attention to budget arrears. At the end of 1994, the volume of arrears in the consolidated budget was 2.4% of annual GDP and the volume of

---

5. Tax breaks were abolished by presidential decree No. 244, "On the Abolition of Presidential Measures Granting Customs Privileges," of 6 March 1995.
6. That is, organizations enjoying privileges relating to the payment of import duties, in accordance with presidential decrees No. 1927, "On the Protectionist Policy of the Russian Federation in the Sphere of Physical Culture and Sport," of 22 November 1993, and No. 2254, "On Measures for State Support of Russian Invalid Organizations," of 22 December 1993.
7. Order No. 763 of the State Customs Committee, "On Recognition of the Invalidity of State Customs Committee Regulations on Questions of Granting Privileges Concerning the Payment of Customs Duties," of 20 December 1995.

Table 8.1
Reconstruction of Revenues and Expenditures of the Russian Federation in 1995

	Federal Budget (% of GDP)	Local Budgets (% of GDP)	Extrabudgetary Funds (% of GDP)	Consolidated Budget (% of GDP)	Consolidated Budget (% of Budget)
TAX REVENUES					
1. Income and profit taxes	2.7	6.6		9.2	27.0
1.1. Income tax	0.2	2.0		2.2	6.4
1.2. Profit tax	2.5	4.6		7.0	20.6
2. Social Security contributions			7.2	7.2	21.2
2.1. Employees			0.2	0.2	0.4
2.2. Employers			7.1	7.1	20.7
Pension Fund			4.8	4.8	14.0
Social Security Fund			1.1	1.1	3.1
Employment Fund			0.3	0.3	1.0
State Medical Insurance Fund			0.9	0.9	2.6
3. Taxes on Wages Fund		0.3		0.3	0.8
4. Property taxes	0.1	1.1		1.2	3.5
4.1. Property tax		1.0		1.0	2.8
4.2. Land tax	0.0	0.2		0.2	0.6
4.3. Securities tax	0.1	0.0		0.1	0.2
5. Domestic taxes on goods and services	6.0	2.6		8.5	24.9
5.1. VAT	4.3	1.5		5.7	16.8
5.2. Excise duties	1.1	0.4		1.5	4.3
(see continuation)					
5.3. Natural resource royalties	0.1	0.3		0.4	1.2
5.4. Mineral replacement tax	0.1	0.0		0.1	0.4
5.5. Special tax	0.4	0.2		0.7	1.9
5.6. Other taxes on goods and services	0.0	0.1		0.1	0.4

Financial Stabilization in Russia

6. Foreign trade taxes	1.5	0.0		1.5	4.3
6.1. Import duties	0.5	0.0		0.5	1.5
6.2. Export duties	0.9	0.0		0.9	2.8
7. Other taxes	0.1	0.9		1.0	2.8
8. Targeted budget funds	0.9	0.2		1.1	3.2
9. Extrabudgetary funds			0.9	0.9	2.6
9.1. Road Fund			0.8	0.8	2.3
9.2. Other extrabudgetary funds			0.1	0.1	0.3
Total Tax Revenues	11.1	11.6	8.2	30.9	90.3
NONTAX REVENUES					
1. Central bank profit	0.2			0.2	0.6
2. Other nontax revenues	2.1	2.5	0.4	2.8	8.3
Total Nontax Revenues	2.3	2.5	0.4	3.0	8.9
CAPITAL INCOME					
1. Income from privatization	0.2	0.1		0.3	0.8
Total Revenues	13.7	14.2	0.4	34.2	100.0
STATE EXPENDITURES AND CREDITS LESS DEBT REPAYMENTS					
State Expenditures	17.0	14.2	8.6	37.6	95.8
1. State services of general character	0.3	0.4		0.7	1.8
2. On defense	2.9			2.9	7.3
3. On law enforcement bodies	1.2	0.4		1.5	3.9
4. On scientific research	0.3			0.3	0.7
5. On social and housing services	1.1	6.5		15.3	39.0
5.1. On education	0.5	2.9		3.4	8.7
5.2. On culture and arts	0.1	0.4		0.4	1.1
5.3. On the mass media	0.1	0.0		0.1	0.4
5.4. On public health and sport	0.2	2.2		2.4	6.2

(continued)

Table 8.1 (continued)

	Federal Budget (% of GDP)	Local Budgets (% of GDP)	Extrabudgetary Funds (% of GDP)	Consolidated Budget (% of GDP)	Consolidated Budget (% of Budget)
5.5. On social policy	0.2	1.0		1.2	3.2
5.6. On social services paid from extrabudgetary funds, including:			7.7	7.7	19.5
Pension Fund			5.3	5.3	13.6
Social Security Fund			1.1	1.1	2.7
Employment Fund			0.4	0.4	1.0
Medical Insurance Fund			0.9	0.9	2.3
6. On state services to the economy	2.2	6.1		9.2	23.5
7. On other functions	9.1	0.7		7.6	19.4
7.1. Other expenditures	2.8	0.7		3.5	8.9
7.2. On foreign trade	1.3			1.3	3.3
7.3. On domestic debt servicing, including:	2.3			2.3	5.9
GKO and OFZ servicing	1.7			1.7	4.4
(see continuation)					
7.4. On foreign debt servicing	0.9			0.9	2.4
7.5. Subsidies to other levels of state administration	1.8	0.0		×	
Credits Less Debt Repayments					
1. Budget loans	1.4	0.4		1.7	4.2
2. State credits to foreign governments	0.7	0.4		1.0	2.7
3. Incomplete transfers of income by the central bank	−0.2			−0.2	−0.4
4. Foreign credits granted to enterprises	0.3			0.3	0.8
	0.5			0.5	1.3
Total Expenditures and Credits Less Debt Repayments	18.4	14.5	8.6	39.3	100.0
Revenues and Subsidies Minus Expenditures and Credits Less Debt Repayments	−4.7	−0.4	−0.1	−5.1	

FINANCING			
1. Domestic financing	3.2	0.4	0.1
1.1. Central bank credits for financing the budget deficit (net)	−0.1		
1.2. Change in monies deposited	−0.1	0.0	0.1
1.3. State short-term obligations (with OFZs)	3.2		
1.4. Savings bonds	0.1		
1.5. Treasury promissory notes	−0.1		
1.6. Treasury bills	0.1	0.1	
1.7. Other government securities (net)	0.0	0.3	
1.8. Other domestic borrowing	0.0	0.0	
2. External financing	1.5		
2.1. Credits from international financial organizations (net)	1.8		
2.2. Other foreign credits	−0.4	0.0	
2.3. Change in monies deposited in foreign currency	0.1	0.4	
Total Financing	4.7		0.1

Sources: Ministry of Finance RF, Goskomstat, IEPPP.

arrears in the federal budget was 1.47% of GDP. There was a notable drop in the volume of arrears as a percentage of monthly GDP at the end of 1994 and a rise at the beginning of 1995. This sudden increase in arrears was partly the result of a measure that granted deferment of payments to the budget.[8] At the end of the year, tax arrears in the consolidated budget were 29% of December GDP (in December 1994 they were 17.4% of monthly GDP).[9] Overall, arrears grew over 1995 to 2.4% of annual GDP. If one includes the arrears accumulated since 1992, then the consolidated budget would have received an additional 3.3% of GDP had these arrears been settled.

The federal budget deficit overall for 1995 was 3.05% of GDP, compared to 10.9% of GDP in 1994. This deficit was financed by domestic sources to the tune of 1.41% of GDP, and by external sources to the tune of 1.53% of GDP.[10] Table 8.1 shows our reconstruction of consolidated state revenues and expenditures for 1995, including the cost of servicing domestic debt and extrabudgetary items.

As is clear from a comparison of Tables 8.1 and 7.3, in 1995 there was a further reduction in the share of tax receipts in the GDP, from 33.8% to 30.9%. The share of state revenues also dropped, from 36.2% of GDP in 1994 to 34.2% in 1995. State expenditures and loans (less repayments) in 1995 were 39.3% of GDP, compared with 47.5% of GDP in 1994.[11] A comprehensive estimate of the federal budget's secondary deficit pegs it at around 4.7% of GDP. In total, the consolidated budget deficit reached 5.1% of GDP.

8.4. Tightening Monetary Policy and the Inertia of Inflation

As a result of the central bank's expansionist policies in the summer of 1994, high levels of inflation continued into the first quarter of 1995

---

8. In a Ministry of Finance and State Tax Service telegram of 14 February 1995.
9. The accumulated volume of arrears to the federal budget at the end of 1995 was 15.8% of December GDP. (In December 1994, the corresponding figure was 11%.)
10. The deficit was 77.3% financed. Domestic financing was 77.9% fulfilled and external financing was 76.7% fulfilled. Among domestic sources of finance, the most important were GKOs and OFZs (1.7% of GDP) and savings bonds (0.06% of GDP). Financing by central bank credits was negative (−0.07% of GDP), as was also the case for Treasury bills and promissory notes (−0.12% of GDP). Loans from international financial organizations amounted to 1.78% of GDP. Net financing through credits from foreign governments, commercial banks, and firms was negative (−0.37%).
11. This cutting of expenditures by 8.2% of GDP was achieved by reducing expenditure on defense by 1.5%, on law enforcement bodies by 0.3%, on scientific research by 0.2%, on the social sphere by 2.7%, and on the economy by 1.7%. Credits (less debt repayment) were cut by 1.9%, while other expenditures grew by 0.5%.

(Table 8.2). The strengthening of inflationary expectations played a part in this. These expectations were provoked by the threat of a sudden devaluation of the ruble at the beginning of the year. The authorities incorrectly hoped that economic agents would be swiftly converted to the idea of rapid stabilization.

From the very beginning of 1995, the central bank adhered to the stringent constraints of the monetary program. There was a sudden drop in the growth of money aggregates, but the central bank did not lend money to the government in excess of the limits agreed to in the monetary program. However, it did purchase government short-term bonds within the limits agreed upon for the increase in net domestic assets. The growth of net domestic assets in the first half-year was only 19%, while the ceiling set by the monetary program allowed for growth of 35% over that period. This tough policy on domestic lending had a certain logic. First, it was necessary for the government and the central bank to demonstrate their commitment to a path of stabilization. Second, a certain reserve was created for increasing net domestic assets in the second half-year. And third, as a result of these actions, there was an unexpected broadening of the monetary base because of foreign reserves accumulated by the central bank.

Throughout 1995 the refinancing rate was prohibitive. It was almost always significantly higher than the rate on the interbank lending market, and from mid-March to the end of the year it was higher than the weighted average GKO yield. The total volume of auctioned credits issued by the central bank to commercial banks was 0.03% of GDP for the entire year.

It is noteworthy that the central bank did not introduce mechanisms either for accepting promissory notes or for providing securitized loans to commercial banks, even though these mechanisms were outlined in the monetary program for 1995. At the same time, the central bank effectively refused to create a discount window in order to exercise influence over short-term interest rates on the money markets. This somewhat narrowed the room for maneuvering in the summer and autumn, a time when the results of the tight credit policy became very clear.

In April, the central bank approved a measure to increase commercial bank reserve requirements that introduced reserve requirements on short-term deposits and hard currency accounts. The motive behind increasing the reserve requirements was to soften the effect of growth in the credit multiplier. The growth of this variable was

Table 8.2
Monthly Data for Selected Financial Indicators, 1995

1995	Official Ruble/ Dollar Exchange Rate (at End of Month, in Rb)	Rate of Growth of Official Exchange Rate (%)	Real Dollar/ Ruble Exchange Rate (June 1992 = 100)	CPI (%)	M2 (bill. of Rb)	M2 Growth Rate (%)	M0 (bill. of Rb)
I	4,048	14.0	33.2	17.8	93,800	−4.1	31,802
II	4,473	10.5	33.1	11.0	101,900	8.6	34,381
III	4,897	9.5	33.4	8.9	107,300	5.3	35,240
IV	5,130	4.8	32.3	8.5	123,200	14.8	41,639
V	4,995	−2.6	29.2	7.9	138,200	12.2	45,459
VI	4,538	−9.1	24.9	6.7	156,600	13.3	54,574
VII	4,415	−2.7	23.2	5.4	165,000	5.4	62,400
VIII	4,447	0.7	21.6	4.6	173,800	5.3	65,794
IX	4,508	1.4	20.7	4.5	179,700	3.4	69,272
X	4,504	−0.1	20.2	4.7	184,200	2.5	69,856
XI	4,580	1.7	19.9	4.5	195,200	6.0	73,995
XII	4,640	1.3	19.5	3.2	220,800	13.1	80,800

Sources: Goskomstat, Ministry of Finance RF, Central Bank RF, IEPPP.

caused by the expansion of ruble investments and the expectation of increased activity on the financial markets. Raising the average reserve norm was combined with the central bank's tough self-restraint on the refinancing of commercial banks. The money multiplier increased at the beginning of the year from 2.04 to 2.13, and remained at roughly that level until the second half-year. In August, there was a drop to 2.02, at which level it remained until the end of the year.

Limiting banks' open foreign currency positions to 30%, increasing reserve requirements, and introducing reserve norms on foreign currency deposits also helped restrain the growth of the money supply. The stabilization of the dollar exchange rate at the same time that interest rates were lowered (which assisted in lowering inflationary expectations) was also important.

Despite the measures adopted for tightening fiscal policy, inflation in the first half-year remained rather high, exceeding 10% per month. This high inflation to a great extent explains the continuing inflationary expectations.

Only in the second quarter did the macroeconomic situation start to change, after the government and central bank confirmed their

M0 Growth Rate (%)	Monetary Base (bill. of Rb)	Monetary Base Growth Rate (%)	Money Multiplier	Net Domestic Assets (trill. of Rb)	Net Foreign Reserves (trill. of Rb)	Net Foreign Reserves (bill. of $)
−12.8	44,000	−8.3	2.132	40.5	3.5	865
8.1	47,600	8.2	2.141	42	5.6	1,252
2.5	49,900	4.8	2.15	40.8	9.1	1,858
18.2	57,300	14.8	2.15	46	11.3	2,203
9.2	64,000	11.7	2.159	44.2	19.8	3,964
20.1	73,700	15.2	2.125	47.5	26.2	5,773
14.3	81,600	10.7	2.022	55.1	26.5	6,002
5.4	86,100	5.50	2.019	59.5	26.6	5,982
5.3	89,300	3.7	2.012	63.8	25.5	5,657
0.8	90,700	1.6	2.031	62.5	28.2	6,261
5.9	95,400	5.2	2.046	70.7	24.7	5,393
9.2	1E +05	8.8	2.127	76.5	27.3	5,884

intention of implementing a tough financial stabilization program in 1995. The financial markets started to reorient themselves accordingly. The preliminary results of the monetary and credit policies in the first quarter somewhat exaggerated the success, but nonetheless provided grounds for optimism. In April there were clear expectations that the dollar exchange rate would slow and the real ruble rate would fall.[12] In the middle of April economic agents undertake a mass conversion of dollar assets into ruble ones, and as a consequence the nominal ruble exchange rate rose. This process of de-dollarization played a key role in all the macroeconomic processes of the spring and summer.

Not until the nominal ruble exchange rate began to grow, at the end of April, did market agents fully realize the consequences of the financial stabilization under way. In a heavily dollarized economy, banks maintained considerable foreign currency assets out of inertia. Because both financial institutions and financial derivatives were underdeveloped, banks restructured their portfolios only very slowly.

---

12. For example, futures contract quotations on the Moscow Commodity Exchange for September 1995 fell from 7,500–7,700 rubles per dollar in the middle of March to 6,300–6,500 in the middle of April.

As a result, dedollarization in the first half-year was not so rapid as simple models of exchange rate "overshoot" assume.[13] Such models do not take into account many important features of stabilization particular to postsocialist economies, including imperfect financial markets, the irrational expectations of economic agents, and limited financial market liquidity. Instead, stabilization in Russia started without "shock" growth of the interest rate and ruble exchange rate. The growth process was fairly smooth, if one ignores the effect of the liquidity crisis on interest rates in August 1995. However, the root causes of the crisis were an entirely different story.

8.5. The Role of the Exchange Rate in Achieving Stabilization

The problem of confidence in anti-inflationary policies can only partly be explained by the inertia of expectations and the delayed reaction of financial institutions. Attitudes toward the authorities' intentions and options should have changed radically soon after the IMF's decision to support the monetary program, at the end of February 1995. However, the currency policy conducted by the central bank in the first four months of the year had a disorienting effect. Whereas in January and February there were good reasons for a smooth devaluation of the ruble, by March and April such a devaluation did not accord with measures for limiting the money supply. The central bank forestalled the change in public expectations by rapidly increasing foreign currency reserves. The only reason for such a policy was to prevent a devaluation of the dollar exchange rate in connection with an expected strengthening of the ruble.

The increase in the dollar exchange rate in February and April slowed the restructuring of financial portfolios and led to a forced growth of the real ruble supply. The increase in real demand for rubles by those participating in the financial markets, along with the anti-inflationary policy and high ruble interest rate, occurred only

---

13. Models of this sort, describing the process of macroeconomic adaptation during sudden changes in the money supply, assume instantaneous changes in the prices of financial assets and the structure of portfolios. A fall in the money supply causes a growth in interest rates and a "shock" increase in the exchange rate of the national currency. After such a leap a new equilibrium is gradually established between interest rates and expected inflation, as a result of which exchange and interest rates fall. See W. Easterly and H. Wolf, *The Wild Ride of the Ruble* (Washington, D.C.: World Bank, July 1995).

after the central bank acquired significant foreign currency reserves. Demand for the ruble grew on the back of a falling dollar exchange rate and decelerating inflation (a result of the tough measures adopted earlier in the year). Thus, growth of the real money supply in the first four months was determined mainly by changes in the supply of money from the central bank and by price rigidity. Only later was it determined by changes in demand for money, above all by the financial markets.

As a result of the artificial raising of the dollar exchange rate in March and April, the central bank acquired more than $5 billion in foreign currency. Net foreign currency reserves grew from $1 billion at the beginning of February to $3.2 billion at the beginning of May. However, a large part of the foreign currency reserves was purchased by the central bank in May and June.

Growth of the monetary base in the second quarter was 48%, instead of the 15% assumed in the monetary program. The money supply for this period grew by 46%, while the forecasted growth was again 15% (see Table 8.2). The accumulation of the above-mentioned sum of external reserves was completely consistent in accord with the aims of financial stabilization because it ensured the stability of the foreign currency market in the second half-year of 1995. However, the absolute size of the reserves accumulated by the central bank should not be exaggerated. In January, the ratio of gross gold and foreign currency reserves to the monetary base was 48%. It reached a high of 92% in May, then dropped in July to 76%, where it stayed more or less until the end of the year. In comparison, in Mexico the ratio of gross external reserves to the monetary base in the period preceding the 1994 currency crisis exceeded 100%.[14] Thus, to suggest excessive accumulation of foreign currency by the central bank in the first half-year of 1995 is hardly justified.

Also unjustified is any exaggeration of the inflation effect of foreign currency reserve accumulation. Money supply dynamics define only the inflationary trend. Deviations from the trend are linked to a large extent to changes in inflationary expectations. In particular, real inflation in the fourth quarter was much lower than that forecast using simple monetary models. This can be explained by the lowering of inflationary expectations in the second half-year because of increasing confidence in governmental and central bank policy.

---

14. M. Obstfeld and K. Rogoff, "The Mirage of Fixed Exchange Rates," *The Journal of Economic Perspectives* 9 (1995): 73–96.

It is possible that a more cautious policy of accumulating foreign reserves would have reduced the need to toughen commercial banks' reserve requirements. According to our estimates, the increase in reserve requirements starting in May averted an additional increase in M2 for the whole of 1995 of about 11 trillion rubles. This is roughly a third of the money printed during the purchase of foreign currency in March and April, because of an exchange-rate spread unfavorable to the central bank. The intensive spring accumulation of external reserves did not result in the expected burst in inflation in the second half-year, but it could have been conducted in a way more beneficial for the central bank itself, with a lower level of inflation during the summer months.

In the second half-year, the growth of net international reserves decelerated to a level of 4.2%. On the other hand, net domestic assets grew by 61%. To a great extent this was linked to the expansion in the supply of GKOs in the second and third quarters, leading the central bank to buy them up on the open market. The monetary program was adjusted to allow for the unforeseen growth of the monetary base in the second quarter.

The introduction on 5 July of an exchange rate corridor with upper and lower limits of 4,300 and 4,900 rubles per dollar stabilized the foreign currency market and contributed to a lowering of inflationary expectations in autumn. Thus, in the second half-year a nominal anchor was in place. This stabilization of inflationary expectations would have been impossible without the anti-inflationary measures adopted in the first half-year, including a tough domestic lending policy and the accumulation of sufficient foreign currency reserves.

The introduction of an exchange rate corridor followed logically from the situation that had emerged in the financial markets by the middle of the year. The fluctuations in the dollar exchange rate from February to June reflected an absence of strategic goals in the currency policy. By accelerating the accumulation of foreign currency reserves, the central bank did not signal its commitment to stabilization, which would have justified a smooth devaluation of the ruble in January and February. Thus, the central bank's behavior was perceived as contradictory and had a negative effect on economic agents' expectations.

The exchange rate corridor reduced uncertainty in dollar exchange rate changes and raised confidence in monetary and credit policies.

The continuation of the policy of uncontrollably floating the exchange rate could have led to a shakeup in the currency markets. At the same time, the exchange rate dynamics and the volume of intervention after the introduction of the corridor attest to the existence of the well-known "honeymoon effect"—a sharp reduction in both the amplitude of exchange rate fluctuations and in the need for intervention.[15] In itself, the central bank's commitment to repel speculative attacks on the borders of the currency corridor discouraged such attacks. The volume of transactions on the currency exchange during the year suggest that in the second half-year, the dollar stopped being considered a speculative asset. The sharp reduction in currency interventions gave the central bank the opportunity to control the money supply more effectively. This was particularly important in a situation where short-term money market interest rates could not be used as an instrument of central bank policy because they did not influence the demand for money.

8.6. The Strengthening of the Real Ruble Exchange Rate

In evaluating the exchange rate policy of the central bank prior to the introduction of the exchange rate corridor, it is important to bear in mind that the real ruble exchange rate grew by 76.5% over the entire year (in comparison, during 1994 the real ruble exchange rate grew by only 14%, and in the first quarter of 1995 it grew by only 4.4%). Initially, the aim of the macroeconomic program was to achieve stable growth of the real ruble exchange rate. However, the growth of real ruble asset yields and the change of expectations in the second quarter led to a rapid dedollarization of the economy and an increase in the supply of foreign currency. As a result, in May the government and central bank were faced with a choice: either to continue the accumulation of foreign currency reserves while preserving the nominal exchange rate at a level above the 5,000 mark, or, with the aim of controlling the monetary base, to limit its growth, at the risk of lowering the dollar exchange rate. The drop in the dollar exchange rate in May changed the expectations of the vast majority of small holders of dollar assets, which further encouraged a lowering of the exchange rate in June.

---

15. P. Krugman, "Target Zones and Exchange Rate Dynamics," *The Quarterly Journal of Economics* 106 (1991): 669–82.

In order to ensure stability of the real ruble exchange rate in conditions of incipient dedollarization of the economy, the central bank had to violate the guidelines of the monetary program. Growth of the monetary base through an increase in foreign reserves did not contradict the basic target requirements of the IMF concerning net internal assets. On the other hand, neither did it accord with the basic aim of stabilization—to lower inflation. And it also conflicted with the IMF's demand that currency interventions to smooth exchange rate fluctuations be restricted.

This was one of the reasons for the central bank's refusal in May to continue its policy of expanding foreign currency reserves sufficiently to stabilize the real ruble exchange rate. This refusal led to some increase in the nominal ruble exchange rate in May and June. As a result of this increase, and also connected with the fall of money market interest rates, the process of dedollarization of the economy slowed down by the beginning of July.

Foreign currency reserves increased to $13 billion by the end of the first half-year. The accumulation of foreign currency reserves led to additional growth in the monetary base, according to the exchange rate then obtaining, of 15 trillion rubles in excess of the guidelines set for the first half-year (see Table 8.2). The decision by the central bank not to take decisive steps provoked a fall in the dollar exchange rate in May and June of 12%. This allowed the central bank to limit growth of the monetary base to approximately 60% for the first half-year. Holding the real ruble exchange rate unchanged in June would have required a much more significant increase in the monetary base by the end of the half-year, with even sharper cuts in interest rates. Such a monetary expansion would clearly have led to inflation by autumn. In the absence of automatic indexation of budget expenditures, higher inflation (than that forecast), increasing the state's budget revenues, would have somewhat eased the fiscal crisis.

Thus, the fall of the nominal dollar exchange rate in May and June can be seen as a compromise policy, a result of the high level of dollarization of the economy and the mobility of capital flows. In other words, there was a trade-off between lowering inflation rates and stabilizing the real exchange rate.

Expansion of the monetary base because of an increase in foreign reserves is less inflationary than growth caused by an expansion of net domestic assets. Insofar as the key role in the collapse of the dollar in May and June was played by the financial markets and not the population, growth of the monetary base occurred because of an increase in the least liquid items on the asset side of the central bank's balance sheet. This fact is confirmed by the increase in the multiplier and in banks' resources on correspondent accounts in the second quarter. Such a change in the structure of the money supply led to a deceleration in money circulation, which was accompanied by a slight increase in prices. The significant increase in money remaining was used for financial market operations. First and foremost this money was used on the market for state obligations, and thus did not threaten the goods markets. The expansion of GKO-OFZs in the second half-year facilitated a further deceleration of monetary circulation.

The increase in the real ruble rate did not have a negative effect on Russia's balance of payments in 1995. According to official data, the annual volume of export operations grew by 25% compared with 1994, while annual imports grew by 12.5%. However, the net increase in exports was influenced by a number of other factors, such as the lowering of export tariffs and the volume of arrears on the domestic market.

At the same time, the strengthening of the real ruble exchange rate stimulated an inflow of capital into Russia. This contributed to the cheapening of credit, a reduction in the profitability of purely speculative operations in the banking sector, and greater attention to investment in industry by financial institutions. In the second half of the year, a number of major Russian banks started to show a strong interest in industry. This phenomenon became evident in the creation of special investment departments and in the intensification of interbank battles for shares in privatized enterprises.

The growth of the real ruble exchange rate led to a considerable increase in the competitiveness of imported products. The government's natural reaction was to raise import tariffs and lower export tariffs (some were simply abolished). However, these measures were clearly not sufficient for those exporters not linked to the fuel and energy complex, such as the few machinery construction enterprises that had been capable of competing on foreign markets.

8.7. The Crisis on the Interbank Market

As with the growth of the real ruble exchange rate, the banking crisis was caused by the success of the stabilization policy. Until 1995,

Russian banks were able to compensate for poor portfolio decisions and high credit risks by failsafe foreign currency operations (offering huge margins, and with inflation hedging against any losses). The start of stabilization required from bank managers first, a rational understanding of stabilization's macroeconomic consequences, and second, changes in competitive strategies. The fundamental error in judgment was the failure to assess the full scale of the relative change in ruble and foreign currency asset yields.

The initial signs of crisis appeared in June, when some banks failed to honor their obligations on the interbank credit market. However, the market continued to work at full intensity right up until 23 August, the day of the crisis, when, as a result of technical problems, trading was effectively stopped. Most market-makers exited the market, fearing an inevitable chain of nonpayments. An almost tenfold reduction in daily turnover followed (from 1.14 trillion rubles to 130 billion rubles), which led to a liquidity deficit. Quotations on 1-day INSTAR credits went up from 77% before the beginning of the crisis to 275%–350% in the last week of August. Judging by individual deals, the price went as high as 2,000% per annum.

The collapse of the interbank market was inevitable, because turnover did not accord with the real level of credit risk. In some respects the crisis was provoked by the central bank's statement announcing the prolongation of the exchange rate corridor at 4,300–4,900 rubles per dollar for an additional three months (to 1 January 1996). The general stabilizing effect of this statement may have affected the commercial banks, which had been expecting changes in the exchange rate regime in autumn and were hoping to reap considerable speculative profits, as they had in 1994. Deprived of this opportunity, the shakiest banks were forced to reevaluate projected profits and consequently their creditworthiness.

The severe liquidity crisis that arose was softened by the actions of the central bank, which started buying up GKOs en masse on the secondary market. As a result of this intervention, the yield on GKO-OFZs fell from 200%–215% at the height of the crisis to 150%–175% at the beginning of September. This was, however, more than twice the precrisis level of yields. Thereafter, the central bank sold the purchased GKOs, which allowed it to distribute liquid assets between banks while at the same time meeting the (revised) limits on the growth of net domestic assets for the second half-year. The interbank loan market, however, effectively stopped functioning as a market providing banks with access to available money resources. Some small segments emerged after the crisis, uniting individual banks on the basis of mutual trust, but these banks still could not resolve the liquidity problem. In general, however, the crisis on the interbank market played a positive role, as it exposed ineffective banks and forced the central bank to strengthen regulations in 1996 and devote much more attention to banks' compliance with regulations.

9 Macroeconomic Stabilization and the Political Process: The Year of the Presidential Elections

Vladimir Mau,
Sergei Sinelnikov-Murylev,
and Georgy Trofimov

A distinctive feature of developments in postcommunist countries in general, and in Russia in particular, is the great dependence of the economy on political processes.

The period around the 1996 Russian presidential election illustrates this relationship. The 1996 election was of key importance to the country's economic as well as political vitality. In the election the country faced a choice between two fundamentally different developmental paths, and the political elite, economic agents, and voters at large were fully aware of it. Furthermore, the election influenced the behavior of economic agents, fueling the major economic policy problems of 1996–1997. The presidential election was the most important factor in Russia's economic life and economic policy throughout 1996, and its impact continued to be felt for years afterward.

9.1. Political Uncertainty and the Economy

The defining feature, and the foremost general problem, of economic and political life in an election period is uncertainty. Moreover, uncertainty as a socioeconomic factor influencing Russia's development in 1996 differed substantially from the normal electoral uncertainty faced by developed, market-based democracies. The difference relates to the lack of experience with electoral participation and therefore with forecasting election results. The difference also involves the absence of confidence in the unshakability of the democratic process that is characteristic of modern Western democracies and consequently makes it possible for each round of elections to be regarded merely as another episode in the country's political life. The sense that the 1996 elections could be the last free elections in Russia's foreseeable future was an important factor influencing people's economic behavior.

Our analysis, however, considers the issue of electoral uncertainty in somewhat narrower terms. We look at electoral uncertainty as a force that impinged on the government's economic policy on the one hand, and on the other, altered the behavior of economic agents. For both influences, electoral uncertainty had at least three manifestations.

The first was the uncertainty of the election results. The standard projection methods, based on a candidate's popularity during a campaign, in no way predicted the outcome of the Russian presidential election. From the very beginning, the only thing that was clear was that the election would probably be a two-way race (excluding the ambiguous position of Alexander Lebed), with the main contenders being Boris Yeltsin and Gennady Zyuganov.

Second, Russia's postelection economic policy prospects were unclear. One could, of course, postulate that in general, a Yeltsin election victory would mean preservation of the existing path and a Zyuganov victory would result in a shift toward a leftist, nationalist model (a combination of strong protectionism and attempts to stimulate demand by pumping money into the economy).[1] However, both candidates' refusal, right up until the end of May, to publish their economic programs, and the contradictory nature of statements made by left-wing advisers in Yeltsin's extremely heterogeneous cabinet, did not provide clarity to the country's prospective economic course.

Third, Yeltsin's pre-election economic policy remained an open question, particularly in the first quarter of 1996. This uncertainty affected not only economic agents but also members of the cabinet, insofar as everything, in the final analysis, depended on the choice of president. Many factors increased uncertainty considerably and placed the government in an ambiguous position. Among these factors were the political heterogeneity of the executive branch, exemplified by the cohabitation within it of advocates not simply of different but of diametrically opposed political and economic doctrines; the contradictory nature of Yeltsin's own statements at the beginning of the year; and the intensifying battle within Yeltsin's

---

1. For a comparison of alternative economic policy models, see *Rossiyskaya ekonomika v pervom polugodii 1996 goda: tendentsii i perspektivy* (Moscow: IET, 1993).

closest entourage, which might have led to the most unexpected outcomes, including the sacking of the prime minister on the eve of the elections.

The economic and political uncertainty had an impact both on the behavior of economic agents and on government policies. It is worth recalling that whereas the 1995 parliamentary elections did not have an appreciable impact on the economic situation, they did send a negative political signal, demonstrating that public opinion had shifted even further to the left and in favor of the nationalists. In the run-up to the presidential elections the legislative process slowed markedly; its ongoing effectiveness, for understandable reasons, was entirely dependent on the outcome of the presidential elections.

9.2. Macroeconomic Problems of the 1996 Electoral Contest

Given the electoral uncertainty and inexperience with how an economy functions during politically significant elections, one could assume that political conditions in Russia would encourage "preelection shortsightedness by the electorate" (including the economic agents examined by us in this case). On the one hand, the electorate lacked any experience in democratic elections and, as it appeared, was not fully cognizant of its electoral responsibility. On the other hand, almost all of the candidates in the presidential race were also electorally inexperienced.

Therefore, voters could not judge candidates' promises by comparing them with past policy efforts. This was true even for the Communist Party, insofar as the Party had no experience in the recent past of running a predominantly market economy. At first glance, the lack of political experience should have resulted in short-sighted behavior, the most important precondition for Nordhaus's political business cycle. However, actual events do not corroborate this thesis, and thus one cannot straightforwardly apply this economic policy-making model. We will examine this situation in more detail.

Based on Yeltsin's pre-election policies and Zyuganov's prospective postelection plans, an inflationary economic policy should have been expected at the beginning of 1996. A number of factors increased the likelihood of a stronger populist tilt to Yeltsin's policies. These factors were apparent among the electorate in general and in economic agents' behavior in particular.

Most instructive among these factors were the personnel changes undertaken by the president in January and February 1996, particularly the removal of Anatoly Chubais, who more than anyone had come to symbolize the government's tough stabilization course, and the weakening of the position of the prime minister, who was implementing the stabilization program. At the same time, Oleg Soskovets and Nikolai Yegorov, adherents of inflationary and protectionist policies, consolidated their political positions. This situation recalled the turn of events in 1994, when, following the left and nationalist parties' strong showing in the Duma elections, the president abandoned the stabilization policies pursued by Yegor Gaidar and Boris Fedorov. It seemed very likely that the situation would be repeated, particularly since it was now Yeltsin himself who was up for reelection. Thus, the logic of pre-election inflationism coincided with the logic of decision making in the so-called Russian "reverse political business cycle."

The results of the Duma elections also supported this conclusion. During the elections the government's macroeconomic stabilization program was opposed by political forces proposing two related but nonetheless different economic policy alternatives—inflationist (the left) and protectionist (the nationalists). Victory was claimed by advocates of the former, which, judging by televised statements, included the Communist Party, the Agrarians, and Yabloko. Inflationary policies also enjoyed substantial support in a number of other parties, including the progovernment Our Home Is Russia party.

Furthermore, the tone of Yeltsin's election campaign, which began in February, clearly demonstrated his inclination toward economic populism. During Yeltsin's trips to the regions he made generous financial promises, proposed a blatantly populist campaign to pay off wage arrears (without differentiating between federal budget arrears, local budget arrears, and enterprises' arrears to their employees), and made the completely unexpected proposal to allot to the war effort in Chechnya 16 trillion rubles over and above what was written into the federal budget. These and other proposals, had they been implemented, would have fueled a new round of inflation.

9.2.1. *The Dynamics of Inflationary Expectations*

The government's statements regarding possible monetary expansion should have led to a rise in expected inflation and to an appro-

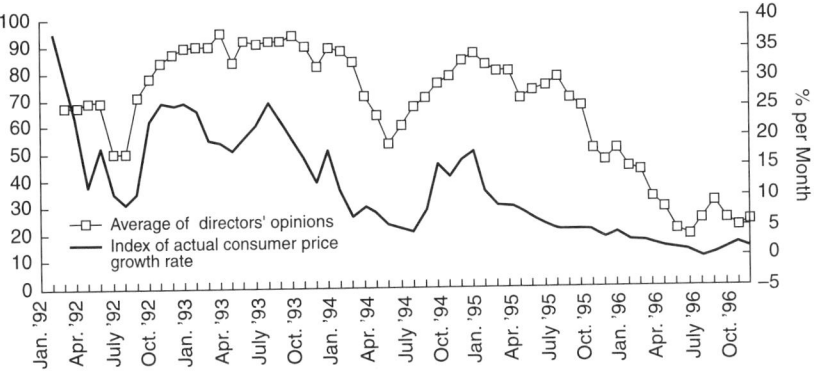

Figure 9.1
Actual consumer price index and directors' expectations concerning price increases, 1991–1992. (Data from Goskomstat and IET surveys.)

priate revision of pricing policy by corporations. However, this did not happen, and enterprises did not follow the usual practice of factoring expected price increases into their contracts.

Thus, surveys of enterprise managers about their own activities and the behavior of their counter-parties throughout the year in question show a steady lowering of expected inflation. Indeed, the actual decline turned out to be greater than expected. This fact does not mean there were not fluctuations over the year. Fluctuations occurred, but they were well within the margin of error associated with such surveys. However, an interesting feature is that expected price growth (as opposed to actual price growth) occurred not in the pre-election period but in the autumn of 1996, reflecting a seasonal increase in the inflation index. The electoral contest had almost no impact on inflationary expectations, suggesting that economic agents had developed rational patterns of behavior, taking their lead from government macroeconomic policy rather than from the promises of politicians. Figure 9.1 shows actual and expected increases in the consumer price index based on monthly surveys of a representative panel of industrial enterprises, conducted by IET from 1992.[2]

Regression analysis shows a significant relationship between this index and actual inflation ($R^2 = 0.65$, $F = 96.8$, t for the variable $= 9.84$, and for the constant $= -4.01$). Throughout 1996 there was

---

2. S. Tsukhlo and R. Gershman, *Konyunktura promyshlennosti: ekonomiko-politicheskaya situatsiya v Rossii, Iyun 1996 goda* (Moscow: IET, 1996), 10.

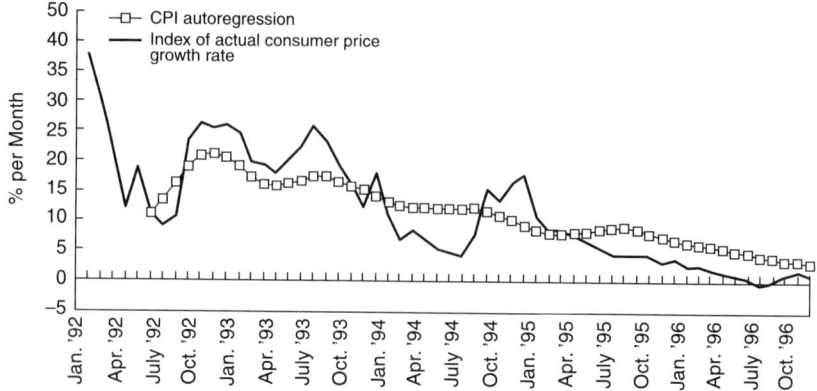

Figure 9.2
Dynamics of consumer prices in Russia, January 1992–December 1996, and an autoregression model.

a steady decline in expected inflation, apart from the autumn burst mentioned above, which coincided with an increase in real inflation.

Comparisons of inflation forecasts based on this regression model with actual price growth rates bear out this observation.[3] In the first half of 1996 there was a steady divergence between inflation forecasts based on money supply dynamics and actual inflation figures, which were lower. Although the deviation of actual inflation from the monetary forecast can be explained by economic agents' demand for real cash balances, the conclusion can nonetheless be drawn that a pre-electoral acceleration of inflation was not expected (Figure 9.2).[4]

---

3. See *Rossiyskaya ekonomika v pervom polugodii 1996 goda*, 57; V. Mau, S. G. Sinelnikov, and G. Yu. Trofimov, "Economic Policy Alternatives and Inflation in Russia," *Communist Economies and Economic Transformation* 8, no. 3 (1996): 307, 313.
An analysis of the link between M2 growth and the actual level of inflation in the period from July 1992 to December 1996 yields the formula $\pi_t = a\pi_{t-1} + bm_{t-6,t-1} + \varepsilon_t$, where π_t is inflation per month in the month t, $m_{t-6,t-1}$ is the average money supply growth rate for the preceding half-year, and ε_t is the random variable representing the impact of inflationary expectations and nonmonetary factors. The following are estimates of the regression parameters: $a = 0.7394$; $b = 0.2771$. The multiple regression coefficient $R^2 = 0.879$. The t-statistic is 11.12 for parameter a and 3.61 for parameter b.
4. In interpreting the deviation of the actual data from the estimates in the retrospective prognosis, it is necessary to take into account that these deviations include not only mistakes resulting from underestimating the demand for money and other factors, but also mistakes linked to the modeling of the structure of lags.

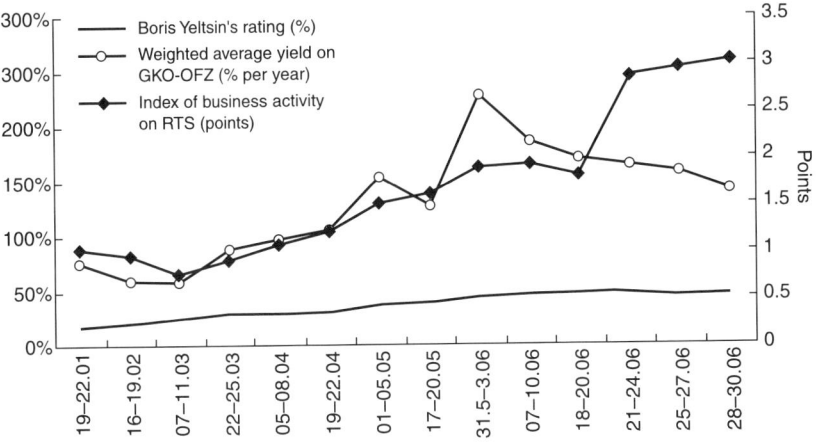

Figure 9.3
Economic indices and Yeltsin's popularity rating, January–June 1996.

9.2.2. The Situation on the Stock Market

The rationality of economic agents' behavior was expressed particularly clearly on the stock market. Because of the political uncertainty, the exacerbation of the investment crisis that characterized the first half of 1996 was no great surprise. However, while economic agents were rather conservative in their investment activities, a willingness to engage in more risky operations is clearly evident from their actions. This presupposes an ability to track the political situation effectively. In this respect, the activity of the stock market from March onward, although unexpected, can be entirely explained by the fact that at this time, Yeltsin's ratings in public opinion polls started to climb (Figure 9.3).

The dynamics of the stock market in the pre-election period reveal two significant points. First, at the end of March, business activity grew slowly, following the publication of public opinion poll results. The second point occurred at the end of May, when a sudden burst in stock market activity coincided with a clear shift in public support in Yeltsin's favor.

Of course, the economic significance of these dynamics should not be exaggerated. The small size of the Russian stock market (in absolute terms and compared with the GKO market) makes it impossible to speak of any serious level of absolute risk. Furthermore, as far as can be judged, the main agents on the market for corporate paper were foreign investors, whose share of investments in Russia were insignificant and whose level of risk was consequently tolerable. But despite these reservations, stock market dynamics are extremely instructive, providing additional evidence of the rationality and appropriateness of economic agents' behavior in conditions of political uncertainty.

We can conclude, based on the actual turn of events, that economic agents' behavior manifested a good understanding of inflation. Economic agents undertook a number of rational measures to secure themselves against risks, hedging against the possible, perhaps delayed, consequences of inflationary policies and political changes that could occur as a result of the presidential elections. They assessed the true macroeconomic situation correctly, taking into account the fact that the monetary authorities had sufficient foreign reserves to keep inflation under control at least until the end of the year and recognizing the balance of political forces in the government and the limited influence of those on the inflationist wing.

Political risk—particularly the possibility of a communist restoration—had a very great impact on the government securities and currency markets. The dynamic of inflationary expectations demonstrated an understanding by economic agents of the government's options and the constraints on its policies. The relative autonomy of inflation from the political process can be explained by the differences in the mechanisms linking risk assessment and the dynamics of other relevant parameters.

9.2.3. *The Situation on the Currency Market*

The high level of political risk in the first half of 1996 led investors to change the composition of their financial portfolios in favor of dollar assets. Economic agents' moved to reduce their share of ruble deposits and government bonds while increasing their hard currency holdings of cash and noncash instruments. These actions led to a sudden growth in interest rates and increased pressure on the exchange rate. This fact is corroborated by data on the purchase of hard currency by the population as well as data on foreign exchange reserves. The share of hard currency cash purchases in the population's expenditures increased from 12.8% in December 1995 to 16.9% in June 1996. At the same time, the share of the population's income saved in the form of deposits or securities decreased from 7.3% in

December 1995 to 3% in June 1996. Also indicative is the fall in net foreign exchange reserves, from $5.9 billion in December 1995 to $4.1 billion in June and $2.5 billion in November 1996.

At the same time, the high risk of a change in monetary policy during the second half of the year in the event that an opposition candidate won the elections had little or no impact on expectations of future inflation, and therefore had little or no impact on the level of real cash balances and prices in the pre-election period. Even though elections were approaching, the demand for money in the first half of the year continued to increase, although more slowly than might be expected in normal political circumstances.

The different intensity in reactions to political uncertainty, in our opinion, was due to the fact that economic agents made initial changes to the composition of their portfolios for the purpose of optimizing their savings structure. A second set of changes in demand for money was connected to the shift in the general demand for consumer and investment products. And whereas precautionary changes in the composition of a savings portfolio can be implemented relatively rapidly and without significant transaction costs, reducing the demand for money (especially when rising inflation is forecast) requires more serious and costly measures, including the carrying out of appropriate operations on goods and financial markets. Also, foreign exchange and money markets react to changes or expected changes in economic policy much faster than goods markets (due to goods stocks, the inflexibility of contracts, and the like). In other words, a crisis on the foreign exchange and money markets can immediately follow the introduction of inflationary policies. This does not, however, mean the sudden and unexpected onset of inflation. The possibility of inflation in 1996 would have been predictable by economically active agents, and thus relatively harmless to them. Therefore, failure to hedge against the sudden implementation of inflationary policies meant that the risk to economic agents of losing savings placed in ruble and hard currency assets was much greater than the risk of losses to real cash balances wrought by an inflation tax.

9.2.4. The Securities Market as an Indicator of the Political Situation

The government bond market proved most sensitive to political uncertainty. Relatively low expected inflation, an understanding of the impossibility of sudden macroeconomic changes in the six months prior to the elections, and fears of a radical change in economic policy following the elections are all clearly manifested here.

At the start of 1996, the sum total of GKOs and OFZs in circulation reached 76.5 trillion rubles. Calculated on the basis of available aggregate data, the average yield at this time was 94% per annum. In the first half of January, GKO-OFZ yields started to fall. The rise in prices is explained by the moderate volume of new bond issues in January in comparison to December, and also by the redemption of some GKO and OFZ issues by the Ministry of Finance prior to their maturity. This signaled that the Ministry of Finance was trying to revise the maturity structure of its GKO portfolio with the aim of reducing expenditure on the servicing of its domestic debt. By the last week of the month, the yield on thirty-day to ninety-day government debt was on average 4.3% per month, similar to the January level of inflation. To some extent this can be explained by the decision taken in February 1996 to allow foreign investors access to the GKO-OFZ market. At the beginning of February, the average annual yield for all issues was 82.7%, while at the end of February it was 56.2%.

However, from mid-March the rise in GKO prices was suddenly reversed. This was connected first to the fall in budget revenues for the first two months of the year, and second to the need to make major redemptions of previous debt issues in March and April (Figure 9.4). This in turn brought a new round of GKO issues. The scale of debt redemption in May was much less than in the preceding months, but at the same time the upcoming elections produced a significant increase in social expenditure. The increased spending raised the cost of borrowing on the domestic market.

The considerable volume of GKO redemptions in April and the need for funds to finance budget spending forced the Ministry of Finance to place new bond issues, which were to be redeemed after the presidential election. As a result, the cost of servicing these debt issues rose sharply. Thus, in the middle of April the auction rate on three-month GKOs rose to 188.9% and the rate on six-month GKOs rose to 235.1%—in essence, back to the December 1995 level. Moreover, the Ministry of Finance was forced to reject up to 90% of competitive bids on GKOs in order to prevent prices from falling even further. In the second half of April yields rose as high as 245% for three-month GKOs and 271% for six-month GKOs.

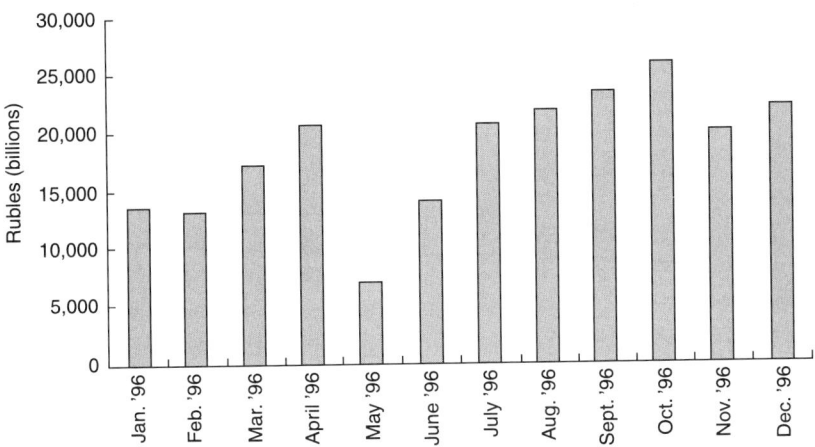

Figure 9.4
Volume of debt repayment and coupon payments on the GKO-OFZ market in 1996.

By April, the yields on GKO issues of differing maturities were reflecting the level of political risk. The weighted average yield of bonds to be redeemed before 16 June was 40.6% per annum. The yield of GKOs to be redeemed between the first and second rounds of the elections was 58.4% per annum, while the yield on those to be redeemed after 10 July was 89.6% per annum (Figure 9.5).

An analysis of GKO-OFZ yields between the end of May and the beginning of June suggests that this time frame can be roughly divided into three periods: 16 to 31 May, 1 to 14 June, and after the first round of presidential elections. The first period saw growth of average yields on all debt issues of 160% to 230% per annum. In the following two weeks, yields continued to grow on the secondary market, although at a much slower pace. The deceleration, in our view, was connected to Yeltsin's rising popularity as a presidential candidate (see Figure 9.3).

Nonetheless, average GKO yield rates continued to climb in accordance with the increase in the share of debt issues to be redeemed after the elections. On 12 June, the average rate reached 240% per annum. The peak yield, 327.4%, was reached at an auction on 13 June to place the 36th series of six-month GKOs. This high yield was related to the ruble deficit caused by the conversion to dollars prior to election day (16 June).

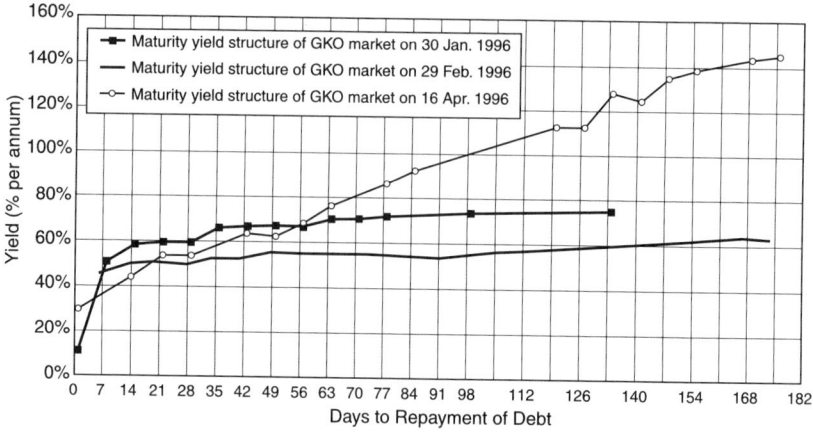

Figure 9.5
Dynamics of the GKO (short-term government bond) maturity yield structure, 1995.

After the first round of the presidential elections, government bond prices started to rise, as did trading volumes. By Monday, 17 June, the average yield of circulating GKO-OFZs in different series fell by 30%–50% per annum, compared with the last day of trading before the election (14 June). The results of secondary trading in the days that followed showed further price growth on these bonds. Thus, by the end of June, yields had fallen to 70%–110% per annum on three-month GKOs and to 110%–150% per annum on six-month GKOs, while at the same time the yield curve had flattened. This situation is illustrated by the GKO maturity yield structure in June 1996 (Figure 9.6).

After the second round of the presidential elections, the price of government bonds increased further. By mid-July, the yield on various GKO series had settled at 60%–100% per annum.

This review supports our contention that the securities market, both state and corporate, was the most sensitive reflector of political developments in the run-up to the election. By the end of May, these markets were already signaling a probable Yeltsin victory, although the two leading candidates' ratings were level at this time. The convergence in June of government bond yields with differing redemption dates further underscored the influence of political factors on this market.

The joint statement of the government and central bank on 16 May, "On the Ruble Exchange Rate Policy," established new princi-

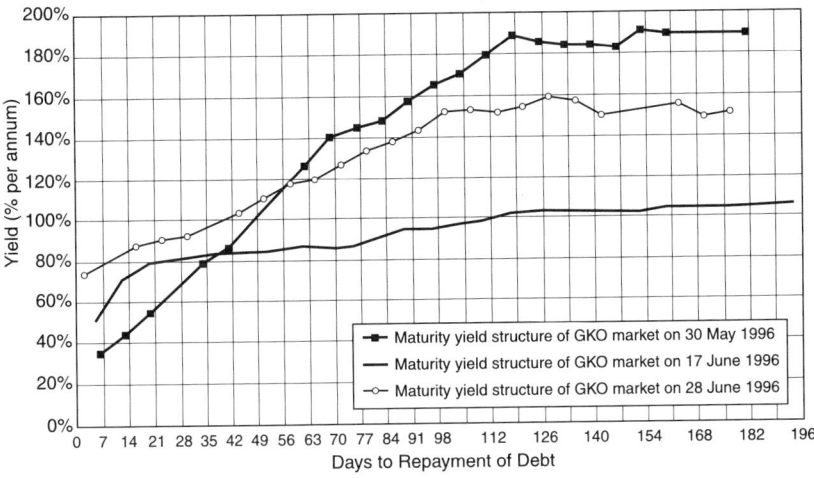

Figure 9.6
Dynamics of the GKO (short-term government bond) maturity yield structure, 1996.

ples for regulating the exchange rate and was a pivotal point in fulfilling the monetary program for 1996. In the second half of the year a sliding corridor was in force, with limits of 5,000–5,600 rubles per dollar on 1 July and 5,500–6,100 rubles per dollar on 31 December 1995. The rate of nominal ruble depreciation in the second half of the year was accordingly set between 1.3% and 3% per month. Thus, for 1996 the devaluation of the ruble exchange rate against the dollar was officially limited to an 18.5%–31.5% range. The exchange rate in fact was 19.8%.

In the run-up to the 1996 presidential election, appreciable redollarization of the economy occurred. In these conditions, the ruble should have depreciated more rapidly than in the second half of 1996. However, the central bank pursued an exchange rate policy aimed at restraining the rate of decline of the nominal ruble exchange rate. The main reasons for this action were first, the danger of strengthening inflationary expectations; second, the possibility of the opposition using rapid depreciation of the national currency for political ends; and third, the need to minimize the growth of the money supply linked to the major purchase of government bonds by the central bank. Net domestic assets grew in the first half by 41.7% as a result of these purchases; thus, for the first half of 1996, net foreign reserves fell by 23%, from 27.3 trillion rubles to 21 trillion rubles.

The steady demand for foreign currency, which ran counter to the trend of summer and autumn 1995 toward a dedollarization of the economy, basically reflected the public's inclination, in times of political uncertainty, to keep its money in hard currency rather than the more lucrative GKOs. These developments also testify to the rationality of economic agents, who accurately assessed the authorities' ability to maintain a general macroeconomic balance until the election. However, these developments also reflected doubts about the stability of the government's course after the election, regardless of whether this was due to the uncertain outcome of the election (the possible victory of Zyuganov) or to the exhaustion of hard currency reserves.

9.2.5 Crisis of the Tax System

Another very important feature of the pre-election economy was the sudden deepening of the tax system crisis. The problem of nonpayment of taxes did not begin in 1996. This problem was neither a reaction to the election nor due purely to the effective collapse en masse of enterprises. Thus, tax evasion cannot be blamed on the lack of funds available for paying taxes. Nonetheless, a detailed study of tax arrears over the past few years reveals a tight link between this phenomenon and political crises in Russia, in particular the weakening of federal authority.

From the summer of 1993 until mid-1994, the volume of tax arrears grew rapidly, from 6% of monthly GDP to 21%. Thereafter the share of arrears in GDP was relatively stable until the beginning of 1996 (Figure 9.7). Substantial growth in tax arrears started in January 1996 and was the result of two interconnected factors. First, the incumbent president could not run a successful election campaign while simultaneously toughening the executive branch's actions toward the electorate. Thus, no tough measures to counteract tax arrears were pushed through. Moreover, nonpayment of taxes provided the government with an alternative means of loosening its monetary policy prior to the election, a practice commonly used in market economies.

Second, the fiscal behavior of enterprises was influenced by CPRF politicians, who openly declared their sympathies for those who did

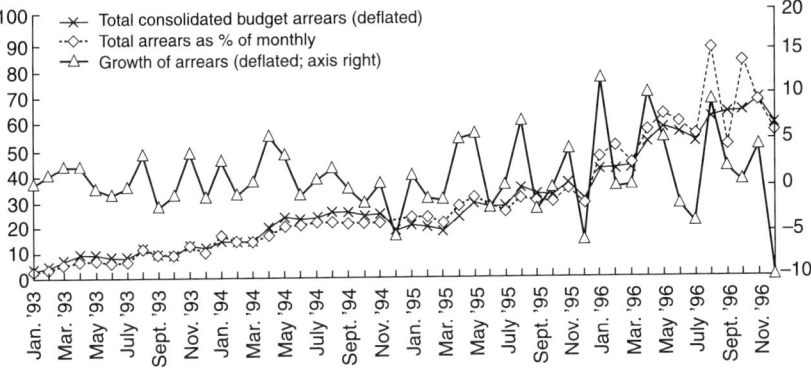

Figure 9.7
Dynamics of the arrears to the consolidated budget, 1993–1996.

not pay taxes to "the government of national betrayal."[5] This, combined with the real possibility of Zyuganov being elected president, encouraged economic agents not to pay taxes. It was understood that in the case of a CPRF victory, there would most probably be an amnesty on tax arrears (this was entirely in keeping with the left's thinking on the need to support enterprises by propping up working capital). Even in the case of a Yeltsin victory, however, prosecution for nonpayment of taxes would be highly unlikely as well.[6]

Thus, in the pre-election period enterprises simply paid less taxes, reckoning both on a softening of tax enforcement during the election campaign for populist reasons and on a probable tax amnesty in case of a communist victory.

From the beginning of 1992, a decline in government revenues in the first few months of each year was characteristic for Russia.[7]

---

5. For example, at the hearings in the State Duma on problems of socioeconomic policy on 9 April 1996, T. Karyagina, economic adviser to Gennady Zyuganov, said, "It should be said to entrepreneurs as well that all those who now deceive and avoid taxes, are in fact Russian patriots, and are etatists [state-minded] by nature; they should not fear [the communists coming to power]."
6. Minister of the Economy E. Yasin explained the tax crisis in the context of the acute electoral battle and the unpredictability of its outcome in the following manner: "Some do not pay because they wait for their own to come to power. Others do not want to create a financial base for the communists in case they come to power."
7. To a certain extent this can be explained by a purely technical factor: the accounting procedure for so-called "final turnover" in the budget assumes that that part of revenues which is received in the first ten days of January is attributed to the revenues for December. The seasonality of tax receipts also plays a role, manifesting in some fall in advance profit calculations as compared with actual profits, and in the low level of foreign trade at the beginning of the year owing to the large number of public holidays.

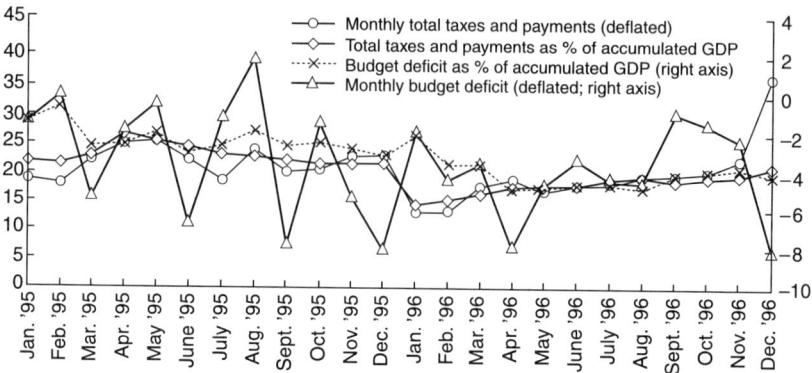

Figure 9.8
Dynamics of tax revenues and revenues to the consolidated budget, 1995–1996.

However, in 1996 government revenues collapsed. Federal tax receipts fell by 3.5% of GDP in January 1996 compared with the end of 1995 (from 10.3% to 6.8%, mainly owing to a decline in profit tax and taxes on goods and services). Tax payments to the consolidated budget fell from 21.7% of GDP in 1995 to 14.4% in January 1996.

Consolidated budget revenues for the first quarter of 1996 were only 69.7% of those planned. Specifically, tax receipts reached only 62.8% of the target level. Tax receipts in the first quarter remained at the January–February 1996 level (16.4% of GDP), or 29% lower than for the first quarter of the preceding year (23% of GDP). In the second quarter, the approaching presidential election continued to affect tax collection, and receipts remained low: 17.9% of GDP for the first half of 1996, compared with 24.7% of GDP in the first half of 1995 (Figure 9.8). The situation with respect to federal budget receipts was similar. Tax payments to the federal budget for the first half of the year were 7.7% of GDP, compared to 10.8% in the first half of 1995.

Several factors explain the fall in tax receipts.[8] The main reason for the drop in budget revenues was an increase in tax arrears. The real

---

8. Changes in tax legislation may have played some role in this. In particular, on 1 January 1996 several changes in the tax legislation adopted in 1995 came into force. In particular, a tax on additional wages above the prescribed norm and a special tax were abolished. By our calculations these changes would have led to a fall in tax receipts amounting to 0.6%–0.7% of GDP. A number of other measures, such as measures to simplify the taxation system and the calculation of small businesses' tax bills, and changes in the list of those enjoying VAT privileges, could not have had a significant impact on the level of tax receipts.

volume of arrears increased by 42.1% in January 1996. However, in January the State Tax Service changed its method for calculating tax arrears. Under the old method, growth of arrears in January is estimated at 18.1%, while under the new method, for comparable months the figure is 35.7%. Cumulative consolidated budget arrears in unadjusted figures grew by 37.4% in January 1996 in comparison with December 1995. It is worth noting that in January 1995, the real volume of arrears to the federal budget grew by 3.5%, and the real volume of arrears to the consolidated budget grew by 7.1%. To a large extent, this seasonal growth of arrears was the result of an increase in the volume of taxes accrued in the first month of the quarter, which in the context of a liquidity deficit led to growth in arrears.

The absence of data on the structure of tax arrears growth complicates a qualitative assessment of their role in the decline of tax receipts. Apart from the taxes not transferred to the budget, arrears in any given month include the sum total of fines for nonpayment of previous tax bills.

The defective mechanism for granting deferrals on tax payments established by a presidential decree of 19 January 1996 also encouraged the growth of arrears. This law allowed approximately 30,000 taxpayers to pay off their arrears in installments.

However, even taking into account the change in the method for calculating arrears, their seasonal character, and the granting of deferrals, it is clear that the growth in arrears in January 1996 was caused by the high level of political uncertainty and was the most prominent feature of the unfolding tax crisis.

Increased tax evasion was another factor in falling tax receipts. Diverse methods of evasion were employed, including the use of cash for business transactions that was not recorded in company accounts. The 2.5% growth in the cash share of M2 in the first half of 1996 indirectly corroborates the use of unrecorded cash payments to settle business transactions.

Third, there was a contraction of the profit and value-added tax base as a result of a significant growth of debts. The volume of debts at the beginning of 1996 increased from 191% of monthly GDP in December 1995 to around 280% in the first half of 1996. One possible factor accelerating the growth of mutual nonpayments was a prohibition on cutting off electricity supplies to delinquent consumers, a policy introduced at the beginning of the year.

Fourth, one of the hypotheses frequently put forth to explain the tax crisis was the increased resort to barter and the spread of multi-link, nonmonetary offsets of debt between suppliers and their clients. The Ministry of Finance became actively involved in nonmonetary offsets in 1996, using promissory notes, tax breaks, commodity credits, and the like. Consequently, many enterprises operated with minimal cash flows, and the lack of funds on their current accounts led to further growth of budget arrears. Price distortions adopted in offsets between taxpayers, the budget, and those receiving budget funds led to a contraction of the tax base. However, existing statistics do not allow accurate estimates of the scale of these operations and their significance for the economy.

Thus, the tax crisis that intensified at the end of 1995 and beginning of 1996 turned out to have rather serious consequences. If the crisis had been confined to the election period, then tax collection should have more or less automatically returned to its previous level in the second half of the year. However, the severity of the tax problem, which eased somewhat in the middle of the year, flared up again in autumn. This phenomenon cannot be explained away simply by reference to the political uncertainty that persisted as a result of Yeltsin's poor health. Likewise, arguments concerning the ineffectiveness of the tax system and the need for fundamental reform are correct, but insufficient.

The scale of tax evasion grew sharply in 1996 and marked the beginning of a qualitatively new stage in the tax crisis. In 1995–1996, the extent of "adverse selection" among taxpayers increased significantly. Previously, tax violations were simply a means for enterprises to reduce their overheads and did not have a significant impact on market competitiveness. However, the rise in tax evasion and the existence of numerous individual tax breaks led to a situation in which honest entrepreneurs who complied with tax legislation found themselves on a blatantly uneven playing field, which undermined the development of an environment conducive to efficient entrepreneurship. Previously, tax evasion or tax privileges provided enterprises with higher than average earnings (which could be seen as a premium for risking being fined). However, as the practice became more widespread, compliance with tax legislation made it very difficult for enterprises to achieve average profit levels. This can be explained by the fact that a significant percentage of tax evasion is factored into prices. The result is negative selection: conscientious taxpayers either are squeezed out of the market or (more often) adopt new rules of the game, such as lobbying for tax privileges, deferrals, and engaging in tax evasion.

9.3. Government Economic Policy in Conditions of Electoral Uncertainty

The pre-election behavior of the government was determined by a number of factors, some of which are common to all market-based democracies, others of which are typical of politically weak regimes with populist inclinations (including both weak democracies and weak dictatorships), and still others that surfaced in the specific situation of economically and politically important elections in post-communist Russia.

In the broadest sense, the government's actions should have been focused on keeping Yeltsin president, which would have enabled the existing cabinet to continue working. This factor should have been particularly dominant in the case of Viktor Chernomyrdin, a man who forfeited participation in the presidential elections in return for certain political guarantees. The prime minister's motivation is crucial and can be viewed as representing the position of the government as a whole.[9]

Loosening monetary policy was a natural reaction by the government to the gravity of the political situation in general and to the situation in the run-up to the 1996 presidential election in particular. The main issue in the election—the issue the electorate was most sensitive to, and which was recognized as such by Yeltsin—was wage arrears at all levels of the budget (approximately 20% of all wage arrears) and enterprise wage arrears to their employees. Wage arrears grew in real terms in the first half of 1996 by more than 85% in comparison to the end of 1995.

---

9. The actual situation was somewhat more complicated. A number of the members of the pre-election government, which in some respects strongly resembled a coalition government, were (at least at the beginning) counting on holding on to their posts even in the case of a change of president—all the more so as Zyuganov and his closest associates gave very clear signals to that effect. However, it quickly became apparent that such a "soft transformation" of the regime would be impossible. On the one hand, when the CPRF leadership team started to take shape, it became apparent that there was no place on this team for members of the existing executive. On the other hand, potential "collaborationists" in the existing cabinet had almost no opportunity to influence economic policy, which was controlled entirely by the prime minister and his economic team.

However, the standard policy of stimulating economic activity and reducing unemployment at the cost of increased inflation acquired a somewhat different aspect. In Russia, as a result of high levels of hidden unemployment, monetary policy has a weak impact on the labor market. Inflationary shocks were targeted toward reducing wage arrears rather than toward bringing down unemployment. Moreover, substituting the fight against nonpayment of wages for the fight against unemployment sharply decreases the period of time between broadening the money supply and realizing the positive effects for the economy. This reality was demonstrated at the beginning of the summer, when budget arrears were suddenly reduced. This process, however, in no way altered the essence of the problem of electoral inflationism.

Actual events developed differently. The government decided not to resort to expanding the money supply to resolve its political problem (ensuring Yeltsin's reelection) and economic problem (overcoming the budget crisis). There were several, predominantly political reasons for this decision.

First, the steady reduction in inflation starting in the spring of 1995 was virtually the only visible success of the government after it overcame the goods deficit in 1992. It was clear that backsliding on inflation would not be electorally wise and could not be compensated for by the payment of pension and wage arrears. The experience of the 1995 Duma elections had already demonstrated that satisfying wage demands in a given region did not automatically lead to an increase in the popularity of the pro-government party there. The logic here is that voters, perceiving the settlement of arrears as their due, then vote against the authorities, particularly since the authorities have sanctioned a new round of inflation anyway.

Second, with the IMF's close monitoring of the implementation of the monetary program, expanding the money supply would have signaled failure of the policy. This failure would be evident not only in the short term but also in the medium term, because it would have unavoidably worsened the government's position after the elections. As Yeltsin's chances of victory grew, the latter argument was more and more persuasive.

Third, the government lacked sufficient experience with fine-tuning monetary policy and the postcommunist economy was not sufficiently forecastable to allow risky experiments with monetary policy. The exchange rate crisis in October 1994 clearly demonstrated the problem of varying time lags in the context of continual changes in market institutions (above all financial market institutions). This understanding strongly influenced Chernomyrdin's economic decision making thereafter.

Under these circumstances, the aim was to construct a monetary policy such that all the positive consequences of its easing would (while taking into account possible uncertainty over the time lag) occur prior to the elections, and all the negative consequences afterward. The government pursued the policy that seemed to it to be the most reliable. Expansion of the money supply was timed to occur as close to the elections as possible and to be brief. In May and June, the monthly rate of M2 growth increased somewhat, reaching on average 3.1% over the two months (Table 9.1). The authorities' impact was limited to monetizing the consolidated budget deficit while remaining within the overall framework of the monetary program. The main channels of money supply were purchases by the central bank of government bonds on the open market and the purchase of foreign currency, precious stones, and metals from the Ministry of Finance.[10]

In the choice between easing monetary policy or easing budget policy, the government chose the latter. This signaled the government's acceptance of the rules of the game, including worsening tax collection together with an expansion of government expenditures and a sharp increase in borrowing on the domestic market. In some respects this option was worse than direct monetary emission, because it deprived the authorities of room to maneuver. However, in some respects it was a better option. With the government's well-known flexibility, this tactic made it possible to preserve the policy of bringing inflation down, while implementing a number of populist measures aimed at winning the election.

9.3.1. The Government's Budget Policy in the Year of the Elections

In the spring of 1996, adherence to the federal budget in the first quarter came under heated debate in Parliament, the mass media, and economic circles. The source of the contention was the extremely

---

10. The purchase of government bonds by commercial banks can also lead to money supply growth if their surplus reserves are reduced, and hence the money multiplier is also reduced.

Table 9.1
Monthly Data for Selected Financial Indicators, 1996

1996	Official Ruble/ Dollar Exchange Rate (at End of Month, in Rb)	Growth Rate of Official Exchange Rate (%)	Real Effective Dollar/ Ruble Exchange Rate (June 1992 = 100)	CPI (%)	M2 (bill. of Rb)	M2 Growth Rate (%)	M0 (bill. of Rb)
I	4,734	2.00	19.4	4.10	216,700	−1.90	75,400
II	4,818	1.80	19.2	2.80	229,200	5.80	80,400
III	4,856	0.80	18.8	2.80	241,800	5.50	86,700
IV	4,940	1.70	18.7	2.20	251,000	3.80	93,100
V	5,014	1.50	18.7	1.60	254,200	1.30	93,700
VI	5,097	1.70	18.8	1.20	266,900	5.00	104,400
VII	5,191	1.80	19	0.70	271,900	1.90	102,800
VIII	5,348	3.00	19.6	−0.20	275,300	1.30	101,100
IX	5,396	0.90	19.8	0.30	276,000	0.30	96,200
X	5,455	1.10	19.7	1.20	278,800	1.00	94,400
XI	5,508	1.00	19.6	1.90	282,300	1.30	95,800
XII	5,560	0.90	19.5	1.40	292,500	3.60	103,800

Source: Central Bank RF, Ministry of Finance RF, Goskomstat RF, IET.

low level of budget fulfillment on both the revenue and the expenditure sides, as well as the specific political situation at the time. The government's opponents tried to use the growing budget crisis to demonstrate that Yeltsin's team was unable to pull the country out of an economic decline. At this time, the president tried to stabilize the situation by setting strict financing priorities (the unconditional clearing of wage arrears before 1 April, the clearing of pension arrears before 1 May, and so forth) while sequestering other expenditure items, and by preparing and implementing measures to raise tax receipts (issuing a number of presidential decrees, mobilizing the State Tax Service to prosecute evaders, and so on).

The reduction in federal budget expenditures at the beginning of 1996 was even greater than the fall in revenues. Only servicing of state debt remained at the same level it had been at the end of 1995, which was motivated by the government's desire to fulfill its obligations to foreign creditors. In January 1996 all other items were cut from 15.2% of GDP to 7.1%.[11] The overall volume of budget expenditures in March increased by almost 2% from February. However,

---

11. In particular, expenditure on defense and law enforcement was cut to 2.4% of GDP, and spending on the national economy was cut to 1.19% of GDP.

M0 Growth Rate (%)	Monetary Base (bill. of Rb)	Monetary Base Growth Rate (%)	Money Multiplier	Net Domestic Assets (trill. of Rb)	Net Foreign Reserves (trill. of Rb)	Net Foreign Reserves (bill. of $)
−6.70	100,800	−2.90	2.15	75.5	25.3	5,344
6.60	106,700	5.90	2.148	82.7	24	4,981
7.80	113,700	6.60	2.127	73.5	40.2	8,278
7.40	120,900	6.30	2.076	89.9	31	6,275
0.60	118,800	−1.70	2.14	98.8	20	3,989
11.40	129,400	8.90	2.063	108.4	21	4,12
−1.50	131,100	1.30	2.074	111.6	19.5	3,757
−1.70	129,000	−1.60	2.134	111.8	17.2	3,216
−4.80	125,600	−2.60	2.197	110.9	14.7	2,724
−1.90	124,000	−1.30	2.248	116.7	7.3	1,338
1.50	125,000	0.80	2.258	111.2	13.8	2,505
8.40	130,900	4.70	2.235	121.4	9.5	1,709

only 75.9% of the quarterly expenditure target was fulfilled, of which a significant share went to pay off wage arrears.

Despite difficulties with adhering to the budget, the State Duma continually strove to approve legislation that increased the budgetary burden, and some of the proposed amendments to the 1996 budget were subsequently adopted. However, the lack of a clear, economically grounded budget policy deterred adherence to budgetary guidelines. The growth of expenditure on servicing the state debt was determined by government bond yields, which in turn, as we have discussed, were largely influenced by electoral forces and by the need for a massive increase in domestic borrowing by the Ministry of Finance during a revenue crisis. Under the circumstances, the Ministry of Finance had to make large GKO tenders despite having to pay high interest rates. As a result, prices for government discount bonds dropped considerably. In the first half of 1996 the volume of GKOs in circulation nominally doubled; in real terms it increased by 89.6%.

9.3.2. The Dilemma: Tax Reform or the Growth of Government Debt?

Our analysis shows that during the election campaign, the government chose to increase government debt further rather than engage in tax reform. This decision was determined by the tax crisis, which worsened during the election campaign, when certain categories of expenditures were absolutely necessary for political reasons.[12] In Russia, owing to the economic and above all political inexpediency of abandoning a tough fiscal policy, budgetary policy was not relaxed. Nonetheless, tax reform continued to be rejected (or, more precisely, the government took a very soft line on tax evasion and collecting tax arrears) in favor of increasing domestic debt.

9.3.3. Monetary Policy

It is worth noting another precondition for the government's cautious fiscal policy. Russian law guarantees the autonomy of the central bank, whose leadership was committed to stabilization. However, the central bank was not entirely neutral in the election. Through its actions on the securities market and its support of the exchange rate corridor, the central bank assisted in Yeltsin's reelection victory. These actions can be justified by two groups of factors. First, the central bank's actions remained within the framework of achieving macroeconomic stabilization.[13] Second, the political opposition clearly conveyed its hostility to stabilization of the national currency. In case of an opposition victory, this hostility could not fail to affect the position taken by the central bank's leadership.

According to the monetary program adopted in 1996, the central bank was supposed to ensure M2 growth over the first half of the year of no more than 20%. In fact, between 1 January and 1 July 1996, M2 grew by 20.9%. On average, during the first half of 1996 M2 grew by 3.2% per month. Thus, central bank emissions between January and June 1996 inclusive were very close to the guidelines in the monetary program agreed upon with the IMF.

As a result of this policy, inflation continued to fall in the first half of 1996. Whereas in January the consumer price index was 4.1%, in

---

12. In A. Cukerman, S. Edwards, and G. Tabellini, "Seignorage and Political Instability" (*The American Economic Review* 82 (1992): 537–55), the authors provide a theoretical basis for, and empirical confirmation of, the fact that political instability and polarization of the main competing parties' political platforms lead to tax reforms being abandoned in favor of monetary emission, increasing the share of seignorage. There is a clear similarity between the described model and the situation in the Russian economy in 1996.

13. When the government's actions were in conflict with this policy in the central bank's opinion, such as in June 1996, when 5 trillion rubles of central bank profits were removed, the central bank resisted strongly.

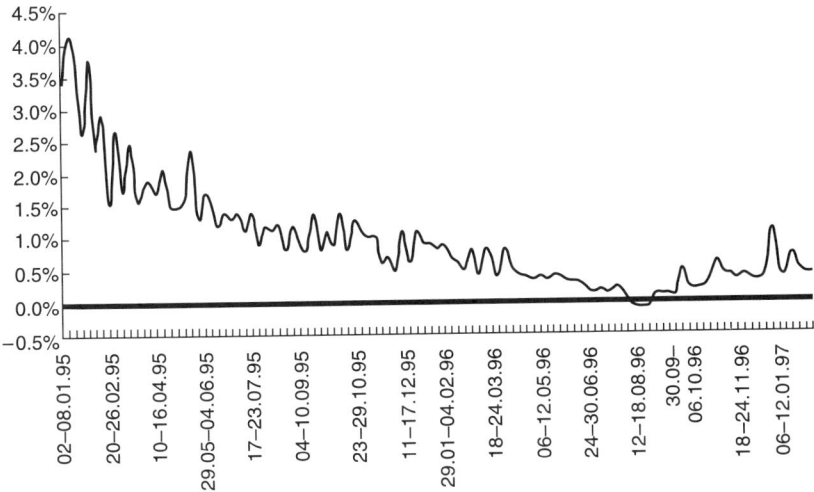

Figure 9.9
Weekly consumer price index, January 1995–February 1997.

June consumer prices grew by only 1.2%. Overall, in the first six months of 1996 inflation was 15.6%, less than the rate of inflation in the first half of 1995 by a factor of five (Figure 9.9).

The pre-election economic policy demonstrated the executive's inclination, when faced with a choice between two evils: Relaxing budgetary policy or monetary policy. The executive branch chose the former over the latter. This choice set the fundamental contours of the economic problems of the postelection period, both in the second half of 1996 and in 1997. The budget crisis was the government's main problem and a source of tension not only in the economic but also in the political sphere.

9.4. Economic Policy After the Presidential Election

Boris Yeltsin's victory ensured continuity in economic policy and created the conditions necessary for the inflow of foreign investment and the repatriation of domestic flight capital. This should have led to a drop in the demand for, and a rise in the supply of, hard currency, resulting in dedollarization of the Russian economy. A similar process had occurred in the second half of 1995. However, Yeltsin's worsening health generated additional political uncertainty, which obstructed these developments. Also, the postelection development of the country occurred during an acute budget crisis.

Under these circumstances, growth in federal budget expenditures to 15% of GDP in July and to 15.5% in August made it impossible to reduce the budget deficit to the level set in the 1996 budget law. Calculated using the Ministry of Finance's methodology, the deficit for July was around 4.1% of GDP, and for August it was 4.2% of GDP. If one includes the cost of servicing government borrowing, the secondary federal budget deficit rises, by our estimate, to 6.1% of GDP in July and 6.5% in August.

The creation of the Temporary Extraordinary Commission on Tax and Budgetary Discipline by a presidential decree on 11 October 1996 demonstrated the executive's understanding of an important fact: the budget crisis was linked not only to imperfections in legislation or the tax system, but first and foremost to the existence of politically influential interest groups whose economic well-being partly depended on tax evasion.[14] The slight increase in tax receipts in the initial period after the commission started operating indirectly confirmed the importance of adopting urgent administrative measures to raise tax collection, as did the rigid resistance that the commission encountered among certain economic and political groups.

In November and December, federal tax receipts as well as consolidated budget tax receipts grew somewhat and arrears fell (boosting tax receipts by 46% in December in current prices). However, the government proved incapable of maintaining this trend. This was partly a result of the sudden increase in political pressure applied to the executive by politically influential economic agents and regions, and partly a result of Yeltsin's new indisposition, which again placed the country's leadership in a situation of political uncertainty.

It is worth noting that there was some reduction in the budget deficit in September and October, which was facilitated by cutting government expenditures in autumn. The decree "On Immediate Measures to Economize on Budget Fulfillment in the Second Half of 1996" of 18 August 1996 had some impact on restricting budget

---

14. The fundamental aims of the commission were to monitor the punctual payment in full of taxes and other obligatory payments; to prepare measures to ensure their collection in full; to ensure the legality and efficiency of tax and customs bodies, as well as the tax police; and to monitor the punctual and accurate use of federal budget funds and extrabudgetary funds.

expenditures because it temporarily froze the implementation of all decisions on increasing the expenditure side of the budget, with the exception of pension payments (covered by decrees of 8 April and 25 January) and expenditures on housing for servicemen. From a macroeconomic perspective, the decision to freeze expenditures helped support fiscal stability. However, this political document was ethically questionable, to say the least, as it violated obligations taken on by the executive, including electoral obligations.

A comparison of the reconstructed budgets of 1995 and 1996 budgets (see Tables 8.1 and 9.2) shows that in 1996 there was an insignificant fall in tax payments made to the consolidated budget (1.7% of GDP) relative to 1995. Most of this figure was in tax payments to the federal budget (1.4% of GDP). Contributions to extrabudgetary funds remained unchanged, even though pension fund arrears, for example, increased by a factor of 2.2 during 1996. Against this background, consolidated budget expenditures and loans (less debt repayments) went up by 2.7% of GDP in 1996, mainly owing to increased extrabudgetary fund expenditures (by 1.3% of GDP), increased local budget expenditures (by 0.8% of GDP), and increased federal budget expenditures (by 0.7% of GDP, excluding nonconsolidated expenditure items). This led to a consolidated budget deficit increase of 2.4% of GDP.

Compared with 1995, there was a substantial increase in 1996 in the secondary deficit of the federal budget. In 1995 it was 4.7% of GDP (servicing the state debt was 3.2% of GDP), while in 1996 it was 7.2% of GDP (5.6% of GDP was expended on state debt servicing). There was also some growth in the primary deficit (from 1.5% to 1.6% of GDP).

9.4.1. Inflation and Central Bank Policy

In August 1996, consumer prices fell by 0.2%. This can be explained not only by a tough monetary and credit policy but also by seasonal price fluctuations. In September and October 1996, the trend of falling inflation rates was reversed (see Figure 9.9). In September 1996, the consumer price index was 0.3% (3.7% per annum), and in October and December 1996 inflation was on average 1.5% per month.

The acceleration of inflation in September and October 1996 suggests that excessive emission in the election period was not being compensated for by an increased demand for money.

Table 9.2
Reconstruction of Revenues and Expenditures of the Russian Federation in 1996

	Federal Budget (% of GDP)	Local Budgets (% of GDP)	Extrabudgetary Funds (% of GDP)	Consolidated Budget (% of GDP)	Consolidated Budget (% of Budget)
TAX REVENUES					
1. Income and profit taxes	1.7	5.1		6.8	19.76
1.1. Profit tax	1.4	2.8		4.3	12.45
1.2. Income tax	0.2	2.3		2.5	7.29
1.3. Other profit and income taxes	0.0	0.0		0.0	0.02
2. Tax on wages fund	0.0	0.3		0.3	0.99
3. Tax on goods and services, including:	6.7	2.5		9.2	26.85
VAT on goods produced within the Russian Federation and services	3.7	1.9		5.6	16.17
VAT on goods imported to the Russian Federation	0.8	0.0		0.8	2.36
Excise duties	2.0	0.4		2.4	6.88
4. Property taxes	0.0	1.6		1.6	4.76
4.1. Securities tax	0.0	0.0		0.0	0.04
4.2. Other property taxes	0.0	1.6		1.6	4.72
5. Mineral resource royalties	0.2	0.7		0.9	2.73
5.1. Natural resource payments	0.1	0.4		0.5	1.36
5.2. Mineral replacement tax	0.1	0.1		0.2	0.51
5.3. Land taxes and lease payments	0.0	0.2		0.2	0.68
5.4. Other mineral resource royalties	0.0	0.1		0.1	0.18
6. Taxes of foreign trade and foreign economic operations, including:	1.0	0.0		1.0	2.94
Import duties	0.7	0.0		0.7	1.91
7. Other taxes and duties	0.1	0.9		1.0	2.91

Macroeconomic Stabilization and the Political Process

8. Social Security contributions			7.3	21.33
8.1. Employees			0.2	0.50
8.2. Employers			7.2	20.82
Pension Fund			4.8	14.08
Social Security Fund			1.1	3.16
Employment Fund			0.2	0.71
Fund of Compulsory Medical Insurance and regional funds of compulsory medical insurance			1.0	2.86
9. Other extrabudgetary funds			0.9	2.54
Total Tax Receipts and Payments	9.7	11.3	29.2	84.80
NONTAX REVENUES			0.0	0.00
1. Revenue from state property	0.2		0.4	1.16
1.1. Remitted central bank profit	0.2		0.2	0.64
1.2. Other revenue from state property	0.0		0.2	0.52
2. Revenue from the sale of state property	0.0		0.1	0.33
3. Revenue from state supplies	0.8		0.8	2.28
9. Other nontax revenues	0.7		1.0	3.24
10. Transfers from other budget levels	0.0		×	
10.1. Subsidies	0.0	0.4	×	
10.2. Grants	0.0	0.4	×	
10.3. Funds transferred in mutual settlements	0.0		×	
10.4. Transfers	0.0		×	
11. Other receipts	0.0		0.0	0.03
12. Other revenues from extrabudgetary funds	0.0	1.7	1.7	4.88
Total Nontax Revenues	1.7	2.9	4.1	12.01
BUDGET FUND REVENUES	1.0	0.2	1.2	3.60
Contributions to targeted budget funds	0.1	0.1	0.1	0.40
Total Revenues	12.4	14.3	34.4	100.00

(continued)

Table 9.2 (continued)

	Federal Budget (% of GDP)	Local Budgets (% of GDP)	Extrabudgetary Funds (% of GDP)	Consolidated Budget	
				(% of GDP)	(% of Budget)
EXPENDITURES					
1. State administration	0.2	0.5		0.8	1.82
2. Foreign activities	1.2			1.2	2.82
3. National defense	2.8			2.8	6.75
4. Law enforcement and security	1.3	0.5		1.7	4.14
5. Research and furthering scientific and technological progress	0.3	0.0	0.0	0.3	0.83
6. The national economy, including:	1.8	6.0	0.9	8.8	20.86
6.1. Industry, power engineering, and construction	1.2	0.6		1.7	4.11
6.2. Agriculture and fisheries	0.4	0.7		1.1	2.66
6.3. Environmental protection	0.1	0.0		0.1	0.31
6.4. Transport, communications, and information science	0.0	0.7		0.8	1.80
6.5. Development of market infrastructure.		0.0		0.0	0.03
6.6. Communal services		3.9		3.9	9.36
6.7. Prevention and dealing with emergencies and natural disasters	0.2	0.0		0.2	0.48
6.8. Regional road funds			0.9	0.9	2.11
7. Social services	1.4	7.1	7.7	16.2	38.67
7.1. Education	0.5	3.2		3.7	8.85
7.2. Culture and art	0.0	0.4		0.4	1.01
7.3. Mass media	0.0	0.0		0.1	0.23
7.4. Public health and sport	0.2	2.3		2.5	5.94
7.5. Social policy	0.6	1.2		1.8	4.28

	Col 1	Col 2	Col 3	Col 4	Col 5
7.6. Extrabudgetary funds			7.7	7.7	18.36
Pension Fund			5.5	5.5	13.21
Social Security Fund			0.9	0.9	2.12
Employment Fund			0.3	0.3	0.71
Social benefits			0.0	0.0	0.01
Fund of Compulsory Medical Insurance and regional funds of compulsory medical insurance			1.0	1.0	2.31
8. Government debt servicing	5.6			5.6	13.38
8.1. Servicing domestic debt, including:	4.7				
GKO, OFZ, KO servicing	4.1				
8.2. Foreign debt servicing	0.9				
9. Replenishment of state supplies and reserves	0.4	0.2		0.4	0.95
10. State-targeted budget funds	0.7	0.7		0.9	2.21
11. Other expenditures	2.9	0.0		2.3	5.45
11.1. Financial assistance to other budgets	2.1		1.3	×	×
11.2. Other expenditures not included elsewhere	0.4	0.7	0.1	1.1	2.63
11.3. Subsidies to extrabudgetary funds	0.4			×	×
11.4. Other extrabudgetary fund expenditures			1.2	1.2	2.82
Total Expenditures	18.6	15.0	9.9	41.1	97.88
CREDITS LESS DEBT REPAYMENTS					
1. Budget credits	1.0			0.9	2.12
2. Government credits to other CIS countries	0.6	0.2		0.5	1.27
3. Credits to foreign governments	−0.1			−0.1	−0.35
4. Foreign credits extended to enterprises and organizations	−0.2			−0.2	−0.59
5. Other credits less debt repayments	0.6	0.2		0.6	1.44
	0.1			0.1	0.43
Total Expenditures and Credits Less Debt Repayments	19.6	15.2	9.9	42.0	100.00
Surplus of Revenues Over Expenditures and Credits Less Debt Repayments	−7.2	−0.9	0.3	−7.5	

(continued)

Table 9.2 (continued)

	Federal Budget (% of GDP)	Local Budgets (% of GDP)	Extrabudgetary Funds (% of GDP)	Consolidated Budget (% of GDP)	Consolidated Budget (% of Budget)
FINANCING					
1. Domestic financing	5.8	0.9	−0.3	−7.5	
1.1. Change in balance of budget monies in ruble bank accounts	0.2	0.0	−0.3		
1.2. Government short-term bonds	4.5				
1.3. Federal debt obligations with variable coupon yield	1.1				
1.4. Federal debt obligations with fixed coupon yield	0.2				
1.5. Savings bonds	0.3				
1.6. Treasury obligations	−0.3				
1.7. Other government bonds	0.0	0.2			
1.8. Budget credits from other levels of the budget	0.0	0.2			
1.9. Other domestic borrowing	−0.3	0.4			
2. External finance	1.5	0.0			
2.1. Credits from international financial organizations	1.0				
2.2. Credits extended by foreign governments, foreign commercial banks, and foreign companies to the Russian Federation	0.5				
Total Financing	7.2	0.9	−0.3	−7.5	

Sources: Ministry of Finance RF, IET.

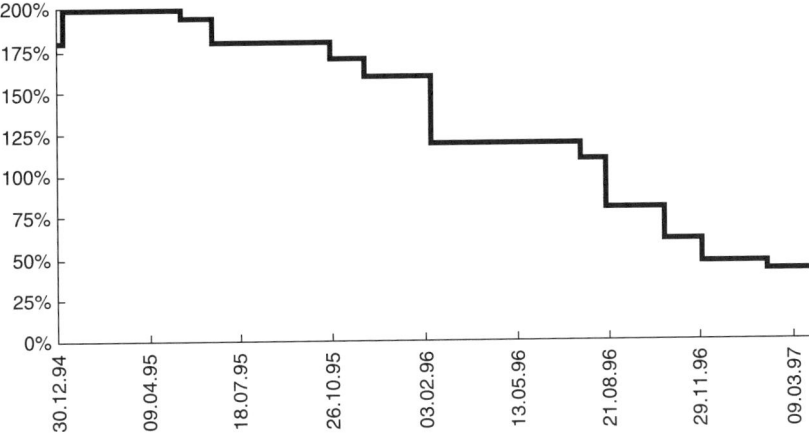

Figure 9.10
Russian Central Bank refinancing rate.

In October, for the second time in 1996, Russia was not granted its IMF credit tranche in line with the Extended Fund Facility (EFF) program. The IMF's tough position was motivated by the deterioration in tax collection in August and September 1996. EFF program financing was resumed only in January 1997.

A significant drop in financial market yields made it possible for the central bank to lower its refinancing rate on 21 October (Figure 9.10). The new rate was set at 60% per annum, which was about 40% per annum in real terms. At this time the weighted average GKO yield was 68%.

In October the refinancing system was further developed. The decision was taken to divide GKO-OFZ dealers into primary dealers and others. Primary dealers, in return for committing themselves to buying up no less than 1% of each issue at primary auctions, had the right to use liquidity windows (one-day noncollateralized central bank credits) and to carry out repo operations.[15]

From 1 November 1996, new normative reserve requirements for commercial banks were brought into force. Thus, on thirty-day current ruble accounts and deposits, the reserve rate was reduced from 18% to 16%, and on ninety-day deposits and accounts it was reduced

---

15. In a repo deal, a primary dealer can sell its securities to the central bank with the obligation of subsequently buying them back; the central bank sets the repo interest rate and the limit on such operations.

from 14% to 13%. For hard currency accounts the requirement was increased from 2.5% to 5%. In December 1996, the volume of refinancing by means of this scheme increased substantially (by as much as 3.5 trillion rubles, or more than 60% of average monthly M2 growth for 1996).

In the second half of 1996, there was some absolute contraction in the cash money supply, accompanied by growth of M2. Thus, in the first four months of the second half of 1996, M0 contracted by 10.2% and the monetary base contracted by 4.2%, while M2 expanded by 4.4%. This reflects an increase in the money multiplier from 2.07 at the end of July to 2.25 at the end of October. The main causes of this were as follows: first, the monetary base contracted as a result of the central bank's exchange rate policy of making hard currency interventions and withdrawing rubles from circulation; second, from 11 June, reserve requirements on commercial bank deposits were reduced by 2%; and third, the political uncertainty resulting from the presidential elections and the president's subsequent infirmity raised public demand for freely convertible foreign currency. This led to a reduction in the volume of cash circulating and accordingly reduced the growth of the credit multiplier, M2.

9.4.2. *The Situation on the Government Bond Market*

GKO-OFZ yield dynamics in the second half of the year were largely determined by underlying factors rather than by short-term liquidity effects and political risk. In contrast to 1995 and the first half of 1996, the volume of bonds issued by the Ministry of Finance had less and less impact on the cost of servicing domestic debt. This can be explained largely by the inflow of foreign investors into this market. Increased foreign access to the market also enabled the Ministry of Finance to eliminate problems of limited liquidity on the financial markets and smooth out interest rate fluctuations. All of this was accomplished while maintaining fairly high rates of government bond issuance.

In September and October 1996, the general yield level dropped from 1.5%–1.6% per week (78%–83% per annum) at the start of September to 1.1%–1.2% per week (57%–62% per annum) in the last ten days of October (Figure 9.11). The brief yield bursts observed in this period were to a considerable extent tied to rumors about Yeltsin's health.

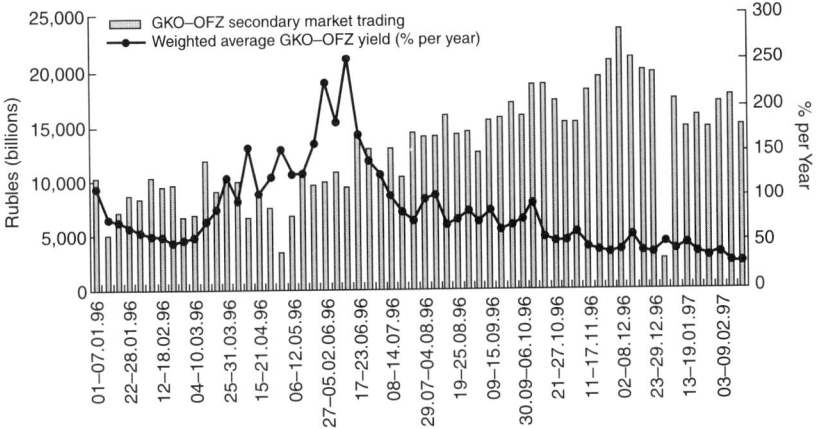

Figure 9.11
Dynamics of the GKO-OFZ market, 1996–1997.

In October, the weighted average yield was 58% per annum, while placement volumes continued to increase. Trading volumes on the secondary market also continued to grow, from 12–15 trillion rubles per week at the start of September to 16–19 trillion rubles at the end of October. In November, prices continued to rise on all series of government bonds. The weighted average yield fell from 80%–90% per annum at the beginning of October to 45%–50% per annum in the second half of the month. Increased political certainty as a result of Yeltsin's successful heart operation brought a further fall in bond yields in November. Trading volumes on the secondary market in October and November remained stable at 16–19 trillion rubles per week.

In November, the Ministry of Finance increased the monthly quota for foreign investors from US $1.5 billion to $2 billion. Substantial demand on the part of foreign investors brought about further falls in government bond yields to 40% per annum by the end of November.

The issuing of the first tranche of eurobonds in the sum of $1 billion on 15 November was an important event both in terms of financing the budget deficit and in terms of creating a reference point for the domestic debt market. These bonds were five-year issues with a coupon interest rate of 9.25% per annum. The issuing conditions on these bonds turned out more advantageous for Russia than expected.[16]

---

16. Given Russia's Standard & Poor's BB− credit rating, the cost of borrowing should have been 1.5%–2.5% higher.

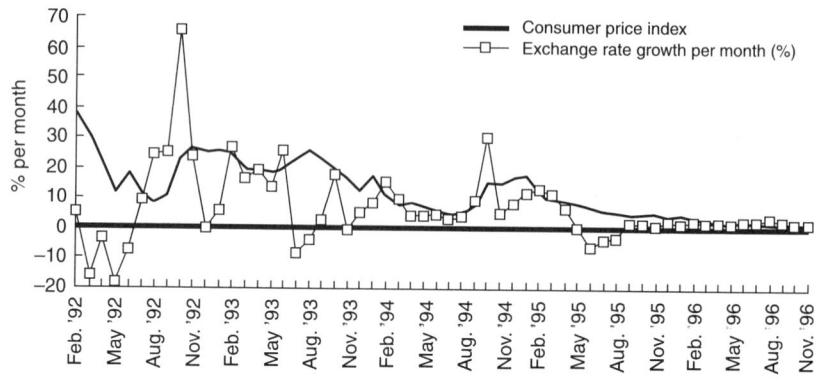

Figure 9.12
Consumer price index and growth of the official dollar/ruble exchange rate per month.

At the end of November, along with a rise in GKO-OFZ prices, there was considerable growth in trading volumes. In December 1996, the government bond market demonstrated further steady price growth. Thus, whereas in November weighted average GKO yields were around 45%–50% per annum, by the end of December they had fallen to 38% per annum. The overall yield drop on the government bond market made it possible for the central bank from 5 December to reduce the guaranteed level of hard currency yield for foreign investors to 13%.

After the election, the central bank rather abruptly changed its behavior on the foreign exchange markets. The volume of dollar interventions was reduced, and the growth rate of the dollar reached 3% in August (Figure 9.12). Average monthly dollar appreciation against the ruble in the second half of the year reached 1.45%. This policy change was dictated primarily by the substantial decline in hard currency reserves in the election period: in the first half of the year, reserves fell by $3.6 billion. After the elections the political need to support low rates of ruble depreciation decreased. Thus, the central bank reduced the extent of its dollar interventions and allowed the dollar to appreciate against the ruble at a faster pace. The official dollar exchange rate for 1996 is shown in Figure 9.13.

Attempts to slow down growth of the real ruble exchange rate may have been an additional factor in accelerating the strengthening of the dollar in the third quarter, although, because of a reduction in inflation, real ruble appreciation slowed sharply in the first half of

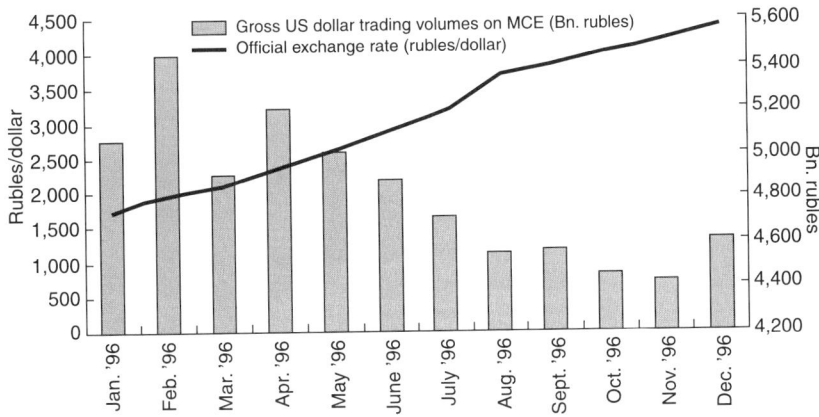

Figure 9.13
Dynamics of the official ruble/dollar exchange rate and gross trading volumes on the MCE in 1996.

the year, amounting to only 5.4% (while over the analogous period for 1995 it was 27.9%). In the second half of the year the central bank switched to a policy of gradual nominal ruble devaluation with the introduction of a sliding exchange rate corridor in July 1996. Nominal depreciation over 1996 was 19.8%. As a result, by the end of 1996 the real ruble exchange rate had virtually returned to the level it had been at the end of 1995 (Figure 9.14).

Strengthening of the real ruble exchange rate occurred as a result of the adoption of a nominal anchor for stabilization purposes in 1995, while relatively high rates of inflation continued by inertia. In 1996, the curbing of inflation brought this to a halt.

In autumn of 1996 the central bank's net foreign reserves continued to diminish. This occurred as a result of the continuing redollarization of the economy brought about by the sustained political uncertainty. The central bank also had to buy up rubles from redeemed GKOs belonging to foreigners. By the end of the year, net foreign reserves had increased somewhat, reaching $2.51 billion at the end of November (compared with $1.34 billion at the end of October).

The central bank's policy aimed at reducing yields on financial and money markets introduced a certain degree of predictability to exchange rates, which reduced the speculative attractions of currency markets for banks. The narrowing of the arbitrage spread between official and market dollar rates in September and October was evidence of stabilization in this sector of the financial markets.

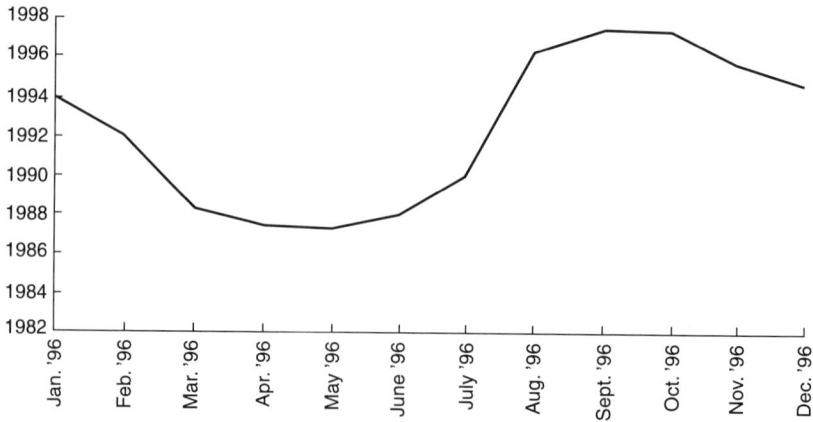

Figure 9.14
Change in the real effective dollar/ruble exchange rate (June 1992 = 100).

Thus, the stabilization of political expectations at the end of 1996 raised economic agents' confidence in the monetary authorities.

9.5. The Phenomenon of Delayed Growth

The search for an appropriate economic growth model has been a central issue in economic and political debates in Russia since the election. Despite the intense polemic of the preceding years between the government and the opposition on the role of macroeconomic stabilization in economic growth, it was in fact the curbing of inflation that focused politicians' attention on the problem of growth. As mentioned in Chapter 4, the link between economic growth and bringing inflation down below 50% per year has been demonstrated convincingly in recent economic literature.[17] This empirical fact was at the heart of the Russian government's economic policy throughout the period of radical economic reforms. This strategy was continually subjected to harsh criticism by the major opposition parties, which attempted to prove the impossibility of maintaining low levels of inflation over a long period of time (Yavlinsky's position) or insisted that radical measures had to be taken "to revive the national

---

17. See, for example, S. Fisher, R. Sahay, and C. Vegh, "Stabilisation and Growth in Transition Economies: The Earlier Experience," IMF Working Paper no. 31 (1996): 11–15.

economy" while rejecting anti-inflationary monetary policies (the CPRF's position).

At the same time, the political battle over economic policy strategy shifted gear. The focus of attention became the issue of whether fairly low levels of inflation were really a necessary condition for growth, or, more precisely, whether, with macroeconomic stabilization effectively achieved, some weakening of monetary policy was required in order to stimulate economic activity.

In many ways this was a repeat of the discussions at the end of 1991 and beginning of 1992. The political decision to conduct liberalization was plagued by doubts over whether the Russian economy would react properly, or whether there were some hidden defects that would prevent liberalization from overcoming the goods deficit and strengthening economic agents' interest in the ruble. Analogous questions relating to inflation and economic growth were posed in 1996.

However, while price liberalization is not only a necessary but also a sufficient condition for wiping out the goods deficit, simply curbing inflation may not be sufficient to stimulate economic growth. As the experience of a number of Latin American and African countries demonstrates, specific mechanisms may be preserved that block economic growth. Indeed, the growth issue in Russia at the moment is not just economic but also political—as political as the formation of anti-inflationary policy was in the battle to achieve macroeconomic stabilization at a time when the level of inflation in Russia reflected the actual balance of forces between the main socioeconomic interest groups.[18]

The absence of officially registered growth throughout 1996 does not in itself contradict those macroeconomic regularities that economists have isolated in analyzing the stabilization experiences of other, primarily postcommunist countries. In postcommunist countries, it has been statistically established that growth comes 1.5–2 years after inflation is brought down below 50% (for Russia, this was 1996). This logic—a cautious monetary policy that factors in expected economic growth—provided the foundation for the government's post-election program.

Sociopolitical stability is critical for restoring economic growth. Yeltsin's victory in the elections created the basic conditions for po-

---

18. For more detail, see *Rossiyskaya ekonomika: tendentsii i perspektivy* (Moscow: IET, 1993, 1994).

litical stability in the country and for stability of postcommunist Russia's constitutional regime. Yeltsin's victory also created the necessary conditions for the start of serious investment in the country. The situation was more complicated in the sphere of institutional reforms, the essence of which is guaranteeing property rights. Legislation regulating property rights and guarantees for foreign investors remain extremely weak.

10 Macroeconomic Stabilization and Fiscal Crisis

Sergei Arkhipov,
Said Batkibekov,
Sergei Drobyshevsky,
Vladimir Mau,
Sergei Sinelnikov-Murylev,
and Alexei Uluykaev

10.1. The Political and Economic Situation: A New Window of Opportunity

The political and economic situation in Russia at the end of 1996 gave cause to believe that the year 1997 would usher in a new—and wide—window of opportunity.[1] By this we mean a situation in which the government, entrusted with the confidence of the President, and the Duma, uninterested in decisive opposition, would act in concert to develop and implement a coherent economic program. The hope was that this program would be above popular sentiments.

Indeed, 1997 became in essence the first year of poststabilization development of the economy. The principal conditions for a transition from delayed stabilization to sustained economic growth had been created. Inflation was brought down to a level that permitted investment in industry, GKO yields came down, and a positive dynamic for a range of social indicators was in evidence. All of these indicators bore witness to the arrival of a new stage in development. At the same time, however, these developments showed that the main factors holding back the start of economic growth were now in the institutional sphere. In particular, budgetary problems and problems associated with stimulating economic growth came to the fore.

In 1996 the authorities changed the form of their "economic reaction" to political infighting: instead of loosening monetary policy, the government softened its budgetary requirements, which gave rise to a severe budgetary crisis. The crisis was aggravated by the fact that as a result of its successful anti-inflation measures, the gov-

---

1. The first such window appeared in late 1991 to early 1992.

ernment had deprived itself of the inflation tax characteristic of all postsocialist countries that had gone through prolonged periods of high inflation. The existing tax system had degenerated. In addition, delays in structural reform of the budget caused a crisis in government expenditure. Cuts in government spending in turn had an extremely negative effect on the social safety net, nonmanufacturing branches of the economy, and the army.

The unfolding of the budgetary crisis in 1997 was the direct consequence of adopting an unrealistic and unimplementable budget for that year. This is unusual for a postelection period, which elsewhere in the world is characterized by a display of a reasonable measure of rigidity on the part of the government. The government formed in August 1996, and particularly the financial block, showed an unprecedented docility when faced with the demands of various lobbies. At the same time, the tax system was being actively destroyed by mutual settlements, which provoked the accumulation of arrears and the reduction of "live money" as a share of budgetary revenue.

The parliamentary opposition majority's interest in the continuation of the sluggish economic crisis, on the one hand, and the coalitional nature of the government that had arisen through a compromise between the executive branch and business elite, on the other hand, caused a policy deadlock, with conflicting private interests impeding the conduct of a coherent economic policy.

At the beginning of 1997 two scenarios for the future were possible. The first consisted in breaking the deadlock and intensifying the reform process. This scenario could be achieved by taking steps toward overcoming the budgetary crisis, restructuring natural monopolies, improving the social sphere, and so forth. The second scenario involved moving toward an oligarchic system. The risk with this scenario was that the state of permanent crisis might in the end lead to a victory for the opposition or to undemocratic developments.

Under these circumstances, the need to move from a coalition government to a team-based government had become patently obvious by spring. The cabinet reshuffle put an end to protracted political uncertainty and was helpful in creating the political preconditions for economic growth. This became a key factor in Russia's economic life in 1997. The gradual removal of some representatives of business interests from the government occurred during that period.

On the whole, the coming to power of a team-based government in the spring of 1997 marked a new stage in the political and economic development of the country, the chief thrust of which was to distance the state from business and to separate national from private interests.

The principal structural problem was the division of the Russian economy (primarily industry) into two large segments. On the one hand, there were export-oriented branches, which were interested in macroeconomic stability, an open economy, and minimal government regulation. On the other hand, there were import-substituting (more precisely, *potentially* import-substituting) branches, which by virtue of their low competitiveness suffered from market liberalization and therefore required protectionism, government subsidies, and "cheap money."

Analysis of the structural shifts under way allows us to distinguish four categories of branches, depending on their characteristics and the type of economic policies required to sustain their development. The structural shifts affected the balance of power between influential interest groups and the ability of the federal government to influence socioeconomic processes.

First, there was a weakening of antimarket groups, which constituted the base of left-wing parties, and proponents of import-substituting orthodoxy (cheap credits, high import tariffs, redistribution of profits from export-oriented branches to machine-building, tight regulation) were gradually squeezed out of the political elite. With these developments the government gained additional opportunities to pursue a more independent policy, one more fully reflecting the real national interests.[2]

The flip side of such a development, however, was the increasingly conflictual nature of the political process. This conflict split the economic elite and the powers-to-be. Only recently, it seemed, this elite had stood united against the communists and in support of Yeltsin in the presidential elections of 1996. The government, cardinally renewed in March 1997, chiefly by the inclusion of Anatoly

---

2. The overcoming of bipolarity and the diversification of economic interests put an end to a situation in which the government had to choose between two conflicting parties. Now the government could base its decisions on broader coalitions while using the conflicting interests of certain groups to further its own agenda (for example, by maintaining an overall liberal regime and by exercising tighter oversight over natural monopolies, which until recently would have been impossible for political reasons, as it required the support of antimarket, antiliberal forces. The government could also manipulate in its own interests the conflicts between financial groups interested in the development of different branches of industry).

Chubais and Boris Nemtsov as first vice-premiers, took a series of consistent steps to strengthen the independence of state institutions from main pressure groups, which by that time had fully consolidated and represented leading financial-industrial groups.[3]

10.2. The Main Areas of Government Activity and the Reaction of the Legislature

After the reshuffle, the government focused its efforts on specific areas, with the aim of achieving a balanced budget.

First, since difficulties in tax collection had become the main factor driving the growing budget deficit and the growing dependence of the government on borrowing domestically, the government took decisive steps to change regulations affecting tax collection and the financing of government expenditures. In addition, it sought to restructure enterprise debts to the budget. The Tax Code brought before the Duma was intended to increase the level of fairness and neutrality of the tax system by reducing tax preferences and fighting tax evasion.

Second, a package of documents dealing with social reform, housing reform, and reform of the army was oriented toward increasing the efficiency of budgetary expenditure.

Third, measures were undertaken to overcome the nonpayments crisis by reforming the system of prices and tariffs. These measures included in particular a number of decrees and resolutions on restructuring the natural monopolies.

Fourth, the first half of 1997 marked a new stage in the fight against corruption. The essential novelty of this stage was that it entailed not only government measures to identify and punish corrupt officials, but also measures to eliminate opportunities for abuse of office by establishing clear rules of the game.

The aforementioned policy was characterized by two fundamental elements. First, the government paid particular attention to tax collection, at a time when the largest debtors were enterprises that, in one way or another, were associated with the leading financial-industrial groups. Second, the government took steps to strengthen the fiscal dimension of privatization; that is, it proposed to abandon

---

3. The leaders of these groups were A. Smolensky, Vladimir Gusinsky, Mikhail Khodorkovsky, Mikhail Fridman, Rem Vyakhirev, Boris Berezovsky, V. Vinogradov, and some other entrepreneurs and bankers.

the by then established principle in relations with the leading groups: property in exchange for political support.

Attempts to add a practical dimension to the search for solutions engendered stiff opposition from all of the interested parties. The ensuing confrontation between business and the government led to losses on both sides. Further separation of business from the state occurred, at least formally, in November 1997, when the last representative of big business, Boris Berezovsky, quit his government post. However, the concomitant increase in political pressure on the executive branch effectively halted the work of the government, which by then was reeling under the weight of mounting conflicts within the cabinet and its apparatus. This situation was all the more dangerous because it coincided with the beginning of the global financial crisis, which required clear, timely, and effective responses from the government.

That the government's program was in crisis was already apparent by mid-1997, when the State Duma rejected a package of social draft laws. The government had by then shown itself to be indecisive in pursuing a consistent reform-oriented policy, as was evident in lower tax revenues, reluctance to take tough measures against debtors unwilling to restructure their debts to the government, the absence of efforts to restructure government spending, and similar lapses in the reform policy.

The erosion of the team-based government's program had several causes. First, the government underestimated the interest of the opposition majority in the Duma in maintaining the sluggish economic crisis. At the same time, in 1997 a new feature of Russia's regional politics came into relief. Elections in the constituent units of the federation in late 1996 and early 1997 placed greater responsibility on the regional authorities toward their electorates and increased the regions' independence from the federal center, since a large number of governors who were formerly appointees were elected. The federal center, as was shown by the experience with the Maritime (Primorsky Kray) Region, did not have effective levers of influence over the regional authorities.[4]

---

4. In this situation the center tried to use confrontation between the regional and municipal authorities. A Council for Local Self-Government was set up. There was a new impetus to develop budgetary federalism (including adoption of the Law on Local Self-Government) and to increase the transparency of financial relations between Moscow and the regions.

Second, the government was weakened by a fight among new interest groups for control over power. And third, there were conflicts within the government itself. In consequence, hopes for the beginning of fast economic growth in Russia in 1997 proved unrealistic.

In 1998, it was clear that yet another reorganization of the government was inevitable. On 23 March 1998, the government formed only a year earlier was sacked by the president.

10.3. Government Finance

From the viewpoint of economic development, the main strategically important problem confronted by the government in 1997 was how to overcome the budgetary crisis.

The first quarter of 1997 was marked by record low tax revenues. This is the case even when seasonal factors are taken into account. In January, federal tax revenues were 5.7%, or 1% lower than in January 1996. Such a fall in tax payments at the beginning of the year can be largely explained by subjective factors, including delayed tax reform, the inability of the 1996 government to tackle budgetary shortfalls, and the absence of measures to counteract the growth in budget deficits.

In the second quarter following the reshuffle, after the government declared its pursuit of a tough tax policy, tax revenues increased noticeably, reaching 9.2% of GDP for the first five months, while total budgetary revenues exceeded 10% of GDP. Nevertheless, despite some growth in tax collection, budgetary revenues, excluding the sequester, were only 64% of the original projection.

As we noted earlier, from summer 1997 on there was a gradual destabilization of the political situation in Russia, as a result of which the influence of the "young reformers" in the formulation of economic policy began to diminish. One of the last serious successes in the fiscal area during 1997 was the adoption, in July, of the Budget Code on only one reading, as well as the adoption of a special section of the Tax Code on first reading. This success, however, could not be sustained.[5]

---

[5]. The Duma changed its decision with respect to the Tax Code by resolving, on 19 November 1997, to carry out a repeat review of it in first reading, thus effectively reducing previous gains along a number of parameters.

Thus, there were no substantial improvements in the budgetary situation during the second half of 1997. In 1997 federal budget tax revenues were 9.1% of GDP.

The positive trend in the first half of 1997 consisted in a gradual reduction, starting in March, in the size of taxpayer indebtedness to the budget. The dynamic of the real size of federal budgetary shortfalls is given in Table 10.1. The main reason for this dynamic was the tough stance adopted by the government in the spring of 1997 and its perseverance in tackling nonpayments. This line of action led not only to a sharp increase in debt repayments but also to an increase in current tax collection. As is evident from Table 10.2, the first half of 1997 saw a dramatic increase in current tax receipts (less debt repayments). The statistics for March are particularly favorable, reflecting in large part the changes in the composition of the government and more decisive measures to increase federal budget revenues.

In July, however, current tax receipts fell significantly and the growth of arrears accelerated, and this situation continued into the autumn of 1997. One reason for the decrease in tax receipts, in our opinion, was that economic agents sensed that the government's stance on nonpayments of tax had softened. This relaxation of the government's line was exhibited in particular in the government's failure to take tough measures against those debtors who did not wish to restructure their debts in accordance with the resolution of the government of the Russian Federation No. 254 of 5 March 1997. The adoption of resolution No. 928 (subsequently partially annulled) provided for an extremely lenient scheme for settling budgetary debts (including debts of budgetary organizations), leniency for settling tax arrears in the energy sector, the forgiveness of arrears relating to fines, and similar relaxation measures across a number of spheres.

In the second half of 1997 the level of shortfalls in real terms grew constantly. In the period from June to November, the size of shortfalls in real terms grew by almost 50%. Only toward the end of the year, with monetary settlements, was the volume of arrears reduced, by almost 7% in real terms.

In 1997, settlements of tax receipts and budgetary obligations were carried out in accordance with the principle of "reverse settlement," whereby the chain of obligations was traced from the enterprise, not from the government, as was done before. Nonetheless, even with

Table 10.1
Federal Budget Tax Arrears in 1997 (in December 1996 Prices, in Billions of Rubles)

Shortfall	1996	1997, Month											
		I	II	III	IV	V	VI	VII	VIII	IX	X	XI	XII
Total shortfall deflated (Rb)	57,886	62,669	63,559	60,169	58,035	57,617	55,891	63,091	68,247	72,199	77,370	82,194	76,647
Total shortfall in % of monthly GDP	31.3	38.8	39.9	37.8	40.2	40.4	37.5	37.90	39.30	39.11	42.87	44.51	40.61
Change in total shortfalls (%)		8.3	1.4	−5.3	−3.5	−0.7	−2.9	12.9	8.2	5.8	7.2	6.2	−6.7

Source: RF Ministry of Finance.

Table 10.2
Federal Budget Tax Receipts in 1997 (in Billions of Rubles)

	I	II	III	IV	V	VI	VII	VIII	IX	X	XI	XII
Accumulated tax receipts	10,000	23,499	46,995	75,794	97,079	123,924	141,234	159,240	173,032	190,775	206,260	249,532
Including repayment of tax arrears owed from beginning of year	1,005	2,824	10,498	19,427	28,976	37,403	42,895	45,681	51,690	56,379	61,078	69,609
Tax receipts by month	10,000	13,499	23,496	28,799	21,285	26,845	17,310	12,600	13,792	17,743	15,485	43,272
Including repayment of tax arrears owed by month	1,005	1,819	7,674	8,929	9,549	8,427	5,492	2,786	6,009	4,689	4,699	8,531
Current payments	8,995	11,680	15,822	19,870	11,736	18,418	11,818	9,814	7,783	13,054	10,786	34,741
Current payments as % of monthly GDP	4.5	5.8	7.8	9.7	5.7	8.6	5.3	4.2	3.2	5.4	4.4	13.6
GDP by month (trill. Rb)	201	200	204	205	207	215	222	234	245	240	247	255

Source: RF Ministry of Finance.

the help of settlements, in 1997 only about 25% of the tax receipts were collected. Such an instrument of budgetary implementation, in conjunction with insufficiently clear organization of the settlement process, led to constant erosion of tax discipline. Taxpayers, anticipating such settlements in the future, tried to reduce current tax payments, and thus increased the shortfall even more.

In the first quarter of 1997, financing of government spending from the federal budget decreased somewhat in comparison with 1996, owing to a sharp fall in revenues. Because full financing of expenditures was not feasible, a proposal to sequester the budget was brought by the government before the Duma as a draft law. Because of the revenue shortfalls, the proposal sought to reduce expenditures by 3.96% of projected GDP. Some expenditures were to be cut by 55%, and even the most important expenditures were to be cut by 30%. In addition, the government proposed reducing the number of protected items. Although the Duma did not adopt the draft law during its spring session, the Ministry of Finance in essence had to adhere to the sequestered budget.

During the whole of 1997 indicators for the budget deficit slightly exceeded the levels set by the law. At the end of the first half of the year the federal budget deficit (according to the statistical methods used by the Ministry of Finance) constituted 4.1% of GDP, which was 0.6% higher than the level allotted for by the law. In the second half of the year there was a trend toward a lowering of the budget deficit to 3.23% of GDP, which was caused by a significant growth in budget revenue (up to 12.1% of GDP in December, compared with 10.8% of GDP in November). Thus the budget deficit turned out to be even lower than the permitted 3.5%.

The sharp rise in the cost of servicing government debt as a result of the financial crisis did not have much effect on the implementation of the 1997 budget; however, it had extremely negative consequences for the 1998 budget and the budgets of the following years.

The domestic government debt of the Russian Federation relative to GDP grew in 1997 in comparison with 1996 by 16%, reaching 18.7% of GDP. The growth of government bond debt, in particular OFZs (by 4.5% of GDP) and GKOs (by 1.1%) contributed the most to this increase. The size of the government debt on all other items had somewhat decreased. The dynamic of the government debt for the years 1994–1998 is shown in Table 10.3.

Table 10.3
Dynamic of Government Debt, 1 January 1994–1 January 1998

Type of Debt	As of 1 January 1994		As of 1 January 1995		As of 1 January 1996		As of 1 January 1997		As of 1 January 1998	
	(bill. of Rb)	(% of GDP)	(bill. of Rb)	(% of GDP)	(bill. of Rb)	(% of GDP)	(bill. of Rb)	(% of GDP)	(bill. of Rb)	(% of GDP)
1. Debt on securities, including:	329.5	0.2	18,917.4	3	85,196.9	5.1	249,034.7	11.04	449,230.8	16.79
Government borrowing 1992	15	0.009	22	0.003	53	0.0	55	0.00	105	0.004
Russian government domestic borrowing 1990	0.35	0.0002								
Government domestic borrowing 1991	80	0.04	80	0.01	80	0.0	79.7	0.00	79.7	0.003
GKO	185	0.1	10,594	1.7	66,118.7	4.0	203,600	9.02	272,612	10.19
OFZ					7,597	0.5	37,300	1.65	163,352.4	6.11
Treasury obligations			6,681.4	1.1	7,348.2	0.4				
Treasury receipts			1,540	0.2						
Gold receipts	49.1	0.03			1,000	0.1				
Government savings bonds					3,000	0.2	8,000	0.35	13,081.7	0.49
2. Debts to Central Bank	29,156.7	18.0	58,752.3	9.30	61,026	3.7	59,583.27	2.64	0.0	0.0
3. Debts to commercial banks (government-issued guarantees)	1,899.8	1.2	1,700	0.3	5,793	0.3	17,057.17	0.76	4,916.8	0.18
4. Debts of former USSR on products, including:	3,204	2	3,100	0.5	2,500	0.2	5,300	0.23	4,237	0.16
Targeted borrowing 1990	2,500	1.5	2,400	0.4	1,850	0.1	2,300	0.10	2,037	0.08
Targeted deposits, automobile checks, debts to employees of the agro-industrial complex (AIC)	704	0.4	700	0.1	650	0.0	3,000	0.13	2,200	0.08

Macroeconomic Stabilization and Fiscal Crisis

5. Debts to AIC, converted into Treasury promissory notes	0		5,441.6	0.9	5,040	0.3	4,480	0.20	3,920	0.15
6. Debts on centralized credits and interest accruals by AIC organization engaged in Northern shipments					25,000	1.5	25,000	1.11	25,000	0.93
7. Debts to JSC KAMAZ converted into Ministry of Finance promissory notes							1,745.5	0.08		
8. Debts to textile enterprises of the Ivanov regions on unpaid interest							560	0.02	560	0.02
9. Debts on financing the formation of mobilization reserves					1,960	0.1	2,389.5	0.11	1,993.5	0.07
10. Others, including:	276.6	0.2	153.6	0.02	2,028	0.1	398.027	0.02	8,233.2	0.31
Debts to State Insurer	23.8	0.01								
Domestic debt of Russian Central Bank inherited from former USSR	330	0.2	335	0.05	335	0.0	335	0.01	191.4	0.007
Difference in agricultural raw materials deals, requiring repayment	61	0.04								
Federal budget in 1991	63	0.04	63	0.01	63	0.0	63.027	0.00		
Central Bank debts on credit resources of the former Sberbank	128.8	0.08	90.6	0.01						
Debts to Pension Fund					1,630	0.1				
Debts on technical credits by Central Bank to CIS countries									2,408	0.09

(continued)

Table 10.3 (continued)

Type of Debt	As of 1 January 1994		As of 1 January 1995		As of 1 January 1996		As of 1 January 1997		As of 1 January 1998	
	(bill. of Rb)	(% of GDP)	(bill. of Rb)	(% of GDP)	(bill. of Rb)	(% of GDP)	(bill. of Rb)	(% of GDP)	(bill. of Rb)	(% of GDP)
Debts to enterprises in energy and other sectors									5,000	0.19
Debts on Central Bank credits (principal and interest) by agro-industrial enterprises of the Chelyabinsk region									93.8	0.003
Bank guarantee promissory notes of Agroprombank									540	0.02
Total government domestic debt	35,196.6	21.7	88,400	14	188,543.6	11.4	365,548.2	16.20	500,959.1	18.73
GDP (trill. Rb)	162.3		630		1,659.2		2,256		2,675	

Source: RF Ministry of Finance.

10.4. A Breakdown of the 1997 Budget

Table 10.4 gives our reconstruction of the 1997 federal and local budgets and the budgets for off-budgetary funds as implemented. (Data for off-budgetary funds were estimated on the basis of reported data for the first nine months of the year.)

10.5. Monetary and Credit Policy

The year 1997 saw the continuation of the tight monetary policy that had begun in 1995. The main causes of a significantly lower rate of inflation in 1996–1997 were control over growth in the money supply within the limits agreed to with the IMF and some reduction in the budget deficit as a result of cuts in government spending.

The growth of the money base over the whole of 1997 was 25.7%, which corresponds to an average monthly growth of 1.92%. Cash in circulation, or M0, increased 32.0% (2.34% per month on average), and the broad money aggregate, M2, increased 28.6% (2.12% per month on average) (Table 10.5). This reflects a decrease in the money multiplier from 2.4 at the end of January 1997 to 2.36 at the end of February 1997. The money base grew by 5.8%.

Growth of the money base in 1997 occurred chiefly because of increases in official external reserves (Figure 10.1). In the first half of 1997 the gross assets of the central bank grew from 130.9 to 167 trillion rubles, or by 27.6%. In the second half they remained practically unchanged (the decrease constituted 1.5%). However, at the end of the year, during the crisis on the financial markets, the central bank was buying government securities en masse. Over the second half of the year the assets of the central bank grew by 33.08%. The net international reserves of the central bank in the second half of 1997 grew from US $1.7 to $10.6 billion, or by 517%. From June to December they decreased by approximately 62%.

The build-up of external reserves by the central bank in the first half of 1997 and the increased pressure for ruble appreciation were called forth not so much by a considerable trade surplus as by foreign capital inflows into Russian financial markets.[6] These capital inflows were primarily into GKO market and were fueled by the

---

6. In 1997 a tendency toward its reduction was already in evidence. In 1996, when the trade surplus was at its peak, net international assets never reached such levels.

Table 10.4
Reconstruction of the 1997 Budget

	Federal Budget (% of GPD)	Local Budgets (% of GDP)	Extrabudgetary Funds (% of GDP)	Consolidated Budget (% of GDP)	Consolidated Budget (% of Budget)
REVENUES					
1. Income taxes, profit taxes	1.3	5.3		6.7	19.1
1.1. Profit tax	1.2	2.6		3.8	11.0
1.2. Income tax on physical persons	0.1	2.7		2.8	8.1
1.3. Other income and profit taxes	0.0	0.0		0.0	0.1
2. Payroll taxes	0.0	0.3		0.3	1.0
3. Taxes on goods and services, including:	6.4	2.8		9.2	26.3
VAT on goods made in the Russian Federation and services	3.3	2.0		5.3	15.3
VAT on imported goods	1.1	0.0		1.1	3.1
Excise taxes	1.9	0.5		2.3	6.7
4. Property taxes	0.0	1.8		1.8	5.1
4.1. Securities tax	0.0	0.0		0.0	0.1
4.2. Other property taxes		1.8		1.8	5.0
5. Payments for use of natural resources	0.3	1.1		1.3	3.8
5.1. Payments for mineral resources	0.1	0.4		0.6	1.6
5.2. Payments for resource reproduction	0.1	0.3		0.4	1.0
5.3. Land taxes and land rents	0.0	0.3		0.4	1.0
5.4. Other payments for use of natural resources	0.0	0.1		0.1	0.2
6. Taxes on foreign trade and external economic operations, including:	1.0	0.0		1.0	3.0
Import duties	1.0	0.0		1.0	2.9

Macroeconomic Stabilization and Fiscal Crisis

	(1)	(2)	(3)	(4)	(5)
7. Other taxes and duties	0.0			1.1	3.1
8. Payments into social insurance funds		1.0	7.6	7.6	21.8
8.1. Employees			0.2	0.2	0.6
8.2. Employers			7.4	7.4	21.3
Pension Fund			5.4	5.4	15.6
Social Insurance Fund			1.1	1.1	3.0
Employment Fund			0.3	0.3	0.8
Fund for Compulsory Medical Insurance and regional funds for compulsory medical insurance			0.6	0.6	1.8
Regional road fund			0.0	0.0	0.0
Taxes and Payments in Total	9.1	12.3	7.6	29.1	83.3
NONTAX REVENUE				0.0	0.0
1. Revenue from state property and operations	0.3	0.2		0.4	1.2
2. Revenue from sales of state property	0.7	0.0		0.9	2.5
3. Revenue from sales of government reserves	0.2	0.0		0.2	0.6
4. Fines	0.0	0.4		0.3	1.0
5. Revenue from external economic operations	0.3	0.0	0.3	0.3	0.9
6. Other nontax revenue	0.1	0.4		0.5	1.3
7. Nonrefundable payments from other levels of government	0.0	1.9	1.4	x	x
8. Revenue from state off-budgetary funds		0.3		x	x
9. Other revenue from state off-budgetary funds			1.5	1.5	4.3
NonTax Revenue in Total	1.6	3.0	3.2	4.2	12.0
REVENUE FROM OFF-BUDGETARY FUNDS	1.4	0.2		1.7	4.8
Revenue in Total	12.1	15.5	10.8	34.9	100.0

(*continued*)

Table 10.4 (continued)

	Federal Budget (% of GPD)	Local Budgets (% of GDP)	Extrabudgetary Funds (% of GDP)	Consolidated Budget (% of GDP)	Consolidated Budget (% of Budget)
EXPENDITURES					
1. Public administration	0.4	0.7		1.1	2.4
2. International relations	0.3			0.3	0.7
3. National defense	3.0			3.0	6.8
4. Law enforcement and national security	1.6	0.5		2.1	4.9
5. Fundamental research and promotion of technoscientific progress	0.4	0.0	0.0	0.4	0.9
6. State services to the national economy, including:	2.0	6.2	1.1	9.3	21.3
6.1. Industry, energy and construction	1.0	0.7		1.7	3.9
6.2. Agriculture and fisheries	0.5	0.7		1.2	2.7
6.3. Protection of the environment and natural resources	0.1	0.1		0.1	0.3
6.4. Transport, road infrastructure, communications and information technology	0.1	0.7		0.9	2.0
6.5. Housing and utilities		4.0		4.0	9.1
6.6. Prevention and liquidation of extraordinary situations and consequences of natural disasters	0.2	0.0		0.3	0.6
6.7. At the expense of territorial road funds			1.1	1.1	2.6
7. Social services	1.8	7.7	10.1	19.6	44.8
7.1. Education	0.5	3.5	0.0	4.1	9.3
7.2. Culture and the arts	0.0	0.4		0.5	1.0
7.3. Mass media	0.0	0.1		0.1	0.3
7.4. Health care and physical education	0.3	2.5	1.2	4.0	9.1
7.5. Social policy	0.9	1.2	8.9	11.0	25.1
8. Servicing of government debt	4.4			4.4	10.1
Including servicing of GKOs, OFZs, and KOs	3.3				
9. Accumulation of government reserves	0.4			0.4	0.8

	1	2	3	4	5
10. Expenditure of state target budgetary funds	1.1	0.2		1.3	3.0
11. Other expenditure	2.2	1.1		1.6	3.7
11.1. Financial assistance to other levels of government	1.9	0.0	0.2	x	3.4
11.2. Other, unclassified expenditures	0.3	1.1		1.5	0.4
11.3. Other expenditure of off-budgetary funds			0.2	0.2	
Expenditure in Total	17.5	16.5	11.4	43.5	99.4
Credits Less Debt Repayments	0.7			0.3	0.6
1. Budget loans	0.9	0.2		0.5	1.1
2. Government credits to CIS countries	−0.1	0.2		−0.1	−0.2
3. Government credits to governments of foreign countries	−0.2			−0.2	−0.4
Expenditures and Loans Less Repayments in Total	18.2	16.7	11.4	43.7	100.0
Excess of Revenue Over Expenditure and Loans Less Repayments	−6.1	−1.2	−0.6	−8.9	
GENERAL FINANCING					
1. Internal financing	4.1	1.2	0.6		
1.1. Changes in residual budget funds on bank accounts in rubles	−0.4	−0.2	0.7		
1.2. GKO, OFZ-PK, OFZ-PD	4.2				
1.3. Savings bonds	0.2				
1.4. Other government securities	0.1	0.2			
1.5. Budget loans from a higher-level budget	0.0	0.6			
1.6. Other internal borrowings	0.0	0.5			
1.7. Credits and loans to off-budgetary funds			−0.1		
2. External financing	2.0	0.0			
2.1. Credits from international financial organizations	0.9				
2.2. Credits from governments of foreign countries, foreign commercial banks, and foreign companies	1.1				
2.3. Changes in residual budget funds on bank accounts in foreign currencies	0.0	0.0			
General Financing in Total	6.1	1.2	0.6		

Sources: RF Ministry of Finance, State Statistics Committee of Russia, IET.

Table 10.5
Changes in Money Aggregates and the Money Multiplier in 1997

1997	M0 (End of Month)		Broad Money M2 (End of Month)		Money Base (End of Month)		Money Multiplier (M2/Money Base)
	(trill. of Rb)	(% Change)	(trill. of Rb)	(% Change)	(trill. of Rb)	(% Change)	
XII '96 December	103.8	8.35	295.2	4.57	130.9	4.72	2.26
I '97 January	96.3	−7.23	297.4	0.75	123.9	−5.35	2.40
II February	102.0	5.92	307.6	3.43	130.2	5.08	2.36
III March	105.2	3.14	315.0	2.41	136.3	4.69	2.31
IV April	115.2	9.51	328.4	4.25	145.7	6.90	2.25
V May	120.4	4.51	339.4	3.35	148.2	1.72	2.29
VI June	136.8	13.62	363.8	7.19	167.0	12.69	2.18
VII July	140.3	2.56	375.5	3.22	171.4	2.63	2.19
VIII August	141.6	0.93	377.7	0.59	174.7	1.93	2.16
IX September	134.8	−4.80	376.2	−0.40	169.8	−2.80	2.22
X October	135.7	0.67	382.3	1.62	170.4	0.35	2.24
XI November	128.7	−5.16	371.1	−2.93	163.8	−3.87	2.27
XII December	137.0	6.45	379.5	2.26	164.5	0.43	2.31

Sources: Russian Central Bank, RF Ministry of Finance.

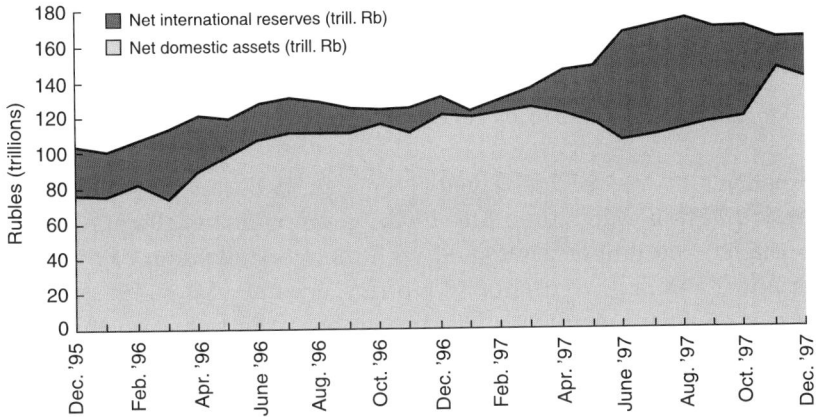

Figure 10.1
Breakdown of sources of the money base in 1996–1997.

dedollarization process, as economic agents partly switched from dollars into rubles.

According to balance-of-payments statistics, foreign investments in federal government securities in 1997 increased by over US $7 billion. Such an influx of foreign capital into the government debt market led to contradictory results. On the one hand, it promoted financial stabilization via a rapid reduction in interest rates, which held in check increases in the cost of servicing government debt. On the other hand, given instability on the world financial markets, a flight of wary investors from emerging markets could lead to a serious crisis engendered by massive sales of government securities, as well as the danger of an attack on the ruble.

Inflation in 1997 was on a steady course of decline. If in January 1997 the consumer price index was 2.3% per month, in the second quarter it came down to approximately 1% a month, and until the end of the year it did not exceed that level. At the end of the first half-year, price inflation was 8.6%, which was a little higher than the projection built into the monetary program for 1997. In the second half-year inflation came down to 2.3% (4.6% on an annual basis). Over the year prices grew by 11%.

As a result of lower inflation in 1997, the real exchange rate of the ruble grew. Over the first six months of 1997 the ruble strengthened against the dollar by 4.14%, while over the second half-year the real value of the ruble decreased by approximately 1%. Over 1997 as a whole it grew by 3%.[7]

10.6. A New Threat to Reforms on the Rise

Financial and economic developments in 1997 fall into two main periods. From March until July 1997, agents on financial markets had positive expectations associated with the reorganization of the government and an invigoration of reforms, and therefore with stronger prospects for economic growth (which led them to bid on the market) and more favorable business conditions. In June, an overheating of the Russian financial markets, particularly the stock market, became evident. This situation arose because investors had overestimated the country's political stability and the government's capacity to push forward economic reforms and overcome the fiscal crisis. However, as noted above, toward the middle of the year there were signs of a new crisis in the reform process, which was manifested in the rejection by the Duma of a reform package of social draft laws and the growing opposition to reform within the government itself.

As a result of growing pressure on the reform wing of the government and a weakening of its position following a series of large-scale political scandals, investors (particularly foreign investors) were reassessing the country's economic prospects. This reassessment worsened the situation on the Russian financial markets.

The crisis on the world financial markets, which had started in October with a devaluation in Southeast Asian currencies, led to instability on the Russian financial markets. In this situation the Central Bank of the Russian Federation took a number of steps to prevent speculative attacks against the ruble in order to stabilize the government securities market. The refinancing rate was increased from 21% to 28%, the mandatory reserve requirement for currency accounts was raised, and Lombard credit rates were reduced. These

---

7. It should be noted that the mobility of international financial flows increased markedly once the elections were held and the restrictions on convertibility of the ruble for current transactions were lifted in June 1996. This created new problems for for exchange-rate policy in 1997, similar to those encountered earlier by some other emerging markets. Sensitivity to political events and to some extent the "herd behavior" of Western investors fuels the potential for speculative attacks without reference to economic fundamentals (so-called self-fulfilling currency crises). That is why, with long-term stability of the currency market in mind, accumulation of considerable currency reserves ($23.8 billion at the end of June) was completely justified.

steps were effective in preventing devaluation of the ruble, which would have had grave consequences for the entire Russian financial system.

An extremely important consequence of the financial crisis was the considerable and unforeseen losses in the banking sector.[8] A significant share of banking assets, which had formerly yielded high profits, was constituted by the instruments most undermined by the financial crisis: corporate shares, GKO-OFZs, eurobonds, domestic currency bonds, and debts to the London Club. At the same time, the growing need for liquidity engendered by the crisis forced the banks to increase the supply of the depreciating assets. This process further decreased their value. All of this led in early December to the first signs of the banking crisis: a number of banks defaulted on their obligations, and the prepayment requirement made its appearance on the financial markets.

In the course of 1997 the nominal size of domestic government GKO-OFZ debt grew by approximately 52%. The nominal value of government securities turning over on the domestic market by mid-December 1997 was 13.9% of GDP.

Over most of the year, up until the autumn, GKO-OFZ yields steadily declined, and therefore the cost of servicing ruble-denominated government debt also declined. However, changes in the internal political situation engendered lower investor confidence in Russian government policies.

The global financial crisis, along with deterioration in the general political situation in Russia, spurred changing trends on the GKO-OFZ market. From November 1997 the cost of servicing government debt grew. In 1997 a decisive influence on the dynamic of lending rates on the interbank ruble market was exerted by such factors as a decline in inflation, a lowering of yield rates on the government securities market, and a decline in the liquidity of the entire banking system.

In January–April 1997, considerable fluctuations in credit rates with different maturities could be observed. The average rate for the period in question was 25%–30% on an annual basis. From May, after the lowering of yields on government securities, the average rate dropped to 15%–20% annually.

---

8. A deterioration in the financial fortunes of many financial groups was an important reason for the growing intensity of the struggle for political influence in the autumn, which in turn contributed to destabilizating the political situation in Russia.

The financial crisis led to significant changes on the interbank credit market as well. Rates for one-day credits, dominant on that market, increased over the following six months from an annual 12%–27% to an annual 30% at the start of December. Among the causes of such a high increase in rates were the "delayed crisis" on the GKO-OFZ market and declining trust among commercial banks.

Despite the December rise in rates and the abolition of mutual credit limits by a number of major Russian banks, a crisis on the interbank credit market did not occur in 1997. The market turnover increased gradually, reaching in March–November Rb 13–15 billion per week, which exceeded by a large margin (in adjusted prices) the turnover on the interbank credit market before the 1995 banking crisis. The stabilizing influences on the interbank ruble market included implementation by the central bank of the mechanism for repo deals and wider opportunities for receiving Lombard credits. However, until the end of 1997, one-day credits predominated on the market. This in large measure was due to the shakier financial position of a number of major Russian commercial banks and the abolition of mutual credit limits.

10.7. The Situation on the Currency and Stock Markets

In the first quarter of 1997 the official and market exchange rates of the dollar grew steadily and at roughly the same rate, 0.6%–0.7% per month (or 7%–8% per annum). At the beginning of the second quarter, market rates began to lag behind official rates. In April the dollar on the Moscow Interbank Currency Exchange (MICEX) grew by only 0.3% (an annualized 3.6%), while on the interbank nonexchange market it dropped by 0.4%. In May–June the official rate stopped growing. However, in July the exchange rate of the dollar grew at a faster rate. The total increment of the official and market rates of exchange in the first half-year were respectively 4% and 3%. In the second half-year the dollar grew at a slower rate. Over the second half-year the official and the market rates of the dollar grew by approximately 3% (Figure 10.2). Data on various financial market indicators in 1997 are given in Table 10.6.

During the first eight months of 1997 the dynamic of the exchange rate of the dollar had to do not only with the seasonal increase in exports earnings, but also with a favorable macroeconomic situation. As capital inflows increased, the central bank had to maintain the

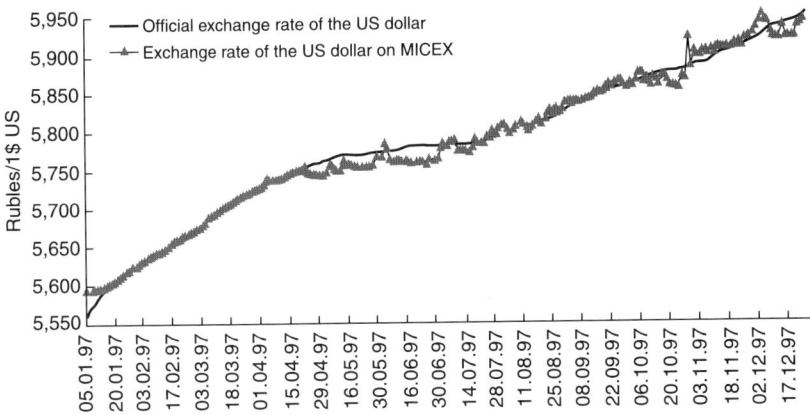

Figure 10.2
Exchange rate of the US dollar, 1997.

exchange rate of the dollar while adhering to the projections of the monetary program.

However, from mid-autumn 1997 the situation changed dramatically. Repatriation of nonresident profits from the government securities market led to an increasing demand for dollars. In these conditions the central bank's priority was to maintain the ruble exchange rate. Any sharp fluctuation in the rate could lead to a Mexico-style development, in which devaluation of the national currency would sharply increase the desire of nonresidents to convert their financial assets into hard currency. On 10 November the central bank announced guiding targets of its exchange-rate policy for 1998–2000, which indicated its stability and continuity while giving it greater room to maneuver in pursuing exchange-rate policy. In particular, the central bank received greater control in the band of fluctuation for the ruble. The rate of growth in the exchange rate would continue to be regarded as an important indicator affecting the rate of inflation, the investment climate, and the prospects for economic growth.

Of all the sectors of the financial market, the stock market is most dependent on the political situation and the dynamic of politico-economic expectations. The Russian stock market in 1997 exhibited several periods that corresponded to the development of the politico-economic situation.

The first period, from January to mid-February, was characterized by a rapidly rising market that attracted significant foreign and do-

Table 10.6
Financial Market Indicators in 1997

	1997, Month											
	I	II	III	IV	V	VI	VII	VIII	IX	X	XI	XII
Monthly inflation, %	2.3	1.5	1.4	1	0.9	1.1	0.9	−0.1	−0.3	0.2	0.6	1.0
Central Bank refinancing rate	48	42	42	36	36	24	24	24	24	21	28	28
Auction rate for GKOs (end of month), %	31.85	31.01	36.55	30.64	27.26	18.64	18.84	18.75	18.44	19.91	28.20	33.55
Auction rate for OFZs (end of month), %	35.12	35.12	43.18	36.65	35.58	25.84	24.63	18.17	17.91	18.81	25.67	25.67
Auction rate for OGSZ (end of month), %	52.7	35.2	35.2	39.70	34.61	20.42	18.22	18.22	18.22	19.00	19.00	19.00
Yields by repayment of GKO issues (% per year) with maturities:												
<1 month, %	30.55	23.9	31.39	27.40	22.00	17.84	17.68	17.5	19.27	21.49	14.45	30.98
1–3 months, %	33.5	28.78	33.69	32.16	24.13	19.61	17.49	18.5	19.52	19.71	23.00	36.19
3–6 months, %	35.71	31.01	33.66	33.62	28.24	21.69	18.93	18.5	18.57	18.44	24.93	31.94
Average rates for all issues, %	34.67	29.35	33.00	32.17	26.65	20.28	18.28	18	18.99	19.60	22.37	33.82
Average for all issues, %	34.67	29.35	33.00	32.17	35.4	31.5	27.1	27.5	28.38	21.67	30.82	36.29
Market turnover in GKOs/OFZs per month (bill. Rb)	64,982	65,586	77,117	90,230	77,011	82,445	71,841	60,000	—	81,660	91,882	52,488

Macroeconomic Stabilization and Fiscal Crisis

MBK-INSTAR rate (% per year at end of month) for credits of the following duration:												
1 day, %	12.82	24.57	14.93	26.49	7.71	15.13	8.97	7.5	26.81	6.57	21.47	36.13
1 week, %	26.13	20.67	27.80	24.06	9.90	20.34	19.51	16	20.74	20.45	25.88	33.93
2 weeks, %	28.0	35.0	29.95	28.56	16.75	21.04	16	15	17.00	25.00	30.00	36.00
1 month, %	25.0	31.0	30.00	30.40	22.13	20.00	23	23	21.00	22.00	24.00	28.00
Turnover of the MBK market per month (bill. Rb)	42,270	50,920	56,625	69,912	67,535	74,768	78,821	95,000	88,843	100,262	109,866	83,258
Average rise in value of US $ per month (% on an annual basis)	15.95	10.3	11.80	7.8	2.32	1.89	3.37	6.17	7.23	5.67	6.29	9.08
Average rise in value of DM per month (% on an annual basis)	−41.3	−23.8	18.92	−27.7	22.1	−1.24	−46.68	40.07	50.82	36.31	−14.38	1.56
Total gross turnover in US $ and DMs on MICEX per month (bill. Rb)	1,495.5	588.3	892.7	1,157.4	1,956	1,700	1,713.8	2,050	2,183	3,077	4,099	10,234
Turnover on RTS per month (bill. USDs):	865.6	818	565.4	575.76	804.0	948.74	1,575.1	1,600	1,398	2,693	926	1,240

Sources: State Statistics Committee, Central Bank of the Russian Federation, Agency Finmarket, IET.

mestic investments. This was a reaction to Yeltsin's recovery and return to active life, which brought political stability and predictability and a lowering of investment risks. As a result, the prices of most shares rose and the volume of deals sharply increased. Average yields on the market by 20 February reached 25% a month.

The second period lasted from mid-February to late April. Investors reacted to the government's lack of will and apparent inability to resolve the country's sociopolitical problems by sharply reducing investment activity. The government's idleness only exacerbated the fiscal crisis it had inherited from the postelection cabinet. In late February the stock market began to fall. Business activity on the stock market declined noticeably. Daily trading volumes on RTS-1 did not exceed US $35–45 million, compared with $55–65 million during the first period of 1997.

The third period lasted from late April to late July. Investors reacted positively to reorganization of the government and a more vigorous pursuit of reform in the areas of tax collection, the budget, and so on. In consequence, business activity on the stock market increased substantially. Daily trading volumes on RTS-1 reached US $45–65 million in May, $60–90 million in June, and $100–200 million in July–August.

In the fourth period, from early August to late October, the market underwent a correction and then stabilized, chiefly as a result of diminishing investor confidence in government policies and investors' desire to avoid political risks.[9] This process was also influenced by a decline in US stock market indices, with which Russian stock market indices closely correlate. Trading volumes on RTS-1 remained high as foreign investors began a massive sell-off of their holdings.

The beginning of the fifth period is closely associated with the crisis on the world stock markets. Significant involvement of foreign capital in the Russian financial markets determined the scale and structure of the crisis, which began on 23 October 1997. Following the October global crisis, in November 1997 the Russian stock market registered a significant decline.

The main cause of this serious fall in Russian share prices was the retreat of Western investors from the Russian market. A large volume of nonresident funds and the absence of barriers against

---

9. The growth of such risks was signaled by the political conflict around the privatization of Svyazinvest.

repatriation of profits—for both European and US stock markets were undergoing a postcrisis correction—set Russian share prices on a persistently declining trend. Overall, from 6 October until 19 December, the fall was 37.8%. This decline far exceeded the declines in US and European stock market indices.

The Russian stock market in 1997 continued to be characterized by a high level of concentration. The seven largest corporations accounted for 70% of the total volume of trades for that period.

The year 1997 should be assessed by looking at how the government used all the opportunities that once again were open to Russia. Progress was made in a number of areas affecting socioeconomic policy, as was reflected in concrete indicators and positive economic shifts.

First, economic growth resumed in a number of sectors of the economy, as well as in the overall dynamic of the GDP. For the first time in eight years the economy registered a small growth (the GDP grew by 0.4%). Industrial growth, up 1.9%, was higher at this time than GDP growth.

Perhaps the main achievement, however, was not even economic growth per se but the beginning of structural shifts, particularly evident in industry (this subject is addressed in Chapter 18). In 1997 the bulk of growth was accounted for by enterprises oriented toward meeting domestic demand—that is, enterprises that competed successfully with foreign producers. Moreover, these processes began to unfold without any protectionist measures. They were chiefly the consequence of an increase in domestic demand (due to macroeconomic stabilization) and the adaptation of enterprises (particularly owners and management) to the market environment.

Second, the activities of the state diverged somewhat from business interests as federal authorities took steps to reduce dependence on business and various interest groups. The growing independence of the state gave rise to a series of intense political conflicts, which will likely continue for the foreseeable future. Privatization and the associated problems of ownership rights are likely to remain at the core of these conflicts.

Third, the government managed to materially weaken the influence of the principal destabilizing factor in the social sphere in early 1997—wage and pension arrears. In the summer the government settled its debt to pensioners, by autumn wages to the military had been paid off, and by the new year the regions had received sufficient federal funds to fully cover the wage arrears in the budgetary sphere. Resolution of these and other problems led to a significant downturn in strike activity. (It should be noted that the government did not fortify these successes by creating a mechanism to prevent mass wage and pension arrears from arising in the future, and in 1998 the situation began to repeat itself.)

Fourth, the government developed and proposed to legislators a number of realistic and effective reforms. These reforms included above all the tax code, the budget code, a package of social reforms, a concept of pension reform, and a series of health care reform proposals. Even though a large part of these proposals were not, for political reasons, approved by the legislature, their appearance was extremely important since it laid the foundation for resolving these acute problems in the future.

Fifth, during a considerable part of 1997 the government succeeded in maintaining stability in the monetary and credit systems. In 1997 inflation in Russia was lower than in countries that had proceeded farther down the path of postsocialist transition, including Poland.

Sixth, an important achievement of the year was Russia's entry into the Paris and London Clubs.

At the heart of the positive shift in economic trends lay two factors: the remonetization of the economy, which determined the positive dynamic of demand by consumers and industry alike, and a revival of crediting of the real sector. In turn, remonetization is an integral indicator of the disinflation potential of the economy that accumulated in 1995–1997 and the effectiveness of a reasonably tight monetary policy.

However, not all of the problems were resolved definitively or consistently. Among the main government failures one should especially note the following:

- Tax collection did not improve.

- Despite a slowdown, interenterprise arrears continued to grow.

- The budget deficit remained at a level detrimental to economic growth, and the cost of servicing government debt became alarmingly high.

- The measures taken by the government to regulate natural monopolies were clearly insufficient.

11 The Crisis of the Russian Financial System: Key Factors, Economic Policies, and Initial Results

Sergei Arkhipov, Said Batkibekov, Sergei Drobyshevsky, Tatiana Drobyshevskaia, Vladimir Mau, Sergei Sinelnikov-Murylev, and Ilya Trounin

The year 1998 was marked in Russia by a dramatic crisis in its economic, political, and social sphere. The crisis, which had been brewing for a long time, assumed an explicit and unambiguous dimension in August. The underlying causes of the crisis remained after August, although their economic and political manifestations were slightly different. The August 1998 crisis will remain a key factor in the economic and political development of Russia for a long time to come.

11.1. Evolution of the Russian Financial Crisis in 1997–1998

The crisis that erupted in August had evolved in four major phases: November to December 1997, January 1998, February to April 1998, and May to August 1998. Throughout the ten-month period the risks associated with doing business in Russia grew steadily worse. We refer to risks related to currency convertibility, changes in the credit ratings of the country and its domestic counter-parties, loss of prestige, changes in the tax system that were not investor-friendly, and a negative transformation of the legal environment. Moreover, actual developments followed the worst possible path.

The first of the aforementioned phases was a sort of prehistory of the crisis of 17 August 1998, discussed in Chapter 10. As concerns the events of 1998, it suffices here to mention that a benign situation on the Russian financial markets in September 1997 (with weighted average yields on the GKO-OFZ market down to 20% per annum and the RTS-1 index at about 500 points) made it possible for Boris

Yeltsin to declare that from 1999 on, Russia would no longer need any financial assistance from the International Monetary Fund. (His statement was also meant to prepare the ground for redenomination of the ruble.)

However, financial stabilization and the explosive development of the Russian financial markets occurred against a backdrop of fundamental economic challenges: a fiscal crisis, a dramatic worsening of the balance of payments, and an increasingly unstable banking system. Serious concern arose over the ratio of short-term government debt held by nonresidents and the external reserves of the central bank. In the wake of a political scandal over a July 1997 tender for a block of shares in joint-stock company Svyazinvest, investors had to downgrade their assessment of Russia's political stability and the possibility of implementing the governmental program proposed in the spring of 1997.

On 27 October 1997 the Dow Jones Industrial Average index fell by a record 554 points, an event that signaled the beginning of a financial crisis in Russia. The crisis eventually vacated all of the macroeconomic successes achieved in 1997 and entailed a change of course in the economic transformation. Obviously, the acute global financial crisis that hit the developed markets and sent prices downward in a number of emerging markets was just one factor triggering a series of destructive processes in Russia.

As early as the first week of the crisis, weighted average yields on the government debt market rose from 22% to 28% per annum. There was a dramatic increase in auction sales, with a more than twofold weekly growth of the secondary market and a concurrent heavy drop in Russian eurobond quotations.

The central bank had to decide between a bad and a very bad option. Its first option was to protect the ruble against a large devaluation by increasing interest rates on the government debt market. Its second option was to keep interest rates at a relatively low level through open market transactions. Regrettably, in November 1997 the central bank chose the latter option and increased its GKO holdings.

It was not until 11 November 1997 that the central bank increased its refinancing rate, from 21% to 28%, which was clearly not enough to maintain equilibrium on the government debt market. Its interventions on the GKO market helped the central bank prevent rates from rising above 30% until the last week in November. Nevertheless, as nonresidents who had sold their government bonds developed an appetite for foreign exchange, the central bank's gold and foreign exchange reserves declined quickly, which jeopardized the stability of its exchange-rate policy. During November 1997 its external reserves plummeted from $22.9 billion to $16.8 billion. The November depletion of reserves resulted in a sharp increase in the ratio of short-term debt to international reserves, from 1.9 to 2.7.

The policy just described appears to have fueled the crisis. Instead of supporting low interest rates on the GKO-OFZ market, the central bank should have allowed interest rates to rise until a market equilibrium was reached. Moreover, it should not have permitted a complete liberalization of the domestic debt market for nonresidents as of 1 January 1998. More specifically, it should not have canceled a guaranteed level of bond yields and a restricted time frame for profit repatriation. Had there been a timely and significant rise in the refinancing rate and an appropriate growth of interest rates on government securities, attacks on the Russian ruble might have been far less aggressive.

The policy of higher interest rates could have been complemented by higher rates of ruble depreciation. Even though this would have signaled to investors that there was a higher risk of devaluation, it could have helped stabilize the currency market, given an adequate level of external reserves and a predictable exchange rate. Such policies could have been implemented by establishing a narrower currency band with a higher slope. However, the central bank failed to take advantage of a possible acceleration in ruble depreciation when it announced, on 10 November 1997, its exchange-rate policy targets for 1998–2000, which provided for a wider currency band. The announcement sent a negative signal to the markets, showing that the central bank was committed to maintaining a low rate of ruble depreciation via foreign currency interventions, which was bound to increase exchange-rate risks.

Apparently, the alternative measures just described—higher interest rates coupled with higher rates of ruble depreciation—would have had a controversial impact on the financial situation. Some investors may have thought that high interest rates would suffice to offset higher risks. More conservative investors would have continued to export their capital out of Russia. Nevertheless, the most likely result of this policy would have been the emergence of a new equilibrium on the Russian financial markets against the background of a moderate decline in external reserves.

At the same time that the central bank was pursuing an inappropriate policy, the government did not have any meaningful program for reducing government expenditures and the size of the fiscal deficit. Another factor responsible for the deteriorating financial situation was the government reshuffle at the end of November 1997. This reshuffle signaled the final abandonment of the program of the "young reformers'" government. Investors no longer believed in the executive authorities' ability to pursue a sound and consistent financial policy.

In the last week of November 1997 the central bank, which had lost over a quarter of its international reserves, gave up its efforts to maintain low interest rates and quit the GKO-OFZ market. Weighted average yields on government debt soared to 40% per annum.

The end of 1997 and the start of 1998 were marked by a growing crisis in Southeast Asia. In this context major investment funds chose to redistribute their investment quotas among various countries, and equity markets saw yet another fall in stock prices, while GKO and OFZ yields increased.

In January 1998, quotations for Russian securities plummeted nearly 30%. The overall decline of the RTS-1 index between 6 October 1997 and the end of January 1998 was 50.9%. The fall in quotations for Russian corporate stock was tantamount to a self-supporting process. Having received clients' orders to sell sizable blocks of shares, investment companies anticipated a heavy drop in the market levels and were themselves eager to sell their liquid shares, thereby aggravating the market crisis.

An outflow of portfolio investments from Russia increased pressure on the ruble, so that at the beginning of the year the official exchange rate of the US dollar grew at a fast pace and forward quotations increased. The central bank's attempts in January to boost the rates of ruble depreciation provoked a dramatic rise in GKO interest rates. The market extrapolated the faster growth of the exchange rate to a broader context and responded by hiking interest rates to offset a drop in foreign currency–denominated yields. The market reaction confirmed that it is generally impossible to attempt devaluation in the context of a confidence crisis, short government debt, a high percentage of nonresidents on the market, and low foreign exchange reserves.

The second half of January was marked by renewed political complications. A substantial reallocation of powers occurred within the government: Chubais's sphere of influence was curtailed to economics, since the financial sphere became Victor Chernomyrdin's domain, and Boris Nemtsov lost control over the fuel and energy complex. The weakening of the reformers' position resulted in even lower investor expectations.

A period of relative market stabilization set in between February and April 1998. The positive trend was largely due to a series of steps taken by the President and the government, steps that clarified the immediate prospects for economic policy. More specifically, Yeltsin advocated a tighter fiscal policy and called for achieving a primary surplus of the federal budget in 1998. Following a series of reshuffles, the government formulated twelve key social and economic policy measures. The document made all members of the government and presidential administration officials personally responsible for implementing specific measures to promote a sound budget, normalize the wage arrears situation, and so on.

Meanwhile, some other developments occurred that sent positive signals to investors. In February the IMF decided to extend a three-year credit to Russia for another year. Michel Camdessus let it be understood that Russia would get another $700 million tranche of the credit and that, subject to compliance with all of the arrangements, Russia would receive loans until 2000. Furthermore, on 24 February, Russia and the United Kingdom reached a complete agreement on the terms of Russian debt restructuring within the framework of the Paris Club.

On 10 March 1998, Fitch IBCA rating agency, despite the ups and downs of the Russian financial markets, confirmed Russia's long-term credit rating for foreign currency–denominated borrowings at BB+ and left its short-term rating at the same B level. On the following day, however, Moody's rating agency downgraded Russia's credit rating for foreign currency–denominated external debt from Ba2 to Ba3, and downgraded the rating for foreign currency–denominated bank deposits to B1.

On 23 March 1998 the Russian Cabinet of Ministers resigned by order of the President, who was striving to consolidate power, and Sergei Kiriyenko was appointed acting prime minister. The financial markets' short-term reaction to the government reshuffle was quite positive. Later, however, economic agents lost their bearings in the political uncertainty that followed this reshuffling, owing to the five-week delay before Kiriyenko's final confirmation as prime minister (the head of the Russian government).

The newly formed government focused on budget recovery as the thrust of its economic policy. An analysis of the fiscal policy pursued by the Kiriyenko government in the spring and early summer of 1998 shows that it succeeded in preventing a further aggravation of the crisis. Tax collections in the first quarter of 1998 proved to be slightly better than in 1997. At the same time the execution of the expenditure side of both the federal and the consolidated budgets in the early half of 1998 was radically different from the previous year. Practically all items in both budgets other than government debt service and government administration expenditures were slashed. The federal budget's defense spending in the first half of 1998 was cut by approximately 1%–1.5% of GDP, compared with the previous year's level.

A reconstructed budget of Russia's enlarged government (including extrabudgetary funds) in the first half of 1998 shows that tax receipts fell in the first half of 1998 in comparison with 1997 (from 32.6% of GDP to 30.7%). There was an even more significant change in total revenues, to 36.5% of GDP, compared with 33.4% of GDP in 1997. A greater decline in consolidated budget expenditure (from 43.2% of GDP to 38.5% of GDP) reduced the deficit of the consolidated budget by 1.6% of GDP.

The final phase of the Russian financial crisis developed as follows: There was a build-up of political instability and greater pressure on foreign exchange reserves in a setting of strained government finances, short domestic debt, a large share of international investors, and an emerging banking crisis. Under such circumstances there is a high probability that problems will worsen even though the government may be pursuing a correct and consistent policy aimed at a sound budget, compliance with investors' rights, and so on. Objectively speaking, the market reaction is asymmetrical: any error in economic policy or bad news has serious adverse effects, while the right steps fail to elicit a positive response from the markets.

In mid-May, right after the new cabinet's confirmation, there was a sharp drop in quotations for government securities. Trading on the secondary market increased, the RTS-1 stock index fell by 40%, and the ruble exchange rate came under heavier pressure. During May the foreign exchange reserves fell by $1.4 billion (nearly 10%).

The government's response to a growing crisis on the Russian financial markets was too slow and made the crisis even worse. It was not until the end of May that the newly formed Kiriyenko government began to develop anticrisis measures. A series of statements was issued between 17 and 19 May: by the government, on its commitment to a policy aimed at macroeconomic stability; the central bank, on the immutability of its currency policy and the inadmissibility of monetary financing of the budget; the Ministry of Finance, on an austerity plan for budget expenditure; and the Federal Securities Commission, on securing investors' rights.

On 29 May, the government issued a statement on immediate measures to stabilize the financial market and on fiscal policy in 1998. A few days after his cabinet appointment, Boris Fedorov outlined major ways of improving tax collection in Russia. Financial markets began to show some degree of optimism after Chubais paid a visit to Washington, D.C., on 29–30 May to discuss the possibility of a large financial aid package for Russia. In the first week of June, yields on government debt dropped to 51%, and in the second week they dropped further, to 46%.

Nevertheless, investor confidence was waning in the absence of consistent anticrisis actions by the government. The June situation was made worse by the slow pace of the Russian government's talks with the IMF on the disbursement of a large aid package.

A massive flight of investors' funds from financial markets led to yet another increase in the GKO interest rate, to 50%, in the second half of June. The stock index fell by 20% during the month of June. All this put much more pressure on the ruble exchange rate and forced the central bank to carry out large-scale interventions on the currency market.

Despite an unfavorable environment, on 10 June Russia floated five-year bonds for the amount of $1.25 billion at the rate of 11.75%. On 24 June, a new $2.5 billion loan was floated at a rate as high as 12.75%. The high cost of borrowing sent a negative signal to investors and reduced quotations for other negotiable eurobonds.

On 17 June, Boris Yeltsin appointed Anatoly Chubais special presidential representative (with vice-premier status) and liaison with international financial institutions—a positive move in the eyes of the players on the Russian financial markets. On 23 June the IMF board of directors approved the disbursement of another $670 million tranche of its Russian credit. Moreover, the IMF issued a statement in support of the Russian government's measures to prop up its national currency and avoid a major devaluation.

During June 1998 the government was busy developing anticrisis program measures. This program notably included (1) a planned reduction in gas prices and electricity tariff rates, (2) amendments to tax legislation (the VAT to be charged at shipment, the introduction of a flat income tax scale, a lower rate of profit tax, higher rates of excise taxes and duties, a limited number of enterprises' settlement accounts, the introduction of a sales tax, and so on), and (3) the selling of government-owned stakes in major Russian corporations (in particular, 5% of the shares in RAO Gazprom and the government stake in joint-stock company Svyazinvest). Sergei Kiriyenko submitted a package of anticrisis bills in installments for consideration by the State Duma early in July 1998.

At the time, weighted average yields on the government securities market amounted to 126% per annum. On 8 July 1998 the Ministry of Finance canceled auction bids for GKOs and OFZs. On 13 July the Russian government announced its intention to offer GKO holders an option of converting the bonds into medium- or long-term dollar-denominated bonds, to be redeemed in 2005 and 2018, respectively. The situation took a turn for the better after an announcement on 13 July 1998 that the IMF, the World Bank, and the Japanese government would give Russia $22.6 billion in financial aid, of which $5.6 billion was to be disbursed right after a meeting of the IMF board of directors. Between 13 and 19 July, weighted average yields on GKOs dropped to 53%. The RTS-1 index rose 34% during the same week. The next GKO auction, scheduled for 15 July, never took place, however, and government debt was serviced at the expense of the federal budget. On 20 July an announcement was made that one-year government securities would no longer be issued.

The State Duma voted down many of the bills in the anticrisis package proposed by the government in June and July 1998. As passage of those bills was part and parcel of the Russian commitment to the IMF and a condition for the provision of financial support, the size of the aid consequently might have been expected to decrease. Nevertheless, as a result of Chubais's talks with the IMF's top management, the first tranche was cut only by a reasonable amount— from $5.6 billion to $4.8 billion. On 21 July the IMF passed a resolution on disbursing a new aid package to Russia.

Notwithstanding the reduced size of the first tranche, the financial markets' response was positive. Yields on government debt fell to 45%. Further developments, therefore, largely depended on whether the market would receive clear signals from the Russian leaders as to their further measures to normalize the situation. The government did not take any steps, however, to show that it had a coherent plan of action.

The Russian government interpreted a temporary stabilization of the market after 20 July as a sustainable trend, and it did not arrange until the following week a meeting, which took place on 27 July, between the prime minister and a number of key investors to explain the government's plan of action with respect to government debt repayment and service in the near future. Even at this meeting, however, the government failed to produce any convincing proof that Russia would be able to meet its commitments before the end of 1998, based on available data on tax revenue and increased international reserves.

In addition to the increasingly obvious political weakness of the government, which failed to push through the State Duma the package of bills agreed upon with the IMF, several additional factors caused a downturn in the overall situation by early August and led to an uncontrollable chain of further reactions. We refer here first to a slump on the international financial markets. Second, there was a seasonal drop in the proportion of risky assets in the portfolios of key institutional investors—a common occurrence shortly before summer vacations. A serious aggravation of the banking crisis was a third major factor, provoked by a worsening situation on the financial markets in the context of the tight monetary policy pursued in the first half of 1998. An acute liquidity crisis occurred in the banking system largely because of decreased quotations for Russian government securities denominated in foreign currencies. Because these securities served as collateral for loans granted by foreign banks to their Russian counterparts, the latter were requested to increase their margin calls. To meet these margin requirements, banks began selling their portfolios of GKOs and OFZs and corporate shares with the goal of converting the proceeds into foreign exchange. Such moves by the banks made the financial markets even more nervous, including the market for Russian paper denominated in foreign currencies. The first two banks to default on their debts to international lending institutions were SBS-Agro and Imperial.

The above factors combined to produce a serious deterioration in the financial situation in the period between the IMF loan disbursement date and early August. Yields on government debt jumped to

56%, and the stock market fell at an accelerating rate. The RTS-1 index plunged nearly 30% between the disbursement of the IMF stabilization loan and 17 August. International reserves were plummeting faster: from $19.5 billion as of 23 July to $18.4 billion as of 31 July to $16.3 billion as of 17 August.

To round off our analysis of developments leading up to the climax of the crisis, it is worth noting that, along with the aforementioned underlying causes, two other major factors were responsible for Russia's failure to avoid ruble devaluation in August—the State Duma's lack of support for the government's anticrisis program and insufficient aid from the IMF. The situation might have been reversed by G-7 countries' aid to the tune of $10 billion to $15 billion. Under the prevailing political situation, however, it would have been unrealistic to expect such help. A devaluation of the ruble, consequently, was the only feasible option.

The government's plan as announced on 17 August provided for three sets of measures: the introduction of a floating exchange rate for the ruble, with its devaluation to roughly Rb 9 per dollar by the end of the year; a three-month moratorium on repayment of Russian banks' external debt; and a compulsory GKO-OFZ debt restructuring scheme.

On 15–16 August the IMF agreed to the government's plan. The program announced on 17 August did not include a domestic government debt restructuring scheme and provoked a negative response from the financial markets. The stock market plunged an additional 29% the following week. A restructuring scheme was finally published by the government with a one-week delay. The amount of frozen domestic sovereign debt totaled Rb 265.3 billion ($42.2 billion at the exchange rate as of 14 August 1998). The only thing that remained in circulation were the OFZs, totaling Rb 75 billion and maturing in 2000–2001.

The Kiriyenko government's program was never implemented as originally announced. On 23 August the Kiriyenko cabinet resigned and Victor Chernomyrdin was appointed acting prime minister. This decision had some serious economic and political implications. First, the cabinet's resignation and the statements about a change in economic policy virtually annulled Russia's arrangements with the IMF in respect to both an enlarged lending facility program and a stabilization loan (with due regard to the IMF-backed measures as announced on 17 August). Second, the political crisis introduced much more uncertainty into economic policy.

The above factors generated a new wave of panic on financial and commodities markets. On 26 August the RF Central Bank, having spent considerable reserves to prop up the ruble at low rates vis-à-vis the dollar, suspended trade at the Moscow Interbank Currency Exchange (MICEX) for an indefinite period in an effort to preserve its gold and foreign exchange reserves. Regional currency exchanges had to suspend their trade as of 28 August. Later, the central bank was no longer able to prevent the ruble from falling, owing to its depleted foreign exchange reserves ($12.46 billion as of 1 September).

September 1998 witnessed a further aggravation of an economic and financial crisis arising from the devaluation of the ruble and eroded confidence in the Russian national currency. A devaluation of the ruble by two-thirds and the skyrocketing velocity of money accounted for a rapid rise in consumer prices. In August prices rose by 3.7%, and in September they rose by 38.4%.

Eventually the rate of inflation slowed down, concurrent with a depreciation of the US dollar. This was largely a result of the monetary policy pursued by the RF Central Bank. There was practically no change in base money in August, even though the central bank then spent US $5.95 billion out of its gold and foreign exchange reserves. Apparently, foreign exchange interventions were sterilized as a result of open market operations with government debt and the disbursement of stabilization loans to commercial banks.

During September, base money increased by 9.5% against a background of dramatically decreased rates of shrinkage of external reserves. At the same time, the inflationary effects of a currency issue were largely offset by a decrease in the monetary multiplier due to the withdrawal of household deposits from commercial banks.

In the absence of a market for domestic public borrowing, the only indicator of interest rates on Russian debt was now the market for foreign currency–denominated domestic bonds (OVVZs) and eurobonds. Quotations for third-tranche OVVZs (maturing in 1998) plunged to 40% of their face value (compared to 90% as of early August), while the prices of the other OVVZ tranches plummeted to 10% of their face value. The eurobonds were rated at 20%–30% of their face value (versus 70%–85% before the crisis).

September 1998 saw marked fluctuations in the dollar exchange rate in the Electronic Lot Trading System (commonly known as SELT, to use the Russian acronym). On 31 August, for example, the exchange rate was Rb 7.905 per US dollar, whereas on 9 September it was as high as Rb 20.825. The need to reduce exchange losses on forward contracts maturing in mid-September accounted for a subsequent drop in the dollar exchange rate to Rb 8.67 per dollar. After the rate was fixed at this level on 15 September 1998, it soared again to Rb 16 per dollar. During September the US dollar rate went up by 102.4%.

Following the August drop in quotations, Russian stock prices declined at a slightly slower pace in September 1998. In August the RTS-1 index dropped by 56.2%, whereas in September it fell by 33.2%. Since the start of 1998 the RTS-1 index had dropped by 89%, and since the beginning of October 1997 it had dropped by 92.3%.

Data on the interbank ruble loan market show that overnight lending rates as of mid-September had reached 450% per annum, and interest rates on three-day loans had reached 130% per annum. High earnings from foreign exchange operations ensured repayment of such loans. The September volume of transactions plunged to one-tenth of the August volume.

11.2. Principal Factors Behind the 1998 Financial Crisis

11.2.1. Fiscal Deficit and Government Debt

The principal reason for the financial crisis was the failure of all the successive cabinets in Russia to adopt and, more important, to execute a realistic budget. The positive trends in 1996 and 1997, such as falling inflation rates, stabilization of the ruble exchange rate, declining interest rates, and an incipient economic rise, were maintained solely by a tight monetary policy pursued against the background of highly unbalanced government finances. The considerable government finance shortages, which pushed up government debt and debt servicing while simultaneously depressing national savings and reducing the current balance of payments surplus, were a major destabilizing factor in the nation's socioeconomic development.

One of the worst performers among the democratic nations in terms of economic growth, Russia stands level with the United States in terms of budget strain. The budgetary crisis in postcommunist Russia has political roots, and not solely because its government lacks the political will to fight tax evasion and tax arrears (see Chapter 9). The political landscape of the budgetary crisis reflects the incompatibility between the level of tax collection by the government, on the one hand, and the democratic character of the political regime and the country's economic development on the other.[1]

Lack of understanding of the underpinnings of the budgetary crisis has led to incorrect decisions to end it. It is arguable to what extent tax revenues correspond to the growth level of the national economy, its sectoral structure, public well-being, public consumption structure, law-abiding traditions, comprehensiveness of the laws, and many more factors. That attainable tax collection does not rise above 30% of GDP, give or take a few percentage points, can be taken as proved by practical economic experience. Restructuring expenditures, not the least by cutting them, is therefore pivotal to a balanced budget—a painful admission in both political and social terms.

Between 1991 and 1997, the government slashed public spending by approximately two-thirds, with spending on social programs dropping by about a third. For all that, the government moved too slowly to cut its spending, reducing expenditures by far less than what was needed to put the budget in balance. Furthermore, budgetary spending was commandeered by an assortment of lobbies (agribusiness, the military-industrial complex, banks, primary industries, and so on), which twisted the structure of budgetary spending tortuously out of shape and left it unable to create conditions for economic growth or to maintain a desired level of sociopolitical stability.

In the period under review (particularly the juncture of 1997 and 1998), the government made repeated attempts to discipline federal and local budgetary spending. In June and July 1998 the Kiriyenko cabinet went so far as to develop and adopt a program tailored to these aims. The measures undertaken in this area were, however, hardly more than efforts to identify and plug the leaks. The problem was far more complex overall: the government had to go back on many of its commitments, which could no longer be honored without piling up a precarious pyramid of public debt.

Beginning in 1995, the internal public debt started running up, above all because of heavy borrowing on the securities market (see

---

1. In principle, a feasible level of tax collection is determined by factors connected to the country's economic development, such as economic structure; the population's educational standards, which allow developed tax legislation and appropriate accounting standards to be applied; the level of tax administration; the general level of the population's law abidance; tax payment traditions; and the population's social and ethnographic homogeneity. Authoritarian regimes can afford to put far greater resources in the government's hands than is possible under democratic rule. That was actually the case in communist countries.

Table 11.1
Dynamics of Federal Foreign Debt, 1992–2000

Year	USSR Debt (in bill. $)	RF Debt (in bill. $)	RF Debt Service as % of GDP
1992	104.9	2.8	0.7
1993	103.7	9.0	0.3
1994	108.6	11.3	0.5
1995	103.0	17.4	0.9
1996	100.8	24.2	0.9
1997	97.8	33.0	0.7
1998	95.0	55.0	1.2
1999	90.0	52.0	2.4
2000*	55.0	68.0	2.9
2000†	15.0	95.0	2.9

*After restructuring the debt to the London Club.

†Assuming the debt to the Paris Club is restructured on terms similar to those agreed upon with the London Club.

Sources: RF Ministry of Finance, RF Goskomstat, IET.

Statistical Appendix, Table 1). By early 1998 the domestic debt had increased to 18.7% of GDP.

The costs of servicing the swelling domestic debt mounted. Between 1995 and 1996 these costs almost doubled, from 2.6% to 4.8% of GDP. In 1997 and the first six months of 1998, the servicing costs dipped to 3.6% and 3.9% of GDP, respectively—still an unacceptably high rate.

At about the same time, 1996 to 1998, the government started borrowing indiscriminately on foreign financial markets. Table 11.1 shows the growth of the federal foreign debt. The total debt load on the country's economy, at 49.8% of GDP (as of 1 January 1998), was relatively light, by the measure of many other countries across the world.[2]

The domestic debt burdening Russia in 1997 was singularly short-termed, with a large proportion of it being nonresident debt. The duration of Russia's domestic debt (the average time before retirement of outstanding GKOs-OFZs) increased from 60 to 90 days over 1995, to 150 days in 1996, to 250 days in 1997. Even though debt duration had crept up to 330 days by August 1998, the funds needed monthly to retire the previous bond issues alone (leaving aside cou-

---

2. Russia's own debt as of 1 January 1998 was 7.6% of GDP, or 25.2% of the total. In the first eight months of 1998, federal liabilities as a proportion of overall foreign debt, including the debts of the former USSR, reached 36.7%.

pon payments on two- to three-year coupon securities, OFZs) had shot up to between 10% and 15% of monthly GDP.

The ratio of short-term domestic debt to household bank deposits, which give an inkling of the total domestic financial savings in Russia, points to a long lead of domestic debt, which continued into the fall of 1997, from spring 1996, when it had topped 1.

This situation forced the decision to open the internal public debt market to nonresidents. Given the persistent fiscal deficit and limited domestic borrowing sources, the government had no alternative to nonresidents: it was either contrive to narrow the fiscal deficit or throw the door to the domestic debt market wide open to nonresidents.

Starting on 1 January 1998, the central bank and the Russian government announced the removal of all restrictions to nonresidents entering the Russian debt market (guaranteed yields were waived and restrictions on profit repatriation periods were lifted). The presence of nonresidents on the GKO-OFZ market grew steadily. According to the Russian Finance Ministry, nonresidents accounted for almost 28% of the market in April 1998.

Another point must be made: The significant easing of foreign capital controls and the consequent decline in government debt servicing costs gave the government an illusion of a trouble-free reality, with enough funds to finance the government fiscal deficit, at least in the mid-term. From this perspective, the admission of nonresidents to the domestic debt market had a disastrous effect on the government's economic policy because it intensified the moral risks of the soft budgetary policy option, which did not anticipate a rapid contraction of the fiscal deficit and hence the need for more public borrowing.

Although foreign borrowings have longer maturity dates than domestic market securities, in 1999 Russia began to repay the credits and loans it had received from international financial organizations in the relatively distant past, while in 2001 it began to retire the eurobonds placed in 1997 and 1998. Over the next ten years, the annual costs of repaying debts to international organizations and meeting interest payments to investors who have purchased Russian eurobonds will range from $3.5 billion to $5 billion. As if that were not enough, the grace period on debt repayment to the London and Paris Clubs ends in 2002, which will significantly boost annual foreign debt repayments.

Still, it is safe to say that the government debt management policy in 1997 and 1998 did not make full use of external borrowings as an alternative to loading up on domestic debt. The advantages of external borrowings include their longer terms and the absence of ruble exchange-rate fluctuation risk for investors, which together make the price of borrowing less dependent on the current exchange-rate policy. In our view, the attempts made in that period to step up external borrowing by floating eurobonds were not consistent enough. A total of $14.9 billion worth of eurobonds was floated in 1997 and 1998. Had consolidation (that is, substitution of long-term debt for short-term debt by altering the ratio of internal to external borrowings) been more forceful, the threat of financial crisis could have been deflated, if not completely averted.

11.2.2. The Balance of Payments

In analyzing the major changes in the balance of payments figures in 1998, it is important to remember the inherent contradictions of Russia's economic situation in the summer of 1997. On the one hand, the plunge in oil prices at the source fed fears that the ruble was overvalued in the changing market conditions, and therefore that devaluation could be expected. These expectations were fomented by the rising cost of foreign debt servicing and repayment. The need for an adjustment in the current exchange-rate policy and a moderate devaluation of the ruble was obvious in the last quarter of 1997. At this time a clear trend emerged for the official gold and foreign exchange reserves to be used as an important source of deficit financing and the forecasts for the world energy markets pointed to a stubborn price downtrend.

On the other hand, in an economic situation highlighted by short-term government debt and the high-profile presence of nonresidents on the debt market, any attempts to tamper with the exchange-rate policy (in particular, attempts to accelerate the gradual devaluation of the ruble) would send foreign investors scampering from the financial markets, interest rates shooting up, demand for foreign exchange soaring, foreign exchange reserves thinning out, and the risk of default on government debt and biting devaluation looming. In the end, the policy of letting the ruble devalue gradually to bring the balance of payments back into equilibrium grinds to a halt. That was what we witnessed in 1997 and 1998.

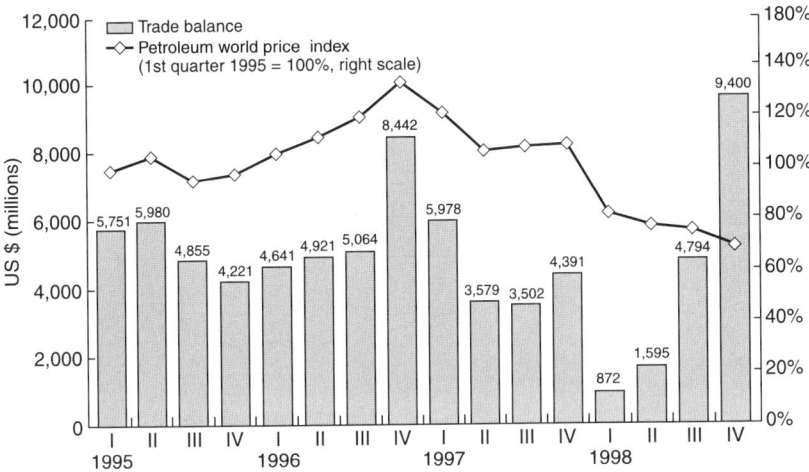

Figure 11.1
RF trade balance and world oil prices, 1995–1998. (Sources: RF Central Bank, International Financial Statistics.)

Starting in the second quarter of 1997, the current account balance was moving solidly into the red (with the sole exception of the fourth quarter of 1997, when the balance stood at no more than $400 million). The key factors accounting for the contraction of the current account balance included the bad market for Russia's main export commodity groups (Figure 11.1 shows Russia's trade balance almost following the fluctuations in world oil prices) and the increased interest payments to nonresidents by the government and the private sector (the 1997 bottom line puts the total revenues paid for capital services at $8 billion, or 1.75% of GDP) (Figure 11.2).

Despite the continued drop in world oil prices, the Russian trade balance surplus surged in the third quarter of 1998, propelled by the ruble's devaluation, to $4.8 billion, largely as a result of a cut in imports (to $13.3 billion, down from $17.2 billion in the second quarter). The balance of payments current account also showed an improvement over the preceding period, to over $777 million. This improvement can be fully attributed to the trade balance growth, with the revenue balance deficit standing at $3.3 billion in the third quarter, a tad below the second quarter's showing. These trends persisted in the fourth quarter of 1998: the trade balance reached $9.4 billion, while the balance of payments current account balance surplus increased to $6.1 billion. After August 1998 the major factor contributing to the growth of the current account balance was an in-

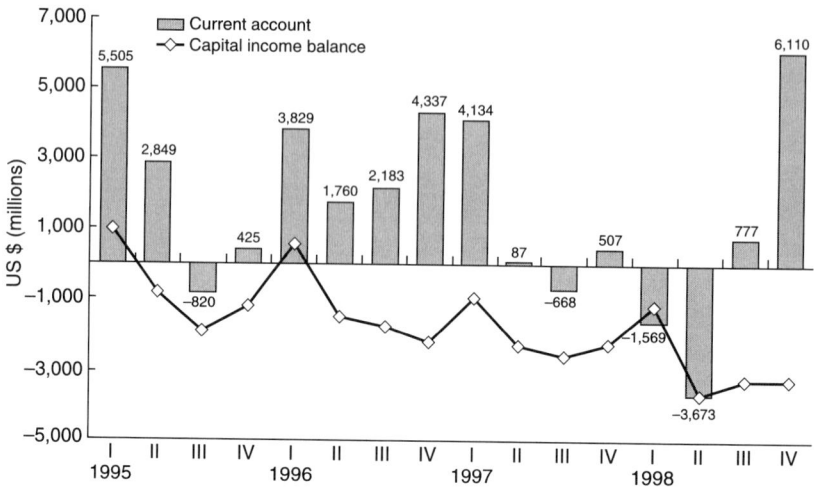

Figure 11.2
RF current account and balance of capital services, 1995–1998. (Source: RF Central Bank.)

crease in exports (up to $19.3 billion in the fourth quarter), as export effectiveness improved and imports dropped (to $9.7 billion) as a result of the ruble's devaluation. Foreign debt servicing by Russian residents remained at about the precrisis level ($3.5 billion a quarter) until year-end.

Despite the poor showing of the current account, the balance of the current capital and financial account in 1997 stayed in the black, at $19.5 billion, or 4.2% of GDP, pulling the total balance of payments into surplus. The 1997 financial account surplus was, however, created by the influx of foreign portfolio investments showing up in the balance of payments,[3] the balance for the remaining items

---

3. In 1993, nonresidents' Russian assets increased only slightly faster than Russia's foreign assets, the latter being smaller than the former in 1994. In 1995, residents' foreign portfolio investments rose faster than nonresidents' investments in Russia as well. This trend reversed in 1996, however: whereas foreign portfolio investments in Russia were equal to 0.03% of GDP all through 1995, versus 0.42% of GDP for Russian foreign investments, the former grew to 2.21% of GDP in 1996, while the latter slid to 0.04% of GDP. The year 1997 could be considered the time of greatest influx of foreign portfolio investments into Russia: at year-end, the difference between the growth of nonresidents' Russian assets and residents' foreign assets topped $46 billion, or 10.02% of GDP, with foreign investments pouring into Russia registering at 10.06% of GDP. In all, foreign portfolio assets in Russia increased to $56.4 billion (4.4% of GDP) over the three years, leaving the Russian portfolio assets abroad far behind, at $1.9 billion (0.15% of GDP).

of the capital and financial account swinging over the year between faded red and grayish black. In the third and fourth quarters of 1998 the capital and financial account negative balance (excluding operations of the government sector) was $16 billion, due to decreasing Russian assets abroad and nonresidents' assets in Russia, which resulted in a deficit in the annual balance of payments. This deficit was financed at the expense of diminishing gold and foreign exchange reserves, increasing overdue repayment of debts, and a new IMF loan (in the third quarter of 1998).

The poor showing of the financial balance of payments account in 1997 was precipitated by the restructuring of Russia's liabilities for the debts of the former USSR to the members of the London Club by a bond issue to cover the principal ($22.1 billion) and interest arrears ($6.1 billion). The restructuring was shown in the balance of payments as a reduction of the debt owed by the public sector on contracted loans (reduction of debt arrears) and a corresponding increase in the debt on nonresidents' portfolio investments (as a result of securities issue). In order to arrive at balance of payments accounts giving a true picture for the fourth quarter of 1997, we adjusted the "portfolio investment" account and the "general government liabilities" account of the Russian balance of payments by reducing residents' liabilities on portfolio investments by the amount of restructured debt and simultaneously increasing general government liabilities (Figure 11.3).

An analysis of Russia's 1997 adjusted balance of payments shows a significant reduction in the balance of the portfolio investment account in the fourth quarter to $906 million (0.72% of GDP) and in the total net balance of payments to $9.9 billion (7.9% of GDP). The movement of foreign portfolio investments reached a critical turnaround point in the fall of 1997. Alongside the sudden collapse of Russian export prices, this factor set off, in late 1997 and the first six months of 1998, a catastrophic swell in the balance of payments deficit, which was held under control by infusions of the central bank's diminishing external reserves.

In the last quarter of 1997, the central bank's gold and foreign exchange reserves dropped by a further $5.9 billion. Even worse, in the second quarter of 1998 Russia posted a trade balance deficit, its first since late 1993, which spread to the nonfactor services as well (at over $300 million); the current account deficit continued to run up (reaching well above $4 billion); and foreign debt servicing costs

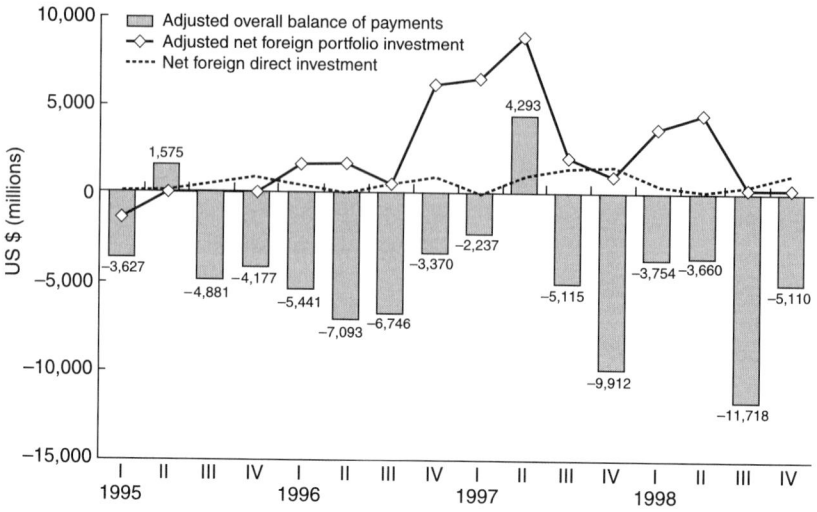

Figure 11.3
Adjusted balance of investment accounts in RF balance of payments and overall balance, 1995–1998. (Source: RF Central Bank. Estimates by the authors.)

were steadily increasing (net capital services passed the $4 billion mark). The situation took a U-turn in the third quarter of 1998, when the growing trade balance pulled up the current account balance at the cost of an insignificant decrease in capital gains. The default on GKO-OFZ debt falling actually on the last month of the quarter and the huge securities payoffs in July and August helped maintain the net gains deficit at a high level.

The net capital and financial account remained in the black through the three quarters of 1998, dipping slightly, to $2.9 billion, in the third quarter. An analysis of third-quarter financial account figures shows that the most shattering changes occurred in the portfolio and other investment accounts. In particular, foreign portfolio assets in Russia shrank by $726 million over this period, a striking contrast to the quarterly growth of foreign portfolio investments by a margin of between $2 billion and $8 billion in the preceding periods.

Among the unfavorable changes in the financial account figures for July to September 1998, the deepest imprint was left by the growth of Russian foreign assets and the dwindling of foreign liabilities, in particular the boom in residents' current accounts and deposits abroad ($83 million), the draining of nonresidents' Russian deposits and current accounts ($1.48 billion), the swelling of Russian export credits and the drying up export revenues ($4.2 billion), the bloating of residents' foreign exchange holdings ($1 billion), and even the flight of loans from the banking sector ($3.25 billion).

In the last quarter of 1998 the financial account deficit surged to $6.7 billion. This development was caused chiefly by growing rates of capital outflow in various forms: residents' current account and deposit balances increased by $1.14 billion, outstanding debt in terms of delayed export revenues and nonrepaid import advance payments grew by $2 billion, trade credits and advance payments reached $4.4. billion, while the balance of loans across all economic sectors was negative at $2.9 billion. Despite outstanding debts at $2.5 billion, the size of capital outflow caused a large deficit in the total financial account.

Whereas in the spring and early summer of 1998 the current balance of payments deficit was contained by attracting foreign portfolio investments and IMF loans and by a run on the central bank's gold and foreign exchange reserves, by August 1998 the foreign exchange reserves as a source of deficit financing had been cleaned out (from July 1997 through August 1998, the central bank's gold and foreign exchange reserves had been left $12 billion short). The crisis shut off all avenues for a continued inflow of portfolio investment, while the first IMF tranche had been spent in record time to support the ruble exchange rate.

Under these conditions, the balance of payments deficit in the third quarter of 1998 was financed from two sources: an IMF loan ($4.8 billion) and, until 25 August, forays into the foreign exchange reserves (the third quarter claimed $2.3 billion in foreign exchange reserves). With the reserves dried up, the only way to maintain a balance of payments equilibrium was to devalue the national currency, which was done on 17 August, followed soon by a contraction of imports.

According to central bank data for 1998, the current account active balance was $1.6 billion, while the trade balance showed a net gain of $16.9 billion, down from $3.56 billion and $17.5 billion, respectively, in 1997. In respect to the balance of payments capital account, the 1998 bottom line showed the net influx of capital into the Russian Federation as $17.8 billion, including a net capital drain of $6.5 billion from the banking sector and an inflow of $7.1 billion into the private corporate sector (in 1997, the corresponding figures were $44.1 billion, $8.9 billion, and $13.5 billion, respectively).

Yet the Russian balance of payments at year-end 1998 raised a question about the sources for repaying the external debt principal and interests due in 1999 as well as how to pay off the third tranche of the external debt on foreign currency–denominated bonds, the OVVZs (a total of about $18 billion, including $9.2 billion owed by Russia proper). Apparently, given the mix of the above factors (the growing current account deficit, contraction of the central bank's gold and foreign exchange reserves, the gloomy outlook for loans from international financial organizations or for any other investment), this amount would not be paid off. The only option still left open to the external debt managers in 1999 was to seek a further restructuring of Russia's foreign debt.

11.2.3. *Vulnerability of the Banking System*

As the dollar raced ahead in 1992–1994, foreign currency–denominated loans predominated in the structure of commercial banks' assets. The rapid devaluation of ruble-denominated liabilities allowed them to be used to finance even those projects that were inefficient in foreign exchange terms. The situation changed once the ruble had plateaued: the high real interest rate on ruble-denominated liabilities required a more efficient commitment of assets. Between 1995 and 1996, therefore, commercial banks built up their foreign exchange liabilities. In the first quarter of 1997, these liabilities outweighed banks' foreign exchange assets (Figure 11.4).

Moreover, at the close of the first quarter of 1998, the foreign exchange liabilities of commercial banks had more than doubled, from $9.5 billion to $19.2 billion, reaching $20.5 billion on 1 July 1998. This jump was a consequence of the precipitous growth in contracted loans against relatively sedate current foreign exchange accounts and deposits (Figure 11.5).

Foreign exchange assets had expanded to about $12.1 billion during that period, primarily as a result of expanded lending (Figure 11.6). This structure of the banking system balance (apart from its financial weakness, induced by the government's protectionism toward most major banks) was the obvious reason for its extreme vulnerability to national currency devaluation. Furthermore, massive foreign loans were collateralized by securities, which plunged in price as the financial crisis raged, requiring extra funds to beef up the deposit accounts and kicking off a banking crisis.

The Crisis of the Russian Financial System

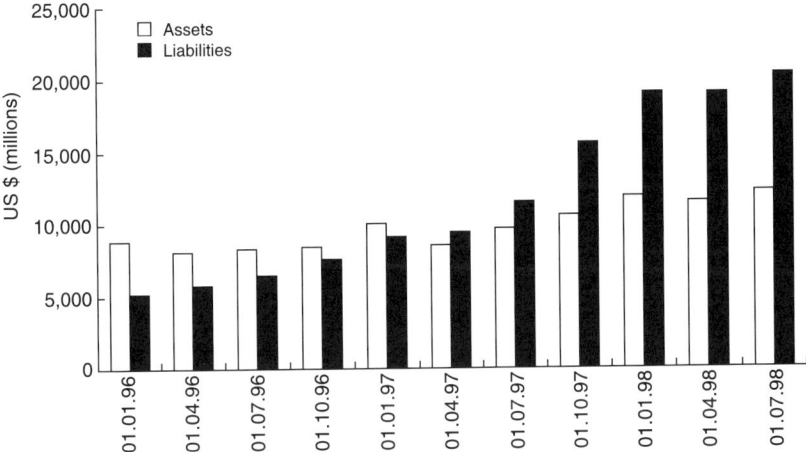

Figure 11.4
Dynamics of foreign exchange assets and liabilities of commercial banks, 1996–1998. (Source: RF Central Bank.)

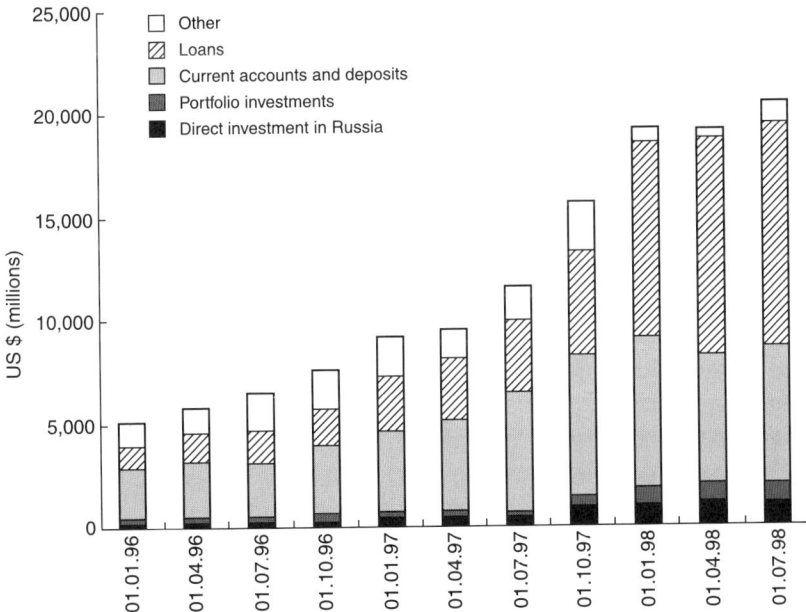

Figure 11.5
Foreign exchange liabilities of commercial banks, 1996–1998. (Source: RF Central Bank.)

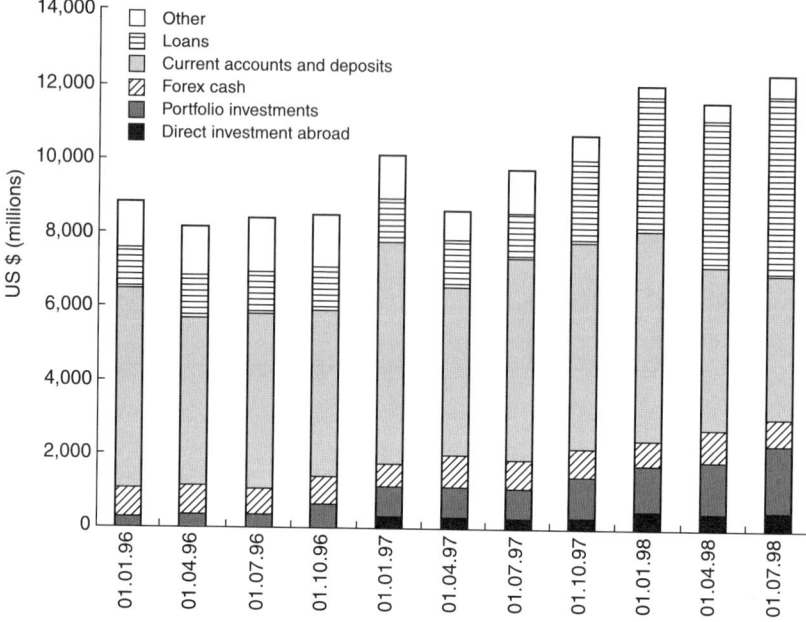

Figure 11.6
Foreign exchange assets of commercial banks, 1996–1998. (Source: RF Central Bank.)

11.3. The Economic and Political Fallout of the Financial Crisis

The financial crisis in Russia, which peaked in August 1998, had the following major economic implications:

• Foreign and domestic investors' confidence in the government, the central bank, and the Russian Finance Ministry was shaken, robbing the government of credibility in the eyes of both foreign and domestic lenders, bringing about an exodus of foreign investments, and dimming the prospects for economic growth.

• With both foreign and domestic sources of financing the fiscal deficit choked off, the country faced the prospect of inflationary budgeting and a return to the old practice of the Russian government being fed out of the central bank's hand—a threat that remains today. Moreover, this recidivism would spur money supply growth rates and, inevitably, consumer price growth, and would sap the strength of the monetary policy.

- The crisis in the domestic banking sector, due both to financial market losses[4] and to the shutdown of the GKO-OFZ market as the principal source of revenues (and the interrelated financial roots), would worsen the crisis of arrears.
- The meltdown of the Russian stock market, which reflected the demise of portfolio investment in the Russian corporate sector (the RTS-1 index fell by 90% between early October 1997[5] and early September 1998), would further undercut Russian manufacturers' chances of attracting funds.
- Expectations of a rebound in the oil and gas industry and in other export-oriented sectors of the economy, thanks to a twist in the ratio of ruble-denominated costs to foreign currency–denominated revenue, may fail to materialize, as the government, squeezed as it continues to be by a budgetary crisis, may be tempted to scoop up surpluses from the sector, either by hitting it with more taxes or by wringing the long-overdue budget arrears out of it. In much the same way, far from all domestic producers can increase production of import-substituting output and so avail themselves of the long fall of the real ruble rate and the consequent decline in the competitiveness of imports. The outlook hangs on the rate of the forthcoming inflation as well.

The sociopolitical aftermath of the 17 August devaluation is too much in evidence to warrant detailed comments here. Its more prominent aspects are as follows:

First, the explosion in inflation intensified social discontent. The worst-hit segments of the population were those that had supported the existing socioeconomic and political system—the new middle class (the employees of the fast-growing service industry), small businesses, and residents of large cities in general.

Second, the President's political standing was critically damaged. By insisting on Kiriyenko's approval as prime minister, Yeltsin actually took the blame for the performance of the new cabinet. The devaluation and default dealt a heavy blow to the President, while the dismissal of the cabinet and the merging of the political crisis with

---

4. At the time of the default, the Russian banks (minus Sberbank) had about 40 billion rubles in GKO-OFZ bonds among their assets. According to various estimates, the losses incurred by Russian banks, which hedged foreign investors' exchange risks, as a result of the ruble's meltdown ranged between $15 billion and $22 billion.
5. The RTS-1 index reached an all-time high of 571.66 on 6 October 1997.

the financial meltdown further dented public confidence in Yeltsin and reinforced the political positions of those who had been calling for a change in the constitutional system and the election of a new president. In all fairness, these developments strengthened the hand of the legislature. Finally, the appointment of Yevgeny Primakov, with solid Duma backing, to lead the cabinet made the new prime minister a powerful and legitimate political player.

Third, there was a conspicuous jockeying for power and shifting of influence wielded by different interest groups. Above all, the political clout of the "oligarchs," particularly those with ties to the banking and energy business, was severely curtailed by the virtual bankruptcy of many large banks and the erosion of the financial might of the energy exporters. The military-industrial complex regained political weight, but at the moment uncertainties remain about the relationships between its export-oriented industries and noncompetitive partners. The chances of the agrarian lobby were improved by the situation.

11.3.1. The Crisis: Economic and Political Alternatives

The cataclysmic economic and political changes in August and September 1998 wrote a new page in Russia's recent history. The current definitions of the developments that followed are largely similar—they spelled the end of the Yeltsin era, an era of liberal reforms, and even forewarned of the restoration of communist rule. All of the definitions have their reasons and can be logically or historically motivated. All these interpretations, most of them rooted in political science thought, are generally divorced from an analysis of economic processes (which always and everywhere, and particularly in the current Russian context, set the mold for the possible and the necessary); guide to a large extent the government's hand; and offer a yardstick with which to gauge the decisions taken and a crystal ball to peer into the medium term.

The Primakov government formed in September 1998 was very clear about its intention to veer decisively off the economic course the country had been steering. No executive had made similar statements, at least since late 1992. And now, in September 1998, a change in tack was discussed in public. What else could be expected under the circumstances?

First, the Primakov government was formed with the active support and close involvement of the left political forces and their respective political factions—the Communists and Agrarians, in the first place. Although Communists and Agrarians were a frequent sight in the previous governments, they had minor roles. The situation changed with the advent of the Primakov cabinet. The familiar leftist heavyweights were awarded key cabinet positions, from where they could pull major strings. Most of them wore two hats—membership in or affinity with the Communist Party, and affiliation with the traditional Soviet economic establishment, which has been a strong lobbying force in the last few decades. Unlike the left and right in most West European countries, which actually converge on common grounds, the leftist views on economics and politics in present-day Russia differ cardinally from the conceptions and backgrounds of noncommunist politicians.

Second, the need for a resolute change of course was dictated by the scale and depth of the economic crisis. The meltdown in August 1998 was not just a financial collapse; there was a disastrous domino effect on the country's social and political fabric. The price spike and the loss of savings by the population, the spiraling unemployment figures (especially among the population groups with the greatest stakes in the market economy), the consumer market crisis, contraction of demand, and deterioration of the business environment were seemingly sprung upon the country without warning. Everybody was demanding "change," even though different sociopolitical forces assigned different meanings to this term.

For all the turmoil, no one bothers to answer the question: How is the change to occur, and what will the current policy be abandoned for? It is not difficult to work out that the real options open to the government are scarce and obvious enough. They logically flow from the hands-on experience in economic politicking in the post-communist period, particularly from 1995 through 1998.

To return to our subject, the Primakov government was from the outset confronted with a tough political choice, one it could not skirt or reduce to a compromise between alternatives. One alternative was a return to the practices of 1992–1994, which combined a soft monetary policy and an equally soft budgetary policy. Another was to hang on to a rigid monetary policy and work toward exchange-rate stabilization, with radical budgetary reforms added for good measure, so that Treasury revenues and expenditures could be put in balance—in other words, to seek compatibility and coordination between the Finance Ministry and the central bank. The choice between these two alternatives had an unmistakably political character.

The first alternative clearly leans toward inflation. The money supply in the economy is built up, sparking price hikes and devaluation of the national currency. The trick is expected to dispose of the heaping social problems, wipe out stagnant arrears, flush businesses with working capital, and jack up demand for domestically produced consumables, giving a boost to domestic consumer industries. This scenario was acted out in Russia in 1992–1994, when a spell of short-lived stabilization of production (which held for two or three months) was followed by a spurt of inflation and a tumbling ruble. Given the stronger Communist pull on the government, the most likely response to the price scramble would have been attempts to freeze prices and introduce a mandatory dollar exchange rate. These attempts would have had fully predictable consequences: a booming black market and snowballing commodity shortages. Given our current circumstances, however, prices would wriggle out of effective control, so we would end up with both inflation and consumer shortages.

The second alternative aims at stabilization (keeping a lid on inflation). It seeks to achieve a rigid budget equilibrium and macroeconomic stabilization, which are the foundation of economic recovery. These aims are to be attained by determined measures to push the government budget into surplus, pursue a restrictive monetary policy (even introducing the currency board regime, if necessary), and continue measured economic liberalization. The structural and budgetary reform next in the pipeline are to brace up businesses for competition and readiness to find a market niche.

Both alternatives were made public literally within days to weeks following the outbreak of the full-scale financial crisis in mid-August. Most of the Economics Division staff of the Russian Academy of Sciences (RAS), led by D. Lvov, were consistently pushing for inflationary and *dirigiste* government policies, giving full voice to their preferences in a published open letter to the government, which spelled out their views and proposals. On the other extreme, a policy of rigid stabilization was formulated in a program put forward by liberal economists rallied around Yegor Gaidar.

The choice between inflationism and a rigid stabilization policy is largely a political one. At the time, the choice of policy was not the government's alone to make, nor did it depend on the government's ideological, political, and social preferences alone; it was also influenced by the logic of events and prevailing circumstances. In particular, as domestic and outside finance sources disappeared with the resignation of the Kiriyenko government, the country was being nudged toward the inflationary option. This option had not, however, been made inevitable by the previous developments; it had to be written by the government on a clean slate.

The chief political problem of choosing between the inflationary and stabilization alternatives was picking the social segments and groups who were to pay most for whichever economic policy the government opted for. The two alternatives differed essentially in social context and payoffs.

An inflationary option benefits the banks above all. Russia's banking sector owes its affluence to the 1992–1994 inflation, and now that many banks are floundering they can be thrown a life belt by the central bank in the form of cheap loans, "cheap money." It would knock down enterprises that have jumped on the market bandwagon, whether exporters or producers of manufactures competitive on the domestic market. The lack of monetary stability erodes their operating base and holds back their investment plans and growth prospects.

Inflation is at its worst in large cities and industrial centers, chiefly because it hurts local enterprises, which have adapted to the market environment. Second, the urban population (particularly the residents of Moscow) depends more heavily on stable commodity flows than rural residents or inhabitants of small towns. As money depreciates, provisions cease flowing from farming regions, which tends to impose restrictions on supplies going out, while foreign imports thin to a trickle. By contrast, people in the hinterlands, in some ways maintaining their links to farming, can more easily adapt to ups and downs in the food supply. The aftermath of 17 August is a vivid demonstration of the vulnerability of large cities (primarily Moscow) to prices running amok and commodity flows thrown into disarray.

The situation is different under a rigid monetary policy scenario. It closely integrates efforts to speed the structural reorganization of Russia's economy and allows inefficient businesses—both manufacturers and bankers—to go bankrupt or change hands. This policy endeavors to retain the country's vibrant ties with world goods and capital markets, encourage competition, and restrict government intervention in the economy.

Understandably, this policy benefits efficient businesses and large cities. With exchange rates holding steady, businesses are afforded favorable opportunities to implement investment programs. City dwellers, in their turn, are offered a wider choice of jobs or enterprise. The numerous labor market options ease the pain of unemployment, the inevitable companion of economic restructuring, for urban agglomerations. Banks and inefficient businesses, however, are confronted by the stark choice of reorganization, not infrequently a very painful surgery. Unemployment is poised to deliver its blow, which would fall more heavily on the hinterlands, where job opportunities are much more limited than in large cities.

The two options share some common and politically unpleasant, yet practically inescapable, consequences. In both options the government's commitments, including social covenants, are reduced. Under a tight financial policy this occurs directly, with budget expenditures cut to the size of budget revenues. Inflation produces the same result, causing a devaluation of budget expenditures. Both options are painful, with the second one being unjust to boot, as rising prices hit the poorest segments of the population first.

11.3.2. *Development of an Economic Program*

The Primakov government was not politically neutral from the outset, nor did it make a clean choice between the two economic policy alternatives. As it was hammered together, the government was expected to opt for inflationism and populism, the likelihood of which was suggested by the dominating presence of proxies of the Agrarian and Communist forces in the cabinet and countless statements from politicians and economists supporting the government. The premier promised to pay off arrears to public sector employees and pensioners within months, if not weeks; cut the knot of inter-enterprise arrears; stabilize the ruble; and clean up the national house in general. Utterances about the need to begin a measured and controlled money issue, nationalize selected sectors of the economy, and introduce a mandatory exchange rate, if not ban foreign exchange possession, and much in the same vein could be heard almost daily from, among other big guns, high-ranking politicians.

The inflation option certainly had firm roots that could not easily be explained by the leftist (Communist) face of the new cabinet. The vast fiscal deficit and the conspicuous absence of external sources to reduce it nudged the government forcefully toward the printing press. Of course, another alternative was to sharply reduce government spending, but that alternative was unacceptable to the government for political reasons, at least in the short term.

The printing press overtures were bolstered by ungainly institutionalist ideas that also raised serious apprehensions about the authenticity of the interpretation which the emerging cabinet was putting on the situation in the country and the possible moves by the authorities.[6]

Had the new government acted exactly as it was expected to, it would not be difficult to guess what would have come next. Actually, the model peddled to the government by advisers from the Duma and the Academy of Sciences was nothing new, having been tested in the decades following World War II in dozens of countries, with the most spectacular results registered in Latin America. The model is called the "economics of populism" in specialist literature and is well known to every economist.[7]

---

6. Typical in this respect were the suggestions made by Gennady Seleznyov, the Duma's chairman, regarding economic policy measures that ostensibly had to be put into effect literally within days. These ideas—actually, planks of a program—were proposed almost immediately after Primakov's appointment. Seleznyov, the Duma chairman, threw his full weight behind the appointee: "It is important to suspend the operations of the currency exchange and have the central bank issue a directive fixing the ruble exchange rate to the dollar at a ratio of seven to one.... Talks are to be held with financial interests in the West with a request to suspend the use of plastic forex credit cards to prevent the flight of foreign exchange out of the country.... A temporary ban is to be imposed on currency exchange offices to sell forex to the population. All they are to do is buy dollars.... The foreign exchange in the hands of commercial banks is to be used exclusively to purchase foodstuffs, daily necessities, and medicines" (quoted in *Kommersant*, 11 September 1998, p. 2). Add to this proposals from the new government's brass to denationalize the loss-making enterprises of the military-industrial complex, which were hardly consistent with the simple logic of government action in the heat of the financial crisis. (Significantly, these ideas of the cabinet's doctrine implied nationalization of loss-making sluggards rather than prosperous export-oriented dynamos.)

7. In practice, the economic policy of populism has four stages. These stages recur from country to country, with slight differences due to local conditions. In the first stage, the government tries to speed up industrial growth by pumping funds from export-oriented industries into "national pride" industries (commonly engineering) and simultaneously expanding the money supply. The economy picks up in response to these measures, and public well-being begins to improve. The government appears to be scoring major points, with the country poised to become yet another "economic miracle." The government's popularity rises.

In the second stage, the economy begins to show signs of getting out of balance. It turns out that the growing production and improving standards of living are accompanied by a worsening in some macroeconomic factors: the trade and balance of payments deficits increase, foreign exchange reserves contract, and foreign debt swells. For a time, these adverse developments are apparent only to professional economists

Faced with stark reality, the Primakov government stepped more cautiously than was expected. The fact that such expectations had been associated with it at all could hardly go unnoticed or put the cabinet in a more difficult position. Indeed, the inflation apprehensions could prove to be a self-fulfilling prognosis, infecting the moods and behavior of the business community. Moreover, these apprehensions had a firm grounding, and were an integral part of the draft schemes pondered by the government as it sat down to draw up its economic program.

The Primakov cabinet's program-making efforts and the premier's own economic ideas have undergone significant modification in the time the cabinet has been in office. Initially, its policy documents were shot with undisguised inflationist and *dirigiste* ideas—extremely to the point, as long you could call a spade a spade and talking about money printing did not make you blush. The documents issued later were swamped with technicalities and fine specifics, with no room left deliberately for money issue or fiscal deficit.

The government started out with the ideas supplied by the Economics Division of the RAS. The no-nonsense approach to the program is evidenced by the fact that its authors were among in the government's first group set up to develop its economic program and that the vice-premier sought regular counsel from the titled academics as group members for about a month after the birth of the new cabinet.

The program inspired by the academics espoused the most consistent and rigid (if not extremist) breed of ideas about populism, inflationism, and *dirigisme* imaginable. In form, it was a fairly integral and harmonious system of measures that could easily be formalized in legislation. According to the program fathers, the crisis

---

(and only to some of them, given the country's protracted detachment from real market economics). The budget is sputtering, but no attention is given to these "trifles" as long as manufacturing continues to chug along.

Well into the third stage, commodity shortages have built up in the public sector, and free prices are inflating. Attempts to rein in prices make commodity shortages even worse, and the inevitable devaluation of the national currency explodes into violent inflation. Tax collection slips, and the budget collapses. Whatever the government is doing, living standards begin to drop, and production falls off.

In the fourth stage, the government falls, and new authorities (not infrequently military or emergency powers) adopt radical measures to calm the socioeconomic turmoil (see R. Dornbusch and S. Edwards, eds., *The Macroeconomics of Populism in Latin America* (Chicago: University of Chicago Press, 1991), 7–13).

was wholly rooted in the economic policy pursued since late 1991, first and foremost in the liberalism of the economic policy, failure to make the best use of the government's broad administrative powers, and exaggeration of the role of macroeconomic regulation in comparison with institutional reforms. Two closely affiliated ideas—jacking up consumer demand and getting the idling industries to work again—formed the mainstay of the constructive planks of the program.

The program advocated considerable cash injections to resolve social problems, stimulate demand as a way to end the slump, expand the payment system, and get the banking crisis under control. It even suggested "automatically" activating the printing press to avoid arrears (of any kind, not just the shortfall in budget revenues) in the future. It viewed the printing press, therefore, as a cure-all for the country's myriad economic problems. It also called for rigid monetary controls, including suppression of the population's yen for foreign exchange.

As soon as it was out, the program was heartily flogged by the public, not so much for its theoretical opportunism (manifest inflationism) as for its glaring detachment from the real economic processes of the day. Many of the measures it marshaled opened the way for abuse of unprecedented scope on the part of both government agencies (through allocation of easy loans) and businesses. The idea of feeding loans to businesses that were developing arrears implied that virtually any entrepreneur could glut himself on "easy money." The blanket guarantee for the population's deposits could lead the banker to lure funds at fantastic interest rates—and file for bankruptcy. Examples of this kind abound.

By early October the government had prepared its own economic program. Deprived of official endorsement, the document outraged the public, including the mass media, which compelled Primakov to disown it. The program merits close scrutiny, though, for unlike its later modifications, it was streamlined and specific.

In form and substance, it was a sibling of the academics' program. It, too, relied heavily on the printing press to heal economic and social problems in record time and advocated more obtrusive government intervention in the economy, including proscription of the dollar for hoarding and saving purposes. It also projected sweeping government regulation of prices and tariffs ("on the output of core manufacturing industries, food and non-food necessities," and so on), protectionism, and government tutelage for import-substituting industries.

All is not old wine in new bottles, though. As a very practical document, the program named agencies responsible for putting the plans into effect. Unlike the academic version, it nearly missed the central bank among the "responsible agents," loading the full burden of responsibility for jacking up demand on the Finance Ministry. The document loses the virgin innocence of the academic program.

The cabinet bosses were clearly frightened by their own inflationist moods and the general anticipations of inflation. The central bank, too, was dragging its feet over the money issue. It had learned its lessons well, and its realization of a direct link between money issue and inflation was vivid enough to immediately translate talk about the bracing effect of more money sloshing around into printing press activation. The central bank chief himself was evidently loath to assume responsibility for fueling a wild inflation and was pressuring the Duma into taking legislative action on the monetary policy.

By downsizing its profile on the money issue, the government was plainly trying to exploit its administrative powers. The ideas of tough exchange controls are set in bold type here. As the program appeared unofficially in the press, Eduard Rossel came out in favor of banning the use of the dollar in Russia, a proposal that, he claimed, had the backing of Yeltsin. Much is to be read into this coincidence, although it was hardly deliberate. The simple reason is that these moods were at the time pervasive among the segment of the political elite most closely tied to the government. Faith in the central bank, exchange controls, and other forms of government intervention was coming on the heels of worries about unrestrained inflationism—even overlapping them, it seemed.

Not surprisingly, a strong government is among the most popular catchphrases today. Its zealots, however, are habitually wrong in tracing the reasons for weak government in postcommunist Russia. It is held that weak government is a by-product of the liberal ideology that sought to put the government beyond the economic framework, depriving the country of an effective tool to implement the economic policy and correct "market failure." To restore the nation's economic and political might, in this view, it becomes necessary to brand the previous doctrine a mistake and to start working to consolidate the government, and particularly to allow it to expand its influence on the country's economy.

The reality is at great odds with this perception of the situation. The weak government in postcommunist Russia cannot be blamed on liberalism, for the liberal ideology upholds a strong government acting within the rigid confines of the law. It is precisely the absence of such a government that stands in the way of a liberal economic policy. The weak government that is the hallmark of present-day Russia was brought about by the array of forces at work in its brief postcommunist history. The first sign of weak government is inability to collect taxes or to place merciless budgetary constraints on businesses. Another sign of weak government is crime—corruption in the civil service, on the one hand, and the omnipresence of powerful criminal cartels usurping many government functions (arbitration, contract enforcement, protection of property) on the other. Greater intervention by government officials in the economy under these conditions would further corruption and bureaucratic abuse rather than facilitate a stronger government.

Beginning in late October 1998, the program grew even more moderate and less specific. More precisely, it absorbed a host of unrelated plans in the social and manufacturing spheres, tax policy, and interbudgetary relations. Just as before, however, it was reluctant to give any solid substance or specifics to the economic policy. Analysts poking around for the reasons of the crisis were now talking less about the fallacious policy of yesteryear and more about the implications of the budgetary crisis and ways to pull out of it. Maslyukov, unbelievably, went on record (in a statement to the delegates of the Davos Forum meeting in Moscow on 4 December) as saying that the new government was going to accomplish what its predecessors wanted but were unable to accomplish.

The core idea suddenly vanished from the program. Hopes no longer rested on money issue. Rather, the revised program exuded a realization of the dangers haunting an economy awash in banknotes, as is evidenced by the recognition of "the critical gap between the necessity of a larger money supply and the possibility of inflation-free currency printing" and the acknowledgment of "the danger of hyperinflation." Hopes for strong and wise government have eventually been reduced to a ritualistic chant about the need to "fortify the nationhood concept as a major source of improved economic performance." Ultimately the program was renamed, on the premier's cue, with the elusive title *Apropos of Measures, etc.*, as though to emphasize that the measures it contained had a loose relation, or none, to one another.

The microeconomic growth concept built into all of the programs surveyed here was a very specific thing. In the first place, it gave negligible attention to the protection of private property, which was accorded only scant attention in most of the documents. "Privatization" did not merit attention at all. Here was a government that tended to parade its preference for direct over portfolio investments.

It would be unfair to reduce the government's program-mongering to a hodgepodge of finished or draft program products. Another two documents, the tax reform conception and the draft 1999 federal budget, certainly played a bona fide program-setting role. They warrant a brief summary, which comes a few paragraphs below.

The bottom line at the end of 1998 was that the government had, after months of program-mongering and pondering the problems confronting the country and ways to resolve them, backed itself into a corner. It had recognized the perils of prescriptions borrowed from the cookbooks of the "economic policy of populism," yet it had failed to come up with a worthy replacement for the initial (populist, printing press-reliant) action program. The cabinet was reluctant, and the premier lacked the will, to accept the unpalatable fact that only two alternatives—rigid inflationism or rigid stabilization—were open to them, and that they had to accept one or the other.

The unwillingness to clinch the choice drove Primakov to opt for evading critical decisions, putting them off until a "better time." The political mandate conferred on the premier and the backing he received from the lawmakers and a large segment of the public justified his tactic. Accelerating economic processes left him increasingly less room for maneuvering. The government's practical moves, no matter how earthly and ideologically barren, were not politically neutral by any measure, and were pushing the government to the edge of the cliff, where it was to take the plunge.

11.3.3. *Practical Economic Policy in Outline*

The Primakov government's day-to-day policy consisted of practical moves in economics and a stream of enactments churned out by the government. Accordingly, the cabinet members in their assorted actions can be divided into two groups. One group gathers measures, hand-me-downs from the Soviet economic establishment, to strike a compromise between the leading Soviet-era interest groups, the Agrarian and engineering lobbies. The other group unites in moves to dismantle the brickwork put up by the preceding cabinets, particularly the Kiriyenko government, mostly in respect to taxes and budget management, and attempts to steer financial flows. The government rescinded legislation that ran against the policy of balancing the main lobbies against one another and embraced whichever side did them a favor. The powerful lobbies were coddled by the endorsement of previous cabinet decisions to cut taxes, allow output to be sold below cost, and a series of other steps that were portrayed as measures to support the real economic sector.

11.3.4. Budgetary Policy

An analysis of the Primakov government's budgetary policy spotlights two essentially different approaches, and therefore two different groups of decisions, that had entirely different effects on prospects for the country's economic development. The first approach entailed decisions that eroded the revenue base of the budget, above all those affecting the tax policy. The second approach advocated preparation of the 1999 budget based on the principle of minimum money issue to finance the deficit. The conflict between these two approaches was largely explained by the evolution of the cabinet's macroeconomic views from inflationism, in September and October, to a recognition of the need for a more rigorous budgetary policy, in November and December. The conflict has a self-evident, practical basis—the cabinet's desire, and the premier's private yearning, to avoid awkward moves and to secure, as a reward, the maximum possible political backing for their decisions, however unpopular.

The government's decisions and actions, therefore, fell into two groups, and accordingly into two phases, in actual practice. The first phase was marked by the populist decisions of the first three months. The second phase was the preparation of a cautious budget for 1999, the publication and adoption of which proved to be a stand-alone factor in the evolution of the economic situation.

The budgetary policy decisions that rolled out in October through December hit federal revenues first. Revenues were dissipating for three principal reasons. First, the budgetary take was undercut by government decision. Second, warning signals had been sounded about the government's intentions, which dampened businesses' enthusiasm for paying taxes. And third, decisions were made to lop off the tax base of the federal budget. The first two reasons for falling revenues were most in evidence during the first few months of the Primakov government. The third reason, a change in the tax base, took more time to make its force felt, as the government had to seek legislative approval of its decisions.

In its early months, the Primakov government made a series of unorthodox decisions that exposed it to the lobbying crowd and showed its readiness to sacrifice federal revenues to please some interests. Typically, most of the government's moves were aimed at rewriting the decisions of previous governments, which had discovered from their own experience the efficiency of netting-out operations, custom-made tax payment schemes, indulging the financial carelessness of big businesses, and so on.

In its search for political support, the government went so far as to sign separate covenants with giant taxpayers over when and how they were going to meet their obligations to the budget. The first covenant was signed with Gazprom and was followed by a declaration of intent to continue this practice. Moreover, according to Federal Tax Service officials, Gazprom was allowed to tie its tax payments to the arrears due to that gas giant from public sector entities.

Simultaneously, decisions were taken to permit wholesale set-offs among enterprises and budgets at all levels, quite in the spirit of the Primakov cabinet's program products. The experience of 1996 and 1997 conclusively showed that the mere mention of legitimacy being given to netting-out operations provoked a steep reduction in government revenues. Revenue denting was fated to happen when the government, notorious for its kid-glove, magnanimous attitude toward real sector businesses, regardless of their financial standing, opted for set-offs.

Significantly, as the government gave the green light to set-offs, it abandoned vigorous efforts to take persistent tax dodgers to court. Summary bankruptcy proceedings were, in effect, outlawed. The annulment of the bankruptcy proceedings against UralAZ (with Maslyukov as the power behind it) was little less than a potent signal to other tax evaders. Frequent statements about the government's intention of announcing a tax amnesty worked to the same end. The government's readiness to collect some taxes in kind further widened the revenue drain hole.

Taking the ax to the tax tree, the government chopped down the ruling for the VAT to be paid on an accruals basis and reverted to the voluminous catalogue of goods slapped with a VAT at a rate of 10%. Although deeper changes in the tax system were tied to budget approval for 1999, the deliberations on the proposed tax relaxation that started in the fall of 1998 were an early signal that, for the lawmakers, keeping businesses busy was more important than collecting taxes, even if that meant collecting fewer taxes.

In an effort to stabilize the ruble, on 11 September the central bank directed a return to the previous requirement for exporters to sell 50% of their foreign exchange proceeds on the home market. This measure yielded a beneficial result in the short run. Over the longer term, it created an irresistible lure to understate the foreign exchange earnings remittable to Russia.

The government's decisions on agribusiness and food provision for the nation were contradictory in essence, yet equally damaging to the budget. Ostensibly, these steps were aimed at easing the situation of farmers and farm produce–processing industries. In the good old communist tradition of four decades' standing, the government restructured, at the cost of 5% per annum for the beneficiaries— that is, practically for nothing—the farmers' arrears to the budget. Tax dodgers took it as a hint that tax evasion would be tolerated and was economically sound, while law-abiding taxpayers had to swallow the shortfall again.

To show its liberal side, however, the government hastened to bring down the import duties that had been increased just months earlier by the Kiriyenko government, to broaden the revenue base of the federal budget. Impatient to get the official endorsement of the "action program," it reduced customs duties on a long list of foodstuffs, above all meat and dairy products. The government's haste could be attributed to the fear, which haunted Soviet-economy bosses, of food shortages (which normally arrived in the train of their economic policies), the blunting of imports' competitive edge as a result of the ruble's devaluation, the pressure brought to bear on it by the interests linked to food imports, and the difficulties of maintaining high tariffs against the rest of the customs union (particularly Belarus). From whatever point it is regarded, the decision works in a twofold way against the budget, throttling revenues and domestic producers, whose competitive positions have been undercut. Obviously, the two decision packages were not motivated by ideological considerations but were squeezed out by lobbying by interest groups with many ties to the corrupt elements in the civil service.

Among the government's other decisions—largely symbolic gestures—the most important were a move to reinstate a system of government guarantees to individual businesses[8] (coupled with an ardent request to Western governments for humanitarian food aid) and cancelation of Kiriyenko's decision to transfer the bank accounts of cultural institutions to the Treasury.

All of the decisions we have cited, and some we have not, had much in common. First, they removed most of the obstacles to continued corruption in the civil service and shadow business. Second, they were an amiable bow to the lobbies. Finally, far from reinforcing government, they undermined it, while at the same time giving more scope to bureaucratic abuse in the interests of individuals and small groups.

It was only natural to expect real budget revenues to dry up, the cash component of revenues to ebb, and therefore the nonmonetary sources available to finance spending to shrink.

The performance of the 1998 budget can tentatively be broken down into three periods—from January to March, March to September, and September to year-end (Table 11.2). The year opened with a seasonal slack in revenue flow to the federal budget and the build-up of a large deficit (4.7% of GDP in January). This alarming deficit had been caused by high federal spending, which (in particular, the "credit less repayment" section) recorded Rb 4.3 billion in revenues that had not been credited to the central bank. In February, this spending item was not present in the budget, bringing the deficit down to a sound 1.8% of GDP.

The second period, from March to September, registered a higher level of takes (an average 0.5% of GDP) than at the start of the year, and a higher rate of federal spending (around 14% of GDP). Spending increased, mostly as a result of larger allocations to service

---

8. The decision was unique. In fact, it was the first example in recent economic history of a decision to *resurrect* legislative acts buried two or three years earlier. It was not merely an economic move, but a political wink as well. Rather than saying that he was introducing government guarantees, Primakov went for an unprecedented reinstatement of repealed acts in an unabashedly demonstrative move.

government debt (about 5% of GDP). Tax receipts in this period occasionally (in May) rose to 9% of GDP.

Beginning in September, federal budget revenues sagged (to just over 10% of GDP), and spending slid further, by almost 1% of GDP. Little or no allocations were made to service government debt in this period. The healthy growth of revenues and the prodigal spending of federal money in December were precipitated by the clearance of arrears, on the one hand, and by repayment of debt to public sector dependents (target financing) on the other, as well as by so-called bottom-line evening (balancing of revenues against expenditures in the first week of January and somewhat later).

Another notable set of figures: According to Finance Ministry data, cash inflows into the federal budget in 1998 amounted to 10.2% of GDP, of which 7.7% of GDP was contributed by taxes. This compared favorably with 1997, when cash receipts were around 7.0% of GDP. To our thinking, the latest improvement in cash receipts as a percentage of GDP was in large measure due to the tough stand taken by the Kiriyenko government, which came out forcefully against irresponsible budget performance. The cash taken in to finance government spending under the budget (less target allocations) was put at approximately 90% (9.4% of GDP).

Spending was more rigidly controlled, without major fluctuations under virtually all headings registered over the year.

In general, government debt servicing (4% of GDP), defense spending (2.1% of GDP), and social spending (2.1% of GDP) were the largest expenditure items of the 1998 budget. In the social expenditure bracket, the biggest sums went to education (0.5% of GDP) and social policy (1.5% of GDP). Allocations to different industries (0.9% of GDP, with manufacturing claiming 0.4% of GDP) were the largest spending items of the remaining federal budget. In 1998, total federal budget expenditure worked out at 14.5% of GDP (18.4% of GDP in 1997), and the deficit bottomed out at 3.3% of GDP (3.9% of GDP in 1997).

With the exception of February, the federal fiscal deficit never slipped below 3.0% of GDP, registering a maximum (3.9% of GDP) in June and July. The deficit financing structure was altered at mid-year 1998, after the government renounced, in May 1998, domestic borrowing, except for refinancing domestic government debt. From mid-August domestic borrowing was abandoned fully in favor of external sources, which had come first beginning in June.

Table 11.2
Federal Budget Execution in 1998 (% of GDP)

	\multicolumn{12}{c}{1998, Month}
	I	II	III	IV	V	VI	VII	VIII	IX	X	XI	XII
REVENUE												
1. Profit tax	0.9	0.9	1.2	1.4	1.4	1.3	1.3	1.3	1.2	1.2	1.2	1.3
2. Value-added tax	4.4	4.2	4.1	4.2	4.1	4.0	4.0	3.8	3.6	3.6	3.6	4.0
3. Excises on excisable goods and selected mineral raw materials produced on RF territory	2.0	1.9	2.0	1.8	1.8	1.9	1.9	1.9	1.8	1.8	1.8	2.0
4. Taxes on foreign trade and foreign economic operations	1.0	1.1	1.2	1.2	1.4	1.4	1.3	1.3	1.2	1.2	1.2	1.4
5. Other taxes	0.2	0.4	0.3	0.3	0.3	0.3	0.3	0.3	0.4	0.3	0.4	0.2
Total Taxes and Payments	8.5	8.5	8.8	8.9	9.0	8.9	8.8	8.6	8.2	8.1	8.2	8.9
NONTAX REVENUE	1.7	1.8	1.9	1.8	1.9	1.9	1.9	2.0	2.0	1.9	1.9	2.5
TOTAL REVENUE	10.2	10.3	10.7	10.8	10.9	10.8	10.7	10.6	10.2	10.1	10.0	11.3
EXPENDITURES												
1. Government administration	0.3	0.3	0.3	0.4	0.3	0.3	0.3	0.3	0.3	0.3	0.3	0.4
2. National defense	2.0	2.0	1.9	1.9	1.8	1.9	1.8	1.7	1.8	1.8	1.9	2.1
3. International activities	0.1	−0.2	0.0	0.0	0.0	−0.1	−0.1	−0.1	−0.1	0.0	0.0	0.3
4. Justice	0.0	0.1	0.1	0.1	0.1	0.1	0.1	0.1	0.1	0.1	0.1	0.1
5. Law enforcement and security	1.1	1.2	1.2	1.2	1.2	1.1	1.1	1.1	1.0	1.0	1.0	1.2
6. Basic research and promotion of scientific and technological progress	0.2	0.2	0.3	0.3	0.2	0.2	0.2	0.2	0.2	0.2	0.2	0.2
7. Government services to the economy, of which:	0.4	0.7	0.6	0.7	0.7	0.8	0.8	0.8	0.8	0.8	0.8	0.9
8. Social services, including:	1.6	1.8	2.0	2.0	1.9	1.9	2.0	1.8	1.7	1.9	1.9	2.2
8.1. Education	0.2	0.4	0.4	0.5	0.4	0.4	0.5	0.4	0.4	0.4	0.4	0.5
8.2. Culture and arts	0.0	0.0	0.0	0.0	0.0	0.0	0.0	0.0	0.0	0.0	0.0	0.0

The Crisis of the Russian Financial System

8.3. Mass media	0.0	0.0	0.0	0.0	0.0	0.0	0.0	0.0	0.0	0.0	0.0	0.0
8.4. Health and physical fitness	0.1	0.1	0.1	0.2	0.2	0.2	0.2	0.2	0.2	0.2	0.2	0.2
8.5. Social policy	1.3	1.3	1.3	1.3	1.3	1.2	1.2	1.2	1.1	1.2	1.3	1.4
9. Government debt service	2.7	3.3	5.0	4.9	5.3	5.2	5.4	5.1	4.5	4.1	4.0	4.0
10. Financial aid to other levels of government	1.5	1.4	1.4	1.6	1.5	1.6	1.4	1.3	1.2	1.2	1.2	1.6
11. Other expenditure	0.6	1	1.1	1	1.1	1.3	1.2	1.3	1.2	1	1.2	1.1
Total Expenditures	10.5	11.8	13.9	14.1	14.1	14.3	14.2	13.6	12.7	12.4	12.6	14.3
CREDITS LESS REPAYMENTS	4.4	0.4	0.4	0.4	0.4	0.4	0.4	0.5	0.6	0.7	0.6	0.4
Total Expenditures and Credits Less Repayments	14.9	12.1	14.3	14.4	14.5	14.7	14.7	14.0	13.2	13.1	13.2	14.7
Surplus of Revenue over Expenditure and Credit Less Repayment	−4.7	−1.8	−3.5	−3.7	−3.6	−3.9	−3.9	−3.5	−3.0	−3.1	−3.2	−3.3
TOTAL FINANCING	4.7	1.8	3.5	3.7	3.6	3.9	3.9	3.5	3.0	3.1	3.2	3.3
Domestic Financing	1.2	0.1	2.5	2.7	2.6	1.0	−0.6	−0.8	−0.8	−0.6	−0.3	−0.1
1.1. Change in bank acccount balances of budget funds, in rubles	−0.3	−1.6	−0.8	−0.7	−0.5	−1.3	−0.1	−0.1	−0.6	−0.5	−0.6	−1.2
1.2. Short-term government debt	1.5	1.9	2.9	0.8	0.6	−0.5	−3.4	−3.4	−3.0	−2.6	−2.3	−2.2
1.3. Federal floating rate bonds	0.0	0.0	0.0	−0.3	−0.2	−0.3	−0.3	−0.3	−0.3	−0.2	−0.2	−0.2
1.4. Nonmarketable government bonds	−0.3	−0.4	−0.3	−0.2	0.0	0.2	0.2	0.2	0.1	0.1	0.0	0.0
1.5. Federal fixed-rate bonds	0.0	0.0	0.9	3.3	2.9	3.0	3.2	3.1	3.0	2.8	2.9	3.4
1.6. Government savings bonds	0.3	0.1	0.3	0.1	0.1	0.1	0.1	0.1	0.1	0.1	0.1	0.1
1.7. Other domestic borrowing	0.0	0.1	−0.5	−0.4	−0.3	−0.3	−0.2	−0.3	−0.3	−0.2	−0.2	−0.2
External Financing	3.5	1.7	1.0	1.0	1.0	2.9	4.5	4.3	3.9	3.6	3.5	3.4
2.1. Loans from international financial institutions	3.2	1.7	1.2	0.9	0.7	1.0	0.7	1.1	1.0	0.7	0.5	0.5
2.2. Foreign government loans to RF	0.3	0.0	−0.2	−0.2	0.0	0.0	0.1	0.1	0.1	0.2	0.0	−0.2
2.3. Loans from foreign commercial banks and companies to RF	0.0	0.0	0.0	0.3	0.3	1.9	3.6	3.1	2.7	2.8	2.9	3.2

Source: The Ministry of Taxes and Charges.

Wage arrears of the federal budget were paid in late 1998 and early 1999. According to estimates by Finance Ministry experts, they had reached Rb 13.3 billion by early December, or 5% of the November GDP. The federal budget arrears to the Pension Fund ran at 1.6% of GDP in early 1999, having grown by only 30% of this amount over 1998.

The consolidated budget performance in 1998 was, in general, similar to the execution of the federal budget, although it does not show the three periods of the latter as distinctly (Table 11.3).

An analysis of real monthly growth rates in tax arrears to the federal budget (Table 11.4) shows arrears to be steadily on the upgrade through most of 1998. Taxes due to the federal budget were in much deeper arrears than the year before: whereas they were 4% of annual GDP in 1997, the figure at year-end 1998 was as high as 6% of GDP. Tax arrears to the federal budget as a percentage of monthly GDP for 1998 are shown in Table 11.5.

A scrutiny of tax revenues at the start of 1999 shows that they had shrunk, in comparable prices, from January–February 1998, outperforming only September 1998 revenues.

Accumulated tax arrears to the consolidated budget stood at 9.6% of GDP as of 1 January 1999.

As of 1 January 1999, the domestic government debt was Rb 751 billion, which amounted to approximately 28% of GDP and was almost 8 percentage points higher than the figure recorded on 1 January 1998. The structure of the government debt also changed. Whereas in 1997 the debt on floated securities was 90% of the government debt, in 1998 this figure rose to 95%. The highest share was accounted for by GKO-OFZ arrears (62% of the debt on securities, or 17.5% of GDP) and OVVZs (32% of the debt on securities, or 8.6% of GDP) (Table 11.6). For comparison, the 1997 arrears in GKOs-OFZs were 16.8% of GDP, and the arrears in OVVZs were 2.62% of GDP.

Among the other domestic debt items, it is worth mentioning the arrears on centralized loans and accrued interest of agrobusinesses in charge of the Northern winter deliveries, which were 0.8% of GDP, or 3% of the domestic debt as of 1 January 1999 (1% of GDP, or 4.4% of the domestic debt as of 1 January 1998). The rest of the domestic debt, apart from arrears on securities and Northern deliveries, amounted to less than 3% of the overall domestic debt, or less than 1% of GDP.

During 1998, domestic debt increased by 7% of annual GDP.

11.3.5. Monetary Policy

The developments in monetary policy after August 1998 can be divided into three phases. The rapid rise in prices and the fall of the ruble exchange rate in September gave fiscal authorities an opportunity to increase the money supply without inflationary consequences and contributed to a perceptible decrease in the foreign currency exchange rate. This made it possible for the central bank to increase its foreign exchange reserves in September and October without a serious devaluation of the ruble and an immediate acceleration of inflation. That was the case up to the end of October. The situation turned around between 10 October and 10 November: the foreign exchange reserves first stabilized and then began to decline, and three weeks later the inflation rate and the decline in the nominal ruble rate both accelerated. However, the central bank's tight monetary policy and intervention on the foreign exchange market made it possible to slow down the inflation rate in January–February 1999. At the same time, the depletion of gold and foreign exchange reserves continued. Let us examine these phases in more detail.

In September 1998, the economic and financial crisis related to the ruble's devaluation and declining confidence in the Russian national currency continued to exacerbate. The over 60% devaluation of the ruble and the sharp increase in the velocity of money caused a rapid rise in consumer prices. In the first week of September alone, the consumer price index rose by 35.7% (Figure 11.7). Later, however, the inflation rate slowed down in concert with the declining US dollar exchange rate.

As has already been noted, the deceleration of the inflation rate in mid-September 1998 can be largely explained by the absence of growth in the money supply in August 1998 (Figure 11.8 and Table 11.7).

In September, the central bank stepped up money printing in order to maintain the banking system's liquidity and ensure payments to clients. In September–October, Rb 26.1 billion was printed, which corresponds to a 16.45% increase in the money supply from the end of August 1998. The beginning of currency issuance did not, however, accelerate the growth in prices. In October 1998 the consumer price index rose by 4.5%, and in November it rose by 5.7%, or 69.6% and 94.5% respectively in annual terms. This can be explained

Table 11.3
Execution of 1998 Consolidated Budget (% of GDP)

	1998, Month											
	I	II	III	IV	V	VI	VII	VIII	IX	X	XI	XII
REVENUE												
1. Profit tax	2.3	2.5	3.0	3.6	3.7	3.7	3.5	3.5	3.4	3.3	3.3	3.6
2. Personal income tax	2.3	2.5	2.5	2.5	2.5	2.5	2.6	2.5	2.4	2.4	2.4	2.7
3. Value-added tax	5.9	5.9	5.9	6.0	5.9	5.8	5.8	5.5	5.3	5.3	5.3	5.9
4. Excises	2.4	2.4	2.5	2.3	2.3	2.4	2.4	2.4	2.4	2.3	2.4	2.6
5. Property tax	0.5	0.6	0.8	1.3	1.6	1.6	1.6	1.7	1.7	1.6	1.6	1.8
6. Taxes on foreign trade and foreign economic operations	1.0	1.1	1.2	1.2	1.4	1.4	1.3	1.3	1.2	1.2	1.2	1.4
7. Other taxes	2.3	3.0	3.0	3.7	3.9	4.0	4.2	4.2	4.1	4.0	4.0	4.2
Total Taxes and Payments	16.2	17.4	18.1	19.3	19.7	19.8	19.8	19.4	18.8	18.5	18.6	20.5
Total Nontax Revenue	2.6	2.7	3.2	3.1	3.2	3.4	3.4	3.4	3.5	3.5	3.4	4.3
Total Revenue	18.8	20.1	21.2	22.4	23.0	23.2	23.2	22.9	22.3	22.0	22.0	24.8
EXPENDITURES												
1. Government administration	0.9	1.0	1.0	1.1	1.1	1.1	1.1	1.1	1.0	1.0	1.0	1.1
2. National defense	2.0	2.0	1.9	1.9	1.8	1.9	1.8	1.7	1.8	1.8	1.9	2.1
3. International activities	0.1	−0.2	0.0	0.0	0.0	−0.1	−0.1	−0.1	−0.1	0.0	0.0	0.3
4. Justice	0.0	0.1	0.1	0.1	0.1	0.1	0.1	0.1	0.1	0.1	0.1	0.1
5. Law enforcement and security	1.4	1.5	1.6	1.6	1.6	1.5	1.5	1.5	1.4	1.4	1.4	1.6
6. Basic research and promotion of scientific and technological progress	0.2	0.2	0.3	0.3	0.3	0.3	0.2	0.2	0.2	0.2	0.2	0.2
7. Government services to the national economy	3.4	4.5	4.6	5.0	5.2	5.5	5.5	5.4	5.3	5.2	5.3	6.2
8. Social services, of which:												
8.1. Education	6.7	7.2	7.7	8.4	8.4	8.8	8.7	8.4	8.0	8.0	8.1	9.0
8.2. Culture and arts	2.6	2.8	3.0	3.4	3.4	3.7	3.7	3.6	3.4	3.3	3.3	3.7
8.3. Mass media	0.2	0.3	0.3	0.3	0.3	0.4	0.4	0.4	0.3	0.3	0.3	0.4
8.4. Health and physical fitness	0.1	0.1	0.1	0.1	0.1	0.1	0.1	0.1	0.1	0.1	0.1	0.1
8.5. Social policy	1.7	1.8	2.0	2.2	2.2	2.3	2.2	2.2	2.1	2.1	2.1	2.4
	2.2	2.2	2.3	2.3	2.3	2.3	2.3	2.2	2.1	2.2	2.2	2.4

The Crisis of the Russian Financial System

9. Government debt service	2.7	3.3	5.0	4.9	5.3	5.2	5.4	5.1	4.5	4.1	4.0	4.0
10. Other expenditures	2.0	2.3	2.8	2.8	2.7	2.9	3.0	2.9	2.9	2.8	2.8	3.0
Total Expenditures	19.4	21.9	25.0	26.1	26.5	27.2	27.2	26.3	25.1	24.6	24.8	27.9
Credit Less Repayment	4.7	0.6	0.6	0.6	0.7	0.8	0.8	0.8	0.9	1.0	0.9	0.5
Total Expenditure and Credit Less Repayment	24.1	22.5	25.6	26.7	27.2	28.0	28.0	27.1	26.0	25.5	25.6	28.4
Surplus of Revenue over Expenditure and Credit Less Repayment	−5.3	−2.4	−4.3	−4.3	−4.2	−4.8	−4.8	−4.3	−3.7	−3.6	−3.6	−3.6
FINANCING												
1. Domestic financing	1.8	0.7	3.3	3.3	3.3	2.0	0.3	0.0	−0.2	−0.1	0.1	0.2
1.1. Change in bank acccount balances of budget funds, in rubles	−0.2	−1.5	−0.6	−0.7	−0.6	−1.1	0.0	0.0	−0.5	−0.6	−0.7	−1.1
1.2. Short-term government debt	1.5	1.9	2.9	0.8	0.6	−0.5	−3.4	−3.4	−3.0	−2.6	−2.3	−2.2
1.3. Federal floating rate bonds	0.0	0.0	0.0	−0.3	−0.2	−0.3	−0.3	−0.3	−0.3	−0.2	−0.2	−0.2
1.4. Nonmarketable government bonds	−0.3	−0.4	−0.3	−0.2	0.0	0.2	0.2	0.2	0.1	0.1	0.0	0.0
1.5. Government (municipal) securities	−0.1	0.0	0.1	0.1	0.1	0.1	0.1	0.1	0.0	0.0	0.0	0.0
1.6. Federal fixed-rate bonds	0.0	0.0	0.9	3.3	2.9	3.0	3.2	3.1	3.0	2.8	2.9	3.4
1.7. Budgetary loans from other-level budgets	0.0	0.0	0.1	0.0	0.0	0.0	0.0	0.0	0.0	0.1	0.1	−0.1
1.8. Government savings bonds	0.3	0.1	0.3	0.1	0.1	0.1	0.1	0.1	0.1	0.1	0.1	0.1
1.9. Other domestic borrowing	0.4	0.6	0.0	0.1	0.3	0.4	0.4	0.3	0.3	0.2	0.2	0.3
2. External financing	3.5	1.7	1.0	1.0	1.0	2.9	4.5	4.3	3.9	3.6	3.5	3.4
2.1. Loans from international financial institutions	3.2	1.7	1.2	0.9	0.7	1.0	0.7	1.1	1.0	0.7	0.5	0.5
2.2. Foreign government loans to RF	0.3	0.0	−0.2	−0.2	0.0	0.0	0.1	0.1	0.1	0.2	0.0	−0.2
2.3. Loans from foreign commercail banks and companies to RF	0.0	0.0	0.0	0.3	0.3	1.9	3.6	3.1	2.7	2.8	2.9	3.2
Total Financing	5.3	2.4	4.3	4.3	4.2	4.8	4.8	4.3	3.7	3.6	3.6	3.6

Table 11.4
Growth of Arrears to the Federal Budget, 1998

1998	Deflated Growth of Arrears to the Federal Budget (mill. of Rb)	Deflated Monthly Tax Receipts by the Federal Budget (mill. of Rb)
January	8,298	15,792
February	−4,381	15,274
March	2,219	18,467
April	10,092	18,527
May	8,386	18,617
June	543	17,011
July	7,172	17,908
August	5,051	14,625
September	3,143	10,500
October	4,498	12,565
November	5,589	14,991
December	−1,256	21,415

Table 11.5
Tax Arrears to the Federal Budget, 1998

1998	Deflated Arrears to the Federal Budget (mill. of Rb)	Growth Rate of Deflated Arrears %	Arrears as % of Monthly GDP
January	81,566		60
February	77,644	−4.8	59
March	78,798	1.5	55
April	85,844	8.9	59
May	91,617	6.7	62
June	91,922	0.3	62
July	96,969	5.5	64
August	97,463	0.5	63
September	72,714	−25.4	57
October	72,863	0.2	58
November	74,136	1.7	58
December	65,515	−11.6	51

Table 11.6
Domestic Government Debt Structure

	1 January 1998		1 January 1999	
	(bill. of Rb)	(% of GDP)	(mill. of Rb)	(% of GDP)
1. Debt on securities, of which:	518,799	20.06	480,175	17.89
1992 government loan	105	0.00	125	0.00
1991 domestic government loan	80	0.00	80	0.00
GKOs	272,612	10.54	14,640[†]	0.55
OFZs	163,352	6.32	448,057[†]	16.69
Government savings loan	13,082	0.51	14,637	0.55
Nonmarketable bonds	1,768	0.07	2,635	0.10
Debt on foreign currency–denominated domestic bonds (OVVZs)*	67,800	2.62	229,649	8.56
2. Arrears to banks (government guarantees)	4,917	0.19	882	0.03
3. Ex-USSR arrears on commodity debt, of which:	4,237	0.16	4,875	0.18
1990 directed loan	2,037	0.08	1,910	0.07
Target deposits, car vouchers, wage arrears to agro-industry workers	2,200	0.09	2,965	0.11
4. Arrears to agro-industry converted into treasury bills	3,920	0.15	3,360	0.13
5. Arrears on centralized loans and accrued interest of agro-industry organizations in charge of Northern winter supplies	25,000	0.97	22,002	0.82
6. Interest arrears of Ivanovo oblast textile industry	560	0.02	490	0.02
7. Arrears on financing reserve stock costs	1,994	0.08	1,755	0.07
8. Other items, of which:	8,233	0.32	7,368	0.27
RF Central Bank's domestic debt inherited from former USSR	191	0.01	191	0.01
Arrears on Central Bank's technical loans to CIS countries	2,408	0.09	2,408	0.09
Arrears to the fuel and energy complex and other industries	5,000	0.19	4,181	0.16
Chelyabinsk oblast agro-industry arrears on centralized loans and interest	94	0.00	94	0.00
Agroprombank guaranteed *veksels*	540	0.02	494	0.02
Total domestic government debt	500,959	21.99	750,556	27.96
GDP (trill. of Rb)	2,586,000		2,684,000	

*Ministry of Finance statistics have referred to foreign currency–denominated domestic bonds as domestic debt since 1998. Data as of 1 January 1998 are based on total negotiable OVVZs valued at $11.3 billion.
[†] Includes bottom-line evening. If bottom-line evening is excluded, GKO arrears amount to Rb 215 billion and OFZ arrears, Rb 258 billion.

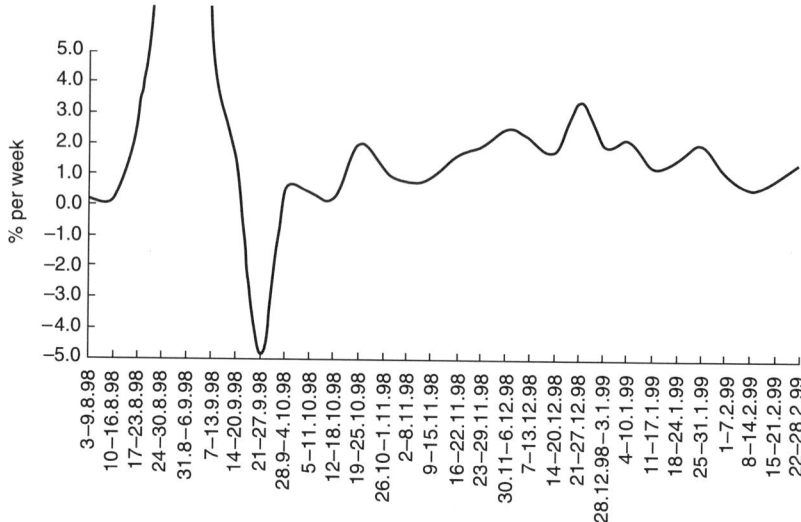

Figure 11.7
Consumer price index, August 1998–February 1999. (Source: Goskomstat.)

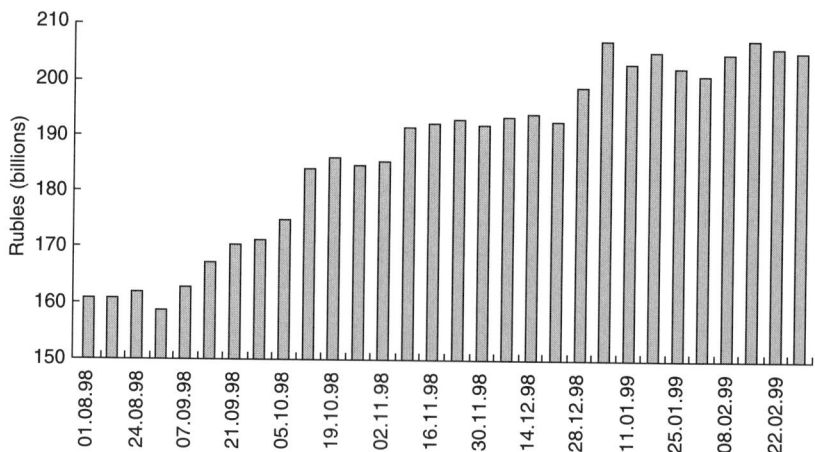

Figure 11.8
Money supply, August 1998–February 1999 (billions of rubles). (Source: RF Central Bank.)

Table 11.7
Changes in Base Money and Gold and Forex Reserves, August 1998–February 1999

Period	Base Money (bill. of Rb)	Rate of Change in Base Money (%)	Gold and Forex Reserves (bill. of US $)	Rate of Change in Gold and Forex Reserves (%)
10–16.VIII.98	160.7		15.1	
17–23.VIII.98	161.8	0.68	13.4	−11.26
24–30.VIII.98	158.7	−1.92	12.7	−5.22
31.VIII–6.IX.98	162.8	2.58	12.3	−3.15
7–13.IX.98	167.3	2.76	12.3	0.00
14–20.IX.98	170.3	1.79	12.0	−2.44
21–27.IX.98	171.2	0.53	12.4	3.33
28.IX–4.X.98	174.8	2.10	12.8	3.23
5–11.X.98	183.9	5.21	13.3	3.91
12–18.IX.98	185.9	1.09	13.1	−1.50
19–25.X.98	184.8	−0.59	13.3	1.53
26.X–1.XI.98	185.3	0.27	13.6	2.26
2–8.XI.98	191.5	3.35	13.4	−1.47
9–15.XI.98	192.3	0.42	13.1	−2.24
16–22.XI.98	192.9	0.31	13.0	−0.76
23–29.XI.98	191.9	−0.52	12.8	−1.54
30.XI–6.XII.98	193.3	0.73	12.1	−5.47
7–13.XII.98	194.0	0.36	12.0	−0.83
14–20.XII.98	192.5	−0.77	11.9	−0.83
21–27.XII.98	199.0	3.38	12.3	3.36
28.X.98–3.I.99	207.3	4.17	12.2	−0.08
4–10.I.99	203.0	−2.07	12.0	−1.64
11–17.I.99	205.4	1.18	11.9	−0.83
18–24.I.99	202.2	−1.56	11.6	−2.52
25–31.I.99	201.1	−0.54	11.6	0.00
1–7.II.99	204.7	1.79	11.6	0.00
8–14.II.99	207.1	1.17	11.3	−2.59
15–21.II.99	205.8	−0.63	11.4	0.88
22–28.II.99	205.2	−0.29	11.5	0.88

Source: RF Central Bank.

by a variety of reasons, including lower inflationary expectations,[9] technical lags between the outset of currency issue and its effect on the inflation rate, and the lower money multiplier that emerged in the course of the banking crisis.

By the end of 1998, inflationary processes in the Russian economy were gradually accelerating (see Figure 11.7). After a significant price leap in September, which ensured price stability over the following month or two, in December 1998 consumer prices rose by 11.6%. This means that in 1998, inflation in Russia was 84.3%, or an average of 5.2% a month. But the price growth throughout the year was uneven: whereas in the first seven months the consumer price index rose by only 4% (an average of 0.56% a month), between August and December prices increased by 77.2%, or 12.1% a month.

The situation began to turn around in November 1998. The dynamic of the central bank's gold and foreign exchange reserves changed direction (Figure 11.9 and Table 11.7). Throughout November, these reserves fell by $800 million, from $13.6 billion to $12.8 billion. In November 1998 the Finance Ministry used central bank money to make payments on foreign debts. On 27 November, the Finance Ministry made payments on the first tranche of five-year eurobonds, in the amount of $46.3 million, and on 2 December it paid $216 million on IAN bonds. During the preceding month or two the central bank had done its best to smooth out the dollar-rate vacillations, but by the end of November to early December, the ruble rate had fallen from 18 rubles to 20–21 rubles to the dollar. In December the central bank's gold and foreign exchange reserves continued to dwindle. In the first three weeks of that month alone, they diminished by $900 million. In late December the government made payments on eurobond coupons in the amount of approximately $330 million.

During 1998, the central bank's gold and foreign exchange reserves decreased by approximately $5.5 billion (from $17.784 bil-

---

9. After a leap in inflation in late August to early September 1999, the new price equilibrium was not adequate to the volume of money in circulation. However, because of a rigid price level, which in this case implied economic agents' (producers' and go-betweens') reluctance to significantly reduce the already increased prices, no adequate deflation took place (see Figure 11.7). As a result, the currency issue that followed (loans to the government and commercial banks) was largely used to support the price proportions established after the inflation leap (the real money stock rose). An important factor behind the lower inflationary expectations and increased real money supply was exchange-rate stability and the gradual increase in the RF Central Bank's gold and foreign exchange reserves that occurred during that period.

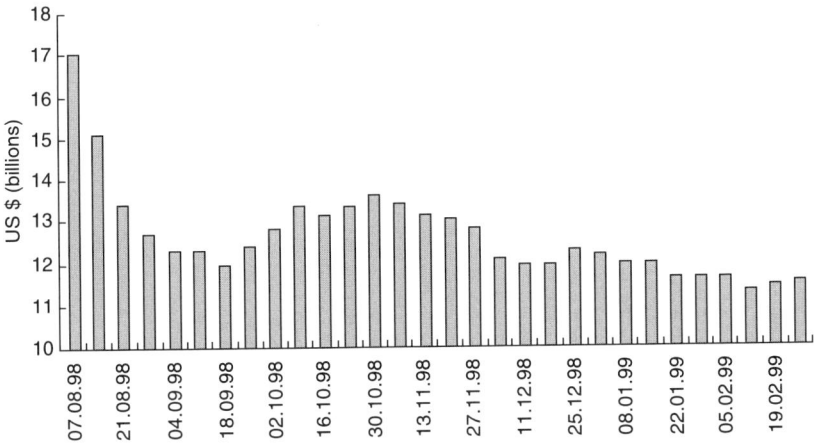

Figure 11.9
The RF Central Bank's gold and foreign exchange reserves, August 1998–February 1999. (Source: RF Central Bank.)

lion to $12.223 billion, a drop of 31.3%). The share of gold in the reserves rose from 27.5% to 36.2%.

Data on the dynamics of monetary aggregates in 1998 (see Statistical Appendix, Table 1) demonstrate that by and large, base money rose by 26% (by 28.5% from 1 August). In that year the money supply M2 increased by 21.0% (25.7% from 1 August) and the amount of broad money (including dollar deposits) increased by 36.3% (by 43.9% from 1 August). The amount of currency in circulation went up by 44.0% (by 45.2% from 1 August). This means that the share of cash in M2 rose from 34.86% to 41.5%. The withdrawal of bank deposits and the stricter rationing of loans owing to the overall crisis of the banking system caused the money multiplier to drop from 2.4 in January to 2.02 in October. In November–December it rose to 2.18. Overall, throughout the year, the real money supply M2 diminished by 34.4%. At the same time, as the GDP deflator lagged behind the growth rate of consumer prices and the rate of decline in real GDP, the monetization of the economy increased, from 14.4% (in 1997) to 16.85%.

Panic buying of foreign exchange between late August and October 1998 caused sharp fluctuations in the US dollar exchange rate (Figure 11.10). To protect the national currency against speculative onslaughts in the context of a floating exchange rate, from Septem-

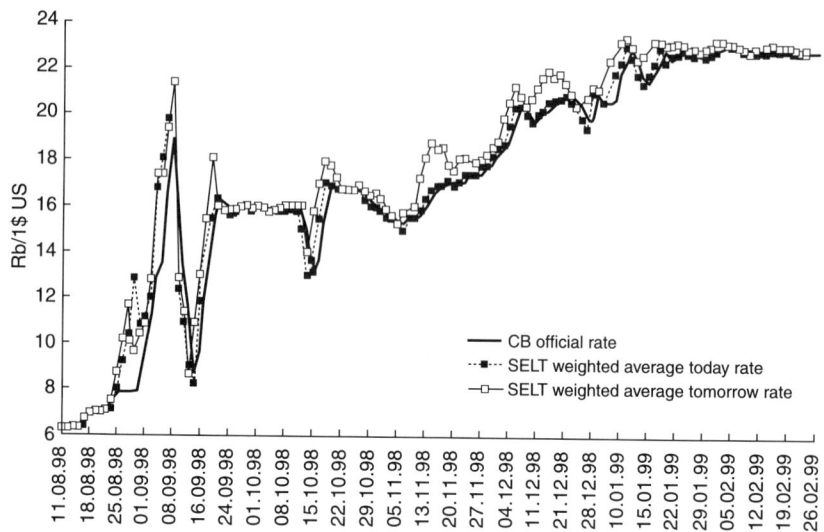

Figure 11.10
US dollar exchange rate, August 1998–February 1999. (Source: Central Bank of Russia, Finmarker.)

ber 1998 to January 1999 the central bank took a number of administrative steps to restrict demand for foreign exchange:

1. Exporters are obliged to sell 50% (from September) and 75% (from 1 January 1999) of their foreign exchange earnings on the interbank currency exchanges that hold central bank licenses.

2. A new sales procedure that envisaged the separation of trading sessions was introduced. During the morning special session, the mandatory sale of foreign currency by exporters and the purchase of foreign currency against import contracts are held, with the transactions implying immediate delivery. Based on the special session, the central bank announces the official exchange rate for the following day. During the afternoon session, foreign currency transactions are conducted by commercial banks for their own needs and for clients. Delivery takes place on the following day.

3. Commercial banks are obliged to submit to the central bank daily reports on their foreign currency transactions. Failure to comply with the central bank's instructions may entail banishment from trading and loss of license.

4. Effective 1 November 1998, a seven-day limit was imposed on how long foreign currency bought against import contracts can be kept

on bank accounts. Upon expiration of this term, the foreign currency not used for the specified purpose is to be surrendered for sale.

5. The purchase of foreign currency at special sessions to pay for the import of services, works, and products of intellectual activity is prohibited.

6. Resale by resident legal entities of foreign currency purchased on the domestic market and deposited in special transit foreign exchange accounts may take place only during the special morning sessions.

Also, the rules for managing C accounts for nonresidents were revised. A government resolution on innovation in respect to government securities aimed at reducing the export of capital envisaged a special procedure for nonresidents' use of cash received by them on innovation terms.

In our view, although these steps cannot be regarded as compatible with market principles, they are justified in the current economic situation. It is indicative that there is practically no spread between the official exchange rate, the SELT dollar rate, and the selling and buying rates at the bureaus de change. This belies the assumption that the official ruble rate is a nonmarket one.

11.3.6. Production Dynamics and Social Stability

The end of the panic on the consumer market, added to the ruble's devaluation, stepped up import substitution, as a result of which the recession in industrial production in October and November was of a smaller scale than had been predicted from an inertial assessment of production dynamics.

In November through January, a number of industries showed growth not only from the previous month but also from the same period in 1997–1998. In January 1999, engineering output rose by 2.3% compared with January 1998, timber and woodworking rose by 5.8%, industrial building materials rose by 2%, glass, china, and earthenware production rose by 2.6%, and microbiology output rose by 0.4%. Of course, this is not much, but the Russian economy had already begun to show signs of growth a year earlier, so the reference point in this comparison is not the lowest level of the postcommunist crisis.

One has to wonder about the reasons for these positive developments. In late 1998 the government managed, for the most part, to ensure macroeconomic stability (chiefly by preventing inflation from skyrocketing) and to more or less normalize the system of payments and settlements.

Generally speaking, two principal groups of factors determined the production growth trend. First, the ruble's devaluation, which sharply undermined the competitive capacity of many imported products, generated a rapid rise in the efficiency of a number of domestic producers. This factor will continue to operate provided that the real ruble rate is maintained—that is, provided that the inflation rate coincides with the rate of decline of the exchange rate. High inflation would by itself cancel the growth potential. Inflation would be curbed (using a fixed or quasi-fixed rate) when the real ruble value rises and the "devaluation" source of the competitive capacity of domestic production has been exhausted.

Second, the growth of the last few months of 1998 was associated with the economy's entering into a high-inflation cycle. The experience of many countries makes it quite clear that the expansion of monetary financing of the economy initially (and for several months) stimulates economic growth, thanks to the emergence of a "monetary illusion." In other words, money injected into the economy creates the illusion of expanding demand. Households have the money to buy goods. Companies perceive the market's signals as an increase in demand and begin to expand production. The demand for intermediary goods (ones used for production purposes) grows. The real level of nonpayments in the economy goes down. This factor is strictly short term and usually soon followed by a new recession.

By early 1999, then, the Russian economy had two mechanisms for stimulating growth that, although compatible in the short term, were bound to diverge in the midterm (over six months). The stability of the December–January favorable trends depended above all on the government's economic policy. Adequate macroeconomic and institutional decisions on the part of the government would be essential for maintaining the favorable trends that came into being in late 1998 to early 1999.

It was also important that the Duma's support for the Primakov government made it possible to pass a law on production sharing that had been blocked for several years. This sent positive signals to investors, especially foreign ones.

The Crisis of the Russian Financial System

Table 11.8
Dynamics of the Strike Movement in 1998

Month	Number of Enterprises and Organizations Where Strikes Occurred	Number of Strikers (thousands)
January	246	19.6
February	78	8.1
March	70	9.7
April	946	52.3
May	362	25.4
June	92	13.9
July	31	5.4
August	47	2.1
September	2,394	78.5
October	4,229	196.1
November	2,135	65.5
December	5,305	134.3

Source: RF Goskomstat.

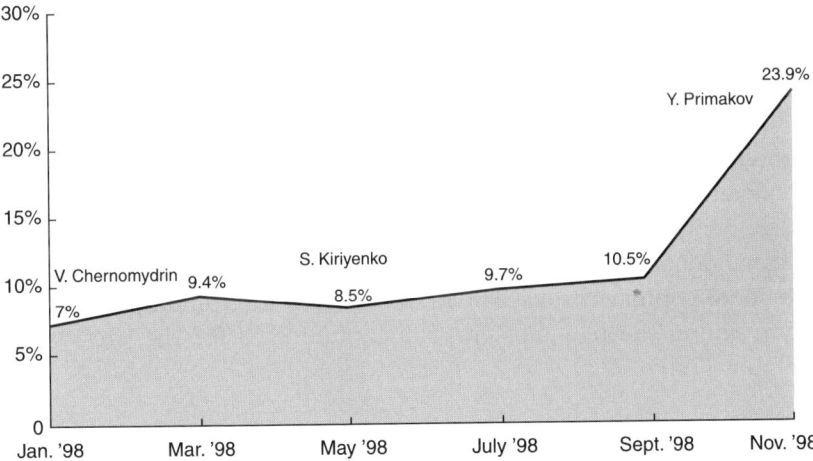

Figure 11.11
The premier as the most trusted political figure (percentage of those who singled out the prime minister in a political credibility poll). (Source: VTsIOM monitoring data.)

Steps were taken to tighten controls over pricing by the natural monopolies. Many tariffs were frozen, and some were even reduced (such as for railroad transportation of some necessities, including foodstuffs).

Statistics and sociological data also testify to stabilization and an improved position of enterprises. After a rapid decline in production in September, output stabilized, demand began to rise, and the share of idle production capacities decreased, especially in the fuel and energy complex and the consumer goods and food-processing industries.

Favorable changes also occurred in the social sphere. The government managed to use monetary sources to address some of the accumulated wage and pension arrears. Although the value of the ruble decreased several times, the public mood was overall in favor of the current authorities. The duality of the economic situation was also reflected in the dynamics of labor strikes. In September the number of striking enterprises increased more than fifty times and the number of strikers rose forty times, and in October both figures doubled again. Although the strike movement began to wane in November, falling to the September level (with 97% of the strikes accounted for by educational establishments), in December it began growing again (Table 11.8).

Nevertheless, according to sociological surveys, in November 1998, 53.2% of the respondents would not have supported protest actions demanding that the government resign. Yevgeny Primakov's personal popularity was also on the rise: public opinion polls placed him among the five most probable candidates for the presidency (Figure 11.11).

12

Financial Policy in 1999

Sergei Arkhipov, Said Batkibekov, Tatiana Drobyshevskaia, Sergei Drobyshevsky, Olga Izryadnova, Sergei Sinelnikov-Murylev, and Ilya Trounin

The events of August 1998 set the course for Russia's economy in 1999. Both foreign and domestic investors' declining confidence in official Russian policy threatened a loss of most reliable sources the government could count on to finance its budget deficit, and pointed as well to a continuing flight of capital from the country.

The pro-Communist government under Yevgeni Primakov, which came to power in September 1998, stirred expectations of momentous change in the country's macroeconomic policy. An inflationary scenario for impending events could be grasped from the public appearances of leading cabinet figures, who called for greater government interference in the economy, compensation for the losses borne by the public from the crisis of autumn 1998, and government support for the banking system. The government appeared to be poised for an open confrontation with international financial institutions and foreign investors. Its statements of intent to ease the tax burden, step up government support for Russian manufacturers, enter into custom-tailored agreements with major corporate taxpayers on their tax arrears to the budget, allow massive set-offs between businesses and revenue authorities, waive its right to initiate bankruptcy proceedings against tax dodgers, revoke the previous government's decision to charge VAT on different principles, and many more "sweeteners" were signals of a relaxed tax policy, which was bound to cut deeply into budget revenues.

From the beginning however, the Primakov government was more cautious than expected. Despite arm-twisting from the Communists, it succeeded in having a tough 1999 budget pushed through the legislature and implemented, with all its restraint in monetary policy. Its practical policy was a blend of pro-Communist rhetoric and "pragmatic liberalism."

We can now recognize the principal factors that kept events from following an inflationary course, despite the government's clear intentions to the contrary. First, the media played a key role by providing space and air time for open, wide-ranging discussion of what the government's measures could lead to. In this way the parliamentarians' populist electioneering zeal was deflated. Second, the alignment of forces among the different interest groups changed, as the banking and energy moguls, better known as "oligarchs," saw their omnipotence severely undercut, while import-substituting producers had their power boosted. Regional business, especially those with links to the real sector and regional markets, suffered noticeably less during the crisis than business connected on a countrywide scale to financial-industrial groups.

The government's 1999 budget bill was submitted to the State Duma on 11 December 1998, passed within record time, and was signed into law by the President on 22 February 1999. The budget's principles were extremely vulnerable—the budget law was based on tax revenues amounting to 10% of GDP, an inflation rate of 30%, and foreign loans contributing 5% of GDP. All of this meant that, given the looming threat of declining tax revenues, the nominal budget figures could be met only by whipping up inflation.

On balance, however, the 1999 performance results proved more pleasant than expected. There were several causes for this phenomenon. First, in 1999 both the government and the central bank stopped sending signals of any easing in tax policy anytime soon, and instead persevered in their efforts to improve tax collection.[1] Combined with greater returns on capital invested in the real sector and a rising percentage of cash payments, this tactic nudged actual tax revenues to 11% of GDP. These two steps also succeeded in marshaling a larger share of taxes into the federal budget. In the absence of major indexation of federal budget spending items, the GDP's overall share of budgetary expenditure slipped to 14.5% in 1998, from 18.4% in 1997, and the budget deficit edged down to 3.3% of GDP (from 3.9% of GDP in 1997).

Second, the central bank's monetary policy was prudently restrained throughout 1999. The financial policy it maintained in November and December 1998 and its intervention on the currency

---

[1]. See also R. Perotti, "Fiscal Policy in Good Times and Bad," *The Quarterly Journal of Economics* 114 (1999): 1437–1467.

market were rewarded with slowing rates of inflation and stabilization of the ruble exchange rate by early 1999. The growth in tax revenues and abandonment of a large-scale rehabilitation of the banking system allowed the central bank to reduce monetary financing despite a substantial drop in loans from international financial organizations to $1.2 billion in 1999, from the $4.5 billion the central bank had expected. As a result, the annual inflation rate only moderately overshot the budget's 30% target, to 38%.

Third, beginning in the autumn of 1998, the Russian economy showed signs of recovery. Following the ruble's devaluation, which reduced the ruble exchange rate to the 1994 level, and the emergence of a more benign situation on international commodity markets, export-oriented and import-substituting industries rebounded. Rather than falling as feared, the GDP showed a healthy growth of 3%.

The successive governments of Primakov, Stepashin, and Putin deserve credit for their efforts through 1999 to bring the country's budget into balance. For the first time in a decade, the budget was in the black and was implemented fully. This achievement was equal in significance to the market equilibrium attained under the Gaidar cabinet (through price liberalization) and the development of a credible monetary policy under Chubais. Finally, the principal elements of macroeconomic stability—a tough monetary policy and a balanced budget—were put in place. More than anything else, it was this macroeconomic success of the left cabinet that was behind the rapid stabilization of basic physical parameters and the improvement in the economy's real sector. The main reasons for this development are examined in more detail below.

12.1. Balance of Payments, Monetary Policy, and Real Ruble Exchange Rate

In the period between price liberalization and the August 1998 crisis, the strength of the ruble grew in real terms. Overall, the real exchange rate of the ruble rose 19.65-fold between 1 January 1992 and 17 August 1998 (Figure 12.1).[2]

Foreign trade liberalization and the opening up of the Russian economy to the world, which helped meet the demand of the con-

---

2. See M. Obstfeld and K. Rogoff, "The Mirage of Fixed Exchange Rates," *Journal of Economic Perspectives* 9 (Sept. 1999): 1–41.

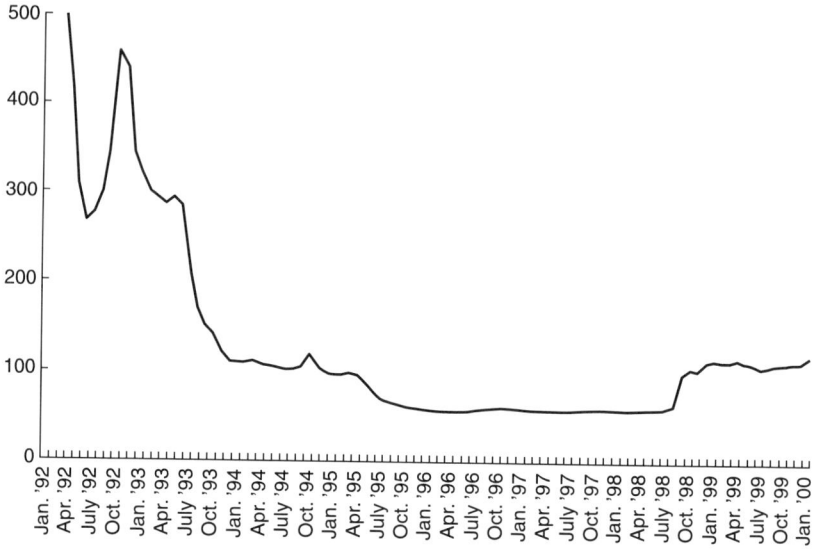

Figure 12.1
Real US dollar/ruble exchange rate, January 1992–January 2000 (December 1994 = 100). (Source: Working Centre for Economic Reforms under the RF Government.)

sumer market within months of the start of market reforms and allowed Russian exporters to increase their presence on the world market, contributed to a convergence of domestic and world prices for identical goods. The growing ruble exchange rate from 1992 to 1997 and the population's rising purchasing power stimulated an influx of consumer imports superior to their domestically produced substitutes. Also, the growth in dollar-denominated production costs reduced the profit-making potential of Russian exports. Many Russian manufacturers found themselves completely unprepared to face growing competition when the benefits of low prices or low costs ceased to play the key role they previously had.[3]

In August and September 1998, the Russian economy was thrown into a shock by a fourfold devaluation of the ruble. Elsewhere a currency crisis of this magnitude is commonly followed by a relatively fast rise in the real exchange rate of the national currency, owing to a growing surplus in the balance of trade.[4] Throughout 1999, however,

---

3. For a comparable experience, see S. Zecchini, ed., *Lessons from the Economic Transition: Eastern and Central Europe in the 1990's* (Boston: Kluwer Academic, 1997).
4. See, for example, B. Eichengreen, A. Rose, and C. Wyplosz, "Exchange Market Mayhem: The Antecedents and Aftermath of Speculative Attacks," *Economic Policy* 21 (October 1995): 249–312.

the real exchange rate of the ruble in Russia was only about half what it had been over the first six months of 1998.

This real exchange rate dynamic is largely explained by the fact that the central bank was lending directly to the Russian Ministry of Finance so that it could service and repay the government's foreign debts and purchase hard cash on the currency market. This process kept downward pressure on the nominal ruble exchange rate through the year, even at the price of rising inflation.[5]

12.1.1. Russia's Balance of Payments in 1999

A close look at Russia's balance of payments shows that its key figures changed drastically in 1999 from what they had been for years, even though the changes were engineered by factors that had previously had a major influence on them. For example, although the balance of payments on the capital account stayed stubbornly in the red, the balance of payments on the current account held just as steadily in the black, at over $5 billion at all times from the first through the third quarter of 1999, while in the fourth quarter it shot up to $10.2 billion, an all-time record for as long as Russia has kept a balance of payments (previously the balance of payments on the current account was below $6.1 billion). This situation was brought about by a buoyant trade balance that was showing a growing surplus, from $6.5 billion in the first quarter to $12.7 billion in the fourth quarter. Moreover, the trade balance surplus grew not only in concert with growing exports (from $15.5 billion in the first quarter to $23.5 billion in the fourth quarter), but also in the absence of substantial import growth (over the year the indicator of merchandise imports fluctuated between $9 and $10.5 billion).

It must be noted that exports forged ahead in the fourth quarter of 1998, chiefly because of their greater efficiency following the ruble's devaluation, a process that continued to pull up the trade balance surplus (as imports declined) by inertia well into the first quarter of 1999. The second quarter of 1999 saw some recovery of the real US dollar versus ruble exchange rate, which was reflected in larger imports. Although exports continued to grow, in conjunction with rising world oil prices, in our view it was the recovery of the real

---

5. See I. M. D. Little, R. N. Copper, W. M. Cordon, and S. Rajapatirana, *Boom, Crisis and Adjustment: Macroeconomic Policy in Developing Countries* (Oxford: Oxford University Press, 1994).

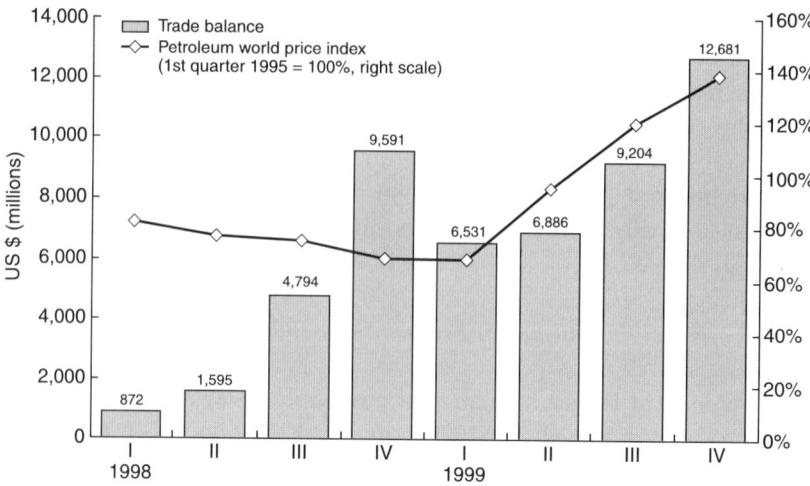

Figure 12.2
RF balance of trade and world oil prices, 1998 and 1999. (Source: RF Central Bank, International Financial Statistics.)

ruble exchange rate that accounted for the trade balance surplus receding in the second quarter. Beginning in the third quarter the trade balance was, as previously, swayed by the behavior of world prices for oil and nonferrous metals. As shown in Figure 12.2, a strong growth in world oil prices boosted the trade balance surplus in the third and fourth quarters of 1999.

The favorable current account balance was used to chop the deficit in the capital and financial account. The balance in this account was driven deep into the red beginning in the fourth quarter of 1998. Against the background of contracting surpluses in the direct and portfolio investment accounts, there was an increase in Russian overseas accounts (growth in outstanding debt, balances in residents' overseas current accounts and deposits, and swelling overdue export receipts from abroad). Foreign liabilities in Russia eased insignificantly in 1999, chiefly because accrued debt was being paid off in the absence of new loans. In this situation, the loan balance could only be maintained in surplus by the public sector piling up its outstanding debt. From January through September 1999, for example, the government paid off $6 billion in government debt on schedule, and another $5.9 billion became outstanding or was deferred. This, combined with the $1.9 billion in foreign loans drawn, pushed the

Financial Policy in 1999

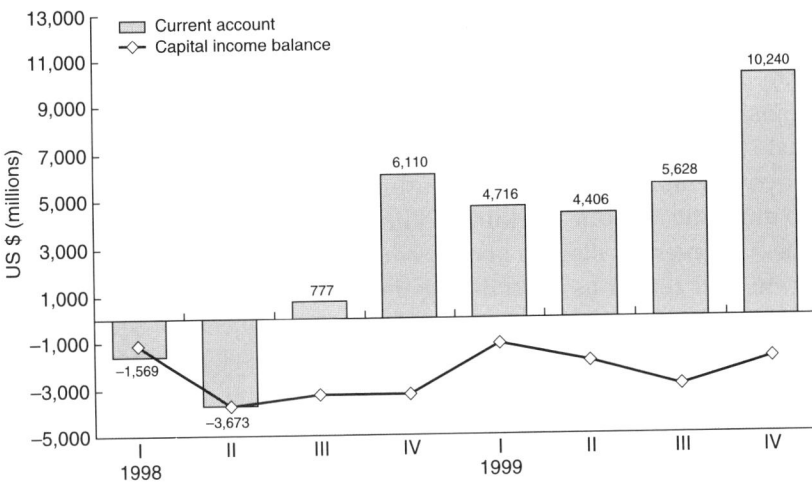

Figure 12.3
Current and capital accounts, 1998 and 1999. (Source: RF Central Bank.)

general government's balance of the above operations into the black (Figure 12.3).[6]

A close examination of a diagnostic cross-section of Russia's balance of payments shows that the overall balance of payments surplus was rising along with the surplus in the current account balance (that is, the surplus less the reserve assets and government sector operations to contract new loans). In late 1998 and the first six months of 1999, the total balance of payments deficit was financed through reserve assets, building up outstanding debts, and deferring payments in the public sector. With the current account surplus rising over 1999 and a loan tranche received from the IMF in the third quarter of 1999, the government was able to chip away at its outstanding debt and rebuild some of its depleted reserve assets. These balance of payments characteristics are evidence of a high demand for foreign exchange by the Finance Ministry, which accounted for the high nominal exchange rate of the ruble despite an abrupt surge in the trade balance surplus.

Within the context of Russia's balance of payments analysis, one should focus attention on capital export from Russia, one of the

---

6. General government operations here include those of the Bank of Russia (involving $454 million to repay the IMF loan in the third quarter) and those of local governments, whose balance of loans received, repaid, past due, or deferred between January and September stood at $43 million.

problems widely discussed by economists and even more so by political figures. Official capital exports are made up of sums channeled into direct and portfolio overseas investments in the form of capital transfers, financial and commercial credits by businesses in the non-state sector, and hard currency taken out of the country. The balance of payments records currency earnings that have not been credited to domestic accounts and unpaid import loans. It is wrong to regard these monies as illegal exports, since no one knows how much of them will return as outstanding debt repayment. In 1998, Russian residents paid around $16 billion (at a monthly rate of $1.3 billion) through these channels, with approximately $11 billion (at a rate of $1.2 billion per month) paid in the first three quarters of 1999. The monthly average of registered capital exports in the first nine months of 1999, therefore, was slightly lower than in the year before, probably because of declining imports more than anything else.

12.1.2. *Monetary and Exchange Rate Policy*

In 1999, the Russian Central Bank adhered to a sufficiently tough monetary policy against the background of the nominal ruble exchange-rate dynamics described in the previous section. Despite major ruble interventions in the currency market, the central bank supported the growth in money aggregates by keeping growth in net domestic assets low. Otherwise, given the expansionist monetary policy, the real exchange rate of the ruble could hardly have been expected to remain stable. This was particularly the case with inflation rising as domestic lending expanded. The ruble would probably have fallen faster, by nominal measure, than prices could rise to keep up with the balance. Alongside the ruble's devaluation the central bank's monetary policy became the second most important factor in the 1999 Russian economic scenario.[7]

The growth rate of the consumer price index declined over the period as a whole (Figure 12.4). On balance, the consumer price index rose by 36.7% in 1999, or at a monthly average of 2.64%. The food price index rose by 35.9%, nonfood goods rose by 39.2%, and services rose by 34.0%.

Several factors should be considered in an analysis of the exchange-rate policy pursued by the Russian government and the central bank

---

[7]. See M. Obstfeld and K. Rogoff, *Foundations of International Macroeconomics* (Cambridge: MIT Press, 1996).

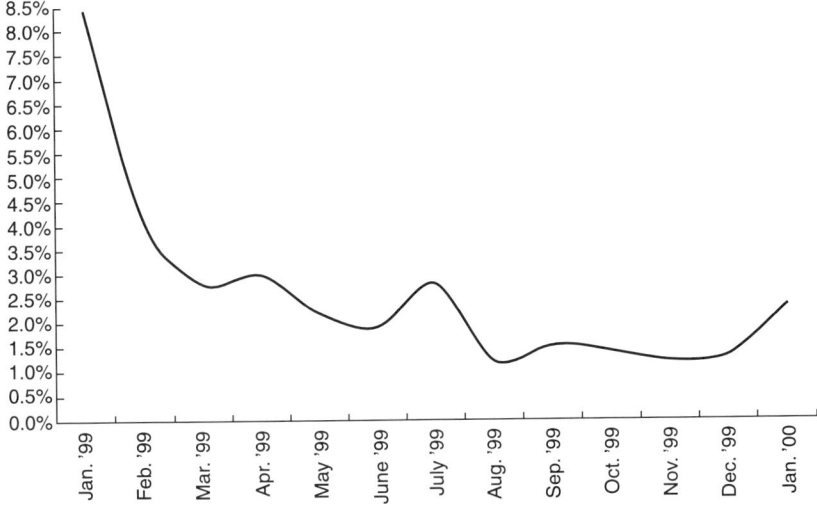

Figure 12.4
CPI between January 1999 and January 2000. (Source: Goskomstat.)

in 1999. First, the spurt in consumer prices in the autumn of 1998 and the inflationary surge that followed in its wake in late 1998 and early 1999 focused the nation's attention on the government's anti-inflationary measures again. The low ruble devaluation rate on the currency market was, under the circumstances, a necessary yet insufficient condition to keep inflation under control.[8]

Second, the imminent repayment of large sums of external public debt in 1999 and 2000 required the central bank to maintain its gold and hard-currency reserves at adequate levels.

Third, the absence of attractive ruble-denominated instruments on Russian financial markets pushed up commercial banks' demand for hard currency. However, existing constraints on banks' investment in hard currency (such as increases in the amount of obligatory reserves for hard-currency deposits and caps on commercial banks' open hard-currency positions) resulted in large ruble-denominated sums piling up in the commercial banks' corresponding accounts with the central bank.

Fourth, a long string of political events in 1999 spurred speculation on the currency market. Under two cabinets, and with the

---

8. See P. Lane, "The New Open Economic Macroecnomics: A Survey," CEPR Discussion Paper no. 2115 (March 1999).

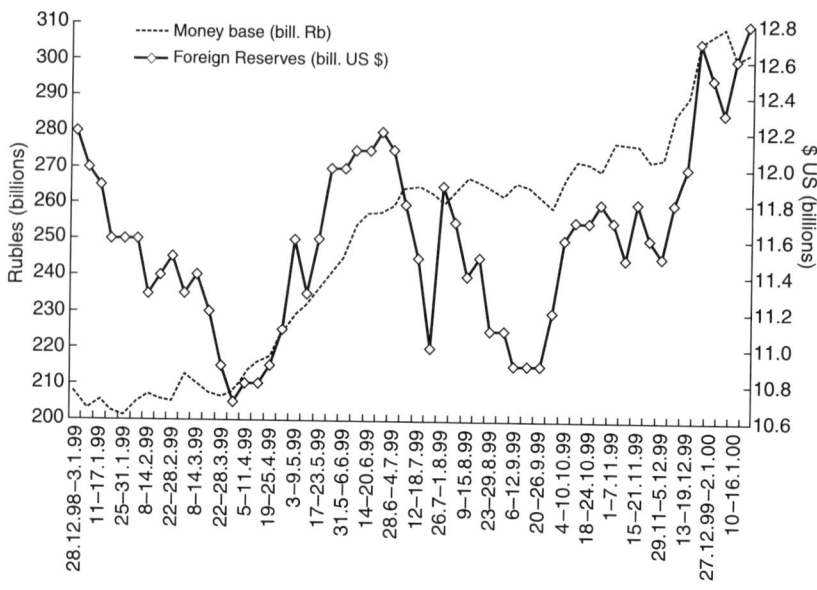

Figure 12.5
Money base and foreign reserve dynamics, 1999–2000. (Source: RF Central Bank.)

Duma elections looming in late 1999, the currency market saw inordinately volatile quotations against a background of swelling trading volumes.

Figure 12.5 helps identify several periods of varying money demand dynamics: a restrained anti-inflationary policy in January to March 1999, monetary expansion in April to June, a restrictive monetary policy in July to November, and rising monetary base growth rates in December 1999 and January 2000. Approximately the same periods can be recognized from the perspective of exchange-rate dynamics, shown in Figure 12.6: year beginning to mid-March, mid-March to early August, and mid-August to the end of 1999.

Year Beginning to Mid-March 1999

Inflation slowed in the first quarter of 1999, largely owing to the government's and the central bank's sufficiently tough monetary policy in late 1998 to early 1999. Despite some fluctuations, the money base held practically stable through the first three months of 1999 (registering a tiny blip of 0.24% only). In January, inflation stood at 8.5%; in February it dropped to 4.1%; and in March it fell again, to 2.8%.

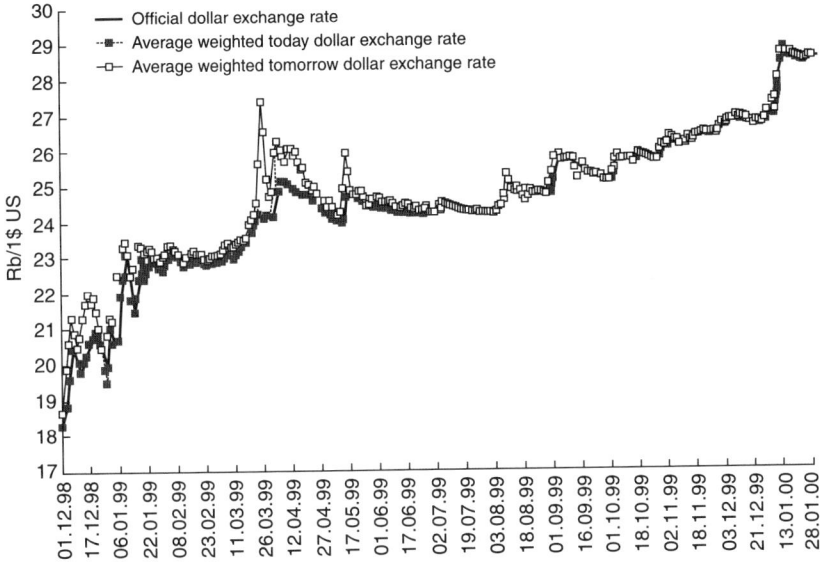

Figure 12.6
Dynamics of US dollar exchange rate, December 1998 through January 2000. (Source: Bank of Russia, "Finmarket" Agency.)

A moderate growth in inflation in late 1998 (see Figure 12.4) sent up demand for dollars by the public and currency-market players. The relatively large amounts of hard currency the Russian Ministry of Finance needed to service the foreign debt in late 1998 and early 1999 hiked up the dollar exchange rate against the ruble in November and December 1998.[9] Early in 1999, the central bank succeeded in achieving relative stability on the currency market. In January 1999, the official exchange rate of the dollar rose against the ruble, from 20.62 to 22.60 (see Figure 12.6). This was equivalent to a 9.60% growth. The central bank cooled the participants' speculative mood with massive dollar interventions. Its gold and foreign exchange reserves diminished by almost $602 million in January 1999 (4.93%), by another $184 million in February (1.58%), and by a further $672 million in March (5.88%). In the absence of any sizable foreign debt repayment,[10] this rapid dwindling of the central bank's gold and

---

9. In the fourth quarter of 1998 as a whole, Russia spent nearly $3 billion to repay its foreign debt.
10. At the end of the first period (25 and 31 March 1999), DM 297 million (around $170 million) was paid on Deutschmark-denominated eurobonds.

foreign exchange reserves through heavy market interventions allowed it to peg the official exchange rate of the dollar against the ruble at 23 rubles through the first three months of 1999.

Consequently, in the first three months of 1999, the central bank's gold and foreign exchange reserves were slashed by about $1.5 billion, or 12.3%. The emerging trend stirred up concern among investors over the consistency of the monetary authorities' exchange-rate policy and Russia's ability to pay off its foreign debts. The plummeting confidence in the government, the Ministry of Finance, and the central bank led to a currency-market squeeze on the ruble. As a result, the ruble exchange rate leaped several times in February through April, and expectations of racing inflation in the near future persisted despite the monetary authorities' continuing tough monetary policy.

An analysis of the situation dominating the currency market during the period under review shows that the beginning of 1999 was marked by a succession of devaluations in countries rated as developing markets.[11] The wave of suspicion over weak currencies that swept the world in early 1999 was therefore a factor that jacked up the risk of investing in ruble assets.

Second Half of March to Early August 1999
After a spell of relative calm in January and February 1999, with typically low dollar gains, the official dollar exchange rate and SELT (Electronic Lot Trading System) quotations picked up again in March. Domestic debt repayment resumed by the Ministry of Finance can be singled out as the principal market factor. In the situation that emerged by late March, the ruble-denominated funds raised by investors put considerable pressure on the ruble exchange rate. The central bank's deeply dented reserves and the prospect of Rb 1.5 billion being paid on internal currency bonds in May buoyed the market players' speculative mood.

In March 1999, the official dollar exchange rate rose by 5.87% (see Figure 12.6). Beginning on 25 March, the central bank intensified its market presence. Its massive interventions stemmed the growth of the official exchange rate and stabilized the market for a time. In the opening days of April, however, speculative demand sent the ruble

---

11. In particular, a wave of financial crises swept Brazil in mid-January 1999, bringing devaluation of the real in its wake.

falling again, with the official dollar exchange rate going up by 4% between 1 and 8 April. This turnaround forced the central bank to waive, beginning on 7 April 1999, the privilege previously enjoyed by authorized banks to purchase dollars on their own behalf and for their own account to pay hard-currency withdrawals by private individuals from their accounts and deposits with these banks.

The central bank's move, combined with Russia's public admission that it would be unable to pay the $1.5 billion on internal foreign currency bonds in mid-May 1999,[12] turned things around on the currency market. Some of Russia's largest companies dumped their dollar holdings as a result, and consequently helped reverse the official dollar exchange rate and SELT dollar quotations in the second half of April.

A certain role in stabilizing the market was played by the rate of obligatory sale of export receipts within seven days being raised from 50% to 75%. In late March, the President signed an enabling decree. For all the concern about the growing capital flight from Russia, the increased hard-currency supply on the market allowed the central bank to build up its reserves and improve its capacity to smooth out ruble exchange-rate fluctuations.

Talks continued in April 1999 over an IMF loan and restructuring of Russia's foreign debts. Toward the end of the month, the parties had basically harmonized their positions, and the IMF agreed to give Russia about $4.5 billion, to be drawn over two years. As the principal condition for releasing the loan, the IMF directors required the Russian government's budget to show an initial surplus of 2% of GDP and a start to be made on realistic reforms in taxation, banking, bankruptcy regulations, and so on.

The official dollar exchange rate rose by 0.21% in April 1999 (at an annualized rate of 2.51%). Actually, however, the dollar jumped

---

12. In late April, the differences between the Russian Finance Ministry and several investors over domestic debt novation resurfaced at a meeting in London between the first deputy finance minister, Kasyanov, and members of the London Club. Kasyanov stated in London that Russia would not be able to repay the $1.5 billion on internal foreign currency bonds in mid-May in full. On the one hand, this admission improved the central bank's chances of keeping ruble exchange rate fluctuations on the open market in hand. On the other hand, the Russian government's unilateral move on its foreign debts dealt a further blow to Russia's reputation on international financial markets. On 20 April, Standard and Poor's reduced the rating of Russian internal foreign currency bonds to CC and confirmed Russia's rating on hard currency liabilities at the SD level, and that of Russian eurobonds at the CCC− level.

almost 4% in the first week of April. After this sharp rise in the official dollar exchange rate, the central bank launched an intervention that brought down the dollar by the end of the month. This seesawing pattern of the dollar exchange rate shooting up within days only to fall, after a longer period of central bank intervention, to where it had been previously, became a typical pattern for the Russian currency market in 1999 (see Figure 12.6).

In April through June 1999, consumer price increases slowed down to a leisurely pace, reaching 1.9% in early June. An important factor contributing to price stabilization was the downscaling of businesses' inflationary expectations. There were several reasons for businesses to feel more confident. The first was the absence of large-scale lending by the central bank to finance the federal budget deficit. Second, the Russian financial markets recovered significantly, and consequently there was a rising demand for cash to be fed into transactions. A third factor was the central bank's success in repelling the attempted attack on the ruble in April 1999: stabilization, and even some strengthening, of the ruble against the dollar is, in the Russian context, read by businesses as an important sign of the monetary authorities' tough policy. Fourth was the gathering process of import substitution in the population's consumer basket (the growth in the ruble-denominated value of imports following the ruble's devaluation was a key force driving prices rapidly up in September 1998 through January 1999).

In a drive to build up its gold and foreign exchange reserves, early in April 1999 the central bank switched to a policy of money supply expansion, with the monetary base growing at a faster pace than it had in the first quarter of 1999. Also at that time, the Duma passed an amendment to the 1999 budget law that raised the ceiling on the amount of gold and foreign exchange reserves the central bank could use to repay the government's foreign debt over the year from $2.1 billion to $4.5 billion.

Meanwhile, the monetary base was expanding without strongly pulling along net domestic assets, drawing instead on the growing net international reserves. With the central bank receiving no loans from international organizations during this period, the growth in its gold and foreign exchange reserves was equivalent to that in net international reserves.

In April and May 1999, the monetary base grew faster than it had in the first quarter of the year (see Figure 12.5). Overall, the monetary base had grown by about 14.2% from the start of the year, which meant that the real monetary base had contracted by 6.3%. The central bank's liabilities grew in April and May chiefly because of the hard-currency purchases it was making to replenish its gold and foreign exchange reserves (see Figure 12.5) and to pay off the federal external debts.

In May 1999, political factors dominated the currency market. The resignation of the Primakov government and voting in the State Duma to impeach the President on 12 May destabilized the currency market for a few days. The failure of the impeachment attempt on 15 May and the rapid endorsement of Sergei Stepashin as prime minister by the State Duma on 19 May combined to lower the political risk level and improve the market situation somewhat. The situation on the currency market stabilized before the month was over.

The currency market remained relatively calm through June 1999. Its composure gave the central bank an opportunity to introduce, beginning on 29 June 1999, a single trading session for US dollars to be exchanged for Russian rubles.[13] The monetary aggregate M2 had grown by 26.6% in the six months of 1999, and cash in hand (M0) had increased by 15.2%. In the absence of developed financial markets, the changes in the money supply structure (the share of cash in hand having fallen to 38.1% from 44.1% in October 1998 and the monetary multiplier[14] having edged up from ca. 2.0 to 2.2–2.3) were expected to be evidence of improved liquidity in the nonfinancial sector of the economy.

The share of claims against nonfinancial sector businesses in total domestic lending (aggregate of all claims by the banking system against the economy) went down from 40.3% to 32.5% in the period between August 1998 and June 1999, while the share of claims against the enlarged government rose from 58.9% to 66.3%. Russian commercial banks had not, therefore, modified their attitude to the real sector despite a visible growth in industrial output and the rising profitability of manufacturing enterprises. Loans were as rigidly rationed as before, and in the absence of financial markets, lending to government at all levels remained the single most important area of business for commercial banks.

---

13. This decision was effected with the central bank's regulation No. 17-P, of 16 June 1999, simultaneously with the repeal of the central bank's regulation No. 57-P, of 28 September 1998, on special trading sessions.
14. The ratio of M2 to the narrow money base.

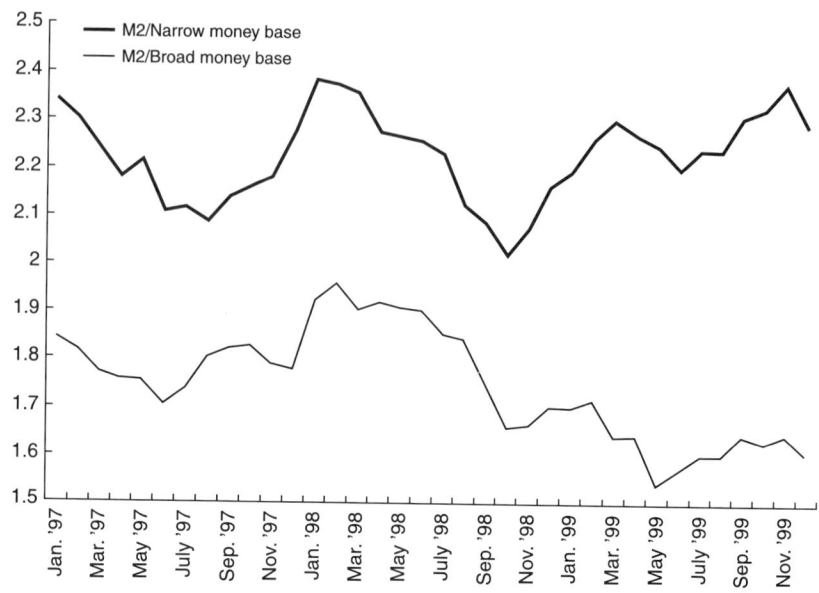

Figure 12.7
Monetary multiplier fluctuation. (Source: Bank of Russia.)

A useful illustration is provided by the ratio of the two monetary multipliers computed from two different bases: the ratio of M2 to the narrow monetary base and the ratio of M2 to the broad monetary base (or reserve money; Figure 12.7). Whereas these two indicators had identical dynamics before the August 1998 crisis, beginning in January 1999 they started to move in different directions: while the narrow monetary base was now growing, the broad monetary base multiplier continued to slump. This difference can be explained chiefly by a wider gap between the narrow and broad monetary bases, that is, the sum of idle reserves (balances in correspondent accounts with the central bank) and funds deposited by commercial banks with the central bank. An analysis of the broad monetary base dynamics shows, therefore, that money is locked up within the banking system. Here it poses a threat to the national currency exchange rate at the slightest hint of uncertainty and is reluctant to flow into the real sector of the economy.

In the first half of 1999, the growth rate of the money aggregates trailed the rate of inflation. As a result, the real money supply (aggregate M2) in early July 1999 was 28%–29% below the precrisis level registered in July 1998 (Figure 12.8).

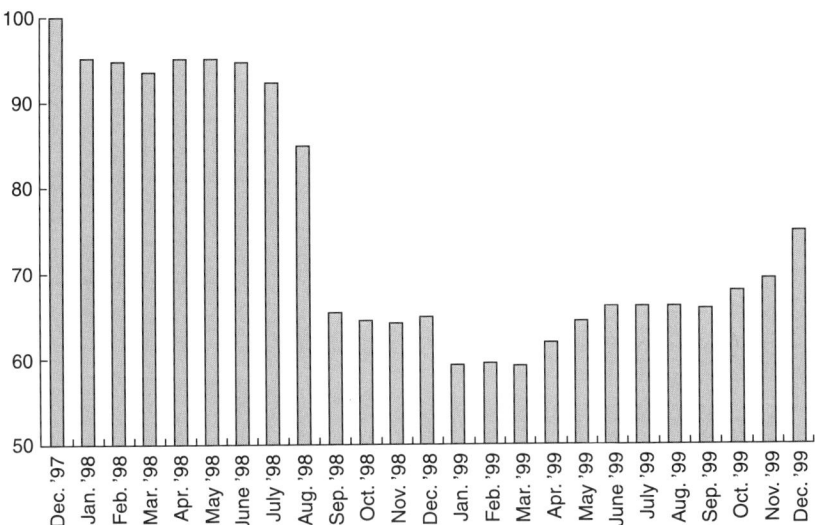

Figure 12.8
Real M2, December 1997–December 1999 (December 1997 = 100). (Sources: Russian Central Bank, Goskomstat, IET.)

On 10 June 1999 the central bank reduced the refinancing rate, for the first time in a year (Figure 12.9), by 5 percentage points, to 55% per annum. In a situation in which the number of the government ruble-denominated bond market participants was limited (see Appendix I), this change in the refinancing rate was a symbolic gesture.

The money the central bank continued to issue through the second quarter of 1999 sped up price growth rates. Because of the time lag of six to nine months (shorter in the absence of financial markets) between a rise in money supply and the time prices begin rising, the impact of this policy was not felt until mid-summer 1999.

In July 1999, the weekly consumer price index growth rates picked up noticeably, bringing inflation to 2.8% for the month. Considerable variations in the relative growth rates of prices for different groups of goods may be cited among the supplementary factors impacting the inflationary processes. In the period 1992–1998, prices for consumer services led those for food and nonfood products, mostly below the consumer price index growth rates. In the first seven months of 1999, however, the food product price index rose 30.0%, nonfoods registered a 26.1% growth, and the services trailed at 23.1% only. To make matters worse, gasoline prices were hiked up sharply in late

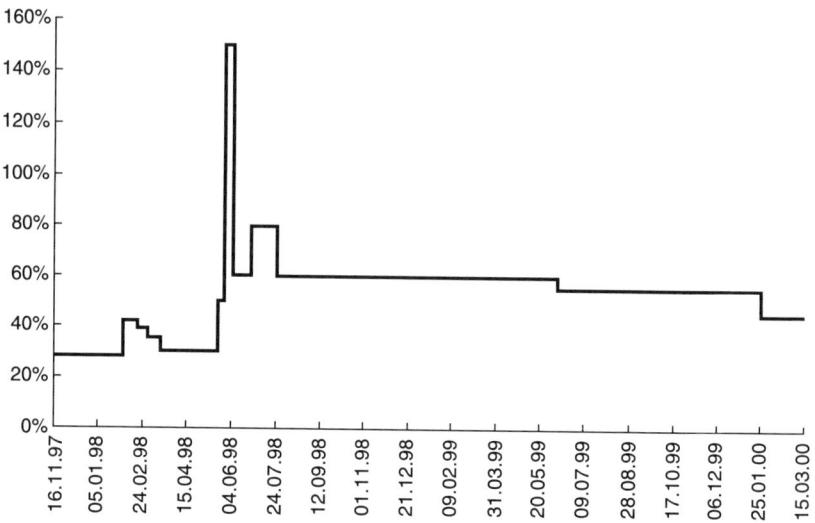

Figure 12.9
Russian Central Bank refinancing rate, 1997–2000.

June and early July.[15] Changes in the tax system were a further contributing factor: a sales tax, effective from 1 July 1999, was introduced in some regions of the Russian Federation, and the list of goods eligible for a reduced VAT was shortened severely.

The narrow money base continued to rise through July 1999, posting an increase of almost 3% in the first two weeks of the month. The actual money issue scale proved even more significant, since the central bank sterilized the money supply growth by expanding its deposit and open market operations. In the third week of July 1999, however, the central bank adopted a tougher monetary policy than it had followed in the preceding three or four months. The money supply growth slowed to a monthly rate of 1% or less through the rest of the year.

The currency market remained calm in July 1999. The official dollar exchange rate was almost flat through the month (see Figure

---

15. Specifically, according to Goskomstat figures, prices for different gasoline grades grew between 7% and 11% in June. In July 1999 they rose by another 15.2%. The prices for motor fuel rose in the wake of rising oil prices on the world markets, combined with coordinated moves by Russian market participants. Moreover, producer prices in April through June outstripped consumer prices by an average of 3.5%–3.6% a month, escalating consumer inflation in the months ahead.

12.6). Toward the end of the month, however, the market players began exhibiting faint signs of speculative activity. They were probably encouraged by the central bank's rapidly dwindling gold and foreign exchange reserves (in July, the gold and foreign exchange reserves were reduced by $231 million, or 1.9%, and in August they shed another $690 million, or 5.8%).

Mid-August to Late 1999
Exactly a year after the crisis of August 1998, the currency market was again reverberating with political events. The population's demand for cash dollars rose sharply within days of Stepashin's resignation as prime minister. Yet the hard-currency purchasing and selling rates went up only insignificantly at exchange offices. The US dollar, for example, gained a paltry one or two rubles.

The central bank's vigorous interventions quelled the rising speculative wave of demand for dollar and calmed the currency market. On 9 August 1999, the today dollar exchange rate at the SELT single trading session rose by 3% over its August 6 showing. It then slid back gradually, reaching 24.75 rubles at the end of the month. The central bank's interventions on 9–15 August dented its gold and foreign exchange reserves by 2.65%, from $11.7 billion to $11.4 billion.

In September 1999 the dollar reached a new peak at the SELT single session, registering Rb 25.89 on 3 September for trades executed tomorrow. Again, the dollar retreated slowly for the rest of the month (see Figure 12.6), yielding to the pressure of the central bank's currency interventions and under the effect of the government's decision to feed nonresidents' funds into the MICEX settlement system.[16] The official dollar exchange rate advanced 1.33% for the whole of September.

In October 1999 the ruble lost more ground to the dollar, slightly faster than the month before. The official dollar exchange rate moved up 4.03%. The deadline for large sums to be repaid on foreign debts

---

16. The central bank's decision of 16 September 1999 applied to nonresidents who kept their funds in C accounts with Russian commercial banks. Under that decision, all ruble-denominated monies in these accounts which their owners received as a result of GKO-Minfin bond novation or from the sale of bonds issued as a result of restructuring on the secondary market were to be transferred into the MICEX settlement system. Since commercial banks relied on liabilities to finance their own operations, the decision increased the demand for liquid assets within the banking system.

at the end of 1999, the IMF's postponement of another tranche, and lack of progress in talks with the London Club of creditors to restructure the debts of the former USSR forced the central bank to review its open market position. The central bank reverted to its policy of building up its gold and foreign exchange reserves. In the first half of the month, it managed to add $0.8 billion to its reserves. A faster growth of the monetary base in October (3.9% for the narrow money base) could largely be attributed to ruble interventions on the currency market. In turn, the increasing money issue sped up inflationary processes, and the ruble resumed wobbling against the dollar.

In August 1999, the increase in the consumer price index was only 1.2%. Seasonal factors typical of this month were behind the slowdown in the consumer price creep. They continued well into September, holding inflation to 1.5%. In October 1999, the consumer price index eased to 1.4%. The relatively low inflation persisting in this period could be attributed above all to slackening money issue by the central bank in the summer and early autumn of 1999. To forestall an inflationary fallout of an expanding money supply, on 12 October 1999 the federal government approved regulations to control money issue and the registration of central bank bonds. This financial instrument was to give the central bank added powers to control the money supply, specifically by sterilizing ruble interventions on the currency market. The auctions, held as late as 14 December, only to place the new instruments, were aborted owing to lack of demand at prices acceptable for the issuer.

The money aggregate dynamics in November, therefore, were typical for several months of 1999: rapid acceleration at the start of the month, followed by a gradual slowdown over the next two or three weeks, a pattern that allowed the central bank to combine its policy of building up gold and foreign exchange reserves and restrain money supply growth. In November and December 1999, consumer prices held steady at a monthly growth rate of 1.2%–1.3%.

In November 1999, the currency market was spared sharp exchange-rate fluctuations. The dollar advanced by 1.26% during the month at the official exchange rate. Nevertheless, devaluationary moods among currency market players edged up a little. Even after the Export-Import Bank of Japan agreed in late November to give $375 million in loan to Russia, some concern over foreign debt repayment persisted: in late November and December, Russia was to pay about $352 million on eurobonds, $800 million to repay the IMF loan, and a further $170 million to the Paris Club. It was very probable that the central bank would soften its exchange-rate policy and that the dollar would shoot up in early 2000 as a result.

In December 1999, days before Russia's foreign debt came due, and with new foreign loans nowhere in sight, the central bank stepped up its ruble interventions on the currency market in an attempt to rebuild its gold and foreign exchange reserves. Over the month, its gold and foreign exchange reserves rose by $1.2 billion (or by about 10%) to $12.7 billion, a record since November 1998. The scale of ruble interventions is reflected in the growth of the monetary base from Rb 272.0 billion to Rb 307.5 billion, or by 13%. As an obvious result of this policy, balances in commercial banks' accounts with the central bank rose sharply, and the ruble exchange rate jumped in the opening days of 2000. In the period from 27 December 1999 to 10 January 2000, the central bank's gold and foreign exchange reserves decreased by $400 million. They rebounded, however, from 10 January 2000 (reaching $12.8 billion by 21 January 2000). Despite a combination of measures undertaken by the central bank (such as resuming deposit operations and operations on the secondary GKO-OFZ bond market), it could not sterilize the money base growth. On 24 January 2000, the narrow money base fell to Rb 302 billion (or Rb 7.2 billion less than it was on 10 January).

In December, the increased supply of foreign exchange as a result of exporters selling their foreign exchange holdings to pay taxes kept the ruble stable against the background of the central bank's ruble interventions. In December, the official exchange rate of the dollar went up by 2.20% (or 29.77% on an annualized basis). The situation was different in January, however. Actually, in its drive to save its reserves during the first two weeks of January only, the central bank allowed the ruble to decline by 5.7%. In this way, the central bank's gold and foreign currency reserves diminished by $400 million between 27 December 1999 and 10 January 2000 (see Figure 12.5). Beginning on 10 January 2000, however, the central bank's gold and foreign exchange reserves started rebuilding again (to $12.8 billion by 21 January 2000). Meanwhile, the official dollar exchange rate climbed by 5.74%.

The narrow money base grew by 48.3% for the whole of 1999 (from Rb 207.3 to Rb 307.5 billion), and the broad money base swelled by 66.8%, from Rb 263.7 to Rb 439.7 billion. In 1999, the money base registered a real growth of 8.5% for the aggregate in its narrow sense, and 22.0% for the aggregate defined broadly.

Other money aggregates grew more slowly in 1999. In particular, the money supply M1 gained 53.7% (or 12.4% in real terms), the money supply M2 expanded by 57.2% (or 15.0% in real terms), and broad money rose by 56.7% (or 14.6% in real terms). Given a drop in the real money supply in January 1999, demand for money (in the aggregate M2) was set to advance by 25.8% for the year. With the GDP deflator lagging behind the consumer price index, the GDP monetization was expected, according to preliminary estimates, to reach 14.6% in 1999—a record for the period since price liberalization.

The Finance Ministry's high demand for foreign exchange versus the central bank's restrictive monetary policy translated into an insignificant growth in the real ruble exchange rate in 1999. The consequences of this real exchange-rate policy for the Russian economy were varied, particularly when the short- and long-term effects of devaluation are separated. An analysis of theoretical constructions measuring the impact of the real exchange rate of the national currency on economic growth, as applied to the development pattern of the Russian economy in September 1998 to December 1999, yields a number of beneficial and adverse effects of devaluation and restraints preventing long-term advantages to be gained from the devalued ruble.

12.2. Trends in the Real Sector of the Economy: Revival of Export-Generating and Import-Substituting Industries

A rapid growth in manufacturing was a distinctive feature of the Russian economy in 1999. The gross industrial output in 1999 advanced by 8.1%, the highest growth rate in ten years. In 1999, industrial output was 2.5% higher than in the memorable year of 1997, when recovery was achieved for the first time since the onset of reforms, and the industrial growth index reached 102.0%. The GDP increased by 3.2% over 1998. Not even these high growth rates in 1999 could offset the consequences of the economic slump triggered by the crisis on the world and domestic financial markets between October 1997 and August 1998. A comparison of key socioeconomic figures for 1998 and 1999 shows that Russia's economy has yet to return to its precrisis level. In 1999, real GDP was 98.1% of the 1997 level.

Financial Policy in 1999

An analysis of structural shifts in the real sector shows that between 1992 and 1998, the slump in the service-providing industries was more moderate than the recession in manufacturing (Table 12.1). Actually, this was a factor restraining the trend toward lower GDP growth rates. In 1997, too, the upwardly trending dynamics of the GDP, propelled by the rising output in both economic sectors, was dominated by the service industries growing at a faster pace than manufacturing output. The situation turned around in 1999: the structural shifts in the GDP were determined by an acceleration in the growth rate in output of goods, while the dynamics of the service sector appeared more gradual.[17]

An analysis of the output proportions of various economic sectors has to allow for the specifics of price formation and dynamics in individual industries and sectors of the economy. Whereas producer prices for manufactured goods rose through 1999 by 67.3% from the beginning of the year and those for farming produce posted an increase of 91.4%, in the service sector, charges paid for consumer services climbed by 34.0%, freightage fees advanced 18.2%, and communications charges rose by 22.8%. Changes in the price structure had an effect on GDP growth proportions. A comparison between GDP growth in current and comparable prices allows the extent of changes in proportions in different economic sectors to be assessed and the real contribution of each industry to be estimated. The manufacturing infrastructure industries intensified their favorable impact on the growth dynamics of GDP generated in 1999. Given a restrained tariff policy, the growth of value added in transport and communications was due both to the larger scale and to the wider range of services provided.

A comparative analysis of the dynamics of different industries shows that manufacturing responded the fastest to changes in the domestic market situation after the August 1998 crisis (Table 12.2). Positive monthly dynamics in manufacturing were registered beginning in the third quarter of 1998, with a slowdown in the uptrend in the second quarter of 1999 being adequately explained by the influence of seasonal factors. Almost all manufacturing firms registered growth in 1999.

---

17. See Richard Caves, Jeffrey A. Frankel, and Ronald W. Jones, *World Trade and Payments* (New York: HarperCollins, 1999) for a discussion of the effect of exchange rate changes on the structure of domestic production.

Table 12.1
Dynamics of Key Macroeconomic Indicators, 1992–1999 (% of Previous Year's Figure)

	1992	1993	1994	1995	1996	1997	1998	1999
GDP	85.5	91.3	87.3	95.9	95.1	100.8	95.4	103.2
Industries	82.0	86.0	79.0	97.0	96.0	101.9	94.8	108.1
Extracting	89.0	90.0	90.0	99.0	98.0	103.0	96.5	
Processing	81.0	85.0	76.0	96.0	95.0	101.8	92.8	
Consumer goods	85.0	89.0	74.0	87.9	93.4	102.1	93.6	
Agriculture	91.0	96.0	88.8	92.0	93.0	100.1	87.7	102.4
Investment in fixed assets	60.0	88.0	76.0	90.0	82.0	94.5	93.3	101.0
Freight turnover	86.0	88.0	86.0	99.0	95.4	96.6	96.5	105.2
Communication services							119.9	133.1
Retail trade turnover	97.0	102.0	100.1	93.0	96.0	101.4	96.7	92.3
Paid services to households	82.0	70.0	62.0	82.0	94.0	103.7	99.5	102.4
Foreign trade turnover	—	90.6	100.3	122.3	108.2	102.9	82.3	
Exports	—	87.9	106.9	118.8	113.9	97.7	84.1	
Imports	—	77.2	90.8	128.2	99.4	107.0	80.2	
Real disposable money incomes	53.0	116.0	112.0	84.0	100.0	106.3	81.9	84.9
Real wages and salaries							86.6	76.8
Unemployment (registered)	—	164.6	202.5	145.2	124.9	88.9	82.1	85.1
Price indices:								
Consumer	2,608.6	939.9	315.1	231.3	121.8	111.0	184.4	136.5
Foodstuffs	2,626.2	904.9	314.1	223.4	117.7	109.1	196.6	134.0
Nonfoods	2,673.4	741.8	269.0	216.3	117.8	108.1	199.5	139.2
Paid services to households	2,220.5	2,411.2	622.4	332.3	148.4	122.5	118.3	134.0
Industrial								
Finished products:	3,380.0	1,000.0	330.0	275.0	125.6	107.4	123.2	167.3
Purchased resources	—	—	305.0	314.4	124.3	106.8		
Capital construction	1,610.0	1,160.0	530.0	270.0	137.3	105.0	112.1	146.0
Freight carriage	2,050.0	1,850.0	760.0	300.0	122.1	100.9	116.7	118.2
Communication services	—	—	—	—	144.7	104.2	106.2	122.8
Agriculture	940.0	810.0	300.0	330.0	140.0	108.0	166.4	191.4

Source: Russian Statistical Agency.

Financial Policy in 1999

Table 12.2
Growth Rates (%) of Industrial Performance Indices

Industry	Jan. 97–Jan. 2000	Aug. 98–Jan. 2000
Total industry	16.60%	23.57%
Fuel and energy complex	2.56	4.68
Electric power industry	3.98	5.08
Oil extracting industry	2.41	2.53
Oil processing industry	−0.61	5.19
Natural gas industry	−0.94	−2.68
Coal industry	5.49	14.22
Ferrous metallurgy	19.46	36.42
Nonferrous metallurgy	18.12	12.20
Machine building	21.22	46.79
Chemical and petrochemical industry	28.61	37.74
Wood, wood-processing, and pulp- and-paper industry	50.44	36.95
Constructing material industry	7.58	11.24
Food industry	22.05	23.48
Light industry	36.14	83.74

Source: RF government's Center for Economic Trend Analysis (seasonally adjusted values).

The growth dynamics of individual sectors were affected by a set of specific factors and conditions. Real ruble devaluation, however, was certainly the most important influence. The beneficial effects of devaluation are widely known. They are, above all, growth in import-substituting output in the real sector of the economy and a higher earning capacity in export-oriented industries.[18]

Concomitant with the ruble's devaluation, favorable changes on the world market for fuel and primary resources boosted growth rates in export-oriented industries of the mining sector. The recovery of the manufacturing dynamics can be traced to growth in demand

---

18. In the following paragraphs we examine the effect of the manufacturers' improved financial position on the declining proportion of nonmonetary settlements in the real sector, reduced arrears among businesses, and improved tax revenues to the budget. Besides, devaluation of the national currency and the accompanying growth in domestic prices cut into the real wealth of businesses denominated in the national currency. In such a situation, current consumption contracts and savings grow, providing the economy with additional funds to step up investment, and the labor supply expands. In the Russian economy, however, the banking crisis and high rates of inflation devalued a considerable proportion of the population's savings and sharply undercut confidence in the banking system—a poor climate for investment resource accumulation. As well, a large proportion of the Russian populace saves in foreign currencies, so the actual effect of wealth cannot be estimated with any degree of accuracy.

for domestically produced manufactured goods on the internal market and to intensified import-substitution processes.

It must be noted that all economic growth forecasts made in the autumn of 1998 underestimated the Russian economy's capacity to respond to devaluation by vigorously stepping up output. It appeared more likely that the niches previously filled by imports would stand empty. What actually happened was that a large percentage of imports were successfully replaced by their domestic equivalents. This situation came about both because of changes in the domestic consumption structure (a shift toward less expensive, sometimes lower-quality goods after the deep plunge in real incomes put more expensive consumer goods out of reach of the general public) and because of the pent-up potential of domestic industries. Regardless of the standards of their technology and labor quality, Russian manufacturing industries proved remarkably capable of turning out a wide range of products, the demand for which had earlier been met almost entirely by imports.

Along with the falling real exchange rate of the ruble, production growth in the manufacturing sector was stimulated by government measures imposed to restrict the import of competing goods (steel pipes, for example) and by greater government support for certain industries (for example, by placing more orders with defense industry enterprises).

The industrial growth in the Russian economy that was awakening in the autumn of 1998 signaled the beginning of the end to the severe crisis brought about by the transition from a planned economy to a market economy. The highest growth rates were posted predominantly by industries (such as consumer goods, food, and engineering) producing for the domestic market (see Table 12.2). Despite a reduction in the population's real incomes,[19] demand for domestically produced goods grew, as consumer imports were largely outcompeted. Obviously, foreign-produced goods were now too expensive for most of the population, even if they were superior to domestic competitors in quality.[20]

---

19. Even though monthly dynamics trended upward from time to time during the course of the year, the population's real incomes amounted, on final tabulation, to 84.9% of the preceding year's average, and real wages were even lower, at 76.0% of the preceding year's average.

20. See also Karen Lewis, "Trying to Explain Home Bias in Equities and Consumption," *The Journal of Economic Literature* 37 (June 1999): 571–608.

Output in the light and food industries grew in 1999, for the first time since the start of reforms. As businesses improved their financial standing enough to be able to make investments, the demand for capital goods and, accordingly, output growth rates rose in the second half of 1999. The rising output of high-quality goods raised the share of value-added industries in the structure of generated GDP from 29.0% in 1998 to 45.7% in 1999.

Industrial growth in turn gave rise to a higher demand for infrastructure services—commercial freight turnover rose by 5.2% over 1998, and communications services went up by 36.3%.

Communications and information technologies remain a leading and dynamically growing industry. Communications services accounted for 1.8% of GDP in 1999, an increase of 1.2 percentage points over the previous eight-year period. The communications sector has been showing a recovery since 1996.

Commercial freight turnover in all modes of transport operations rose 5.2% from 1998, with railroads, which carry over a third of total freight, posting an 18.1% growth. Growing freight carriage rates have been stimulated both by rising demand for domestically produced goods on the internal market and by steadily climbing exports, both in volume and share of the total freight.

The retail turnover had a negative impact on the dynamics of market services in trade during 1999. The downward trend in retailing began early in 1998, fueled by falling personal incomes. Retail turnover shrank by 10.8% from the year before. The growth in the retail gross income under the effect of value factors, however, acted to increase its share in the GDP.[21]

A factor to be reckoned with in analyzing retail trade dynamics is that the period of 1998–1999 was accentuated by a downtrend in the share of imports in the structure of commercial inventories. Whereas domestically manufactured goods accounted for 52% of retail inventories in the first and second quarters of 1998, their share had risen to 71% by the fourth quarter, at the expense of imports, which had fallen proportionally. This trend continued into 1999, with preliminary estimates from the Russian Ministry of Economy putting the

---

21. An analysis of changes in the GDP share of trade should take account the specific methods used to compute this indicator, especially estimates of the foreign trade gross income at basic prices. As the level and structure of domestic prices changed with ruble devaluation, foreign trade became a more lucrative operation, with the GDP share of trade rising by 4.0 percentage points from 1998.

shares of imports and domestically produced goods in the retail turnover structure at 27% and 73%, respectively. The gloomy predictions of a possible crisis on the consumer market following the August 1998 crisis proved utterly incorrect. The growing output of domestically produced consumer goods was a stabilizing factor in the consumer sector.

Another specific of 1999 was that manufacturing infrastructure services were growing at a higher rate than services provided to the public. The continued reduction in the volume of nonmarket services paid for out of the government's budget and off-budget funds had a significant effect on the situation on the public services market. The share of these services in GDP dropped by 3.7 percentage points compared with 1998. The declining scale of service provision was generally in line with dwindling consumer demand.

The growth in output raised the demand for labor, which somewhat eased the tight labor market. Beginning in February, employment grew steadily, and the total jobless figures, including the number of people registered with the employment service, showed a strong falling trend. Employment started to rise for the first time in the many years of reform. Total unemployment decreased by 1.3 million in absolute figures over the year, and the number of people on official jobless lists of the employment service fell by 0.6 million. The ratio of the jobless registered with the employment service to one advertised vacancy dropped from 6.5 in November 1998 to 2.4 in November 1999. As a result, total unemployment was back to its precrisis figures, which helped ease social tensions, particularly at the regional level. Despite these favorable changes on the labor market, the situation remains unstable, as evidenced by persisting stagnant unemployment, widespread involuntary part-time employment, and related overstaffing.

12.2.1. Profitability of Production and Changes in the GDP Structure According to Incomes

The ruble's devaluation significantly improved the earning capacity of exporting manufacturers. The growing output in import-substituting industries improved earnings and profit margins as well, owing to a considerable percentage of fixed costs in the cost structure. In January through November 1999, the economy made an

Table 12.3
GDP Formation Structure by Revenue Source

	1995	1996	1997	1998	1999
Wages and salaries (including concealed) of employees (% of total)	45.2	49.6	49.3	49.3	40.2
Net taxes on production and imports (% of total)	11.9	13.5	14.2	14.8	15.7
Gross economic profit and gross mixed incomes (% of total)	42.9	36.9	36.5	35.9	44.1
Total GDP	100.0	100.0	100.0	100.0	100.0

Source: Russian Statistical Agency. Calculations based on Rosstatagentstvo and Ministry of the Economy data.

aggregate profit of Rb 279.9 billion, a threefold improvement over the previous year's profit (or nearly twofold in real terms). With respect to performance results for January through November, the share of unprofitable enterprises dropped by 10.0 percentage points from the period January–November 1998. Profitability for all industries showed an improvement of 7.2 percentage points over 1998, reaching 15.3%. Financial performance actually improved in all manufacturing industry groups. The GDP share of gross economic profit and production and import taxes rose as well (Table 12.3).

The beneficial combination of devaluation and rising prices on the world market for fuel and primary commodities gave a healthy boost to profit margins in export-oriented extractive industries and primary processing enterprises. Also headed in the same direction on the domestic market was a trend for prices of intermediate products to stay ahead of price dynamics in capital and consumer goods. The share of extractive and primary processing industries in total industrial profits expanded by almost 30.0 percentage points.

Assuming the share of foreign exchange costs of Russian exporting manufacturers to be in the range of 10%–20% of total production costs,[22] the falling exchange rate of the ruble translates into profit a significant proportion of receipts resulting from the higher ruble-denominated value of products sold for foreign currency. This effect stimulates investment of company assets, broadens opportunities for borrowing from banks at higher interest rates, and helps increase budget tax revenues at all levels.

---

22. These estimates were prepared by the Economic Expert Group of the Russian Finance Ministry.

The government's regulation of prices and tariffs for the output of natural monopolies was a further factor stimulating industrial growth. Gas prices, which were held stable from late 1996 to October 1999, were responsible for the low-keyed dynamics of prices in power engineering: electric power sold to industrial consumers registered a price rise of 20.7% for all of 1999. Wholesale prices for natural gas were raised by 15% on 1 November 1999.

The restrained prices for the output of natural monopolies produced significant disproportions between their prices and tariffs in consumers' favor. At midpoint of the first half-year, price dynamics revealed new trends toward a considerable slowdown in prices for consumer goods and capital goods and higher growth rates of prices for intermediates.

Manufacturing industries, reeling under the constraints of lower domestic demand, reverted to a restrained pricing policy in the second quarter of 1999. In our estimate, about 80% of profit growth in industries producing capital and consumer goods is contributed by pricing policies and the remaining 20% is contributed by reductions in material inputs.

Inflation was much higher in manufacturing as a whole in 1999 than on the consumer market—67.3%. Prices were rising at high rates under the pull of demand for domestically produced goods, the greater efficiency of exports, lower competition from significantly curtailed imports, the growth of world prices for oil and petroleum products and several other Russian exports, and the rising costs of imported primary materials.

Improvements in the financial standing of manufacturing enterprises and their growing profits were also made possible by positive shifts in production and technologies—cost reductions, the adoption of resource-saving technologies, restructuring, and the manufacture of competitive products. In the nine months of 1999, manufacturing costs fell by 13.7% from the same period in the preceding year. Profit margins, however, rose to 27.1%, up from 9.7% for the nine months of 1998. The fuel industry posted the greatest cost reduction (24.8%) of all manufacturing industries.

Costs fell in all categories of assets except primary materials. Fuel and power costs were forced down by the government's policy of holding up prices for the output of natural monopolies. Depreciation charges dropped as well, because producers and offices failed to revalue their fixed assets as of 1 January 1999.

12.2.2. Investments in the Real Sector of the Economy

The dynamics of investment in fixed assets showed an upswing in 1999, for the first time in eight years. The slump in investment slowed over the first half of 1999, with July seeing a bottom and the beginning of an upturn in fixed capital investment. Over the whole of 1999, organizations and enterprises under all forms of ownership invested Rb 598.7 billion in fixed assets, 1% more than the year before. Production in investment industries posted a growth for the first time since the reforms had started.

Investment in housing construction and utilities accounted for about a third of the total investment made in social and civilian projects. After a five-year lull, investment in housing construction started to grow again in 1999, with more ready housing commissioned. In 1999, enterprises and organizations under all forms of ownership built 32.0 million square meters of housing, or 4.3% more than in the preceding year. In sixty-three of the eighty-nine regions, more housing was built in 1999 than in 1998. Business activity in housing construction continued to finish previous startups and to expand building operations.

To assess the effect of this process on general economic conditions, we need to see its specific aspects in perspective. An unprecedented curtailment of investment is a striking specific of Russian reforms (Figure 12.10). In 1999, investment in fixed capital entailed a low 26.3% of outlays in the prereform year of 1991. The investment slump in the period 1992–1999, however, was structural in nature, exposed as it was to the combined effect of such factors as shifts in the sectoral, technological, and reproductive forces in the national economy.

Sectoral Structure of Investment in Fixed Capital

Changes in the GDP structure were accompanied by a reshuffle of fixed capital investment flows from manufacturing into the service sector. In 1998, investment in services accounted for 59.0% of the total investment made in the national economy, compared to 43.0% immediately before the start of reforms. The channeling of investment flows into the services went along with an increase in the share of infrastructure industries. Between 1997 and 1999, transportation, communications, and trade claimed, on average, a fifth of the total investment in fixed capital, almost double the 12% average for the period 1992–1996.

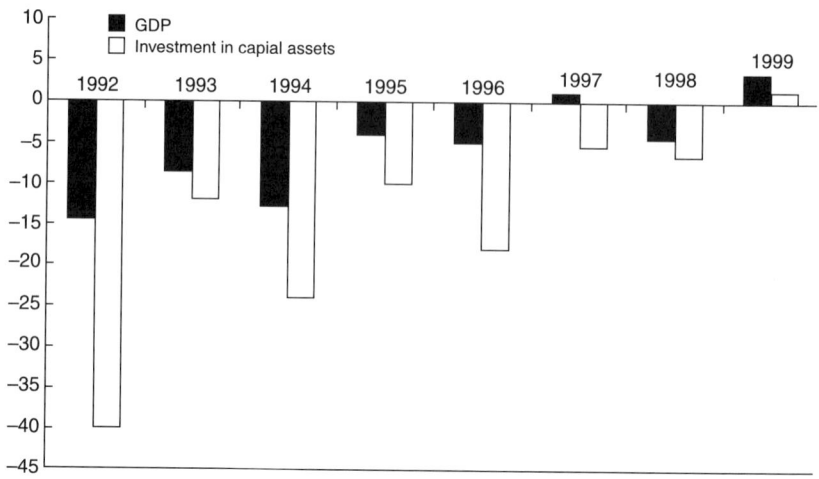

Figure 12.10
Change in rate of GDP and investment in capital assets between 1992 and 1998 (percentage of prior year's figure). (Source: Goskomstat of RF.)

The dynamic growth of communications and information technologies was maintained by heavy investing. Whereas investment in communications accounted for less than 1% of the total for the national economy in 1994, it reached 3.8% in 1999, despite the dampening effect of the financial crisis. Expanding investment activity in the industry and growing demand for communications services tend to trigger economic recovery. Notably, the investment policy in the industry aims to solve long-term problems. Typical for 1999 was a trend toward expanding the market and structure of communications services provision while at the same time restraining the tariffs charged for communications services. As a result, communications companies were able to maintain or expand their presence on the services market and develop a foundation for future growth.

With a change in the institutional structure of the economy and reduced government presence on the capital market, the share of investment in agriculture declined from 10.8% in 1992 to 2.5%–3.0% in the period 1996–1999. Between 1994 and 1998, investment in manufacturing averaged approximately a third of total investment in fixed capital.

As the slump in industrial production abated, the decline in investment slowed down as well. This process was acutely differentiated according to periods and industries. In 1997, for example, a revision of tax privileges caused a considerable slowdown in investment in industrial construction. For a 5.0% reduction in investment in fixed capital in the economy in general, investment in industrial construction stood at 99.0% of the preceding year's level. This trend did not survive, however, in 1998, when a crisis exploded in the financial sector of the economy, and investment activity dropped sharply again. A change in the economic climate in 1999 brought about an 8.8% growth in investment in industrial fixed capital in comparison with the preceding year.

A notable development of 1998 and 1999 has been significant changes in the investment structure of industrial complexes. The situation in 1999 was radically different from the period of 1992–1997, when the share of investment in the fuel and energy complex was steadily rising and that in the industrial complex was falling correspondingly. According to tentative figures from the Russian Ministry of Economy, investment in engineering in 1999 rose by 36.9% from 1998, in comparison with a 2.2% fall in investment in the fuel industry and a 21.4% drop in investment in the power industry.

A vigorous growth of investment in the consumer complex was another characteristic development of 1998 and 1999. The food industry, which in 1997 accounted for 9.5% of the total investment in industrial fixed capital, saw its share rise to 15.9% in 1999. The expanding investments in the fixed capital of the food and medical industries—35.7% and 94.8%, respectively—reflected the trend to substitute domestically produced goods for consumer imports.

The structural change in investment from industry to industry reflects the Russian business community's response to shifts on the domestic market and the growing demand for domestically produced manufactures. Despite sturdy growth, however, current investments are too little to sustain steady economic growth.

Structure of Financial Investment Sources

Corporate funds are the principal sources enterprises and organizations can rely on to finance investment in fixed assets. In 1999, the share of such funds in the fixed assets of enterprises stood at the preceding year's level of 53.6% (Table 12.4). The percentage of enterprise-owned funds differs significantly by industry and sector. In the power industry, enterprise-owned funds account for around 90% of investments. In the gas industry they amount to 82%, in the oil industry 74%, and in pipeline operations 55%.

Table 12.4
Investment in Fixed Assets, by Financing Source
(Prices in Respective Years)

	1997	1998	1999 (Jan.–Sept.)
Investment in fixed assets	100.0	100.0	100.0
1. Internal and borrowed funds		80.2	83.3
a. Internal funds of enterprises	60.8	53.6	53.5
i. Accumulation fund	13.2	13.3	14.2
b. Borrowed funds	18.5	25.2	28.9
i. Commercial banks' loans			5.7
—Funds borrowed from other sources			5.5
ii. Extrabudgetary funds			9.5
—Other			8.2
2. Consolidated budget funds	20.7	19.2	17.6
a. Federal budget funds	10.2	6.6	4.8

Source: Russian Statistical Agency.

Given the high risks involved, the lending and banking sector shows virtually no interest in investing in the real sector of the economy. Lending institutions give clear preference to short-term operations, their share of long-term loans standing at less than 5.0%.

The share of bank loans and foreign direct investments in the structure of sources drawn upon to finance investment in fixed capital in 1999 registered an uptick under the impact of favorable changes in general economic conditions.

Foreign direct investments rose significantly in 1999 compared with 1998, to $2.4 billion in the first half-year, up from $1.5 billion for the first six months of the previous year. Actual investments were made, however, as a result of talks that had been ongoing for several years and the launch of projects discussed during the talks. The heaviest flow of direct investments went into the fuel industry (oil above all) and the food industry, for logical reasons: fuel is the most efficient industry in strategic terms, while food has a short payback period.

The talks with the international financial organizations that went on throughout the year showed that, in an atmosphere in which a lack of confidence in the Russian authorities prevailed, repayment of outstanding loans could be deferred and new loans granted only through political expediency. Domestic political uncertainty in the run-up to parliamentary and presidential elections, as well as growing tensions with developed countries (first over Kosovo, and lately over Chechnya), had a discouraging effect on foreign creditors' co-operation with Russia in 1999.

The restrained budgetary policy reinforced the trend toward further cuts in the share of budgetary funds among the sources available to finance investment in fixed capital. As a result, the share of budgetary funds in fixed capital investments shrank to 1.5% of GDP in 1999.

The share of private investments in the total funds invested in the fixed capital of businesses under various forms of ownership declined to 26.4% in 1999, from 31.6% in January–September 1998. Since the bulk of private investments are made by private home builders, reductions in personal incomes and savings reduced investment capacities and the number of prospective investors. Moreover, public confidence in savings institutions, deflated by the financial crisis, is rebuilding too slowly. With the share of circulating cash (rather than in bank accounts) remaining high, and in the absence of a mechanism to transform circulating paper money into investments, the national economy is suffering heavy losses from the underutilization of the population's accumulated investment potential.

Investments packaged according to forms of ownership had a specific property that came to the surface in 1999. The change in the domestic market situation following the ruble's devaluation spurred foreign capital into activity. Foreign direct investments rose by 56% over the period January–September 1998, with 64.0% of those investments being funneled into manufacturing. In contrast to 1998, the share of investments made by enterprises with foreign capital and fully foreign-owned enterprises increased by 2.0 percentage points, to 10.0% of the total investment made in fixed capital between January and September 1999. The growth of investment from enterprises with foreign capital was due to a greater emphasis on the production of competitive import-substituting goods in the economy in general and the desire of these enterprises to retain their positions on a potentially vast market.

12.2.3. *Reduction in Nonpayments and Nonmonetary Settlements*

After the start of economic recovery, the second most important positive effect of the ruble devaluation in August 1998 included more money available to enterprises, reduced arrears, and fewer deals settled in ways other than money payment. Swelling circulating assets in the real sector of the economy and money used in all links of the producer-consumer chain stirred demand for industrial output at every stage of production, and therefore led to a rise in aggregate demand in the economy as a whole.

This process was initiated by exporting enterprises, which were deriving larger profits, and by import-substituting product manufacturers, which improved their financial standing on the rising wave of domestic demand for their output. Another circumstance that played a prominent role later on was improved tax collection, which augmented budget revenues and allowed the government to meet its liabilities to the full extent required under the 1999 budget law. The flat growth in businesses' arrears in payments to the budget was a major factor contributing to the reduction in total arrears in the greater economy.

Beginning in late 1998, the deflated scale of debts receivable and payable that enterprises owed to one another declined steadily. For all of 1999, therefore, the absolute amount of nominal arrears rose at a rate below that of inflation. To assess the dynamics of arrears, however, it is useful to examine series reflecting deflated increments in outstanding receivables and payables or debt increments as percentages of the industrial output for a respective period. As shown in Figure 12.11, the deflated default increments were falling during the entire period under review, at times even becoming negative. Similar dynamics are displayed by the default increment ratio to the industrial output volume.

Arrears and nonmonetary settlements were falling as real cash balances were rising. On the one hand, an expanding real money supply is equivalent to growing liquidity, which facilitates settlements. On the other hand, more frequent monetary settlements raise demand for real cash balances and accordingly cause the real money supply to swell. Moreover, arrears are influenced directly by enterprises' real cash balances rather than by the total volume of the real money supply. Figure 12.12 shows that real cash balances in the ruble-denominated accounts of enterprises increased by nearly 50% in the period between November 1998 and December 1999. Meanwhile, the real money supply (aggregate M2) did not grow by more than 15% or 20% in the same period (see Figure 12.8). Besides, the near absence of income-yielding instruments in the postcrisis period

Financial Policy in 1999

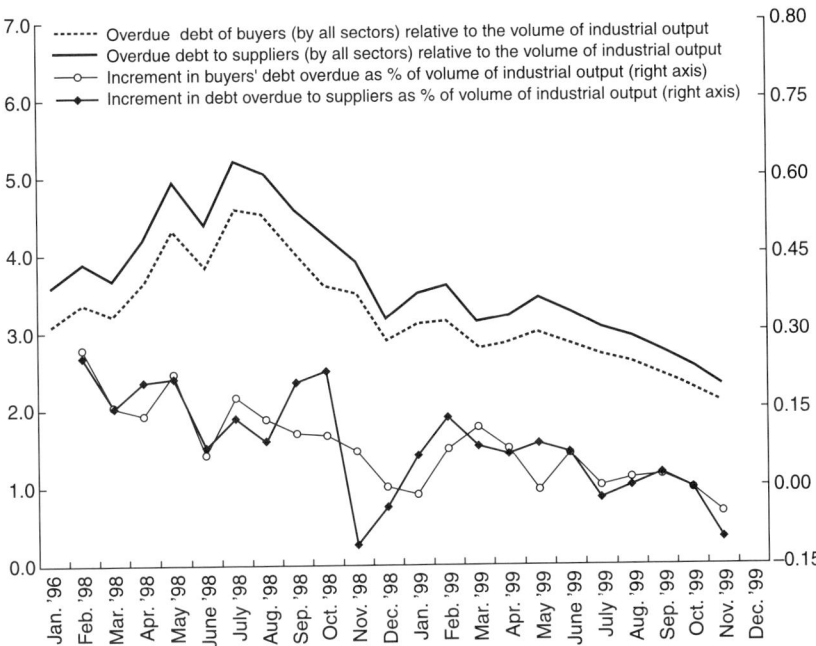

Figure 12.11
Dynamics of enterprises' arrears, January 1998–December 1999. (Source: Goskomstat of RF.)

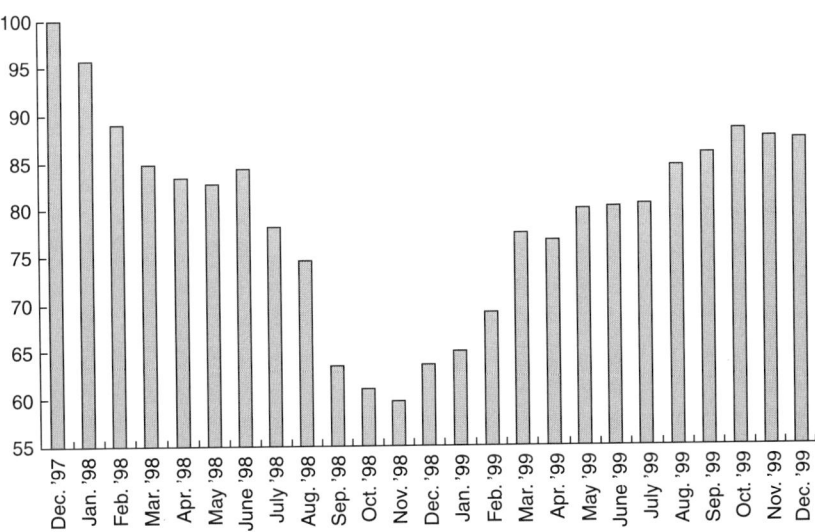

Figure 12.12
Real balances on enterprises' ruble accounts, December 1997–December 1999 (December 1997 = 100). (Sources: RF Goskomstat, Russian Central Bank, and IET calculations.)

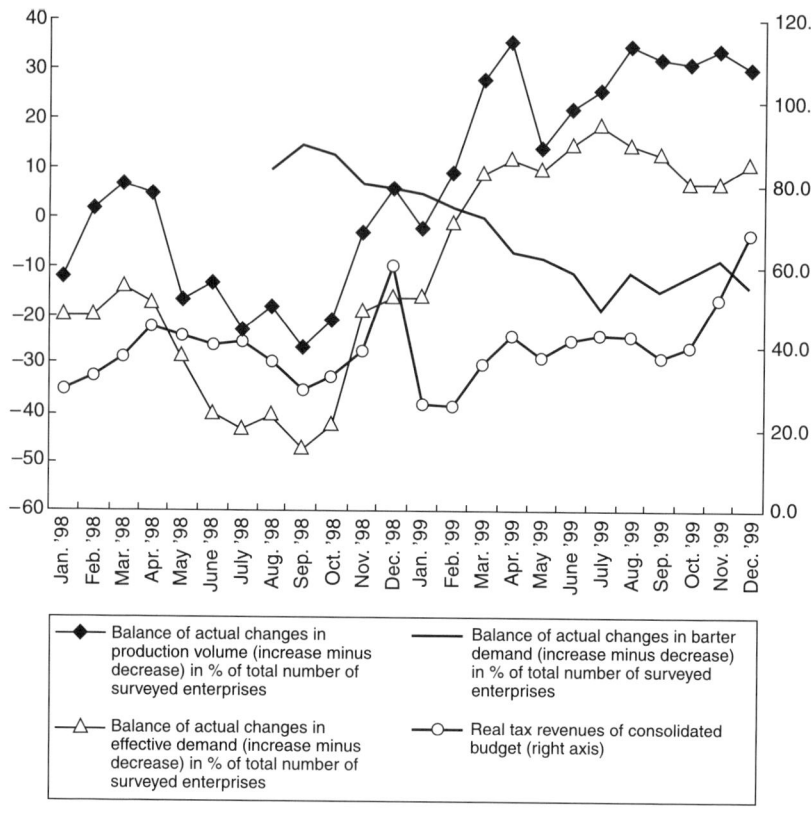

Figure 12.13
Monthly enterprise surveys, January 1998–December 1999 (Source: IET.)

caused (in combination with low inflation) a drop in the alternative value of money saving, depressing incentives to pile up arrears.

Rising effective demand and a diminishing scale of barter in settlements between enterprises are evident in the surveys conducted monthly by the Institute for the Economy in Transition (IET) among enterprises. Figure 12.13 shows the dynamics of balanced responses regarding changes in production volume, changes in effective demand and demand for output paid for with goods (barter demand) rather than money, and real tax revenues of the consolidated budget in 1998–1999.[23]

---

23. The balance of actual changes in production volume is the share of excess of enterprises that have increased their production volume over enterprises whose production volume has decreased from the preceding month in the total number of enterprises (according to survey returns).

Beginning in February 1999, the balance of survey responses regarding changes in production volume became positive, and, from March 1999 on, so did the balance of responses as regards changes in effective demand. Survey returns also show that barter demand fell in the same period (the balance of responses turned negative beginning in April 1999).

12.3. The Budget

12.3.1. *Budget Revenues*

The recovery in production improved the financial standing of enterprises, reduced tax arrears, and set off a growth in tax revenues (1.9% of GDP in 1999 compared with 1998), producing a surplus over the revenue figures provided for in the 1999 budget law and ensuring its use almost entirely in monetary form (according to the Ministry of Taxes and Duties, less than 5% of federal budget revenues in 1999 were drawn in by target financing).

This favorable federal budget situation was largely achieved by redistributing tax revenues from regional budgets to the federal budget. Beginning on 1 April 1999, regions of the Russian Federation could transfer 15% of VAT revenues collected in their respective territories, instead of the 25% previously mandated. Also from that date, the portion of income tax collected at a rate of 3% has been transferred to the federal budget, and federal and regional profit tax rates have been reduced from 13% to 11% and from 22% to 19%, respectively. The balance of revenues received from principal federal taxes weighed upon the regional budgets: the proportions of VAT and income tax revenues transferred to regional budgets contracted, with the profit tax distribution remaining unchanged, provided the tax is collected at a maximum regional rate.

The consolidated budget tax revenues in 1999 amounted to 22.2% of GDP, or 1.9% more than their GDP share in 1998 and at the 1997 level. The total revenues of the federal and regional budgets in 1999 amounted to 26.6% of GDP, or 2.1% more than their GDP share in 1998 and steady at the 1997 level. The federal budget revenues in 1999, however, rose by 2.3% of GDP over 1998 revenues and by 1.1% of GDP over 1997 revenues. In the end, the share of the federal budget revenues in the consolidated budget revenues rose from 47.1% in 1997 and 46.1% in 1998 to 51.2% in 1999.

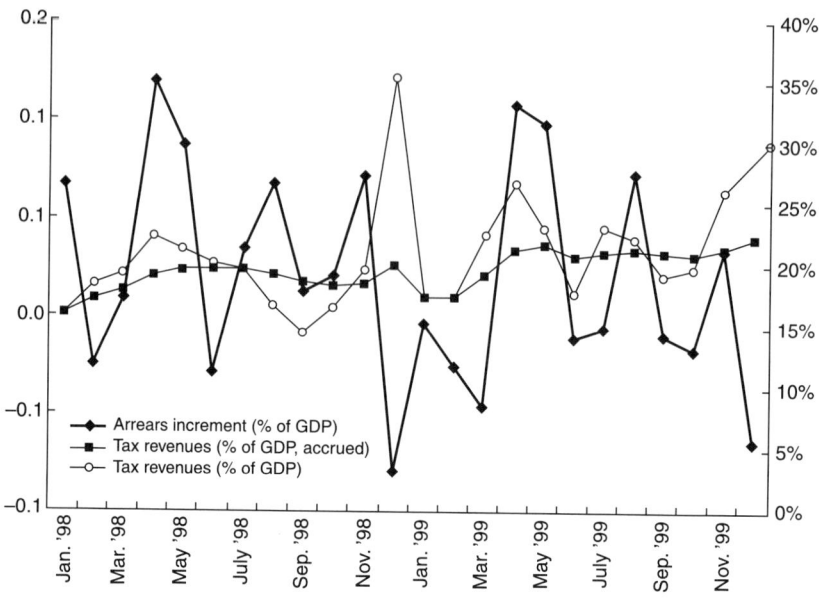

Figure 12.14
Tax revenues and arrears increment as percentage of GDP, January 1998 through November 1999. (Source: Ministry of Taxes and Duties.)

A major positive effect on the fulfillment of current tax liabilities to the budget by taxpayers was produced by an almost complete abandonment of set-offs at the federal level, a practice that was outlawed by the recently enacted general part of the Tax Code, which requires taxes to be paid in cash only, and by a certain reduction in the scale of set-offs at the regional and local levels.

Figure 12.14 shows the monthly dynamics of tax revenues, arrears, and assessment of tax liabilities (amount of tax revenues and growth in arrears per month) in the federal and consolidated budgets. Monthly tax revenues and tax liabilities in both the federal and consolidated budgets tended to grow throughout 1999, despite seasonal fluctuations (down at the beginning of the year and up in April, when the deadline for past year settlements arrives). The drop in tax revenues in September was largely caused by diminishing tax revenues from foreign trade.

The change in the dynamics of macroeconomic parameters led to a shift in the structure of tax revenues flowing into the consolidated budget (Table 12.5). Despite a lowering of the profit tax rate from 35% to 30%, the share of this tax rose significantly, from 17.7% of the

Table 12.5
Tax Revenue Structure of Consolidated Budget, 1998–1999

	1998	1999, Month											
		I	II	III	IV	V	VI	VII	VIII	IX	X	XI	XII
Profit tax	17.7	12.1	12.3	15.3	17.3	19.3	20.2	19.9	20.9	21.2	20.8	21.7	22.0
Personal income tax	13.1	12.2	13.1	13.0	12.5	12.1	12.0	12.1	11.9	11.9	11.8	11.6	11.7
VAT	28.8	36.1	33.8	31.1	29.8	28.4	28.0	28.7	28.1	28.4	29.0	28.5	28.6
Excises on goods and certain mineral raw materials	12.5	19.6	17.6	16.5	14.9	13.7	12.7	11.8	11.4	11.2	11.1	10.6	10.8
Sales tax	0.1	0.9	1.3	1.4	1.5	1.6	1.6	1.7	1.8	1.9	2.0	2.0	1.9
Property taxes	8.6	2.3	2.4	2.9	4.3	5.5	5.4	5.2	5.6	5.4	5.2	5.4	5.2
Fees for use of natural resources	4.1	2.5	3.4	3.4	3.4	3.2	3.6	3.7	3.7	4.1	4.2	4.3	4.4
Taxes on foreign trade and foreign economic operations	6.7	7.4	9.3	9.5	9.0	8.7	9.4	9.9	9.5	8.7	8.9	8.9	8.6
Other taxes, fees, and duties	7.1	5.3	5.3	5.6	6.0	6.3	6.0	5.9	6.1	5.9	5.8	6.0	5.6
Total Taxes and Payments	100	100	100	100	100	100	100	100	100	100	100	100	100

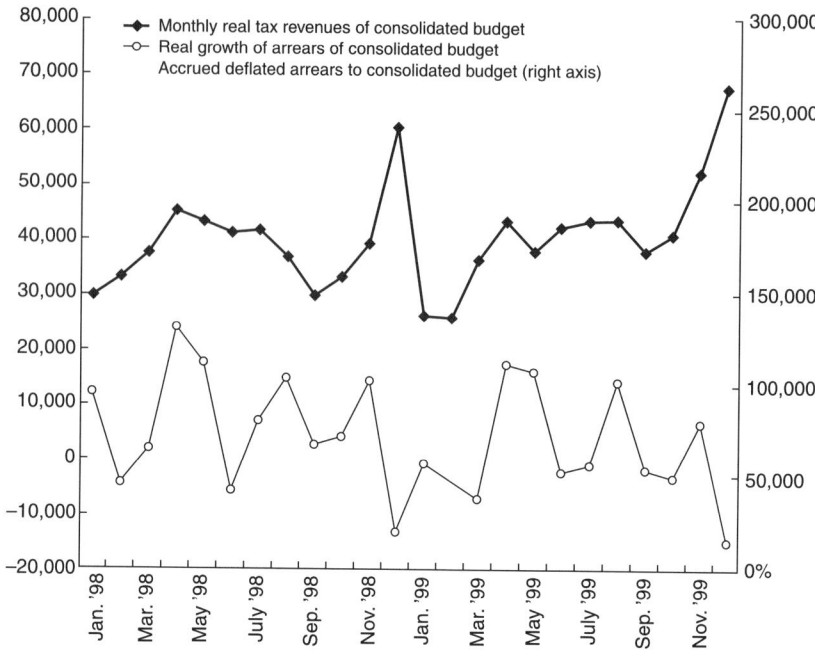

Figure 12.15
Real tax revenues and arrears, 1998–1999. (Source: Ministry of Taxes and Duties, Tax arrears to consolidated budget.)

budget revenues in 1998 to 22% in 1999. One percentage point was shaved off the income tax share, and the share of excises lost 2.7 percentage points. But then, VAT revenues moved 0.5 percentage point up, and the share of the foreign trade tax added 1.8 percentage points.

In 1999, manufacturing industries in general paid slightly more taxes than they had in 1998 (by approximately 1 percentage point of GDP). The highest growth was posted by the fuel industry (0.6 percentage point of GDP more than in 1998). In the nonferrous and food industries, tax revenues grew by 0.4 percentage point of GDP and 0.2 percentage point of GDP, respectively, in 1999. At the other extreme, tax revenues from power industry enterprises went down a little (0.3 percentage point of GDP). In some other industries, such as communications, construction, and finance, tax revenues declined, reducing their combined GDP share by about 2 percentage points.

The growth in tax arrears subsided somewhat in 1999 (Figure 12.15 and Table 12.6). Accrued arrears showed an absolute decrease

Table 12.6
Growth of Arrears to the Federal and Consolidated Budgets, 1996–1999

	1996	1997	1998	1999
Growth of arrears to the federal budget (% of GDP)	1.1	1.3	2.1	0.9
Growth of arrears to the consolidated buget (% of GDP)	3.0	2.4	2.9	0.7

in February, March, and October 1999. In real terms, arrears to the federal budget dropped by 9.2% and arrears to the consolidated budget dropped by 18.1%.[24]

As percentages of GDP for the respective period, arrears to the federal budget in 1999 grew more slowly than they had in 1998 by a factor of 2.3, and arrears to the consolidated budget rose at a rate that was lower by a factor of 4.1. These arrears had a similar growth pattern in real terms.

The improved tax collection can be partly attributed to the stronger financial position of enterprises and a larger share of money-based settlements. It must be admitted, however, that the absence of a clear downward trend in real arrears growth that could signal a consistently tougher government line toward tax dodgers or a measure of independence of the arrears dynamics from macroeconomic parameters can be explained by tax collectors approaching major taxpayers discreetly to work out individual tax arrangements.

Tax revenues were 28.2% greater than planned in 1999. More specifically, profit tax receipts were 126.6% higher than planned, VAT revenues were 54.6% higher, and payments for the use of natural resources were 10.6% higher. Income tax collection was 20.6% short of the requirement under the 1999 budget law, excises were 6.8% short, and international business taxes were 5% short (Table 12.7).

The federal budget revenues totaled Rb 611.7 billion, or 13.6% of GDP,[25] a rise of 2.3 percentage points over 1998. Tax revenues surpassed the preceding year's performance by an even higher figure, 2.6 percentage points. Growth was achieved chiefly through improved collection of VAT revenues (up 1 percentage point); it was less notable in the profit tax and foreign trade tax (0.5 percentage

---

24. As in the case of arrears, this indicator reflects the real extent of encumbrance of enterprises with debts to the budget.
25. Preliminary estimates put the GDP for 1999 at Rb 4.5 trillion.

Table 12.7
Execution of the Federal Budget and Law on Budget, 1999

	Budget balance in 1999 (% of GDP)	Budget balance in 1998 (% of GDP)	Law on budget for 1999		Budget balance in 1999 (% of the law)
			(% of targeted GDP)	(% of actual GDP)	
REVENUES					
Profit tax	1.8	1.3	0.9	0.8	226.6
Personal income tax	0.4	0.0	0.6	0.6	79.4
VAT	4.9	3.9	3.6	3.2	154.6
Excises on excisable goods and selected mineral raw materials produced in RF territory	1.8	2.0	2.2	1.9	93.2
Fees for use of natural resources	0.2	0.1	0.2	0.2	110.6
Taxes on foreign trade and foreign economic operations	1.9	1.4	2.3	2.0	95.0
Other taxes, fees and duties	0.2	0.2	0.2	0.1	150.1
Total Taxes and Payments	10.8	8.8	10.0	8.9	128.2
Nontax Revenues					
Revenue from government property or activity	0.2	0.2	0.2	0.2	85.6
Revenue from foreign economic operations	0.8	0.6	0.6	0.5	149.0
Total Nontax Revenues	1.0	0.8	0.8	0.7	123.2
Receipts from Government Budgetary Funds	1.2	0.9	1.0	0.9	123.9
Total Revenues	13.1	11.3	11.8	10.5	124.3
EXPENDITURES					
1. Government administration	0.3	0.4	0.3	0.3	107.9
2. National defense	2.6	2.1	2.3	2.1	123.9
3. International activities	1.3	0.3	0.9	0.8	158.7

Financial Policy in 1999

4. Law enforcement, security, and justice	1.3	1.3	1.4	1.2	107.6
5. Basic research and promotion of scientific and technological progress	0.2	0.2	0.3	0.3	96.2
6. Government services to the national economy	0.8	0.9	0.9	0.8	106.2
6.1. Industry, power engineering and construction	0.4	0.4	0.4	0.3	116.0
6.2. Agriculture and fisheries	0.2	0.1	0.2	0.2	97.7
6.3. Protection of the environment and natural resources, hydrometeorology, mapping and geodetic surveying	0.1	0.1	0.1	0.1	99.7
6.4. Transportation, road maintenance, communications and information technology	0.0	0.0	0.0	0.0	104.4
6.5. Preventing and/or eliminating the effects of emergencies and natural disasters	0.2	0.2	0.2	0.2	100.4
7. Social services	1.9	2.1	2.0	1.7	108.9
7.1. Education	0.5	0.5	0.5	0.5	100.4
7.2. Culture and arts	0.1	0.0	0.1	0.1	93.9
7.3. Mass media	0.0	0.0	0.1	0.0	95.9
7.4. Health and physical fitness	0.2	0.2	0.3	0.2	99.0
7.5. Social policy	1.1	1.4	1.0	0.9	117.3
8. Expenditure by target budgetary funds	1.3	0.9	1.1	1.0	136.9
9. Government debt service	3.6	4.0	4.2	3.7	97.4
Domestic debt			1.7	1.5	
External debt			2.5	2.2	
10. Financial aid to other levels of government	1.3	1.6	1.1	1.0	131.5
11. Other expenditure	1.6	2.4	−0.1	−0.1	−1672.0
Total Expenditures	15.0	14.5	14.4	12.8	117.8
Surplus of Revenues over Expenditures and Credits Less Repayments	−1.2	−3.2	−2.5	−2.3	52.2

353

point each). Income tax transfers to the federal budget raised the federal budget revenues by 0.4% of GDP. Excise tax revenues alone dropped, by 0.2 percentage point.

12.3.2. Budget Expenditure

Nominal federal budget expenditure overshot the appropriation levels approved by the 1999 budget law by 17.8%, to Rb 664.7 billion (or 14.8% of GDP). The budget deficit went down to Rb 52.9 billion (or to 1.2% of GDP, versus the 2.5% of GDP under the budget law). Noninterest budget expenses reached Rb 514.6 billion, or 11.4% of GDP. Federal budget spending was 1 percentage point lower than it had been in 1997, and 0.3 percentage point above the 1998 figure. Noninterest expenditure was reduced by 2.9 percentage points from the 1997 level, rising 0.8 percentage point above the 1998 level. In particular, defense spending rose by half a percentage point, and spending on social programs went down by 0.2 percentage point.

The execution of Russia's consolidated budget revealed somewhat different trends. Major reductions were made expenditures to be borne by the regional budgets. Spending under the consolidated budget ran to 27.8% of GDP, or 0.4 percentage point below the 1998 figure and 2.7 percentage points less than in 1997. Noninterest spending rose insignificantly over 1998 (by 0.1 percentage point of GDP), falling by 4.4 percentage points of GDP from the 1997 figure, and expenditure on social programs shrank by 0.8 percentage point of GDP from the 1998 level and by 1.7 percentage points of GDP from the 1997 level.

The expenditure figure stipulated in the 1999 budget law was exceeded by 17.8%. Other spending items that exceeded the appropriation levels included international business (58.7%), financial aid to regional and local authorities (31.5%), and defense spending (23.9%). Spending on social programs was 8.9% beyond the limit set in the budget law, the largest excess being posted in the Social Policy item (17.7%). Government services to the economy were 6.2% above the appropriation limit, with manufacturing accounting for 16.0%. Government debt servicing received 2.5% less than budgeted.

The Russian budget may be said to be conspicuously lacking regular indexation in the period when inflationary processes accelerated sharply after the crisis of August 1998. A scrutiny of the budget figures at constant prices produces a similar picture. Consolidated budget revenues at comparable prices rose by 17% over 1998 revenues (including a 21% growth in tax collection) and dropped by 34% from 1997 (of which tax revenue declined by 25%). Real spending under the consolidated budget fell by 31% from 1997 (with noninterest expenditure decreasing by 37%) and rose by 13% over the 1998 level (of which noninterest expenditure climbed 13%).

The problem of debts payable under budgets at all levels lost some of its sharp edge in 1999, owing to plan targets being generally attained with a wide margin. Considering, however, that accrued payables for the preceding years added up to an impressive amount (according to Finance Ministry statistics for 1 January 1999,[26] the results of an inventory of federal budget debts payable, accrued payables amounted to Rb 92.6 billion, with those due under the budgets of federation members for 1998 alone amounting to Rb 85.7 billion), it is still premature to speak of their full repayment.

12.3.3. Interbudgetary Relations in Russia in 1999

The reformation of interbudgetary relations initiated in 1997–1998 continued apace in 1999. We recall here that the "Conception of Reform in Interbudgetary Relations," approved in 1998, set guidelines for reform in the relationships between budgets at all levels of government up to the year 2001.

The resources of the Federal Fund for Financial Aid to the Regions (FAR) were allocated by new methods developed and approved by the government. Consequently, the shares of the regions in the fund, computed by the Ministry of Finance and submitted to the State Duma for approval, were passed, on an unprecedented first vote, by the Duma in its debates on the draft budget.

In general, the federal government took a firm line in its relations with federation members beginning early in 1999. During the tenure of the Primakov cabinet, there were repeated calls to abolish the election of regional administration heads, to continue the centralization of power over revenues, and for greater supervisory authority over the performance of regional authorities. In February the government adopted a directive on reform in housing and utilities that set a rate schedule of limits on the price of housing and utility services differentiated according to economic regions, to be adhered to

---

26. Government directive No. 600 of 17 June 1998, *On Approval of the Program of Public Spending Reductions.*

in allocating financial aid to the regions. For all the imperfections of the rate schedule, it was one of the few attempts made to put relations with the regions within a legal framework.

All of these changes reflected on the qualitative aspects of relations between the federal center and the regions. Beginning in 1998, loans from the federal budget could not, in general, be viewed as financial aid. Specifically, in both 1998 and 1999 these loans showed a negative balance, which meant that more debts were repaid than new loans were made. The share of outstanding federal budget loans in the total federal budget funds transferred into the federation members' budgets in 1996 and 1997 equaled 10% and 25%, respectively. In 1999 the Ministry of Finance discontinued its practice of making transfers from the FAR Federal Fund as a set-off against the federal share of VAT receipts. Previously, the transfers made in this way amounted to 17% of all federal financial aid (including outstanding budget loans), creating a favorable setting for bargaining between federal and regional authorities over VAT amounts to be set off against transfers.

The total scale of financial aid transferred into regional budgets dropped to 1.4% of GDP, or to 1.11% if one takes into account the balance of federal budget loans granted and repaid. There was, however, an insignificant but steady growth in the share of transfers from the FAR fund in the general context of federal financial aid to the regions: on the 1999 bottom line, it registered at 71.4%.

12.3.4. Deficit and Government Debt

The 1999 budget deficit came out at 1.2% of GDP, significantly smaller than in either 1998 (3.2%) or 1997 (6%). The budget deficit was reduced by rising budget revenues and large cuts in the budget interest spending during 1999 (3.6% of GDP, down from 4% of GDP in 1998 and from 4.5% of GDP in 1997).

In 1999, the net annual budget deficit financing took up 1.2% of GDP,[27] of which foreign financing accounted for 1.1% of GDP, the

---

27. According to data provided by the Economic Expert Group of the Federal Finance Ministry, the 1999 federal budget deficit was equal to 1.7% of GDP, of which foreign financing claimed 0.2% of GDP and domestic financing 1.5% of GDP. This discrepancy with the figures given in the table can be attributed to a different classification of financing sources. In particular, the Economic Expert Group's report placed IMF loans among domestic financing sources, included proceeds from privatization projects, and so on.

remaining 0.1% of GDP falling on domestic financing (Table 12.8). Compared with 1998, total net financing came to 3.2% of GDP (with 3.4% of GDP for foreign financing and 0.2% for domestic financing). In 1997 this same figure was 6% of GDP (2% of GDP and 4% of GDP, respectively).

In all, the funds attracted in 1999 claimed 4.3% of GDP, including 4.2% of GDP from foreign financing sources. The Russian Ministry of Finance included loans from the federal central bank used to pay off foreign debt (around $4.5 billion, or 2.6% of GDP) among foreign financing sources. This amount is shown as loans from foreign commercial banks in the budget.

The government's domestic debt in 1999 was reduced by Rb 170 billion (at comparable prices, by 70%, or by 15 percentage points of GDP), even as bond liabilities increased to Rb 70 billion (in terms of GDP share, bond liabilities decreased by 6 percentage points of GDP, or by 55% at comparable prices). Domestic government debts servicing required 1.2% of GDP in 1999.

12.3.5. Domestic Debt Market

The market for ruble-denominated government bonds (GKO-OFZ bonds) recovered slowly but steadily throughout 1999. Regular secondary market trading in bonds maturing after 31 December 1999 resumed on 15 January 1999. Bonds issued within the framework of reissuance of bonds frozen in August 1998 were floated on the market on 28 January. Since then, regular trading sessions have been held five days a week. Throughout the year, trading was contained by a ceiling on the yield-to-maturity rate equal to double the refinancing rate of the central bank, or 110%–120% per annum. Consequently, transactions in many, mostly long, OFZ series were invalidated, so that these bonds remained illiquid.

12.3.6. Domestic Debt Restructuring Program

Under the Russian government's directive of 12 December 1998, "Novation of Government Securities," novation (restructuring) involved government bonds maturing between 17 August 1998 and 31 December 1999 and was to go on for a period between 15 December 1998 and 15 March 1999. The novation period was then extended to 30 April 1999. Restructuring was applied to GKOs and OFZs with

Table 12.8
Financing of the Federal Budget Deficit in 1999 (% of GDP)

	I	II	III	IV	V	VI	VII	VIII	IX	X	XI	XII
1. Domestic financing	-5.7	-2.3	-1.1	-0.9	-0.7	-1.1	-1.0	-0.6	-0.3	-0.1	-0.5	0.1
1.1. Change in bank account balances of budget funds (in rubles)	-5.5	-2.2	-1.8	-1.9	-1.4	-2.0	-1.8	-1.1	-0.8	-1.1	-1.2	-1.1
Balance at beginning of period	2.7	1.4	1.2	0.8	0.6	0.5	0.4	0.3	0.3	0.3	0.2	0.3
Balance at end of period	8.2	3.5	2.9	2.7	2.1	2.5	2.2	1.4	1.1	1.3	1.4	1.4
1.2. Short-term government debt	-0.1	-0.1	-0.7	-0.8	-0.6	-0.8	-0.7	-0.6	-0.5	-0.4	-0.4	-0.3
Borrowings	0.0	0.0	0.0	0.0	0.0	0.0	0.0	0.0	0.0	0.0	0.0	0.0
Repayment of principal	0.1	0.1	0.7	0.8	0.6	0.8	0.7	0.6	0.5	0.4	0.4	0.3
1.3. Nonmarketable government bonds	0.0	0.0	0.0	0.5	0.4	0.8	0.5	0.4	0.3	0.2	0.1	0.0
Borrowings	0.0	0.0	0.0	0.5	0.4	0.8	0.7	0.6	0.5	0.4	0.4	0.3
Repayment of principal	0.0	0.0	0.0	0.0	0.0	0.0	0.1	0.2	0.2	0.2	0.3	0.3
1.4. Federal fixed-rate bonds	0.0	0.0	0.9	1.0	0.8	0.9	0.6	0.3	0.5	1.1	1.2	1.2
Borrowings	0.0	0.0	0.9	1.0	0.8	1.1	1.9	1.9	2.0	2.4	2.3	4.8
Repayment of principal						0.2	1.3	1.6	1.4	1.2	1.1	3.6
1.5. Government savings bonds	0.0	0.0	-0.1	-0.3	-0.3	-0.3	-0.2	-0.2	-0.2	-0.2	-0.2	-0.2
Borrowings	0.0	0.0	0.0	0.0	0.0	0.0	0.1	0.1	0.1	0.1	0.1	0.1
Repayment of principal	0.0	0.0	0.1	0.3	0.3	0.3	0.3	0.2	0.3	0.3	0.3	0.3
1.6. Other domestic borrowing	-0.1	-0.1	0.6	0.5	0.5	0.3	0.6	0.5	0.3	0.3	0.3	0.5
Borrowings	-0.1	-0.1	0.6	0.6	0.5	0.4	0.6	0.5	0.3	0.4	0.2	0.7
Repayment of principal	0.0	0.0	0.0	0.0	0.0	0.0	0.0	0.0	0.0	0.1	0.2	0.3

Financial Policy in 1999

2. External financing	5.6	3.6	3.6	3.3	3.5	3.5	3.1	2.5	1.9	1.3	1.1	1.1
2.1. Loans from international financial institutions	-3.4	-2.4	-2.1	-2.4	-2.3	-1.9	-1.3	-1.2	-1.2	-1.3	-1.4	-1.2
Loans received:	0.2	0.2	0.2	0.2	0.2	0.2	0.9	0.9	0.8	0.7	0.7	0.7
Tied	0.2	0.2	0.2	0.2	0.2	0.2	0.2	0.2	0.2	0.2	0.2	0.2
Untied	0.0	0.0	0.0	0.0	0.0	0.0	0.7	0.7	0.6	0.5	0.5	0.5
Repayment of principal	3.6	2.7	2.3	2.6	2.5	2.1	2.2	2.2	2.0	2.1	2.0	1.9
2.2. Foreign government loans to RF	0.2	-0.3	-0.1	-0.1	-0.3	-0.4	-0.3	-0.3	-0.2	-0.2	0.0	0.1
Borrowed (used)	1.3	0.9	1.0	1.0	0.9	0.7	0.7	0.7	0.7	0.7	0.9	0.9
Principal repaid	1.1	1.2	1.0	1.1	1.2	1.2	1.1	1.0	0.9	0.9	0.9	0.8
2.3. Loans from foreign commercial banks and companies to RF	8.8	6.3	5.7	5.8	6.1	5.9	4.7	4.0	3.3	2.9	2.5	2.2
Borrowed (used)	8.8	6.3	5.7	5.8	6.1	6.2	5.2	4.4	3.8	3.3	2.9	2.6
Principal repaid	0.0	0.0	0.0	0.0	0.0	0.3	0.5	0.4	0.5	0.4	0.4	0.4
Total Financing	-0.1	1.3	2.5	2.4	2.9	2.5	2.1	1.8	1.5	1.2	0.7	1.2

a total value of almost Rb 281 billion. The share of nonresidents invested in these bonds amounted to 30.42%.

The Russian government divided GKO-OFZ holders into four categories, according to different debt novation conditions:

1. Individuals who were residents of the Russian Federation, press periodicals, obligatory medical insurance funds, and insurance companies
2. GKO-OFZ holders who were required to make obligatory investments in government bonds at specified rates
3. All other investors
4. The Central Bank of the Russian Federation

Special conditions were offered to investors in the first and fourth categories. Investors in the first category were refunded the par value of their bonds in cash within terms corresponding to the bond redemption date. Bonds held by the central bank did not explicitly meet the novation conditions, and their restructuring procedures were negotiated under separate arrangements between the Ministry of Finance and the Central Bank.

The remaining investors were offered new discount and coupon bonds along with repayment of certain cash amounts. In particular, a majority of investors in the third group received 3.334% of the bond par value in money, 6.67% in discount (GKO) bonds with maturities of three to six months, 20% as zero-coupon OFZs with three-year maturities, and 70% as OFZs with a fixed coupon rate of 15%–30% per annum and maturities between four and six years. Investors in the second group received 10% of the amount due in money, 20% in GKOs, 20% in zero-coupon OFZs, and 50% in OFZ bonds.

Bonds worth Rb 170.5 billion were issued within the novation framework, including Rb 15.5 billion in GKOs, Rb 35 billion in zero-coupon OFZs, and Rb 120 billion in OFZ bonds with fixed coupon payments. On balance, novation slashed the total domestic debt by almost Rb 110.5 billion (or 4.12% of GDP for 1998).

12.3.7. Enlarged Government Budget

The revenues of the enlarged government budget in 1999 ran at 36.2% of GDP, or approximately as much as in 1997 and 1.4 percentage points more than in 1998. More taxes were collected in 1999

Table 12.9
Tax Revenue Structure by Taxable Base and Percent of GDP, 1997–1999*

	% of Tax Revenues			% of GDP		
	1997	1998	1999	1997	1998	1999
Personal incomes	9.5	9.1	8.3	3.1	2.8	2.8
Revenues of enterprises	12.0	11.6	15.2	3.9	3.6	5.1
Labor cost	24.7	24.1	20.4	8.1	7.5	6.8
Merchandise cost	32.2	31.8	33.8	10.5	10.0	11.3
Other production costs	21.6	23.3	22.3	7.0	7.3	7.5

*The taxable base included personal incomes, for income tax assessment and 1% of earnings withheld into the Pension Fund; corporate incomes, for assessment of profit tax and aggregate income tax; payroll tax, for transfers into social off-budget funds; and inventory value, for VAT assessment, excises, and customs levies and duties.

than in each of the preceding two years, or 33.4% of GDP, up from 31.3% of GDP in 1998 and 32.6% of GDP in 1997.

The growth in budget revenues was largely a result of increased receipts flowing into the federal budget in 1999, at 13.7% of GDP (up from 11.3% of GDP in 1998 and 12.4% of GDP in 1997), or 38% of the total receipts in the budget system (compared with 34% in 1997 and 32% in 1998). The budget revenues of the Federation members in 1999 were, however, the smallest for three years—14.5% of GDP (down from 14.9% of GDP in 1998 and 15.9% in 1997)—as also were off-budget fund revenues, at 10.1% of GDP (a fall from 10.9% in 1997 and 11.1% of GDP in 1998) (Table 12.9).

The year 1999 saw an increase in the share of taxes based on corporate incomes (3.6 percentage points up from the 1998 level and 3.2 percentage points up from the 1997 level), while the share of personal income tax dropped (by 0.8 percentage points from 1998 and 1.2 percentage points from 1997), as did the share of payroll taxes (by 3.7 percentage points from 1998 and 4.3 percentage points from 1997).

The expenditure of the general government budget in 1999 fell to a level equivalent to 36.5% of GDP (down from 1998, when the expenditure reached 38.1% of GDP, and from 1997, when spending was 43.1% of GDP). Accordingly, noninterest expenditure was 32.9% of GDP in 1999, 34.1% of GDP in 1998, and 43.1% of GDP in 1997.

As in previous years, the bulk of the expenditure under the enlarged government budget went to social programs, which accounted for 41.2% of the total spending (15.4% of GDP, compared to

17.9% of GDP in 1997 and 17.3% of GDP in 1998). Government economic services claimed 19.3% of the total expenditure in 1999 (down from 20.7% in 1998 and 22.4% in 1997), or an equivalent of 7.2% of GDP (down from 8.0% of GDP in 1998 and 9.6% of GDP in 1997). Defense spending in 1999 was 6.9% of total expenditure (up from 5.4% in 1998 and down from 7.1% in 1997), or an equivalent of 2.6% of GDP (up from 2.1% of GDP in 1998 and 3.1% of GDP in 1997).

According shown by the data in Table 12.9, the structure of tax revenues flowing into the enlarged government budget did not change much in the three years 1997 to 1999. A point to be made, however (see Table 12.10), is that the share of deductions into off-budget funds, particularly social off-budget funds, fell to 20.9% in 1999 (from 24.2% in 1997 and 24.7% in 1998), along with that of property taxes assessed to federation members' budgets, which fell to 3.5% in 1999 (from 5.6% in 1998 and 1997). Simultaneously, the share of the foreign trade tax in government revenues rose to 5.8% in 1999 (from 3.3% in 1997 and 4.4% in 1998), and in the share of the profit tax in revenues rose to 14.7% (from 12% in 1997 and 11.5% in 1998).

Table 12.10
Tax Revenue Structure of Enlarged Government Budget, 1997–1999

	1997	1998	1999
1. Profit (income), capital gains taxes	21.0%	20.0%	22.5%
1.1. Profit tax	12.0	11.5	14.7
1.2. Personal income tax	8.9	8.5	7.8
2. Taxes on goods and services, license and registration fees	28.9	27.5	28.0
2.1. VAT	20.1	18.6	19.2
2.2. Excise taxes on excisable goods and selected mineral raw materials produced on RF territory	7.4	8.1	7.2
2.3. Sales tax	0.0	0.1	1.3
2.4. Other taxes on goods and services	1.3	0.7	7.5
4. Property taxes	5.6	5.6	3.5
5. Fees for use of natural resources	4.2	2.7	3.0
6. Taxes on foreign trade and foreign economic operations	3.3	4.4	5.8
7. Other taxes, fees, and duties	3.4	4.6	3.8
8. Extrabudgetary fund receipts	27.4	30.2	26.5
8.1. Extrabudgetary social insurance fund receipts	24.2	24.7	20.9
9. Revenue of target budgetary funds	5.2	4.9	6.5
Total Taxes and Payments	100.0%	100.0%	100.0%

12.4. Social Effects of the Stabilization Policy

The crisis in autumn 1998 was followed by a plunge in living standards for all segments of the population, including the wealthiest 20%. Goskomstat statistics from January 1999 show that 38.2% of the population were thrown below the poverty line. By February 1999, real average monthly pensions had been halved from the precrisis period, and real wages per employee had been reduced by more than 42%. In early 1999, the ratio of average money income per capita to the subsistence minimum had dropped to less than 1.5. In August 1999, real personal incomes barely amounted to 80% of those in August 1998.

Interestingly, official and subjective subsistence levels did not track each other exactly (Figure 12.16). Beginning in November 1998, the subjective subsistence level began to edge downward, and between January and July 1999, the subjective subsistence minimum—the income that respondents in polls conducted by the Public Opinion Research Institute (VTsIOM) were ready to recognize—proved slightly lower than the official subsistence minimum arrived at by Goskomstat.

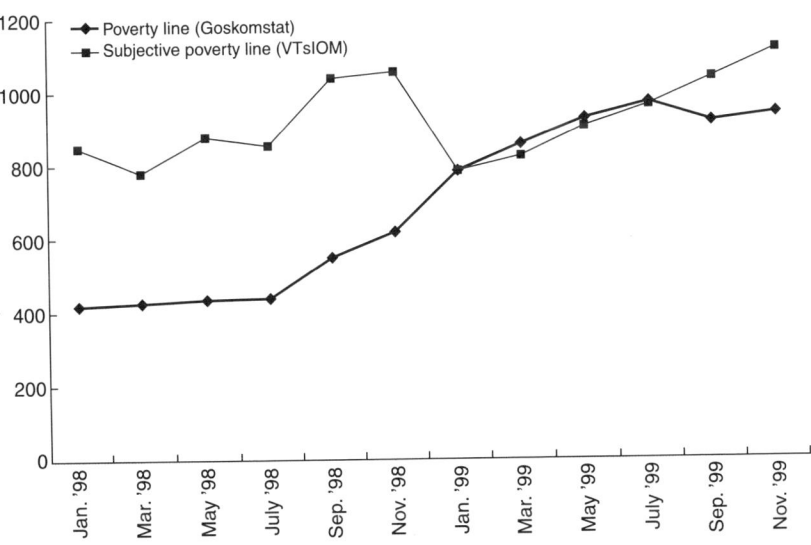

Figure 12.16
Official and subjective subsistence minimums. (Sources: Goskomstat and VTsIOM.)

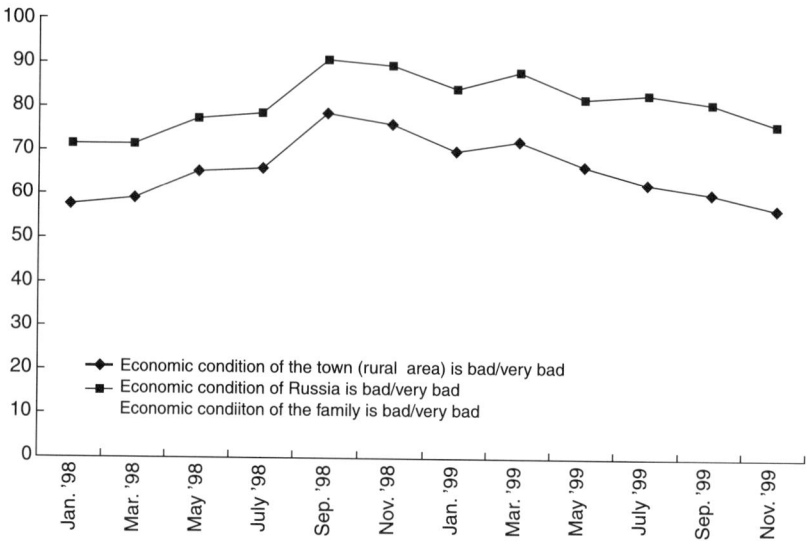

Figure 12.17
Trends in proportion of survey respondents reporting economic conditions of town, country or family as bad/very bad. (Source: VTsIOM.)

The following factors might explain this discrepancy. First, the economic collapse prophesied by many economists and politicians—paralysis of the financial system, hyperinflation, a throwback to the times of general shortages and rationing cards—did not arrive. Figure 12.17 shows, with reference to VTsIOM figures, that after the peak in early autumn 1998—that is, hot on the heels of the crisis—the share of respondents describing the economic situation in their area and in Russia as bad/very bad generally declined.

Second, the dollars that people kept as the overwhelming part of their savings appreciated at the expense of the ruble. This occurred despite the trend, already evident early in 1998, for saving modes to diversify, and dollar savings attained greater subjective value in the eyes of their owners.

Third, the recovery in production took hold and barter declined in importance (with growth in the economy's monetization). This was one of the many aftereffects of the ruble's devaluation in the second half of 1998 and somewhat compensated in turn for the plunge in

Financial Policy in 1999

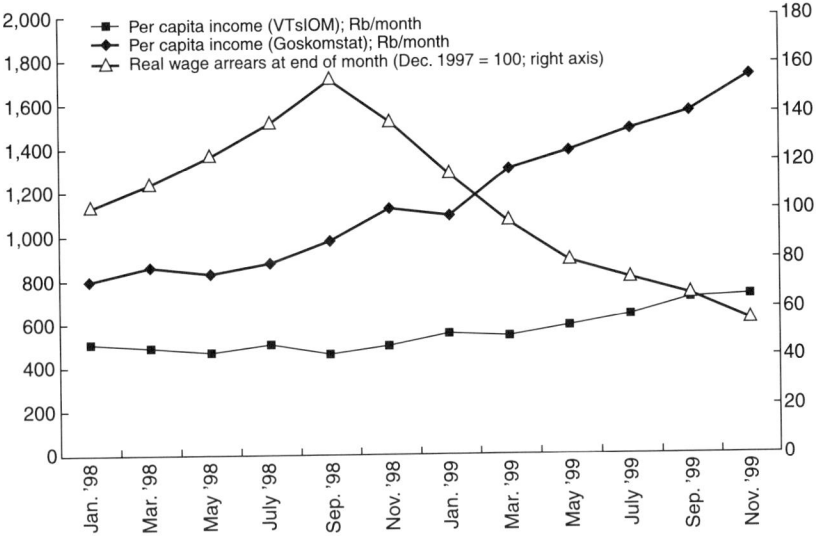

Figure 12.18
Trends in wage earners' finances, January 1998–November 1999. (Sources: VTsIOM, Goskomstat.)

real personal incomes, with wages paid mostly on time and in cash, and wage arrears tapering off (Figure 12.18).[28]

As wage arrears were progressively being reduced and real earnings went up together with output, labor strikes, which peaked in autumn 1998, fell off, and work time losses diminished.

The increasing portion of wages paid in cash to compensate for falling personal incomes might explain the phenomenon of growing public confidence in government leadership even as standards of living deteriorated. Figure 12.19 illustrates the dynamics of confidence in the prime minister in comparison with real wage arrears from January 1998 to December 1999. Except for the deep drop in confidence set off by the retirement of Prime Minister Stepashin and the appointment of the previously unknown Putin in his place, confidence in the prime minister grew as wage arrears went down. The income "compensation effect" enabled the government, despite a re-

---

28. There is a close link between falling real wage arrears and industrial output growth: the correlation coefficient is negative and equal to 0.98. The correlation coefficient between the industrial production intensity index and the size of the subjective average per-capita income is positive, reaching 0.73.

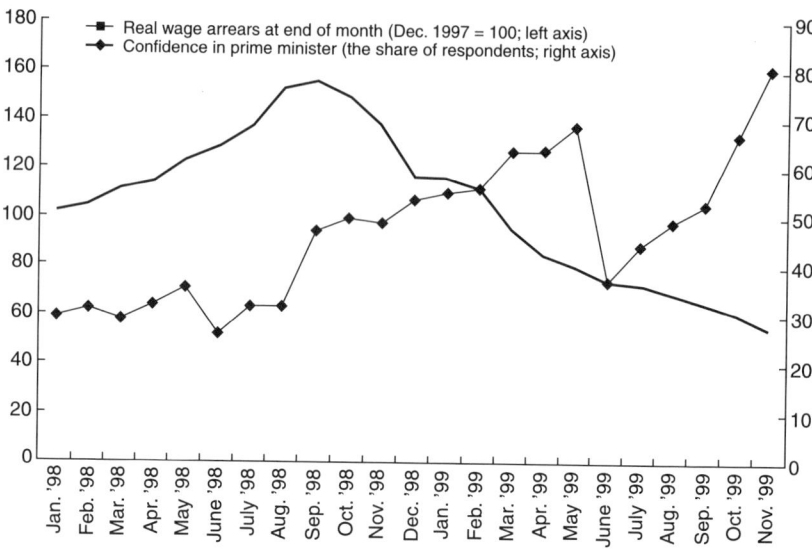

Figure 12.19
Dynamic of wage arrears versus confidence in prime minister, January 1998–November 1999. (Sources: VTsIOM, Goskomstat.)

duction in its social liabilities in real terms, to raise public confidence in the government to a higher level.[29]

12.5. Medium-Term Limitations of the Economic Policy

The ruble's devaluation in August 1998 gave Russia a few short-term advantages, chiefly by underwriting the beginning of recovery in its export-oriented and import-substituting industries. Accordingly, our starting point in the scenarios we sketched out earlier was that the monetary authorities would continue their policy of preventing rapid growth in the real ruble exchange rate.

Along with some important boons from the national currency's devaluation, the country's economy has found itself face to face with a set of undeniably negative aftereffects. Ignoring these effects could, in varying degrees, threaten the country's economic growth. These aftereffects include (1) warning signals of a "low economic growth level," (2) a more expensive foreign debt, (3) the probability of over-

---

29. See A. Alesina and A. Drazen, "Why Are Stabilizations Delayed?" *The American Economic Review* 85 (1991): 1170–1188.

protection for domestic manufacturers, (4) a decline in the real worth of national companies, (5) profit redistribution and possible unfavorable shifts in the economy, and (6) more expensive foreign equipment and technologies required for making investments. Let us take a closer look at these factors.

Warning Signals of a "Low Economic Growth Level"
This effect is more a psychological result of devaluation than a reflection of real changes in the economy. Today, the ratio of the nominal exchange rate of the ruble to the dollar, related to the purchasing power parity of the two currencies, stands at approximately 2.5. Although no formal economic model exists to show the extent of damage caused to the national economy by this high ratio,[30] the worldwide economic record suggests that this situation is characteristic only of countries at a very low level of development. As the national economy ascends to a higher development level, the ratio of the exchange rate to the purchasing power parity of the currency falls, such that deviation from unity does not exceed 10%–15% for economically developed countries.

A More Expensive Foreign Debt
A more expensive foreign debt owed by Russian businesses (including the country's government) and the growing costs of servicing the debt portion denominated in foreign currency together constitute one of the most serious negative effects of the ruble's devaluation.

Russia has already come to grips with this problem: its foreign debt has risen from 30%–35% to 70%–80% of GDP as a result of the August 1998 devaluation. It will have to spend between 4% and 10% of GDP every year to service its debts and repay the principal in the years 2000 to 2005. This obviously represents a very heavy burden on its economy (federal budget revenues worked out to be 13.3% of GDP in 1999).

As well as weighing down the federal government, more expensive foreign debts also heavily hamper some regional admin-

---

30. The existing models of Balassa-Samuelson and Bhagwati-Kravis-Lipsey explain the causes of differences in price levels between countries, but they do not show how an economically justified ratio is to be determined. The problem of finding an equilibrium real exchange rate for a national currency in a transitional economy is discussed, for example, in L. Halpern and C. Wyplosz, "Equilibrium Exchange Rates in Transition Economies," IMF Working Paper no. 96-125 (1996).

istrations (Nizhny Novgorod's and Moscow's, for example), giant Russian companies (Moscenergo, Tyumen Oil Company, and Tatneft Oil Company), and commercial banks (Alfa Bank, Russian Credit, and UNEXIMbank). Nonetheless, the total share of foreign debt in the private sector of the Russian economy is sufficiently low, and the situation in this area is markedly better in Russia than in a number of developing countries (such as the Republic of Korea, Thailand, and Mexico).

It must be said, though, that the Russian banking system had, by August 1998, been encumbered with enormous contracts to deliver money in foreign exchange (up to $78 billion at the current exchange rate). But all was not as bad as it looked. First, these liabilities were outweighed by a slight margin by the counterclaims the banking system had on money deliveries in foreign exchange (nearly $79 billion at the current exchange rate). Second, many fixed-term contracts had already been made between Russian banks themselves. And third, no direct foreign exchange deliveries were to be made under most contracts, for they were overwhelmingly futures and options contracts. In our view, therefore, there is no reason to assert that the Russian banking system has been crippled by external liabilities having gone up in value because of the ruble's devaluation rather than because of poor management and massive runs on the banks.

Probability of Overprotection for Domestic Producers
The ruble's devaluation stimulated industrial growth by giving domestically produced goods a price advantage over imports. We should distinguish, however, between the substitution effects engendered by demand switching from imports to domestically manufactured substitutes within identical price groups and the price barriers thrown up to inhibit entry into the domestic market for foreign-produced goods. Extensive devaluation makes the price differences between imported and domestic goods prohibitively large for imports. As a result, competition weakens, the quality of domestic goods remains poor, and eventually the living standards of consumers decline, depriving domestic producers of incentives to make their products competitive.

Decline in the Real Worth of National Companies
The next adverse effect of devaluation is a decline in the real worth of national companies. Falling real worth makes companies more

attractive for foreign investors, who see a chance to acquire real assets at low prices. An inflow of foreign capital into the stock market is the more probable, the deeper stocks plunge under the pressure of factors unrelated to the revaluation of future earnings in foreign exchange in the period preceding devaluation (for example, in consequence of country risk fluctuations). In fact, a fall in a stock market index (including one denominated in US dollars) before devaluation may be related to a revaluation of future company profits. In particular, since a large number of national corporations operate on the domestic market (indeed, growth in the output of import substitutes targets specifically domestic demand), their foreign exchange-denominated value falls, depreciating the present worth of future earnings (denominated in the national currency) of companies.

A fall in a corporation's stock price and capitalization (in foreign exchange terms) reduces the corporation's chances of attracting external loans. This handicap appears to be particularly important for the Russian economy, because for domestic companies, modernizing operations and the purchase of modern technologies and machinery requiring heavy investment are critical factors in the transition to sustainable long-term industrial growth. In a situation where opportunities to borrow on the domestic market are limited, fewer chances of contracting loans on foreign markets may constrain the beginning of economic growth.

Profit Redistribution and Possible Unfavorable Shifts in the Economy

The ruble's devaluation and growing profitability in the export industries lay the groundwork for major structural shifts in the economy, whose impact was far from always desirable.

Rising profitability in the export-generating sector causes the profit derived in the economy to be redistributed in favor of export industries, even if output is growing in the import-substituting sector. Besides, exporting enterprises derive their profits in foreign exchange, their worth remains high on the stock market, and they have more opportunity to borrow on external loan markets (domestic loans, too, are within easy reach for them because of their high profit margins).

All financial resources, therefore, are flowing into a limited number of industries. Commonly, these are capital-intensive industries that drain the economy of wage-related funds in labor-intensive sectors (above all in the service industries) and encourage labor outflow from these sectors. Moreover, "excessive" devaluation leaves the bulk of industries outside the financial flows. A result of these processes is an economy with an accentuated focus on primary material production, one that is dangerously exposed to fluctuations in world prices and has a small share of services, as is typical of countries at a low level of economic development.

The problem should not, of course, be overdramatized in Russia's case. The danger of this kind of change in the economic structure would be great in the absence of a large and diversified manufacturing sector. The results of the economy's performance in 1999 show, however, that devaluation has stimulated growth both in primary industries and in manufacturing, such as engineering and the food industry (see Table 12.2).

More Expensive Foreign Equipment and Technologies

The modernization of domestic industries is an important condition for transforming the recovery of import-substituting industries in the wake of devaluation into a sustainable economic growth.[31] Industrial modernization is ultimately aimed at giving Russian goods a greater competitive edge on the domestic and world markets. The quality of many domestically produced goods launched on the wave of the import-substitution drive is still very poor. They sell mostly because of their relatively low prices compared to imports, and their producers can only survive in the present state of protectionism, which shields them from competition. Apart from imposing a heavier debt burden on the economy, devaluation of the ruble reduces opportunities for enterprises to purchase imported machinery and technologies to replace and modernize their manufacturing equipment. In today's conditions, this limitation appears to be a very serious one.

The Choice of a Real Ruble Exchange-Rate Policy in the Short Term

The growth sparked by the ruble's devaluation can be sustained, therefore, if it is fueled by investment. To speed up modernization and replace machinery and technologies, the surplus profits compa-

---

31. For more detail, see Ye. Gaidar, *Anomaly of Economic Growth* (Moscow: Eurasia, 1997).

nies derive in the period immediately following devaluation must be channeled into long-term investment projects instead of current consumption. Russia today, regrettably, has only very limited possibilities for accumulating savings. Moreover, industrial managers are mostly preoccupied with expanding domestic demand and meeting it using whatever manufacturing equipment they already own. This is yet another argument for improving the investment climate in Russia.

It is still an open question as to which exchange-rate policy is to be pursued in the short and medium terms. An analysis of possible variants of a real ruble exchange policy in the short term (up to two years) shows that a rapid revaluation of the ruble today would be undesirable, and hard to implement in practice. Despite the negative effects of the low exchange rate, maintaining the existing balance between domestic and world prices is beneficial to Russian manufacturers, the central bank, and the government of the Russian Federation.

At a time when exporting enterprises are contributing a fifth of the country's tax revenues (see Statistical Appendix, Tables 3 and 4), their falling profits would cut into the budget revenues and, in turn, complicate yet more seriously the foreign debt servicing problem for Russia. Consideration, however, is to be given to a certain degree of externality of Russian exports. Indeed, Russian exports are structured in such a way that prices for most categories of commodities (such as oil, gas, and metals) are set on world commodity markets and are binding on all trading partners.

The antidumping lawsuits against Russian metal producers in the European Union and the United States show that Russia cannot make full use of its relative competitive advantages by selling its commodities below world prices. This means that world prices actually determine the profit margins of Russian exporting enterprises, which have little control over their own efforts to cut production costs. The financial "cushion" formed at current prices is sufficiently large to discourage production cost reductions (as in primary industries). If and when the prices of Russia's principal commodity exports fall, profit margins may again be reduced to zero in manufacturing. The government's response to such a situation will most likely be another devaluation of the ruble.

In regard to the prospects for economic growth driven by import-substitution efforts, thought must be given to yet another aspect, related to the ratio of income elasticities in exports and imports. As shown by P. Krugman,[32] the ratio of elasticities that exists in Russia today (low elasticity for exports and high elasticity for imports) means that long-term growth of the national economy is possible only if the national currency is devalued from time to time. The scale of primary exports is limited by the relative price inelasticity of fuel and by few opportunities to influence world oil and natural gas prices. On the other side, as living standards rise, demand for imports of better quality than domestically produced items grows. As a result of this the trade balance deteriorates. If this process is combined with worsening conditions for the country's foreign trade and a hurried flight of capital, the economy descends into a crisis like the one experienced in 1998. Under these conditions, the country's government is compelled to devalue the national currency periodically to sustain the rates of domestic economic growth and a favorable trade balance.

The short-term growth prospects for the Russian economy are constrained by the need to raise foreign exchange funds to repay the country's foreign debt, which restricts the central bank's ability to pursue a monetary and currency policy capable of strengthening the ruble. Demand for foreign exchange by the central bank and the Ministry of Finance heightens expectations of a continued fall in the nominal exchange rate of the ruble. This action as well as measures that could possibly be taken to sterilize ruble interventions on the currency market would contribute to a further slowing of inflationary processes and a reduction in the real exchange rate of the ruble. Attempts to increase the foreign exchange supply (such as a mandatory requirement for exporting enterprises to sell 100% of their foreign exchange proceeds, or levying higher taxes on them, along with other foreign trade–related payments) in the absence of more efficient currency controls would only force more capital to flee the country, and their net effect on the foreign exchange supply on the domestic market is unpredictable.

On the other hand, because of the inflow of foreign capital that began in late winter of 1999 and its possible intensification in the foreseeable future, the government and the central bank may face a dilemma: to allow a fast revaluation of the national currency, as was

---

32. P. Krugman, "Differences in Income Elasticities and Trends in Real Exchange Rates," *European Economic Review* 33 (1989): 1031–54.

done in some Latin American countries[33] and in Russia in the summer of 1995, or to undertake protective measures aimed at restraining capital inflows, mainly short-term portfolio investments. These measures may include the following[34]:

• Restrictions on the amounts (or growth rates) of foreign liabilities of commercial banks.

• A bar against the purchase of ruble-denominated corporate (and bank) bonds by nonresidents of Russia.[35]

• The introduction of a mandatory reservation system for certain foreign liabilities (to include bank credits and portfolio investment used for investing in ruble assets [shares, government bonds]. Trade credits and direct foreign investment shall be exempted from the mandatory reservation[36]). Mandatory reserve rates shall be set in inverse proportion to investment terms.

• Issuance of foreign exchange–denominated CBR bonds[37] and deposit certificates.

• Ruble interventions on the foreign exchange market aimed at the repurchase of surplus foreign exchange supply, and a broader set of monetary policy measures aimed at their sterilization (CBR bonds, higher mandatory reservate rates, sales of government securities).

• Suspension of government foreign borrowings (in the form of eurobonds).

• Taxation of repatriated profits (at 25%–30%).

These measures shall be aimed at sustaining a low real exchange rate of the ruble for the next year or two. In the medium term (up to five years), it will probably be desirable to work for a gradual rise in

---

33. S. Edwards, "Capital Inflows into Latin America: A Stop-Go Story?" NBER Working Paper no. 6441 (1998); idem, "Capital Flows, Real Exchange Rates, and Capital Controls: Some Latin American Experiences," NBER Working Paper no. 6800 (1998).
34. Based on the experiences of a number of countries (Chili, Colombia, Malaysia, Brazil, the Czech Republic). See Edwards, "Capital Flows"; idem, "On Crisis Prevention: Lessons from Mexico and East Asia," NBER Working Paper no. 7233 (1999); R. B. Johnston and N. Tamirisa, "Why Do Countries Use Capital Controls?" IMF Working Paper no. 98-181 (1998); *World Economic Outlook and International Capital Markets: Interim Assessment, December 1998* (Washington, D.C.: IMF, 1998).
35. Nonresidents will purchase eurobonds.
36. An option: only direct foreign investment for over 12 to 18 months shall be exempted from mandatory reservation (mandatory reserve rate at 20%).
37. Similar to tesobonds in Mexico.

the real ruble exchange rate. Several factors support this path. First, the peak period of foreign debt repayment will have passed by the year 2005, and the need to raise foreign exchange for government expenditures will have declined. A lower demand for foreign exchange in the setting of a favorable trade balance will lift restrictions on a stronger ruble. Second, the anticipated economic growth will make Russia more attractive for investors and push both the current account balance and capital account balance into the black sooner. Third, as industrial production goes up, it will be vitally important to gradually lift barriers to penetration of the Russian market, in this way stimulating replacement of machinery and technologies and sharpening the competitive edge of Russian companies.

In regard to the prospects for long-term growth of the Russian economy based on import substitution, it is necessary to note yet another aspect related to differences in income elasticities of exports and imports. As P. Krugman has shown, sustainable long-term growth of a national economy is possible only under conditions of regular devaluation of the national currency at the ratio of income elasticities between exports and imports that is like the one currently observed in Russia (low elasticity of exports and high elasticity of imports).[38] Raw material exports are constrained by the relatively low price elasticity of fuels and the limited possibilities of influencing world oil and natural gas prices. At the same time, as living standards improve, the demand for imported goods of a better quality than domestically made substitutes grows. Therefore, the trade balance deteriorates. Should this process coincide with deteriorating terms of trade and an intensifying capital flight caused by growing country-specific risks, it may result in an economic crisis like the one that occurred in 1998. In this situation the government has to regularly devalue the national currency in order to maintain domestic economic growth rates and a positive trade balance.

---

38. Krugman, "Differences in Income Elasticities."

13 The Fallout of Russia's Financial Crisis on Its Neighbors

Marek Dabrowski

13.1. Overview

The financial crisis that hit Russia in August 1998 was not without serious consequences for its near and more distant neighbors. The shock waves swept both the real sector of their economies (above all, rocking their foreign trade) and their financial markets.

Central European and Baltic countries, which had advanced farthest in reforms and had installed a more shock-resistant macroeconomic foundation over the preceding years, recovered relatively quickly from the effects of the "Russian shock" on their financial markets. In the Baltics, speculation against their currencies, tumbling prices on their stock markets, and mounting risk premiums went on for only a few weeks. Also, the banking systems of those countries escaped heavy losses (with the exception, perhaps, of a few Latvian banks that traded on the government short-term bond (GKO) markets in Russia and several other CIS countries). The Baltic countries evidently rode out the storm on their fully operational currency boards.

The aftershocks, however, lasted longer in the real sector of the economies. This was especially the case in the Baltic countries and Poland, which had retained relatively strong commercial ties with Russia and other CIS countries (particularly Belarus and Ukraine). In Poland, for example, exports fell and GDP growth slowed. In the first quarter of 1999, GDP growth rates plunged to 1.5%, their lowest level in recent years (having previously registered a breezy annual 5%–7% expansion). Even though Poland has shown, beginning early in the second quarter of 1999, an upswing in growth rates (in the first six months of 1999, real GDP posted a 2.3% rise over the same period of 1998), the country will nonetheless take some time to recover fully from the backwash of the Russian crisis in the real sector. The 1999 GDP was expected to show a growth of about 3.6% (*Polish Economic Outlook* 1999). Downtrends also continue to hold in Poland's exports.

Similar problems confront the Baltic countries, which also saw a marked slowdown in growth rates in 1999. In Estonia and Latvia, exports dipped by 10% in the first half of 1999 from the corresponding period of the year before. In Lithuania exports dived by 25% overall, with that country's exports to Russia sinking to 25% of pre-crisis levels. On balance, all three Baltic nations saw their GDP performance deteriorate in the first six months of 1999 (down by about 4% in Estonia and Lithuania) from the first half of 1998 (*World Economic Outlook* [*WEO*] 1999, 71). For all of 1999, the IMF predicted a GDP growth of 0.5% for Estonia and Lithuania and 2% for Latvia. By way of comparison, in 1997 GDP growth raced ahead at 10.6% in Estonia, 7.3% in Lithuania, and 6.5% in Latvia, easing off to 4.0%, 5.1%, and 3.8%, respectively, in 1998 (*WEO* 1999, 32).

The fallout of the Russian crisis has been much more detrimental to CIS countries in both the real and financial sectors. Within a few months following the August 1998 crisis, the majority of these countries began to share Russia's experience, on a scale and in forms that differed from country to country.

The Ukrainian hrivna collapsed two weeks after the onset of the Russian crisis, with its devaluation creeping on for a few more months afterwards. The Belarussian ruble, which had been losing value rapidly from early 1998, fell precipitously after the Russian crisis in the last quarter of 1998 and early 1999. The Moldovan leu was devalued between late October and early November 1998, followed, in mid-November, by the Kyrgyz som and, in early December, the Georgian lari. The devaluation of the Uzbek sum gathered speed; the Tajik ruble took some time to tumble down as well.

The Kazakh tenge staved off devaluation the longest. The decision to depreciate it came relatively late, in April 1999. It provoked another wave of speculative pressure on Central Asian currencies, particularly the Kyrgyz som and Tajik ruble. A full-scale banking crisis, the second in three years, broke out in Kyrgyzstan (see Brudzynski, Dabrowski, and Mogilewski 1999; Kloc 1999). Armenia came in last, with a limited devaluation of its dram in early July 1999. Among the CIS countries, Azerbaijan alone has so far managed to avoid scaling down its currency (the manat) against the US dollar.

Several reasons can be suggested for this precipitous chain reaction. First, almost all CIS countries (with the exception of Turkmenistan and Tajikistan) have maintained strong commercial and industrial ties with Russia. In the aftershock of the Russian crisis (which spread to other CIS countries as well), much of the real sector in CIS countries depended, and continues to depend, on markets affected by the crisis. To an extent, strong ties remain between the CIS countries' financial markets as well.

Second, the CIS countries' economies shared the fundamental drawbacks and problems of the Russian economy—above all large budget deficits, growing government debts, narrow monetization of their economies, fragile banking systems, and inadequate progress in institutional and structural reforms.

Third, psychology played a key role, as many foreign and domestic entities anticipated a replay of the Russian scenario in CIS countries.

This chapter takes a closer look at the factors that contributed to the far-reaching effects of Russia's crisis on other CIS countries.

13.2. Fundamental Flaws of the Transformation Process in CIS Countries

Unlike its course in Central European and Baltic countries, transformation in the CIS countries has been less consistent and slower. Following the political disintegration of the USSR in 1991, the majority of the newly emergent states hesitated instead of launching radical economic reforms immediately. Those that attempted to begin reforms forthwith, like Russia in late 1991 and early 1992, failed for political reasons, abandoning their attempts prematurely.

Thus, most CIS countries ended up, for many years, with an intermediate economic system, one that was no longer subject to the discipline of the planned economy (which actually decayed spontaneously in the years of perestroika) and was only marginally exposed to market forces, usually with a brutal twist. Excessive administrative regulations hindered the spontaneous rise of a new private sector (as in East European and Baltic countries), on the one hand, and encouraged corruption and administrative rent seeking by old and new oligarchies on the other. Regardless of the approach—fast or slow—taken to privatization, a majority of undertakings fell into the hands of old-breed "red directors" and the "new oligarchs." The former had a large stake in maintaining the status quo; the latter

Table 13.1
Annual Inflation in CIS Countries, 1992–1998 (% of Previous Year's December Figure)

Country	1992	1993	1994	1995	1996	1997	1998
Armenia	1,241.2	10,896.1	1,884.5	32.1	5.8	22.0	−1.1
Azerbaijan	—	1,293.8	1,788.0	84.5	6.7	0.4	−7.8
Belarus	1,557.8	1,994.0	1,957.0	244.2	39.1	63.4	181.7
Georgia	1,178.5	7,484.1	6,473.0	57.4	13.7	7.2	10.7
Kazakhstan	2,962.8	2,169.1	1,160.3	60.4	28.6	11.3	1.9
Kyrgyzstan	1,257.0	766.9	95.7	32.0	34.9	14.7	18.3
Moldova	2,198.4	836.0	116.0	23.8	15.1	11.1	18.4
Russia	2,321.6	841.6	202.7	131.4	21.8	11.0	84.5
Tajikistan	—	7,343.7	1.1	2,133.3	40.5	163.6	2.7
Turkmenistan	—	—	1,328.5	1,261.5	445.9	21.8	19.8
Ukraine	2,001.0	10,155.0	401.1	181.4	39.7	10.1	20.0
Uzbekistan	910.0	884.8	1,281.4	116.9	64.4	50.0	26.0

Source: IMF and EBRD data.

were obsessed with parking corporate profits and liquid assets in overseas accounts rather than with boosting their businesses' profits or growth prospects. Unsurprisingly, this microeconomic environment did little to reverse the continuing collapse of the real economies (at least in their official sectors) in the majority of CIS countries.

The flaws of the structural and institutional reforms and the unending plunge of the officially reported GDP, as well as the strong populist trends in domestic policies, were bound to affect government finances. Nearly all CIS countries are currently running a large consolidated budget deficit, and some of them—Belarus, Uzbekistan, and Turkmenistan—are also engaging in quasi-fiscal operations through their central banks.

At the outset of transformation, fiscal and quasi-fiscal deficits were financed predominantly by central bank loans—that is, by money printing. The cost of this practice was very high inflation, even hyperinflation in some cases. Beginning in 1994 and 1995, some CIS countries (Moldova, Kyrgyzstan, Russia, Georgia, Armenia, Kazakhstan, Ukraine, and Azerbaijan) secured the cooperation of the International Monetary Fund in fighting inflation in earnest. Initially, they made considerable headway in their efforts. Most of them managed to beat down annual inflation rates to single-digit or low two-digit figures in 1997 (Table 13.1). In the first six to nine months of 1998, some of them succeeded in reducing inflation still further.[1]

---

1. It must be said, however, that falling prices for primary resources, especially oil and other fuels, played a key role in sharply lowering inflation in 1997 and 1998.

Table 13.2
Monetization Levels of CIS Countries' Economies, 1993–1996 (Ratios of Aggregate Money Supply to GDP)

Country	1993	1994	1995	1996
Armenia	23	11	6	7
Azerbaijan	27	18	11	9
Belarus	20	16	12	13
Georgia	7	4	2	4
Kazakhstan	20	11	9	9
Kyrgyzstan	11	10	14	14
Moldova	11	10	13	20
Russia	20	14	11	10
Tajikistan	42	32	20	7
Turkmenistan	13	5	6	6
Ukraine	20	18	13	10
Uzbekistan	29	20	14	14

Source: Jarocinski (1998).

Their success was short-lived, however, chiefly because of the continuing budgetary crisis. Progress in this area was either nonexistent or far too little. The only improvement was in the sources of budget deficit financing. Candid money printing was replaced with wide-scale borrowing on the commercial market through government securities (Dabrowski 1998). A contributing role was played by foreign loans from official creditors (that is, international organizations and governments of developed countries), particularly in countries with low per capita GDP (Kyrgyzstan, Tajikistan, Georgia, Armenia, and Moldova), which were granted such loans on easy terms.

Extensive government borrowing on the securities market and from official creditors could not go on indefinitely, for many reasons. First, the very low level of monetization of the recipient economies (under or within 12%–14% of GDP; see Table 13.2 and Jarocinski 1998) and the institutional fragility of the banking system limited the capacity of the domestic financial market to finance government debt. Experience shows that opportunities for floating Treasury bonds on the domestic market are exhausted within approximately a year of the start of their large-scale issue. Second, the opening of the Treasury bond market to nonresidents and the tapping of international financial markets (by issuing eurobonds, for example) broadened the range of potential deficit financing sources for a short time only. Foreign investors soon began to have doubts about the solvency of the borrowing countries. The Asian crisis in 1997 was a

Table 13.3
CIS Countries' Consolidated Budget Balances, 1992–1997 (% of GDP)

Country	1992	1993	1994	1995	1996	1997
Armenia	−37.3	−54.3	−10.1	−11.1	−9.3	−6.7
Azerbaijan	−27.9	—	−11.4	−4.3	−2.6	−1.3
Belarus	0.0	−1.9	−2.5	−1.9	−1.6	−1.2
Georgia	−62.3	−26.1	−16.5	−4.5	−4.4	−3.7
Kazakhstan	−7.3	−1.2	−7.2	−2.0	−2.5	−3.6
Kyrgyzstan	−14.8	−14.4	−11.6	−17.3	−9.5	−9.4
Moldova	−23.9	−7.4	−9.1	−5.8	−6.6	−6.8
Russia	−18.2	−7.3	−10.4	−5.8	−8.1	−7.5
Tajikistan	−30.5	−23.4	−5.1	−11.2	−5.8	−3.3
Turkmenistan	13.3	−0.5	−1.4	−1.6	−0.8	−0.4
Ukraine	−23.2	−9.7	−8.2	−5.0	−3.2	−5.1
Uzbekistan	−18.4	−10.4	−6.1	−4.1	−7.3	−2.3

Source: IMF data.

major catalyst for this process, but it was not the only or the main trigger. Confidence in Russia and other CIS countries would have wavered regardless of the Asian crisis, perhaps only with a time lag. Third, growing government debt service costs swelled budget expenditure, augmenting the budget deficit still more. The classic debt trap took hold.

Table 13.3 shows that virtually all CIS countries have been steadily running budget deficits above 5% of GDP. This means that, in terms of quality, the macroeconomic foundations of these countries were no different from Russia's, so a devaluation crisis could visit these countries regardless of what was happening in Russia. Kyrgyzstan was hit by a crisis of this type (with the som depreciating by more than 50%) in 1996, and the ruble in Belarus started falling in early 1998.

13.3. The Shock in Foreign Trade and the Real Sector

The Russian crisis drew in the real sector of neighboring economies, essentially through foreign trade conduits, in three ways.

First, across-the-board, real, no-nonsense devaluation of the Russian ruble (with inflation and labor costs growing far more slowly than devaluation) sharply reduced the prices of Russian goods imported by CIS countries. CIS countries' own exports to Russia lost in competitiveness on the Russian market. On third countries' markets, too, Russian goods now had a competitive edge over similar products from other CIS countries.

Second, GDP and domestic demand, including demand for imported goods, contracted in Russia. The fall in GDP and domestic demand was particularly striking when translated into foreign currency. Moreover, some Russian importers, anticipating the ruble's devaluation, had built up speculative inventories of foreign-made goods in the spring and summer of 1998. This further cut into demand for imports in the first few months after the crisis. Administrative restrictions on the currency market and foreign trade depressed imports still further.

Third, ruble devaluation was accompanied by a tremendous banking and payments crisis. The gridlock in the banking system halted payments on many trade deals and, as a result, frustrated the signing of many more.

These forces inflicted the greatest damage in the early months after the crisis. After a while, demand for imported goods in the Russian economy recovered partially, restrictions on the currency market were gradually lifted, and the banking system resumed normal operation. Also, importers and exporters found other payment channels (including barter).

The extent to which the foreign trade balance deteriorated was closely linked to the share of Russian exports and imports in the overall trade and GDP of a particular country. According to data from the European Bank for Reconstruction and Development (EBRD 1998), while exports from Turkmenistan and Tajikistan to Russia were respectively 5% and 8% of these countries' total exports in 1997, levels of exports to Russia were much higher in other CIS countries, ranging from 21% in Kyrgyzstan to 59% in Belarus and 63% in Moldova. Outside the CIS, Latvia was involved the most, with 21% of its exports going to Russia.

If we include exports to Ukraine and Belarus as well, the picture changes perceptibly, with Belarus (sending 74% of its exports to Russia and Ukraine) coming first, followed closely by Moldova (70%). The pair were trailed by Kazakhstan (42%), Uzbekistan (39%), Georgia (34%), Azerbaijan (28%), Ukraine (27%), Armenia (26%), and Kyrgyzstan (23%). Across CIS borders, Lithuania and Latvia relied more than any other nation on combined exports to Ukraine, Belarus, and Russia (28%), far ahead of Estonia (13%), Macedonia (11%), and Poland and Bulgaria (10% each). These figures, however, under-represent the actual scale of trade flows, for they leave out "suitcase" trade and exports via third countries (these two factors accounted for a considerable share of Polish exports).

By correlating these export performance figures with GDP, we get Belarus in first place, with 41%, Moldova in second place (26%), Kazakhstan third (13%), and Uzbekistan fourth (10%). Outside the CIS, Lithuania alone had a two-digit result (12%).

These figures show the initial exposure of individual economies at the outbreak of the Russian crisis. The amount of exposure and the chain reaction effect equaled falling GDP and devaluation of national currencies in countries touched by the Russian crisis. Because of the different sizes of the individual economies, crisis-like developments in Kazakhstan and Uzbekistan, apart from developments in Ukraine and Belarus, have extracted a heavy toll from their neighbors, with serious implications for other countries of post-Soviet Central Asia as well. With Uzbekistan and Kazakhstan resorting to various protectionist measures, trade problems in the region have grown.

Thus, the strong commercial and production links among CIS countries, regardless of the continuing economic and political instability in Russia, made their economies perilously vulnerable to a crisis of any caliber in their largest neighbor. These commercial links are both a legacy of the past and a consequence of regional geography, reinforced by the absence of alternative transport corridors. It is unreasonable to expect the close neighbors of Russia, Ukraine, or Kazakhstan to give up trade with one another only to spite the others. Some of the trade links inherited from the command system are hardly justifiable from the viewpoint of economic efficiency, however, and are most likely a result of slow structural reforms, the inability to find other markets, low product quality, technological backwardness, and other factors. It is more the drag of the past than a deliberate choice among relative advantages that has led to the current situation. In comparison, radical structural reforms in the Baltic countries helped those countries rapidly diversify their trade options and successfully break into world markets, even though their economies had been firmly tied to Russia's.

Apart from their shared geographic handicap, another reason for the structural weakness of some CIS countries' economies is the single-product nature of their exports, dominated by primary resources or unsophisticated intermediate products. For example, oil, natural gas, metallic ores, and metals account for much of Russian exports. Oil is the core product of Azerbaijan's exports, Turkmenistan earns most of its export receipts from natural gas, Uzbekistan exports cotton, oil, natural gas, and gold, and Kazakhstan's exports are made up largely of oil and ferrous and nonferrous metals. In the wake of the 1997 Asian crisis, demand and world prices for primary resources and fuels dropped swiftly (by 30% for some products). In addition to accelerating the crisis in Russia itself, these developments exacerbated the economic situation in Kazakhstan, Uzbekistan, Turkmenistan, and Azerbaijan. In contrast to the primary exporters' woes, importers of fuels and primary resources enjoyed a temporary boom, at least until the Russian crisis overwhelmed them. This applied particularly to Central European and Baltic countries, as well as Ukraine, Georgia, and Armenia.

13.4. Contagion Effect on Financial Markets

The spread of the Russian crisis through financial channels was driven by several key factors.

First, a large part of the balance of payments in some countries, primarily Georgia and Armenia, consisted of private transfers from nationals of those countries working in Russia or from relatives living in Russia. The ruble's devaluation sharply reduced the dollar-denominated value of these transfers, while the paralysis of Russian banks made money transfers out of Russia physically impossible.

Second, investors placing their money in CIS countries' government securities were exposing themselves in Russia as well. Those affected included Western investment banks and speculative funds, Baltic (above all Latvian) banks, and Russian investors (including offshore entities). Each time speculators attacked the Russian ruble (the strongest jolts to the Russian financial market prior to the August meltdown were registered in November 1997 and May 1998), nonresidents (and often residents, too) fled the treasuries markets in Ukraine, Moldova, Kazakhstan, and Kyrgyzstan. Their behavior was at times attributed to an attempt to make up for their losses on the Russian market, but more often than not it was simply instinctual.

Third, banks in CIS countries did have links with their Russian counterparts, although this was not always evident from their formal ownership structure (indeed, CIS countries also host subsidiary or joint banks established by Russian banks). Some interbank links were used by Russian (offshore) investors to maintain their presence in a particular country's treasuries market (via loro or interbank deposits). Other links served the purpose of financing and settling bilateral and multilateral commercial operations (through correspondent accounts). There are also a variety of informal or indirect links. As a result, commercial banks in CIS countries responded violently to convulsions on the Russian financial market, even when the situation in their own countries did not entirely warrant panicky behavior.

The situation in the CIS countries' banking system merits further comment. The low monetization level mentioned earlier testifies to the minuscule role banks play in the economies of these countries. Given the low level of savings, a large share of barter and cash transactions, and extensive use of raw commodities and dollars as surrogate legal tender in their economies, banks have little room to grow. In turn, their weakness and fragility do little to inspire confidence among the population and businesses and restrict growth in the demand for the national currency—a vicious circle indeed.

In the past few years, the CIS countries' banking systems have sustained two major crises. Kyrgyzstan illustrates this cycle very well. Following a basic macroeconomic stabilization in the mid-1990s, large state banks,[2] which had piled up huge portfolios of politically motivated loans, began to pose a major problem. Previously such loans had been issued, on orders of the Parliament, government, or central bank, to the so-called priority industries (such as agriculture, the fuel and energy complex, and housing construction) at low interest rates and frequently with long maturities. High inflation or hyperinflation rapidly depreciated the liabilities under these loans. At the critical stage of inflation control, however, when new targeted loans were to be scaled down abruptly and automatic depreciation of the old liabilities stopped, the financial situation of the hitherto privileged debtors and their financing banks deteriorated drastically. This circumstance forced the governments and central banks in many countries to make adjustments to the banking system, particularly banks engaged in the agrarian sector.

In Kyrgyzstan, readjustment ended, in 1996, in a liquidation program for two large banks, Sberbank and Agroprombank (see Kloc

---

2. In some countries they were no longer owned by the state, after spontaneous privatization.

1999). The radical restructuring of the banking system succeeded at the time, but the banking crisis reemerged two years later. This time the crisis originated in new private banks, including those with foreign and offshore capital stakes, which had been engaging in high-risk deals or pure fraud. Weak regulation of the banking system and effective political lobbying by bankers (many of whom had personal ties to members of the legislature and executive branch) blocked preventive measures that could have forestalled a crisis.

In contrast to the banking system, the shock waves of the Russia crisis had little effect on the stock market, for the simple reason that Russia was the only country to have a developed stock market without equal elsewhere in the CIS. Some countries (such as Georgia, Moldova, and Kyrgyzstan) have token stock markets, with nothing to show in the way of practical results.

13.5. The Psychological Factor

The effect of the psychological factor should be looked at separately for foreign and domestic entities. In regard to the former, in previous crises international speculative investors showed a tendency to generalize to the region any economic turn of events in a single country, even in the absence of conclusive economic evidence. This tendency stems from speculators' expectations of large short-term margins, the weaknesses of their own analytical services, and their inclination to imitate the behavior of market leaders. This herd behavior was especially to be anticipated in a situation where the macro- and microeconomic foundations of CIS countries' economies did not differ much from country to country (see Chapter 2).

The reaction of domestic entities was more surprising. The vast majority of them, whether political figures, bankers, entrepreneurs, or ordinary people, expected an inevitable replay of the Russian scenario at the macroeconomic level in their own countries. Such expectations were most evident in Kazakhstan, where the government and the central bank had long resisted pressure to devalue the tenge, a move that certainly did not appear unavoidable from an economic perspective. Finally, however, the general expectation of devaluation turned into a self-fulfilling prophecy. This psychological pressure was undoubtedly reinforced by the calculated actions of exporters and producers manufacturing import-substituting output, who stood to gain from devaluation.

13.6. Economic Implications of the Crisis

The currencies of CIS countries affected by the crisis lost much of their previous value. In a majority of countries, particularly Ukraine, Moldova, Georgia, Kyrgyzstan, Tajikistan, and Kazakhstan, the US dollar rose 80%–100% against the national currency between August 1998 and August 1999. This devaluation of the national currency was less profound than in either Russia or Belarus, but more than strong enough to wreck the fragile macroeconomic stability these countries had achieved in the preceding years.

Rising inflation was the first visible result of devaluation. Very soon, however, in late 1998, the trend suddenly changed: from a low rate, below 10% (in Russia, Ukraine, and Kyrgyzstan), or even a negative one (as in Georgia and Moldova), posted in the first seven months, annual inflation shot up to 84.4% in Russia, 20% in Ukraine, 18.4% in Moldova, 18.3% in Kyrgyzstan, and 10.7% in Georgia in December 1998.

The outlook for 1999 was different for different countries. It was by far the bleakest in Belarus, where inflation had been running at a three-digit clip for over a year (and still showing an upward trend) and was accompanied by shortages of consumer goods (provoked by a return to pricing by government fiat). In Russia and Kyrgyzstan, annual inflation forecasts still stood at relatively high two-digit levels, about 50% and 40%, respectively. In Moldova, Ukraine, and Kazakhstan, annual inflation was not expected to exceed 20%, and possibly as low as 10% in Georgia. These estimates allow a cautious forecast to be made: these countries have succeeded in coping with the immediate inflationary pulls of their currencies' devaluation, or at least in keeping them limited.

The shock in foreign trade and finances pushed the officially registered GDP to a new low. After a moderate rise of 0.9% in Russia in 1997, the GDP slumped by 4.6% in 1998. In Ukraine, incipient growth in late 1997 and the first half of 1998 gave way to a deep plunge in the second half of 1998 and early 1999 (for the whole of 1998, the GDP fell by 1.7%). In Moldova, the GDP retreated by 8.6% in 1998 (after a 1.3% recovery in 1997). In Kazakhstan, the GDP receded by 2.5% in 1998—months before the devaluation.[3] In Geor-

---

3. A drop in world prices for oil and other primary resources was a major contributing factor in Kazakhstan and Russia.

gia and Kyrgyzstan, the two fastest growing CIS countries in 1997, the growth rate slowed rapidly in 1998, from 11.0% to 2.9% and from 9.9% to 2%, respectively. Armenia and Azerbaijan, which sustained only a glancing blow from the Russian crisis, stepped up their growth rates in 1998, from 3.1% to 7.2% and from 5.8% to 10.0%, respectively. Very high growth rates were posted in Belarus (8.3%), although strong doubts exist about the quality of the GDP statistics and the stability of this growth trend.

In 1999, the economic slump rolled on in Ukraine, Moldova, and Kazakhstan, and set in in Belarus as well. Kyrgyzstan and Georgia were expected to register modest GDP growth, within 2%–3%. According to IMF forecasts, the GDP of Armenia and Azerbaijan was expected to grow 3%–4%, down from the year before.

Once again, Russia is the odd man out. Estimates worked out in late 1998 predicted a significant decline in GDP, by as much as 5%–7%, in 1999. Gross industrial output, however, registered growth throughout 1999 (from the respective period of 1998), and the pessimistic outlook for GDP growth gradually brightened. The latest IMF forecast suggests zero GDP growth (*WEO* 1999, 74).

Stabilization of the GDP and growth of the gross industrial output in Russia are due to two factors: first, the increase in world prices for oil and some other primary resources during 1999, and second, the extensive devaluation of the ruble, which created a niche for domestic import-substituting industries. Unless these hopeful developments are followed up with vigorous structural and institutional reforms, however, this slow recovery may prove brief. Regrettably, reforms in the Russian economy have been making little progress, and in some cases reversing course, since the August 1998 crisis.

Tenuous recovery also has been registered in some of Ukraine's import-substituting industries. This development is a far cry from signaling the beginning of real GDP growth in that country, though.

Poor statistics make it difficult to gauge the full impact of the crisis in foreign trade. Imports, particularly consumer goods and investments, have doubtless dwindled dramatically in all countries hit by devaluation. Exports to Russia, and selectively to other CIS countries, have declined as well. A key role in this downturn has been played by falling demand for imported goods in Russia and changes in real currency exchange rates (the real purchasing power of the ruble has dropped more steeply than that of other CIS currencies). In some places, protectionist policies were invoked in foreign trade, as, for example, in Kazakhstan and Uzbekistan against imports from Kyrgyzstan. In most countries, exports across CIS borders improved somewhat, but this is hardly a good time to make guesses about whether or not this tentative recovery will keep up. Continued growth of exports beyond the CIS may be checked by, above all, the very slow pace of structural reforms and of normalization of formal commercial relations between CIS countries and the world community. Up to this point, Kyrgyzstan alone has succeeded in gaining membership in the World Trade Organization, although Georgia, Armenia, and Moldova stand a good chance of joining WTO soon. All other CIS countries, Russia and Ukraine among them, are so far only in the opening phase of negotiations.

If the devaluation has been beneficial to selected real sector industries, particularly import-substituting manufacturing, the cost has been a steep decline in real wages, pensions, and all social benefits. The population has again paid a heavy price for the inefficiency of manufacturers.

Nor has devaluation been able to resolve such problems as budgetary imbalance, government debt overhang, or the tenuous state of the financial sector. Rather, it has considerably added to the debt burden of the government, manufacturers, and banks. It has also added to current debt servicing costs, with the bulk of liabilities being denominated in foreign currencies. In the same vein, the GDP slump, dwindling foreign exchange reserves, and occasionally thinning exports have adversely affected outstanding liabilities, regardless of how they are calculated.

Russia has failed to reverse the default of its government and some of its biggest banks since the default was announced, on 17 August 1998. Its short- and medium-term prospects for fully mending its relations with creditors and returning to legitimate creditworthiness are not good.

Ukraine does not appear to have fared any better. Although its government and national bank have attempted to steer clear of open default and have prevailed again and again to convince their domestic and foreign creditors to consent to "voluntary" debt consolidation, the country is broke. Ukraine has virtually no hope of repaying its debts on time in 2000 and 2001.

Countries with a low per capita GDP (Moldova, Kyrgyzstan, Georgia, and Tajikistan) are probably immune to an immediate default, for the bulk of government debt is owed on long-dated (10 to 35 years) bonds issued on easy terms to international financial organizations and other official creditors. Liabilities, however, are piling up at an alarming rate, particularly in Kyrgyzstan and Moldova, while the devaluation of national currencies is adding to their debt burden.

Kyrgyzstan and Russia must also wrestle with the consequences of systemic banking crises. This is a very tall order, especially for Russia. Ukraine and the other countries discussed in this overview have, for the time being, avoided a full-blown banking crisis, although the situation in their banking sectors is precarious. In particular, Ukrainian banks keep most of their assets in domestic government bonds, which have turned out to be illiquid in practice. Another part of their banking assets consists of the foreign exchange liabilities of manufacturing enterprises. These liabilities have swelled alarmingly in the wake of devaluation and may prove very hard to service.

The crisis has shaken confidence in both the national currency and the banking system.[4] Personal and corporate deposits waned. They recovered slightly in some countries (in Ukraine, for example) after a while, but have not regained their precrisis strength. This means that the banks' potential to issue new loans to businesses is extremely curtailed even in countries that have been spared a systemic banking crisis and whose banking systems have not sustained damage to the same extent as Russia's has.

The stock market in Russia has rallied only partly, while the stock markets of other CIS countries are as good as dead. This fact, and the startlingly low international ratings of CIS countries after the near-default crisis, seriously obstruct efforts to complete monetary privatization of the so-called strategic industries (power, communications, air freight, oil and gas, among others). The crisis has pushed into the background any attempts to speed up privatization and urgent structural reforms in Russia, Ukraine, and Kyrgyzstan, and still poses a danger for future efforts in these areas. Crisis, of course, often proves a convenient pretext, whereas the actual causes of a slowdown in reforms lie in internal politics. This is particularly manifested in the lack of support for the executive among the parliamentary majority and the ongoing election campaigns.

---

4. In this situation, too, a psychological factor is at work. The deplorable condition of the banking system in Russia and the slow pace of its restructuring have bred general mistrust of commercial banks in all CIS countries, even if a particular country has managed to avert a banking crisis of its own.

13.7. Summary and Conclusions

The succession of financial crises provoked in CIS countries by the August 1998 meltdown in Russia has revealed the inherent weakness of reforms in those countries. It has also borne out, once again, the poor efficiency of slow, gradual reforms. Moreover, it has exploded the commonly held myth about the allegedly strict position of the IMF and World Bank toward reforms in transition economies. Nearly all countries affected by the crisis (with the exception of Belarus) had been implementing programs endorsed by the IMF and World Bank. Some of the beneficiaries, for example Georgia, Kyrgyzstan, Kazakhstan, and Moldova, were even considered leaders in the reform process in the post-Soviet space. These programs, however, failed to be radical enough or consistent enough to avert a crisis.

The crisis has widened the gap between the health of the economies and economic institutions in Central European and Baltic countries, on the one hand, and the condition of CIS countries on the other. The CIS countries and some Balkan countries (Romania is the best example) are beginning to form a second or even a third (Belarus) league of economies in transition, with hopes of joining the first league fading with each passing year.

To break the deadlock without squandering the assets the CIS countries have built up over the past five years, such as relative price stability (as in Georgia, Moldova, Kazakhstan, and Ukraine) or incipient economic growth (as in Georgia or Kyrgyzstan), these countries will have to drastically boost their structural and institutional reforms and put in order public finances, particularly their tax and welfare systems. Unless they do so, they will have little hope of reversing the slump or stagnation in the real sector of their economies or of maintaining inflation at low rates and enjoying any stability in their national currencies. In respect to finances, they will have to take more meaningful steps to restore confidence in their monetary and banking systems. Essentially, small countries with a large share of foreign trade in the GDP and a low monetization level should consider introducing a currency board or adopting a foreign currency (the dollar or euro) as the sole legal tender. Possibly large countries too, like Russia or Ukraine, that are unable to create conditions for a stable monetary system should abandon single-handed efforts in this area and "import" stability from across their borders.

Regarding a revival of the banking system, the only workable way, and one that has been corroborated by the experience of Hungary, Poland, and Estonia, is to cultivate an environment attractive to foreign prime banks that could take on the burden of restructuring and honing the existing banking system. This option is open first and foremost to large countries (Russia, Ukraine, and Kazakhstan) that offer alluring prospects for a burgeoning financial market. Such an option is less likely to be available to smaller and poorer countries such as Georgia, Moldova, Armenia, and Kyrgyzstan.

Bibliography

Brudzynski, Robert, Marek Dabrowksi, and Roman Mogilewski. 1999. *Economic Crisis in Kyrgyzstan in Late 1998: Causes and Routes of Escape.* Warsaw: Center for Social and Economic Research (CASE), *Research and Analysis*, no. 174.

Dabrowski, Marek. 1998. *Fiscal Problems During the Period of Transformation.* Warsaw: Center for Social and Economic Research (CASE), *Research and Analysis*, no. 122.

European Bank for Transition and Development (EBRD). 1998. *Transition Report 1998.* London: EBRD.

Jarocinski, Marek. 1998. *Demand for Money and Monetization in the Economy of Countries in the Process of Reforms.* Warsaw: Center for Social and Economic Research (CASE), *Research and Analysis*, no. 159.

Kloc, Kazimierz. 1999. *The Banking Systems of Ukraine, Kyrgyzstan and Georgia in 1991–1998: Institutional Analysis.* Warsaw: Center for Social and Economic Research (CASE), *Research and Analysis*, no. 179.

PEO—Polish Economic Outlook: Trends, Analyses, Forecasts. 1999. Warsaw: Center for Social and Economic Research (CASE), *Research and Analysis*, no. 2.

World Economic Outlook. 1999. Geneva: International Monetary Fund.

III

Institutional Reforms in the Russian Economy

14

Privatization, Ownership Redistribution, and Formation of the Institutional Basis for Economic Reforms

Alexander Radygin

14.1. Ownership and Privatization: Preliminary Methodological Notes

14.1.1. Ownership

Although there are many different theoretical approaches to and explanations of the role ownership plays in social and legal organization and the functioning of the economic system in any society, most researchers recognize as axiomatic that property, specifically property rights, is the base of any modern economic system. A few examples illustrate this principle.

The civilizations of antiquity, starting with the Greek states in the Classical period (fifth and fourth centuries B.C.), comprehended ownership in a social and economic context. Democritus treated private property as a necessary condition of the natural struggle to survive, a position that may be better understood by his viewing property as the basis of the economic system of his time. Plato in his *Laws* also saw the inviolability and stability of property as an important condition of the ideal state.

The British philosopher and economist David Hume stated in his *Treatise on Human Nature* (1740) that a contract on the distribution of property and on the stability of such ownership is the most necessary condition for the organization of human society. Hume further asserted that there remains little to do after this contract has been made. The founder of British positivism, John Stuart Mill, noted that among the methods applied to the distribution of the fruits of the land and of labor, the institution of private property was to be considered the most important fundamental institution on which the economic systems of society are always based. With a few exceptions, however, this institution in its secondary manifestations varies and is susceptible to change (Mill 1980, 339).

Orthodox Marxism lacks a detailed and clear definition of ownership, which suggests that the subject is difficult and multifaceted. Marx's understanding of property as a relation to a thing—a purely legal or a purely economic relation to the complex of bourgeois relations—is evident in his writings from different periods (see, for example, the Introduction to *A Contribution to the Critique of Political Economy*, *The Poverty of Philosophy*, *Capital*, and *Theories of Surplus Value*). At the same time, Marxist theorists recognized private property as the basis of the capitalist method of production and appropriation. A similar approach was a characteristic of the political economy of socialism. According to this approach the socialist economic system was defined as a "planned organization of the social production based on public ownership of means of production" (Abalkin 1979, 600).

In the current economic literature, well-defined property rights—more specifically, clarity, stability, and predictability of property rights—are regarded as a major factor in economic growth and are closely linked to successful economic development (Coase 1960; Demsetz 1967; North 1981). Nevertheless, the role of property rights may vary, depending on the size of the entities, whether they are public or private, access to information, and other factors (Arrow 1974; Stiglitz 1975, 1994; World Bank 1998).

Theoretical approaches aside, the importance of well-defined property rights to institutional reform cannot be overestimated. As early as 1912 the Russian philosopher Vasili Rosanov noted, "In Russia all property was either 'obtained by begging,' or 'given,' or 'cheated.' Property is earned in a very few cases. Therefore it is not stable, and is not respected" (Rosanov 1990). If this statement is adopted as "Rosanov's theorem," then the failure of the Russian institutional reforms of 1990s may be explained by "incomprehensible Russian specifics."[1] A serious analysis of the Russian reform of property relations, of course, requires us to look much deeper.

Under the socialist economic system, legal sanctions for the protection of public property were prominent. In the transitional Russian economy the zone of uncertainty in respect to property rights

---

1. At the end of the 1990s, many Western critics of the Russian reforms in essence confined themselves to this approach. See, for example, Mau (1999).

has become wider. This phenomenon has unfolded since the protections for public property began to be eroded. A new, clear system of private property rights does not yet exist.[2]

The erosion of property rights also leads to paralysis of corporate investment activity. This is the case because the better property rights are defined, the less risk there is on the capital markets (Grossman and Hart 1986; Hart and Moore 1990). However, Russia still lacks clear economic and legal boundaries between public and private property, with all the resultant problems (including the protracted absence of bankruptcy as a mechanism of corporate control). Problems stemming from imperfect information in the field of ownership relations are also apparent in the Russian transition.

The problem of transforming property relations and ownership structure is one of the most important problems faced by a country undergoing economic transition. The role of property rights as the basis for an economic system determines both the systemic character of the transformation in this sphere and the character of reforms in general in the course of transition.

14.1.2. Two Types of Privatization

The privatization process, understood in the most narrow sense as a transfer of some property (assets) from the state to the private sector, has a very long history—probably as long as the history of property itself.

In ancient Egypt, the utilization of private mechanisms (use, ownership, and property) was conceived on the basis of and in counterbalance to the use of state property. The "property" of Egyptians included state property that could be used by private persons and property possessed by administrators during the tenure of their administrative positions. In general, researchers have noted a nonlinear relation between the strength of the central authority and private property ownership: as the former weakens, the latter grows (at the expense of state property), and vice versa (*Vsemirnaya istoriya* 1:47–48).

More than two centuries ago Adam Smith analyzed the advantages of privatization of state (crown) lands. Smith clarifies:

---

[2]. See Radygin and Entov (1999). On the problem of poor defined property rights in transition economies, see Shleifer (1994).

> In every great monarchy in Europe the sale of crown lands would produce a very large sum of money, which, if applied to the payment of the public debts, would deliver from mortgage a much greater revenue than any which those lands have ever afforded to the crown.... When the crown lands have become private property, they would, in the course of a few years, become well improved and well cultivated.[3]

In simplest terms, privatization can be defined as any sale (transfer) of state property to private owners, occurring in any age. The modern sense of privatization began to emerge only at the end of the 1970s—and the modern concept of privatization differs fundamentally, in its social and economic processes, from the concept of private property in ancient Egypt and in nineteenth-century Britain. To understand the nature of contemporary privatization, we must peruse some general and specific features of the privatization process.

In the general civilization approach (based on Kondratyev cycles), the difference lies in the quantitative degree of privatization across various spatial aspects. From the point of view of systemic transition in a transitional economy, the problem is much more complicated and includes a radical transformation of all system-forming elements of this economic system.

To clarify, the first type of privatization is related to shifts in the mechanism of reproduction, and to the structural reconstruction of the economy of developed Western countries. This reconstruction began in the second half of the 1970s and required a considerable reexamination of the structure of the state regulation of the economy, which was formed in the period of the 1950s and 1960s. In practically all Western countries there took place a serious reappraisal of the place and role of state property and state entrepreneurship in the economy, a reappraisal that was manifested in privatization processes during the 1980s and 1990s. This phenomenon was observable not only in most West European countries with a traditionally high degree of state interference in the economy, but also in such countries as the United States, Japan, and Switzerland, where the state plays a relatively minor role. Neoconservative shifts in ideology, general economic theory, and the economic policies of industrially developed countries were later exported to developing countries, both as ideas transferred through the global scholarly community and as pressure directly exerted by the West as a precondition for assistance.

---

3. Cited in Yarrow (1986, 324).

These radical changes in theories of economic development of Third World countries occurred in the 1970s and 1980s, when "market failure" theories were replaced by opposing concepts of "state failure." At the end of the 1980s and the beginning of the 1990s, more than eighty industrially developed Western countries and developing countries across Asia, Africa, and Latin America had completed or were in the process of conducting various programs of privatization of state property.[4]

In the framework of the technological paradigm, including neoclassical economic theory as adumbrated by O. E. Williamson (1990), the effectiveness of an enterprise—its economic results—is poorly correlated with ownership type. Rather, market structure and competition are much more important for an enterprise's effectiveness than are differences between those who control the assets in question. At the same time, G. Yarrow has noted that "the competitive and regulatory environment is more important than the question of ownership per se. In competitive markets there is a presumption in favor of private ownership. Where there is a natural monopoly, vigorous regulatory action is required" (Yarrow 1986).

In light of these positions, evaluating the advantages of private enterprises over state-owned ones becomes a separate problem. In a narrow sense, the question has to do with the positive influence of privatization on enterprises' effectiveness. Most researchers are inclined to answer this question positively. However, a common point of view has not been agreed upon.[5] Several approaches favor private enterprises:

- *Social:* State-owned enterprises are an instrument for "curing" market shortcomings via price policies, taking into account social marginal prices (Shapiro and Willig 1990). Such functions and costs negatively affect an enterprise's efficiency.

---

4. There are so many works on the problems of privatization that any number of references would not be sufficiently complete. On problems of privatization in Western and developing countries, see, for instance, Bizaguet (1988); Hanke (1987); Kikeri, Nellis, and Shirley (1992); Nellis and Shirley (1991); Shapiro and Willig (1990); UNCTAD (1993); Vickers and Yarrow (1988); and Vuylsteke (1988). Some principal works on problems of privatization in transition economies are cited in the next paragraph, when basic models are compared.

5. For a detailed overview of works on this problem, see Perevalov, Grimadi, and Dobrodey (1999). The problem of the effectiveness of privatized enterprises in transition economies is reviewed in the following paragraphs.

- *Political:* Political (bureaucratic) interference in enterprises' operations results in redundant employment, nonoptimal placement, shortage of investment, and unclear signals to managers. These enterprises are more susceptible to pressure from interest groups, which negatively affects profit maximization (Shleifer and Vishny 1994).
- *Competition:* Privatization enhances competition, which forces enterprises to work more effectively. Private enterprises must be responsive to the discipline of commercial financial markets (Kikeri, Nellis, and Shirley 1992).
- *Stimulation:* Managers of state-owned enterprises do not have necessary incentives for effective work, or are insufficiently controlled (Vickers and Yarrow 1988).

No doubt opposing points of view could be expressed to each of these reasonings. For instance, at a certain point, long-term political interference may be better for improving enterprises' operations. This situation may arise if (1) legal protection of ownership rights is lacking *ex ante*, or (2) the interests of private owners become speculative in the short term. Arguments supporting the stimulating approach may fail if the government as the holder of the controlling interest is better able to control managers than dispersed stockholders of private corporations can (Dewenter and Malatesta 1998). Arguments supporting the competitive approach are sound only if private firms prove to be truly more effective than state-owned ones.

Although levels of development, concrete motives for privatization (budgetary revenues and healthier state finances, improvement in the economy's effectiveness, the revival of competition, and management reform, as well as specialization and demonopolization, ideological motives such as "people's capitalism," investment attraction, and so forth), legal and economic traditions, and political and ideological doctrines vary across countries, all of them share key common features: (1) privatization is conducted within the framework of an existing market and competitive environment, (2) the private sector is dominant, and (3) all of the countries are developing economically.

The second type of privatization emerged somewhat later, since about 1989, in the course of the systemic transformations that began in former socialist countries, first in Russia and then in the countries of Eastern and Central Europe. Simultaneously with the development of systemic reforms in these countries, economic transition theory became the fastest developing branch of economic theory. In the context of a transition from a command and administrative (socialist, planned, or centralized) economy to an economy based on market and competitive principles (at least in accordance with economic theory), privatization acquired a special role.

The concept of property as the basis of any economic system requires (1) the systemic character of transformation related to ownership as a country switches from one economic system to another, and (2) the systemic character of reforms as a whole in the framework of an economy in transition. The systemic nature of the changes is the principal difference between the privatization process in a country in transition to a market economy and any measures toward privatization undertaken by Western and other developing countries.

The trio of stabilization, liberalization, and ownership reform became a classic calculus for determining the direction of systemic transformations in transitional economies, at least in their first stage. Of course, pivotal to ownership reform in transitional economies is a set of privatization policies and practices. In Russia, the ownership reform process did not begin suddenly; it was preceded by a range of preparatory measures of an ideological and legal nature. Similarly, ownership reform in transitional economies does not end after privatization programs have been completed, but just gets a powerful start, since only after "primary" privatization has occurred can truly effective property rights begin to take shape.

14.1.3. Short-, Medium-, and Long-Term Stages of Privatization in a Transition Economy

The experience of Russia in the 1990s represents the systemic form of privatization as a relatively prolonged, formative phenomenon, occurring in two parallel processes. First, the state gradually withdrew from performing its functions as an economic agent. These functions were not appropriate for the state to perform in a competitive market economy. The state's opportunities to exercise property rights were correspondingly reduced. The process can be called "de-etatization" in the framework of systemic transition. Second, there was the process of creating new economic and legal mechanisms and institutional structures, without which the institution of private property cannot be fully realized.

It is very important to bear in mind that in the early stages of market reforms, the process of creating new legal mechanisms and institutional structures can occur only as the state withdraws from the economy. Indeed, the institutions, which initially emerge passively, occupy the spaces vacated by the state's withdrawal. For example, most Russian corporations created during the privatization initially differed little de facto from their former state-controlled predecessors. As a result, it is hard to overestimate the importance of a well-grounded and competent government policy for stimulating and regulating this process and providing conditions conducive to the systemic transformation of property relations.

The first stage was a noneconomic act of will: formal privatization, the success of which depended entirely on balancing interests. There were two reasons for the noneconomic character of this stage. First, before the beginning of formal privatization and even during its course, spontaneous privatization occurred. This spontaneous privatization took legal, semilegal, or potentially illegal forms. The initial formal privatization, therefore, simply legalized previously existing informal ownership rights (manifested, for instance, in relations between the state and managers of state-owned enterprises). Second, it was the political will of the authorities that provided the impetus for the developments of this stage. In the case of mass privatization, in addition to legalization of already existing informal property rights, there was a formal dispersion of ownership rights throughout society.

The most important features of this stage were the emergence of a critical mass of private and quasiprivate enterprises and the intense quantitative formation of new institutions.[6] In this respect, a deceleration in the quantitative transformation process and the first appearance of nascent qualitative institutional change should be regarded as marking the completion of the first stage.

In the second stage there occurred (1) an intense redistribution of property rights after the initial formal privatization, and (2) a stream-

---

6. "In the period of rupture of regularities, society loses its orientation, as it were ... regulatory mechanisms weaken which in normal circumstances maintain the rates and level of consolidated reproduction within certain boundaries usually found in a given country. The condition of weakness or 'powerlessness' of developmental mechanisms, the confusion and disorientation of economic agents last for a more or less prolonged period, *until new institutions emerge* (emphasis added), capable of transforming individual impulses for a better life into an effective social movement of production, exchange, distribution and consumption" (Kuznetsov 1994, 5–6).

lining of the state's chaotic intervention in the redistribution process at the microlevel. Thus, some stabilization of the new system of property rights and the qualitative and quantitative stabilization of the new institutional structures, which is a necessary condition for the functioning of a new property rights system, can be understood as marking the completion of the second stage.

In the third stage, a stable system of property rights should emerge. For such a stable system to be in place, the systemic reforms must be fully completed.

To gain some perspective on Russia's progress through these three stages, it is important to understand the aims of privatization in the different stages and to develop some criteria for assessing the effectiveness of the process as a whole. In general, the aim of privatization is to ensure the basic conditions for the normal functioning of the market system. According to a prevailing theory, formal privatization "leads to the permanent redistribution of control from bureaucrats to firm insiders and outside shareholders. Privatization has very clear advantages for economic efficiency because it establishes initial private property rights" (Shleifer 1994). Accordingly, the ultimate goals of privatization, viewed systemically, are

1. To ensure the stability of the new system of property relations (as manifested in the formation of a stable structure of property rights and all necessary infrastructure components and mechanisms).

2. To create conditions—mechanisms and institutions—for the self-sustainability of this system.

3. To raise the economic efficiency of management at micro and macrolevels.

The basic criterion for evaluating the effectiveness of privatization in its systemic sense can be applied only after the final goals have been achieved. In essence this entails the assessment of whether or not conditions have been created in which the new system of property rights can operate and which are oriented toward an efficient economic system. It is also important to take into account the fact that privatization (in the narrow or broad sense, formal or systemic) is a process with a definite time structure. Therefore, any criterion for evaluating the effectiveness of privatization should not be applied freely but rather in freeze-frames at certain stages of the systemic transformation.

It is also possible to elaborate on the general criterion by introducing a set of subcriteria of effectiveness (in the same sense as above) and evaluating whether or not they have been achieved in the short-, medium-, and long-term stages of privatization. Table 14.1 offers a set of subcriteria that may be useful in this regard.

The positive impact of any privatization program relies on a number of measures, such as financial stabilization, liberalization of prices, demonopolization of production, the development of financial markets, active antimonopoly policies, and the opening of the economy to foreign goods and capital. Privatization in and of itself does not automatically lead to the emergence of stable, viable enterprises. It merely creates the necessary legal and economic conditions that permit such enterprises to emerge. Thus, the presence of an appropriate economic environment to some extent determines the effectiveness of privatization. In turn, privatization is a necessary condition for the transformation of a transitional economy into a market economy.

14.2. Privatization Models in Transitional Economies: A Comparative Analysis

The rather extensive literature on the problems of privatization in transitional economies[7] will not be surveyed here. Instead, we will consider only the most general tendencies. Currently three main privatization models have appeared in postsocialist economies in transition: the mass privatization program, the insiders' model (management and employee buyouts), and the model of initial majority shareholdings. Table 14.2 identifies the privatization model used by each of the former Soviet republics and their economic neighbors, along with the resulting public- versus private-sector shares. Of note, almost all countries adopted a model of mixed (private-state) ownership. There are also models specific to individual countries, such as the "socially oriented ownership" model and the "case-by-case" model.[8]

---

7. For comparisons of different privatization models, see, for example, Blaszczyk and Woodward (1996); Böhm (1997); Earle, Frydman, and Rapaczynski (1993); EBRD (1997, 1998); Ernst, Alexeev, and Marer (1996); IET (1998); OECD (1995); Railean and Samson (1997); World Bank (1996); and World Bank–OECD (1997).

8. I refer to the originally realized models (at the first stage of privatization), without regard for how the property was subsequently redistributed. It is also assumed that although one or another model was dominant in a given country, combined models could also occur.

Table 14.1
Proposed Subcategories for Evaluating the Results of Privatization in Various Stages of a Systemic Transformation

	Short-term	Medium-term	Long-term
Political results:			
Impossibility of restoring the former political and economic system	−	+	+
Assistance in the creation of democratic institutions	−	+	+
Ideological results:			
Perceptions of the institution of private property	±	±	+
Perceptions of the ideology of "people's capitalism"	±	−	±
Economic results:			
Efficiency at the microlevel	−	±	+
Macroeconomic efficiency	−	−	+
Fiscal stabilization	−	−	Does not apply
Restructuring	−	±	+
Demonopolization and a competitive environment	−	∓	+
Attraction of investments	−	±	+
Social results:			
Significant social conflicts	−	−	−
Property inequality	+	+	+
Unemployment	+	+	−
Growth of wages	−	±	+
Existence of a stable middle class	∓	±	+
Legal results			
Formal distribution of property rights	+	Does not apply	Does not apply
Redistribution of property rights	−	+	Does not apply
Stable system of clear property rights which are defended	−	−	+
Stable and detailed legislation	−	∓	+
Institutional results:			
A private sector	+	+	+
A private corporate sector	+	+	+
A system of corporate governance	−	∓	+
Mechanisms and infrastructure of the securities market	∓	±	+
A stable system of institutional investors	∓	±	+
A clearly defined role for the state as owner	−	±	+

Table 14.1 (continued)

	Short-term	Medium-term	Long-term
Psychological results (understanding of new incentives and new behavioral customs):	∓	±	+
Ecological results	−	−	+
Criminal results:			
"Wild," spontaneous privatization	+	−	−
Corruption, swindling	+	±	∓
Laundering criminal money	+	±	∓
High transaction costs	+	∓	−

Note: + and − signs merely signify the existence (or absence) of a given result at a given stage, and in no way attach a positive or negative appraisal of the said effect. The evaluations primarily refer to the Russian transition.

Mass Privatization Model

The principle of charge-free distribution of state ownership did not become common in Eastern Europe, and therefore the significance of mass privatization for subsequent corporate governance of privatized enterprises has been unequal across the various countries. This model was widely applied in Russia and Czechoslovakia (and, after the disintegration of the single state, in the Czech Republic), Latvia, Lithuania, and Mongolia. In many other countries mass privatization as the base model was implemented later (Armenia, Azerbaijan, Georgia, Kazakhstan, Kyrgyzstan, Moldova, Ukraine). In other countries this model became an auxiliary to other methods of privatization, or was applied to a very small part of shares in a narrow circle of enterprises (Albania, Bulgaria, Poland, Slovenia, Tajikistan, Estonia). In several countries, nevertheless, its implementation was stopped at the stage of acceptance of appropriate legislation (Romania) or in connection with a crisis (Albania in 1997).

In some countries such schemes were not used at all (the former East Germany, Hungary, Macedonia). Nevertheless, the Hungarian project, for example, allowed each adult citizen to obtain an interest-free credit of 100,000 forints for five years, similar to the system of crediting of employees. In some parts of former Yugoslavia there was a transfer of shares to various social funds as a special variant of mass privatization.

The distribution of vouchers (bonds, checks, points) in mass privatization programs would, it was assumed, result in the emergence of both small shareholders and large outsiders (investment funds). The practice was expected to boost the development of the capital market, increase the consequent concentration of ownership in the hands of active investors, and finally increase the efficiency of corporations. On the whole, the effect of mass privatization on how corporations in former Soviet bloc countries are run is unknown. In the short term it is probably negative; in the intermediate term much depends on how the dichotomy between diffusion of vouchers and ownership concentration is resolved.

Insiders' Model
The insiders' model, or management and employee buyout model, is based on purchase of enterprises (assets of enterprises) or of controlling blocks of shares by employees and managers (jointly or separately), with the formal right of a subsequent sale or purchase. This practice has been rather widely adopted in Albania, Belarus, Poland, Romania, Slovakia, Tajikistan, Turkmenistan, and Uzbekistan. In Russia and Georgia this model has in fact become an official submodel (with employees having large legal privileges) within the mass privatization framework. In Lithuania and Mongolia a similar situation developed spontaneously: employees and members of their families used the vouchers to purchase shares in enterprises on the open market, that is, without closed subscription.

Specific insiders' models have also developed in Slovenia, Croatia, and Macedonia but should be considered separately within the context of the general Yugoslavian development. Most of the models in use in the countries of former Yugoslavia are submodels of socially oriented ownership.

Critical evaluations show that the various countries differ very little in the actual participation of employees and managers in the privatization of enterprises. Nevertheless, employee ownership has established a particular niche for itself in transitional economies. The influence of employee ownership on corporate governance, as a rule, is relatively negative, although some contributors argue that insiders' improved access to information helps them monitor the activity of managers, and therefore is beneficial. Obviously, in transitional economies a benefit from monitoring is only theoretical, especially if we remember that managers are the most influential insiders.

Table 14.2
Privatization Results in Some Transitional Economies

Country	Privatization Methods		SOE Total Assets Privatized, 1997 (%)	Number in 1994–1997 (or Share, by End of 1997, in %) of Medium/Large Firms Privatized	Number in 1994–1997 (or Share, by End of 1997, in %) of Small Firms Privatized	Total Private Sector Share in GDP (%), Mid-1998
	Main	Secondary				
Albania	OS, MEBO	MP1 (interr. in 1997)	≤25	71	5,600	75
Bulgaria	OS (DS)	MP1	20.0	NA	(21.1)	50
Czech Republic	MP1	OS (DS)	>50	1,680 (74.2)	NA	75
Slovak Republic	MEBO (DS)	MP1, SF	62.0	1,281 (79.4)	NA	75
Bosnia and Herzegovina	Uncertain (MP, MEBO, OS, restitutions—mainly in laws)		NA	NA	NA	35
Croatia	MEBO	SF	≤50	1,600 (67.5)	NA	55
Macedonia	MEBO	DS, SF	≤50	(70.8)		55
Slovenia	MEBO	SF, MP, OS, IP	>50	(72.0)		55
Hungary	OS (DS)	PC, MEBO	>50	1,566 (35.7)	(87.7)	80
Poland	MEBO	MP1, OS (DS)	>50	(28.4)	NA	65
Romania	MEBO	OS (DS)	≤50	1,010 (72.3)	(95.5)	60
Armenia	MP1	MP2, MEBO	≤50		(77.8)	60

Privatization, Ownership, and Economic Reforms

Country	Main	Secondary	70% of 3,200 enterprises' assets by mid-2000		
Azerbaijan	MP1	DS, MEBO	>50	(71.0)	45
Georgia	MP2	MEBO (DS)		876 (73.1)	60
Kazakhstan	MP1	OS (DS)	70	NA (100.0)	55
Kyrgyzstan	MP1	MEBO	≤50	NA (63.8)	60
Estonia	OS (DS)	MEBO, MP	>50	(99.0) (99.6)	70
Latvia	MP1	OS (DS)	38.2	1,351 NA	60
Lithuania	MP1	MEBO, DS	≤50	1,034 NA	70
Belarus	MEBO	MP	NA	(25.5)	20
Moldova	MP2	OS (DS)	≤50	1,100 NA	45
Russia	MP2	OS, MEBO	>50	35,000 115,000	70
Ukraine	MP1	MEBO	≤25	7,800 NA	55
Tajikistan	MEBO	MP	≤25	(72.4) (11.3) (50.0)	30
Turkmenistan	MEBO	DS	NA	15 1,779	25
Uzbekistan	MEBO	MP, DS, IP	≤50	18,264	45
Mongolia	MP	MEBO	NA	470 (70.0) NA	NA

Abbreviations: SOE, state-owned enterprise; MP1, mass (voucher) privatization with significant concessions to insiders; MEBO, management and employee buyouts; OS, sale to formally outside owners; DS, direct sales; PC, preferential credit; IP, through insolvency proceedings; SF, transfer of shares to social funds. Main and secondary privatization methods indicate the contribution (importance) of the concrete methods to the privatization of SOE assets.

Sources: Böhm, ed. (1997); EBRD (1997, 1998); IET (1998).

Model of Initial Majority Control

This model is based on one-stage, or at least not temporally extended, obtaining of a majority control (more than 50% of the voting shares) by outsiders. This practice was characteristic of a rather small group of East European countries, but it did not occur in Russia. Although it is the slowest privatization method, it has several advantages in terms of effective corporate governance. The Western analogue of this model is the case-by-case method, which has been well-tested in Great Britain and Chile.[9]

The outsider initial majority control model has been widely applied only to Hungary and Estonia. In the former East Germany this model could be considered the dominant one for more than 8,000 enterprises, but only in a combination with management buyouts and liquidation. In the Czech Republic this model was a second-best choice after mass privatization (32% of the enterprises, but only 5% of the total value of privatized enterprises).

The further development of enterprises in the case of outsider initial majority control depends on how privatization manifests itself. As a rule, it is carried out through auctions, tenders, or direct sales, where preference is typically obtained by "external" investors, who have often established connections with these enterprises. A special variant of this method (which is limited by the state of the stock market) is the public offering of shares, including offerings on stock exchanges.

Another important factor is the nature of investors or owners of majority blocks of shares. In many cases the outsiders are really pseudo-outsiders representing the interests of an enterprise's management.

Certainly, each country's choice of one or another privatization model and whether that model was the primary or the secondary model—with correspondingly different expectations of the outcome of privatization—depended on the balance between political forces and ideological traditions. At the same time, most countries (with any model, legally adopted or spontaneous) aimed at reaching a certain level of concentration of ownership. It was supposed that concentrated ownership is the basis for effective corporate governance, which in turn should increase the efficiency of enterprises.

---

9. This method has been widely applied (in its pure sense) in transitional countries only since the mid-1990s, to sell strategic enterprises and natural monopolies.

In almost all countries undergoing economic transition, the state proved incapable of effectively managing property that has remained under state ownership. The following issues are relevant in almost all countries undergoing economic transformation: the link between privatization and a change in the political regime (in particular the problem of restitution); the scale of privatization; the absence of a rational, competitive market environment; major technical problems; the need to take an ideological stand; absence of the requisite institutional structure in the initial stage; and a high level of corruption and criminal activity.

Although Russia did not have to resolve such problems as restitution or serious regional separatism in the course of privatization, developing and implementing a privatization policy under the conditions prevalent in Russia at the time was particularly difficult. Several factors weighed more heavily in Russia than in many other countries undergoing transition. First, during the process of choosing an all-embracing model at the microlevel, state enterprises and property were spontaneously converted into other forms of property (collective and private or quasicollective and quasiprivate). Second, a very high level of monopolization, together with backwardness, in many sectors of Russian industry obstructed the implementation of efficient and socially "soft" structural reforms before and during privatization. Third—and particularly important—privatization and the problems of ownership reform are the area of economic reforms in which political and populist pressures have been felt most strongly.

The political factor in privatization policy directly intensifies the contradictions in the legislative base. This intensification becomes manifest in many ways, including: (1) the lack of universally applied laws, (2) contradictory regulatory acts being in force, (3) frequent changes in tactics, and (4) the adoption, in a number of specific instances, of acts giving one or another party exclusive rights outside the legislative framework or the ability to cancel decisions that have already been made. Moreover, the highly politicized and therefore contentious nature of the privatization process in Russia has had a major influence on the choice of privatization model, which is biased toward achieving maximum social compromise. This politicization in turn has led to extremely high transaction costs, both in the course of implementing the privatization program and later, in specific privatization deals.

14.3. The Russian Privatization Model

14.3.1. Preconditions of the Reforms and Spontaneous Privatization (1985–1991)

The wave of privatization that swept the world in the 1980s reached Russia only in the early 1990s.[10] Whereas in the 1980s the theme of privatization interested only a narrow circle of scholars, and only as applied to Western and developing countries, around autumn of 1990 there began a heated discussion of privatization models that would meet the domestic requirements of Russia. The very term privatization became one of the trendiest terms in economic circles, even as it remained the subject of fierce political and populist clashes. However, this discussion attempts to abstain from political appraisals, focusing instead on actual economic processes.

If the period from 1985 to 1989 may be characterized as the period of cosmetic changes in the existing system, when alternative types of ownership could be considered only within the master framework of the "socialist economy based on multiple economic models," with the public sector dominating, the years 1990–1991 were a time of more systematic reforms, or, to be more exact, of more systematic conceptualization of pro-market transformations. There was a noticeable change in ideological approaches to ownership issues in general and to reform of ownership patterns in particular. The latter was evident both in the content of the programs being considered and in the legislation that was adopted during this period.

At the same time, while discussion about the permissibility of alternative types of ownership and privatization methods went on, the momentum of the spontaneous transfer of ownership increased sharply (this process was referred to by many names—nomenclatural, bureaucratic, nomenclature-territorial, "collective," and "managerial" privatization; see Hanson 1990; Johnson and Kroll 1991; Radygin 1992, 1996). The greatly increased momentum was linked to the lack of uniform and legal privatization procedures, the adoption of leasing and cooperative legislation, and new legislation for state-owned enterprises.

---

10. For simplicity, I have used the name Russia in describing events that occurred before the collapse of the Soviet Union. The term USSR is used only when official Soviet documents or institutions are referred to.

Thus, the USSR law, *On State-Owned Enterprises (Associations)*, effective since 1 January 1988, introduced a principle of "full business independence" (*polnoye hozyastvennoye vedeniye*), which afforded managers of state-owned enterprises a unique opportunity to gain opportunistically, while being inconsistent in legal terms. This principle still remains in the Russian legal system (*RF Civil Code* 1995). In fact, this legal innovation created certain favorable conditions for legal security (irresponsibility) of enterprise managers; however, it was also necessary to secure private ownership rights in legal terms.

The spontaneous privatization of state property became evident as managers were granted control over state assets (by leasing, creating independent enterprises from structural subdivisions of larger enterprises, creating various associations, and the like). As the system of state control over enterprises collapsed, while the legal basis of private property was missing, new owners to a considerable degree secured their control over enterprises by force, using criminal structures and bribing state officials traditionally responsible for controlling enterprises. The first truly new owners on the scene were foreign investors and pseudo-investors, whose goal was control over financial flows.

14.3.2. Mass Privatization Model of 1992–1994 as the Basis of the Corporate Sector Formation

Preparations for large-scale privatization began in the autumn of 1991. Having declared from the very beginning that privatization was one of the key elements of economic reform, the government formed in November 1991 pushed hard for the development of privatization legislation, but it was not immediately able to gain operational control over the course of privatization. One of the peculiarities of the economic reform program, therefore, was that prices were liberalized before large-scale privatization began—out of step with the reigning orthodoxy on transition to a market economy. There were important underlying factors for this sequence of events:

- It was not possible to wait for major privatization to be conducted along the lines of classical economic theory (that is, over a number of years) because of severe goods shortages at the end of 1991.
- Without the liberalization of prices, all state enterprises were essentially state institutions for the administrative distribution of deficit goods, which resulted in serious social conflict.

- Intense spontaneous privatization was taking place regardless.

On 29 December 1991, the president signed a decree, "On Accelerating the Privatization of State and Municipal Enterprises," in accordance with which the "basic principles of the privatization program for state and municipal enterprises in the Russian Federation for 1992," based on the draft state privatization program for 1992, were approved. Their implementation commenced on 1 January 1992. The document on basic principles was the first regulating the privatization process and marked the start of programmatic (as opposed to spontaneous) privatization in Russia.

The first privatization program (in 1992) became the keystone document for the subsequent large-scale privatization of 1992–1994. It represented a compromise between money privatization and free (voucher) privatization, and between a model of privatization for all and the dividing up of property among enterprise employees. This compromise resulted in such blatant—from an economic perspective—shortcomings as the book valuation of property; ignoring the problems of restructuring enterprises before and during privatization; failure to address the problems of enterprises' social infrastructure; ignoring demonopolization and the need to preserve technological links; failure to address a lack of investment; and a host of other problems.

Among its other negative aspects, Russian privatization was marked by a high degree of corruption and criminalization. At the same time, it would be wrong to promulgate (any further) the view that privatization was responsible for the wave of criminal activity that overwhelmed Russian society. It is true that privatization created numerous objects of criminal interest; however, the active expansion of criminal activities to the sphere of privatization (as well as to other spheres) was related chiefly to the general conditions in all gather fields.

Notwithstanding differing evaluations of the qualitative character of this process, 1992 was the year in Russian history when the widescale reform of ownership took off, on the basis of the elaborate privatization legislation.[11] At the core of the Russian privatization program was the mass privatization model, which encompassed

---

11. For more details on the first (voucher) stage of Russian privatization, see Boyko, Shleifer, and Vishny (1995); IET (1998); McFaul and Perlmutter (1995); Radygin (1994, 1995a,b); and Vassilyev (1995). For details on the second (money) stage, see Böhm (1997); IET (1995–1999); and Radygin (1996).

widescale corporatization (on the supply side) and the distribution of privatization vouchers among Russian citizens (the demand side). The important elements of the system were the closed subscription for stocks among insiders, the system of voucher auctions, and the network of intermediaries—voucher investment funds.

Critics and advocates of privatization by voucher (which officially ended on 30 June 1994) agree on one thing only: in formal, quantitative terms, the success of the mass privatization program is indisputable. Beyond simple quantitative assessments, however, the results of the mass privatization program were and remain the subject of debate.

From the perspective of the ideologists of Russian privatization, an important motive for implementing the voucher scheme arose from a pragmatic assessment of the real situation at the time when formal privatization commenced. This situation was characterized by:

- Lack of effective demand from the population.
- Lack of interest on the part of foreign investors.
- The existence of more than 240,000 state and municipal enterprises, all of which would require standard privatization procedures.
- The need for extremely rapid, legal privatization (in the initial stage) in order to limit the spontaneous privatization, which was already well under way.

The behavior of "red directors," aimed at formalizing their control within the new system of private property, became a prerequisite to the mass privatization of 1992 through 1994. Even at that time, however, a contradiction between the idea of mass privatization and reality was apparent. From the point of view of the ideologists, privatization was necessary for the formation of orthodox market capitalism with clearly defined (in Coase's sense) ownership rights. Simultaneously, the formalization of ownership rights was considered by ideologists as a way to keep assets from being plundered in the course of spontaneous privatization. Paradoxically, in that situation—the absence of state control—privatization became the last attempt at reviving such a control.

This ideology was alien to the concrete goals of both the managers of state-owned enterprises and the opponents of the government in the Supreme Soviet (it was the latter who insisted on granting property to the populace for free, and on selling it to employees at low prices). At the same time, corporatization and privatization became necessary for managers so that they could legally formalize their rights as "first usurpers" of corporate control over finances. More narrowly, it meant the creation of legal guarantees freeing them from criminal prosecution.

Finally, the interests of reformers and of state managers, their partners, coincided at the point of formalizing ownership rights; however, they viewed the goals of this process differently. In the end, the practice vanquished the ideology. In other words, the ideologists' notion of the mass privatization was adequate to Coase's theory, but it did not completely work in the Russian political environment, in which formal ownership rights became only a screen hiding the legalized consumption of the assets and resources of enterprises.[12]

Obviously, the privatization technique per se was not enough to prevent the consumption of assets. Political will, an integral legal system, and (initially) strict enforcement were also necessary.

So, the paradox of this situation was that whereas privatization was necessary for market reforms in terms of strategy, and strict enforcement (in the sense of a tough legal framework and restraints on enterprises' managers) was needed at first for its maximal effect, at the same time, in the framework of the state-owned enterprise model existing at the time, there were no alternatives to "directors' forces" that would be able to launch privatization of concrete enterprises in the general interest of facilitating market reforms. Thus, privatization would be impossible without directors' support, but there would be no directors' support if stringent measures against their "spontaneous" activities were introduced simultaneously with privatization.

Besides, since 1993 the situation had become irreversible, as by that time powerful lobbying groups, which had been undermined

---

12. As Ye. Gaidar said in an interview, "We intended to privatize for money after having first achieved a certain financial stabilization, after having formed market elements so that the country could finally accumulate some funds that could be used to purchase enterprises.... However, it very soon became clear that in the situation of an uncontrolled economy, it would be naive to count on financial stabilization; therefore we had to comply with the law on privatization approved by the Supreme Soviet.... Today, those who had fought for lower prices for those enterprises severely criticize the reformers for the free granting of property. It is a natural result that the country got not effective owners, but people having the right to uncontrollably dispose of other people's property" (Gaidar 1999, 8–9).

after the collapse of the USSR, were reestablished. To suggest the strength of these lobbies, it suffices here to recall attempts to create superholdings on an all-Russian scale in August 1993 and the budgetary failure of 1994.

No less important was an awareness of the real (and realistically achievable) aims of privatization in the transition economy at different stages of transformation. It is rather naive to judge the results of privatization by its formal targets written into the privatization program. There was only one real aim: the temporary mass distribution and consolidation of formal rights of private property in Russia with minimal social conflict, in hopes that subsequent transactions would work in favor of effective and responsible owners. In other words, the quantitative stage ended with the completion of mass privatization—the first stage of privatization as a system-forming phenomenon.

With respect to developing a new system of property rights, the most important result was the formation of new economic and legal mechanisms and institutional structures. The following are of particular note:

- The corporate sector of the economy (more than 30,000 joint-stock companies)
- The corporate securities market, including a trading infrastructure and a secondary market for shares in privatized enterprises
- A system (still in transition) of institutional investors
- A social class that, despite its extreme heterogeneity and lack of legal recourse, can be called a class of owners (there were about 40 million formal shareholders by the end of mass privatization)

According to the estimates of the Russian Ministry of State Property and Ministry of Economy, in 1994 the total share of the public sector in GDP was 38%, and in 1998 it was 30%. In the same years the share of privatized enterprises (including corporations in which the government held a stake) was 47% and 49%, respectively, while the share of the originally private enterprises was 15% and 16%. To understand why the share of privatized enterprises changed so little, we should bear in mind that by the end of 1994, practically all of the largest Russian enterprises had been transformed into joint-stock companies, and therefore the share of the private sector in GDP could not have changed significantly in the following years. As can be seen from Table 14.3, privatization proceeded most intensely (or at least the applications were submitted most actively) in 1993, while in 1994–1997 there was a stable and continuous decrease in new enterprise participation. This trend continued through 1998–2000.

Between the first and second stages of privatization, the following specific contradictions in the privatization program came to the fore:

• The contradiction between the formally eliminated disproportionality between different types of property and the de facto preservation of the state's dominant role as both an economic agent and a regulator of property rights.

• The contradiction between the need to restructure Russian enterprises, at the very least during the implementation of the privatization program, and the restraints placed on restructuring by the sociopolitical compromise (specifically, the system of privileges for employees as well as the voucher scheme).

• The contradiction between the need to halt spontaneous privatization prior to and during the official privatization, and the role of spontaneous privatization as a preparatory phase in the implementation of the official program.

• The contradiction that the very same authorities (from the federal level to the municipal) were at one and the same time legislating universal procedures and serving as the source of spontaneous privatization.

• The historical and logical contradictions between the preconditions and results of privatization in a transition economy, in which the privatization initiated creates the necessary environment for its realization (the securities market, investment institutions, and so on).

• The contradiction between the initial dispersion of property rights (by mass privatization) and the need to attract strategic investors, and also the dispersion of property rights in the absence of institutions to monitor management.

• The contradiction between speed and the standardization of privatization procedures in accordance with the specific economic and political aim of maximizing revenues.

• The contradiction between maintaining chaotic state intervention in the economy and in ownership (which is perhaps a preparatory stage in the state's withdrawal from this sphere) and the increasing

Table 14.3
Basic Indicators of Russian Privatization

Cumulative total starting 1 January 1992	As of 1.I.1993	As of 1.I.1994	As of 1.VII.1994*	As of 1.I.1995	As of 1.I.1996	As of 1.I.1997	As of 1.I.1998
1. State-owned enterprises (units)	204,998	156,635	138,619	126,846	90,778	89,018	88,264
2. Applications submitted (units)	102,330	125,492	137,501	143,968	147,795	149,008	155,660
3. Applications refused (units)	5,390	9,985	11,488	12,317	13,295	13,642	15,607
4. Applications at the implementation stage (units)	46,628	24,992	19,308	17,491	13,214	12,327	10,305
5. Implemented applications (units)	46,815	88,577	103,796	112,625	118,797	123,744	126,825
6. Sale price of property (bill. of old rubles)†	57	752	1,107	1,867	2,510	3,230	5,723
7. Price at which property was sold (bill. of old rubles)†	193	653	958	1,092	1,618	2,205	2,875
8. State enterprises which have been transformed into JSCs, whose shares have been put on sale (units)	2,376	14,073	20,298	24,048	27,040	29,882	30,900
9. Enterprises leased, including hire-purchase (units)	22,216	20,886	20,606	16,826	14,663	14,115	11,885
	13,868	14,978	15,658	12,806	12,198	11,844	10,413

*Official date of completion of the voucher privatization phase.
† Excluding the largest, "nonstandard" deals with stakes.

Sources: Data base of the Ministry of State Property RF, and the Russian Federal Property Fund.

need for targeted state regulation of the economy (and of the general transition process as a whole).

14.3.3. The "Money" Stage of Privatization (1995–2000)

If the period of 1992–1994 saw the rapid build-up of a "critical mass" of the requisite quantitative transformations, the years 1995–2000 were characterized by attempts—largely unsuccessful—to switch to money-based privatization. The goals, which were not achieved within the framework of the 1992–1994 model, and preeminently the goals of restructuring the enterprises and mobilizing investments, demanded the formation of such a privatization model, which might at least partially compensate enterprises for the methods used during the sale of their stocks in the first stage of privatization—methods not based on economic considerations.

At the same time, as a result of mass privatization the government was left with an unprecedented number of shareholdings in privatized enterprises, and the problem of selling them became a key issue both for the privatization policy and for the intense lobbying in this field. By the beginning of 1995 the state still owned about 14,000 residual shareholdings (from small holdings to controlling interests) that had not been sold for one reason or another, and about 5,000 shareholdings (including the "golden shares") that were officially fixed as federal property. By 2000, the state still owned 3,100 blocks of shares (via golden shares) and 7,000 to 8,000 unsold ones.

For the liberal wing of the government, an additional incentive to sell these shares was the generally accepted fact that the state was incapable of managing federal property, given the volume involved and contemporary economic realities. Furthermore, the task of organizing the sales of these shares was clearly unmanageable, for a number of reasons: lack of demand, the blatant undervaluation of assets, the impossibility of selling major loss-making enterprises in order to reduce the expenditure burden on the budget, and various purely political factors.

The new law, *On the Privatization of State Property and Guidelines for the Privatization of Municipal Property in the Russian Federation* (No. 123-F3, signed by the President Yeltsin on 21 July 1997) formally went into effect on 2 August 1997. Among its major innovations several can be singled out. The law, even in its name, emphasized not enterprises but property (particularly the state's share of property). The program of privatization provided a general projection of entities that were to be privatized during the year (depending on the current market situation) and strategic entities for which privatization was prohibited (they can be privatized only on the basis of a federal law). A wider range of privatization methods was offered (through legalizing the sale of derivatives, which had already happened). Benefits for employees were still allowed (a 5% or 10% discount from the selling price of stocks) but could be revoked or made more flexible. The value of a property ("property complexes") was to be calculated according to the combination of the property's capital, balance sheet value, and market price. Commercial tenders with investment conditions were introduced, and the investment tenders were canceled. The notion of "leasing with the right of redemption" was reintroduced, but at market price. It is also assumed that unitary enterprises can be transformed into joint-stock companies with 100% state ownership. The state thereby acquires the opportunity to sell this property.

In 1992–1994, not selling enterprises to strategic investors could be easily justified by the voucher program, which had other priorities. Nonetheless, from the beginning of the money-based phase (despite the statements of those in charge of the State Property Committee about the "investment era" in Russian privatization beginning after June 1994), the key criterion for choosing the basic method of sale, regardless of the economic sector or region, was the maximization of federal budget revenues. To a large extent this reality owed to political expediency. The precedence given to this short-term tactical goal clearly meant that the state lost out in the long term.

Thus, the new privatization policy was transformed into

• an essentially spontaneous process of residual privatization of the shares retained by the state after mass privatization;

• the utilization of privatization (or quasiprivatization) instruments for the purpose of attracting political allies among the regional elites and major financial groups;

• the noticeable "regionalization" of the privatization process, including for political purposes; and

• the process of consolidation and further distribution of property among the major financial groups and natural monopolies.

The years 1995–1997 were also characterized by the use of non-standard methods of privatization, such as loans-for-shares auctions, the transfer of federal shares to the regions in payment of federal debts, conversion of debt into equity, and so on.

The loans-for-shares auctions, which took place at the end of 1995, are well-known. The chronic budget crisis and failure to meet budget targets for privatization in 1995 were among the most important reasons for the implementation of this scheme. The twelve auctions of major Russian enterprises that took place raised a total of 5.1 trillion rubles for the budget, including 1.5 trillion rubles of enterprise debts paid to the state. Two major Russian banks—UNEXIMbank and Menatep—dominated these auctions.

Despite the legal facade of these auctions, they were to a considerable extent either the veiled purchase of shares by the enterprises themselves or the direct, noncompetitive sale of shares to interested banks. The numerous court hearings and examinations of the legitimacy of these deals in 1996–1997 did not uncover any evidence of legal violations committed during the loans-for-shares auctions and the subsequent sale of the shares. However, this is proof more of imperfections in the regulatory and legal base at the time than of transparency in the loans-for-shares auctions.

It is clear that almost all collateral-holders were interested in acquiring the shares as their own property as well as in minimizing the cost of the transaction. The preferred method was to organize a quasi-open sale of the collateralized shares and their acquisition through an affiliated company. By the beginning of 1998, this method had already been used to acquire shares in the oil holding company, YUKOS (45% initially, 33.3% after dilution; qualified control went to Menatep), Sidanko (51%; control went to UNEXIMbank), Sibneft (51%; formally control went to Neftyanaya finansovaya kompaniya), Surgutneftegaz (40.12%; de facto the company bought up its own shares), Lukoil (5%; de facto the company bought up its own shares), and RAO Norilsk Nickel (38%; control went to UNEXIMbank). The scandals surrounding most of these deals are well-publicized. The least contentious auctions were of shares in Surgutneftegaz and Lukoil, in which the companies bought up their own shares through the management companies of their pension funds. In all these tenders the final price minimally exceeded the starting price, and consequently the state's earnings were insignificant. The main reasons for this were the lack of real competition, the collusive character of a number of the auctions, and the unsatisfactorily formulated demands and conditions of the privatization deals.

According to data from the Ministry of State Property, about 130,000 enterprises (58.9% of the total number of enterprises in Russia at the beginning of privatization) had been privatized by 1 January 2000.

The slowdown in the privatization process was due to many factors, but mostly to lack of demand for the majority of "residual blocks of shares" on sale (either because of principal lack of interest in these shares or because of the established formal and informal levels of corporate governance of the individual enterprises). The main objective in continuing the privatization sales was to establish, or to complete establishing, control—as was typical of the post-privatization period in all of the former Soviet bloc transitional economies. Unsolved problems of land plots, noncommissioned objects, mobilization capacities, and large state-owned blocks of shares (which were in fact managed by no one) also slowed the privatization process and led to fewer completed transactions.

It should be also noted that in the regions, two other trends are also constraining the privatization process: recently approved decisions on privatization are not being implemented, and the regional authorities are striving to maximize control over the number of regional enterprises, including those in federal ownership.

In 1997 and 1998, the emerging financial crisis became another negative factor militating against the effectiveness of privatization transactions, which were crucial for the budget. As investors lost interest in oil companies in the wake of the unfavorable world business situation, the possibility of implementing a budget-oriented privatization policy was especially limited (at least until mid-1999).

With respect to formal budget criteria (that is, fulfilling budget targets without resorting to schemes such as loans-for-shares), 1997 was the first successful year in the history of money-based privatization (Table 14.4). In 1999 revenues from privatization were excluded from budget revenues and listed among the sources of financing the budget for the first time. It then became possible to avoid a tougher budgetary orientation and to make decisions on transactions with more attention for the real business situation.

Table 14.4
Revenues from Privatization, 1995–1999

	1995	1996	1997	1998	1999	2000
Number of privatized enterprises	6,000	5,000	3,000	2,583	595	320
Approved budget	4.991 trillion[a]	12.3 trillion	6.525 trillion	8.125 billion[c,d]	15 billion[c,f] (total 18.5)	18 billion[c] (total 23.7)
Actual revenues	7.319 trillion	1.532 trillion	18.654 trillion[b]	14.005 billion[e]	8.33 billion[c] (total 17.3)	31.4 billion (total 50.6)
Dividends on blocks of shares in federal ownership	115 billion	118 billion	270.7 billion	574.6 million	6.15 billion	Planned 3.5 billion

[a] The approved budget was adjusted in December 1995; 70.8% of the actual revenues were derived at the expense of loans-for-shares auctions.
[b] Including $1.875 billion for shares in Svyazinvest.
[c] Only for property sold.
[d] Adjusted to Rb 15 billion in April 1998 (at the governmental level).
[e] Including Rb 14.5 billion for 2.5% of shares in Gazprom.
[f] Not included in budgetary revenues.

Source: RF State Property Ministry.

In 1999 the actual privatization revenues amounted to Rb 17.3 billion (planned revenues were targeted at Rb 18.5 billion). The revenues derived from sales of enterprises (shares) was almost two times less than planned: Rb 8.33 billion, as compared with Rb 15 billion planned for 1999. The amount was so much less than planned because the government refused to sell a number of blocks of shares (25% plus one share in Rosneft, 19.68% of shares in Slavneft, small blocks of shares in Gazprom and United Energy Systems of Russia, 25% minus two shares in Svyazinvest). In the end, the funds were obtained by several individual sales (as in previous years).

Nonetheless, other revenues from sales of state-owned property were considerably above the planned level (Rb 8.99 billion versus Rb 3.5 billion). Thus, according to the federal budget for 1999, dividends on shares in state-owned property, which were projected to be Rb 1.5 billion, in fact reached Rb 6.15 billion. Revenues from leasing federal real estate were Rb 2.165 billion (Rb 2 billion had been planned). Revenues from Russian Federation property abroad amounted to Rb 315 million (Rb 200 million had been planned).

At the same time, the success in the area of dividends came from squeezing the largest companies. In 1999 in particular the basis of this source was expanded: 600 joint-stock companies paid dividends to the state, compared with 200 joint-stock companies in 1998. It was much more difficult to realize revenues from federal property in Russia and abroad because the properties were scattered, and it was difficult to peg the real beneficiaries.

In 2000 many problems related to privatization persisted. These problems may prove troublesome to investors who are true outsiders, or "bona fide purchasers." Among the most acute problems the following should be mentioned:

• The problem of reprivatization in Russia at large dimmed the attractiveness of the country for investors. In 1999, unofficial appraisals put the proportion of enterprises privatized in violation of the law at 40%.

• The normative and legal basis for nationalization was lacking (that is, a set of procedures for compensating investors, and procedures that would take into account multiple resales, for defending the interests of bona fide purchasers).

• A dual approach to the evaluation of privatization transactions with respect to offenses committed is necessary: (1) an indefinite term of prosecution (including criminal prosecution) for offenses committed by officers and their counteragents (if such offenses can be discovered and proven), and (2) ensuring the absolute principle of inviolability of bona fide purchasers' property (as would be suitable for the state's noninterference in the existing structure of ownership). The only permissible alternative may be compensation for losses suffered by a bona fide purchaser.

• The informally adopted ten-year period of claim limitation for privatization transactions is a separate problem (based on Article 181 of the RF Civil Code). It will likely be necessary to reduce and to adjust legally the period for claims on the invalidity of a null and void transaction.

• The problem of transparency persists for most privatization transactions. Outsiders do not understand the terms of the investment process.

• Sales of minority (up to 25%) blocks of shares, especially to foreign investors, often result in minority owners having little influence on companies' decision making.

• Discrimination against insiders and outsiders persists in regard to the terms of transactions. For instance, the sale of 9% of shares in Lukoil in 1999 obviously discriminated against outsiders, who had to pay $6 per share, compared with the $3 per share paid by insiders. The sale of TNK shares and many other such transactions during previous years offer similar examples of bias.

• Discrimination against insiders and outsiders persists in regard to the degree of prosecution for failure to meet the terms of the privatization transactions.

• The problems related to approving decisions on privatization while at the same time managing state-owned property have persisted since 1991, when the State Property Committee and the Fund for Federal Property were created. Thus, the RF State Property Ministry tried to find new avenues for its activities in 1999 and 2000 (by initiating projects, which would allow it to control the Federal Agency for Financial Recovery, the Federal Commission for Securities, the evaluation of activities, and so on). The Fund for Federal Property strives for the status of a state investment bank, with the right to operate on the securities market, although the need for it is not clearly justified.

What are the prospects of the privatization policy?

It seems that *The Concept of Managing State-Owned Property and of Privatization in the Russian Federation*, approved by RF government decision No. 1024 on 9 September 1999, may be considered a policy document for the next few years. Moreover, it is highly probable that this document will be a guideline until 2010 (both because it was approved by the most probable candidate for the presidency (now the President) and because it is obviously impossible to make radical amendments to it). The general aims and principles of privatization are traditionally of a declarative nature; however, new approaches to sales organization deserve attention, in particular:

• A differentiated approach to the privatization of enterprises depending on their liquidity: (1) highly liquid enterprises shall be privatized, taking into account the balance between the amount of attracted investment and funds due to the budget, based on real price evaluation maximally close to world levels; (2) enterprises having liquidity problems may be sold to "effective owners" at minimal prices upon submission of business plans and the implementation of measures to control enterprises' operations.

• In case soundly liquid blocks of shares are privatized, with the goal of realizing substantial budgetary revenue, the remuneration of financial advisers shall depend on the revenue amount.

• The creation of a broader range of privatization instruments: (1) issuance of derivative securities backed by state-owned property, permitting their placement on foreign security markets (deferred right to purchase state-owned shares); (2) the purchase and sale of shares at exchanges and off-board, aimed at optimization of state participation; (3) sales resulting from direct negotiations with investors, including cases in which auctions (tenders) were declared void (in such cases the price of the entity shall not be less than the starting price at the void auction); (4) sales of state-owned property payable on installment plans guaranteed by banks.

• Decisions on privatization shall be made on the basis of plans for the long-term development of enterprises submitted by potential investors and privatization agreements minutely regulating investors' obligations.

• Presale preparation of enterprises, including the services of financial advisers, auditors, surveyors, legal advisers, business advisers.

- Commercial tenders, including social conditions.
- Determining the optimal number of unitary enterprises (approximately 1,500–2,000, compared to the 13,786 existing in 1999) and their conversion into joint-stock companies (excluding socially important cases).
- The sale of not yet commissioned buildings and structures unused for state purposes, mainly to create new production capacities (on the condition that the new owners assume obligations in accordance with the system of controlled indicators that is under development).
- Determining the expediency of creating vertically integrated industrial structures using state-owned property on trust.
- The sale of property (if investment conditions permit) mainly for industries with a fast return on investment (investment programs shall be as compressed in time as technology permits).

Many of these innovations require the law on privatization to be amended (for instance, the Federal Property Fund's idea of selling 9% of shares in Lukoil through securities exchanges or direct sales), and therefore these methods may remain unused for a time. It is also difficult to issue derivative securities backed by state-owned property in legal terms. The budget has to be amended, and discordances between the law on privatization and the law *On Specifics of the Issuance and Circulation of State and Municipal Securities, etc.* will have to be resolved.

The problem of unsold minor blocks of shares (less than 25%) persists both in the area of privatization and for state management. Although in 1997 and 1998 the intention to sell them off practically for free was voiced, their number remains considerable. The following decisions concerning these blocks of shares are likely:

- They may be included in the charter capital of other joint-stock companies.
- State-owned blocks of shares may be increased in order to obtain a blocking interest by including state-owned property in the charter capital of companies or by purchasing shares in those companies on secondary markets, with the goal of selling such blocks of shares to strategic investors.
- State-owned blocks of shares may be transferred to issuers or to subjects—municipal entities—of the Rusian Federation in lieu of

budgetary financing. This could be done with the condition that wage arrears would be paid off, there would be no new wage or budgetary arrears, and other such parameters would be met.

- State-owned blocks of shares may be sold to employees at lower prices.

At present, Russia needs a new, comprehensive privatization model, one geared toward resolving all of the problems of enterprise operations. Without such a comprehensive model, it is difficult to set any further goals for privatization.

Although views differ drastically regarding the proper privatization model, various approaches and the principles behind them are already included in present law. Most likely, a combination of such approaches will be applied.

The fundamental goal of privatization is to optimize ownership structure so as to secure stable conditions for economic growth. However, privatization as an element in economic reform is becoming less urgent, both in its system-forming role (the focus of interest in the first half of the 1990s) and in the budgetary orientation of privatization sales (which dominated the second half of the 1990s). The declining importance of privatization to the development of transitional economies is apparent in, for example, the increasing criticism of the applied privatization models (not only the Russian model but also the Czech coupon scheme, which had been a point of reference for the West).

With regard to the increase in budget revenues (or, since 1999, the financing of a budget deficit), the effective management of state-owned property has become a priority. With regard to systemic transformation, privatization evidently became less important than problems of corporate governance and of restructuring the privatized enterprises. In this connection, the next section examines problems that have arisen in the postprivatization redistribution of property, as they are of key importance for understanding the prospects for further institutional development.

14.4. Major Stages and Results of the Postprivatization Ownership Redistribution

The complex and controversial formative process of the postprivatization structure of ownership in Russia had as its general positive outcome the gradual stabilization (streamlining) of ownership: from an amorphous and dispersed structure to the emergence of apparent (formal, based on the title to the property) or hidden (informal, based on the real authority within a corporation) hubs of corporate control. According to Federal Commission for Securities Markets (FCSM) estimates, in 1996 the struggle for control was over in 25% of the Russian corporations, and by the beginning of 1998 it was over in 50%. Although it is impossible to speak about the real economic effect of such stabilization even in 1997–1998 (especially since the redistribution was still going on and the system in general remained unstable), nevertheless, we believe that the stabilization of ownership did have an economic impact. The financial crisis of 1998, however, significantly changed the situation.

14.4.1. Major Features, Stages, and Tools of the Establishment of Corporate Control

The postprivatization redistribution of property in the 1990s occurred in different ways:

• By aggressive or "coordinated" buying of shareholdings of different sizes on the secondary market (from employees, investment institutions, brokers, banks).

• By lobbying for specific transactions, with the stocks remaining in the ownership of the federal or regional authorities (residual privatization, trust management).

• Through the voluntary or administratively enforced joining of holdings and financial and industrial groups.

During the first years of the postprivatization redistribution of ownership (1993–1996), the most widely used methods of redistribution involved transactions on the primary (privatization) and secondary markets. Although 1997–1999 saw no significant improvement in regard to the protection of shareholders' rights, it was during 1993–1996 that the violations of corporate law resulting from the struggle for control were most savage (undesirable shareholders were deleted from the registers, voting during the general assembly was done by raising hands and not according to the principle of "one share—one vote," and so on).[13]

It should be pointed out that these processes were typical mostly of those Russian enterprises where the potential for competition between insiders and outsiders existed (that is, the potential for profit-making) and where the board had concrete strategic plans for the future. If the managing board continued a passive course, paying little attention to the future of the company, in the best possible case such a company could only expect a takeover by an outsider, and in the worst case it could expect its assets to be opportunistically used by managers.

Actually, the key conflict during all of these years was the conflict between old managers trying to defend their positions and the newcomers, who could potentially seize control. This was true for the majority of Russian enterprises. However, many different reasons for this struggle arose, including: financial flows and profits, accounting, export orientation, the site or other real estate, the market segment or branch specialization of interest to a foreign company with the same production profile, and so on.

In Russia, managers adopted the following tactics (apart from purely criminal ones) in their fight for control:[14]

---

13. Here are some examples of violations of shareholder rights typical for the managers of Russian joint-stock companies in 1994–1996: the minimum size of a shareholding was introduced, which allowed its owner to pretend to be elected to the governing bodies of the company; the information about the general shareholders' meeting was either withheld or delayed on purpose; various high fees and commissions were introduced (to participate in the meeting, to register transactions, to buy and sell stock, to obtain copies of documents, and so forth); instead of voting according to the principle of "one share—one vote," voting by raising hands was introduced; "special" (different from the privileged stocks envisaged by the law) shares were issued that entailed the right to "special" dividends; "pocket" boards of directors were set up, consisting of the director (manager), chief accountant, and other top people of the company; sales of stock to outsiders were obstructed; company shares were bought from small shareholders at a low price at the company's expense; new issues were floated and placed at low price with individuals who served as fronts, without the shareholders being informed; the register of shareholders was manipulated before shareholder meetings, and registration was denied; and the assets of companies were sold through individuals or companies that served as fronts, without the shareholders being notified.
14. Some of the methods listed here lost their usefulness once the privatization procedures were completed, and others could not be used in 1996–1998 because legal restrictions appeared.

- Managers acquired options for 5% of the stock and closed subscription (first type of benefit) or closed subscription (second type of benefit) in the process of privatization.[15]
- The shares of joint-stock companies were bought during privatization tenders and auctions.
- Stock was purchased by firms (funds) owned by management.
- The company's shares were redeemed by the company itself for subsequent sale to employees and administrators (or to companies under the administration's control) in order to increase the proportion of inside relative to outside shareholders.
- Managers held control over part or all of the stock belonging to employees (through a collective trust in the closed joint-stock companies).
- Trusts were established for the management of government shareholdings.
- Managers controlled the register of shareholders (especially in the case of joint-stock companies with fewer than 500 shareholders) and limited access to or manipulated the register.
- The capital base of companies was changed through the targeted dilution of the share of specific "outsider" shareholders by making newly issued shares available on preferential terms to administration and employees, as well as to "friendly" outsiders and pseudo-outsider shareholders.
- A general strategy of dispersion of the share capital was adopted in order to make a potential takeover through buying up shares more difficult.
- "Residual" shareholdings were bought in the course of money privatization (many managers increased their stakes even while was no competition from outsiders).

---

15. According to a poll conducted by the FKTsB (FKTsB 1996b), in 1995, out of 172 polled joint-stock companies, 41% of respondents said they bought up their own shares. Of the companies that bought their own shares, 62% indicated that the shares were subsequently sold to their employees and administration. According to the official figures of the RF Goskomstat, as of 1 January 1997, 5,474 surveyed joint-stock companies (only with the government stake, including RAO UES of Russia and Rostelekom) issued 67.6 billion shares, of which 16.8 million shares, or 0.02%, were redeemed by the company from the shareholders, 656 million shares, or 1%, were transferred into a trust or holding, and 3.5 million shares, or 0.005%, were used as collateral (Kobrinskaya 1997).

- Various material and administrative sanctions were levied against employee-shareholders intending to sell their shares to outsiders.
- Manager-shareholders formed alliances with "friendly" outsiders.
- Local authorities were involved in introducing administrative limitations on the operations of "alien" middlemen and firms that were buying up employees' shares.
- Managers engaged in lawsuits, supported by the local authorities.
- Limitations (quotas) on the size of a shareholding in the company's charter were introduced.
- Managers established control over the market for shares of the company (by rigging the infrastructure, for example).
- Asymmetrical information was used to fend off raiders and reduce the power of existing outside shareholders.
- The placement of additional issues was organized on the basis of the "bottleneck" principle (at inaccessible places and within an attenuated time period).
- Companies were put through fictitious bankruptcies, with the managers subsequently buying up the assets.

The strategies and the motives behind them differed significantly, depending on who was interested in a particular shareholding. For example, the largest Russian oil and gas companies resorted to completely different strategies for cutting off outside shareholders during the initial stage. Lukoil tried to disperse the shares issued to the maximum extent possible, subsequently buying them up through affiliated and friendly companies; Gazprom introduced rigid limits for outsiders and organized a dual (domestic and foreign) market for its stocks; Surgutneftegaz used its own pension fund for the "self-buyout" and tried to dilute the influence of outsiders' stake through new issues; and the oil company YUKOS resorted to a "friendly" takeover by the bank, with a subsequent legalized dilution of the government's stake through a restricting of the company's arrears to the federal budget.

Most of these ploys were also used by outsiders interested in seizing control of a corporation. If from the issuers' standpoint the securities market preeminently offers an opportunity to consolidate their own control, the outsiders' motivations may be quite varied. For example, the motives for investing in the corporate securities of commercial banks in 1992–1998 (given all known legal and financial limitations) can be assorted as follows:

• To establish control over the concrete perspective enterprise being privatized (usually for the purpose of bookkeeping, achieving control over the financial flows and export revenues, and so on)

• To purchase shares as a means of gaining a foothold for expanding into certain branches

• To get the commission or the price margin from the resale of stocks of privatized enterprises bought on behalf of large foreign and domestic investors

• As part of a takeover policy for the purpose of the minimum restructuring and resale

• To obtain a stake in the company as repayment of debt

• To redistribute (in their own favor) part of the proceeds from the sale of the government's shareholdings

• To establish ownership of a kind of "insurance fund" (since the government would not allow the industrial giants to go bankrupt and would resort to subsidies or some other benefits that could be used by an outside shareholder as well)

• To establish ownership of the stocks of the largest companies in order to pass as a serious investor[16]

In regard to the other institutional investors, corporate securities did not constitute a significant part of their investment portfolios.[17] Insurance companies and pension funds (except those of the affiliates of some large insurance companies) were traditionally oriented toward government securities. The voucher investment funds offered some exception since, owing to their origins, they became the holders of rather large stakes in privatized enterprises. Mostly these funds performed a broker's functions: they resold stocks specifically

---

16. For more details, see Radygin (1999). According to data provided by the Russian Central Bank, at the beginning of 1998, 3.9% of commercial banks' total assets were invested in the corporate securities and equities of other organizations. It is impossible to precisely estimate the investments made through the subsidiaries of the banking holdings (initial attempts to introduce consolidated statements were made in July 1998). The most serious problems are encountered when a bank is not the parent company of the holding, but just one of the members of the financial-industrial group at some level of control.

17. For more details, see FKTsB (1997).

to managers of enterprises or handed the shares over to them in trust, and structured the portfolios of foreign investors. Some of the funds acted as speculative portfolio investors. Only a very small proportion of these funds, which were also set up by large corporations, became long-term holders of a stake in the parent company in order to preserve control over corporations. Mutual funds and bank-managed mutual funds are a relatively new type of collective investor, and so far they cannot be regarded as playing a serious role in the redistribution of ownership rights.

Based on this background of consolidation of control in the Russian corporate sector, and within the framework of this process, at least two significant substages arise. First, the period from the end of 1995 until 1997 was a very specific stage in the postprivatization redistribution of property, when reshaping of the ownership structure in a number of key Russian companies was already finished. In some of them the major loci of influence had already reached agreement, and the consolidation of control was painless (Lukoil and Surgutneftegaz are examples). In other companies the final stage of consolidating control was protracted, owing to the ongoing struggle between interested parties (federal and regional authorities, natural monopolies, large banks, industrial enterprises), intense lobbying, and the state ownership of large shareholdings. Because of the protracted mess and conflicting interests, some of the largest transactions of this period were tainted by well-publicized scandals (Svyazinvest, Norilsk Nickel, and some large oil companies).

In practical terms, this rancorous process was evident in the loans-for-shares schemes of 1995 and in the buying back of stocks used as collateral in 1997–1998; in the "oligarch" wars of 1997; in the legalized dilution of the government's stakes; in trust schemes; in the buying up of drafts; in the manipulation of dividends on privileged shares, and so on.[18] Both the presidential elections of 1996 and 2000 and the long-term financial and economic interests of the rival groups energized these developments.

The second substage had a different flavor. After the law *On Joint-Stock Companies* went into effect, along with a number of other legislative and regulatory actions, and law enforcement improved,[19] in

---

18. For more details, see IET (1998), and Radygin (1999).
19. In this context I do not have in mind any real achievements in the field of enforcement or positive shifts in the judicial system, but rather threats to apply the screw to violators and certain demonstrative measures (because of the impossibility of controlling all the violations).

1996–1999 purely procedural methods began to be used more frequently. These included methods that violated many facets of corporate law. We list a few here:

• Shareholders were not being notified at all about shareholder meetings, or were not notified on time, or were not notified about the substantive issues on the agenda.

• Boards of directors were not elected at the general meeting, as required by law.

• Under different pretexts, outside investors were disallowed membership on the board, which was "closed" to outsiders.

• There was opposition to independent audits of the financial activity of the company, although outside shareholders insisted on such measures.

• The procedural requirements concerning voting during the general meetings were not observed.

• The rights of small shareholders were infringed upon in the distribution of dividends.

• The rights of shareholders were violated during the exchange of shares (when shares of the holding alone were introduced).

Nevertheless, the best way to get rid of outsiders is still to dilute the outsiders' share—both their share on the board of directors and their share in the issuer's equity—in favor of the majority shareholders.

Derivative mechanisms may also be used for this purpose, such as convertible bonds, fractionalization or consolidation of shares, and the transition to a single share. In holding companies, if an outsider has a veto right (controls more than 25% of the voting stock) and can block additional issues, so-called transfer prices are used. In this method the assets are redistributed between the parent company and its affiliates without regard for the interests of minority shareholders.

The better-known conflicts of 1997–1998 took place in the oil sector. YUKOS transferred funds from its subsidiaries, SIDANCO attempted to issue convertible bonds at a price lower than the market price and to place them with friendly entities, and Sibneft transferred assets to the holding company and discriminated against minority shareholders of subsidiaries during the transition to a single share status.

Among the common violations of shareholders' rights is the widespread practice of managers unrestrainedly pumping the assets of the company they work for into their own companies and their own accounts, both in Russia and abroad, or, in the best possible case, fixing exorbitantly high salaries for themselves, while rank-and-file employee-shareholders do not receive wages or dividends for months on end. Such managerial behavior generally follows from an unstable corporate governance situation, which provides an incentive for managers to create golden parachutes for themselves.

The financial crisis of 1997–1998 led to a serious shift in ownership redistribution. Some investors were attracted by the steep devaluation of corporate securities. Some of the shareholders, including the issuers, took the reverse path and tried to maximize their financial situation by dumping stocks. Many commercial banks and financial groups, which found themselves on the verge of bankruptcy or already in bankruptcy, considered ceding their stakes in the real sector, or attempted to dump nonliquid holdings. Within the framework of the privatization sales, some of the stakeholders attempted to consolidate their holdings in the interest of seizing control at minimum cost.

At the same time, the crisis spawned the more active use of additional issuance of shares and derivatives, debt schemes (securitization of debt), bankruptcy, and corporate reorganization. Under such conditions, attempts by the regional elite to establish control over the major enterprises of their regions became more vigorous and successful. These trends are expected to continue, which may increase the instability of property rights and require a more stringent policy for protecting investors' (shareholders') rights.

14.4.2. Structure of Stock Ownership

In countries that adopted the course of attracting external (or quasi-external) investors right from the start, a struggle for control has not been much in evidence. The struggle for control of joint-stock companies is also less intense in countries in which the model of mass privatization resulted in concentrated ownership with a transparent structure.

The most acute struggle was developing in countries where diluted property rights dominated, as a result of mass privatization or the insiders' model. Large shareholders, including insider-managers, continued to buy up shares. In Albania, which accorded few privileges to insiders, immediately after mass privatization, the wave of share reselling by small shareholders to larger ones began (mainly informally, circumventing registration of the shares). In Macedonia, the struggle for control and therefore for ownership concentration has happened fastest in joint-stock companies, where the ownership structure is not "amorphous" but gravitates to managers (their "teams"). In Poland, in the 853 companies that were created by insiders in the framework of "direct sales," capital has tended to become concentrated in the hands of the managers. In Slovenia, managers have started a "war" against outsiders, to the extent of entering various restrictions of outsiders' rights into charters of joint-stock companies.

The direct consequences of an intense struggle for corporate control are the following:

1. Conditions conducive to conflict of interest and violation of the rights of shareholders are maintained over the long term.
2. The shaping of a model of corporate control and governance is set on a protracted course.
3. Therefore, a tighter centralized state policy becomes necessary.

In general, the process of ownership redistribution in Russia has been characterized by two parallel trends: the strengthening of managers (in their capacity as shareholders or as persons who exercise real control over enterprises) and the growing "invasion" of outsiders. Moreover, redistribution is taking place while at the same time a further concentration of ownership occurs.

It would make sense to apply in the Russian practice (in the spirit of the US Securities and Exchange Commission's interpretation of insider transactions) the following categories:

• "insiders" (internal shareholders), "managers," and "large shareholders."
• "Small shareholders" (up to 10% of the stock; hence, they cannot exert procedural pressure, and managers and large shareholders can simply ignore them).

One of the nuances of the Russian situation is that the monitoring of large transactions is exercised with low efficiency, and only for the sake of complying with antimonopoly regulations. However, monitoring, or the transparency of participation, has evolved beyond that of determining compliancy with regulations. It is also important as a means of preventing insider transactions detrimental to external or small shareholders, who, unlike managers and large shareholders, do not have access to full information about the company.

A scrutiny of the stock ownership structure in Russian joint-stock companies over the period 1994–1999 shows the following trends (Table 14.5):

• A decrease in the employees' share, the rate of which slowed down in 1995–1998.[20]

• Stabilization or growth of the administration's (management's) share.[21]

• A significant increase in the share of outside majority investors (whose, have in 1996–1998 nevertheless was growing slower than in 1994–1995).

• Stabilization or a decrease in the share of external minority investors (individuals).

• A consistent decrease in the government's share.

In general, internal shareholders' aggregate share fell during the period (owing to the decrease in employees' interest), while external and pseudo-external shareholders' aggregate share in companies' equity grew.

The stock ownership structure of the largest Russian companies differs from the typical one (Table 14.6). It is characterized by the following features:

• The large participation of financial and industrial groups and holdings, including government entities.

• The considerably smaller (compared with the typical corporation) share of employees of all kinds

• A relatively large share held by nonresidents of different types

---

20. The increase in employees' share in 1995–1996 indicated in Survey 3 (Table 14.5) was probably a result of a policy consciously pursued by management in order to disperse the additionally issued shares among the employees and to prevent the establishment of outside control.

21. The tendency toward a formal decrease in managers' share identified in Survey 1 in Table 14.5 is probably connected to the dispersion of equity in 1995–1996. We can also presume that some of the shares obtained by managers under the closed subscription or on the secondary market were "transferred" to other companies in order to avoid social tension (or were in fact sold to outside shareholders). However, in general, that does not mean that managers lost control.

Table 14.5
Stock Ownership Structure in Russian Joint-Stock Companies, 1994–1999 (%) (Data Obtained in Different Surveys)

	(1)			(2)				(3)			(4)		
	After privatization	1994	1996	1994	1995	1996	1994	1995	1996	1995	1997	1999
1. Insiders, total	66	66	58	62	56	56	65	55	58	58.5	51.6	51.3
Employees	47	44	43	53	43	40	56	39	40	48.5	39.5	36.3
Managers	19	22	12	9	13	16	9	16	18	10	12.1	15
Collective trusts	—	—	3	—	—	—	—	—	—	—	—	—
2. Outsiders, total	10	16	33	21	33	34	22	33	33.6	31.7	41.3	45.3
2.1. Juridical persons			23	11	21	25	—	23	24.5	20.7	23.6	22.8
Banks	—	—	2	—	1.5	—	—	1	1.6	1.6	1.2	1.7
Investment funds	3	5	5	—	6	—	—	6	5	7.2	4	5.2
Suppliers, buyers, other firms	—	—	3	—	3	—	—	5	3	8.1	12.9	11.8
Holdings and FIGs	—	—	3	—	1	—	—	1	2.6	3.5	4.9	3.4
Others	—	—	10	—	9.5	—	—	10	12.3	0.3	0.6	0.7
2.2. Individuals	3	6	8	10	11	9	—	9	6	9.6	13.2	15.6
2.3. Foreign investors	—	—	2	—	1	—	—	1	1.6	1.7	5.1	7.6
3. State	20	12	9	17	11	10	13	13	9	9.5	6.5	2.7
Total*	100	100	100	100	100	100	100	100	100	100	100	100

Notes: (1) The survey of 1994 covered 88 privatized enterprises in Moscow, St. Petersburg, Urals, and Nizhny Novgorod. The survey of the fourth quarter of 1995–first quarter of 1996 covered 312 privatized enterprises (across 12 branches of industry) in Moscow, St. Petersburg, Urals, and Nizhny Novgorod. Collective trust was not mentioned in other surveys for other years as well. Data supplied by the University of Nottingham. Source: Afanasyev, Kuznetsov, and Fominykh (1997), p. 87. (2) The summary evaluation of the author on the basis of the results of 1994–1996 surveys conducted by the RF State Property Committee (400 enterprises), FKTsB and the securities market monitoring group of FKTsB (250 and 889 enterprises), and IET (174 enterprises), which together covered all regions of Russia. For the entries "Juridical persons" and "Individuals" the real data on large and small outside shareholders are shown. It should be remembered that in 1994 and 1995, "small shareholders" meant less than 5% of equity; whereas in 1996 it meant up to 1% of shares. The figures in the table were calculated as unweighted arithmetic averages, but the absence of weights should not, presumably, play any significant role, since the size of the enterprises in the sample is almost comparable (no small or very large companies were included). For more details, see Radygin, Gutnik, and Mal'ginov (1995); Radygin (1996). (3) Surveys of the Blasi group of 1994 and 1996. Sources: FKTsB (1996, May); Blasi, Kroumova, and Kruse (1997), p. 193. Data for 1995 differ across quarters. Here the fourth quarter data are shown; see FKTsB (1996, May). (4) Surveys of the Russian Economic Barometer, conducted upon request of IET, covered 138 industrial enterprises in 1995 and 139 in 1997; of these, 46 enterprises were covered in both surveys. Data for 1999 represent the respondents' forecast. Source: Aukutsionek, Kapelyushnikov, and Zhukov (1998).

*Strictly speaking, many of the figures are not consistent from the standpoint of analysis of annual changes in ownership structure because even the annual data are based on different data arrays (in survey (1)) or data arrays with little repeated coverage (surveys (2) and (4)). For survey (3), there is no exact information about the annual samples used. Nevertheless, a high degree of coincidence in the results for one and the same period in different surveys allows us to draw a conclusion about the reliability of these figures, which are summarized in the table from the standpoint of general trends in changes in stock ownership of large and medium privatized enterprises in Russia. It also important that all of the surveys focused mainly on "typical" Russian industrial enterprises (medium and large), which also allows us to extrapolate (with some reservations) these trends to the whole of Russian industry.

Table 14.6
Stock Ownership Structure of the 100 Largest Russian Companies, 1997*

Type of Shareholder	Ownership (%)
All employees of the company	22
Including employees	20
Administration	2
Share of managers of all levels among all employees	5
Including general manager	0.5
Shares sold to employees in previous 12 months	6
Issuer (issuer's representatives)	21.8
All outside shareholders	57.6
Including the state or state holding	20.6
Including the state	6.5
State holding	14.1
Average shares of all large outside shareholders (including the one out of all outsiders, from large to small)	
Russian commercial enterprises, total	16.7 (10.5)
Russian investment funds, total	11.7 (10.5)
Foreign companies, total	11.7 (11.1)
Of which (individual types):	
Russian enterprises: suppliers of the company	10.0 (22.8)
Russian financial-industrial groups or nonstate holdings	10.0 (33.0)
Russian commercial banks	6.7 (17.0)
Foreign banks	6.7 (9.3)
Russian enterprises: buyers of the company's output	3.3 (16.4)
Foreign investment/pension funds	3.3 (14.0)
Russian pension funds	1.7 (1.0)
Additional Data	
% of companies with a large outside shareholder (>5%)	88
Average no. of large outside shareholders	2.5
Average share of large outside shareholder's ownership	15.3
Mean value of average share of large outside shareholder	12.6

*The average data on sample groups of shareholders were used, and so do not add up to 100% of the companies' capital.
Source: Khoroshev (1998).

Of course, any quantitative estimate is immediately seen to be artificial if we consider that among the formally external shareholders of the companies, a considerable number of shares are directly or indirectly owned by the managers of a company or by those friendly toward them. In fact, among the holders of large or controlling stakes, a considerable number own commercial enterprises. In practice, such commercial enterprises or holdings are often nothing more than companies set up by the management as trade intermediaries and created to mobilize the company's profits, which are being used, among other purposes, to buy the company's shares during the privatization process and on the secondary market. Similar mechanisms are well-known in, for example, Slovenia and other countries.

Any evaluation of the efficacy of managers as holders of corporate control in a postprivatization period is necessarily two-pronged. Such an arrangement is certainly effective for preserving and consolidating corporate control. However, if we are trying to evaluate the efficacy of the "managerial model" of control not only for strategic development, but also for the elementary survival of enterprises, the efficiency of managers' activity remains open to discussion.

According to some studies, the concentration of control in managers' hands ensures a significant increase in enterprise efficiency. According to other studies (Frydman, Gray, Hessel, and Rapaczynski 1997), the managerial-control model shares some weaknesses with the employee ownership model. Nevertheless, corporations controlled by managers were characterized by much higher efficiency than enterprises owned by employees.

Employee-insiders in all countries with a transitional economy do not, as a rule, represent an independent faction with respect to corporate control. Their shares are controlled by managers,[22] or are diluted and form an amorphous structure of stockholdings. The activity of small shareholder-insiders is traditionally low, and their interests are focused mainly on various wage payments. For example, at general shareholders' meetings in Moldova, the typical conflict expressed between shareholder-employees and managers has to do with terms of employment and various money payments.

In a survey of 312 Russian joint-stock companies conducted in 1996, only 7.5% of the managers indicated that employee-shareholder participation on the board and supervisory council was important, 19% said that discussing strategic and current problems at general meetings of shareholders was important, and 21% said it was desirable to grant managers the right to vote at general meetings of shareholders (Afanasyev, Kuznetsov, and Fominykh 1997, 3:96).

The major problem with foreign investors is to identify the real origin of the investment capital. In many cases it is repatriated capital, which was taken out of Russia.

The state's share in the equity of the majority of enterprises (with the exception of the strategic branches of the economy and the

---

22. In such cases there is a direct analogy with American employee stock option plans as a way for managers to protect themselves from hostile takeovers (Williamson 1985).

Table 14.7
Changes in Ownership Structure in Six CIS Countries, 1995–1997 (% of total (Means))

	Georgia		Kazakhstan		Kyrgyzstan		Moldova		Russia		Ukraine	
	1995	1997	1995	1997	1995	1997	1995	1997	1995	1997	1995	1997
Managers	41.5	53.6	23.1	29.4	28.1	34.4	7.2	18.3	25.4	36.3	14.6	46.2
Employees	9.4	10.4	10.7	8.2	38.3	36.4	21.6	19.7	26.0	23.3	23.6	15.3
State	41.0	23.3	34.8	16.1	12.4	5.6	38.6	23.8	23.5	14.7	42.6	15.4
Local outsiders*	4.9	8.0	23.6	30.2	16.8	18.9	24.7	22.6	23.4	21.5	18.9	17.7
Foreign outsiders	1.0	2.2	4.4	6.8	2.2	2.3	0.3	2.1	1.6	3.8	0.3	0.9
Individuals	2.0	2.2	3.4	9.3	2.2	2.4	7.6	13.5	0.1	0.4	0.2	4.5

*Including investment funds.
Source: Djankov (1999).

largest companies) does not play a key role. If management and some large outside shareholders are included in the "active" groups of stockholders, the most "passive" group would include the government and the rank-and-file employees of enterprises (see Chapter 13).

In general, notwithstanding the gradual concentration of stock ownership and the increase in outside stockholders' share in the capital of companies, their role in the management of the companies is so far inadequate to their growing proportion of equity. Of course, with the growth of outsiders' share in the company's capital, outsiders' positions (including the opportunities provided by legal protection) should strengthen.

14.4.3. Ownership Concentration, Enterprise Performance, and the Myth of an "Efficient Owner": Some Intercountry Comparisons and Results

By the end of the 1990s a number of empirical studies on ownership structure in various countries in economic transition had been conducted. The conclusions of practically all of them are somewhat conditional and incomplete for the purpose of intercountry comparisons, owing to such problems as sampling, the different sizes of the enterprises, the reticence of respondents, the impossibility of revealing affiliated entities and the real locus of corporate control, and so on. Nevertheless, they allow us to evaluate most general and characteristic tendencies with a relatively high level of reliability. In the second half of the 1990s several attempts also were made to evaluate the correlation between ownership structure and enterprise performance after privatization.[23]

In almost all countries with a transitional economy, a high level of ownership concentration is observed during or after privatization. In the Czech Republic, Hungary, and Poland, by the middle of the 1990s 98% of the inspected medium-sized companies had a single dominant shareholder (Frydman et al. 1997). The average

---

23. See Afanasyev, Kuznetsov, and Fominykh (1997); Aukutsionek, Kapelyushnikov, and Zhukov (1998); Blasi, Kroumova, and Kruse (1997); Carlin, Fries, Schaffer, and Seabright (1999); Claessens, Djankov, and Pohl (1997); Djankov (1999); Earle, Estrin, and Leshchenko (1995); Entov (1999); Frydman, Gray, Hessel, and Rapaczynski (1997); Klepach, Kuznetsov, and Kryuchkova (1996); Leontieff Center (1996); Pohl, Anderson, Claessens, and Djankov (1997); Radygin and Entov (1999); and Radygin, Gutnik, and Mal'ginov (1995).

Table 14.8
Comparison Between the Integral Financial and Economic Indicators of the Efficiency of the Public and Privatized Enterprises in Russian Industry by Branch for 1995*

	Integral efficiency		
Branches	Public Enterprises	Enterprises (Companies) with Government Share >25%)	Enterprises (Companies) with Government Share <25%)
Ferrous metals	0.384	0.644	0.505
Nonferrous metals	0.534	0.259	0.726
Chemical industry	0.309	0.533	0.895
Mechanical engineering	0.128	0.696	0.922
Construction materials	0.178	0.807	0.775
Light industry	0.292	0.461	0.681
Food industry	0.229	0.488	0.852
Pharmaceuticals	0.288	No data	0.727

*The actual sample included 2,438 enterprises from the RF Goskomstat Register: 575 public enterprises, 596 privatized enterprises with a state shareholding of more than 25%, and 1,267 privatized enterprises with a state shareholding of less than 25%.

The integral efficiency was calculated on the basis of four indicators of economic efficiency (productivity, profit margin on the products, use of fixed assets, current assets turnover) and four indicators of the financial situation (autonomy coefficient, maneuverability, supply of internal working capital, and current liquidity). The integral indicator was calculated for each group of enterprises and allowed evaluation of the general situation in this group on the basis of a number of parameters. In essence, the integral indicator represents the level of parameters (individual indicators) achieved in this group. The level of each individual indicator is rated for the groups of enterprises under comparison from 0 to 1, where 0 is the worst value of the average indicator and 1 is the best. The detailed method is described in Addendum 2 in the source below.
Source: Leontieff Center, 1996.

share of the main shareholder varied from 50% to 85% (except for the state and Czech investment funds). The dominance of the main-shareholder ownership structure is due chiefly to the fact that owners cannot afford to rely on other institutions and arrangements to monitor and discipline managerial performance (although the separation of ownership and management is common in the region).

In the CIS countries the tendency toward concentration is also marked. The available data on six countries (Table 14.7) point clearly to the stable growth in the share of managers. In Russia, postprivatization redistribution of ownership led to the concentration of dispersed stocks in privatized enterprises since 1993 as the most common process. Along the way, this process saw the loans-for-shares schemes of 1995, the "oligarch" wars of 1997, and the transition from the wildest forms of redistribution to the legal procedural technologies of corporate control and redistribution of equity, in 1996–1999.

Nevertheless, according to many recent studies, privatized enterprises are more effective than state-owned ones. They exhibit sharper economic growth and faster increases in investments. Data from the Leontieff Center in St. Petersburg indicate a higher level of efficiency in privatized enterprises than state-owned ones in Russian industry (Table 14.8). Examination of the data shows the following traits: (1) "deeply privatized enterprises" are more efficient than "medium-privatized enterprises", and both types of privatized enterprises are more efficient than public enterprises. (2) The efficiency indicators of the enterprises privatized in 1993 are higher than those of enterprises that underwent privatization in 1994–1995. If we assume that stock ownership is more concentrated at enterprises that became involved in the privatization process earlier (which in general corresponds to the trend observed throughout Russia), then we may also assume that enterprises with concentrated ownership are more efficient.

Similar conclusions were published in 1998 by the RF Ministry for State Property. The ministry study found a direct correlation between an increasing state share in the authorized capital of joint-stock companies (in the range of 25% to 50%) and poor management and financial situation in those companies. To a certain extent the poorer efficiency of such companies is connected to the reluctance of private shareholders to conduct reorganization and to invest in such joint-stock companies where the property rights to a significant block of shares remain uncertainly tied to the state's intentions.

At the same time, firms adapt to market demands more vigorously if property rights are well-protected in general and if the principle of soft budget constraints is nontypical for the current economic policy.

Nevertheless, in a number of studies of Russian enterprises no stable relation between postprivatization ownership structures and the intensity of transformation was detected (Earle and Estrin 1997; Linz and Krueger 1998). A study of Ukrainian enterprises also did not confirm a clear relation between ownership structure and restructuring (Estrin and Rosevear 1999). In a recent survey of 3,000 enterprises in twenty transitional economies, Carlin and colleagues found no clear relation between privatization model, ownership type, or structure, and the restructuring and transformation of enterprises (the lack of information on state-owned enterprises prior to their privatization was addressed as an explanation for the unclear results) (Carlin et al. 1999). Yet another comprehensive survey of 7,534 industrial enterprises in Russia[24] drew the conclusion that on average, firms with all sorts of ownership structures are transforming poorly; however, private firms are transforming worse than state-owned ones (Brown and Earle 1999). The authors make the final conclusion that privatization negatively affects economic effectiveness, but note that it would be wrong to attribute such a poor showing solely to privatization, because state-owned enterprises do not demonstrate better results.

The advantages of privatized companies become ever clearer as the concentration of ownership in the hands of external private holders increases. New private firms are the most effective. Among privatized companies, firms in which strong external control has been installed have the best results. Data on the turnover of top managers of Czech firms support this point: the executives who had been recruited by external holders (for the first time) were much more successful than executives appointed by state entities (Claessens and Djankov 1999). Djankov (1999) observes that further empirical research should separate ownership effects according to different concentration levels.

The mere appearance of external owners adds dynamism to the postsocialist economy (Carlin and Landesmann 1997). At the same time, some studies that have evaluated the correlation between ownership and efficiency have found that ownership by outside local investors is not significantly correlated with successful restructuring (Djankov 1999). It has also been suggested that the ideal form of corporate governance is ensured for companies with foreign owners (Brada and Singh 1999, 14). Foreign ownership is positively associated with enterprise restructuring when the ownership levels are high—above 30% of shares (Djankov 1999).

Can we assert, then, that it was ownership concentration in the postprivatization period that led to effective corporate governance and corporate performance?

---

24. An important shortcoming of this research is that only officially registered primary privatization transactions are considered in appraising the ownership structure. If the further redistribution of shares were taken into account—and further redistribution through collateral arrangements, trusts, and so forth was typical of the overwhelming majority of Russian enterprises—the picture would change considerably. We readily concede the difficulties of penetrating the real ownership structure of many enterprises, not the least of which is lack of information.

Concentrated ownership (concentrated control), in different forms, is often cited as the major economic mechanism for effective corporate control. Concentrated ownership provides the basis for investors' real influence, which in itself strengthens legal protections and minimizes recourse to the courts for problem solving. The majority of the transitional economies were oriented toward the concentrated ownership model, with different degrees of success, whether success is measured legalistically or ideologically, and whether success was achieved by applying mandatory schemes or through some form of spontaneous activity. It was hypothesized that the corporate relationship model, based on a more concentrated structure of ownership and an insignificant role for insiders (both employees and managers), would also stimulate the entity's financial progress and economic efficiency. This hypothesis established a solid link between the corporate governance (control) model, the efficacy of such governance, and the efficiency of the enterprise itself under such a model.

The question of what form of corporate control would underwrite the most efficient corporate performance in a transitional economy has no single answer. According to some existing evaluations, studies attempting to correlate ownership concentration, control over management, and growth in the price of a company's stock, even in countries with a stable market economy, have come up with ambiguous results (Gray and Hanson 1994). Some studies show that concentration of ownership results in the better operation of corporations in the developed branches of industry with relatively simple technologies. Other research has suggested that the structure of ownership is a dependent rather than an independent variable. It has also been proposed that highly concentrated ownership may be useful in some branches of industry but not in others, and that the market will always push the company toward the optimum solution. More nuanced positions that take into account the size of the corporation exist as well (Demsetz and Lehn 1985).

At the same time, there are drawbacks to the concentration of ownership in a corporation, largely due to the potential conflicts of interest between large and small shareholders—the problem of common versus private interest that has been described in literature. Thus it is not possible to draw any conclusion with certainty, especially for an unstable transitional economy.

In practice, the resolution of this common versus private interest debate had extremely controversial results, and the preliminary assessments cannot be generalized. We take as an example the situation in the Czech Republic. This example is especially indicative, in that the Czech Republic has traditionally been considered the standard (sample) for effective privatization.

According to data from the Czech Fund for National Property, during 1995 it became increasingly obvious that the conclusion of voucher privatization had to be followed relatively quickly by a further massive redistribution of property, resulting in a substantially greater concentration of share capital. This process began spontaneously, independent of state authorities. Its initiators were several large private industrialists and financiers (IPFs). Their objective was to obtain major financial stakes in promising companies from small investors, and then to sell these interests to other, mostly foreign, investors (Böhm 1996, 143–4). Those who expected that the new shareholders (mainly IPF representatives appeared on the boards of directors and the supervisory boards of privatized companies) would immediately begin to perform their functions as owners were probably disappointed. IPFs and all other shareholders whose existence originated in the voucher privatization behaved in most cases as passive investors. As a rule, they were mainly interested in selling their shares as profitably as possible, and in obtaining money from transactions on the capital market. These shareholders participated to a relatively small extent in the company's business growth.

Obviously, the concentration of shares for the purpose of resale and the passive behavior of majority shareholders hardly promote an increase in management efficiency or contribute to the strategic development of a joint-stock company.

Data from the Czech Ministry of Finance also display a number of ways for handling the property of IPFs and investment trusts, the consequences of which are a decrease in property value and harm to both shareholders and unit holders. These methods of asset management are combined in practice and are very difficult to demonstrate and to penalize. The practices include the following (for details, see OECD 1998, 118–24): formal and informal interconnection of several companies, large conventional fines, purchases of worthless shares, concluding unfavorable options and futures contracts, transfer of the advances for purchase of securities, long settlement periods for securities sold, loans of securities, poorly drawn-up agreements on the transfer of securities, irrational movements of securities, trading in securities at overblown prices, disadvantageous purchases and sales of securities, trading by management on its own account, the concentration of considerable amounts of cash in the bank accounts of IPFs, failure to comply with limits for restricting and spreading risks, different methods of funnelling funds from the company ("tunneling" into companies), and so on.

The reverse point of view also exists, and is also reinforced by statistical analysis. The sample of 706 Czech enterprises in 1991–1995 shows that concentrated ownership resulted in higher market value for the enterprise and therefore in greater profitability. The authors surmised the existence of a positive influence, which rendered the enterprise its own main bank through indirect control of the investment fund (Claessens, Djankov, and Pohl 1997). An indirect confirmation of such a point of view is to be found in the tendency of corporations worldwide in the 1970s to 1990s to reduce the number of individual shareholders and increase the number of institutional ones, at least until the financial crisis of 1997.

Data from the Leontieff Center in St. Petersburg indicate a higher level of efficiency of privatized enterprises in Russian industry than in Czech enterprises. To repeat what was said earlier, if we assume that stock ownership is more concentrated in enterprises that became involved in the privatization process earlier (which in general corresponds to the trend observed throughout Russia), then we can also maintain that enterprises with concentrated ownership are thus more efficient.

Indirect confirmation of the observation that enterprises with highly concentrated ownership are more efficient can also be found in comparative studies on the operation of enterprises with different types of predominant owners during 1995–1997. In many cases the best economic performance was turned in by those small and medium-sized enterprises whose ownership was concentrated in the hands of managers, and by large enterprises owned predominantly by certain types of outsiders. However, there are figures supporting the opposite conclusion as well (see Aukutsionek et al. 1998; Earle et al. 1995; Klepach et al. 1996).

The numerous cases in which majority shareholders (both managers and outsiders) acted against the interests of their corporations' development are also well-known. There is an almost standard set of accusations, which can be leveled equally as well against owners in other transitional economies. Such accusations include a desire to control only financial flows and export transactions; the unjustified splitting of an enterprise by selling or leasing the assets, to the detriment of shareholders and the enterprise itself; a "free rider's" attitude during the search for strategic solutions; owners' treatment of their stake as an object of speculation or as collateral for loans, and so on. It was especially relevant in the case of financial institutions, which became large stockholders in the course of and after privatization.

Among the explanations for this situation, at least in respect to Russia, the following dominate. If the "amorphous" system of corporate control (that is, the absence of any visible signs of control, even if there is an informal system in place) is preserved, medium-term development objectives may be lost sight of, and investors may consequently not be attracted. The problem is that with the amorphous system, even if the real control is concentrated in someone's hands, both responsibility for the corporation's current situation and shareholders' control over those who bear this responsibility simply disappear. At the same time, there are no external mechanisms of control (legal and market) to provide for such a responsibility. Mechanisms to protect investors' rights, which are so important for attracting investment, are also nonexistent.

In regard to further institutional changes, the problem of the "efficient (responsible) owner," who in the last few years has achieved almost mythical status in official programs, needs to be resolved.

In general, the concept of an efficient owner is one that is connected in large degree to macroeconomic conditions, taxation, an effective system for implementing contractual obligations, and so on. It is paradoxical that in a number of transitional economies, including Russia, a dual concept of an efficient owner has developed.

The most primitive interpretation, and one that is typical of the official ideology of government, is to equate "efficient owner" with "owner (private) of a large or controlling interest in a company." The problem then becomes the simple bureaucratic one of "mechanically constructing" new responsible owners. At a certain stage of this construction it turns out that the efficient owner (whether the owner of a certain interest or the manager who retained his position of control) does not meet the government's original plan: he doesn't pay wages to employees, doesn't pay taxes, is not interested in the enterprise's development, and establishes subsidiaries in order to drain the assets of the company while leaving only an empty shell.

At the same time, however, the same owner is functioning efficiently as a specific economic agent in the specific environment in which he has to operate, an environment that may be characterized by exorbitant and very complicated taxes, barter, cash settlements, criminal activities, the desire of potential outside shareholders to seize control only for the purpose of controlling the financial flows of the company, and so on. In this case the owner is efficient because he maximizes profits by carrying out his functions as owner under the specific conditions imposed on him, and by protecting the company from external destabilizing factors.

Of course, the picture would not be complete without taking into account the financial ambitions of the individual who retains or establishes control over the company. The degree of his criminal behavior depends on many economic, legal, social, and psychological factors. The range of different types of behavior is extremely wide, from the setting up of "profit centers" outside of the company but for the purpose of its development right on up to different schemes for pumping the corporation's assets for their subsequent transfer to his personal accounts abroad. In this context it becomes clear that in order to realistically implement the official governmental concept of efficient owner, adequate measures on the part of the state are needed in practically every aspect of the economic reform.

In this connection, we turn to the results of a Harvard University study comparing the legal systems of forty-nine countries with respect to investors' rights protections (La Porta, Lopez-de-Silanes, Shleifer, and Vishny 1997, 32–35, 40–43). The authors concluded that concentrated ownership was a reaction (or adaptation) to the weak legal protection of investors within the framework of the national model of corporate governance. High accounting standards, legal mechanisms to protect investors' rights, and a high level of enforcement of legislation correlate negatively with ownership concentration. At the same time, a high level of concentration signals the weak operation of the capital market. The authors' analysis shows that weak legal protection of investors denies companies the opportunity to mobilize the necessary capital.

This conclusion is also valid for the Russian situation. With this in mind, we assume that the problem of attracting investment to privatized enterprises will not be resolved even when the struggle for control of the new corporations is over. The concentration of ownership typical of the struggle for control may be regarded as the new owner's way of adapting, but it offers no guarantees to potential new investors under the predominant conditions of weak legal regulation.

In Russia, the process of ownership concentration is closely connected to the activity of managers (or large shareholders who become insiders). Accordingly, ownership concentration is by no means a tool for adapting to the weakness of external mechanisms of corporate governance. On the contrary, ownership concentration becomes a tool for violating the rights of other shareholders.

In this context, another crucial conclusion is that attempts to create a favorable investment climate (including development of the corporate segment of the securities market) in Russia and other transition economies will not be very effective until ongoing improvements to protect external investors and improved law enforcement system take hold.

Bibliography

Abalkin, L. I. 1979. "Sotsialisticheskaya systema khozaistva." In *Ekonomicheskaya entcyklopediya. Politicheskaya ekonomiya*, Vol. 3, p. 600. Moscow.

Afanasyev, M., P. Kuznetsov, and A. Fominykh. 1997. "Korporativnoye upravleniye glazami direkorata (po materialam obsledovaniy 1994–1996)." *Voprosy ekonomiki* 5: 84–101.

Arrow, K. J. 1974. *The Limits of Organization*. New York: Norton.

Aukutsionek, S., R. Kapelyushnikov, and V. Zhukov. 1998. "Dominant Shareholders and Performance of Industrial Enterprises." *The Russian Economic Barometer* 1: 8–41.

Bizaguet, A. 1988. *Le secteur publique et les privatisations*. Paris: PUF.

Blaug, M. 1994. *Ekonomicheskaya mysl' v retrospektive*. Moscow.

Blasi, J., M. Kroumova, and D. Kruse. 1997. *Kremlin Capitalism: The Privatization of the Russian Economy*. Ithaca, N.Y.: Cornell University Press.

Blaszczyk, B., and R. Woodward, eds. 1996. *Privatization in Post-Communist Countries*, vols. 1–2. Warsaw: Center for Social and Economic Research (CASE).

Böhm, A., ed. 1996. *Economic Transition Report 1995*. Ljubljana: CEEPN.

Böhm, A., ed. 1997. *Economic Transition Report 1996*. Ljubljana: CEEPN.

Böhm, A., and M. Simonetti, eds. 1996. *Privatization—95*. Ljubljana: CEEPN.

Boyko, M., A. Shleifer, and R. Vishny. 1995. *Privatizing Russia*. Cambridge, Mass.: MIT Press.

Brada, J., and I. Singh. 1999. "Corporate Governance in East Central Europe: Issues and Summary of Case Studies." In *Corporate Governance in East Central Europe: Case*

Studies of Firms in Transition, edited by J. Brada and I. Singh. Armonk, N.Y.: M. E. Sharpe.

Brown, J. D., and J. S. Earle. 1999. "Privatization and Restructuring in Russia: New Evidence from Panel Data on Industrial Enterprises." Manuscript, 7 December draft.

Carlin, W., S. Fries, M. Schaffer, and P. Seabright. 1999. "Competition, Soft Budget Constraints and Enterprise Performance in Transition Economies." Proceedings of an international conference, "Ten Years After: Transition and Growth in Post-Communist Countries." Warsaw: CASE.

Carlin, W., and M. Landesmann. 1997. "From Theory to Practice? Restructuring and Dynamism in Transition Economies." *Oxford Review on Economic Policy,* pp. 77–105.

Claessens, S., and S. Djankov. 1999. "Enterprise Performance and Management Turnover in the Czech Republic." *European Economic Review,* pp. 1115–24.

Claessens, S., S. Djankov, and G. Pohl. 1997. "Ownership and Corporate Governance: Evidence from the Czech Republic." World Bank Policy Research Working Paper no. 1737.

Coase, R. H. 1960. "The Problem of Social Costs." *Journal of Law and Economics* 3 (no. 1): 1–44.

Demsetz, H. 1967. "Towards a Theory of Property Rights." *The American Economic Review* 57 (no. 2): 347–59.

Demsetz, H., and K. Lehn. 1985. "The Structure of Corporate Ownership: Causes and Consequences." *Journal of Political Economy* 93: 1155–77.

Dewenter, K., and P. Malatesta. 1998 (August). "State-Owned and Private-Owned Firms: An Empirical Analysis of Profitability, Leverage, and Labor Intensity." Financial Economics Network Working Papers.

Djankov, S. 1999 (February). *Ownership Structure and Enterprise Restructuring in Six Newly Independent States.* Washington, D.C.: World Bank, Technical Paper no. 2047.

Earle, J., and S. Estrin. 1997. "After Voucher Privatization: The Structure of Corporate Ownership in Russian Manufacturing Industry." Stockholm Institute of Transition Economics (SITE) Working Paper no. 120.

Earle, J., S. Estrin, and L. Leshchenko, 1995. "The Effects of Ownership on Behavior: Is Privatization Working in Russia?" Presented at a World Bank workshop, "Are Russian Enterprises Restructuring?" April 11–12.

Earle, J., R. Frydman, and A. Rapaczynski, eds. 1993. *Privatization in the Transition to a Market Economy.* London: Pinter.

Entov, R. M. 1999. *Korporativnoye upravleniye: teoreticheskiye i empiricheskiye obsledovaniya.* Moscow.

Ernst, M. M. Alexeev, and P. Marer. 1996. *Transforming the Core: Restructuring Industrial Enterprises in Russia and Central Europe.* Boulder, Colo.: Westview Press.

Estrin, S., and A. Rosevear. 1999. "Enterprise Performance and Ownership: The Case of Ukraine." *European Economic Review,* pp. 1125–36.

European Bank for Restructuring and Development (EBRD). 1997. *Transition Report 1997: Enterprise Performance and Growth*. London: EBRD.

———. 1998. Transition Report 1998: *Financial Sector in Transition*. London: EBRD.

Ericson, R. 1998. "Restructuring in Transition: Concept and Measurement." *Comparative Economic Studies* 40: 103–8.

FKTsB. 1996 (Spring). "Korporativnoye upravleniye v Rossiskoi Federatsii: 1994–1995." Moscow: Federal'naya komissiya po rynku tsennykh bumag.

———. 1996 (May). "Vladeniye aktsiyamai kompaniy i korporativnoye upravleniye v Rossiskoi Federatsii." Moscow: Federal'naya komissiya po rynku tsennykh bumag.

———. 1997. "Razvitiye rynka tsennykh bumag v Rossii." Moscow: Doklad Federal'noi komissii po rynku tsennykk bumag.

———. 1998. "Godovoi otchet za 1997 god." Moscow: Doklad Federal'noi komissii po rynku tsennykh bumag.

———. 1999. "Godovoi otchet za 1998 god." Moscow: Doklad Federal'noi komissii po rynku tsennykh bumag.

Frydman, R., C. W. Gray, M. Hessel, and A. Rapaczynski. 1997. "Private Ownership and Corporate Performance: Some Lessons from Transition Economics." Washington, DC: The World Bank. Working Paper No. 1830, September.

Gaidar, Ye. T. 1999. "Izbavleniye ot illuziy i zabluzhdeniy: pervy shag k vyzdorovleniyu." *Chelovek i trud* 11: 4–11.

Goskomstat, RF. 1999. "Sotsial'no-ekonomicheskoye polozheniye Rossii—1998 god." Moscow.

Gray, C. W., and Hanson, R. 1994. "Korporativnye othnoshenia v Centralnoy i Vostochnoy Europe. Uroki Rynochnoy ekonomiki Razvitykh Stran." In *Korporativnoye upravleniei i prava aktsionerov*. Mimeo.

Grossman, S. J., and O. D. Hart. 1982. "Corporate Financial Structure and Managerial Incentives." Pp. 123–55 in *The Economics of Information and Uncertainty*, edited by J. J. McCall. Chicago: University of Chicago Press.

———. 1986. "The Costs and Benefits of Ownership: A Theory of Vertical and Lateral Integration." *Journal of Political Economy* 94: 691–719.

Hanke, S. H., ed. 1987. *Privatization and Development*. San Francisco: International Center for Economic Growth.

Hanson, P. 1990. "Ownership issues in Perestroika." Pp. 67–79 in *Perestroika and the Private Sector of the Soviet Economy*, edited by J. Tedstrom. Boulder, Colo.: Westview Press.

Harte, O., and J. Moore. 1990. "Property Rights and the Nature of the Firm." *Journal of Political Economy* 98: 1119–58.

Heine, P. 1991. *Ekonomicheskiy obraz myshlenia* (Russian edition). Moscow.

Institute for the Economy in Transition (IET). 1992–1999. Annual Reports on the Russian Economy: Trends and Prospects. Moscow: IET.

IEPPP/IET. 1998. "Ekonomika perekhodnovo perioda." Moscow.

———. 1998. "Rossiskaya ekonomika v yanvare–sentyabre 1998 goda: tendentsii i perspektiviy." Moscow.

Johnson, S., and H. Kroll. 1991. "Managerial Strategies for Spontaneous Privatization." *Soviet Economy* 7 (no. 4): 281–316.

Khoroshev, S. 1998. "Reforma sobstvenosti." *Zhurnal dlya aktsionerov* 2: 44–46.

Kikeri, S., J. Nellis, and M. Shirley. 1992. *Privatization: The Lessons of Experience*. Washington, D.C.: World Bank.

Klepach, A., P. Kuznetsov, and P. Kryuchkova. 1996. "Korporativnoye upravleniye v Rossii v 1995–1996." *Voprosy ekonomiki* 12: 73–78.

Kobrinskaya, L. 1997. "Emissionnaya deyatel'nost' aktsionernykh obschestv." *Zhurnal dlya aktsionerov* 11: 13–15.

Kuznetsov, V. I. 1994. K teorii perekhodnoi ekonomiki. Mirovaya ekonomika i mezhdunarodnye otnosheniya 12.

La Porta, R., F. Lopez-de-Silanes, A. Shleifer, and R. W. Vishny. 1997. "Law and Finance." HIID, Development Discussion Paper no. 576. Cambridge, Mass.: Harvard University.

Leontieff Center. 1996. "Sraunitel'ny analiz ekonomicheskikh rezul'tatov raboty rossiskikh predpriyatel razlichnykh form sobstvennosti." Moscow and St. Petersburg: Mezhdunarodni tsentr sotsial'no-ekonomicheskikh issledovaniy "Leont'yevskii tsentr."

Lin, J. Y., and J. B. Nugent. 1995. "Institutions and Economic Development." In *Handbook of Development Economics*, Vol. III, chap. 38, pp. 2301–2370.

Linz, S., and G. Krueger. 1998. "Enterprise Restructuring in Russia's Transition Economy: Formal and Informal Mechanisms." *Comparative Economic Studies* 40: 5–52.

Marx, K., and F. Engels. *Sochineniya*, 2nd. ed.

Mau, V. 1999. "Rossiskiye ekonomicheskiye reformy glazami zapadnykh kritikov." *Voprosy ekonomiki* 11: 4–23; 12: 34–47.

McFaul, M., and T. Perlmutter, eds. 1995. *Privatization, Conversion, and Enterprise Reform in Russia*, with a foreword by Kenneth Arrow. Boulder, Colo.: Westview Press.

Mill, J. S. 1980. *Osnovy politicheskoi ekonomii*. Book II, "Raspredeleniye," chap. 1, "O sobstvennocti" (Russian edition). Moscow.

Nellis, J., and M. Shirley. 1991. *Public Enterprise Reform: The Lessons of Experience*. Washington, D.C.: World Bank.

North, D. 1978 (September). "Structure and Performance: The Task of Economic History." *Journal of Economic Literature* 16: 963–78.

———. 1981. *Structure and Change in Economic History*. New York: W. W. Norton.

North, D., and R. Thomas. 1973. *The Rise of the Western World*. Cambridge: Cambridge University Press.

OECD. 1995. *Mass Privatisation: An Initial Assessment*. Paris: OECD.

———. 1998. *Capital Market Development in Transition Economies: Country Experience and Policies for the Future*. Paris: OECD.

Perevalov, Yu., I. Grimadi, and V. Dobrodey. 1999. Vliyaet li privatizatsiya na deyatel'nost' predpriyatiy? *Voprosy ekonomiki* 6: 76–89.

Pohl, G., R. E. Anderson, S. Claessens, and S. Djankov. 1997. *Privatization and Restructuring in Central and Eastern Europe.* World Bank Technical Paper no. 368. Washington, D.C.: World Bank.

Radygin, A. 1992. "Spontaneous Privatization: Motivations, Forms, and Stages." *Studies on Soviet Economics* 3 (no. 5): 341–7.

———. 1994. *Reforma sobstvennocti v Rossii: na puti iz proshlovo v buduschee.* Moscow: Respublika.

———. 1995a. "The Russian Model of Mass Privatization: Governmental Policy and First Results." Pp. 3–18 in *Privatization, Conversion, and Enterprise Reform in Russia,* with a foreword by Kenneth Arrow. Boulder, Colo.: Westview Press.

———. 1995b. *Privatisation in Russia: Hard Choices, First Results, New Targets.* London: CRCE–Jarvis Print Group.

———. 1996. *Securities Market Development and Its Relationship to Corporate Governance in Russia.* Paris: OECD, DAFFE/MC/EW 25.

———. 1998. "Corporate Securities Market Development in Russia." Pp. 161–88 in *Capital Market Development in Transition Economies: Country Experience and Policies for the Future.* Paris: OECD.

———. 1999. "Ownership and Control in Russian Industry." *Proceedings of the OECD/World Bank Global Corporate Governance Forum.* Paris: OECD.

Radygin, A., and R. Entov. 1999. "Institutional Issues of Corporate Sector Development: Ownership, Control, Securities Market." Moscow: IET.

Radygin, A., V. Gutnik, and G. Mal'ginov. 1995. "Struktura aktsionernovo kapitala i korporativny kontrol': kontrrevolyutsiya upravlyayuschikh?" *Voprosi ekonomiki* 10: 47–69.

Railean, V., and I. Samson, eds. 1997. *Post-Privatization Period in Eastern Europe: A Chance for Enterprises and Shareholders.* Chisinau.

Rosenbaum, E., F. Bonker, and H.-J. Wagener, eds. 1999. *Privatisation, Corporate Governance, and the Emergence of Markets.* London: Macmillan.

Rozanov, V. 1990. *Uyedinennoye* (1912). Moscow.

Shapiro, C., and R. Willig. 1990. "Economic Rationales for the Scope of Privatization." In *The Political Economy of Public Sector Reform and Privatization.* London: Westview Press.

Shleifer, A. 1994. "Establishing Property Rights." Presented at the World Bank's Annual Conference on Development Economics, Washington, D.C., April 28–29.

Shleifer, A., and R. Vishny. 1994. "Politicians and Firms." *Quarterly Journal of Economics* 109: 995–1025.

Stiglitz, J. 1975. "Incentives, Risk, and Information: Notes Toward a Theory of Hierarchy." *Bell Journal of Economics* 6: 552–79.

———. 1994. *Whither Socialism?* Cambridge, Mass.: MIT Press.

World Bank. 1996. *From Plan to Market: World Development Report 1996.* Oxford, England: Oxford University Press.

———. 1998. *Knowledge for Development: World Development Report 1998/1999.* Washington, D.C.: World Bank.

World Bank–OECD. 1997. *Between State and Market: Mass Privatization in Transition Economies,* edited by Ira W. Liberman, Stilpon S. Nestor, and Rai M. Desai. World Bank–OECD.

UNCTAD. 1993. *Public Enterprises: Restructuring and Privatization. An Annotated Bibliography.* UNCTAD Secretariat. Geneva: UNCTAD.

Vassilyev, D. 1995. "Privatization in Russia—1994." Pp. 343–85 in *Privatization in Central and Eastern Europe 1994,* edited by Adreja Böhm. CEEPN Annual Conference Series no. 5.

Vickers, J., and G. Yarrow. 1988. *Privatization: An Economic Analysis.* Cambridge, Mass.: MIT Press.

Vuylsteke, C. 1988. *Techniques of Privatization of State-Owned Enterprises.* Vol. 1, *Methods and Implementations.* World Bank Technical Paper no. 88. Washington, D.C.: World Bank.

Williamson, O. E. 1985. *The Economic Institutions of Capitalism: Firms, Markets, Relational Contracting.* New York: Free Press.

———. 1990. "A Comparison of Alternative Approaches to Economic Organisation." *Journal of Institutional and Theoretical Economics* 146 (no. 1).

Yarrow, G. 1986. "Privatization in Theory and Practice." Pp. 324–56 in *Economic Policy.* Cambridge, England: Cambridge University Press.

15

Main Corporate Governance Mechanisms and Their Specific Features in Russia

Alexander Radygin and
Natalia Shmeleva

15.1. Corporate Governance in a Transition Economy: Preliminary Methodological Notes

The crystallizing structure of ownership rights and corporate governance is important both for the postprivatization development of enterprises and for the economy in general, for a number of reasons:

• The optimal organization of ownership rights in a corporation (as well as the delegation of authority over those rights) provides an incentive for restructuring and increasing microeconomic efficiency.

• The historically (or traditionally) formed structure of ownership distribution in a corporation defines specific national models of corporate governance and accordingly shapes concrete legislative concepts and models of government regulation.

• A transparent (clearly defined) model of corporate governance in which the rights of all types of investors (shareholders, creditors) are protected is requisite to attracting investment.

• The corporate governance model and the structure of the capital market together determine differences in how corporations are organized and financed, as well as the industrial structure of the corporation and the relationship between employers and employees.

• At the microlevel, the corporate governance model is one of the major institutional components of economic growth.

If we interpret a firm as an institution, an organization, or a network of contracts (Alchian and Demsetz 1972; North and Thomas 1973; Williamson 1985) and assume a similar approach to corporate governance, we can draw some practical conclusions for an economy in transition. In particular, the absence of a developed system, of a long-standing culture, and of standardized mechanisms for contract implementation as means for transferring property rights opens opportunities for large-scale violations of shareholders' rights, biased enforcement of property laws for political purposes, the development of nonmarket relationships between economic players, increased rent-seeking, and corruption (for details, see Radygin and Entov 1999).

Consequently, conflicts between managers and outside shareholders, both large and small, within the framework of the "principal-agent" relationship become acute. Problems related to the monitoring of managers by shareholders (see Hart 1995) are aggravated by the fact that managers, either directly or through proxy, are acting both as the insiders and the outsiders of the corporation.[1] In such a scenario, the problem of an issuer's transparency becomes crucial not only for potential investors but also for de facto outside shareholders of the corporation.

The corporate governance problem is no less important from the standpoint of the financial system, which is understood as certain institutional arrangements that provide for the transformation of savings into investments and for allocating resources among alternative users in the industrial sector (Tobin 1984). In a transition economy, the development of an efficient system of financial institutions, especially banks, within the overall framework of the financial system becomes especially important for shaping a national model of corporate governance and the financing of industrial development.

As the overall weakness of financial institutions in Russia became absolutely clear during the financial crisis of 1998, theoretical discussions about the applicability of any particular country's model of corporate governance (such as the American model versus the German one) became useless. Similarly, discussions of the potential role

---

1. Numerous constructions of "insiders" and "outsiders" exist in the literature: (a) internal (employees, managers) and external (banks, funds, other corporations) investors of a corporation; (b) from the standpoint of their involvement in the system of intercorporate ownership (in holdings or in cross-ownership schemes); (c) from the standpoint of the diffusion of the ownership (insiders as large controlling shareholders and outsiders as small portfolio shareholders); and (d) as "internal executives" and "independent" directors in the unitary or two-chamber governing body. Some scholars of Russian legislation include in the insider category board members, members of the collegiate executive body of the company, the person performing the function of single-person executive body, and majority shareholders who can shape the decisions made by the company.

of banks as an alternative mechanism of corporate control when other mechanisms that might have forced managers to act not solely in their own interests have failed (see Stiglitz 1994, 77–78, 189–90) and also turned out to be of little relevance.

From the standpoint of corporate control issues, the situation in the transitional economy is unclear. On the one hand, the "manager's revolution" concept, known since the 1930s (Berle and Means 1932), suggests there are reasons to place formal owners outside the framework of the real authority relationships involving control and management in Russian joint-stock companies. This model was typical of the first postprivatization years, before the law *On Joint-Stock Companies* was enacted. On the other hand, there is also evidence to claim that the process of ownership—corporate control—corporate governance does exist. The latter makes sense when it is possible to identify different types of the "hard-core" shareholders exercising control either directly or through affiliated entities ("coalitions," in the language of organizations theory). In this respect the key problem becomes one of identifying the hubs of real control (Aghion and Tirole 1996) in a corporation with a formally dispersed ownership structure.

It should also be pointed out that when a market is illiquid, the choice between the mechanism of "vote" and the mechanism of "exit" loses all meaning (Hirschman 1970, 15–54), since there is essentially no alternative: if it is impossible to sell one's shares, then the voting mechanism must be upgraded. One way to implement this mechanism in a transition economy is suggested by the self-enforcing model of corporate governance (Black, Kraakman, and Hay 1996; Black, Kraakman, and Tarasova 1997).

Corporate governance theory describes a number of mechanisms to ensure the realization of shareholder rights and to form a system of relations among shareholders, managers, employees, creditors, and other participants in firm operations with respect to the order in which assets are disposed of and income is distributed.[2] Economic theory, jurisprudence, sociology, psychology, and other avenues approach the operation of these mechanisms. In general, there is a tendency to use an interdisciplinary approach in develop-

---

2. See, for example, Andreeff (1995); Charkham (1994); Clark (1986); Monks and Minow (1995); OECD (1999); Prentice and Holland (1993); Radygin and Entov (1999); and Wouters (1973).

ing theories about corporate governance (see Prentice and Holland 1993).

The mechanisms of corporate governance are traditionally differentiated into internal and external mechanisms. Internal mechanisms include procedural mechanisms of governance within the corporation; external mechanisms refer to influential factors in the external environment. External mechanisms of corporate governance usually include the following:

- Corporate legislation (codes, special company laws, conjugate laws, departmental acts, rules, instructions) and its executive infrastructure (enforcement)
- Financial markets (for example, if the securities of ineffective corporations are dumped on liquid financial markets, managers face the insurmountable problem of finding new resources in a climate of declining investor interest in the corporation's securities)
- The threat of bankruptcy owing to managers' poor policies (in the most extreme case, bankruptcy results in the transfer of control to creditors)
- The market of corporate control (the threat of a hostile takeover and the replacement of managers)

This chapter reviews the key mechanisms necessary for the development of a national model of corporate governance in Russia and other CIS members, and obstacles to their implementation. The discussion is mostly concerned with open joint-stock companies set up in the industrial sector, generally medium-sized and large public enterprises, and with the course of their development and privatization. The data used in analyzing trends in Russia are current through 1 January 2000; for other countries the data may vary, depending on what sources were available.

15.2. Internal Mechanisms

Following the work of Tirole (1999), at least three internal mechanisms regulate the coordination of decisions made within the corporation with the interests of shareholders:

1. Retaining a managerial post for the manager (and upholding management's business reputation when a corporation proves successful)

2. Maintaining an incentive for effective management (from the shareholders' point of view) by means of special systems of payment
3. Direct monitoring, mainly by large shareholders and their representatives

In different countries the role played by each of these mechanisms can differ fundamentally. Nevertheless, despite all the differences in existing structures of corporate governance, in each developed country a system of checks and balances safeguards the interests of investors while allowing managers some independence and initiative.

In countries with a transitional economy, the weak development of external mechanisms of corporate governance makes internal mechanisms especially important (Table 15.1).

In all developed countries, a two-tiered system of governance is in place. One tier consists of the executive board or managing board and the other tier consists of the board of directors or the supervisory council. The existence of a board of directors may be tied to a company's size (Russia, Latvia, Poland). In some countries the board can be dissolved at the discretion of shareholders (Bulgaria, Romania). On the other hand, in other countries the two-tiered system is mandatory (the Czech Republic, Hungary). The board of directors (supervisory council) is usually considered the main internal or direct mechanism of control.

With respect to the executive management of a joint-stock company, a primary problem in a transitional economy is getting rid of the concept of "principal owner." Retaining the concept of principal owner generally results in a fierce struggle for control (in "amorphous" or "insider" models), or resistance to new owners.

One more principal trend should be noted. The second half of the 1990s was characterized by a very specific process of merging the functions of managers and outsiders in Russian corporations. The managers gradually became stockholders in corporations, while the outsiders, consolidating their control, started function as managers. This is a conflict-ridden process, and so far it has not played a decisive role. However, in perspective this process is very important for its potential to smooth over bitter corporate conflicts and further stabilize ownership control in a corporation.

Data on the replacement of managers in the hundred largest Russian corporations provide some indirect confirmation of ownership

Table 15.1
Standard Elements of Corporate Law and Their Presence in Some Transition Economy Countries at End of 1996*

	Russia	Czech Republic	Hungary	Bulgaria	Poland	Romania
Main legal acts	Civil Code (1994), Law on JSC (1995)	Commercial Code (1991)	Law VI on commercial societies (1988)	Commercial law of 1991 and 1994	Commercial Code (1934 with amend.)	Commercial Societies Act (1990)
1. Clear distribution of decision-making authority	Weak	Exists	Exists	Weak	Exists	Weak
2. Governance structure (two-tier, i.e. management and board of directors)	Two-tiered if more than 50 shareholders	Always two-tiered	Always two-tiered	According to shareholders decision	Two-tiered if capital is more than 50 mln zloty	According to shareholders decision
3. Nomination of directors (necessary number of votes)	More than 50%	More than 50%	More than 50%	More than 50%	n.m.—some directors can be appointed by large shareholders	Competence of the board
4. Removal of directors	More than 50%	More than 50%	More than 50%	More than 50%	More than 50%	More than 50%
5. Control over votes (proxies)†	Exists	Exists	Exists	Exists	Exists	Exists
6. Rules for disclosure of information and audit	Standards rapidly developing	Low level	High standards	Low level	High standards, close to EC	Low level
7. Rights of minority shareholders						
a. Preemptive right	Exists 75%	Exists 66%	Exists 75%	Exists 2/3 of chartered capital	Exists	No data
b. Qualified (or higher) majority during important decisions					May be 50%, 2/3, 3/4, 4/5	2/3 of quorum 75%

Corporate Governance Mechanisms in Russia

c. Takeover rules	Exists	No	Exists	No	No data	No data
d. Cumulative voting	Exists	No data	No data	No data	Exists	No data
e. Limitations on number of votes per 1 shareholder	NM	May be	May be	NM	May be	May be
f. "Independent" directors	Exists	No data	No data	No data	No data	No data
g. Rules for important transactions	Exists	No data	No data	No data	No data	No data
8. Participation of employees in supervisory board	NM	1/3–1/2, if more than 50 employees	1/3, if more than 200 employees	NM	NM	NM
9. Minimum quorum for meeting	More than 50%	30%	More than 50%	According to the charter	NM	50%
10. No. of votes per 1 share	As a rule, 1	1	Not limited	1	1–5	1
11. Insider dealing prohibited	Yes	Yes	Yes	Yes	Yes	Yes
12. Enforcement	Weak	Weak	Weak	Weak	Weak	Weak

*Data may be obsolete. According to the EBRD (1997), in 1997 a number of countries enacted modern company laws (the Czech Republic, Estonia, Hungary, Lithuania, Poland, Slovak Republic, Slovenia, and Uzbekistan). NM, not mentioned in the legislation.

†In reality, depends on: (a) rules of excess to shareholder registers and (b) prospects of the formation of a depository system resembling that in Germany (where depository banks vote for shareholders who do not express their opinion on the subjects of agenda). This directly contradicts the rules in the United States, where such votes are cancelled.

Sources: RF laws; Böhm (1997); Gray and Hanson (1994); *Aktsionernoye obschestvo* (1995); EBRD (1998).

stabilization (Khoroshev 1998). Fifty percent of the general managers of these companies assumed their position after 1992, while 25% of those assumed their position in 1997. Before assuming office, a minority (36.4%) had no prior experience at the company at all, but the majority had, either as deputy general managers (45.5%) or in some other position (18.2%). The study also found that the average age of general managers was between 50 and 65 years; 19% of them were younger than 40.

On the whole, the problem of a board's (managers', executive directors') loyalty to joint-stock companies and their shareholders is acute in all countries undergoing transition. The most draconian measures to ensure such loyalty are stipulated in Latvia's law on joint-stock companies. This law states that members of the executive board are elected at general meetings, and in the first month following the election each member of the board must acquire a certain percentage of shares in the company (usually 0.1%–5%, but since 1996 up to 25%) without the right to sell them. Should a joint-stock company suffer losses because of the activities of a board member, that individual's shares will be sold to cover the loss. If this is not adequate to cover the loss, the individual is forced to sell personal property.

In this connection, problems of representation of external shareholders in different bodies of joint-stock companies become more important. In particular, in Russian joint-stock companies there is a significant stratum of shareholders who, while participating in the capital investment, are neither represented in any corporate governance body nor participate in current management. Most affected are shareholder—employees and individual external shareholders, while commercial banks and industrial enterprises (suppliers and buyers) are least affected. That commercial banks and industrial enterprises are not much affected is not surprising, because both kinds of entities have more possibilities of ensuring their shareholder rights by using other financial and trade mechanisms.

15.3. General Legislative Situation

After the achievements of the first half of the 1990s, Russia made little progress in the development of new legislation and legal institutions. In 1996, the World Bank noted that "there was some progress

Corporate Governance Mechanisms in Russia

in legislation and insufficient in institutions." This reality placed Russia in the third group of countries in the World Bank's classification, a group that included Kyrgyzstan, Moldova, Armenia, Georgia, and Kazakhstan. Russia lagged seriously behind the leaders—the countries of the first group (Poland, Slovenia, Hungary, Croatia, Macedonia, the Czech Republic, and Slovakia)—where there was "significant progress both in legislation and in institutions" (World Bank 1996).

By the end of the 1990s the situation had changed markedly (EBRD 1998). In regard to addressing commercial laws, Russia joined the group of leaders, being granted the "expert" grade of 4− (Bulgaria, the Czech Republic, Hungary, Poland, Romania, Lithuania, and Croatia have been given a grade of 4, and industrially developed countries are graded as 4+). The lag is greater in regard to the "efficiency" of commercial laws (Russia received the "expert" grade of 2, while the leaders are graded 3 or 4). As a result, according to this classification, Russia holds an intermediate position among the countries in transition.

Of course, not a single country in transition has legislation on corporate governance (in the broad sense—encompassing all the necessary regulatory documents) that could be considered highly developed. This legislation "does not so much reflect what already is but what should be or, in the best possible case, what is emerging" (Aktsionernoye obschestvo ... 1995, VIII–IX).

The federal law *On Joint-Stock Companies*, adopted in 1995 and in force since 1 January 1996, became the landmark piece of legislation in the field of commercial law in Russia. In principle, it could be considered quite progressive, at least at the moment of its adoption, because it included a generally accepted set of traditional provisions for corporate governance.

The major objectives of corporate governance regulations cover several areas relevant to the protection of shareholder rights:

- To fill in the legal gaps characteristic of Russian corporate legislation (such as regulations on insiders' transactions, affiliated persons and relationships, corporate reorganizations, and so on)
- More rigid regulation of relations between legally independent but economically connected companies (an example is the definition of a "group" in French law)

- To clarify procedural issues bearing on corporate relationships (authority and procedure of shareholders' meetings, boards of directors, new securities issues, and so forth)
- To establish requirements for an issuer's transparency (at present the quantitative approach to disclosure of information prevails; however, qualitative aspects—the reliability of the information—are no less important)
- To strengthen the sanctions against violating the provisions of corporate law
- To enhance the authority of the governmental regulatory bodies
- To widen the scope of judicial control over a company's "activity"

Moreover, a new, systemic approach to the development and updating of legislation is needed, as well as conciliation between the provisions of the different branches of law (administrative, civil, civil procedural, criminal, and criminal procedural) regulating the activity of corporations. Another crucial factor now is the general legal environment in which companies function. Another important element is the systematization of the related regulatory documents: on the securities market, bankruptcy, mergers and takeovers, protection of investors, investment institutions, banks, and so on.

In countries in transition, the process of developing regulations for this broad range of problems is usually stepped up when reforms have reached a certain qualitative stage. All of the above-mentioned considerations allow us to conclude that at present, there is no real need for any radical changes in the corporate law. Under normal conditions, a policy of gradual improvement and filling in the legal vacuum is probably the optimal solution.

The key problem today is that the efficient regulation of corporate relationships demands not only active (or even leading) legal regulation of the developments in this sphere, but also the creation of a system of state control and enforcement that would bring companies into compliance with existing legislation. The "self-enforcing" model of internal protective mechanisms cannot be strengthened indefinitely, nor does it work under conditions of continuing struggle for control within corporations. Such external mechanisms of protection and control as a liquid securities market and a well-functioning bankruptcy mechanism are weak in Russia. In such a situation, internal methods of control and enforcement of existing laws become much more important.

No single law on companies can cover the whole spectrum of corporate problems. Thus, a governmental regulatory body that could efficiently and legally intervene in corporate governance disputes would become the most important element of the law enforcement system. The role of such factors as political will in establishing such an efficient regulatory body is self-evident.

15.4. The Corporate Securities Market

The importance of the securities market to shaping the model of corporate governance needs no comment. When a developing market is illiquid and the major objects of trade are securities issued by ten to fifteen entities, the mechanism of "exit" (sale of stock) as an element of corporate governance in the absolute majority of cases simply does not work. The market for the shares of a specific issuer may be liquid for only a short period of time, and it is only one-way: small shareholders may only exit, and only during periods of consolidation of a controlling interest or times of corporate conflict between large shareholders and managers. In many cases small shareholders are unable to sell, either because absolute control of the company has been established or because the enterprise is of no interest to investors.

Thus, there is almost no alternative to the currently forming corporate governance model: if the exit mechanisms do not work—if you simply cannot sell your shares—then there should be a natural tendency to strengthen the voting mechanism. If problems arise in this connection as well (resulting from the ideology of a "principal owner" still supported by the managers), the only way left is the intervention of state executive and judiciary authorities. Some inter-country comparisons of this process are presented in Table 15.2.

However, the opposite type of relationship also exists. According to many estimates, violations of corporate governance rules in Russian corporations were a major factor leading to the withdrawal of investors and the collapse of the securities market in 1998.[3] An excellent example in this respect is the adoption of federal law No. 74-FZ of 7 May 1998, *On Specific Aspects of Disposal of the Shares of the*

---

3. According to various estimates, this factor accounted for between 30% (FCSM of Russia) and 100% (Brunswick Warburg) of the decrease in market capitalization in 1998, although estimates are obviously very artificial.

Table 15.2
Comparative Corporate Securities Market Development Data, End of 1996 to End of 1997

	Czech Republic	Hungary	Poland	Russia	Romania	Slovenia	Slovakia
Capitalization: US $ (bill.) / % of GDP	18.1 / 39	5.3 / 12	8.4 / 7	68 / 11	0.9 / 2	2.5 / 15.9	2.2 / 12
Trading volume: US $ (bill.) / % of capitalization	8.4 / 47	1.6 / 31	5.4 / 64	3.0 / 8	0.5 / 55	0.7 / 33	2.3 / 106
No. of listed shares	1,000 tot., 50 liquid	50 (types A and B)	129 (incl. NIFs)	30,000 tot., 150 liquid	60 (two tiers)	73	19
No. of securities dealers	460 licensed	98 licensed	50 (incl. 16 banks)	1,561	100	42	ND
% of shares trading on stock exchange market	3	86	OTC since 1997	2	BSE and RASDAQ	100	ND
Universal banking	Yes	Since 1997	Yes	Yes, with restrict.	No	Yes	Yes, with restrict.
Central depository (or central clearing and settlement entity)	Yes	KELER (all clearing and settl. for BSE)	Yes	No	Central Company for clearing and settlement	Central clearing corp.	Yes

Corporate Governance Mechanisms in Russia

Independent securities commission	Since 1998	Integrated office for banking and securities under government	Since 1991	Since 1993, under President	Yes, under Parliament	Yes	No, control office within MF
Securities law	Act on Securities; Act on Stock Exchange; new law (1997)	Law on Securities Issues and Stock Exchange (1990)	Law on Securities Trading and Investment Trusts (1991)	1996 Law on Securities Market	1994 Securities Law	1994 Law on Securities Market (new law will be close to EC)	New (1998)
Insider laws, investor protection, disclosure and compliance regulation	Yes, with weak enforcement	Well-developed standards (close to IOSCO)	Well-developed standards (close to IOSCO)	Yes, with weak enforcement	Yes, with weak enforcement	Standards developed, with weak enforcement	Yes, with weak enforcement

Sources: OECD, 1998a; Thiel (1998); RF FCSM; various countries' legislation.

Russian Joint-Stock Company in the Field of Energy and Electrification "Unified Energy System of Russia" and the Shares of Other Joint-Stock Companies in the Power Sector Under Federal Ownership. Article 3 of this law permitted foreign states, international organizations, foreign legal persons and their affiliated Russian legal persons, and foreign individuals to own up to 25% of all types of an RAOs' shares (RAO is the abbreviation for *rossiskoye aktsionernoye obschestvo* or Russian government-controlled corporation). At the time the law was adopted, 30% of shares in RAOs were already owned by foreigners.[4] The adoption of this quota, which hypothetically meant a demand for nationalization of a certain percent of shares, became one of the key factors in the Russian stock market crash of 1998.

The Russian corporate securities market was developing robustly during 1996–1997. The global financial crisis that began in 1997 dealt an especially severe blow to emerging markets, including Russia (the overall decrease in capitalization was 90% between October 1997 and September 1998). Nevertheless, even if we take into account the sharp drop in the stock market indices in 1997, Russia at the time was still the global leader in the growth of its stock index (which by the end of 1997 had increased by 88% compared with 1996). To a considerable degree the growth in the index was explained by significant legislative progress, development of the securities market infrastructure, and the increasing attractiveness of Russian corporate securities in the setting of decreasing yields on other financial instruments during 1995–1997.

Nevertheless, the Asian crisis and lower world prices for raw commodities were just external factors contributing to the financial crisis in Russia, which had its own specific features. The catastrophic crash of the Russian stock market in 1998 cannot be explained solely by the unfavorable global financial situation. The latter only aggravated the accumulated internal negative trends in the Russian economy, and it

---

4. Limiting foreigners' share to 25% was essentially a psychological factor, because it was not realistic to expect that the foreigners' share could be legally brought down to the required level. There is only one legal way to decrease this share—by issuing additional shares, which becomes possible only after a decision made at a general shareholders' meeting (foreigners have a blocking interest, the government has a controlling interest), after which the issue must be registered with the FCSM, which has the right to refuse to do so in accordance with the RF Civil Code. According to some data, by February 1999 the share of foreign investors increased to 33%, which was explained by the expectations (apparently mistaken) that the prohibitive quota would be canceled and the companies' stock prices would significantly increase.

was these internal trends that proved fatal in 1998. The significant drop in stock prices and liquidity between the autumn of 1997 and the autumn of 1998 was linked to a whole range of different macroeconomic and institutional factors.[5]

The financial crisis uncovered several shortcomings of the domestic securities market:

• The market players were speculators and not interested in long-term investment.

• Individual domestic investors had an insignificant presence on the securities market, which is inexcusable.

• Issuers had little interest in opening the market (because of ongoing struggle within corporations, among other reasons).

• Issuers had insufficient knowledge of market opportunities to mobilize capital.

• There was loose coordination between governmental agencies that regulate the securities market, and a permanent conflict of interest between governmental agencies.

• Gaps and contradictions in the normative and legislative base of the securities market persist.

The persisting postcrisis economic growth in 1998 and 1999 (the GDP increased by 3.2% and industrial output rose 8.1%), the relative stability of the macroeconomic situation (contrary to some predictions, hyperinflation did not occur), and political changes at the end of 1999 and the beginning of 2000 positively affected the situation on the Russian securities market. According to most rating agencies, the Russian stock market in 1999 was among the three fastest growing markets in the world. The value of Russian debts increased by 60%–70% of the nominal value. The annual yield of Russian bonds was 130% (Brazilian bonds yielded 39%). The capitalization of blue chip companies increased by 182% during the year. The RTS-Interfax index was the second fastest growing national stock market index in the world, after Turkey's. In January 2000, investors again began showing interest in "second-echelon" companies, a sign that investors were starting to turn to a more long-term strategy from purely speculative short-term investment.

---

5. For more details see FKTsB (1997, 1998, 1999); IEPPP/IET (1998); and Radygin (1998, 1999).

The profitability of mutual investment funds increased substantially. Most profitable were the mutual funds that invested in state securities and utilized the results of the novation and growing OVVZ quotations (Ilya Muromets showed a profit of 1,877%, and Templeton Funds a profit of 854%). Although several funds were liquidated in the wake of the crisis, their total number reminded almost the same, since new corporate equity funds were created. Moreover, the number of depositors in many mutual funds increased by a factor of four or five. However, the flood of private funds into the securities market (including money invested through mutual funds and the Moscow Stock Center) was linked not to the advantages of one or another investment method but to the absence of alternative high-profit instruments on the financial market in 1999.

Foreign funds that invested in Russian equities in 1999 ended the year up 150%. These results led experts to anticipate that investors would continue to be interested in Russia after the presidential elections in March 2000. Although political stability is an important factor in this case, for many funds the market's growth rate is no less important, as it is the fund manager's mandate to invest in the fastest growing markets.

In 1999, for the first time since the financial crisis, some large Russian corporations (Sibneft, Unified Energy System of Russia) announced their intention of issuing depository receipts. It is also significant that a majority of Russian corporate borrowers strove to meet their current liabilities on the eurobond market on time. The year 1999 also saw renewed interest in the Russian corporate securities market. Some of the largest companies issued securities in 1999 (including those linked to the novation of governmental securities), while others planned their issues for 2000.

In the short term, the Russian securities market could probably be characterized by the following main tendencies:

• Fewer (as a result of mergers) and larger companies, and greater competition among professional securities market players

• The postcrisis redistribution of ownership in financial groups and corporations, which, together with low prices on the weak stock market, could result in widescale abuses and violations of shareholder rights

• The appearance of instruments not typical for the Russian market, owing to the attempts of real sector enterprises to find alternative sources of financing (corporate bonds, warehouse receipts, mortgages)

• The development of new forms of collective investment (real estate investment trusts, for example)

• A more active role for self-regulatory organizations of professional participants in the securities market and investors (shareholders)

The Russian securities market has a significant potential for further development. This potential is based on such factors as the large number of open joint-stock companies that were created in the course of privatization, the substantial number of enterprises with good prospects, the interest many enterprises have in additional issues, and the desire of many regional and municipal authorities to place their loans (bonds). To a considerable degree, the prospects for growth in the Russian market depend on reasonable policies for financing the deficit of the federal budget through the issuance of various types of government securities.

Favorable conditions for the medium-term development of the securities market are determined by a number of qualitative characteristics unrelated to the current business situation:

• A considerable understatement of assets (although this factor may remain hypothetical in the absence of effective management or the greater transparency of issuers)

• The inflow of funds from large Russian investors into the corporate segment of the Russian securities market

• The appearance of conservative foreign investors on the Russian market

• An increasing share of long-term investment by global mutual funds in Russian corporate securities

• Favorable shifts in the development of the securities market infrastructure

• Increasing transparency of the Russian market

• Removal of political risks

• Removal of the ruble devaluation risk

• Decreasing tax-related risks

• Decreasing risks related to protection of stockholders' rights and "anti-outsider" policies of companies' managers

- The reduction of risks by creating a central depository linking regional depositories
- The development of a system of collective investors

In general, the securities market in a transitional economy can perform four major functions: attract investment, fill the portfolios of speculative investors, achieve the postprivatization redistribution of ownership rights within corporations, and serve as a mechanism of outside corporate governance (to put pressure on managers).

Throughout the 1990s, attracting investment in enterprises remained the weak link in the market that was taking shape during this time. The possibility of an efficient start-up of the market mechanisms of corporate governance is definitely limited in such a market. Probably in the next few years the major function of the market will remain, as it has been all along, the redistribution of ownership in Russian corporations. However, this redistribution will take into account the specifics of the postcrisis situation. Correspondingly, the problem of shareholder rights protection and strengthening governmental regulation in this field become especially urgent.

15.5. Bankruptcy Procedures

The role of potential bankruptcy as a mechanism for putting pressure on corporate managers in a market economy is well-known. The threat of bankruptcy managers face when they adopt an incorrect market policy (and, in the most severe cases, the transfer of control to creditors) is usually regarded as a major external instrument of corporate governance control. Regardless of the specific country model and regardless of whether bankruptcy favors creditors or debtors, bankruptcy should alleviate the financial situation of the corporation, and the corporate operations should thus become efficient.

At the same time, in a transitional economy there are objective limitations to the broad implementation of bankruptcy as a means of external control:

- The traditionally soft budget restrictions
- The existence of a large number of corporations with state shareholding
- The lack of an adequate executive and judicial infrastructure

- Social and political obstacles to conducting real bankruptcy procedures in the case of loss-making corporations, especially if they are very large corporations or located in one-employer towns
- Numerous technical difficulties in evaluating the financial situation of candidates for bankruptcy
- Corruption and other criminal aspects, including problems connected with the redistribution of ownership

Under these conditions, since the time of its appearance and during the 1990s the institution of bankruptcy in Russia has performed two major functions: the redistribution (obtaining, retaining, privatization) of property, and as a way for the state to apply permanent political and economic pressure, which has been extremely rarely and very selectively applied.

The number of bankruptcy petitions during the period of 1993–1997 when the law *On Insolvency (Bankruptcy) of Enterprises* (adopted by the RSFSR Supreme Soviet on 19 November 1992 and in force since 1 March 1993) was valid is very insignificant.[6] From 1993 to 1 March 1998, arbitration courts saw altogether 4,500 cases. As of 1 March 1998, the courts were engaged in proceedings involving 2,900 cases, an increase in the annual docket. (Table 15.3).

A new law, *On Insolvency (Bankruptcy)*, No. 6-FZ, was adopted on 8 January 1998 and became effective on 1 March 1998. We will not try to evaluate its innovations and content here (but see, for example, *Kommentari* ... 1998), but will only point out that this law is more detailed and progressive than the earlier one. The problem can be condensed to the following points. First, all political, social, and economic obstacles to the widescale application of this law still remain (and have become even more relevant after the crisis of 1998). According to Goskomstat, 55.2% of small and medium-sized Russian enterprises were in the red in 1998.

Second, in an environment of high levels of corruption and the continuing redistribution of ownership, alternative solutions envisioned by the law and the procedures for their adoption become a convenient tool for manipulation and applying pressure in the inter-

---

6. According to the Single State Register of the enterprises and organizations of all forms of ownership, the number of registered businesses in Russia as of 1 January 1999 (including affiliates and remote subdivisions) was about 2.7 million units, including more than 1.6 million joint-stock companies and partnerships (RF Goskomstat 1999).

Table 15.3
Bankruptcies in Some Transition Economy Countries

Country	1990	1991	1992	1993	1994	1995	1996	1997	1998
Russia									
No. of bankruptcies filed	—	—	—	100	240	1,108	2,618	5,810*	12,781*
No. of companies recognized as bankrupt	—	—	—	50	ND	ND	1,035	2,600[†]	4,747[†]
Czech Republic									
No. of bankruptcies filed	—	—	350	1,098	1,816	2,393	2,990	ND	ND
No. of bankruptcies completed ([‡])	—	—	5	61	290	482	725	ND	ND
			(0)	(1)	(2)	(2)	(6)		
Hungary									
No. of bankruptcies filed	—	—	14,060	8,229	5,900	6,461	7,477	ND	ND
No. of bankruptcies completed ([‡])	—	—	1,302	1,650	1,241	2,276	3,007	ND	ND
			(740)	(510)	(90)	(21)	(9)		
Poland									
No. of bankruptcies filed	151	1,327	4,349	5,936	4,825	3,531	3,118	ND	ND
No. of bankruptcies completed ([‡])	29	305	910	1,048	1,030	1,030	984	ND	ND
	(1)	(8)	(98)	(179)	(235)	(287)	(173)		

* Applications filed with arbitration courts.

[†] In 1997, external management was instituted in 850 cases. During the first months of the new law enforcement (in March–June 1998), 800 applications were submitted (80 were rejected). By the beginning of November 1998 the number of applications had grown 10 times, to 8,000, and arbitration courts had appointed 3,000 arbitration managers. In general, according to the figures of the Federal Insolvency Agency (FIA), in 1998, 12,781 applications were filed demanding the pronouncement of debtors as bankrupts, including 4,573 cases involving the bankruptcies of industrial enterprises (out of which monitoring was instituted over 1,462 enterprises, external managers were appointed in 472 cases, bankruptcy proceedings were begun in 2,006 cases, and in 80 cases an amicable settlement between creditors and managers was achieved).

[‡] Including reorganizations.

Sources: RF FIA; EBRD (1997); *Kommentari* (1998).

ests of different participants of this process. Of importance here is the type of arbitration manager appointed, as well as the choice between liquidation and rehabilitation (reorganization).

In this connection, any significant simplification in the procedure for initiating bankruptcy (at the level of arrears equal to 500 minimum wages for legal persons) would make it much easier to put this procedure into operation for the liquidation of property. From the Russian experience it is well-known that the appointment of a "friendly" arbitration manager (whether temporary, specifically for the liquidation process, or an external one) almost automatically means that the problems of "the manager's friend" will be settled in his or her favor, whether it is protection against aggression or aggression.[7]

Third, if the number of bankruptcy petitions is compared with the total number of Russian enterprises and the number of debtor companies, this figure, instead of impressing, will rather alarm. Apparently the overwhelming majority of private creditors are not in a hurry to use the legal schemes offered by the new law. Instead, they prefer the traditional "private enforcement." Bankruptcy as an institution has not yet gained wide recognition and become a universal and uniform system but remains largely a tool to apply selective pressure on debtors, and its application is quite often motivated by the political interests at the federal and regional level.

Fourth, the problem of legal and practical support for the protection of rights and interests of all types of shareholders within the framework of the bankruptcy procedure remains unresolved. In particular, the threat of forced bankruptcy of many large corporations in arrears to the federal budget became a factor in the rapid withdrawal of portfolio investors from the corporate securities market in 1998.

Consequently, it is hardly possible today to regard the institution of bankruptcy in Russia as a stable and efficient external mechanism that improves the management and finances of a company. The increase in the number of bankruptcy petitions apparently does not indicate an enthusiastic response by creditors to the new legal avenues open to them. Rather, it seems simply to provide a trial run of new methods of privatization, protection of managers against hostile takeovers, or, conversely, a way to hostilely take over assets of in-

---

7. For detailed descriptions of different schemes for taking property away by appointing arbitration managers, see Volkov, Gurova, and Titov (1999).

terest. It is not accidental that this process co-occurred with the general rise in ownership redistribution around the time of the 1998 crisis.

15.6. The Market of Corporate Control (Takeovers)

Along with bankruptcy, the market of corporate control, which bears the threat of a hostile takeover and the replacement of managers, is considered to be a key external mechanism for effective of corporate governance. Many researchers believe that an active takeover market is the only way to protect shareholders from the arbitrary actions of managers. Coffee (1988) has pointed out that this method of corporate control is most efficient when it is necessary to break the opposition of a conservative board of directors not interested in listening to reason, which might call for splitting up a company, or when a company is already highly diversified. The numerous theoretical writings on the subject have also noted the relationship between takeovers that have provided a "private" (special) benefit to large shareholders and an improvement in the economic efficiency of the corporation after the new owner took control.

At the same time, the effectiveness of a takeover threat from the standpoint of subsequent improvement in corporate governance has been increasingly questioned. In particular, many commentators stress that the threat of a takeover pushes managers toward near-sightedness because they are afraid of stock prices going down in the near term. Other critics believe that takeovers serve only the interests of shareholders and do not take into account the interests of all "accomplices." Finally, there is always the possibility that the takeover will destabilize both the buyer company and the company that is taken over (see Gray and Hanson 1994).

Estimates of the amount of takeover activity depend on the methodological approach chosen. If a broad definition is used, many large privatization transactions may be characterized as friendly or hostile. If narrower definitions are applied, only the following may be singled out as not possibilities for takeovers in the Russian situation: (1) companies in the postprivatization period, (2) individual secondary transactions, and (3) large companies. Both mergers and takeovers are limited in all three cases by the need for large amounts of money, typically acquired through loans, which are available only to largest companies (banks), or by mobilizing sizable blocks of shares in order to exchange them.

Corporate mergers in the strict sense of the term—that is, friendly transactions between equal (large) firms that are not accompanied by the buying up of small stockholders' shares but do involve an exchange of shares or establishment of a new company—are not yet common in Russia. This process is traditionally common at the stage of economic growth in which share prices increase. However, in Russia corporate mergers are more often regarded as a potential anticrisis mechanism, or as political maneuvering, or as the institutional formalization of technological integration.

Thus, the oil company Lukoil's transition to a single-share company is deemed to be the final stage of integration in the full merger of the company into a single financial and economic entity (the subsidiary companies have merged with the holding company).[8] Among the better-known examples from 1998–1999 are the noncompleted merger of oil companies YUKOS and Sibneft, the announced merger of joint-stock company Izhorskie zavody (St. Petersburg) and Uralmash zavody (Yekateriburg), and the announced merger of Neftekamsky automotive plant (Bashkiria) and Kamsky automotive plant (Tatarstan).

In essence, mergers and friendly takeovers can be regarded as synonyms. The capital market is unnecessary for friendly takeovers (which are initiated on agreement between the parties), and there is no visible connection with the problems of corporate governance. Mergers have been the most typical form of takeover for postprivatization Russia. They have occurred in a large number of newly established corporations and were motivated primarily by technological reasons: to reestablish old business ties, to control market share, and to integrate vertically.

The oil company Surgutneftegaz, for example, as opposed to Lukoil, completed the process of technological integration through a series of takeovers (of joint-stock company KINEF and a number of refined-product supply companies). Typically, such a process followed the establishment of financial and industrial groups repre-

---

8. At the same time, the shares of Lukoil remained relatively attractive and liquid (for more details, see Lyapina 1998), as happened similarly in a number of cases involving full takeover with the withdrawal of the company's shares that was taken over (Surgutneftegaz), but as is not typical of takeovers in which only the controlling interest is purchased, such as the takeover of Chernogorneft by the oil company SIDANKO.

senting a cross-ownership system around large corporations (especially in the chemicals and construction industries). It should also be pointed out that this process is highly politicized, and federal and regional authorities play an active role in it (especially in Bashkiria and Tatarstan).

In fact, only hostile takeovers hypothetically compensate for faulty corporate governance through the enforced replacement of managers. This market—the market of corporate control as such—has not yet developed to any considerable degree in Russia, and the transactions that actually take place are usually not advertised. Among the major factors limiting wider development of this market, the following can be singled out:

• The need to consolidate large shareholdings. In Russia the share capital (notwithstanding the trend toward concentration) still remains rather dispersed; even at the peak of market activity, in 1996–1997, no more than 5%–7% of shares in blue chip companies were bought and sold on the market.

• The structure of ownership within a corporation should be relatively clear and should remain fixed. In Russia in 1998–1999 the process of ownership rights redistribution once again intensified (simultaneously providing an incentive for takeovers).

• Insufficient liquid capital in case of financial crisis.

Nevertheless, the first hostile takeovers in Russia date back to the mid-1990s (see Radygin 1996). There was a well-known attempt (that ultimately failed) by Menatep Bank to take over confectionary factory Krasny Oktiabr through a public tender offer in the summer of 1995. In another well-known case, the holding company of Inkombank purchased a controlling interest in the confectionary company Babayevskoye. Many of the largest banks (financial groups) and portfolio investment funds engaged in takeovers of companies in completely different branches of industry for their subsequent resale to nonresidents and strategic investors. In 1997–1998 the food industry once again saw takeovers of regional beer brewing companies by the Baltika group; takeovers also occurred in the pharmaceutical and tobacco industries and in consumer goods production companies.

An interesting example of a takeover attempt was the conflict between Gazprom and ONEXIMbank, the international financial corporation of the Renaissance group, in 1997. The latter was intensely buying up stock and hunting for voting proxies in order to participate in the general meeting of Gazprom's board. The objective of the group was to get one out of the eleven seats on the board of directors of Gazprom, since at that time one seat practically equalled a blocking vote (the rest were divided equally between Gazprom and the state). Nevertheless, this attempted takeover failed, and the group had to retreat.

According to some estimates, the postcrisis financial situation of 1999–2000 may accelerate the tempo of mergers and takeovers in those sectors of the economy that were susceptible to takeover even before the crisis. These are chiefly the food and pharmaceutical industries, ferrous and nonferrous metals, cellular telephone communications, and the banking sector (Kamstra 1998).

The following features of this potential process can be singled out:

• A significant stepping up of these developments in the branches, where takeovers do not require a serious concentration of financial resources, can be expected.

• In the takeover policy, major emphasis should be placed on companies that are relatively cheap today and that may strengthen the buyers' independence from the environment.

• A high degree of rationalization of these processes is to be encouraged (as opposed to the general precrisis policy of taking over any potentially profitable entities).

• There is the possibility of an increasing number of international mergers and takeovers due to the low share prices and financial problems of Russian companies in the situation of financial crisis.

• Opposition from regional authorities can be expected when the "aggressors" are not connected to the local-regional elites.

• Favorable incentives (the threat of hostile takeovers) may appear for whole branches to streamline the structure of their share capital.

15.7. Existing Instruments of Corporate Governance in State-Owned Enterprises and Their Effectiveness

As of November 1999, there were 13,786 unitary state-owned enterprises (SOEs) and 23,099 agencies in Russia. The Russian Federation is a participant (shareholder), having over 25% interest in the charter capital of 2,500 joint-stock companies representing basic sectors of the national economy (including 382 joint-stock companies in which the state has 100% interest, 470 joint-stock companies in which the state has over 50% interest, and 1,601 joint-stock companies in which the state has 25%–50% interest). In addition, the state has a "golden share" in 580 joint-stock companies.

Blocks of shares in 697 joint-stock companies producing goods and services of strategic importance for national security (the list of such joint-stock companies was approved by RF government decision No. 784 of 17 July 1998, "On the List of Joint-Stock Companies Producing Products (Goods, Services) of Strategic Importance for Ensuring National Security, Shares in Which Fixed in the State Ownership Are Not Subject to Anticipatory Sale") were fixed in federal ownership. According to other acts, shares in 847 joint-stock companies are fixed in the RF's ownership.

Dividends on federally owned blocks of shares amounted to Rb 574.6 million in 1998, Rb 270.7 million in 1997, Rb 118 million in 1996, and Rb 115 million in 1995 (in 1998 prices).

It is impossible to analyze in detail here all the aspects of managing the state's property. The section that follows is limited to a short survey of existing instruments and an appraisal of their effectiveness.[9]

As the major element of the state policy in this area, the *institution of state representatives* may be singled out. Presidential decree No. 1200 of 10 June 1994, "On Some Measures for Ensuring State Management of the Economy," envisioned (1) framework requirements applicable to contracts between the government (a federal agency) and the chief executive officer of a federal SOE, and (2) framework requirements applicable to private individuals representing state interests in joint-stock companies. These representatives were divided into two categories: government officials, and other RF citizens (working on contract to represent the state's interests in joint-stock companies).

At present there are about 2,000 state representatives, of whom 92% are officials of federal executive bodies and 8% are officials of different agencies. In only a few cases were professional managers invited to manage state-owned blocks of shares. The major reasons

---

9. See also "Papers of the All-Russian Conference 'On the System of Managing State Property in the Russian Federation'" (photocopy, November 1999).

behind this fact include that the state pays irregularly for services and has a complicated mechanism for transferring blocks of shares held in trust.

Available appraisals indicate that the institution of state representatives is ineffective, for the following reasons: simultaneous common representation in several joint-stock companies, lack of expertise, lack of material (legal) incentives, lack of clear (contractual) aims of representation, lack of mechanisms of property accountability aimed at lowering risks for the state, lack of reports on the situations of joint-stock companies, lack of approved decisions, and so on. However, the same requirements are applied to joint-stock companies with a different proportion of state shares, although the degree of the state's influence is unequal.[10]

The experience of federal shareholdings management in 1993–1996 proved that officials are incapable of effectively managing shareholdings in five to ten joint-stock companies located in different regions and often operating in different sectors of the economy. It is not only technical and time considerations but also the lack of necessary qualifications (primarily knowledge of the specific enterprises) and lack of material incentives that prevent such management from being effective. To illustrate the dimensions of the problem, two of the most common types of behavior found among state representatives in joint-stock companies are the following:

1. "Indifferent behavior": State representatives to joint-stock companies show no interest in the companies, despite the state having controlling stakes and the companies sometimes being major budget debtors. In fact, such a position allots joint-stock company management an absolutely free hand.

2. "Self-interested behavior": Officials intentionally ignore joint-stock companies' debts to the government during their tenure as

---

10. The dilution of state-owned blocks of shares approved by state representatives inflicted considerable losses on the state budget. According to various estimates, the dilution of federal shareholdings led to losses for the state to the tune of hundreds of billions of rubles. It happened at a number of strategically important enterprises for ensuring national security: at joint-stock companies NII Delta (from 25.5% to 17%) and Irkutskoye Aviatsionnoye PO (from 25.5% to 14.5%) in 1996, and at joint-stock company Permskiye Motory (from 14.25% to 6.7%) in 1997. Of course, in a few instances state representatives actively influenced the behavior of respective enterprises. For instance, they initiated the resignations of CEOs who were responsible for wage and budgetary payment arrears at twenty-two joint-stock companies across different sectors.

state representatives and as a payback receive highly paid jobs at these joint-stock companies later on; and officials vote on behalf of the state at shareholder meetings of joint-stock companies for secondary share issues, as a result of which the state's proportional holdings are significantly reduced.

The shareholdings that are still held in state property funds and that for some reason have not been sold tend to become the object of bargaining between the fund, the management, and other interested parties. The fund itself or state representatives to joint-stock companies typically do not have a position concerning the management of specific enterprises.

Among the instruments the state used selectively or on a limited basis in 1992–1999 were the following:

• Individual arrangements with strategically important entities (for instance, a personal trust agreement concerning 35% of state-owned shares in Gazprom)

• Installing boards of state representatives at the largest holdings

• "Strengthening" enterprises (holdings) with state participation by contributing to their charter capitals state-owned blocks of shares in other enterprises (coal joint-stock companies, Svyazinvest)

• The transfer of state-owned blocks of shares in trust (oil, coal, electric power engineering in 1992; general "Rules of Transferring Blocks of Shares Fixed in the Federal Ownership in the Process of Privatization in Trust, and on Concluding Trust Contracts for These Shares," promulgated in 1997–1998)

• The transfer of blocks of shares in trust of managing (central) financial-industrial group companies, or in the management of holding companies (FIG Ruskhim, Russian joint-stock company Biopreparat, Nosta-Gaz-Truby, joint-stock company Rosmyasmoltorg, special construction)

• Personal appointments to boards of directors by a decision of the RF government or on instruction from the President (Gazprom, Norilsk Nikel, oil companies)

• Allowing the order of voting at shareholders' meetings to be determined by state-controlled blocks of shares (for oil companies, by RF governmental decisions; for Russian joint-stock companies EES Rossii and Rosgazifikatsia, by the decision of state representatives' boards)

Corporate Governance Mechanisms in Russia 489

• "Re-attestation" of state representatives and investigation of instances when federal blocks of shares were diluted

Currently, the main complaints of the state as a shareholder about the operations of these joint-stock companies coincide with the complaints of other categories of shareholders. The major complaints include the following:

• Lack of transparency, both for ordinary shareholders and for the state.

• Without their consent, outside shareholders in joint-stock companies see their share reduced by additional issuances of shares in favor of inside investors.

• Tangible and financial assets are transferred from parent to daughter companies (the daughter companies as a rule are controlled by managers) or to companies connected to them.

At *unitary SOEs* (including "quasiholdings" controlling daughter unitary enterprises), there are specific problems of management:

• There is no complete register of unitary enterprises with information on their assets and the major results of their financial and economic operations.

• The number of unitary enterprises exceeds the state's ability to manage them and to control their operations.

• Clear criteria concerning the functioning of unitary enterprises are lacking.

• The major lines of business of unitary enterprises do not always coincide with or complement the state's interests (many of them retain their status because their property is insufficiently liquid for privatization).

• Functions concerning the management and regulation of unitary enterprises are not clearly divided between different federal executive bodies.

• A number of unitary enterprises created before the Civil Code became effective are not in line with current legislation in organizational and legal terms.

• No contracts were concluded with a majority of the chief executive officers of unitary enterprises. The contracts in force do not include the terms of the CEO's accountability. Whereas labor legislation effectively protects the rights of CEOs, it creates considerable difficulty in applying measures making CEOs responsible for the results of enterprises' operations.

- The legal construction of full economic jurisdiction grants to its subjects (in reality, the CEOs of enterprises) broad authority in regard to ownership rights, including the independent management of financial flows and utilization of profits,[11] while the authority of the owner is exhaustively detailed.

- No mandatory regular audits are envisioned, which makes it more difficult to control their financial and economic operations.

In practice, the broad authority of CEOs of unitary state-owned enterprises (particularly in the situation in which the state lacks effective means of managing and controlling the enterprises and incentives for the CEOs are generally of their own devising) results in the redirection of some financial flows to satellite firms, as well as in insider deals in the CEO's interests, and in loss of budget revenue. In this connection, it is not surprising that the law *On State- and Municipally-Owned Enterprises in the RF*, which was intended to amend the respective provisions of the Civil Code, has not yet been approved.

When the new privatization law (Article 20) was adopted in 1997, it was expected that unitary SOEs would be reorganized as joint-stock companies, with 100% of shares transferred to state (municipal) ownership. Via this instrument, the state would enjoy an additional opportunity to sell certain property, although that situation would remain hypothetical should unitary enterprises preserve their right of "full economic jurisdiction."

The situation we have outlined with respect to SOEs clearly shows the desirability of achieving positive changes in the system of managing the property owned by the state, within the framework of a comprehensive reform of the system of managing state property at large.[12] The political and economic constraints on such a reform program are also well-known.

---

11. Government officials' lack of interest in settling this question officially (in the framework of the charter) should be included among the reasons for uncontrolled utilization of profits. This right was granted to them by Articles 294 and 295 of the RF Civil Code, which stipulate that the owner has the right to receive a share of the profits.

12. Certain measures are envisioned in "Concept of Managing State Property and Privatization in the Russian Federation" (approved by RF government decision No. 1024 on 9 September 1999). See also Chapter 12.

15.8. State-Owned Holdings and Financial-Industrial Groups

Integrative processes in Russia are driven by the desire for stability in business relations and by the desire to increase the business's economic importance, thus ensuring survival both through the mutual support of business associates and through the inevitable state subsidization. This is particularly important, given the uncertainty of the market in its formative phase. The process of financial-industrial integration, despite its contradictions and negative aspects, should be viewed as an important element in the postcommunist transformation of the Russian economy. At the same time, however, many holdings and financial-industrial groups (FIGs) are artificial, political creations and are not effective from an economic perspective.

The establishment, functioning, and legal regulatory procedures of holding structures in the Russian economy are among the least developed economic matters. The first holding structures in modern Russia were established in the 1980s and 1990s.[13] They can be divided into four large groups, according to origin:

• Pseudoholdings, which were created on the basis of the former USSR's and Russia's ministries and government agencies, follow the interests of high-ranking authorities. These holdings initially emerged as various concerns, unions, and associations (with such distinctive features as a vague system of ownership relations, a high level of management centralization, and low efficiency of management—the latter something they inherited from the former bureaucratic structures).[14]

• Industrial holdings, which were created voluntarily either (1) in the process of developing horizontal links between SOEs (with an initially low level of management centralization, which grew in the course of capital concentration, and scarce capital as their distinctive features), or (2) on the basis of state-owned (industrial and/or re-

---

13. See, for example, Radygin (1992, 1995).
14. The first well-known example of a pseudoholding in the form of joint-stock company (a closed type of joint-stock company) on the basis of a ministry is Avtoselkhozmash Holding, established in October 1991. The company was headed by the former minister. That structure was characterized by all of the typical legal collisions of that time: the holding comprised state-owned enterprises of the whole former USSR, the enterprises had a right to acquire the holding's stocks, the holding was prohibited from possessing the enterprises' assets, and so forth. On the whole, by early 1992 there were approximately 3,100 associations, 227 concerns, 189 unions, and 123 consortiums in Russia.

search) associations, or (3) in the course of separating structural subdivisions.

• Combined (production-finance-trading) holdings, which were established in particular under large SOEs (and where a strict "mother company-daughter company" relationship is characteristic).

• Banking, financial, and exchange holdings (characterized by attempts to optimize control over accumulated capital).

The emergence of classic "combined" holdings (that is, holdings characterized by the combination of production activity plus control over the daughter companies) distinctly coincided with the incorporation and privatization of enterprises after 1992. Financial holdings ("pure" in the classic sense: they participate only in joint-stock capital) began to emerge in Russia after mass privatization. Until the 1998 crisis, they were characteristic of the organization of banks' expansion to the real sector.

The emergence of holdings, like the emergence of other forms of corporate ties, can be traced to the disintegration of the Soviet economic system after the collapse of the USSR, the liquidation of sectoral management in the national industry, and the cessation of subsidization of the real sector from the state budget. Those factors resulted in broken links in production, an imbalance in the activities that take place over a product's life cycle (research and development, production, marketing, sales), and a crisis in enterprises' finances.

As was mentioned earlier, the former ministries (or their departments) are also maintained in a form of holding, which is why holding is often perceived as a modified element of the administrative system of state governance. At the same time, the main reason for the emergence of holdings in Russia was the protective reaction of enterprises to the dissolution of their accustomed environment and previously established links.

The general advantages of a holding structure are well-known. They include: (1) the possibility of exercising control over capital that substantially exceeds the mother company's capital; (2) securing the necessary conditions for the vertical (and horizontal) integration of enterprises; (3) economizing on trade operations; (4) price control; (5) consolidating the financial reporting of enterprises for taxation purposes; (6) optimizing production capacities; (7) centralizing participation in other companies' capital; (8) penetrating commodity markets; (9) optimizing large companies' strategy, finance, and governance; (10) manipulating the prices of the mother and daughter companies' stocks; (11) eliminating destructive competition; (12) the possibility of establishing a relationship between the holding's subsidiaries as legal entities; (13) maintaining the daughter companies' formal independence to buttress their managers' prestige; and (14) increasing the immunity to external factors.

Nevertheless, not all enterprises favor being incorporated into holding structures, private or mixed. The data available on Russian corporations' ownership structure for the period 1994 through 1999 show an extremely low share of holdings in the authorized capital of "standard" Russian corporations (Radygin 1996, 1999). According to a 1996 survey of 160 enterprises, only 11% reported the attractiveness of holding structures (Vinslav 1996). For some, that is related to the lack of capital to acquire stakes, while others either are reluctant to become a daughter company or encounter difficulties in the course of registering with several government agencies. The majority of enterprises are focused on a "softer" form of cooperation. Holding as a form of relationship between enterprises is most characteristic of those enterprises that (1) find themselves in the "stabilization" or "growth" phase and (2) are industries with relatively high profits or clear vertical integration patterns.

It should also be noted that the formation of holding structures may be motivated by a number of considerations: control over financial flows, control and redistribution of state property, capital resources, political and budgetary interests of federal and regional authorities, and so on. These considerations also apply to the formation of state-owned holdings (SOHs).

Here we consider the main types of SOH that emerged in the country during the 1990s.[15]

1. The first type of SOHs were created simply by the transformation of SOEs into joint-stock companies without any preliminary reorganization or compulsory integration into larger structures. Their control (large) stake was fixed as government property (see Section 3 of this chapter for the statistics). In this group we can also include companies whose authorized capital included a "golden share" (which provided the government with possibilities to influence the joint-stock company's activities) and joint-stock companies in which the government owned the remaining stake. The holdings were

---

15. See also IET (1998).

formed spontaneously, by separating subdivisions of the mother company and acquiring daughter companies.

2. The second type of holding structure is represented by the largest companies, mostly monopolies, which were established by special decisions. The first of these became Russian joint-stock companies UES Russia and Gazprom, which were created as early as autumn of 1992. Their authorized capital was established with the total amount of capital (assets) of their industries in total (in this case, the largest producers of electric power and gas), plus controlling stakes in their daughter joint-stock companies. For all of those companies, Gazprom and UES Russia have become powerful holding companies.

Among the key corporate governance problems of the electric power holding UES Russia are the holding's control over regional companies and its relationship with local authorities. During the 1990s, many daughter companies of the holding became notorious for abrogating shareholders' rights. For example, some daughter companies required that an increase in a shareholder's stake by over 1% of voting shares first had to pass the preliminary consent of the board of directors—an illegal and discriminatory provision. Another example was the attempt made in 1998 to restrict foreign shareholders' share of a holding to 25%, through the introduction of new legislation. However, in October 1998 UES Russia attempted to remedy matters by proposing changes to the charters of forty-five (out of more than eighty) daughter regional companies that would bring them into line with the law *On Joint-Stock Companies*.

In 1998–1999, because of anticipated difficulties with domestic gas supplies, power plants' transition to coal fuel became an urgent matter. Projects were developed to create energy power–coal companies by integrating enterprises in the electric power sector and coal-mining companies (to date, only in those regions where coal is produced by open mining). The first company of this type was LuTEK (in Primorsky krai, currently in operation); BurTEK (Byryatia) and UralTEK (Chelyabinsk oblast) are in the planning stages. Projects to establish power-metallurgical companies (such as the merger of the Sayano-Shushenskaya hydroelectric power plant with Sibirsky Aluminum) are also being considered.

As for Gazprom, entrenched management successfully lobbied for a number of measures that would benefit management at the cost of the state and minority shareholders:

- On 20 January 1999, the State Duma passed in a second reading the law, *On Gas Supplies in the RF*. In particular, the law fixes the blocking share of the holding (25% plus one share) in the state's ownership, provided that the share of nonresidents is 25% minus one share (versus the 9% stipulated by presidential decree No. 529 of 28 May 1997). That provision of the 20 January 1999 law unquestionably maximizes the interests of Gazprom's managers: the smaller the state's share in an SOH, the less effective is the government's pressure on the board of directors, given that other shareholders are affiliated, controlled, dispersed, or are strategic partners of the parent company. Furthermore, statute 15 of the law prohibits division of the "single system of gas supplies," which implies that any reform of Gazprom as a natural monopoly is legally impossible.[16]
- Some sources note that by way of applying additional political pressure (against attempts to change top management and impose reorganization), Gazprom considered selling part of the stake controlled by the RJSC and using the funds for the pre-election campaign (according to some estimates, Gazprom's management controls ca. 7% of the company's stake, yet 15% is controlled by the parent company itself).
- Management successfully blocked in the State Duma passage of amendments to the law *On Joint-Stock Companies* that would have changed corporate governance procedures in favor of minority shareholders.

The process of institutional transformation in the oil sector started with the establishment of single oil-extracting corporations and their privatization in 1992–1993. Then the state-owned blocks of shares were accumulated in the respective holdings, and between 1995 and 1997 the newly established structures were privatized. Since then their authorized capital has consisted of several controlling blocks of enterprises. These enterprises were incorporated into those amalgamations. A similar process occurred with stakes in oil-refining and other related companies. The largest oil companies (Lukoil, YUKOS, Surgutneftegas), oil transportation companies (Transneft), and companies that transport petroleum derivatives (Transnefteproduct)

---

16. Nonetheless, in 1999, Gazprom's seventeen daughter companies were transformed into joint-stock companies with their own financial reporting and all nonprofile structures eliminated. It is envisioned that this reorganization will meet the World Bank's requirement of transparency.

occupied a special position vis-à-vis other structures. Their distinctive feature was that their authorized capital consisted of controlling stakes in joint-stock companies that had been created in the course of amalgamation.

Buyers during the "second wave" of privatization, who obtained a majority control over holdings, inevitably entered into conflict with the minority shareholders, who were buyers of the "first wave." According to some estimates, such conflicts delayed the appearance of "efficient owners" in the oil sector for at least three years. (Lukoil, which adopted the single share in 1995, was an exception.) The conflict between the "two privatizations" became one of the symbols of the corporate wars of 1997–1999 and a permanent source of economic destabilization.

By 1999, the majority of the SOHs had been privatized. Some oil companies have undergone numerous structural changes as a result of organizational and legal reorganizations and the realignment of "influences" as a consequence of multilateral lobbying. Typically, stakes in single enterprises that were fixed in the government's ownership were transferred from one company to another. In addition, there were some well-known instances of attempts to change some companies' management that were dictated by financial and political interests (Gazprom and Transneft in 1999).

3. The third type of state-owned holding structure consists of state-owned enterprises (companies) that were established for the specific purpose of governing the stakes (fixed in the state's ownership) of some industries' amalgamations and enterprises. Such state-owned companies, although not formally capital owners (as Gazprom's), were designated to exercise, on behalf of the government, the functions of holding companies in respect to those joint-stock companies in which the government had a stake. At the same time, the companies were required to carry out the provisions of state support for enterprises and to implement industrial policy. Examples of such companies are Rosneft (in addition to the said tasks, the company also sells the state's share of hydrocarbons received according to the production-sharing agreements and is the general commissioner of research and development); Rosugol (which also distributes budget funds to support the subsidized coal-mining industry, mine construction, and the production of equipment); and Roslesprom.

In 1995, Rosneft became a vertically integrated oil company in the form of an OJSC. The company's authorized capital was established on the basis of thirty-two companies' stakes fixed in federal ownership, and Rosneft was entrusted with the government's stake in ninety-eight additional companies. At the same time, Rosneft became a symbol of the failure of the "cash privatization" policy of 1998–1999. Rosugol also attained OJSC status, but the company was liquidated shortly thereafter.

4. Holdings with unitary SOEs' participation became a special kind of SOH structure. These holdings are established by special acts. An example is the OJSC Industrial Company Antei (a 51% stake is owned by the state). In the course of establishing the company, the participating SOEs and joint-stock companies were granted daughter company status.

Holdings in which unitary enterprises participate are not corporations per se. Created as a rule to maintain the research, industrial, and export potential in the metallurgical-industrial complex, they are used to achieve a certain level of competitive strength. In organizational terms, such structures are created as follows: the parent enterprise of the "corporation" is granted the ownership of the SOEs, which become daughter unitary enterprises. Simultaneously, blocks of shares in joint-stock companies that are part of a production chain and are temporarily owned by the state are transferred to the parent enterprise.

The idea of the sectoral organization as a few state-owned concerns dominates the metallurgical-industrial complex at present. In 1999 a first step in this direction may become the merger (and issuance of common shares) of two existing holdings producing military aircraft, VPK MAPO (part of which is ANPK MIG) and AVPK Sukhoi. At the end of June of 1999, the RF government approved the merger of the ANTK (named after A. N. Tupolev) and Aviastar (Ulianovsk); the state's share in the new holding was 50% plus one share. Another holding, interstate aircraft-construction company Ilyushin, was organized only in December 1998. At present, the Tashkent Aircraft Industrial Association is expected to join this organization. The creation and reorganization of holdings in this industry will likely go on for a long period of time.

5. An example of a "financial" SOH (and of an ineffective management strategy) was the formation of Rossiyskaya Metallurgia in 1995. The charter capital of this holding was formed of 10% blocks of shares in several Russian metallurgical joint-stock companies, including the largest integrated iron-and-steel works in Cherepovets,

Lipetsk, and Magnitogorsk, as well as in some other property (including a number of research institutes and centers).

These blocks of shares should have been transferred in the trust of the new joint-stock company, or purchased by selling 49% of the company itself, with 51% remaining in the ownership of the state. According to available appraisals, the real purpose for creating this holding was to prevent outside shareholders from buying blocks of shares. The liquidation of the holding in 1997 was yet another example of an ineffective privatization strategy (an attempt to sell 49% of the shares in the holding) in a situation in which a relatively formed ownership (control) structure already existed at the majority of the metallurgical enterprises.

Another example of a financial SOH is Svyazinvest, created for the mixed aims of preserving sectoral control and increasing budgetary revenues via privatization. First, regional communications companies were created and privatized (including Rostelekom), then controlling interests (38% of shares) were transferred to Svyazinvest. As a result, the principal problem Svyazinvest now faces is improving corporate governance in order to overcome trends toward disintegration and the possible sale of a block of shares in 2000. For instance, in order to strengthen control over the property transfer of daughter joint-stock companies to third parties, it has been suggested that representatives of the largest shareholders (beginning with the Mustcom Ltd. consortium) be included on the boards of directors of daughter regional electric communications companies. It is also possible that the most profitable lines of business will be amalgamated into special daughter companies.

In 1998–1999, the holding's shareholders also discussed the possibility of a merger of Svyazinvest with its daughter company Rostelekom, 50.67% of whose shares are owned by the holding. In 1999 the holding's charter was amended in favor of minority shareholders. (One amendment stipulated that appointment of the general director was to be approved by a three-quarters vote.) Other amendments implied that the issue of new shares in the daughter joint-stock companies was to be approved by the holding's board of directors. The creation of ten to fifteen large daughter companies based on existing regional companies was likewise discussed in 1999.

6. Another kind of SOH structure is represented by newly created companies with mixed capital and a certain amount of state investment. Such a structure can be created in several ways, but chiefly

(1) by implementing investment projects, real estate and equipment operations, and some commercial activities; and (2) privatizing an enterprise by contributing its property to the charter capital of other economic entities (there were two such cases in 1998).

7. Finally, an SOH can be formed by the contribution of state-owned property in financial-industrial groups. The law on FIGs does not set a quantitative limit on the share of state property in FIGs. Moreover, presidential decree No. 141 of 1 April 1996 allows FIG participants to contribute state-owned property to charter capitals of FIGs' central companies, to lease this property, and to mortgage it. Central FIG companies may be entrusted with state-owned blocks of shares.[17]

The common flaws of SOHs are well-known: a trend toward monopoly (oligopoly) behavior, additional costs for procedural questions and the audit of integrated companies, difficulty controlling the redistribution of resources (assets) and revenues, a trend toward politicization, bureaucratization, and so on. However, three points require special attention for a deeper understanding of the flaws of Russian holding structures:

• At the stage of initial and essentially noneconomic reorganization of the largest SOEs, there was no possibility of creating optimal market-oriented management structures aimed at economic efficiency.
• The chronic inability of public authorities to manage effectively is coupled with the general problems of corporate governance of, and control over, Russian corporations.
• There was general economic, financial, and political instability in the 1990s.

The combination of these factors resulted in two processes characteristic of the 1990s. The first was the permanent reorganization of holding structures (state-owned, private, mixed) accompanied by violations of property rights, a struggle for control, transfers of blocks of shares, and so on. In this process, economic effectiveness and rational management did not always hold sway. Here we should distinguish between the motives for reorganizing state and

---

17. The RF Goskomimuschestvo letter of 17 October 1994 states that FIG status is incompatible with holding company status. A holding company cannot be a FIG participant in case (1) tangible assets make less than 50% in the structure of its total assets and (2) the share of state-owned property in its charter capital exceeds 25%.

private holdings. Motives in the first case were dominated by political considerations, lobbying, different types of ownership transfers, budgetary considerations, IMF pressure, and corruption. Motives for reorganizing private holdings were dominated by an interest in optimizing management, an interest in mergers, the disposal of companies operating at a loss, banishing outside shareholders, expansion, tax avoidance, and export of capital. In reality, however, the two sets of motives are often interwoven.

The second result of the three factors listed above was the use of a holding scheme (including holdings with state participation) to serve the narrow interests of government officials and private interests and to place financial resources out of reach (through offshore holdings, the use of transfer prices, creating profit centers outside the formal SOH, infringing the rights of shareholders in holdings and daughter companies, and so on). The 1998 financial crisis further intensified these processes (see Radygin 1999).

By 2000, about 100 officially created holdings existed in Russia. In evaluating the entire process of creating holding structures, the compulsory integration dictated by the state can be considered justified in regard to the fuel and energy complex, some other industries (atomic power engineering, communications, the metallurgical-industrial complex, and other special enterprises (such as the Russian space company NPO Energia and aircraft holdings formed around major design offices).

This allowed the state to maintain formal control over the largest natural monopolies and some strategic industries. This fact prevented the disintegration of traditional economic relations and full degradation of unique R&D projects, and sustained the manageability of link "enterprise associations" in the framework of integrated industrial-technological complexes.

At the same time, there is some doubt over the degree to which the creation of state-owned holding companies in other sectors of the economy (construction, civil engineering, textile and light industries, wholesale trade) is justified during the transition to a market economy. As practical experience has shown, "voluntary" affiliation in holdings and the economic rationale for affiliation in terms of corporate management have not always been high on the list of considerations.

It should also be noted that the formation of new structures of this type may act to the detriment of the existing corporations, established ownership relations, and shareholders' rights. Redistribution of the ownership structure of the existing holdings is often dominated by political decisions. Thus, the importance of this trend depends heavily on the pragmatism and common sense of the executive authorities.

A principal problem with SOHs in Russia is that these structures are used for political interests (elections, the financing of certain political elites) and to influence crucial budgetary decisions. Such an approach, when combined with high levels of corruption, leads to general ineffectiveness of the state as an owner, and therefore poor maximization of available assets.

Russian legislation, even as it has elaborated certain concrete issues, does not provide a comprehensive framework for regulating holdings. It is obvious that approval of the law *On Holding Companies* (or considerable amendments to the law *On Competition*) will be necessary. Fragmented legislation, however, is not the only problem. From our point of view, the following interrelated issues must be addressed:

• The antimonopoly approach in registering transactions must be rejected. While we recognize the importance of ensuring competition, protecting shareholders' rights, including the rights of the state as a shareholder, is no less important. What is needed is a *more comprehensive* approach.

• Transparency of the holding in regard to its organization, financing, structure, and the information it disseminates must be improved.

• Stricter requirements regarding disclosure of information about ownership control are needed. This information should reveal affiliated and interwoven structures and detail their accountability.

• Regulation is needed to ensure control over the redistribution of resources (assets) and to clarify the actual results of holdings' operations, which may result in losses for participants.

• Taxation appropriate to the holdings' structures must be introduced and enforced.

In addition to comprehensive legislation on holdings, the following are also necessary:

• Serious reform in how state property is managed (to include a set of instruments, identification of entities to which these instruments shall be applied, and some means of enforcement)

- Transparency in privatization policies (in this case as an element of corporate governance)
- A transition from the system of "hierarchical bargaining" between the state and the largest SOHs to strict budgetary discipline
- Rejection of extra-economic motives in reorganizing, redistributing ownership, financing, and changing top management at SOHs

Many of these recommendations may seem trivial or naive in light of Russian realities. The overarching goal, however, is to place the development of the Russian economy securely on a global trajectory.

The first regulatory act covering FIGs was presidential decree No. 2096 of 5 December 1993, "On the Creation of Financial-Industrial Groups in the Russian Federation." Although formally catering to the interests of the *nomenklatura* and major branch and bank lobbyists, this decree was essentially an attempt to obstruct the process of FIG formation, which began during the mass privatization phase and amounted to spontaneous distribution of state property. The decree was also a reaction to the scheme proposed in August 1993 to create hundreds of giant FIGs in Russia by administrative means, encompassing the majority of enterprises in the industrial processing and extractive sectors, the chief aim of which was to reproduce the previous centralized system of economic management.

FIG operations are currently regulated by the law *On Financial-Industrial Groups* (signed by the president on 30 November 1995). According to Article 2, a FIG is defined as a collection of legal entities, functioning as parent with subsidiary companies, either wholly or partly integrated in terms of their material and intangible assets. Companies are permitted to participate in only one FIG officially registered in the state register. Subsidiary companies can only join a FIG together with the parent company. A key concept in the law is the "central company of the FIG," which is usually an investment institution but may also be a production company, association, or union. There are two main methods of creating a FIG:

1. According to the holding company model, which includes a "central company" with subsidiaries. This method is most commonly used for FIGs created by commercial banks and their subsidiary investment companies.

2. According to the FIG model, in which the "central company" is established by all members of the group, by signing an appropriate agreement.

The number of official FIGs has been growing: in 1993 there was only one FIG in Russia; in 1994 there were six; in 1995 there were twenty-one. At the beginning of 1998, seventy-two FIGs were registered in the state register (about 1,500 enterprises and organizations, and about 100 credit organizations).

The mechanisms for managing and monitoring enterprises in FIGs have not proved particularly effective. The hopes that they would facilitate the flow of investments from FIG financial institutions (primarily commercial banks, which many experts considered to be the "structure-forming" element of the FIG itself) have not been justified. Banks have shown themselves unwilling to submit to "intergroup discipline" and to invest in unprofitable projects. The most common motive for forming a FIG is to strengthen lobbying leverage, and consequently to benefit from preferential treatment. It is rather obvious, moreover, that despite attempts to observe antimonopoly law, many of the FIGs created have made the Russian economy more monopolistic.[18]

The technological benefits and economy of transaction costs achieved by the integration of enterprises work predominantly in the case of vertical integration. However, there are very few examples of vertically integrated FIGs, except for companies such as Lukoil, which are not officially registered as FIGs. Horizontal (sectoral) integration has primarily been a product of the monopolistic aspirations of those involved. The majority of FIGs have attempted, and evidently will continue to attempt, to create highly diversified holdings, uniting a number of enterprises that are individually powerful but that have weak synergies.

There are also examples of FIGs being used as a cover for attempts to prevent outside shareholders from gaining control over company operations. This has particularly been done by creating a more strictly hierarchical structure within already existing associations and concerns. Constituent enterprises tend to have their own "branch" banks and have no intention of cooperating with "alien" banks. These measures have not only obstructed the development of a competitive market and the free flow of capital in pursuit of investment opportunities; they have also, in some respects, preserved the old structural production patterns and hindered structural reform of the economy overall.

---

18. For details, see, for example, TACIS (November 1998).

According to available estimates, it is expected that in the near future, ten to twenty particularly powerful universal FIGs will emerge in Russia, along with 100 to 150 major groups, comparable in size to their foreign counterparts and together accounting for more than 50% of industrial production. However, state policy with regard to financial-industrial integration requires some correction, primarily to remove inefficient restrictions, to switch from permissive to required registration of FIGs, to renounce declarations concerning unrealistic privileges, and to strengthen monitoring of antimonopoly law observance in FIG formation.

Broadly speaking, the issue here has to do with developing organizational and managerial structures for the Russian economy. Although the most probable outcome is somewhere in between, here we highlight two polar scenarios:

- either there will be genuinely efficient associations of diverse economic units that (1) are created voluntarily or on the basis of mergers and takeovers, or (2) are based on genuinely effective management of shareholdings, or (3) are oriented to reducing their costs and increasing revenues through operations in a civilized marketplace; or

- in the next few years several dozen giant conglomerates and branch monopolies will emerge that enjoy "cozy" relations with the state and will succeed by virtue of these relations. This scenario could result in the revival of a form of centralized management of the economy but under rather different conditions.

15.9. Conclusion: New Institutional Reform for Long-Term Economic Growth

The most general conclusion that can be drawn from this study is that Russia is not an exception to the rules of transitional economics. There is no unique path in this transitional process. All more or less typical trends accompanying the emergence of the corporate control and governance model, including the struggle for ownership, apply in one way or another to Russia as well. We believe that Russia, all its problems notwithstanding, is among the pioneers and, compared to some other transitional countries, has made significant progress in this field.

With regard to further objectives in the formation and regulation of the national model of corporate governance, we suggest very simply that there are neither special obstacles to nor special recipes for the formation and emergence of such a national model. All of the transition economies have encountered most of the problems Russia has faced. Both the problems and the means of their resolution are well-known. The formation of a national model of corporate governance presumes that it is necessary (first of all for the state) "only" to recognize the *need* for the following preconditions to be satisfied:

• Understanding the special role of the state (as a "creative destroyer") in a transition economy

• Understanding the long duration of this process, roughly comparable to the duration of the transition period itself

• The exercise of political will in developing and enforcing efficient legislation to screen the interests of special groups (political, populist, criminal)

• The need not for radical interventions, but for the daily regulatory operation of a single body capable of pursuing a rigid centralized policy

In many countries undergoing economic transition, privatization did not result in any sizable enterprise investment. This places greater pressure on corporate governance practices. However, in the legislation of many countries the necessary mechanisms have not been sufficiently developed yet. The problems that need to be addressed by such mechanisms are those we have discussed: how additional shares are to be issued, the problem of transparency, ensuring that different categories of shareholders are protected, and so on.

In the short term, speculative portfolio investments, which drove the market in 1996 and 1997, are unlikely to retain their previous allure. However, it would be a mistake to ignore the potential for market development through portfolio investments. The problem is not the lack of prospects for this type of investment but whether these financial resources can be directed for the benefit of developing the national economy, while at the same time being secure. It is precisely portfolio investments that are paving the way for the emergence of direct investment funds and the participation of long-term conservative investors. Considerable household resources, which at the moment are outside of the economic turnover, are another substantial source of portfolio investment.

In a study of efficiency in ten sectors of the Russian economy conducted in 1998 and 1999 by the McKinsey Company (with the participation of Nobel prize laureate R. Solow), the key conclusion was that the working efficiency of the Russian economy is unrelated to profitability. Medium-sized enterprises are not interested in restructuring and increasing productivity; more productive enterprises lose out to less productive ones and have no incentives to invest (even with opportunities to do so).[19] This phenomenon is based on the unequal conditions under which they must function (compete): different rates and schedules of taxation; different tariffs on energy resources; different debt requirements; unequal administrative requirements and access to export; inequality in legal terms; local authorities' resistance to restructuring (the problem of social tension); unequal access to land and state procurement orders; unequal access to economic information; corruption, and so forth.

However, the situation is not desperate; at least no purely economic obstacles that could prevent economic growth (up to 8% annually, with a consequent twofold increase in per-capita GDP) were uncovered by the McKinsey study. Moreover, it was noted that 75% of Soviet enterprises created before 1992 would be viable if they were restructured and modern management systems were introduced. Renewing those companies could bring about a growth in production of 40% on average if spot investments were made at less than 5% of GDP over five years (about $7.5 billion at the exchange rate of early 2000—considerably less than the investment requirements of Russia as claimed, for instance, by the Ministry of the Economy). In other words, the principal conclusion was that economic growth, at least in its initial stage, should be based not on very large investment (understood by many as a hard-to-reach panacea, and often as a self-sufficing goal) but on tough and to a considerable degree political efforts to create a generally favorable environment for the operation of enterprises.

These conclusions are important to determining the future path for reform of the Russian economy. The institutional climate necessary

---

19. In 1997 labor productivity in Russian industry was 17% of the US figure, whereas in 1991 it was 30%. Although productivity fell by 50%, employment decreased by a mere 10%.

to attract investment mandates renewed emphasis on appropriate and comprehensive legislation, protection of ownership rights, equal access to financial markets, equal terms of competition, and enforcement of legislation. The paltry achievements of Russia in this field in the 1990s were the most serious breakthrough for long-term economic growth.

At the same time, in modern Russia the external mechanisms of corporate governance, such as the control exercised through the financial markets and the institutions of takeover, merger, and bankruptcy, do not work. Such a situation is typical both for countries with a concentrated ownership structure and for those with an amorphous (nontransparent) structure of corporate control. This means that active control by shareholders (by voting) should become the predominant form of corporate control (as opposed to passive control through the sale of shares). This also creates a special burden for external (legislative) and internal (boards of directors) mechanisms of corporate control. The problems of enforcement become especially relevant.

It should be noted that the increasing instability in the arena of property rights following the August 1998 crisis led to the conservation of an unstable and intermediate corporate governance model in Russia, and this model will probably remain in place at least for the medium term. In this context, there is currently no alternative to the development of legal mechanisms of corporate governance and their enforcement in the medium run.

The fact that during the 1990s Russia moved toward market economy institutions and democratic values is undeniable. At the same time, besides periodic financial crises, "investment hunger," and regular scandals about the property-immanent features of this movement, we cannot ignore the chronic incompleteness of institutional reforms; the system of soft budget constraints and hierarchic bargaining between the state and large corporations; the stages of property redistribution following one another; the absolute insecurity of ownership rights; noncompliance with contracted terms; inefficiency and corruption of the system of state authority; state enforcement as a measure of selective influence; and private enforcement as a variant of the criminal fight to sort things out.

The progress achieved in certain important areas—and here we note the progressive corporate legislation after 1996, a potentially effective bankruptcy mechanism in place since 1998, a system for regulating the corporate securities market, and antimonopoly legislation in place since 1998—was limited by all sorts of constraints, and therefore these mechanisms could not function as intended and needed. This situation became patently obvious by early 2000. Most of the institutional reforms adopted in the second half of the 1990s exist on paper only. Russia must either accept this legacy of the 1990s or prepare for a new stage of tough institutional reforms.

Progress in surmounting these problems depends to a considerable degree on the volumes, efficiency, and intensity of the institutional regulation. In the wake of the financial crisis, and with the country in a new stage of the redistribution of ownership rights, activities to protect investors' rights must be sharply stepped up to restore the investment attractiveness of the country. It scarcely needs mentioning that a real change can be achieved only in conjunction with other macroeconomic and institutional changes.

Bibliography

Aghion, P., and J. Tirole. 1996. "Real and Formal Authority in Organizations." *Journal of Political Economy* 105: 1–29.

Alchian, A. A., and H. Demsetz. 1972. "Production, Information Costs, and Economic Organization." *American Economic Review* 62 (no. 6): 777–95.

Andreeff, W. 1995. "Le controle des enterprises privatisees dans les economies en transition: Une approache theorique." *Revue Économique* 46 (no. 3).

Aktsionernoye obschestvo i tovarischestvo s ogranichennoi otvestvennost'yu: sbornik zarubezhnovo zakondatel'stva. V. A. Tumanov, Managing Editor. 1999. Moscow: BEK.

Berle, A. A., and G. C. Means. 1932. *The Modern Corporation and Private Property.* New York: Macmillan.

Black, B. S., R. Kraakman, and J. Hay. 1996. "Corporate Law from Scratch." Pp. 245–302 in *Corporate Governance in Central Europe and Russia,* edited by R. Frydman, C. W. Gray, and A. Rapaczynski. Vol. 2, *Insiders and the State.* Central European University Press.

Black, B. S., R. Kraakman, and A. Tarasova. 1997. "Kommentari federal'novo zakona ob aktsionernykh obschestvakh." Manuscript.

Böhm, A., ed. 1997. *Economic Transition Report 1996.* Ljubljana: CEEPN.

Charkham, J. 1994. *Keeping Good Company: A Study of Corporate Governance in Five Countries.* Oxford, England: Clarendon Press.

Clark, R. C. 1986. *Corporate Law.* Boston: Little, Brown & Co.

Coffee, J. C. 1988. *Shareholders Versus Managers.* Oxford, England: Oxford University Press.

Demsetz, H., and K. Lehn. 1985. "The Structure of Corporate Ownership: Causes and Consquences." *Journal of Political Economy* 93: 1155–77.

Entov, R. M. 1999. *Korporativnoye upravleniye: teoreticheskiye i empiricheskiye obsledovaniya.* Mimeo, Moscow.

European Bank for Research and Development (EBRD). 1997. *Transition Report 1997: Enterprise Performance and Growth.* London: EBRD.

———. 1998. *Transition Report 1998: Financial Sector in Transition.* London: EBRD.

FKTsB. 1997. "Razvitiye rynka tsennykh bumag v Rossii." Moscow: Federal'naya kommissiya po rynku tsennykh bumag.

———. 1998. "Godovoi otchet za 1997 god." Moscow: Federal'naya kommissiya po rynku tsennykh bumag.

———. 1999. "Godovoi otchet za 1998 god." Moscow: Federal'naya kommissiya po rynku tsennykh bumag.

Goskomstat RF. 1999. "Sotsial'no-ekonomicheskoye polozheniye Rossii—1998 god." Moscow.

Gray, C. H., and R. G. Hanson. 1994. "Korporativnoye otnosheniya v Tsentral'noi i Vostochnoi Evrope: uroki rynochnoi eknomiki razvitykh stran." P. 1.3 in *Korporativnoye upravleniye i prava aktsionerov* (Russian edition). Moscow.

Hart, O. D. 1995. "Corporate Governance: Some Theory and Implications." *The Economic Journal* 105 (no. 430): 678–89.

Hirschman, A. O. 1970. *Exit, Voice, and Loyalty: Response to Decline in Firms, Organizations, and States.* Cambridge, Mass.: Harvard University Press.

IEPPP/IET. 1998. "Ekonomika perekhodnovo perioda." Moscow.

IET. 1992–1999. Annual Reports on the Russian Economy: Trends and Prospects. Moscow: IET.

IMEMO et al. 1999. "Zaschita prav aktsionerov v rossiskom biznese." Materialy konferentsii. Moscow, October 1999.

Kamstra, M. 1998. Makroekonomicheskiye faktory integratsii kompaniy. *Ekspert,* 16 November, no. 46, p. 24.

Khoroshev, S. 1998. "Reforma sobstvennosti." *Zhurnal dlya aktsionerov* 2: 44–46.

Kommentari k zakonu RF "O nesostoyatel'nosti (bankrotstve)." 1998. Moscow.

Latynina, Yu. 1998. "Modernizatsiya bol'shoi dubinki." *Ekspert,* 27 April, no. 16, pp. 10–12.

Lyapina, S. 1998. "Sliyaniya i pogloscheniya: priznak razvitoi rynochnoi ekonomiki." *Rynok tsennykh bumag* 8: 17–20.

Monks, R., and N. Minow. 1995. *Corporate Governance.* London: Blackwell.

North, D., and R. Thomas. 1973. *The Rise of the Western World.* Cambridge, England: Cambridge University Press.

OECD. 1998a. *Capital Market Development in Transition Economies: Country Experience and Policies for the Future.* Paris: OECD.

———. 1998b. *Corporate Governance: Improving Competitiveness and Access to Capital in Global Markets*. A Report to the OECD by the Business Sector Advisory Group on Corporate Governance. Paris: OECD.

———. 1998c. "General Principles of Company Law in Transition Economies." *Private Sector Development Journal* Suppl. 1.

———. 1999. *Principles of Corporate Governance*. Paris: OECD.

Prentice, D., and P. Holland. 1993. *Contemporary Issues in Corporate Governance*. Oxford, England: Clarendon Press.

Radygin, A. 1992. "Spontaneous Privatization: Motivations, Forms, and Stages." *Studies on Soviet Economics* 3 (no. 5): 341–7.

———. 1994. *Reforma sobstvennosti v Rossii: na puti iz proshlovo v buduschee*. Moscow: Respublika.

———. 1995. *Privatisation in Russia: Hard Choices, First Results, New Targets*. London: CRCE–Jarvis Print Group.

———. 1996. *Securities Markets Development and Its Relationship to Corporate Governance in Russia*. Paris: OECD, DAFFE/MC/EW 96-25.

———. 1998. "Corporate Securities Market Development in Russia." Pp. 161–88 in *Capital Market Development in Transition Economies: Country Experience and Policies for the Future*. Paris: OECD.

———. 1999. "Ownership and Control in Russian Industry." Presented at an OECD/World Bank Global Corporate Governance Forum, Paris.

Radygin, A., and R. Entov. 1999. *Institutsional'nye problemy razvitiya korporativnogo sektora: sobstvennost', kontrol', rynok tsennykh bumag* (Institutional Issues of Corporate Sector Development: Ownership, Control, Securities Market). Moscow: IEPP.

Stiglitz, J. E. 1994. *Whither Socialism?* Cambridge, Mass.: MIT Press.

TACIS. 1998 (November). "Financial Industrial Groups." Obzorny otchet. Moscow: TACIS.

Thiel, E. 1998. "The Development of Securities Markets in Transition Economies—Policy Issues and Country Experience." Pp. 13–36 in *Capital Market Development in Transition Economies. Country Experience and Policies for the Future*. Paris: OECD, 1998.

Tirole, J. 1999. "Corporate Governance." CEPR Discussion Paper no. 2086. London.

Tobin, J. 1984. "On the Efficiency of the Financial System." *Lloyds Bank Review* 153: 1–15.

Vinslav, Y. 1997. "Gosydarstvenuoye Rogueirovanie i proektikovanie karporativnykh structur." *Rossiyskiy Economicheskiy Journal* 9.

Volkov, A., T. Gurova, and V. Titov. 1999. "Sanitary i marodery." *Ekspert*, 1 March, no. 8, pp. 18–25.

Williamson, O. E. 1985. *The Economic Institutions of Capitalism: Firms, Markets, Relational Contracting*. New York: Free Press.

World Bank. 1996. *From Plan to Market. World Development Report 1996*, New York: Oxford University Press.

Wouters, H. 1973. *Le droit des societes anonymes dans les pays de la CEE*. Brussels.

16

Russian Banks in the Transition Period

Igor Doronin and
Alexander Zakharov

16.1. The Emergence of the Contemporary Banking System in Russia

Reform of the banking system in Russia began with the adoption by the Russian Supreme Soviet of the resolution *On the State Bank of the RSFSR and Banks on the Territory of the Republic,* on 13 July 1990. On 2 December 1990 the Russian Supreme Soviet adopted the laws *On the Central Bank of Russia* and *On Banks and Banking Activity on the Territory of Russia.* These two laws provided the legal foundation for the formation of a two-tier banking system.

Among the main tasks of the Russian Central Bank was to assist in the formation of a network of independent commercial banks. The central bank's policy toward commercial banks at this time consisted in "simplifying the procedure for setting up commercial banks." The liberal and in large measure encouraging approach of the Russian Central Bank at the outset of economic reforms led to the formation of a network of commercial banks.

The majority of commercial banks were created by transforming the branches and departments of former state specialized banks (Promstroybank, Zhilsotsbank, Agroprombank, and Vneshtorgbank) into independent commercial banks. The exception to this was Sberbank, which largely preserved its branch network.

A not insignificant number of new banks were formed under the aegis of ministries and departments (for example, Promradtechbank, Morbank, Aviabank, and Khimbank). The creation of such banks made it possible to monitor the movement of intrabranch financial flows and ensured ministries' and departments' control over enterprises in their branch via control of their accounts and lending them money.

Table 16.1
Credit Organizations and Their Branches in Russia, January 1996 through January 2000

	1 Jan. '96	1 Jan. '97	1 Jan. '98	1 Jan. '99	1 Jan. 2000
Credit organizations	2,295	2,029	1,697	1,476	1,349
Branches of credit organizations*	5,581	5,123	6,353	4,453	3,923
Total no. of credit organizations and their branches	7,876	7,152	8,050	5,929	5,272

*Excluding Sberbank.
Source: Internet: www.cbr.ru

Some banks were created by enterprises and organizations. This gave the founder-enterprises the opportunity to attract funds for their own needs and to get credits on preferential terms from "their own" bank. A major portion of the charter capital of most of these banks came from enterprises' own funds.

The number of credit institutions and their branches continued to grow until 1996, and the increasingly stricter central bank requirements placed on the banks did not impede the emergence of new banks. The number of credit organizations and branches decreased during the financial crisis, from 1,573 on 1 August 1998 to 1,389 on 1 September 1999 (Table 16.1).

Compared with the situation in leading Western countries, there are relatively few bank branch networks in Russia. Banks with a developed branch network (by Russian standards) are the exception. The reasons for this situation include not only the weakness of the overwhelming majority of banks, which have proved incapable of maintaining an extensive branch network, but also such factors as the uneven distribution of financial resources across Russia.

The liquidity deficit of the regions limits banks' potential development, and often they are forced to depend on a limited number of local clients (frequently these clients are also shareholders in the bank).

The period of extensive growth in commercial banks, which ran from the beginning of the market reforms until 1996, had its pluses and minuses. The fact that over a comparatively short period of time a fairly extensive network of commercial banks emerged (more than 2,000), a development crucial to the very development of the market, was clearly a plus. However, the quality of the banking system, and of the banks themselves, was poor. Rapid growth in the number of banks led to dispersed banking capital, while the emergence of a large number of small and medium-sized banks created difficulties in managing and ensuring the stability of the banking system and in raising the quality of banking services.

Russian commercial banks can be divided into four groups. Sberbank and Vneshtorgbank, both large, state-controlled banks, are in a group by themselves. At the start of 1997 Sberbank held approximately 24% of the total assets of the Russian banking system, and Vneshtorgbank held 3.3%. Furthermore, Sberbank's branch network is much larger than that of any other Russian commercial bank. Sberbank's special status is also due to the fact that it holds around 70% of all household deposits.

The second group comprises the largest private commercial banks. The third and most numerous group of banks is made up of small and medium-sized banks. Roughly one-quarter of these banks have capital of less than $500,000. Finally, the fourth group of commercial banks consists of foreign banks and banks established with the participation of foreign capital. At the end of 1996, there were fifteen representative offices of foreign banks and 133 commercial banks that were partly foreign-owned. The role of foreign commercial banks has been relatively insignificant: whereas the law limits foreign ownership of capital in the banking sector to 12%, the actual figure is closer to 3%.

In order to regulate the influx of foreign banks into Russia, two transitional periods were established during which Russia had the right to set restrictions on the operations of foreign banks. The conditions were set down in an agreement on partnership and cooperation with the European Union that was signed by the Russian President in June 1994.

During the first period, which ended on 1 January 1996, all banks from European Union member states, with the exception of those banks that had acquired their license from the Russian Central Bank and started servicing Russian residents before 15 November 1993, were prevented from working with Russian residents. A separate agreement was reached for banks that had received their licenses prior to 15 November 1993, and this agreement was strengthened by the presidential decree of 10 June 1994.

In the second transitional period, from 1 January 1996 to the end of June 1999, restrictions on foreign banks involved in particular operations with shares of Russian companies, and the establishment of a minimum balance of 55,000 ECUs for Russian residents' private accounts. Furthermore, during this period the Russian authorities were entitled to restrict the number of branches foreign banks could open in Russia. Finally, the Russian Federation reserved the right, without limits or conditions, to maintain a ceiling on the maximum share of foreign equity ownership in the Russian banking system.[1]

As of 1 January 2000, the share of nonresidents in the banking charter capital amounted to 10.7%, compared to 6.4% in January 1999. There were 177 Russian banks registered that were partly foreign-owned and twenty banks that were 100% foreign-owned.

According to estimates provided by the Expert Institute, at the end of 1993 there were about 480 "banking centers" in Russia—that is, populated areas in which there was at least one independent commercial bank. Of these, 114 banking centers had more than one bank, while more than half the country's banks were concentrated in thirty populated areas.

Between 1993 and 1995, the number of banking centers declined both in the country as a whole and in the majority of Russian regions. In a number of regions, such as Kareliya, Ryazan, and Tula, the number of banking centers fell to a minimum: the whole regional banking system was controlled either by banks of the regional (or republican) centers or by banks of other regions (mainly Moscow). Figures on bank branches in the regions for 1997–1999 are given in Table 16.2.

There were more appreciable changes in the regional banking system in 1996, when the process of bank consolidation and expansion got under way. During this process, small and medium-sized banks in the regions were closed and liquidated or became branches of banks based in other regions. In 1996, the number of independent banking institutions in the regions fell by 21%. The closing of regional banks' branches in their own regions occurred at a slower rate. This suggests that banks that had branches were more stable and capable of maintaining their branch networks, and possibly also indicates that independent banks were becoming branches of regional banks.

---

1. *Vestnik Banka Rossii*, 27 September 1994, p. 2.

Table 16.2
Distribution of Commercial Banks and Their Branches Across the Regions of Russia

	As of 1 January 1997			As of 2 January 2000		
	1	2	3	1	2	3
City of Moscow	823	198	159	604	106	60
City of St. Petersburg	43	53	60	41	34	68
Northern zone	48	109	118	26	37	138
North-western zone (excluding St. Petersburg)	18	31	85	12	9	92
Central zone (excluding Moscow)	133	145	541	99	81	460
Volgo-Vyatsky zone	65	98	166	37	61	178
Central black earth zone	24	85	182	16	27	154
Povolzhsky (Volga) zone	144	318	231	91	134	297
North Caucasian zone	244	401	258	135	197	305
Urals zone	141	396	228	96	209	335
Western Siberian zone	150	247	261	93	161	253
Eastern Siberian zone	64	148	191	34	38	186
Far Eastern zone	110	240	144	46	79	179
Baltic zone	23	21	17	14	6	24
Total in Russia	2,029	2,482	2,641	1,344	1,179	2,719

Key: *1*—number of banks in the region; *2*—number of branches of these banks in the region; *3*—number of branches of other banks in the region.
Sources: *Byulleten' bankovskoy statistiki* no. 2 (1997); Internet: www.cbr.ru

The reduction in the number of small and medium-sized banks continued in 1997 and clearly will continue further. According to representatives of a number of major Russian banks, the number of merger proposals is on the rise. However, most such proposals are not particularly attractive, as they come from banks that have already accumulated debts and have a significant portion of unprofitable assets. Frequently it is simpler for a major bank to open its own branch than to take on the debts of a bankrupt bank.

16.2. Concentration of Capital in the Banking Sector

Increasing banks' capital is one of the fundamental problems in developing and stabilizing the Russian banking system. Although the total capitalization of the banking system has grown throughout the years of economic reform, it has not kept up with the needs of the economy. The percentage of banks with declared charter capital exceeding $4 million grew from 1.4% on 1 January 1994 to 9.3% on 1 January 1997. At the same time, the percentage of banks with

Table 16.3
Capitalization of Russian banks

	1 Aug. '98	1 Mar. '99	1 Sept. '99
Total declared charter capital			
In billions of rubles	102	41.2	83.5
In billions of dollars*	16.35	1.80	3.36
Number of registered credit organizations	1,573	1,456	1,389
Average declared charter capital per registered credit organization			
In millions of rubles	65.0	28.3	60.1
In millions of dollars*	10.0	1.2	2.4

*Calculated at the dollar exchange rate on the given date.
Source: Internet: www.cbr.ru

declared charter capital of less than $1 million on 1 January 1997 was 61%, down from 93% in 1994. (Figures on the capitalization of banks in 1998–1999 are given in Table 16.3.) Growth in the capital base was most common among major banks.

The main consequence of the financial crisis of 1998 was loss of banking capital. The declared charter capital was halved. Several months later it had somehow regained its previous level.

The general level of bank capital concentration in Russia remains low compared with Western countries (Table 16.4). In countries with a developed market economy, the overwhelming majority of banking assets are concentrated in several large commercial banks. A high level of concentration is necessary for the formation of a stable national payments and settlements system, for the development of national capital markets, and to ensure links with the international payments and settlements system.

In Russia, there are no major credit institutions comparable to those in Western countries.

The move toward the concentration of banking capital in Russia came about not so much as a result of competition between commercial banks to improve the quality of their services but because of stringent central bank requirements concerning bank stability. These requirements have largely determined the way in which the concentration of banking capital has occurred. In particular, this has been done through mergers, takeovers, and liquidations, as opportunities for increasing banking capital in conditions of low average incomes and decreasing profitability of financial market operations are distinctly limited.

Table 16.4
Comparative Analysis of Commercial Banking Indicators in Russia and Countries with a Developed Market Economy

	Russia*	USA	Japan	England	Germany	France	Italy
Total assets (bill. of $)	73.8	3,707.2	6,130.2	2,189.4	963.2	1,379.4	964.1
Bank assets per unit of GDP	0.21	0.59	1.46	2.33	0.50	0.91	0.97
Total deposits (bill. of $)	42.2	2,754.1	3,914.8	1,558.6	411.9	279.7	526.5
Ratio of deposits to assets (%)	57.2	74.3	63.9	71.2	42.8	20.3	54.6
Loans made (bill. of $)	55.8	2,151.0	4,275.3	1,502.8	631.9	477.4	402.3
Ratio of credits to assets (%)	75.6	58.0	69.7	68.6	65.6	34.6	41.7

*Data on Russia are calculated as of the end of 1995 using IMF, *International Financial Statistics* (February 1997). Conversion to dollars was done using the exchange rate at the end of 1995 (Rb 4,640/$1 US). The authors' calculations correspond to estimates of Western experts. Thus, according to the April 1997 issue of *Banker*, the sum total of Russian banking assets was US $60 billion, or 15% of GDP.

Source: J. Barth, D. Nolle, T. Rice (1997): Commercial banking structure, regulation, and performance: An international comparison. Economics Working Paper 97-6, Offce of the Comptroller of the Currency (Washington).

Banks can be roughly divided into three groups, based on banking capital concentration.

The first group comprises banks with a relatively high level of liquidity that seek to diversify the range of services they provide and to restructure their balances and meet the norms established by the central bank. The business of these banks is concentrated mainly in major financial centers, principally Moscow, while the business of their branches is predominantly in the regional financial centers, where they operate on the regional foreign exchange, interbank credit, and securities markets.

The second group comprises banks that are experiencing a liquidity deficit and thus are forced to limit their activities. The majority of these banks have difficulty meeting central bank requirements. Their business tends to be concentrated in regions where small firms and agriculture dominate, and their strongest competition comes from branches of major banks based elsewhere.

The concentration of funds in the branches of banks based in other regions increases the stability of the regional banking system overall, but it also has a negative side: the strengthening of the position of branches of banks based in other regions is frequently attended by an outflow of financial resources from the regions to major financial centers.

Finally, the third group comprises "problem" banks that are struggling to keep afloat. Banks in this group may be experiencing considerable growth or very little growth, and their fortunes are largely tied to the economic situation prevalent in a specific region.

The creation of informal banking unions and associations has had some impact on the process and character of bank ownership concentration. The majority of associations were created to lobby on behalf of banks or for the realization of specific programs and projects. Later on, associations were set up for the purpose of uniting banks' efforts in the development of specific markets.

A number of banking groups and bank holding companies have also been created. The interest of commercial banks in forming these groups and holding companies is founded on the belief that it will facilitate access to investment, including foreign investment.

Another factor spurring banks to create holding companies has apparently been their unsuccessful involvement in financial-industrial groups, in which banks have often been demoted to the position of the settlements department and a source for cheap credit.

16.3. The Functions of Russian Commercial Banks

According to the federal law *On Banks and Banking Activity* (in the version of 3 February 1996), "a bank is a credit organization which has exclusive right to carry out all of the following banking operations: attracting deposits from individuals and legal entities; investing these deposits in its own name and on its own account on conditions of repayment within the terms specified; opening and handling the accounts of individuals and legal entities." The law specifies banking operations that can be carried out by banks not only in rubles but also in foreign currency (given the appropriate license), and also operations with precious metals (with the appropriate license). Banks can also carry out trust, guarantee, and leasing operations and can provide consultative and informational services. Production, trade, and insurance are among the activities that banks are barred from undertaking. If we compare Russian bank legislation with that of other countries, it becomes clear that commercial banks in Russia enjoy virtually the same rights to conduct business as commercial banks in any other country with a market economy.

According to the law *On Banks and Banking Activity*, banks can obtain a central bank license giving them the right to work with securities, either to make payments (on checks and promissory notes, for example) or to confirm deposits (savings and deposit certificates). Professional activities on the securities market are regulated by other federal laws. Particularly important is the law *On the Securities Market*, which delegates regulatory functions in this sphere to the Federal Securities Commission (FKTsB).

Although at first glance the data on Russian banks' operations appear generally comparable with analogous data on the operations of banks in developed market economies, it is important to bear in mind that in the latter, a significant portion of financial resources is accumulated by various investment funds, pension funds, insurance companies, and other institutions. These funds consequently bypass banks altogether. Investments, including financial market investments, can be made through these institutions. Thus, the relatively modest role of commercial banks in the economy of more progressive countries is a result of the development of a parallel financial sector, whereas in Russia the majority of household deposits are in banks. In this respect Russia is similar to other states with a developing market economy, in which the share of banking assets in the sum total of financial institutions' assets is 75%–95%.[2]

Russian banks differ from banks in developed countries in the structure of their balance sheets. The balance sheets of Russian banks have a small portion of interest-bearing obligations on the liabilities side, around 17.1% of total liabilities, while the share of non-interest-bearing or virtually non-interest-bearing obligations is around 70%.[3] Among the latter obligations are funds on current accounts, budget and fund money, funds on Loro correspondent accounts, and so on. In developed countries the ratio of interest-bearing obligations to non-interest-bearing obligations is the reverse.

The relatively small volume of deposits has a significant influence on the structure of Russian banks' obligations. Moreover, the overwhelming majority of household deposits in Russian banks are short-term, while in Western banks most deposits are either demand or savings deposits. In the United States, the volume of savings deposits is on average double that of current account deposits.

In the structure of Russian banks' obligations, correspondent accounts make up 18% of liabilities, compared to 0.9% in American banks. This relatively high proportion of liabilities in the form of correspondent accounts can be explained by the hypertrophied development of the interbank credit market in a situation of sustained currency and financial instability.

A significant portion of Russian banks' assets do not generate income. Some examples are cash, ruble payments in transit, correspondent accounts with the central bank, mandatory reserves in the central bank, nonperforming loans, equity capital, inventory, intangible assets, and other ruble receivables. Their share is estimated at about 50% of total banking assets, which exceeds analogous assets in US banks by a factor of 3.5.

Also specific to Russian banks is the structure of performing assets. Among the performing assets are freely convertible hard currency, correspondent accounts in hard currency, sundry hard-currency receivables, short-term credits, long-term credits, interbank credits,

---

2. *Economist*, 12 April 1997.
3. *Finansovye izvestiya*, 26 November 1996.

investments in securities, and the like. Whereas for Western banks the main business activity is lending money to industrial and trade companies, for Russian banks the share of such business is considerably lower. The share of Russian banks' loans to the nonfinancial sector constitutes about 30% of active operations, as opposed to 50%–60% in American banks. The share of government securities among Russian commercial banks' assets varies substantially.

After the financial crisis the structure of commercial banks' balance sheets started changing, but not radically.

16.4. Commercial Banks and the Real Sector of the Economy

The role of commercial banks in the development of the economy largely depends on how effective the banks are at performing their role as intermediaries, mobilizing funds and lending them to enterprises and to the public.

In Russia the problem of banks' interaction with the real economy is particularly severe. A number of factors can be offered to explain why banks have so far not effectively performed their role as intermediaries. Aside from the fact that neither the public nor enterprises have exhibited an interest in keeping their money in banks, as inflation has been higher than interest rates on deposits for much of the transition period, one of the major obstacles was the policy followed in 1992–1994 of financing the budget deficit through central bank credits. As long as the state provided substantial credits and subsidies on privileged terms to enterprises and banks, the latter did not have to concern themselves with attracting enterprise and household deposits.

Banks did not have to concern themselves with profitable and careful investments, which require constant evaluation of the creditworthiness of the borrower, minimizing credit risk, securing the loans as far as is possible, developing and maintaining effective, long-term credit relations with borrowers, and the like. A significant portion of central bank credits were targeted, and the credits were granted at below-market interest rates.

Although the central bank's lending policy was set in order to support production, nonetheless, throughout the years of central bank lending, the economic recession continued. Moreover, the policy of central bank lending did not facilitate resolution of the long-term structural problems in industry, without which banks could not start developing credit relations with enterprises on a commercial footing.

The end to centralized credits in 1995, the introduction of financial stabilization policies, stabilization of the exchange rate, and the decreasing profitability of money market operations all forced commercial banks to review their policies with regard to attracting deposits and lending to the public, enterprises, and other organizations. However, banks were still not able to develop effective credit relations with the real sector.

The hypertrophied development of the financial sector was another side effect of the policy of central bank lending during high inflation. Here we will just mention that the development of the Russian financial sector went through a number of stages. The first was a period of intense operations on foreign exchange markets by banks and their clients, both of which speculated on a weakening of the ruble. According to banks' accounts, at this time 70%–80% of banks' profits were generated by speculative foreign exchange operations.

The interbank credit market developed in parallel, and operations on this market provided a significant portion of the funds for speculating on the foreign exchange market. Cheap central bank credits to a large extent subsidized operations on the interbank credit market and stimulated demand for foreign currency.

In May 1993, the government bond market started operations. Although the volume of operations grew, the profitability of the bonds largely depended on the profitability of foreign exchange operations in general.

Bank operations on the financial markets continued to dominate in 1997, despite the fact that the financial market structure underwent serious changes. Beginning in 1995, the state abandoned its policy of covering the budget deficit through central bank credits. Consequently, the situation on the foreign exchange market gradually stabilized. After the introduction of a foreign exchange rate corridor in July 1995 and a managed exchange rate in May 1996, profits from foreign exchange operations fell considerably. Bank operations were gradually displaced by the market for government bonds. The large budget deficit forced the government to borrow money, and bank lending to the state was more profitable and less problematic than lending to enterprises.

The dynamics of enterprise deposits in commercial banks and the volume of bank loans to enterprises serve as an indicator of the interaction between banks and the real economy. As shown in Table 16.5, the volume of funds on enterprises' and organizations' accounts decreased somewhat in 1994. This resulted from a considerable fall in production, on the one hand, and from substantial speculation on the foreign exchange market on the other ("Black Tuesday"—11 October 1994—is an example).

In 1995, following the curtailment of central bank credits, the volume of enterprise and organization deposits increased; at the same time, bank lending also increased. These positive shifts can be explained by the decline in speculative activity on the foreign exchange market, the strengthening of the ruble exchange rate, and the slowing of inflation. All of these processes made it easier for banks to attract deposits. The volume of funds on enterprises' clearing and current accounts grew by 65%. Stabilization of the economy in 1995 led to a 37% increase in the volume of credits extended to enterprises and banks.

The situation in 1996 was more ambiguous. It is difficult to assess the change over the year, because in the second half of 1996 the central bank changed its methodology for calculating individual items on the balance sheets of commercial banks. Thus, comparable data are available only for the first five months of 1996. These data show that in the first half of 1996 the volume of enterprise deposits fell, as did the volume of bank lending. Moreover, bank lending dropped even further than the volume of bank deposits during this period.

Substantial growth in profits on operations in the government bond market in this period may provide an explanation for this trend. In the second half of the year government bond yields fell. However, it was difficult to turn around these negative trends in the second half of the year because of the ongoing economic recession and the general worsening of enterprises' financial positions.

One indicator of banks' involvement in the real economy is the ratio of enterprises' and organizations' bank balances to lending by commercial banks to the real economy (Table 16.6). This coefficient of business activity serves as a rough indicator. It changes depending on the dynamics of the component parts—the volume of enterprise funds in bank accounts and the volume of loans to enterprises and organizations.

Table 16.5
Volume of Funds on Current Accounts of Enterprises and Organizations and Volume of Bank Loans to Enterprises and Organizations (mill. of $)

	As of Jan. 1994	As of Jan. 1995	As of Jan. 1996	As of Jan. 1996 (New Method)*	As of Jan. 1997 (New Method)*	As of Jan. 1999 (New Method)*
1. Balances of enterprises' and organizations' current accounts	6,600	6,412	10,603	42,116†	49,380†	2,746‡
2. Bank credits to enterprises and organizations	24,302	23,382	32,130	46,932‡	46,762‡	13,647‡

*Data calculated by the Central Bank according to a new method for calculating specific balance sheet items; also with the inclusion of Sberbank data in the combined data on commercial banks, but without Vneshekonombank data.

†Funds attracted from enterprises, organizations, and households in rubles and foreign currency; in 1997, excluding budget funds for financing capital investments.

‡Loans made to the economy, banks, and the public in rubles and foreign currency (including overdue debt, without interest). In 1997, excluding long-term credits for financing capital investments.

Sources: Calculated using central bank data published in *Byulleten' bankovskoy statistiki* no. 6, 1994; no. 6, 1995; no. 6, 1996; no. 3, 1997, and no. 6, 1999. Conversion to dollars was calculated using the exchange rate on the relevant date.

Table 16.6
Coefficients of the Relative Business Activity of Commercial Banks in the Regions (%)*

	As of 1 Jan. 1994	As of 1 Jan. 1995	As of 1 Jan. 1996	As of 1 May 1996	As of 1 Jan. 1999
City of Moscow	61	49	64	55	36
City of St. Petersburg	94	96	98	75	44
Northern zone	19	22	29	20	17
Northwestern zone (excluding St. Petersburg)	45	62	68	56	32
Central zone (excluding Moscow)	45	43	49	41	30
Volgo-Vyatsky zone	37	29	37	28	21
Central black earth zone	34	54	55	34	30
Povolzhsky (Volga) zone	27	36	41	35	31
North Caucasian zone	24	28	56	41	35
Urals zone	21	33	46	30	25
Western Siberian zone	13	39	53	35	33
Eastern Siberian zone	22	31	49	27	21
Far Eastern zone	13	15	48	31	18
Baltic zone	55	29	60	54	25
Average across the regions	32	36	55	43	30

*The coefficient of business activity is calculated as the ratio of balances on current and deposit accounts of enterprises to loans made by banks. In the second half of 1996, the Central Bank changed its methodology for calculating balances of enterprises' accounts. As a result, the data starting from the second half of 1996 were excluded from the table.

Sources: Calculated using Central Bank data published in *Byulleten' bankovskoy statistiki* no. 6, 1994; no. 6, 1995; no. 6, 1996; and no. 6, 1999.

The situation with bank lending to enterprises and organizations remained complicated. Here a trend toward reduced bank lending is clearly visible.

Although the general trend toward a decreasing volume of bank lending continued throughout the period under review, nonetheless, the rate of decline slowed down. At the beginning of 1996, in individual regions, after a substantial decline in the volume of bank lending, some growth was registered. One can conjecture that as favorable economic conditions emerged in 1997—falling inflation, falling interest rates, and declining government bond yields—certain positive shifts occurred in lending to the real economy.

In banks' credit portfolios, the overwhelming majority of loans have short maturities, up to three months. Long-term lending, which in Russian practice includes any loan with a maturity of more than a year, makes up an insignificant share of credit portfolios. On the positive side, this share of long-term credits is growing, although

Table 16.7
Relative Proportion of Short- and Long-Term Bank Loans to the Economy (Enterprises, Organizations, and Households), in Rubles and Hard Currency

	Total (%)	Short-Term (%)	Long-Term (%)
As of 1 Jan. 1993	100	95.0	5.0
As of 1 Jan. 1994	100	97.0	3.0
As of 1 Jan. 1995	100	95.0	5.0
As of 1 Jan. 1996	100	83.8	16.2
As of 1 Jan. 1997	100	90.7	9.3
As of 1 Jan. 1998	100	92.0	8.0
As of 1 Jan. 1999	100	97.0	3.0
As of 1 Jan. 2000	100	95.0	5.0

Sources: Calculated using Central Bank data from *Byulleten' bankovskoy statistiki* no. 2, 1994; no. 2, 1995; no. 2, 1996; no. 2, 1997; no. 2, 1998; and no. 2, 1999. The data have been adjusted for ruble depreciation by converting ruble data to dollars at the exchange rate on the respective date.

slowly (figures for 1993–1999 are shown in Table 16.7). The most significant growth occurred in 1995 as a result of the loans-for-shares auctions, one condition of which was that banks that acquired enterprise shares in the auctions had to provide investment loans to those enterprises.

Interest-rate dynamics played an important role in the creation of conditions conducive to the development of lending to the real sector of the economy. In 1999–2000, there were some positive shifts in the cost of borrowing.

However, many obstacles need to be overcome for bank lending to develop in Russia. One obstacle is the considerable volume of overdue debts owed to banks by enterprises and organizations. Since 1994, when there was an appreciable decline, caused by the distribution of substantial central bank credits and a sharp increase in inflation, overdue debts have been growing. This fact is a serious impediment to further bank lending to enterprises.

It is virtually impossible to resolve the problem of overdue debt through radical measures. Because of their grave financial positions, many enterprises are incapable of servicing their debts, including the accumulated interest payments. Moreover, because of their relative financial weakness and lack of necessary reserves, banks cannot afford to write off even part of the accumulated debt. If an enterprise goes bankrupt, the losses sustained by certain banks could also lead to the banks' bankruptcy. The problem can be resolved only gradually: on the enterprise's side, by increasing its profitability, and on the bank's side, by building up reserves to cover nonperforming loans. In some cases it may be possible to securitize enterprise debts and establish an enterprise promissory note market. This market, however, would require the creation of the appropriate infrastructure.

One of the main aims of a bank's credit policy is to keep nonperforming loans to a minimum. This position explains the cautious and balanced approach of most banks to lending to industry. Money is lent to enterprises on the basis of carefully prepared business plans and strict monitoring of the loans by the bank. Banks may also in many cases demand collateral for their loans.

One of the main factors obstructing industrial growth is the lack of managers who are capable of implementing a market-appropriate strategy. In some financial-industrial groups, bank employees take up management positions in the companies to which they lend, providing a sort of guarantee that bank loans will be efficiently utilized.

16.5. Stability of the Russian Banking System

All that has been said to this point should help explain why, at the current stage of transition from extensive to intensive development of the Russian banking system, problems of supervision, regulation, and increasing the reliability of commercial banks have taken on such significance. The transition stage began in 1995 and is directly linked to the implementation of financial stabilization. After the banks were deprived of cheap central bank credits and the opportunity to use the inflation tax to their advantage, the financial position of many banks deteriorated rapidly. One indicator of this deterioration is the number of banks that had their licenses revoked: as of 1 January 1996, 303 licenses had been revoked; as of 1 January 1997, 570 had been revoked.[4]

According to various estimates, in the middle of 1997 only 40%–60% of banks were more or less financially stable, while more than 750 credit organizations were candidates for liquidation. In these conditions, the importance of measures undertaken by the Central Bank to regulate and monitor banking activities increased in value.

The federal law of 2 December 1990, *On the Central Bank of the Russian Federation* (with amendments of 27 December 1995, 20 June

---

4. *Byulleten' bankovskoy statistiki*, no. 3, 1996; no. 3, 1997.

1996, and 27 February 1997), provides the legal basis for the central bank's role as supervisor and regulator of commercial banks' activities. In Chapter 10 of the law *On the Central Bank of the Russian Federation* it is stated that the main aim of banking regulation and supervision consists in "supporting the stability of the banking system and defending depositors' interests."

Currently the central bank issues two kinds of licenses. The general license permits banks to conduct all kinds of banking operations, with the exception of those operations requiring a special license, such as operations with precious metals or foreign currency. Apart from the general license there is also the restricted license, which permits banks to conduct deposit operations—that is, to accept household deposits in rubles and foreign currency. Furthermore, restrictions on the operations that a given bank may conduct can be included in the bank's license.

According to central bank data, on 1 January 2000 the total number of registered credit organizations was 2,376, of which 2,342 were banks and thirty-four were nonbank credit organizations. Two hundred forty-two Russian credit organizations held general licenses, 1,264 held licenses to work with household deposits, and 669 held licenses to conduct foreign currency operations. One hundred thirty-four credit organizations had licenses to conduct operations with precious metals, and another eighteen credit organizations had been granted permission.[5]

The central bank monitors whether a bank is meeting capital and reserve requirements; the observance of mandatory norms; whether internal reserves are correct; liquidity; the quality of a bank's credit portfolio, and other indicators. Observance of established requirements is checked against accounts that the banks regularly provide, and also by inspections and targeted audits. Sanctions are applied to banks that violate these requirements, including the refusal to register increases in charter capital, restrictions on operations that a bank can conduct, and revocation of licenses.

The banking norms provide an instrument for regulating the activities of commercial banks, making it possible to check their stability and liquidity. The procedure for calculating norms and their parameters is established in the central bank's directive No. 1, adopted on 30 January 1996 and amended on 23 May 1997.

---

5. *Byulleten' bankovskoy statistiki,* no. 1, 2000. *Vestnik Banka Rossii,* no. 39, 18 June 1997.

First Group of Norms

The first group of norms comprises two absolute indicators: minimum charter capital for newly established commercial banks and minimum shareholder equity for commercial banks. One relative indicator also falls in this group: the ratio of a bank's equity capital to its total risk-weighted assets. This norm is intended to maintain some minimum permissible percentage of a bank's own resources that it can use for investments.

The minimum charter capital required for newly established credit organizations has gradually increased. In particular, it increased from 2 million ECUs on 1 April 1996 to 5 million ECUs on 1 July 1998. For existing credit organizations, minimum shareholder equity, defined as the sum of the charter fund of the organization and retained profits, is set at a sum equivalent to 5 million ECUs (starting from 1 January 1999).

The capital adequacy norm is defined as the ratio of a credit organization's capital to its total assets, weighted to take into account counter-party risk. The procedures for weighing assets according to risk and capital adequacy norms are consistent with international standards.

At the beginning of March 1997, the central bank's board of directors toughened its capital adequacy requirements. For banks with capital in excess of 5 million ECUs, the capital adequacy norm from 1 February 1998 was set at 7%; from 1 February 1999 at 8%, and from 1 February 2000 at 11%.

For banks with capital of 1 to 5 million ECUs, the capital adequacy norm was set at 7% in 1998, 9% in 1999, and 11% in 2000. Banks with capital between 1 and 5 million ECUs will be restricted in their activities; in particular, they are not allowed to conduct operations abroad, apart from opening correspondent accounts; restrictions are also imposed on opening branches and on participating in the charter capital of other organizations.

For banks with capital of less than 1 million ECUs, the capital adequacy reserve requirement was set at 7% for 1998. After this year it was assumed that these banks will either grow their capital or they will cease to be banks.

The policy of toughening central bank capital adequacy requirements is in line with world practice concerning the regulation of commercial banks. The Basel Agreement of 1988 set the minimum capital adequacy norm at 8%. This became a mandatory requirement for banks in countries that signed the agreement and a guideline for those that did not. Although this initiative was taken by states with a developed market economy, it was also approved by many states undergoing economic transition (Table 16.8).

Norms are viewed as one of the effective instruments for ensuring the stability of a banking system. In 1996, central bank representatives from a number of developing countries and countries undergoing economic transition noted that the standard set by the Basel Agreement, while probably corresponding to the needs of banking systems in developed countries that are quite stable, was inappropriate for countries in which the macroeconomic and financial situation was undergoing significant fluctuation. A number of countries consider the Basel requirements to be a necessary minimum for maintaining bank stability, and some countries introduced even higher requirements; in particular, in Argentina the capital adequacy norm was set at 11.5%, and in Colombia it was set at 9%.

Second Group of Norms
The second group of norms comprises *liquidity norms*, which are required to force banks to balance outgoing and incoming financial flows by volume and term:

• The *current liquidity norm* is the minimum necessary ratio of liquid assets to demand deposits up to a period of thirty days.

• The *instant liquidity norm* is the minimum necessary ratio of high liquidity assets to demand deposits.

• The *long-term liquidity norm* is the maximum permitted ratio of long-term financial investments of a bank to the sum total of shareholder equity and long-term obligations.

• The minimum necessary share of liquid assets in the sum total of a bank's assets is another liquidity norm.

Third Group of Norms
The third group of norms comprises risk norms. The aim of these norms is to encourage banks to ensure maximum diversification of their assets and liabilities. Risk norms establish the following:

• The maximum permissible risk linked to one borrower or group of connected borrowers

Table 16.8
Comparison of the Procedure for Weighing Assets for Risk in the Basel Agreement and in the Normative Requirements of the Russian Central Bank for Russian Commercial Banks

Basel Agreement	Central Bank Directive No. 1
CAPITAL	
Tier 1: Common shares; retained profits; capital revaluation; preferred shares not providing for the accumulation of dividends; noncontrolling stakes in consolidated daughter companies less intangible capital. Tier 2: Reserves to meet unforeseen loan or leasing losses, and also subordinated debt instruments.	(There is no division of capital into tiers): Officially registered charter capital; retained profits; retained earnings reserves; less debts with a maturity of more than 30 days; less incomplete capital investments; and less bank's own shares, purchased from shareholders.
ASSETS	
The following weights are attached to the various elements: 0%—Cash; and claims on the central government and central bank. 20%—Deposits in other banks; claims on domestic public-sector entities, excluding central government. 50%—Loans fully secured by a mortgage; claims on local governments and loans with a maturity of over 1 year. 100%—Claims on the private sector; real estate and other investments.	Assets, weighted for risk. 0%—Funds on central bank accounts, claims on the government. 2%—Cash. 10%—Credits guaranteed by the government, with government securities, or precious metal bullion as collateral. 20%—Local government securities, and loans collateralized with these securities; funds on the accounts of foreign banks which are OECD members in foreign currency, and loans made to these banks. 70%—Funds on the accounts of foreign banks which are not members of the OECD (except banks in the near abroad), traded securities, real estate (apart from that used as collateral). 100%—Commercial credits and all other assets.
INDICATORS OF CAPITAL ADEQUACY	
The ratio of first-tier capital to risk-weighted assets should not be lower than 4%. The ratio of total capital (i.e., tiers one and two) to total risk-weighted assets should not be lower than 8%.	The ratio of capital to risk-weighted assets should not be below: 5% as of 1 July 1996 6% as of 1 Feb. 1997 7% as of 1 Feb. 1998 8% as of 1 Feb. 1999

Source: Analytical report *Rossiyskaya bankovskaya sistema* (Agency Praym, 1996): 31.

- The maximum permissible risk linked to one of the bank's creditors (depositors)
- The maximum permissible risk linked to one borrower who is also a shareholder in the bank
- The maximum permissible risk linked to one borrower who is also an "insider" of a given bank
- The maximum permissible risk linked to investment in the charter capital of one organization
- The maximum permissible volume of household deposits
- The maximum permissible size of major credit risks.

In August 1996, the central bank decided to add to directive No. 1 another (the thirteenth) mandatory norm, to regulate the issuance by banks of their own promissory notes. This was called the "Risk norm for own promissory note obligations" (No. 13), which is calculated as the ratio of total promissory notes issued by a credit organization to bank acceptances in rubles and foreign currency plus 50% of the total balanced obligations of a credit organization from the endorsement of promissory notes, banker's guarantees, and promissory intermediation to a credit organization's own capital. The maximum permissible No. 13 norm was set at 200% of the balance sheet as of October 1996 and lowered to 100% of the balance sheet as of 1 March 1997.

The central bank also established a series of norms from 1 July 1996 to 1 February 1999, with each successive norm more stringent than its predecessor.

Verification of Norm Observance
The effectiveness of introduced norms largely depends on observance of established reporting requirements, which excludes the possibility of manipulating various items on the balance sheet. The central bank intends to devote considerable attention to issues of reporting. At the Sixth International Bank Congress, held in St. Petersburg on 3–7 June 1997, it was noted that out of the 643 credit organizations audited, shortcomings in account reporting were found in 565. The central bank has started to develop a method for supervising multibranch banks and banking groups working in and outside of Russia.

Verification of norm observance is also carried out by the central bank in the issuance of credit support. Banks can hope to qualify for central bank support only if they observe the norms set in the documents regulating the procedure for lending to commercial banks.

16.6. Monetary and Credit Instruments for Regulating Banks' Liquidity

In 1995, following the establishment of control over the growth of the money supply and reduced financing of the budget deficit by central bank credits, instruments of monetary and credit market intervention started to become increasingly important. These instruments had an impact on the liquidity of the banking sector, on money market interest rates, and on the yields of various financial instruments. From 1995 there was a continuous process of renewal and strengthening of the role of previously functioning instruments (for example, obligatory reserves, and the granting of refinancing credits). New regulatory instruments were developed and introduced (for example, lombard credits, deposit operations, open market operations, repo operations, and one-day settlement credits).

The use of instruments of monetary and credit regulation was made possible by the development of the financial market and its developing liquidity.

Operations on the open market include central bank operations for the sale and purchase of government bonds on the secondary market, including repo operations.

The central bank's role on the secondary market for government bonds started to increase from 1995 with the start of financial stabilization. Operating on the open market, the central bank can resolve a number of problems. First, it can smooth out fluctuations in the liquidity of the banking sector. Second, it can regulate the money supply by removing money from circulation through the purchase or sale of government bonds on the secondary market. Third, it can exert influence on other segments of the market by influencing operations on the foreign exchange market, and also on the interbank credit market by regulating banking sector liquidity.

Refinancing credits in Russia have been granted on an auction basis since 1994. The interest rate on auctioned credits depends on existing refinancing rates and commercial banks' demand for these credits.

When granting refinancing credits, the central bank takes into account growth in net domestic assets and the movement of funds on commercial banks' correspondent accounts. The central bank issues refinancing credits as an instrument for supporting banks, and also for encouraging commercial banks to observe established norms and strengthen financial discipline.

Lombard credits are a form of short-term lending by the central bank to commercial banks that was first used in Russia in April 1996, in which government bonds were used as collateral. According to central bank data, at the end of April 1997, around 900 banks held government and other securities that could be used as collateral. From the end of August 1996, the central bank started to extend Lombard credits at fixed interest rates at banks' request. The purpose of these operations is to maintain commercial bank liquidity. Banks that have met central bank obligatory reserve requirements in a timely fashion and in full and that have no overdue debts to the central bank are eligible for lombard credits.

Deposit operations are central bank operations to attract commercial banks' surplus liquidity. In Russia they were first carried out in the middle of 1995, and at the beginning of 1996, the provision for conducting these operations was institutionalized. They are conducted on an auction basis or directly in the form of a deposit at a fixed interest rate. In the first seven months of 1996, the central bank attracted a total of Rb 1,860 billion of commercial banks' surplus funds. The deposit rate, as a rule, is lower than the current market interest rate, which should spur commercial banks to invest their resources on the market.

Mandatory reserve requirements in world practice are considered one of the strongest means of regulating banking sector liquidity, and thus of influencing the money and credit markets. In contrast to operations on the open market and altering refinancing rates, changing mandatory reserve requirements directly affects the liquidity of credit organizations. In countries with a developed financial market infrastructure, this instrument is utilized in exceptional circumstances. In less developed countries, however, it is considered to be one of the more effective ways of regulating liquidity.

In Russia, the importance of this monetary and credit policy instrument grew considerably in 1995–1996. Commercial banks' deposits are also included in reserve requirements. The reserve procedure is defined in the provision on commercial banks' mandatory reserves, which came into force on 1 May 1996. This provides for the exaction of funds from any credit organization that fails to transfer funds in full to the mandatory reserve fund, together with the enforcement of a fine, which should spur banks to observe the requirements.

Since the middle of 1996, the central bank has been conducting a policy of gradually reducing mandatory reserve norms for commercial banks' ruble deposits, which has assisted in increasing commercial banks' liquidity and their relative stability.

One of the aims of the mandatory reserve fund is to create liquid reserves for the support of commercial banks, as the central bank can use these funds to lend to banks. If a bank goes bankrupt, funds from the mandatory reserve fund are transferred to the account of the liquidation commission and to the fund for meeting competing creditors' demands.

Despite the importance of the profound changes in the central bank's monetary and credit policy, involving a broader range of instruments for monetary and credit regulation, it should be recognized that the effectiveness of these instruments remains limited. This situation is not a reflection of central bank capabilities or the degree to which these instruments can affect the liquidity of the banking system. Rather, to a considerable extent, their effectiveness is limited by a host of unresolved problems, primarily structural ones. It can hardly be described as normal that around 70% of household deposits are concentrated in one bank, Sberbank, and that the trend toward the concentration of deposits in this bank is continuing. Whereas in 1994 Sberbank's share of total household deposits was around 50%, by the middle of 1997 it had grown to 74%. Another manifestation of structural problems is the sustained high level of dollarization of the economy. This reality is explained by the fact that the public prefers not to keep the bulk of savings in banks but to exchange it for foreign currency.

Aside from the structural problems, there are also general economic problems.

First, the problem of improving the level of coordination in conducting budgetary, monetary, and credit policies is a serious one. Monetary and credit policies can be effective only if the government's finances are balanced. Under these conditions, tightening or loosening these policies should have an even impact on the behavior of market participants. If budgetary imbalances, tax privileges, changes in the tax regime, and the like exist, then tightening monetary and credit policies can create an excessive burden for some, while barely affecting others.

Long-term strengthening of the stability of the banking system can be achieved only by consistently keeping the budget deficit low, increasing tax collection, and spreading the tax burden evenly across all market participants.

Second, further efforts must be undertaken to develop financial market infrastructure, in part by increasing guarantees that operations are settled. Another important task is to ensure the balanced development of major segments of the financial markets, to lower and level out the yields of market instruments and to redirect market participants to long-term instruments.

Third, the system of interbank settlements and payments needs improving and developing. Economic agents' lack of confidence in the payments system, due to the long time it takes to process payments and the high risk level, as well as the severe financial positions of economic agents has been one of the factors encouraging the proliferation of various forms of barter and the widespread use of foreign currency to settle accounts. The creation of an effective payments and settlements system would make it possible to carry out mutual interbank and other settlements, and to calculate the net financial position of banks and other economic agents much more rapidly.

On 1 April 1996, the Central Bank's Board of Directors approved a strategy for developing the payments system of Russia. It was directed at "creating a modern, automated settlements system, working chiefly in real time, by the beginning of the next century."[6]

According to the adopted strategy, initially the system of real-time settlements between credit organizations would be based on carrying out settlements exclusively through commercial banks' balances' on central bank correspondent accounts. At the same time, the central bank planned to develop its capabilities in granting short-term credits to banks for the purpose of completing payments in timely fashion.

---

6. *Vestnik Banka Rossii*, no. 17, 23 April 1996.

As monetary and credit policy instruments are improved and the Russian banking system is strengthened, it will become possible to switch to the automated extension of such credits while remaining within the limits set for the banks' mandatory reserves held in the central bank.

16.7. The Creation of a System for Regulating and Monitoring Bank Activities

The central bank document, "On the Fundamental Aims of the Central Bank's Monetary and Credit Policy and Principles of Banking Sector Regulation," was promulgated in May 1995.[7] This document stated, first, that the regulatory system should be built on a coherent combination of direct central bank regulation and the self-organization and self-restraint of members of the banking community. Second, the creation of interbank institutions to manage banks in crisis was identified as a promising area of bank cooperation. This process would enable the adoption of joint measures to stave off chains of nonpayments and thus to support the stability of the whole financial system. The document also stated that it was important to create a national system for checking the solvency of borrowers, as banks lack full and objective information on potential bank and nonbank borrowers. And finally, the document pointed to the need to develop principles for establishing mutual correspondent relations, insofar as the lack of relevant universal rules increased systemic risks to the banking system. According to the document, the central bank was to increase the level of commercial bank supervision significantly in the near future.

In 1997, the central bank prepared a draft document on organizing internal, commercial-bank risk management. The system included three elements: first, clarifying the distribution of powers and duties within the bank; second, defining a bank's policy in various segments of the market; and third, ensuring that there are checks on the implementation of the first two elements.

In the final analysis, the investment preferences of the public are the best criterion for evaluating confidence in the stability of the banking system. The dynamics of household deposits compared to other investments can provide an indication of general confidence.

---

7. *Vestnik Banka Rossii*, no. 22, 30 May 1995.

In financially stable conditions, in which interest rates on deposits are positive in real terms, the major factor constraining the growth of deposits is generally lack of confidence in the stability and reliability of banks. In many countries with developed market economies, this problem has been resolved through the establishment of household deposit insurance.

In the presidential decree of 10 June 1994, "On Improving the Work of the Banking System," the central bank was instructed to "accelerate the setting-up of a federal fund for insuring the assets of Russian banking institutions that handle the deposits of citizens of the Russian Federation." The decree specifically stated,

> to ensure the protection of Russian citizens' savings the central bank must accelerate the setting-up of a federal fund for insuring the assets of Russian banking institutions that handle Russian citizens' deposits. To establish that in cases provided for in Russian legislation, the safety of deposits can be guaranteed by the state using funds from the federal fund for insuring the assets of Russian banking institutions, handling the deposits of Russian citizens.[8]

The central bank expounded its position on this issue in April 1995 in a document entitled "Information on Measures Undertaken by the Central Bank Toward Commercial Banks Not Fulfilling Their Obligations to Creditors and Depositors." In this document it was noted that "creating a federal fund without the participation of the Russian government, and in particular, the Ministry of Finance, the State Property Committee, the Federal Bankruptcy Committee, Rosstrakhnadzor [the state insurance supervisory body], is impossible." However, the Ministry of Finance, citing budgetary constraints, refused to participate in the creation of this fund—even though, as world practice has shown, the costs of undermining confidence in the banking system could be considerably greater than the possible expenditure on the state's participation in this fund at the current time.[9]

Nonetheless, a Russian banking publication has identified a solution to this problem:

> Before the adoption of the law on mandatory insurance of household deposits, commercial banks and bank associations can set about creating

---

8. *Vestnik Banka Rossii*, no. 14, 21 June 1994.
9. As indeed was demonstrated in the 1998 financial crisis in Russia.—*Translation editor.*

funds for insuring household deposits on the basis of voluntary participation of banks through the creation of tax-deductible reserves.[10]

The problem of bank insolvency is another major obstacle to improving supervision and monitoring of credit institutions' activities. Some 1,035 credit organizations have gone bankrupt, while external management has been introduced to 430 credit organizations. However, a special law on insolvent credit institutions does not exist. In the current law, *On Enterprise Bankruptcy*, adopted in 1992, only one article is devoted to the peculiarities of bank bankruptcy. This article provides that a bank can be declared bankrupt only after its banking license has been revoked by the central bank. Otherwise all the norms of enterprise bankruptcy are applied in full to bank bankruptcy. This approach does not take into account the specific position of banks, and the fact that bankruptcy of a bank can lead to the insolvency and bankruptcy of many other organizations. For this reason, in practice, bank bankruptcy in many countries, independent of whether or not there exist any special laws, is viewed as an extreme and exceptional measure.

In Russia, revocation of a bank's license forces the bank into bankruptcy. However, as follows from Article 6 of the *Law on Banks and Banking Activity*, a banking license can be revoked not only because of bankruptcy but also on other grounds that are not directly linked to insolvency. Furthermore, a bank that has had its license revoked is not capable of conducting its professional activities, and consequently goes bankrupt. Simply having its license revoked can turn a solvent bank that has committed some minor violations into an insolvent bank. A situation is created in which a bank is deprived of its license but does not cease to exist as a legal entity. As a result, the claims of bank depositors and creditors are not satisfied, and the bank's capital is plundered. As of 11 April 1997, the central bank had revoked the licenses of 714 credit organizations; against 335 of these organizations, no one (out of those who were entitled to) had initiated bankruptcy proceedings. The central bank itself does not have this right.

At the beginning of 1997, a draft law was prepared, *On the Bankruptcy of Credit Organizations*, which granted broader powers to the central bank. This bill allots the central bank the right (and even the obligation) to undertake any actions aimed at "preventing the bank-

---

10. *Vestnik Banka Rossii*, no. 13, 4 April 1995.

ruptcy of credit organizations with the purpose of preserving depositor and creditor confidence." In this case, if the central bank has doubts about the solvency of a bank, it is entitled to:

- Require the founders of the bank to provide financial assistance.
- Propose to the bank that it decrease its dividend payments to founders and not to make loans to them.
- Demand that the bank change its organizational structure, including closing branches and representatives' offices.
- Introduce temporary administration if central bank requirements concerning maintenance of solvency are not adhered to.

Bank bankruptcy and liquidation are enforced as a last resort. In the draft law, the procedure is preserved in which the central bank strips the bank of its license in order to initiate bankruptcy. However, a new addition is the central bank's right to initiate bankruptcy procedures if a bank displays signs of insolvency—if creditors' claims on the bank are more than 1,000 minimal wages and these claims are not met within a period of three months.

According to the bill, founders are responsible if their bank is put into bankruptcy. There is a provision that arbitration courts may hold the founders of a bank that has been declared bankrupt responsible for its debts. Thus, if the bill is adopted, the role of the central bank in maintaining the stability of the banking system will increase significantly.

One aspect of the problem of increasing the stability and reliability of the banking system that is relevant not only to Russia is bad debts. Suffice it to say that the share of bad debts in the sum total of commercial bank loans in countries undergoing economic transition is 14%.[11] Moreover, as has been noted in studies by the International Monetary Fund, from year to year there has been an alarming growth in such debts.

In Russia, the figure is estimated to be around 9%. This level of bad debts has been a harbinger of serious banking crises in a number of countries. On the eve of the banking crisis in Argentina at the end of 1980, the figure was 9%; in Finland at the end of 1992, it was 9%; in Mexico in September 1994, it was 11%; in Norway at the end of 1991, it was 6%; in Sweden at the end of 1992, it was 7%; and in

---

11. *World Economic Outlook* (Washington, D.C.: International Monetary Fund, October 1996), 98.

Venezuela at the end of 1993, it was 9%.[12] It is worth adding that the real situation in the banking sector of countries undergoing economic transition, including Russia, is considerably more serious than the data on bad debts as a share of loans suggest, insofar as these countries are just beginning to switch to international standards for classifying assets, and to international accounting standards.

A serious deficiency in policies to increase the reliability and stability of the banking system is that they are carried out through a regime of special measures in the absence of a clearly formulated long-term systemic approach. In Russia in particular, the main method is "market-based": if banks cannot meet established norms and requirements for increasing capital and reserves, their licenses are revoked, and the banks cease operating. This approach is justified if banks are capable of fulfilling established requirements; however, it is also risky, for if banks are unable to fulfill the established requirements, this policy could precipitate a systemic banking crisis.

Developing and implementing a long-term program is a preferable method for tackling the task of bank restructuring. Such a program would require the allotment of necessary funds for bank sanitation, possibly the creation of special institutions and the development of appropriate regulatory documents; in parallel, it would also require the implementation of measures for the structural reform of industry as a necessary addition to the program of bank sanitation. This presupposes close coordination between the government and the central bank.

The chief task of the program would be to reduce the share of bad debts in bank loan portfolios and prevent their increase in future. There are two approaches to this—decentralized and centralized. In the first approach, the bulk of responsibility for regulating the problem of bad debts is placed on the banks themselves, which would have to set up special departments for this purpose; in the second instance, this task falls to a special agency that would take on banks' bad debts and regulate them. Such an agency should have the appropriate status and sufficient capital for the purchase of bad debts from banks. As the international experience of bank restructuring has shown, in most countries at some stage in the sanitation process, government funds of one kind or another are necessary.

---

12. Ibid.

The bank restructuring program should include provisions to encourage effective work by banks, such as the creation of a self-regulating mechanism, to prevent subsequent weakening of the banking system. For this reason it is necessary that commercial banks be able to act exclusively on a commercial basis, minimizing the possibility of pressure or interference from federal or regional regulators. It is also necessary to strengthen risk management, in addition to strengthening external supervision and creating a system of deposit insurance.

17 Institutional Reforms in the Agro-Industrial Complex[1]

Natalia Karlova, Irina Khramova, Eugenia Serova, and Tatiana Tikhonova

17.1. Reform of the Agricultural Sector and the Fundamental Aims

State agriculture under central planning was characterized not simply by a high level of state regulation but also by direct state management of agricultural production. Investment was centrally allocated by the state, as also, to a considerable extent, was working capital for agricultural producers. The state also set production goals, which in turn determined the branch and regional structure of agricultural production.

Kolkhozy and *sovkhozy* (collective and state farms) were the form of agricultural enterprise appropriate to the Soviet system. In the last years of the Soviet Union they did not differ from one another significantly in terms of their economic and organizational structure. They were major state enterprises with appointed managers, accountable to state bodies, and with a significant collective of workers. The basic features of this system concretized in the USSR at the end of the 1930s, and all changes thereafter occurred based upon this framework.

Six decades of development demonstrated the internal stability of the system of state agriculture while revealing two fundamental problems that proved impossible to resolve without making fundamental changes to the very core of the system. The first problem was the lack of endogenous economic incentives in the functioning of these enterprises. The second problem was the lack of an effective mechanism for motivating workers on collective farms.

---

1. The chapter draws on the material of O. Melyukhina of IET, and R. Yanbykh of the Russian government administration.

Both of these problems were recognized as early as the 1950s, and in the years that followed attempts were made to resolve them without changing the core foundation of the system. In the final analysis, however, the whole process of "improving the economic mechanism of the agro-industrial complex" amounted to attempts to introduce quasimarket conditions to a fundamentally nonmarket system. Consequently, all innovations were distorted.

As a result of the lack of incentives for enterprises and workers in the agrarian sector, Soviet agriculture fell behind much of the rest of the world. This lag became all the more apparent as the "green revolution" took hold in Third World countries, enabling them to make a sudden leap in productivity. Soviet agriculture, despite the ongoing process of reform, gradually fell into stagnation.

In order to stimulate production in the agrarian sector, the state increased subsidies to producers in the form of differentiated price increases, doubled tariffs on agricultural machinery, reduced interest rates on loans, periodically wrote off debts, and provided direct budget support, among other measures. By the end of the 1980s, on about one-third of the collective farms wages exceeded gross income. In other words, the farms were supported by the state through guaranteed wages.

By the beginning of the 1990s the system of state agriculture had reached the limits of its development. It had become an obstacle to technological progress in the sector, and reform required the replacement of its "system-forming" principles.

The situation in agriculture was aggravated by the state's policy of supplying the population with foodstuffs. The key principle here was "cheap foodstuffs for the Soviet people," which was laudable from a social perspective but had absolutely no economic grounding. For many years, even as incomes rose steadily, prices for basic foodstuffs were kept artificially low, and agricultural production grew only minimally.

Despite all the expenditure on agriculture, agricultural production could not hope to meet the increasing needs of the population, as evidenced by worsening problems with the supply of meat and dairy products, rationing, queues, and other symptoms of severe deficit. Because of its commitment to maintain stable, low food prices, however, the state went on subsidizing domestic consumers to an ever greater degree. In 1989 subsidies for food consumption

Table 17.1
Proportion of Retail Price of Food Staples Subsidized by the State, USSR, 1989

Foodstuff	Proportion of Retail Price Subsidized (%)
Bread	20
Beef	74
Pork	60
Mutton	79
Poultry	36
Milk	61
Butter	72
Cheese	48
Sugar	14

Source: *Food and Agricultural Policy Reforms in the Former USSR: An Agenda for the Transition* (Washington, D.C.: World Bank, 1993), 253.

amounted to one-third of the Russian budget, and the retail prices of staple products were 80% subsidized (Table 17.1).

Thus, the state simultaneously subsidized the agricultural producer and the consumer. Such subsidies tend to be progressive, and the national budget can cope with the situation in only two cases: if reserve agricultural production can be drawn on to increase food supplies or if state revenues grow constantly and adequately to cover the progressively increasing subsidies. However, agriculture did not increase productivity, and the returns on utilized resources were extremely low. With regard to budgetary revenues, in the 1970s they were replenished to a considerable degree by sales of natural resources. However, from the beginning of the 1980s, world prices for oil and gas, the country's main exports, fell sharply, which led to cuts in budget expenditures and also restricted the possibilities for subsidizing agriculture.

At the end of the 1980s the governments of Nikolai Ryzhkov and Valentin Pavlov made some timid attempts to raise food prices, but those efforts were clearly insufficient to solve the problem of growing subsidies. The monetary overhang in the hands of the population was so large that it was like trying to put out a fire with a teaspoon.

By the beginning of the 1990s the agrarian and food sectors stood in acute need of radical reform. The goals of the reforms included changing the agricultural system in fundamental ways, establishing more effective production relations in the food sector, and alleviating the burden of the agricultural and food sectors on the budget.

Reforming Soviet agriculture effectively required a reconfiguration of the whole system: pricing, financing and credit mechanisms, and the supply and marketing system. It also required significant social and psychological adaptation by the population. For these several reasons it was inescapable that agricultural reform would result in recession, imbalances, and the breakdown of existing ties.

17.2. Institutional Reforms in Agriculture

The transition to a market economy in agriculture required first the formation of market-oriented productional entities, since all previous development had demonstrated that state and collective farms could not be reconciled with a market economy. Worldwide, the form of agricultural enterprise most appropriate to a market economy is the private family farm. However, right from the start of post-Soviet reforms in Russia it was clear that a switch from Soviet-style agriculture to the family farm model could not be realized quickly. Surveys conducted in the countryside at the end of the 1980s revealed that only 10%–15% of rural inhabitants were interested in running their own farms. The lack of interest in part reflected mass beliefs, but it was also the result of a long period of specialization in agricultural production, during which former rural workers had become narrow specialists. Such specialization is unsuitable for a family farm; a broad set of skills is required. Moreover, the rapid development of a fundamentally new infrastructure and reform in agricultural machinery production was constrained by budgetary shortages, while the division of state and collective farms into family farms under existing conditions would have condemned the majority of farm workers to primitive technology and a primitive way of life. Another consideration was that during an economic crisis, it would not have made sense to destroy the existing production potential, however inefficiently used, of major agricultural enterprises, which often could not be divided up into small farms for technical reasons.

Thus, even before the start of reforms, the question was raised about the creation of production units—farms—in the agricultural sector that would be appropriate to market conditions and capable of functioning independently.

In 1987, experiments with farming were begun in Orel Region and in the Pytalovsky district of Pskov Region. Following the adoption of legislation in 1988, family farms started to appear in the guise of agricultural cooperatives. These and other private agricultural entrepreneurs rented land held by state and collective farms, and as a result found themselves dependent on their landlords. Subsequently it became possible to acquire plots of land for lifelong inherited possesion (a special land title was introduced to Union land legislation in 1989 and written into the Russian land code that gave all the rights associated with ownership, except for the rights to sell the land or use it as collateral). However, once again, state and collective farms were supposed to divide up their land, but they were in no hurry to do so. In villages, conflicts arose over land, and family farms remained somewhat exotic in the countryside, as the rest of the rural population tended to resist their formation. State and collective farms remained the main producers, and the main problem was to transform them into market agents capable of functioning under the new economic conditions.

At the end of 1991, some important measures were adopted that marked the start of the modern phase of agricultural reform. In 1992, the so-called campaign to reorganize state and collective farms began. The campaign, which was to last for one year, proposed the following: (1) the transfer of land and property to the ownership of the work collectives of agricultural enterprises, (2) the dividing up of property into individual shares, and (3) the re-registration of farms as legal entities provided for in the legislation of that period.[2]

The press rapidly declared this reorganization an exclusively formal procedure that in no way affected the core structure of the agricultural system. Those who expressed such views failed to see the fundamental changes occurring in the agricultural sector behind the formality of renaming *kolkhozy* and *sovkhozy* as joint-stock companies and partnerships.

First, the state monopoly of land was discontinued. The ownership of more than 85% of state-owned agricultural land was transferred to the collectives of agricultural enterprises. Of note, the land that state and collective farms had formerly used was not transferred to the ownership of the collective farms as legal entities but to the common ownership of a group of people, that is, the employees and

---

2. The Russian law *On Enterprises and Entrepreneurial Activity*, adopted at the end of 1991 did not include among enterprises such legal entities as a *kolkhoz* (collective farm) or *sovkhoz* (state farm). Thus the requirement to reorganize *kolkhozy* and *sovkhozy* had a formal, legal basis.

pensioners of the agricultural enterprises. In legal practice such common property usually belongs to a family, and indeed, after the reorganization of the agricultural enterprises, the land became the property of a larger "family," with four hundred to a thousand members. Although such joint ownership was an unusual legal form, it certainly worked as a transitional and temporary measure.

The co-owners were supposed to divide up the land they jointly owned into "conditional shares." A conditional share is a kind of security with special rules governing transferability. The owner of such a share has the unconditional right to a plot of land of a size specified in the share certificate and in a location determined jointly with other owners. Furthermore, a conditional share can be sold, leased, used as collateral, exchanged for a property share, and bequeathed. Until October 1993, such transactions were possible only between members of the original work collective; however, after the relevant decree was issued by the President, in October 1993, shares could be put into general circulation outside of the work collectives.

The most significant result of the reorganization was that peasants started to leave collective farms in large numbers to run their own farms. Whereas there were about 50,000 family farms in Russia at the beginning of 1992, over the next two years the number quadrupled. Furthermore, while before the reorganization three-quarters of private farmers were urban and most of the rest composed the rural elite, after land shares were distributed to rural workers the situation was reversed: private farms founded by former employees of collective farms who had used their land shares to leave the collective became predominant. In other words, the reorganization significantly simplified the process of leaving a collective farm to set up a private farm.

The land shares, by Russian standards, were not very large—about six to ten hectares per person. To avoid fragmentation of land use, the possibility of selling and leasing shares within the work collective of the *kolkhoz* or *sovkhoz* was established. Thus, a rural worker who wanted to set up his own farm could increase the size of his plot by buying or leasing shares from his neighbors. Moreover, he did not acquire a land plot but a kind of option allowing him to acquire a plot of land in accordance with the number of land shares held. Thanks to this system of shares, a former *kolkhoz* worker who had acquired land shares from the other owners of *kolkhoz* land

Table 17.2
Indicators of Family Farms, 1991–1998

	1991	1992	1993	1994	1995	1996	1997	1998
No. of farms at year end (thousands)	49	182	270	279	280.1	279	274	270
Average size of farm (ha)	41	42	43	43	43	44	48	51
Share of family farmlands in total farmlands (%)	—	3.4	4.9	5.0	5.0	5.3	5.8	5.8
Share of family farms in output of selected agricultural products (%)								
GAO	—	1	2	2	2	2	2.1	2
Grain	0.2	2.1	5.2	5.1	4.7	4.6	6.2	6.6
Sunflower seeds	0.4	5.8	9.9	10.2	12.3	11.4	10.6	11.0
Sugar beets	0.03	2.0	3.9	3.5	3.8	3.3	3.5	4.0
Potatoes	0.3	0.8	1.0	0.9	0.9	0.9	1.0	1.0
Meat (live weight)	0.1*	0.7*	1.1	1.4	1.7	1.8	1.6	1.6
Milk	0.1	0.5	1.1	1.3	1.5	1.8	1.5	1.6

*Carcass weight.
Source: Data of the Goskomstat.

could acquire land in one consolidated area, independently of how many land shares he had purchased or leased, and from whom.

Despite the rapid expansion of the private farm sector in the first years of the reform, however, as a percentage of agricultural production it remained insignificant (Table 17.2).

In the space of two years almost all state and collective farms in the country were reorganized. There were three basic options in the reorganization: first, state and collective farms could become joint-stock companies or production cooperatives; second, they could preserve their former status[3] (even under this option collective farms acquired ownership of the land and property and divided it up into shares); and third—the most difficult option—the collective farm could be dissolved entirely and divided into smaller, technologically independent farms, private or cooperative production enterprises,

---

3. At the start of the reforms a certain amount of opposition to the reorganization process arose, mainly because little work had been done to explain the reforms. Opponents interpreted the reorganization measures as an attempt to forcibly dissolve collective farms, although all procedures were voluntary as far as possible. Having encountered resistance from rural workers, the government in the spring of 1992 permitted farms that had no desire to reorganize to preserve their prior status. About one-third of farms chose to confirm their prior status.

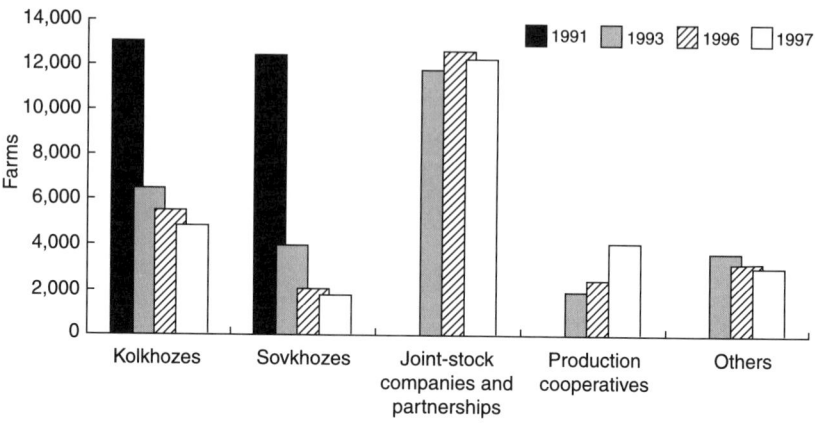

Figure 17.1
Number of large farms of various forms, 1991–1997 (year-end data). (Data from Goskomstat.)

and the like (Figure 17.1). There were only about 1,000 such cases out of 27,000 state and collective farms.

The various terms applied to the reorganized state and collective farms should not mislead. The majority of them, despite their names, were transformed into production cooperatives in which the major property belonged to the work collective on the basis of shared property, and management was carried out according to cooperative electoral principles (one member, one vote; the distribution of profits primarily on the basis of work done, not of shares owned; an elected governing body with a chairman; and the like). Genuine joint-stock companies do exist, but so far they have proven to be an exception rather than the rule.

As a result of the changes of the past few years, the basic form of agricultural enterprise in Russia changed considerably. The number of family farms, which serves as a catalyst for the real market in the agricultural sector, has grown substantially. In 1993–1995 fewer private farms were set up, primarily because those 10%–15% of rural workers who wanted to leave the state and collective farms had already done so, but also because of the difficult situation in which farmers found themselves when the large-scale state support that had been promised did not materialize.

There is, however, a more profound reason for the declining pace of family farm sector formation. Small farms turned out to be incapable of competing with the larger collective farms, not because of lower efficiency—available indicators suggest the opposite—but because of lack of access to market infrastructure. Processing enterprises and procurement agencies by and large prefer to do business with larger producers, as transaction costs are lower. Surveys have found that large farms can command higher prices for their products than small farms. Major enterprises in the Soviet downstream sector have had difficulty adapting to working with small producers, and the ramified layers of intermediaries such as those found in developed countries do not yet exist in Russia. In the transition period, a possible solution to the problem could be the farm cooperative, which could take on intermediary functions and make family farms more competitive with large agricultural enterprises. For a variety of social, psychological, economic, and legal reasons, however, very few cooperatives have been established.

A propos of the transformation of agricultural enterprises, certain socioeconomic consequences of the first stage of reorganization have already made themselves felt. Primarily, the increased economic independence of former state and collective farms has made them more sensitive to market signals. Thus, in 1992, for the first time in many decades, the decline in the acreage of cereals planted halted, as these crops were highly profitable at the time. The traditional (for the Soviet period) buckwheat deficit was eliminated in one year due to consumer demand. Sunflower crops have been expanding for several years and have been among the most profitable crops (mainly because of their export potential). The natural decline in effective demand for livestock products after the abolition of state consumer subsidies led to the sudden disposal of livestock on former collective farms, where during the Soviet era the livestock count was one of the most easily checked indicators of *kolkhoz* and *sovkhoz* activity. In other words, the emerging structure of production was largely shaped by consumer demand.

Today, three main stimulators of real transformation in former state and collective farms are already clearly identifiable. The first will ultimately lead to the division of farms into smaller, autonomous production units—family farms, partnerships, production cooperatives, and so forth.

The second is characteristic of areas with large-scale, extensive cereal production with high-tech, well-equipped, efficient enterprises. Generally, these farms have retained competent and energetic managers who are capable of increasing productivity. On these farms property is gradually being concentrated in the hands of a small group of owners by means of purchase, exchange, or lease of shares. In the near future, these holdings could become major commercial farms controlled by a small group of efficient owners (or even one owner), who would lease land from local people and hire significant number of workers, particularly for seasonal work. After the initial "transformation shock," many managers of such holdings have been inclined to repeat re-registration to become partnerships.

The transformation of collective farms into commercial farms that emerged during the initial reorganization can also be achieved through other mechanisms. Frequently, a successful neighboring farmer, through the acquisition of land and property shares, gradually (although sometimes all at one go) purchases a part—usually the most viable and efficient part—or the whole of an agricultural enterprise. In such cases, what started as a family farm can turn into a major agricultural enterprise of an entrepreneurial rather than collective type.

The third route to commercial farming entails the purchase of a former state or collective farm by a nonagricultural company. Today this process is developing fairly intensely in the southern regions of Russia, which are the most productive agriculturally. Corporations such as Gazprom, Rosenergo, major financial companies, or the railways purchase bankrupt collective farms at the cost of their debts to creditors. In the majority of cases, the aim of the purchase is not to acquire a farm subsidiary in order to ensure food supplies but to make an investment in production: the purchaser does not require food deliveries for itself, but at its own expense makes the necessary (and often significant) capital investments in the acquired holdings. Under such a purchase, the land most often remains the property of the former owners, although until recently lease agreements (or other contracts) for land shares have not been concluded in such deals because of lack of legislative clarity and the absence of legal recourse.

Finally, there is one less desirable, but evidently unavoidable (in the current situation), method of transforming former state and collective farms. This method will likely become fairly typical for marginal regions in the "non-black soil" area of Russia, which face a serious economic crisis in the agrarian sector. The majority of holdings in this area will probably nominally retain the form of a collective farm (regardless of the legal appellation—*kolkhoz* or joint-stock company) but in fact will be divided up into personal subsidiary plots for use by farm workers. Collective property will be used to service these personal plots. Production will be cut to the subsistence level for rural farm families (two or three cows, suckling pigs, and poultry). If demand for agricultural produce grows in the medium term, the most viable portion of these personal plots may form the basis for the rapid emergence of commercially oriented family farms in these regions.

The importance of household subsidiary holdings has increased dramatically during the agrarian reforms. This reality has developed as all restrictions on this sector have been removed and villagers have been given sufficiently large plots of land. The abolition of the "first commandment of the *kolkhoznik*"—supplies of agricultural products to the state are obligatory and take priority over all other needs—has made it possible for farms to distribute an ever greater share of agricultural produce to workers as payment in kind, or to sell produce to workers at discounted prices. This process has also created an environment conducive to the growth of household holdings (Table 17.3).

However, the transformation of single-household holdings into family farms depends, in our opinion, on the form of transformation undergone by the "parent" agricultural enterprise. If a collective farm has truly been turned into a private, commercial farm, then the new owners will strive to limit household holdings in order to reduce the potential for theft of produce and to limit distractions from work.

Table 17.3
Share of Households' Agricultural Production in GAO and Output of Selected Products (%)

	1991	1992	1994	1995	1996	1997	1998
GAO	31.2	31.8	43.8	47.9	49.1	51.1	58.6
Grain	NA	0.5	0.7	0.9	0.8	0.8	1.0
Sugar beets	NA	0.2	0.7	0.7	0.7	0.8	0.8
Sunflower seeds	NA	1.2	1.6	2.0	1.6	1.4	1.5
Potatoes	72	78.0	88.1	89.9	90.2	91.3	91.1
Vegetables	46	54.7	67.0	73.0	76.8	76.4	79.6
Meat	31	39.5	43.2	48.6	51.6	55.9	56.9
Milk	26	31.4	38.7	41.4	45.4	47.2	48.3
Eggs	28.2	26.0	28.8	30.2	31.2	30.4	30.1

Source: Russian Statistical Yearbook. Goskomstat, 2001.

Owners of household holdings, in their turn, are not interested in independence from the parent agricultural enterprise. Such independence could lead to their being cut off from important inputs and social services, which would increase uncertainty and risk. Thus, it would be incorrect to interpret the growth of household holdings as an indication of the growth of family farming in the near future.

The further development of land relations in the course of reforms depends on strengthening owners' and users' legal rights and on the free transfer of land shares, which would allow land ownership to be consolidated in the hands of efficient owners. It is important to note the key role of family farms in this process. Shares and land plots are unlikely to move en masse from one large farm to another, but small-holders create a certain environment around major agricultural enterprises, by means of which land transfer is possible even today: a prosperous farmer can gradually acquire land shares from major agricultural enterprises; a bankrupt farmer may try to sell his holding to the party that offers the higher price, whether it is the prosperous neighboring farmer or the efficient large farm. In this way a competitive market would be created, with free entry and exit for producers.

However, another solution to the land conflict has emerged. The managers of holdings, who are keenly aware of the problem, are proposing to effectively consolidate the land worked by major agricultural enterprises under their ownership as legal entities. Without a doubt, this would fundamentally resolve the contradiction in the existing land tenure. However, it would also result in the expropriation of land shares from all of those owners who two to three years ago put their shares into collective agricultural enterprises. From an economic perspective, this would halt further land reforms in the agrarian sector. In other words, the main factor in agricultural production—land—would be withdrawn from the market mechanism for redistribution between economic agents. The principal features of this approach are formulated in the provisions of the new land code that has been proposed by the State Duma over the past few years. This land code stands in blatant contradiction to the Constitution of the Russian Federation.

In March 1996 the President signed a decree, "On Guaranteeing the Constitutional Land Rights of Citizens," that sought to resolve the contradiction in land relations caused by the incomplete reforms. The decree proposed that within a year, all users of agricultural land (that is, all collective farms), as legal entities, conclude legally registered contracts with owners of land shares and land concerning the right to use this land. According to existing legislation, such contracts can take the following formats: (1) a lease for a fixed period and with conditions defined; (2) the addition of one's land share to the share capital of an agricultural enterprise or the sale of the land share to an enterprise as a legal entity; and (3) the addition to the share capital of the right to use the land share.

In the first and third cases, the owner of a land share remains the owner and has the right to terminate the contract if the conditions of the contract are violated. In the second case, the share owner loses ownership rights, and the land passes over to the agricultural enterprise as a legal entity.

The decree of 7 March 1996 has not been implemented in full, but it is already possible to draw certain conclusions about how its present implementation is affecting the development of land relations. First, it is clear that in the developed agricultural regions, rural workers prefer to lease out their land; in other words, they value land. In marginal regions land shares are sold to agricultural enterprises, which points to the rural population's belief that the marginality of their property is a stable condition, and also points to a lack of confidence in the imminent growth of demand for agricultural land in the region. Such beliefs, and the consequent willingness to sell, may partly be laid to lack of information on the part of rural farmers about the process taking place and to insufficient understanding of the deals that are made.

Lease contracts are concluded, as a rule, in one copy with all members of the collective of owners and for short periods of one to three years, or in exceptional cases for five years. This gives an indication of the underdevelopment and instability of the market for land shares, and of the lack of alternatives for owners of shares. Payment on lease contracts is most frequently made in kind, using the produce of the tenant or social services provided by the tenant.

Third, a certain quasimarket in land shares has appeared that allows land resources to be redistributed from inefficient owners to efficient ones, although this market is still operating on a small scale. However, in the most productive agricultural regions there are registered instances of owners of land shares leasing out the shares not to their enterprises but to a neighboring collective of family farms, because of more profitable contract terms. Conversely, there are also instances of farms refusing to lease land from owners of land shares, which leads to diminished land utilization—and land utilization is an important factor in strengthening agrarian production under the conditions prevailing in Russia. In such a case a social problem arises as well: What should be done with the unclaimed shares and their owners (in case the farms' refusal to lease the share is accompanied by refusal to employ the owner, which often is an interdependent decision)? This problem has not yet been successfully settled by the state.

The land market is just emerging in Russia, and is quite small. Currently less than 0.5% of land is available for transactions, and an additional 1.4% of land is leased. But the absolute majority of transactions have occurred in townships; farmlands are poorly engaged in the open turnover. With falling agricultural production, the demand for land is insignificant, and although the federal land legislation is quite liberal, development of the land market is much delayed (see Table 17.5).

17.3. Institutional Reforms in the Downstream Sector

Whereas land reform and the transformation of state and collective farms were carried out as part of a well-defined concept, other reforms in the agro-industrial complex have occurred in a more spontaneous and ad hoc fashion. The state simply withdrew from the distribution of produce, without making focused efforts to create the necessary market infrastructure. Previously, the planning center set production volumes and regional production specifics, established prices, and provided the link between suppliers and state procurers. The state provided the working capital.

Price liberalization and the reorganization of agricultural producers eliminated this concrete mechanism. The independence of producers made mandatory deliveries at fixed prices impossible, while the abolition of state supply of productive resources and party discipline eliminated the levers for enforcing deliveries to the state at below-market prices. The process of transforming this system of agricultural procurements started in 1992.

The majority of former organizations for state procurements were privatized and demonopolized, including Roskhleboprodukt, Potrebsoyuz, and others. Thus the old system of state procurements effectively ceased to exist.

Most important, however, was that the state ceased to monopolize the market for agricultural produce and foodstuffs, as alternative

Institutional Reforms in the Agro-Industrial Complex

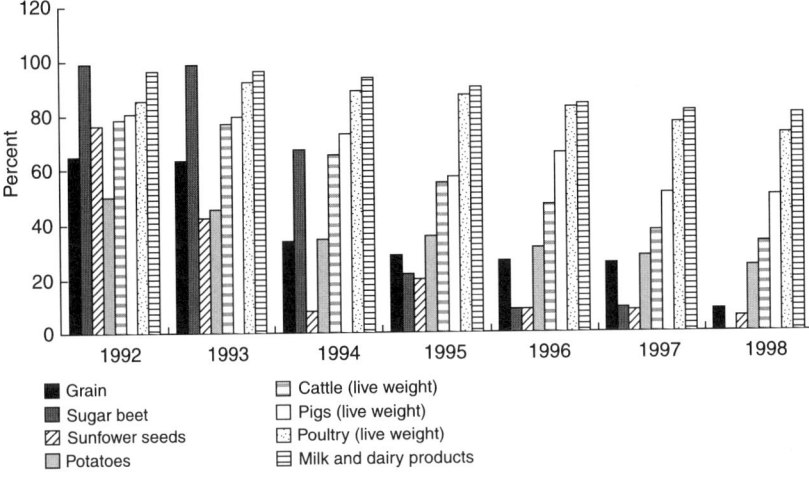

Figure 17.2
Share of state purchases in the total sales of major agricultural products. (Source: Goskomstat.)

intermediaries appeared and a real market started to form. The state's presence on agricultural and food markets has diminished over the past few years and the share of state procurements has steadily decreased, although the decreases have not been even across all product groups. The share of state procurements has declined most rapidly in the cereals market, while in the livestock market it still remains high (Figure 17.2).

However, it should be noted that deliveries of livestock to the state are measured using formal criteria, such as deliveries to enterprises and organizations that have been selected as state procurers for these kinds of products. As a rule, these are local, privatized milk- and meat-processing factories. All deliveries to these factories are recorded statistically as "state procurements." Consequently, the relatively high figures for state purchases of livestock production, while reflecting this fact, do not convey the actual participation of the state in the distribution of these products.

The decline in procurements by the federal food reserve has been the sharpest. This is illustrated most clearly by the cereals market (Figure 17.3).

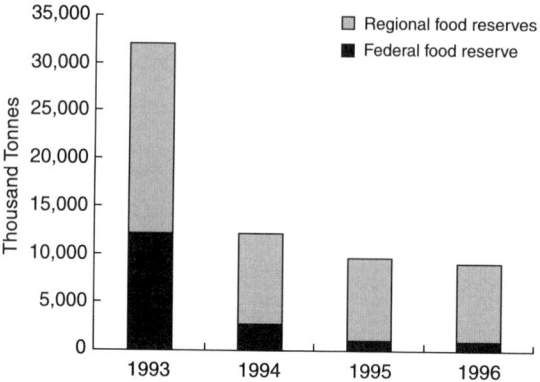

Figure 17.3
Dynamics of grain procurements for state food reserves. (Data from SovEkon.)

At the same time the volume of procurements by the regional food reserves also declined, by a factor of about 2.5 compared with 1993 (the year that regional funds were established). This decline in volume of procurements is evidence of the weakening influence of local administrations on producers, given limited local budget funds.

Besides the privatization of the network of state procurement organizations and the substantial decline in the volumes of produce held in state food stocks, the method of purchasing has also changed. Currently, a contractor for the delivery of produce to the state funds (especially for cereals and sugar) has access to cheap budget credits to cover the full volume of the operation. These credits (especially in conditions of high inflation) are in themselves a significant source of profit. Moreover, they are distributed on a nontransparent, noncompetitive basis, which is conducive to corruption, abuses of all kinds, and the use of budget funds for purposes other than those intended. The system of state procurements has become one of the most corrupt subsectors of the economy.

As the state withdrew from the markets for agricultural produce and foodstuffs, a market infrastructure gradually emerged in its place. Food exchanges, which reached the peak of their development in 1991–1992, were among the first experiments in this sphere. At the time, the main traded goods were cereals and white sugar. The share of exchange trade in the general turnover of each good was extremely small, but nonetheless in a number of regions it determined market prices (in particular in Rostov oblast, where interviews revealed that reports of trading on the exchange, which were disseminated to the districts by computer, were used as guidelines for grain deals, including state procurements).

Until autumn 1992, cereal prices on the exchanges persistently exceeded declared state procurement prices (and at that time, state procurements continued to dominate the market). In September 1992, however, under pressure from the agrarian lobby, the government raised state prices above exchange prices. The immediate impact of the price change was to divert business from the food exchanges to the "shadow" economy (opening the door to financial standardization), and this became an important factor in the decline of trading on the exchanges.

The second factor in the decline of trading on the grain exchanges was the widespread practice of restricting the export of production beyond regional boundaries, a practice that was enforced by regional administrations. Currently, trading on the food exchanges does account for a significant share of the market.

In 1992, the Ministry of Agriculture and Food set up a special department for the development of wholesale markets, and the first World Bank agricultural loan (ARIS) included financing for wholesale markets; also, a number of wholesale market projects have been developed with technical assistance from the European Union and a number of West European countries in Moscow, St. Petersburg, Rostov-on-Don, and other cities. Nonetheless, this form of organized trade of agricultural produce has not developed significantly.

It would appear that wholesale markets will not become a significant element of the agricultural market infrastructure in Russia. Following the reorganization of agricultural enterprises in Russia, the main producers of agricultural produce are still large-scale farms, for which direct deliveries as well as direct association with a major wholesaler entail lower costs than selling on the wholesale market.

Potato and vegetable production are an exception to this rule. Currently, small producers, growing produce on private plots, dominate this sector (accounting for 75%–90% of total gross product), and they require a wholesale market. Therefore, it is reasonable to assume that wholesale markets for the sale of fruit and vegetables will become more widespread.

The system of seasonal food trade fairs, common in the Soviet period, at which contracts were concluded for the delivery of produce in the current season, has been revived. At the outset of the reform period, when inflation was high, such contracts were often concluded without setting prices, making them more an agreement of intent than a genuine contract for delivery. Therefore, the development of trade fairs only really became possible at the onset of financial stabilization.

The private intermediary is a completely new element in the system of agricultural trade. Such an intermediary can be a large company, not necessarily one specializing in the purchase of agricultural produce, or an individual. Powerful intermediary structures are already operating on the cereal and sunflower markets. (Indeed, most major financial groups in the country have departments which deal with the purchase of these products.)

Because of the widespread use of commodity credits and barter, oil companies have acquired significant volumes of grain and as a result have themselves become intermediaries. New, specialized wholesalers have also emerged, and a grain union has been established, uniting grain wholesalers.

The intermediary sector of the livestock market is not so large. Small, private intermediaries are fairly common on the meat market and play a particularly significant role in buying livestock from households (for large farms the volumes involved are too small to be of commercial interest). The major milk- and meat-processing enterprises, confronted with the problem of acquiring raw materials in the absence of mandatory state deliveries, have started to develop their own procurement networks.

New economic realities have provided a stimulus for vertical integration in the agro-industrial complex. Processing enterprises, particularly those working with dairy and meat products, conserves, and sugar, have started to establish more long-term contracts with suppliers as a result of competition. Moreover, there is a clear trend toward investing in the development of supplier facilities, providing credits (including commodity credits), and building livestock housing, although the nature of these deals is not always very clear. For example, a milk factory may equip a number of its main supplier farms at its own expense but may not register this deal either as an investment in the enterprise or as a lease—or in any other clear, legal manner.

Major food-processing enterprises are starting to buy up smaller ones to use as primary collectors or processors of raw ingredients.

These trends are similar to current global trends and will intensify as demand for agricultural produce starts to increase inside Russia.

Whereas the features mentioned above follow the general theories concerning transitions to a market-oriented economy, the development of barter deals on the market for agricultural produce is a direct consequence of the deficit of funds and tax avoidance. On this level, considerable volumes of agricultural production are distributed within farms as wages in kind, dividends, payment for land rental, and so forth.

As with the reform of the system of state procurements and the formation of food markets, the privatization of the processing industry has faced serious problems during reform.

The agricultural sector in the USSR was always a bottleneck in the food production chain. Numerous attempts to redirect some of the funds earmarked for the agro-industrial complex away from agriculture to the tertiary sector were unsuccessful. Furthermore, in accordance with the planned economy doctrine of the "impermissibility of parallelism," only one milk enterprise was established in each district, one meat-processing enterprise per several districts, and so on. Together with the radial communications system (for example, the district center was at the center of the road network), conditions were created for the emergence of local food-processing monopsonies, which presented a major problem when it came time for privatization.

As early as the perestroika years, work collectives were taking control of food-processing enterprises under hire-purchase agreements. The federal privatization program made their privatization a priority area. However, at the end of 1992 a government decision was taken concerning special procedures for the privatization of enterprises for the primary processing of agricultural produce.

The incorrect interpretation of the fall in purchase prices for agricultural produce as a result of the "local monopoly" of processing enterprises (although it was the result of the incorrect state subsidies policy) led to the adoption of a series of antimonopoly measures against the entire system of processing. Chiefly affected was the privatization scheme, under which half of shares offered by closed subscription were distributed among agricultural producers. Because a significant proportion of these enterprises were bought up under the preceding hire-purchase scheme, agricultural producers were not always able to acquire controlling stakes in processing enterprises. In turn, agricultural producers' inability to acquire control of processing enterprises was utilized as an explanation for the ineffectiveness of the special privatization procedure implemented. This argument was supported by the growing disparity in prices between the agricultural sector and the downstream sector. In fact, the cause of the price disparity can be found in the fundamentally incorrect approach that was adopted. Agricultural producers, even if they gained control of food processors, had little influence, and many suppliers sold their produce to enterprises other than those in which they were shareholders. Nonetheless, the battle against "the monopoly position of processors" intensified in 1994 with the adoption of a measure requiring a secondary share issue at all primary processing enterprises for purchase at a discount by agricultural producers, so that suppliers of raw ingredients could acquire controlling stakes. This secondary issue of shares turned into a fiasco: either it was not conducted at all, or agricultural producers refused to acquire the shares even at extremely favorable rates. In some regions the undistributed shares in processing enterprises were transferred to the administration for management in trust, thus in some respects amounting to "deprivatization."

Besides privatization restrictions, other methods were employed to tackle local monopolies. In most regions, prices (or "norms of profitability") are established for processing enterprises. Until 1995, processors reported the price of products to the local authorities and had to justify every price increase. There were even some attempts made to put a cap on the wages paid to enterprise managers.

As a result, the processing industry, which should have been the engine of the foodstuffs sector, suffered a greater decline than agriculture itself. The difficulty of accumulating sufficient funds (because of the many restrictions) meant that investment in production was minimal, and profits had to be used to pay wages.

The transfer of control over processing to financially weak agricultural producers did not equal a growth in output. However, the food industry is of interest to both domestic and foreign investors. Consequently, according to investment figures for the Russian economy, this sector is the third most important (although by a wide gap) after the gas and oil sectors. Unfortunately, the government's policy with respect to the food sector is obstructing the potential inflow of necessary capital.

17.4. Formation of an Agricultural Credit System

Soviet agriculture, because it was a component of the centrally planned economy, did not enjoy a system of market-based credit. State and collective farms received short-term and long-term loans from the regional branches of the state-owned Agroprombank, and state farms also received capital investment from the state budget. The loans were not of a commercial nature—that is, the bank was not trying to make money on the difference between deposit and lending interest rates (the interest was generally insignificant in any case).

The national budget was a source of long-term loans to agriculture, while seasonal loans were extended using the funds held in Agroprombank by agricultural producers on their settlement accounts. So-called "plan loss-making farms"—farms that were loss-making within the norms set for them by the state—received special credits with a two-year maturity in order to support working capital.

In line with the economic paradigm of the time, debts of agricultural enterprises were periodically written off or extended (the most significant write-offs occurred in 1965, 1978, and 1982). Write-offs were performed by transferring budget funds to Agroprombank in the sum of the bad debt. In 1990, the written-off debts of state and collective farms were for the first time explicitly included in the state's debt accounts.

This system encouraged financial irresponsibility and subsidy dependence in agricultural producers and had a formative influence on collective farm management. At the start of market reforms, the agricultural sector lacked an appropriate credit system, and those involved in the Soviet lending process were completely unprepared to adapt to new commercial conditions.

Liberalization of the economy seriously aggravated the so-called "long-term farm problem," whose essential proposition was that farms' income would always lag behind incomes in other sectors of the economy. Thus, 1991 was fairly successful in financial terms for agricultural producers, and the income earned should have been sufficient to cover work in preparation for the following year's harvest. However, price liberalization at the start of 1992 resulted in the rapid growth of price disparities that hindered the agriculture section. The agricultural sector had no funds for the spring planting season, and the inflation that followed the liberalization of prices made the problem chronic.

Furthermore, owing to the high inflation that accompanied the first stage of the reform, only short-maturity credits of two to three months were extended, which was less than a third of the maturity required for seasonal lending to agricultural producers. The lack of loans meant that even the most profitable sectors could not function if high seasonal costs were involved. For example, in the south of Russia vegetable growing is highly profitable, but farms prefer grain production because it requires substantially lower investment.

Lending to agricultural producers is also made problematic by their dependence on climate and weather. Because uncontrollable natural factors can cause a sharp drop in production, the guarantee on loans made to agricultural producers is relatively low, and therefore commercial banks tend to demand major collateral for such loans. In the agricultural sector, collateral itself, excluding real estate (mortgages are not used in seasonal lending), has its peculiarities. Because a poor growing season resulting from natural factors affects not just individual producers but whole regions, the collateral value of special equipment and livestock is marked down, as serious costs would have to be incurred in transporting it to other regions for sale. In 1994, many banks that traditionally extended credit to Russian agricultural producers made seasonal loans to enterprises that utilized agricultural machinery and livestock as collateral. These assets, which had a certain liquidity at the time the credit contracts were concluded, were almost totally illiquid by the end of the agricultural year (the year was particularly difficult in financial terms for Russian agriculture). The banks, consequently, found themselves in a very difficult position.

From the start of the radical economic reforms, Russian agricultural producers, regardless of their legal form, specialization, or location, have encountered serious problems because of the lack of appropriate credits, primarily seasonal credits. By this point the commercial banking system was already fairly well developed, but because of the factors mentioned earlier the agrarian sector could not avail itself of banks' services to a significant degree. With the planting season approaching and agricultural producers lacking funds to sow crops, the federal government decided to solve the problem in the same way it approached all problems in the agrarian sector: with ad hoc measures. Subsidized credit turned out to be the simplest measure to implement, although not necessarily the best. And so subsidies were adopted, and to a large extent they determined the development of the system of agricultural lending over the following years.

We will now examine this system as it has developed up to the present time. As noted, from the outset the state offered agricultural producers cheap central bank credits. In 1992, agricultural enterprises—former and still functioning state and collective farms—were provided with credit from federal sources at an interest rate of 28% per annum, while family farmers were offered credit at 8% per annum. These interest rates included a 3% margin for the commercial banks that were actually performing the lending. In 1993, the borrowing rate was set at 28% per annum for all agricultural producers.

Although these credits were distributed by "authorized" banks (mainly Agroprombank, its regional branches, or former regional branches that had become independent institutions), de facto distribution to borrowers was carried out by the agricultural administration. There is no need to prove the inefficiency of the bureaucratic method of distributing funds—the whole experience of the Soviet system is evidence enough. However, the first thing that almost all regional administrations did was to link central bank credits to the delivery of produce to federal and regional food reserves. As a result, the only source of credit for agricultural producers at that time became a lever for restraining the commercialization of production, its structural reform, the emergence of other channels for sales, and in general the transition to the market.

Central bank credits were designed in such a way that "authorized" banks received their margins monthly, while the principal and interest were paid at the end of the agricultural year. Thus, the bank simply functioned as a conduit for these credits, and had no interest in the loans being repaid. A selective investigation of Agroprombank branches in several regions of the European part of Russia also showed that the 3% margin was insufficient to cover all of the banks' costs incurred during these operations. Therefore, it would seem that banks' interest in participating in the distribution of loans was based on two factors. First, these banks were primarily oriented toward agricultural borrowers and for the most part had a limited clientele, and thus the central bank credits they received were their main source of commercial funds. Second, having received state funds for crediting farms, banks could use these funds for short-term and more profitable operations on the money markets in their own commercial interests. That activity initially was difficult to monitor.

Central bank credits were provided for specific aims, and banks were responsible for confirming that funds were used as intended. However, it is clear that under the circumstances, this condition was not fulfilled. Furthermore, farmers learned to sell cheap state credits to other sectors of the economy. Because the central bank refinancing rate fluctuated between 180% and 230%, these operations could be fairly profitable, particularly in comparison with agricultural production.

There is no need to rehash here the problems of corruption and the growth of criminality in agro-industrial complex lending that came about as a result of the aforementioned central bank–subsidized credits. These credits clearly demonstrated the ineffectiveness of cheap credit in general and for the agricultural sector above all.

At the end of 1993, all forms of cheap credit were abolished, and at the federal level at least, this decision has been adhered to so far. However, it is also important to understand that the credits were preferential not only in terms of interest rates but also in terms of maturity. Credits were extended for a year at a time when the average maturity of short-term loans across the country was two months. Only the subsidized interest rate was abolished, so central bank credits were maintained throughout 1994, but at an interest rate equal to the central bank's refinancing rate.

The lending scheme also underwent some changes. Although officials, as before, were most important in the distribution of credits, "authorized" banks were given the right to turn down farms that appeared to be insolvent. Furthermore, banks started to take collateral on seasonal credits (mainly livestock and agricultural machinery). Thus, the main problems of central bank credit transfers, with some exceptions, were preserved under the new procedure.

The year 1994 was the most difficult year financially for agricultural producers. It was already clear in the summer that agricultural producers would not be able to pay back the credits they had already received. There were several possible ways of resolving this problem. The bad debts could have been used to strengthen the results of the institutional reforms, to further inculcate in farm managers the norms of financial discipline and responsibility. For this purpose, it would have been sufficient to make the restructuring or even the write-off of the debts of each individual farm conditional, first, on them declaring bankruptcy (mainly a psychological measure), and second, on specific obligations to undertake more profound reorganization, liquidation, or to accept the appointment of a state manager (depending on the specific case).

In fact, the government reverted to indiscriminately writing off debts. At the end of 1994 and the beginning of 1995, decisions were made that extended the due date of agricultural producers' debts on central bank credits between 1992 and 1994 in the sum of more than Rb 20 trillion. For comparison, federal spending on agriculture in the 1995 budget amounted to Rb 12 trillion. The Rb 20 trillion was categorized as state debt and is to be paid off in installments by the year 2005, with 10% of the debt paid off per year. Banks have issued promissory notes backed by this debt, as it is permanent on their balance sheets.

The restructuring of debts in the first half of 1995 marked a reversion to the Soviet period, but in an even worse form: in the past, such write-offs were expected, but today write-offs negatively affect the orientation of the economically strongest farms, which were striving to pay back their outstanding loans. From the beginning, it was obvious that restructuring over a ten-year period in the existing economic climate was tantamount to writing off the debts.

Besides federal credits, regional governments implemented their own credit subsidies financed from their own budgets or from the fund for the support of very important sectors of the economy. The consequences were just as deleterious.

In the first years of reform, owing to inertia in the thinking of the political leadership, attempts were made to subsidize agricultural credits not out of the budget, but by forcing certain decisions on banks, many of which by that time had become independent commercial banks. Thus, in 1992 Orel oblast administration instructed the regional branch of the central bank to explore the possibility of providing cheap credit in the sum of Rb 410 million to poultry farms for the purchase of grain fodder. In 1993, commercial banks were advised to provide cheap credit to trade companies at their own expense, and also to restrict credits to organizations "importing" foodstuffs and agricultural produce that was "produced in sufficient quantities on the territory of the oblast." In Pskov, in 1993, similar "recommendations" were given to commercial banks to credit farms that were "close to bankruptcy," using their produce as collateral and under guarantee from the oblast administration.

So-called commodity credits became another form of seasonal crediting of the agricultural sector. After crisis-ridden 1994, the Ministry of Finance proposed a commodity credit scheme for agriculture. The proposal was made that oil companies clear their debts to the federal budget by supplying agricultural producers with fuel. Agricultural producers, therefore, were supplied with a resource that was crucial for the sowing season, and were obliged to pay the debts to the budget at the end of the season. This can be viewed as a form of interest-free credit to the agricultural sector at the expense of the revenue side of the federal budget (because revenue payments to the budget were conveniently delayed).

As with the central bank credits of previous seasons, regional officials immediately tied the provision of this new credit to farms to the farms' deliveries to state food reserves. Fuel supplies were distributed to regions and districts, and then to farms, under contractual agreement. Oil companies were assigned to specific regions. All this could not but have negative consequences, first and foremost for the agricultural producers themselves. Produce was delivered to the state food funds at set prices (no matter how they were referred to: agreed, minimum, guaranteed, maximum, and so on). Thus, one side of the produce-for-fuel exchange was not actually set by the borrower. The assignment of oil companies to specific regions had, almost without exception, a monopoly effect and led to the inflation of fuel prices by 20%–30% above average market prices. Thus, the other side of this exchange was excessively high.

Therefore, the agricultural producer that received fuel for state commodity credits actually paid interest in the amount of the difference between the relative prices of the agricultural produce and fuel established in the credit contract and the real difference between the value of these products on the market.

IET, together with the Agrarian Institute, has conducted research into the real value of commodity credits at the end of 1995 in a number of oblasts (districts) in the European part of the country. Preliminary results show that agricultural producers were actually paying annual interest of 120%–130% on the state commodity credits, or a rate comparable to the central bank's refinancing rate.

That agricultural producers pay interest on the loans they receive is entirely normal, but in the case of the state commodity credits, the state was the creditor, while the interest de facto accrued to the oil companies. Commodity credit debts, as was the case with central bank credits of 1992–1994, were not paid. These debts are being restructured and indeed are not likely ever to be paid off.

Commodity credits in the form in which they were implemented were a hidden subsidy to the agricultural sector. In 1995–1996, the total volume of expenditure on the agro-industrial complex written into the budget was almost the same as the volume of subsidies from the revenue side—that is, from commodity credits. The great danger of such hidden forms of subsidy is the uncontrolled growth of expenditures.

In 1997, the state changed its scheme for the seasonal crediting of agriculture, as a result of which commodity credits were abolished as the main form of credit. Instead, a fund for preferential crediting of the agro-industrial complex was established. Credits were supposed to be provided to agro-industrial enterprises at one-quarter of the central bank's refinancing rate, and the banks through which the crediting was done were entitled to levy a 4% surcharge.

The fund was financed from the budget and also from the repaid debts of the commodity credits given in 1995–1996, which totaled more than Rb 9 trillion. Since agricultural producers were incapable of repaying these debts at the beginning of the year, and because cheap credits were required for the sowing season, a special scheme was developed. Regional administrations, wishing to get cheap credits for their agricultural enterprises, could register the debt of agricultural producers located on their territory as agricultural promissory notes (agrobonds) quoted on the stock market. The earnings from the sale of these promissory notes were to be transferred to the fund for preferential crediting.

SBS-Agro was appointed as the main distributor of credits from the fund. Alfa Bank was also involved to a lesser degree.

It would be incorrect to say that this scheme for seasonal lending was run on an entirely commercial basis (low interest rates, and with the Ministry of Agriculture and Food setting the credit limits for each region). Nonetheless, under this scheme the banks involved could determine the solvency of borrowers and decide whether or not to lend money, without interference from state officials. The regional limits established were not particularly strict. In a number of regions the limit was not reached because the banks could not find a sufficient number of solvent borrowers, and in other regions credits were extended above the established limit. SBS-Agro and Alfa Bank, being commercial banks from their inception and also powerful banks, were not so susceptible to the influence of officials as Agroprombank had been prior to its acquisition by SBS. As a result, the rate of repayment of agro-industrial complex debts increased sharply, reaching almost 100%.

A tender was conducted between banks for the right to participate in the program for preferential lending to the agro-industrial complex in 1998. Twelve banks were selected, including SBS-Agro and Alfa Bank. In 1999 the commodity credit was reused again, although the fund is still alive.

Cooperative credit in market economies is one of the main forms of agricultural credit. Unfortunately in Russia cooperatives have not become a mass phenomenon, or an economic necessity for the producers themselves. Until now, in the agricultural sector it has only been possible to speak of the partial use of some individual cooperative principles in order to resolve specific credit problems.

The concentrated efforts of the state are required for credit cooperatives to really take off, including the creation of an appropriate regulatory base and the establishment of an education for the rural population in cooperative principles. Some financial aid might even be appropriate for emerging cooperatives, but this would have to be undertaken with extreme care, so that budget subsidies would not be used as a means of bribing people to join cooperatives.

The most widespread and rapidly developing form of short-term commercial, agricultural credits is not bank loans but credits within the framework of vertical integration in the agro-industrial complex. One of the most interesting varieties of this is commodity credits from commercial firms,[4] the essence of which is as follows: companies interested in a guaranteed supply of agricultural produce after the harvest supply resources to producers in advance under contract for future deliveries. In contrast to state commodity credits, commercial deals of this kind have proven to be better adapted to the needs of the village. First, they are not tied exclusively to fuel, but

---

4. Commodity credits are often viewed by agricultural producers themselves as a variety of barter.

depend on the farmers' needs. Second, these credits, for obvious reasons, are distributed to the most reliable producers, and not according to bureaucratic parameters; the latter often results in even distribution to all parties (not to mention the inherent opportunities for corruption). Third and finally, in a number of cases the real interest rate on such credits was lower than the 120%–130% on state credits mentioned earlier.

The companies that provide such commodity credits make up a rather diverse group. First and foremost this group includes processing enterprises, such as sugar factories, that work directly with raw agricultural products. Financial groups are also involved in providing commodity credits; many have foodstuff companies (involved in processing or trading) that provide seasonal production resources, such as fuel, fertilizers, and so on. Many oil companies that have accumulated grain on forward contracts are major retailers of cereal on the grain exchanges.

Besides providing short-term credits in the form of various types of commodities, financial lending by the companies mentioned above to their agricultural partners is quite common. These companies have their own financial resources, but they can also use bank credits, as it is easier for them to borrow from commercial banks than for agricultural producers.

However, commercial commodity credits to the agricultural sector do have a negative side. The prevalence of these schemes makes the agricultural market less transparent. Thus, for example, despite the free market, grain prices are below world prices, unquestionably as a result of commodity credits and other forms of barter.

While commodity credits are a contractual form of a loan, both sides to which agree on the conditions of borrowing, growing farm arrears to suppliers are a spontaneous, compulsory (for the creditor) form of loan.

Capital investment in the agricultural sector today is less of a problem than seasonal credits, but its minimal presence creates long-term problems for the sector. Capital investment in the agricultural sector is declining faster than investments in other sectors of the economy, while construction and the purchase of equipment and machinery in this sector have fallen to extremely low levels (Table 17.4).

Currently, this problem is partially resolved by means of budget funds and money from various funds organized by various foreign

Table 17.4
Output Dynamics Across Major Types of Resources for Agriculture

	1991 (thous. pcs.)	1998 (thous. pcs.)	1998/1991 (%)
Tractors	178	9.8	5.5
Grain harvesters	55.4	1	1.8
Forage harvesters	7.4	0.2	2.7
Flax harvesters	2.7	0.2	7.5
Tractor ploughs	81.7	1.1	1.3
Tractor seeders	41	1.3	3.2
Tractor cultivators	72	3.3	4.6
Mowers and threshers	20.4	6.5	31.9
Milking equipment	17.7	0.4	2.3

Source: Goskomstat.

and international institutions to provide technical assistance to Russia. Usually credits are provided on a competitive basis on submission of a business plan and with some degree of self-financing of the given project. However, the vast majority of loans are provided for projects connected with food processing and services for the agricultural sector rather than for agricultural production itself. This can be largely justified by the fact that enterprises in the primary and tertiary sectors of the agro-industrial complex are the main potential creditors of agricultural producers.

The creation in 1994 of the so-called leasing fund marked a new form of state support for direct investment in the agricultural sector. Under this scheme, Rosagrosnab purchased agricultural machinery and equipment using earmarked funds from the federal budget and supplied the equipment to agricultural producers on the condition that it be paid for in installments. At first glance, the program provided substantial assistance in re-equipping agricultural producers (in 1994 more than Rb 1 trillion was allotted), but the program as it was actually implemented benefited machine-building factories and Rosagrosnab above all.

Rosagrosnab, selected to be the government's authorized agent without any kind of tender, ordered machinery and equipment from machine-building factories and distributed it among Russia's regions. The regions in turn distributed the equipment received among the districts, which in turn distributed it among farms. The machinery and equipment was ordered centrally, and therefore did not necessarily meet the needs of local agricultural producers. In

Table 17.5
Dynamics of Regional Land Redistribution Funds

	Agricultural Land in Regional Land Redistribution Funds (thous. of ha)
1 Feb. 1992	9,490
1 Mar. 1993	6,636
1 Mar. 1994	13,095
1 Jan. 1995	13,758
1 Jan. 1996	14,621

Source: Data from the Agrarian Institute.

particular, in 1994 half of the funds were used to purchase equipment from Rostselkhozmash, with the aim of keeping this giant enterprise afloat. The whole program was reminiscent of the old Soviet system.

As a result, the leasing scheme did little to facilitate the acquisition by agricultural producers of needed agricultural equipment. In 1994, the leasing scheme accounted for a minority of the total volume of agricultural machinery acquired by producers.

Besides state leasing, private leasing companies have started to emerge in the agricultural machinery market. The best-known example is a company set up by Vladimir Tractor Factory. Leasing of agricultural machinery is of interest not only to producers of the machinery, but also to universal leasing companies: agricultural machinery is relatively inexpensive (compared with equipment for the fuel and chemical industries, and machine-building), while the market for it is potentially huge.

Considerable attention has been devoted to the problem of mortgage borrowing. In our opinion, this problem has been somewhat artificially exaggerated. Mortgage borrowing is undoubtedly one of the main sources of funds for agricultural producers in market economies. However, it requires a developed market for agricultural land. Furthermore, in Russia, agricultural production has declined by one-third, mainly due to the decline in effective demand; and in line with this the demand for land has also fallen. Thus, in the majority of regions, land redistribution funds (fertile plots that can be acquired for free within limits set by the districts) are not decreasing, and at certain times have even been increasing (Table 17.5). In other words, land in most regions of the country is not a liquid asset, which means it cannot properly be used as collateral. Therefore, mortgage borrowing only applies to a few, specific regions in which land transfer is already taking place, for example in Moscow oblast (where, in fact, a mortgage borrowing pilot program was initiated).

17.5. The System of State Support for Agriculture

The financing of state agriculture suffered from a whole series of systemic problems, as a result of which productivity growth did not materialize. The liberalization of consumer prices and abolition of consumer subsidies on staple products in 1992 immediately decreased the effective demand of the population for foodstuffs. The meat and dairy sectors of the agro-industrial complex were the first to encounter problems with selling their produce. First, livestock production is delivered to the market relatively evenly throughout the year, and by spring of 1992 the decline in demand was already apparent. Second, the demand for meat and dairy products in Russia appears to be highly elastic: when incomes fall, the population ceases to purchase these products first. It was in this context that the financial crisis in the livestock sector occurred.

Under pressure from agricultural producers, one of the first erroneous measures of the reform period entailed a subsidy of livestock production at the primary producer level. An analysis of 1992 demonstrates that twice in the course of the year—in March, when the subsidies were introduced, and in August, when they were increased—the purchase prices of meat and milk fell. This was because subsidies to producers had created false market signals, raising the product price above its genuine equilibrium price, which in turn delayed the pull-back in production necessary to meet lower demand. However, the processing enterprises, having a direct link to the consumer, received market signals about real demand and held their prices accordingly. However, the supply of raw materials for meat- and dairy-processing factories remained higher than necessary. Under these conditions, the purchase price fell, a process that was in no way connected to monopolization of the sector.

Thus, the government puts additional strain on the budget by seeking funds to support livestock production, and with great difficulty transfers these subsidies to the producers, only to discover that through the purchase price, the processing industry becomes the main beneficiary of these subsidies.

In 1993, livestock subsidies were transferred to the regional level. Our research, conducted in a number of regions, found that this phenomenon of livestock subsidy transfer from producers to processors is repeated at the level of individual regions. But in addition to this, the regionalization of subsidies provided a stimulus for the breakdown of the single market across the Russian Federation. A region that subsidizes its own livestock producers for reasons unrelated to market logic strives to prevent the "export" of production beyond its territorial boundaries (throughout the world, producer subsidies are combined with support for the export of production and restrictions on imports, while consumer subsidies are combined with the regulation of exports). Thus, one of the characteristic features of agricultural financing in Russia, livestock subsidies, was created.

Minimum guaranteed prices have become another popular method of supporting producers in Russian agriculture. In 1995 an attempt was made to establish guaranteed prices for grain and other staple products, chiefly livestock products. However, the minimum prices were set below the level of market prices over all the following years, and consequently were ineffective (Figure 17.4).

The situation with respect to minimum prices is not unique to Russia. Attempts to establish minimum guaranteed prices in other countries undergoing transition have had similar consequences. The establishment of minimum prices at an inefficient level suggests a predominantly political rather than economic function. The mechanism of minimum guaranteed prices is not unambiguous in economically developed countries. However, in countries undergoing

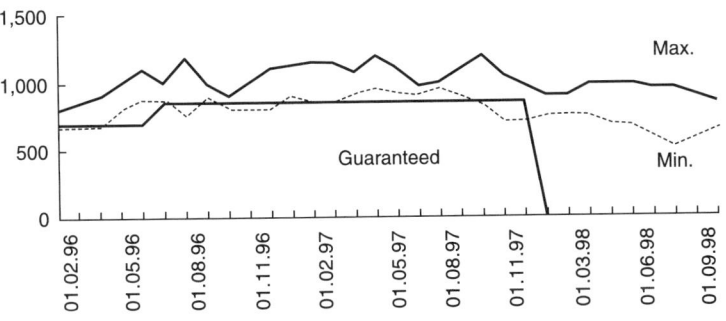

Figure 17.4
Guaranteed minimum prices of wheat and actual sale prices, 1996–1997 (thousands of rubles/ton). (Source: *Protocols on Price Coordination* [RF government document].)

economic transition, this mechanism, as we will try to demonstrate, operates in a fundamentally different fashion; furthermore, establishing effective guaranteed prices—that is, at a level at which there is real intervention—does more to obstruct the process of agricultural reform than to support the agricultural sector.

Earlier we noted the high degree of elasticity in demand for livestock production in transition economies. On the basis of quarterly data on the average monthly consumption of a number of livestock products and the average quarterly retail prices for them between 1991 and the first half of 1995, we have estimated the elasticity coefficient for these products in Russia as a whole (elasticity varies considerably by region, but unfortunately, we do not have access to regional per-capita food consumption data). The elasticity in demand for beef is 2.75%; for pork, 3.74%; and for milk, 3.67%. The elasticity in demand for these products is 0.67%. The elasticity in demand for these products by income was estimated on the basis of per-capita income dynamics in unadjusted 1991 prices. The elasticity in demand for milk by income was around 0.7%, and for eggs, 2.74% (the average elasticity in demand for food by income in OECD countries does not exceed 0.3%).[5] The high level of elasticity can be explained by the population's low income and accordingly the high share of family budget expenditures on foodstuffs. Under these conditions, in the short term and with the same minimum guaranteed price level, the state has to buy up more via an intervention stock than in conditions of nonelastic demand (Figure 17.5).

In the medium term, state purchases increase demand and lead to supply growth, which in turn leads to an increase in the volume of government purchase interventions. In economically developed countries, the demand reaction to state-driven pseudodemand is restrained by means of production quotas and land conservation programs. In Russia, the Ministry of Agricultural Production proposed its version of production quotas: a quota on the right to sell production to the state at minimum prices. It is clear that under these circumstances, the guaranteed price mechanism begins to mimic the traditional Soviet system of state procurements, in which part of production is delivered to the state at a guaranteed price and the rest is sold at low prices on the unregulated market. As a result, a two-tiered market is revived with two price systems that involve certain developmental idiosyncracies. The country already experimented

---

5. The income elasticity of demand for beef and pork has a very complicated dynamic requiring special analysis.

Institutional Reforms in the Agro-Industrial Complex

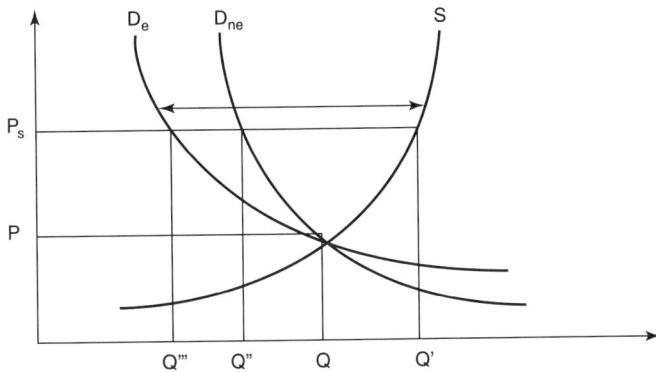

Figure 17.5
Maintenance of guaranteed prices under conditions of elastic and inelastic demand. Note: D_e is the elastic demand curve, D_{ne} is the inelastic demand curve, and P_s is the guaranteed price. In order to support a guaranteed price level established in the case of elastic demand, the size of the purchase intervention is $(Q' - Q''')$. In the case of inelastic demand, it is $(Q' - Q'')$.

with such a system in 1990–1991, with rather negative consequences. The EU model of agricultural quotas in the current socioeconomic conditions is not possible: given the substantial decline in per-capita consumption of basic food staples, government restrictions on production would have negative social and psychological consequences.

Therefore, under the traditional model of guaranteed prices in a transition economy, the problem arises of restraining the growth of purchase interventions resulting from supply expansion. On the other hand, due to high demand elasticity, the required purchase interventions are greater than in developed economies.

In other words, in a postsocialist transition economy, minimum guaranteed prices result in the steady growth of state purchase interventions in the medium term. This policy is an obstacle to the emergence of a market infrastructure in the foodstuff sector. As a result, one of the most important elements of agricultural reform is in danger. The private farmer, lacking access to the appropriate market infrastructure, cannot function as an independent entrepreneur and unavoidably becomes a "state worker." In this way institutional reforms in the agricultural sector are rendered useless.

Besides livestock subsidies, there is a whole series of programs to support flax production, wool, and pedigree cattle production. However, in cost terms these programs cannot be compared with the livestock program, and therefore we will not consider them in this chapter.

Compensation for the increase in agricultural production costs has been another area of state assistance to agriculture and one that was initiated almost immediately after price liberalization. Compensation has been and continues to be effected in various ways, but the principle is the same: to amortize the growing price disparity faced by agricultural producers.

In the Soviet economy, the ratio of agricultural produce prices to capital stock prices was considerably higher than the world average. Price liberalization resulted in the rapid leveling of relative prices, bringing them in line with world prices. Furthermore, demand restrictions in the initial phase of reforms hampered sectors that were closest to the consumer, including agricultural and foodstuff sectors. Capital stock–producing sectors did not initially experience problems and circumvented the price freedoms that forced other sectors to raise their selling prices. As a result, the price growth of agricultural produce up to the end of 1992 lagged far behind that of capital stock. By 1993, the wave of limited demand had passed through the agricultural and food-processing sectors and reached the capital stock–producing sectors, as a result of which the growth in the price disparity slowed down somewhat. Had it not been for state price intervention, in 1994 it would have been realistic to expect a leveling out of price growth trends. In practice, this occurred only in the first half of 1995 (Figure 17.6).

The state's attempts to compensate for this natural process of leveling out of relative prices only resulted in capital stock–producing

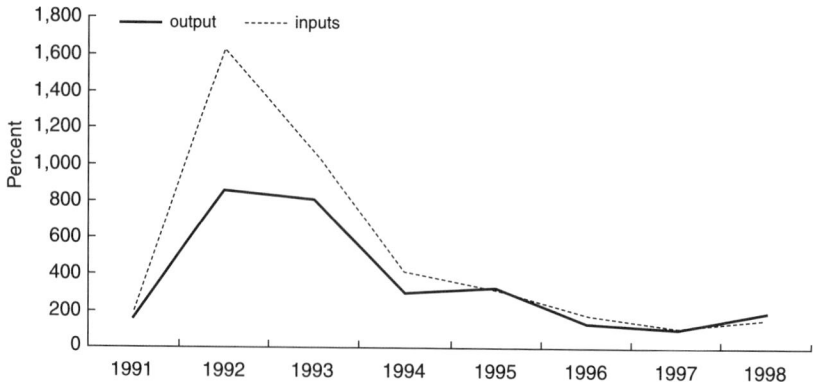

Figure 17.6
Annual price index for agricultural output and inputs, 1991–1998. (Source: Goskomstat.)

sectors once again receiving exaggerated signals concerning the demand for their production. These sectors reacted by raising prices, not by initiating structural reforms in production. Supply on the agricultural capital stock market is fairly nonelastic. Examples of this fact abound. First, prices have remained significantly lower than world prices (Table 17.6), and imports cannot compete on the domestic market. Second, there is a high degree of monopoly in the capital stock–producing sectors (for example, the main enterprises often are not only the sole producer of one or another piece of equipment or machinery, they also provide 50%–60% of total employment in their regions). And third, the production of these sectors can be stored fairly easily.

Until 1995, opportunities for exporting mineral fertilizers were fairly broad, which was an additional factor in the nonelasticity of the supply of this product on the domestic market. Under these conditions, and with the contraction of demand on the part of agricultural producers, these sectors were able to compensate for the decline in demand by raising their prices. However, a point is reached at which the limits of demand are stretched and further price growth is impossible. At this point the opportunity to implement structural

Table 17.6
Relative Agricultural Prices in Russia and the USA

	1992	1993	1994
Tractor (70–90 hp)/grain			
Russia	29–34	67–72	91–135
USA	No data	243	228
Lorry/grain			
Russia	36	61	107
USA	195	208	198
Mineral fertilizer/grain			
Russia	0.2	0.5	1.2
USA	1.5	1.4	1.3
Diesel fuel/grain			
Russia	0.7	1.6	2.4
USA	2.2	2.1	1.7
Petrol/grain			
Russia	0.9	1.8	2.7
USA	3.5	2.8	2.4
Petrol/beef			
Russia	0.3	0.3	0.4
USA	0.3	0.2	0.2

Source: Data from the Ministry of Agricultural Production.

reform and accordingly reduce prices is lost. Capital stock prices then cease to outstrip purchase prices, and capital stock producers face the problem of implementing radical reforms.

If the state at this point provides compensation to agricultural producers for the growth in capital stock prices, then intersectoral relations revert to square one: the monopolist enterprises start to raise prices again. As a result, the price disparity started to shrink, which is what happened at the start of 1994 (see Figure 17.6).

It is worth noting that relations between the upstream sector and agriculture and between agriculture and the downstream sector are asymmetrical. While in the case of livestock subsidies we have come to the conclusion that it is desirable to shift subsidies from the producer to the end consumer, applying this scheme to the input manufacturers does not work. It is clear that this is connected to the nonelasticity of input supply, in contrast to the relative elasticity of supply in the food industry. Therefore, the following paradox arises: The more the state compensates for the increasing input prices in agricultural production, the more rapidly the price disparity grows. Initially, compensation was effected mainly by means of direct payments to producers. However, from 1994 the practice of what can more or less be referred to as leasing was introduced. In reality this practice was a form of state assistance to the agro-industrial complex that had only a superficial resemblance to real leasing. In reality this was a typical attempt to revive the system by which the state supplied cheap capital transfers to the villages (discussed in the previous section).

Thus, these measures of state assistance to the agricultural sector, as in the case of livestock subsidies, are not appropriate to the actual situation and have largely been counterproductive. In our opinion, in the context of the economic transition, state assistance should be targeted at stimulating the development of market interaction between agricultural producers and input manufacturers. Commodity credits and leasing are effectively deployed not by the state, but by private firms.

The mechanism of so-called double tariffs has been retained from the arsenal of the Soviet economy. This mechanism entails a situation in which agricultural producers pay reduced prices for machinery and equipment and for the services of electricity companies, which are then subsidized by the budget. Today, reduced tariffs for the agricultural sector have been preserved only for electricity, and

Table 17.7
Tariff on Electricity for the Agricultural Sector and the Total Economy (Rubles/kw·hr)

	Reference Prices for Electric Power (Rb/kw·hr)	
	Economy as a Whole	Agriculture
1994	62.7	34.1
1995	185.0	98.0
1996	254.0	146.0
1997	241.0	169.0

Sources: Ministry of Agriculture and Food, Ministry of the Economy.

the mechanism is somewhat different: The difference in tariff is not compensated by the budget but by the electricity company. The difference between the average tariff and the special tariff for agricultural enterprises is displayed in Table 17.7.

The maintenance of this reduced electricity tariff may be one of the reasons why electricity consumption, compared with other resources in agricultural production, has declined the least over the reform years (and, compared with 1985, has even grown), despite the decline not only in agricultural output but also in labor productivity. Indeed, when this preferential tariff rate was rescinded in 1994, electricity use in agricultural production fell rapidly.

17.6. Reform of Foreign Trade Regulation of the Agro-Industrial Complex

Radical economic reform has significantly changed foreign trade regulation of the agro-industrial complex. The new institutional structure of the agro-industrial complex, which included abolition of

Table 17.8
Dynamics of Consumption of Certain Inputs in the Agricultural Sector (% of Previous Year's Figure)

	1991	1992	1993	1994	1995	1996	1997	1998
Diesel	97.0	85.1	77.6	60.9	91.0	87.3	112.9	84.3
Gasoline	93.8	88.7	66.0	59.7	89.2	87.9	96.6	85.7
Fertilizers	91.0	55.0	68.0	48.8	71.4	100.0	100.0	86.7
Electric power	104.8	99.1	99.0	88.7	86.3	91.9	86.4	91.2

Calculated by the authors on the basis of *Sel'skoe khozyaystvo Rossii* (Moscow: Goskomstat, 1995), 42, 45; *Proizvodstvenno-ekonomicheskie pokazateli APK RF v 1995 g.* (Moscow: Minsel'khozprod RF, 1996), 53.

the system of mandatory deliveries to the state and price and trade liberalization, has had a significant impact on exports and imports of agricultural produce and foodstuffs and on domestic producers and consumers. While the Soviet economy was characterized by permanent food shortages, as a result of which the state's policies involved significant subsidization of imports and prevented exports, after the start of reforms this system was replaced by system defined by agricultural protectionism, in which the state protects the domestic market from imports of foodstuffs and raw ingredients.

In 1992, centralized imports of food and resources for agricultural production were preserved, and the government continued to regulate the prices of imported goods. According to our estimates, import subsidies in this period exceeded by threefold open transfers to the agricultural sector from the federal budget.

The importance of protectionism and protection from imports became apparent to domestic producers only at the end of 1993. The agrarian lobby fought hard for the introduction of import tariffs on staple agricultural products; such tariffs were established for the first time in the summer of 1994. From that point on, the issue of so-called "food security" has become one of the most sensitive ones in discussions of the country's agricultural policy.

The August 1998 crisis revived some export barriers to agrifood trade. Thus, in the fall, the license for sunflower seeds was reestablished, and in January 1999 an export tax on this item was imposed.

To what extent have food imports grown over the past few years? Our calculations show the following: (1) the share of imports in percapita consumption has not grown a great deal (Table 17.9); (2) this growth in the share of imports has been determined more by the decline in domestic production than by the growth of imports per se; and (3) the increased imports of specific foodstuff groups are evidence of a rise in the quality of the food Russians consume. In particular, the share of imported fruits has risen: previously exotic bananas, pineapples, and the unknown kiwi fruit are now sold in the most far-flung corners of the country. The growth of meat imports, attended by the complete curtailment of fodder imports, merely points to the rationalization of foreign trade. Import of fodder is clearly inefficient, given that the productive yield of fodder is two- or threefold lower in Russia than in the countries from which meat and meat products are imported. Therefore, liberalization has led to the rational substitution of meat imports for fodder imports.

Table 17.9
Share of Net Imports of Specific Products in Total Volume of Personal Consumption, and the Share of Grain Imports in Gross Grain Output (%)

	Share of Net Imports in Total Volume of Personal Consumption					Wheat
	Meat	Milk	Potatoes	Vegetables	Eggs	
1991	13.8	13	5.2	25.9	1.2	44.0
1992	14.8	7.1	1	25.2	−0.7*	41.6
1993	15.8	13	0.4	13.6	−0.8*	17.3
1994	19.2	11.2	0.5	26.8	−0.2*	7.6
1995	27.7	15.8	0.1	10.9	0.2	28.4
1996	27.9	11.8	0.2	14.8	0.7	13.5
1997	40.4	18	0.6	16.5	7.5	12.3
1998	32.3	14.3	1.2	14.9	2.5	7.5
1999	32.2	14.4	9.7	14.6	2.6	33.8

*Russia was a net exporter of the particular item.
Source: Figures calculated based on Goskomstat and Ministry of Agriculture data.

17.7. Conclusions

The widespread opinion that agrarian reform in Russia is lacking is somewhat exaggerated. Such an opinion arises on the one hand from unjustified expectations that agricultural and food output would start to grow immediately in response to the transformations under way. As we have demonstrated in this chapter, the prerequisites for agrarian reform in a country like Russia and the very direction of reforms did not allow hope for an increase in agricultural production. Furthermore, growth in agrarian production is impossible without macroeconomic stabilization and an increase in real household income.

On the other hand, attempts are often made to take the number of created family farms as a criterium of reforms. That only 5% of land in Russia is cultivated farmland is a decisive indicator of the marginality of farming in the structure of agriculture. However, the real difference between old-model entities and market-oriented ones is increasingly recognized in terms of their organizational and legal forms. Large enterprises have appeared with a sufficiently transparent structure of ownership of fixed production assets, including land, that are already engaged in commercial production. At the same time, a considerable proportion of family farms are subsistence entities characterized by underdependence on produce markets and separation from both product and resource markets.

In sum, the agrarian structure of Russia has undergone considerable transformation. Its further market evolution requires time and, more important, an adequate market environment. In this relation, the major problem in agrarian reform today is not institutional transformation, it is not the land market or the next redistribution of land, but the formation of a market infrastructure for existing economic agents. However, the government's agrarian policy in this respect is contradictory, lacks an internal concept, and often puts a brake on the creation of the necessary infrastructure rather than helping it. The government's most effective strategy would be to minimize its regulation of the agro-industrial complex and allow the "invisible hand" of the market to develop the real agrarian and food market in the country.

18

Institutional Reforms in the Sociocultural Sphere

Irina Rozhdestvenskaya
and Sergei Shishkin

18.1. The Need for Reform in Sociocultural Fields

The sociocultural sphere is a relatively large sector of the Russian economy. According to Goskomstat, the number of people employed in health care, education, culture, and social welfare amounts to more than 18% of the country's total workforce.

In the Soviet period, official ideology emphasized achievements in this area in drawing comparisons between the USSR and other countries. One frequently cited fact was that, according to World Health Organization estimates, for satisfactory medical care to be supplied, a country needed to have twenty-eight doctors per 10,000 population. In 1985 the USSR had forty-two doctors per 10,000 population. The USSR also led all other countries in terms of hospital beds per 10,000. In the prereform decades, the country was among the world's leaders in higher and secondary education, with 206 college students per 10,000 population in Russia in 1985, compared to 112 in Britain, 138 in Germany, and 142 in Japan. The United States, the only country ahead of Russia, had 257.

In the centrally planned economy, however, the sociocultural sphere enjoyed the lowest priority for funding. Toward the end of the socialist period, Russia was far behind countries with developed market economies in the share of GDP spent on this sphere. The spending gap was widest in health care (Table 18.1). In health care, Russia was behind developed market economies and nearly all European socialist countries, and stood even with non-communist countries with close or similar per-capita GDP.

The combination of the high proportion of doctors and high percentage of students at institutions of higher learning, on the one hand, and the low level of spending on sociocultural facilities on the

Table 18.1
Public Spending on Health and Education in Individual Countries in 1990

	Health Care (% of GDP)	Education (% of GDP)	Per-Capita GDP (in US $)
US	5.6	5.2	21,967
UK	5.2	4.9	16,930
Sweden	7.9	5.6	26,844
Russia	2.4	3.5	6,539
Romania	2.4	3.0	1,648
Portugal	4.3	4.3	6,814
Poland	4.1	4.8	1,547
Nigeria	1.2	0.8	337
Mexico	1.6	3.6	2,888
Japan	4.8	3.6	23,734
Italy	5.8	5.2	20,192
Indonesia	0.7	1.0	581
India	1.3	4.6	360
Hungary	5.0	4.5	3,442
Germany	5.8	4.1	24,485
France	6.6	5.1	21,077
Czechoslovakia	5.0	4.4	2,359
China	2.1	2.6	341
Chile	3.4	2.5	2,310
Brazil	2.8	4.5*	3,219
Argentina	2.5	0.9	4,343

*1989.

Sources: *World Development Report 1993* (Geneva: World Bank); *Investing in Health* (Oxford: Oxford University Press), 210–1; *Statistical Yearbook* no. 39 (New York: United Nations, 1996), 149–65; *Education at a Glance: OECD Indicators* (Center for Education Research and Innovation, 1997), 66; *Economies in Transition Studies: Regional Monitoring Report* no. 3 (1995), 124.

other was a fundamental specific of the socialist economy: an imbalance between labor and capital. The shortage of investment in equipment and fixed assets essential to provide quality services in the sociocultural sphere was "offset" by a relative surplus of labor. Typically, their pay amounted to 65%–75% of the average for other sectors of the country's economy. The material and technological standards of the sociocultural sphere were very low in comparison with those of developed market economies.

The disadvantages of the existing public system of providing sociocultural services to the population came into sharp focus in the 1980s. During the perestroika years, the central authorities attempted to initiate mild reforms in this system. The idea was to di-vest the government authorities of the right to approve budgets for public sociocultural institutions, which were to be funded partly through receipts for specific performance results, and to give the institutions the right to manage these funds to meet their expenses. The budgetary allocations were to be viewed as revenue and were to be made at stable rates linked to performance results.

It was proposed, for example, that budgetary financing of health services be based on per-capita rates. This would place the funds in the hands of polyclinics (small, community-based health care facilities), which were to pay hospitals for diagnostic services and the treatment of patients.

The early results of the experiments were encouraging, in general, and in late 1988, the Commission on Improvement of the Economic Mechanism, created by the USSR Council of Ministers, adopted "Principles of the New Economic Mechanism in Non-Manufacturing Industries," followed by a series of sectoral regulations. These regulations applied the new budgetary financing principles tested during the experiment to all institutions in health, education, and culture.

In practice, however, only some institutions were granted of the status of independent economic agents. According to the Russian Ministry of Culture, for example, the new management model had been adopted by only 46% of public libraries and 33% of community centers in 1991. As late as 1997, the Russian Ministry of Vocational and General Education put the proportion of schools that had acquired the status of legal entities and opened their own current accounts at 10%.

The 1988 adoption of the new budgetary financing principles, on the basis of stable rates, were true to reality on paper only. The central and local financial authorities held back the development and adoption of such rates or just ignored them, citing in their defense the mounting revenue collection problems in 1989.

18.2. The State and Special Interest Groups in the Sociocultural Sphere

Many activities in health service, education, and culture produce a significant social effect, even though they are not net public goods in the full sense of the term.[1] Medical assistance, higher education, the dissemination of artistic culture, and a number of leisure activities, in Russia as in many other countries, have traditionally been regarded as public goods. Meeting their respective needs has been the responsibility of the government. The government was the authority that measured the resulting social effect, and provided the funds and directly arranged for sociocultural services to be supplied to achieve the social good.

In the 1990s, these ideas underwent significant transformation.[2] The radical political and economic reforms of the early half of the 1990s put sociocultural problems on the back burner, far out of the Russian top authorities' concerns. Sociocultural issues became subordinated to the needs of the current economic policies and a plaything in the hands of political rivals. The government was keen to reform the funding sources for the sociocultural system and was not averse to reducing its size.

As reform of sociocultural services dropped to the bottom of the list of priorities for the government, Parliament, and the public, worried as they were by other headaches of the transition period, the key role in pursuing institutional reform in this area was taken over by special interest groups. By Russian standards, "special interest groups" are the central and local government authorities in charge of individual sectors and professional communities.

The central authorities have no desire for major changes in the content of the activities they oversee: the broader the functions of bureaucrats in the distribution of budgetary resources, the more opportunity they have to capitalize on their positions as managers of limited resources.

By the time economic reform got under way, local government authorities, the second interest group, were preoccupied with halting the deterioration in their socioeconomic situation relative to that of their counterparts in production. The kinds of reforms they wanted were those that established a link between the amount of funding for sociocultural institutions, particularly pay for their personnel, and

---

1. N. Barr, *The Welfare State*, 5th ed. (Stanford, Calif.: Stanford University Press, 1993).
2. In the poll conducted by the Central Institute for Opinion Studies (VTsIOM) in November 1991, 51% of the respondents came out for the coexistence of both paid and free medical care. Paid or free school and university education were supported by 37% of respondents each, 11% were in favor of basically paid medical services, 5% approved of paid school education, and 9% favored a paid university education. L. G. Zubova, "Public Opinion about Social Guarantees. Economic and Social Changes: Public Opinion Monitoring," *Information Bulletin*, VTsIOM, Moscow, no. 3 (1996): 35.

the actual quantity and complexity of work in comparison with the work performed by the workforce in other economic sectors.

18.3. The Switch from Free Care to Health Insurance: The Ideology and Aims of Health Reform

The crisis of Soviet society, the outburst of criticism of the Soviet political and economic system, and the efforts launched to wreck it led to important shifts in the ideas that medical community leaders held about the direction of the long-overdue reforms in the funding and organization of health care. Health insurance in particular was at the forefront of their concerns.

The need for a switch from free care to health insurance was debated throughout Eastern and Central Europe in the early 1990s. Those years were dominated by a negative attitude toward the Soviet health system. There arose the belief that once it was replaced with a market system, both the quality of medical services and the efficiency of the health system would change for the better.

Efforts to reform the health system were led by Hungary, Russia, the Czech Republic, and Estonia. However, these countries quickly discovered that all was not as simple as it had seemed at the outset.

These countries' proposals to initiate market reforms in health care sought to incorporate the following principles:

• Financing medical assistance to the population from insurance contributions made by businesses, government, and the population

• Separating organizationally those who provided medical services to the population from those who paid for them (that is, dividing service providers and purchasers)

• Allowing competition among providers for funds offered by purchasers

• Encouraging competition among purchasers ready to mediate between the population and medical institutions for funds contributed by the population

• Giving patients a choice of doctor, medical institution, and a go-between

• Giving preference to nonpublic providers and buyers over public ones

Here the postcommunist countries followed the lead of Western countries, which in the 1980s had introduced a quasimarket health financing system, which they viewed as a way to improve the efficiency of the health service.[3]

The health insurance initiative in the USSR was launched by the heads of the Union Ministry of Public Health. It was endorsed by the leaders of special interest groups in the service—doctors serving as members of the Supreme Council of the Russian Federation, the heads of some regional health authorities, and a majority of medical workers.

In the 1990s, efforts to reform the health care system in Russia focused on two principal objectives: decentralizing decision making and using insurance as a way to boost funding.[4] Health insurance also was viewed in other postsocialist countries as, above all, a policy of creating sources of guaranteed funding.[5]

As work went on to develop health insurance projects in Russia and other postsocialist countries, the following important circumstances were overlooked:

1. Possible changes in external economic conditions for the future operation of the health service as a whole: changes in the paying capacity of businesses, budgetary possibilities, and incomes of the population. Reform plans were drawn up on the vague assumption (self-evident to the plans' developers) that an economic crisis would not occur, and in the firm belief that local authorities and businesses would finance health care after they had shaken off centralized control.

2. Weakening of the government and crippling of the central authorities' power to enforce enacted laws. In this scenario, organizational changes can only be completed in part, and after some delay. Moreover, such changes would fare differently in different areas, depend-

---

[3]. OECD, *Health Policy Studies*, no. 2, *The Reform of Health Care Systems: A Comparative Analysis of Seven OECD Countries* (Paris: OECD, 1992); *European Health Care Reform: Analysis of Current Strategies*, edited by R. Saltman and J. Figueras (Copenhagen: World Health Organization, 1997).

[4]. D. Rowland and A. Telyukov, "Soviet Health Care from Two Perspectives," *Health Affairs* 10, no. 3 (1991): 85.

[5]. C. Davis, "Eastern Europe and USSR: An Overview," in *Radio Free Europe/Radio Liberty Research Report* 2, no. 40 (1993): 34; and T. Ensor, "Reforming the Health Sector in Former Socialist Countries of Europe" (paper presented at the IRISS Congress, York, 1994), 7.

ing on the administrative expertise, involvement, and determination of their bosses.

3. The interests of bureaucrats stripped of their clout. The question is whether the loss of leverage can be remedied by other benefits, and if the answer is no, whether bureaucrats' official discipline and fear of administrative penalties would be sufficient to drive them to execute decisions infringing on their interests.

4. Finally, no thought was given to the time needed for real competition to emerge in the health insurance market, or to the situation that could exist until such competition became a major factor, or to the kind of effect the change in financing principles would have on the quality and efficiency of health services during that period.

No alternative scenarios were prepared, and no comparisons were made between the different reform blueprints.

The draft reform in Russia was drawn up within a short time, and the law *On Health Insurance of the Population in the Russian Federation* was enacted as early as June 1991. The idea of the health insurance model defined in the law included some of the following. Health care was to be financed by compulsory and voluntary contributions. The working population was to be covered by compulsory health insurance (CHI) paid for by their employers, while the nonworking population and public servants were to be insured through budgetary appropriations. The scale and terms of free medical assistance within the CHI framework were defined in the CHI core program, to be approved by the government, and in territorial programs adopted by local authorities on the basis of the core program. Medical services supplied to the population would be paid for by nongovernmental health insurance organizations. The involvement of private insurance companies was expected to add to the health insurance system free market competition among purchasers.

At the same time, government health management agencies were to be retained to exercise supervisory functions and to develop and implement target programs, the objectives of which lay beyond the framework of medical services provided by the CHI system. This was a dichotomy of power from the start, which created a two-track system in financing medical institutions.[6]

---

6. A. Mironov, A. Taranov, and A. Cheida, *Health Insurance* (Moscow: Nauka, 1994), 163, 169.

The changes in health financing principles were a follow-up on previous attempts to transform financial flows into the sector. The CHI model had entirely novel ideas about the organization of financial flows within the sector. However, new agents and health insurance organizations made their appearance in the health care system. Businesses and government offices, given the role of policyholders, were to sign contracts with insurers, who in turn would select medical institutions and pay for the therapeutic and preventive services provided to insured persons.

The law *On Health Insurance of the Population in the Russian Federation* decreed a switch to health insurance to be made in 1992-1993. This short period very quickly proved to be unrealistic. Establishing insurance companies and adopting the necessary legislation took far longer than the lawmakers had anticipated. To avoid putting off the introduction of CHI and delaying decisions on compulsory contributions to health care by employers, the reformers decided to modify the CHI model. Major amendments were enacted into law in 1993.

Under the 1991 health insurance law, the functions of insurers were to be exercised by health insurance organizations independent of health service authorities and medical institutions. The law did not designate any specialized organizations to collect and accumulate CHI contributions. An amendment to the law in 1993 provided for the establishment of such organizations: federal and territorial compulsory health insurance funds. In status, they were defined as independent, nonprofit financial institutions. They are cofounded by bodies of representative and executive government at the federal and local levels, respectively. In addition, branches of territorial CHI funds were given a temporary right not only to enter into health insurance contracts with health insurance organizations, but also to perform the functions of insurers and enter into direct relations with medical institutions. In 1994, 52% of territorial CHI funds doubled as insurers. The structure of the CHI system in the years 1993-1998 is shown in Table 18.2.

The health service financing model created under the law therefore acquired a two-stage format, with money initially flowing into public CHI funds and then channeled into nongovernmental health insurance companies authorized to sign direct contracts with health service providers. Analogous two-stage models operate in the Netherlands, Israel, and the Czech Republic. The Russian model is specific in that the first-stage entities, the territorial CHI funds, are permitted

Table 18.2
Structure of the Compulsory Health Insurance System, 1993–1998*

	1993	1994	1995	1996	1997	1998
CHI territorial funds (no.)	86	86	88	88	89	90
Branches of CHI territorial funds (no.)	1,058	1,103	1,122	1,160	1,160	1,193
Health insurance organizations (no.)	164	439	536	538	461	415

*Year-end data.
Source: Federal CHI Fund.

to exercise the functions of insurers. If an area does not have enough insurance companies, the funds themselves are authorized to enter into contracts with medical institutions.

The law did not draw a clear line between the rights and responsibilities of the health service management bodies and CHI funds. This oversight led to a flare-up of serious tensions when the time came for the CHI system to be introduced in practice.

The deadline for introducing CHI was moved forward by a year. By the start of 1994, however, many pieces of legislation had not been drawn up or passed. The preparatory phase was centered on reforming the external funding channels for the service, as medical community leaders were in a hurry to have a target tax levied on CHI contributions to finance health care. A payroll tax of 3.6% was indeed imposed on employers in 1993, its effect being cushioned by a proportionate reduction in contributions to the Pension Fund. A small share of the tax receipts, 0.2% out of 3.6%, was to be paid into the Federal CHI Fund, and the bulk of the revenues, 3.4%, was to be accumulated by regional CHI funds.

18.4. Practical Introduction of the New System to Finance the Health Service

Government weakness was the most decisive factor affecting the character and progress of the health reform. Bureaucrats across Russia took different attitudes toward the reforms. Consequently, the results were very patchy. In this situation, neither the Health Ministry nor the Federal CHI Fund had sufficient authority to monitor enforcement of the health insurance law in the constituent members of the Russian Federation. The law did not set the order in which the

Table 18.3
Health Care Share of Budget Expenditure, 1993–1998 (%)

	1993	1994	1995	1996	1997	1998
Federal budget (%)	1.7	1.6	1.3	1.2	2.2	1.5
Budgets of the RF constituent members (%)	17.5	15.7	15.3	15.1	14.8	14.4

Source: RF Goskomstat.

elements of the health insurance system were to be adopted, so the process was held hostage by the regional officials.

Major differences, therefore, developed from region to region in the sequence, rates, and extent of reform. In its final form, CHI was a long departure from what was intended by the law. Instead of a consistent shift from one health service financing system (from public budget revenues) to another (sustained by insurance payments), the end result was an eclectic grab bag of elements from both. According to the Federal CHI Fund, in 1994, insurance companies alone acted as insurers in twenty-three members of the federation, CHI funds only in another fourteen, and both in a further thirty-four. In some regions, CHI money is spent only on hospitals, while in others it goes only to polyclinics; in still others it covers only some kinds of medical care; in yet others it is expended on specific items only, and so forth.

What actually occurred was not that extra funds from CHI contributions supplemented the budget, but that only a partial substitution of one for the other occurred. After CHI was introduced in 1994, the respective share of federal spending began to shrink. In the meantime, local authorities slashed their health service budgets, alluding to the new financing source—CHI contributions paid by legal entities (Table 18.3).

In 1993, 85% of the expenditure on health care came from the budget and 15% came from compulsory insurance contributions by businesses. In 1994 the respective figures were 82% and 18%, and in 1998 they were 77% and 23% (Table 18.4).

If, however, we compare the dynamics of health service financing from the budget and CHI contributions with the dynamics of government spending on education and culture, we find that health care has fared much better than other areas of the social sphere.

Whereas the GDP contracted by 39% in the period 1991–1998, the real health service funding from the budget and insurance

Table 18.4
Structure of Public Health Expenditure, 1992–1998 (%)

	1992	1993	1994	1995	1996	1997	1998
Federal budget (%)	11	9	10	7	6	10	7
Budgets of the RF constituent members (%)	89	76	72	75	74	71	70
Total budgetary expenditure (%)	100	85	82	82	80	81	77
Employers' contributions to compulsory health insurance (%)	—	15	18	18	20	19	23
Total (%)	100	100	100	100	100	100	100

Source: Calculated from RF Goskomstat data.

contributions fell only by 33%. This means that the introduction of insurance medical service has had a positive, stabilizing effect on the financing of the service under crisis conditions. To an extent, the reform has helped redistribute dwindling public resources, to the health service's advantage.

An imbalance has, however, developed between the amount of financial flows entering the health service and the government's liabilities, inherited from the socialist system, to provide free medical services. Citizens' rights to free medical assistance were written very broadly into the constitution of the Soviet state. The law did not, however, list the kinds of health care to which every citizen was entitled. In fact, this law implied an individual's right to free health care in medical institutions to which he or she could get access. People of different social standing and residents of different areas thus received medical assistance of varying kind and quality, according to their access to different therapeutic and disease prevention institutions. The current federal laws have retained the old approach to a citizen's right to free health care in that citizen guarantees are unspecified as to extent or cost. Nonspecific government guarantees are typical of the paternalistic practice prevalent in the provision of social services. The enactment of citizens' rights to free medical assistance is dictated by ideological considerations and political factors, without regard for economic realities.

In political and economic terms, this implies a commitment to financially maintain the existing network of public, municipal therapeutic, and preventive care institutions so that these institutions can continue providing the historically free medical services to the population. As health care funding falls below the level assuring the normal operation of the existing network of therapeutic and preventive care institutions, an imbalance emerges, and automatically grows, between the government's commitment to health care and the resources it has to back up such a commitment.

According to estimates from the Russian Health Ministry, the expenditures required to provide medical services in fulfillment of the state guarantees amounted to 4.0% of GDP in 1998. The basis for this estimate is the Ministry of Health's calculation of the current expenditures necessary to provide medical assistance at existing levels, if the structure of medical assistance is preserved (that is, if there are no changes in the ratio of in- to outpatient assistance). The actual total costs incurred by the government for the health service were 3.3% of GDP in 1998 (including 2.4% of GDP coming from budgetary appropriations, 0.8% derived from businesses' contributions to the CHI, and 0.1% from other revenues of the CHI funds). This underfunding prevents the new system from demonstrating its advantages in full. There is a shortage of money to pay medical institutions at current rates for their health care services or at per-capita rates (provided that the rates can reasonably cover all necessary costs, such as labor, drugs, equipment, utility services, and so on). It has proved impossible to completely scrap the old selective principle, according to which funds were allocated to medical institutions to cover some of their expenses only. The shortage of funds means that some expenses are financed only in part, or not at all.

Now, if the old principle of financing medical service providers survives through economic necessity, there is no rush to transfer budgetary resources to CHI funds. As things turned out, medical institutions in most regions were financed, to carry on their current business, by both CHI funds (out of contributions paid in by legal entities) and health service authorities (from budgetary appropriations). Moreover, the resources accumulated in the hands of CHI funds had either to be spent on some (not all) hospitals and polyclinics or to cover some (not all) of their services only.

The CHI system mandated by law has not, therefore, been executed in full. The reform has been fragmentary and partial. Despite certain structural changes in health care financing approaches, some key principles of health insurance have not been established:

- There is no competition between insurers. In many regions no health insurance companies have been set up, and where they have been set up, the areas have been carved up into spheres of influence among the companies rather than becoming a competitive market.
- There is no competition between medical service providers.
- Few patients are able to choose their own doctor or medical service provider.
- Insurers, medical service providers, and doctors alike have no incentive to improve the efficiency of the funds at their disposal. The financing mechanism is, as always, based on the so-called "затратный" principle.[7]

In most regions health insurance reform has been stalled by a conflict of interests. When CHI was launched on a large scale, flaws were discovered in its legislation. CHI funds and insurance companies, on the one hand, and service providers on the other have clashed on countless occasions over financing terms and priorities.

Far more serious, however, are the clashes between health authorities and CHI funds. The reforms conducted to this point have cut deeply into the funds that health bureaucrats directly control. Even worse, some money flows have bypassed them, through CHI funds and insurance companies. We point out again that the rights and responsibilities of the health authorities and CHI funds have not been clearly defined, making the problem even more messy, with CHI making only minimal progress.

All of these facts underlay the conflict of interest between regional health authorities and CHI funds. Health bureaucrats and medical institution employees reacted violently to the CHI funds' financial policies. According to reform critics, the upkeep costs of the executive echelons in the federal and territorial CHI funds are prohibitively high: 4.4% of businesses' total insurance contributions in 1994 and 4.8% in 1998. In 1994, health insurance organizations put aside 5.6% of their turnover funds to handle CHI cases; by 1998, the figure had dropped to 3.3%.

It must be said that this level of administrative cost is not very high in comparison with other countries' administrative costs. In 1990,

---

7. I. Sheiman, "From Beveridge to Bismarck: Health Finance in the Russian Federation," in *Innovations in Health Care Finance: Proceedings of a World Bank Conference*, March 10–11, 1997, World Bank Discussion Paper no. 365.

administrative costs averaged about 5% of health spending in OECD countries[8] and about 15% in the United States[9]; in Britain, in 1992, they nearly reached 7% of the regional health budgets.[10] In Russia, however, with funding contracting, the inevitable growth of administrative costs to put the reform in place appears to be an unjustified diversion of funds.

In the spring of 1995, the Russian Health Ministry tried to push through amendments to the health insurance law. Had those amendments been adopted, the federal and territorial CHI funds would have been stripped of their independence and placed under health authority control. Such a step would have retracted reforms and placed Russia back under the public health system. The bill was killed by the State Duma.

In 1996 another attempt was made to overhaul the existing CHI model. In the fall of that year, the government took to Parliament a new bill seeking to amend the health insurance law. The bill was lobbied for by the health authorities speaking for their employees. It proposed substituting government regulation for the elements of market regulation in the CHI system. Nonpublic insurance organizations were to be thrown out of CHI membership. Territorial CHI funds, which were independent within the CHI system, were to be reorganized into institutions taking orders from executive government bodies. In essence, the bill aimed at reconstituting the government-controlled health service in a different format. All problems caused by the inconsistency and patchiness of the health reform were to be resolved by abandoning the health insurance principles as a basis of health service organization in a market economy.

The new special interest groups in health, health insurance companies and CHI funds, together succeeded in undermining the bill. Discussion of the bill in Parliament was suspended due to their efforts. However, in the summer of 1999 the draft was approved by the State Duma in the first reading. The legislative future of health insurance remains unclear.

As things stand now, there is a near equilibrium of forces in the health service between three special interest groups: health bureau-

---

8. OECD, *Health Policy Studies*, no. 7, *New Directions in Health Care Policy* (Paris: OECD, 1995), 35.
9. *World Development Report: Investing in Health* (Washington, DC: World Bank, 1993), 122.
10. A. Maynard and K. Bloor, "Introducing a Market to the United Kingdom National Health Service," *New England Journal of Medicine* 344, no. 9 (1996): 604–608.

crats, CHI funds, and health insurance organizations. The future course of the reform will depend on the fighting and cooperation among these groups. Almost no one seems to care much about the interests of the population, or even those of medical workers.

18.5. Institutional Changes in Education

In the Soviet era, education was the highest priority area in the social sphere in general. The reason was that the natural and physical sciences could not thrive unless they stood on a solid educational foundation, starting in the earliest grades. Education was the foundation on which to build the military-industrial complex. The coming of perestroika was received in education as an opportunity to free it from the deadly grip of ideology, which tightened in the years of stagnation. The education sphere did not view it as an opportunity to initiate radical economic reforms. This perception of the necessary change survived into the period of drastic economic reforms of the 1990s.

The positive developments in Russian education were associated with the emergence of new types of educational establishments, the introduction and dissemination of innovative and tailor-made curricula, the adoption of alternative principles, and scrapping of the one-size-fits-all approach in education, and, at the same time, continued reliance on the beneficial experience of the Russian educational system.

Unfortunately, these developments have not been accompanied by adequate improvements in education's infrastructure. The slashing of investment has led to increasingly more children attending a second and even a third session. Higher schools are not allocated any budgetary funds in order to purchase new equipment or educational and scientific literature, to improve staff skills, or to exchange experience.

Recently new forms of general education institutions have emerged, such as grammar schools, lyceums, and nonpublic schools, as an alternative to public schools. As a rule, such schools are much better equipped technologically to support their educational programs than most public schools, and offer superior services to their students.

There is, however, a certain contradiction in the general direction of reform in education: (1) the rise of the nonpublic sector has been accompanied by a strict ban on the privatization of public educational institutions, (2) the government pledges to finance education coexist with widespread and lengthy delays in paying salaries, (3) innovative educational programs live side by side with the appallingly outdated equipment and facilities in the majority of schools and universities, and so on. This situation has resulted from the special interest groups in education pulling in opposite directions. The dynamics and the direction of reform in the educational system as a whole largely depend on the ability of these groups to influence decisions made at the federal, regional, and local levels.

The legislative framework for reform in education was stated in the Russian President's decree No. 1, "Priority Measures to Develop Education in the RSFSR," issued on 11 July 1991, and the federal education law of 10 July 1992, which recapitulated and developed the key points of the presidential decree. In socioeconomic terms, the most notable aspects of these documents were the affirmation of education as a priority area in public policy and the significantly higher status of education workers. This higher status was to be achieved by giving education workers considerable pay increases. Salaries for high school employees were to be raised and kept even with the average pay level in manufacturing, and salaries for university and college faculty were to be raised to twice that level.

These provisions of the law have not been enforced, and the real pay of education workers falls considerably short of stated figures (see Table 18.10, p. 611). Furthermore, this low pay is delayed systematically. Similarly, the declared priority of education is still wishful thinking in terms of both the scale of budgetary appropriations and the share of GDP spending on education.

The 1992 education law is notable for more than a failed attempt to commit the government to financing education as a whole. It authorizes the establishment of nonpublic educational institutions and provides licensing and official accreditation processes for them. Nonpublic educational institutions were, upon official government accreditation, entitled to budgetary financing. They were funded at rates determined on a per-student-capita basis. Public financing was therefore to be in proportion to the actual number of students at a particular educational institution, regardless of its status.

Passage of the federal law, *On Amendments to the Federal Education Law*, in January 1996 was an important step in developing and strengthening legislation on new educational establishments. The more notable provisions of the law included such key principles as reaffirmation of the universal availability of free education at all levels of general education; abolition of competition for admission to public and municipal educational institutions providing complete general secondary and initial vocational education; and the right for orphans and children deprived of parental care, as well as persons with disability Categories 1 and 2 who have passed entrance examinations, to enroll in public and municipal institutions of secondary vocational and higher professional education.

The law confirmed the right of educational institutions to provide extra pay for educational services outside the obligatory educational programs and government standards, and to enter into contracts with the following: legal entities and individuals for the provision of fully paid education, and sponsors in order to admit students and provide skill improvement facilities to graduates. The right to incorporation in the centralized public financing system is now accorded to general educational institutions rather than just those that have been accredited by government authorities.

The desire to stabilize the financial standing of the postsecondary institutions gave further direction to efforts to promote paid education. In 1996, Russian public universities and colleges supplied cost-effective education to 326,100 students, or 11.6% of the total student enrollment (3.7% in 1993). In contrast to manufacturing, construction, and other industries, the nongovernmental sector in education arose by the opening of new secondary and postsecondary institutions, instead of through privatization of public educational establishments. These institutions supplement, do not replace, public schools and universities.

The growth of the nongovernmental sector in education, which is in fact the sole example of real institutional reform in this area, suffered a major setback in 1996, when a new version of the education law was passed. Among the important amendments incorporated in the new version of the law that seriously affected the position of nonpublic educational institutions, the following deserve close scrutiny:

- The right to enter institutions of higher learning is now accorded to graduates of nonpublic schools that have been accredited by government authorities in addition to holding a license.

- The right to defer induction into military service applies only to students at institutions of higher education accredited by government authorities. The number of these institutions in the nonpublic sector is very small.
- The law no longer refers to the right of nongovernmental institutions of higher learning, duly accredited by government authorities, to receive budget funds, and also removes the clause about personal education loans being granted by the government. This amounts to governmental refusal to finance nonpublic institutions from its budget.
- The privatization of educational institutions has been banned.

These amendments have tightened the nongovernmental educational institutions' political dependence on authorities, worsened their economic position by compelling them to raise tuition, abridged the legal and social guarantees of their students, and made nonpublic education less compelling to students.

18.6. Institutional Reforms in Cultural Institutions

In the totalitarian system, creative unions served above all to impose ideological control on people in the arts. To a certain degree, such unions also benefited their members. With the onset of perestroika, when ideological pressure on workers in culture and the arts started to relax, the creative unions remolded themselves from organizations used by the authorities to promote their interests among the professional communities of creative workers into organizations used by the professional communities to put pressure on the authorities and to lobby for their interests. Thus, the unions have made a U-turn in their political functions.

It was the film-makers' union that first developed and won approval, in 1988, for its new model of film industry organization, in which government control of film production and distribution was abandoned and replaced by market regulation. (Of course, the consequences of the reform were nowhere near those expected by the professional community.) Film studios and directors became independent in picking subjects for their films. Film distributors were also now free to decide on the kind of pictures they wanted to buy and screen. Film directors suddenly found domestically produced films unpopular in movie theaters across Russia. In 1995, only 8%

of the films screened in Moscow cinemas were Russian-made; 73% were American productions and 6% were French films.[11] Indeed, it was much cheaper to purchase and show foreign productions.

The Theater Workers Union played a tremendous role in the reform of culture. It succeeded in having a very suitable management model adopted to run public theaters. The model is based on the principle of government provision of funds for theaters no matter what the circumstances, while the theaters assume no specific obligations and have complete freedom of choice in performance and business. While remaining formally nonprofit organizations and enjoying tax benefits, public theaters can now engage in business and distribute proceeds to their members.

During the transition period, special interest groups in culture as in education pressured lawmakers to enact a guaranteed minimum spending on culture from the public purse. In 1992 they succeeded in pushing through Parliament Basic Laws on Culture, which set the minimum level of funds appropriated for culture at 2% of the federal budget and at least 6% of local budgets. Caught in a conflict with the executive branch, the legislators and the Russian Supreme Council had no second thoughts about saddling the government with extra responsibilities. The government in turn found it just as easy to ignore many of the lawmakers' decisions.

In 1993, however, the share of spending on culture, the arts, and the media in the aggregate federal budgetary expenditure, far from equaling the 2% required by the law, dropped significantly from the previous year's level, to 1% from 1.5%. The professional communities and sectoral authorities at that time lacked the necessary strength to enforce the existing law.

The shortfall in federal appropriations was offset in part by boosting spending under the budgets of the federation's constituent members. The share of funds allocated to culture in the regional budgets rose from 2.4% in 1992 to 2.7% in 1998. The weight of support for culture was therefore off-loaded from the federal budget to the regional budgets (Table 18.5).

The parliamentary elections in December 1993 revived some of the concern over the situation with respect to the country's culture. The election programs of nearly all parties paid lip service to the need to

---

11. *The Cultural Policy in the Russian Federation: Report of the European Group of Experts*, prepared by J. Renard (Strasbourg, 1996), 127.

Table 18.5
Budget Financing of the Cultural Sphere, 1992–1998

	1992	1993	1994	1995	1996	1997	1998
Spending on culture, arts, and mass media as a share of budgetary expenditure (%):							
Federal budget	1.5	1.0	1.1	1.0	0.6	0.6	0.5
Budgets of the RF constituent members	2.4	2.6	2.7	2.7	3.1	2.9	2.7
Cultural spending ratio of the federal budget and the budgets of the RF constituent members (%):							
Federal budget	51	33	36	29	17	16	16
Budgets of the RF constituent members	49	67	64	71	83	84	84

Source: RF Goskomstat.

preserve the cultural heritage and bring culture back to life. Capitalizing on the situation, special interest groups in culture stepped up their pressure on the government and Parliament. The presidential decree issued in late 1993 gave public cultural institutions, creative unions, and their members a string of tax and customs advantages. A turnaround began from this point.

In the parliamentary debates over the 1996 and 1997 federal budgets, members of Parliament voiced their intent to increase the share of spending on social programs, culture in particular. Culture, however, was the worst hit by the budgetary crisis. In 1998, spending on culture, the arts, and the media was cut, in comparable prices, by 27% from 1995 levels. The key development in *television and radio broadcasting* in the transition period was the giddy haste with which public funding was replaced by nonbudgetary funds, predominantly revenues from advertising. According to the Federal Television and Radio Broadcasting Service, as early as 1994 the funds appropriated under the federal budget for TV Channel One would only provide five hours of daily air time. In the presidential election year of 1996, budgetary appropriations for public television were enough for six hours of broadcasting a day.

In 1995 the public TV company Ostankino, broadcasting on Channel One, surrendered its frequency band to a nongovernmental company, Russian Public Television (known by its Russian acronym, ORT). The startup's sponsors included, apart from the government, a few nongovernmental private organizations. This set a precedent for the merging of public and private funds for the production of "net public goods."

By contrast, the *printed word media* faced a situation of low demand and small revenues from advertising to cover the growing costs of printing newspapers and magazines. Beginning in 1992, subsidies have been allocated from the federal budget to some publications on a list approved by Parliament.

Control over the mass media, especially television, by the power elite has increased, not decreased. Traditional government regulation, which combines budgetary financing and influence within the framework of the administrative law system, has been transformed into the influence peddling typical of clan relations.

18.7. Shadow Privatization in the Social Sphere

In contrast to productive industries, privatization in the sociocultural sphere has not made spectacular progress. To begin with, privatization of public and municipal institutions in health, education, and culture was banned, except for drugstores and movie theaters. The ban was, however, lifted in the privatization program for public enterprises adopted in 1994. The intention was to develop appropriate federal laws that would establish guidelines for privatization in the various areas of the sociocultural sphere. These laws have failed to materialize.

The privatization ban does not apply to sociocultural institutions owned by public undertakings. Historically, these so-called departmental institutions did not have public status, even though they were carried on the balance sheets of public undertakings. As privatization went on, some of these facilities were transferred to municipal ownership, while others continued to be held by privatized entities. In the latter case, they were only formally privatized. "Formal" implies that a sociocultural facility was turned over to the private sector without acquiring the rights of a legal entity, and remained on the balance sheet of the same for-profit organization outside the public domain. Government statistics, however, placed such institutions in the privatized category.

In another aspect of legal privatization of sociocultural facilities, religious buildings nationalized after 1917 have been handed over to religious organizations.

While the direct ban on privatization of public and municipal sociocultural institutions was in force, the heads and employees of sociocultural institutions were subtly appropriating some assets.[12] Some researchers refer to this process as spontaneous privatization.[13] *Shadow privatization* might be a more accurate description, because this process basically involves formally illegal appropriation of powers—an appropriation that is, however, authorized by informal mutual agreement between bureaucrats at different levels and the employees of such institutions. "Illegal" in this context means only that such appropriation of title to property may not be authorized in the long term. The duration of the informal social authorization is not specified.

A common feature shared by the various forms of property appropriation is that no rent is paid to the owner for use of the property and no taxes are assessed on personal incomes, so that such facilities are very profitable. Hence the owners' interest in being able to obtain, retain, and expand the scale of such appropriation.

In their turn, central and local sociocultural authorities and the heads and employees of sociocultural institutions resist privatization and any reorganization of their institutions, in part because they have actually privatized most of the ownership rights to the public assets. Keeping the services free serves the interests of both the bureaucrats and the employees of service-providing institutions, for it provides the former with grounds to have public funds placed at their disposal and the latter with an opportunity to receive fees for their services directly from their customers.

This is not to say that shadow privatization was first discovered in the transition period. The widespread practice of using the equipment, premises, and other public assets of industrial enterprises by employees of such enterprises for personal gain in the pre-perestroika period must be construed as shadow privatization.

Shadow privatization in the centrally planned economy and its present-day replica rest on different foundations, however. In the planned economy, shadow privatization derived from the prohib-

---

12. V. Ivanov, T. Kliachko, B. Rosenfeld, G. Shvyrkov, and T. Shirokova, "The Sociocultural Sphere: Current Problems of Government Policy," *Economic Forecasting* 4 (1993): 112–25; A. Markov, "Institutional Aspects of Renewal of Russian Higher Education," in *Introduction to Institutional Analysis* (Moscow: Teis, 1996), 165–70.

13. V. Tambovtsev, "Spontaneous Privatization in Research Organizations," *Forecasting Issues* 4 (1995).

itively high cost to the government, under conditions of total public ownership, to monitor the way its property was utilized. Today, shadow privatization originates in unclear distributions of ownership rights. For example, shadow privatization is far more extensive in public research institutions than in institutions that have been transformed into joint-stock companies.[14]

In this connection, the government is to take special note of another alternative, nonprofit privatization, or reorganization of public and municipal institutions into nonprofit organizations of other ownership forms.[15] This form specifically allows the nonprofit function of educational institutions to be combined with the principles of efficient commitment to limited resources. The existing federal laws on charities and nonprofit organizations, together with the Civil Code of the Russian Federation, provide a firm legal basis for nonprofit privatization to be carried out in the sociocultural sphere.

18.8. Commercialization of Sociocultural Institutions

In their desire to perform their functions in the changing economic conditions and to raise the incomes of their employees to keep pace with prices, sociocultural institutions have adapted to the emerging market economy by commercializing their work.

The process takes four principal forms:

1. The charging of actual (shadow) fees for standard "free" services provided to the population

2. A reduction in the selection of free services, and erosion of the traditional roll of free services

3. The provision of new core services for a fee

4. The provision of new noncore services for a fee, using the undertakings' facilities for purposes for which they are not designated

Opportunities to commercialize their business in one form or another are different for different institutions and sectors of the sociocultural complex. Factors responsible for the spread of these various forms notably include loopholes—or, to put it another way, direct bans—in the laws governing activities in each specific sector of the

---

14. Ibid.
15. B. Rudnik, S. Shishkin, and L. Jacobson, "Privatization in the Sociocultural Sphere: Problems and Possible Forms," *Economic Issues* 4 (1996): 18–32.

sociocultural sphere, income differentiation, and consumer preferences of the groups of the population targeted with sociocultural services. Thus, for different reasons, the scale and rates of commercialization have been vastly different from sector to sector in the sociocultural sphere.

An outstanding example is the fee charged for nursery care at preschool institutions, which rose 266-fold between 1993 and 1996, while the aggregate consumer price growth rate stood at 83. The skyrocketing charge for nursery care was largely due to the fact that the enterprises and organizations that formerly owned and subsidized the nurseries were for the most part unable to continue subsidies with the onset of reforms.

In health care, where market factors worked most closely together, the classic form prevailed. Indeed, beginning in the mid-1970s, shadow fees for medical services were widely accepted in health facilities. Today, health care institutions have purchased modern equipment, which enables them to provide the population with new, quality services—at, of course, higher prices.[16] Health care was exposed to the force of some of the above factors as well.

In culture, particularly in the performing arts and exhibitions, there has been a stable effective demand by certain population groups for specific services. Even before market reforms were launched, these cultural sectors had developed an affinity for market economy principles. To make their life easier, experiments were initiated in 1987 to commercialize public theaters and the entertainment industry. According to the Russian Ministry of Culture, public theaters earned 27.7% of their funds from nonbudgetary sources in 1995.

18.9. Evolution of the Sociocultural Sectors in the Years of Reform

In 1992–1997, the network of health, education, and cultural institutions financed out of the budget was largely left intact. The scarcity of government revenues in the transition period led to a reduction in the number of new sociocultural institutions and deterioration of the

---

16. In January 1997, the price charged for computed tomography by several of Moscow's health institutions providing this service to all in need of it ranged between 500 and 600,000 rubles.

Table 18.6
Public Expenditure on Sociocultural Sectors (in Real Terms), 1991–1998

	1991	1992	1993	1994	1995	1996	1997	1998
Health care	100	80	108	98	72	71	81	67
State budget	100	80	91	81	59	57	65	51
Compulsory insurance premiums from employers	—	—	17	17	13	14	16	16
Education*	100	79	79	76	56	58	64	52
Culture, arts, and mass media*	100	91	81	87	63	54	60	46

*Government budget expenditure.
Source: Calculated from RF Goskomstat data using GDP deflators.

facilities of existing ones. The gradual emergence of a nongovernmental sector in this area was not, as a rule, accompanied by adequate investment in facilities: private schools, nurseries, hospitals, and theaters continued to occupy their old buildings. An overall characteristic of the gathering processes is given in Tables 18.6, 18.7, and 18.8.

Serious problems arose over social infrastructure facilities owned by industrial and agricultural undertakings. In the centrally planned economy, a considerable proportion of cultural, recreational, health, and preschool institutions were maintained by these enterprises. Their maintenance costs were paid out of the enterprises' budgets, and their status differed from that of public institutions. The rise of the market economy and the onset of an economic crisis made maintaining such facilities an insupportable burden for enterprises.

Table 18.7
Public Expenditure on Sociocultural Sectors (% of GDP)

	1991	1992	1993	1994	1995	1996	1997	1998
Health care	2.9	2.5	3.7	3.9	2.9	3.1	3.7	3.1
State budget	2.9	2.5	3.1	3.2	2.4	2.5	3.0	2.4
Compulsory insurance premiums from legal entities	—	—	0.6	0.7	0.5	0.6	0.7	0.7
Education*	3.6	3.6	4.1	4.5	3.4	3.7	4.3	3.6
Culture, arts and mass media*	0.5	0.6	0.6	0.8	0.6	0.5	0.6	0.5

*Government budget expenditure.
Source: Calculated from RF Goskomstat data.

Table 18.8
Newly Commissioned Sociocultural Facilities

	1985	1990	1991	1992	1993	1994	1995	1996	1997	1998
No. of hospital beds (in thousands)	31	212	17	8	14	12	10	9	8	7
Outpatient centers, no. of visits per shift (in thousands)	76	86	63	40	47	39	36	21	27	21
General education schools, no. of seats (in thousands)	520	515	396	303	296	194	218	152	155	123

Source: RF Goskomstat.

In many instances, the facilities were either closed outright or leased or sold to commercial interests, which used them for different purposes. As a result, between 1991 and 1998 the total number of preschool institutions declined by 35%, the number of public libraries declined by 12%, and the number of community centers declined by 21%.

In the same period, the workforce in the sociocultural sectors, far from decreasing, rose by 6.2% between 1992 and 1996 (Table 18.9). This occurred despite the growing gap between salary levels in the sociocultural sphere and in other sectors (Table 18.10). A possible explanation is that the salary gap was compensated for by stable earnings: in contrast to many enterprises in other sectors, salaries in the sociocultural sectors were paid regularly and without much delay until the end of 1995.

Table 18.9
Number of Employees in Sociocultural Sectors (in thousands)

	1985	1990	1991	1992	1993	1994	1995	1996	1997	1998
Health care, physical training and sports, social security	3,747	4,238	4,305	4,227	4,243	4,394	4,446	4,531	4,412	4,453
Education	5,340	6,066	6,138	6,413	6,164	6,245	6,179	6,191	6,019	5,919
Culture and arts	1,040	1,165	1,135	1,108	1,075	1,138	1,137	1,122	1,125	1,114

Source: RF Goskomstat.

Table 18.10
Average Wages and Salaries in Sociocultural Sectors

	1985	1990	1991	1992	1993	1994	1995	1996	1997	1998
Total economy, avg.	100	100	100	100	100	100	100	100	100	100
Health care, physical training and sports, social security (% of avg.)	71	67	76	66	76	76	74	77	70	69
Education (% of avg.)	78	67	71	61	68	69	65	70	65	63
Culture and arts (% of avg.)	65	62	67	52	62	62	61	65	62	62

Source: RF Goskomstat.

In late 1995, the budget started running up wage arrears in the sociocultural sphere. Workers responded by striking. In 1997, education was the focus of striking activity, accounting for over 80% of all walkouts across the country.

A trend showed up toward a polarization of sectors offering services to the general public and the sectors providing services to high-income consumers. Whereas service providers catering to high-income groups are largely well-off, the overwhelming majority of sociocultural institutions continue to struggle, and in fact are dangerously balancing on the edge. With the budget chronically underfinanced and the population short of cash, this sector is slowly being degraded. These developments are typical of all sociocultural sectors.

In the 1990s, the overall health of Russia's population deteriorated. Mortality crept up, and the average life expectancy fell constantly until 1995. In 1994, it reached a low 64 years, down from 69.2 years in 1990. The year 1995, however, witnessed a rebound, and life expectancy sprang back to 67 in 1998. General morbidity among the population went up between 1990 and 1994, then started to subside beginning in 1995. For the whole period of 1991–1998, the incidence of infectious and parasitic diseases rose by 32%, the incidence of diseases of the blood and blood-producing organs shot up by 100%, diseases of the circulation increased by 40%, digestive organ diseases increased by 14%, the incidence of tuberculosis increased by 120%,

Table 18.11
Indicators of Human Health and Health Care

	1985	1990	1991	1992	1993	1994	1995	1996	1997	1998
Incidence of first diagnosed disease (per 1,000 persons)	NA	651.2	667.5	615.6	654.3	653.2	678.8	648.5	674.2	670.4
Morbidity (per 1,000 persons)	11.3	11.2	11.4	12.2	14.5	15.7	15.0	14.2	13.8	13.6
Life expectancy (at birth)	69.3	69.2	69.0	67.9	65.1	64.0	64.6	65.9	66.6	67.0
No. of hospital-type institutions (in thousands)	12.5	12.8	12.7	12.6	12.6	12.3	12.1	11.8	11.5	11.1
Beds therein (per 1,000 persons)	13.5	13.8	13.5	13.1	12.9	12.7	12.6	12.4	12.1	11.8
Average period of inpatient treatment (days)	17.0	16.6	16.7	17.0	16.8	18.0	16.8	16.9	16.6	16.5
No. of outpatient centers (in thousands)	19.4	21.5	20.9	20.7	20.9	21.6	21.1	22.1	21.7	21.1

Source: RF Goskomstat.

Table 18.12
Indicators in the Educational Sphere

	1985	1990	1991	1992	1993	1994	1995	1996	1997	1998
No. of preschool children's institutions (in thousands)	81.8	87.9	87.6	82.0	78.3	72.8	68.6	64.2	60.3	56.6
No. of daytime general education schools (in thousands)	67.1	67.6	67.9	68.3	68.1	68.2	68.4	68.3	67.9	67.3
No. of students therein (in thousands)	18,574	20,328	20,427	20,503	20,565	21,104	21,521	21,682	21,683	21,429
No. of teachers (per 1,000 schoolchildren)	63.0	70.6	73.0	76.1	79.0	78.9	78.4	80.5	80.6	81.4
No. of nonpublic general education schools	—	—	—	—	368	447	525	540	570	568
No. of students therein (in thousands)	—	—	—	—	33	40	46	47	50	50
No. of public higher education establishments	502	514	519	535	548	553	569	573	578	580
No. of nonpublic higher education establishments	—	—	—	—	78	157	193	244	302	334
No. of college and university students (per 10,000 persons)	206	190	186	178	176	179	189	202	222	247
No. of college and university graduates (per 10,000 persons)	33	27	27	29	30	28	27	29	31	34

Source: RF Goskomstat.

Table 18.13
Network Status and Operational Parameters of Government-Sponsored and Municipal Cultural Institutions

	1985	1990	1991	1992	1993	1994	1995	1996	1997	1998
Total no. of theaters	338	382	393	421	439	460	470	489	506	523
Theater attendance (per 1,000 persons)	507	375	340	298	279	235	213	198	188	189
Total no. of museums	964	1,315	1,379	1,425	1,478	1,547	1,725	1,814	1,871	1,942
Museum visits (per 1,000 persons)	724	971	770	639	538	424	509	470	475	457
Total no. of libraries (in thousands)	62.7	62.6	59.2	57.2	56.9	54.8	54.4	53.5	52.9	52.2
Community centers (in thousands)	76.3	73.2	70.6	66.0	63.7	61.3	59.9	58.6	57.4	56.1
Average no. of movie theater visits per resident	16	11	9	n.a.	n.a.	n.a.	0.5	0.4	0.3	0.3

Source: RF Goskomstat.

and the incidence of syphilis increased 32.7-fold. The health statistics of the Russian population are much worse than those of developed market economies.

Deterioration in the population's health was attributed to the difficult socioeconomic and environmental situation, not least to the declining standards of health services. This is evidenced in particular by the increase in mortality from infectious and parasitic diseases (158% in 1991–1998) compared to the incidence rates of these diseases (an increase of 32% over the same period) (Table 18.11).

Meanwhile, some structural changes are developing in the health service itself. The abolition of administratively planned development of the network of therapeutic and disease prevention institutions and the curtailing of government funding for health led to the closing of 9% of hospitals and a 13% reduction in the number of hospital beds per 1,000 population between 1991 and 1998. Given the surplus of hospital beds in comparison with many other countries, this reduction is not overly concerning. Besides, it was offset by an expansion of outpatient facilities: the number of beds at day hospitals of outpatient clinics had risen by 60% toward the end of 1996 from 1989.

The changes in *education* throughout the 1990s were primarily related to the rise of new types of educational institutions, the application and dissemination of tailor-made curricula, the introduction of alternatives, and the abolition of universal educational standards. This was all done without, however, overlooking the best of the accumulated experience in the Russian educational system (Table 18.12).

The various areas of the *cultural sector* evolved differently. Although the total number of libraries, community centers, amusement parks, and movie theaters shrank, the network of theaters and museums expanded. However, attendance at cultural institutions of all types dropped (Table 18.13).

19

Reform in Housing and Public Utilities

Irina Starodubrovskaya

The reform process with respect to housing falls into two distinctly different segments: reforms applicable to new housing construction and growth of the housing market, on the one hand, and reforms in the maintenance, operation, and utility of the existing housing stock on the other. Whereas new housing has experienced good growth rates and rapid institutional reforms, existing housing has become the setting for a gradual, muted model of reform. In this chapter the phrase "reform in housing and utilities" will refer to reforms specifically in the second segment, the already existing housing infrastructure.

19.1. General Characteristics of Housing and Public Utilities in the Soviet Period

In a sense, housing and public utilities are a nation's economy in microcosm. Producers and providers of housing and utility services operate in both potentially highly competitive markets (primarily housing maintenance) and in areas dominated by natural monopolies (most utility services).

The base from which reform in housing and utilities was launched was typical of the centrally controlled system in regard to its technological characteristics, institutional structure, relationships between producers and consumers, and pricing mechanism. It suffered from the same flaws that were responsible for the overall inefficiency in the country's economy: the overbearing dominance of public ownership; a high centralization of control, even where this was unwarranted technologically; artificial market monopolization; and a high reliance on subsidies. All of these factors helped shape the motivation of economic agents in this industry, encouraging them to adopt what is known as "cost-maximizing mechanisms."

Table 19.1
Structure of the Housing Sector in the Russian Federation and Moscow as of June 1990 (%)

Housing Stock Ownership	Russia	Rural Settlements	Urban Settlements	Moscow
Total housing stock	100	100	100	100
Public housing stock	67	37	79	90
Local councils	25	2	35	70
Companies and organizations	42	35	44	20
Communal (e.g., collective farms)	3	9	1	0
Housing co-ops	4	0	5	10
Private	26	54	15	0

Source: Raymond Stryke and Nadezhda Kosareva, *Reform of the Russian Housing Sector 1991 Through 1994* (Moscow, 1994), 9.

Table 19.1 shows the structure of ownership rights in the housing sector of the Russian Federation in June 1990. The figures reflect the dominant role of public ownership in this industry, particularly in large cities.

The housing management structure was a highly centralized system. The management echelons—from top to bottom, the RSFSR Ministry of Housing and Public Utilities, regional housing and public utilities authorities, and municipal housing and public utilities authorities—allowed the central government to control all basic processes in the housing industry. However, this industry was simultaneously under the control of the local councils. The organizations that provided housing and utility services lacked the required independence. Services were supplied on monopolistic principles, not only when this was justified technologically (as in heating and water supply), but even when extensive opportunities existed for competition (as in housing maintenance). Housing and utility rates were deliberately maintained at very low levels, the government paying 80%–90% of the real costs. Rent, including utility services, amounted in 1990 to about 2.5% of the average family income of an industrial worker or civil servant.[1] This low figure was viewed as one of the most important social achievements and one of the social guarantees provided to the population.

---

1. Raymond Stryke and Nadezhda Kosareva, *Reform of the Russian Housing Sector 1991 Through 1994*. (Moscow: The Institute of Urban Economics and USAID. 1994), 10.

The technological patterns in building design and utility service provision were intended primarily to facilitate centralized control of these systems. For this reason, priority was given, regardless of economic efficiency, to vast, concentrated, large-scale projects, such as a centralized heating system that would supply heat to a city from a single source. The possible advantages of decentralized heating were never considered.

19.2. The Concept of Reform in Housing and Public Utilities

Three key factors favored a gradualist approach to reform in housing and public utilities. First, in late 1991, the Supreme Council of the Russian Federation adopted the resolution, "On the Separation of Public Property into Federal Property, Government Property in the Constituent Republics of the Russian Federation, Territories, Regions, Autonomous Regions, Autonomous Areas, the Cities of Moscow and St. Petersburg, and Municipal Property." Under the resolution, the public housing stock, previously managed by local councils, was handed over to municipal authorities, along with the respective engineering infrastructure facilities and housing operation, maintenance, and construction organizations. A series of statutory orders subsequently confirmed that departmental housing, too, was to be removed from privatized enterprises and taken over by municipalities. Thus, the foundations were laid for housing-related decisions to be made at the municipal, local level.

This dealt a death blow to the centralized housing and utility management pyramid and fostered the emergence of multifarious local management authorities. It became the norm for several large municipal housing maintenance enterprises (housing trusts) to be set up in a large city. These trusts combined the functions of both customers and contractors: they drew up their own work plans, collected payment from the population, and received subsidies from the local budget, without having any direct responsibility to the housing-stock owner, the municipality, or the end consumers. Tangled housing management hierarchies, without clear dividing lines between the different levels of control, arose in many areas.

In utility services, municipal enterprises responsible for water supply and sewage systems and for heating[2] were commonly set up to

---

2. Most of the heating supply facilities are out of municipal control.

operate both service-generating and service-distribution facilities. Consequently, an unwieldy multiple structure emerged in which rights and responsibilities were distributed irrationally between the different management levels while the monopolization of housing and utility services remained untouched.

A second factor favoring gradual reform was that as prices were freed, on 1 January 1992, the government simultaneously decided that liberalization should not apply to the rates charged for the housing and utility services provided to the population. Far from being freed, housing and utility rates were not even raised appreciably. A chance was thereby lost for housing- and utility-cost-recovery mechanisms to be created and for consumers to be given an incentive to press for fast institutional reforms in the industry. Moreover, when in 1992 and 1993 price and financing levels were adjusted to the new conditions, the share of housing and utility operation costs paid for by the population dropped sharply.

A third factor favoring gradual reform in housing was the existing privatization practice, which hindered radical reforms. The relevant Russian laws required free privatization. However, they also held that privatization was optional, they placed no time limits on free privatization, and they did not require the owners of privatized apartments to assume any obligations regarding the management of the building in which their apartments were located. Thus, the pace of reforms in the management and maintenance of existing housing was left up to the whim of the owners of privatized apartments to form homeowners partnerships and assume responsibility for shared common property. In the absence of a general consensus, a house remained in municipal ownership, even if most of its apartments had been privatized. Any other alternative paths for reforming ownership rights in existing municipal buildings were constrained by the indefinite right of tenants to opt for privatization of their apartments. As a result, privatization basically stimulated the formation of a housing market without having a significant impact on the organizational principles of housing management and maintenance.

Although legislation relating to housing and utility reforms continued to be churned out throughout 1992, key approaches in this area acquired definite outlines beginning in December 1992. At this time the law *On the Basic Principles of Federal Housing Policy* went into effect, and key approaches were subsequently specified in a number of follow-up statutory acts. The main ideas of the housing and utility reform concept boiled down to the following.

A strategy was adopted to have housing and utility charges raised, but gradually. At the city level, the gradual increase was intended to provide a social safety net for low-income families who were unable to pay their share of housing and utility costs. Subsidies were to be granted selectively on a means-tested basis. It was assumed that subsidies would be issued only if a family's housing and utility costs exceeded a statutory proportion of the family's income. This provision allowed a socially reasonable floor rate to be adopted in the housing sector.[3]

Initially, it was intended that 100% cost recovery by the population would be phased in over five years in equal steps. This rigid plan was subsequently abandoned, leaving only the deadline of five years for the housing and utility system to begin unsubsidized operations. The State Duma extended the deadline first to ten years, then to fifteen. Now full cost recovery is scheduled to be reached by 2008.

Simultaneously, the reform concept set the goal of carrying out institutional changes to reduce costs and improve the quality of housing and utility services. A streamlining of the housing and public utilities management structure was proposed that would reduce the number of its echelons and separate the functions of customer and contractor. Where technologically possible, and particularly for maintenance services, contractors were to be chosen by tender (bids), so that the costs of a service would be competitive and quality would be improved. The regulation of local natural monopolies was not specifically addressed in the housing-related by-laws.

A batch of by-laws was adopted to govern the establishment of homeowners partnerships. Housing partnerships were to be set up on a voluntary basis, provided, however, that where a resolution to establish a partnership was adopted, all owners of dwelling and nondwelling premises in the building were required to participate. In respect to local budget subsidies, partnerships were to be on a par with municipal housing, so that joining a housing partnership would not result in higher rent and utility charges for the tenants. Also,

---

3. The rate is established in square meters of floor area per person at the regional level on the basis of the average availability of housing in a given territory and generally differentiated for different family size and composition.

partnerships could bring in extra revenue by leasing unoccupied premises, and spend the revenue on improving living conditions.

Institutional reforms spilled over into yet another housing sector, the housing stock of privatized enterprises. Although different documents placed different interpretations on the sources of financing for the housing stock divested from enterprises and accepted by municipalities, the country in fact now had two real sources. First, a 1.5% turnover tax could be imposed at the municipal level to maintain housing and sociocultural facilities. The actual assessment was deductible by the amount an enterprise spent on upkeep of the social facilities on its books. Enterprises that had never had any social facilities or that had divested them to the municipality were to pay the tax in full. Second, funds were allocated from the federal budget to vest control of enterprise housing.

A general overview of the housing reform program shows that it typically embraced gradualist reform in most sectors. It was assumed that municipal authorities would, of their own free will or under budgetary constraints, carry out the required institutional reforms, which would undercut their ability to behave arbitrarily in housing and utility services and lead to more profound changes. It was also held that commitment to relatively low rates for housing and utility services, allowing them to rise only gradually, would help defuse the social tensions generated by radical reforms in other areas, and so would act as a kind of social safety valve.

19.3. Results of the Reform in Housing and Utilities: 1994–1997

In practice, the reform concept was pursued, with only minor amendments, for more than three years. This period of time affords researchers an extensive opportunity to assess the practicability and efficiency of the reforms. The following conclusions can be drawn from the experience amassed over this period.

The first thing that catches the eye is that Russian cities have split along deep lines over the rates, trends, and comprehensiveness of housing reforms. In this regard, a key role has been played by the extent of the problem and the real interests of local authorities, which, from all available evidence, were far more important than objective realities (size of the population, financial standing, and so forth). For example, the local authorities in some cities where virtually all housing stock had been owned by major enterprises displayed intense zeal in taking over property, despite occasional financial battles. For instance, the housing stock in the small town of Volkhov, Leningrad Region, tripled after the acceptance of enterprise housing between 1992 and 1996. The municipality of another town, Cherepovets, Vologda Region, which owned only 11.5% of the town's housing stock, started taking over housing from four giant enterprises as early as 1992, with the takeover almost finished by the end of 1995. Such fervor can be chiefly attributed to municipal authorities' desire to have real freedom of action and to lay their hands on assets they could actually manage.

The larger population areas, which boasted a more diverse complement of industries and were not driven by this incentive, took their time in taking over housing from their enterprises. The deadline of six months prescribed in the regulations for municipalities to take over the social assets of privatized enterprises passed unmet nearly everywhere.

Even if we disregard the abundant instances of local authorities ignoring housing reform and sticking instead to the old organizational system of housing and utility services, we arrive at the conclusion that the changes implemented in different cities produced entirely different principles and structures of housing and utility management. Moreover, where the reform concept was embraced halfheartedly and one-sidedly, the end result could well fly in the face of the underlying principles of reform.

It is extremely difficult today to find examples of housing reform having been carried through consistently and comprehensively. The following conclusions, therefore, are based on the experience of cities in which the reforms have been pursued without excessive deviation from the initial concept.

The first conclusion that can be drawn after more than three years of housing reform in cities that took a no-nonsense approach to the task is that all of the components of the reform have proved to be realistic and feasible. The more favorable conditions for housing reforms existed in the administrative centers of republics and regions. In smaller towns (with populations under 100,000) and in single-industry towns, more effort is needed to get reforms off the ground. Illustrative examples are provided by two towns: Volkhov (approximately 50,000 population) and Gus-Khrustalny (about 80,000). By late 1997, Volkhov held three tenders from housing service providers, and 28% of the municipal housing was operated on a competitive basis. In Gus-Khrustalny, more than 25 homeowners partnerships have been established, a customer service organization has been put into operation, and housing services have been demonopolized.

Most fears over the practicability of some aspects of the housing reform have proven unfounded. In particular, the assumption that competition in housing service was a bleak prospect of no interest to private firms and that tenders were a waste of time has proved false. On the contrary, experience has shown that where tenders are wisely organized and corruption is not rampant, companies will enter this market. Particularly high activity is displayed by privatized and private construction undertakings and firms whose managers used to be in housing and utilities. There are instances of tenders attracting over a dozen bidders, but the typical number is between five and seven. In February and March 1998, over 70% of the housing stock in Moscow was managed under contracts won through tenders, almost 45% in Nizhny Novgorod, 28% in Ryazan and Volkhov, 23% in Orenburg, about 20% in Novgorod, 16% in Petrozavodsk, and 8%–10% in Novocherkassk and Cherepovets.[4]

The shortage of qualified managers has not become an unassailable barrier to the spread of homeowners partnerships. The process is well under way in cities where it is supported by the municipal authorities. Some cities have between 60 and 70 registered partnerships each (Table 19.2).

There was more validity to apprehensions that higher housing service rates would stir social discontent. In St. Petersburg, for example, a sharp increase in housing and utility charges sparked public unrest that continued for several days. However, this experience is far from the norm. In general, housing and utility charges rose considerably in 1995–1996. Moreover, the share of cost recovery rose from 2%–3% to 20%–40%. By spring of 1998 it had increased to 40%–50% in many cities.

Serious public relations campaigns, backed by a fine-tuned safety net for the population, have permitted service rates to be painlessly revised upward, even where the price hikes were inordinately high. In Cherepovets, for example, service rates for the population were raised by 160% in November 1995, followed by another exorbitant hike in August 1996. In late 1997, the share of cost recovery by the population in the city topped 40%, yet public unrest was minimal.

---

4. Data are from the Institute for Urban Economics and the Foundation for Enterprise Restructuring and Financial Institutions Development.

Table 19.2
Number of Homeowners Partnerships in Selected Russian Cities

City	Jan. 1996	Dec. 1996	June 1997	Apr. 1998
Moscow	18	49	57	144
Nizhny Novgorod	16	44	61	74
Ryazan	29	38	49	54
Novocherkassk	6	21	28	41
Gus-Khrustalny	0	11	21	n/a
Orenburg	2	10	15	31
Novgorod	4	6	9	17
Petrozavodsk	0	2	5	17

Source: Based on data from the Urban Economics Institute Foundation.

Typically, the segment of the population charged extra rates responds by increasingly withholding payments. In a standard situation, between 20% and 30% of families (or even more) fail to pay service fees on time at current rates. This level of arrears is often taken as a signal to stop raising rates. Far better results are achieved in cities that attempt to address the arrears problem. In Novgorod, for example, the arrears index is maintained at 12%–16%, and in Orenburg it dipped to 10% and less. Overall, the majority of cities exhibit a significant potential for continued growth in the share of housing and utility services covered by the population. In fact, even if arrears grow, funds to pay housing subsidies expand, and administrative expenses for developing the housing allowance service rise, the higher service rates for the population do not fail to save a considerable part of the budget subsidies. Even where the share of cost recovery by the population has been raised to 40%, the cost of the housing allowance program varies between 7% and 10% of the amount paid by the population (disregarding the arrears), rising to 17% only in cities where the cost coverage level reaches 60%.

The ongoing reforms in the housing sector, while confirming the feasibility of the reform concept adopted, failed to produce more rational service provision or to lower costs. Furthermore, the growth in housing and utility service costs exceeded the rate of inflation in 1994 and 1995.[5] This fact can be explained by the slow pace of reforms in this area across Russia. But an analysis of the reforms conducted even in cities that have been reasonably consistent in

---

5. More about this can be found in "Concept of a Housing and Utility Reform in the Russian Federation," approved on 28 April 1997.

adhering to the approaches developed at the federal level reveals the same picture: in most cases the reforms in housing and utilities that are already in place have not produced the immediate financial effect that was expected. Several underlying reasons can be identified. First, inadequate attention was given to efforts to rationalize the provision of utility services, which account for the bulk of expenses borne in housing and utilities. Without the appropriate machinery in place to regulate natural monopolies, including Integrated Power Network, which operates the majority of the country's cogeneration plants, control over the power costs in the housing sector will remain inadequate.

However, costs are not going down appreciably in housing maintenance and management either, although the reform concept concentrated on this aspect of the housing sector. The continuing high costs appear to be more than a coincidence; they logically follow from the general approach to the reforms. In many cities with ample opportunity to shift the burden of housing costs to the population itself, local authorities refused to do so, regardless of the catastrophic underfinancing of their housing and utility services. The figures in Table 19.3 demonstrate that even in the European part of Russia, the

Table 19.3
Implementation of a Housing Subsidy Program in Selected Cities in the Russian Federation (Data Current as of Spring 1997)

City	Standard Apartment* Rent (Rb)	Percentage of Families Receiving Housing Subsidies	Maximum Permissible Proportion of Expenditure on Rent and Utilities in Aggregate Family Income (%)
Moscow	148,890	11.4	12.5
Nizhny Novgorod	114,738	8.4	12.5
Ryazan	78,150	1.2	15
Novocherkassk	135,750	13.0	15
Novgorod	166,431	4.8	16
Petrozavodsk	148,194	18.5	5–10–15 (depending on family income)
Samara	218,547	32.0	10
Cherepovets	160,000	2.0	15
Orenburg	138,300	9.8	10

*The term "standard apartment" means an apartment with a total area of 54 sq m and three tenants using 150 kW·hr of electricity per month.

Source: Based on data from the Urban Economics Institute Foundation.

population's payments for housing and utility services in 1997 differed from city to city by as much as 150%, with the share of families receiving housing allowances varying from 1.5% or 2% to 32%.

It should also be remembered that reform in housing and public utilities goes against the interests of some members of the local elite, often those wielding tremendous power. Reorganization of the housing management system, in particular the dissolution of housing management trusts, has proven to be a rather risky undertaking.

It is no surprise, therefore, that management reorganization exercises in housing and utilities have not, except in very rare cases, cut labor and costs in the industry. The opposite effect has been much more common.

Management costs are rising not just because the selfishness of the local authorities but also because of the reform concept itself, in particular the separation of the customer (customer service as a municipal structure) and the consumer (the population). In this situation, control over the performance of housing operators is not maintained in a natural way but has to be enforced "from above." This requires a large staff to regularly check on the quantity and quality of the work done by contractors and their compliance with contractual obligations.

A management option that has grown very popular in practice is to set up an integrated customer service structure for a city as a whole (with branches in districts of a large city), having the status of a municipal institution. This option places housing management in the hands of a single authority, a much more powerful and wicked monopolist than the one that used to run the service before. In such a situation the contractor must be guided by the interests of the customer service institution, not the interests of the tenants, and both municipal and private firms suffer under the same obligation. Moreover, contract awarding by tender would tie the contractor's hands even more firmly, because his resistance to paying just attention to customer service may cost him the job should he fail to win the tender.

Similar problems arise in the case of homeowners partnerships. Their formation and operation also have, in many respects, been placed at the mercy of municipalities, for which partnerships represent a surrender of some of their own housing stock. Besides, partnerships have to be subsidized from the budget, and their housing allowances are also to be compensated on the same terms as allowances to municipal tenants. The spread of partnerships would therefore divert more and more funds from the municipal budget. Not surprisingly, the local budgets in many cities owe months in arrears to their partnerships.

Not infrequently, the customer service structures perceive partnerships as their rivals in the fight for control of resources and as a pernicious example of a more rational management scheme, and obstruct their formation and registration in every way. Or else they attempt to "hang" partnership onto municipal housing service providers, thereby depriving the partnerships of decision-making powers and funds, taking sense out of the partnership idea itself.

The intensifying local budgetary crisis and its related arrears problem are no obstacle to an intrinsically logical housing reform scheme. Local budgetary crisis only brings into sharper focus the contradictions that were built into the housing reform scheme from the start. In most situations, municipal authorities make their own life easier by just refusing to hand out subsidies to housing and utility operators and homeowners partnerships. They also abandon their hunt for cost-slashing options, especially under the threat of losing their savings when next year's budget comes up for approval. The quality of housing and utility services plunges and public opposition to higher service rates mounts. The contradictions embedded in the reform concept will increasingly come to the surface. This had become evident by early 1997, when the reform process had ground to a halt almost everywhere, and even started to regress in some areas.

19.4. A New Stage of Reform: 1997–1999

In his April 1997 decree,[6] President Yeltsin approved a new "Concept of a Reform in Housing and Public Utilities," calling for acceleration and extension of reforms in this sector and for tighter federal control over the progress of housing reform at the local level. The decree gave first priority to rationalization of the housing and utility services and reducing their costs. To this end, it proposed expanding

---

6. Presidential decree No. 425 of 28 April 1997, "Concept of a Reform in Housing and Public Utilities in the Russian Federation."

the scale of changes in the traditional housing reform areas and offered some new ideas.

The new concept advanced the idea of three federal standards in housing charges: (1) a federal standard of housing and utility charges per 1 square meter of total floor area, (2) a federal standard for the public's share of payments in the total housing operation and maintenance costs and utility services, and (3) a maximum allowable share of tenants' expenditures on housing and utility services in the aggregate family income. Regional and local authorities reserved the right to independently establish key guidelines for switching to a new housing payment system. However, funds from the federal budget had to be transferred according to federal standards. If any federation members wished to charge low rates to their tenants, they had to cover the costs involved from their internal resources.

The federal standards were oriented toward gradually increasing the share of housing and utility costs covered by the population, thereby reviving the approach taken in government resolution No. 935 of 22 September 1993 (Table 19.4). There were three basic differences, however. First, the costs to be covered by the population included major repairs; second, the shift to 100% coverage of costs by the population was moved forward to the year 2003; and, third, the proposals provided for more dynamic variations in the maximum share of costs of housing and utility services in the family budget.

Table 19.4
Schedule for Switchover to a New Scheme of Rental and Utilities Charges on Tenants According to the Concept of Reform of Housing and Utilities in the Russian Federation

Year	Tenants' Charges as a Proportion of All Utility Costs (Federal Standard, in %)	Maximum Permissible Proportion of Expenditure on Rent and Utilities in Aggregate Family Income (Federal Standard, in %)
1997	35	16
1998	50	18
1999	60	19
2000	70	20
2001	80	22
2002	90	23
2003	100	25

The federal standard for the social floor area quota was now a uniform countrywide standard: 18 square meters of total floor area per member for a family of three or more, 42 square meters for a family of two, and 33 square meters for one-person households. The federal standards of housing and utility costs were altered in 1997[7] according to regions, varying from 6,000 to just under 17,000 rubles per 1 square meter of total floor area, with the average for all of Russia working out to 8,200 old rubles.

The new concept also envisioned faster institutional reforms, in particular, demonopolization and privatization. The 1997–1998 plans provided for raising the share of housing services on a competitive basis to 60%, with a further increase of the full 100% by 2000. In addition, more attention was to be given to competition in housing management. Approaches were outlined to regulate and rationalize the operation of public utilities, although no specific mechanisms were developed. A more structured and thorough approach to the housing and utility management system was proposed, to replace the initial "customer-contractor" scheme. The approach was based on

[a] rational distribution of functions and establishment of relations between the homeowner, management organization, contractor organizations under various ownership forms providing housing and engineering system servicing, and the agency authorized to exercise government control over the provision of housing and utility services of required quality to the population, and over the operation and preservation of the housing stock irrespective of ownership.[8]

In other respects, the concept largely reaffirmed the principles previously articulated in the housing and utility management reform plan. In particular, the concept supported all-around support for emerging homeowners partnerships, the introduction of contractual relations in housing and utility services, the need to complete the transfer of departmental housing into municipal ownership, and so forth.

In sum, the new stage of housing reform retained the basic approaches of the preceding stages. Nothing changed in the guidelines and principles of reforming. As previously, the reforms were to be executed gradually, step by step. The close dependence of local

---

7. Resolution No. 621 of the Russian government of 26 May 1997, "Federal Standards for a Transition to a New Housing and Public Utility Service Payment."
8. "Concept of a Reform in Housing and Public Utilities in the Russian Federation."

budgets on the housing reform rates continued to be viewed as a strong motivation for local authorities to expedite reforms in this sector, and this approach was strengthened with the introduction of the federal standards. Although this sphere of reforms was considered among the key priorities of the federal policy, the gradualist approach has remained unshaken.

Accordingly, all contradictions intrinsic to this approach were also maintained. Although the introduction of federal standards provided an external impetus to implement the reform, the internal motivation of municipalities continued to be inadequate to the demands made on the housing sector. Although competition in management was heavily stressed, there were no obstacles to the establishment and maintenance of customer service organizations at the city level that could monopolize housing stock management and merge directly with the authorities' political interests. Although homeowners partnerships were, under the reform concept, to become the dominant form of apartment houses by 2003, it was unclear what forces would drive this process forward and what organizational interests would support it. There was a real danger of private firms, which had entered the housing and utility market, transforming into an exact copy of municipal enterprises in this area: no different in motivation or rationalization of management, and winning tenders because of their "special relationships" with the authorities. In other words, there were no guarantees whatsoever that the new elements would gradually transform the old institutional relations, rather than the old system "digesting" the new approaches.

The practice of the next three years to a considerable degree confirmed apprehensions about housing and public utilities reform. This period is conventionally divided in two stages according to the different attitudes the authorities took toward the problem of transforming housing and public utilities.

Until mid-1998, federal authorities seriously concerned themselves with accelerating the reforms. This pressure probably led to real progress in housing and public utilities reform. However, at the same time, it mainly addressed the external formal aspect of the reform and seldom involved real changes in institutional relations and structural transformations. The control over simple, quantitatively measurable indicators overshadowed the necessary work on improving the efficiency of housing and public utilities operations.

In the second period less attention was paid to reform of housing and public utilities. Moreover, arguments that it was necessary to stop the transformation began to be heard. This trend was manifested in the Duma's postponing yet again the transition to full coverage, without subsidized financing, of the housing and public utilities, until 2008. Lack of proper attention to this aspect of reform and contradictory signals from the federal level did not facilitate the acceleration of proper transformation.

A negative environment for housing and public utilities reform also grew up because of unregulated fiscal arrangements between the subjects of the Federation and municipalities. The federal center controlled the rate of reforms of the housing and public utilities and employed fiscal incentives and sanctions at the regional level, whereas real reforms were implemented at the municipal level. So, leaders of the reform who achieved real financial results at the municipal level not only went unrewarded, they were regularly punished by a Federation incentive program that left at their disposal less and less fiscal revenue, allegedly in accordance with "real needs."

At the same time, an acute deficit in local budgets, up to 70% of which were eaten away by the housing and public utilities, did not allow the transformations to be stopped for good, at least in the sphere directly affecting the amount of subsidies (an increased portion of payment for housing and public utilities services by households). It is precisely this aspect of reform that has been most successful: in some towns and regions actively involved in the housing and public utilities transformation, household payments made about 40%–45% of cost recovery. However, a considerable difference persists, and in some localities households have been covering less than 30% of costs.

On the whole, deep-going transformations along other lines were not carried out. In some cities and towns, the dynamics of certain indicators have been positive. Thus, in Moscow, Nizhny Novgorod, Arzamas, and Novocherkassk, over half of housing stock is maintained on a tender basis. St. Petersburg, Novocherkassk, and Novgorod succeeded in almost doubling the number of condominiums; in Nizhny Novgorod, Krasnoyarsk, and both capitals this number came to more than a hundred.[9] However, individual achievements should not mask the scope of the remaining problems. The country

---

9. Data from the Institute for Urban Economics Fund.

at large has been unable to resolve the most important qualitative problem, that of exposing the housing sector to market relations.

No substantial progress was observed in the ownership sphere. Municipal authorities clearly demonstrated their inability to be effective owners of the bulk of the housing stock. Condominium associations have formed more slowly than was stipulated in the program of reforms and have involved less than 1% of households in the country as a whole. Even in the case of newly constructed housing, condominiums are by no means common, while municipalities sometimes become owners of newly commissioned houses even though they own no share in them. Thus, condominiums will not be able to solve the effective owner problem in housing in the near term.

When effective owners are lacking, the quality of housing stock management becomes especially important. In practice, such management has been of administrative rather than business character. Privately owned structures have almost always been kept out of the management sphere; tenders are not effective. As a result, management organizations do not see a higher efficiency in housing and public services and an increase in property values as their primary goals. Owners' indifference and managers' administrative zeal create wholly inadequate incentives for producers and providers of housing and public services.

The flaws in the reform program in regard to the control of local natural monopolies providing public services have been clear. The creation of an adequate regulatory system that would concern itself with balancing interests and equilibrating demand and supply across individual municipalities and regions was replaced by ad hoc actions, such as auditing public utilities, of ambiguous purpose and uncertain prospect. In response to the growing demands of monopolists and mounting arrears in payments for heat and water on the part of local budgets,[10] there appeared the notion of lowering tariffs, even if the price undermined the sound operation of public utilities. The lack of a normal regulatory system has allowed the implementation of neither market nor administrative measures that would increase the efficiency of housing and public utilities by increasing their transparency to regulating authorities, influencing the investments made by public utilities entities (and therefore influencing

---

10. In some municipalities debts exceed annual budgets.

their aims), or effectively managing budget resources channeled through the housing and public utilities.

In order to complete the reform of housing and public utilities, then, three main objectives must be met:

1. The reform of household payments for housing and public utilities should be completed. Once housing and public utilities are no longer subsidized, normal mechanisms of financing of housing can start to emerge.

2. Housing management should be exposed to market relations, which should turn it into an efficient business involving enterprises with all forms of ownership.

3. A regulatory mechanism should be put into place that would both enable regulatory authorities to control key parameters of housing and public utilities operations and at the same time allow housing and public utilities to operate independently in a predictable environment.

Without these measures, all attempts to improve the efficiency of housing and public utilities, to form a sound basis for housing to operate and develop on, or to stop pumping budget resources into the black hole of subsidizing housing and public utilities seem to be futile.

IV Real Sector of the Economy: Adaptation Problems

20

General Trends in the Real Sector in the Reform Period

Evgeni Gavrilenkov and Olga Izryadnova

20.1. Principal Development Tendencies and Factors of Economic Restructuring

Economic growth rates in the USSR, including Russia, began gradually slowing in the second half of the 1970s, in association with a steady decline in the efficient utilization of key factors of production. The end of the seventies brought into particularly sharp focus the discrepancy between the production machinery and technologies and the proportion of investment in basic sectors of the country's economy. Imbalances piled up in production, consumption, and financing, and producers' innovative zeal subsided. The structural crisis in the economy was brought about by natural development processes and by the impact of destructive long-term trends in the operation of the Soviet economy as a closed, administratively managed system. The years 1990 and 1991 saw a real meltdown, not simply a slowdown in growth, as social production plunged to hitherto unknown depths. In 1990, industrial production in the USSR dipped 1.2% from 1989, and in 1991 it dropped by as much as 8% from its 1990 level. In the last quarter of 1991 industrial production was down 21% from the analogous period a year before, and off by a quarter from the peak it had reached in 1989. The plummeting production figures signaled that the economy could not be put back on the growth track unless radical economic reform was carried out and new economic regulation forms and tools were found.

Without repeating what was said in the preceding chapters, we emphasize here that the economic situation in the first stage of reform was shaped by several groups of factors:

1. Factors rooted in the structural deformity and technological backwardness of the Russian economy, which was geared toward

the extensive utilization of resources and preservation of a heavy extraeconomic burden

2. Factors aimed at restructuring the traditional political government and economic setups, which were most evident in the late 1980s and early 1990s

3. Factors associated with the implementation of radical economic reform in 1992, liberalization of economic activity at home and abroad, and budgetary and lending policies

Whereas the first group of factors largely accounted for the sluggishness of economic development, factors in the second and third groups powerfully influenced changes in the economic structure.

In 1992, the economic situation remained tense under the weight of large macroeconomic imbalances and the problems that unavoidably arose during the opening moves toward a market economy. The contraction in aggregate production was caused by a fall in domestic effective demand as real incomes were depressed by the 1992 price liberalization and producers' slow pace of adaptation to the new price relations. Changes in the government spending structure and scale strongly affected investment in fixed capital and defense. A factor of no little consequence was the breakdown of traditional economic links with East European countries and the rest of the Commonwealth of Independent States.

The breakdown in production and technological ties led to problems in providing producers with funds and technologies as well as problems with output marketing, thereby aggravating the producers' financial position. The share of inventories in the working capital structure was steadily rising. Moreover, to cushion the impact of inflation, enterprises were building up reserves of raw and other kinds of materials, without heed for the sagging demand for their output. Enterprises' economic strategies continued to be centered on boosting output, with no attention paid to marketing, demand, or structural analysis. The producers' inadequate response to the changing economic conditions and pricing policies was one of the reasons why they defaulted and triggered a financial crisis. The ratio of their own assets to borrowed funds changed too, particularly in highly cooperative industries, such as mechanical engineering and the light industry.

As a result of privatization and the formation of joint-stock companies, the nonpublic sector rapidly captured a dominant position

Table 20.1
Ownership Patterns of GDP Production, Employment, and Fixed Capital Investment (% of total)

Ownership Type	GDP			Employment			Investment		
	1993	1996	1998	1993	1996	1998	1993	1996	1998
Public (state and municipal)	48.0	30.0	25.4	53.0	42.0	38.1	63.2	33.4	27.4
Private	17.5	24.7	27.3	28.1	35.6	43.2	12.1	16.0	25.7
Mixed, without foreign participation	33.0	43.5	45.3	17.6	21.0	16.4	22.1	48.5	40.6
Mixed, with the participation of foreign capital	0.6	0.8	1.2	0.4	0.8	1.6	2.5	3.0	4.0
Total	100	100	100	100	100	100	100	100	100

Source: Calculated from RF Goskomstat data.

and went on to strengthen its influence in all business areas. This process stimulated structural changes at both the macro- and microlevel (Table 20.1).

The gradual adaptation of the economy to the changing management practices proceeded against the background of a continuing slump in industrial production and a downturn in business activity. The emerging economic situation was strongly influenced by the currency market. The high margins on the financial and currency markets severely limited possibilities for investing capital in the real sector. The fiscal regulation measures helped restrain inflation and gradually stabilize production. They were not enough, however, to produce a recovery of the real sector of the Russian economy. Finance remained the most attractive business area.

The existing economic situation worsened some of the problems that had been fermenting in the Russian economy for a long time. The most serious problem was that the reform of the structurally deformed economy had failed to have any effect on the technical and technological structure of production. This was evidenced, above all, by the mining industries acquiring a greater role in production. The share of mining rose from 12.8% in 1992 to 16.4% in 1997, while that of the manufacturing industries slipped, and the socially oriented sectors continued their downward slide. This was due, on the one hand, to the still high share of GDP contributed by natural resources, and on the other hand, to renewed growth in exports of minerals and fuels and their preprocessed products at accelerating rates. In this situation, a significant increase in foreign trade became a factor restraining the rate of decline of the national economy.

It was not until early 1995 that conditions had evolved for enterprises to gradually shift their priorities from pricing policies to the formulation of a strategy to promote and establish goods markets.

In the conditions of a consistent, moderately tough monetary policy, the dynamics and structure of macroeconomic indicators were favorably influenced by a slowdown in the rate of decline in manufacturing, a stronger ruble against the dollar, a larger share of Russian currency in the aggregate money supply, and a continuing foreign trade surplus.

Inflation rates were steadily decreasing. The growth in consumer prices slowed down, with prices for finished products in manufacturing and material and investment resources continuing to spearhead the growth trend. Power- and fuel-price regulation was having a restraining effect on producer prices.

Measures to rein in inflation by limiting the money supply, without adequate control over payments in the economy, encouraged negative developments in the payment system. In 1996, especially in the first six months of the year, "surrogate money" in various forms (bills of exchange, tax exemptions, commodity credits) and barter between enterprises had reached alarming proportions in the circulation structure, reducing still further the taxable base and diluting the real flow of revenues into the budget.

The consistent, rigid fiscal policy was a major factor in the economic situation that unfolded in 1997. The GDP and industrial production rose, while the agriculture and transport sectors slowed down. These trends advanced as inflation was steadily losing momentum, the ruble was strengthening against the dollar, and foreign trade was continuing in surplus. In 1997 the GDP increased by 8.8% and industrial output rose by 1.9%. The output of the manufacturing and extracting sectors of industry grew as well. As inflation rates slowed down and real household incomes increased by 6.3%, household demand rose somewhat. The increasing household demand in turn spurred growth in domestic production. The prerequisites for economic growth were gaining momentum in the national economy.

However, these positive trends were weakened and later completely neutralized by changes on the world financial markets. Beginning in October 1997, signs of a recession were evident in the

Russian economy. Although the government and the central bank succeeded in temporarily stabilizing the situation, from 1998 onward, permanent and growing negative trends were registered both in the real and in the financial sectors of the economy. Over the years of reform, the Russian economy had become somewhat integrated into the world's economy, and therefore the crisis on the international financial and commodity markets inevitably affected the dynamics of Russia's economic development. With the financial crisis of August 1998, the Russian economy experienced a new slump. Nevertheless, the pessimistic forecasts made at the time proved to be incorrect, as by the end of 1999 the GDP had increased by 3.2% and industrial output had increased by 8.1%, thus returning the Russian economy almost to the levels of the last precrisis year (1997). As a result of the ruble's devaluation and shifts in the structure of effective demand, the development of import-replacing and export-oriented businesses progressed. Domestic producers successfully used favorable changes in the competitive environment and began to generate growth. Apparently, over the past few years the economy was able to realize a certain production potential on a scale that was unexpected. This may be attributed both to the specifics of economic development under conditions of a hypertrophied system of nonmonetary payments and barter and to inaccurate statistical monitoring of economic processes (Tables 20.2 and 20.3).

Table 20.2
Structure of Gross Output Allocation, 1991–1998, in Basic Prices* (% of total)

	1991	1992	1993	1994	1995	1996	1997	1998
Total gross output in basic prices	100	100	100	100	100	100	100	100
Intermediate consumption	44.5	42.0	40.1	39.0	41.6	41.9	40.7	39.2
Expenditure on final consumption	30.1	18.9	28.6	34.2	33.4	34.7	36.8	37.4
Gross accumulation	17.8	13.5	12.4	12.6	11.9	11.9	11.3	8.0
Exports of goods and services	6.5	24.4	17.6	13.7	13.0	11.9	11.6	15.6
Statistical discrepancy	1.1	1.2	1.4	0.4	0.0	−0.4	−0.4	−0.2

*Basic prices, in terms of allocation, include subsidies for food and imports and exclude taxes thereon.
Source: RF Goskomstat.

Table 20.3
Performance of Key Macroeconomic Indicators, 1992–1999 (% of Preceding Year's Figure)

	1992	1993	1994	1995	1996	1997	1998	1999
Gross domestic product	85.5	91.3	87.3	95.9	95.1	100.8	95.4	103.2
Industry	82.0	86.0	79.0	97.0	96.0	101.9	94.8	108.1
Extractive	89.0	90.0	90.0	99.0	98.0	103.0	96.5	—
Manufacturing	81.0	85.0	76.0	96.0	95.0	101.8	92.8	—
consumer goods	85.0	89.0	74.0	87.9	93.4	102.1	93.6	—
Agriculture	91.0	96.0	88.8	92.0	93.0	100.1	87.7	102.4
Investment	60.0	88.0	76.0	90.0	82.0	94.5	93.3	101.0
Transportation companies' freight turnover	86.0	88.0	86.0	99.0	95.4	96.6	96.5	105.2
Communication services	—	—	—	—	—	123.6	119.9	133.1
Goods turnover	97.0	102.0	100.1	93.0	96.0	101.4	96.7	92.3
Paid services	82.0	70.0	62.0	82.0	94.0	103.7	99.5	102.4
Foreign trade	—	90.6	100.3	122.3	108.2	102.9	82.3	86.6
Exports	—	87.9	106.9	118.8	113.9	97.7	84.1	100.2
Imports	—	77.2	90.8	128.2	99.4	107.0	80.2	69.5
Balance	—	—	94.4	1190.2	112.0	76.0	99.5	219.9
Real disposable cash income	53.0	116.0	112.0	84.0	100.0	106.3	81.9	84.9
Real wage	67.0	100.4	92.0	72.0	106.0	105.0	86.6	76.8
Officially registered unemployed	—	164.6	202.5	145.2	124.9	88.9	82.1	85.1
Price Indices*								
Consumer prices	2,608.6	939.9	315.1	231.3	121.8	111.0	184.4	136.5
Foodstuffs	2,626.2	904.9	314.1	223.4	117.7	109.1	196.6	134.0
Nonfoods	2,673.4	741.8	269.0	216.3	117.8	108.1	199.5	139.2
Paid services to households	2,220.5	2,411.2	622.4	332.3	148.4	122.5	118.3	134.0
Industry prices								
For finished products	3,380.0	1,000.0	330.0	275.0	125.6	107.4	123.2	167.3
For acquired resources			305.0	314.4	124.3	106.8	—	—
In major construction	1,610.0	1,160.0	530.0	270.0	137.3	105.0	112.1	146.0
For freight transportation	2,050.0	1,850.0	760.0	300.0	122.1	100.9	116.7	118.2
For communication services	—	—			144.7	104.2	106.2	122.8
Agriculture (produce sales)	940.0	810.0	300.0	330.0	140.0	108.0	166.4	191.4
Official dollar exchange rate*	—	300.0	280.0	131.0	119.8	107.6	346.5	130.8

*End of period.
Source: RF Goskomstat.

Table 20.4
Direct Material Input Coefficients by Economic Sector and Dynamics of GDP Power Consumption, 1991–1998 (%)

	1991	1992	1993	1994	1995	1996	1997	1998
Total national economy	48.4	52.2	48.9	46.1	49.0	48.8	47.5	46.5
Production of goods	53.4	61.4	53.7	49.5	58.3	56.8	56.3	55.2
Industry	59.9	65.6	57.5	51.3	61.9	59.7	59.1	57.3
Agriculture	37.4	48.5	43.3	51.3	52.1	52.9	53.2	53.5
Construction	39.5	44.1	43.8	41.3	48.4	48.4	47.8	47.6
Provision of services	36.2	37.0	42.3	42.1	37.3	39.3	37.9	37.5
Transportation	26.8	36.9	42.1	35.0	35.9	36.0	33.5	37.1
Trade	19.1	26.4	28.6	31.8	27.0	31.0	30.8	29.6
Other services	48.2	54.3	52.4	52.0	45.1	45.4	43.1	42.6
Power consumption	105.6	111.1	104.1	104.2	101.1	99.4	97.1	102.7
Capital to output ratio	108.8	119.2	110.1	114.2	104.5	103.4	98.7	104.3

Source: RF Goskomstat.

20.1.1. Utilization of the Main Factors of Production

The development of a labor-intensive segments of the services market (Table 20.4), in which service charges tend to race ahead of prices for finished products and prices for material and technical resources, lowers the share of intermediate consumption in the gross output. A similar effect is caused by structural changes in industrial production, where the growth of service-intensive mining industries is clear. The technical and technological conditions of fixed capital and low investment activity delay attainment of the practical objective of lowering the consumption of materials and power in production (Table 20.5).

The economy continues to be dominated by mining and pre-processing industries. An upward trend in power consumption in the economy was observed between 1991 and 1995. In 1996–1997, power consumption systematically diminished, demonstrating a trend toward stabilization (see Table 20.4). This trend ended in 1998 as a result of the sharp decline in the GDP following the financial crisis. However, as economic growth rebounded in 1999, the power consumption per GDP unit reached 5.4%. An analysis of the efficient use of material resources has to take into account changes in the end consumption structure. As domestic demand contracted, export resources swelled, so that estimates of the material capacity of the GDP took into account changes in the dynamics and structure of

Table 20.5
Distribution Patterns of Fixed Capital Investment and of Employment, by Economic Sector, 1992–1996 (%)

	Employment					Investment				
	1992	1993	1994	1995	1996	1992	1993	1994	1995	1996
Total	100	100	100	100	100	100	100	100	100	100
Production of Goods	54.9	54.1	52.4	50.3	49.2	76.6	70.7	63.4	66.7	64.6
Industry	29.6	29.4	27.1	25.9	24.7	40.9	37.0	32.3	34.4	37.0
Agriculture	14.0	14.3	14.5	15.0	15.0	10.8	7.9	5.0	3.6	3.3
Construction	11.0	10.1	9.9	9.3	9.7	24.4	25.5	25.3	27.8	23.2
Provision of Services	45.1	45.9	47.5	49.7	50.8	23.4	29.3	36.6	33.3	35.4
Transportation and communications	7.8	7.6	7.8	7.9	8.0	8.8	11.0	12.8	14.6	15.8
Trade	7.9	9.0	9.5	10.1	10.0	1.0	0.9	1.6	2.0	1.1
Credit and national insurance	0.7	0.8	1.1	1.2	1.3	—	—	—	—	—

Source: Calculated by the authors from RF Goskomstat data.

foreign trade. In this case, the upward trend in the resource capacity of the GDP reflected, more than anything else, the low technical and technological level of production, because, with outputs contracting and with structural shifts (especially those due to the conversion of the defense enterprises), it could be expected that, all other conditions unchanged, material consumption would at least remain stable.

The transformation of the GDP dynamic was accompanied by changes in the ratio of the principal factors of production—fixed assets and labor. An entirely new production structure is shaping up in the economy.

The number of employed in the economy fell by 13.8% over the years 1992–1998, while fixed capital investment fell by more than 80%. In a situation of shrinking demand for major factors of production, the growth in demand for services and, accordingly, the gradual reallocation of resources into these industries ease somewhat the situation in the labor and capital markets. In 1998, 52.6% of the workforce was employed in the services, up from 44.1% in 1992, with the share of investment in the services sector having gone up from 44.4% to 58.5% over the same period. In 1999, as production recovered, a growing demand for labor and an increase in fixed capital investment were registered for the first time in the entire reform period. The employed population increased by 1.3% over 1998 figures. This process occurred against the background of a stable decrease in the number of unemployed during 1999 and facilitated the gradual easing of social tensions, especially in the regions.

20.2. Production and Use of the GDP

The structural changes in the national economy are most vividly reflected in changes in the relative proportions of the economic sectors. With the transition to a market economy, the services have acquired greater weight, while manufacturing's share has declined (Tables 20.6 and 20.7).

The growth dynamics of the Russian economy have traditionally been greatly influenced by agriculture. An analysis of the gross farming output dynamics in 1992 through 1994 reveals a smaller slump than that suffered by manufacturing. In 1995, for the first time in the period under review, farming output fell more than manufacturing output. Whereas agriculture accounted for 15.4% of GDP in 1990, its share in GDP had dropped to 6.7% by 1999.

Table 20.6
Sectoral Structure of the GDP, 1990–1999 (% of Total)

	1990	1991	1992	1993	1994	1995	1996	1997	1998	1999
Gross domestic product	100	100	100	100	100	100	100	100	100	100
Production of Goods	65.1	62.8	48.4	50.9	48.9	45.2	49.6	50.0	47.2	40.9
Industry	37.8	38.2	33.7	34.4	32.8	11.8	13.5	14.5	15.2	16.0
Construction	9.5	9.4	6.3	7.9	9.1	7.8	8.5	8.7	8.7	10.3
Agriculture	15.4	13.7	7.2	8.1	7.0	43.0	36.9	35.5	37.7	43.1
Provision of Services	34.9	37.2	51.6	49.1	51.1	19.8	23.8	—	—	—
Transportation and communications	10.0	7.2	7.3	8.2	9.6	23.2	14.1	—	—	—
Trade	5.7	11.8	28.9	18.3	18.0					
Finance, credit, insurance	0.8	2.2	4.6	5.2	4.4					

Source: RF Goskomstat.

The dynamics of the value were particularly adversely affected by the serious deterioration in investment parameters, and the volume of construction fell by about 66% over the past eight years. The construction industry showed a decline from the previous year. Only in 1999, after a long period of decline in the volume of construction works, did investment begin to recover, and the volume of works in the industry increased by 5.4% compared with 1998.

Structural shifts in the economy are occurring against the background of a rising share of the infrastructure in GDP. Dynamic communications and transportation are an integral component of the emerging market economy. Transportation and communications dynamics must match the growth rates of the productive industries of the national economy. In 1991–1994, there was a growing gap between the slowdown rates in freight carriage and GDP dynamics. As the GDP decline decelerated, demand for transport service went up. In 1995, for example, freight carriage slipped by 2% from 1994, while output plunged by another 4%; in 1999 the commercial freight turn-

Table 20.7
Structure of Services, 1990–1999 (% of Total)

	1990	1991	1992	1993	1994	1995	1996	1997	1998	1999
Total provision of services:	100	100	100	100	100	100	100	100	100	100
Market services		63.3	67.5	84.3	74.5	73.4	76.4	75.2	73.2	75.4	80.7
Nonmarket services		36.7	32.5	15.7	25.5	26.6	23.6	24.8	26.8	24.6	19.3

Source: RF Goskomstat.

over increased by 5.2% compared with the previous year's figures, while the GDP rose by 3.2% and industrial output was up by 8.1%.

The share of transportation in the GDP shot up from 7.3% in 1992 to 9.1% in 1998 and from 8.2% in 1992 to 11.7% in 1998 in the structure of investment in the economy.

Along with information and computing services, communications remained among the most dynamically developing sectors of the national economy. In 1999, communication services accounted for 1.8% of the GDP, an increase of 1.2 percentage points in eight years. Growth in communications has been registered since 1996 as a result of qualitative changes in the management system; the development of new segments of the market for financial, credit, and insurance services; real estate transactions; and growth in market-servicing industries. Although these industries accounted for only 5.6% of the GDP, an increase in demand is having a positive effect on the volume and structure of communication services.

However, underdevelopment of the transportation system and communications continues to inhibit the formation of an entirely new distribution system of productive forces in the Russian economy.

The arrival of new services leads to changes in the existing structure of market and nonprofit services. The share of services provided by financial and insurance institutions in the total services is steadily growing. As the new institutional economic structure takes shape, the application of market services expands to include health care, education, housing, and public utilities, among others.

An analysis of the structure of the GDP has to take into account the differences in the dynamics of prices for manufactures and service charges, and the dynamics of changes in the catalogue of services provided.

20.2.1. GDP Structure According to Income

The ongoing institutional reforms in the Russian economy have been accompanied by changes in the ratio of the wages of hired labor to incomes derived from entrepreneurial activity (Table 20.8).

After the share of wages in the GDP fell to 36.7% in the first year of reform (1992), as inflation rates gradually slowed down and a system of governmental measures in the field of social policy was being implemented, by 1996 the share of wages in the GDP had increased to 49.6% and remained at about the same level until 1999.

Table 20.8
Structure of the GDP at the Revenue-Generating Stage, 1992–1999 (% of Total)

	1992	1993	1994	1995	1996	1997	1998	1999
Total GDP	100	100	100	100	100	100	100	100
Compensation to employees	36.7	44.5	49.3	45.2	46.9	50.0	47.2	40.9
Net taxes on production and imports	3.4	10.6	9.6	11.8	13.5	14.5	15.2	16.0
Net taxes on foodstuffs and imports	1.8	9.1	7.9	7.8	8.5	8.7	8.7	10.3
Gross profit and gross mixed revenue	59.9	44.9	41.1	43.0	36.9	35.5	37.7	43.1
Use of fixed assets	13.2	14.9	18.2	19.8	23.8	—	—	—
Net profit and net mixed revenue	46.7	30.0	32.9	23.2	14.1	—	—	—

Source: Calculated from RF Goskomstat data.

With the repeal, on 1 January 1997, of the payroll tax exceeding the fixed rates, wages and transfers to the pension and medical insurance plans grew. The share of wages (accrued) of the hired workforce went up from 45.9% in 1996 to 49.0% in 1997.

After the financial crisis of 1998, the share of payments to employees in the GDP began to decline. This decline can be explained by the operational specifics across different sectors of the economy, a growing gap between the rates of increase in profits and nominal wages, and changes of the ratio of wages paid to those employed in extracting versus manufacturing sectors. Furthermore, as institutional changes in the economy develop, a greater proportion of household income comes from earnings from business ventures and property. Whereas in 1992 the share of earnings from business and property in the aggregate money income was 7.4%, in 1996 it increased to 19.1%. Nearly half of the mixed income structure is contributed by trade and intermediary operations and about 40% comes from agricultural earnings. As paid services spread, an increasingly larger share is contributed by persons earning their incomes from private practice (in health and education).

A rather illustrative bit of evidence of the new economic environment is the fact that despite the financial crisis of 1998, earnings from business and property grew rapidly, and their share in total household income reached 21.8% in 1999. Consequently, the recovery of income for the lowest income groups lags behind income recovery for higher-income groups, since the relative growth of real incomes over the previous years resulted mainly from higher earnings. It should be noted that since 1994, lesser differentiation across incomes has occurred: the Gini coefficient was 0.289 in 1992, peaked at 0.409 in 1994, and fell to 0.379 in 1998.

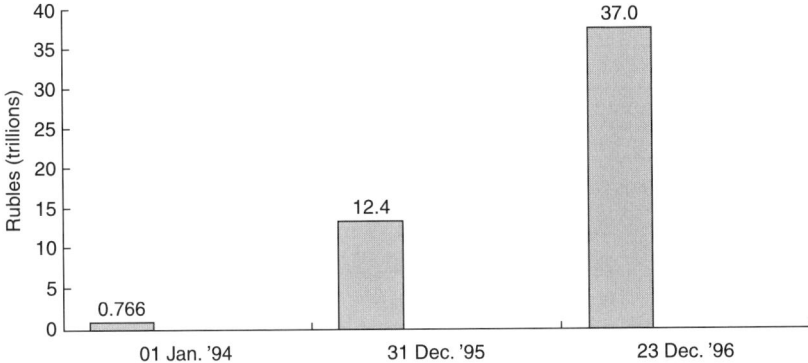

Figure 20.1
Growth in arrears on wage payments from companies' funds (in trillions of (old) rubles).

In analyzing household incomes, however, we should consider that wages remain the main source of household income for most of the population. Wages account for 40% of the GDP and over 60% of total household income.

A serious problem in evaluating the share of wages in the GDP income structure is the concealed forms of remuneration for work—that is, unofficial, unreported wages. According to estimates from the RF Ministry of the Economy, the amount of concealed labor remuneration, outside the statistical data, reached 12% of GDP. It is chiefly small businesses and financial and commercial organizations that are responsible for the concealed labor remuneration. These commercial entities seek to evade tax transfers to budgets and extrabudgetary funds in order to avoid the high rates set by the fiscal system of that time.

Another serious problem is irregular payment of wages. Deterioration in enterprises' financial position, the growth of defaults in the economy, and wage arrears undermined income growth. In 1996, a significant increase was observed in the implicit indicators and estimates of real money flows in the economy. As a result, wage arrears for the year rose by more than 2.5 times the pay growth rate in the year before (Figure 20.1). In 1999, as production grew and the financial results of operations improved, a trend toward diminishing wage arrears became noticeable.

Irregular wages and social transfers, being in most cases the only source of household income, provoke destabilization of the social

Table 20.9
Production Profitability by Key Economic Sector, 1992–1996 (%)

	1992	1993	1994	1995	1996
Total production profitability	31.7	26.3	14.5	15.8	4.8
By economic sector:					
Industry	38.3	32.0	19.5	20.1	9.2
Agriculture	37.5	31.6	−10.0	−3.2	−22.2
Construction	20.0	27.8	23.2	23.3	11.6
Transportation	5.7	15.4	10.3	15.1	2.9

and political situation. Among others, the low-income groups react most severely to wage and social benefit arrears.

In 1996, for the first time since the start of reforms, the nominal aggregate mass of profits slid in manufacturing, transportation, and construction. Profits in 1996 stood at 50% of the 1995 level. This shortfall was attributed to the continuing slump in production, a reduction in the inflationary part of the profits, growth of the depreciation share after the productive fixed assets were revalued beginning on 1 January 1996, and the asynchronous dynamics of prices for end products and intermediates. Profits in 1996 were higher than the year before only in gas transportation and transmission of electricity. In all other industries, prices plunged considerably.

In analyzing the changes in the proportions among GDP-forming revenues and the trends in production profitability (Tables 20.8 and 20.9), it should be noted that indicators of gross profits and gross mixed earnings include changes in the total depreciation allowances. After a revaluation of fixed capital, the share of depreciation in the GDP rose from 20.2% in 1994 to 23.8% in 1996. Less depreciation, the share of gross profit in the GDP dropped from 41.1% to 36.9% over the same period.

Enterprises' financial position deteriorated because of a sharp drop in profitability. For example, the profitability of marketable output in manufacturing was 9.2% in 1996, down from 20.1% in 1995 (see Table 20.9).

The favorable international trade conditions allowed the industries manufacturing intermediate products (metals, chemicals and petrochemicals, pulp and paper) to raise the prices for their output in 1995 by more than they had to pay for the material resources they used. Profitability in these industries jumped sharply, to between 30% and 45%. This trend continued until most domestic prices in Russia reached world levels, in late 1995.

Table 20.10
GDP Allocation Structure, 1991–1999

	1991	1992	1993	1994	1995	1996	1997	1998	1999
Total GDP	100	100	100	100	100	100	100	100	100
Expenditure on final consumption	62.6	49.9	64.2	69.6	71.1	71.4	74.8	76.6	68.2
Households	41.4	33.7	40.9	44.1	49.2	48.8	50.0	54.6	51.6
General government	16.9	14.3	17.9	22.5	19.7	20.2	21.3	18.7	14.4
Individual services	6.5	7.2	8.3	9.9	9.5	9.5	9.6	8.1	6.1
Collective services	10.4	7.1	9.6	12.6	10.2	10.7	11.7	10.6	8.3
Nonprofit organizations providing services to households	4.3	1.9	5.4	3.0	2.2	2.4	3.5	3.3	2.2
Gross accumulation	37.1	35.7	27.8	25.8	24.7	24.5	22.3	16.2	15.0
Fixed assets	23.8	24.7	21.0	22.0	21.2	21.1	19.0	17.7	15.8
Change in inventories	13.3	11.0	6.8	3.8	3.5	3.4	3.3	−1.5	−0.8
Net exports of goods and services	0.3	14.4	8.0	4.6	4.2	4.1	2.9	7.2	16.8

Source: RF Goskomstat.

A comparison between the growth of profitability and marketable output volume in 1996 suggests that prices for consumable material resources were racing ahead of prices for the end output in most industries. This was evidence that effective consumer demand had reached its limit.

With the start of reforms, a significant shift in the relationship between demand and supply got under way in the Russian economy. An analysis of the structure of the GDP illustrates this relationship clearly (Tables 20.10 and 20.11).

As emphasis has shifted to the foreign market, the gross output structure has begun to show a greater share of exports. The change in the output structure in favor of mining industries has occurred alongside a continuing slump in the output of capital and consumer

Table 20.11
The Structure of End Use of GDP, 1997 (% of Total)

	1997
Total GDP	100.0%
Expenditure on final consumption	73.9
Including by households	49.9
Gross accumulation	23.0
Net exports of goods and services	3.1

Source: RF Goskomstat.

goods. Whereas industrial output dropped more than twice over the period 1991–1996, the output of capital goods made about 23% of the prereform levels, and the output of consumer goods was at 41.5%. (For the 54.6% decline in industrial output, the production of capital goods fell by 77.0% and the manufacture of consumer goods by 41.5%.)

A change in production proportions sets the main trends in the final consumption structure of the GDP. The share of spending on final consumption in GDP equaled 71.4% in 1996. Final consumption by households rose to 48.8% in 1996, from 33.7% in 1992, and public administration costs climbed 5.9 percentage points over the same period. The gradual rise in the share of households' final consumption spending in the GDP is logical in the light of reductions in the hypertrophied spending on defense.

Compared with 1992, spending on manufactures in household expenses went down. In 1996, retail sales increased by 88.4% over their 1991 level. This was accounted for by the restrictive fiscal policy, which caused the population's money incomes to grow slightly slower than consumer prices. The dynamics of real household incomes fluctuate considerably in the situation of persisting high inflation rates. The decrease in real incomes by 47% in 1992 was replaced by an upward trend. Real household incomes increased by 9.1% in the period 1993–1996, but reached only 57.8% of the prereform level. This cut into households' purchasing power.

The drop in households' purchasing power in turn had a negative effect on consumer industries that targeted the domestic market (such as the food industry and light industry). The production of many durables continued to slide, as the market was glutted with imported goods. Whereas in 1992 domestically produced goods accounted for 71% of retail sales, the remaining 29% being imports, in 1996 the ratio was 48% to 52%.

The decline in real consumption of pay services by the population slowed down in 1995. At the same time, the population was spending more on services calculated as a share of GDP because the prices and charges for housing, utilities, and transportation services were increasing much faster than any other consumer prices. The share of spending on services in the final consumption structure of households was also growing.

Major shifts are observable in the final consumption structure in respect to spending purposes, specifically an increasing trend to save

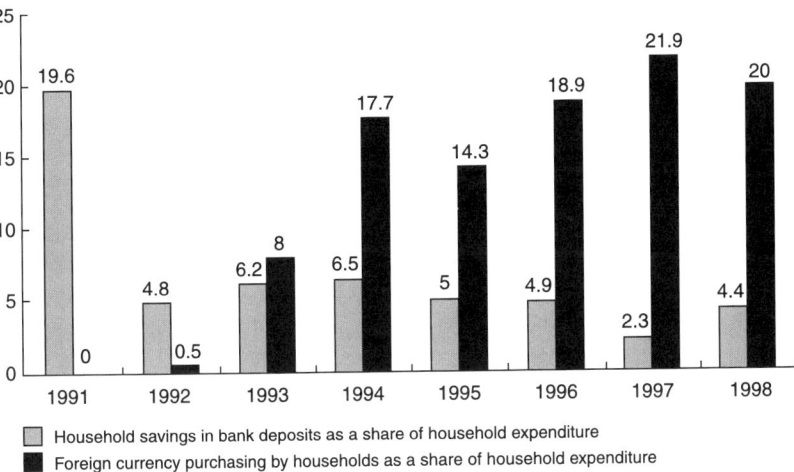

Figure 20.2
Dynamics of household savings, 1991–1998. (Calculated by the authors from RF Goskomstat data.)

earnings and spend less on consumer products. The share of the population's resources used for accumulation in all forms rose to 23.7% in 1996, from 5.3% in 1992 (Figure 20.2). According to Sberbank (Russian Savings Bank), on 1 January 1997 the population's deposits were valued at Rb 96.4 trillion, a 90% increase over the year before.

An analysis of households' final consumption structure shows that the public responds rapidly and flexibly to changes in the economic situation and adapts relatively quickly to financial market fluctuations.

The gradual climb in domestic effective demand in the consumer market was the principal factor impacting the dynamics and structure of the use of the GDP in 1997.

In 1997, the real disposable incomes of the population moved up 3.5%, and the real accrued wage per worker rose by 4.3%. Real pensions stood at 94.6% of the 1996 level.

The share of final consumption spending by households, including free services, edged up 1.1 percentage points in 1997. Beginning in the second half-year, the spending structure showed a steady increase in purchases of nonfood items and a decline in spending on food. The share of nonfoods in total retail sales, after dropping from 52% in the first quarter of 1997 to 49.7% in the third quarter, rebounded in August, reaching 51.7% in the fourth quarter. The rise in the share of population spending on goods and services was due in part to reasonable apprehensions in expectation of impending money redenomination. The consumer market remained steady through 1997, glutted with commodities and backed by full inventories.

In 1997, the volume of services paid to the population registered its first increase over the five years of reform. The structure of pay services was persistently dominated by three kinds of services, which together accounted for more than two-thirds of services consumed by Russia's population: housing and utilities, passenger transportation, and paid medical services.

Social parameters fluctuated through 1997, pushed up or down by the high level of pay arrears accumulated by the government and businesses, which were not worked off until year-end.

Changes in the population's spending structure were accompanied by a fall in the share of the population's savings in deposits and securities, a clear drop in its investment potential. This savings structure was in no small measure explained by low investment demand, which fact, combined with declining margins on the government securities market, forced lenders to curtail cash borrowing and scale down cash investment conditions for the population.

Despite the dive in the real purchasing power of the US dollar in 1997 on the Russian market, it retained its allure as a store of value. The population's savings were structured to increase purchases of foreign exchange, a policy that somewhat contributed to the downward trend of inflation.

The gross accumulation in GDP in 1996 fell to 24.5%, from 35.7% in 1992 (Figure 20.3). Moreover, the patterns of accumulation continued to show a diminishing share of gross fixed capital accumulation (from 24.7% in 1992 to 21.1% in 1996). This occurred despite the completed revaluation of fixed capital and modifications of the depreciation policy.

The current economic situation does not favor an influx of investment. The continuing reduction of investment in fixed capital reproduction is made even worse by the enduring trend toward a reduction of net accumulation in the national economy (Figure 20.4).

Contraction of effective demand despite some recovery in industrial production boosted inventories and unfinished construction, against a downward trend in stockpiles of primary and material resources.

General Trends in the Real Sector

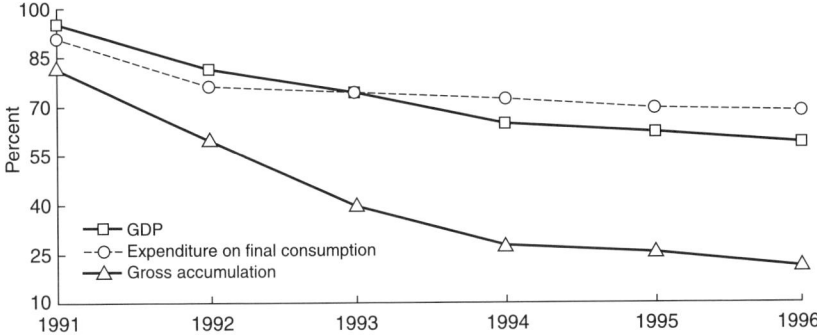

Figure 20.3
Dynamics of GDP and expenditure on final consumption versus gross accumulation.

Over the years of reforms, gross accumulation was brought down both by a reduction in new investment in fixed capital and by changes in material inventories. The investment slack was much greater than the industrial slump and GDP decline. Beginning in 1993, the figures for net fixed capital accumulation have been negative, particularly in production. A further drop in investment would curtail reproduction prospects (more on that subject later).

As the economic recovery picked up in 1997, the share of accumulated material working assets in GDP fell off. In fact, as inflation slowed down, the share of inventories and stock in trade in the structure of accumulated working assets dwindled, which had a stabilizing effect on the economy in general. In mid-1997, finished

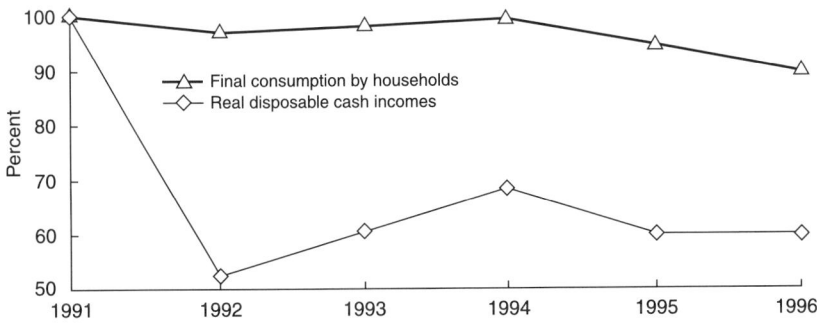

Figure 20.4
Change in final consumption and in households' real disposable cash income (1991 = 100%).

products were shipped at slightly higher rates than the output was produced. This was certainly influenced favorably by the steady increase in the share of paid-for products in the total sales. Obviously, economic agents' priorities in formulating their market expansion strategies, combined with a price-restraining policy, were beginning to take effect. As the payment crisis took a new turn in the fourth quarter, however, stocks in trade started to build up again.

The domestic market was experiencing the negative effect of diminishing demand for capital goods. The share of new investment in fixed capital was 15.3% of GDP in 1997. One of the causes responsible for the scale-back of investment in the first half of 1997 was the sharp reduction in government funds to finance investment and construction programs of enterprises because of an acute shortage of working capital.

The dynamics of investment in fixed assets were positive in 1999 for the first time in eight years. The investment sphere reacted adequately to the intensifying business activity in the real sector. In 1999, organizations and enterprises of all forms of ownership invested Rb 598.7 million in fixed assets, that being by 1.0% over the level of the previous year. However, the share of investment in fixed assets remained flat, at the minimal level it has sustained for the last ten years.

The share of net accumulation in the gross national accumulation structure continued to fall. The slowdown in fixed capital renewals and deteriorating age and technological characteristics of the assets initiated irreversible processes in capital reproduction. It was extremely important in this situation to set priorities and strategies for fixed capital reproduction, taking into account the ongoing structural changes at all levels of the economy.

20.3. Restructuring the Real Sector of the Economy

In 1997, industrial production registered a 1.9% recovery, the first in years. This positive dynamic notwithstanding, the contraction of industrial output by more than 50% over the years of reform merits comment, if not a detailed analysis of the root causes and consequence. To this end, we will briefly analyze the industrial production structure and the nature of economic ties that had formed over the decades of administrative economic management and that were set on a course of reforms in the 1990s.

Table 20.12
Sectoral Structure of Industrial Production in the Russian Federation, 1991–1996, in Actual Prices (%)*

	1991	1992	1993	1994	1995	1996
Electricity	4.0	6.4	9.2	13.5	13.1	16.0
Fuel	7.3	18.5	17.2	16.0	17.4	18.6
Ferrous metals	4.9	8.2	9.0	9.4	9.9	9.2
Nonferrous metals	6.3	8.6	8.1	7.2	7.2	6.0
Chemicals and petrochemicals	6.5	8.0	7.2	7.5	8.1	7.2
Machine building	24.9	20.1	19.9	19.1	18.4	19.0
Forestry, woodworking, pulp and paper	5.8	4.8	3.9	4.2	5.0	3.8
Building materials	3.7	3.3	3.3	3.8	3.6	3.6
Light industry	16.2	7.1	5.2	3.1	2.5	2.0
Food processing	14.4	10.3	12.4	11.9	11.1	10.7
Other sectors	5.9	4.9	4.6	4.4	3.7	4.1
Total industry†	100	100	100	100	100	100

*Exclusive of small businesses and joint ventures.
† Adding up sector data may produce a different total number due to rounding.
Source: RF Goskomstat.

By the time reforms were initiated, the Russian economy had become notorious for a series of imbalances that were probably not fully evident in the conditions of the centrally planned economy. Table 20.12 illustrates the structure of industrial production in the Russian Federation in nominal prereform 1991 prices and the changes it has undergone since 1992.

Judging from the data in the table, two industries, light goods and food, which were oriented basically toward domestic final consumption, together generated about a third of the aggregate industrial output (the structure of industrial production in the USSR was little different from that of Russia). This fact undermines the notorious speculation that heavy industry had received top priority in the USSR. In fact, this productive structure characterized the Russian (or Soviet) economy as one preeminently serving the needs of the population rather than its own requirements. Nevertheless, the consumer market was perpetually plagued by shortages of foodstuffs and durables, particularly in the late 1980s and early 1990s, and the country was compelled to import these goods. For comparison, the share of the food industry in the total industrial output of Finland, which exported foodstuffs, clothing, and footwear to Russia, was about 14%, while that of the light industry was a mere 3%.

Table 20.13
Russian Prices Versus World Market Prices for Selected Goods in 1991 (per ton, in %)

	Russia	World markets
Oil	100	100
Gas	19	67
Rolled ferrous metals	640	292
Aluminum	3,220	1,058
Copper	6,401	1,917
Wheat	600	147
Ammonia	221	83
Phosphorus fertilizer	800	33
Cotton fabric*	5,333	533

*For 1,000 sq m.
Source: RF Goskomstat.

The share of the energy sector (power and fuel) in Russia was just above 11%, as much as in Finland. Russia, however, exported energy and fuel, while Finland imported them. This paradox can be explained by the contorted Russian domestic prices in comparison with world market prices. First, with prices for raw materials and energy sources understated relative to prices for manufactured products, the value of manufacturing output was overstated, and the value of energy-producing and primary industries was understated. Second, the low-price policy in respect to capital goods (particularly armaments) in comparison with consumer prices hopelessly distorted the value proportions in the economy.

Table 20.13 illustrates relations between the prices for some goods on the world markets and in Russia in the prereform years. Structural relationships between the prices for these goods are shown, for convenience of analysis, with the price of a ton of crude oil assumed to be 100% and the prices for other goods calculated in tons of oil as a base product, instead of rubles or dollars. This approach avoids the complexity of the numerous exchange rates that existed before the reforms, the relation between the exchange rate and purchasing power parity, and so on.

As shown in Table 20.13, Russian industrial goods related to basic energy resources were much more expensive than their world counterparts. A ton of metal valued in tons of oil, for example, was two to three times as expensive in Russia as on the world markets. Wheat was four times as expensive. A vast gap existed between Russian and world prices for chemical, light industry, and engineering goods.

Table 20.14
Sectoral Structure of Industrial Production in the Russian Federation in 1991, in World Market Prices (%)

	Russia	Finland (For Reference)
Power engineering	38.1	11.0
Metals	7.9	7.0
Chemicals and petrochemicals	2.2	7.2
Machine building	19.0	22.6
Forestry, woodworking, pulp and paper	13.5	25.0
Building materials	5.4	3.6
Light industry	2.9	2.9
Food processing	8.2	14.6
Other sectors	2.8	6.1
Total industry	100	100

Source: Authors' estimates.

Moreover, the higher the processing degree, the more costly Russian goods were compared to their world counterparts.

The valuation of the prereform structure of industrial output measured in world market prices[1] gives a different picture (Table 20.14). The table shows an entirely different economic structure, one designed not to meet consumer needs but to keep up the production of energy and raw materials and intermediates. Table 20.14 shows, for comparison purposes, the industrial structure of a country (Finland) whose climate resembles Russia's.

Table 20.15 lists the per-capita production of some types of industrial output in Russia and the United States in the late 1980s, before the general industrial collapse in Russia. In per-capita terms, Russia mined three times as much iron ore as the United States, made nearly twice as much steel, and produced four times as many tractors. Regardless of these multiples, Russia's per-capita grain production was only 30%–50% that of the United States, and Russia manufactured only a quarter of the total US automobile production.

The price structure in the centrally planned economy resulted basically from extensive development, which was itself evidence of the very low efficiency (with a few rare exceptions) of industrial technologies. The abundance of energy and raw material resources

---

1. Evgeni Gavrilenkov, "Russia: Out of the Post-Soviet Macroeconomic Deadlock Through a Labyrinth of Reforms," Bank of Finland, *Review of Economies in Transition* 3 (1994): 39–58.

Table 20.15
Output of Selected Industrial Products in Russia and the USA in 1989 (Per Capita)

	Russia	USA
Iron ore (tons)	726	
Steel (tons)	630	364
Motor vehicles (no.)	0.0072	0.0274
Tractors (no.)	0.0159	0.0043
Mineral fertilizer (tons)	119	94
Wheat (tons)	711	1,152
TV sets (no.)	0.0302	0.0592

Source: RF Goskomstat.

in the country and the low prices, which were seldom adjusted, hardly encouraged their frugal use or stimulated higher production efficiency in the 1970s and 1980s. And although the volatile world prices spurred the development of new technologies and the manufacture of revolutionary products, these processes were actually stifled in the USSR. As in any economy, distorted prices gave wrong signals to both consumers and producers and, in large measure, were responsible for the economic malaise into which the Soviet economy was being steered. The established price structure, therefore, reflected the country's technological advance as well as the distribution of financial flows among the economic sectors, regions, and social groups.

The development potential the Russian economy possessed was customarily rated very high. For all that, it has not been realized in full to this day. In fact, production slid relentlessly in the first half of the 1990s.

One of the Russian government's strategic aims was to correct the existing price imbalances, primarily by raising the relative prices for energy resources. The government's practical policy included continued regulation of energy prices, the absolute level of which has been raised more than fivefold since 2 January 1992.

As early as January 1992, prices for the majority of industrial products rose in the wake of rising energy prices and at approximately the same pace. Since energy and fuel prices are regulated by the government, while prices for all other industrial products have been freed, producers started raising them at their own discretion, little concerned about demand limitations. Prices were normally raised by a wide margin above the growing costs. The producers were motivated by old associations, in the hope that the government, after having severely slashed its centralized procurements (military technology and farming machinery), would regain its good sense and abandon its reform plans. The inventories of components and primary resources built up at the time of general shortages allowed the manufacturers to keep up production of output that no one wanted anymore and to ship products to their old consumers.

This compelled the government, after a few months' respite, to pull up energy prices again to correct the deteriorating, rather than improving, price structure, which had been distorted by the prices for manufactures outpacing those for energy and fuel. After another short period of calm, energy prices were jacked up again to fix the imbalances.

The spontaneous price race, in nearly total disregard of demand limitations by intermediate producers, and the relatively tough fiscal policy triggered a blizzard of mutual defaults. Accordingly, this situation put a considerable restraint on budget fulfillment, for the government was forced to finance its spending plans at the current prices, while its revenues (in real terms) declined sharply as arrears took on the role of noncash money. Prepayment for product shipments, which was required beginning in mid-1992, went some way toward disciplining the defaulters, but at the same time it set off a deep plunge in industrial production, as many fewer goods unwanted by consumers were produced.

The fall in investment activity and therefore in effective demand for investment products was yet another major factor triggering an industrial slump at the outset of the reforms.

Industrial production took another dive in 1994. Its causes, however, were totally different from those behind the contraction of production in 1992 and 1993. By early 1994, following the structural adjustment in the relative price system and growth of the real value of the national currency, an overwhelming majority of Russian producers had had their first ever experience of competition. Already in 1993, prices for some Russian-made goods were edging up to world levels, and the prices of many more did so in 1994.

Light industry enterprises were the first producers to confront competition from importers. Starting out in specific conditions, light industry producers had less leeway to raise prices than other industries, so they were the first to bump their heads against the world price ceiling. This was followed by a massive expulsion of Russian

Table 20.16
Price Indices by Industry, 1991–1997 (Previous Year = 1)

	1991	1992	1993	1994	1995	1996	1997
Electricity	2.1	55.1	13.6	3.3	3.0	1.4	1.087
Fuel	2.3	92.7	7.3	3.0	2.9	1.4	1.111
Ferrous metals	3.4	36.3	11.9	3.4	2.9	1.2	1.011
Nonferrous metals	3.3	52.2	6.6	4.0	2.2	1.1	1.031
Chemicals and petrochemicals	2.7	38.9	9.5	3.6	2.7	1.2	1.065
Machine building	3.1	27.2	10.5	3.3	2.8	1.2	1.087
Forestry, woodworking, pulp and paper	3.4	20.2	9.9	3.7	2.7	1.1	1.075
Building materials	3.1	28.1	12.5	3.1	2.7	1.3	1.085
Light industry	4.7	12.6	7.8	3.4	2.6	1.2	1.101
Food processing	4.1	27.3	10.7	3.1	2.6	1.2	1.114
Total industry	3.4	33.8	10.0	3.3	2.8	1.3	1.074

Source: RF Goskomstat.

producers from the market. Over 1994 alone, light industry output was nearly halved.

Table 20.16 shows the dynamics of domestic prices by industry, confirming the fact that the major shifts in the relative price structure occurred during the opening phase of the reforms and that, beginning in 1995, changes in relative prices were less striking.

Because of higher production costs and lower product quality, Russian producers began to retreat from other commodity markets as well (automobiles, home appliances, other durables, and foodstuffs).

However, signs of a recovery in Russian manufacturing were spotted in 1995. Some industries made up for the decline in domestic demand by rushing to the world market. Raw material and energy producers were now joined by exporters of some industrial semi-manufactures. There was a surge in Russian exports of metals (ferrous and nonferrous metals), chemicals, forestry and woodworking products, and pulp and paper. According to 1995 statistics, ferrous metal production rose 10% and nonferrous metals went up by 3%. Chemicals were pushed up 8% by exports. These early hints of a rebound in some industries were due not only to a general improvement in the economy but to an evolution in business mentality as well (Table 20.17).

During a general increase of 1.9% in industrial output in 1997, the fastest growth rates were posted in nonferrous metals (thanks to exports) and engineering (mostly auto manufacture, to meet rising

Table 20.17
Indices of Physical Volumes of Production by Industry, 1990–1997 (% of Previous Year's Figure)

	1990	1991	1992	1993	1994	1995	1996	1997
Electricity	102	100.3	95	95	91	97	98	97.9
Fuel	97	94	93	88	90	99.2	99	100.3
Ferrous metals	98	93	84	83	83	110	98	101.2
Nonferrous metals	98	91	75	86	91	103	96	105.0
Chemicals and petrochemicals	98	94	78	79	76	108	93	102.0
Machine building	101	90	85	84	69	91	95	103.5
Forestry, woodworking, pulp and paper	99	91	85	81	70	99.3	83	101.2
Building materials	99.1	98	80	84	73	92	83	96.0
Light industry	99.9	91	70	77	54	70	78	97.6
Food processing	100.4	91	84	91	83	92	96	99.2
Total industry*	99.9	92	82	86	79	97	96	101.9

*As adjusted by an estimated informal sector.
Source: RF Goskomstat.

domestic demand). Production rose significantly (15%) in the medical industry as well. The light and food industries, too, were sending tentative recovery signals. Domestic food producers were successfully taking on their foreign competitors, above all meat-packing and dairy plants, which had installed new technologies, and improved the quality and marketability of their products.

To sum up, the Russian industrial structure was considerably transformed after six years of reform. In the wake of changes in the domestic price structure and physical volumes of output, the share of the energy-producing sector reached about a third of total industrial output. The shares of engineering and light industry products dropped significantly. Statistics now show that the relative price structure in Russia is very near that of the world market.

Our analysis also shows that whereas in the initial phase of the reforms, changes in the sectoral structure of industrial output were largely due to a change in the domestic price structure rather than to differences in the production volume dynamics in different industries, beginning in 1995, shifts in physical output volumes have contributed increasingly to transformations in the Russian industrial structure. The domestic price structure has remained largely unchanged in recent years and has been relatively stable in comparison with the abrupt fluctuations typical of 1992 and, in part, of 1993.

This means that it is practically impossible to significantly reallocate financial resources among the industries by juggling prices only. Whether industries and enterprises are making profits or suffering losses will in the future depend on the real volumes and efficiency of production, instead of relative price dynamics. This also implies that the output volume dynamics are now fully controlled by effective demand. In these conditions, a search for a compromise between maintaining positive domestic demand dynamics and containing inflation is one of key tasks to be addressed by macroeconomic policy.

Given the growing integration of the Russian economy in world economic affairs, the dependence of the consumer market on imports may have a negative effect on the stability of the national economy. The recent shake-down on the world financial markets has seriously destabilized the Russian economy. If the Russian consumer market continues to fully depend on imports, likely fluctuations in exchange rate dynamics with variations in world commodity and capital markets may have a destabilizing impact on this country's socioeconomic establishment as a whole.

In fact, the Russian real sector has been, and will in the short-term be, developing along two tracks. First, large companies (essentially, in the energy sector) are expected to gain strength and consolidate, becoming concentrated and merging with the banking capital, and second, the future of Russia's economy will in no small measure be staked on the advance of small and medium-size business. According to Goskomstat, small and medium-size businesses have been gaining in weight and stature in total industrial output. Support for this trend and the creation of a favorable macroeconomic and legal environment for small-scale producers would improve social stability in the regions and benefit the general macroeconomic dynamics.

20.4. Investment in the Period of Market Reforms

The consequences of the socialist state's investment policies are notoriously deplorable.

Evidence of the economy moving slowly but surely toward a critical line beyond which qualitative changes should occur is provided by data on the age structure of fixed capital (Table 20.18) and the dynamics of the share of the GDP put aside for investment projects (Figure 20.5). The chart is based on data on capital outlays and the GDP in fixed 1990 prices. The chart shows that the share of invest-

Table 20.18
Age Structure of Production Equipment in Industry, 1970–1996 (%)

Year	Total Equipment (at Year-End)	≤5 yr	6–10 yr	11–15 yr	16–20 yr	>20 yr	Average Age, yr
1970	100	40.8	30.0	14.0	6.9	8.3	8.42
1975	100	37.5	29.7	14.8	9.0	9.0	8.34
1980	100	35.5	28.7	15.6	9.5	10.7	9.47
1985	100	33.1	28.2	16.0	9.8	12.9	10.11
1990	100	29.4	28.3	16.5	10.8	15.0	10.80
1991	100	26.6	28.9	17.1	11.3	16.1	11.30
1992	100	22.8	29.4	18.2	12.0	17.6	11.98
1993	100	19.0	29.5	19.5	12.8	19.2	12.69
1994	100	14.7	29.8	20.7	13.8	21.0	13.41
1995	100	10.9	29.5	21.7	14.9	23.0	14.13
1996	100	8.7	27.0	23.0	15.9	25.4	14.90

Source: RF Goskomstat.

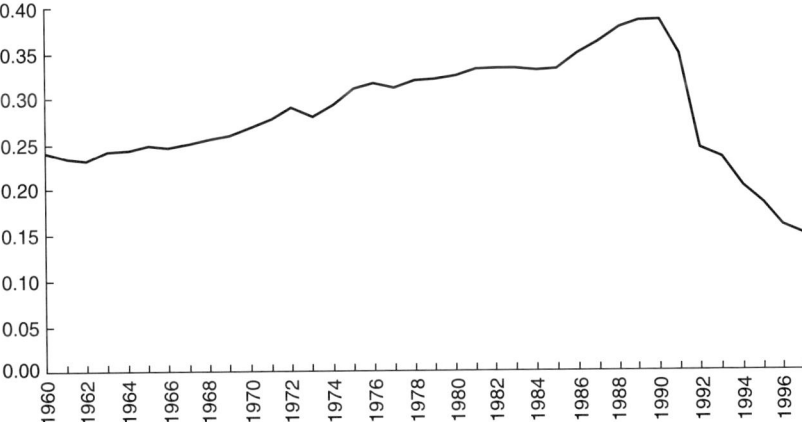

Figure 20.5
Ratio of investments to GDP, 1960–1997. (Source: RF Goskomstat.)

ment in the GDP was steadily rising since the early 1960s. Nevertheless, the age composition of fixed capital continuously deteriorated, so that at the start of market reforms Russian industry enjoyed fixed capital with an average age of 11 years. Worse still, the share of relatively modern productive equipment (less than five years old) was under 30%.

20.4.1. Promotion of Investment

To understand the changes in investment activity and the transformation of investment policy during the market reforms, the state of capital construction in 1992 needs a closer look. Business liberalization was followed by changes in long-standing capital construction financing practices. The drastic curtailment of centralized investment assumed an expansion of investment efforts by enterprises from their own and borrowed funds. The radical economic reform in the Russian economy made the choice of investment decisions totally dependent on purely economic factors and economic agents' financial strength.

In that period, the investment environment was shaped by the following factors:

- Changes in the structure and sources of investment financing
- Institutional changes in the national economy as the government divested its property
- A relative reduction in effective demand with changes in the level and structure of prices for investment products
- Changes in the structure of investment demand and its inconsistency with investment sector capacities
- Delays in measures to modify indexation techniques in the depreciation and revaluation of productive fixed assets

From the start, the lack of incentives for accumulation was due to the constantly rising cost of living and to priority being given to meet the social claims of the workforce engaged in production, which functioned to expand latent unemployment, to the detriment of progress in production.

The crisis in Russia's economy was followed by an unprecedented reduction of investment in the real sector (Table 20.19).

Table 20.19
Dynamics of New Fixed Capital Investment, 1990–1997 (% of Preceding Year's Figure)

	1990	1991	1992	1993	1994	1995	1996	1997
Total new investment in fixed assets	100.1	85.0	60.0	88.0	76.0	90.0	82	95.0
Productive assets	99.0	82.0	56.0	81.0	67.0	89.0	82.0	98.9
Nonproductive assets	103.0	91.0	70.0	101.0	89.0	91.0	82.0	88.5
GDP	97.7	95.0	85.5	91.3	87.3	95.9	94.4	100.4

Source: RF Goskomstat.

Another major factor was the continuing high level of production monopolization, which worked against the cultivation of a competitive environment. As a result, the majority of industrial producers lacked the motivation to invest.

As production slumped and inflation heated up, the principles of investment regulation were governed by the priorities given to current problems. Even with priorities followed faithfully, investment in industries critical to structural reform in the economy (power engineering, mechanical engineering, the fuel industry) was too small to reverse the negative trends in fixed capital reproduction.

The contraction of noncentralized investment in fixed capital from enterprise-owned funds highlighted consumers' preference to accumulate savings. The scarcity of investment opportunities was worsened by the fact that the indexation of depreciation allowances failed to make up for the shortage of financial resources. The exploding prices for investment in engineering products and civil engineering projects frustrated efforts to create conditions for a simple reproduction of fixed capital. Consequently, the scale of major repairs expanded. Whereas the ratio of major repairs to new construction was approximately 1:5 in 1990, in terms of costs, it reached 2:1 in 1992.

The hypertrophied scale of major repairs involving long-outdated production machinery (see Table 20.18) added to the imbalance of fixed capital reproduction processes. With the launch of radical reforms, the scale of fixed capital renewals plunged to 2.5% in 1992, from 6.6% in 1990. Wear and tear on equipment led to a further decline in production and helped sustain the growth of the power and material to output ratios.

As the institutional structure of the economy underwent changes, enterprises came to play a dominant role in capital construction.

Table 20.20
Structure of Fixed Capital Investment by Source of Financing, 1992–1997 (% of Total)

	1992	1993	1994	1995	1996	1997
Total investment	100.0	100.0	100.0	100.0	100.0	100.0
Investments financed from budgetary funds	26.9	34.3	26.0	21.8	18.8	19.2
Federal budget	16.6	19.2	13.4	10.1	9.2	9.5
Budgets of RF constituent members and local budgets	10.3	15.1	10.6	10.3	9.6	9.7
Investments financed from extrabudgetary funds	73.1	65.7	74.0	78.2	81.2	80.8
Companies' and organizations' own funds	69.3	57.4	64.2	62.8	66.3	71.2
Individual developers	0.9	2.6	2.3	2.5	3.2	4.2
Joint ventures and foreign companies	—	2.4	1.7	2.7	2.5	5.4

Source: RF Goskomstat.

Public sector investors accounted for 22.3% of the investments made in 1998 (down from 81% in 1992) and for 12.7% of investments in civil engineering projects.

The government's greatly reduced share of investment cut deeply into the market's capacity and aggravated the market conditions. Ultimately, underinvestment in the economy set off a further slump in production. So far, nongovernment investors have been unable to compensate for the government's withdrawal from the investment market, since industrial construction financed from centralized sources is, as a rule, expensive and holds little attraction in terms of return on capital invested in industrial projects.

The enterprises' and businesses' own funds are turning into the dominant source of financing (Table 20.20). Although steps have been taken to improve the accounting of productive fixed capital movements, depreciation allowances do not exert an appreciable effect on the financial support for investment projects: With spare funds in short supply and an effective machinery to supervise their uses lacking, depreciation allowances are frequently funneled into making urgent payments. As a result, the potentially powerful financial effect of fixed capital revaluation and indexation of depreciation allowances has not been used properly. Reduction of operating industrial capacity to between 40% and 50%, on average, for the economy as a whole is another factor curbing investment. The growth of capacity maintenance costs affects the volume of enterprises' own funds earmarked for investment. In this situation, many enterprises, having lost any hope of getting centralized investment funds, started looking for alternative investment sources. First many enterprises sold unfinished construction projects, surplus fixed assets (buildings, uninstalled machinery, and so forth), and land. Second these enterprises began attracting investment into specific projects.

The drop in investment activity was triggered by the specifics of the institutional economic reform programs of the transition period. Because the status of enterprises was in a sense indefinite, they could not be expected to invest funds in production development and modernization from the outset. As problems associated with ownership rights reforms are resolved and investors consequently have a greater choice for investment, healthy conditions are created to invigorate investment. Proposals to stimulate investment included allowing a tax exemption on profits used to develop and modernize production or building and renovating social facilities, or lowering the VAT from 28%–20%, or lifting it altogether from residential housing construction. Enterprises' own funds can be expanded through revaluation of their fixed assets and indexation of depreciation allowances following the creeping prices for investment industry products. Such measures can yield beneficial results only if depreciation allowances are used appropriately. The trouble is, a trend has emerged in recent years to switch them to consumption purposes, which wastes the accumulated potential.

20.4.2. *Gross Savings and Investment in Fixed Capital*

In the period 1992–1996, investment fell further than the GDP. By the early 1990s, the share of gross domestic accumulation had surpassed a third of GDP. Despite the slump in production, gross investment in fixed capital remains relatively high. In 1995, gross accumulation amounted to 28% of GDP. As inflation slows down, accumulation in working capital decreases fastest in the gross accumulation parameter. Despite some fluctuations caused by fixed capital revaluation and changes in depreciation accounting, gross accumulation stands at around 22% of fixed assets. For all that, the share of new investment in fixed capital in the GDP fell off significantly from the prereform period, to 17.2% in 1995 from 38.7% in 1990 (Table 20.21).

Table 20.21
GDP Share of Gross Savings, 1990–1996 (%)

	1990	1991	1992	1993	1994	1995	1996
Gross savings	31.0	38.8	52.2	39.3	31.4	33.5	30.9
Gross domestic accumulation	31.0	37.1	35.7	27.8	25.8	24.7	23.8
Gross accumulation of fixed assets	28.7	23.8	24.7	21.0	22.0	21.2	20.9
New investment in fixed assets	38.7	15.1	12.9	16.3	17.9	17.2	16.3
Credit (+), debt (−)	0.9	2.5	16.5	11.5	5.6	8.8	7.2

Source: RF Goskomstat.

20.4.3. Structure of Investment in the Real Sector of the Economy

Structural changes in investment in the real economic sector were prevalent in the Russian economy between 1991 and 1996 (Table 20.22).

The structural distribution pattern of the operating fixed capital reflects the survival of the extremely conservative, ponderous economic structure. The sectoral structure of fixed assets has not in fact experienced major changes, despite frequent revaluations of the fixed assets.

The reduction in fixed capital growth rates and the drop in capital retirement rates are accompanied by steadily growing depreciation. The small decrease in the depreciation rate in 1995 from the 1991

Table 20.22
Structure of Fixed Assets and Depreciation, by Industries, 1991–1996

	Book Value of Fixed Assets						Depreciation	
	1991	1992	1993	1994	1995	1996	1991	1996
Total fixed assets	100	100	100	100	100	100	100	100
Goods Sectors	49.2	63.0	63.6	50.2	45.1	42.9	41.0	37.4
Industry	33.7	40.3	41.3	34.8	31.2	28.9	44.7	47.8
Agriculture	11.4	16.2	16.9	11.6	10.4	10.6	22.6	40.9
Construction	3.8	6.0	5.2	3.6	3.4	3.2	40.2	36.8
Market and Nonmarket Service Sectors	50.8	37.0	36.4	49.8	54.9	57.1	32.2	30.7
Transportation and communications	14.2	17.1	16.6	13.8	10.5	12.5	38.1	40.6
Trade and material and technical supplies	2.9	3.8	3.1	3.1	2.6	2.4	39.0	34.1

Source: RF Goskomstat.

Table 20.23
Renewal and Retirement Rates for Fixed Assets (in 1990 Comparable Prices)

	1991	1992	1993	1994	1995	1996	1997	1998	1998
Renewal rate (%)	6.0	3.2	2.1	1.7	1.9	1.3	1.1	1.1	1.2
Retirement rate (%)	1.8	1.1	1.4	1.7	1.6	1.3	1.2	1.1	0.9

Source: RF Goskomstat.

figure was due to changes in the fixed assets revaluation technique rather than to a higher quality of the reproduction process. In the years from 1991 to 1998, the renewal rate of fixed assets fell consistently, from 5% in 1991 to 1.3% in 1998 (Table 20.23).

Given the shortage of capital resources, it is reasonable policy to alter the investment structure so as to speed up technological renewal rates and commit the renewed assets swiftly to the aims of economic restructuring.

However, an analysis of the investment reproduction structure shows new construction expanding at the expense of technological renovation (Table 20.24). Enterprises maintaining idle assets in their balance sheets have found their financial state overburdened which, following the Soviet tradition and mentality, they consider a complementary instrument securing their development as soon as the state of affairs becomes more favorable. This compels them to claim for unnecessary investments. From the macroeconomic point of view, the problem is not so much determining the scale of financing as identifying areas for investing the available resources.

The industry-based investment utilization pattern has clearly shifted toward social and civilian applications. This shift likely reflects both an effort to maintain business activity in the social and civilian areas at a practicable level and a noticeable trend toward underinvestment in fixed capital reproduction in productive indus-

Table 20.24
Investment Reproduction Structure (by Productive Asset, % of Total)

	1991	1992	1993	1994	1995	1996	1997	1999
Total investment	100	100	100	100	100	100	100	100
Retooling and upgrading of existing enterprises	54	53	51	46	47	47	78	40
Extension of existing enterprises	15	15	14	14	12	12	10	7
New construction	26	27	29	34	36	36	37	44

Source: RF Goskomstat.

Table 20.25
The Structure of Fixed Capital Investment (by Economic Sector, % of Total)

	1990	1991	1992	1993	1994	1995	1996	1997
Total investment in fixed assets	100	100	100	100	100	100	100	100
Housing construction	16.6	18.1	21.7	23.1	23.7	22.8	20.3	18.5

Source: Calculated by the authors from RF Goskomstat data.

tries. The data in Table 20.5 (investment distribution structure) are here supplemented with data on housing construction dynamics (Table 20.25).

Government investment in social and civilian construction is diminishing against the background of a surge in private capital activity in the housing market and construction of sociocultural projects. Private investment in housing construction is running ahead of investment in the economy.

Although new housing construction financed from all sources tapered off in 1990 through 1994, it staged a vigorous comeback in 1995 (Table 20.26). Moreover, the low housing construction rates in the public sector, depressed as a result of a change in the economy's institutional structure, were partly compensated for by the increasing pace of housing construction financed by private investors. The share of private residential houses in the new housing sector built

Table 20.26
Newly Commissioned Housing (by Ownership), 1994–1997

	Newly Commissioned Housing (mill. of sq m)				Newly Commissioned Housing Structure (% of total)			
	1994	1995	1996	1997	1994	1995	1996	1997
Total residential buildings	39.2	41.0	34.3	32.6	100	100	100	100
Public	10.0	9.1	5.9	4.6	25.6	22.1	17.1	14.1
Federal	7.8	7.1	4.7		19.9	17.2	13.6	
RF constituent members'	2.2	2.0	1.2		5.7	4.9	3.5	
Municipal	4.3	4.0	2.9	2.8	11.0	9.8	8.5	8.5
Private	11.8	14.8	14.6	15.9	30.0	36.0	42.7	48.8
Individual developers'	7.1	9.9			18.2	23.2		
Mixed	13.0	13.0	10.8	9.2	33.2	31.8	31.5	28.2

Source: RF Goskomstat.

using own and borrowed funds has been rising steadily, from 5.8% in 1987 to 10.9% in 1991 to 22.0% in 1995 and 43.1% in 1999. It should also be noted that intensive construction financed by individual developers compensated for the state's withdrawal from the housing market and the decreasing business activity of non-state-owned structures.

The current high interest rates on loans are a factor discouraging many potential investors. Restoring the population's confidence in savings can, to a certain degree, positively affect housing construction prospects. It will also be necessary to improve the normative and legislative basis, which will help commit the resources accumulated and saved by the population, attract funds into housing construction, and secure owners' rights to real estate and business deals.

The decrease in gross accumulation of fixed assets in the GDP structure is due to a persistently low investment demand. Although the financial situation of the real sector improved in 1999 and the investment potential grew as profits increased, producers are still very reluctant to invest and cautious in making investment decisions. The persistently positive dynamics of production in 1999 were mainly due to increasing utilization of active and reserve capacities. Investments for the reproduction of fixed assets in the real sector were generally "spot" investments and oriented toward the short term, to quickly recoup projects targeted at the production of competitive products. In the first half of 1999 the share of new investment in fixed assets was 12.0%, the lowest level in the past eight years. In the second half of the year, as investment demand grew briskly, the share of expenditure for the reproduction of fixed assets increased by 1.3 percentage points compared with the previous period. However, it did not compensate for negative trends at the end of 1998 and in the first half of 1999. During this period the share of gross accumulation in the GDP structure fell by 2.8 percentage points. The 30% fall of the share of gross accumulation can be explained by the decrease in expenditure for overhauls of fixed assets.

In the investment sphere it is very important to monitor the process of import-replacing demand for capital goods on the basis of available statistical data. The necessary condition for the transformation of import-replacing postdevaluation growth of production is modernization of the domestic industry. In the initial period, extra profits earned by companies should be channeled not into current consumption but into long-term investment projects. Unfortunately, opportunities to accumulate savings in Russia at this time are very limited. Besides, the ruble's devaluation makes it increasingly difficult for enterprises to purchase modern imported equipment and technologies for the technical modernization of production. In 1998 and in 1999, the growth in production was achieved mainly by engaging reserve capacities and using them better. However, worn-out fixed assets and aging machinery are tough constraints. The modernization of industry is aimed at increasing the competitiveness of Russian-made products on domestic and world markets. At the same time, the lack of investment in production and high price barriers hindering the access of foreign-made products to the Russian market delay resolution of this problem. Obviously, the quality of a large number of domestic products whose output increased in the wake of import substitution remains very poor. These products are in demand only because of their relatively low prices (compared with imported goods) and their producers can operate only in the current favorable environment, in which competition is nonexistent and limited.

The level of per-capita expenditure for gross accumulation in Russia is below that of all developed countries. A low level of accumulation is a key factor limiting the recovery of sustainable economic growth.

21 Development Specifics of Real Sector Industries

Yuri Bobylev and
Eugenia Serova

Among the structural specifics of Russia's economy responsible for the industrial slump, the most important was an extensive inefficient sector.[1] This sector included thousands of enterprises in mechanical engineering, a varied superindustry, and especially the oversized defense industry, which had many intersectoral ties to industries commonly regarded as nonmilitary. In the planned economy, inefficient operation of the industrial sector was maintained by arbitrary pricing policies, centralized intersectoral distribution of resources, and tough restrictions on imports. The price liberalization that signaled a switch to a market economy (and which occurred virtually in one fell swoop), the axing of defense industry orders, and the breakdown of countless production links that occurred with the collapse of the USSR radically altered industrial development conditions in this sector.

Production slumped in all industries, but the dynamics of the slump differed considerably among key industries (Table 21.1). The highest production rates were in the fuel and energy complex. In power, the 1996 production figure was 80.7% of the 1989 figure, and in the fuel industry it was 64.8% (Figure 21.1). The relatively good showing in the fuel and energy complex can be explained by the ongoing high domestic demand for energy. This high demand was determined by several factors: (1) an increasing energy consumption in

---

1. The existence of a large inefficient sector in Russia's prereform economy, in which costs exceeded the value of the output produced at domestic prices measured in world terms (that is, profits were negative), was theoretically shown in a number of independent studies that used an intersectoral balance model. See A. Cherniavsky, Y. Bobylev, and S. Smirnov, "Material Production: Dynamics, Structure, Development Forecast," *The Economist* 4 (1993): 13–22; and A. Pitelin, V. Popova, and V. Pugachev, "Inter-Industry Analysis of Russia's Economy in World Prices," *Economics and Mathematical Methods* 1 (1994): 61–75.

Table 21.1
Dynamics of Physical Volumes of Industrial Output, 1990–1996 (% of Previous Year's Figure)

	1990	1991	1992	1993	1994	1995	1996	1997	1998	1999
Electric power industry	102.0	100.3	95.3	95.3	91.2	96.8	98.4	98.0	97.5	100.2
Fuel industry	96.7	94.0	93.0	88.4	89.8	99.2	98.5	100.3	97.5	102.4
Ferrous metallurgy	98.1	92.6	83.6	83.4	82.7	109.6	97.5	101.0	91.9	114.4
Nonferrous metallurgy	97.6	91.3	74.6	85.9	91.1	102.8	96.4	105.0	95.0	108.5
Chemical and petro-chemical industry	97.8	93.7	78.3	78.5	75.5	107.6	92.9	102.0	92.5	121.7
Machine-building and metal processing	101.1	90.0	85.1	84.4	69.2	90.9	95.4	104.0	92.5	115.9
Forestry, wood-processing, pulp and paper industries	98.8	91.0	85.4	81.3	69.5	99.3	82.5	101.0	99.6	117.2
Construction materials	99.1	97.6	79.6	84.0	72.7	92.0	82.7	96.0	94.2	107.7
Light industry	99.9	91.0	70.0	77.0	54.0	69.8	77.5	98.0	88.5	120.1
Food industry	100.4	90.5	83.6	91.0	82.5	91.8	95.8	99.0	98.1	107.5
Total industry	99.9	92.0	82.0	85.9	79.1	96.7	96.0	102.0	94.8	108.1

Source: Rosstatagentstvo.

Development Specifics of Real Sector Industries

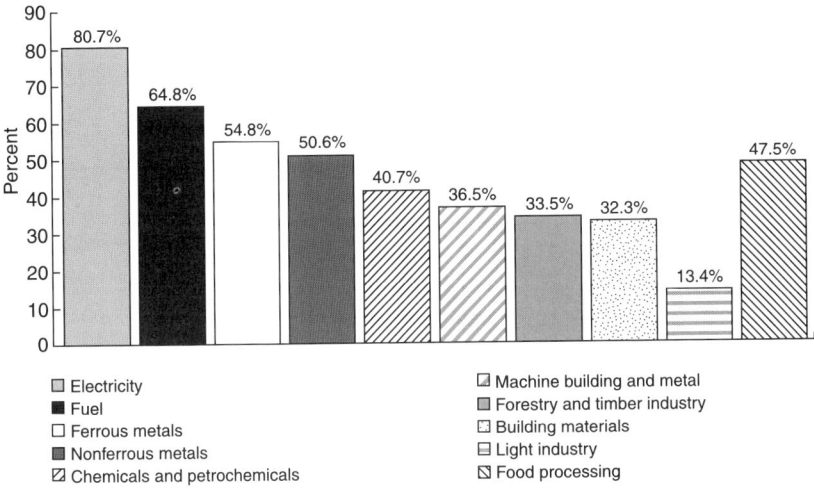

Figure 21.1
Output by key industrial sectors in 1996 relative to their precrisis levels (%).

the nonproductional sphere, which was responsible for a significant share of the total energy consumption, (2) a relatively attenuated fall in production in energy-consuming industries (metallurgy) compared with industries that consumed less energy (engineering, light industry), (3) the decreasing effectiveness of energy resource utilization originating in declining productional capacities, and (4) the very slow technological reconstruction of production.

The relatively high output levels in the fuel industry have largely been maintained by export opportunities. Net oil exports (of both crude and processed oil) accounted for 56.9% of total oil output, while natural gas exports accounted for 32.3% of extracted volume.

Despite the high competitive advantage and considerable export opportunities, however, the oil industry succumbed to a crisis in production. Oil production in Russia plunged from 568.8 million tons in 1988 to 301.3 million tons in 1996, or by 47% (Table 21.2). The principal factors behind the drop in oil output were not deteriorating field conditions or decreasing investment in production, which are commonly cited as the main causes, but a sharp decline in domestic demand for oil and on the markets of Eastern Europe and the former Union republics. The drop in effective demand was an inescapable consequence of the general economic slump and the convergence of domestic and export prices (for oil delivered to the former Union

Table 21.2
Russia's Energy Resources, 1990–1998: Production, Consumption, and Exports

	1990	1991	1992	1993	1994	1995	1996	1997	1998
Oil (mill. tons)									
Production	516.2	462.3	399.3	353.9	317.8	306.8	301.3	305.6	303.4
Total exports	220.3	173.9	137.7	122.6	129.8	122.3	126.0	126.9	137.1
Exports to non-CIS countries	99.7	56.5	66.2	79.9	91.7	96.2	105.4	109.8	117.9
Exports to CIS countries	120.6	117.4	71.5	42.7	38.1	26.1	20.6	17.1	19.2
Net exports	201.5	155.8	127.0	112.2	121.6	113.8	117.2	119.0	129.2
Domestic consumption	269.9	266.2	231.4	196.5	151.4	150.4	129.7	130.0	123.2
Net exports as % of production	39.0%	33.7%	31.8%	31.7%	38.3%	37.1%	38.9%	38.9%	42.6%
Oil Products (mill. tons)									
Total exports	50.6	46.1	43.0	47.4	47.3	47.0	57.0	60.6	53.8
Exports to non-CIS countries	35.0	27.0	25.3	35.3	39.1	43.5	55.0	58.4	51.2
Exports to CIS countries	15.6	19.1	17.7	12.1	8.2	3.5	2.0	2.2	2.6
Net exports	44.8	40.3	40.9	45.2	44.8	42.6	54.4	56.6	51.0
Oil and Oil Products (mill. tons)									
Net export of oil and oil products	246.3	196.1	167.9	157.4	166.4	156.4	171.6	175.6	180.2
Net export of oil and oil products as % of oil production	47.7%	42.4%	42.0%	44.5%	52.4%	51.0%	56.9%	57.5%	59.4%

Natural gas (bill. m³)								
Production	640.6	643.4	641.0	618.4	607.2	595.4	601.1	571.1	591.0
Total exports	249.2	246.8	194.4	174.4	184.3	192.2	198.5	200.9	200.6
Exports to non-CIS countries	96.0	91.0	87.9	95.9	109.3	121.9	128.0	120.9	125.0
Exports to CIS countries	153.2	155.8	106.5	78.5	75.0	70.3	70.5	80.0	75.6
Net exports	179.2	177.8	187.4	168.4	180.3	188.3	193.9	196.4	197.6
Domestic consumption	461.4	465.6	453.6	450.0	426.9	407.1	407.2	374.7	393.4
Net exports as % of production	28.0%	27.6%	29.2%	27.2%	29.7%	31.6%	32.3%	34.4%	33.4%
Aggregates									
Oil and gas production (mill. tons, oil-equivalent)	1092.7	1041.4	976.2	910.5	864.3	842.7	842.3	819.6	835.3
Net export of oil, oil products, and natural gas (mill. tons, oil-equivalent)	407.6	356.1	336.6	309.0	328.7	325.9	346.1	352.4	358.0
Domestic consumption of oil and natural gas (mill. tons, oil-equivalent)	685.1	685.3	639.6	601.5	535.6	516.8	496.2	467.2	477.3
Net export of oil, oil products, and natural gas as % of oil and gas production	37.3%	34.2%	34.5%	33.9%	38.0%	38.7%	41.1%	43.0%	42.9%

Note: Data on the geographic distribution of exports in 1990 and 1991 reflect exports both outside the former USSR and to former Soviet republics.

Sources: Rosstatagentstvo, OECD International Energy Agency, RF Fuel and Energy Ministry, State Customs Committee of RF, author's calculations.

republics), on the one hand, and world market prices on the other. According to our estimates, real domestic oil consumption, measured as the difference between oil output and net exports of oil and petroleum products, shrank from 269.9 million tons in 1990 to 130.6 million tons in 1996, or by 51.6%. During this same period, oil exports to CIS countries fell from 110.6 to 20.6 million tons, or to less than 20% of what they had been.

Unlike oil, the decrease in domestic demand for gas in the years of reform was much less severe, with a relatively high demand for it supported by the power industry and households and the rise in the share of gas in the fuel and energy balance as the most efficient fuel in both economic and environmental terms. Moreover, the drop in domestic demand and in exports to CIS countries was offset by exports of gas to other foreign countries, whose share in natural gas exports reached 65.1% in 1996. As a result, in 1995, which was a record-low year for the gas industry, gas production fall was a mere 7.5% from the prereform level.

The dynamics of Russia's energy exports over a long period of time show that aggregate net oil and oil product exports still remain considerably below prereform levels, although showing a growth pattern in recent years. Aggregate net exports fell from 246.3 million tons in 1990 to 180.2 million tons in 1998, or by 26.8%. At the same time, the share of oil and oil product exports in oil production rose from 47.7% to 59.4% as a result of a sharp decline in domestic consumption over the same period. As for natural gas, both the physical volume of exports and the share of exports in production grew. At the same time, aggregate net oil, oil product, and natural gas exports fell from 407.6 million tons in oil-equivalent units in 1990 to 358 million tons in oil-equivalent units in 1998, or by 12% in our estimate. At the same time, the share of net exports in the aggregate production of oil and natural gas increased from 37.3% to 42.9%. Thus, the export intensity of the oil and gas sector appears to be strengthening; however, this is related not to an increase in absolute export volumes (which in fact have decreased) but to the lower output of hydrocarbons in the wake of falling domestic consumption and exports to neighboring countries.

External demand is becoming an increasingly important factor affecting the dynamics of raw materials production in Russia. For some products it has had a decisive influence on the current volume and output dynamics. Growth in the exports of primary materials against a background of falling investment in production and a drop in consumer goods slanted industrial production in general toward exports. According to our estimates, which take into account the purchasing power of the ruble and the dollar, the share of exports in industrial output went up from 6.9% in 1992 to 22.6% in 1996, or more than threefold.

Mechanical engineering has been among the worst-hit industries. The chief reason for the fall in engineering output was the sharp decline in investment activity. The decline in investment was due above all to steep inflation and contracted investment opportunities in inefficient industries, particularly those catering to the military-industrial complex. Investment activity in the other CIS countries also slackened, with a corresponding reduction in demand for Russian engineering products. Unlike the primary industries, however, the engineering industry was unable to competitively adjust to producing for the markets of other foreign countries. On the domestic market, engineering producers surrendered more and more of their position to foreign competitors. As a result, the output of machinery and equipment in 1996 amounted, by our estimates, to a low 21.5% of the prereform level.

The production of consumer goods also took a steep dive. To an extent, this can be attributed to a drop in the population's effective demand, which was particularly marked at the outset of reforms. But there is another point to be made: whereas in 1996 retail sales recovered to 88% of the prereform level, in 1991 the production of consumer goods had plummeted to 45.8%. In other words, the drop in effective demand accounts for only 22% of the total decline in consumer goods production. In our view, the principal cause of the slump in the consumer industry is the noncompetitive quality of consumer goods produced domestically, whether for foreign or for domestic consumption. As a result, the share of imports in sales jumped abruptly, and domestic producers had to scale down production. The share of imports in total sales rose from 14% in 1991 to 52% in 1996, while the share of domestically produced goods tumbled from 86% to 48% over the same period (Table 21.3). For some items, such as tape recorders, video cassette recorders, and color televisions, imports accounted for more than 90% of total sales. With regard to the products of light industry and the food industry, the share of imports in household consumption in 1995 reached 84.2% and 34.3%, respectively. Passenger car production remains at a rela-

Table 21.3
Percent Contribution of Domestic Goods and Imports to Retail Trade Structure, 1991–1996

	1991	1992	1993	1994	1995	1996
Domestic goods (%)	86	77	71	52	46	48
Imports (%)	14	23	29	48	54	52

Source: RF Government's Working Center for Economic Reform.

tively high level (auto production in 1996 stood at 78.7% of the 1990 level), a statistic that can be attributed to the government's tough protectionism in this area.

The factors responsible for the dynamics of industrial production include an enormous reduction in government spending on defense, which led to the closing of defense plants and to corresponding reductions in the output of related industries. In the estimates of the Federal Economy Ministry, three years of ebbing defense orders (1993–1995) reduced overall industrial production by 20%–25%. The volume of defense production in 1996 was a meager 15% of its prereform, 1991 level.

Our analysis of the sectoral structure of the industrial slump in 1992 prices reveals that engineering and light industry contributed the most to the general meltdown of industrial production in Russia. The collapse of production in these industries accounted for almost 40% of the industrial slump. Moreover, the fall in effective demand for the products of these industries dragged down output in the metal and chemical industries, and indirectly in the fuel and energy complex. This justifies the claim that engineering and light industry were the principal driving forces behind the industrial slump. There were significant differences between these industries, however: whereas production in light industry fell largely because of the inefficiency of the industry, the meltdown in engineering was brought about by a combination of all the key factors behind the industrial slump—primarily inefficiency, the investment crisis, and demilitarization. An important factor depressing industrial output, particularly in engineering, chemicals, and the food industry, was the sharp reduction in demand for farming machinery and mineral fertilizers and the contraction of primary materials for the food industry. According to the Academy of Sciences' Institute for National Economy Forecasting, farmers' demand for industrial output (real purchases of industrial inventories) was estimated at 14% of the 1990 level.

Table 21.4
Industrial Output Structure in Comparable Prices (1995 Prices) (%)

	1990	1991	1992	1993	1994	1995	1996	1997
Fuel and energy complex	20.4	21.2	23.4	24.8	28.5	29.1	30.9	29.8
Metallurgical complex	14.4	14.2	13.3	13.1	14.3	15.9	16.4	16.6
Wood chemistry	14.1	14.1	13.9	12.9	11.8	12.8	11.7	12.1
Machine-building complex	22.6	21.9	22.4	22.0	19.3	18.1	17.5	18.8
Light industry	7.0	6.8	5.6	5.0	3.4	2.5	2.0	2.0
Food processing	12.0	11.7	11.4	12.1	12.7	12.1	11.9	12.1
Total industry	100.0	100.0	100.0	100.0	100.0	100.0	100.0	100.0

Source: Rosstatagentstvo; author's calculations.

Data on the structure of industrial output, investments, and employment testify to the growing role of fuel, energy, and metals in the industrial output structure at the same time that the share of engineering and light industry continued to slip relentlessly (Tables 21.4 to 21.6 and Figures 21.2 to 21.5).

The large increase in the share of the fuel and energy complex and metals in the industrial structure highlights the pronounced structural character of the industrial slump. This conclusion reflects both the logical continuation of the relatively high production levels in power and the fall in the output of investment products, and also the widely varying competitiveness of different Russian industries. The fuel and energy industries (except coal) are the most competitive from the viewpoint of the international division of labor (by various estimates, these industries would remain highly profitable even at world prices, that is, in open market conditions). In other

Table 21.5
Capital Investment in Industry from All Financing Sources (in Current Prices) (%)

	1990	1991	1992	1993	1994	1995	1996	1997
Fuel and energy complex	39.1	39.7	52.8	55.7	57.6	61.7	62.4	61.3
Metallurgical complex	8.2	9.1	11.1	10.7	11.0	12.3	10.4	9.7
Wood chemistry	9.3	10.1	9.3	6.9	5.0	7.2	7.2	7.1
Machine building complex	23.1	20.0	11.9	12.2	11.7	8.3	8.3	8.4
Light industry	3.3	3.4	2.5	1.7	1.2	0.7	0.6	0.7
Food processing	8.1	9.1	6.4	8.1	7.8	6.1	7.4	8.6
Total industry	100.0	100.0	100.0	100.0	100.0	100.0	100.0	100.0

Source: Rosstatagentstvo; author's calculations.

Table 21.6
Structure of Industrial Personnel, 1991–1997 (%)

	1990	1991	1992	1993	1994	1995	1996	1997
Fuel and energy complex	6.4	6.8	7.4	8.2	9.0	10.0	11.0	11.7
Metallurgical complex	6.0	6.5	6.7	7.1	7.2	7.9	8.5	8.5
Wood chemistry	13.9	14.1	14.8	14.6	14.6	14.6	14.6	14.5
Machine building complex	46.0	45.2	43.8	42.1	40.3	38.7	37.7	37.6
Light industry	10.9	10.7	9.2	9.0	9.2	8.3	7.6	7.2
Food processing	7.4	7.6	7.8	8.2	8.9	9.4	10.0	10.4
Total industry	100.0	100.0	100.0	100.0	100.0	100.0	100.0	100.0

Source: Rosstatagentstvo.

industries and in agriculture, with the products they use and their output priced at world prices, production would be either unprofitable or minimally efficient (this conclusion applies, of course, to vast industries, not excluding competitive individual subindustries and plants operating within their framework). As a result, with the existing technological structure of the Russian economy, a convergence of domestic and world prices would inevitably cut the profitability of production in noncompetitive industries and cripple the respective enterprises.

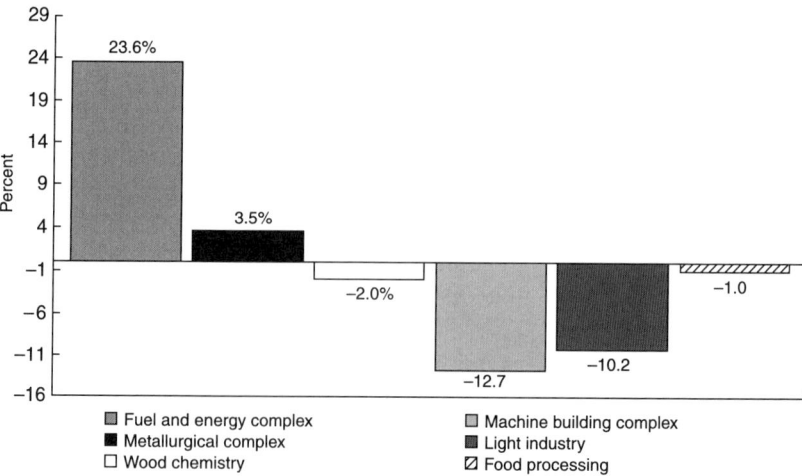

Figure 21.2
Changes in relative shares of key industries in the overall industrial production structure, in current prices, 1991–1996 (%). (Source: Goskomstat.)

Development Specifics of Real Sector Industries 685

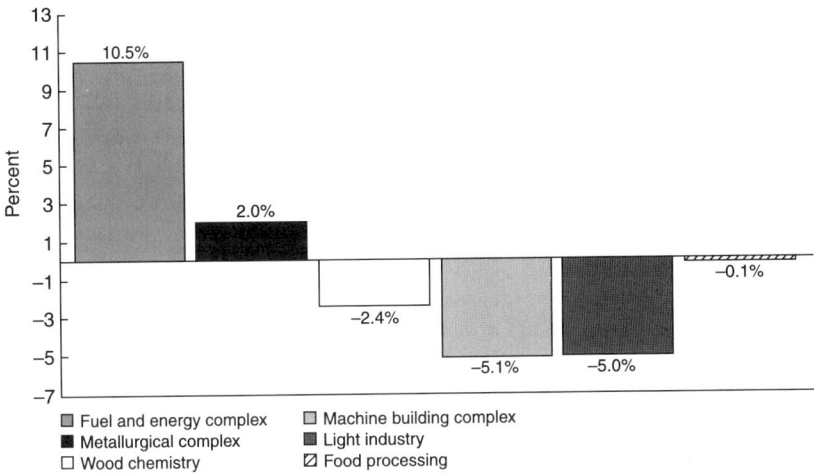

Figure 21.3
Changes in the relative shares of key industries of the overall industrial production structure, in comparable prices, 1991–1996 (%). (Source: RF Goskomstat.)

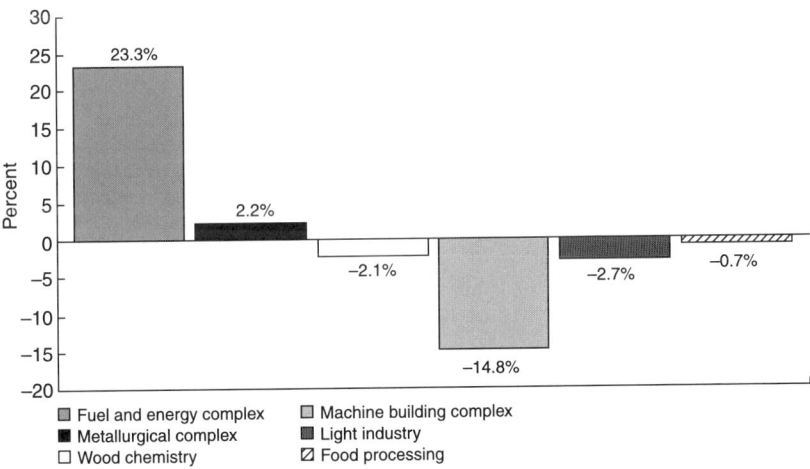

Figure 21.4
Changes in the relative shares of key industries in the industrial investment structure, 1991–1996 (%). (Source: RF Goskomstat.)

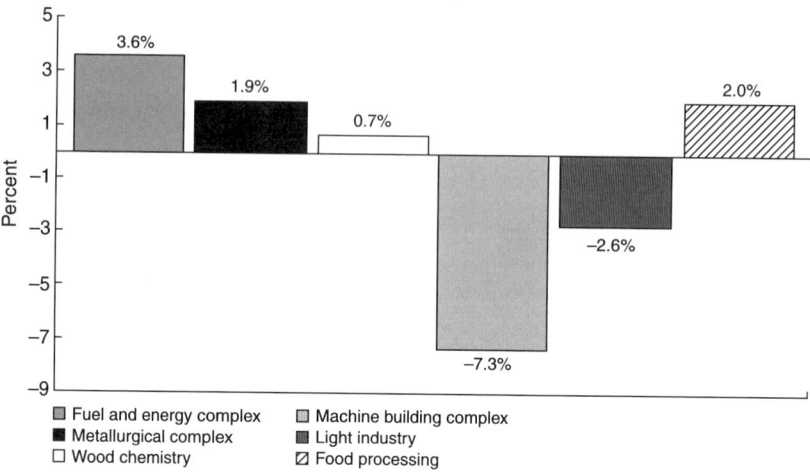

Figure 21.5
Changes in the relative shares of key industries in the industrial personnel structure, 1991–1996 (%). (Source: RF Goskomstat.)

Industrial dynamics in the reform period were determined by an array of factors, chiefly the collapse of inefficient industries and agriculture. This in turn led to a sharp contraction in aggregate domestic demand, which led to a fall in the output of the more competitive industries. Recently, however, a gradual stabilization of industrial output has occurred, and a redistribution of output, investment, and labor in favor of the most competitive industries has been taking place as well. Considering the positive general economic processes at the macrolevel, this suggests that the period of crisis-bound restructuring of Russian industry has ended. Favorable conditions have therefore been laid for the firm stabilization of production and the resurgence of industrial growth, and, in the longer term, for the gradual formation of a new and more efficient industrial structure.

22

International Business in the Period of Market Reforms

Natalia Leonova,
Sergei Prikhodko,
and Nadezhda Volovik

Control over international business ties in the USSR was linked to the nature of the Soviet economy, which was based on the centralized allocation of resources. The state monopoly of foreign trade led to an administered distribution of international business. The principal objective of this system was to compensate for imbalances in the national economy. Imports provided resources the country needed, and exports produced the funds needed to pay for the imports. Pressure from outside competition was neutralized by the autarchic structure of the economy. Producers shielded from the external market produced noncompetitive output. Because the right to carry on foreign trade was accorded only to specialized government organizations, 95% of the country's foreign trade was in the hands of the various departments of the Ministry of Foreign Trade.

By the mid-1980s, exports consisted predominantly of fuel and raw materials, while imports were largely made up of consumer goods.

The economic crisis that struck in the late 1980s and early 1990s adversely affected the country's foreign trade (Figure 22.1). Already in 1989 there was no growth in the value of Russian exports, and the physical volume of exports fell. What followed next—a slump in production, the breakdown of economic ties with former eastern bloc countries and the former republics of the USSR, and errors in trade policies and organization at the federal and regional levels—cut deeply into Russian foreign trade in 1991. The government's attempts to reform its foreign trade practices were unsuccessful, without any practical result to show for those efforts.

22.1. Liberalization of Foreign Trade: Results and Prospects

The beginnings of a new mechanism for regulating Russia's economic relations with the rest of the world, appropriate for a market

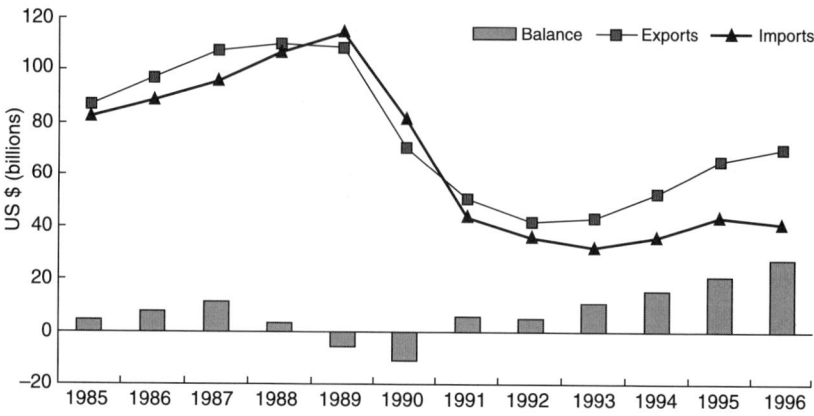

Figure 22.1
Key parameters of Russian foreign trade with non-CIS countries (billions of dollars). (Source: RF Goskomstat.)

environment, were established by presidential decree No. 213, "Liberalization of External Economic Relations," of 15 November 1991. From that time on, all economic agents, regardless of ownership form, were, in principle, given the green light to engage in foreign trade.

Initially, from late 1991 to mid-1992, the liberalization measures included the following:

• The removal of restrictions on the export of finished products (with rigid quantity and tariff restrictions retained on fuels and raw materials)
• Partial freeing of the exchange rate (with a special rate introduced for budget payments, and subsidies for critical imports left in place)
• The lifting of all restrictions on imports

Beginning in January 1992, exporters were required to sell 40% of their hard-currency receipts at a special exchange rate and 10% at the market rate. The application of an export tariff helped prevent a furious surge in domestic prices for energy and manufactured goods to world levels, which could have hurt Russian manufacturing industries. Until mid-1992, no duties were imposed on imports, which strongly boosted consumer imports.

The liberalization of imports was essential to create a competitive environment in the overmonopolized domestic market and to offset the steep fall in Russian industrial output. The ceilings fixed by administrative writ on fuel and raw material exports were a forced measure in a situation in which domestic prices for these goods were significantly lower than world prices. Removal of restrictions at that time could have swept the domestic market catastrophically clean of products.

The crowding of a vast number of Russian enterprises, many of them without a background in foreign trade, onto the world market led to rivalries and to a loss of bargaining power over contract terms. Russian exporters were aiming for foreign exchange at any price, ignoring both the actual costs and world prices. Loss of parity between contract prices and world prices cost Russian exporters much foreign exchange and caused world prices for some goods to slip. This process gave Russia the reputation of a trading partner that tended to depress prices on the world markets.

In these conditions, the Russian government was compelled to tighten its control over exports. In the second phase of foreign trade liberalization, during the second half of 1992, the government introduced special rules for exporters of strategically vital raw materials. These rules applied to 70% of Russian exports.

An interim customs tariff on imports was introduced early in the second half of 1992 and was soon followed, in September, by a permanent tariff. The first Russian tariff was little differentiated, applying identical rates to nearly all commodities. After repeated modifications, it became a flexible and selective tool, offering protection to some industries and ushering in international competition for others.

The measures to restrain exports (duties, licenses, quotas, mandatory sale of foreign exchange) proved more effective than incentives. Efforts to prevent a plunge in exports failed. This meant a reduction in the foreign exchange receipts needed to finance imports.

The country's foreign trade in 1992 closed at $79.4 billion, down 17% from 1991 and lower by a factor of 2.1 than in 1990 (Table 22.1).

From 1 June 1992, exporters were ordered to sell 50% of their foreign exchange receipts, with the share of receipts to be sold at market rates (rather than the central bank's fixed rate) subsequently being raised from 20% to 50%.

During the third phase of international business liberalization (1993–1994), regulation by tariff continued to spread and the role of quotas gradually decreased. Centrally controlled export and import

Table 22.1
Key Parameters of Russian Foreign Trade with Non-CIS Countries, 1991–1996 (ex Unorganized Trade, in Billions of Dollars)

	1990	1991	1992	1993	1994	1995	1996
Foreign trade turnover	163.8	100.3	69.2	71.1	79.8	97.6	103.7
Exports	80.9	54.7	42.4	44.3	51.5	64.3	71.9
Imports	82.9	45.6	37.0	26.8	28.3	33.3	31.8
Balance	−2.0	9.1	5.4	17.5	23.2	31	40.1

Source: RF Goskomstat.

operations shrank to 30% of foreign trade in 1993. Enterprises under all forms of ownership were acquiring a pivotal role in external economic relations and foreign trade.

In 1993 some important legislation governing Russia's foreign trade was enacted, in particular the Customs Code and the Federal Customs Tariff Law. The Customs Code, the final version of which was passed by the Russian Supreme Soviet on 18 June 1993, defined the legal status of customs authorities. This law outlined the types of customs regimes and duties; rules for assessing, paying, and collecting duties; clearance rules for goods and vehicles; and documents justifying imports and exports.

The Federal Customs Tariff Law of 21 May 1993 established rules for imposing customs duty rates, contingency measures to regulate foreign trade through the imposition of seasonal and special duties, rules for assessing the customs value and country of origin of a commodity, and rules for applying tariff preferences.

As a singular Russian specific, the customs regime provided for levying export taxes to balance domestic and world prices, especially the prices of raw materials, and to gain revenue for the budget. The new export customs tariff went into force on 1 November 1993, and was amended in July and September 1994. The Russian export tariff was highly differentiated. A large selection of goods was exempted (unlike the import tariff, the export tariff was drawn up as a list of individual goods, which did not include duty-free commodities). Export duties were levied in ECU per ton (this was their unique specific), with ad valorem duties being imposed only very rarely.

For some time after the export customs tariff went into effect, it was common practice to exempt individual exporters from duties by government resolution. The presidential decree No. 406 of 27 March

1993 curtailed this practice significantly, limiting it to preferences specified in the Customs Tariff Law and to those granted by presidential decrees.

Toward the end of 1993, export duty rates were cut by 50% on average, and the list of goods subject to levies was almost halved. Foreign exchange receipts from exports proved much smaller than expected. The quotas and export privileges granted to centrally controlled exporters did not live up to the promise.

The year 1993 was a difficult period for Russian imports. Subsidies for centralized importers were withdrawn, and customs and tax policies hardened. Imports fell by 27% through 1993.

Starting on 1 February 1993, a value-added tax (VAT) and excise duties were placed on goods imported into the Russian Federation. These levies are paid concurrently with other customs levies, that is, before or at the time the goods are delivered for customs inspection. The VAT was applied at the same rate of 20% to both imports and Russian-made products. Excise duty rates for imported goods are set by resolutions of the federal government and may be different from those imposed on similar Russian goods.

With the breakup of the USSR, Russia was left without a fully guarded border, which made smuggling of goods into or out of the country a major problem. According to the State Customs Committee, nearly 85% of cigarettes and alcohol entered Russia illicitly, and up to one-half of electronic goods were smuggled in or entered in violation of customs rules. Skirting customhouses was the easiest way to take goods into Russia. Various schemes involving "false transit" and "false re-export" were also very popular. To stop offenses of these kinds, the State Customs Committee issued a directive, "Some Specifics of Re-export as a Customs Regime," which authorized the re-export of goods on payment of customs duties by pledge, the presentation of bank guarantees, or the deposition of cash with customs. As a result, smugglers rarely use the re-export mechanism today.

To improve the collection of excise taxes and to prevent excisable goods (alcohol, wines, vodka, tobacco and tobacco products) from being brought into and sold in Russia, on 14 April 1994 the Russian government adopted resolution No. 319, "Introduction of Excise Stamps in the Russian Federation," which established the practice of collecting excise duties on imports by selling excise duty stamps of official design.

The Russian government's resolution No. 863 of 18 July 1994, "Changes in Excise Duty Rates for Selected Goods Brought into the Territory of the Russian Federation," effective from August 1, introduced new excise duty rates on some goods brought into Russia. The existing approach to excise duty assessment as a percentage of the customs value was replaced with excises levied in ECU per commodity unit. This provided a mechanism to end customs value understatement, one of the most widespread methods of minimizing obligatory customs duties.

Infringement of the exchange laws caused serious damage. Foreign exchange escapes from the country through the following illegal channels:

• Foreign exchange is not repatriated, under the pretext of *force majeure* or other adverse circumstances.

• Unwarranted advance payments are made by importers against the future delivery of commodities, which frequently are not supplied.

• Price manipulations leave foreign exchange abroad, under the cover of barter operations.

• Accounts of foreign firms are credited with payments for fictitious services.

• The contract price is understated on export and overstated on import.

• Bail is deposited with a foreign bank for a loan to be obtained, but in fact no loan is contracted.

In January 1994, the central bank of Russia and the State Customs Committee jointly issued the "Order on Control Over the Repatriation of Foreign Exchange Receipts for Commodity Exports to the Russian Federation." Today, exchange controls cover almost 100% of Russian export operations. According to the Ministry of the Economy, while the export of strategic goods by specialized exporters has risen 20% in volume, contract payments have grown by 60%, in general, following the introduction of exchange controls in 1994.

In 1994, goods taken out of Russia's customs territory under export quotas for federal needs were exempt from customs duties. Since 1 January 1994, customs duties have not been levied on oil, petroleum gas, and petroleum products that are exported under quotas for government needs. Also, exemptions from import duties were granted for productive material resources purchased by oil-producing enterprises for cash received from the oil export, petroleum gas, and petroleum products.

New import tariff rates were introduced in the Russian Federation on 1 July 1994. Whereas the import customs tariff rates in 1993 were ad valorem duties only, the 1994 tariff listed both ad valorem and specific duties. In contrast to the 1993 tariff, which exempted the majority of food products, ores, lead, tin, cotton wool, books, railroad locomotives, tram cars, tankers, fishing vessels, and a variety of other goods, the 1994 list was much shorter. Under pressure from industrial lobbies, import duties were raised on manufactured goods that competed with domestic products (autos, rugs, and the like), and the taxation level rose to 25%–30%. The application of combined rates under the new tariff contributed to a general increase in the duty level.

A special tax was introduced on imported goods on 1 January 1994. The VAT was lifted from exported goods produced or purchased by the manufacturer, exported services and jobs, and some imports.

In January 1994, the retailing of goods and services to the public for foreign exchange was discontinued. Changes were introduced in the rules governing the movement of goods across the customs border to be used for purposes other than production or any other for-profit business by individuals. The new rules allowed individuals to carry only 40% of the value of their cargoes duty-free.

The Russian executive decree No. 1007, "Abolition of Quotas and Licenses on Exports of Goods and Services," of 23 May 1994, was a major milestone in the liberalization of foreign trade. Export quotas on oil and petroleum products were retained, however, until the end of the year.

As a result of all these changes, at year-end 1994, Russia had the following five export regimes in operation:

- Export of oil and petroleum products
- Export of strategic raw materials
- Export of goods under Russia's international commitments
- Export of special goods (arms, dual-purpose goods, medicines, nuclear materials, and so on)
- Exports requiring registration of contracts

Beginning on 1 January 1995, quotas were applied to around 5% of export volumes (these quotas applied to goods exported under Russia's international commitments), and another 8% of goods were subjected to special regulation (arms and military equipment, dual-purpose goods, precious metals and alloys and articles made from them, and so on).

Control was exercised by registering export contracts on application by exporters. The list of goods requiring export contract registration included fifteen commodity groups (among them oil, oil distillation products, natural gas, fertilizers, and timber), which accounted for around 50% of the total volume of exports.

Until 1995, the number of exporters of some commodities (such as oil and petroleum products, natural gas, electric power, nonferrous, alkali, alkaline-earth and rare-earth metals and raw materials for their production, nitrogen and phosphorus fertilizers, pulp, softwood timber and boards, and wheat) had been restricted. These goods could only be exported by special exporters, that is, entities registered for this purpose with the Ministry for External Economic Relations (MEER). This approach was required to ensure a high level of professionalism from the exporters and to guarantee repatriation of foreign exchange receipts to Russia. Surveillance of these special operations, however, exposed numerous violations. In particular, checks of the lumber industry in 1994 revealed that 50% of foreign exchange receipts earned by Russian lumber exporters were concealed, and 30% of Russian lumber products were exported at dumping prices. Countless financial infringements, particularly in barter operations, were uncovered. Surveillance of oil exporters turned up similar problems. The idea of special exporters (like any other bureaucracy-inspired project) was hardly worth the effort. In the spring of 1995, another step was taken to liberalize exports: the special exports scheme was discarded as worthless by presidential decree No. 245 of March 6, effective from March 25 of that year.

The law *On Government Regulation of Foreign Trade* was adopted in July 1995 and went into effect in October. The law defines the functions of the Russian President, government, and the MEER. The exclusive role of the MEER is emphasized by the undivided right it has to issue export and import licenses for goods to which quotas are applied or for which permits are required.

The Russian government is bound, under the law, to submit a foreign trade development program, along with a federal budget bill, to Parliament for approval. The program must show, among other things, the customs tariff rates for the respective year and the range of their possible variations, a feature that should make foreign trade behavior more predictable. The government may introduce quotas on exports and imports to safeguard the country's national security, discharge its international obligations, or protect the domestic market, on giving at least three months' notice. The program provides for the possibility of a state monopoly being imposed on trade in selected commodities. This would specifically require a change in the rules that apply to the issuance of export and import licenses to government-controlled businesses only.

Upon entry into force, the law *On Government Regulation of Foreign Trade* lent full legitimacy to the Government's Commission on Measures to Protect Foreign Trade. This commission received, in late December 1995, the "Rules of Investigation Preceding the Introduction of Protective Measures," approved by the Russian MEER. Protective measures against competitive imports are common the world over. In fact, Russia lagged behind other nations in developing and applying protective measures. This lag was particularly telling insofar as Russian exports are frequently, and usually without justification, discriminated against in international markets.

Work continued through 1995 to reduce and gradually abolish export duties. The final phase of Russian export liberalization ended in 1996. Beginning on 1 April 1996, customs duties were abolished on all export goods except oil, and oil's turn came on 1 July.

When the financial crisis broke out in the summer of 1998, the Russian government had to change its foreign trade policy dramatically. A sharp fall in imports resulted in less revenue being derived from customs duties. In this situation the practice of imposing duties on Russian exporters, whose incomes had begun to grow after the dollar-to-ruble exchange rate increased, was forcibly renewed. Thus, based on the Russian government's resolution No. 17 of 4 January 1999, "On the Approval of Export Customs Duties on Commodities Exported from the RF Territory," export duties were introduced on nonferrous scrap, timber, leather, and pelts, among other products.

On 23 January 1999 the government approved a resolution linking the level of state duties on oil operations with changes in world market prices. For oil exports at prices from $9.5 to $12.5 per barrel, the duty was set at 2.5 euros per metric ton; at prices of over $12.5 per barrel, the duty was 5 euros per metric ton. If oil prices fall below $9.5 per barrel, as occurred in March 2000, no export duty shall be imposed.

During 1999 the government constantly added to the list of commodities subject to export duties: fish, crab, ethyl alcohol, ferrous scrap, ammonium nitrate, wood and wood products, paper, cardboard and products thereof, precious and semiprecious gems and metals, and other commodities.

Beginning in May, export duties were imposed on a large number of commodities exported both outside and inside the CIS, excluding the Customs Union member countries. From 1 August the export duty was imposed on crude oil exports from Russia to all countries outside the Customs Union.

At first the duties were intended to remain in effect for six months, but this period was later extended. Thus, the Russian government's resolution No. 798 extended the 5% export duty on copper, nickel, and coal-processing products until the approval of the next resolution, thus effectively removing the original six-month limit.

Export duties at 5% of customs value were set on unprocessed nickel, nickel matte, and other intermediary products of nickel metallurgy, as well as on any items made of nickel.

During 1999 the price of oil increased by about $100 per metric ton; therefore the government approved a resolution increasing export duties on oil up to 7.5 euros per metric ton from 23 September 1999 and up to 15 euros per metric ton from 8 December.

In 1994 and 1995, Russian importers enjoyed relatively wider preferences than exporters, in the absence of exchange control over their operations. According to central bank experts, in the absence of exchange control over imports, an equivalent of $8 billion in foreign exchange was illegally parked overseas. The central bank and the State Customs Committee (SCC) issued a directive, effective from 1 January 1996, "Exchange Control Over Justification of Payment in Foreign Exchange for Imported Goods." Its chief purpose was to stop illegal transfers of foreign exchange from Russia in import operations.

In order to recover the losses the budget suffered from the abolition of export duties, controls over goods carried by individuals into Russia were tightened. The Russian government's resolution No.

808, of 18 July 1996, "Movement of Goods Used for Purposes Other Than Production or For-Profit Business Across the Customs Border of the Russian Federation by Individuals," lowered the value of duty-free goods that individuals could take into Russia from $2,000 to $1,000, provided that the total weight of the goods did not exceed 50 kilograms.

In 1996, measures were adopted to protect Russian producers. Under the government's resolution No. 413, of 11 April 1996, customs duty rates were raised, starting on 15 May 1996, on a number of commodities, in particular buses, trucks, refrigerators and freezers, washing machines, microwave ovens, electric motors, aluminum articles, linoleum, polyvinyl chloride, chicken meat, and several other goods.

Barter operations continue to beset foreign trade. Barter contracts did not follow any officially established form. Russian exporters used barter as a loophole, to report minimum details about their deals. Improperly executed contracts created an avenue for foreign exchange to flee Russia and gave foreign partners a pretext to renege on their obligations. To illustrate, in 1995, Russian exports involved in barter trade with countries other than the former Soviet republics were $1.5 billion greater than imports. To fight these violations, the President issued the decree "On Government Regulation of Barter in Foreign Trade," which introduced, beginning on 1 November 1996, a mandatory form of barter contract, to be made in writing and containing information about the export and import sides of the deal. The parties are to show each commodity item, both export and import, its price, and the delivery deadline. The foreign partner's obligations are to be lawfully signed and validly formulated in accordance with the laws of his country.

The mechanism for regulating foreign economic activities that has been put in place in recent years has not as yet facilitated progressive shifts in the export and import structure. The profound raw-material component of Russian exports makes the import-export structure dependent on the situation on world markets, thus precluding an opportunity to adjust the Russian economy to changing world market situations quickly and painlessly. Russia satisfies almost half of its demand for food at the expense of imports that present a real threat to the economic security of the country. The need to improve the mechanism for regulating foreign economic activities remains urgent.

22.2. Consequences of the Policy of Foreign Trade Privileges and Preferences

Some businesses managed to obtain privileges in their international operations. For example, presidential decree No. 1973 of 22 November 1993, "Protectionist Policy of the Russian Federation in the Area of Physical Culture and Sport," exempted the National Sports Foundation from customs duties. Another executive decree of 22 December 1993, "Measures of Government Support for Russian Public Associations of Disabled People," granted similar exemptions to the Russian Society of Disabled People, the Russian Society of the Blind, the Russian Afghan War Veterans Foundation, and similar organizations. The idea was to use the funds saved to promote Russian sport and provide a safety net for disabled people.

The total worth of the privileges was estimated at $2–$3 billion a year. It is common knowledge now that many of the organizations accorded foreign trade privileges and preferences were involved in crime and association with the criminal world.

The overall amount of customs benefits dispensed by the Russian government's Commission on International Humanitarian and Technical Aid in 1996 exceeded Rb 1 trillion. In a great majority of cases, privileges were granted on alcoholic beverages and cigarettes, commodities hardly fitting the concept of humanitarian aid.

A decisive step toward completely abolishing all foreign trade privileges except those specified in the current laws was made in 1995. The opening move came in presidential decree No. 244 of 6 March 1995 and was followed up by the special law, *On Some Aspects of Privileges Accorded to International Business Participants*, passed on 13 March 1995. The special law revoked all previous privileges except those covered by the customs tariff, VAT, and excise duties laws and by the Customs Code. The revocation took effect immediately in part, to become effective in full in mid-May. It ran into fierce opposition and was not always implemented consistently.

22.3. Commodity Composition of Russia's Foreign Trade

The foreign trade sector of the Russian economy has been least affected by the deep structural crisis the economy has been going through to this day.

Table 22.2
RF Trade Balance, 1990 and 1991 (in Billions of Dollars, ex Inter-republic Economic Transactions)

	1990				1991			
	Hard Currency	COME-CON	Clearing	Total	Hard Currency	COME-CON	Clearing	Total
Exports	26.1	40.7	14.1	80.9	24.8	17.0	12.9	54.7
Imports	−24.1	−46.3	−12.5	−82.9	−20.0	−17.5	−8.1	−45.6
Trade account balance	2.0	−5.6	1.6	−2.0	4.8	−0.5	4.8	9.1

Source: RF Goskomstat.

Russia's foreign trade balance has been in surplus since 1991, and the surplus has been growing with each passing year (Table 22.2). The revenues from export and import duties have contributed greatly to the budget, accounting for almost a quarter of revenues.

In the days of the Soviet Union, international settlements were made in hard currency with developed market economies only. The transferable ruble, a closed regional accounting unit that had limited foreign exchange functions, was used in settlements and payments between Russia and CMEA countries. The purchasing power of the transferable ruble was expressed in terms of foreign trade prices, which assumed the application of an exchange rate of the transferable ruble to foreign currency on the basis of a currency basket containing nine principal currencies of developed capitalist countries.

Settlements with such countries as Finland, Yugoslavia, Egypt, Syria, Iran, Iraq, Afghanistan, India, China, North Korea, Laos, and Cambodia were affected by currency clearing, or intergovernmental agreements on set-offs of reciprocal claims and obligations arising from the value parity of goods and services supplied.

An analysis of Russia's balance of trade in 1990 and 1991 shows that its trade shrank in 1991 largely because of the sharp drop in mutual deliveries to and from former member countries of the CMEA (see Table 22.2).

The disintegration of the CMEA touched off a geographic reshuffling of export and import flows in favor of developed market economies. Assured payment in hard currency makes these countries more attractive partners than East European and some developing economies. The reshuffle helped maintain, and even step up, exports paid for in hard currency, despite a decline in Russia's export potential. In

Table 22.3
Exports as a Share of Production, 1991–1996 (%)

	1991	1992	1993	1994	1995	1996
Oil	38.6	36.2	32.8	37.4	39.1	40.9
Gasoline	10.3	9.3	7.9	6.9	8	19.6
Diesel fuel	27.4	21	23.8	29.1	38.6	45.1
Furnace fuel oil	16.5	16.3	16.8	18.5	23.3	22.0
Rolled ferrous metals	17.6	22.2	31.9	49	54	61
Aluminum	—	39.5	52.8	80.5	80.5	88
Copper	—	—	—	62.9	64.9	56.6
Nickel	—	—	—	78.3	79.9	79
Mineral fertilizer	—	51.6	54.1	65.2	72.5	74
Commercial timber	—	7.5	8.5	16.3	20	19
Lumber	—	16.8	18.4	19.8	21.4	24.2
Commercial pulp	—	74.4	56.6	74.6	74.6	80
Paper and cardboard	—	—	—	44.1	47	49

Source: RF Goskomstat.

particular, whereas exports earned around $12.5 billion for the USSR in 1973, $30 billion in 1983, and $26.1 billion in 1990, Russia alone netted $42.4 billion in 1992, when all its goods were exported for hard currency.

22.3.1. Exports

Aside from bringing home foreign exchange, exports today keep Russian enterprises in business and provide jobs for Russian labor. As arrears between Russian producers mount, many producers are redirecting their output to the world market. In fact, the proportion of the output devoted to export is rising for nearly all competitive products (Table 22.3).

Russian exports basically consist of *fuel and energy products*, which account for almost half of all exports (Table 22.4). This structure reflects the growing dependence of primary industries on world markets and adds to the uncertainty of Russian exports supported by primary materials. After a 19% drop in oil and gas condensate in 1992, these products have plateaued at around 120 million tons in recent years. Domestic oil prices are steadily increasing, closing the wide gap that existed between domestic and world prices in the early 1990s. Of late, oil exports to CIS countries have tapered off because of persistent defaults. Exports have found new markets in other foreign countries.

Table 22.4
Exports of Oil, Oil Products, and Natural Gas from Russia, 1990–1996

	1990	1991	1992	1993	1994	1995	1996
Oil exports (mill. of tons)	220.3	173.9	137.7	122.6	129.8	122.3	125.6
Exports of oil products (mill. of tons)	50.6	46.1	43.0	47.4	47.3	45.4	56.5
Natural gas exports (bill. of cu m)	249.2	246.8	194.4	174.4	184.3	192.2	196.5

Source: RF Goskomstat.

The growth in physical volume and in average export prices for countries other than CIS members in 1996 over 1995 was 9% and 21%, respectively, for oil; 26% and 25% for petroleum products; and 5% and 11.6% for natural gas. The share of these products in total exports to other countries, excluding CIS countries, was 18.2%, 9.8%, and 15% in 1996 versus 16.1%, 7%, and 14.8% in 1995.

The strong growth in ferrous and nonferrous metals production since the launch of the reforms has turned *metal fabrication* into one of the most export-oriented industries in Russia, with 37% of the output sent to other countries. In terms of value, the metal industry is the second most important sector of the Russian economy (Table 22.5).

Between 1991 and 1996 as domestic demand for ferrous metals steadily sank, Russian producers persisted in expanding their presence on the world markets. In particular, rolled ferrous metals posted a vigorous growth, from 18% to 63% of output. The export of cold-rolled sheet steel nearly trebled, and the export of hot-rolled sheet steel went from 24% to 63% of output. The exports of more sophisticated products, such as steel pipes, dropped by more than half

Table 22.5
Structure of Ferrous Metal Exports

Component	%
Ores and concentrates	6
Merchant shapes	13
Steel ingots	5
Cast and rolled billets	25
Pig iron	5
Rolled sheet	23
Ferroalloys	4
Other	19

of total sales because of a significant reduction in deliveries to CIS countries.

The bulk of Russian exports consists of raw materials and intermediates.

By late 1995, domestic prices for most ferrous industry products had drawn level with or surpassed world prices. As of 1 December 1995, domestic prices, including VAT, special taxes, and freight charges, were 24% higher than world prices for cold-rolled sheet steel, 50% higher for hot-rolled sheet steel, and 56% higher for zinc-plated sheet steel, while the export of rolled ferrous metals, sheet steel, and steel pipes had become a losing business by the end of 1995.

From 1991 to 1995, domestic demand for primary aluminum plunged by a factor of 2.9. The principal causes of the low demand were the scaling down of defense orders and a recession in mechanical engineering and construction projects. In this situation, aluminum producers were able, with government backing, to win a niche in the world aluminum market within a relatively short time, at virtually the same production and payroll levels.

The stunted demand for *chemical industry* products on domestic commodity markets forced producers to step up exports. In particular, polystyrene exports have climbed 120% since 1991, polyethylene exports have increased by 220%, and mineral fertilizers have increased by a more modest 57%. Faced with depressed domestic demand for mineral fertilizers, mineral fertilizer producers switched their attention to exports. Whereas in 1991 they exported 30% of their output, by 1995 that figure had risen to 78%.

To offset limited domestic demand for chemical and petrochemical products, a prominent place was given to the export of these commodities in 1996 (Figure 22.1). In value terms, chemical exports earned $5.5 billion, or 6.3% of Russia's total exports. The fall in world prices for some products, however, cut into the exports of Russian chemical products. International sales retreated about 7% from the 1995 showing. Over 40% of chemical exports are accounted for by mineral fertilizers and organic products (methanol). Producers' wholesale prices for all chemical and petrochemical products have reached or surpassed world prices.

The *lumber industry*, which relies on Russia's enormous renewable forest resources, is also an export-oriented industry. Its products are

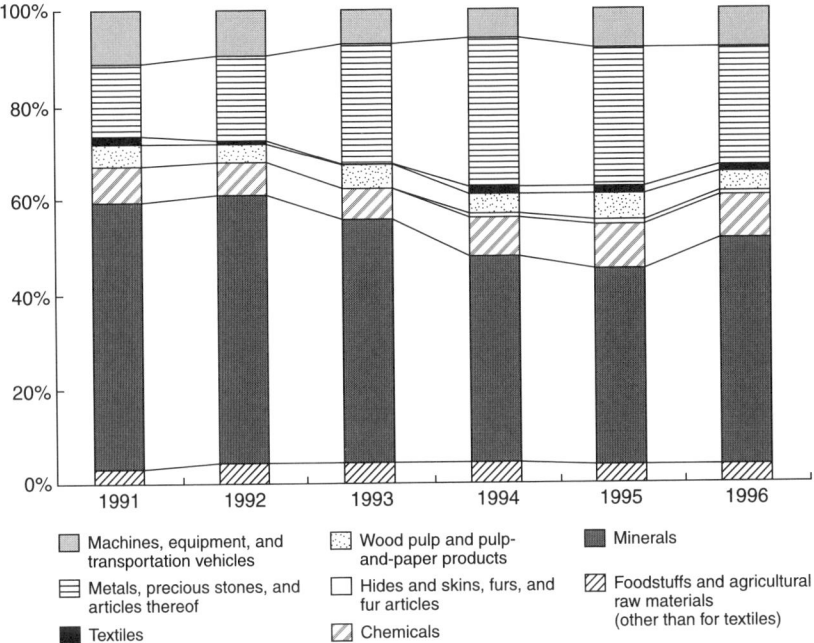

Figure 22.2
The structure of Russian exports. (Based on RF Goskomstat data.)

competitive on the world market, and exports account for 50% of the total output. Vibrant demand for lumber from foreign consumers made up for the declining domestic demand, and as a result, the share of exports in the total output went up significantly. The structure of lumber exports is beginning to lean toward cruder products, like round timber (34%) and wood pulp (14%).

In the Soviet era, the share of *machinery and equipment* in the USSR's total exports was almost 25%. Most of the deliveries consisted of products to CMEA countries that were produced under interstate protocols and specialization agreements.

A slackening in machinery and equipment trade was already evident by the late 1980s. Exports took a deep plunge in 1991 (when they fell to just over a third of the 1990 figure). Several factors were responsible for the decline in engineering exports. First, Russia's decision to abandon ideological benchmarks in foreign policy was reflected in the geographical distribution of Russian exports, a growing share of which now went to industrial countries. Russia's smaller presence on its traditional markets in Eastern Europe, which absorbed 20% of its engineering exports in the late 1980s, cannot be compensated for by deliveries of machines and equipment to industrial countries, which are mostly interested in Russia's primary materials and fuels.

Second, radical changes have occurred in Russia's capacity to extend technological and economic assistance to other countries, which used to be a prime mover in getting Russian-made machines and equipment to foreign markets. In the late 1980s, cooperation of this sort accounted for nearly a third of Russian exports of engineering products for civilian applications. In 1992, deliveries under technological assistance programs fell to less than a quarter of the 1990 figure. This reduction was caused by a drastic cut in credits, more than 60% of which had gone to countries that were subsequently unable to repay them.

Third, the freeing of prices and liberalization of Russia's foreign trade suddenly made primary material and fuels more attractive exports. Primary material exporters spend little to promote and market their products, in contrast to the sizable marketing costs incurred by exporters of machinery and equipment.

The USSR was one of the biggest arms exporters in the world. In 1990 it exported $14 billion worth of arms, of which Russia accounted for at least $9 or $10 billion.

International and domestic conditions have changed dramatically since that period. There is virtually no demand for arms from the Soviet Union's former Warsaw Treaty partners. The UN has invoked a ban on arms exports to Iraq, Libya, and a few other states that formerly were major arms customers of the USSR. Finland has stopped buying military aircraft. Today, Russia exports defense technologies only. It fulfills its obligations under the nuclear nonproliferation treaty and prohibits exports of commodities and technologies likely to violate the treaty. Western markets remain virtually closed to Russian arms exports. New competitors from among CIS countries, particularly Ukraine, have joined the field. These adverse developments notwithstanding, Russian arms exports in 1992 were estimated at $5 billion, or some 15% of total export earnings for that year. Arms came third, after natural gas and oil, in the total volume of Russian exports. Russia supplied military hardware to around fifty countries. About half of its exports were warplanes and helicopters of various types, considerable quantities of missile and antimissile systems, and

Table 22.6
Ratio Between Domestic Buying Prices and World Market Prices, 1991–1996 (as %)

Commodity	1991	1992	1993	1994	1995	1996
Natural gas	3	13	9	22	57	65
Oil	13	25	30	42	62	69
Gasoline	9	28	43	92	170	180
Diesel fuel	9	25	34	83	170	157
Aluminum	71	41	54	71	113	116
Copper	45	45	38	70	107	111
Nickel	31	50	51	44	90	108

Source: Calculated from RF Goskomstat and Central Institute of Economics data.

land warfare equipment such as tanks, armored troop carriers, and artillery systems. Some naval equipment was exported as well.

A government arms company, the Russian Arms Company, or Rosvooruzhenie, was set up in 1993. It now handles around 95% of Russian arms exports. The RAC earned $1.7 billion from arms exports in 1994, nearly $2.8 billion in 1995, and $3.4 billion in 1996.

An analysis of prices for the main groups of commodities shows that the average price level is just below world prices. In particular, whereas the ratio of domestic to world prices was 70% in the early 1990s, it rose to 90% in 1995 (Table 22.6).

22.3.2. Imports

The reform years have not seen dramatic changes in imports (Figure 22.3). Foodstuffs and industrial equipment remain the two principal groups of imports, and their share increased considerably in 1996 (Table 22.7). This fact reflects the crisis in the country's economy (which continues to this day). The slump in agricultural production, with the ensuing shortages of domestically produced foodstuffs and raw materials for some industries, called for imports of commodities in this group to be expanded. Specifically, while in 1989 imports met 20% of domestic demand, they accounted for over 50% in 1996.

The decline in the share of clothing and footwear in 1996 is due to the fact that these commodities are mostly brought in by "suitcase" dealers, who account for up to 70% of inexpensive clothing and footwear, the bulk of cheap bijouterie, about half of leather goods, and up to 30% of audio and video equipment imported into Russia (Table 22.8).

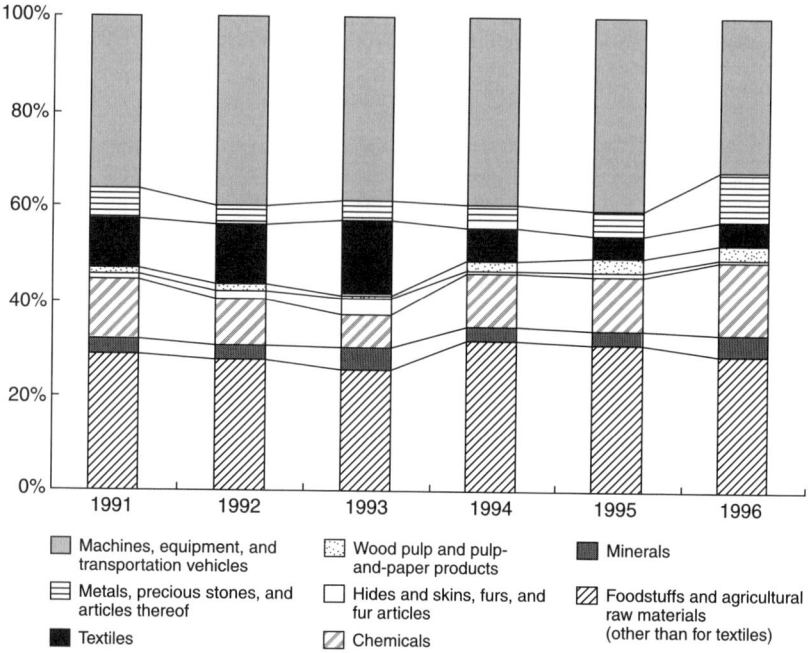

Figure 22.3
The structure of Russian imports. (Based on RF Goskomstat data.)

Table 22.7
Russian Import Structure (%)

	1989*	1996[†]
Foodstuffs and agricultural raw materials	16.6	25.0
Quick-frozen meat	0.75	2.3
Grain crops	3.8	1.0
Vegetable oil	0.34	0.2
Raw sugar	6.2	1.9
White sugar	0.11	0.2
Chemicals	2.85	14.4
Medical drugs	2.53	3.4
Clothes	3.77	1.0
Shoes	1.64	0.9
Ferrous metals	2.02	0.7
Steel tubing	2.55	1.1
Machinery and equipment	25.2	36.8
Other goods	42.84	16.7
Total imports	100	100

*Excludes interrepublic supplies
[†] The structure of imports from non-CIS countries, exclusive of unorganized trade.

Table 22.8
Unorganized Imports (in Billions of Dollars)

	1995	1996					1997		
	Total	Q1	Q2	Q3	Q4	Total	Q1	Q2	First 6 months
Total	14.2	3.7	4.0	3.6	3.1	14.4	3.9	2.7	6.6
Non-CIS	11.0	2.8	3.0	2.7	2.5	11.0	2.9	2.6	5.5

Source: Calculated from RF Goskomstat data.

The principal factors boosting the role of imports in the Russian economy include the convergence of domestic and world prices as a result of the ongoing domestic price liberalization policy. High freight, energy, and fuel costs and harsh loan terms have raised the average producer wholesale prices for staple commodities on the domestic market above the costs of purchasing them under import contracts. In 1997, the average price of an imported product was 7%–34% below the average price of the same product purchased from a domestic producer for rolled ferrous metals, steel pipes, polyethylene, car tires, beef, butter, sunflower oil, and sugar. Despite the raising of import customs duties beginning on 1 July 1995, the share of many imported goods in their total sales has expanded, since imports are economically convenient and financially less expensive. To illustrate, the share of imported vegetable oil in total domestic sales rose from 15% in 1994 to 29% in 1995, the share of imported butter rose from 21% to 38%, and the share of imported meat products rose from 19% to 24%.

The low quality and extremely narrow range of home and electronic equipment, electrical appliances, clothing, and footwear are offset by the swelling share of imports of these goods in total domestic sales. In particular, while the share of imported televisions amounted to 8% in 1991, it shot up to 60% in 1995. The share of imported knitwear skyrocketed from 14% to 78% over the same period, and the share of footwear rose from 8% to 82%.

The glut of commodities on the domestic market, mounting arrears, sluggish investment activity, falling effective demand at home, and measures to control imports combined to restrain imports in 1996. The imports (including suitcase trade) in that year ended at $59.8 billion (including $42.3 billion worth from countries other than the CIS), a decline of 2% over the whole of 1996 and 4% below the 1995 figure.

As investments in Russia weakened in 1996, the share of machinery and equipment in total imports dropped to 31.8%, from 33.7% in 1995, and the share of machinery and equipment imported from non-CIS countries fell to 37%, from 39%. The value of engineering imports was 8% lower in 1996 than in 1995, primarily because of less importing of machines and technology from non-CIS countries, which fell by 9%.

Imported food and nonfood consumer goods are flooding the domestic market as production plummets in Russian agribusiness and light and textile industries. The high level of dependence on imports requires safeguards for domestic producers in the form of special, antidumping, and compensatory duties on unfair imports, quotas on some imports, and any other measures that could help prevent or minimize damage to domestic producers.

22.3.3. Import-Export Dynamics After 1996

In 1997, Russian foreign trade edged up 2.4% from the 1996 level, to $155 billion. For the first time since 1993, foreign trade figures were helped by growing imports, at $67.6 billion, or up 8.6% from 1996. Exports, however, dipped 2%, to $84.4 billion.

The share of the "far-abroad," or non-CIS countries, in Russian trade in 1997 rose to 77.2%, from 76.6% in 1996. Trade with far-abroad countries (including suitcase trade) was $119.6 billion, an increase of 3.2% over the prior year, with imports increasing by 13.8% to $50.1 billion. For the first time since 1992, exports dropped by 3.3%, to $69.5 billion.

Rising imports and falling exports cut the balance of trade surplus in 1997 to $19.4 billion, which was 30.5% below the previous year's level.

The buoyant behavior of exports (which posted rates well above the pace of imports) between 1993 and 1996 was largely attributable to the foreign trade liberalization measures that had been put into effect. By 1997, the inventory of liberalization tools had been almost emptied. Imports, in their turn, were stimulated in 1997 by an increase in real incomes, with a large proportion of the increase going toward purchases of imported goods and services. Imports were also aided by the turnaround of investment in Russian manufacturing, which had reached a nadir in the early part of the year. The business rally that started in mid-1997 nudged up productive investment demand for imported products.

The fast growth of Russian exports in 1993–1996 was further stimulated by the strong world market for raw materials, which exerts a powerful pull on Russian exports, 46.9% of which consist of fuel and energy. The 1997 weakness on the world markets hit Russia painfully. The financial crisis in Southeast Asian countries, the principal consumers of nonferrous metals, sent prices for these metals tumbling. The decision by OPEC to raise oil production quotas by 10% and news of an impending increase in Iraq's export quotas under the UN Oil for Food program depressed prices for oil and petroleum products.

By 1997, Russian exports of key commodities had reached the maximum quotas allocated for most primary industries. During the year, Russian exports continued to be heavily weighted toward raw materials. The bulk of exports still consisted of fuel and energy resources (45.1%) and ferrous and nonferrous metals (19.6%). The share of machines and equipment remained low (8.1%), although it edged up by 0.3 percentage points over the course of the year.

Instruments alone showed an improvement in export rates. Little or no growth was posted by the biggest export items, such as heavy and general engineering products, electrical engineering and electronic goods, and motor vehicles. Airspace exports were shaky.

No changes occurred in the composition of imports, which continued to be dominated by engineering products (38.5%). Most of the growth in imports at this time is contributed by machines and equipment. The import of these items was stimulated by the lifting of the VAT on commodities (except for excisable goods) intended for integration in fixed productive assets imported by foreign investors as their contribution to the authorized capital of enterprises with foreign capital, and by exemptions from customs duties on equipment brought in under credit arrangements with foreign states and international financial institutions. These credit arrangements are in accordance with international agreements signed by the Russian Federation.

Noncompetitive domestically produced home appliances were elbowed out completely by imports. To prevent a total collapse of domestic production, the Russian government moved in with protectionist measures. Import licenses for color televisions were introduced, effective from 1 January 1998, to save domestic production from extinction, after it had plunged in 1996 to a minuscule 5% of its 1993 figure. Even as the industry was going under, some 2.5 million televisions were imported illegally in 1996. The license requirement will enable the State Customs Service and the State Tax Service to register all video equipment importers and improve the collection of duties and taxes from them. The market erosion caused by "gray" import of the least expensive models will, however, send retail prices up. This may compel importers to step up the import of components for televisions to be assembled by local enterprises.

In 1997, Russia's trade with CIS countries was valued at $35.4 billion in current prices, down 0.2% from 1996. Throughout the year, trade with CIS countries remained in surplus ($0.4 billion at year-end). The downward trend in trade with this group emerged in the second half of 1996 and continued into 1997. The share of CIS countries in Russia's foreign trade as a whole dropped to 22.8% (from 23.4% in 1996).

In 1998, Russian foreign trade turnover decreased for the first time in five years. The primary reasons behind this phenomenon included extremely unfavorable external conditions and growing internal difficulties; the importance of foreign trade as a stabilizing factor in production and as a material basis for market reforms weakened.

The foreign trade turnover of Russia, including unorganized exports and imports, fell in 1998 by 19.3% from the 1997 figure, to $130.6 billion. Exports fell by 18.3% (to $72.1 billion) and imports fell by 20.3% (to $58.6 billion).

Russia's foreign trade turnover with CIS countries, including unorganized imports, fell by 18.9%, reaching $102 billion in 1998.

The unfavorable situation for the staple commodities of Russia's exports on the world markets in 1997 continued to worsen in 1998. The instability of the world's economy due to the financial crisis experienced by a number of countries led to a further decrease in world prices for raw material commodities (energy resources, non-ferrous and ferrous metals, chemicals and timber). In consequence, the value of Russia's exports fell.

In 1999 the world business situation improved. The increase in domestic aggregate demand in Asia and Europe in the setting of OPEC's decision to limit oil extraction led to a significant increase in the price of energy resources. Oil prices increased in 1999 almost as fast as they had previously fallen.

Russia's foreign trade turnover with countries outside the former USSR was $91.6 billion in 1999, a decrease of 12.3% compared with the previous year's figure. Exports were valued at $61 billion (an increase of 3.6%) and imports at $30.6 billion (a decrease of 32.7%). The volume of unorganized trade in 1999 was estimated at $8 billion (a decrease of 37%).

The share of countries outside the former Soviet Union in the total foreign trade turnover of Russia was 80.2% (compared with 78% in 1998).

In 1999 Russia enjoyed a positive balance of trade. Exports exceeded imports by about $30 billion, or almost by two times more than in 1998. However, no qualitative positive shifts in foreign trade were observed over the year: the growing prices of raw materials and a falling effective demand for imported products after the ruble's devaluation caused a spontaneous shift in the structure of foreign trade. The volume of exports decreased by 3% compared with the previous year (making, according to preliminary estimates, about $75 billion), while imports fell by 30% (to about $40 billion).

The commodity structure of Russia's exports to countries outside the former USSR did not change substantially. The major role was played by fuel and energy commodities and metals, which accounted for about 65% of total exports to countries outside the former Soviet Union.

The decrease in imports in 1999, while positively affecting the competitiveness of Russian commodities on the domestic market, also improved certain sectors of the economy. On the other hand, decreased imports lead to certain economic and social problems, as some imported goods cannot be replaced with domestically manufactured goods in such a short period of time.

Russia's economy depends to a considerable degree on imports of food and the raw materials necessary for food production; the share of food products in imports is stable at about 26%. At the end of 1999, food imports from countries outside the former Soviet Union decreased, to $6.3 billion (a decrease of 28% from the previous year's figure). The value of meat imports fell by 45.6% on average (including a decrease in poultry imports by 3.8 times), while grain imports grew by four times. About 70% of grain imports were used for food aid.

Another important imported commodity is medicines, as Russia imports two-thirds of their required volumes. In 1999 medical imports from countries outside the former USSR fell by 1.6 times.

The decrease in imports of these various commodity groups could not be replaced quickly with domestically manufactured products. Market saturation is being achieved by the gradual restoration of imports of a number of foodstuffs and food raw produce (grain, unrefined sugar, meat, oil) and medicines.

Machinery and equipment account for about 40% of imports from countries outside the former Soviet Union. In 1999 imports of these goods fell by 40%. A decrease in the purchase of equipment not manufactured in Russia but necessary for the development and modernization of domestic production is a rather negative trend.

According to the federal law, *On State Regulation of Foreign Trade*, a "Register of Instances of Discrimination and of Violation of Bilateral and Multilateral Obligations in Regard to Russian Persons on Markets as Broken Down by States and on the List of Measures Undertaken or Planned in Order to Protect Lawful Trade and Economic Interests of the Russian Federation" was introduced in 1999. As of 6 January 2000, ninety-seven cases of the application of restrictive measures in regard to Russia had been entered into the register, of which sixty-seven (about 77%) were antidumping procedures. In the period 1992 through December 1999 the number of cases of restrictive measures being applied had grown from thirteen to ninety-seven, including twenty-two cases in 1999. The export of ferrous metallurgy products suffered the most, accounting for about 77% of applications of restrictions.

The situation of some other industries, especially the chemical industry, is also grave. At this time twenty-one restrictive measures are applied to the products of the chemical industry, of which ten procedures were started in 1999, including eight antidumping procedures.

The losses Russian exports suffer because of unjustified and discriminatory measures are estimated at about $2 billion annually, with losses from antidumping restrictions accounting for about $1.5 billion. With regard to export restrictions, Russia is among the most discriminated-against countries in the world.

Across countries, the most restrictions are imposed on Russian exports by the European Union (fifteen), the United States (thirteen), India (nine), and Turkey (eight). There are a number of reasons why antidumping measures, which are legal measures to protect domestic markets, are of a particularly discriminatory nature when it comes to Russia, which is not a member of the World Trade Organization. The legal basis lies in the national legislation of the United States and a number of other countries, until recently including those in the European Union, which regard Russia as a country with a nonmarket economy. Such a label means that stricter norms in antidumping investigations are applied to Russian exporters.

While the issues of Russia's accession to the World Trade Organization are being settled, work is under way that would allow the Russian Federation to be recognized as a country with a market economy even before it joins the World Trade Organization. One alternative is to gain recognition of discrete sectors in the Russian economy as market sectors. As a result of Russia's efforts to gain sector-by-sector recognition, Thailand, Indonesia, and Canada have begun applying a market paradigm in their antidumping surveillance of Russian exporters.

V

The Social Price of Reforms

23

Certain Trends in the Evolution of the Labor Market

Alexander Smirnov

23.1. Forecasts That Went Wrong

Economic and political publications of the late 1980s and early 1990s were furiously engaged in forecasting the effect the coming market reforms might have on labor markets in Russia. The oracles were particularly worried by the ghost of officially recognized unemployment making its first appearance since 1930, when the last labor exchange was shut down in the USSR. The majority of divining academics and political scientists warned of the possibility of mass unemployment erupting in the country immediately upon the launch of reforms.

As early as April 1991, a law, *Population Employment in the RSFSR* (hereinafter the Federal Employment Law), was enacted in Russia. Under the law, the government recognized an individual to be the owner of his abilities to engage in creative work and, in the same breath, disowned any responsibility for maintaining full employment of the population. The government, however, committed itself to giving material support (through the payment of unemployment benefits) and social assistance (by providing vocational retraining facilities, filling job vacancies, and so forth) to a worker having the status of an officially registered unemployed person. To fulfill its promise, the government put in place, in accordance with the law, a labor market infrastructure consisting of two components, institutional (the Federal Employment Service) and financial (a population employment fund independent from the federal budget). By January 1992, the government had girded itself for the hard decisions it was facing to regulate the labor market.

Reality, however, has overturned both the expectations of the optimists and the apprehensions of the pessimists. Between 1992 and

Table 23.1
Dynamics of Numbers of Registered Unemployed During the Russian Reform Process

Year	Registered Unemployed (as at Year-Start) (thous. of persons)	Yearly Increase (thous. of persons)	Increase in Numbers of Registered Unemployed per 1% of GDP Decrease (thous. of persons)
1992	61.5	516.2	36.9
1993	577.7	257.8	28.6
1994	835.5	800.3	66.7
1995	1,635.8	691.2	172.8
1996	2,327.0	179.0	29.8
1997	2,506.0	−507.3	—*
1998	1,998.7		

*The Russian GDP increased by 0.4% in 1997.
Source: Calculated from data provided by the RF Ministry of Labor and Social Development.

1998, employment in Russia dipped much less precipitously than the country's GDP. For every 1% of GDP decline in Russia from 1992 to September 1999, the workforce employed eased down by 0.3%. Over the years of reforms, employment in Russia was reduced by 9.2 million in all, or 12.5%. On the bottom line, unemployment has not exploded in staggering numbers on a countrywide scale.

Indeed, the country's jobless register showed slightly over 1.3 million unemployed at the start of October 1999 (compared to 61,000 in early 1992), that is, fourteen out of every 100 workers left without a job were put on the official list. The remaining eighty-six persons (excepting, first, retirees on old-age pensions; second, people who had quit working, encouraged by big pay hikes won by other family members; and third, those who died while still in the workforce) joined the category of the unemployed, whose numbers were calculated by the technique developed by the International Labour Organization (ILO).[1]

The numbers of registered unemployed (Table 23.1) during the reform process have been affected by both objective factors (GDP dynamics) and subjective ones (registration rules for jobless workers and rules for granting and paying unemployment benefits).

---

1. The difference between these categories of unemployed is that support for the registered jobless requires allocation of funds from the consolidated government budget, while the unregistered unemployed can only claim the attention of politicians because of their unofficial status.

Table 23.2
Dynamics of Officially Registered Number of Unemployed in Russia, 1994–1997 (%)

Period	1994	1995	1996	1997
1st quarter	29.67	17.43	15.00	1.74
2nd quarter	16.26	4.34	−2.65	−9.80
3rd quarter	13.18	4.98	−5.18	−10.30
4th quarter	14.74	10.59	1.46	−3.10
Yearly total	95.79	42.25	7.69	−20.23
For reference: average monthly increase in number of unemployed (thous. of persons)	66.7	57.6	14.9	−42.3

Source: Calculated from data provided by the RF Ministry of Labor and Social Development.

The rapid 9.4-fold increase in the number of registered jobless in 1992 can be ascribed both to the abrupt contraction of the GDP during the "shock therapy" stage of the reforms and to certain material advantages that an individual acquired by signing up with public employment service agencies as a registered unemployed.

In 1997, while the GDP edged up only insignificantly, the roster of the registered unemployed was reduced by over 20%—the first reduction in all of the reform years (Table 23.2). The drop in the number of registered unemployed—and therefore, with the economically active population stable, in the unemployment level—was nothing new. It had already been experienced before, even if for only a brief period of time.

Clearly, the onset of economic stabilization was one of the factors contributing to a reduction in the number of unemployed. In a situation in which many enterprises maintain inflated payrolls, however, there must be other reasons to account for the reduction. This assumption is justified primarily by the fact that the decline in total unemployment figures determined using the ILO technique in 1997 was fully consistent with the decrease in the absolute number of registered jobless.

In addition to economic stabilization, other reasons accounting for the decline in the number of unemployed in 1997 include (1) the growing arrears in unemployment benefits, a typical ingredient of the budgetary crisis in government employment policy; and (2) continued enforcement of the revised version of the Federal Employment Law passed in 1996, which toughened the criteria for putting jobless on the register and taking them off, and related the amount of unemployment benefits to the average pay in a respective member of the Russian Federation.

After eight years of reforms, registered unemployment has held at a socially acceptable level, peaking in February to April 1997 (at 3.5% of the economically active population) and falling to 1.7% in early 2000.

The financial and economic crisis of 1998 did not tangibly affect the situation on the registered labor market. Despite declining effective household demand and the resulting bankruptcy of many small and medium-sized businesses, accompanied by cuts in the workforce, far from all of those so left unemployed applied to the public employment service agencies seeking employment. As a result, the number of registered unemployed continued to decrease, until by early 2000 it was 1,263 thousand. This process was accompanied by increasing general employment in the economy, from 63.3 million in early 1999 to 65.1 million in early 2000.

23.2. Part-Time Employment: Objective Data and Subjective Interpretation

The figures for so-called full unemployment, which is measured by the ILO technique, have been at the center of endless economic and political speculations. From early 1997 through 1998, the number of fully unemployed individuals was 4.3 to 4.4 million larger than the number of registered unemployed. Not all of the fully unemployed have any real claim to getting employed, and because they do not sign up with the public employment service, the government does not, under the current laws, bear any financial responsibility (in respect to employment guarantees).

The total number of unemployed calculated by the ILO technique includes many persons working part-time or laid off. As a specific phenomenon of the Russian labor market in the period of transition, the two latter categories of employees in aggregate numbered 3.7 million people in September 1995, 5 million in September 1996, 4.2 million in September 1997, 3.4 million in September 1998, and 1.8 million in June 1999.

Part-time employment can be explained by several factors, and it is advantageous to both the employers and, strange as this may seem, the unemployed themselves.

Employers' motivations had largely financial underpinnings: the one-time social benefits that, under the current legislation, are to be paid to an employee fired under a downsizing plan cost the employer more than part-time wages paid for a considerable period of time, and still more than placing the employee on leave without pay. This situation logically led some employers to maintain surplus labor. A mere 20% of all employers found downsizing the best solution to payroll redundancy.

The advantages some employees saw in part-time work were both economic (the possibility of moonlighting, and plenty of free time under the cover of official employment) and social (an opportunity for women to care for their children while maintaining uninterrupted service as a safeguard in case the earnings of other household members proved insufficient, and, not least, an opportunity for part-time workers to avail themselves of the employer's social infrastructure services).

Hired workers who did not draw pay from their employers had three principal sources of livelihood: their small subsidiary plots, earning on the side, and living on relatives' earnings. The surveyors were satisfied by a high proportion of respondents citing work on the side as a source of livelihood at a time when their core work earned them nothing. In the final analysis, it is sideline work that provides a new and vigorous work motivation for an employee (in the final phase of the USSR, some 10%–15%, at most, of the workforce earned on the side).

As a result, about one in four employees did not quit their jobs because they were content with the situation that obtained, which gave them a chance to moonlight or work on the side. It may be assumed that the problem of transforming unofficial employment and workplace relations into official ones is one of the greatest challenges in a period of economic stabilization in a country and a key factor leading to stabilization.

The choices of sideline business were limited, however, by the reigning economic depression, and the large numbers of hitchhikers among the economically active population were a cause for concern.

A serious consideration against dismissing any part-time employees was that they could not subsequently be rehired; this reason was cited as a restraint on dismissals by 47% of the employers.

The onset of economic recovery, employers believed, would fully resolve the part-time employment problem: more than 60% of the employers believed they did not have on their payrolls anyone who could not be hired back once the economy was set on a recovery course. The conclusion that suggests itself is that the market reforms have not altered the structure of demand for labor at large and medium-sized enterprises anywhere to the extent feared before the start of reforms.

In all probability, the managers of many enterprises did not, four years into the reforms, adequately understand the idea of the reforms and counted on resuming production of "prereform" output, relying on their old technologies, as the economy surged back to life. This delusion, found chiefly among "old-guard" managers, could only be dissipated as economic proficiency rose in general and as new blood in the form of "efficient owners" was injected into the economy.

23.3. Registered Labor Market Indicators

Apart from demand on the registered labor market, which in this situation is expressed in the number of registered unemployed, the supply to demand ratio is an important characteristic describing the behavior of the labor market. Demand is expressed by the number of job openings, information about which is accumulated by employment service agencies. The number of registered unemployed per one vacancy is called market pressure in Russian statistics. The dynamics of this indicator were unfavorable in the early years of reforms.

Indeed, if we disregard professional skills, age, and gender, an unemployed person could, in the opening weeks of 1992, pick one out of 13.6 job openings to get employed. In the next quarter the number of vacant jobs per unemployed person fell to 3.8, and in September of that year the number of unoccupied jobs per registered unemployed person dropped to 0.9.

The supply and demand relation on the registered labor market worsened continuously. Whereas the pressure on the Russian labor market was two persons per job opening in early 1993, that figure rose to 2.4 in 1994, five in 1995, 7.5 in 1996, and 9.8 in early 1997.

Subsequently, as the number of registered unemployed started to go down, the labor market pressure started to ease too, and by early 1998, each opening could be claimed by an average of 5.8 unemployed job seekers. This sudden relaxation of pressure was certainly

Table 23.3
GDP Performance and Dynamics of Job Openings Filed with Government Employment Agencies, 1992–1997

Year	GDP (% of Previous Year)	No. of Openings (thousands)		Change in No. of Openings (%)	GDP Decline Elasticity of Decrease in Jobs
		As of 1 January	As of 31 December		
1992	86	841.0	306.9	36	4.6
1993	91	306.9	351.7	115	Not calculated
1994	87	351.7	325.6	93	0.6
1995	96	325.6	309.4	95	1.3
1996	95	309.4	254.6	82	3.0
1997	100	254.6	369.3	145	Not calculated
1992–1997	62	841.0	369.3	44	1.5

Source: Calculated from data provided by the RF Ministry of Labor and Social Development.

affected by the seasonal factor, but there is statistical evidence that the background trend had also made a U-turn. In early August 1996 there were on average 7.3 jobless individuals per opening, but by the start of 1998, the labor market pressure had softened to 5.4 jobless individuals per opening.

The financial and economic crisis of 1998 did not principally affect this trend. Thus, in early 1999 there were 5.9 registered unemployed per opening, while in early 2000 the ratio was 2.1 per opening. These data indirectly confirm the growth of the real sector of the national economy observed in 1999.

It is interesting to look at the way the economic slump influenced the job opening dynamics (Table 23.3).

In 1992 there was a wild scramble to shed job openings—one of the simplest of employers' responses to the changing situation arising in the course of the economic reform. No financial exertion was required on the part of employers to plug redundancies, while at the same time the exercise allowed them to scale down their obligations to take on persons referred to them by the employment service to fill job openings. Also, a reduction in the number of openings gave the impression of "overfull" employment, a typical fact of life in the Soviet-era economy.

Employers' behavior with respect to job openings was later significantly modified: for an average 319,600 openings in the period from late 1992 to 1997, the largest absolute deviation from the average was 65,000, or 20%, which was registered in late 1996.

The jerky spurt of almost 50% in the number of job openings in 1997 could be viewed as additional confirmation of Goskomstat's official claims that the GDP paused in its downward slide and registered a modest rally.

Since early 1999 the number of openings announced by employers has grown steadily except during the winter months, when the seasonal decrease has persisted.

The demand and supply proportions on the labor market are a key factor influencing the length of unemployment. An increase in the average length of unemployment, along with a rising proportion of persons with a long unemployment record among the jobless, is an undesirable development both economically and politically, as it will eventually swell the size of marginal groups of the population. Russia's reform record shows that long-standing unemployment is a problem that has not been resolved against the background of the economic slump.

Specifically, in December 1994, 146,900 registered persons, or 9% of the registered unemployed, had been without a job for over a year. In December 1995 that figure jumped to 326,200, or 14% of the registered unemployed, and in December 1996 it climbed to 457,500, or 18.2%. Despite a decrease in the total number of jobless persons, the number of unemployed who had been on the register for more than a year rose further, to 459,800, or 23% of all unemployed. Later this proportion stabilized, and in 1999 the share of unemployed on the register for over a year fell slightly, to 22.6%, while the average duration of unemployment was 7.6 months.

The nonuniform composition of the chronic unemployed category is a factor mitigating the impact of long-standing unemployment (in excess of one year). Some of the jobless are really hopeless prospects, no matter how much they thirst for a job, while others are happy to accept chronic unemployment as a way of life.

There is a ray of hope, however, in the fact that the average length of unemployment among young people, the most prized category on the labor market, is below the overall average. In early October 1997, for example, it was 6.8 months, or 9.5% below the national average.

23.4. Regional Labor Markets

In addition to the social stratum of marginal unemployed that has formed, and is growing, in Russia, a solid group of regions have developed their own depressed labor markets. Registered unemployment in seventeen of the eighty-eight constituent members of the Russian Federation was at least twice the countrywide average in early 2000. In contrast to these continuously depressed regions, however, some regions' unemployment levels have bettered the countrywide average (Table 23.4).

Significantly, instability in the rankings of regions according to their unemployment levels reflects the influence of subjective factors on the registered labor market. Uncertainty complicates the operation of employment service agencies in the regions, which are confused about the measures they should adopt to adequately regulate the regional labor markets in response to changes in the local situation (Tables 23.5 and 23.6).

The numerical associations between the key indicators characterizing the labor markets in the constituent regions of the Russian Federation are described in terms of Spearman's rank correlation coefficients and shown in Table 23.7 (the ranks were represented by slots occupied by regions according to the values of labor market indicators).

In 1997, as in previous years, the following three associations proved to be the closest: (1) unemployment level and number of jobless per one job opening at year-end, (2) unemployment level at year-end and length of unemployment in December, and (3) the number of jobless per one opening and the length of unemployment in December. The remaining associations were, by tradition, minor.

Some background climb in correlation coefficients in 1997 merits special attention. This likely reflects the declining role of subjective factors in shaping registered labor market trends.

23.5. Workforce Movement: Sectoral Aspects

Even as total employment fell throughout the years of reform, from 73.8 million in 1991 to 64.6 million in September 1999, the workforce was overflowing from sector to sector (Table 23.8). In the period surveyed, the largest reductions in employment occurred in manufacturing (from 30.3% to 24.7%) and construction (from 11.5% to 9.5%), while the highest spikes were registered in retailing and catering, logistics, marketing, and procurements (from 7.6% to 10.4%), agriculture (from 13.5% to 14.9%), and in education, culture, and the arts (from 9.8% to 11.2%).

Table 23.4
Top 10 Regions with the Highest and Lowest Unemployment Levels, 1994–1998 (as of 1 January in Respective Years)

Region	1998	1997	1996	1995	1994	No. of Times in the Top 10 Group
Regions with the highest unemployment level						
Ivanovo oblast	+	+	+	+	+	5
Ingush Republic	+	+	+	+	+	5
Vladimir oblast	76	+	+	+	+	4
Republic of Daghestan	+	+	75	+	+	4
Kalmyk Republic	+	+	+	+	75	4
Pskov oblast	77	+	+	+	+	4
Arkhangelsk oblast	+	+	+	77	78	3
Kirovskaya oblast	+	+	76	+	76	3
Kostroma oblast	50	66	+	+	+	3
Udmurtian Republic	+	+	+	75	77	3
Yaroslavl oblast	33	71	+	+	+	3
Komi-Permyak autonomous okrug	68	60	77	+	+	2
Republic of Mordovia	74	+	74	78	+	2
Republic of Karelia	+	72	66	63	67	1
Komi Republic	+	61	67	73	64	1
Koryak autonomous okrug	+	75	64	56	54	1
Nenets autonomous okrug	75	76	+	74	71	1
Chuvash Republic	57	77	78	76	+	1
Regions with the lowest unemployment level						
Belgorod oblast	+	+	+	+	+	5
Moscow	+	+	+	+	+	5
Orenburg oblast	+	+	+	+	+	5
Smolensk oblast	+	+	+	+	+	5
Volgograd oblast	+	13	+	+	+	4
Rostov oblast	+	+	+	+	11	4
Republic of Sakha (Yakutia)	17	+	+	+	+	4
Lipetsk oblast	+	+	+	17	19	3
Republic of Tatarstan	27	11	+	+	+	3
Aghin-Buryat autonomous okrug	72	70	23	+	+	2
St. Petersburg	+	+	24	34	56	2
Stavropol krai	+	20	11	21	+	2
Karachayevo-Circassian Republic	+	46	55	47	15	1
Kursk oblast	12	15	+	28	21	1
Novosibirsk oblast	15	+	19	31	40	1
Samara oblast	58	39	21	11	+	1
Ust-Ordynsky Buryat autonomous okrug	18	+	17	19	29	1
Chita oblast	78	73	44	+	13	1

Note: Data were evaluated for 88 RF constituent members exclusive of the Chechen Republic. A region's presence in either group is marked with a +. If a region does not belong with either group, it is identified by its unemployment ranking among 88 constituent members of the Russian Federation.

Source: Calculated from data provided by the RF Ministry of Labor and Social Development.

Table 23.5
Distribution of Subfederal Regions by Variation in Registered Unemployment Numbers

Growth (reduction) in Registered Unemployment Numbers During a Calendar Year	1995	1996	1997
<0.5	0	1	3
0.51–0.75	1	6	30
0.76–1.00	3	26	39
1.01–1.25	19	31	15
1.26–1.50	26	13	1
1.51–2.00	33	8	0
2.01–3.00	5	3	0
≥3.01	1	0	0

Source: Calculated from data provided by the RF Ministry of Labor and Social Development.

Table 23.6
Distribution of Regions by Supply and Demand on the Labor Market*

No. of Unemployed per Job Opening	1 Jan. 1995	1 Jan. 1996	1 Jan. 1997	1 Jan. 1998
<1.00	3	1	1	1
1.01–2.00	3	0	1	4
2.01–5.00	25	19	6	17
5.01–10.00	23	17	20	18
10.01–25.00	21	26	27	22
25.01–50.00	9	14	17	13
>50.00	4	11	16	13

*Excludes the Chechen Republic.

Source: Calculated from data provided by the RF Ministry of Labor and Social Development.

Table 23.7
Spearman's Rank Correlation Coefficients for Selected Indicators of the Russian Labor Market in 1996 (Top Figure in Cell) and 1997 (Bottom Figure in Cell)

	Growth Rate for Numbers of Unemployed	Unemployment at Year-End	Unemployment Numbers per Job Opening at Year-End	Length of Unemployment in December	Newly Employed as a Share of Total Unemployed Stricken off the Register in December
Growth rate for unemployment numbers	1 1	−0.26 0.31	−0.15 0.29	0.32 0.51	−0.02 0.14
Unemployment at year-end	−0.26 0.31	1 1	**0.81** **0.78**	**0.50** **0.56**	0.08 0.10
Unemployment numbers per job opening at year-end	−0.15 0.29	**0.81** **0.78**	1 1	**0.46** **0.56**	0.21 0.26
Length of unemployment in December	0.32 0.51	**0.50** **0.56**	**0.46** **0.56**	1 1	0.03 0.26
Newly employed as a share of total unemployed stricken off the register in December	−0.02 0.14	0.08 0.10	0.21 0.26	0.03 0.10	1 1

Source: Calculated from data provided by the RF Ministry of Labor and Social Development.

Table 23.8
Sectoral Structure of Employment in Large and Medium-Sized Companies in 1991 and 1996

	Sectoral Structure of Employment, January–December 1995	Sectoral Structure of Employment, January–December 1996	Increase (reduction), in percentage points
Total	100	100	
Industry	30.3	24.7	−5.6
Agriculture and forestry	13.5	14.9	1.4
Construction	11.5	9.5	−2.0
Education, culture, and arts	9.8	11.2	1.4
Trade and public catering, material and technical supply, marketing and procurement	7.6	10.4	2.8
Transportation	6.6	6.6	0.0
Health care, physical training, and social security	5.8	7.0	1.2
Housing and community amenities, nonproductive consumer services to the population	4.3	5.0	0.7
Science and research support	3.7	2.4	−1.3
General government staff	2.3	2.9	0.6
Communications	1.2	1.3	0.1
Credit, finance, and insurance	0.6	1.4	0.8
Other sectors	2.6	2.7	0.1

Source: RF Goskomstat.

In the mid-1990s, the bulk of employment was provided, as before, by large and medium-sized enterprises. However, even their employment level was falling faster than the countrywide average.

In 1996, the drive toward downsizing at large and medium-sized enterprises swept through the majority of industries. Most contractions due to redundancy occurred in four industries—manufacturing, construction, agriculture, and retailing/catering. These industries shed 3.2 million employees, and actually reduced the companies' payrolls.

The downsizing in other industries was in part offset by higher employment figures in six industries, including some in the nonproductive sector. This phenomenon, by itself, was a welcome de-

Table 23.9
Distribution of Full-Time Small-Company Employees by Sector, 1996

Sector	Average Payroll	
	Thousands of Persons	% of Total
Total	6,269.1	100
Trade	1,901.4	30
Construction	1,612.8	26
Industry	1,427.0	23
Other sectors	1,327.9	21

Source: RF State Regional Planning Committee.

velopment for the prospects of a postindustrial economy emerging in Russia.

As is shown in Table 23.9, small businesses have a slightly different employment pattern. A comparison of the sectoral employment structure in small businesses versus large and medium-sized enterprises shows at least three clear differences. First, small businesses have a much greater proportion of people employed in the nonproductive sector: in 1996, the proportion of the workforce employed in trade in the total employment at small businesses was four times as high as the proportion of trade-related employment in the total number working at large and medium-sized enterprises.

Second, small businesses may prove to be more competitive than larger undertakings in material production sectors as well. For example, the respective proportions of employment in construction were 26% and 7%, respectively, or a 3.7-fold difference in 1996.

Third, a considerable differentiation in activity types was typical of large and medium-sized enterprises. For example, the three biggest employers (manufacturing, agriculture, and public education) accounted for 55% of the total workforce, leaving the remaining industries with 45%. The proportion was different for small businesses. Enterprises in the three largest industries (trade, construction, and manufacturing) employed 79% of the total full-time workforce, with the remaining industries accounting for the 21% left over.

Industries also differed sharply in the workforce turnover rate (Table 23.10). All industries can be broken down into several groups according to workforce turnover rate. By far the most interesting groups are those with the highest and lowest rates of turnover.

Table 23.10
Workforce Turnover by Economic Sector, 1995–1996

Sector	Ratio of the Sum Total of Newly Hired and Newly Redundant Employees to Average Annual Workforce Numbers (%)		Change, in Percentage Points
	1995	1996	
Total	48.3	40.1	−8.3
Real estate business	125.9	149.6	23.7
General commercial market supply	88.8	73.8	−15.0
Construction	84.5	58.0	−26.5
Housing and community amenities, nonproductive consumer services to the population	69.9	65.4	−4.5
Forestry	64.3	54.1	−10.2
Geology and mineral resource exploration, surveying, and hydrometeorological services	63.3	51.6	−11.7
Trade and public catering	61.5	48.9	−12.6
Communications	57.9	54.6	−3.3
Procurement	51.0	46.2	−4.9
Transportation	50.7	42.1	−8.6
Material and technical supply and marketing	50.3	40.8	−9.5
Industry	49.5	39.9	−9.6
Credit, finance, insurance	45.0	40.0	−5.0
IT support	43.8	37.7	−6.1
Health care, physical training and sports, social security	42.5	37.1	−5.4
Culture and arts	37.6	34.7	−2.9
Science and research support	35.1	26.7	−8.5
Public education	32.4	29.3	−3.1
Agriculture	31.3	28.0	−3.2
General government	29.6	33.0	3.4
Other sectors	69.6	57.8	−11.7

Source: Calculated from RF Goskomstat data.

In 1995, the high-turnover groups included organizations in the real estate business, in which staff turnover was 30% (it was 50% in 1996); organizations engaged in general commercial market supply business, whose staff turnover was 88.8% (73.8% in 1996); and construction enterprises, where staff turnover was 84.5% in 1995 (falling considerably, to 26.5%, in 1996). In 1996, housing and utilities and businesses providing nonproductive consumer services, with a 66.6% workforce turnover (69.9% in 1995), came third in staff turnover rates.

It may be assumed that the high staff turnover rate at enterprises in the first two industries was due to the unstable financial standing of a majority of them and the lack of adequate social safeguards for their employees. The substantial staff turnover in construction apparently was related both to the specifics of the construction cycle, which is heavily exposed to seasonal factors, and to the investment crisis. High staff turnover in housing and utilities and nonproductive consumer services may be explained in part by the orientation of some of them toward the public's effective demand, which so far is limited (in 1996, for example, the sales of services to the public dropped by 7% in comparable prices), and in part by the technological specifics and working conditions prevailing in housing and utilities.

Among the industries with the lowest staff turnover rates in both 1995 and 1996 were enterprises and organizations in government, agriculture, and public education, which replaced only 29.6%, 31.3%, and 32.4% of their respective payrolls in 1995. The corresponding figures for 1996 were 33%, 28%, and 29.3%.

The extremely low staff turnover rates in these industries can be attributed to various causes. In government, for example, an employee enjoys the benefit of a social safety net, despite the relatively low pay. For the majority of farm workers, on the other hand, low turnover more likely reflects the absence of alternative employment. Finally, education workers may be anchored to their jobs by, apart from the lack of professional alternatives, the prospects of nonbudgetary financing sources for educational institutions.

It is important to note that enterprises in virtually all industries (except for real estate) registered a significant, almost 20%, slowdown in staff turnover rates in the period in question. This fact may be chiefly associated with the financial limitations restricting intersectoral work force overflows.

The fastest rates of new staff hiring in 1995 were posted by enterprises and organizations in real estate, general market supply commerce, housing and utilities, nonproductive consumer services, and construction. Construction alone dropped off this list in 1996. At the other extreme, the slowest rate of new hirings in both 1995 and 1996 was registered in agriculture, information and computer services, government, and public education.

Enterprises in different industries had different staff cut rates. Whereas in 1995 the number of redundancies at real estate businesses was 24.6% of the average payroll, staff reductions involved a mere 0.5% of the payroll in organizations in health care, physical culture and sport, and social services.

As a general trend in 1996, layoffs typically rose to 2% of payroll, or 0.4% above the 1995 figure.

Unsolicited dismissals as an employment restructuring factor had different importance for different industries. Whereas 8.9% of the workers on the government payroll quit government service of their own free will in 1996 (9.4% did so in 1995), 42.7% (42.4% in 1995) of workers in real estate quit voluntarily, or 4.8 (4.5) times as many as had left government service voluntarily.

The causes behind the high rates of voluntary exits were, in principle, identical for all industries similar to real estate (real estate, general market supply, retailing and catering, construction): the insecure market position of enterprises in such industries (an uncertain market niche), dissatisfaction with material and other working conditions, the strength of the social safety net, and so on. However, the high rate of voluntary departures probably testifies to the competitiveness of the employees who quit the industries in question.

On the other hand, the lower rate of voluntary departures in some industries may have different causes. Government employees, for example, have fewer incentives to quit because of their reliable safety net, while people in public education and science and science services may lack employment alternatives, or may combine salaried government work with a side job.

23.6. Employment Policy Financing

Between 1992 and 2000, the government's employment policy in Russia was financed by the nonbudgetary State Employment Fund (SEF). In the years it has been in existence, the SEF has developed into a major financial entity. Nevertheless, it has not been formally institutionalized, and its current business has been run by the former Federal Employment Service of Russia (and, after it was disbanded in 1996, by the Ministry of Labor and Social Development of the Russian Federation). The SEF consists of the so-called federal pouch formed from a specified proportion of employers' insurance contributions collected in the regions and by employment funds in the regions.

In 1995, the insurance contributions paid by most employers (at a rate of 2% of the payroll) added up to Rb 6.17 trillion, or 0.37% of the country's GDP. Considering the SEF carryovers at the beginning of 1995 (Rb 0.81 trillion), the SEF's total financial resources were estimated at Rb 6.98 trillion, or 0.42% of GDP.

Beginning on 1 January 1996, employers' insurance contribution rates were cut by 0.5% (one of the chief factors prompting the cut was the systematic excess of SEF's receipts over spending in the years 1992–1995). As a result, the SEF's receipts of Rb 7.01 trillion in 1996 lowered the SEF's share in Russia's GDP by 0.06%, to 0.31%. Together with the carryovers (Rb 0.58 trillion), the share of the SEF's total resources (Rb 7.59 trillion) dropped to 0.34% of GDP, a decline of 0.08%. At a 23% growth rate in 1996, the SEF's resources rose by a very modest 0.82% in real terms. In the first half-year of 1997, the SEF collected Rb 3.82 trillion, or 0.31% of GDP. Less the carryovers, the SEF ran up a budget deficit of Rb 56 billion in the first half of 1997. In 1998 the receipts of the SEF budget were Rb 8.7 billion (in denominated rubles), or 0.32% of GDP.

Among all extrabudgetary social funds, the SEF ran the biggest budget deficit in the first quarter of 1997. It spent 2.9% more than it collected. This is significantly higher than the 0.5% spending overrun by the Federal Pension Fund or the tiny 0.1% excess of spending over collection of the Social Insurance Fund (the Federal Obligatory Medical Insurance Fund spent 6.8% less than it collected). Later, the SEF budget stabilized, chiefly because of rising arrears in unemployment benefits. Thus, by year-end 1998, it made almost Rb 3 billion (in denominated rubles), or 64% of the SEF expenditure for payment of unemployment benefits.

Saddled with a budget deficit, the SEF (which was turning a profit in the early years of business) kept switching priorities between the spending items of its budget. The SEF allowed spending to grow in areas of passive employment policy financing and to decline in areas of active employment policy measures.

In particular, there was a considerable growth in spending on programs of material support for the unemployed (income support). Whereas spending under this item amounted to 37.2% of the SEF's total expenditures in 1995, in 1996 it rose to 52%, an increase of 14.8 percentage points. In the second half of 1997 the figure jumped by another 9 percentage points, to 61%. Later, the share of these expenditures in the CEF's budget stabilized, amounting to 57.9% in 1998. In the grip of its budget crisis, the SEF is increasingly functioning as a financial institution fulfilling government social guarantees (primarily by paying unemployment benefits).

These developments are further confirmed by changes in the spending structure of the "income support" item (Table 23.11). In 1998, the share of funds used to pay unemployment benefits was 16.8 percentage points higher than in 1995, while that of spending on early pensions, one of the most expensive methods of providing social support for the jobless, decreased by a factor of 4.2. The situation existing at the time restrained an active employment policy, which had a most painful effect on regions with high registered unemployment levels.

On the other hand, the share of spending on such active employment policy programs as financial support, vocational training, retraining, job counseling, and public works dropped from 26.5% in 1995 to 16.8% in 1996, and fell further to 14.3% in 1998 (Table 23.12). Already in 1995 it was smaller than the share of spending on material support for the unemployed, or 0.71 rubles under the active employment policy programs per 1 ruble of direct material support paid to the unemployed. In 1996, this spending item plunged to 0.32 rubles, and in 1998 it fell again, to 0.25 rubles.

Table 23.11
Structure of SEF Expenditure on Income Support for the Unemployed (%)

Payment Type	1995	1996	1st Half of 1997
Total	100	100	100
Unemployment benefits	77.1	90.3	94.2
Lump-sum benefits	1.4	1.2	0.8
Pre-retirement age pensions	21.5	8.5	5.0

Source: Calculated from data provided by the RF Ministry of Labor and Social Development.

Table 23.12
Structure of SEF Expenditure on Active Employment Policy Programs (%)

Expenditure	1995	1996	1st Half of 1997
Total	100	100	100
1. Financial support	67.1	43.3	33.5
Compensatory payments	2.3	2.0	1.3
Retention of jobs	37.2	13.0	4.4
Creating new jobs	26.1	26.3	25.8
Subsidies for setting up new businesses	1.5	1.9	2.0
2. Vocational training and retraining and job counseling	25.1	43.3	55.6
3. Public works	7.8	13.4	10.9

Source: Calculated from data provided by the RF Ministry of Labor and Social Development.

Out of the eighty-seven regions (less the Republic of Bashkortostan and the Chechen Republic), only three—St. Petersburg, Moscow, and Vladimir oblast—began fiscal year 1999 without unemployment arrears. Overall, by the start of 1999, the unemployment benefits per one registered jobless were 1,549 rubles in arrears. For comparison, enterprises and organizations owed 1,216 rubles in back pay per person employed in the economy by the beginning of 1999.

The existing budgetary restrictions on benefit payments became a key factor in the steady decline in the number of registered jobless in 1997–1999, many of whom had lost material inducements to register with state employment service agencies.

Whatever the future institutional and financial fate of the State Employment Fund, people making the final decisions would be well-advised to note that socialization of the SEF's expenditures and a refusal to use SEF resources to finance active employment policy programs would strengthen the formation of a stable group of social dependents—the unemployed, whose financial claims would eventually, given the activity of the able-bodied population, force the question of raising unemployment benefits. This debate could spur the search for sources to finance this dependent population.

24

Household Income in the Period of Economic Reforms

Igor Kolosnytsyn

24.1. Socioeconomic Differentiation of the Population in Russia, 1992 Through 1999

The postcommunist transformation in Russia resulted in momentous changes in the income distribution pattern among various population groups. Income differentiation is unavoidable during an economic transition that aims, among other tasks, to establish a meritocracy. Moreover, the redistribution of property in the course of privatization gives certain segments of the population an opportunity to derive income from property. Where wealth has been accumulated in a lawful way, a growing differentiation resulting from property distribution is a legitimate outcome of reform as well. At the same time, the absence of legislative restraints on the processes involved can lead to countless abuses in the course of the accumulation of capital. These abuses frequently cause an absurdly rapid growth in income differentiation, which incites extreme social tensions.

As the number of high- and superhigh-income earners increases, so also does the number of low-income earners. This polarization is often a natural result of reform: low-skilled workers who do not have the proficiency required by the market have an incentive to seek retraining and more taxing employment, but far from all of them have the necessary ability to adjust to new conditions. Spreading unemployment and poverty appear to be an inevitable fallout of economic reform, at least at the outset.

Welling ownership stratification and increasing poverty have become particularly acute since the launch of the reforms in Russia. Consider the following:

- Compared with 1991, the size of the population earning incomes below the subsistence level more than doubled in the period 1992–1994.
- The proportion of the economically active population rose among the poorest segments.
- A group of territories with high concentrations of the poor emerged.

A large body of work by Western economists on income inequality problems bears out the conclusion that individual wage distribution explains up to 80% of variation in the final per capita income distribution. This is not exactly the situation in Russia, where the share of earned wages in the total income of the population has contracted sharply in the past five years. Consequently the explanatory power of individual wage distribution is significantly weaker than in other countries (in Russia, wages and self-employment compensation generally account for between two-thirds and three-quarters of all personal income).

A useful illustration of the role of wage inequality in the resultant inequality of population incomes is provided by the growth of intersectoral wage differentiation (Table 24.1). These data show that personal incomes have risen fastest, relative to the countrywide average, in the fuel and energy sector (more precisely, in extractive industries with a clear export orientation).

As economic restructuring continued, the wage differentiation between leading industries and manufacturing enterprises and the economy in general was somewhat blunted. The handicap initially borne by export-oriented industries because of the gap between domestic and world prices was attenuated. But wages then plunged to extremely low levels in lame-duck industries that enjoyed only limited potential to adapt to market conditions, in particular mechanical engineering, light industry, and agriculture. In 1996, the average wages in the last two sectors dropped below the subsistence level for the able-bodied population. Wages in the publicly financed sector remained very low, even when compared with the 1991 figures.

The current intersectoral wage differentiation is giving rise to interregional income differentiation. Moscow's money income is five times higher than the average for the regions of the Central Economic Area and eight to ten times as high as those of outside regions. Toward the end of 1999, when the per capita income in Moscow topped Rb 6,800, the Russian average stood at about Rb 1,700. This

Table 24.1
Ratio of Average Accrued Monthly Wages and Salaries of Employees in Companies and Organizations to Average Russian Level, by Economic Sector, 1991–1997 (%)

	1991	1992	1993	1994	1995	1996	1997*
Total economy	100	100	100	100	100	100	100
Industry	111	118	108	104	114	115	119
of which:							
Electricity	167	221	210	205	212	198	199
Fuel	183	290	255	237	248	236	250
Oil production	202	336	311	282	289	279	306
Oil refining	121	242	204	207	221	201	205
Gas	206	429	402	448	398	383	400
Coal	198	293	250	230	233	186	179
Ferrous metals	127	170	143	121	134	139	134
Nonferrous metals	176	250	216	197	223	195	194
Chemicals and petro-chemicals	108	128	101	94	105	101	107
Machine building and metal working	97	87	83	80	84	78	83
Forestry, woodworking, pulp and paper	107	110	90	83	102	92	91
Building materials	118	116	115	114	109	100	99
Light industry	105	85	71	54	54	52	53
Food processing	119	127	130	122	124	120	118
Agriculture	84	67	61	50	47	45	40
Construction	127	134	133	129	136	138	138
Transportation	120	146	151	150	157	144	143
Housing and community amenities and nonproductive consumer services	80	82	92	96	107	—	—
Health care	76	66	76	76	71	75	70
Education	71	61	68	69	63	68	64
Science and research support	94	64	68	78	75	81	87

*January–September 1997.
Source: RF Goskomstat.

gap was largely due to the concentration of financial and lending institutions and foreign currency investments in Moscow.

The specific qualities of interregional and intersectoral income differentiation are important in estimating trends in population income differentiation. Statisticians commonly use two indicators for this purpose—the Gini coefficient and the fund index, which characterizes the gap between the incomes of the richest 10% of the population and the poorest 10% (Tables 24.2 and 24.3).

Income inequality, therefore, peaked in 1994, diminished slowly until 1997, then increased again in 1998–1999, mainly due to the

Table 24.2
Dynamics of the Gini Coefficient in Russia, 1990–1997 (%)

Year	Gini Coefficient
1990	23.3
1991	
1992 (June)	27.5
1992 (Dec.)	32.7
1993 (June)	32.5
1993 (Dec.)	35.5
1994 (June)	36.5
1994 (Dec.)	40.9
1995	38.1
1996	37.5
1997 (Jan.–Sept.)	37.0

Sources: Data provided by the RF Government's Central Institute of Economics and the RF Goskomstat.

financial and economic crisis of August 1998. A possible explanation for this income inequality pattern is that a financial stabilization program that aims to eliminate the source of inflationary incomes can check the growth of inequality. During a crisis period, however, other factors begin to alter the income structure in such a way as to increase inequality. Meanwhile, the interregional income differentiation in Russia continued to broaden, regardless of low inflation rates.

Changes in income inequality in the 1990s become clearer if we look at income data by quintiles (Table 24.4). The tougher monetary policy and lower inflation rates negatively affected the poorest 20% of the population, whose relative position had tangibly improved in 1995 and 1996. The concentration of resources in the hands of the

Table 24.3
Dynamics of the Fund Index, 1991–1997 (Ratio of Income of the Richest 10% and the Poorest 10% of Households)

Year	Ratio of Richest/Poorest
1991	4.5
1992 (Dec.)	8.0
1993	11.2
1994	15.1
1995	13.5
1996	13.0
1997 (Jan.–Sept.)	12.5

Source: RF Goskomstat.

Table 24.4
Distribution of Total Household Cash Incomes by 20% Quintiles, 1991–1997

	1991	1992	1993	1994	1995	1996	1997*
Total cash income	100	100	100	100	100	100	100
Group I (lowest income)	11.9	6.0	5.8	5.3	5.5	6.5	6.3
Group II	15.8	11.6	11.1	10.2	10.2	10.9	10.6
Group III	18.8	17.6	16.7	15.2	15.0	15.5	15.5
Group IV	22.8	26.5	24.8	23.0	22.4	22.4	22.5
Group V (highest income)	30.7	38.3	41.6	46.3	46.9	44.7	45.1

*January–September.

most affluent 20% paused briefly (probably because of both the narrowing of the intersectoral income differentiation and fewer opportunities for high-yielding investment). Growth in the share of income attained by the most affluent 20% of the population turned positive only at the end of the 1998–1999 period. The changes in the relative standing of the three quintiles in between were less conspicuous. Between 1994 and 1996, the share of the three intermediate groups in the total population income was around 48%, with a slight rise in 1997.

An analysis of interregional differentiation over the past few years highlights two opposite trends. In an overwhelming majority of regions, the income differentiation indicators (Gini coefficient) fell even faster than the Russian average, which stayed within the brackets of 0.3 to 0.35. The growing gap between the country's leading regions and outsiders, however, resulted in some regions posting an explosive increase in income differentiation, with the interregional component of the resultant differentiation indicator rising and the share corresponding to intraregional differentiation falling.

Income inequality indicators such as the Gini coefficient are commonly measured on the basis of household budget surveys. The survey results are not to be taken at face value; respondents are often vague about the real size of their incomes or intentionally understate them (by at least 15%–20%). The final results derived for different countries are not directly comparable. Nevertheless, their comparison may be useful for rough conclusions.

Interregional and intersectoral differentiation of incomes contributes to a much faster growth of income differentiation in Russia than in any other economy in transition. In Poland, for example, the Gini coefficient rose from 0.19 in 1990 to 0.24 in 1992; in Romania it crept up from 0.23 in 1989 to 0.25 in 1993; and in Hungary the fund index rose from 4.7 to 6.3 between 1986 and 1992.

It is generally accepted that the growth of average per-capita income initially pushes up the Gini coefficient and the income differentiation level somewhat. This process then allows the differentiations to drop, in conformity with the classic hypothesis formulated by S. Kuznets in his 1955 paper, "Economic Growth and Income Inequality." This trend does not, of course, apply always and everywhere. The distribution of the population according to income for Russia as a whole is close to income distribution figures recorded in low-income countries (Ghana), medium-income countries (Tunisia), and even some high-income countries (Switzerland and Britain). In the case of a high-income area such as Moscow, however, the figures are more similar to those for countries notorious for their high income differentiation (Brazil).

24.2. Poverty Line Changes

The growth of income inequality and the corresponding increase in the proportion of individuals with relatively low incomes lead to widespread poverty. During an economic slump, poverty intensifies because of declining real incomes and because the widening gap in income levels pushes increasingly more families out of the middle class and into poverty.

According to an accepted definition, poverty exists in a country when a certain group of the population cannot attain a level of well-being equal to the reasonable minimum in that country, or to meet its "basic needs." Available statistics do not allow a comprehensive evaluation of the situation of the poorest segments of the population in terms of basic needs. On the brighter side, Goskomstat is soon to launch, in cooperation with some international organizations (the World Bank and Eurostat), special surveys of households to obtain more complete estimates of a family's economic potential.

Meanwhile, we have to be content with a simpler approach that identifies as poor families whose incomes have dropped to the "poverty line," or subsistence level. It is extremely difficult to use the subsistence level as an objective measure, for people can, in general, survive if they drastically reduce their expenses. An alternative to a subsistence-level definition of poverty is a social definition: Poor families are those that cannot achieve for themselves the minimum standard acceptable in their area at a particular time. In a psychological sense, poor families are those that feel they are deprived of the benefits enjoyed by another stratum of society, the reference group with which they compare themselves.

The official cost of living in Russia has been computed since 1992 by a technique developed by the Labor Ministry (and identified with the poverty line in official statistics). The input parameters entail dietological factors. Specifically, the minimum caloric requirement in a diet is determined and a minimum food basket is designed whose structure reflects the actual food consumption structure of the poor segments of the population. The data on the spending structure of the least-provided-for groups of the population (determined by Labor Ministry techniques developed in 1990 and 1991) are then used to develop "standards" for measuring the other components—nonfoods and services—of a subsistence budget. It is accepted that spending on food products amounts to 68% of the subsistence budget, and the consumer basket has been differentiated according to eight climatic zones, as well as sex and age. The figures characterizing the cost of living dynamics and the poverty line for 1992 to 1997 are shown in Table 24.5.

It is tempting, on the basis of Table 24.5, to draw an optimistic conclusion about the steady contraction of the poverty scale in 1995–1997 as a result of slowing rates of inflation (inflation takes its greatest

Table 24.5
Dynamics of the Subsistence Minimum and the Poverty Line, 1992–1997 (per Capita, in Thousands of Rubles)

	1992	1993	1994	1995	1996	1997*
Total population	1.9	20.6	86.6	264	369	412
Working-age population	2.1	23.1	97.4	297	415	463
Pensioners	1.3	14.4	61.0	186	260	291
Young children	1.9	20.7	87.4	269	373	416
Ratio of average per-capita income to subsistence minimum (%)	210	213	234	202	211	214
Population with incomes below subsistence minimum (mill. of persons)	50.2	46.9	36.2	36.6	31.9	31.3
Poor population (%)	33.5	31.5	24.4	25.0	21.6	21.2

*January–September.
Source: RF Goskomstat.

Table 24.6
Consumer Spending Structure in the Subsistence Budget and According to Survey Data on Consumer Spending by Russia's Poorest 10% of Households, 1993–1996

Consumer Spending Structure	Subsistence Budget	1993	1994	1995	1996
Food	72	56.4	61	64	63
Nonfoods	20	40.0	29	22	21
Services	8	3.6	10	14	16

Source: RF Goskomstat.

toll on poor, fixed-income families) and narrowing of the income distribution gap. Actually, however, these statistics are not completely reliable, chiefly because of the techniques used in estimating the poverty line. The crisis of 1998–1999 caused a dramatic bulge in the lowest income quintile, and the relevant indicators of 1999 were rather close to the levels of 1992. The year 1992 was a critical year in social terms.

It is inappropriate to use the 1992 yardstick today. Profound changes have occurred since 1993 in the spending structure of the poorest 10% of the population, while calculation of the subsistence minimum remains tied to outdated figures from 1990 and 1991 (Table 24.6). Moreover, the consumer spending structure of the poorest groups is changing dramatically, with expenses on services growing particularly fast. These changes will probably become more radical in the future as the reform in housing and utility services goes on. In this situation, continued reference to a poverty line tied to the price of a fixed food basket would result in serious underestimations of the poverty calculation.

Looking only at the share of families subsisting on incomes below the poverty line is clearly insufficient to make a comprehensive judgment about poverty as a socioeconomic phenomenon. This yardstick is increasingly dismissed in research papers as unreliable. For this reason, two other indicators, poverty depth and poverty acuteness, are commonly used in addition to this core indicator.

Poverty depth is defined as the amount by which the income of a family is less than the subsistence minimum (as a percentage of the relative cost of living). *Poverty acuteness* is calculated as the sum of squared deviations of poor families' actual incomes from the cost of living, applied to the total number of families in the population. In the latter case, the more significant the individual deviations are, the higher is the index.

Table 24.7
Composition of the Poor Population in 1992 and 1994

Age	1992	1994
Total population	100%	100%
Children < 6 years	9.9	9.6
Children 6–15	18.4	20.3
Young people 16–30	17.7	19.3
Women 31–54	17.4	20.1
Men 31–59	16.8	19.7
Women > 55	15.2	6.0
Men > 60	4.6	2.1

Source: RF Goskomstat.

Because of wide regional differences in poverty in Russia, it makes sense to use all of these indicators to obtain a comprehensive characterization of poverty. For example, the share of poor families in the Nizhny Novgorod and Bryansk regions was identical in 1995, yet the poverty acuteness index in Bryansk region was 50% higher than in Nizhny Novgorod region (0.051 versus 0.033).

The poorest regions are particularly prone to stagnant poverty, or temporary poverty that develops into chronic poverty. Gradually, the initially loose groups of the poor acquire clearly defined outlines. According to T. V. Yarygina, the very fact of living in a particular area or being employed in a particular occupation is an indicator of poverty.[1]

Certain changes are taking place in the demographic composition of the poor population as well, with the share of the working-age population rising and that of old-age pensioners declining somewhat, and the proportion of children remaining approximately the same (Table 24.7).

Families with children under six years of age are the worst off: in 1994, over 60% of children in this age bracket lived in poverty-stricken families. In comparison, only 28% of old-age pensioners subsisted in poverty.

In the specific situation in Russia today, traditionally vulnerable segments of the population—large families, the disabled, single-parent families, old-age pensioners, and students—are being joined by new and large groups of jobless individuals, child-care workers,

---

1. T. V. Yarygina, "Poverty of the Population, Poverty of the State," in *Income Policy and the Social Security of the Population* (Moscow: Labor Institute, Russian Labor Ministry, 1995), 33–46.

and armed forces personnel. These new groups are economically active, and have traditionally been able to achieve an adequate standard of living through work.

It is very difficult today to forecast changes in the scale and acuteness of poverty in Russia. Poverty could not be contained during the period of reforms: real incomes fell throughout almost the entirety of that period. A sustainable reduction in the scale of poverty can only be realized with economic recovery, when incomes are distributed impartially or redistributed in favor of the poorer segments of the population. International experience suggests that investment in human capital among the least secure population groups is one of the vital prerequisites for a successful fight against poverty.

Organization of targeted assistance to the poor (so-called program targeting) must become a key area for such efforts. Yet there is nothing in Russia today like an integrated methodology to provide social assistance to poor families, or a common approach to assessing their needs. Various privileges are enjoyed by around 100 million people. Yet, whereas the list of privileges accorded at the federal level has been systematized, the privileges, subsidies, indemnities, and benefits payable at the regional and local levels have not been organized. Beginning in 1997, pilot social assistance programs got under way in three federation members—the Republic of Komi and the Voronezh and Volgograd regions. Each of these areas is testing a possible needs-assessment technique. The results of this testing are then used to draw up extreme poverty benefit payment schemes. In the Republic of Komi, for example, a benefit is paid, under the republic's Subsistence Minimum Law, when the full per capita income of a family falls below the so-called guaranteed per capita monetary income, amounting to between 40% and 50% of the subsistence minimum. The full per capita income of a family is determined on the basis of its economic potential, which is measured as the income that the family members could achieve by using their property rationally and the family's earning potential. (In practice, the share of the additional "imputed" income calculated by the technique accepted in the republic is not great, the economic potential being just 5%–10% higher than ordinary income.) No formalities, such as references or certificates, are required for a family to be put on the needy register, although the information provided by the applicant may be verified by social service workers. Interestingly, the registration results turned out to be very remote from official statistics, which place the number of people living below the poverty line at more than 30% of the republic's population. In 1997, a tiny 4% of the Komi population was placed (in the absence of any administrative qualifications) on the needy register. The gap was just as wide between the percentages of "statistically officially poor families" in the other pilot regions and the number of actually registered families. The introduction of destitution monitoring and a uniform poverty allowance to be provided on a targeted principle to population groups living in extreme poverty can, in the long term, significantly reduce the amount of social spending and allow budget funds to be used more efficiently.

Recently, pressure has been building for a technique to be developed for use in appraising the efficiency of poverty-control programs at a time when such programs are in the works. In the future, the spread of poverty will have to be assessed on the basis of various factors. Hopefully, a new calculation will replace subsistence level as the sole (and far from irreproachable) indicator of the poverty line.

Finally, poverty-control programs to be developed for the long term should take into account the existing gap between monetary and gross family incomes, particularly in view of the growing role of revenues from subsidiary farms, which amount to 50%–60% of the included monetary incomes of rural families and families living in small towns.

24.3. Impact of Inflation on Nominal Assets of Households; Inflation and Poverty

This section looks at the relationship between the observable income differentiation and poverty level, on the one hand, and the inflation rate, on the other. The calculations made by the author of this section confirm the existence of a stable statistical relationship between these processes during a period of high inflation. At the same time, as inflation rates fall, income differentiation begins to be affected by a significantly different set of factors than those we discussed in the previous section.

The burden of the inflation tax on a particular population group (conventionally understood as decile or quintile groups in this context) depends on the structure of its assets and liabilities, the speed with which it spends its earnings, methods used to make provisions, and the proportion of savings.

We could try to model the effect of inflation on the demand for money in circulation, the demand for ruble-denominated deposits with savings banks and commercial banks, and average wages (this last indicator is used as an approximate estimate of cash income). In particular, in the period between 1992 and 1996, the short-term elasticity of real demand for money relative to the inflationary variable (price level) was equal to 0.07; thus, the appropriate relationship cannot be considered to be statistically significant. (The model is described in paragraph 1 of the postscript to this chapter.)

The amount of inflation tax on ruble-denominated deposits depends on whether the real interest rate is positive or negative. The inflation tax on bank deposits has varied significantly, acquiring negative values in some months of 1994 and 1995. Calculations made using regressive equations to estimate the dependence of deposits with the Sberbank savings bank and commercial banks on the inflation variable in the period between February 1992 and July 1996 show that whereas inflation has a negative effect on bank deposits in real terms, this effect is not statistically significant for commercial banks.

The results of the calculation show that the share of inflation tax in monthly incomes in the period 1992–1996 grew almost in proportion to the inflation rate. In particular, for the monthly inflation rate of 10.6% in February 1994, the inflation tax came to about 5% (with payment made once a month). In March 1993, when monthly inflation ran at around 20%, the share of the inflation tax in incomes almost doubled from the month before, to 9.17%. When payments are made twice a month, the share of the inflation tax is halved.

Which groups carried the main burden of the inflation tax at a time of high inflation in Russia? To answer this question, we must consider the structure of real assets of the different income groups of the population.

Portfolio structure is affected by a variety of factors. Having deposits with Sberbank was an attractive option for certain groups of the population, as the deposits were guaranteed by the government. During the period 1992–1996, however, Sberbank's interest rates were significantly lower than the rates offered by commercial banks, so that Sberbank's share in the (growing) total bank deposits slid until early 1996. After a sharp cut in the refinancing rate in mid-1997, Sberbank's share in total bank deposits rose again, as the interest rates of both Sberbank and commercial banks stabilized at a low level, even though Sberbank's rates were very near the inflation rate, while commercial banks accepted deposits at slightly higher rates.

Until 1 October 1993, the minimum deposit accepted by Sberbank was 10 rubles, and after 1 August 1995, the minimum deposit rose to 300,000 rubles. It is generally held that access to high-yielding deposits is easier for people earning higher incomes and for more mobile population groups (inflation tax regression).

The results of surveys conducted by the Union Center for Public Opinion Studies (VTsIOM) allow us to estimate the share of savings in the total sum of incomes earned by population groups enjoying different income levels. From this we can guess whether or not high-income groups can "evade" paying the inflation tax by keeping some of their income in savings accounts. Low-income groups tended more frequently than medium- and high-income groups to keep their savings in ruble-denominated deposits. This means, of course, that, given the low elasticity of demand for cash and the high inflation rates in 1992–1994, the inflation tax fell most heavily on the low-income groups of the population. The medium-income group had a considerable part of its savings with Sberbank, while the highest-earning groups of the population spent much of their incomes to purchase hard currency, or placed them on deposit with commercial banks. In 1993, the low-income groups were more inclined to place their savings on deposit with Sberbank, although their cash savings in rubles were smaller than the cash savings of the other groups.

There is then a strong relationship between income level and savings structure: low-income groups more often than the other groups prefer to keep their rubles in cash and less often use their savings to buy foreign exchange. The choice of methods used by different income-level groups to keep their savings contributes to a higher inflation tax regression.

Therefore, the low-income groups of the population pay the highest inflation tax (in relative terms). The explanation is simple enough: higher-income groups have easier access to income-bearing (or at least indexable) assets. Moreover, the poorer segments of the population cannot shield their wages from "sudden" inflation, which has a more destructive impact on them, since they have few additional sources of income or financial assets.

We have examined the effect of inflation rates on the dynamics of real wages. (Because of seasonal real wage variations in Russia, we first had to carry out a seasonal smoothing.) We have discovered a statistically significant correlation between the growth of the real wage logarithm and the inflation rate logarithm (with a one-month lag). The correlation coefficient was found to be −0.45. Changes in real wages are sufficiently closely related to inflation rates. In particular, a 1% change in the inflation rate causes the real wage to move in the opposite direction by 0.06%. In other words, as inflation subsides, real wages rise, and conversely, as inflation rates rise, real wages fall. This is why the poorest segments of the population, whose wages are not indexed, suffer the heaviest losses from growing inflation.

In a situation in which money incomes, wages, and pensions are subject to an inflation tax, the growth of inflation spurs poverty. A regressive analysis of the relationship between the poverty level and inflation rates from data for 1994 and 1995 is complicated by certain circumstances associated with the approach used by Goskomstat to calculate poverty indicators during that period. The budget surveying technique was altered in 1995, making the 1994 and 1995 data on the numbers or proportions of the population subsisting on incomes below the subsistence level hardly comparable at all.

In a very general form, the results of the economicostatistical investigation of the relationship between inflation and poverty can be summed up as follows. If the 20% segment of the population having incomes below the subsistence line is taken as the base, a 1% reduction in the inflation rate must reduce the proportion of the poor by 0.5%. It must be emphasized again that this relationship is only typical of periods of fast inflation rate drops. In more stable periods, the numbers and proportion of the poor population may also be affected by other socioeconomic factors, with the explanatory power of the inflation factor becoming increasingly less significant.

24.4. Postscript

This section presents the mathematical calculations used to derive the regression data on the impact of the inflation tax.

1. *Inflationary losses* (or, otherwise, the government's gain) are measured in the form of inflation tax on the money base (cash plus reserve claims plus extra reserves). They are represented by the following equation:

$$it = \left[\frac{\pi_t}{\sqrt{1+\pi_t}} \right] \left(\frac{MB_t}{GDP_t} \right) \tag{1}$$

where MB = the average monthly value of the money base, GDP = the GDP value for a month, π = inflation rate, and it = inflation tax.

To measure the inflation tax on money in circulation, the demand for money in circulation is estimated (in real terms) on the basis of equation (2):

$$\frac{M0}{P} = F\left(i, \frac{E}{P}, \frac{\text{Income}}{P}, \left(\frac{M0}{P}\right)_{-1}, \varepsilon\right),$$

$$F_i < 0,\ F_{\text{Income}/P} > 0,\ F_{E/P} > 0,\ F_{(M0/P)_{-1}} > 0 \qquad (2)$$

where M0 = cash in circulation, P = price level, i = nominal interest rate, E = nominal exchange rate (in rubles per US dollar), and Income = nominal income of the population (index$_{-1}$ – preceding period). The income figure includes wages, social benefits, rent on property, and dividends. The GDP in real terms and real wages are used to represent the population's real incomes approximately.

Variations in the real interest rate are shown by the equation parameter corresponding to external "disturbances." The regressive equation was estimated by the least common squares method, using monthly data for the period between February 1992 and July 1996. The t-statistic values are given in parentheses (the exchange-rate factor was found to be statistically insignificant):

D (LRM0) = −0.00 + 0.23*D (LRM0(−1)) − 0.07*D (LINF)
(−0.11)   (2.38)   (−2.27)

+ 0.33*D (LRW) + 0.28*D (LRGDP) (3)
    (3.27)   (3.14)

where D (LRMO) = the first difference between the logarithms of the amount of money in circulation (in real terms); D (LINF) = the first difference of the inflation level logarithms; D (LRW) = the first difference of the logarithms of average wages in real terms; and D (LRGDP) = the first difference of the GDP logarithms in real terms.

In accordance with equation (3), therefore, the short-term elasticity of real demand for money, in terms of the inflation level, was 0.07 in the period from 1992 to 1996. In other words, demand for real money in circulation is not very sensitive to inflation.

2. *Calculation of the share of inflation tax in the total amount of wages.* Assume that an employee has saved nothing in the preceding period, draws his monthly wages in cash, and spends the income over a calendar month. On this assumption, the current cash balance is equal to half his monthly income, and the inflation tax, which he

pays every month, is equal to:

$$it_m = 0.5y_m(\pi_m/\sqrt{1+\pi_m}) \qquad (4)$$

Now assume that the employee has no money in savings, receives her wage twice a month, and spends the money evenly over two weeks. In this case the cash balance must be equal to half the two-week income, $y_{m/2}$, and the inflation tax, which the employee will pay every two weeks, will be:

$$it_{m/2} = 0.5y_{m/2}\left(\pi_{m/2}/\sqrt{1+\pi_{m/2}}\right) \qquad (5)$$

If $\pi_{m/2}$ designates the inflation level over the two-week period, calculated as $\pi_{m/2} = (1+\pi)^{1/2} - 1$, then the ratio of the annual inflation tax to the annual income (if the latter corresponds to average annual wages) would be:

$$26[0.5y_{m/2}\left(\pi_{m/2}/\sqrt{1+\pi_{m/2}}\right)] / 26\pi_{m/2} = 0.5\left(\pi_{m/2}/\sqrt{1+\pi_{m/2}}\right) \qquad (6)$$

VI Economic Reform and Public Opinion Dynamics

25

Key Trends in the Population's Attitudes Toward Market Reforms

Tatiana Koval

25.1. On the Threshold of Reforms

The need for far-reaching economic reform was appreciated by Russian society—the common man—in the heyday of perestroika. Perestroika was perceived not only as one of the greatest events in the history of Russia but also as a global event. Most people, however, saw it as an effort to improve the socialist system and socialist method of managing the economy. According to polls conducted by the Sociology Institute in the late 1980s, perestroika was most frequently understood as a genuine social revolution and a return to Leninist principles (40.5%). A large proportion of the respondents, however—29%—took a more skeptical view of perestroika, considering it no more than a "papering over" or a "facelift" of socialism that changed nothing of substance. A mere 7% viewed perestroika as Gorbachev's departure from communist principles. However, as time went on, disappointment both in perestroika at large and in its pace and methods in particular increased.

The proportion of workers in Moscow dissatisfied with the advance of reforms was 38% in 1987 and as high as 56% in 1988. In the autumn of 1992, almost half of all Russian citizens considered perestroika "an effort not worth making."[1] For positive changes to be tangible, it was essential, according to many respondents (38%), to seek "stabilization of life," an idea associated with the "imposition of firm law and order." Moreover, the realization of social justice and a return to the socialist principles of social equity was interpreted by one in four respondents as "stripping the bosses of their privileges."

---

1. For more, see T. I. Zaslavskaya, "Transformation of Russian Society as a Process to Be Monitored," *Information Bulletin*, VTsIOM, Moscow, no. 2 (1993): 6.

A substantial minority—10%–15% at most—linked the success of perestroika with the continued expansion of freedom, openness, and a broader choice of business options.[2]

Yet in the perestroika years a peculiar "hybrid" social consciousness, an ability to combine opposite opinions, came to the surface. Thus, the same person could approve of both a market economy and a planned economy, desire democracy and the rule of a "firm hand," and express communist beliefs and be sympathetic to the idea of monarchy at the same time. Therefore, on the one hand, more than a third of Russian citizens (36%) were reported by the Union Center for Public Opinion Studies (VTsIOM) to believe, to the last day of the Gorbachev era, that socialism was the "right system," with an additional 11% firmly against public discussion of the very possibility of "our" system being replaced by capitalism. On the other hand, more than half of survey respondents advocated the transition to a market economy, with about one-fourth of respondents supporting the idea of preserving a planned economy. On the whole, by the early 1990s Russian society appeared to be ready for resolute steps toward the transformation of economic life. However, this readiness to a considerable degree originated in an idealization of market relations and in a utopian hope for an "economic miracle"—a better life for everyone that was to be achieved quickly and painlessly.

25.2. The First Stage of Economic Transformation

25.2.1. Price Liberalization

Strong anticommunist feelings were a conspicuous feature of public attitudes in the early years of independent Russia. "Democracy," "market," "private ownership," and "privatization" were readily embraced by the public as "anti-communist" values. When these concepts assumed a definite form, however, the public began to be tormented by contradictions. In 1991 and 1992, a considerable pro-

---

2. Yu. A. Levada (ed.), "Soviet Common Man: Experience of the Social Portrait at the start of the 90s" (Author, photocopy). These data are entirely consistent with data obtained in a survey by the Sociology Institute and the Philosophy Institute of the USSR Academy of Sciences. In the late 1980s 48.7% of respondents expressed support for a market economy, and only 20.4% supported the planned economy. See *The Socium in Crisis: Our Society in Three Dimensions*, ed. N. I. Lapin and L. A. Belyaeva (Moscow: 1994), 231.

Figure 25.1
Survey Responses

Having a relatively low but guaranteed wage/salary and feeling secure about your future	45%
Working hard and earning much, even with no prospect of a secure future	27%
Having a relatively low wage/salary but less intensive work or more time to spare	10%
Running your own business at your risk	10%

Source: Yu. A. Levada, ed., *A Common Soviet*, 45.

portion of Russian society supported the overall policy of Boris Yeltsin and his government. While supporting the course of radical economic reform in general, however, people did not approve of specific economic transformations. Only a small fraction—between 10% and 15%, by most estimates—approved of the specific steps taken to reform the country's economy. The pivotal issue was the freeing of prices.

The majority of Russian citizens viewed price liberalization negatively and were nostalgic for regulated prices. Probably many of them did not, in their minds, relate market relations to free prices. Every Soviet citizen knew from practical experience that low prices can only be regulated by government and that high prices are rigged, unjust, and extortionate.

Finding themselves in a post-Soviet environment, many continued to prefer guaranteed poverty over uncertainty with the promise of affluence (Figure 25.1). According to VTsIOM data, as early as 1990–1991, when the country faced a choice between free prices and rations, a tiny 6% opted for free trade, while around 60% supported rationing. Having learned the Soviet lesson well, the public feared price increases above all.[3]

According to Public Opinion Foundation (FOM) data, the freeing of prices in 1992 was received favorably by only 15% of Russian citizens, with 71% disapproving of it (Table 25.1). Fifty percent were "dead set" against liberalization. In 1992, 58% wanted controlled prices back; a year later that figure had risen to 63%. True, the

---

3. Levada, Soviet Common Man, 45.

Table 25.1
Attitudes Toward Price Liberalization and a Possible Return to Price Controls

Social Group	Price Liberalization		Return to Price Controls	
	Pos. (%)	Neg. (%)	Pos. (%)	Neg. (%)
Pensioners	5	89	80	9
Employees in spending organizations	14	75	80	9
Collective farmers	15	75	62	22
Workers	15	66	60	24
Unemployed	20	65	55	25
Government administrators	22	60	29	49
Military officers	27	57	45	40
Private farmers	37	61	27	55
Government company managers	38	46	27	55
Entrepreneurs	49	38	23	64
Total population	15	71	58	24

Public Opinion Foundation data. See *Polis* 4–5 (1993).

number of free price supporters rose slightly, to 20%, thanks to those who had been noncommittal a year before (Figures 25.2 and 25.3).[4]

In general, price liberalization was an extremely unpopular move, and the erstwhile eagerness to advance toward a market economy evaporated in its wake (Figure 25.4). Instead of an alluring prospect, the harsh contrast of the market to the socialist environment turned out to be a rude reality for many.

Even though about half of the population did not believe that price liberalization could have positive results, the appearance of all staple foods on the shelves was evidence that the most acute problem—overcoming the supply deficit—had been resolved. In April 1993, between 70% and 90% of respondents noted the ease with which all food staples could be purchased.[5]

Interestingly, these VTsIOM data look more encouraging than the official statistics on the consumer market. A point to be made is that Goskomstat (the Federal Statistics Board) released the official figures

---

4. Public Opinion Foundation, "Russian Society on the Eve of September 21: Evaluation of the Freeing of Prices and Their Possible Return to Government Regulation," *Polis* 5 (1993); "Russian Society: Value and Priorities. Privatization in Russia," *Polis* 6 (1993): 54–59.

5. *Information Bulletin*, VTsIOM, Moscow, no. 2 (1996).

Figure 25.2
Survey Responses

Which of the following propositions regarding government price controls would you subscribe to?			
	December 1990	December 1991	December 1992
The government should establish fixed prices for most goods.	44%	45%	45%
The government should establish fixed prices for a relatively narrow range of goods.	38	30	30
The government should control prices as little as possible.	6	11	10
Hard to say.	13	13	15

Source: *Information Bulletin*, VTsIOM, Moscow, no. 1 [1993]: 29.

Figure 25.3
Survey Responses

Which system of economic management is better, the market-oriented one or the planned one?						
	1992			1993		
	Feb.	Mar.	Dec.	Mar.	June	Oct.
The market is better.	52%	42%	42%	33%	39%	33%
Planning is better.	27	32	30	35	34	33
Hard to say.	21	25	28	32	26	34

Source: *Information Bulletin*, VTsIOM, Moscow, no. 1 [1995].

Figure 25.4
Survey Responses

> *Responses to a 1992 poll*
> **If you had known in 1985 what it would be like today and where the changes that had just started in this country would lead, would you or would you not have supported them then?**
>
> | | | |
> |---|---|---|
> | Yes, I would. | 36% | (57% of those selecting this response were university and higher school students; 80% were cooperators and entrepreneurs) |
> | No, I would not. | 46% | (71% of those selecting this response were pensioners) |
> | Hard to say. | 18% | |
>
> Source: Polls conducted by the Institute for Social and Political Studies of the USSR Academy of Sciences. See *Reforming Russia: Myths and Realities*, 120.

about the real situation in the market for particular products. People answering polltakers were not so unbiased in their responses, for they compared the current situation with the dreary days when store shelves stood almost empty.

On the other hand, those who did not believe that food supplies had improved were right, to a certain extent: the consumer market was flooded largely because the public's purchasing power had contracted. The proportion of people who noted a wider variety of products in the free market was immeasurably greater than the proportion of those who could purchase such products.

The VTsIOM polltakers attempted, within the framework of their sociological surveys, to compare the public's estimates of actual consumption by households to the officially adopted minimum food product consumption standards. Their calculations showed that poor diets, insufficient to maintain full physical human development, were becoming the norm for an increasingly larger proportion of the country's population. Over half of the population lacked the officially established minimum of meat and meat products, fruit and vegetables (except potatoes), fish products, and confectionary. About half (47%) lacked the resources to purchase sufficient milk and dairy products. A third (33%) were short of bread, cereals, and pasta. According to experts from the United Nations Food and Agriculture

Figure 25.5
Survey Responses

How has your family diet changed recently?										
	1991		1992				1993			
	Feb.	Mar.	Mar.	Apr.	May	June	July	Sept.	Oct.	Nov.
For the better.	4%	4%	3%	4%	5%	5%	6%	4%	4%	5%
No change.	22	26	37	37	36	36	36	38	37	36
For the worse.	71	69	57	56	55	55	55	55	55	51

Data cited in *Information Bulletin*, FOM, Moscow, no. 1 [1993]: 34, no. 1 [1994].

Organization (FAO), in 1993 Russia moved to the last group of developing nations, where the consumption of animal proteins was between 25% and 40% of the daily requirement.[6]

25.3. Privatization and Private Property in Russians' Eyes

In the early 1990s the social consciousness retained many stereotypes and attitudes inherited from the Soviet past, including a negative attitude toward private owners and private ownership, which Marxist ideology had for decades presented as the root of all social and economic suffering.

According to VTsIOM figures, in 1991, 36% of rural dwellers, 18% of city dwellers, and 12% of the residents of the capital cities of Moscow and Leningrad (St. Petersburg) were opposed to private ownership in principle. Almost twice as many rural dwellers renounced, across the board, the privatization of small businesses, large plants and factories, and any private ownership in general. The attitude toward private ownership of land was perfectly consistent with this general "anti-ownership" philosophy.

The attitude toward private ownership and entrepreneurship gradually improved, however. In 1999, half of Russia's citizens considered the freedom to engage in entrepreneurial activities to be an important positive result of reforms.

At the same time, the attitude toward Russia's entrepreneurs ("cooperators") first, and later toward the "new Russians," was neg-

---

[6]. T. Yarygina, "Poverty in Rich Russia," *Social Sciences and Our Time* 2 (1994): 25–36.

Table 25.2
Enrichment Factors

Factor	Aug. 1992	May 1994
Penchant for commerce	16%	10%
Business connections	20	13
Profiteering	58	39
Aptitude for business	13	16
"Mafia" money laundering	28	17
Public property embezzlement		34
Gifts and talents	5	6
Hard to say	5	4

Source: *Reforming Russia: Myths and Realities* (Moscow: Analytical Center of the Institute for Social and Political Studies of the Russian Academy of Sciences), 325.

ative. Surveys conducted by the Institute for Sociopolitical Studies (ISS) of the Russian Academy of Sciences captured the public's attitudes toward the very rich people, popularly known as the "new Russians," who were emerging in Russia. Moreover, society significantly changed its views on accumulating wealth within two years, from 1992 to 1994. Whereas the 1992 survey responses suggested a feeble hope that the game might be played by fair rules, and named a commercial streak, proper connections, and the ability to do business as among the factors underlying the ability to accrue resources, in 1994 there was a shift toward a belief that negative political factors such as "embezzlement of common public property" were the main causes (Table 25.2).

At the beginning of the radical economic reforms the issue of privatization arose. Different social strata had different attitudes toward privatization. Moreover, opposing attitudes toward the privatization of small shops, diners, enterprises, and small plots of land, on the one hand, and large factories, plants, and plots of land on the other were registered.

The FOM published a series of sociological information bulletins expressly devoted to privatization in Russia. The figures in these bulletins fully reflect the attitudes of different social groups toward the privatization of large, medium-sized, and small enterprises, plots of land, retailers, and services (Tables 25.3 through 25.6).[7]

---

7. The data are from "Privatization in Russia: 1993–1995," in *Sociological Information Bulletin* (Moscow: FOM, 1995), and I. Klyamkin, V. Lapkin, V. Pantin, and E. Petrenko, "Privatization in Russia: 1992–1993," *Sociological Information Bulletin*, FOM, Moscow (1993).

Table 25.3
Evolution of Social Groups' Attitudes Toward Privatization of Small and Medium-sized Companies, 1992–1995

	1992		1993 Spring		1993 Fall		1994 (Spring)		1995 (Winter)	
Social Group	Pos. (%)	Neg. (%)	Pos. (%)	Neg. (%)	Pos. (%)	Neg. (%)	Pos. (%)	Neg. (%)	Pos. (%)	Neg. (%)
Farm chairmen	78	14	69	21	62	22	58	29	47	—
Collective farmers	61	23	56	21	47	30	46	23	38	29
Pensioners	39	26	37	30	34	34	31	34	27	40
Government administrators	78	6	84	9	75	16	71	17	71	19
Government company managers	86	7	78	11	80	11	81	12	68	21
Employees in spending organizations	66	7	63	18	62	17	58	18	49	23
Military officers	82	6	68	15	67	19	65	19	63	26
Workers	58	21	59	22	60	20	53	23	45	30
Unemployed	71	13	59	17	65	11	49	19	54	25
Entrepreneurs	93	1	88	7	92	4	90	6	81	9
Private farmers	85	8	90	4	84	8	71	10	80	12
Total population	64	17	57	20	55	22	51	21	45	

Sources: "Privatization in Russia: 1992–1993," and "Privatization in Russia: 1993–1995," in *Sociological Information Bulletin: The People and Politics Series* (Moscow: Public Opinion Foundation, 1993, 1995).

Judging by the results obtained by the FOM researchers, the public's attitudes toward privatization changed between the fall of 1992 and the fall of 1993. Initially, privatization was expected to change many things, and was viewed with enthusiasm. The euphoria evaporated, however, as the privatization program went ahead (Figures 25.6 and 25.7).

Public interest in privatization sagged significantly in 1993–1995, specifically in relation to the privatization of large enterprises, and the lowest levels of interest were registered primarily among the groups that were most closely involved in the privatization process. These groups consisted of industrial managers in control of enterprises, and top local government officials, who were burdened with the problem of salvaging and developing the social infrastructure. The greatest disappointment, however, was expressed by entrepre-

Table 25.4
Evolution of Social Groups' Attitudes Toward Privatization of Large Companies, 1992–1995

Social Group	1992 Pos. (%)	1992 Neg. (%)	1993 Spring Pos. (%)	1993 Spring Neg. (%)	1993 Fall Pos. (%)	1993 Fall Neg. (%)	1994 (Spring) Pos. (%)	1994 (Spring) Neg. (%)	1995 (Winter) Pos. (%)	1995 (Winter) Neg. (%)
Farm chairmen	22	53	37	56	28	57	20	67	16	71
Collective farmers	31	49	35	43	26	51	20	50	19	56
Pensioners	27	39	19	49	17	51	15	51	10	57
Government administrators	35	40	42	48	39	48	34	51	26	56
Government company managers	30	50	34	54	42	48	39	41	33	59
Employees in spending organizations	27	40	33	43	36	39	24	48	22	52
Military officers	29	49	29	53	28	57	26	55	25	63
Workers	29	44	35	44	37	40	31	46	25	49
Unemployed	30	37	29	41	33	40	28	39	30	45
Entrepreneurs	52	26	58	31	72	19	58	29	41	39
Private farmers	36	41	56	32	56	24	34	35	40	42
Total population	31	41	33	42	32	42	28	43	23	51

Sources: "Privatization in Russia: 1992–1993," and "Privatization in Russia: 1993–1995," in *Sociological Information Bulletin: The People and Politics Series* (Moscow: Public Opinion Foundation, 1993, 1995).

neurs, who saw no chance of laying claim to large industrial enterprises as they underwent privatization.

The overwhelming majority of the population had next to nothing to gain from the privatization of enterprises, in particular retailing and services, the privatization of which had been a popular idea from the start. And although some segments of society that rejoiced in the fact that consumer goods were readily available on the market because of the privatization of retailing, the success of the undertaking lost its luster in the wake of prohibitively rising prices.

The highest interest in and the most positive attitude toward privatization were initially expressed by entrepreneurs and industrial managers. These were the "new entrepreneurs" and the old-style administrators, the two groups most bitterly embroiled in a fight among themselves. The managers were not of one mind about privatization. Some of them (42%), thirsting for economic indepen-

Table 25.5
Evolution of Social Groups' Attitudes Toward Privatization of Trade and Services, 1992–1995

	1992		1993 Spring		1993 Fall		1994 (Spring)		1995 (Winter)	
Social Group	Pos. (%)	Neg. (%)	Pos. (%)	Neg. (%)	Pos. (%)	Neg. (%)	Pos. (%)	Neg. (%)	Pos. (%)	Neg. (%)
Farm chairmen	60	19	52	29	48	35	51	33	43	50
Collective farmers	38	41	41	34	36	39	38	32	31	46
Pensioners	27	41	23	43	22	44	23	41	20	47
Government administrators	60	19	65	26	53	36	56	32	53	36
Government company managers	70	18	59	25	64	31	69	20	62	24
Employees in spending organizations	43	34	47	32	47	26	46	31	38	35
Military officers	57	27	50	31	48	30	51	25	47	36
Workers	39	39	41	34	36	39	41	35	36	41
Unemployed	49	29	39	35	53	17	48	20	47	32
Entrepreneurs	76	9	75	16	83	9	87	7	77	11
Private farmers	73	15	75	15	73	15	60	20	69	20
Total population	43	30	41	33	42	31	43	29	37	38

Sources: "Privatization in Russia: 1992–1993," and "Privatization in Russia: 1993–1995," in *Sociological Information Bulletin: The People and Politics Series* (Moscow: Public Opinion Foundation, 1993, 1995).

dence, were solidly behind the privatization of large-scale industry. Most of the rest (48%) leaned toward government control and were hostile to privatization. Moreover, whereas the entrepreneurs wanted privatization to gather speed, the managers and such public servants as supported privatization thought it was proceeding too quickly.[8]

Senior public servants and collective and state farm chairmen felt no evident animosity toward privatization—at least, they had no reason to. By the fall of 1993, however, it appeared to be working against their vested interests, and therefore they took an aggressive stand against it. Officialdom was thick with people who thought privatization was unneeded, but once there was no escaping it, their sentiments hardened. There was logic in this stand, for these public

---

8. Ibid.

Table 25.6
Evolution of Social Groups' Attitudes Toward Land Privatization, 1992–1995

	1992		1993				1994 (Spring)		1995 (Winter)	
			Spring		Fall					
Social Group	Pos. (%)	Neg. (%)	Pos. (%)	Neg. (%)	Pos. (%)	Neg. (%)	Pos. (%)	Neg. (%)	Pos. (%)	Neg. (%)
Farm chairmen	51	30	58	42	34	56	31	62	28	69
Collective farmers	68	23	56	26	46	40	33	48	35	50
Pensioners	55	28	43	34	32	41	26	49	31	41
Government administrators	63	18	69	20	57	35	52	39	47	41
Government company managers	72	16	65	24	68	23	58	29	57	36
Employees in spending organizations	63	22	63	21	56	23	52	31	49	32
Military officers	77	14	61	24	59	30	48	38	57	31
Workers	66	19	64	22	58	24	52	27	50	30
Unemployed	71	12	63	19	62	15	54	24	51	30
Entrepreneurs	87	6	81	11	89	7	81	11	77	14
Private farmers	90	7	86	11	81	11	79	14	87	9
Total population	68	18	60	23	55	26	47	32	48	31

Sources: "Privatization in Russia: 1992–1993," and "Privatization in Russia: 1993–1995," in *Sociological Information Bulletin: The People and Politics Series* (Moscow: Public Opinion Foundation, 1993, 1995).

servants were particularly concerned about losing assets and about their own lack of leverage to impose their own divestiture option. As for farm chairmen, turning land over to private individuals boded complete ruin for them.[9] For their part, workers initially counted on getting their "share" of privatized property and were optimistic about the privatization plans for their enterprises. A year later, their enthusiasm had waned appreciably.

Opinion studies have analyzed attitudes toward privatization according to the real owner of a privatized enterprise. (This applies to the situation in which the majority of shares are held by the work group.) According to the FOM, shareholding drives a wedge between managers and administration officers, on the one hand, and workers and budget-fed employees on the other.[10]

---

9. Ibid.
10. I. M. Klyamkin, "Parliamentary Elections: Before and After," *Polis* 6 (1993): 39–53.

Figure 25.6
Survey Responses

What is your attitude toward the idea of individuals in this country owning:*

	1990		1991		1992		1993	
	Pos. (%)	Neg. (%)	Pos. (%)	Neg. (%)	Pos. (%)	Neg. (%)	Pos. (%)	Neg. (%)
Small-Scale Property								
Small enterprises, shops, cafes	57	27	62	22	69	22		
Small plots of land					86	6	87	7
Large-Scale Property								
Large factories	29	47	23	54	27	51		
Large plots of land			39	39	33	45		
What Is Your Attitude Toward the Idea of Foreign Nationals Owning in This Country:								
Large factories			14	70	13	72		
Small enterprises, shops, cafes			44	45	45	44		

Data from *Information Bulletin*, Moscow, VTsIOM, no. 1 [1993].
*Data on those who found it hard to answer the question are not cited.

Figure 25.7
Survey Responses

General evolution of attitudes toward privatization (% of those polled).
Russia does not need any privatization at all.

Autumn 1993	15%
Spring 1994	18%
Winter 1995	28%

From "Privatization in Russia: 1992–1993" and "Privatization in Russia: 1993–1995," *Sociological Information Bulletin—People and Politics Series* (Moscow: Public Opinion Foundation, 1993, 1995).

Figure 25.8
Survey Responses

Who is the actual company owner?		
Actual owner is:	As perceived by employees	As perceived by management and directors
The director	24%	6%
The management	32	15
The work collective	21	49
Source: *POLIS* 6 (1993).		

Broadly, there were no striking differences in the positions of ordinary workers over anything to do with privatization. The picture was different for their bosses: the managers of joint-stock companies were, by and large, in favor of privatization, while their counterparts at public enterprises were noticeably cooler toward the prospect.

Specifically, the rank-and-file at privatized enterprises and their boards held conflicting views on who was the real owner of the privatized enterprise. FOM and VTsIOM data help put this problem into focus.

Figure 25.8 shows FOM data on who the rank-and-file and management of an enterprise considered the real owner to be. These results are worth comparing with the figures utilized by S. P. Shpilko of VTsIOM in his paper, "Privatization of Enterprises: Hope and Reality." Shpilko's figures are based on the responses given by employees of enterprises already privatized or about to be placed under private ownership within six months (autumn of 1993) (Figure 25.9).

There is, therefore, a glaring difference between the real state of things and desirable prospects. In the view of enterprise employees, their enterprise was, in most cases, owned in reality either by the former management or by the former boss (Figure 25.9). To the rank-and-file, these individuals were particularly reprehensible as owners.

According to VTsIOM, the general expectations excited by privatization scarcely resembled optimism.[11] Around half (45%) of employees of joint-stock (privatized) enterprises expected their own situation to change little, 21% hoped to gain, and 11% were expect-

---

11. *Information Bulletin*, VTsIOM, Moscow, no. 1 (1993); no. 8 (1993).

Figure 25.9
Survey Responses

	Who actually owns the company you work for?	Whom would you like to see as your company owner?
Who actually owns the company you work for, and whom would you like to see as its owner? [Company employees' perceptions]		
The current director	22%	8%
The current management	31	2
The work collective	16	42
The shareholders meeting	9	16
A new boss from among Russian entrepreneurs	5	10
A foreign businessman	2	3
Hard to say	14	18

Source: *Information Bulletin*, VTsIOM, Moscow, no. 8 (1993).

ing worse things to come. Nevertheless, 24% of employees expected to earn more. Overall, however, few (a low 16%) believed that the situation of their enterprise would stabilize. Almost no one (3%) expected to see an improvement in the shop floor climate, and 23% feared that privatization would bring an adverse result—either greater redundancy (23%), or more labor hours (13%), or smaller wage packets (13%).

25.4. Evolution in Attitudes Toward the Economic Reform and Government (1993–1997)

25.4.1. *From the April Referendum to October 1993*

The period between the spring and fall of 1993 was an eventful time in the country's reform effort, and one that culminated in the tragedy of the October turmoil.

In the spring of 1993 a referendum was held, among other purposes, to uncover Russian citizens' attitudes toward the economic reforms. Sixty-four percent of the population took part in the referendum, with 53% of the voters voicing support for continued reforms and 43% voting against.

What was the attitude toward economic reform among people who did not take part in the referendum? The Sociology Institute asked them the question, "If you had voted in the referendum, how would you have answered its questions?" The responses were 59.9% against giving a vote of confidence to Boris Yeltsin and 68.7% against the socioeconomic policy conducted by Boris Yeltsin and his government.[12]

Thus, in the spring of 1993, Russian society was roughly equally divided over confidence in Boris Yeltsin and his policy of market reforms.

Between the spring and fall of 1993, public opinion polls uncovered four principal trends. First, the public felt alienated from government and expressed consistently negative views regarding politics and politicians in general. Second, a certain stabilization in the public mood occurred. Cataclysmic prophesies declined, but pessimistic views on both economic and political developments remained steadily high: between the beginning of the year and autumn, 70%–85% of the Russian public feared a turn for the worse in political and economic life. Pessimism rose in the traditionally "optimistic" cities of Moscow and St. Petersburg, to 72%, and among private sector employees, of whom 67% expressed a dim view regarding the future of reforms.

Third, in September, the level of pessimism over the future of the economy rose. Compared with April, the number of people who anticipated deteriorating economic conditions surpassed those who would not make predictions.

Fourth, general uncertainty about the future mounted, particularly among people of lower educational rungs, public servants, and retail workers.

The number of people who feared a worsening political situation was nearly the same as the number of people who feared economic deterioration. This gives us reason to assume that

> what we are tracking is not politics or economics, but rather an integral, syncretic attitude of the mass consciousness to social realities. It is a fusion of perception of the consumer market and the threat of unemployment, political conflicts, and confidence in government institutions.[13]

---

12. Sociology Institute, Russian Academy of Sciences, *Opinions in the Mirror* (Moscow: June 1993).
13. *Information Bulletin*, VTsIOM, Moscow, no. 6 (1993): 23.

Figure 25.10
Survey Responses

Responses to a 1993 poll
How much of your family income goes toward food?

	March	July	November
Less than half	3%	4%	5%
Nearly half	17	14	15
Nearly two-thirds	17	21	21
Almost all	59	57	55

Data from *Information Bulletin*, VTsIOM, Moscow, no. 1 (1994).

The bleak outlook affected the public's social feelings in general. Over half of Russian citizens (54.3%) reported low emotional states.[14]

The public moods and views on the overall situation were largely rooted in the harsh economic conditions. In the spring of 1993, the cash earnings of 85% of the Russian population trailed consumer prices, and 76% of households spent over two-thirds of their budget on food (59% of them spent almost all they had on food) (Figure 25.10). For the country as a whole, the actual per capita income was only one-third of the subsistence minimum. It was no accident, therefore, that 34% of survey respondents spoke about possible mass protests against rising prices and deteriorating living standards in their cities, with 25.9% suggesting the possibility of their (highly likely) involvement in protests.[15]

Probed for views about the speed of the reforms, enthusiasts of a blitz to capitalism were considerably fewer in number.

In late 1991, shortly before the launch of radical economic reforms, many took the President's exhortations to "have patience for a half-year" at face value, hoping that quick and resolute measures to transform the economy would produce remarkable results. Accordingly, around 30% of the population were in favor of fast-track reforms. In the spring of 1993, supporters of a gradual transition to a market economy were 2.6 times as numerous as supporters of a

---

14. S. P. Shpilko, "Privatization of Enterprises: Hope and Reality," *Information Bulletin*, VTsIOM, Moscow, 8 (1993): 20–22.
15. Ibid.

"shock therapy" approach. In October 1993, however, the gradualists outnumbered the fast-pacers 4 to 1.

The October events left a deep scar on society, the pain of which was felt for some time to come. Those events proved a turning point in public attitudes toward Boris Yeltsin and toward democrats in general.

In the fall of 1993, two processes occurred in parallel, but in opposite directions. Interest in politics waned, but awareness of dependence on politics grew. The divide between government and society widened without parallel in recent history.

Disappointment with politics and politicians showed up, in particular, in 45% of the public denying confidence in all political leaders, parties, and movements. A similar proportion of the electorate boycotted the parliamentary elections in December 1993 (and therefore evaded the referendum on the draft Constitution of the Russian Federation).

25.4.2. *From the 1993 Parliamentary Elections to the Presidential Elections of 1996*

The results of the 1993 parliamentary elections and the 1996 presidential elections were an indirect indication of society's attitudes toward reforms in general, and toward the economic renovations in particular.

In an article titled "Parliamentary Elections: Before and After," an analysis of the outcome of the 1993 parliamentary elections and the defeat of the democrats, I. M. Klyamkin wrote, with good reason, that Zhirinovsky had been unmatched in filling "the niches of pent-up ideological and political demand."[16] In his view,

The political behavior of the population has, for a long time, been loosely correlated with its socioeconomic interests and values: many, for example, voted for Yeltsin, even if they were dissatisfied with his policy. Yeltsin was a symbol of anticommunism, a symbol of victory over communism. While they seriously feared a return of communism, therefore, those who dreaded this prospect supported the president, irrespective of their attitude to his reforms. After the shelling of the Parliament's White House and the dissolution of the Soviets of People's Deputies, after the anticommunists had themselves split into several election camps, society stopped believing in the

---

16. I. M. Klyamkin, "Before and After the Parliamentary Elections," *Polis* 5 (1993).

danger of a communist comeback. People's political behavior was beginning to match their socioeconomic interests and values.[17]

The new phase adhered to the formula of the preceding period that anticommunism invariably implied democracy. The black-and-white scheme and the line drawn between "us" and "them" gave way to a more variegated vision of the world and of social processes in general.

Beginning in December 1993, and continuing right up to the 1995 parliamentary elections, the mainstream trend gained force in the public's attitude toward the government and its economic policy. This trend was characterized by disappointment, disbelief, rejection, and bitterness. It was perfectly in tune with the negative trends that were developing in economics and the social sphere.

VTsIOM reports assert that the economic situation played a greater role in the public's negative attitudes. Again, two distinct trends can be recognized. The first reflects diverging estimates of the economic situation in different spheres—in the country as a whole, in the city or rural district of the respondent, and in the respondent's family. Russian survey respondents have always had better opinions about the situation in their families than in their home towns or rural districts, not to mention the country in general. The other trend was toward a more or less even evaluation of the financial position of the respondents' families throughout that period. There was, however, a small increase (within 2%–3%) in the proportion of respondents who described the situation of their families as "very bad." Also notable is that approximately equal proportions of people saw their families' situation as "average" and as "bad" or "very bad" (Table 25.7).

25.4.3. *Rating of Problems of Public Concern*

How did society's attitudes toward market reforms develop after the 1995 parliamentary elections? The presidential election in 1996 became a major political event that marked a milestone in the life of postcommunist Russia. In particular, it shed light on many important aspects of society's attitude toward the government and its social and economic policies.

Fluctuations in the rating of problems worrying society allow us to see the results of the economic reform through the eyes of Russians.

---

17. Ibid.

Table 25.7
Evolution of Survey Responses Regarding the Current Economic Situation in Russia and in the Respondent's City (Rural District) and His or Her Family's Financial Standing Between Spring 1993 and Fall 1995

	1993			1994				1995			
	Mar.	June	Dec.	Mar.	June	Nov.	Mar.	May	July	Nov.
How Would You Assess Russia's Economic Situation?										
Very good and good	0.7%	1.2%	2.1%	0.9%	1%	1%	0.5%	0.6%	0.8%	0.8%
Average	10.1	19.9	17.6	14	15.3	15.6	11.9	16.4	15	14.3
Bad and very bad	77.6	64.2	68.2	73.1	68.7	69.5	76	68	72.3	71.8
Hard to say	11.4	14.7	12.2	11.7	15	14	12	15	12	13
How Would You Assess the Economic Situation in Your City (Rural District)?										
Very good and good	2.1	2.5	2.7	1.2	2.1	2.2	2.1	2.8	2.3	1.6
Average	28.7	36.7	32.9	29.3	29.3	29.2	26.6	33.7	32	30.4
Bad and very bad	54.1	46.1	50.5	58.5	53.6	54.9	59.4	49.9	54.2	55.8
Hard to say	14.9	14.4	13.2	10.6	14.8	13.5	12	13.1	11.4	14.7
How Would You Assess Your Family's Financial Standing?										
Very good and good	6.8	7.7	6.8	4.7	4.8	5	4	5.7	5.1	4.2
Average	48.1	48.4	48	44.5	48	48.8	42.3	44.6	46.5	46.6
Bad and very bad	43.4	41	42.8	48.7	44.8	43.4	51.2	46.8	46.2	46.7
Hard to say	1.7	2.8	2.4	2	2.3	2.8	2.5	2.8	2.2	2.5

Source: *VTsIOM Information Bulletin* 3 (1996): 41.

Table 25.8
Ranking Issues of Greatest Public Concern, 1993–1997

Which of our society's problems are worrying you most?	1993 Mar.	1993 Sept.	1994 Sept.	1995 Sept.	1996 Sept.	1997 Apr.
Shortages	28%	19%	11%	11%	8%	5.6%
Growing prices	84	83	81	77	63	55
Unemployment	30	32	56	48	63	61
Economic crisis, production slump	45	45	51	47	54	55
Growing crime	64	63	67	58	60	59
Crisis in morals, ethics, and culture	25	26	29	27	28	27
Environmental problems	29	27	29	31	27	22
Worsened ethnic relations	20	16	16	25	20	20
Renunciation of ideals of social justice	7	7				
Unfair income distribution	—	—	37	33	37	43
Corruption, bribery	19	24	24	23	26	28
Weak government	33	31	30	35	29	36
Conflicts within the country's leadership	30	28	11	12	10	14
Armed border conflicts	13	13	15	35		
The threat of fascism and extremism				6	3	4
The war in Chechnya					51	
Instability and crises in Chechnya						14
Arrears on wages, salaries, pensions, allowances, etc.						66

Source: *VTsIOM Information Bulletin* 7 (1993); 5 (1994); 5 (1995); 6 (1996).

The question, "Which of our society's problems worry you most?" asked by the VTsIOM for several years in succession, elicited different responses. Some of the problems bore directly on economics, while others, although not strictly of an economic variety, were intrinsically tied to the economic situation (Table 25.8).

The problem of consumer shortages was completely resolved over the first two years of reforms. Store shelves were filled, and queues were a thing of the past. Understandably, the number of those who had previously identified shortages as the most serious problem fell by a factor of 3.5. Shortages as a problem dropped to ninth place among all the problems concerning society. Over time, it faded from view altogether: in 1996, it was remembered by only 8% of respondents. This alone can be counted as an indisputable achievement of the economic reforms.

Turning now to the ratings of other major problems, we see that five problems predominated:

- Constantly rising prices (inflation)
- Unemployment
- A slump in production
- Rising crime rates
- Wage arrears

The collapse of living standards linked to these problems was an important indicator of Russians' attitude toward economic reforms. In this regard, the gap between Russians' notions of the income necessary to support the "normal life," the level of their incomes, and the subsistence minimum is illustrative.

Asked about the subsistence minimum, three-quarters of the respondents in 1993 and again in 1997 considered it an income that ensured them a modest yet more or less dignified existence. The suggestion that the subsistence minimum was to ensure a person's physical survival was accepted by only 13% of respondents in 1993 and by 18% in 1997. T. I. Zaslavskaya had these comments at the time:

> Having learned to lead an unassuming but tolerably comfortable life, the majority of Russian citizens cannot, and do not want to, reconcile themselves to the onset of poverty or give it some kind of legitimacy. Despite their present economic difficulties, they consider themselves entitled to human dignity and, therefore, to certain social boons.[18]

This assessment holds today as well.

Table 25.9
Evolution of the Wage Arrears Problem Between 1993 and 1997

	1993		1994		1995	1996			1997
	Mar.	Dec.	Mar.	Nov.	Mar.	Mar.	June	Sept.	May
Yes, I drew my full wage on schedule	62%	48%	38%	40%	43%	31%	34%	32%	27%
My wage got behind schedule	26	31	28	32	29	31	24	24	18
It was not paid in full	2	4	5	3	4	5	5	5	5
I was paid an incomplete wage behind schedule	2	6	10	5	6	8	9	8	10
I drew no wage at all	7	11	19	19	17	24	27	32	40

Source: *VTsIOM Information Bulletin* 6 (1996).

---

18. T. I. Zaslavskaya, "Incomes of the Working Population," *Information Bulletin*, VTsIOM, Moscow, no. 1 (1994).

The sociological concept of a "subsistence minimum" (reflected subjectively in the mass consciousness) is hard to correlate with an economic definition. In official economics, the subsistence minimum is a conventional quantity that conforms to a country's real budget, even though it reflects some human claims. As a result, the economic subsistence minimum occupies a middle ground, below the social subsistence minimum and above the subsistence pension and subsistence wage. Should the official subsistence minimum, which is certainly less than enough to survive on, be replaced by the social subsistence minimum, it would turn out that almost everyone in Russia lives below the poverty line.

Another sociological indicator, "normal per capita income," is a level of livelihood that, according to common views, allows people to live "normal lives." This indicator reflects an income level that is socially established and subjectively accepted as "equitable" by the general citizenry.[19]

It is instructive to look at the pattern of changes that have occurred in the years of radical economic reforms in the correlations between a family's cash income, the subsistence minimum, and the income that respondents believe is good enough to lead a "normal" life.

According to Table 25.10, the "normal" income was about four times as high as the actual income in all periods from 1993 to 1997. The varying assessments of "normal per capita income" by the population illustrates a trend for Russian citizens to gradually reduce their expectations to a socially acceptable or "adequate" level of affluence.

It was only natural for economic problems to be prominent in making the choice at the ballot box. This is borne out by the following statistics from the VTsIOM.

The constituents who voted in the second round, between Yeltsin and Zyuganov, differed considerably in their economic orientation, moods, and views. These differences were especially evident in regard to market reforms (Table 25.11). Whereas over half of Yeltsin's supporters came out for continued reforms, almost half of Zyuganov's followers voted for an end to reforms. Many more people in the communist electorate were living below the poverty line. Significantly, Zyuganov's supporters enjoyed much lower economic re-

---

19. T. I. Zaslavskaya, "Incomes of Social Groups and Strata: Levels and Dynamics," *Information Bulletin*, VTsIOM, Moscow, no. 2 (1996).

Table 25.10
Cash Income, Subsistence Minimum, and Income Fit for "Normal Life" (in Thousands of "old" Rubles)

	Size of Income Fit for What Respondents Perceive as "Normal" Life	Income That, in the Respondent's Opinion, Currently Provides a Subsistence Minimum	Respondent's Aggregate Family Income for the Previous Month, per Family Member
1993			
March	41	23	10
June	94	50	21
December	226	120	52
1994			
March	257	154	84
June	295	198	104
November	461	255	166
1995			
March	536	323	187
May	720	358	228
July	774	453	257
November	865	516	311
1996			
January	920	570	331
March	1,067	581	354
May	1,224	492	389
July	1,427	542	410
September	1,479	528	413
1997			
April	1,399	568	422

Source: VTsIOM data, quoted in *Information Bulletin* 6 (1996); 2 (1997).

sources. The difference between an income small enough "to live a decent life" and the income of Yeltsin's followers was about 200,000 "old" rubles. The difference in personal wealth between Yeltsin's and Zyuganov's supporters is estimated at a million rubles.

25.4.4. General Trends of 1997–1999 in Public Opinion and Dynamics in Assessments of Economic Reforms in Ten Years

The last period of the Yeltsin era, which ended in December 1999, was marked by new political and economic upheavals. After the

Table 25.11
Opinions and Assessments as a Function of the Way People Voted in the Second Round of Presidential Elections

Voters	Total	For Yeltsin	For Zyuganov
HOW WOULD YOU DESCRIBE YOUR FAMILY INCOME?			
We are below the poverty line	12%	7%	16%
We can hardly make ends meet	46	41	48
We economize and live a fairly decent life	34	43	33
We have no financial problems to speak of	5	7	2
Per capita income necessary for what the respondent perceives as normal life (thous. of Rb)	1,398	1,489	1,260
Respondent's aggregate per capita income (thous. of Rb)	421	497	370
Average monthly per capita cash income which is, in the respondent's opinion, the lowest reference point for a family to be seen as rich (thous. of Rb)	4,900	5,142	4,157

Source: VTsIOM data, quoted in *Information Bulletin* 2 (1997).

presidential elections of 1996, when the election fever had abated, it became clear that the many hopes of Russians were not to be met. Within three years, the majority of those who had voted for Yeltsin thought they had voted incorrectly.

In all of the ten years of reforms, 1997 was the most tranquil and stable year. Throughout the entire year a trend persisted of growing hopes for a "better future," as indicators of positive expectations in the economy and politics, appraisals of the economic situation in the country, etc. grew. The year 1998 brought new shocks: four changes in government, and the financial crisis of August 1998. According to VTsIOM data, 83% of Russians said 1998 was more difficult than all of the preceding years of reform.[20]

The August crisis caused real household incomes to diminish considerably. According to Goskomstat data, in September through December real incomes fell by about a third, compared with incomes in September through December of the previous year. In respondents' subjective estimates, incomes fell by a half. From August 17 until mid-October, society was in panic. Indicators of social well-being deteriorated dramatically, and attitudes toward the reform were in-

---

20. *Information Bulletin*, VTsIOM, Moscow, no. 1 (1999).

creasingly negative. The general social well-being began to improve gradually only after November.[21]

The results of polls conducted immediately after the August crisis, in September 1998, indicated that more than half of the populace would prefer long queues and food rationing to a wide range of choices at unaffordable prices. The lack of money even to purchase food was mentioned by 42% of respondents.

The Russian mood stabilized somewhat in 1999. A certain economic recovery and the payment of wage and other arrears increased the public's optimism about the economy. The general mood of the Russians, their attitude toward their personal economic situation and toward the economic situation of the country at large, improved perceptibly, and indicators of social tension and the readiness to protest fell. However, as O. Savelyev of the VTsIOM PR service has noted,

> improving mood indicators originate rather in growing hopes for better characteristic of the "pre-election optimism" similar to that already noted at VTsIOM's polls during the elections of 1995 and 1996. When no real improvement in the living standards of the majority of Russians occurred after the presidential elections of 1996, a mood hangover was registered, and the level of appraisals of living standards, reforms, and hopes for the future fell sharply. Therefore, we shall not delude ourselves: there have been very few objective signs of an economic recovery as yet.[22]

The general dynamics of the populace's attitude to the economic reforms over ten years will be analyzed next.

How did the public's general appraisal of the economic reforms change? Much depended on how people could adapt to the changes in the country. At the end of 1999, one-third of Russian citizens claimed they could not adapt to the new realities. Moreover, this proportion had increased considerably over the preceding five years (from 23% in 1994 to 33% in 1999[23]). The proportion of those who thought that the majority of Russian citizens would never be able to adapt to the changes had also grown steadily, from 32% in 1995 to 46% in 1998.[24]

---

21. For more on this see M. Urnov, "Certain Factors in the Adaptation of Russian Society to the Situation After the August 1998 Crisis. *Information Bulletin*, VTsIOM, Moscow, 2 (1999).
22. VTsIOM Press Service, "Can't dampen our optimism!" (February 2000).
23. For more on this see Yu. A. Levada, "'Soviet Man' Ten Years: 1989–1999," *Information Bulletin*, VTsIOM, Moscow, 3 (1999).
24. *Information Bulletin*, VTsIOM, Moscow, 6 (1998).

This sentiment is accompanied by nostalgia for the Soviet past: in 1999 over half of Russian citizens (59%) agreed with the statement, "It would be better if everything in the country [had] remained the same as before 1985." Only young people less than 25 years old and the highly educated preferred changes.[25]

Difficulty in adjusting to changes and nostalgia for the past determine to a considerable degree the choice of priorities of Russian citizens in their economic behavior.

Over the past ten years a stable and growing majority preferred the "Soviet" choice of a modest but guaranteed income. The orientation toward "much work at a good wage" remained attractive for a quarter of Russian citizens, on the average, peaking at 32% for the age group 25–40 years and falling to 8% for seniors (over 55).

What changes do people appraise as positive or negative? Let us compare the polls of 1994 and 1999.

Between 1994 and 1999, the appraisal of free speech, multiparty elections, and rapprochement with Western nations deteriorated, while the appraisal of free enterprise improved. In this context the attitude toward market reforms on the whole becomes clearer.

The results of surveys conducted by the Institute for Sociological Studies before 1995 to clarify society's attitudes to market reforms show variations in views on the transition to a market economy. Typically, despite the overall negative assessment of Russia's economic and political situation, society continued to be consistently divided into people who thought the transition to a market economy was a correct step, those who thought it was wrong, and the uncommitted (Figures 25.11 and 25.12).

Approximately the same proportions held in responses to questions about the soundness of the general strategy of the country's development. There was, however, a downward trend in the proportion of those who thought Russia was moving in the right direction and an upward trend in the proportion of those who considered the general strategy to be a mistake (Figure 25.13).

These assessments generally agree with VTsIOM surveys. They show that about a third of Russian citizens (32%) in 1994 supported the continuation of reforms. But only 10% of them believed this to be the only way to prosperity. Another 14% of the reform backers embraced the reforms only because they rejected a return to the past.

---

25. Levada, "'Soviet Man.'"

Figure 25.11
Survey Responses

Have the changes referred to below done more good or more harm?

	1994		1999	
	More Good	More Harm	More Good	More Harm
Freedom of speech and of the press	53%	23%	47%	32%
Free enterprise	44	28	50	25
Freedom of exit from Russia	45	23	43	23
Multiparty elections	29	33	21	50
Rapprochement with Western nations	47	19	38	23

Source: *Information Bulletin*, VTsIOM, Moscow, no. 1 (1995) and no. 3 (1999).

Figure 25.12
Survey Responses

Transition to a free market economy: Is it right or wrong for Russia?

	1993		1994		1995
	June	Nov.	June	Nov.	June
Right	42.8%	45.9%	41.9%	38%	44%
Wrong	28	27.4	33.4	33	30
Hard to say	29.3	26.7	24.7	29	27

Sources: Institute for Sociological Studies of the Russian Academy of Sciences, *Socio-Express: Opinions in the Mirror* (1993, 1994, 1995 issues).

Discontent peaked in May 1995, when a low 26% held that the reforms should be continued, while 30% advocated a halt to reforms, with 43% being unspecific. In 1997 a critical attitude toward the reforms prevailed.

In the September panic following the August 1998 crisis, the number of opponents of reforms grew dramatically. However, at the end of 1998 and in early 1999, the pro-market mood surged again. At the same time, notions about what capitalist and socialist economic systems entail remained very vague.

Thus, over the years 1997–1999 the proportion of proponents of the socialist economic model (one based on state ownership, state

Figure 25.13
Survey Responses

Are things in Russia moving in essentially the right or wrong direction?			
	1993	1994	1995
	June	Nov.	June
Right	12.8%	6%	7%
Partly right, partly wrong	44.7	46	47
Wrong	28.4	35	35
Hard to say	14.2	13	11

Sources: Institute for Sociological Studies of the Russian Academy of Sciences, *Socio-Express: Opinions in the Mirror* (1993, 1994, 1995 issues).

planning, and state distribution) almost doubled. The proportion of proponents of a market economy fell from over half of respondents to just above one-third of respondents in the same period. These opinion changes correspond to the data on the notion of a better model of political system.

The idealization of the Soviet system depends to a considerable degree on one's personal appraisal of changes in the country. Two-thirds of the populace think that they personally and their families are worse off because of the changes. Such a deep perception of personal loss corresponds to the general appraisal of the Yeltsin era, which disappointed many Russian citizens.

In the summer of 1998, a third of Russian citizens (34%) thought that the main result of Yeltsin's presidency was "collapse"—of the country, the economy, industry, and values. Twenty-eight percent of respondents identified the economic crisis and its consequences (slump, unemployment) as the chief result, and 20% of respondents identified impoverishment of the populace as the chief result. Positive results such as democratic transformations and liberties were mentioned by only 8% of respondents, while establishing the market, reducing the budget deficit, and an abundance of goods were mentioned by a mere 3% of respondents. This low valuation of the importance of the democratic transformations over the past decade and of the market breakthrough closely correlates with their low valuation in the general population's hierarchy of urgent future goals.

A few general conclusions can be drawn about the dynamics of public opinion on economic reforms over the ten-year reform period as a whole.

First, the ten years of economic reforms can be divided in several stages, each with a specific social consciousness. Thus, the social consciousness of perestroika was within the socialist mind-set. Since the start of the radical economic reform, the social consciousness has changed considerably. On the whole, the economic mentality of the "post-Soviet" individual differs little from that of "*Homo sovieticus.*" It would be fitting to speak of "the mentality of *Homo sovieticus* in the post-Soviet environment." This mentality is characterized first by multiplicity or "hybridity," an ability to match the unmatchable, and second by a sort of spontaneity, in which each judgment is made independently of any other, without a clear logical link between them. Thus, what has really changed are the political values and ideological orientations rather than the intrinsic aims and concepts of individuals.

Second, the evolution of social attitudes toward economic reform was determined not only by objective social and economic realities but also by social and psychological factors. According to the multi-dimensional sociological research of S. Grebenichenko, the most important factors are the following:

1. Faith in a better tomorrow, deeply rooted in the history and culture of the Russian spiritual tradition

2. The influence of the political opposition on the official course of economic and social development

3. The populace's immunity to economic cataclysms

4. The economic, social, and reformist role of consumers

5. The need for an authoritarian regime to rule over the national economy

1. *Faith in a better tomorrow.* This faith, which did not manifest itself in the perestroika years, surged in 1991 and 1992. However, as hopes for an immediate economic miracle faded, it weakened. It peaked in periods of abundant political promises such as the presidential campaign and before the parliamentary elections, and shrank after the elections. In 1997–1998 it seemed to be growing at a stable rate. However, the crisis of 17 August 1998 undermined this process for a long time.

In periods when it was waxing, this faith positively influenced the economic and political enthusiasm of the populace, causing higher appraisals of the general economic situation of the country. Conversely, when "faith in a better tomorrow" waned, the appraisal of the situation in the country on the whole deteriorated sharply. It may seem surprising, but fluctuations in this faith affected neither the current appraisal of individual well-being nor consumer behavior.

2. *The influence of the political opposition on the official course of economic and social development.* The increasing influence of the opposition on the official course of social and economic development of Russia in certain periods (from the end of 1994 until mid-1995, during the election campaign of 1996, and in the period October 1997 through mid-1998) led to growing confidence in public and parliamentary activity on the whole. Specifically, it led to growing confidence in G. Yavlinski and G. Zyuganov, while confidence in Yu. Luzhkov and B. Nemtsov waned. At the same time, the opposition's influence constrained the possibility of mass protests against price increases and falling living standards, which is of special importance for this topic. When the opposition's influence on the official course of developments was weak (such as in the summer of 1996, after the presidential elections), discontent with economic reforms and the potential for mass protests increased.

3. *The populace's immunity to economic cataclysms.* Russian society, like a living organism, showed an ability to develop a certain psychological immunity to the political and economic cataclysms of the 1990s. According to S. Grebenichenko, this immunity determines the "reserve of strength" the populace has (the ratio between "not so bad," "patience stretched to the limit," and "beyond endurance"), the everyday mood of the people, and the potential for mass protests against price increases and deteriorating living standards.

Up until October 1994, the immunity to economic cataclysms strengthened, and from the end of 1994 until August 1995 it weakened. Before the presidential elections the defense system strengthened again as hopes for a better future grew. However, seeing no substantial economic recovery after the election of 1996, society again began to lose its immunity to the difficulties of the transition period. In the summer of 1997 the immunity somewhat stabilized, only to be undermined again in 1998. In June 1998 the state of immunity was close to critical. The August 1998 crisis utterly destroyed it.

4. *The economic, social, and reformist role of consumers.* To a considerable degree, the populace's various consumer functions determine its attitudes toward economic reforms on the whole, determine the number of proponents and opponents of reforms, and determine the populace's appraisal of households' situation at a given moment in time. The better the political and legal environment suits the realization of the economic role of consumers, and the more tangible this role is, the larger is the share of proponents of continuation of reforms, and the less is the share of those requesting to cease them, the higher is the integrated index of Russian consumer moods. The shrinking role of consumers in the development of the national economy leads to a shrinking social basis for reforms and a deterioration in households' living standards. People do not wish to (and often cannot) make plans to buy expensive things; the majority of households lose faith in savings and loan operations. Whereas from the beginning of the reforms until September 1993 the role of consumers (that is, common people) in the national economy grew steadily larger, after the events of October 1993, and especially since early 1994, this role has been steadily losing in importance. In June 1998 the role of ordinary people who consume goods and services on an everyday basis became minimal, reaching the null point after the August crisis. However, in the course of 1999 it gradually gained in importance.

5. *The need for an authoritarian regime to rule over the national economy.* This need manifested itself twice in the past decade: in 1994–1995 and again at the end of 1996. As the need for an authoritarian rule over the economy is more and more supported, it influences the general psychological climate, and people feel less irritated and afraid.

Third, the society experiences great difficulties while attempting to adapt to modern political and economic realities. In this situation people generally strive first for personal, individual survival. As a result, stability, security, and confidence in the future become priorities. At the same time, such values as ownership, professionalism, having a career, the state of the market, and reform become secondary. The conflicts between social, economic, and political realities, the difficulty of realizing changes in the country, and the difficulty of choosing among preferences facilitate an enduring ambiguity in the social consciousness.

We conclude our discussion with the following quotation from Y. A. Levada:

The ease of sharp turns always arouses suspicion. The collapse of the Soviet system was followed not by the coming of the legendary champion, but by the emergence of a new man ready to compromise to survive. Ready to trumpet his loyalty to democracy because of his aversion to the old system of government, but in no way accustomed to democratic institutions. Ready, as he did until recently, to follow, in times of emotional uplift, the new leaders in the hope that they will prove to be the bosses, fathers, and saviors of the nation. And, incidentally, prone to turn away from these leaders if they betray his hopes. Ready to demonstrate his preferences for the market and privatization, but only little adjusted to independent economic behavior.[26]

In the final analysis, this duplicity and contradictoriness lie at the root of public opinion in general.

---

26. Levada, ibid. p. 266.

26

Some Conclusions

Yuri Bobylev, Revold Entov, Olga Izryadnova, Vladimir Mau, Sergei Prikhodko, Alexander Radygin, Eugenia Serova, Sergei Sinelnikov-Murylev, and Sergei Tsukhlo

26.1. Russia's Economic Policy at the Beginning of the New Phase of Economic Reforms

26.1.1. *Political and Economic Stabilization*

The main feature that distinguished the year 2000 was the stability and even predictability of the chief characteristics of Russia's economic and political development. The final surprise of 1999, Boris Yeltsin's early resignation, launched the process of establishing a system of steady relationships between the main political players. This, in turn, became one of the most important factors contributing to economic stability.

Such a development bears out the conclusion we have repeatedly stressed in this book—the political nature of the Russian economic crisis. The main source of economic instability throughout the nineties was the permanent political crisis, fueled by the failure of leading political forces and interest groups to come to terms on the fundamental issues and goals of economic policy. The surmounting of a political crisis should, of course, lead to economic stabilization. However important and complex are the problems of structural adaptation of the old Soviet system to the requirements of the market, however important are external shocks, the very ability of economic agents to adequately respond to them depends on the political elite coming up with clear and stable "rules of the game," and implementing those rules.

The first signs of political stabilization came as early as 1999. The firing of Ye. Primakov's government (which came off without trouble, despite the backing of this government by the Duma majority), the failure of the impeachment attempts, and the ease with which the new premiers, S. Stepashin and V. Putin, were appointed all were signs of the new realities of political life. Still, those events might have meant only a change of tactics by the opposition parties as they lost interest in Kremlin intrigues and decided to focus on preparing for more important events, the parliamentary and presidential elections.

However, the Duma election campaign showed that there were more serious grounds for the intensity of the conflicts to decline. The pre-election documents of the leading political groups showed an unquestionable convergence of their positions on issues of social and economic development, including microeconomic and fiscal policies, property relations, and so forth.[1] Although their specific proposals could be widely different, the parties represented at the Duma stayed within the paradigm of the market economy, and their differences were no greater than the usual differences between the right and left poles of the political spectrum.

Such a trend rested on an objective economic foundation. One of the important consequences of the 1998 financial crisis and the sharp devaluation of the ruble was the resolution of the conflict between the exporting sector of the Russian economy and the industries with the potential for import substitution. Favorable conditions on the world markets helped boost exports, while the low exchange rate protected Russian producers on the domestic market, thus encouraging their development. Conflict that seemed impossible to resolve in the mid-nineties, and that constituted the greatest danger to the stability of postcommunist Russia, virtually ceased to exist. That had an inevitable impact on the positions of the political forces that acted in the interests of economic groups.

After the 1999 elections, the Duma is so structured that the executive branch can vote any bill it needs through the lower house. The spectrum of the political parties and blocs represented in the Duma can be broken down into three parts of roughly equal strength: the left-wing bloc, the pro-government bloc, and the center with the right wing. In such a situation, almost any proposal by the President or the government will get the backing of the Duma: the pro-government factions vote for it almost automatically, with either the right wing's or the left wing's votes added. Differences between the right wing and the left wing matter only when a constitutional majority is

---

1. For details, see *Rossiyskaya ekonomika v 1999 godu: tendetsii i perspektivy* (Moscow: IET, 1999), 313–319.

required to pass a bill. However, even in these cases the executive powers always succeed in finding common ground with the Duma. Thus, the kind of parliamentary mechanism that has developed in Russia can be considered a voting machine.

This became evident as early as the first sessions of the state Duma in January 2000, when the key posts in the lower house were carved up between the left-wing and pro-government factions, with the interests of the right wing and the center all but ignored. There was concern that this alliance would end up as a long-lasting bloc reflecting the political preferences of the new administration, but this concern proved to be unfounded. Throughout the course of 2000, the executive branch struck up temporary coalitions, now with some factions, now with others, to achieve its goals. Moreover, there was a pattern to the coalitions: in resolving social and economic issues, the executive powers relied on the center and center-right forces, while with regard to "symbolic" issues they looked to the left wing.[2]

Such political maneuvering is in principle only natural for a regime that is pulling out of a long period of instability. It drastically decreases the political and financial costs of passing the bills, as in most cases there is no need to work out compromises in getting the ideological opponents to vote for the proposed document. Practically all the groups can vote consistently with their ideological preferences. This system is conducive to taking responsible economic decisions, as was evident in the voting on the Tax Code and the 2001 budget: it was the first time in the postcommunist period that the budget was approved without support from the Communist Party and the Agrarian Party, whose votes previously had to be secured at the expense of macroeconomic stability.

At the same time, the current situation is fraught with danger, as decisions that are approved automatically may turn into obstacles once the political conditions or goals change. For example, the compromise reached between the left and pro-presidential groups in forming the governing bodies of the Duma in January of 2000, when all the committees on the social issues were handed to the left-wing factions, seriously impeded work on the relevant laws.

One could also say that the development of federative relations is entering a new phase, characterized by the stabilization of politi-

---

2. The fact that legislators work closely with the executive branch does not mean that their actions are fully coordinated. In 2000, the President used his right of veto twelve times, each time with respect to a law dealing with social and economic issues.

cal processes. The main features of change in this area are first, the equalization of conditions in which the regional political institutions operate; second, the enhancement of federal control over the situation in the regions and establishment of uniform rules of the game; and third, a clearer division of responsibilities and levels of government. The political crisis of the nineties gave rise to "special relations" between some regions and the federal center, in which the politically weak center had to pay for political support at the cost of violating federal legislation and an expansion of its responsibilities to an extent that often ran counter to the Constitution. These practices were formalized through the adoption of bilateral agreements ("agreements on the division of responsibilities") between the federal center and the regions, which was made possible by the first chapter (not subject to amendment) of the Russian Federation's Constitution.

A step toward the development of a stable economic and political system is the establishment of equal economic conditions for all regions. What is meant is not absolute equalization of these conditions, for, according to the regions' status, they should be allowed sufficient room to compete for investors. Rather, it is equalization as opposed to the situation in which some regions enjoy more favorable treatment than others, as happened with the special tax regimes for Tatarstan and Bashkiria, which were allowed to retain a greater proportion of tax revenues than other regions. This situation, which even quite recently seemed impossible to resolve, was changed in March 2000. Moreover, the leaders of those republics initiated the revision of their special status ostensibly on their own.

General regulation and the stabilization of relations between the center and the regions called for deeper political reforms. Those reforms became the object of the first laws President Putin initiated during his first month in office. Constitutional bills that changed the rules for making up the Federation Council and entitled the President to depose the regional leaders and dissolve their legislatures, if those violated the federal legislation, had two important potential consequences. First, the regions were encouraged to act on their own to bring their laws in line with federal legislation, as there were too many regional laws for the center to revise. Second, the heads of the regional administrations were stripped of immunity and made subject to deposition for failure to comply with lawful decisions of the federal authorities.

The uniformity of law was to be further enhanced by the institute of the President's representatives in the federal okrugs (consolidated regions), formed simultaneously with the reform of the upper house. Initially, the achievement of legal uniformity was deemed to be the primary reason for creating representatives. In addition, representatives of the President were to coordinate the activities of the federal authorities in the regions, taking those activities out of the regional authorities' control. This was one of the most serious political and economic problems of the nineties, for the regional leaders, who had a lot of political clout, were able to influence the operation of the institutions that were supposed to be out of their sphere of influence in principle—chiefly the courts, prosecutors' offices, and the tax authorities.

Finally, Putin himself began to act much more actively, initiating the cancellation of undoubtedly unlawful decisions that had been taken by the authorities of some regions (Archangel, Vladimir, Orenburg, Voronezh, Tver). This was to demonstrate the federal authorities' commitment to bringing regional laws in line with the federal legislative framework. Most of the regional laws that were repealed had imposed excessive and unlawful restrictions on businesses at the behest of regional authorities.

The reform of fiscal relations between the center and the regions is also crucial. The federal government has renounced the practice of expanding "nonfinanced mandates," which is a code term for shifting the responsibility for financing certain expenditures (social, as a rule) to the regions. The federal center took upon itself the implementation of the programs that were prescribed by the legislation, simultaneously substantially increasing the share of taxes going to federal coffers. It is noteworthy that the legislators proved willing to go along with such a redistribution of financial resources.

At the same time, the reform of fiscal relations between the center and the regions has been accompanied by actions intended to alleviate the effect of the drastic measures on the regions. In parallel with the change of Tatarstan's and Bashkiria's fiscal status, special mechanisms (programs) are being adopted that allow those regions to adapt to the reduced tax revenues that remain at their disposal. With this in view, the federal government pledged to return to them at the first stage of the reform most of the financial resources transferred to the federal budget, and to approve special programs for those republics' development. In addition, amendments to the legislation that effectively extend the terms of office for a number of influential regional leaders (including the President of Tatarstan) for almost a decade were approved. A mild procedure for rotating members of the Federal Council has been adopted. Finally, a State Council, made up of the regional governors, has been established that is meant to cushion the blow of losing parliamentary status for them.

Stabilization has changed the role of privatization and its place in Russia's political and economic life. On the one hand, privatization has shed its importance as a major factor in securing political support for the regime, which was its predominant role throughout the period of 1992 to 1997. On the other hand, the favorable economic situation and growth in tax revenues have sharply decreased the importance of the fiscal function of privatization, which was especially essential in 1997–1998. As a result, it has become possible to focus on the economic objectives of privatization, on implementing it for the purpose of increasing the efficiency of the economic system. Discussions about approaches to further privatization continued in 2000, but the element of political fighting was hardly discernible in them.

Finally, stabilization has caused substantial shifts in the structure of the Russian elite, changing the balance of economic and political influence groups and the role and status of oligarchs. One of the distinctive features of the nineties was the direct influence wielded by economic interest groups on the executive branch. In contrast to stable democracies, such influence was exerted without relying on political intermediaries (parties, Parliament). Now the situation is changing. Political institutes are acquiring a weight of their own and are gradually becoming equal parties in a dialogue with business, even beginning to play the leading role in this dialogue. To a certain extent, this is part of a general trend toward strengthening the political system, but this transformation also rests on a serious macroeconomic basis.

In the second half of the nineties, the inability of the authorities to balance the budget and the need to constantly rely on the resources of the financial market to close the gap made the authorities vulnerable to the main players on the financial market. The fate of the government, and even the stability of the political system, hinged on the situation in the GKO market, which in practice meant their dependence on the actions of a few owners of major financial entities. The way these owners operated in the financial markets—primarily, their decisions to buy or sell securities—could have brought about the fall of the ruble, the cabinet, or the entire political system of the country. It was precisely this power to stave off or incite chaos that made them oligarchs. Thus, dependence on the oligarchs was not only personal but also institutional, and each new budget that ran a deficit strengthened the oligarchs' effective control over the authorities' course of actions.

Now all this has ceased to exist. The balanced budget has put an end to the authorities' dependence on business, and banks' political role has weakened substantially. The government has finally proved capable of promising what it can really provide; hence there is no need to run into debt. Thus, the government has the necessary leeway now. Social support is, of course, important, but now there is an opportunity to lean on various interest groups, taking advantage of conflicts between them to stabilize political power.

Of course, all of this does not mean that corruption or opportunities to maintain "special relations" between business and authorities have abated. Now, however, the problem is more of a personal than an institutional one. In other words, individual politicians and officials may be susceptible to the influence of individual entrepreneurs, but the state as an institution is not directly manipulable by the organized actions of business.

The new political environment means that a new phase of Russia's social and economic development has begun, which paves the way for developing a new program for the nation's social and economic development.

26.1.2. Strategic Program for Russia's Social and Economic Development

An immediate impulse to the development of the new strategic program of Russia's development and reform was afforded by the emergence of a new administration headed by Vladimir Putin. There were, however, deeper causes, which were associated with the actual (not merely formal) completion of the first stage of the postcommunist reform and the emergence of objective and subjective circumstances pointing to the beginning of a new phase.

The first program of the postcommunist reform was outlined in 1991–1992 and reflected the Gaidar government's general intentions with respect to the reform of the Russian economy. The main goals set by this program were liberalization of the economy (chiefly the freeing of prices and the liberalization of foreign trade), macroeconomic stabilization (fiscal and monetary), and, finally, privatization, which was regarded as the most important goal of institutional transformation as part of the development of a market economy. Implementation of this program took much longer than was originally planned, but by the end of the nineties, the goals of the program had been achieved. This set the stage for moving on to the next phase of the postcommunist development, that of structural and institutional reform to secure sustainable growth.

Political stabilization, the gradual overcoming of the power crisis, and the consolidation of power, with the convergence of the elite groups' stances on fundamental issues, made it possible to start a discussion about Russia's long-term development. The result was the drawing up of the Strategic Program, also known as the Gref[3] program. The program was supposed to set the main goals of Russia's social and economic development and to identify key mechanisms for achieving a rate of growth that would bridge the gap between Russia and the most advanced countries of the world. In other words, the program was intended to set the goal, and find the means, of securing high rates of growth in a postindustrial economy.

In the course of the economic and political discussions of 1999–2000, three main avenues to achieving these goals took shape. The first was the statist model, typical of the left-wing groups. In this model, the state is the main economic agent, and only the state can assume responsibility for investment. This implies maximum concentration of resources in the hands of the state (primarily rent and export revenues) and the redistribution of these resources according to national priorities. Protectionism is important in this model as a way of defending domestic producers from the competition of stronger foreign companies.

The second approach called for growth based on the encouragement of business and on proactive measures on the part of government to create an environment favorable for investors, both domestic and foreign. This approach required establishing an adequate system of institutions, along with appropriate legislation and efficient enforcement.

The third approach involved drastic cuts in budget spending as a share of the economy, making it comparable with the parameters

---

3. German Gref, then head of the Center of Strategic Studies, later Minister of Economic Development and Trade of RF.

typical of countries with a similar level of development (i.e., a reduction in the budget's share of the economy from 35%–36% of GDP to 20%–22% of GDP).

In the course of developing the Strategic Program, all possible alternatives were discussed, including the statist approach (even its mobilization-oriented version). The nonexclusionary discussion reflected the principles of the new administration, which is willing to consider all kinds of proposals without rejecting them on ideological or political grounds. The discussion mainly unfolded between adherents of the second and third approaches. This fact in itself became a significant event in the political and economic life of postcommunist Russia. Both approaches are closely related and are in effect liberal. The establishment of a new institutional environment implies a certain reduction in budget spending as a share of GDP, which would leave economic agents more resources for investment. The reduction in budget spending as a share of GDP as a key problem of growth in turn implies the establishment of the same kind of institutional environment, that is, an environment characteristic of a market-based democracy (with property-rights guarantees of chief concern). Throughout the nineties, the difference between these two approaches was practically indiscernible at the political level, for their adherents were united in opposing the statist (and populist) alternative. Only in 2000 did their separation in the framework of the liberal model become evident to everyone, and differences between the two approaches moved out of the sphere of purely economic debate and into the political sphere.

The beginning of this debate itself indicated a new phase of economic reform. The focus of the economic and political debate shifted to the right (liberal) end of the spectrum, whereas the doctrines of the left were increasingly displaced from the sphere of practical discussion and relegated to the arena of abstract speculation.

The Gref program was mainly drawn up in the first half of 2000. The key feature of this document was its political and ideological consistency, a consistency not seen since the 1992 program. The key concept of the program is the establishment of an institutional environment conducive to entrepreneurship as a basis for sustainable growth.

President Putin's approval of the fundamental approaches of the Strategic Program in April 2000 meant that the conceptual choice was made in favor of the politico-economical model proposed by this document. The full text of the program was not approved as an official document that year. However, for a period of 18 months, spanning the years 2001–2003, it was used as the basis for more technical documents, such as the Program of Measures, and for government-drafted laws and regulations.

Such a development is only natural. It is not only through formal approval that an ideologically consistent document can lend credibility to a policy; rather, credibility also depends on how accurately the document reflects actual trends in the development of social and economic processes.[4] At the same time, formal approval implies tedious coordination between numerous agencies, which either protracts the process substantially or results in inconsistency. The latter is inevitable and only to be expected in the real political process, as the various interest groups interact.

The heart of the Strategic Program is a package of institutional and structural reforms, including political reforms, to be implemented as overall macroeconomic stability (primarily fiscal and monetary stability) is maintained. The key components of the institutional reforms that, under the Gref program, Russia is to carry through, are the following:

1. Tax reform and alleviation of the tax burden.

2. Reform of the budgetary system. What is meant is not formal spending cuts but deep structural reforms of the public sector that would secure more efficient management of public funds.

3. Deregulation of business, or what amounts to the same thing, improving the efficiency of the government regulation of business. Deregulation involves lowering barriers to entry, simplifying the systems of registration, licensing, and supervision of private businesses, and simplifying the implementation of investment projects.

4. Guaranteeing property (including intellectual property) rights, and improving the efficiency of state property management.

5. Lowering and unification of customs tariffs.

6. Development of the financial market and financial institutions. Increasing the stability and efficiency of the banking sector is a special problem.

---

4. For example, the 1992 program was never officially approved. It was severely criticized by most of the political groups. The program was, however, implemented, as it reflected real needs of the Russian economy, even though its implementation took much longer than was originally planned.

7. Reform of natural monopolies to improve their investment attractiveness, which involves splitting up the monopoly and competitive sectors, enhancing their transparency, and encouraging competition to the maximum possible extent.

8. Reform of the social support system to concentrate resources on providing benefits to the poor.

9. Reform of the pension system along the lines of developing savings-based pension plans.

The key feature of the Strategic Program is that it does not envisage any sectoral priorities, which is the most important characteristic of the document aimed at addressing the problems of the post-industrial era. In fact, two circumstances are recognized here. First, the time has not yet come to speak about the comparative advantages of the Russian economy in terms of specific industries and the competitiveness of those industries on the world market. Second, it might be individual companies rather than industries that will prove to be the most competitive. The latter is generally more characteristic of countries facing the challenges of "catch-up industrialization."

Finally, the Strategic Program addresses a number of key issues that go beyond socioeconomic policies as such. Two of them are especially important: administrative reform and judicial reform. The achievement of practically all economic goals hinges on the reform of these two systems, as entrepreneurial activity will be impeded by corruption among government officials and unfair court rulings. This foregrounds the problem of enforcement, which, in the current situation in Russia, is even more important than the adoption of new laws and regulations.

26.1.3. Economic Policy

Practical implementation of the Strategic Program began even before it was formally approved. As early as 2000, bills aimed at fundamentally reforming the tax system were introduced in the Duma. The 2001 budget drafting was also based on these laws.

Tax Reform. Having proposed tax cuts in 2000, the government decided against building an expectation of higher revenues into the following year's budget projections, despite criticism by some deputies. This decision reflected not so much skepticism about the Laffer curve or even the conservatism of the new government's budget planning as a firm commitment to alleviating the tax burden on the economy. In other words, alleviating the tax burden as a means of encouraging economic growth is one of the government's key goals. The flat rate (13%) income tax was introduced. Taxes based on enterprises' turnover (the tax on maintenance of housing and items of the social infrastructure and the tax on motor road users) were dramatically reduced.

Another peculiarity of the tax reform is that it is oriented toward bringing financial demands in line with the actual potential for tax collection. The proposed system (the flat personal income tax and the unified payroll tax) recognizes as a given the paucity of administrative resources available to the weak state. In other words, the authorities are trying to avoid laying claims that they cannot enforce.

The new tax system clearly targets certain social groups. It is undoubtedly attractive to the public at large, but it is especially important to entrepreneurs, on whose support the government counts in the first place.

Customs Regulation. Action taken to reform import tariffs was based on similar logic. It was decided to cut the number of tariff rates and to amalgamate commodity items as much as possible. This approach departs from prevailing world trends, for, thanks to the development of information systems, there are now new opportunities for monitoring goods crossing borders and, accordingly, for using more subtle and diversified methods of customs regulation. However, the limited administrative resources of the Russian authorities do not allow them so far to exercise efficient customs control, and the government is demonstrating willingness to concede this in its customs policies.

Discussion of the new customs tariffs has testified to the somewhat contradictory position of the government in the system of economic interests being formed. Proposals for customs tariffs cuts received wide support from the political elite. The government had no influential forces in its ranks that would insist on the "protection of domestic producers" through customs regulation. That might have been due to two circumstances. The first is the still low real exchange rate of the ruble, which is a barrier to foreign goods. The second is that nascent economic growth made the import of technologies, equipment, and components vital to many companies. Hence the importance of cutting tariffs on the relevant products.

However, the developments in the autumn of 2000 were not as straightforward as that. Delays in the final approval and publication of the new customs regulations resulted in increased pressure from groups that were not interested in the liberalization of foreign trade policy. It became clear that those groups included companies operating in Russia under investment agreements (such as car assembly companies) and light industry. This pressure mounted in direct proportion to the real appreciation of the ruble.

Budget Expenditures Reform. Whereas in 2000 the revenue base issues (the tax reform, revision of revenue sharing between the federal budget and regional budgets) were the focal point of the financial system reform, in 2001 more attention was paid to restructuring federal budget spending.

So far, budget spending has never been reformed in a systematic way. Expenditures are planned, to a large degree, on an ad hoc basis and are oriented to possible revenues instead of being part of a thought-out system of economic and political priorities or a vision of the nation's strategic development. Practice demonstrates convincingly that without systemic transformation of this area, not only the budget but the entire economic, social, and political life of the country will remain potentially (and actually) unstable. Thus, the system of budget spending is a complex theme in which all the problems of macroeconomic policy and structural reform as well as political problems proper are intertwined.

On the one hand, transformation of the system of expenditure planning and management is prerequisite to overcoming Russia's dependence on the fluctuations of world economic conditions and alleviating the debt burden on the economy. Without such a transformation, even budget balancing cannot be carried out, as the budget will remain vulnerable to all kinds of unfavorable circumstances.

On the other hand, this reform paves the way for improving the business climate and is one of the components of structural reform. It should put things into the right perspective for budget recipients and, more important, set priorities for using the state's financial resources in the medium term.

Changes in and refinements of mechanisms for allocating budget funds are another area of budget expenditure reform. Improved methods of allocation should help combat corruption and improve the business climate in Russia.

Finally, the reform of budget expenditures involves the resolution of a number of political problems. The establishment of strategic priorities and transparent procedures of budget financing should help restrain the populist tendencies in the authorities' course of action, especially when additional resources become available to them as a result of favorable economic conditions.

Business Climate and Deregulation. A major test of the government's efficiency is whether it is able to secure official approval for, and practical implementation of, the deregulation program. Deregulation was outlined in the Strategic Program, with top-priority activities set forth in a list of priority measures. At the end of 2000, the first package of laws and regulations was drafted and presented for the government's approval. The package deals with simplifying rules and procedures for business registration, licensing, and supervision by inspecting authorities. Each of these areas is important from both economic and political standpoints.

They are important economically because registration, licensing, and supervision are where the most serious obstacles to entrepreneurship are concentrated. The absolute power of bureaucracy is primarily reflected in the barriers that a business runs into when it is started, and it is also displayed when all kinds of inspections are held. There are about three dozen inspecting authorities, the duration and periodicity of inspections are not specified by regulations, requirements are often impossible to meet, and the penalties and fines are so heavy that they may cause a business to close down. Small and medium-sized businesses are, of course, especially vulnerable, and not only because of bureaucratic pressure and bribe extortion. Excessive regulation may be used to squeeze competitors out of the market and to square the authorities' accounts with entrepreneurs who are not loyal enough.

From the political standpoint, approval of the deregulation package is important as an indicator of the government's ability to concentrate on priority areas and to attain its goals, overcoming the bureaucracy's resistance. Despite the overall awareness of the importance of the proposed measures, however, each of them will meet with serious bureaucratic resistance, as they all trespass on the rights of a host of important agencies, both federal and regional.

Reform of the Natural Monopolies. In 2000, a fundamentally new tendency emerged in this sector. Whereas earlier the management of the relevant sectors of the national economy put up strong resistance to the government's attempts to implement their restructuring, now they are themselves becoming the driving force of change. This trend is especially notable in the railway system and among the electric utilities. We do not at all mean that the government is becoming a hindrance to change. On the contrary, it is certainly interested in implementing reform. However, unlike in previous years, the natural monopolies themselves not only do not resist the government's proposals, they are eager to lead the process of reform themselves. There are at least three factors behind this development.

First, the overall economic and political stabilization allows and necessitates greater attention to the prospects of those sectors' development. To achieve growth, investment is required, and it has become obvious to everyone that government resources are not to be counted on in the foreseeable future. It should be private investment, then, but given their current financial position and organizational status, the natural monopolies are not attractive to big private investors.

Second, a new type (and even new generation) of managers has taken over the relevant companies. In recent years individuals who are able and willing to work in the logic of the marketplace have emerged at the helms of companies, and not only natural resources companies such as UES or Transneft. There has been substantial change in the Railway Ministry's style of management, which is today radically different from what it was only three years ago. Hence the conceptually new level of discussions (both political and economic) which the managers of the natural monopolies are having with the government.

Third, the new managers are interested in enhancing their control over companies "of their own," being well aware that this is best achieved through restructuring and privatization. If top managers keep information and financial flows under control, they exercise much more efficient control over the situation in their industries, which also strengthens their position in the process of any structural reforms.

It should be added that companies' minority shareholders and potential investors in the relevant sectors of the Russian economy have also become much more active. They, too, want to have terms of restructuring adopted that would allow them to gain control with minimum cost. In part, this position is justified by shareholders' willingness to invest in the development of particular industries, but to a considerable degree, such investments represent speculative capital seeking to take advantage of share price fluctuations.

The new situation changes the role of the government in implementing reform of the natural monopolies. Today, the main objective of the government is careful appraisal of various interest groups' proposals for reforming these sectors rather than encouragement of reformist steps. The government now should act chiefly as a supreme arbiter in discussions. However, it cannot do so straightforwardly, by discussing the incoming proposals. In a situation of information asymmetry, the optimum tactic is to encourage conflict between various alliances interested in reforming this sector, so that the debate between them can be used as a basis for careful and realistic analysis of the recommendations presented.

As specific as the individual natural monopolies are, a number of general principles for their reorganization can still be identified. First, it is important to secure continuity of operations, which suggests that the management of those sectors has responsibility for implementing reorganization measures. Second, reorganization should involve separation of the state management and business functions, especially in reference to the Railway Ministry and the Nuclear Energy Ministry. A third principle is to secure financial transparency, which implies adopting international accounting standards. Fourth, reorganization should involve separation of monopolistic businesses from potentially competitive businesses. A fifth principle is to secure equal access to the services or products of these sectors.

Reform of the Financial Markets. Finally, reform of the financial system, chiefly the banking system, is of critical importance. It is this element that is one of the main obstacles to channeling savings into investment. The lack of consensus between the government and the central bank on the principles of banking sector restructuring and improving its stability is a serious problem of the current political process. Still, however difficult this problem is, it should not be resolved by crippling the central bank's independence. That would be the wrong thing to do, because of general theoretical considerations: the central bank's independence is one of the most important gains of the first postcommunist decade and is a factor in the monetary system's stability. In fact, the main source of the instability of the financial system is not so much its legal framework or organizational structure, however important they are, as the low level of economic agents' confidence in one another—depositors' confidence in banks, and vice versa. This creates a situation in which private depositors prefer Sberbank to other banks, while commercial banks prefer to keep funds in the accounts of the central bank at a negative real interest rate, or to invest them in government securities, which have a very low yield compared to commercial loans.

Better legislation can alleviate the confidence problem only to a limited degree. A good credit history is much more important here, and this takes time. For this reason, the stability and predictability of the economic and political course are now the primary prerequisite for improving the operation of the financial markets, even though the government, of course, should take serious steps to improve the situation in this sector. Especially important are steps toward merging banks and enhancing their stability, demonopolizing the lending services market (especially retail services), and allowing entry of foreign banks.

26.1.4. Factors of Destabilization

Despite the reconciliation of interests predicated on the Gref reform program, at the end of 2000, factors that could become a source of destabilization of the economic and political situation in Russia were readily discernible.

Growth of real exchange rate is, in principle, a natural phenomenon of a society pulling itself out of a long period of macroeconomic instability. Undervaluation of the national currency cannot be a constant phenomenon; it gradually comes to an end with a sustainable economic recovery. However, it was the low exchange rate that was one of the factors of the economic and political consensus in 1999–2000, which allowed the interests of exporting industries and those with import substitution potential to be reconciled. Now the impact of this factor is petering out. It would not be so dangerous in itself if it were occurring against the background of investment growth, and especially the inflow of foreign capital.

The national economy remains extremely dependent on high world prices for the raw materials exported by Russia, especially oil.

Prices that are too low or too high present a serious problem. The adverse impact of low prices (less than $10 a barrel) on Russia's situation and the government is obvious. However, extremely high prices are no less detrimental to the economic and political process in present-day Russia, and the year 2000, especially the second half of it, provides ample evidence of this. Three negative effects of the developing situation could be highlighted.

First, high prices create excessive pressure for the ruble's appreciation, with the adverse consequences mentioned above. For sustainable economic growth, it would be preferable to retain the low exchange rate, or at least to contain real exchange-rate appreciation.

Second, the inflow of foreign currency in a situation of limited investment growth accelerates inflation, for, as the monetary authorities try to hold back real exchange-rate appreciation, they are forced to buy hard currency and issue rubles. In addition, in the specific Russian situation, with the "August syndrome" still persisting, the instruments of ruble supply sterilization are limited: policymakers, scared by the GKO collapse, are shying away from reestablishing the government securities market. As a result, the central bank has to perform a balancing act between containing inflation and restraining exchange-rate appreciation, drawing fire from all sides.

And third, high oil prices make it difficult for the government to pursue a responsible fiscal policy, and the problem is incrementally worse than when oil prices were low. Additional budget revenues prompt various lobbies into action. There are difficulties in all the sectors, and all are demanding money, even those that got out of the habit of laying claims to the budget in recent years. In autumn of 2000, pressure was mounting week by week. As a result, the danger of taking the same road as the USSR in the seventies or of Russia in the mid-nineties began to increase.

The problem is not confined to pressure from industrial and agricultural lobbies. All the branches of power are facing temptation to increase their popularity by raising wages, pensions, and all kinds of social payments. Given the current low level of such payments, such decisions would be understandable, but economically and politically dangerous. They would be dangerous economically because they would set a level of government commitments that would be impossible to live up to if the foreign markets changed. In addition, greater consumer demand in a situation of real appreciation of the ruble might be largely oriented to imported goods, and thus would not contribute to growth in Russia.

This is where a potentially serious political problem arises, namely, a possible divergence between the President's and the government's positions. The President, exposed to the pressure of factors making for political stability and the maintenance of his popularity, may prove to be more inclined to make populist decisions than the technocratic government. A likely consequence is greater tensions within the executive branch itself. In the face of such a development, implementing a deep restructuring of budget spending and adopting a special mechanism for using additional budget revenues flowing in because of favorable conditions in the foreign markets (in other words, revenues that do not depend on economic activity within Russia) acquire great importance. Such a mechanism might take the form of a special stabilization fund that would allow accumulating resources and protecting them from inefficient use as a result of pressure from lobbyists.

The dependence of Russia's economic development on world economic performance is not, however, related only to the movement of prices for the exported primary resources. Russia's postcommunist economy is becoming closely tied to the world economy and will henceforth be affected by the world market conditions. Thus, the slowing down of the developed Western countries' growth, predicted for 2001 and later, would also affect the performance of the Russian economy. The cyclic development characteristic of the market system in general will gradually start playing its role, too. All this has yet to make up an integral system of factors that would affect the performance of the Russian economy and gradually replace the specific features of the postcommunist development. In this particular case, we only want to draw attention to the fact that the role of the postcommunist features is gradually receding to the background, while the standard factors of a market economy operation are becoming the main determinants of socioeconomic performance.

One of the factors holding back the development of entrepreneurship and economic growth is the weakness of the enforcement system, and especially the judiciary. Stronger laws and mechanisms to enforce contracts are a major factor in reducing transaction costs, and thus in achieving sustainable growth. In the current situation, better enforcement of existing laws and contracts is even more important than new legislation.

26.2. Russia's Economic Development in the Year 2000: Major Outcomes

26.2.1. Macrostructure of Production

GDP Production. The Russian economy in the year 2000 was characterized by exceptionally high growth rates, higher than at any time in the previous decade. By year-end 2000, the GDP had grown by 7.7% in comparison with year-end 1999, while investments in fixed assets increased by 17.7% and gross industrial output grew by 9.0%. Commercial freight increased by 4.8%, wholesale trade grew by 8.5%, and communication services rose by 13.1% in comparison with 1999. The output of goods increased by 8.6%, and market services grew by 8.0%. The sector of services oriented toward the consumer market demonstrated a smoother dynamics of growth (Table 26.1).

Changes in intersectoral proportions were a distinctive feature of years 1998 to 2000. The share of goods in GDP increased from 42.9% in 1998 to 46.7% in 2000. In 2000, the positive contribution of industrial production and construction in the faster rates of economic growth increased. Whereas in the first half of 1999, growth in industrial output only made up for the previous year's setback in production, the next half-year showed a trend toward the economy's emerging on a path of economic growth (Figure 26.1).

Two phases may be singled out in the economic growth recovery:

- Active import substitution observed from the end of 1998 through the first six months of 1999, caused by the ruble's devaluation

Table 26.1
Dynamics of Key Macroeconomic Indicators, 1997–2000 (% of Previous Year)

	1997	1998	1999	2000
Gross domestic product	100.9	95.1	103.5	107.7
Output of goods and services by base industries	—	94.2	104.6	108
Industrial output	102.0	95.1	108.1	109.0
Investment in fixed assets	95.0	93.3	105.3	117.7
Agricultural produce	101.3	86.8	104.1	105.0
Freight turnover	96.6	96.6	105.8	104.8
Retail trade turnover	104.7	96.7	92.3	108.9
Foreign trade turnover	101.7	84.7	86.7	129.7
Real disposable cash incomes	106.3	81.9	85.8	109.1

Source: RF Goskomstat.

against a background of relatively low prices for the products of the natural monopolies, a sharp shrinkage of imports, and restrained growth in wages and salaries.

• Expansion of domestic and external demand since the second half of 1999, related to a more favorable world business situation and the growth of household and business incomes.

During the first stage, consumer sectors traditionally oriented toward the domestic market found themselves in a better situation. Consumer sectors contributed 13.2% of the growth of industrial output in 1999, compared with 8.4% in 1998. In 2000, the impact of consumer sector industries was at approximately the same level as in 1999. A comparison of the monthly dynamics of growth rates observed in the light and food industries outputs and the dynamics of retail trade turnover shows that the potential of import substitution and ruble devaluation in these industries was gradually becoming exhausted (Table 26.2).

The second phase of the economic growth recovery was characterized by a transition to an investment growth model. From the second half of 1999 on, as the financial standing of enterprises improved and savings accumulated, the demand for capital goods increased. This trend grew stronger in 2000 as a result of expanding investment demand on the part of export-oriented industries for

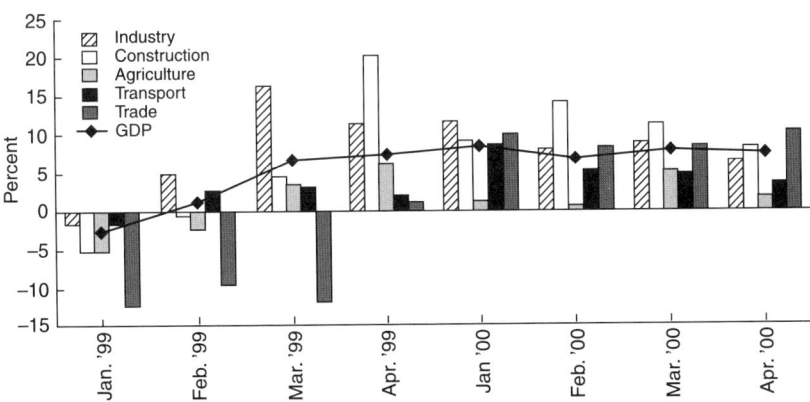

Figure 26.1
Change in the real GDP and gross added value across sectors of the economy, as a percent of the respective quarter of the preceding year. (Sources: RF Goskomstat, RF Ministry for Economic Development.)

Table 26.2
Dynamics of Gross Industrial Output by Production Complexes, 1998–2000 (% of Preceding Year)

	1998	1999	2000
Industry	98.4	108.1	109
Fuel and energy complex	97.5	101.7	104.0
Metallurgy complex	93.5	111.3	113.4
Chemistry and forestry complex	95.3	119.8	112.3
Investment complex	92.8	114.6	114.4
Consumer complex	97.1	108.7	108.6

Source: Calculated based on RF Goskomstat data.

the products of domestic mechanical engineering. In 1999–2000, the output of the investment complex increased by 31.3% over 1998 figures. The increased output of the mechanical engineering and construction materials industry was a factor in the increasing output of related industries. Mechanical engineering contributed 30% of the growth of industrial output in 1999–2000, while the metallurgy complex was responsible for 25% (Table 26.2).

GDP Formation by Revenues. In 2000, the aggregate revenues generated by the economy made Rb 1186.8 billion, which was 1.62 times the aggregate revenues of the preceding year. The share of loss-making enterprises and organizations in the economy at large decreased from 53.2% in 1998 to 41.6% in 2000. The improvement in indicators of financial operations was observed across almost all sectors of the economy. On the whole, in 2000 the profitability of production in the economy was 17.7%. For industry, this indicator was 27.7%. Growth of output and increasing revenues were responsible for increasing tax revenues of the budget. Net taxes on production and imports as a share of GDP grew by 2.7 percentage points over 1999 figures (Table 26.3).

The share of industry in the aggregate profits of economic sectors increased from 56.1% in 1998 to 65.8%. The key specific of the structural shift registered in the formation of gross profit of industry in 1999–2000 was its redistribution from processing industries to the fuel and energy complex and raw materials industries. According to some estimates, the share of extracting industries and the primary processing sector in total industry-generated profits expanded by almost 35 percentage points (Table 26.4).

Table 26.3
Formation of GDP Structure, by Revenue Sources (% of Total)

	1995	1996	1997	1998	1999	2000
Total GDP	100.0	100.0	100.0	100.0	100.0	100.0
Wages and salaries of employees (including concealed remuneration)	45.2	49.6	50	47.6	42.3	41.3
Net taxes on production and import	11.9	13.5	14.5	14.2	14.6	17.3
Gross profits of the economy and gross mixed revenues	42.9	36.9	35.5	38.2	43.1	41.4

Source: RF Goskomstat, RF Ministry for Economic Development.

Table 26.4
Profitability of Production Across Key Sectors of the Economy and Industry, 1993–2000 (%)

	1993	1994	1995	1996	1997	1998	1999	2000*
Economy, total	26.3	14.0	15.8	4.8	6.3	8.1	18.5	17.7
Industry	32.0	19.5	20.1	9.2	9.0	12.7	25.5	27.3
Power engineering	25.5	18.6	17.5	14.3	14.1	12	13.7	16.9
Fuels	19.0	9.4	20.8	11.7	13.1	15.7	44.5	75.8
Ferrous metallurgy	48.5	20.8	22.1	5.0	3.6	10.3	28.2	27.3
Nonferrous metallurgy	43.6	33.2	32.7	10.4	11.4	33	57.4	58.3
Chemistry and petro-chemistry	38.5	25.1	19.5	5.0	2.8	7.8	21.4	18.9
Mechanical engineering and metal working	43.5	26.3	20.8	10.9	8.0	10.0	17.3	15.7
Forestry, woodworking, pulp and paper industry	32.8	16.1	21.8	−5.5	−5.5	5.0	23.9	19.2
Construction materials industry	31.3	19.9	17.9	8.0	5.6	5.2	8.6	13.3
Light industry	36.2	18.9	9.3	1.0	−1.5	0.9	9.5	11.1
Food industry	23.5	16.6	16.3	5.5	8.4	12.8	13.0	10.8
Construction	27.8	23.2	23.3	11.6	11.2	6.8	9.2	12.6
Transport	15.4	10.3	15.1	2.9	6.8	10.6	27.3	32.0
Communications	28.1	26.2	39.2	27.3	27.4	29.4	33.6	56.6
Trade	15.6	2.0	9.8	0.5	0.2	2.6	4.9	9.7

Source: RF Goskomstat.
*Calculated according to RF Ministry for Economic Development estimates.

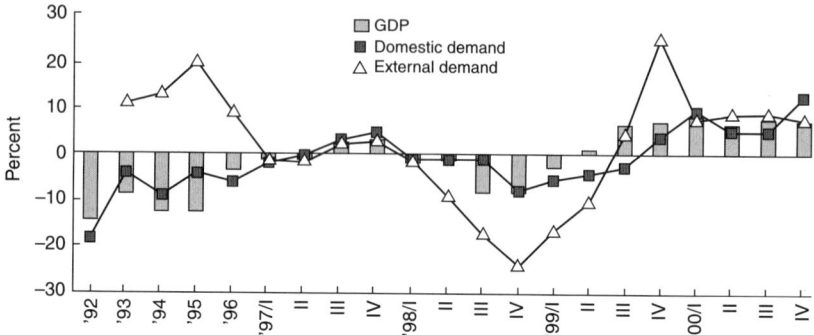

Figure 26.2
Changes in dynamics of GDP and domestic and external demand, 1992–2000, in comparable prices, as a percent of the respective quarter of the preceding year. (Source: Author's calculations based on RF Goskomstat and RF Ministry of Economic Development data.)

The profits of export-oriented (oil, natural gas, ferrous and nonferrous metallurgical) industries increased substantially, and their share in the aggregate profit of the economy overall increased from 26% in 1999 to 45% in year 2000.

The situation was less favorable for processing industries oriented toward the domestic market. Because these industries are generally cost-intensive, the hike in prices for intermediate goods contributed to their decreasing profitability.

GDP Utilization. The dynamic development of the world market for raw fuel and energy resources gave a new impetus to the growth of the domestic economy in 2000. An analysis of changes in GDP dynamics and structure over the years of reform reveals that whereas in 1992 through 1996, increasing external demand helped compensate for a contracting domestic market, the situation changed in the following years (Figure 26.2).

Domestic demand and external demand grew hand in hand in 1999–2000. This situation can be attributed to two factors. First, an almost twofold contraction of imports, as compared with pre-crisis levels, provided the space for intensive expansion of domestic production of goods and services. Second, increasing export-generated revenues were behind substantial changes in the structure and dynamics of final demand (Table 26.5). An active balance of external trade registered in 2000 made over US $61 billion, compared with US

Some Conclusions   813

Table 26.5
Dynamics of GDP Utilization, by Components (% of Previous Year)

	1998	1999	2000 (est.)
Gross domestic product	−4.9	3.2	7.6
Expenditures for final consumption	−2.3	−3.5	7.9
Households	−3.6	−5.3	10.3
Government	0.6	0.9	1.6
Gross accumulation	−31.3	9.3	16.2
Capital accumulation	−11.2	2.4	15.0
Net exports	111.0	60.2	−1.9
Exports	−0.3	9.4	8.4
Imports	−11.0	−15.6	14.3

Source: RF Ministry of Economic Development; customs statistics on RF foreign trade.

$34 billion in 1999, and growth in net exports accounted for almost one-third of the increased volume of GDP in year 2000.

In analyzing the strength of the Russian economy, we should remember that the combination of external factors affecting the growth in production was different in 1999 and 2000. Whereas in 1999 the key factor behind the growth in production was devaluation of the ruble, which enhanced the effectiveness of external operations, rising prices for energy resources and nonferrous metals on the world market were a driving force in 2000. The effects of the ruble's devaluation began wearing off in the second half of 1999, while the influence of the rising world prices for energy resources had noticeably weakened by the end of 2000.

In 2000, the volume of imports again grew at a faster rate than exports and GDP. While some deceleration of the increase in volume of exports may be explained by developments on the world markets for raw materials, internal factors accounted for an intensive growth in imports. In 2000, the expansion of domestic demand initiated by the export-oriented sectors of the economy was based on the continued growth in production of a rather narrow segment of the national economy.

Underlying the poor competitiveness of domestic products is the fact that economic growth in 1999–2000 mainly reflected more comprehensive utilization of operating and reserve production capacities. The commissioning of new capacities was flat, which accounted for the failure to consistently implement import substitution policies and to diversify export flows. From the beginning of 2000, a trend toward a greater share in imports was observed in the structure of commodity resources, both on the consumer market and on the market of material and technical products. The specific weight of imported consumer goods in the total commodity resources (in comparable prices) increased from 38% in the first quarter of 2000 to 43% in the fourth quarter. Growth in imports was also facilitated by real appreciation of the ruble. As a result, according to the Ministry of Economic Development, in 2000 net exports were at 98.9% of the previous year's level.

Growing profits from foreign trade have considerably affected the proportions of final consumption in the GDP. Over the course of 2000, growth rates of gross capital accumulation outpaced the growth rates of other elements of final GDP utilization. Brisk business activity in the Russian economy accounted for the fact that growth in investment demand generated almost one-fourth the volume of GDP. However, the redistribution of GDP resources in favor of the investment component and the rest of the world resulted in a distinct trend toward a falling share of expenditure for final consumption of goods and services in 2000 (Table 26.6).

In 1999, production expanded against a background of low consumer demand. As a result, the aggregate expenditures for final consumption fell by 3.5% over the year, and household expenditures decreased by 5.3%, while real household incomes reached only 85.8% of the previous year's level. In 2000, real household incomes, driven by a steady growth in wages and pensions, increased by 9.1%. An increase in final consumption accounted for almost two-fifths of the increment in GDP in 2000. However, the sharp deterioration in living standards caused by the crisis of 1998 persisted, despite the positive dynamics registered over the year.

Increasing production profitability, coupled with growing export receipts (since 1999), accounted for the fact that for the first time since the beginning of reforms, an upward trend in the share of accumulation was evident. In 2000, savings accounted for 36.2% of the GDP, compared with 29.4% in 1999 and 22.1% in 1997.

The character of investment operations is most illustrative of the mixed developments that took place in 2000. The increase in investment in 2000 was mainly a result of the exceptionally favorable external situation of Russian exporters. Accordingly, the share of the fuel, energy, and transportation complexes in the structure of investment expenditures for reproduction of fixed assets increased by almost 8 percentage points over 1999 figures. As investment de-

Table 26.6
GDP Utilization Structure by Quarter, 1998–2000 (% of Total)

	1998				1999				2000			
	I	II	III	IV	I	II	III	IV	I	II	III	IV
Utilized GDP	100	100	100	100	100	100	100	100	100	100	100	100
Expenditure for final consumption	77.8	77.6	72.7	80.1	72.8	70.7	62.6	70.0	65.0	63.9	57.6	64.2
Households	55.9	52.5	53.6	55.4	58	51.4	46.4	48.9	48.7	44.4	42.1	44.1
Government	18.5	21.2	16.3	20.8	12.1	16.4	13.8	18.1	14.2	16.8	13.2	17.3
Gross accumulation	22.4	22.1	22.6	0.4	11.4	16.0	15.4	22.7	10.9	14.6	24.3	16.0
Capital accumulation	15.2	17.9	18.0	17.7	13.7	15.2	15.4	18.0	13.7	16.1	18.3	21.4
Net exports	−0.2	0.3	4.7	19.5	15.8	13.3	14.7	20.4	24.1	21.5	18.1	19.8

Source: RF Goskomstat.

mand expanded, it became obvious that the domestic mechanical engineering complex could not supply the market with sufficient high-quality materials and technical resources. The lack of modern equipment significantly constrains industrial growth. Consequently, the import of machinery and equipment competitive with domestically produced equipment, with an emphasis on second-hand resources, also increased in 2000.

26.2.2. The Real Sector: Specific Components

Processing Sector. Faster growth in the processing industries than in extracting industries was a distinctive feature of the economic surge of 1999–2000. The output of the processing sector increased 23.0% over the 1998 level, while the output of the extracting industry increased by 12.1%. For the first time since the start of reforms, processing industries' share in the structure of industrial output increased.

An increase in the share of capital-forming industries in the structure of production positively affected the investment environment of the national economy. Whereas in 1992 through 1998, the dynamics of mechanical engineering depended on the rate of output of the motor industry, in 1999 and 2000 the situation changed. Production increased across almost all subindustries of the mechanical engineering complex (Table 26.7). Growth was greatest in the instrument-making industry, in communications facilities, in basic engineering industries that supply the market with investment goods for transport, in agriculture, and in the oil-extracting industry.

An economic recovery was also observed in the defense industries. Whereas the output of the defense complex grew by 25.2% compared with 1999 levels, the output of civilian products increased 21%. The production of civilian products salable on the domestic and foreign markets increased across all industries of the defense complex. The output of the aircraft construction industry grew by more than 37.5% compared with 1999 figures, civilian shipbuilding increased by 9.3%, and the civilian airspace industry experienced a 22% growth. Civilian exports of the defense complex reached US $645 million in 2000.

Despite the positive developments observed in mechanical engineering, however, the contribution of this sector to the growth in industrial output was considerably less than the contribution of the raw materials complex. This fact may be explained both by the

Table 26.7
Output Dynamics Across the Mechanical Engineering Industries, 1995–2000 (% of Previous Period)

	1995	1996	1997	1998	1999	2000
Industry, total	97	96	102	94.8	108.1	109.0
Mechanical engineering	91	95	104	92.5	115.9	115.5
Railroad	73	97	81.1	87	108.9	107.4
Metallurgy	95	93	85.2	70.6	91.8	130.2
Electrical engineering	93	79	93.5	85.7	127.0	130.1
Chemical and oil engineering	96	76	95.6	96.1	120.7	119.5
Machine tool and equipment engineering	87	66.6	84.9	82.3	99.6	111.5
Instrument making	110	70	105.8	103.4	140.8	118.4
Motor industry	97	100.2	112.6	88.5	114.7	103.3
Communications facilities industry	42	33.5	123.2	93.7	95.7	330.0
Tractor and agricultural mechanical engineering	64	59	91.9	70.7	159.3	148.4
Mechanical engineering for light and food industries, household appliances	65			90.6	115.8	109.5

Source: RF Goskomstat.

legacy of the Soviet period and by the specifics of the evolving business situation.

The technical and economic condition of fixed assets of enterprises and the lack of equipment have emerged as factors that seriously affect the potential for a further growth in production. In 2000, capacity utilization was at its peak for the first time in the last decade, reaching 50% for industry as a whole, 77% for the oil industry, 69% for the electric power industry, and 66% for ferrous metallurgy, lumber, woodworking, and the pulp and paper industry. An intense use of reserve capacities was behind the economic recovery; however, there is a limit to capacity utilization. The technical and economic condition of production capacities are a factor constraining growth rates and the competitiveness of domestic products.

Oil and Natural Gas Sector. In 2000, the situation in the Russian oil and natural gas sector was determined by prices on the world oil market. Extremely high world oil prices and the ruble's devaluation resulted in a very favorable situation for the Russian oil and natural gas sector.

Output, profits, and investment in the oil industry all increased substantially (Table 26.8). The total extraction of oil and natural gas

Table 26.8
Russian Energy Resources: Output, Consumption, and Exports, 1990–2000

	1990	1991	1992	1993	1994	1995	1996	1997	1998	1999	2000
Oil (mill. tons)											
Output	516.2	462.3	399.3	353.9	317.8	306.8	301.3	305.6	303.4	305.0	323.2
Total exports	220.3	173.9	137.7	122.6	129.8	122.3	126.0	126.9	137.1	134.5	144.5
Export outside CIS	99.7	56.5	66.2	79.9	91.7	96.2	105.4	109.8	117.9	115.7	127.6
Export to CIS	120.6	117.4	71.5	42.7	38.1	26.1	20.6	17.1	19.2	18.8	16.9
Net exports	201.5	155.8	127.0	112.2	121.6	113.8	117.2	119.0	129.2	128.5	138.7
Domestic consumption	269.9	266.2	231.4	196.5	151.4	150.4	131.3	132.2	125.1	120.5	123.0
Net exports, % of output	39.0	33.7	31.8	31.7	38.3	37.1	38.9	38.8	42.4	42.1	42.9
Oil products (mill. tons)											
Total exports	50.6	46.1	43.0	47.4	47.3	47.0	57.0	60.6	53.8	56.9	61.9
Export outside CIS	35.0	27.0	25.3	35.3	39.1	43.5	55.0	58.4	51.2	53.9	58.4
Export to CIS	15.6	19.1	17.7	12.1	8.2	3.5	2.0	2.2	2.6	3.0	3.5
Net exports	44.8	40.3	40.9	45.2	44.8	42.6	54.4	56.6	51.0	50.3	61.5
Oil and oil products (mill. tons)											
Net exports (oil and oil products)	246.3	196.1	167.9	157.4	166.4	156.4	170.0	173.4	178.3	184.5	200.2
Net exports (oil and oil products), % of oil output	47.7	42.4	42.0	44.5	52.4	51.0	56.4	56.7	58.8	60.5	61.9

Some Conclusions

Natural gas (bill. cu. m)										
Output	640.6	643.4	641.0	618.4	607.2	595.4	601.1	571.1	591.0	590.7	584.2
Total exports	249.2	246.8	194.4	174.4	184.3	192.2	198.5	200.9	200.6	205.4	193.8
Export outside CIS	96.0	91.0	87.9	95.9	109.3	121.9	128.0	120.9	125.0	131.1	133.8
Export to CIS	153.2	155.8	106.5	78.5	75.0	70.3	70.5	80.0	75.6	74.3	60.0
Net exports	179.2	177.8	187.4	168.4	180.3	188.3	193.9	196.4	197.6	201.3	189.7
Domestic consumption	461.4	465.6	453.6	450.0	426.9	407.1	407.2	374.7	393.4	389.4	394.5
Net exports, % of output	28.0	27.6	29.2	27.2	29.7	31.6	32.3	34.4	33.4	34.1	32.5
Aggregate indicators											
Oil and natural gas output, mil. t. (oil equivalent)	1092.7	1041.4	976.2	910.5	864.3	842.7	842.3	819.6	835.3	836.6	849.0
Net oil, oil product, and natural gas exports, mil. t. o. e.	407.6	356.1	336.6	309.0	328.7	325.9	344.5	350.2	356.1	365.7	370.9
Domestic consumption, oil and natural gas, mil. t. o. e.	685.1	685.3	639.6	601.5	535.6	516.8	497.8	469.4	479.2	470.9	478.1
Net oil, oil product, and natural gas exports, % of oil and natural gas output	37.3	34.2	34.5	33.9	38.0	38.7	40.9	42.7	42.6	43.7	43.7

Note: Data on the geographical distribution of exports in 1990–1991 reflect export outside the former Soviet Union and export to former Soviet republics.

Source: RF Goskomstat, RF Energy Ministry, RF State Customs Committee, OECD International Energy Agency, authors' calculations.

condensate increased by 6.0% over the previous year's level, reaching 323.2 million metric tons, while primary oil processing grew by 2.7%. The output of gasoline increased by 3.6% and that of diesel fuel increased by 4.9%, while fuel oil output decreased by 1.7%. Investment activity sharply intensified: oil well production and surveying for drilling increased by 67.5% and 27.8%, respectively, while the commissioning of wells grew by 53.7% in comparison with the previous year's figures. There was also some improvement in the quantitative and qualitative indicators of oil processing. The degree of processing increased from 68.7% in 1999 to 70.0% in 2000.

Data on the production and export of oil and oil products show that the bulk of the extra oil output in 2000 was exported, either directly or as oil products. Net oil and oil product exports reached 200.2 million metric tons, an increase of 15.7 million metric tons over the previous year's figure (reflecting an increase of 10.2 million metric tons in oil exports and 5.5 million metric tons in oil product exports). Thus, the key factor in the increase in oil output in 2000 was the growth in exports, which accounted for more than 80% of the increase in oil extraction. By specific weight, oil and oil product exports took 61.9% of the total oil production. At the same time, the overall economic recovery resulted in an increase in domestic consumption, which we estimate grew by 2.1%, or 2.5 million metric tons, over the course of the year.

Expanding domestic demand stimulated a hike in domestic prices for oil and natural gas products, which trended upward noticeably over the year. As a result, domestic oil prices in dollar terms were practically at the pre-devaluation level by year-end, while oil product prices exceeded that benchmark. At the same time, extremely high world oil prices resulted in a ratio between domestic oil (producer) prices and export prices of less than 25%–29% over the whole year (with the exception of December).

The export of oil and oil products expanded from 191.4 million metric tons in 1999 to 206.4 million metric tons in 2000, or by 7.8% (7.1% for oil and 8.8% for oil products). Natural gas exports contracted by 5.6% as a result of falling exports to CIS countries. The major share of energy resources (88% of oil, 94% of oil products, and 69% of natural gas) was exported outside the CIS.

The hike in world oil prices resulted in sharply growing forex-denominated proceeds for Russia's oil exports. The aggregate value

Table 26.9
Oil Industry: Financial Indicators, 1997–2000 (US $billion)

	1997	1998	1999	2000
Proceeds from oil and staple oil product exports	21.09	13.96	18.82	34.89
Profits (balanced proceeds)	3.52	0.60	6.32	10.42
Overdue payables (by year-end)	6.79	2.41	1.61	1.35
Including to the budget	2.53	0.66	0.43	0.27

Source: Calculated based on RF Goskomstat data.

of Russian oil exports and staple oil products—gasoline, diesel, and fuel oil—increased from US $18.82 billion in 1999 to US $34.89 billion in 2000, or by 85%. Compared with the pre-crisis 1998 level, when this indicator was a mere US $13.96 billion, the value of oil and oil product exports grew by 150% (Table 26.9). As a result, the specific weight of oil and oil products in Russia's total exports was 33.2%.

Analysis of the long-term dynamics of the Russian energy sector exports reveals that aggregate net oil and oil product exports, although demonstrating some upward trend in 2000, still were considerably below the levels observed in the late 1980s and early 1990s. Over the past decade, net oil and oil product exports decreased 19%, from 246.3 million metric tons in 1990 to 200.2 million metric tons in 2000. At the same time, a sharp contraction in domestic oil consumption (according to our estimates, consumption fell from 269.9 million metric tons in 1990 to 123 million metric tons in 2000, or more than twofold) was behind an increase in the specific weight of oil and oil product exports in total oil production, from 47.7% to 61.9%, over this period, while natural gas showed some growth both in volume of exports and in the specific weight of exports in the total output.

Agro-industrial Complex. The Russian agrarian sector grew in 1999–2000. In 2000, this growth was registered at 5%, although production was below the level of 1997, a relatively successful year. A growth rate of 5% was exceptionally high by comparison with the previous 15 years (Figure 26.3). Gross output grew mainly because of crop production, which expanded by 8.9%, while livestock production increased insignificantly.

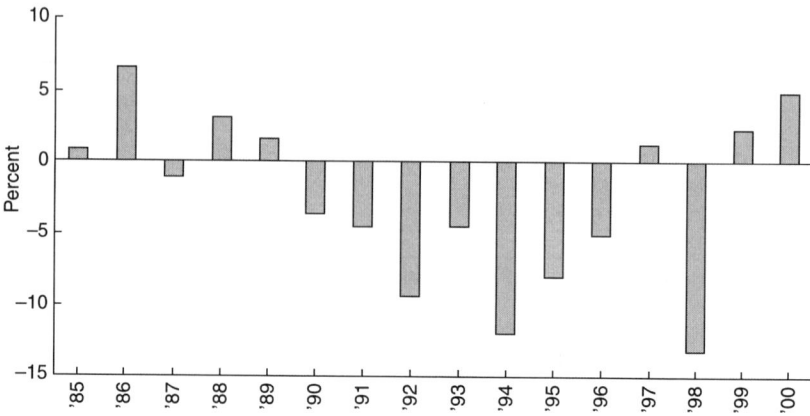

Figure 26.3
Russian agrarian output: growth rates, 1985–2000. (Source: RF Goskomstat.)

All other components of the Russian agricultural and food sector showed growth as well. The food industry output followed the trend of 1999 and increased by 7.1%. Tractor and agricultural machinery production also held on to the unprecedented growth rates of the previous year, growing by 48.4% in 2000. The output of mineral fertilizers expanded by 6.3%. Only the microbiological industry and flour milling declined (Table 26.10).

The undervaluation of the ruble, which has persisted since the 1998 crisis, still favors economic performance of the agri-industrial sector, which remains quite profitable and attractive for investors. In mid-2000, the Concept of Agri-Food Policies for Years 2001 Through 2010 was adopted, and the first efforts were made to implement it. The developments of late 2000 and early 2001 provided evidence of the strengthening of government regulation of agri-food markets. In contradistinction to previous attempts, these efforts brought real results, positively influencing the market situation. With the discontinuation of humanitarian aid supplies, restrictions on the exports of Russian agrifood commodities were lifted. All of these factors, to which we should add favorable weather conditions, fostered a notable growth in agriculture and the agro-industrial sector at large.

The bulk of gross output growth was provided by crop production, chiefly grains. The production of basic livestock products (except milk) also grew. Output increased against a background of a continuing decline in livestock, evidencing a higher productivity of

Table 26.10
Dynamics of Output of Producer Goods in Agriculture, 1990–2000

	1990	1997	1998	1999	2000	2000 as % of 1999	2000 as % of 1990
Tractors (thous.)	214	12.4	9.8	15.4	19.2	124.8	8.97
Tractor ploughs (thous.)	85.7	1.3	1.4	1.8	2.5	137.7	2.9
Tractor seed drills (thous.)	51.1	1.5	1.3	3.3	5.1	156.9	10.0
Tractor cultivators (thous.)	101	3.0	3.2	3.2	4.5	141.8	4.4
Grain harvesters (thous.)	65.7	2.3	1.0	2.0	5.1	By 2.5 times	7.8
Tractor mowers (thous.)	22.6	4.2	6.1	6.7	6.4	96.1	28.55
Feed grinders (thous.)	0.4	1.1	1.5	1.5	0.9	64.2	By 2.3 times
Mineral fertilizers (thous. metric tons)	15,979	9,546	9,380	11,496	12,221	106.3	76.5

Source: RF Goskomstat.

Table 26.11
Production of Basic Foods (Thous. Metric Tons)

	1990	1998	1999	2000	2000 as % of 1999	2000 as % of 1990
Meat	6,629	1,336	1,129	1,153	102.1	17.4
Sausage products	2,283	1,113	948	1,061	111.9	46.5
Butter	833	276	262	265	101.1	31.8
Milk products	20.8	5.6	5.7	6.158	108	29.6
Vegetable oil	1,159	782	881	1,354	153.7	116.8
Sugar powder	3,758	4,745	6,808	6,058	88.98	161.2
Flour, mil. metric tons	20.7	12	12.7	11.9	93.7	57.5
Groats	2,900	1,089	868	919	105.9	31.7
Macaroni	1,038	554	679	691	101.8	66.6
Margarine products	808	185	377	455	120.7	56.3
Canned meat (mill. standard cans)	8,202	344	490	437	89.2	5.3

Source: RF Goskomstat.

animals. The output of livestock products continues to grow faster than the amount of sales, which suggests that the process of eliminating shadow turnover is not yet completed.

Growing proceeds from sales of agricultural produce enable producers to purchase more farm machinery. The growth in tractor and agricultural machinery output continued. At the same time, it is necessary to note that some part of the increase in the output of farm machinery is exported, mainly to the CIS countries. In 1999 Russia became a net exporter of tractors. However, the bulk of agricultural machinery is sold to domestic consumers. In a situation in which agricultural production is growing, the domestic demand for Russian farm machinery will depend on its price-to-quality ratio and, accordingly, on the exchange rate of the national currency.

The food industry also continued to grow, with the output of certain foods (sugar, vegetable oil) exceeding prereform levels (Table 26.11). The production of some commodities is still constrained by low household demand and underdeveloped exports.

According to preliminary estimates, in 2000 the revenues from agriculture amounted to Rb 24 billion (as of 1 October 2000), which was 30% above the level registered in 1999. The sector was profitable for the second year in a row (in 1998 it lost Rb 34 billion). The number of farms with net losses declined from 54% in 1999 to 48% in 2000.

As of 1 November 2000, federal budget outlays for agriculture equaled Rb 10.3 billion—only 66% of the targeted amount (industry, power engineering, and construction received an even smaller percentage of targeted funds, 47%). After a relatively full financing of the agro-industrial sector in 1998, the practice of sequestering expenses thereon is being restored. Nevertheless, in real terms the federal budget outlays for the sector grew by 8% (with the index of agricultural prices taken as a deflator), while agricultural produce increased by 5%.

Investment in agricultural production is growing, especially direct foreign investment in primary farming. At the same time, however, the sector's increased profitability does not solve the problem of agricultural producers' accumulated debts. In November of 2000, producers' debts amounted to nearly Rb 180 billion, including Rb 143 billion in outstanding debt. Almost 65% of the outstanding debt is owed to various budgets and extrabudgetary funds. Agricultural growth necessitates a rational restructuring of these debts, which noticeably hinder the sector's development.

The situation on the food markets began to improve in 1999, with improvement persisting throughout 2000. The more favorable situation was primarily due to the increasing demand for food and changes in the demand structure related to increased real household incomes. The growing consumption of foods expands the possibilities for further growth in the domestic production of foods and agricultural produce. For two years after the crisis of 1998, the gap between the retail prices for a number of major domestic foodstuffs and prices for imported food products persisted. Average retail prices of major domestically produced foodstuffs remain below the prices of imported products.

26.2.3. Public Finances

In 2000, the budget was in an exceptionally favorable situation. For the first time since 1992, the level of tax revenues to the federal budget exceeded 15% of GDP, while total revenues topped 16%. At the same time, the budgetary expenditures were at the lowest level of the preceding decade (Table 26.12).

Several factors were behind such a positive situation of the federal budgetary revenues. A key factor was a price situation that favored

Table 26.12
Administration of Revenues and Expenditures of the Federal and Territorial Budgets (% of GDP)

	1992	1993	1994	1995	1996	1997	1998	1999	2000
Federal budget									
Tax revenues	16.6	12.4	11.5	11.6	9.9	10.9	9.6	12.6	15.2
Revenues*	16.8	14.0	13.1	14.3	12.7	12.5	11.2	13.7	16.2
Expenditures	44.8	23.2	25.2	19.2	20.1	18.5	14.4	14.8	13.7
Deficit	−28.0	−9.2	−12.1	−4.9	−7.4	−6.0	−3.2	−1.1	2.5
Territorial budgets									
Tax revenues	12.0	13.5	13.5	12.2	11.6	12.9	12.1	12.0	12.6
Revenues*	12.3	16.9	18.2	14.8	14.7	16.0	14.8	14.5	15.2
Expenditures	12.0	13.1	17.9	15.2	15.6	17.3	15.1	14.5	14.7
Deficit	0.3	3.8	0.3	−0.4	−0.9	−1.3	−0.3	0.0	0.5

*Including revenues of targeted budgetary funds.
Source: RF Finance Ministry; authors' calculations.

traditional Russian staple exports—oil, natural gas, nonferrous metals, and timber.[5] A second factor was a broader tax base, achieved with general growth of the economy. The broader tax base resulted in higher tax revenues, both in nominal and in real terms. Thus, the real profits of enterprises grew by 50% compared with 1999 figures, while the real increase in tax revenues was 82%. In 2000, real household incomes grew by 9.1%, while wages and salaries increased by 22.5%. The aggregate personal income tax revenues of the federal budget were up by 14%. Aggregate indirect tax revenues of the federal budget increased by 36% compared with 1999 figures (VAT revenues grew by 40%). Third, regulating taxes were redistributed between the federal and territorial budgets. Fourth, tax administration improved. According to Revenue Ministry data, better tax administration increased tax revenues by one-fourth. This growth was mostly generated by large taxpayers (262 enterprises). For instance,

---

5. According to our estimates, in 1998–2000 the fluctuations in federal budget revenues related to changes in oil prices exceeded 4% of GDP (i.e., 40% of the total amount of revenues of the federal budget). For instance, in 1998, when oil prices were below US $12 per barrel, the value of the cyclic (caused by oil price fluctuations) deficit of the federal budget reached 2.2% of GDP. On the other hand, according to preliminary estimates, in 2000 the amount of extra revenues received by the federal budget due to high oil prices was about 2% of GDP. It is necessary to note that over the past 10 years, oil price levels were above the long-time average (calculated over 15 years) only in 1996, 1997, and in 2000, when the industry generated extra revenues for the budget.

Some Conclusions

Table 26.13
Annual Increase in Tax Arrears, 1996–2000 (% of GDP)

	1996	1997	1998	1999	2000
Federal budget	1.1%	1.3%	2.1%	0.8%	0.1%
Consolidated budget	3.0	2.4	2.9	0.7	0.5

Source: RF Revenue Ministry; authors' calculations.

Table 26.14
Rate of Increase in Arrears in Real Terms, 1996–2000 (Real Annual Increase in Arrears as % of Amount of Arrears in Previous Year)

	1996	1997	1998	1999	2000
Federal budget	41%	42%	30%	18%	2%
Consolidated budget	100	46	24	9	10

Source: RF Revenue Ministry; authors' calculations.

Gazprom increased its cash payments by 50%, while UES nearly tripled its cash payments.

Fifth, the growth rate of arrears in taxes due to the federal budget decelerated considerably (Table 26.13). In 2000, the annual increase in tax arrears was only 0.1% of GDP, while the real increment of the balanced tax arrears for 2000 was only 2% (Table 26.14).

And sixth, the level of nonmonetary budget administration declined. For instance, the amount of target financing was Rb 16.6 billion (0.2% of GDP) in 2000.

The declining federal budget expenditures relative to the GDP may be explained by the fact that the GDP grew in real terms by 7.5% over the year, exceeding by 12.5% the amount of nominal GDP (Rb 5,350 billion) set by the budget.

For the first time since 1992, there was a surplus in the enlarged government budget. At 4.9% of GDP, this surplus was rather considerable. At the same time, the total amount of revenues reached the levels registered in 1992 and 1993, while the level of expenditure was the lowest of the preceding nine years (Table 26.15).

An analysis of the administration of the enlarged government budget in 2000 compared with 1999 permits the following conclusions to be drawn. First, in 2000, the federal budget accounted for almost all the increase in the revenues of the enlarged government. Thus, in 2000, tax revenues of the enlarged government made 37.9% of GDP (they were 34.4% of GDP in 1999), while total revenues were

Table 26.15
Administration of the Enlarged Government Budget, 1992–2000

Indicators	1992	1993	1994	1995	1996	1997	1998	1999	2000
Budgetary revenues	40.4	40.6	36.3	35.8	36.7	36.5	34.8	36.2	40.4
Budgetary expenditures	65.1	48.6	47.5	41.1	43.0	43.1	38.1	36.5	35.4
Deficit	−24.7	−8.0	−11.2	−5.3	−7.7	−6.7	−3.3	−0.3	4.9
Domestic financing	13.7	6.1	10.3	3.8	6.2	4.6	−0.1	−0.8	−2.0
External financing	11.0	1.9	0.9	1.5	1.5	2.1	3.4	1.1	−2.9
Total financing	24.7	8.0	11.2	5.3	7.7	6.7	3.3	0.3	−4.9

40.4% of GDP (36.9% of GDP in 1999). At the same time, the increase in the revenues of the federal budget amounted to 2.6 percentage points (up to 15.2% of GDP), while territorial budgets accounted only for a growth of 0.6 percentage points (up to 12.6% of GDP), and revenues of the extrabudgetary funds increased by 0.3 percentage points (up to 10.1% of GDP).

This unevenness may be chiefly attributed to the fact that the favorable prices for oil and natural gas did not directly affect the revenue base of the territorial budgets and extrabudgetary funds.

Second, the uneven growth of revenues resulted in some structural changes: the share of federal budget revenues in the revenues of the enlarged government increased from 37% to 40%, while the revenues of the territorial budgets decreased from 39% to 37.5%, and the revenues of extrabudgetary funds fell from 29.3% to 27.7%.

Third, a decrease in the expenditures of the enlarged government (down to 35.4% of GDP), accompanied by a growth in revenues, resulted in an increase in the primary profit of 6.3 percentage points. The expenditures also diminished unevenly: whereas expenditures of the federal budget and the extrabudgetary funds decreased by 1.1 percentage points and 1.5 percentage points, respectively, the expenditures of the territorial budgets increased by 0.2 percentage points.

Tax Policy. The year 2000 saw serious changes in the tax legislation that affected the structure of the tax system. For instance, four articles of the second section of the Tax Code were approved, to take effect in 2001, which seriously changed income taxes and social taxes, VAT, and excise taxes.

At the same time a number of novations affecting the tax revenues of the budgetary system in 2000 were approved, including the following measures:

- CATE (Closed Administrative Territorial Entities)—related tax privileges were considerably limited.
- A new income tax scale was introduced. Aggregate incomes up to Rb 50,000 became subject to a 12% tax, while the maximum rate was reduced to 30%. The federal law applies to incomes received after 1 January 2000.
- New tariffs for insurance contributions to the RF Pension Fund were approved (at 28% for employers [organizations] and special tariffs at 20.6% and 14% for certain industries; 20.6% for entrepreneurs for business-related or other incomes excluding expenditure borne in the process of deriving such incomes).
- In 2000, the new tariff for insurance contributions to the Social Insurance Fund for employers (organizations and citizens [individuals]) hiring labor via labor contracts was set at 5.4% of remuneration paid in cash or in kind; contributions to the State Employment Fund of the Russian Federation were set at 1.5% for employers (organizations); and payments due to compulsory health insurance funds were set at 3.6% (including 0.2% due to the Federal Compulsory Health Insurance Fund).

26.2.4. Monetary Policy

In general, during the year 2000, a certain stabilization of the inflation rate was evident, in the range of 1%–2% per month; the annual inflation rate for the year overall was 20.2%. By the end of the year the nominal exchange rate of the ruble against the US dollar had dropped by 4.3%, while the ruble gained 4% against the euro. Our calculations indicate that on average, the exchange rate of the ruble against the US dollar over the year 2000 was Rb 28.15.

The main source of the money supply in the Russian economy in 2000 was represented by export receipts, which were transformed into rubles through the mechanism of the compulsory sale of 75% of the receipts on the monetary exchange. An indirect evidence of the fact that the supply of currency on the domestic market considerably exceeded the demand for it (with all of the external operations also taken into consideration) is the growth of the gold and foreign exchange reserves of the CBR. Over the year, the gold and foreign exchange reserves grew more than 2.2 times, from US $12.5 billion to US $27.95 billion. The growth of the gold and foreign exchange reserves and the consolidation of the nominal exchange rate of the national currency due to an increase in the export surplus are typical of countries that have experienced a currency crisis as serious as the one Russia experienced in August and September of 1998.[6] Nevertheless, in Russia in 2000, the real exchange rate of the ruble versus the US dollar was approximately two times less than in the first half of 1998.

The Bank of Russia had only limited means to regulate the ruble rate on the market. The absence of any other liquid sectors of the financial market precluded an effective sterilization of ruble interventions. Any further issue of money could only have resulted in an accelerated price rise, and its aggregate influence on the real ruble rate could not have been altogether positive. On the other hand, the departure of the CBR from the currency market could have resulted in a sharp rise in the ruble rate, as had already happened in the period between May and July of 1995.

The main form of growth of the monetary base in the postcrisis period turned out to be the balances on the correspondent and deposit accounts of the commercial banks with the Bank of Russia, that is, the spare liquid funds not used by the banks in their conduct of active profitable operations (including the funds for servicing the current payments of their clients).[7] The aggregate share of these two components of the monetary base in the years 1999 and 2000 amounted to 30%–35%, while in the years 1997 and 1998 it did not exceed 15%–20%.

This tendency has resulted from several processes observed in the monetary sphere. First, a certain segment of the growth of balances on the correspondent accounts can be attributed to the need to increase the volume of spare funds available for servicing the current payments of the clients. With an allowance made for the change in price levels in the years 1998–2000 and for an increase in the share of monetary payments, both on an enterprise-to-enterprise basis and in

---

6. See, for example, B. Eichengreen, A. Rose, and C. Wyplosz: "Exchange Market Mayhem: The Antecedents and Aftermath of Speculative Attacks," *Economic Policy* (1995): 249–312. In order to stabilize the market it is necessary either to reduce the currency demand (such as by canceling the compulsory selling of currency on the Moscow International Stock Exchange) or to increase the internal demand for currency (such as by replacing the external debt from the budget surplus). Choosing an appropriate policy regarding the real ruble rate is still an important problem.

7. The deposit operations with the CBR are also placed in the category of nonprofit operations because the interest on them is set below the market rate.

relations with the budget at all levels, the volume of balances on correspondent accounts of the commercial banks with the CBR just slightly exceeded in real terms the level of the first six months of 1998.[8]

Second, the absence of risk-free financial instruments and the low attractiveness of the existing financial markets have limited the opportunities of commercial banks to conduct active operations. Under these circumstances, deposits with the CBR virtually play the role of financial investments, despite the low interest they bear. At the same time, the money remaining within the banking system is not used, for example, for crediting the real sector of the economy.

Third, the real sector is still characterized by high credit risks in relation to the crediting of enterprises. Actually, Russian commercial banks are still unable to perform the function of creating money in the economy; they ration credit. This process can be illustrated by the dynamics of the money multiplier calculated on the basis of the ratio between M2 and the broad money base (the reserve money).

The money multiplier started to decrease prior to the crisis, in March 1998, and continued to fall throughout 1999 and 2000. Thus, in 2000, the multiplier of the reserve money had dropped to 1.4–1.5 (from 1.95 in February 1998 and 1.75 in September 1998). This indicates that the attitude of the Russian commercial banks to the real sector has not changed, despite the obvious rise in production and the increased profitability of enterprises. The money multiplier started to grow only in the second half of 2000 (up to 1.55).

Among the possible explanations for the continuing fall of the money multiplier are first, the curtailment of operations on financial markets (the government securities market, the interbank market); second, the fact that the Bank of Russia does not conduct operations on the open market (on the GKO-FSB market), which precludes any reduction of the aggregate surplus reserves by purchasing securities from the Central Bank; and third, a reduction in short-term crediting of the real sector as a result of falling demand for short credits against current assets, import transactions, and trade operations caused by the rise in volume of internal funds of enterprises and the decline of imports. At the same time, the ineffective system of enforcement, coupled with low financial discipline, produced

---

8. This point of view is reflected in a number of publications, including *Obzor rossiiskoi ekonomiki v 1999 godu* (*A Review of the Russian Economy in the Year 1999*) (Moscow: BEA, 2000).

extremely high risks in the sphere of long-term crediting, where no improvements have been made in this respect.

The absence of effective interest rates in the economy and the rationing of credit imply the absence of interest and credit channels of money transmission in the economy.[9] The only working mechanism of money transmission is the exchange-rate channel dealing with the inflow of money from abroad into the accounts of export enterprises and its subsequent sale (especially the compulsory share) on the domestic currency market to the Bank of Russia.

The expansion of the money supply due to currency purchasing by a central bank can exert a rather negative influence on the real sector of any economy. The monetary expansion leads to an acceleration of inflationary processes. In a situation in which the nominal exchange rate of the ruble is kept at a stable level by the high volume of the currency supply on the market, the rise in domestic prices results in an increase in the real exchange rate of the ruble, and consequently in a decrease in the volume of net exports. Accordingly, the government and the RF Central Bank either have to solve the problem of limiting the currency supply on the market, or they have to create some additional (but unrelated to the speculative behavior of economic agents) sources of demand for currency. In particular, it is important to be ready to undertake some curbing of the inflow of short-term foreign capital, which does not increase the volume of investments inside the country but goes primarily to the financial markets, and also to be ready to start sterilizing export receipts.[10]

One of the most important results of the devaluation of the ruble in August 1998 that became evident once business recovery had begun was an increase in the volume of internal funds of enterprises, the downscaling of nonpayments, and a decline in the share of transactions serviced by nonmonetary forms of payments. The rise in volume of current assets in the real sector of the economy and the passage of money along the entire production chain guaranteed a demand for products at every stage of production, thus resulting in

---

9. A similar situation has been observed in many countries that have suffered from twin crises in currency and banking (see A. Garcia-Herrero, "Monetary Impact of a Banking Crisis and the Conduct of Monetary Policy," IMF working paper, 97/124).

10. The Hungarian experience indicates that an attempt at sterilizing the capital inflow by means of open market operations or other monetary instrument results in excessive tightening of the monetary policy, which creates a threat to the prospects of growth in the real sector (see P. Siklos, "Capital Flows in a Transitional Economy and the Sterilization Dilemma: The Hungarian Experience, 1992–1997," *Policy Reform*, 3:

Some Conclusions 833

the growth of the aggregate demand in the economy in general. The factors behind this process are the improved economic situation and the rise in the volume of profits of both export enterprises (caused, among other things, by the situation on the world raw materials markets) and import substitution industries, because of increased domestic demand for their products. The absence of growing indebtedness of the budget to economic agents is a major factor reducing the scale of nonpayments in the economy.

The reduction in nonpayments and nonmonetary forms of payments is conducive to a growth of real cash balances. On the one hand, an expansion of the real money supply implies more liquidity, which is beneficial for effecting payments. On the other hand, the growth of monetary payments implies an increase in the demand for real cash balances and, accordingly, an increase in the real money supply. At the same time, a direct influence on nonpayments is exerted not by the whole volume of the real money supply but only by the real cash balances of enterprises. By year-end 2000, their volume in real terms amounted to approximately 145% of the December 1997 level, while the growth as related to the trough (in November 1998) was more than twofold. At the same time, the real volume of personal assets in commercial banks remained considerably below the precrisis level. Thus, balances on personal ruble deposits at the end of 2000 amounted to only 70% of the December 1997 level and approximately 60.5% of the peak value (in June 1998). By the beginning of 2001, the real money supply, M2, was 101% of the level registered in December of 1997.

It should be noted that both at the end of 1999 and at the end of 2000, the demand for cash decreased. Whereas the share of M0 in M2 amounted to approximately 44% in October 1998, shortly after the crisis, in the second half of 2000 it stabilized at a level of 33%–35%, which corresponded to the situation observed in 1996 and 1997. At the same time, the share of ruble-denominated payments in the economy remained at a much lower level than in the postcrisis period. Between September 1998 and November 2000, the share of the ruble supply M2 in the broad money (M2 plus the balances on forex accounts plus the forex-denominated deposits) fluctuated around 70%, whereas in 1997 and 1998 it exceeded 80%. This phenomenon reflects the preservation of a high extent of dollarization of the economy despite the fact that the effective yield on the currency holdings was negative (Table 26.16).

Table 26.16
Indicators of Money and Financial Markets: Dynamics in Year 2000

	Base Money (bill. Rb)	Base Money Growth Rate (%)	NDA (bill. Rb)	NIR (bill. Rb)	Reserve Money (bill. Rb)	Reserve Money Growth Rate (%)	M0 (bill. Rb)	M0 Growth Rate (%)	Money Multiplier (M2/Broad Money)	CPI (% per mo.)	Official Ruble Exchange Rate (Rb/$1 US)	Ruble Exchange Rate Growth Rate (Rb/$1 US)	Forex and Gold Reserves (mill. $)	Real Exchange Rate (Rb/$1 US; Dec. 1997 = 100)
Jan 00	297.8	−3.15	355.4	−57.6	430.7	−2.06	695.0	−1.38	1.61	2.3	28.55	5.74	12,948	51.70
Feb 00	309.2	3.83	334.3	−25.1	449.4	4.34	726.6	4.55	1.62	1.0	28.66	0.39	13,657	51.95
Mar 00	318.9	3.14	284.6	34.3	491.0	9.25	751.4	3.41	1.53	0.6	28.46	−0.70	15,532	52.50
Apr 00	349.6	9.63	259.7	89.9	513.8	4.65	787.9	4.86	1.53	0.9	28.40	−0.21	17,091	53.66
May 00	365.0	4.41	207.9	157.1	558.4	8.70	831.6	5.55	1.49	1.8	28.25	−0.53	19,570	55.16
Jun 00	397.2	8.82	194.9	202.3	602.8	7.94	892.2	7.29	1.48	2.6	28.05	−0.71	20,996	56.53
Jul 00	417.3	5.06	141.5	275.8	654.7	8.61	931.2	4.37	1.42	1.8	27.80	−0.89	23,302	57.20
Aug 00	427.6	2.47	122.9	304.7	648.2	−1.00	960.1	3.10	1.48	1.0	27.75	−0.18	23,731	57.64
Sep 00	437.6	2.34	97.8	339.8	671.1	3.53	992.4	3.36	1.48	1.3	27.75	0.00	25,007	58.58
Oct 00	449.0	2.61	78.9	370.1	662.5	−1.27	1001.2	0.89	1.51	2.1	27.83	0.29	25,880	
Nov 00	455.2	1.38	48.3	406.9	684.2	3.27	1036.4	3.52	1.51	1.5	27.85	0.07	27,667	
Dec 00	519.6	14.15	—	—	739.2	8.04	1144.3	10.41	1.55	1.6	28.16	1.11	27,951	

Note: NDA, net domestic assets; NIA, net international reserves.

Sources: RF Goskomstat, RF CBR, RTS, IA Finmarket, RETsEP, International financial statistics.

26.2.5. The Social Sphere

The year 2000 saw certain positive changes in the living standards of Russia's population. Real disposable cash incomes increased by 9.1% over the year; however, they were still 10% below the precrisis level (in the first half of 1998). Income growth was positively affected by increases in pensions and wages of those employed by organizations financed from the budget, and by a further decrease in wage arrears (by 27.6% as of December 2000). In 2000, the average per capita monthly cash income was Rb 2,112 (the average for the month of December alone was Rb 3,112).

With regard to the inter-regional differentiation of incomes, in November of 2000 average cash household incomes in Moscow were five to ten times higher than respective indicators calculated for regions in the Central Economic Region. By comparison, in 1999 average cash household incomes in Moscow were seven to ten times higher than in the Central Economic Region, and in 1998 they were six to nine times higher.

The increase in wages was more substantial than the increase in average total income. Average wages and salaries grew by 22.5% over 1999 figures. Average monthly gross wages and salaries made Rb 2,268 in 2000, compared with Rb 1,523 in 1999 (Table 26.17).

Although in 2000, average monthly wages across the majority of Russia's regions exceeded average per capita incomes, in Moscow average monthly wages were only 38% of average per capita income (42% in 1999, 48% in 1998, 41% in 1997).

Table 26.17
Structure of Cash Household Incomes, 1999–2000 (%)

	1990	1991	1992	1994	1995	1996	1997	1998	1999	2000
Cash incomes, total	100	100	100	100	100	100	100	100	100	100
Wages and salaries, including concealed payments	74.1	69.7	73.6	64.5	62.8	65.9	65.7	64.9	65.5	65.6
Social transfers	14.7	16.3	14.3	13.5	13.1	14.0	15.0	13.6	13.2	13.4
Property-based incomes	2.5	2.8	1.0	4.5	6.5	5.4	5.7	5.5	7.2	7.2
Business-related incomes	3.7	4.1	8.4	16.0	16.4	13.6	13.0	14.2	13.2	12.6
Other incomes	5.0	7.1	2.7	1.5	1.2	1.1	0.6	1.8	0.9	1.2

Source: RF Goskomstat.

Table 26.18
Total Household Cash Incomes Across Income Groups, Coefficients of Differentiation, and Concentration of Incomes, 1991–2000 (%)

	1991	1992	1993	1994	1995	1996	1997	1998	1999	2000*
Cash incomes, total	100	100	100	100	100	100	100	100	100	100
Group 1 (lowest incomes)	11.9	6.0	5.8	5.3	5.5	6.2	6.2	6.2	6.2	6.1
Group 2	15.8	11.6	11.1	10.2	10.2	10.7	10.6	10.5	10.6	10.3
Group 3	18.8	17.6	16.7	15.2	15.0	15.2	15.1	14.9	14.9	14.5
Group 4	22.8	26.5	24.8	23.0	22.4	21.5	21.4	21.0	21.0	20.5
Group 5 (highest incomes)	30.7	38.3	41.6	46.3	46.9	46.4	46.7	47.4	47.3	48.6
Decile coefficient of differentiation (funds)	4.5	8.0	11.2	15.1	13.5	13.0	13.2	13.2	14.5	14.1
Gini coefficient	0.260	0.289	0.398	0.409	0.381	0.375	0.381	0.379	0.394	0.400

*Third quarter of 2000.

Some Conclusions

Table 26.19
Population Groups, by Amount of Per-Capita Cash Income (Thous. of Rb) (% of Total)

	1999	2000
Total population	100	100
Including groups with per-capita cash incomes (Rb):		
<400.0	3.4	1.4
400.1–600.0	8.1	4.3
600.1–800.0	11.0	6.9
800.1–1,000.0	11.6	8.4
1,000.1–1,200.0	10.8	8.8
1,200.1–1,600.0	17.5	16.5
1,600.1–2,000.0	12.2	13.4
>2,000.0	25.4	40.3

The intersectoral differentiation of wages and salaries continued to increase. In May of 2000, wages differed by 8.4 times across sectors. In November of 2000, the average wage in the fuel industry was 3.2 times higher than the all-Russia average (it was 2.95 times higher in 1999 and 2.37 times higher in 1998), while relatively underpaid sectors financed from the budget sank even more compared with the national average. For instance, the average monthly wage in the public health sector was 58% of the all-Russia average (it was 60% in 1999 and 67% in 1998), and the average monthly wage in education, culture, and the arts was 54% of the national average (55% in 1999, 60% in 1998).

In 2000, the average monthly gross pension, adjusted for compensatory payments, was Rb 694.2. The amount of real pension increased by 28% compared with 1999 figures.

The ratio between the average pension and the subsistence minimum for pensioners improved somewhat. Whereas in 1999 the average pension was 31% below the subsistence minimum for a pensioner, in the third quarter of 2000 it was 74% of the subsistence minimum for a pensioner. The ratio between average wages and the subsistence minimum for the employable population also improved somewhat during the year. In the third quarter of 2000 the average wage was 168% of the subsistence minimum, whereas in the previous year it was less than 156% of the subsistence minimum.

Despite some economic growth, the differentiation of household incomes remained at the same level. Changes in the decile coefficient of differentiation of funds (which decreased by 0.4%) and in the Gini coefficient (which increased by 0.006%) registered at the end of the third quarter of 2000 were insignificant. In 2000, the distribution of the total amount of household incomes among 20% income groups also changed insignificantly in comparison with 1999 figures (Tables 26.18 and 26.19).

In 2000, the social psychological climate was positively affected by a change in the labor market situation and a growing sense of employment security on the part of the population. The unemployment figure calculated according to ILO methods decreased by almost 1.8 million people, to about 6.9 million, while the number of officially registered citizens out of work decreased by almost one-third over the same period. As the economy recovered, demand for labor increased. The number of vacancies that enterprises reported to employment agencies amounted to about 751 available jobs by the end of 2000, compared with 588 vacancies reported in the previous year. The number of job-seekers per vacancy decreased from 6.6 in January 1999 to 1.6 in December 2000.

Appendix I

Modeling Inflation Dynamics, 1992 Through 1998

Sergei Drobyshevsky

The dynamics of the consumer price index (CPI) in the period between 1992 and August of 1998, according to the records of Goskomstat (the Federal Statistics Board), are shown in Figure I.1. Two distinct subperiods of inflation are evident in the figure. The first, spanning 1992 to 1994, was characterized by jumping inflation with a wide volatility amplitude (the standard deviation reached 7.93%). The second subperiod, which began in early 1995 and ended in the summer of 1998, was marked by a gradual reduction in CPI growth rates to virtually zero, at a low dispersion value. The mean was 2.8%, with a standard deviation of 3.54%. In modeling the dynamics of inflationary processes, therefore, one must consider both the general pattern of changes in inflation over the whole period under examination and the specifics of each subperiod. The specifics of the subperiods are particularly important in forecasting future CPI values, for the prominence of different factors in different periods may lead to bias in the estimates and affect the forecast error of the regression model.

For this reason, we have assumed a set of hypotheses that must be verified before developing an approach to forecasting inflation in the short run.

- *Hypothesis 1:* Price growth rates either are persistent or exhibit a deterministic trend overtime. Persistence in this case denotes a stable relationship between the current inflation rate and previous CPI values. The deterministic trend assumes an obvious trend toward lower or higher inflation rates, along with a random pattern of variations.
- *Hypothesis 2:* In evaluating future inflation, economic agents give overwhelming preference to adaptive expectations.

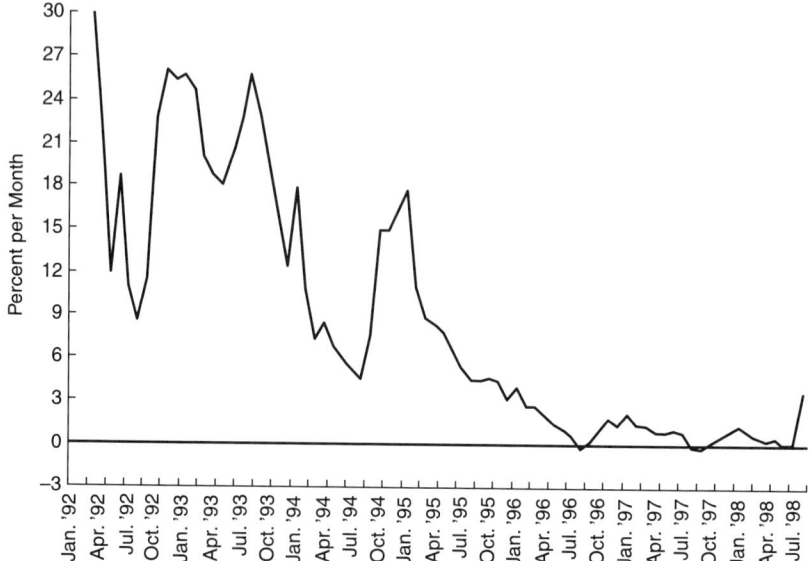

Figure I.1
The CPI in Russia, 1992–1998.

- *Hypothesis 3:* In the long run, inflationary processes in the Russian economy are determined by the dynamics of changes in the money aggregates (M0, M2, broad money) and fluctuations in the demand for cash.
- *Hypothesis 4:* Over the first period (from 1992 to the first half of 1994), excessive money emission and a falling demand for money played dominant roles in the developing inflationary process. In the second period, inflationary persistence and a growing demand for money dominated.

The results of testing these hypotheses are described below.

Specification of the equation for the dynamics of consumer price index rates. The equation we have chosen to describe the dynamics of inflationary process is based on the standard model of demand for money:

$$\frac{M_t}{P_t} = L_t(i, Y, \ldots)$$

where M_t is the nominal money supply at time t, P_t is the price level at time t, i is the nominal interest rate, Y is the real GDP, and the error term represents other factors affecting the demand for money.

In order to estimate the equation, we proceed to the discrete form of representation of demand for money. After some mathematical calculations, and having taken into account the hypothesis that economic agents have adaptive expectations (that is, expectations of price increases in future periods are formed on the basis of previous price dynamics: $E_{t-1}(\dot{p}_t | \Omega_{t-1}) = f(\dot{p}_{t-1, t-m})$, and representing nominal interest as a sum of real interest and expected inflation (according to the Fisher hypothesis), we can write the equation as follows:

$$\dot{p}_t = c + a_1 f(\dot{p}_{t-1, t-m}) + a_2 \dot{m}_{t-1, t-n} + a_3 \dot{Y}_t + \varepsilon_t$$

where $\dot{p}_t$ is the monthly CPI increase at time t, c is a constant term, $f(\dot{p}_{t-1, t-m})$ is a function depending on lagged inflation values over m previous months, $\dot{m}_{t-1, t-n}$ is the rate of increase in the monetary aggregate over n previous months, $\dot{Y}_t$ is the rate of increase of the real GDP, ε_t is a random error that is independently and normally distributed over time, and a_1, a_2, and a_3 are regression coefficients.

The first term, therefore, shows the persistence of inflationary processes, or the adaptive nature of inflationary expectations. The second term reflects the monetary nature of inflation and the effect of the growth rates of nominal monetary aggregates on the price level in the economy. The third term reflects the fluctuation in transactional demand for money resulting from changes in the real GDP.[1]

We deliberately chose August 1998 as the terminus of our observations. Beginning in the fall of 1998, the forced abandonment of the currency corridor, which had been characterized by a relatively slow ruble depreciation relative to the US dollar, along with the ensuing collapse of the market exchange rate of the ruble, resulted in the rapid growth of prices of imported goods and a panic explosion of inflationary expectations. In consequence, the structure of the process under investigation changed considerably. The experience with inflationary developments after the explosive financial crisis has not been long enough to allow adequate analysis. Therefore the period from February 1992 to August 1998 was chosen for the appraisal of parameters of the aforementioned equations.

---

1. Here we disregard the volume of transaction demand for money for conducting operations on financial markets. For a more exact evaluation one would want to take into account an indicator reflecting the availability of financial markets (for instance, the turnover of key financial market segments).

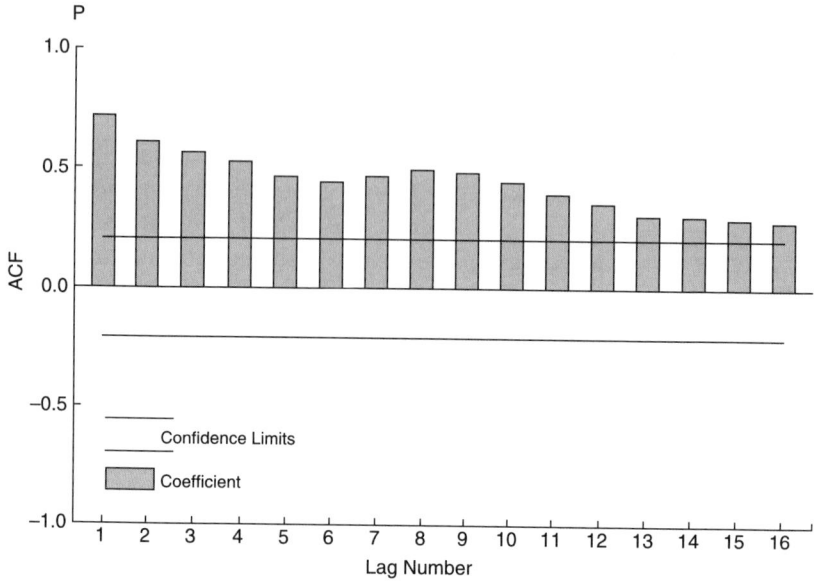

Figure I.2
Autocorrelation function for CPI rate time series.

1. **Price Inertia.** This hypothesis assumes that the dynamics of inflationary processes are largely determined by the dynamics of inflation in the past.

To test this hypothesis, we analyzed the autocorrelation functions (ACF) and partial autocorrelation functions (PACF) of the CPI rate time series, tested the CPI rate time series for unit roots, and estimated regressions of the type $p_t = c + a_1 \cdot f(t) + \varepsilon_t$.

Analysis of the ACF and PACF[2] of the CPI rate time series. The ACF and PACF for the initial CPI rate time series are shown in Figures I.2 and I.3.

Analysis of the ACF and PACF shows that the time series are first-order autoregressive processes (only the first coefficient of the partial autocorrelation function is significant), or AR 1.

Result of the Dicky-Fuller test for unit roots. The augmented Dicky-Fuller test[3] statistic for the time series $\dot{p}_t$ is equal to -4.0556 at the

---

2. See J. Johnston and J. DiNardo, *Econometric Methods*, 4th ed. (New York: McGraw-Hill, 1997).
3. See T. Mills, *The Econometric Modelling of Financial Time Series* (Cambridge: Cambridge University Press, 1993).

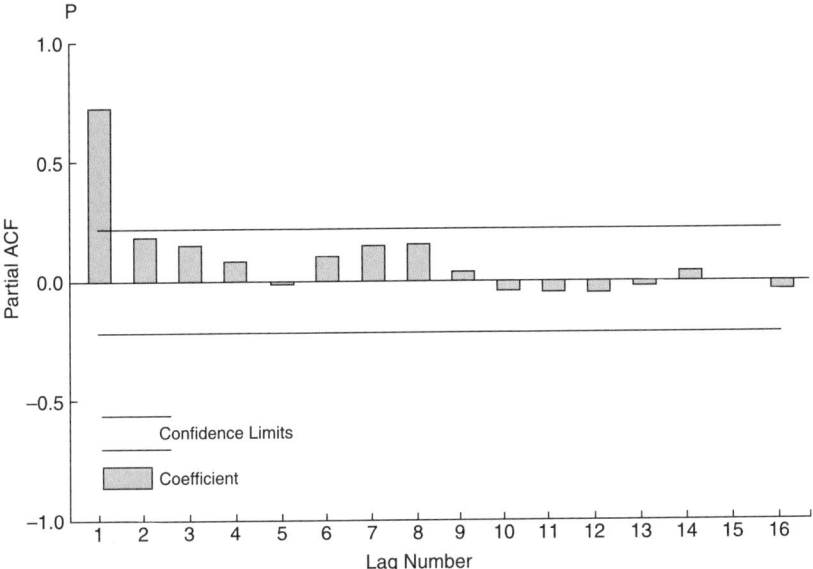

Figure I.3
Partial autocorrelation function for CPI rate time series.

critical value for rejecting the null hypothesis of a unit root at a 95% significance level equal to −3.4704. The test therefore shows that the initial time series of monthly CPI growth rates is stationary and can be used in the regression equation without additional variable transformation.

2. **Economic Agents' Expectations.** Whereas the persistence of inflation is determined by the changing expectations of economic agents, current inflation would largely be determined by the preceding values of the price growth rates. Analysis of the initial CPI time series using a PACF showed a strong dependence of the current CPI growth figure on the previous month's value. Our assumption, however, was that economic agents' expectations are based on the inflation dynamics over several preceding months. Therefore, we chose to model expectations using not only the autoregressive model, but also distributed lags (including Charles Almon's lags[4]) of different specifications:

---

4. See G. Judge, W. Griffiths, R. C. Hill, H. Luetkepohl, and T.-C. Lee, *The Theory and Practice of Econometrics*, 2nd ed. (New York: John Wiley & Sons, 1985).

(a) First-order autoregressive model
   Equation 1:

   $$\dot{p}_t = c + a_1 \cdot \dot{p}_{t-1} + \varepsilon_t$$

(b) Polynomial distributed lag
   Equations 2 and 3:

   $$p_t = c + \sum_{i=0}^{n} a_1 w_i p_{t-i-1} + \varepsilon_t$$

   where $n =$ depth of the lag, twelve months for equation 1 and six months for equation 2;

   $$w_i = b_0 + b_1 i + b_2 i^2 + b_3 i^3 + b_4 i^4$$

   where $i =$ number of the lag, the fourth degree of the polynomial being chosen to take into account the number of observations and the required number of degrees of freedom.

(c) Lag with linearly decreasing weights
   Equation 4:

   $$p_t = c + a_1 p_{t-1} + 0.8 a_2 p_{t-2} + 0.6 a_2 p_{t-3} + 0.4 a_4 p_{t-4}$$
   $$+ 0.2 a_5 p_{t-5} + 0.01 a_6 p_{t-6} + \varepsilon_t$$

(d) Lag with hyperbolically decreasing weights
   Equation 5:

   $$p_t = c + a_1 p_{t-1} + 0.5 a_2 p_{t-2} + 0.33 a_2 p_{t-3} + 0.25 a_4 p_{t-4}$$
   $$+ 0.2 a_5 p_{t-5} + 0.17 a_6 p_{t-6} + \varepsilon_t$$

(e) Lag with weights for individual months.
   Month numbers were chosen based on the results of estimating equations 2 and 3.
   Equation 6:

   $$p_t = c + a_1 p_{t-1} + 0.5 a_2 p_{t-3} + \varepsilon_t$$

The results of the equation evaluation are shown in Table I.1.

As was expected, the CPI model with a polynomial distributed lag follows most closely the model for economic agents' behavior with changing expectations and describes the current inflation dynamics better than any other type of relationship. As shown in Figure I.4, economic agents frame their expectations on the basis of inflation

Table I.1
Coefficients Derived from Equations 1 Through 6 Using Various Time Lags*

Lag (months):	Equation					
	1	2	3	4	5	6
1	0.874	0.724	1.075	1.215	1.148	0.988
	(23.240)	(9.970)	(10.211)	(10.949)	(10.634)	(12.766)
2		0.250	−0.043	−0.483	−0.774	
		(13.152)	(−0.404)	(−2.425)	(−2.872)	
3		0.012	−0.188	0.185	0.336	−0.146
		(0.427)	(−3.352)	(0.776)	(1.053)	(−1.042)
4		−0.069	−0.017	−0.068	−0.109	
		(−2.326)	(−0.246)	(−0.193)	(−1.539)	
5		−0.061	0.089	−0.741	−0.974	
		(−2.830)	(1.956)	(−1.052)	(−1.400)	
6		−0.014	0.034	19.481	1.145	
		(−0.854)	(0.546)	(2.169)	(2.850)	
7		0.033				
		(1.730)				
8		0.058				
		(2.989)				
9		0.050				
		(3.300)				
10		0.015				
		(1.100)				
11		−0.028				
		(−1.369)				
12		−0.049				
		(−2.376)				
Adjusted R^2	0.875	0.907	0.901	0.901	0.901	0.871

*Coefficients were calculated as $a_i w_i$ for a polynomial distributed lag, a_i for other equations. t statistics are shown in parentheses.

values for the preceding two or three months, but the weights of more remotely past months tend to zero.

3. Linear Autoregressive Monetary Model of Inflation. Our study of the effect of money supply growth rates on current CPI growth rates focused on two points. First, we sought to determine which of the money aggregates (M0, M2, or broad money as a sum of M2 and foreign exchange deposits) most affects the growth of inflation in the Russian economy. Second, we measured the influence of changes in the nominal money supply on the current price level.

To address the first problem, we performed a correlation analysis of CPI dynamics and average growth rates of the monetary aggre-

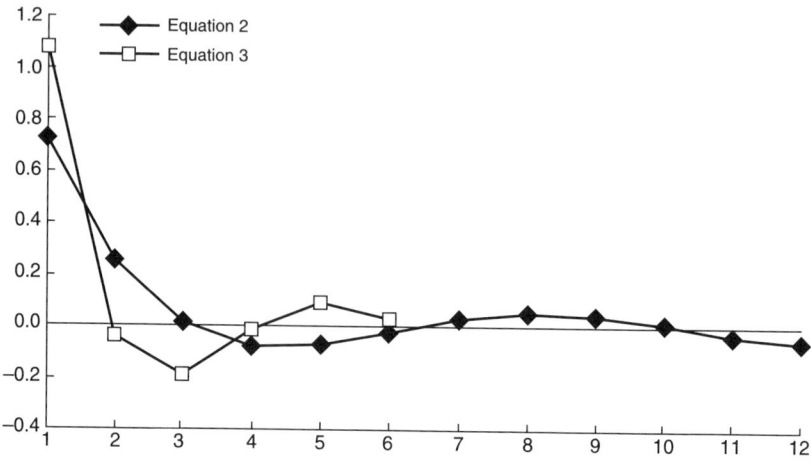

Figure I.4
Structure of weights of polynomial distributed lags.

gates for two to ten months. The following formula was used to calculate the average money supply growth rates:

$$\dot{m}_{t-1,t-n} = \left(\frac{M_{t-1}}{M_{t-n-1}}\right)^{1/n} - 1$$

where n = number of months.

The values of the paired correlations of CPI and money aggregate growth rates are shown in Table I.2. We found that the closest relation exists between inflation rates and increases in the money supply M2.

In order to ascertain the lag by which M2 affected the inflation level, we first applied the Granger-Sims test for causality[5] to CPI rates and M2 growth rates across different numbers of lags. We then estimated regression equations of the type $\dot{p}_t = c + a_1 \dot{p}_{t-1} + a_2 \dot{m}_{t-1,t-n} + \varepsilon_t$, using average money supply growth rates for three to ten months. The test results and the results of estimating the regression equations are shown in Tables I.3 and I.4.

The final choice of lag depth was based on the acceptance of causality between M2 and CPI, and statistical significance of the regression coefficient of the monetary aggregate. The Granger-Sims

---

5. See R. Pindyck and D. Rubinfeld, *Econometric Models and Economic Forecasts*, 3rd ed. (New York: McGraw-Hill, 1991).

Table I.2
Paired Correlations of CPI and Money Aggregate Growth Rates

		P	M0	M2	BM2
P	Pearson correlation	1.000	0.545*	0.522*	0.485*
	Sig. (2-tailed)		0.000	0.000	0.000
	N	84	79	79	79
M0	Pearson correlation	0.545*	1.000	0.834*	0.743*
	Sig. (2-tailed)	0.000		0.000	0.000
	N	79	79	79	79
M2	Pearson correlation	0.522*	0.834*	1.000	0.907*
	Sig. (2-tailed)	0.000	0.000		0.000
	N	79	79	79	79
BM2	Pearson correlation	0.485*	0.743*	0.907*	1.000
	Sig. (2-tailed)	0.000	0.000	0.000	
	N	79	79	79	79

*Correlation is significant at the 0.01 level (2-tailed).

Table I.3
F-Statistics and Significance Level for the Granger-Sims Causality Test*

	Number of Lags of the CPI and M2 Growth Rates (months)							
	3	4	5	6	7	8	9	10
"CPI does not Granger cause M2"	8.91	6.54	5.97	3.67	2.66	2.09	1.87	1.51
	(0.000)	(0.000)	(0.000)	(0.004)	(0.019)	(0.054)	(0.079)	(0.164)
"M2 does not Granger cause CPI"	8.20	8.44	5.89	5.10	6.19	5.64	5.03	5.14
	(0.000)	(0.000)	(0.000)	(0.000)	(0.000)	(0.000)	(0.000)	(0.000)

*t statistics are shown in parentheses.

Table I.4
t Statistics for the Coefficient of the Money Aggregate, and Coefficients for Estimations of the Regression Equations

	Depth of Average M2 Growth (months)							
	3	4	5*	6	7*	8*	9	10
t Statistics for coefficient a_1	4.25	4.98	5.17	4.95	5.29	6.20	2.06	2.01
R^2	0.878	0.896	0.881	0.890	0.888	0.898	0.905	0.904

*Corrected for autocorrelation in residuals by the Prais-Winsten method.

causality test allows one not to reject a joint hypothesis about the existence of causality between CPI and M2 growth rates starting at a lag depth of eight months. Most statistically significant are coefficients of the average money growth rate over five, seven, and eight months. At the same time, the highest values of R^2 are observed at four, eight, nine, and ten months.[6] Thus, we chose the M2 influence depth to be equal to eight months.

4. Nonlinear Monetary Model of Inflation. The Lagrange multiplier test for autoregressive conditional heteroscedasticity[7] reveals that the residuals of the linear regression model of inflation are heteroscedastic. To adjust for this property of the residuals, we estimated the nonlinear regression model for CPI growth rates with autoregressive conditional variance of residuals, or ARCH 1, as follows[8]:

$$\dot{p}_t = c + a_1 \dot{p}_{t-1} + a_2 \dot{m}_{t-1, t-9} + a_3 \dot{Y}_t + \varepsilon_t$$
$$\sigma(\varepsilon)_t^2 = b_1 + b_2 \varepsilon_{t-1}^2 + \eta_t$$

The results of estimating the equations are shown in Table I.5. Estimated coefficients of the first-order autoregressive term, money supply growth rates, and real GDP rates are statistically significant at the 5% level and have the expected signs.

Use of the nonlinear model allowed us to improve the characteristics of the regression equation (the R^2 and information criteria) and to estimate fluctuations in error variance in periods of higher inflation rates. The assumption of the preconditional form of variance (ARCH) also allowed estimated coefficients of exogenous variables to be cleaned of random noise in the periods of high inflation fluctuations. Over the whole period under scrutiny, two subperiods with different error variance can be distinguished (Figure I.5). These periods fully coincide with the subperiods characterized by different inflation regimes that we mentioned at the beginning of the discussion.

---

6. Serial autocorrelation observed in equation residuals is considered evidence of the absence of other significant variables (for instance, GDP).
7. See R. Engle, "Autoregressive Conditional Heteroskedasticity, with Estimates of the Variance of United Kingdom Inflations," *Econometrica* 50 (1982): 987–1008.
8. See A. Harvey, *Time Series Models*, 2nd ed. (Cambridge, Mass.: MIT Press, Harvester Wheatsheaf, 1993).

Table I.5
Nonlinear Monetary Model of Inflation: CPI Growth Rates Estimated with Autoregressive Conditional Variance of Residuals (ARCH)

	c	a_1	a_2	a_3
Coefficient	−0.004	0.805	0.131	−0.023
t-statistics	−2.44	22.98	3.90	−2.10
R^2			0.904	
Adjusted R^2			0.897	
F-statistics			122.5	
Number of observations			71	
AIC			−8.14	
BIC			−7.95	

ARCH	b_1	b_2
Coefficient	0.000	2.013
t statistics	1.58	2.97

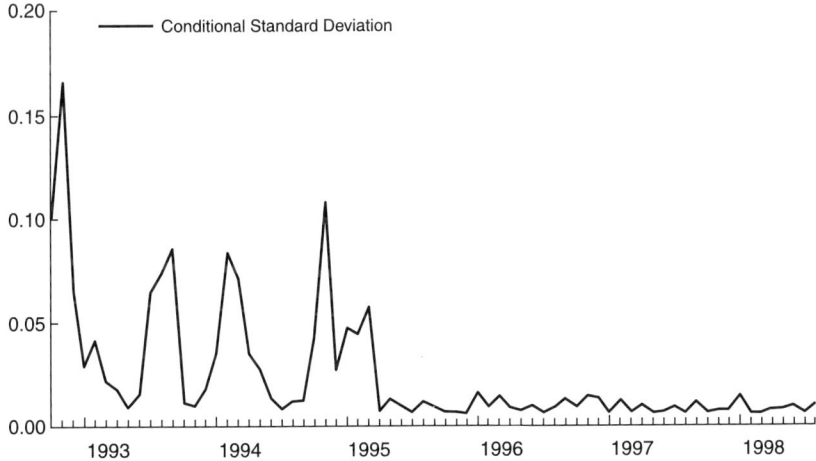

Figure I.5
Two subperiods of different error variance in nonlinear model of inflation. These subperiods correspond temporally with the different inflation regimes discussed earlier in the Appendix.

In a situation of high inflation rates, the volatility of CPI values is also high, owing to various shocks (related to exchange rates, money, and so on). Therefore, the likelihood that current inflation values will deviate from the trajectory determined by fundamental factors (average money growth rate for several previous months, changes in demand for real money balances) increases, thus introducing greater error variances into the model.

In respect to low inflation values—and at times inflationary processes abated, when the currency corridor and a relatively tough monetary policy obtained—the ratio between actual current inflation rates and fitted values was more stable. The error variance was not considerable.

Various factors contributed in different proportions to the CPI growth rate variance. For the simple first-order autoregressive model, the coefficient of multiple determination (R^2) is equal to 0.876. In other words, the sluggishness of price adjustments explains more than 87% of the variance. When averaged M2 growth rates are included in the equation, the proportion of variance explained by sluggish price adjustments increases to 89.8%.

At first glance, the monetary factor appears to be responsible for over 3% of the CPI variance in 1992 through 1998. However, we must take into account that the influence of a growing money supply includes its growth over all eight previous months. Thus the first-order autoregressive term included in the equation also informs about changes in the nominal quantity of money in the economy, and so the actual proportion of inflation variance explained by monetary factors is considerably higher. For instance, the coefficient of multiple determination of the paired regression equation linking CPI and M2 growth rates over eight months is 0.83, although this estimate is obviously biased because of violation of some requirements of the regression model estimated by OLS (the time series is the first-order autoregressive process, while the corresponding term is excluded).

5. The Stability of Coefficients Across Different Periods.

Estimation of the nonlinear model of inflation $\dot{p}_t = c + a_1 \dot{p}_{t-1} + a_2 \dot{m}_{t-1,t-n} + \varepsilon_t$ in the specified subperiods (1992 through February 1995 and March 1995 to August 1998) yielded the results shown in Table I.6. The average depth of the M2 growth rate was

Table I.6
Results of Estimating Nonlinear Model of Inflation in Two Subperiods*

	February 1992– February 1995	March 1995– August 1998
R^2	0.799	0.914
First-order CPI coefficient	0.680 (6.26)	0.853 (13.15)
Coefficient of average M2 growth rate for 6 or 8 months	0.477 (4.19)	−0.016 (−0.21)
Coefficient of real GDP change rate	−0.038 (−0.73)	−0.032 (−2.73)
Coefficient of ARCH (1)	−0.221 (−1.33)	−0.454 (−1.70)

*t statistics are shown in parentheses.

six months in the first period and eight months in the second period.[9]

It is clear from these results that the contribution of the monetary factor in the first subperiod to the dynamics of inflationary processes was considerably greater, as is typical in a period of high mean inflation. At the same time, changes in the transaction demand for money (represented as changes in the real GDP) were statistically insignificant. The elasticity of CPI change in terms of money supply growth rates in 1992 to early 1995 was 1.20, and it was 0.62 in 1995 to 1998. Thus, it is possible to conclude that in general, inflationary processes in Russia developed in accordance with general concepts of causes and fluctuations of inflation over periods of price liberalization and consequent disinflation.

In the period following price liberalization, inflation rates were very high. In this situation, economic agents systematically underestimated inflation levels (the estimated coefficient of the first-order autoregressive model equals 0.68 and is significantly different from 1), and the demand for real money balances declined. At the same time, any fluctuations in the money supply caused sharp fluctuations in price growth rates.[10] The test for causality between CPI and M2

---

9. Nonlinearity of the model does not allow the use of standard procedures to check for the stability of coefficients (Chow test, recursive estimates of coefficients).
10. Since we regarded smoothed-out money supply growth rates over a number of months as the explanatory variable, individual monetary shocks are responsible for fluctuations in the error variance in the model.

Table I.7
F Statistics and Significance Level for the Granger-Sims Causality Test Between M2 and CPI Growth Rates During Two Subperiods*

	February 1992–February 1995	March 1995–August 1998
"CPI does not Granger cause M2"	3.31 (0.050)	2.86 (0.098)
"M2 does not Granger cause CPI"	1.98 (0.156)	0.37 (0.546)

*The number of lags was six in the subperiod February 1992–February 1995 and eight in the subperiod March 1995–August 1998. t statistics are shown in parentheses.

dynamics based on the Granger-Sims test (Table I.7) confirms a unilateral influence: from M2 to prices.

Over the second period the coefficient of the money supply term was not significant, while changes in the real GDP began to significantly affect the demand for money and therefore price growth rates. Thus, as average inflation rates slowed down, the influence on inflation levels of factors related to the sluggishness of price adjustments and to the transaction demand for real money balances increased, while the effect of growth in the money supply slackened. The growing demand for money (Figure I.6) allowed for an increase in real money supply in ruble terms, and the dynamics of M2 and CPI growth rates did not coincide.

When the Granger-Sims test for causality between CPI and M2 is applied, the absence of influence of either variable on the other (or their mutual influence) is not rejected, at the 5% level of significance. Moreover, at the 10% level of significance the influence of the price growth rate on M2 dynamics is not rejected.

The statistical insignificance of the estimated coefficient in the equation of the conditional error variance is evidence that the heteroscedasticity of residuals is principally related to the levels and fluctuations of inflation in each period. While individually estimated for the equation in each period, the residuals may be considered heteroscedastic in each individual case.

In summary, the accelerated inflation rate during the first subperiod of our study was related to the monetary overhang (which had accumulated over a long period), price liberalization, money emission, and gradually growing inflationary expectations. In this process, each percentage point of additional money supply generated an average increase in consumer prices of about 1.2%.

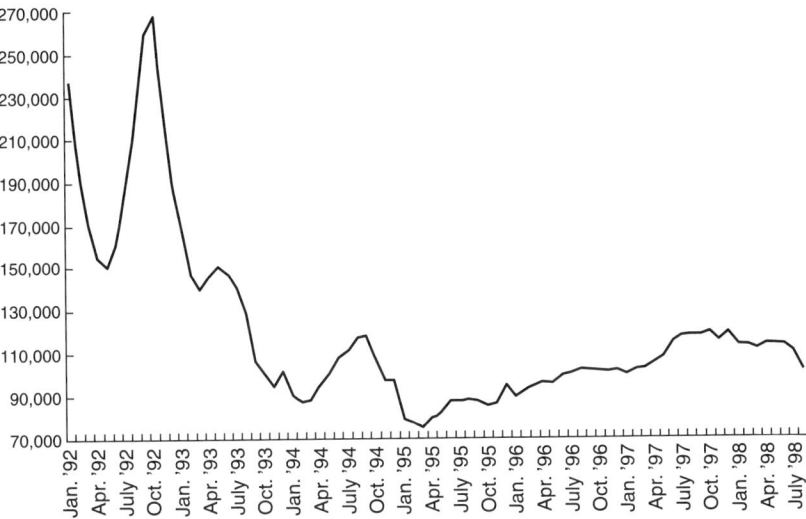

Figure I.6
Real M2 (millions of rubles, in December 1994 prices).

Despite the relatively small number of observations for the second subperiod, we are able to divide it into at least three different stages: a stage of relatively high inflation rates (over 3% per month) until spring of 1996, substantial stabilization of the macroeconomic situation (from spring of 1996 through autumn of 1997), and the consequent ripening and explosion of the financial crisis in 1998. The above-mentioned joint calculation for two first stages reveals the growing role of sluggish adjustment mechanisms, which did not allow inflation to be addressed and fought off quickly. By autumn of 1998 price growth rates had significantly slowed (compared with the period 1993–1995), although the inflationary expectations of economic agents did not entirely abate,[11] as was revealed in the market panic and the consumer price surge during the financial crisis (in September of 1998 consumer prices grew by 38.4%). The abandonment of the currency corridor (meaning, in essence, that the economy lost its last nominal anchor) and the consequent devaluation of the ruble in relation to the US dollar helped reanimate inflationary processes.

---

11. In this connection the growth of the coefficient of the lag variable characterizing price persistence is noteworthy (see Table II.6).

Appendix II Arrears: A Macroeconomic Analysis

Oleg Lugovoy

By late 1997, mutual arrears in the Russian economy had reached enormous proportion, which significantly slowed economic recovery.[1] The growing liabilities put the brakes on the development of the financial markets, including the corporate debenture market, thereby increasing the risk that outlays made would never be repaid.

Appendix II offers an approach to explaining the dynamic of the arrears. This approach to analyzing the causes of the emergence and spread of the arrears phenomenon in the Russian economy, and therefore ways of getting it under control, identifies some of the macroeconomic parameters that can influence the scale of outstanding accounts payable. Also, this approach allows an assortment of hypotheses illuminating the relationship between the variables examined to be made.

II.1. Macroeconomic Model of Arrears

The variables affecting the behavior of arrears[2] examined here include outstanding accounts receivable, business activity (dynamics of the GDP), money supply growth rates (M2), actual spending under the federal budget, borrowing methods practiced by the Federal Ministry of Finance on the financial markets, and real and nominal interest rates on short-term government bonds (GKOs).

Each of these factors is examined in more detail below.

---

[1]. Arrears are understood as overdue outstanding payables. This variable in Russia is calculated by the RF Goskomstat and includes interenterprise arrears, wage arrears, and tax arrears.

[2]. From this point onward the consumer price index was used as a deflator; January 1990 is the base period.

II.1.1. Dynamics of Business Activity

A critical factor setting the pace for variations in outstanding payables is the combination of seasonal fluctuations in business activity and the general GDP dynamic. In 1991 through 1997, falling domestic demand for goods manufactured in Russia, held down by prices, quality, or quantity, led to considerable structural changes in the real economic sector and to a wholesale slump in manufacturing. As a result of cutbacks in production, quite a few producers could not pay their suppliers. We can assume, therefore, the existence of an inverse relationship between variations in outstanding payables and the behavior of the real GDP (or the volume of industrial production). A lag of one to three months is to be expected; this lag is consistent with the length of the production cycle at some major undertakings and with the average finance turnover period of enterprises. Furthermore, a surge in business activity signals a relatively smaller rate of growth of accumulated debts that gradually degenerate into arrears (on average, within three months).

II.1.2. Money Supply in the Economy

Explanations for swelling arrears frequently refer to a "money shortage" in the economy or to a low GDP monetization level. Advocates of this explanation normally favor printing more cash to boost the money supply, as a way of reducing outstanding liabilities. In our view, this is a lopsided approach that takes into account only the short-term effects of printing more money and the pull that monetary expansion may have on other factors (particularly arrears). Growth in the nominal money level does not always signal a long-term expansion of the money supply. Rather, faster growth of the nominal money supply more often than not stimulates inflationary processes, sends interest rates higher, and consequently undercuts demand for real money balances.

II.1.3. Return on Government Securities

High yields on the GKO-OFZ (government bonds) market are yet another factor often proposed to account for arrears in the real economic sector. The more common hypothesis runs as follows. From

1994 to early 1997, real interest rates on the government bond market soared, vastly exceeding the profits that could be expected in the real economic sector. Succumbing to the temptation, many businesses rushed to invest their own (and borrowed) funds in the GKO-OFZ market to reap superhigh margins, siphoning money from, and raising a wave of arrears in, the real sector.

Climbing nominal interest rates may whip up a tide of arrears for two more reasons—rising expectations of an impending inflation and escalating liquidity problems. Puzzled by the first prospect, business executives may choose to hold off paying outstanding debts and current liabilities, in order to pay off debts with devalued money later. Overrun by the second prospect, they cannot meet their liabilities on time because of lack of liquidity.

Whatever the case, we must not leave out the feedback, the causal link between arrears and interest rate. This is best illustrated by the interbank liquidity crisis of August 1995, when the banks, cornered by creditors, had to sell their own assets, including their GKO-OFZ holdings, which boosted the return on these government bonds. Another probability is for the interest rate on loans issued to grow in parallel with rising arrears, as a higher risk premium. In this situation, therefore, it is logical to view lending interest rates, rather than GKO returns, as an exogenous variable. Because such statistics are hard to come by, we will confine ourselves to testing the hypothesis of the reciprocal influence of GKO interest rates and outstanding payables, on the assumption that GKO interest rates are favorably affected by swelling arrears, which force debtors to unload their assets.

II.1.4. Formation of an Arrears Chain and the Payment of Budget Liabilities

A business, even one that is diligent about repaying its debts and strives to conduct itself professionally, can be burdened by a heavy load of outstanding payables for reasons not of its own creation. It is, in fact, pushed to the wall by its business partners.

Firms plan their money flows in the expectation that payments for the products they have supplied to customers will show up on their ledgers on time. Betrayal of this expectation by even one customer can set the stage for a firm's defaulting on some of its liabilities.

The situation that had arisen by the end of 1997 took on a special cast because of the involvement of the government in the chain of arrears. The government too, with an interest in budgets at all levels, can find itself on the list of "unscrupulous" entities. The government's failure to meet its budget obligations, in particular its scheduled spending plans, paralyzes producers and their partners, depriving undertakings of money they could use to repay their debts to creditors and, to complete the payment cycle by thinning out budget revenue.

The bottom line (hypothesis) is that outstanding receivables and the extent to which the government meets its budget liabilities (scheduled expenditures) are the key factors in an analysis of outstanding payables.

II.2. Empirical Testing of the Hypotheses[3]

The above hypotheses can be tested statistically by evaluating the following model:

$$\begin{cases} \left(\dfrac{\Delta C}{P}\right)_t = \alpha_0 + \alpha_1 \cdot \left(\Delta \dfrac{Y}{P}\right)_{t-3} + \alpha_2 \cdot r^f_{t-1} + \alpha_3 \cdot \left(\dfrac{B_F - B_P}{P}\right)_{t-1} \\ \qquad + \alpha_4 \cdot \left(\dfrac{\Delta D}{P}\right)_{t-1} + \alpha_5 \cdot \dot{R}^{3m}_t + \varepsilon_1, \qquad (1) \\ \dot{R}^{3m}_t = \beta_0 + \beta_1 \cdot \dot{P}^e_{3m} + \beta_2 \cdot X_1 + \cdots + \beta_{n+1} \cdot X_n + \beta_{n+2} \cdot \left(\dfrac{\Delta C}{P}\right)_t + \varepsilon_2 \end{cases}$$

where

$\left(\dfrac{\Delta C}{P}\right)_t$ = the first difference of overdue payables (arrears) in real prices;

$\left(\dfrac{\Delta D}{P}\right)_t$ = the first difference of overdue receivables in real prices;

$\left(\Delta \dfrac{Y}{P}\right)_t$ = the first difference of the real product (GDP);

---

3. The author would like to thank Dr. Vladimir Nosko for valuable comments on economic analysis.

$\left(\dfrac{B_F - B_P}{P}\right)_{t-1}$ = the excess of the actual federal budget spending in the preceding month over the plan targets (in real prices)[4];

r^f_{t-1} = the real three-month GKO interest rate observed in the previous month (in percent per annum);

$\dot{R}^{3m}_t$ = the growth rate of the nominal three-month GKO interest rate (averaged for the month);

$\dot{P}^e_{3m}$ = anticipated inflation (the three-month interest rate being modeled, the anticipated inflation variable is estimated three months ahead as well); and

$X_i \{i = \overline{1, n}\}$ = additional factors affecting the return on government securities (which will be introduced in the description of the interest-rate model).

Model 1 consists of two equations, one describing the behavior of arrears and the other describing the GKO interest rate. Both explicable variables are also explicatory variables. The independent variables in the arrears equation include, in accordance with our hypotheses, the real product difference, the real GKO interest rate, federal budget spending, and overdue receivables. All of these variables are used with a lag, reinforcing their exogenous nature.

The interest-rate modeling is based on the assumption that the nominal interest rate is formed by economic entities as a product of the expected inflation and assumed (desired) real return on investment (the Fisher effect). In addition to the expected inflation, "external" factors affecting the interest rate are included in the model as explicatory variables. These factors are described below.

II.2.1. Interest-Rate Modeling

According to the Fisher effect, the nominal interest rate is made up of anticipated inflation and the desired real rate of return:

$$1 + R_t = (1 + r^*_t) \cdot (1 + \pi^e_t), \tag{2}$$

or, to simplify the conclusions,

---

4. The plan target for budget spending in the current month is calculated as 1/12 of the aggregate expenditures appropriated under the budget law for the current year (in 1995 it was 1/4 of the quarterly spending).

$$R_t \approx r_t^* + \pi_t^e \qquad (3)$$

where

R_t = the nominal interest rate observable in the current period;
r_t^* = the "desired" real interest rate (for the current period); and
π_t^e = the anticipated inflation in the current period.

The nominal return on government securities represents the risk-free rate of return as compared with the return on any other instrument (in a given country). Government securities are not entirely risk-free, however. Among the risks they are subject to are the risk of fluctuating inflation, liquidity risk, and, in periods of political instability, the risk of default, as was typical of the pre-election period, when the difference in returns on issues redeemed before and after the elections was very significant. If the nominal interest rate were broken down into two components, real return and inflation, the real risk premium would be the real "desired" rate of return. This is only natural, for a nominal interest at or below the level of inflation cannot be considered a "premium," because it is equivalent to a real return of zero. Similarly, there is always a hedge against inflation, such as investing in a stable foreign currency, which would provide protection from internal inflationary processes and devaluation. The return on this operation would be equivalent to a nominal interest equal to the inflation rate. It may be argued, therefore, that the risks lie in the real rate of return, and that the nominal interest rate cannot fall below the anticipated rate of inflation. A drop below the anticipated rate would provoke arbitrage involving, among other things, transactions in the hard-currency market. It may also be argued that the desired real return is anything but negative, and is much less volatile than the actual return. This is explained by the fact that there is a link between the change in the desired return and the change in risks of variable nature, whereas a change in the actual real return is related to an error in the inflation forecast, which is always in the picture.

Another determining factor in the Fisher effect is anticipated inflation. In most situations there is an error in inflation forecasts, systematic or random, that is revealed at the end of a period. Where expectations are adaptive, this error is probably considered by investors in their future inflation forecast:

$$\pi_t^e - \pi_{t-1}^e = \gamma \cdot (\pi_{t-1} - \pi_{t-1}^e) \tag{4}$$

where

π_t^e = inflation in the period t expected toward the end of the period $t - 1$;

π_{t-1}^e = inflation in the period $t - 1$ expected toward the end of the period $t - 2$;

π_{t-1} = actual inflation in the period $t - 1$; and

γ = the correction factor characterizing the degree of self-learning from errors ($0 \leq \gamma \leq 1$).

The expression $(\pi_{t-1} - \pi_{t-1}^e)$ would then be the inflation forecast error for the period $t - 1$. If this number is negative, inflationary expectations were too high, and investors obtained a real return that was higher than the expected $r_{t-1} > r_{t-1}^*$. If, however, the inflationary expectations were unjustified (if, that is, the number $(\pi_{t-1} - \pi_{t-1}^e)$ turned positive), the actual real return would work out to be less than the expected $r_{t-1} < r_{t-1}^*$.

However, since the nominal interest can be shown as the sum of the actual inflation and real return values:

$$R_t = r_t + \pi_t \tag{5}$$

then, in accordance with the inequality (2):

$$(\pi_{t-1} + r_{t-1}) = (r_{t-1}^* + \pi_{t-1}^e) \tag{6}$$

or

$$(\pi_{t-1} - \pi_{t-1}^e) = (r_{t-1}^* - r_{t-1}) \tag{7}$$

Equation (4) for adaptive expectation can then be presented differently:

$$\pi_t^e - \pi_{t-1}^e = \gamma \cdot (r_{t-1}^* - r_{t-1}) \tag{8}$$

or, with the parentheses removed:

$$\pi_t^e - \pi_{t-1}^e = -\gamma \cdot r_{t-1} + \gamma \cdot r_{t-1}^* \tag{9}$$

The result is that a change in anticipated inflation is negatively related to the actual real interest in the preceding period. Indeed, in certain situations, anticipated inflation can be so much less than actual inflation that the real return is negative. This was observed, for example, in 1993, and in some measure again in 1994, when actual inflation outpaced the nominal interest. Subsequently, this led to a growth in the nominal return. It further follows from equation (9) that the desired return and the anticipated inflation are negatively correlated. This appears reasonable, too, for the expected real return includes the premium on the risk of changes in inflation, which is likely to grow along with the growth of inflation itself.

If equation (2) is now presented in differences, the result is:

$$R_t - R_{t-1} = (r_t^* - r_{t-1}^*) + (n_t^e - n_{t-1}^e) \tag{10}$$

which means that the change in inflationary expectations is reflected in the nominal rate of return.

As we said earlier, the real expected return is much less volatile than the actual return. It may be argued, therefore, that the actual real return is the determining factor for adjusting adaptive expectations.

It follows, then, that a high rate of real return (above the expected level) in the preceding period helps scale down inflationary expectations and, in conformity with the Fisher effect, helps hold down nominal interest. Conversely, a low (below expectations) or negative rate of real return in the preceding period sends up inflationary expectations, and therefore pulls up the nominal interest.

II.2.2. Return on GKO-OFZ Auction Sales

The floating of new issues (on top of those to be retired) increases the supply of bonds on the financial market. It boosts interest rates and reduces liquidity. Moreover, if the return on the freshly floated issues differs sharply from that on similar series maturing in the secondary market, it means that the issuer's moves were not very predictable. In most cases, the market response is not unlike a shock, a convulsive urge to jolt the interest rate abruptly out of balance.

The extent of unpredictability of the issuer's moves at auction sales can be measured on the basis of a primary market analysis. Dealers enter purchase bids at bond-placing auctions, where the minimum satisfied price (cut-off price) is set by the issuer. The tighter the bunch of bids made at the auction sales, the smaller is the spread of the bidders' expectations regarding the sale results. The auction outcome depends on the issuer. If only bids with a return close to the market performance are accepted, the market is not exposed to a shocklike pressure. In the absence of benchmarking to the market interest rate, with only those bids offering returns well above the market level being accepted, expectations of a higher interest rate arise, and a still higher interest is asked at the next auction sale.

A factor is introduced here to show the extent of cut-off return and the average weighted return:

$$S = \left(\frac{i_{max}}{i_{avr}}\right)$$

where

i_{max} = maximum return at an auction sale (at the cut-off price); and

i_{avr} = average weighted return at the auction sale (at the average weighted price).

This factor is not negative, because the maximum return is always higher than or equal to the average weighted value. The higher this factor is, the wider the gap between the cut-off return and the average return, and the smaller the proportion of bids with "correct" expectations in the total accepted bids. Accordingly, the Finance Ministry behaved less predictably at the auction. This factor correlates positively with interest rate growth. In essence, the more unexpected the maximum return at the auction is, the higher the average interest rate at succeeding auction sales.

II.3. Growth Rates of the Money Supply

Rising growth rates of the nominal money supply in the economy enhance liquidity in the short term and stimulate a decline in the nominal interest rate; in the longer term they boost prices and therefore spur the growth of interest rates.

It is worthwhile taking a look at the effect of additional money emissions on prices and business activity in a standard macroeconomic model. The growth of the nominal money supply means (in the short term) an expansion of the real money supply in the economy. This process consequently pulls up aggregate demand. Given surplus capacity and labor, the shift of aggregate demand can then, in the initial phase, trigger growth in real production. Over a longer term, however, with prices for the factors of production going up and conduction costs swelling, this inevitably must set off inflationary processes, against a background of a drop in production.

Two hypotheses—the short- and medium-term effect of variations in the nominal money supply growth rates on interest rates—will therefore be verified concurrently:

- Short-term effect: The nominal interest rate initially declines in response to rising growth rates in the nominal money supply. The decline is set in motion by the effect of rising liquidity.
- Medium-term effect: The nominal interest rate then rebounds under the effect of rising inflationary expectations and variation in the nominal return.

Evaluation of the coefficients in the macroeconomic model of arrears and interest rates. The above-described factors influencing the interest rate are introduced into model (1):

$$\begin{cases} \left(\frac{\Delta C}{P}\right)_t = \alpha_0 + \alpha_1 \cdot \left(\Delta \frac{Y}{P}\right)_{t-3} + \alpha_2 \cdot r^f_{t-1} + \alpha_3 \cdot \left(\frac{B_F - B_P}{P}\right)_{t-1} \\ \qquad + \alpha_4 \cdot \left(\frac{\Delta D}{P}\right)_{t-1} + \alpha_5 \cdot \dot{R}^{3m}_t + \varepsilon_1, \\ \dot{R}^{3m}_t = \beta_0 + \beta_1 \cdot r^f_{t-1} + \beta_2 \cdot \dot{M2}_t + \beta_3 \cdot \dot{M2}_{t-3\ldots6} + \beta_4 \cdot S_t \\ \qquad + \beta_5 \cdot \left(\frac{\Delta C}{P}\right)_t + \varepsilon_2 \end{cases} \qquad (11)$$

where

$\dot{M2}_t$ = growth rate of the nominal money supply M2 in the current month;

$\dot{M2}_{t-3\ldots6}$ = geometric mean of the nominal money supply growth rates in the periods $t-3,\ldots,t-6$; and

S_t = auction premium (geometric mean for a month).

Turning now to an evaluation of the factors in the model, the above discussion of the hypotheses can be summed up in respect to the signs of the factors given. The increase in outstanding payables is influenced:

- negatively—by the preceding growth in business activity $\left(\Delta \frac{Y}{P}\right)_{t-3}$
- positively—by the high real return on bonds in the preceding period r^f_{t-1}
- negatively—by the excess of the actual budgetary expenditures over the targets (that is, un-spent funds, or a negative difference, lead to a growth in arrears) $\left(\frac{B_F - B_P}{P}\right)_{t-1}$
- positively—by the growth in outstanding receivables in the preceding month in real prices $\left(\frac{\Delta D}{P}\right)_{t-1}$
- positively—by the growth in the nominal (three-month) GKO interest rate $\dot{R}^{3m}_t$

The increase in the nominal GKO interest rate is affected:

- negatively—by the high real return on bonds in the preceding periods, also interpreted as an error in the inflation forecast for the preceding period in adaptive expectations r^f_{t-1}
- negatively—by a rise in the growth of the nominal money supply in the current period $\dot{M2}_t$
- positively—by the preceding rise in the nominal money supply growth rate as a result of the price growth $\dot{M2}_{t-3\dots6}$
- positively—by an unexpectedly high auction premium S_t
- positively—by growth in the outstanding payables $\left(\frac{\Delta C}{P}\right)_t$ in consequence of the sale of liquid assets by debtors and debtors' demand for liquid funds

As we said earlier, the explicable variables in one equation become explicatory factors in the other. The model, therefore, assumes a relationship between arrears and the interest rate, the interest rate and arrears being determined concurrently and having no effect on the remaining (exogenous) variable. To take into account this relationship, a two-stage least squares (TSLS) method is employed. Tables II.1 and II.2 show the coefficients obtained in the second TSLS stage.

It is clear from the tables that far from all coefficients are statistically significant. The percentage of explained dispersion (R^2)

Table II.1
Estimation Results for Model Coefficients in the Arrears Equation (February 1994 Through September 1997, Monthly Data, 44 Observations)

Variable	Coefficient	SE	t Statistic	Probability
Constant	1.172	1.302	0.900	0.374
$\Delta(Y/P)_{t-3}$	−0.027	0.090	−0.306	0.762
r^f_{t-1}	0.013	0.007	1.857	0.071
$(B_F - B_P)/P|_{t-1}$	−0.199	0.081	−2.454	0.019
$(\Delta D/P)_{t-1}$	0.118	0.239	0.492	0.625
$\dot{R}_t^{3m}$	1.693	1.447	1.171	0.249

R^2	0.307	Mean of dependent variables	4.242	
Adjusted R^2	0.216	SD of dependent variables	1.717	
SE of regression	1.520	Akaike information criterion	0.963	
Sum of squared residuals	87.770	Schwartz criterion	1.207	
F statistic	3.879	Durbin-Watson statistic	1.936	
Probability (F statistic)	0.006			

is rather low, particularly in the arrears equation. The partial correlation charts show "surges" that adversely affect the quality of regression.

To account for the influence of other economic and political factors that probably affected the outliers, conditional[5] variables were introduced into the model.

The following variables were added to the arrears equation:

• *September 1994:* Situation preceding Black Tuesday. The accumulation of funds to purchase hard-currency diverted funds from the real sector. In addition, at that time expectations of the ruble's devaluation had the same effect as inflationary expectations.

• *October 1996:* The illness of President Boris Yeltsin increased investment risk.

• *February–April 1997:* Presumably, expectations of budget sequestration and a cabinet reshuffle.

Conditional variables are included in the interest-rate equation:

• *July–August 1995:* An escalating interbank arrears crisis caused funds to flee liquid assets.

---

5. The values of each dummy variable are equal to unity for t equal to the respective period in question. In the remaining instances, the variable had zero values. That is, the dummy variable for September 1994 ($D_{sep.94}$) equals 1 in September 1994 and zero in other months.

Table II.2
Estimation Results for Model Coefficients in the Interest-Rate Equation (February 1994 Through September 1997, Monthly Data, 44 Observations)

Variable	Coefficient	SE	t Statistic	Probability
Constant	−2.085	1.317	−1.583	0.122
$\dot{M2}_t$	−2.077	0.884	−2.348	0.024
$\dot{M2}_{t-3...6}$	2.437	1.294	1.883	0.067
r^f_{t-1}	−3.52E−03	9.84E−04	−3.579	0.001
S_t	2.766	0.718	3.851	0.000
$(\Delta C/P)_t$	−0.030	0.048	−0.617	0.541

R^2	0.517	Mean of dependent variables	0.990
Adjusted R^2	0.453	SD of dependent variables	0.332
SE of regression	0.245	Akaike information criterion	−2.684
Sum of squared residuals	2.288	Schwartz criterion	−2.440
F statistic	8.359	Durbin-Watson statistic	1.686
Probability (F statistic)	0.000		

• *January 1996:* The government and the RF Central Bank pursued a vigorous policy to depress the return on government bonds in the period between the presidential elections and the elections to the State Duma.

• *May 1996:* The situation obtaining before the presidential elections, when the gap in the return between issues redeemable before and after the election was the widest ever. Issues (such as three-month bonds) that were redeemable after the election carried more risk, which had a positive effect on their return.

Tables II.3 and II.4 show the coefficients for the model with the dummy variables added. The new evaluations have a higher significance, with the determination coefficient rising to between 0.70 and 0.90.

All of the coefficients are significant at a level of 1%, and their signs agree with the hypotheses we have advanced. The only exception is the coefficient of outstanding receivables in the arrears equation, which casts into doubt the effect arrears may have on the GKO interest rate. The negligibility of the coefficient of the outstanding receivables is most likely due to the correlation of this variable with the budget spending variable. In a paired regression, these series explain 20% of the dispersion of each other ($R^2 = 0.2$). To specify the extent of influence of each factor, we evaluated each of the coefficients separately, with the other factor deleted from the equation. The specified coefficients are shown in Tables II.5 and II.6 (the

Table II.3
Estimation Results for Model Coefficients in the Arrears Equation with Logic Variables (February 1994 Through September 1997, Monthly Data, 44 Observations)

Variable	Coefficient	SE	t Statistic	Probability
Constant	0.960	0.605	1.586	0.122
$\Delta(Y/P)_{t-3}$	−0.148	0.058	−2.579	0.014
r^f_{t-1}	0.016	0.004	3.864	0.002
$(B_F - B_P)/P|_{t-1}$	−0.181	0.047	−3.889	0.000
$(\Delta D/P)_{t-1}$	0.000	0.126	0.002	0.998
$\dot{R}^{3m}_t$	1.742	0.596	2.925	0.006
$D_{sep.94}$	6.777	1.019	6.649	0.000
$D_{oct.96}$	2.866	0.953	3.007	0.005
$D_{feb.-apr.97}$	2.311	0.588	3.932	0.000

R^2	0.758	Mean of dependent variables	4.242	
Adjusted R^2	0.703	SD of dependent variables	1.717	
SE of regression	0.936	Akaike information criterion	0.048	
Sum of squared residuals	30.678	Schwartz criterion	0.413	
F statistic	14.131	Durbin-Watson statistic	2.547	
Probability (F statistic)	0.000			

Table II.4
Estimation Results for Model Coefficients in the Interest-Rate Equation with Logic Variables (February 1994 Through September 1997, Monthly Data, 44 Observations)

Variable	Coefficient	SE	t Statistic	Probability
Constant	−1.786	0.703	−2.540	0.016
$\dot{M2}_t$	−1.917	0.510	−3.759	0.001
$\dot{M2}_{t-3\ldots6}$	1.819	0.755	2.409	0.022
r^f_{t-1}	−3.02E−03	5.76E−04	−5.244	0.000
S_t	2.839	0.396	7.161	0.000
$(\Delta C/P)_t$	−0.015	0.015	−0.968	0.340
$D_{jul.95}$	0.638	0.144	4.418	0.000
$D_{aug.95}$	0.355	0.145	2.453	0.020
$D_{jan.96}$	−0.614	0.159	−3.858	0.001
$D_{may.96}$	0.858	0.148	5.817	0.000

R^2	0.860	Mean of dependent variables	0.990	
Adjusted R^2	0.823	SD of dependent variables	0.332	
SE of regression	0.140	Akaike information criterion	−3.741	
Sum of squared residuals	0.663	Schwartz criterion	−3.335	
F statistic	23.178	Durbin-Watson statistic	1.875	
Probability (F statistic)	0.000			

Table II.5
Estimating the Budget Variable Coefficient in a Model Eliminating Deflated Incremental Outstanding Receivables

Variable	Coefficient	SE	t Statistic	Probability
$(B_F - B_P)/P\vert_{t-1}$	−0.181	0.038	−4.768	0.000
R^2		0.758		
Akaike information criterion		0.003		
Adjusted R^2		0.711		

Table II.6
Estimating the Coefficient of Deflated Incremental Outstanding Receivables in an Equation with an Eliminated Budget Variable

Variable	Coefficient	SE	t Statistic	Probability
$(\Delta D/P)_{t-1}$	0.244	0.123	1.990	0.054
R^2		0.660		
Akaike information criterion		0.344		
Adjusted R^2		0.593		

remaining coefficients did not change much and are not shown in the tables).

As is evident from the tables, the significance of both factors increases, although the coefficient of the outstanding receivables still remains insignificant (at a level of 5%), but has the assumed sign. Moreover, exclusion of the outstanding receivables variable from the model (Table II.5) improves the statistical characteristics of the model (the adjusted R^2 rises, while the Akaike information criterion drops). However, exclusion of the federal budget spending variable from the model (Table II.6) significantly affects the quality of the model. The suggested conclusion, then, is that nonfulfillment of budgetary obligations plays a greater role in the emergence of arrears than do outstanding receivables. This is probably due to the fact that enterprises that depend on budget allocations have less freedom of choice (including solvency) than those running their own business.

II.4. Stability of Coefficients and Forecast Qualities of the Model

Tables II.7 and II.8 show the results of the Chow breakpoint tests and the Chow forecast test. Since the interval under investigation is

Table II.7
Chow Test Results for the Arrears Equation

Chow Breakpoint Test: January 1996	
F statistic: 1.162	Probability: 0.359
Chow Forecast Test: Forecast from January 1996 to September 1997	
F statistic: 0.770	Probability: 0.714
Chow Forecast Test: Forecast from January 1997 to September 1997	
F statistic: 0.551	Probability: 0.823

Table II.8
Chow Test Results for the Interest-Rate Equation

Chow Breakpoint Test: January 1996	
F statistic: 2.472	Probability: **0.034**
Chow Forecast Test: Forecast from January 1996 to September 1997	
F statistic: 1.598	Probability: 0.193
Chow Forecast Test: Forecast from January 1997 to September 1997	
F statistic: 0.956	Probability: 0.497

not too large, we have broken it down into two intervals to test the hypothesis about the variation of coefficients. The forecast test (forecast quality) was undertaken for two subperiods, 1996–1997 and 1997.

As shown in the tables, the arrears equation does not repudiate all the coefficient stability hypotheses. In the interest-rate equation, however, beginning in January 1996 the coefficient stability hypothesis is repudiated at the 95% significance level. This period saw a major structural shift (break) in the pressure of the explicatory variables. Accordingly, we reevaluated the coefficients in the interest-rate equation for the two subperiods, before and after January 1996 (Tables II.9 and II.10).

Basically, all of the coefficients retain a high significance for both subperiods, although their weights vary considerably. The decline in the significance of some coefficients could well be due to the smaller number of observations made.

The emergence of a significant coefficient with a rise in outstanding payables is notable. Moreover, the dependence exhibits different directions: before 1996, interest rates depended negatively on the growth of arrears, whereas in 1996 and 1997 the dependence turned

Table II.9
Estimation Results for Model Coefficients in the Interest-Rate Equation for a Subperiod of February 1994 Through December 1995 (23 Observations)

Variable	Coefficient	SE	t Statistic	Probability
Constant	−5.272	1.901	−2.773	0.014
$\dot{M2}_t$	−1.106	0.578	−1.915	0.075
$\dot{M2}_{t-3\ldots 6}$	3.074	1.556	1.976	0.067
r^f_{t-1}	−1.34E−03	1.38E−03	−0.974	0.345
S_t	4.142	0.565	7.329	0.000
$(\Delta C/P)_t$	−0.067	0.019	−3.437	0.004
$D_{jul.95}$	0.814	0.153	5.317	0.000
$D_{aug.95}$	0.354	0.129	2.730	0.016
R^2	0.915	Mean of dependent variables	1.039	
Adjusted R^2	0.875	SD of dependent variables	0.348	
SE of regression	0.123	Akaike information criterion	−3.923	
Sum of squared residuals	0.227	Schwartz criterion	−3.528	
F statistic	23.176	Durbin-Watson statistic	2.261	
Probability (F statistic)	0.000			

Table II.10
Estimation Results for Model Coefficients in the Interest-Rate Equation for a Subperiod of January 1996 Through September 1997 (21 Observations)

Variable	Coefficient	SE	t Statistic	Probability
Constant	−2.379	3.362	−0.708	0.492
$\dot{M2}_t$	−2.857	1.374	−2.079	0.058
$\dot{M2}_{t-3\ldots 6}$	4.062	3.347	1.214	0.247
r^f_{t-1}	−3.52E−03	6.42E−04	−5.476	0.000
S_t	1.937	0.723	2.681	0.019
$(\Delta C/P)_t$	0.035	0.013	2.811	0.017
$D_{jul.95}$	−0.547	0.175	−3.120	0.008
$D_{aug.95}$	0.826	0.132	6.250	0.000
R^2	0.917	Mean of dependent variables	0.936	
Adjusted R^2	0.872	SD of dependent variables	0.313	
SE of regression	0.112	Akaike information criterion	−4.095	
Sum of squared residuals	0.163	Schwartz criterion	−3.697	
F statistic	20.202	Durbin-Watson statistic	2.466	
Probability (F statistic)	0.000			

positive. The negative dependence in 1994 and 1995 was probably due to the high rate of return prevailing on the short-term government bond market, which provided a strong incentive for liabilities to be left unpaid for a time in order to earn extra revenue. These facts are in accord with the hypothesis about the flow of funds from the real sector to the GKO market. Hence the aggravation of the liquidity problem (and therefore the arrears problem) in the real sector and the decline in the rate of return on the GKO market. The swelling arrears could cause a reduction in loans issued to the real sector and investment of the funds released elsewhere, including on the GKO market (thereby undercutting the yield of GKOs). Starting in 1996, the interest rate showed a positive dependence on arrears. In 1996 and 1997, nonresidents entered the market and steadily pushed down the rate of return. This downturn reduced the incentive to park funds (including borrowed money) in government bonds. In such a situation, arrears—the liquidity squeeze—can encourage debtors to sell their liquid assets. On balance, this may give rise to a trend for capital to flow back to the real sector.

The influence of the auction premium on the interest rate weakened considerably. The following explanation may account for this: the auction premium itself had dwindled in the preceding period, largely because nonresidents were snapping up bonds at average prices. This kept demand for the securities at a moderately high level, holding the auction premium and its influence on interest-rate growth to a low level.

Conversely, the dependence of variations in the interest rate on the real observable interest rate (in the previous month) shot up to a significant level in the second subperiod. This was evidence both of a lowering of the risk rate and scaled-back inflationary expectations (indicative of a drop in the absolute value of the coefficient), and of a favorable trend toward greater control over the rate of real return, that is, a higher predictability of inflation (according to the theory about the real rate of return as a characterization of the error in the forecast of adaptive expectations).

Interestingly enough, the second interval (1996–1997) registered a significant rise in the effect of the nominal money supply growth rates on the interest rate in the current period. The coefficient is insignificant in the medium-term period, however, which may indicate attenuation of inflationary pressures. In both instances, however, the variation in the coefficients may be caused by an easing of inflationary processes and a slowdown in the nominal money supply growth rates themselves.

It would be more correct to evaluate the effect of variations in the real money supply. In general, the real money supply may expand with a growth in the money demand. In this situation, expansion of the money supply would not, eventually, lead to an accelerated growth of prices. If, however, the inflationary processes are sluggish and the money supply surpasses the demand for real cash balances, an equilibrium can set in through price rises. Therefore, substituting the growth rates of the real money supply for those of the nominal money supply in our model, we can evaluate the lagging inflationary effect of the nominal money expansion in a situation where the short-term money supply is at variance with real cash balances.

$$\begin{cases} \left(\frac{\Delta C}{P}\right)_t = \alpha_0 + \alpha_1 \cdot \left(\Delta \frac{Y}{P}\right)_{t-3} + \alpha_2 \cdot r^f_{t-1} + \alpha_3 \cdot \left(\frac{B_F - B_P}{P}\right)_{t-1} \\ \qquad + \alpha_4 \cdot \left(\frac{\Delta D}{P}\right)_{t-1} + \alpha_5 \cdot \dot{R}^{3m}_t + \varepsilon_1 \\ \dot{R}^{3m}_t = \beta_0 + \beta_1 \cdot r^f_{t-1} + \beta'_2 \cdot \left(\frac{\dot{M2}}{P}\right)_t + \beta'_3 \cdot \left(\frac{\dot{M2}}{P}\right)_{t-3\ldots 6} + \beta_4 \cdot S_t \\ \qquad + \beta_5 \cdot \left(\frac{\Delta C}{P}\right)_t + \varepsilon_2 \end{cases} \quad (12)$$

Tables II.11 and II.12 show estimates of the coefficients in the interest-rate equation of system (12), arrived at by the two-stage least-squares method (system (12) was obtained by replacing the growth rates of the nominal money supply in system (11) with the growth rates of the real money supply). The result this gives is that the growth rates of the real money supply are insignificant in both periods, while, given a lag of three to six months, the significance was even greater than with the nominal money amount used. Moreover, the coefficient β'_3 rises more than fivefold (from 1.7 to 9.5) in the second period. This jump in the coefficient reveals a build-up of inflationary pressure on the interest rate of the expanding money supply. The conclusion that emerges, therefore, is that the nominal expansion outstripped the demand for money, which had actually been falling before 1995. This is most in evidence in the period starting in 1996, when the demand for money was positive, but short of having the growth of the nominal money supply cause inflation.

Table II.11
Estimating Coefficients in the Interest-Rate Equation Set (12) on the Interval February 1994 Through December 1995 (23 Observations)

Variable	Coefficient	SE	t Statistic	Probability
Constant	−3.769	0.963	−3.913	0.001
$(\dot{M}2/P)_t$	−0.679	0.443	−1.533	0.146
$(\dot{M}2/P)_{t-3\ldots6}$	1.667	0.591	2.820	0.013
r^f_{t-1}	−1.40E−03	1.30E−03	−1.074	0.300
S_t	3.753	0.590	6.355	0.000
$(\Delta C/P)_t$	−0.041	0.017	−2.429	0.028
$D_{jul.95}$	0.790	0.132	5.967	0.000
$D_{aug.95}$	0.395	0.120	3.297	0.005

R^2	0.925	Mean of dependent variables	1.039	
Adjusted R^2	0.890	SD of dependent variables	0.348	
SE of regression	0.115	Akaike information criterion	−4.054	
Sum of squared residuals	0.199	Schwartz criterion	−3.659	
F statistic	26.451	Durbin-Watson statistic	2.176	
Probability (F statistic)	0.000			

Table II.12
Estimating Coefficients in the Interest-Rate Equation Set (12) on the Interval January 1996 Through September 1997 (21 Observations)

Variable	Coefficient	SE	t Statistic	Probability
Constant	−9.569	3.445	−2.778	0.016
$(\dot{M}2/P)_t$	−1.244	1.316	−0.946	0.362
$(\dot{M}2/P)_{t-3\ldots6}$	9.479	2.898	3.271	0.006
r^f_{t-1}	−3.26E−03	4.97E−04	−6.553	0.000
S_t	1.995	0.387	5.152	0.000
$(\Delta C/P)_t$	0.048	0.019	2.549	0.024
$D_{jan.96}$	−0.322	0.178	−1.816	0.093
$D_{may.96}$	0.850	0.109	7.793	0.000

R^2	0.940	Mean of dependent variables	0.936	
Adjusted R^2	0.908	SD of dependent variables	0.313	
SE of regression	0.095	Akaike information criterion	−4.427	
Sum of squared residuals	0.117	Schwartz criterion	−4.029	
F statistic	28.848	Durbin-Watson statistic	2.639	
Probability (F statistic)	0.000			

II.5. Elasticities

Now we turn to the sensitivity of the variable to changes in the effective factors. For this task we will calculate the elasticities involved. To improve the interpretation of elasticities, they will be calculated in mean values (of the period) for most of the series, except the following:

- Instead of the mean value of real product first differences, elasticity was calculated for the mean value of the product itself $(Y/P)_{t-3}$.
- Instead of the mean value of the real interest rate r^f_{t-1}, we calculated the elasticities of the dependent variables according to variations in the real interest rate per 1 percentage point (that is, we used the variation r^f_{t-1} by 1, irrespective of the mean value, instead of variation by 1% from the mean value, which is equal to 0.3, if the mean value r^f_{t-1} is 30% per annum.
- Instead of the mean value of the variable characterizing the differential between actual and targeted expenditure of the federal budget, the elasticity was calculated for the mean value of targeted expenditure.
- The elasticities of the interest growth rates $\dot{R}^{3m}_t$ (and according to the interest growth rates) were calculated for rates equal to 1, in which case a variation of the growth rates by 1% would signify a change in the interest rate by 1% from the current figure.

Tables II.13 and II.14 show elasticities calculated for the period as a whole and for the two subperiods. The coefficients obtained for each period individually were used in calculating the elasticity of the

Table II.13
Effective Variable Elasticities of Incremental Outstanding Payables

Variable	1994–1995		1996–1997		1994–1997	
	Value	Elast.	Value	Elast.	Value	Elast.
$(\Delta C/P)_t$	4.378*		4.094*		4.242*	
$(Y/P)_{t-3}$	39.094*	−1.325	35.112*	−1.273	37.194*	−1.301
r^f_{t-1}	—	0.358	—	0.383	—	0.369
$(B_F - B_P)/P\vert_{t-1}$	57.348*	−2.371	39.893*	−1.763	49.017*	−2.091
$(\Delta D/P)_{t-1}$	3.215*	0.179	2.440*	0.146	2.845*	0.164
$\dot{R}^{3m}_t$	1	0.398	1	0.426	1	0.411

*Period average.

Table II.14
Effective Variable Elasticities of Growth Rates for the Three-Month GKO Interest Rate

Variable	1994–1995		1996–1997		1994–1997	
	Value	Elast.	Value	Elast.	Value	Elast.
$\hat{R}_t^{3m}$	1		1		1	
$\dot{M2}_t$	1.084*	−0.941	1.026*	−4.003	1.056*	−2.134
$\dot{M2}_{t-3\ldots6}$	1.095*	3.204	1.034*	5.126	1.064*	2.455
r_{t-1}^f	—	−0.153	—	−0.531	—	−0.407
S_t	1.073*	4.699	1.056*	1.636	1.065*	2.786
$(\Delta C/P)_t$	4.378*	−0.181	4.094*	0.195	4.242*	—
$(\dot{M2}/P)_{t-3\ldots6}$	1	1.667	1	9.479	1	1.925

*Period average.

interest rate according to the effective variables. The coefficients proved stable in the arrears equation, and therefore they were not reevaluated for the subperiods.

II.6. Money Supply and Arrears: An Analysis Using Distributed Lags

According to a widely held view, growth in the money supply reduces the backlog of arrears. What is frequently overlooked, however, is the meaning attached to money supply growth. If the real money supply is implied, its growth enhances liquidity, stimulates demand, speeds up payments, and can help reduce the backlog of outstanding receivables. If, however, nominal monetary expansion is advocated as a way to mend arrears, a steady climb in its growth rate intensifies inflationary processes. In this situation, higher price growth rates would favor the debtor, the real value of whose debts declines. This would give the debtor an extra stake in delaying payment. Moreover, the escalating inflationary processes would jack up the nominal interest rate and contract the real money supply, thus pushing the liquidity problem to the brink. This relationship is clearly confirmed by the results of our previous analysis. An alternative analysis using polynomial distributed lags (Almon lag) strengthens our argument. This analysis shows more explicitly the structure of the effect of monetary expansion on arrears and interest rates.

Figure II.1 shows a plot of coefficient estimates of growth rates of the nominal money supply M2 according to lags in the paired re-

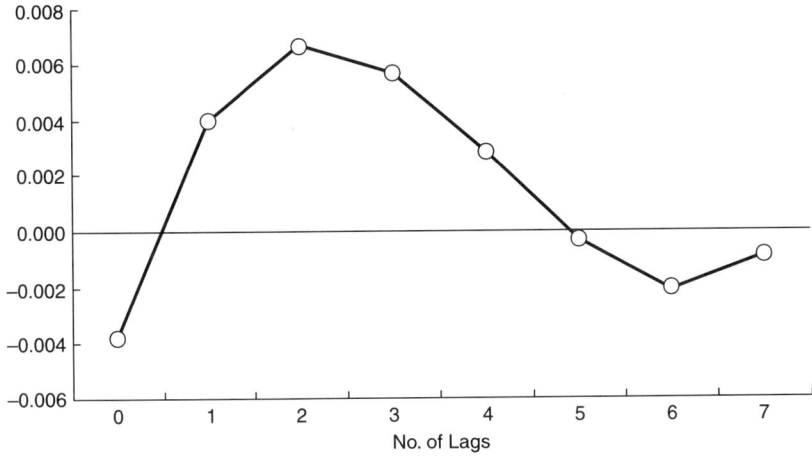

Figure II.1
Distributed lags for nominal supply growth rates for deflated incremental outstanding payables.

Table II.15
Distributed Lags for Nominal Money Supply Growth Rates for Deflated Incremental Outstanding Payables in a Paired Regression (Degree of Polynomial: 3, No. of Lags: 8)

Lag	Coefficient	SE	t Statistic
0	−3.79E−03	3.45E−03	−1.010
1	4.05E−03	2.11E−03	1.923
2	6.67E−03	2.24E−03	2.976
3	5.71E−03	1.87E−03	3.053
4	2.83E−03	1.75E−03	1.618
5	−3.40E−04	2.06E−03	−0.166
6	−2.15E−03	1.96E−03	−1.095
7	−9.50E−04	2.86E−03	−0.333

gression of the deflated first differences of arrears on the growth rates of M2. The values of the coefficients corresponding to each lag are plotted on the y-axis. The values of the coefficients, their standard errors, and t-statistics are shown in Table II.15.

At time zero (without a lag), the dependence between the arrears and growth rates of M2 is negative. This agrees with the hypothesis that a rise in the growth rate of the nominal money supply may initially boost the real money supply and, consequently, mitigate the liquidity problem somewhat. It should be noted, however, that the first coefficient displays a low statistical significance. At the same

Table II.16
Distributed Lags for Nominal Money Supply Growth Rates for Growth Rates for the Nominal Three-Month GKO Interest Rate (Degree of Polynomial: 3, No. of Lags: 8)

Lag	Coefficient	SE	t Statistic
0	−1.528	0.760	−2.011
1	0.255	0.450	0.566
2	1.005	0.469	2.143
3	1.031	0.400	2.581
4	0.642	0.397	1.618
5	0.144	0.469	0.307
6	−0.154	0.443	−0.348
7	0.055	0.670	0.083

time, the dependence acquires a positive character, in accordance with the hypothesis about the intensification of inflationary processes and the growth of the nominal interest rate. We will now verify this hypothesis by constructing analogous distributive lags for the growth rates of the nominal interest rate. As in the case of arrears, the distributive lags for the growth rates of the nominal interest rate are shown in Table II.16 and Figure II.2. Similar results are obtained. According to the hypothesis, the initial moment of rising growth rates of M2 registers a reduction in the nominal interest rate (through the pull of the liquidity effect). Subsequently, from the second to the fourth lags, adaptation to the intensifying inflationary processes occurs.

II.7. Conclusions

As shown in our analyses, changes in nominal interest rates play a major role in originating arrears. Proof of this is their high statistical significance in the models and the high elasticity of interest repayment arrears. According to our evaluations, a 1% increase in the nominal interest-rate growth rate results in a 0.4% rise in the first difference of arrears. In all probability, the mechanics of this dependence are related to the aggravation of liquidity problems as nominal interest rates grow. Liquidity contraction makes payment transfers more difficult and hinders lending to the real sector, which consequently increases its costs. As a result, higher interest rates undermine enterprises' solvency and facilitate the payment arrears chains.

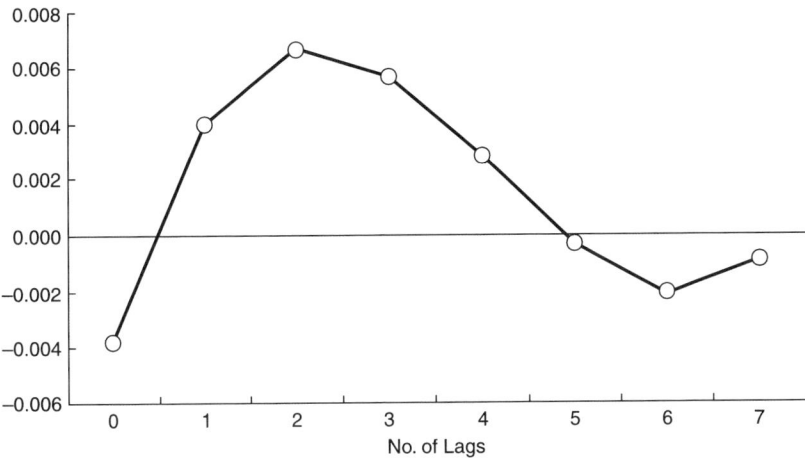

Figure II.2
Distributed lags for nominal money supply growth rates and for the nominal three-month GKO interest-rate growth rates.

Since GKO interest rates were used in this analysis, the government debt market plays an important role in the payment arrears problem. This is confirmed by the significance of GKO real interest rates (in the previous month) in the payment arrears model. Growing real interest rates render government bonds more attractive and attract additional financial resources to the government debt market, crowding out investments in the real sector of economy. The increasing cost of servicing the debt caused by additional borrowing aggravates the budgetary crisis, thus engendering payment arrears chains. The growth of real interest rates may also be related to increasing political and economic risks. Political and economic confusion in turn is a major factor contributing to the build-up of arrears. It affects both the growth of arrears proper and the climb of the nominal (and real) interest rate (which indirectly affects arrears). It is not difficult to see that the political confusion, such as the type that occurred during Yeltsin's illnesses and the resignation of the government, resulted in "unexplainable regressions" of arrears by an average of 50%.

The influence of the liquidity effect that we have demonstrated agrees well with the results of our analyses. Our analyses illustrate the impact of the growth rate of the nominal money supply on both the nominal interest rate and arrears (the impact is similar for both variables). A reduction in the demand for real cash balances can therefore be considered an important factor in the growth of arrears. The preceding fierce inflation can be blamed for the transition to a lower demonetization. Attempts to resolve the problem by significantly increasing the money supply can only augment arrears. A more reasonable policy would entail suppressing inflation, lowering the interest rate, and encouraging demand for real cash balances.

Unrealized federal budget spending has a considerable effect on the growth of arrears. A 1-ruble increase in arrears in budget liabilities in the preceding month results in outstanding payables growing by an average of 0.18 rubles. A 1-ruble increase in debtors' arrears in the preceding month causes outstanding payables to increase by 0.24 rubles on average. This process fosters a string of arrears in liabilities.

Thus, the payment arrears problem in the period under consideration was to a considerable extent caused by such factors as liquidity, political and economic uncertainty, and an overextended government debt market. Its resolution will require effective measures aimed at attracting investment in the real sector of the economy.

Appendix III Modeling Tax Revenues and the Tax Liabilities of Russian Taxpayers, 1992 Through 1998

Pavel Kadotchnikov and
Sergei Sinelnikov-Murylev

III.1. Key Factors Determining Tax Liability Dynamics

On average, taxes accounted for about 85% of budget revenues in 1992 through 1998. At the same time, budgetary tax revenues fluctuated with a considerable amplitude, and sharp shifts in the tax return structure were observed. During the initial period of economic reforms such a dynamic depended mainly on changes in the tax legislation and on normative acts regulating taxation techniques. As legislation developed and taxpayers adapted, economic factors affecting both the size of the tax base and the effective tax rates began to play a major role in determining the amount of state tax revenues. Therefore, our analysis focuses on the influence that economic factors had on tax revenues.

The problem of modeling tax revenues can be largely reduced to one of modeling tax base dynamics according to various macroeconomic and microeconomic parameters.[1] However, Russia lacks data on the tax base of major taxes for the period 1992–1994. Goskomstat (the Federal Statistics Board) has been gathering this information only since 1995 (originally on a quarterly basis, and since 1996 biannually). Therefore GDP volumes (monthly data in constant prices as of the end of December 1993) had to be used not only as an indicator of economic activity, but also as an indicator reflecting tax base fluctuations (Figure III.1).[2] Such an approach is possible be-

---
1. For instance, this approach was used in Manchester (1973); Bayar and Frank (1987); Browing (1989); Boskin (1990); Falvey and Gemmell (1996); Grapperhaus (1996); and Sobel and Holcombe (1996).
2. The somewhat conditional character of monthly nominal and real GDP indicators published by Goskomstat should be taken into account. Both monthly and annual GDP estimates were frequently revised, at times by as much as 20%–25%, which is evidence of their low reliability; wide discrepancies were sometimes found between

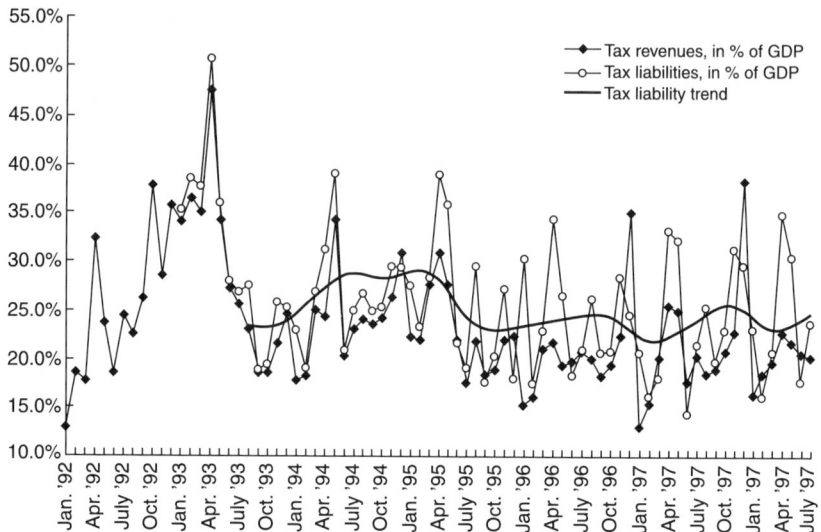

Figure III.1
Tax revenues and liabilities (% of GDP).

cause there is a close connection between the GDP and the tax base of major taxes. Modeling the GDP as a tax base and establishing its dependence on different indicators (such as the dynamics of capital and labor, technological progress, inflation, and the real exchange rate) would be a somewhat different task and is beyond the scope of this study.[3]

Insofar as income taxes accounted for between 8.9% (in 1992) and 13.1% (in 1997) of total tax revenues, we decided not to use the available estimates of unemployment as an indicator of business activity.[4] And because of unreliable statistics on investment and savings, we did not estimate the influence of these indicators on tax revenues.[5]

The next key factor to be considered in modeling tax dynamics is inflation dynamics. If all prices and costs grow evenly, if there are

---

the sum of monthly values and the final annual total. Therefore, the consumer price index was used as a deflator for nominal indicators (for instance, for the GDP), tax return amounts, tax arrears, enterprises' debtor indebtedness, and so on.
3. On taxation and economic growth, see, for example, Engen and Skinner (1996) and Clemens and Soretz (1997).
4. On the effect of taxes on employment, see, for example, Mark, McGuire, and Papke (2000).
5. See, for example, Jorgenson (1963); Hall and Jorgenson (1967); Boskin (1978); Summers (1981); and Hubbard and Skinner (1996).

no intertemporal redistributions of income and stocks, and if the relationship between price growth and nominal incomes is linear, then inflation does not affect the real incomes of economic agents. In such a case the inflationary effect on values of real taxes would be reduced to an influence on the effective income tax rate (assuming that an ascending tax scale exists) and on the real excise tax rate (if specific rates are applied). In practice, however, prices grow unevenly, and products are not produced and consumed instantly. Therefore, inflation distorts the tax base in a number of ways, depending on concrete taxation techniques.

The asymmetrical influence of inflation on production costs and outputs results in the depreciation of costs of material resources and fixed assets used by enterprises in the course of production, and subtractable from the profit tax base, between the time such materials are purchased and the time profits are realized from the sale of finished products. Similarly, because prices grow in the period between the time that the goods used in the process of production are purchased and the time that the VAT credit is granted, there is an inflationary depreciation of the permitted exemption. If the cost of taxable assets is not systematically revalued in a situation of price growth, the base of the tax on the property of individuals and enterprises shrinks. As prices grow, the real value of the tax-exempted minimum income of individuals diminishes. In real terms, all specific tax rates fall during inflation. At the same time, inflation affects different taxes differently; therefore it is difficult to determine the integrated effect a priori, especially in periods of high inflation.

Whereas the distorting effect of inflation on the tax base and scale can influence the amount of taxes collected both downward and upward, another inflationary mechanism affects budgetary tax revenues only unilaterally: tax revenues depreciate between the time that taxpayers' liabilities arise and the time tax revenues are received by the budget.[6]

Statistical analysis confirms that these asymmetrical trends in the inflationary effects on revenues from various taxes result in unstable coefficients in the corresponding regression equations.

The choice of debtor indebtedness as a factor determining the amount of tax revenues can be explained by a number of considera-

---

6. The effect of this mechanism was considerably heightened by the fact that the majority of Russian enterprises in 1992–1997 used the cash basis accounting method to account for sold products and profits, in contradistinction to the accrual method generally used in market economies.

tions. First, liabilities for profit and VAT taxes arise as enterprises are paid by customers for their products and services. Therefore, payment arrears on the part of buyers result in lower sales and profits, and consequently in lower real tax revenues. However, it should be remembered that increasing debts to suppliers, which grow along with the debts of buyers, lower the amount of tax exemptions for the purchase of materials used in production while determining VAT payments that partially compensate for lesser amounts of taxes. In a similar situation no expansion of the profit tax base occurs, since costs incurred before the sale of finished goods can be deducted from the tax base irrespective of whether the payment has been made.

Second, the total amount of enterprises' budgetary arrears depends to a considerable degree on the amount of inter-enterprise indebtedness. This can be explained by the fact that the insolvency of enterprises directly affects the solvency of their creditors, and therefore their relations with the budget.

Third, enterprises' arrears are an indirect indicator of the scale of barter operations in the economy. Barter operations distort price proportions and are used for tax evasion.

The direct use of debt variables in the regression equation is impossible, since series of these indicators are nonstationary even in real terms. Therefore, in estimating the equation, we will use the first differences of the series.[7]

The large-scale tax evasion in the period under observation underscores the importance of testing hypotheses about a relationship between tax collection dynamics and the scale of evasion characterized by various indirect measurable parameters.

In theory, it may be assumed that as actual inflation and inflationary expectations abate, the share of cash money M0 in the money aggregate M2 should decrease. However, this was not observed in practice. In 1992–1993 the share of cash money in M2 increased, while in 1994–1998 it remained at approximately the same level (about 35%). A possible explanation for this phenomenon is that cash-based operations in the shadow economy increase the demand for cash. At the same time, a considerable number of shadow economic transactions are conducted for the purpose of tax evasion. Cash payments allow economic operations to be conducted without

---

7. All of the time series used were tested with the Dickey-Fuller test for unit roots. Nonstationary variables were used in the regression equations in differences.

appearing on enterprises' accounting statements, and therefore no tax liabilities arise.

The macroeconomic parameters used to explain revenue dynamics mostly affect tax liabilities. Tax revenues, by contrast, depend to a considerable degree on tax discipline, and often on political factors. At the same time, monthly statistics on tax revenues include not only payments of tax liabilities incurred in the current month but also payments of liabilities incurred earlier, plus fines and penalties. Therefore, in a number of cases it is more expedient to use tax liabilities due in the current period rather than tax revenues as the modeled variable. An approximation of tax liabilities due in a current month can be computed by summing up the tax revenues and the increase in tax arrears in this period.

For the purposes of this study it was necessary to identify periods in which patterns of tax revenues were radically altered by such factors as the macroeconomic situation of the country and bursts of legislative innovations concerning taxation. One of these periods (1992–1993) was characterized by high inflation rates and numerous changes in tax legislation. Beginning in 1994 the situation was more stable, both politically and economically. However, after a financial crisis was sharply aggravated in the summer of 1998, many economic trends changed seriously. Therefore, the period from January 1994 to July 1998 was chosen as the base interval for computations.

During the period under observation (1992–1998), four major taxes—the profit tax, VAT, income tax, and excise taxes—accounted for 72.1% (in 1997) to 85.7% (in 1993) of total annual tax revenues. Because receipts from excise taxes depend on a number of factors that are outside the framework of this study, we have confined ourselves to analyzing the dynamics of profit tax, VAT, and income tax liabilities. The results are then used to model the dynamics of aggregate tax revenues and liabilities.

III.1.1. *Profit Tax on Enterprises*

The tax on enterprises' profits is a substantial source of tax revenues in the RF consolidated budget.

In this section we use available statistics to evaluate the profit tax base. The GDP may be considered to be an initial approximation. For a more exact evaluation, we also consider the share of indirect taxes in GDP. Furthermore, because the available statistics allow us to evaluate the amount of social payments and the deduction of wages and salaries from the tax base, adjustment for these two components allows us to test the effect of salary and wage payment peaks (vacation pay in summer and a payment peak in December) on profit tax liabilities. According to the hypothesis being tested, the characteristics of equations that describe the dependence of profit tax liabilities on the evaluation of the tax base should improve as the tax base becomes clearer.

According to actual quarterly results, for the first three quarters of the year, deadlines for paying the profit tax are the second month of the quarter following the quarter to be accounted for. The annual adjusted payment deadline is April of the year following the year in which the liability is incurred. To statistically describe the adjusted amounts, quarterly liabilities were assumed to be proportional to the quarterly tax base. The liabilities arising in certain months will be assigned to two dummy variables: the first variable, for adjustments in the first, second, and third quarters, is equal to 1 in May, August, and November and is zero in the other months. The second dummy variable, for the adjustment in the fourth quarter, is zero in all months except April, when it equals 1.[8] All nominal values were converted into constant prices as of the end of December 1993 via the consumer price index. If serial correlation occurred in the estimation residuals, the Prais-Winsten method was applied for correction, and the equation statistics in Table III.1 are shown after removing the serial correlation in residuals; F statistics, Durbin-Watson statistics, and the Schwarz criterion value for the original equation are given for reference. t statistics are shown in the cells of the table immediately below the value of the coefficients. (The equations themselves are not shown.)

The purpose of analyzing these equations was to test the hypothesis about the influence of various indicators characterizing the tax base and the level of economic activity (various GDP adjustments) on tax liabilities. Although the functional form of the equation was kept the same, the explanatory variables were replaced. A

---

8. The coefficients of the auxiliary variables (see Table III.1, equations 1–4) allow an estimation of quarterly payments. It should also be remembered that they correspond to quarterly values of the base; that is, the respective effective monthly rate is threefold for quarterly payments.

Table III.1
Explained Variable—Real Profit Tax Liabilities

	Equation No.					
	1	2	3	4	5	6
Period of evaluation	01/94–07/98	01/94–07/98	01/94–07/98	01/94–07/98	02/95–07/98	01/94–07/98
No. of observations	55	55	55	55	42	55
Constant	−1.276 (−1.680)	−1.241 (−1.586)	−0.901 (−1.194)	−0.217 (−0.716)	−0.076 (−0.276)	1.234 (2.316)
GDP	0.101 (3.220)					
GDP − indirect taxes		0.121 (3.086)				
GDP − indirect taxes − social payments			0.120 (2.743)			
GDP − indirect taxes − social payments − wages and salaries				0.109 (4.537)	0.061 (2.125)	0.063 (2.611)
Adjustments for I–III quarters	0.021 (10.070)	0.025 (9.978)	0.029 (9.774)	0.040 (10.271)	0.046 (7.852)	0.041 (9.417)
Adjustment for IV quarter	0.021 (7.998)	0.025 (7.921)	0.028 (7.743)	0.040 (8.386)	0.044 (7.675)	0.044 (8.711)
Inflation rate (CPI)					11.821 (5.414)	
Share of loss-making enterprises						−2.652 (−3.195)
R^2	0.736	0.732	0.726	0.774	0.824	0.814
R^2 adjusted	0.715	0.710	0.704	0.756	0.805	0.795
F statistic	21.297*	18.393*	17.466*	60.651*	43.292	64.625*
Durbin-Watson statistic	0.615*	0.565*	0.558*	1.216*	2.086	1.727*
Schwarz criterion	−0.816*	−0.737*	−0.710*	−1.523*	−1.846	−1.751*

*Statistics before removing serial correlation in residuals by the Prais-Winsten method.

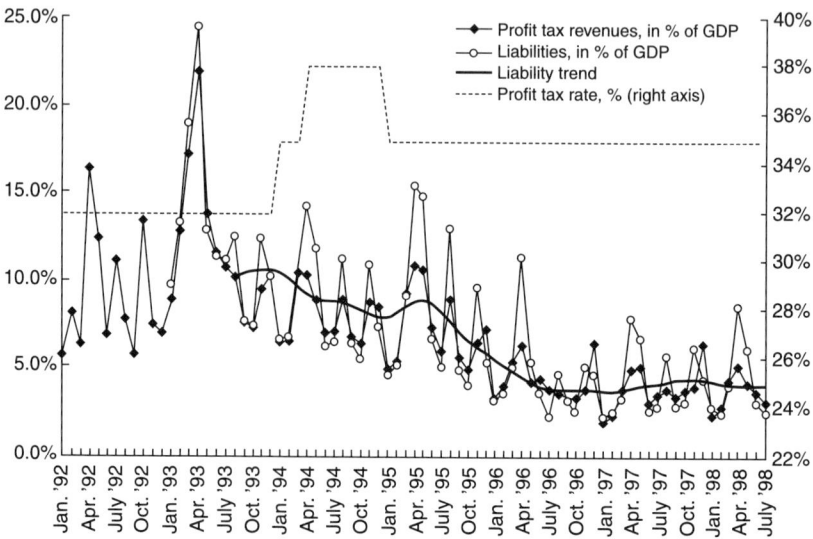

Figure III.2
Profit tax revenues and liabilities (% of GDP), graphed against profit tax rate.

key indicator for comparing equations in such a case is the share of explained variance of tax liabilities—the coefficient of R^2. The comparison was also based on values of the Schwarz information criterion.[9]

As Table III.1 shows, the GDP adjusted for wages and salaries results in better characteristics of coefficients and the equation at large. This may be explained by the fact that in early 1996, the limitation on deducting wage and salary costs from the profit tax base was abolished, and consequently taxable profits fell. Figure III.2 shows that the downward trend in profit tax liabilities occurred exactly in 1996.

The inflationary effect on real profit tax revenues means that price growth depreciates enterprises' costs between the time the respective goods are purchased and the time they are apportioned to production costs. Moreover, real profit tax revenues diminish owing to the lag between the time tax liabilities arise and the time taxes are

---

9. Because all explanatory variables in the equation are replaced, and because the construction of a general model that included all variables would be improper owing to apparent multicollinearity, it is impossible to statistically test the significance differences in R^2. Therefore, the comparison based on the Schwarz information criterion was used.

received in the budget. Sales and profits accounted for on a cash basis result in inflationary depreciation of enterprises' debtor indebtedness, sales proceeds, and enterprises' profits, and therefore in an inflationary depreciation of the profit tax over the period between the shipment of goods and payment for them. The advance payment of the profit tax partly counteracts the inflationary depreciation of tax revenues.

This set of factors does not allow one to unambiguously predict the sign of the dependence of profit tax liabilities on inflation rates. For purposes of statistical testing, an additional explanatory variable, the monthly rate of CPI growth, was added to the equation, which produced the most satisfactory evaluations of the profit tax base (see Table III.1, equation 5). No significant dependence of profit tax on the CPI growth rate could be established for the period of high inflation. The second period of data evaluation was set from February of 1995 to July 1998, thus allowing exclusion of the peak inflation rate, which occurred in January 1995 (17.8%, the highest rate in 1994–1995). The equations show that a positive dependence of profit tax liabilities on the monthly inflation rate (CPI) persisted in the period under observation (February 1995 to July 1998). "Positive dependence" means that in this period, current and capital costs depreciated in the time elapsed between the purchase of goods and accounting for them as production costs more than tax revenues depreciated in the time required for their transfer to the budget. Moreover, for the interval from 1997 through the first half-year of 1998, the positive dependence of liabilities on inflation rates cannot be completely explained by the proposed hypothesis, and in part results from similar dynamics of respective time series—liabilities diminish due to declining taxable profits and a growing proportion of loss-making enterprises against a background of falling monthly inflation rates.

When we tested the hypothesis that cash payments were used to evade paying profit taxes (because the use of bank accounts and cash registers was avoided), we discovered no statistically significant dependence on the share of cash at the 5% level of significance.[10] Thus,

---

10. In the case of tax evasion through unaccounted-for cash turnover, the statistically registered added value and the profit tax base also diminish. However, in computing GDP statistics, various adjustments to account for such operations are often made. Therefore, the dependence of GDP on the share of cash in the economy was excluded from this study.

it may be assumed that in the case of the profit tax, other tax evasion methods were actively used.

To test the effect of the profit tax base dynamics on liabilities, the share of loss-making enterprises in the total number of enterprises can be used as an indicator, since if enterprises move from this category or otherwise, it results in changes in taxable profits,[11] and therefore in a change in liabilities. This indicator can also be used for characterizing the general trend of evading taxes by means of reporting lower profits. The dependence of profit tax liabilities on the share of loss-making industrial enterprises was evaluated for the base period (1994–July 1998), with the equation including the respective explanatory variable (see Table III.1, equation 6). A significant negative coefficient of the share of loss-making enterprises confirms our assumptions that the increasing share of loss-making (loss-showing) enterprises resulted in a reduction in profit tax liabilities.

According to our hypothesis, the effect of the dynamics of enterprises' interindebtedness (the amount of debtor indebtedness) on profit tax liabilities should manifest first in declining balances and taxable profits (due to greater debtor indebtedness) for enterprises that use the cash basis accounting method. Second, in a situation of inflation, debtors' indebtedness (and therefore crediting of enterprises' real profits and profit taxes) depreciates over the period between the time the debt is incurred and the time it is repaid. Therefore, a negative dependence of profit tax liabilities on debtor and overdue debtor indebtedness would be expected. As mentioned above, the use of levels of accumulated indebtedness for the modeling is improper due to nonstationarity; therefore, increments of indebtedness were used in the regression equations. Econometric estimations showed that the coefficient of the indebtedness variable insignificantly differed from zero.

Using the special variables listed above to describe advance payments and quarterly adjustments, we tested the hypothesis that advance payments of profit tax are insufficient to ensure regular tax receipts. Taxpayers deliberately understate profit estimates, striving to obtain interest-free credits in this way, since the principal amount is paid after being adjusted to actual quarterly results. The evalua-

---

11. The test of the share of loss-making enterprises and of the evaluation of the profit tax base for multicollinearity proves that it is permissible to use them in the same equation.

tions given in Table III.1 show that deferments in payment of the principal tax amount actually occurred. If all enterprises estimated their profits close to the amounts actually paid to tax agencies, there would be no peaks in the months in which the adjustments were made. Although the t statistics of the coefficients of the special variables used to describe the adjustments are considerably above the critical value, the coefficients do allow us to evaluate the monthly effective rates of quarterly payments. As it turns out, these rates are approximately equal to the effective rates of monthly payments.

Evaluations of the tax base by means of adjusting the GDP for the amount of allowed deductions show that the adjustment for the allowed deduction of wages and salaries (until 1996 the deduction was limited: to four minimal wages in 1992–1993 and to six minimal wages in 1994–1995) is most significant.

In this section we have attempted to state and test a number of hypotheses about the character of profit tax liability dependence on various factors. Still, a large number of such factors remain outside the framework of this study. The general fall in profitability of the bulk of taxpaying enterprises, the active use of barter, overestimated costs entered into accounting documents, and various techniques of tax evasion were factors contributing to lower amounts of profit tax due to the shrinking actual tax base. Yet another factor that could have lessened profit tax liabilities might be the deteriorating effectiveness of export-oriented sectors caused by the policies of a quasi-fixed exchange rate, which resulted in constantly rising real ruble exchange rate. Unfortunately, the lack of authentic statistics for the dynamics of these several indicators prevents us from performing econometric estimations of the respective equations and testing these hypotheses.

III.1.2. VAT

An analysis of VAT revenue dynamics shows certain periods standing out in the general series (Figure III.3):

• January 1992 to December 1993: During this period VAT revenues and liabilities fluctuated the most, owing to changes that improved taxation techniques. Therefore, the period from January 1994 to July 1998 was chosen as the base period for the purposes of statistical evaluation.

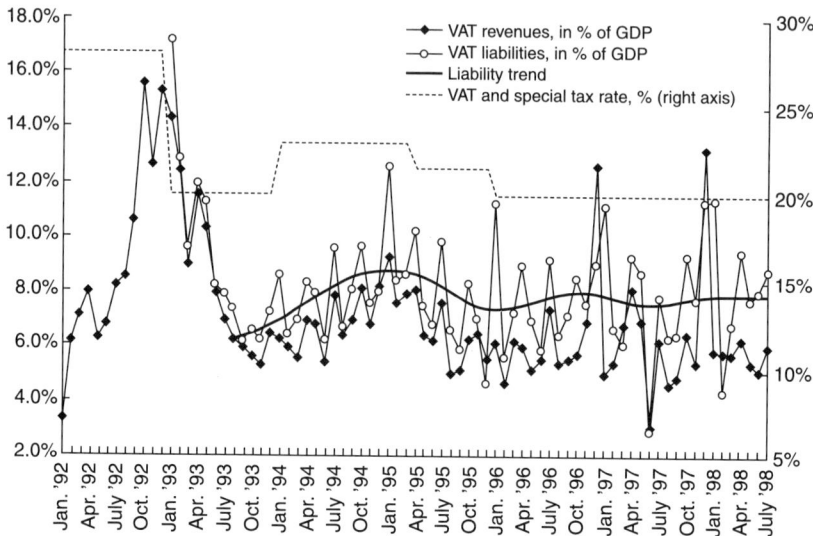

Figure III.3
VAT revenues and liabilities (% of GDP), graphed against VAT plus special tax rate.

- December 1996 to January 1997: VAT revenues peaked owing to reciprocal offsets. Since this effect was mostly due to the diminishing amount of tax arrears, the use of tax liabilities removes this peculiarity.

- June 1997: The most probable explanation of an "outlier" in this month is improper statistics. To avoid errors during the special adjustment of the data in this month, a dummy variable ($dummy_{0597}$) was introduced (the variable equals zero in all cases except June 1997, when it equals 1).

- December 1997 to January 1998: Revenues peaked in this period due to reciprocal offsets. Because the use of liabilities in evaluating tax arrears dynamics does not sufficiently compensate for this peak, a dummy variable ($dummy_{1297}$) was used for adjustment (the variable equals 1 for December 1997 and zero otherwise).

A special tax for the support of certain industries, in force in 1994–1995, was collected on the VAT base; therefore, the dynamics of the VAT plus special tax aggregate were observed for purposes of quantitative analysis. The VAT liability dynamics were observed over the period starting in 1993 (the statistics on VAT arrears before 1993 are not available).

For the purpose of computing monthly data, the GDP was used as a proxy for the tax base. For a more precise evaluation, state expenditure on wages and salaries, gross investment, and net exports should be deducted. Statistics on the first two indicators are not available. The deduction of net exports as a possible adjustment will be analyzed below.[12] To compute the base of liabilities arising in a current period, it is necessary to include the total liabilities, both those due for the current period and those acquired from previous periods (for large taxpayers this portion represents about one-third). Small businesses and taxpayers liable for small monthly payments (up to Rb 3,000) must pay the VAT on a quarterly basis. It is advantageous for taxpayers to pay the VAT immediately before the allowed term of payment expires, as arrears are penalized. Respective liabilities are included in VAT budgetary liabilities in the first month of the next quarter.

To take into account the aforementioned considerations, a statistical analysis of the effect of the tax base dynamics on tax liabilities should include the following indicators among the explanatory variables: GDP, GDP with a lag of 1, and GDP for the three previous months (the term of the quarterly tax payment). However, the variables GDP and GDP with a lag of 1 are highly colinear, and therefore they cannot be simultaneously included in the equation. Since a larger portion of the liabilities arise during the current period, the GDP without a lag was included as an explanatory variable.

As Figure III.3 demonstrates, the tax liability trend to a certain degree reflects changes in VAT rates, and thus confirms a relationship between revenues and tax rates (as long as rate changes are small). In order to discover the dependence of VAT liabilities on rates, we used the following approaches:

1. Linear regression of VAT liabilities on the basic rate set by legislation.

2. The introduction of certain dummy variables for each period in which VAT and special tax rates were above 20%.

---

12. Retail trade turnover can also be used as an evaluation of the tax base. This approximation helps to account for export tax offsets and import taxation. However, the turnover time series shows an explicit seasonal factor (manifested, for example, in the sharp peaks in December caused by consumer demand dynamics), and serious export adjustments were made by Goskomstat. Therefore it would be improper to use the respective statistics in an econometric analysis.

3. Ideally, tax liabilities equal the product of the tax base and the tax rate. Thus, we evaluated linear regressions of logarithms of the tax base and a constant over periods in which different rates existed. The constant in the regression equation, being significant, must coincide with the logarithm of the current rate, and since we assumed that a proportional dependence of tax liabilities on the tax base existed, the coefficient at the logarithm of the base must correspond to the assumption of linearity; in other words, it must be about 1 (since in the multiplicative form it is the power to which the base is raised).

4. Multiplication of the tax base by the changing tax rate: If not just the dependence of liabilities on the base is analyzed in the linear model but also the dependence of liabilities on the product of the base and rate, the results of the equation should improve.

The fourth approach yielded the best results. When the first two approaches were used, no significant relationship between liabilities and the VAT tax rate could be discovered. Unsatisfactory evaluations of equations with "steplike" variables resulted, apparently because a considerable unexplained variance of liabilities does not allow isolating statistically significant changes in the level of revenues depending on changes in rates, although fluctuations in the liability trend and in the rate are close, as Figure III.3 shows.[13]

When the third approach was tried—that is, the equation was evaluated in logarithms—the coefficients in the equation describing the dependence of VAT liabilities on GDP and the tax rate significantly differ from zero. However, this approach assumes that there is a nonlinear dependence, whereas quarterly VAT payments are additional tax payments made by certain categories of taxpayers in certain terms. Therefore, it is preferable to use an additive model for their description.

In order to take into account the changes in the tax rate and at the same time retain the comparability of the effective rate (the coefficient of the tax base in the equation) with actual tax liabilities measured in percent of GDP, the tax base (GDP) was multiplied by the ratio of tax rates in the current month to 20%. This ratio equaled 1

---

13. Moreover, major changes in the tax rate occurred in 1992 through 1994. Over the base period we used for our econometric estimations (January 1994 through July 1998), no such fluctuations in tax liabilities were observed, and the fluctuations in the tax rate were insignificant. (Beginning in 1994 there was a special 3% tax on the VAT base. This tax was later lowered to 1.5%, and finally abolished in 1995.)

for 1993 and for 1996–1998; for 1992, when the rate was 28%, and for the period the special tax existed (1994–1995), this ratio was greater than 1, reflecting an increase in liabilities as a result of an increase in the tax rate.[14]

All nominal values were converted into constant prices as of end of December 1993 by applying the CPI. If serial correlation occurred in the estimation residuals, the Prais-Winsten method was applied for correction. The equation statistics in Table III.2 are shown after removal of the serial correlation in residuals. F statistics, the Durbin-Watson statistic, and the Schwarz criterion value for the original equation are provided for reference.

It should be noted that in testing the dependence of tax revenues on the tax base, some deterioration in the evaluation of the equation occurs (DW, R^2 after removing serial correlation in residuals) as net exports are deducted (see Table III.2, equations 8 and 9). This may be accounted for by a number of factors, among them the difference between the effective rates at which the VAT is reimbursed for exports (the rate is close to 20%) and the effective rate of import taxation, which is significantly lower, since a considerable part of exports are foodstuffs taxed at a preferential rate. Moreover, the statistics on imports are adjusted for about 10%–20%. Therefore, deducting net exports, while formally permitting a more precise evaluation of the VAT base, may not in fact improve the results.

In analyzing the dependence of VAT revenues on inflation proceeding from qualitative considerations, it can be assumed that in 1992, the decline in VAT due to depreciation of payments over the time required to complete their transfer to the budget should have exceeded the effect produced by the growth of the tax base caused by depreciation of deductions. This phenomenon can be explained by the rather significant lags that occurred between economic operations and tax transfers to the budget. In 1992 taxation techniques were improved in order to shorten these lags. As a result, the negative effect of inflation on VAT revenues and liabilities should have waned. The order of reimbursing VAT payments only as current assets were charged off for production, which existed in 1993–1994,

---

14. If various macroeconomic indicators are used as explanatory variables along with the tax base and rate, it is more proper to interpret GDP not as an evaluation of the tax base, but as an indicator of economic activity. Therefore, when additional variables are included in the equation (such as the price index, the share of M0 in M2, or mutual indebtedness), no GDP adjustment is made.

Table III.2
Explained Variable—Real VAT Liabilities

	Equation No.					
	7	8	9	10	11	12
Period of evaluation	01/94–07/98	01/94–07/98	01/94–07/98	01/95–07/98	06/93–06/96	02/95–07/98
No. of observations	55	55	55	43	37	42
Constant	0.238 (0.741)	0.541 (1.112)	0.687 (2.525)	0.398 (1.113)	1.647 (2.805)	1.601 (2.319)
GDP	0.060 (4.425)			0.048 (3.105)	0.058 (4.916)	0.071 (3.705)
Quarterly payment base	0.009 (9.302)			0.009 (7.748)	0.009 (6.454)	0.009 (7.490)
GDP adjusted for VAT rate		0.050 (2.285)				
Same for quarterly payments		0.009 (9.713)				
GDP – net exports adjusted for rate			0.041 (3.585)			
Same for quarterly payments			0.009 (9.044)			
Inflation rate				2.893 (2.826)		
Share of cash in M2					−3.597 (−2.135)	−4.617 (−1.929)
dummy0697	−0.916 (−3.780)	−0.920 (−3.807)	−0.913 (−3.653)	−0.857 (−3.575)		−0.790 (−3.232)
dummy1297	1.084 (4.384)	1.075 (4.076)	1.167 (4.625)	1.255 (5.106)		1.083 (4.306)
R^2	0.748	0.740	0.731	0.771	0.668	0.764
R^2 adjusted	0.722	0.713	0.704	0.741	0.637	0.731
F statistics	34.782*	37.444*	30.969*	24.977	22.097	23.278
Durbin-Watson statistics	1.594*	1.690*	1.523*	1.872	1.709	1.995
Schwarz criterion	−2.529*	−2.583*	−2.445*	−2.524	−2.489	−2.536

*Statistics before removing serial correlation in residuals by the Prais-Winsten method.

led to a stronger positive inflationary effect on tax revenues that was especially noticeable for enterprises with long production cycles. Similarly, a long process of crediting VAT for investments in fixed and intangible assets led to overestimation of the effective tax rate, especially for capital-intensive enterprises. As a result, the influence of inflation on tax revenues in 1993 should probably change from negative to positive. Our statistical analysis, although producing some ambiguous results, proved the validity of some of these considerations.

Monthly statistics on VAT arrears in 1992 are not available; therefore, evaluations for the period 1992–1993 were carried using not liabilities but actual tax revenues. In our analysis of the influence of real GDP and monthly inflation rates on VAT revenues from January 1992 through December 1993, after serial correlations in the residuals in the equation were removed, the coefficient of inflation rates turned out to be insignificant. Using econometric estimations, we were able to confirm the positive character of the relationship between inflation and tax liabilities only since 1994, as the positive coefficient of monthly inflation rates is significant (see Table III.2, equation 10).

In testing the hypothesis about the dependence of tax revenues on the share of cash money in M2 aggregate, it should be remembered that whereas the coefficient of liabilities from the tax base in the regression equation reflects the effective VAT tax rate, the introduction of the explanatory variable (the share of M0 in M2) makes the coefficient of the tax base reflect the value of the potential effective rate in a situation of no tax evasion. The ratio between the evaluated (7.1% of GDP) coefficient of the tax base including the variable (the share of M0 in M2) and excluding it (6.0% of GDP) reflects the amount of evasion.

Evaluations of the dependence on the M0 share for different periods (see Table III.2, equations 11 and 12), which demonstrate an increasing elasticity of VAT liabilities in respect to the share of cash money in M2, prove the thesis that in the process of adapting to new taxes, managers learn to use tax evasion techniques involving cash turnover.

Because VAT liabilities arise at the moment of payment for enterprises using the cash basis accounting method, enterprises' reciprocal payment arrears may influence the amount of tax liabilities. If all other things are held constant (constant price growth rates, constant base), increasing payment arrears under the present accounting system result in fewer economic operations being completed, and hence in a decrease in VAT liabilities. On the other hand, VAT credits for purchased goods cannot be deducted from the tax charged to the amount of the sale until payment is made, which results in an equivalent increase in VAT liabilities. Thus, changes in the reciprocal indebtedness of enterprises should not influence VAT liabilities. This conclusion agrees with our econometric evaluations: the coefficient remains insignificant, while buyers' debts and debts to suppliers increase in real terms.

In contradiction to the profit tax, for VAT liabilities the coefficient of the share of loss-making enterprises insignificantly differs from zero. This result may be explained by better VAT taxation techniques than profit taxation techniques, which allows enterprises to evade the tax via a fictitious increase in costs and transition to the loss-making category.

III.1.3. Income Tax on Individuals

Due to the time and method of taxation (for instance, wages are taxed at the source), there are almost no income tax arrears. In recent years some small deviations have been observed in July, the last month for paying income tax declared for the previous year. Even in these periods, however, arrears account for only a small portion of total revenues. Therefore, unlike profit and VAT taxes, income tax arrears will not be analyzed in relation to tax liabilities.

During the period under consideration (1992–July 1998), income tax was charged based on an ascending tax scale, with the monthly payments being determined as the difference between the income tax due since the beginning of the year and the amount of tax paid to date. Therefore, as incomes accrue from January to the end of the year, and as more and more taxpayers move to higher-accrued-income groups, the individual income tax rate also increases. Moreover, this process is not linear but intensifies as the end of the year approaches. To account for the effective income tax rate increasing over the year, we introduced into the regression equation a special saw-toothed dummy variable that increases quadratically from zero in January to 1 in December of each year and is multiplied by the evaluation of the tax base.

Available statistics allow us to use accrued wage, paid wage, and cash household incomes less mandatory payments to evaluate the income tax base. Because wages and salaries accounted for 80%–90% of household incomes in the early years of reform, both wage and cash income dynamics—or either one alone—adequately describe changes in income tax revenues during that period. In 1994–1995 the situation changed: the share of wages and salaries decreased to about one-half of cash household incomes. If we consider the greater effectiveness of the wage tax compared to the (poorly) effective taxation of nonwage income (income from property, including interest income and dividends; entrepreneurs' incomes; tax-exempt pensions, benefits, and grants), it is evident that wages better describe income tax dynamics.

Since the statistics of the equations describing income tax revenues from differently evaluated tax bases are close, two partially coinciding periods (January 1993 through December 1996, and July 1996 through July 1998) were additionally studied.

The models (see Table III.3, equations 13 through 20) demonstrate that in 1993 through 1996, paid wages were a better evaluation of the income tax base than cash household incomes. This confirms that income taxation is unfair: the major income taxpayers are those whose compensation comes only in the form of wages and salaries, whereas high-income individuals can take advantage of a number of ways, legal and illegal, to evade taxes. When data for more recent years were used in the models, the situation changed slightly: wages and salaries only insignificantly better explained the income tax revenue dynamics. This suggests that the taxation of previously nontaxable incomes prompts the use of other evasion tactics whereby cash income is not recorded.

Income tax is paid when wages and salaries are paid, and therefore modeling using paid wages instead of gross accrued wages and salaries is better (paid wages are evaluated as the difference between the gross wage fund and the increase in wage arrears). The influence of wage arrears on tax revenues, as an indirect characteristic of the interenterprise payment arrears crisis, also should not be excluded. Therefore it seems reasonable to evaluate the equation that includes paid wages and to add an explanatory variable representing the real increase in wage arrears. The expected dependence is assumed to be negative, since increases in wage arrears result in lower budget

Table III.3
Real income tax revenues

	Equation No.									
	13	14	15	16	17	18	19	20	21	22
Period of evaluation	01/93–12/96	01/93–12/96	07/96–07/98	07/96–07/98	01/94–07/98	01/94–07/98	01/94–07/98	01/94–07/98	01/95–07/98	01/94–07/98
No. of observations	48	48	25	25	55	55	55	55	43	55
Constant	−0.008 (−0.101)	−0.038 (−0.292)	−0.650 (−3.404)	−0.596 (−2.595)	−0.116 (−1.157)	−0.113 (−1.629)	−0.425 (−3.844)	−0.016 (−0.251)	−0.545 (−4.586)	−0.150 (−1.417)
Accrued gross wages and salaries					0.098 (6.198)			0.091 (9.554)	0.217 (8.439)	0.101 (6.266)
Same, as adjusted for higher income group					0.036 (6.277)			0.023 (5.681)		0.033 (5.235)
Paid wages	0.087 (7.036)		0.190 (5.939)			0.103 (9.031)				
Same, as adjusted for higher income group	0.022 (4.706)		0.017 (2.140)			0.028 (6.155)				
Cash incomes		0.047 (4.721)		0.086 (4.666)			0.072 (8.419)			
Same, as adjusted for higher income group		0.008 (2.247)		0.007 (1.307)			0.006 (2.096)			

Modeling Tax Revenues and Tax Liabilities

	(1)	(2)	(3)	(4)	(5)	(6)
Real increase in wage arrears				−0.217 (−6.402)	−0.249 (−6.997)	
Share of loss-making enterprises					−0.538 (−3.272)	
Real increase in purchasers' outstandings						−0.013 (−1.755)
R^2	0.873 / 0.762	0.860 / 0.815	0.733 / 0.823	0.817	0.857	0.815 / 0.748
R^2 adjusted	0.862 / 0.745	0.840 / 0.789	0.717 / 0.813	0.806	0.848	0.801 / 0.728
F statistics	74.653*	128.008*	111.825*	101.694	57.177	50.350*
Durbin-Watson statistics	1.545*	1.622*	1.303*	1.839	1.968	1.438*
Schwarz criterion	−4.973*	−5.399*	−5.288*	−5.490	−5.385	−4.924*

*Statistics before removing serial correlation in residuals by the Prais-Winsten method.

revenues, either through direct shrinking of the tax base due to the deteriorating effectiveness of economic activities or through the increased wage arrears owed by enterprises to their employees, which also diminish the tax base (see Table III.3, equation 21).

To evaluate the influence of payment arrears dynamics on the amount of income tax revenues, we used an additional explanatory variable, the real increase in aggregate buyers' debts. Using this variable with the tax base was aimed at elucidating how changes in reciprocal payment arrears between enterprises influence tax revenues at a given tax base.[15] In other words, we wanted to uncover the relationship between the tax discipline and the condition the payment system is in. Our econometric estimations demonstrated that a negative coefficient of the increase in aggregate buyers' debts significantly differs from zero at the 10% level of significance (see Table III.3, equation 22).

To test the hypothesis about the dependence of income tax revenues on the share of cash turnover, we added the share of M0 in M2 as a variable to the equation estimated. However, the respective coefficient insignificantly differs from zero at the 5% level of significance.[16]

When enterprises strive to maximally lighten their tax burden, remuneration for work may be granted in the form of other benefits (such as catering, transportation by car, housing, and recreation) that are disguised as production costs, thus permitting the enterprise to evade paying income tax and making payments to social funds. To test the hypothesis that such evasions exist, we used the share of loss-making enterprises, on the assumption that it is more characteristic of loss-making enterprises to represent some of the income of individuals as costs. When we added the share of loss-making enterprises in industry to the equation, the coefficient of this variable turned out to be negative and significant at the 5% level (see Table III.3, equation 21), and consequently confirms our thesis.

---

15. An assumption that increases in aggregate buyers' debts do not affect wages and salaries is permissible in this case, for in respective pair regression the hypothesis that coefficients equal zero is not rejected.

16. By varying the period over which estimations are made, in a few cases a negative coefficient at M0/M2 is obtained that significantly differs from zero at the 10% level of significance.

III.2. Modeling Aggregate Tax Revenues, Taking Into Account the Specifics of Major Tax Payments

Our analysis of individual taxes revealed their specific nature caused by taxation techniques, which must be taken into account in studying aggregate tax revenue dynamics.

- The real GDP for the current month is used as the base of all taxes. The respective coefficient in the equation reflects the relationship of the effective tax rate to the GDP.
- Tax liabilities computed as the sum of revenues in the current month and the increase in arrears are used for the analysis.
- Profit tax and VAT account for over half of total tax revenues; therefore the peaks of adjustments of profit tax and VAT quarterly payments significantly increase revenues in the respective months. To take into account these specifics, the respective quarterly variables described above are included in the equations.
- The integral effect of individual factors were studied by including various macroeconomic factors (inflation rates, the share of M0 in M2, the share of loss-making enterprises, debtor indebtedness, buyers' debts) in addition to the tax base.

In 1994–1995 there was an increase in tax revenues (Figure III.4). The major factors contributing to this increase were higher profit tax rates and the introduction of the special tax. Later on, rates were lowered somewhat, and this fact, together with the decrease in profit tax liabilities we mentioned earlier, resulted in a shrinking of the total tax revenues.[17] The period 1996–1998 was characterized by relative stability of tax liability and tax revenue levels.

To test the hypothesis about the effect changes in profit tax and VAT rates have on tax revenues, we included the respective independent variables in the equations; however, on testing, the coefficients of these variables turned out to be statistically insignificant, and therefore these variables were not further used in the equations. When a variable characterizing quarterly VAT payments is added to

---

17. In recent years a trend toward oscillation has appeared, owing to insufficient data for proper neutralization of the seasonal factor. No special attention was paid to this circumstance, since the trend component was not used in regression equations, while the seasonal factor was explained in substantive terms proceeding from the terms of major tax payments.

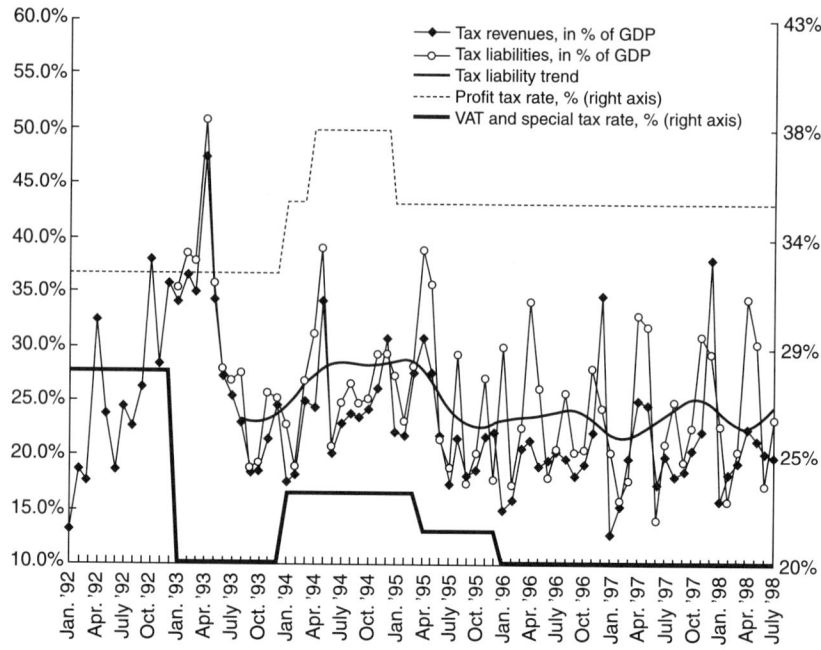

Figure III.4
Tax revenues and liabilities (% of GDP), graphed against profit tax and VAT rates.

the equation, the respective coefficient turns out to be insignificant as well.

The effect of other factors was evaluated by including additional explanatory variables to equation 23 in Table III.4.

Equation 24 in Table III.4 reflects the dependence of tax liabilities on inflation rates, with a significant positive coefficient. It's consistent with our hypotheses about the prevailing positive inflationary effect on state revenues as formulated for individual taxes. It should be noted that our estimations, including inflation rates and the share of cash money, were made for a period characterized by low inflation rates (since February 1995). In periods of high inflation (more than 10%–15% per month), the effect of depreciation of payments over the time required for their transfer to the budget is expected to dominate, and therefore a negative dependence on inflation levels may be assumed; however, the attempt to statistically test this dependence failed.

The significant negative coefficient of the share of cash money (see Table III.4, equation 26) reflects the fact that tax evasion by

Table III.4
Explained Variable—Aggregate Tax Liabilities

	Equation No.				
	23	24	25	26	27
Period of evaluation	01/94–07/98	02/95–07/98	02/95–07/98	02/95–07/98	01/94–07/98
No. of observations	55	42	42	42	55
Constant	−0.140 (−0.140)	1.096 (1.089)	−0.846 (−0.945)	5.160 (2.786)	1.700 (1.269)
GDP	0.221 (5.172)	0.143 (3.214)	0.162 (4.606)	0.220 (4.099)	0.178 (3.834)
Profit tax base – adjustments for I–III quarters	0.078 (6.846)	0.097 (8.825)	0.097 (8.911)	0.098 (8.919)	0.078 (7.108)
Profit tax base – adjustment for IV quarter	0.084 (6.614)	0.092 (8.628)	0.097 (9.774)	0.097 (9.038)	0.083 (6.718)
Inflation rate		9.104 (2.527)			
Real $ exchange rate			2.561 (4.853)		
Share of cash money in M2				−15.852 (−2.501)	
Share of loss-making enterprises					−2.486 (−1.985)
dummy0196	1.830 (2.070)	1.846 (2.856)	1.933 (3.352)	2.048 (3.176)	1.504 (1.720)
dummy1297	2.029 (2.282)	2.732 (4.115)	2.999 (5.200)	2.179 (3.188)	2.467 (2.768)
R^2	0.719	0.831	0.879	0.831	0.740
R^2 adjusted	0.690	0.802	0.854	0.802	0.708
F statistics	25.080	28.703	34.186*	28.596	22.811
Durbin-Watson statistics	1.953	2.074	2.309*	1.900	2.165
Schwarz criterion	0.037	−0.488	−0.636*	−0.485	0.031

Table III.5
Augmented Dickey-Fuller Unit Root Test

Augmented Dickey-Fuller Unit Root Test	ADF Statistics
MacKinnon 5% critical value for rejection of hypothesis of a unit root	−3.492
Real overdue debtor indebtedness	−2.821
Real arrears	−1.664

Table III.6
Results of the Johansen Cointegration Test

Likelihood Ratio	Critical Level (5%)	Cointegration Equation	Hypothesis
39.588	19.96	None	Is rejected
8.558	9.24	At most one	Is not rejected

unaccounted-for cash turnover takes place not only for profit and income taxes, but also for other taxes that are components of the aggregate budgetary tax revenues.

The increasing share of loss-making enterprises, the coefficient of which turned out to be positive (see Table III.4, equation 27), characterizes the general contraction of economic activity—the shrinking profit tax base—and is evidence that the current situation allows the use of this method for tax evasion.

No significant dependence of aggregate tax revenues on overdue debtor indebtedness and buyers' debts could be discovered. This may be related to the fact that increasing overdue debtor indebtedness directly affects the availability of funds for paying taxes at enterprises, thus causing arrears to climb and tax revenues to decline under constant conditions.[18]

The study of the relationship between debtor indebtedness and tax arrears requires a comparison of sums of real increases deflated according to the CPI at the time of the increase instead of deflated cumulative values, which reflect payment arrears at various points in time from the standpoint of payers' debt burdens or creditors' assets.

However, the respective series are nonstationary. The unit root hypothesis (see Table III.5, the equation with the trend and the constant) is not rejected for the series of real debtor indebtedness and real tax arrears; therefore, in order to study the relationship between them, it is necessary either to use the first differences or to test series for cointegration. The latter approach was used, since a long-run relationship between overdue debtor indebtedness and arrears is assumed to exist.

The results of the Johansen cointegration test (Table III.6) confirm that a long-term positive relationship exists between overdue debtor

---

18. We discovered no relationship to the profit tax. For the VAT, the negative coefficient of the real increase in overdue debtor indebtedness was significant at the 5% level, while the t statistics were (-2.19).

indebtedness and real tax arrears. In substantive terms, such a relationship means that both processes originate for similar reasons, the main factor, in our view, being the lack of an effective way to force Russia's economic agents to carry out their obligations.

III.3. Conclusions

An analysis of models of tax revenue dynamics shows that modeling using tax liabilities is better than modeling using actual tax revenues. This fact proves that the arrears dynamics are determined by discretionary decisions of the tax administration and reflect its tax effort in a greater degree than tax revenue dynamics do.

In analyzing profit tax, we noted sharp peaks in tax receipts in months when tax amounts were adjusted for actual quarterly financial results. These peaks mean that the applied tax payment order in fact allowed enterprises to use understated advance tax payments as credits during quarterly periods. Our analysis confirms the hypothesis of a positive dependence of profit tax liabilities on inflation rates, which is explained by the fact that costs depreciated over the time elapsed between the purchase of goods and accounting for them as production costs more than tax revenues depreciated in the time required for their transfer to the budget over the whole period under observation. It can be said that the negative dependence on the share of loss-making enterprises characterizes the general contraction of business activity and the deliberate understatement of the profit tax base by enterprises.

Evaluations of equations for the VAT confirmed our thesis that there exists a negative dependence of liabilities on the share of M0 in M2 and the corresponding assumption that tax evasion via unaccounted-for cash turnover results in shrinking tax liabilities. The positive dependence of VAT liabilities on inflation rates (as in the case of the profit tax) allows us to state that the increase in liabilities caused by the inflationary depreciation of credits on purchased goods exceeded the tax revenues depreciation occurring over the time required for their transfer to the budget in 1994 through the first half of 1998.

The modeling of income tax revenues demonstrated that paid wages were a better evaluation of the income tax base than cash household incomes in 1993 through 1996. The results we obtained do not allow rejection of the hypothesis of a negative dependence of income tax revenues on wage arrears, increases in buyers' debts, and the share of loss-making enterprises.

Our investigation of the integral effect of macroeconomic indicators on the aggregate tax revenues of the consolidated budget seems to favor the hypotheses of a positive dependence of tax liabilities on inflation rates and their negative dependence on the share of loss-making enterprises and the share of M0 in M2. Quarterly profit tax payments turned out to be significant for tax dynamics. A long-term positive relationship between real overdue debtor indebtedness and real tax arrears was also observed.

Bibliography

Bayar, Ali, and Max Frank. 1987. "The Erosion of the Different Tax Bases." *Public Finance* 42 (no. 3): 341–56.

Boskin, Michael J. 1978 (April). "Taxation, Saving and the Rate of Interest." *The Journal of Political Economy* 86 (no. 2, Pt. 2): S3–S27.

———. 1988 (May). "Issues in the Measurement and Interpretation of Saving and Wealth." Stanford Center for Economic Policy Research Discussion Paper no. 132, p. 35.

———. 1990. "On Some Recent Econometric Research in Public Finance." Pp. 486–95 in *Readings in Public Sector Economics*, edited by Samuel H. Baker and Catherine S. Elliot. Lexington, Mass.: Heath.

Browning, Edgar K. 1989 (March). "Elasticities, Tax Rates, and Tax Revenue." *National Tax Journal* 42 (no. 1): 45–8.

Clemens, Christiane, and Susanne Soretz. 1997. "Macroeconomic Effects of Income Taxation in a Model of Stochastic Growth." *Finanz/Archiv* 54 (no. 4): 471–93.

Engen, Eric, and Jonathan Skinner. 1996 (December). "Taxation and Economic Growth." *National Tax Journal* 49: 617–42.

Falvey, Rodney E., and Normal Gemmell. 1996. "Are Services Income-Elastic? Some New Evidence." *Review of Income and Wealth* 42 (no. 3): 257–69.

Grapperhaus, Ferdinand H. M. 1996 (November–December). "The Tax Base: Changing the Tax Base: Moving from a Tax on Yields to a Tax on the Use of the Factors of Production." *Bulletin for International Fiscal Documentation* 50 (nos. 11–12): 490–5.

Hall, Robert E., and Dale W. Jorgenson. 1967 (June). "Tax Policy and Investment Behavior." *American Economic Review* 57 (no. 3): 391–414.

Hubbard, R. Glenn, and Jonathan S. Skinner. 1996 (Fall). "Assessing the Effectiveness of Saving Incentives." *Journal of Economic Perspectives* 10: 73–90.

Jorgenson, Dale W. 1963 (May). "Capital Theory and Investment Behavior." *The American Economic Review* 53 (no. 2).

Manchester, P. B. 1973. "An Econometric Analysis of State Cigarette Taxes, Prices, and Demand, with Estimates of Tax-Induced Interstate Bootlegging." Ph.D. diss., University of Minnesota.

Mark, Stephen T., Therese J. McGuire, and Leslie E. Papke. 2000 (March). "The Influence of Taxes on Employment and Population Growth: Evidence from the Washington, D.C. Metropolitan Area." *National Tax Journal* 53 (no. 1): 105–23.

Sobel, Russell S., and Randall G. Holcombe. 1965 (December). "Measuring the Growth and Variability of the Tax Bases over the Business Cycle." *National Tax Journal* 49 (no. 4): 535–52.

Summers, Lawrence H. 1981. "Taxation and Corporate Investment: A q-Theory Approach." Brookings Papers on Economic Activity no. 1. Washington, D.C.: Brookings Institute.

Appendix IV   Monetary Policy and the Expectations Hypothesis on the Russian Government Bond Market

Sergei Drobyshevsky

In contradistinction to similar studies of developed financial markets, an analysis of the term structure of Russian government short-term bond (Russian abbreviation: GKO) yields faces certain difficulties and must make a number of assumptions, as noted here.[1]

1. *Observation frequency.* Because the period of observations encompassed less than four years (1994 to early summer 1998), we mainly reviewed the data with weekly (or monthly) frequency, in order to ensure a sufficient number of degrees of freedom in the econometric models. By contrast, most studies of the term structure of interest rates on Western markets use quarterly data. The greater frequency of the observations may cause a stronger influence of random noises and market fluctuations related more to short-term variations in market liquidity and the actions of individual significant actors than to macroeconomic factors. In this case, the results of analyzing yield dynamics across individual GKO tranches, in particular the results of testing hypotheses on the term structure, may lead to the rejection of certain hypotheses (expectations, preference for liquidity) in favor of others (time-varying term premium, market segmentation, "preferred habitat").

2. *Term classification.* Because the longest maturity of discount bonds on the Russian market was less than one year, the classification of GKOs into short-, medium-, and long-term securities that we use is a convention. Similar instruments on developed markets

---

[1]. It should be noted that this analysis cannot state normative conclusions in strict terms. The subject of our study is the Russian T-bill and federal loan bond (Russian abbreviation: GKO/OFZ) market, which currently does not exist in its former form. Thus, our conclusion that the term structure of GKO yields can be used as an indicator of monetary policy pertains only to the conditions *observed* on the government securities markets until August 1998. Whether these characteristics will prove valid for Russia's internal (or foreign) debt market either currently or in the future is outside the framework of this study.

would be classified as shortest-term (up to three months) or short-term (up to one year) bills. Because of the specifics of the Russian domestic market, however, investors considered GKO tranches with maturities of more than three months to be long-term securities whose risk premium included a unique term component (compared with short-term GKOs). It is possible that over most of the period examined here (but probably excluding 1997), short- and long-term GKOs were in demand by different groups operating on the market. Thus, it is assumed that GKOs can be divided into short-term (up to three months), medium-term (from three to nine months), and long-term (from nine to twelve months) government securities.

3. *Effect of variable maximum duration of bonds.* Because the maximum duration of GKOs varied from three to twelve months during the years 1994–1998, we were not able to analyze the dynamics of long-term (in our definition) bonds over the whole of that period. From our perspective, the most acceptable solution to this problem was to evaluate ratios between GKOs with different maturities over each time interval.

4. *Approximation of yield curve.* More frequent observations lead to a greater number of gaps in the data actually observed. With the exception of certain brief periods in 1997 and 1998, there was no week in which bills maturing at all terms, from one to fifty-two weeks (or from one to twelve months), were simultaneously on the market. Thus, to create continuous time series of yields across GKOs of different maturities, we approximated weekly and monthly yield curves. Such an approximation somewhat distorts the term structure of interest rates by smoothing the yield curve; however, it does not change the shape of the yield curve.

5. *Use of nominal interest rates.* Most theoretical models of term structure (including stochastic models) either are based on an analysis of real interest rates or do not specify a division into nominal and real interest rates. However, empirical studies of the term structure of yields on developed and emerging markets deal with nominal rates. This is chiefly related to the fact that in developed countries, inflation is low over short (monthly or quarterly) periods, and the transition to real *ex post* rates affects the general market patterns insignificantly, while the economic interpretation of real *ex post* rates is ambiguous. Furthermore, even if we assume that the real rate is constant (over short periods), variations in inflationary expectations and in the risk premium randomize the dynamics of nominal interest rates, thus making it possible to model them as a stochastic pro-

cess. Information on expected price growth rates may be important for elucidating term premium values. Therefore, this study also analyzes the term structure of nominal GKO yields (except in specifically mentioned cases).

IV.1. The Data for the Study

The source data for the study of the term structure of interest rates on the GKO/OFZ market came from the database of Finmarket information agency. Even though coupon bonds (mainly with varying coupon yields) have been present on the Russian government securities market since 1995, we worked with discount securities (GKOs) only.[2]

In order to compare rates for bills of different maturities, we computed continuously compounded GKO yields over all tranches for each trading day, i.e.:

$$I_d = \frac{-\ln P_t}{T/365}$$

where P_t is the bond price in portions per 1.

A law on the taxation of government securities yields, approved in late January 1997, apparently affected the prices of new bill tranches.[3] The discount yields were taxed at a fixed rate of 15%. In

---

2. This limitation does not significantly affect the results of analyzing the dynamics of interest rates and the term structure of government security yields. In most studies of term structure, the interaction of interest rates, and other macroeconomic variables, only discount bond rates (such as US Treasury bill rates) are examined. The study of coupon bonds does not change the principal conclusions reached in studies of discount bonds (see T. Coleman, L. Fisher, and R. Ibbotson, "Estimating the Term Structure of Interest Rates from Data That Include the Prices of Coupon Bonds," *Journal of Fixed Income* 2 (1992): 85–116).
3. The influence that changes in taxation have on the prices of government securities is outside the framework of this study. Although we do not have calculations confirming a price decrease in new taxable tranches of GKOs compared with previously issued tranches of similar maturities, such a hypothesis is based on the results of the analysis of consequences of tax reforms on the market of US government bonds (see S. Eijffinger, H. Huizinga, and J. Lemmen, "Short-Term and Long-Term Government Debt and Non-resident Interest Withholding Taxes," LSE Discussion Paper no. 275 (1997); R. Green and B. Odegaard, "Are There Tax Effects in the Relative Pricing of U.S. Government Bonds?" *The Journal of Finance* 52 (1997): 609–33; T. Koch and D. Stock, "An Analysis of Implied Tax Rates on Long-Term Taxable and Tax-Exempt Bonds," *The Journal of Business Research* 38 (1997): 171–6; and E. Elton and T. C. Green, "Tax and Liquidity Effects in Pricing Government Bonds," *The Journal of Finance* 53 (1998): 1533–62).

computing the yields of taxable GKO tranches, we assume that a purchased bill is held until maturity. In this case the tax equals 15% of the difference between the nominal and current prices of a bill. To make yield time series comparable with previous government bill tranches, this sum is added to the price, and this new value is used in computing the continuously compounded yield, i.e.:

$$I_d = \frac{-\ln \tilde{P}_t}{T/365}$$

$$\tilde{P}_t = P_t + 0.15 \cdot (100 - P_t)$$

The term structure of GKO yields to maturity is shown in Figure IV.1.

The weekly weighted average GKO yield is determined according to the formula:

$$I_d^a = \frac{1}{V} \sum_t \sum_i I_d^{i,t} V^{i,t}$$

where V is the total amount of trade on the secondary market across all GKO tranches for a week (month), $I_d^{i,t}$ is the yield of bill i on day t

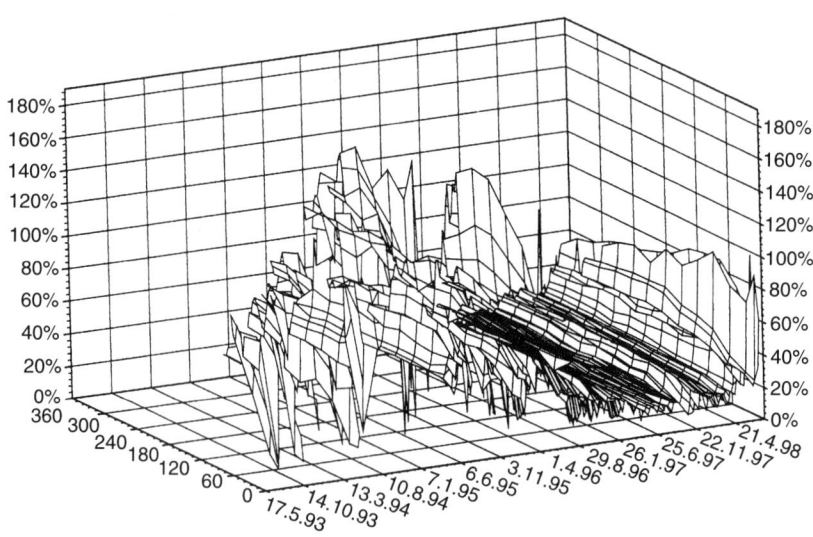

Figure IV.1
The term structure of GKO yields to maturity.

in continuously compounded terms, and $V^{i,t}$ is the amount of trade in bill i on day t.

The yield in real terms is determined as the ratio between the nominal yield to maturity and the consumer price index (CPI) as computed by RF Goskomstat, in accordance with the following formula:

$$R_t = \frac{I_t - \pi_t}{1 + \pi_t}$$

An important problem is that gaps appear in the observed data, owing to the absence of bills of the requisite maturity on the market in certain weeks (months). In many cases even the aggregate method we applied did not help. A method commonly used to solve this problem is to plot yield curves based on the approximation of actual data via various functions (such as polynomial functions or exponential splines[4]). In using this approach an economist chooses between goodness-of-fit and smoothness of analytical curves. Moreover, analytical curves cannot be used for the study of effects observed at the ends of the yield curve, which are the most interesting for our purposes.[5] Because the figures for yield to maturity for each month are averaged, the resulting yield curves are smooth enough. Therefore we used the method of simple interpolation between either the observed GKO rates with close maturity dates, or (for corner points) between rates of bills of the same maturity observed before and after the current week (for gaps of less than two weeks):

$$r(t,m) = \frac{r(t, m+1) + r(t, m-1)}{2}, \text{ in case the observation for } m \text{ is lacking;}$$

$$r(t,m) = \frac{r(t-1, m) + r(t+1, m)}{2}, \text{ in case the observation for } t \text{ is lacking,}$$

where t is the current period of time (week or month) for which the observation is lacking and m is the maturity term (in weeks or months).

---

4. N. Anderson, F. Breedon, M. Deacon, A. Derry, and G. Murphy, *Estimating and Interpreting the Yield Curve* (Chichester, UK: John Wiley & Sons, 1996); and D. van Deventer and K. Imai, *Financial Risk Analytics: A Term Structure Model Approach for Banking, Insurance and Investment Management* (Chicago: Irwin, 1997).

5. Because of imposed boundary conditions for the numerical estimate of parameters, the analytical curves have smooth ends.

GKO forward rates are calculated according to a formula similar to the yield-to-maturity expression:

$$f_t(n,m) = \frac{(m-n)r_t(m) - nr_t(n)}{m-n}$$

where m is the term before the maturity (in months) of a long-term bill and n is the term before the maturity (in months) of a short-term bill. The designation of forward rates is assumed to be $f_t(n,m)$. For instance, $f(1,2)$ means the forward rate of a one-month bill computed on the basis of yield to maturity for bonds due in one and two months.

Other macroeconomic indicators are as cited in official documents of the RF Central Bank and the RF Goskomstat.

IV.2. Analyzing the Properties of GKO Rate Time Series

An analysis of statistical characteristics of GKO rate time series (yields to maturity, forward rates) allows us to compare the behavior of variables under observation and to demonstrate ratios between average rates, volatility (dispersion), and inertia (serial autocorrelation) across series of different rates. The analysis is based on comparing sample statistical moments that characterize the distribution of rates.

IV.2.1. Analyzing the Term Structure of GKO Yields

Statistical Characteristics of Yields Across Maturity Terms. For key statistical characteristics of time series of GKOs of different maturities (the number of observations, mean value, standard deviation, values of first three autocorrelation coefficients), see Table IV.1. These indicators (except the autocorrelation coefficients) were computed from actual observations; interpolated values were not included in the computations.

In order to analyze the fluctuation in statistical indicators of the GKO yield term structure over the whole time interval (1993 through 1998), we divided the interval into three subperiods in which different dynamics of the average GKO yield level were observed[6]:

---

6. The period from May 1993 to August 1994 was excluded in order to ensure continuity of actual yield values for shortest-term GKO tranches.

- *September 1994 to July 1996:* A period of market turbulence resulting from higher inflationary and political risks and the emergence of the GKO/OFZ market.
- *August 1996 to November 1997:* A period of low average level of yields characterized by declining risk and high liquidity.
- *December 1997 to August 1998:* A period of emerging financial crisis, diminishing confidence of market operators in government securities, and intense support of bond prices by the central bank.

To get a clearer picture of the relation between yields and volatility of GKOs of different maturity, Figures IV.2 and IV.3 show mean yield curves and mean standard deviations of GKO yields for the whole of the observation period and each subperiod separately.

As these results demonstrate, the GKO yield term structure over the whole of the period has a complex shape. At the short end (up to three months) the slope of the yield curve is positive. The yield curve is flat for GKOs with a maturity of three to six months, followed by a negative slope for yields of longer-term issues. A more detailed investigation of each subperiod reveals that the shape of the yield curve is affected by fluctuations in the average yield level and by the number of observations made at different time intervals.[7]

The yield curve for the first subperiod (1994–1996) has an apparent positive slope. However, at that time short- and medium-term bills dominated the market, thus facilitating the rise of the short and medium segment of the term structure over the whole period since they represented risky securities. Bills with maturities exceeding six months had begun to be traded on the market only since 1997, when the average yield level fell dramatically. In the third subperiod, late 1997 and early 1998, the crisis developed rapidly over a short interval. Average GKO yields over this period, although outpacing their values in 1996–1997, remained at rather low levels. So, although the GKO yield term structure has a primary positive slope, in real terms the yield curve was stable for terms of up to six months.

The volatility of GKO yields across different maturity terms, estimated as a standard deviation of rates, indicates that the general pattern of the Russian market is consistent with general economic

---

7. For similar results of an analysis of the level and volatility of GKO yields in different periods, see V. Barinov, A. Pervozvanski, and T. Pervozvanskaya, *The Policy of the Government Debt Floatation and the Behavior of the Government Securities Market*. EERC Scientific Report no. 99/05 (1999).

Table IV.1
Key Statistical Characteristics of Time Series of GKOs of Different Maturities

	Y1W	Y2W	Y1M	Y2M	Y3M	Y4M	Y5M	Y6M	Y7M	Y8M	Y9M	Y10M	Y11M	Y12M
17 May '93–16 Aug. '98														
No. of observations	212	221	266	269	270	212	222	213	127	104	97	83	80	73
Mean value (%)	39.75	47.76	52.17	63.39	66.70	60.64	61.98	61.81	40.42	32.63	34.18	31.63	30.09	29.61
SD (%)	31.48	33.55	32.29	36.20	37.68	38.52	38.29	37.21	26.43	22.28	31.26	27.80	23.52	25.28
AR(1)	0.720	0.849	0.851	0.943	0.945	0.960	0.956	0.980	0.977	0.969	0.990	0.988	0.986	0.989
AR(2)	0.691	0.809	0.760	0.898	0.891	0.923	0.918	0.952	0.924	0.926	0.978	0.972	0.969	0.975
AR(3)	0.585	0.769	0.739	0.869	0.856	0.895	0.881	0.929	0.906	0.883	0.967	0.958	0.960	0.963
5 Sept. '94–28 July '96														
No. of observations	99	100	108	108	108	96	99	92	26	9	7	5	5	5
Mean value (%)	56.07	70.92	70.56	84.35	89.76	89.83	89.93	91.69	78.23	89.33	139.3	133.3	113.8	117.5
SD (%)	34.53	31.90	28.52	29.82	31.42	31.22	30.95	26.53	17.13	27.51	4.33	7.30	5.79	12.77
AR(1)	0.605	0.707	0.767	0.893	0.856	0.916	0.887	0.940	0.936	0.986	0.783	0.929	0.768	0.706
AR(2)	0.592	0.645	0.658	0.780	0.705	0.807	0.776	0.845	0.625	0.965	0.832	0.778	1.000	0.659
AR(3)	0.424	0.592	0.618	0.707	0.595	0.698	0.665	0.744	0.629	0.950	0.360	1.000	1.000	1.000

29 July '96–30 Nov. '97														
No. of observations	61	61	61	61	61	61	61	61	61	58	53	41	39	40
Mean value (%)	17.71	21.17	20.76	23.52	24.50	25.14	25.34	25.25	25.08	23.57	21.55	19.32	19.16	19.07
SD (%)	6.27	6.42	5.99	8.17	8.81	9.65	10.40	10.12	11.04	9.18	6.36	4.22	3.82	3.51
AR(1)	0.257	0.759	0.783	0.955	0.967	0.977	0.981	0.932	0.980	0.984	0.969	0.959	0.948	0.769
AR(2)	−0.107	0.692	0.656	0.924	0.939	0.952	0.950	0.922	0.947	0.957	0.926	0.899	0.862	0.676
AR(3)	0.014	0.647	0.572	0.897	0.913	0.932	0.924	0.919	0.928	0.933	0.876	0.778	0.724	0.547
1 Dec. '97–16 Aug. '98														
No. of observations	36	37	37	37	37	37	37	37	37	37	37	37	36	28
Mean value (%)	29.04	27.48	28.77	30.45	31.85	32.40	32.13	32.66	32.56	33.04	32.39	31.54	30.30	28.96
SD (%)	21.20	15.58	16.33	15.41	16.62	15.86	14.34	14.61	13.20	13.49	12.51	11.23	9.72	8.13
AR(1)	0.627	0.485	0.630	0.495	0.558	0.668	0.765	0.806	0.835	0.820	0.856	0.861	0.850	0.926
AR(2)	0.362	0.152	0.291	0.198	0.338	0.457	0.575	0.644	0.687	0.669	0.734	0.741	0.736	0.865
AR(3)	0.233	0.105	0.194	0.182	0.325	0.461	0.544	0.601	0.642	0.649	0.681	0.716	0.757	0.841

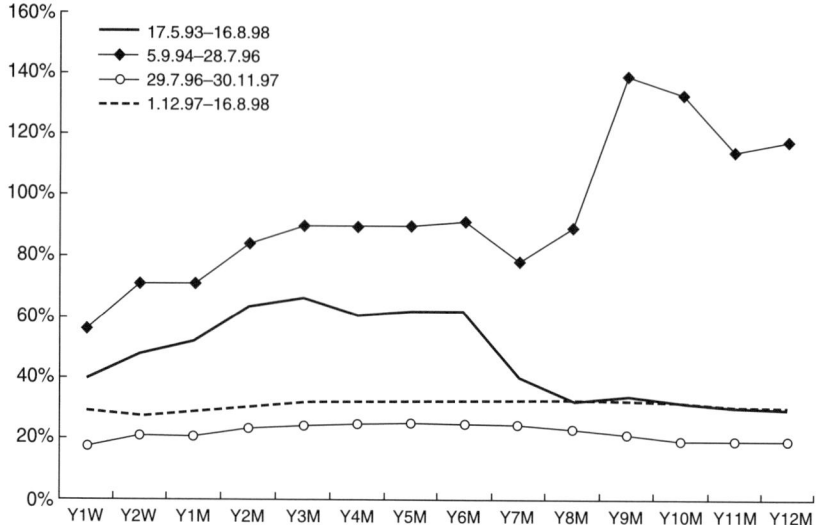

Figure IV.2
Mean GKO yields over different periods.

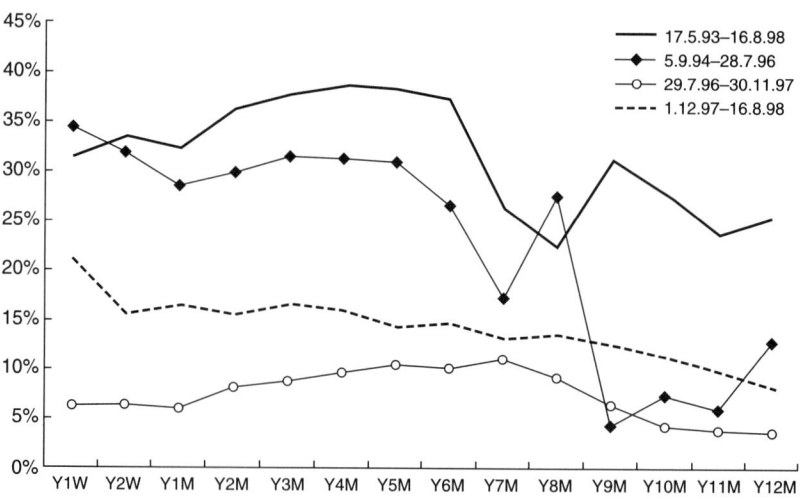

Figure IV.3
The volatility of different-termed GKOs.

principles.[8] Over almost all of the observed periods, short-term rates were more volatile than long-term rates. However, the lower volatility of GKOs maturing after six months relates mostly to the small number of observations (less than half of all business weeks), the relatively low liquidity of these issues, and the Russian Central Bank's actions toward supporting the required yield level. An obvious example is supplied by estimates for the subperiod of August 1996 through November 1997, when the CRB and primary dealers had to "clamp" the ends of the yield curve[9]: as Figure IV.3 shows, the lowest volatility in this period was observed at the ends of the yield curve, while the yield on bonds of intermediate maturity exhibited much more volatility.

The first three coefficients of autocorrelation of GKO yield time series (as shown in Table IV.1) also confirm the conclusion that longer-term bonds are less volatile. The values of autocorrelation increase almost to 1 as the maturity becomes longer. At the same time, the values of all coefficients, including third-order coefficients, are high. The yields to maturity of the shortest-term GKOs (one to two weeks, one month) are considerably less autocorrelated, while the spot rate of week-termed GKOs is not correlated over the period from August 1996 through November 1997. In 1998 the evolving crisis caused a sharp decrease in the "memory" of yields' time series: over this subperiod, coefficients of autocorrelation have lower values for the majority of terms than averages of this period on the whole and averages over other subperiods; moreover, values of autocorrelation coefficients of the second and third order drop considerably.

Stationarity of Time Series. For several reasons, analysis of the stationarity of time series of bills' yields is outside the usual test-

---

8. See, for instance, R. Shiller, J. Campbell, and K. Schoenholtz, "Forward Rates and Future Policy: Interpreting the Term Structure of Interest Rates," *Brookings Papers on Economic Activity* 1 (1983): 173–217; N. G. Mankiw and L. Summers, "Do Long-Term Interest Rates Overreact to Short-Term Interest Rates?" *Brookings Papers on Economic Activity* 1 (1986): 223–47; N. G. Mankiw, "The Term Structure of Interest Rates Revisited," *Brookings Papers on Economic Activity* 1 (1986): 223–42; N. G. Mankiw and J. Miron, "The Changing Behavior of the Term Structure of Interest Rates," *Quarterly Journal of Economics* 101 (1986): 211–28; K. Salyer, "The Term Structure and Time Series Properties of Nominal Interest Rates: Implications from Theory," *The Journal of Money, Credit, and Banking* 22 (1990): 478–90; and G. Duffee, "Idiosyncratic Variation of Treasury Bill Yields," *The Journal of Finance* 51 (1996): 527–51.

9. Clamping was necessary to support certain yield levels at the ends of the yield curve.

ing of the hypothesis about the presence of a unit root in the time series.

First, time series of interest rates of bills with different maturity terms are not independent: the random deviations of interest rates for different terms are correlated with each other.[10] In evaluating the unit root test statistics, the number of lags can be chosen to take into account the correction for autocorrelation in the residuals, in accordance with the Newey-West method.[11]

Second, as Enders and Granger demonstrate,[12] asymmetry in rate dynamics is typical for time series of the term structure of bill rates. In this case, the usual Dickey-Fuller and Phillips-Perron tests are not effective enough. The transformation of the Dickey-Fuller test proposed by Enders and Granger increases its effectiveness in testing the hypothesis about asymmetry in the stochastic process of bill rates.

Third, theoretical studies of random processes modeled similarly to relationships between time series of the term structure of interest rates do not provide a definitive answer about the number of unit roots in the term structure of interest rates.[13] Empirical studies of the term structure of bill yields in different countries confirm that actual time series of rates are of different orders of integration. Eugene Fama[14] noted that the hypothesis about the random walk of time series of financial assets, which appears to be true for stock prices,

---

10. Salyer, "The Term Structure and Time Series Properties of Nominal Interest Rates."
11. W. Newey and K. West, "A Simple, Positive Semi-Definite, Heteroskedasticity and Autocorrelation Consistent Covariance Matrix," *Econometrica* 55 (1987): 703–8. The number of lags is approximately $\sqrt[3]{n}$, where n is the number of observations.
12. W. Enders and C. Granger, "Unit-Root Tests and Asymmetric Adjustment with an Example Using the Term Structure of Interest Rates," *The Journal of Business and Economic Statistics* 16 (1998): 304–11.
13. See, for instance, M. Bradley and S. Lumpkin, "The Treasury Yield Curve as a Cointegrated System," *The Journal of Financial and Quantitative Analysis* 27 (1992): 449–63; H. Zhang, "Treasury Yield Curves and Cointegration," *Applied Economics* 25 (1993): 361–7; P. Johnson, "On the Number of Common Unit Roots in the Term Structure of Interest Rates," *Applied Economics* 26 (1994): 815–20; T. Engsted and C. Tanggaard, "Cointegration and the US Term Structure," *The Journal of Banking and Finance* 18 (1994): 167–81; T. Engsted and C. Tanggaard, "A Cointegration Analysis of Danish Zero-Coupon Bond Yields," *Applied Financial Economics* 4 (1994): 265–78; and K. Cuthbertson, S. Hayes, and D. Nitzsche, "Interest Rates in Germany and the UK: Cointegration and Error Correction Models," *Manchester School of Economic and Social Studies* 66 (1998): 27–43.
14. E. Fama, "Efficient Capital Markets: A Review of Theory and Empirical Work," *The Journal of Finance* 25 (1970): 383–417.

Table IV.2
Results of Tests for Unit Root Hypothesis and Asymmetry Hypothesis for Weekly Time Series of GKO Yield Term Structure

	Interval, No. of Observations	Dickey-Fuller Test	Phillips-Perron Test	Enders-Granger Test	Asymmetry of the Process
Y1W	12.9.94–16.8.98, 205	−4.60	−4.74	18.52	34.24
Y2W	5.7.94–16.8.98, 206	−2.26*	−3.38	15.13	20.65
Y1M	12.7.93–16.8.98, 266	−3.41*	−5.44	1.14*	1.74†
Y2M	12.7.93–16.8.98, 266	−3.25*	−3.73	2.79*	5.34
Y3M	12.7.93–16.8.98, 266	−1.84*	−2.49	8.11	24.59
Y4M	18.4.94–16.8.98, 226	−1.91*	−2.37*	2.38*	6.31
Y5M	18.4.94–16.8.98, 226	−1.96*	−2.27*	4.00	10.26
Y6M	6.2.95–16.8.98, 184	−2.24*	−2.62*	1.32*	0.91†
Y7M	17.6.96–16.8.98, 113	−0.40*	−1.60*	4.39	9.70
Y8M	11.11.96–16.8.98, 92	−0.45*	−0.81*	12.78	31.65
Y9M	25.11.96–16.8.98, 90	−0.42*	−0.32*	5.82	11.73
Y10M	3.2.97–16.8.98, 80	−0.07*	−0.69*	7.64	19.50
Y11M	24.2.97–9.8.98, 76	−1.27*	−1.71*	4.49	13.87
Y12M	24.2.97–12.7.98, 72	−0.19*	−0.24*	3.82*	9.79

*The unit root hypothesis is not rejected at the 5% significance level.
†The hypothesis about the asymmetry of the process is rejected at the 5% significance level.

requires economic justification when applied to yields on Treasury bills with different maturities.[15]

The results of unit root Dickey-Fuller, Phillips-Perron, and Enders-Granger tests (for unit root and the asymmetry of the process[16]) for weekly time series of the GKO yield term structure are shown in Table IV.2. These time series include both actual values and values interpolated in order to bridge the gaps. For each series, continuous time intervals of actual and calculated values and the number of observations over these intervals are given.

On the whole, the results do not contradict the most frequent cases of properties of the term structure of government bond yields. The tests reject the hypothesis about the presence of a unit root for

---

15. Here it should be noted that nominal rates contain inflationary expectations, and the inflation time series has (as a rule) a unit root. Thus, if expectations are not biased, and assuming a constant real interest rate, the time series of the nominal bill yield will also be nonstationary.
16. The asymmetry of the process presupposes that interest rates usually deviate from mean values nonuniformly (for example, they may increase more than decrease), which may be considered the nonstationarity of the process during the usual tests for a unit root.

the series of the shortest-term bills (one- and two-week GKOs), and the hypothesis about asymmetry is confirmed over practically all terms (except for one and two months). Of note, the Dickey-Fuller test more often than the other two tests tends not to reject the unit root hypothesis. The influence of asymmetry on the evaluation of a series order of integration is most noticeable for longer-term tranches: both symmetric tests (the Dickey-Fuller test and the Phillips-Perron test) do not reject the presence of a unit root, while the Enders-Granger test rejects the hypothesis at the 5% level of significance. Thus, the time series under observation are more consistent with an autoregressive process than with a random walk.

Similar evaluations were obtained when we analyzed monthly series of the term structure of GKO yields. Because these series mostly represent aggregated values, in order to ascertain whether they were stationary we applied the Phillips-Perron test (Table IV.3).

Thus, the assumption that the time series of differently termed GKO yields are nonstationary cannot be rejected, at least in analyzing a system that includes several time series, or in analyzing them with the inclusion of other variables of the first order of integration.

IV.2.2. Analysis of the Term Structure of GKO Forward Rates

We computed the values of implicit GKO forward rates across all terms from one to twelve months, for a total of sixty-six time series of forward rates. These series are not continuous, since only actual observations of GKO yields were used, in order to ensure the correctness of the computation. Moreover, we excluded negative values of forward rates (thereby excluding twenty-three cases, or 0.29% of the sample). The statistical characteristics of the term structure of GKO forward rates are shown in Table IV.4.

Since forward rates are determined based on a comparison of yields to maturity of two different bills and are indicators of future GKO yields to maturity, the parameters of their distribution must correspond with the parameters of distribution of GKO yields to maturity. However, the results of tests for the equality of the first two moments of distribution, shown in Table IV.5, do not confirm this assumption.

The hypothesis about the equality of mean values of forward rates and yields was not rejected only for the longest-term GKO tranches, the yields of which were most tightly controlled by the central bank.

Table IV.3
Phillips–Perron Test for Stationarity for Monthly Time Series of GKO Yields

	Y1W	Y2W	Y1M	Y2M	Y3M	Y4M	Y5M	Y6M	Y7M	Y8M	Y9M	Y10M	Y11M	Y12M
Test statistics	−3.97	−3.57	−3.17	−3.47	−2.91	−4.35	−2.02	−1.75	−1.03	−0.21	−0.67	−0.34	−0.72	−0.29
Critical values (5%)	−2.51	−3.48	−3.48	−3.48	−3.48	−3.49	−2.91	−2.91	−3.59	−3.61	−3.65	−3.69	−3.69	−0.71

Table IV.4
Statistical Characteristics of the Term Structure of GKO Forward Rates*

	No. of Observations	Mean Value (%)	SD (%)		No. of Observations	Mean Value (%)	SD (%)
$f(1,2)$	265	68.90	40.49	$f(2,7)$	127	41.20	27.00
$f(2,3)$	264	72.89	43.69	$f(3,8)$	104	32.94	22.25
$f(3,4)$	208	63.77	45.77	$f(4,9)$	97	33.33	29.48
$f(4,5)$	196	60.06	43.88	$f(5,10)$	83	30.70	25.71
$f(5,6)$	194	62.84	47.32	$f(6,11)$	80	28.45	19.68
$f(6,7)$	122	38.36	29.58	$f(7,12)$	67	22.40	6.16
$f(7,8)$	101	31.66	21.72	$f(1,7)$	127	41.05	27.00
$f(8,9)$	89	26.52	20.11	$f(2,8)$	104	33.14	22.66
$f(9,10)$	78	24.26	14.03	$f(3,9)$	97	33.97	30.67
$f(10,11)$	75	24.10	13.62	$f(4,10)$	80	27.20	17.95
$f(11,12)$	66	22.05	11.95	$f(5,11)$	78	27.33	17.58
$f(1,3)$	262	70.81	40.75	$f(6,12)$	71	25.35	16.47
$f(2,4)$	212	64.07	42.37	$f(1,8)$	104	33.04	22.74
$f(3,5)$	220	62.99	40.32	$f(2,9)$	97	34.39	31.44
$f(4,6)$	190	59.22	39.60	$f(3,10)$	83	31.02	25.85
$f(5,7)$	124	40.92	29.76	$f(4,11)$	78	28.01	20.88
$f(6,8)$	104	31.78	22.20	$f(5,12)$	70	25.42	18.34
$f(7,9)$	88	26.23	10.57	$f(1,9)$	97	34.44	31.62
$f(8,10)$	77	23.68	6.72	$f(2,10)$	83	31.53	27.01
$f(9,11)$	75	23.10	5.90	$f(3,11)$	80	30.38	24.66
$f(10,12)$	65	21.30	6.35	$f(4,12)$	73	28.78	24.20
$f(1,4)$	211	62.65	40.42	$f(1,10)$	83	31.81	28.06
$f(2,5)$	221	64.47	40.62	$f(2,11)$	80	30.24	23.64
$f(3,6)$	213	63.49	39.17	$f(3,12)$	73	29.33	25.19
$f(4,7)$	124	40.46	26.80	$f(1,11)$	80	30.25	23.75
$f(5,8)$	103	31.92	20.70	$f(2,12)$	73	29.47	25.12
$f(6,9)$	94	29.78	24.89	$f(1,12)$	73	29.66	25.35
$f(7,10)$	76	25.07	7.80	$f(1)$	1658	54.36	42.18
$f(8,11)$	74	23.62	5.84	$f(2)$	1417	51.43	38.55
$f(9,12)$	67	21.93	4.82	$f(3)$	1183	48.37	36.56
$f(1,5)$	222	63.62	39.69	$f(4)$	982	45.51	34.80
$f(2,6)$	213	63.95	39.19	$f(5)$	771	41.11	32.03
$f(3,7)$	126	40.44	26.20	$f(6)$	557	32.43	24.02
$f(4,8)$	103	32.20	21.83	$f(7)$	432	30.81	24.76
$f(5,9)$	95	30.90	24.62	$f(8)$	333	31.50	27.30
$f(6,10)$	82	28.42	21.08	$f(9)$	236	30.51	25.65
$f(7,11)$	74	24.14	7.01	$f(10)$	153	29.88	24.34
$f(8,12)$	67	22.11	5.02	$f(11)$	73	29.66	25.35
$f(1,6)$	213	63.28	38.46				

*$f(n)$ is the forward rate for n months calculated across all possible combinations of bill maturity terms.

Table IV.5
Results of Tests for Equality of Mean Value and Variance of Multiple Samples (GKO Forward Rates on Bills of Different Maturity)

	Y1M	Y2M	Y3M	Y4M	Y5M	Y6M	Y7M	Y8M	Y9M	Y10M	Y11M
17 May '93–28 July '96											
Equality of mean values	7.53	2.53	2.20	2.19	4.25	5.52	17.33	6.30	12.28	5.36	0.43*
Equality of variances (Bartlett)	56.68	19.11	16.40	17.56	28.77	33.66	17.98	12.00	6.89*	3.18*	2.01*
Equality of variances (Levene)	2.34	2.73	2.40	2.45	3.43	4.29	2.63	3.22	3.20*	5.53	9.87
Equality of variances (Brown-Forsythe)	1.59*	1.70*	1.75*	2.01*	2.72	3.63	1.02*	1.12*	1.52*	0.91*	1.12*
29 July '96–30 Nov. '97											
Equality of mean values	5.85	5.94	6.77	7.72	9.17	10.41	10.66	8.04	3.13	0.04*	0.01*
Equality of variances (Bartlett)	268.63	267.60	309.39	327.24	271.16	263.13	225.42	137.66	24.25	1.82*	0.17*
Equality of variances (Levene)	13.44	14.82	17.88	19.78	19.94	21.54	23.83	18.36	14.79	2.49*	0.51*
Equality of variances (Brown-Forsythe)	8.12	8.28	10.22	12.19	12.69	14.27	16.24	14.62	10.71	1.18*	0.24*
1 Dec. '97–16 Aug. '98											
Equality of mean values	2.69	2.79	2.24	2.07	1.46*	1.24*	1.18*	1.11*	0.87*	0.69*	0.34*
Equality of variances (Bartlett)	59.06	71.58	70.85	48.87	39.61	37.94	27.65	19.75	10.80	4.91*	1.27*
Equality of variances (Levene)	3.08	4.08	4.83	4.58	5.03	5.17	4.70	4.26	3.48	2.82*	1.97*
Equality of variances (Brown-Forsythe)	1.51*	1.89	2.23	1.92*	2.06	2.00*	1.82*	1.70*	1.32*	1.12*	0.92*

*The hypothesis about equality is not rejected at the 5% significance level.

Note: The table contains values of statistics of tests for equality of the mean value (ANOVA F test; see Johnston and DiNardo, 1997) and of variance (Bartlett's test, Levene test, and Brown-Forsythe test; see Judge, Griffiths, Hill, Luetkepohl, and Lee, 1985) of two and more samples. Since different tests for the equality of variance are of different power across cases, we show statistical values for all three cases.

The distribution of both GKO rate values differs markedly from the normal one, as the results of the Bartlett test for the equality of distribution variance demonstrate. This test is highly sensitive to deviation of the sample distribution from normal. The Levene and Brown-Forsythe tests, which are less sensitive to the normal distribution requirement, often do not reject the null hypothesis about the equality of mean values. In particular, a more powerful Brown-Forsythe test demonstrated identical volatility of GKO yields and forward rates over the first subperiod (from May 1993 to July 1996) and the last subperiod (from December 1997 to August 1998). In our view, the results we obtained reflect the fact that in periods of increasing general instability, fluctuations in the forward and spot rates are symmetric. Over the second subperiod (from August 1996 through November 1997) current GKO yields fell steadily, thus causing greater volatility of yields to maturity over the whole subperiod as compared with forward rate fluctuations.

IV.3. Monetary Policy Shocks and the Term Structure of GKO Yields

In analyzing the effects of monetary policies on GKO yield term structure, two lines of research can be singled out, each examining a different target of monetary policy. The first is the study of the ratio between targeted interest rates (such as Federal Reserve rates for short-term instruments on the US money market) set by the monetary authorities and the yields of bonds with different maturities. This approach came into being as a number of countries started to monitor interest rates as targets of monetary policy.[17]

The second line of investigation examines the direct impact of money supply shocks on the term structure of interest rates. The theoretical principles of such an analysis include not only standard macroeconomic models, but also special macroeconomic approaches

---

17. For studies in the framework of this approach see L. Svensson, "Estimating and Interpreting Forward Interest Rates: Sweden 1992–1994," IIES Seminar Paper no. 579 (1994); B. McCallum, "Monetary Policy and the Term Structure of Interest Rates," NBER Working Paper no. 4938 (1994); J. Campbell, "Some Lessons from the Yield Curve," NBER Working Paper no. 5031 (1995); P. Balduzzi, G. Bertola, and S. Foresi, "A Model of Target Changes and the Term Structure of Interest Rates," *The Journal of Monetary Economics* 39 (1997): 223–49; and H. Dillen, "A Model of the Term Structure of Interest Rates in an Open Economy with Regime Shifts," *The Journal of International Money and Finance* 16 (1997): 795–819.

to the study of the term structure of interest rates.[18] Because the RF Central Bank targeted the dynamics of various money aggregates in conducting its monetary policy, the second approach seems more appropriate for examining the Russian government bond market.

In analyzing the effect of money supply shocks on the yields of GKOs of different terms, it is important to choose suitable money aggregates. Chari, Christiano, and Eichenbaum[19] noted the difference in the signs of correlation coefficients between time series of short-term rates and various money aggregates: nominal short-term rates correlate positively with the money base and with money aggregates M0 and M1 and correlate negatively with the amount of nonborrowed reserves. The positive dependency can be explained by endogenous changes in both variables: at higher interest rates, the FRS intensifies its activity on the open market, increasing narrow money aggregates. On the other hand, the growth of nonborrowed reserves is connected to sluggish decision making with respect to enhancing the active operations of commercial banks after shocks to the positive money supply have resulted in lower interest rates.

Thus, the effects of monetary policy shocks can be studied first by considering emerging inflationary expectations and second by considering changes in liquidity on the market. These effects can also be divided according to the type of financial instrument (in our case it is GKO term of maturity) and the money aggregate under observation.

To analyze the relation between the money aggregate dynamics and interest rates on GKOs of different terms, we chose yields of GKOs maturing in one week and one, three, six, and nine months. One-week GKOs were defined as shortest-term bonds, one-month GKOs as short-term bonds, and three- and six-month GKOs as long-term bonds. Four money aggregates were analyzed:

- Narrow money base (MB, cash plus required reserves)
- Money supply M0 (cash outside the banking system)
- Money supply M2 (cash outside the banking system plus RF residents' ruble-denominated current deposits and other balances in credit organizations)

---

18. See, for example, O. Blanchard, "Output, the Stock Market, and Interest Rates," *American Economic Review* 71 (1981): 132–43; and S. Turnovsky, "The Term Structure of Interest Rates and the Effects of Macroeconomic Policy," *The Journal of Money, Credit and Banking* 21 (1989): 321–47.

19. V. Chari, L. Christiano, and M. Eichenbaum, "Inside Money, Outside Money and Short Term Interest Rates," NBER Working Paper no. 5269 (1995).

Table IV.6
Coefficients of Correlation Between Changes in GKO Yields to Maturity and Rates of Change in Money Aggregates

	MB	M0	M2	BM
D(Y1W)	0.128	0.045	−0.017	−0.012
D(Y1M)	0.051	0.011	−0.027	0.067
D(Y3M)	−0.098	−0.085	−0.300	−0.042
D(Y6M)	−0.184	−0.140	−0.432	−0.182
D(Y9M)	−0.201	−0.111	−0.479	−0.201

- Broad money (M2 plus all foreign exchange–denominated deposits)

Table IV.6 lists the coefficients of correlation between changes in GKO yields to maturity and rates of change in money aggregates.

The results we obtained are consistent with the correlation we mentioned earlier between interest rates on GKOs of different terms and the dynamics of money aggregates. The Russian money market in this case behaved similarly to developed markets, such as that of the United States. Changes in the yields of shortest- and short-term GKOs correlated positively with money base and cash M0 growth rates and correlated negatively with the broader money aggregates, M2 and broad money (the case of one-month GKOs and broad money is an exception). Changes in the yields of longer GKO tranches (over three months) demonstrate negative values of the coefficients of correlation with growth of all money aggregates. The highest absolute values of correlation coefficients for medium- and long-term rates were observed for the series of M2 increments. For shortest- and short-term rates the highest correlation coefficients occurred as the money base grew.[20]

The interpretation of these results may be similar to that offered by Chari, Christiano, and Eichenbaum.[21] Substantial increases (or reductions) in the shortest-term rates chiefly reflected the liquidity of the banking system before the primary GKO auctions. If the amount

---

20. Similar findings, although without qualitative interpretation, were presented by Mishkin for the US T-bill market (F. Mishkin, *Money, Interest Rates and Inflation* (Aldershot, UK: Edward Elgar, 1993).)

21. A theoretical background for these conclusions based on the model of money supply influencing interest rates with endogenously segmented markets was presented in F. Alvarez, A. Atkeson, and P. Kehoe, "Money and Interest Rates with Endogenously Segmented Markets," NBER Working Paper no. 7060 (1999).

of liquid funds diminished, many banks would start selling shortest-term GKO tranches. After the central bank began taking responsibility for supporting liquidity on the GKO/OFZ market through open market operations and crediting dealers on repo terms over a considerable part of the period under observation, then, when liquidity deteriorated, the money base grew. It is likely that some portion of the funds obtained by commercial banks due to the increasing money base was converted into cash, thus facilitating increases in M0. Taking into account the frequency period we have chosen (one month), such fluctuations in the money base and M0 coincide with changes in yield.

Signs of the coefficients of correlation between medium- and long-term rates and all money aggregates, and between short-term rates and broad money aggregates, reflect the effects of growing liquidity: interest rates decreased as the money supply expanded. Moreover, as average yield levels fell as the result of a growing volume of transactions on the market (and correspondingly accelerating rates of growth of broad money aggregates), the volatility of GKO yields abated in the second half of 1996 through 1998. So, over the whole period under observation, the estimation of correlation coefficients was primarily affected by the general trend toward a decreasing amplitude of fluctuations in yields across all GKO tranches at the same time that the growth of broad money aggregates accelerated.

To estimate the dynamic consequences of monetary policy shocks, we used vector autoregression models to model the growth rate of four money aggregates and the first differences of nominal yields of GKOs maturing at the terms we chose. Such an approach is often used to analyze the effects of monetary policy on the dynamics of the term structure of interest rates.[22] In particular, our approach is close to the one presented by Evans and Marshall.[23] CPI growth rates were included as the endogenous variable in the vector autoregression models. At the same time, to take into account cointegrating equations between inflation rates and nominal GKO yield levels, we

---

22. See, for example, C. Sims, "Are Forecasting Models Usable for Policy Analysis?" *Federal Reserve Bank of Minneapolis Quarterly Review* 10 (1986): 2–16; McCallum, "Monetary Policy and the Term Structure of Interest Rates"; and N. Roubini and V. Grilli, "Liquidity Models in Open Economies: Theory and Empirical Evidence," NBER Working Paper no. 5513 (1995).
23. C. Evans and D. Marshall, "Monetary Policy and the Term Structure of Nominal Interest Rates: Evidence and Theory," *Carnegie-Rochester Conference Series on Public Policy* 49 (1998): 53–111.

estimated vector error correction (VEC) models, which allowed us to evaluate the reaction of interest rates to a growing money supply while accounting for simultaneous changes in inflation rates. A VEC model can be formally presented as follows:

$$\begin{pmatrix} \Delta i_t^n \\ \Delta \pi_t \\ \dot{M}_t \end{pmatrix} = \begin{pmatrix} \Phi_p(\Delta i_{t-p}^n) & \Phi_p(\Delta \pi_{t-p}) & \Phi_p(\dot{M}_{t-p}) \\ \Phi_p(\Delta i_{t-p}^n) & \Phi_p(\Delta \pi_{t-p}) & \Phi_p(\dot{M}_{t-p}) \\ \Phi_p(\Delta i_{t-p}^n) & \Phi_p(\Delta \pi_{t-p}) & \Phi_p(\dot{M}_{t-p}) \end{pmatrix} \cdot \begin{pmatrix} a_i & b_i & d_i \\ a_\pi & b_\pi & d_\pi \\ a_M & b_M & d_M \end{pmatrix}$$

$$+ \begin{pmatrix} \gamma_1 \cdot CE(\pi) \\ \gamma_2 \cdot CE(i^n) \\ 0 \end{pmatrix} + \begin{pmatrix} \varepsilon_t \\ \eta_t \\ \delta_t \end{pmatrix}$$

where Δi_t^n is the first difference of nominal yields of GKOs of maturity n; $\Delta \pi_t$ is the first difference of the CPI growth rates; $\dot{M}_t$ is the growth rate of a money aggregate; $\Phi_p(\cdot)$ is the linear function of values of variables with lags from $t-1$ to $t-p$; **a**, **b**, and **d** are vectors of estimated coefficients at lag values of the respective variables for each equation; $CE(\cdot)$ are cointegrating equations for equations of yields and inflation[24]; γ_1 and γ_2 are coefficients of cointegrating equations; and ε_t, η_t, and δ_t are random errors for each equation.

Figure IV.4 shows the impulse response functions of the first differences of nominal yields of differently termed GKOs in response to positive shocks in monetary policies. That is, at accelerating growth rates of the respective money aggregates, Δ equals 1 SD.

As the graphs in Figure IV.4 demonstrate, the rates react to shocks somewhat differently, depending on the money aggregate under observation. Increases in the money supply (accelerating rates of growth of the money base and M0) cause yields across all GKO tranches to grow (except for the longest, nine-month GKOs), with a lag of about four to five months. This fact is related to evolving inflationary expectations, which intensify when monetary policy becomes softer over several months in a row. For about a year thereafter, the rates of one-, three-, and six-month GKOs remain high, reflecting the growth of nominal GKO yields at accelerating inflation

---

24. Since money aggregate series are stationary in levels (the value of the Dickey-Fuller test statistics for time series H is -4.05, for M0 it is -4.32, for M2 it is -5.86, and for BM it is -4.13, while the critical value for rejecting the null hypothesis about unit root is -3.48), they are included in the model in levels and do not appear in cointegrating equations.

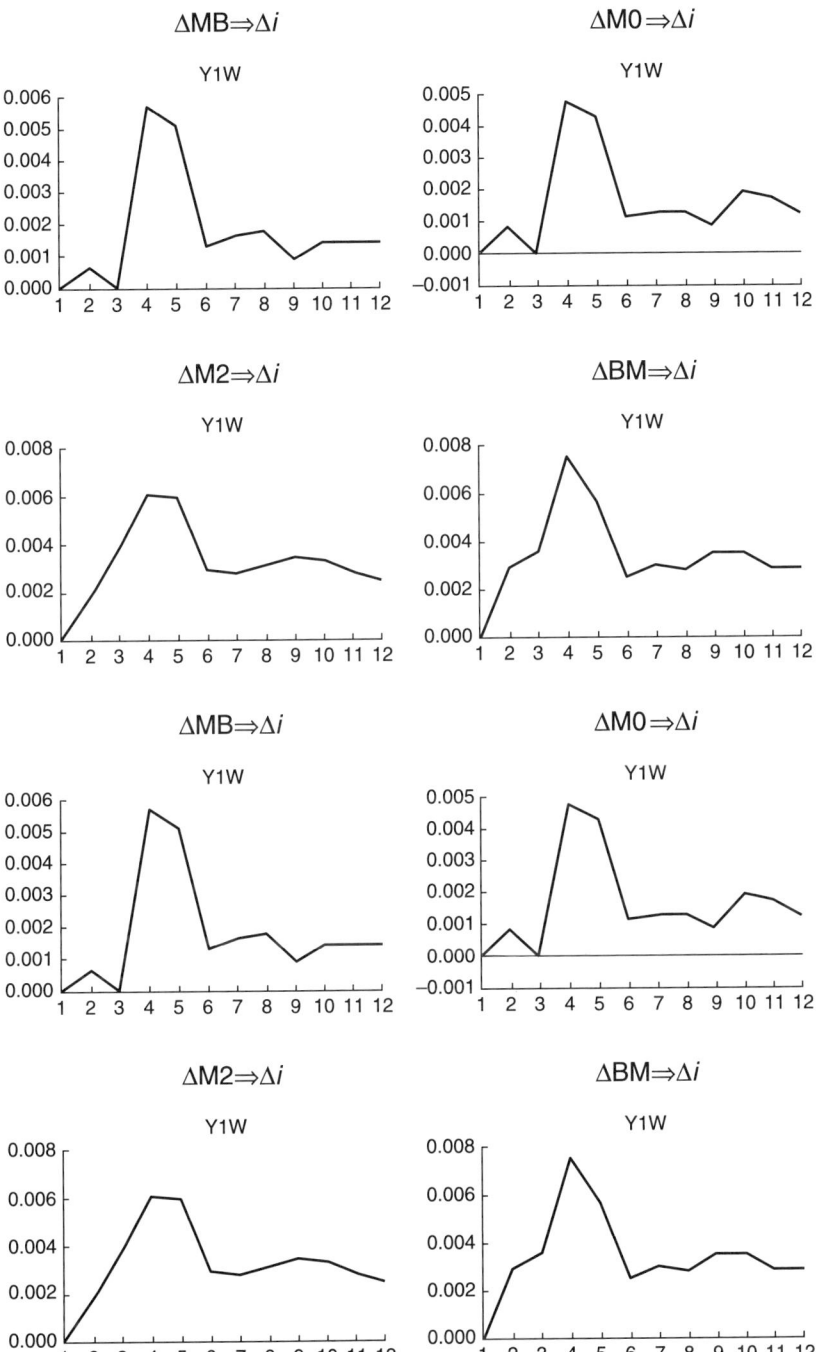

Figure IV.4
Impulse response functions of GKO spot-rates to money supply shocks.

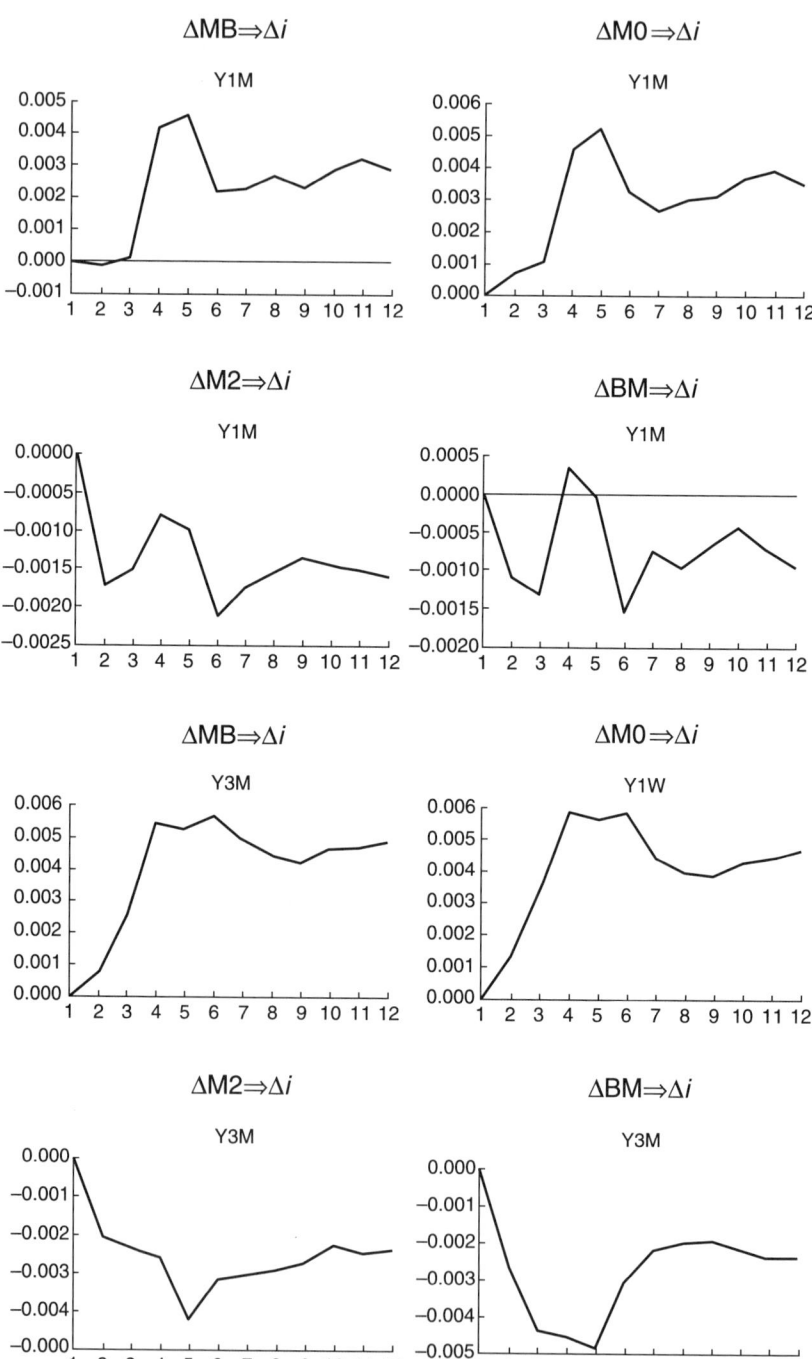

Figure IV.4 (continued)

Expectations of the Russian Bond Market

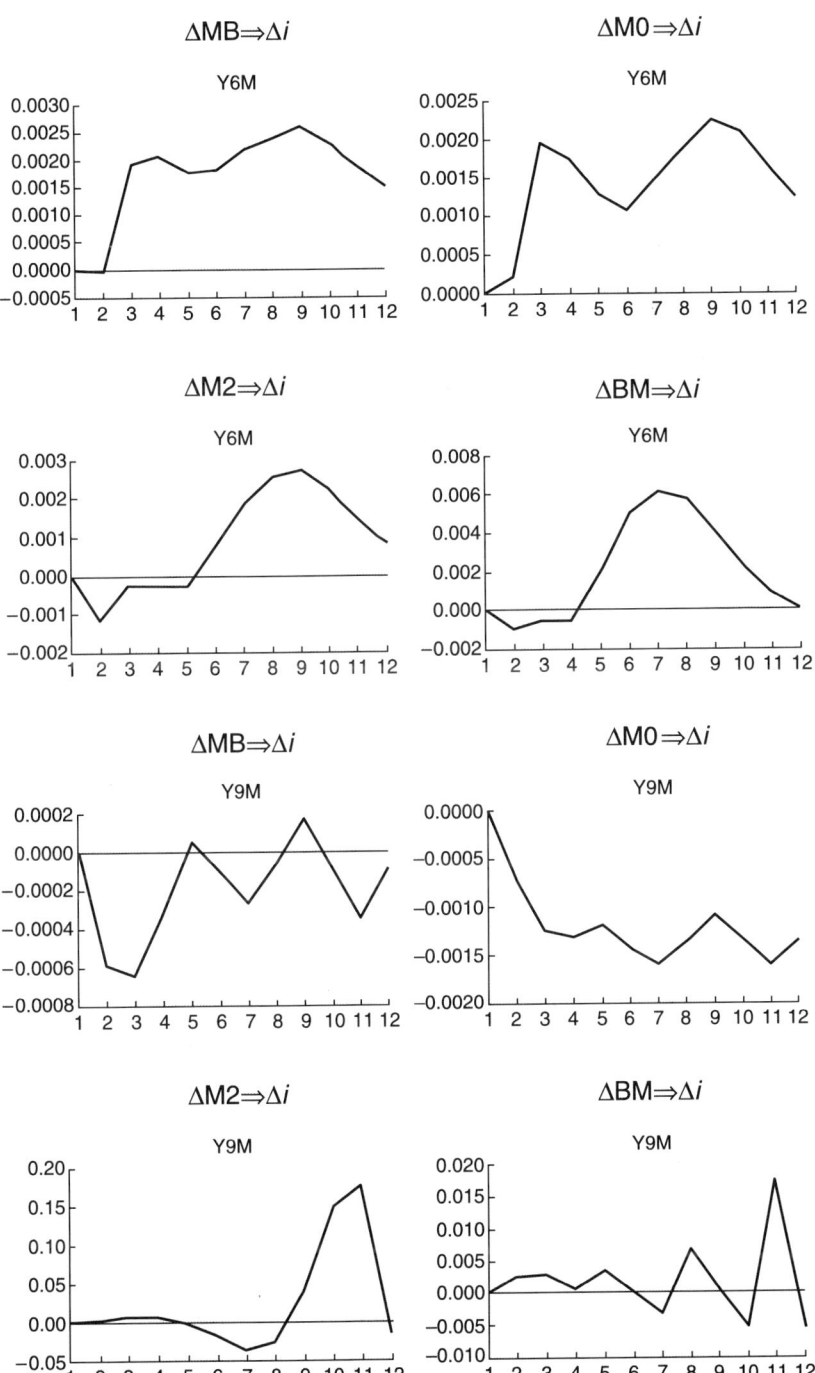

Figure IV.4 (continued)

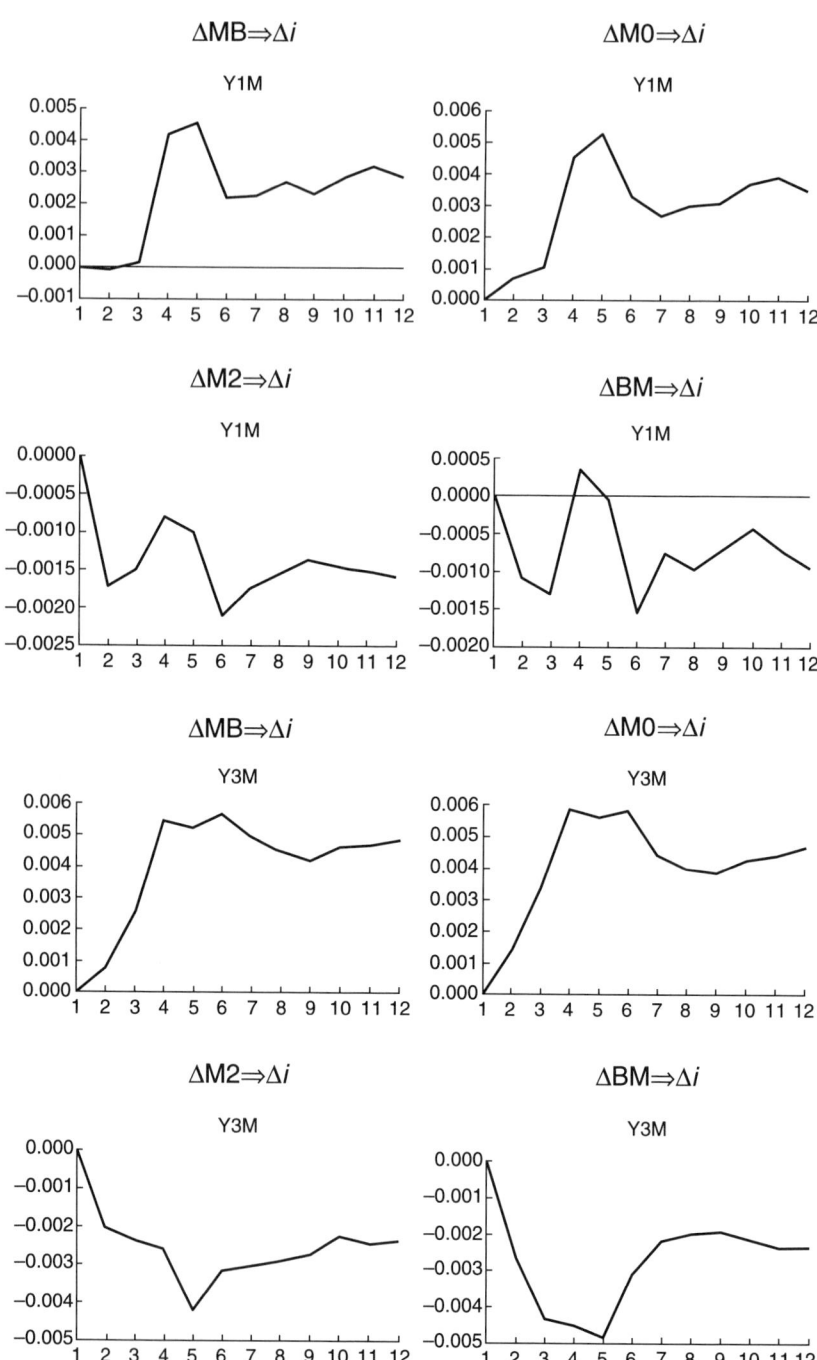

Figure IV.4 (continued)

Expectations of the Russian Bond Market

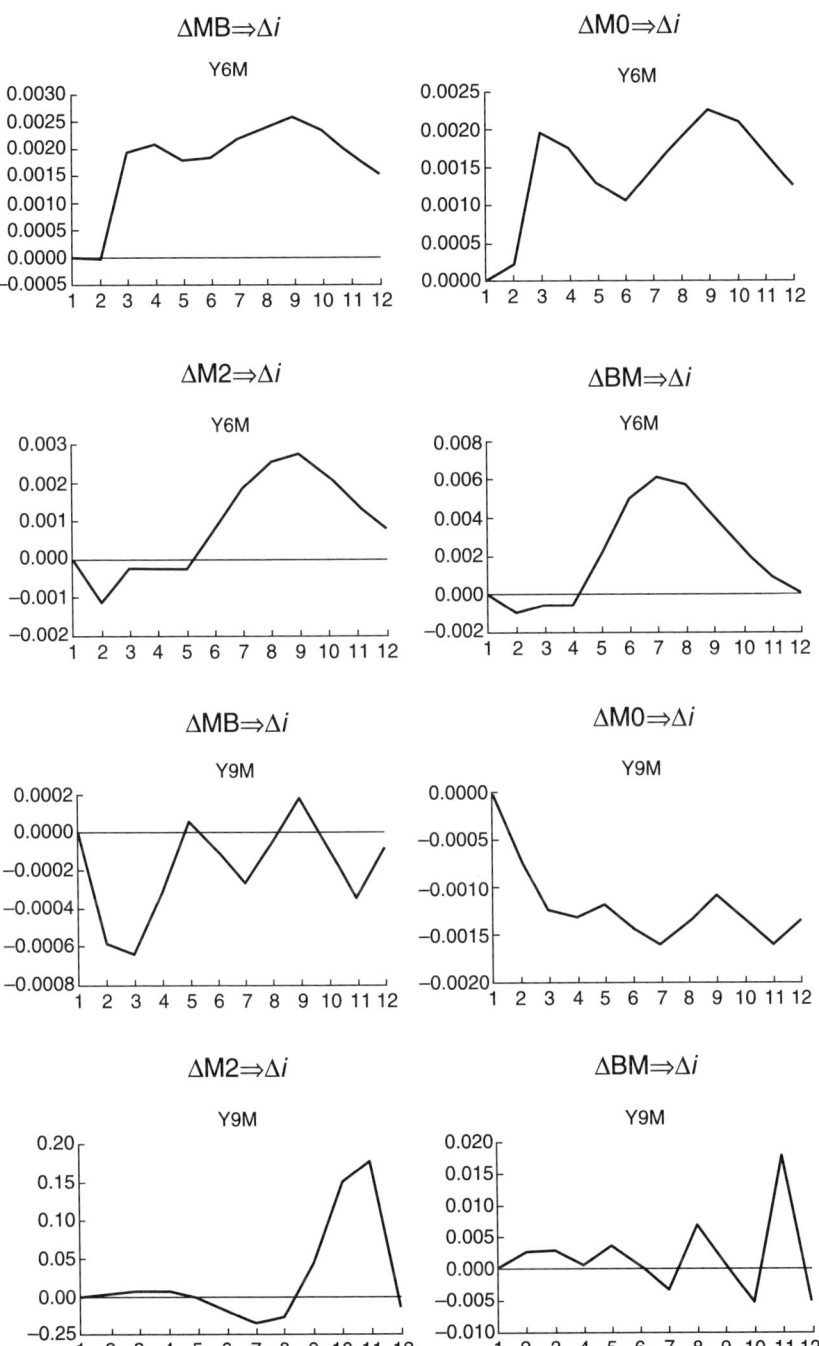

Figure IV.4 (continued)

rates. It is worth noting that the reaction of the shortest-term rates ceases (becoming indistinguishable from zero, in statistical terms) in six months, since they least take into account inflation outside the current moment in time and stabilize at a new, higher level.[25]

A similar reaction of shortest (week) rates to accelerating rates of growth of broad money aggregates, on the other hand, reflects instead the absence of the direct influence of the latter and may be explained by the simultaneous processes of increased interest rates and money expansion in the economy caused by the dynamics of the narrow money aggregates.

Accelerating M2 and broad money growth rates, indicating an increasing amount of money in the economy and an increasing amount of liquid funds on the market, result in lower GKO yields, which are reflected in negative changes in short- and medium-term GKO tranches. At the same time, yields on longer-term bills (six and nine months) barely react to changes in the broad money aggregates (nine-month GKOs do not react even to changes in the money supply). The transition to a new yield level occurs with a lag of about six to ten months, which coincides with the lag between the start of money issuance and acceleration of the CPI growth rate, thus reflecting the inflationary effect. This conclusion corresponds to an assumption that rates on longer-term issues are less volatile.

Since real interest rates reflect the liquidity effect more than nominal rates do, in order to distinguish between the effect of inflationary expectations and the effect of liquidity we reviewed simple vector autoregression models that included money aggregate growth rates and real *ex post* GKO interest rates. Since the influence across the pairs of narrow and broad money aggregates is similar, we analyzed

---

25. At the same time, the duration of the shock effects and the lagged reaction of rates may be related to fluctuations in the inflation level and mean growth rates of money aggregates. Kim and Limpaphayom and Goodfriend have demonstrated that fluctuations in the term structure of interest rates are extremely sensitive to changes in the inflation regime and monetary policy. In particular, as high inflation gives way to low inflation, the reaction of interest rates on issues of different maturities to a tougher monetary policy becomes less distinguished by regression methods (K. Kim and P. Limpaphayom, "The Effect of Economic Regimes on the Relation Between Term Structure and Real Activity in Japan," *The Journal of Economics and Business* 49 (1997): 379–92; and M. Goodfriend, "Using the Term Structure of Interest Rates for Monetary Policy," *Economic Quarterly (Federal Reserve Bank of Richmond)* 84 (1998): 13–30). Unfortunately, our small number of observations does not allow us to analyze the impulse response functions for each subperiod under different inflationary regimes.

only models that included money base and M2 growth rates. The impulse response functions for these models are shown in Figure IV.5.

The dynamics of real GKO yields in response to monetary policy shocks are not so transparent as the dynamics of nominal yields. The behavior of longer-term GKOs appears most readily explainable: the real yields of nine-month GKOs barely react to fluctuations in money aggregate growth rates, while the real yields of six-month GKOs fall over the first four months and start to rise somewhat only after the reaction of the respective nominal rates becomes evident (see Figure IV.4).

The reaction of real rates for shorter-term GKOs is more contradictory. Nevertheless, the impulse response function of real yields of three-month GKOs is close to the graph typical for other medium-term bills (such as six-month bills); however, the initial decrease and subsequent increase are not so statistically significant, chiefly because of the shorter time these fluctuations exist (this period is limited by the securities' time of circulation). The real rates of shortest- and short-term issues react very little to not at all.

To study changes in the pattern of the term structure of nominal GKO yields to maturity, we reviewed the relationship between money aggregate dynamics (money base and M2) and the time series of the term structure characteristics based on the impulse response functions of the vector autoregression models. To describe the movements in the term structure, we performed a quadratic approximation of yield curves for each month, based on the three-factor models of term structure proposed by Dai and Singleton and by Bliss.[26] Thus, we estimated regression equations of the following type:

$$i_m(t) = C(t) + A(t)m + B(t)m^2 + \varepsilon_t$$

where i_m is the yield of GKO with maturity m at time t. Since an individual yield curve for each observation is considered, regression coefficients are functions of time.

---

26. Q. Dai and K. Singleton, "Specification Analysis of Affine Term Structure Models," NBER Working Paper no. 6128 (1997); and R. Bliss, "Movements in the Term Structure of Interest Rates," *Economic Review (Federal Reserve Bank of Atlanta)* 82 (1997): 16–33. The quadratic shape of the yield curve appears in a number of theoretical models of term structure (see, for instance, O. Vasicek, "An Equilibrium Characterization of the Term Structure," *The Journal of Financial Economics* 5 (1977): 177–88).

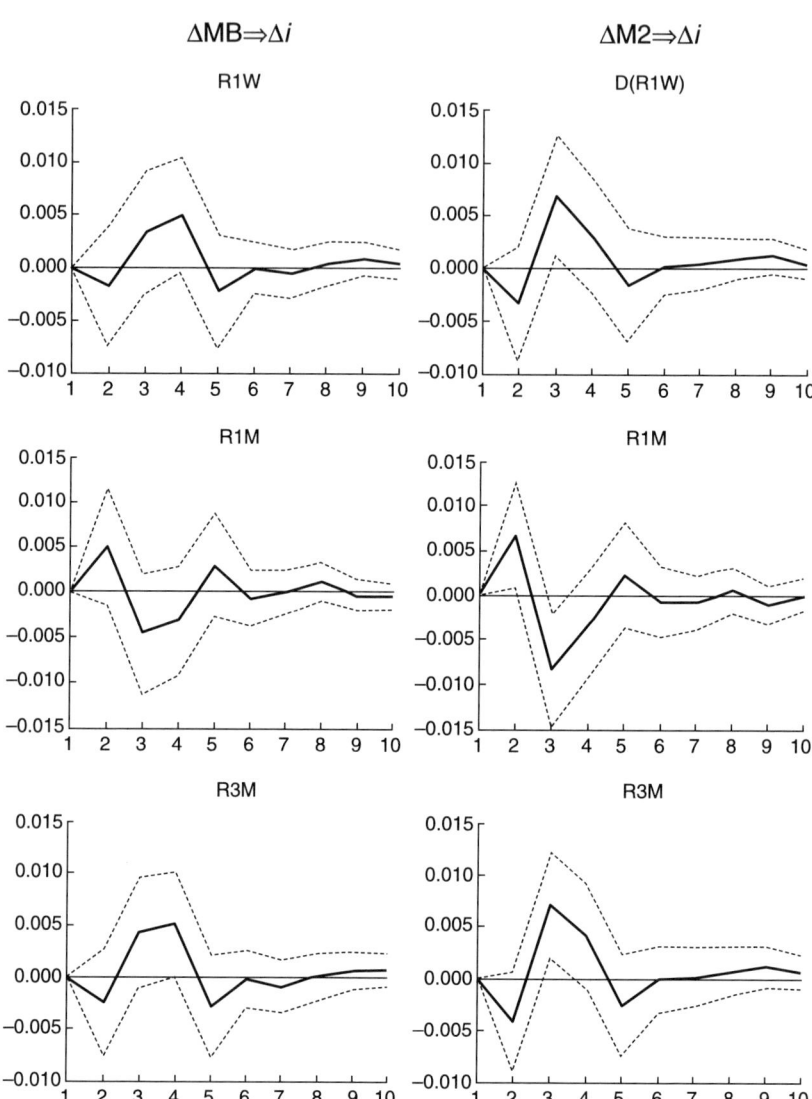

Figure IV.5
Impulse response functions of real GKO rates to money supply shocks.

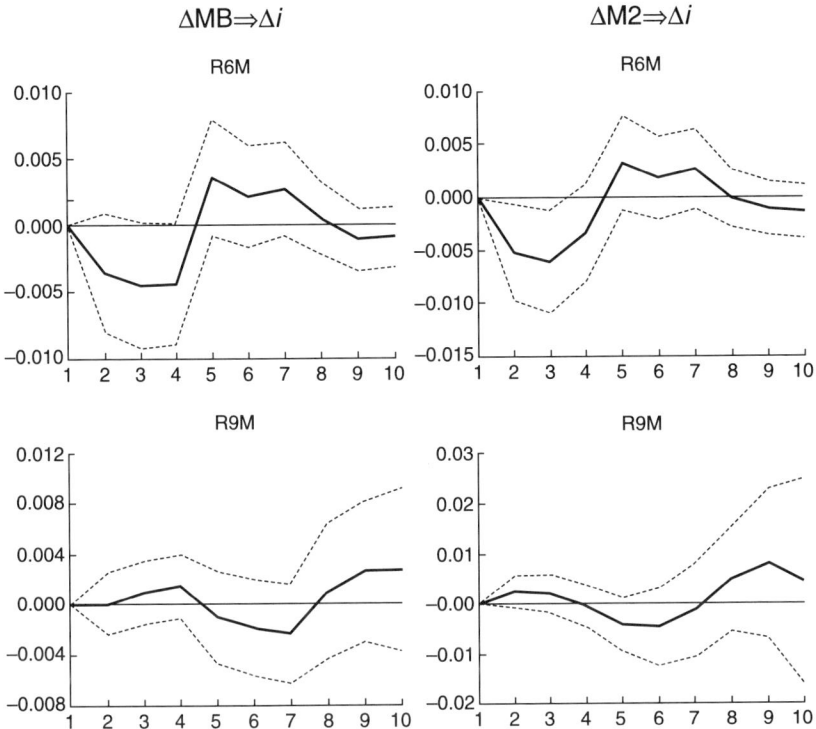

Figure IV.5 (continued)

Coefficients of the quadratic approximation $A(t)$, $B(t)$, and $C(t)$ are reviewed as three parameters describing the yield curve at any given time and are, respectively, intercept, slope, and curvature. To analyze the effects of monetary policy shocks, we estimated vector regression models, including money aggregate growth rates and the time series of these three indicators.[27] The impulse response functions are shown in Figure IV.6.[28]

As the graphs demonstrate, monetary policy shocks raise the intercept, steepen the slope, and increase the degree of curvature of the yield curve, since the negative response of curvature means an increase in the concavity of the yield curve (the mean yield curve for

---

27. The Dickey-Fuller test rejects the hypothesis that there is a unit root for all three time series at the 5% significance level.
28. The impulse response functions are similar for interest rate spreads between three-month, six-month, and one-week GKO tranches.

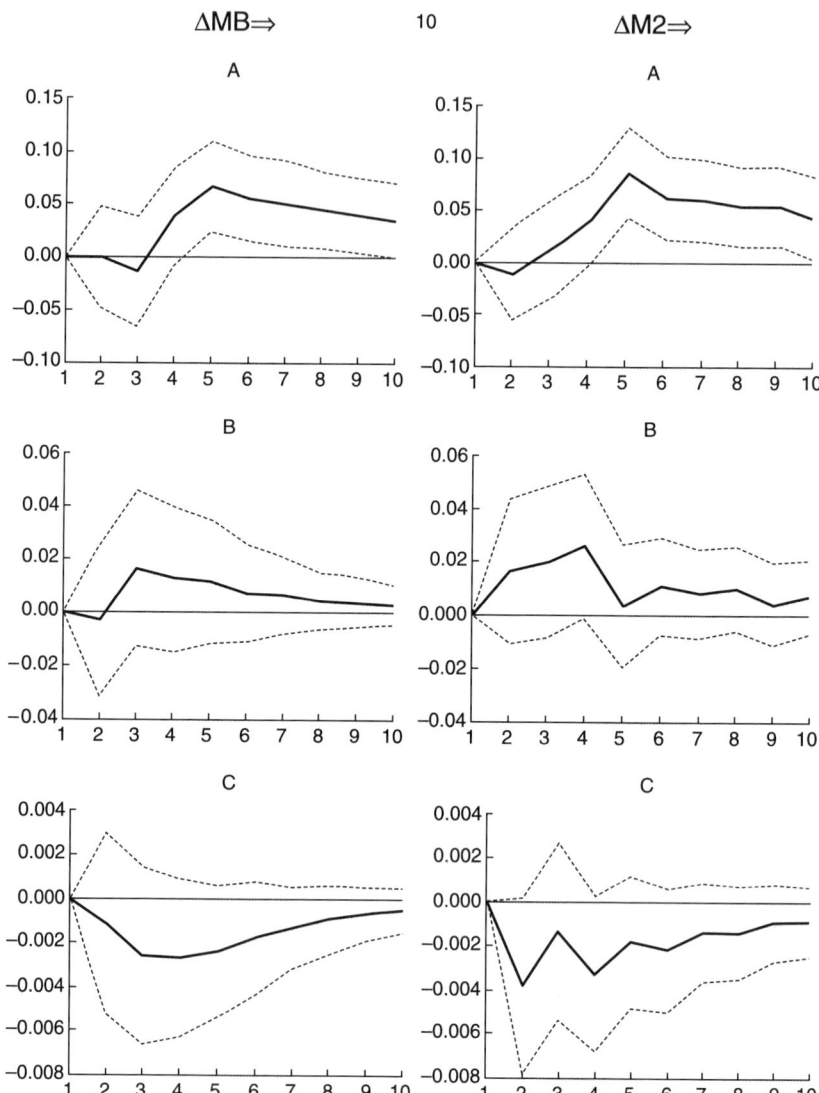

Figure IV.6
Impulse response functions of yield curve parameters to money supply shocks.

the period is concave; that is, the curvature value is negative).[29] The positive response of the intercept is similar to the response of short-term GKO rates (see Figure IV.4). As in the case of nominal yields, the parameters of the yield curve react to monetary policy shocks with a lag of about four to five months, reflecting the predominance of the inflationary effect compared with the liquidity effect. In this case the responses of the intercept, slope, and curvature become muted after six to seven months. This dampening is especially apparent in the case of M2.

The results we obtained are compatible with the term structure models based on macroeconomic approaches worked out by Blanchard, McCafferty, or Turnovsky.[30] The impulse response functions of nominal and real GKO yields across maturity terms correspond to theoretically determined changes in interest rates (nominal and real) for a case of expected increase in money supply.

IV.4. Testing Hypotheses About the Term Structure of GKO Rates

Testing of the expectations hypothesis is most interesting from the viewpoint of monetary policy goals. The hypothesis assumes (in terms of rational expectations[31]) that the term structure of bond yields contains information on future interest rates if market operators use all available information (including measures of the monetary policy being undertaken). The other hypotheses about the term

---

29. Evans and Marshall have obtained similar results based on monthly data on the US Treasury bill market (C. Evans and D. Marshall, "Monetary Policy and the Term Structure of Nominal Interest Rates: Evidence and Theory," *Carnegie-Rochester Conference Series on Public Policy* 49 (1998): 53–111). The only difference was in the lag of term structure response to monetary shocks (one to two months). In our view, the latter fact reflects the difference in market development and in the government's ability to control the situation. Lynch and Ewing, analyzing the situation in Japan, also noted that greater money growth variability resulting from monetary policy shocks leads to a steeper slope of the yield curve (G. Lynch and B. Ewing, "Money Growth Variability and the Yield Spread in Japan," *The American Business Review* 16 (1998): 61–67).

30. Blanchard, "Output, the Stock Market, and Interest Rates"; S. McCafferty, "Aggregate Demand and Interest Rates: A Macroeconomic Approach to the Term Structure," *Economic Inquiry* 24 (1986): 521–33; and Turnovsky, "The Term Structure of Interest Rates."

31. T. Sargent, "Rational Expectations and the Term Structure of Interest Rates," *The Journal of Money, Credit and Banking* 4 (1972): 74–97; F. Modigliani and R. Shiller, "Inflation, Rational Expectations and the Term Structure of Interest Rates," *Economica* 40 (1973): 12–23.

structure—liquidity preference, time-varying term premium, market segmentation, "preferred habitat"—are considered either as explanations of the negative results of the expectations hypothesis testing or as additional aspects influencing the behavior of bond yield curves.

Our study of the reaction of interest rates to monetary policy shocks revealed that the formation of yields of GKOs across maturity terms corresponded to GKO market operators having rational expectations. Therefore, we a priori assume that market operators' expectations are rational and that confirmation or rejection of the expectations hypothesis does not constitute an evaluation of the rationality of their behavior.

IV.4.1. Expectations Hypothesis

In this study two methods of testing the expectations hypothesis are reviewed: (1) the cointegration analysis of time series of the term structure of bill yields, and (2) the estimation of regression equations in the specification for the expectations hypothesis.

Cointegration Analysis. If interest rate dynamics agree with the expectations hypothesis, the term structure must have either one common stochastic (in the case of nonstationary separate time series) or a deterministic trend.[32] Thus, the existence of one cointegrating equation determining a long-term trend toward the convergence of differently termed rates may be interpreted as confirmation of the expectations hypothesis.

To evaluate the number of cointegrating equations for the GKO yield term structure, we studied a system consisting of six time series of yield to maturity of GKOs maturing in one to six months. Yields of longer-term tranches were excluded from the system since the number of observations available for them was considerably (by a factor of two or three) less than the number of observations for shorter-term tranches. Moreover, as we discussed earlier, the reaction of long-term rates to economic policy shocks was ambiguous. These circumstances make it more difficult to interpret the results of

---

32. A. Hall, H. Anderson, and C. Granger, "A Cointegration Analysis of Treasury Bill Yields," *Review of Economics and Statistics* 74 (1992): 117–26; P. Johnson, "On the Number of Common Unit Roots in the Term Structure of Interest Rates," *Applied Economics* 26 (1994): 815–20.

Table IV.7
Results of the Johansen Cointegration Test

Eigenvalue	Likelihood Ratio*	Critical Value (5%)	Critical Value (1%)	Hypothesized No. of CE(s)
0.405358	175.5429	94.15	103.18	0†
0.308326	107.9694	68.52	76.07	≤1†
0.245381	60.04607	47.21	54.46	≤2†
0.091644	23.44565	29.68	35.65	≤3
0.079716	10.95014	15.41	20.04	≤4
0.001158	0.150589	3.76	6.65	≤5

*The LR test indicates three cointegrating equations at the 5% level of significance.
† The hypothesis is rejected at the 5% (1%) level of significance.

their evaluation. The results of the Johansen test for cointegration are shown in Table IV.7.[33] The number of observations was 130, and the number of lags is six.

According to the results, the term structure of GKO yields has three common stochastic trends. A similar result was obtained by Zhang[34] for the US Treasury bills market, and three cointegrating equations were interpreted as the intercept, slope, and curvature of the term structure. However, Johnson[35] proved that Zhang's conclusions resulted from the evaluation of a mixed system that included both discount and coupon bonds. In our case only discount bills were reviewed. Therefore, the existence of three cointegrating equations does not permit rejection of the hypothesis of a long-term trend toward the convergence of yields of differently termed GKOs, while at the same time the expectations hypothesis is challenged.

---

33. Similar methods of testing for cointegration permitting to determine the number of cointegration relations were used in Zhang, "Treasury Yield Curves and Cointegration"; Engsted and Tanggaard, "Cointegration and the US Term Structure"; Engsted and Tanggaard, "A Cointegration Analysis of Danish Zero-Coupon Bond Yields"; and Cuthbertson et al., "Interest Rates in Germany and the UK." For testing the hypothesis about cointegration between individual time series of differently termed rates, see Bradley and Lumpkin, "The Treasury Yield Curve as a Cointegrated System." Cuthbertson and Nitzsche applied the Phillips–Hansen test (P. Phillips and L. Hansen, "Statistical Inference in Instrumental Variables Regression with I (0) Processes," *Review of Economic Studies* 57 (1990): 99–125), while U. Hassler and D. Nautz ("Der Zusammenhang zwischen kurz- und langfristigen Zinssätzen in Deutschland," *Jahrbücher für Nationalökonomie und Statistik* 217/2 (1998): 214–26) used the Engle–Granger test.
34. Zhang, "Treasury Yield Curves and Cointegration."
35. P. Johnson, "On the Number of Common Unit Roots in the Term Structure of Interest Rates," *Applied Economics* 26 (1994): 815–20.

Estimation of Linear Regression Equations. The most common (and historically the first) method of testing the expectations hypothesis is the estimation of linear regression equations specified in compliance with the rational expectations hypothesis of the term structure of interest rates. In this study we chose the following specification of regression equations:

$$i_{t+\tau}(m) - i_t(m) = \alpha + \beta[f_t(t+n,m) - i_t(m)] + \gamma\varepsilon_{t-1} + \varepsilon_t \quad (1)$$

where $i_t(m)$ is the current monthly rate of GKOs maturing in m, $i_{t+\tau}(m)$ is the monthly rate of GKOs maturing in m, observed after τ weeks, and $f_t(t+n,m)$ is the current forward rate of GKOs for the period $[t+n,m]$, $n < m$. If the rational expectations hypothesis is true, $\alpha = 0$, $\beta = 1$, and $E(\varepsilon_t) = 0$. The choice of equations specification is based on the following presumptions.

1. Forward rates as explanatory variables are preferred to interest-rate spreads for monetary policy analysis.[36] Forward rates express future interest rates *ex ante* anticipated of the observed yield curve. Equations with interest-rate spread in the right part serve to test the expectation hypothesis *ex post*.[37]

2. Forward rates may be interpreted as expectations of future interest rates. This formulation makes it possible to use this specification for testing the expectations hypothesis by considering rational expectations instead of pure expectations.[38]

3. The additional term (the MA 1 term) was included in the equation to correct for autocorrelation in residuals originating as a result of the linear approximation of the rational expectations model and errors of expectations measurement on the basis of forward rates.[39]

The number of equations for $m = 1\ldots6$ months is fifteen. To allow for a greater number of observations, we reviewed the weekly time series. In order to ensure compatibility with the periodization of maturity terms ($n = 1\ldots5$) values of $\tau = 4, 9, 13, 18, 22$ weeks.

---

36. See Shiller et al., "Forward Rates and Future Policy"; Svensson, "Estimating and Interpreting Forward Interest Rates: Sweden 1992–1994"; and M. Dahlquist and L. Svensson, "Estimating the Term Structure of Interest Rates for Monetary Policy Analysis," *Scandinavian Journal of Economics* 98 (1996): 163–83.
37. See Mankiw, "The Term Structure of Interest Rates Revisited"; Mankiw and Miron, "The Changing Behavior of the Term Structure of Interest Rates"; and Anderson et al., *Estimating and Interpreting the Yield Curve*.
38. See R. Shiller, "Alternative Tests of Rational Expectations Models: The Case of the Term Structure," *The Journal of Econometrics* 16 (1981): 71–87.
39. See Mankiw, "The Term Structure of Interest Rates Revisited," and Anderson et al., *Estimating and Interpreting the Yield Curve*.

The computation of forward rates is based on the comparison of GKO yields across maturity terms, so that the same bill transits from one category of securities to another as its maturity approaches. In this case, residuals of regression equations will be autocorrelated and estimates obtained by the OLS method will be ineffective. To ensure the effectiveness of estimates, we applied the seemingly unrelated equations technique.[40] Estimates of seemingly unrelated equations (equation 1) are shown in Table IV.8. The period of observation is from 26 July 1993 through 26 July 1998.

On the whole, the results we obtained contradict the expectations hypothesis. With the exception of one or two cases (for yields to maturity of three- and five-month bills and forward rates of one to four and six months respectively), the null hypothesis corresponding to the expectations hypothesis is rejected with a very low probability of error.

At the same time, the constant term in almost all of the equations does not differ statistically significantly from zero, thus corresponding to a zero term premium. Estimates of the coefficient β, although different from 1 (at the 5% significance level), have the expected signs (positive). The majority of the equations ensure a high percentage of explained variance of changes in GKO yields ($R^2 > 0.5$).[41]

Thus, despite certain inconsistencies with the expectations hypothesis, the evaluations indicate that forward rates contain some information about future spot rates. However, the accuracy of such forecasts is low, and forward rates, although not biased ($\alpha \approx 0$), are ineffective estimates of future spot rates[42] (forward rates vary more than spot rates; see Tables IV.1 and IV.4).

---

40. The presence of the first-order moving average is a sufficient condition for eliminating the autocorrelation in residuals of individual equations (see A. Zellner and F. Palm, "Time Series Analysis and Simultaneous Equation Econometric Models," *The Journal of Econometrics* 2 (1974): 17–54; and G. Tiao and G. Box, "Modeling Multiple Time Series with Applications," *The Journal of the American Statistical Association* 76 (1981): 802–16). An alternative method to estimate systems of this type is to apply convergent-parameter regression models (B. Rosenfeld, "Random Coefficients Models: The Analysis of a Cross Section of Time Series by Stochastically Convergent Parameter Regression," *Annals of Economic and Social Measurement* 2 (1973): 399–428).
41. High values of R^2 may be also explained by the influence of strong serial autocorrelation in residuals and a correlation between residuals across equations.
42. Similar results that were obtained from testing the expectations hypothesis (based on similar specifications of equations) on the GKO market were presented in *Development of the Russian Financial Market and New Investment-Attracting Instruments* (Moscow: IET, 1989). However, that study analyzed equations individually (not as a system of simultaneous equations) over a shorter observation period (January 1994 through January 1998). The authors' estimates of relevant coefficients were within the margin of our evaluations, and the null expectations hypothesis was rejected at the 5% level of significance.

Table IV.8
Estimates of Seemingly Unrelated Equations*

Dependent Variable	Explanatory Variable	α	β	$H_0: \alpha = 0, \beta = 1$	R^2
$i_{t+4}(1) - i_t(1)$	$f_t(1,2) - i_t(1)$	-0.076 (-2.63)	0.470 (8.78)	132.15†	0.335
$i_{t+9}(1) - i_{t+4}(1)$	$f_t(2,3) - i_{t+4}(1)$	-0.068 (-1.64)	0.398 (11.37)	312.28†	0.458
$i_{t+13}(1) - i_{t+9}(1)$	$f_t(3,4) - i_{t+9}(1)$	-0.076 (-2.09)	0.230 (5.71)	408.43†	0.235
$i_{t+18}(1) - i_{t+13}(1)$	$f_t(4,5) - i_{t+13}(1)$	-0.048 (-1.42)	0.275 (6.57)	320.91†	0.345
$i_{t+22}(1) - i_{t+18}(1)$	$f_t(5,6) - i_{t+18}(1)$	-0.029 (-0.97)	0.081 (2.88)	1107.89†	0.220
$i_{t+9}(2) - i_t(2)$	$f_t(1,3) - i_t(2)$	-0.038 (-0.86)	0.764 (9.45)	9.74†	0.659
$i_{t+13}(2) - i_{t+4}(2)$	$f_t(2,4) - i_{t+4}(2)$	-0.090 (-1.86)	0.664 (18.34)	92.04†	0.676
$i_{t+18}(2) - i_{t+9}(2)$	$f_t(3,5) - i_{t+9}(2)$	-0.061 (-1.40)	0.472 (12.21)	193.13†	0.650
$i_{t+22}(2) - i_{t+13}(2)$	$f_t(4,6) - i_{t+13}(2)$	-0.016 (-0.21)	0.294 (7.11)	292.15†	0.698
$i_{t+13}(3) - i_t(3)$	$f_t(1,4) - i_t(3)$	-0.048 (-0.90)	0.910 (11.55)	2.21	0.766
$i_{t+18}(3) - i_{t+4}(3)$	$f_t(2,5) - i_{t+4}(3)$	-0.024 (-0.42)	0.734 (16.35)	35.89†	0.774
$i_{t+22}(3) - i_{t+9}(3)$	$f_t(3,6) - i_{t+9}(3)$	0.014 (0.14)	0.613 (11.29)	50.79†	0.804
$i_{t+18}(4) - i_t(4)$	$f_t(1,5) - i_t(4)$	-0.044 (-0.70)	0.458 (2.76)	11.43†	0.856
$i_{t+22}(4) - i_{t+4}(4)$	$f_t(2,6) - i_{t+4}(4)$	-0.020 (-0.22)	0.813 (15.14)	12.12†	0.887
$i_{t+22}(5) - i_t(5)$	$f_t(1,6) - i_t(5)$	0.181 (1.24)	0.809 (7.61)	4.96	0.897

*t statistics in parentheses.
† The hypothesis is rejected at the 5% level of significance.

IV.4.2. The Liquidity Preference Hypothesis and Time-Varying Term Premium Hypothesis

A possible explanation for the rejection of the expectations hypothesis for the GKO market is the varying term premium (or liquidity premium). As both Campbell and Longstaff[43] have demonstrated, time-varying term premiums are a common cause for rejecting the expectations hypothesis in empirical studies. Engsted[44] reviewed a case in which the expectations hypothesis was rejected in favor of the liquidity preference hypothesis; that is, the term premium depended on the bond maturity term.[45]

To test the liquidity preference hypothesis and time-varying term premium hypothesis, we analyzed the dynamics of time series of different premiums (assuming unbiased rational expectations of market participants):

1. Liquidity premiums (interest spread):

$$s_t(n,m) = i_t(m) - i_t(n)$$

2. Term premiums:

$$\Phi_t(n,m) = f_t(t+n,m) - i_{t+n}(m)$$

3. Holding period term premiums:

$$H_t(n,m) = h_t(t-n,m) - i_{t-n}(n)$$

---

43. J. Campbell, "A Defense of Traditional Hypothesis About the Term Structure of Interest Rates," *The Journal of Finance* 41 (1986): 183–93; and F. Longstaff, "Time-Varying Term Premia and Traditional Hypothesis About the Term Structure," *The Journal of Finance* 45 (1990): 1307–14.
44. T. Engsted, "The Term Structure of Interest Rates in Denmark 1982–1989: Testing the Rational Expectations / Constant Liquidity Premium Theory," *Bulletin of Economic Research* 45 (1993): 19–37.
45. We do not review other term structure hypotheses in this study. Although compliance with the conditions of the market segmentation hypothesis may lead to rejection of the expectations hypothesis (see M. Taylor, "Modelling the Yield Curve," *Economic Journal* 102 (1992): 524–32; N. Baldini and U. Cherubini, "Yield Curve Movements and Market Segmentation: A LISREL Analysis of the Italian Case," in *Economic Notes*, edited by Banca Monte dei Paschi di Siena, no. 27 (1998): 35–54), this explanation is of little use for a monetary policy analysis of the term structure. On the other hand, Mishkin has demonstrated that the conditions of the "preferred habitat" hypothesis may be complied with within the framework of the expectations hypothesis in the form of rational expectations (F. Mishkin, "Is the preferred habitat model of the term structure inconsistent with financial market efficiency?" *Journal of Political Economy* 88 (1980): 406–11).

Table IV.9
Characteristics of Representative Time Series of GKO Premiums

	Mean Value	SD	ADF	PP	p_1	p_2	p_3	Q(16)
$s(1,2)$	0.112	0.150	−6.23	−10.04	0.580	0.111	0.202	379.73
$s(1,3)$	0.149	0.195	−4.35	−8.62	0.616	0.063	0.171	351.44
$s(2,4)$	0.046	0.102	−3.30	−4.49	0.799	0.171	−0.137	464.14
$s(3,6)$	0.020	0.105	−4.28	−7.51	0.520	−0.162	0.031	68.15
$s(1,6)$	0.147	0.188	−2.57*	−4.76	0.695	0.173	0.103	459.84
$\Phi(1,2)$	0.170	0.276	−4.93	−8.23	0.621	0.107	0.114	277.77
$\Phi(1,3)$	0.077	0.245	−4.71	−6.99	0.643	−0.078	−0.021	165.63
$\Phi(2,3)$	0.207	0.402	−3.28	−5.74	0.731	−0.010	0.123	377.67
$\Phi(3,4)$	0.182	0.446	−3.38	−3.88	0.710	0.120	0.151	351.65
$\Phi(3,6)$	0.062	0.345	−1.86*	−2.69*	0.813	−0.053	0.136	475.86
$H(1,1)$	0.722	0.813	−4.11	−5.30	0.858	0.143	−0.040	937.00
$H(1,3)$	1.403	3.641	−3.43	−3.87	0.819	−0.241	−0.142	233.58
$H(2,1)$	0.631	0.756	−3.80	−4.12	0.888	0.177	0.137	1042.30
$H(3,1)$	0.538	0.802	−3.36	−3.61	0.859	0.030	−0.049	556.63
$H(3,3)$	0.782	1.420	−2.25*	−3.43	0.793	0.142	−0.028	399.41

Note: ADF, the Augmented Dickey-Fuller test statistics; PP, the Phillips-Perron test statistics; p_1, p_2, p_3 = first three coefficients of the serial correlation; Q(16) = the Box-Lyung test statistic (the number of lags is 16).
*The unit root hypothesis is not rejected at the 5% significance level.

where $i_t(m)$ is the current yield to maturity of GKOs maturing in m, $f_t(t+n,m)$ is the forward rate of GKOs n to m months in the future, and $h_t(t-n,m)$ is the holding period for GKOs maturing in m months over n months.

The Liquidity Preference Hypothesis. According to the liquidity preference hypothesis, security yields depend only on the term of maturity. The longer the maturity term, the higher are bond yields. Thus, interest-rate spreads and term (holding period) premiums of bonds are constant for each maturity pair and have strictly positive values.

Table IV.9 gives the statistic characteristics of time series of individual GKO premiums that in our view are most representative. As the table demonstrates, the time series of all premiums are stationary (except the term premium for the period from three to six months), have positive mean value, and have high serial correlation (values of the first-order autocorrelation coefficients are within the range of 0.5 to 0.9).

Nevertheless, these results do not allow us to state that the liquidity preference of market operators explains the rejection of the expectations hypothesis for the GKO time structure, for several reasons. First, premium values have large variation (the absolute value of the standard deviation considerably exceeds the mean for all series). Second, the premium magnitudes do not always increase with bill maturity. This property is quite evident in comparison with the holding period term premium. At the same time, the results of comparing interest rate spreads and term premiums are less obvious. Third, small values of autocorrelation coefficients of higher orders (above the first) in many cases have different signs, which is evidence of considerable fluctuation of premiums.

Time-Varying Term Premium Hypothesis. The time-varying term premium hypothesis is an alternative to the liquidity preference hypothesis. According to the liquidity preference hypothesis, the sign and the amount of premium may vary depending on changes in observed or implicit (nonmeasurable in quantitative terms) factors. The influence of implicit factors is often the main reason why the expectations hypothesis is rejected, since observed factors (such as macroeconomic variables) can be directly considered in the specification of regression equations for testing the expectations hypothesis.[46]

Insofar as the character of premium dynamics is a priori unknown, we reviewed two functional forms presupposing different characteristics of this process.

1. The time series of premiums is represented as an autoregressive–moving average process with autoregressive conditional heteroscedasticity of residuals[47]:

$$\phi_t(n,m) = \text{ARMA}(p,q) + \varepsilon_t$$
$$\sigma_t^2 = x\text{GARCH}(1,1)$$
(2)

where $\phi_t(n,m)$ is any premium (liquidity, term, holding period), p and q are determined based on an analysis of the autocorrelation and partial autocorrelation functions of the time series, and $x\text{GARCH}(1,1)$ denotes different specifications of the autoregressive conditional variance of residuals.

---

46. K. Cuthbertson, *Quantitative Financial Economics* (New York: John Wiley & Sons, 1996).
47. Similarly in R. Engle and V. Ng, "Time-Varying Volatility and the Dynamic Behavior of the Term Structure," *The Journal of Money, Credit, and Banking* 25 (1993): 336–49.

2. It is assumed that the degree of the time series mean reversion (the first-order autoregressive term in model AR 1) corresponds to a stochastic process, being a "random walk"[48]:

$$\phi_t(n,m) = c + a_t\phi_{t-1}(n,m) + \varepsilon_t$$
$$a_t = a_{t-1} + \eta_t \tag{3}$$

Such a specification of the risk premium puts less constraint on the character of the stochastic process than the ARMA-GARCH model.

To test the aforementioned hypotheses concerning the type of functional form describing the dynamics of premium stochastic processes, we estimated the parameters of equations 2 and 3 for three time series—the interest spread $s(1,2)$, the term premium $\Phi(2,3)$, and the holding period term premium $H(1,1)$. Table IV.10 gives the results of estimation of best (in terms of information criteria) specifications of model 2 for each of the selected time series. Estimations of model 3, made using the Kalman filter technique, are shown in Table IV.11.

The results obtained confirm the aforementioned hypothesis about strong fluctuations of premiums and reflect features of each premium pattern. As Tables IV.10 and IV.11 demonstrate, the mean values of the interest rate spread and the term premium are close to zero, while deviations from the mean are proportional to the conditional variance[49] (both series are better described by equations of the ARCH-M type). The variances of these series are stationary (the sum of the coefficients of the conditional variance equation is close to 1). The asymmetric response of the term premium (the specification of conditional variance as TARCH) to negative and positive values of residuals may be caused by nonidentical changes in the expectations of market participants concerning future rates in response to "good" and "bad" news. Estimates of random coefficients in the autoregressive term obtained by means of the Kalman filter are less than zero. So, both series have the property of reversion to the mean.[50] How-

---

48. Similarly in R. Bhar, "Modelling Australian Bank Bill Rates: A Kalman Filter Approach," *Accounting and Finance* 36 (1996): 1–14.
49. A similar property of the time-varying term premium on the US Treasury bill market was noted in R. Engle, D. Lilien, and R. Robins, "Estimating Time-Varying Risk Premia in the Term Structure: The ARCH-M model," *Econometrica* 55 (1987): 391–407.
50. The property of mean reversion of term premium series of US Treasury bills was noted in T. Park and L. Switzer, "Mean Reversion of Interest-Rate Term Premiums and Profits from Trading Strategies with Treasury Futures Spreads," *The Journal of Futures Markets* 16 (1996): 331–52.

Table IV.10
Results of Estimating Model 2 for Three Time Series*

	$s(1,2)$ GARCH-M(1,1) $s_t(1,2) = c + a s_{t-1}(1,2) + \lambda \sigma_t + \varepsilon_t$ $\sigma(\varepsilon)_t^2 = \delta + \alpha \varepsilon_{t-1}^2 + \beta \sigma_{t-1}^2 + \eta_t$	$\Phi(2,3)$ TARCH-M(1,1) $\Phi_t(2,3) = c + a\Phi_{t-1}(2,3) + \lambda \sigma_t + \varepsilon_t$ $\sigma(\varepsilon)_t^2 = \delta + \alpha \varepsilon_{t-1}^2 + \beta \sigma_{t-1}^2 + \gamma \varepsilon_{t-1}^2 d_{t-1} + \eta_t$ $d_t = \begin{cases} 1, \varepsilon_t < 0 \\ 0, \varepsilon_t \geq 0 \end{cases}$	$H(1,1)$ GARCH(1,1) $H_t(1,1) = c + aH_{t-1}(1,1) + bH_{t-2}(1,1) + \varepsilon_t$ $\sigma(\varepsilon)_t^2 = \delta + \alpha \varepsilon_{t-1}^2 + \beta \sigma_{t-1}^2 + \eta$
λ	0.657 (6.05)	0.281 (2.71)	—
δ	$2.64 \cdot 10^{-5}$ (0.78)	0.000 (1.83)	0.000 (0.59)
α	0.356 (7.04)	0.192 (2.37)	0.789 (6.25)
β	0.736 (28.86)	0.716 (22.99)	0.533 (10.37)
γ	—	0.368 (2.38)	—
R^2	0.441	0.564	0.742

*The form of conditional variance is shown immediately below the time series. t statistics are shown in parentheses.

Table IV.11
Estimations of Model 3 (with Kalman Filter) for Three Time Series*

	$s(1,2)$	$\Phi(2,3)$	$H(1,1)$
c	0.423	0.352	0.131
	(0.15)	(0.00)	(5.62)
a_t	−0.312	−0.597	0.061
	(−34.22)	(−2.14)	(0.114)
$\sigma^2(\varepsilon)$	0.022	$1.60 \cdot 10^{-27}$	0.034
	(5.06)	$(9.58 \cdot 10^{-50})$	(5.09)
$\sigma^2(\eta)$	$3.13 \cdot 10^{-20}$	0.078	0.281
	$(3.57 \cdot 10^{-35})$	(36.26)	(9.37)

*t statistics are shown in parentheses. For coefficient a_t the statistics of its mean value are shown.

ever, the stochastic character of the premiums results from different causes: whereas in the case of the term premium it is caused by random fluctuations in the autoregressive term, in the case of the interest rate spread the respective coefficient is stable, and the fluctuations are caused by random additive errors (according to the significance of variances of the observation equation and the state equation).[51]

The characteristics of the holding period term premium differ considerably from the characteristics of the interest rate spread and the term premium. First, the value of the term premium is stable and positive (the mean is above zero and is statistically significant). Second, the mean of this premium is relatively constant (estimates of the coefficients of the autoregressive term in model 3, or of the coefficients of conditional variance in the observation equation, are not significantly different from zero). Third, the variance of the $H(1,1)$ time series is not stationary (the sum of the coefficients in the equation of conditional variance is more than 1). Moreover, the variance of this time series is the sum of the premium random deviation variances and fluctuations in the a_t coefficient.

These differences can be explained in relation to the formation of premiums. The interest rate spread reflects current evaluations of

---

51. A similar result for series of interest spreads between one-, two-, and six-month GKOs over a shorter observation period was obtained in evaluating a somewhat different specification of the observation equation and the state equation by the Kalman filter: the observation equation presupposed not the autoregressive process, but a constant with random errors. See Ye. Paltseva, *Modeling Inflationary Expectations: The Russian Case* (Moscow: NES, 1998).

bill risks, which depend on maturity and market liquidity, while the term premium expresses conditional expectations of future rates. Therefore, the interest rate spread dynamics reflect fluctuations in ratios between the riskiness of bills of different maturity and changes in market liquidity (via short-term rates). At the same time, the term premium may take into account the systematic bias of market participants' forecasts, the value of which changes depending on the mean yield, changes in the economic environment, and so on. The holding period term premium expresses the actual extra revenues derived at the moment of sale compared with the short-term rate prevalent on the market at the time of investment.

Because the character of the dynamics varies considerably across premiums, the choice of a concrete hypothesis to explain their behavior is difficult, and is sensitive to the premium type. Both hypotheses (liquidity preference and time-varying term premium) can explain the negative results that are obtained when the expectations hypothesis is tested for the GKO market. If the dynamics of the holding period term premium are of interest, the liquidity preference hypothesis may be preferred. The character of the term premium stochastic process is more consistent with the conditions of the time-varying term premium, while the results of the study of interest rate spreads were ambiguous.

IV.5. Conclusions

Analysis of the statistical characteristics of GKO rates in different subperiods reveals that the character of GKO yield curve over the whole period under observation changed considerably, depending on the degree of institutional development of the GKO/OFZ market. Over the first subperiod (1993 through 1996), the shape of the yield curve is unstable. The ratio between yields of short-, medium-, and long-term bills was determined by fluctuations in outstanding volumes of differently termed bills, the appearance of new GKO types, and political risks. Primary yield curves over the second subperiod (August 1996 through November 1997) are smooth, with a positive slope. For the third period (1998), which coincided with the evolving financial crisis in Russia, the average mean yield curve is high for short- and long-term GKOs, but flat for medium-term issues. It was characteristic of the term structure of GKO yields to maturity that short-term bill rates were more volatile than rates of long-term bills. Tests for a unit root reveal different integration orders (zero or first) of time series of differently termed rates.

Expectations of market operators were unstable over the whole period under observation; at the same time, the possibility of arbitrage between GKOs maturing at different times was not used enough. This conclusion is confirmed by the fact that term structures of GKO forward and holding period rates have statistical characteristics differing from the term structure of GKO yields to maturity. In particular, the hypothesis about the equality of the distribution of GKO spot and forward rates is rejected at the 5% significance level. The values of forward rates and holding period rates vary more than values of GKO yields to maturity.

The study of the GKO term structure provides important information about the effects of monetary policy shocks on the yields of government securities. The impulse response function to monetary policy shocks plotted based on the estimation of vector autoregression models reveals that the reaction of GKO yields depends both on bill terms and on the choice of a money aggregate. Estimates for the GKO yield term structure do not contradict the results of empirical studies of developed financial markets, or conclusions arrived at on the basis of theoretical macroeconomic approaches to the analysis of the term structure of interest rates. The reaction of both the yields of short- and long-term bills and the parameters of the GKO yield curve (intercept, slope, and curvature) to shocks in the narrow and broad money aggregate supply are consistent with theoretical conclusions and indicate the rationality of market participants' expectations. Thus, the influence of monetary policy on the bill yield curve in a transitional economy is similar to that observed on developed financial markets and is distinguishable even over a short period.

Our study of the term structure of GKO rates for monetary policy goals revealed that current forward GKO rates contain some information on future spot rates, although on the whole, the expectations hypothesis (in the form of the rational expectations hypothesis) for the Russian government discount bond market is rejected. To explain this result we reviewed the liquidity preference hypothesis and the time-varying term premium hypothesis. Estimation of dynamics equations across different premium types (liquidity, term, holding period) does not permit rejection of either of the latter hypotheses. In our view, the factors determining premium dynamics might be the insufficient use of arbitrage between differently termed bills by market participants,[52] systematic bias in forecasting future rates in a situation of falling GKO yields, and fluctuations in the default risk premium across differently termed GKOs.[53]

---

52. Such a conclusion may be evidence either of market segmentation or of the validity of the "preferred habitat" hypothesis.

53. On the effect of the bond default risk premium on the analysis of the term premium see J. Clinebell, D. Kahn, and J. Stevens, "Time Series Estimation of the Bond Default Risk Premium," *Quarterly Review of Economics and Finance* 36 (1996): 475–84.

Appendix V Leading Indicators of the Russian Currency Crisis in August 1998

Sergei Drobyshevsky

An important aspect of studying currency crises is analyzing the dynamics of leading macroeconomic and financial indicators over the precrisis periods. Before embarking on such an analysis, however, we will first scrutinize developments on the Russian exchange market for signs of an impending crisis. To do so, we use the index of "exchange market pressure," authored by Eichengreen, Rose, and Wyplosz.[1] The authors of this index reviewed two critical thresholds that, if exceeded, would signify the threat of a currency crisis: the mean value of the index over the whole period and a value equal to three standard deviations (3 SD). Across different countries and currency crises, either threshold value is significant.

As Figure V.1 shows, the mean value of the index pointed to a currency crisis threat in November 1997 through January 1998 and once again starting in May 1998, while in November 1997 and in January, June, and August 1998, the level of 3 SD was also exceeded. The index of exchange market pressure peaked by 14 August 1998, just before the ruble's devaluation.

In order to analyze economic developments in Russia during the precrisis period, we selected a set of macroeconomic and financial indicators of a currency crisis from among those identified by IMF experts Kaminski, Lizondo, and Reinhart,[2] who studied twenty-eight empirical works on currency crises. Our work follows the methods used by Kaminski and colleagues for each indicator, with a few exceptions that will be noted. Altogether fifteen indicators divided into four groups were reviewed:

---

1. B. Eichengreen, A. Rose, and C. Wyplosz, "Exchange Market Mayhem: The Antecedents and Aftermath of Speculative Attack," *Economic Policy* 21 (1995): 249–312.
2. G. Kaminski, S. Lizondo, and C. Reinhart, "Leading Indicators of Currency Crises," IMF Staff Paper no. 45 (1998): 1–48.

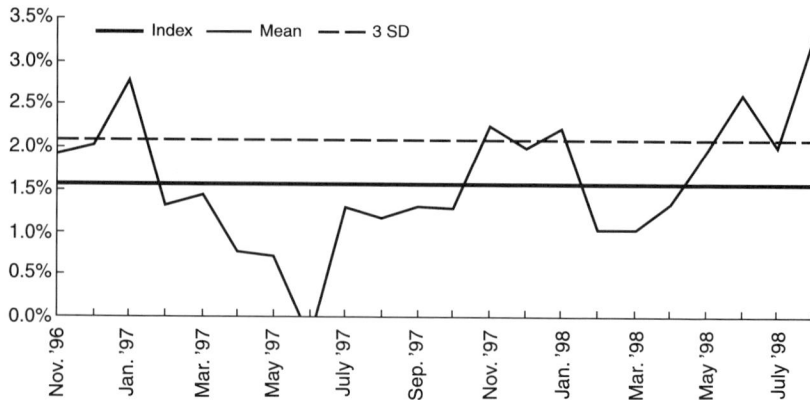

Figure V.1
Index of exchange-market pressure, November 1996–July 1998.

1. Indicators related to the external sector and the balance of payments
2. Financial market indicators
3. Monetary indicators
4. Real sector indicators

The methods and specifics of computing each indicator for the Russian case, their dynamics in November 1996 through July 1998, and intercountry comparisons are given below.

External Sector and Balance of Payments Indicators

1. **International reserves.** The annual growth rate of CBR international reserves (in US dollars) was observed. The indicator started to decelerate ten months prior to the crisis, while CBR international reserves began declining six months before the crisis (March 1998; Figure V.2). Similar developments are characteristic of most currency crises around the world.

2. **Exports.** Figure V.3 shows import and export growth dynamics (in US dollars) as compared with the same periods in the previous year. Negative growth rates in exports were observed beginning in January 1998, or seven months before the crisis. The key factor contributing to the decrease in exports was the drop in oil prices on world markets.

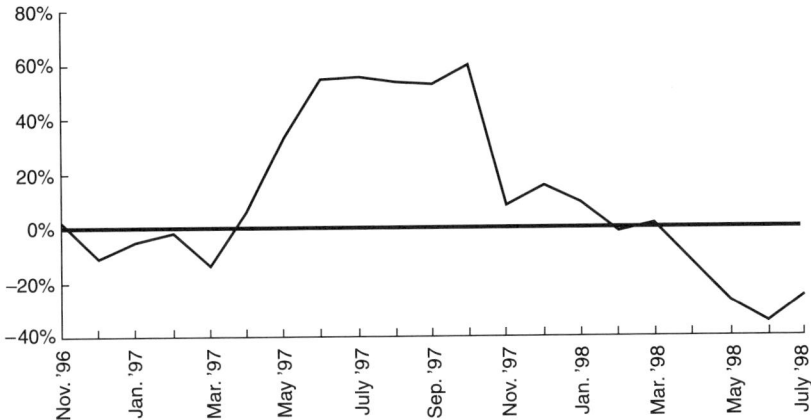

Figure V.2
Dynamics of RF Central Bank's international reserves, November 1996–July 1998.

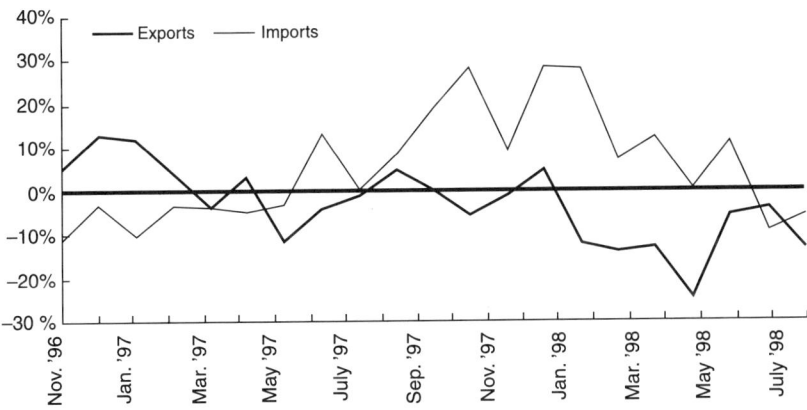

Figure V.3
Import and export dynamics, November 1996–July 1998.

3. **Imports.** This indicator is computed similarly to exports: the import growth rate (in US dollars) is compared with the growth rate in the same month of the previous year. In contradistinction to exports, however, the dynamics of imports differed from those observed in other countries. Import growth rates began decelerating in December 1997 and actually declined in the two months immediately preceding the crisis, whereas in most other cases of currency crises imports grew before the crisis.

4. **Terms of trade.** In the work by Kaminski and colleagues this indicator represents the ratio of the price of exports to the price of imports. Owing to the lack of export and import price indices in the RF balance of payments statistics, however, it was impossible to compute this indicator for the Russian case. Oil price dynamics were chosen as a substitute indicator (based on the data on crude oil prices in the United States). Since oil is a staple of Russian exports, the index of change in oil prices may be a reasonably reliable indicator of the terms of trade in the country (assuming that the prices of imported goods remain relatively constant). A sharp decline in oil prices was registered beginning in September 1997 (eleven months prior to the crisis). After February 1998, prices stabilized at an extremely low level, about 60%–65% of the levels observed in early 1996 (Figure V.4).

5. **Real ruble exchange rate.** The real exchange rate is determined based on the ratio of the nominal exchange rate growth to the con-

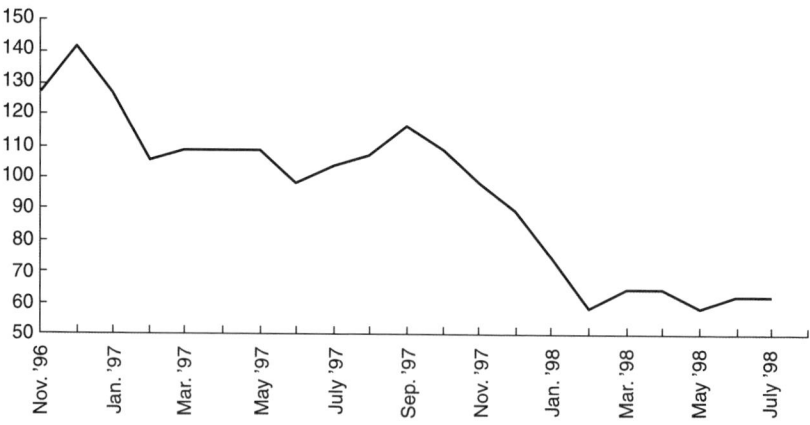

Figure V.4
Crude oil prices, November 1996–July 1998 (price in January 1996 = 100).

sumer price index (CPI) in such a way that the growth of this indicator means an appreciation of the national currency. Figure V.5 (real ruble-US dollar exchange rate growth over the previous year) demonstrates that real ruble exchange rate dynamics were not a good indicator of the future currency crisis. The real ruble exchange rate began to grow only in March 1998 (five months prior to the crisis); it had declined over the four previous months.

Financial Market Indicators

6. **Spread between domestic and external interest rates.** The spread between average weighted GKO/OFZ yields to maturity and the three-month LIBOR (both rates in monthly terms) was monitored. As Figure V.6 shows, a trend toward a wider spread was registered beginning in August 1997, twelve months before the crisis.

7. **Real interest rates on the domestic market.** Figure V.7 shows changes in real ruble-denominated government bond interest rates calculated using average weighted GKO/OFZ yields and the CPI. The real interest rate dynamics closely follow changes in the domestic to external interest-rate spread. Real interest rates began to grow in July 1997 (thirteen months before the crisis); however, the sharpest increase occurred after May 1998.

8. **Lending to deposit interest-rate spread.** In a number of currency crises the gap between lending and deposit interest rates has

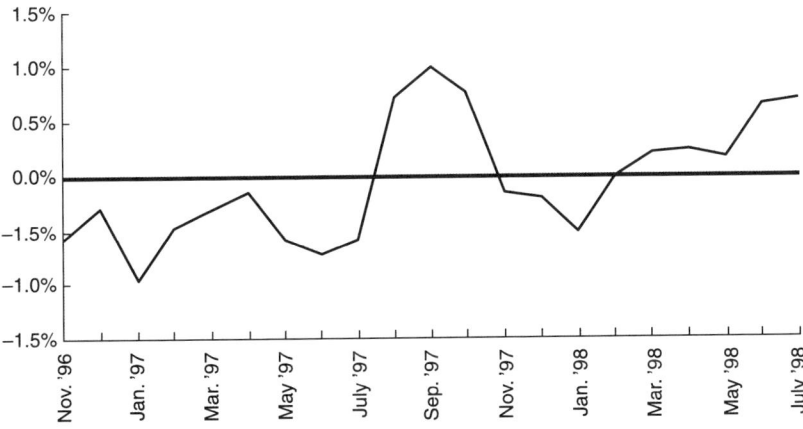

Figure V.5
Real ruble exchange-rate dynamics, November 1996–July 1998.

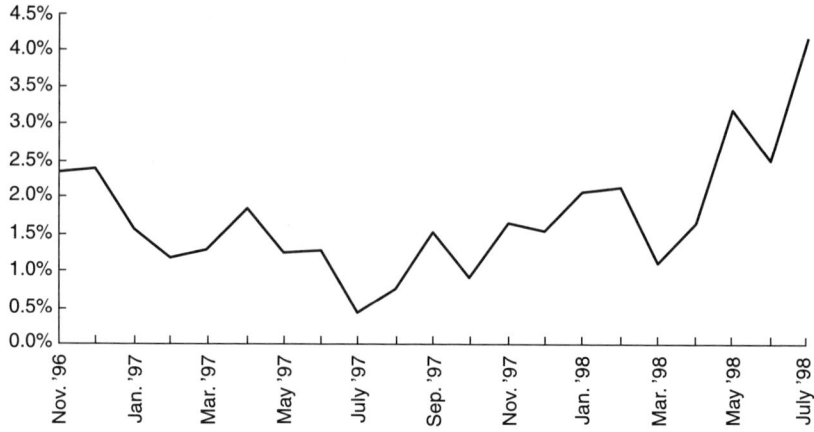

Figure V.6
GKO YTM/LIBOR spread (% per month), November 1996–July 1998.

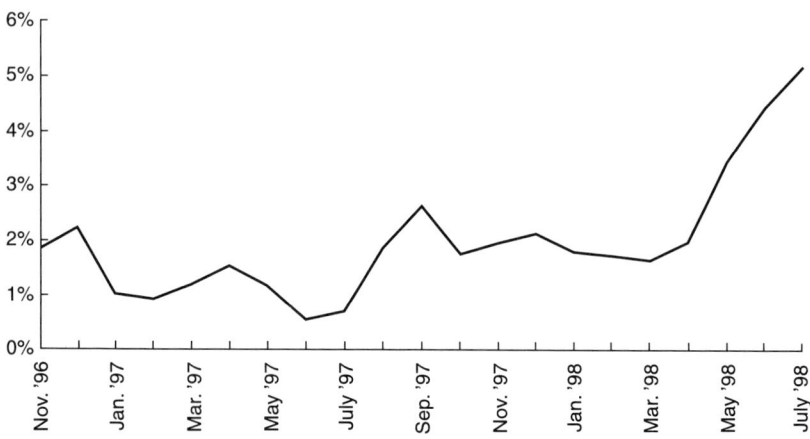

Figure V.7
Real GKO-OFZ interest rates (% per month), November 1996–July 1998.

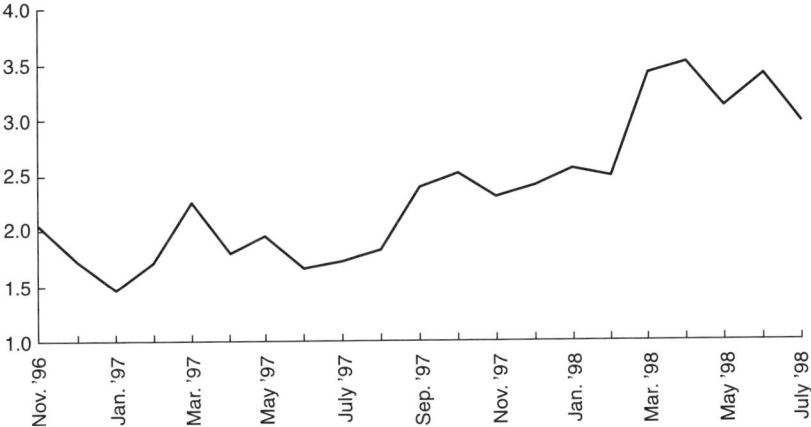

Figure V.8
Lending to deposit interest-rate ratio, November 1996–July 1998.

widened in the run-up to the crisis. It may be assumed that currency crises are preceded by an expansion of domestic lending. In this situation the share of "bad" credits increases, and banks raise interest rates, seeking to compensate for probable losses from loan defaults. Deposit rates also rise, although to a lesser degree.

In Russia, the "usual" widening gap was observed from June 1997 through April 1998 (Figure V.8). However, in the three months immediately preceding the crisis, the lending to deposit interest rate ratio decreased. The decreasing gap in interest rates might have been related to the small share of credits to the real sector in the consolidated balance of the banking system, rather than household deposits playing a major role. In this situation, increasing the interest rates on deposits in order to attract extra funds had a stronger effect.

9. **Growth of bank deposits.** On the threshold of a crisis, deposits are expected to flow out of the banking system. However, this phenomenon was not registered in Russia, as the growth rate of bank deposits compared with growth rates in the respective periods of the previous year (in real terms, adjusted for inflation) remained positive over the whole precrisis period (Figure V.9). Moreover, in the months immediately preceding the crisis the growth rate stabilized, after some growth in winter of 1997–1998. The growth of bank deposits might be related to the fact that households responded to rising deposit rates by increasing deposits in commercial banks.

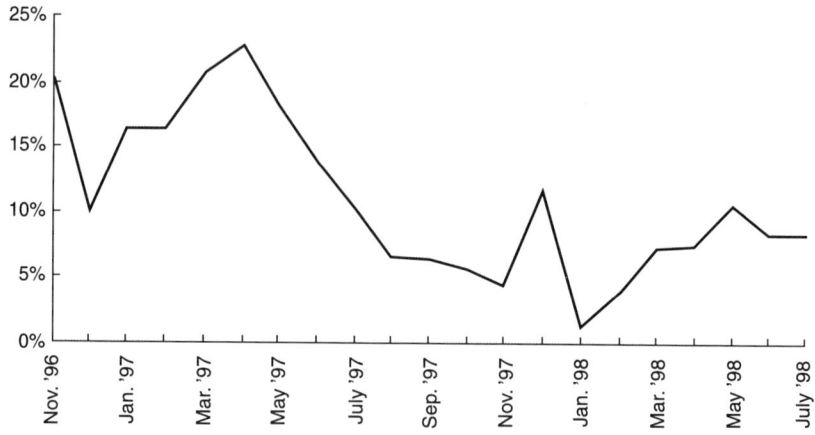

Figure V.9
Bank deposit growth rate, November 1996–July 1998.

10. **Stock market index.** The dynamics of the RTS-1 index growth rate compared with the dynamics in the respective periods of the previous year demonstrate that the Russian stock market had begun to fall by January 1998, seven months before the crisis (Figure V.10). At the same time, it is assumed that a precrisis period is characterized by rapidly growing markets, resulting in a speculative bubble (Figure V.11).

Monetary Indicators

11. **"Excess" real M1 balances.** According to the methods described by Kaminski and colleagues, "excess" real M1 balances are defined as the difference between estimated demand for M1 and actual M1 in real terms. This difference can be shown as a regression equation of the following type:

$$\frac{M_t}{GDP_t} = a_0 + a_1 Y_t + a_2 \dot{p}_t + a_3 t + \varepsilon_t$$

where M_t is the broad money M2, GDP_t is the nominal GDP, Y_t is the real GDP, $\dot{p}_t$ is the consumer price index, and t is time. Positive balances are interpreted as an indicator of "excessive" crediting of economies preceding crises.

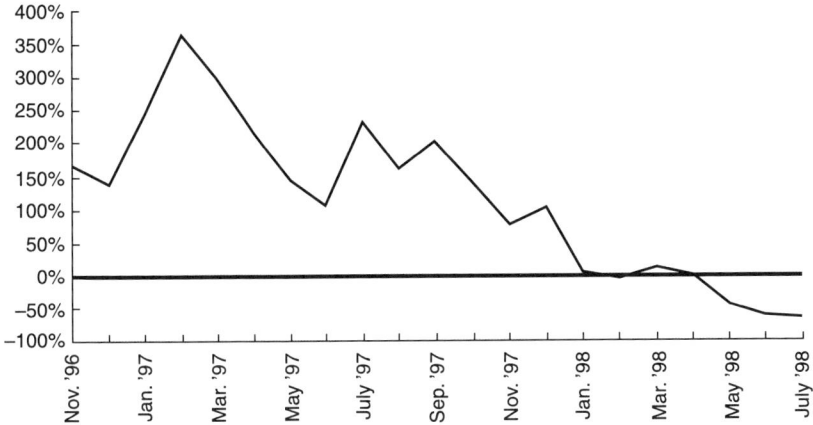

Figure V.10
Rate of change of RTS-1 index, November 1996–July 1998.

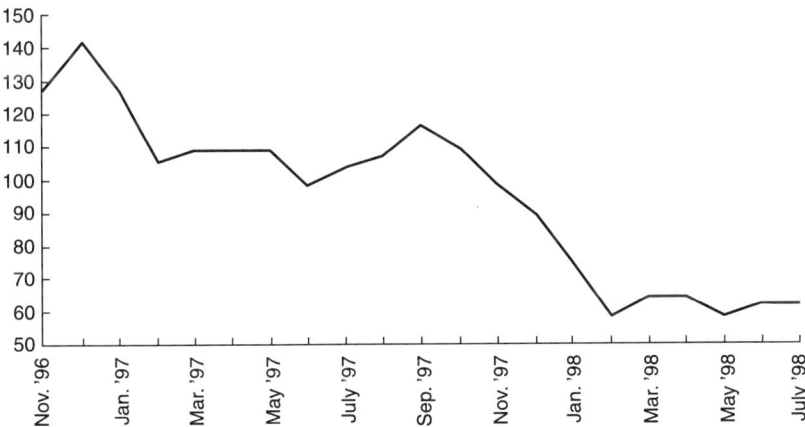

Figure V.11
Crude oil prices, November 1996–July 1998 (January 1996 = 100).

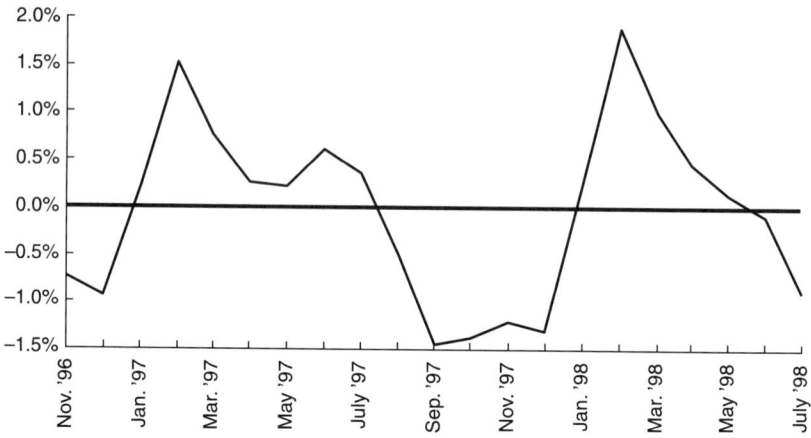

Figure V.12
"Excess" M2 balances (% of GDP).

No such situation was observed in Russia. Beginning in February 1998, real M2 contracted (Figure V.12). Apparently, along with CBR policies aimed at the withdrawal of money from the economy, it was affected by a gap between the financial and real sectors of the economy and by a lesser scope of credits to the real sector than in other countries that have sustained a currency crisis.

12. **The money multiplier.** The multiplier of M2 (M2 to money base ratio) changed similarly to the "excess" money supply. It began declining in early 1998, contrary to the assumption of this indicator's behavior prior to a crisis (Figure V.13).

13. **M2 to GDP ratio.** Like the other monetary indicators, the M2 to GDP ratio was not a leading indicator of the currency crisis in August 1998. The coefficient of monetization of the economy began to decline in July 1997, stabilizing only in 1998 (Figure V.14).

14. **Broad money to international reserves ratio.** The ratio of broad money (M2 plus foreign exchange–denominated deposits) to CBR international reserves also is among the "poor" indicators of the situation in Russia. On the one hand, in November 1997, nine months prior to the crisis, this ratio surged as expected; however, in the last few months preceding the crisis it fluctuated sharply while exhibiting a general downward trend (Figure V.15). That behavior is inconsistent with the hypothesis that this indicator should grow in a precrisis period.

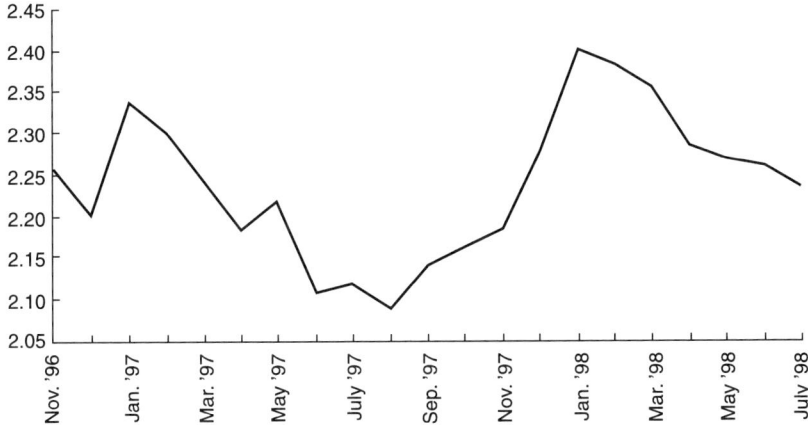

Figure V.13
M2 multiplier.

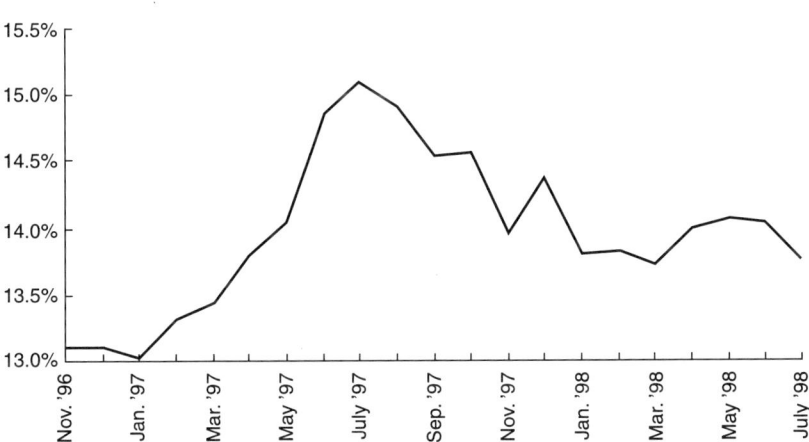

Figure V.14
M2/GDP ratio.

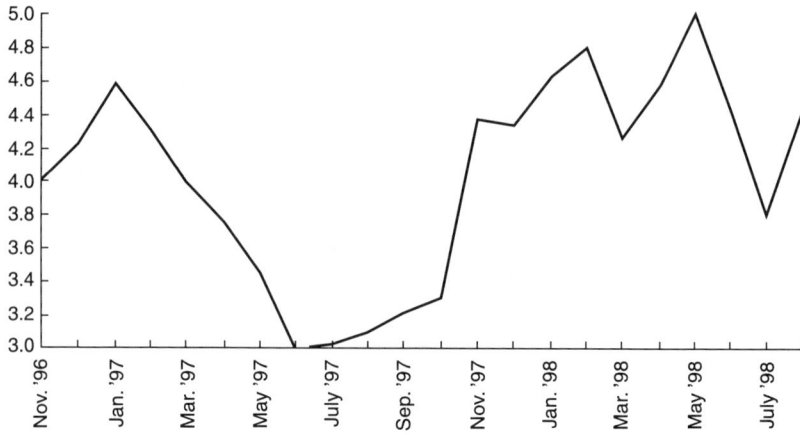

Figure V.15
Ratio of broad money to international reserves.

Real Sector Indicators

15. **Industrial output.** In the precrisis period, the Russian industrial output index behaved as expected. In November 1997 (nine months prior to the crisis), the industrial output index been to grow at a slower rate than in the respective months of the previous year, and beginning in April 1998 (four months prior to the crisis) it turned negative (Figure V.16).

The aggregate results of evaluating the adequacy of the observed leading indicators of currency crises as applied to the August 1998 crisis in Russia are presented in Table V.1. Fundamental indicators related to the real sector of the economy (including the external sector), balance of payments, and financial market indicators seemed to be the best indicators of the crisis in Russia. Indicators of monetary policies, the banking system, and imports were the least informative.

In order to explain these results, the following hypotheses may be advanced:

1. The August 1998 currency crisis was caused by fundamental factors related to the real sector of the economy and the narrow export orientation of production.

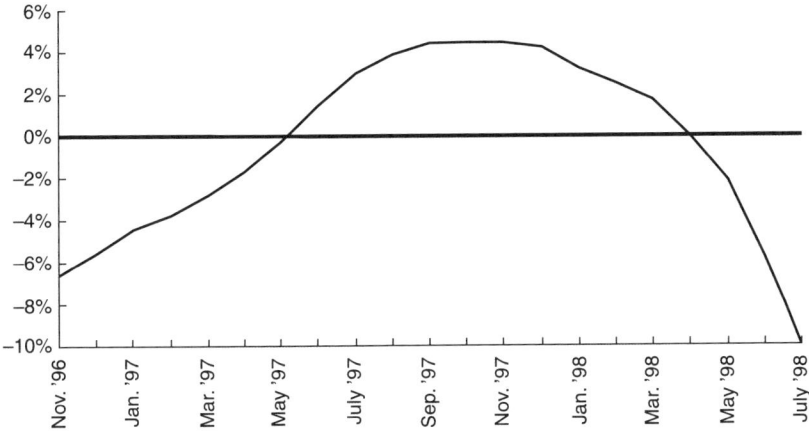

Figure V.16
Industrial Output Index: rate of change, November 1996–July 1998.

Table V.1
Macroeconomic and Financial Indicators of the August 1998 Currency Crisis

"Good" Indicators	Ambiguous Indicators	"Bad" Indicators
1. International reserves	1. Real ruble exchange rate	1. Imports
2. Exports	2. Lending to deposit interest rates ratio	2. Change in banking deposits
3. Oil price index	3. Stock market index	3. "Excess" real M2 balances
4. Spread between domestic and external interest rates	4. Broad money to international reserves ratio	4. M2 multiplier
5. Real domestic interest rates		5. M2 to GDP ratio
6. Industrial output index		

2. Capital (both national and foreign) flowed mostly to financial markets and did not deeply penetrate the real sector and the banking system.

3. The monetary policy pursued by the CBR was aimed at holding crisis developments in check.

4. However, budgetary problems and a gap between the financial sector and the real sector weakened the effect of the anticrisis measures.

5. The emerging budgetary crisis, indicators of which are outside the framework of this study, together with external factors, was the second major cause (after the worsening situation of the real sector) of the August 1998 currency crisis.

Statistical Appendix

Table 1
Weekly Dynamics of Russia's Financial Market Indicators, August 1997–December 1998

Week	Inflation (% per Week)	MICEX Ruble Rate (Rb/1$ US)	$ Exchange Rate Growth (% per Week)	RTS-1 Index, by End of Week	Rate of Change in RTS-1 Index (% per Week)	GKO-OFZ Weighted Average Yield (% per annum)	GKO/OFZ Secondary Market Trade (bill. Rb)	GKOs/OFZs in Circulation by End of Week (bill. Rb)	GKO-OFZ Auction Rate (% per annum)	GKO-OFZ Market Portfolio Duration, by End of Week (days)
4–10 Aug. '97	0.00	5,813	0.14	569.23	11.57	20.12	11,885.204	312,050.128	20.54	214.93
11–17 Aug. '97	−0.10	5,813	0.00	563.14	−1.07	21.47	15,453.983	313,550.869	19.06	216.39
18–24 Aug. '97	0.00	5,825	0.21	525.25	−6.73	19.23	10,617.683	315,627.115	18.71	217.77
25–31 Aug. '97	0.00	5,839.5	0.25	474.80	−9.60	19.50	11,257.131	317,008.224	18.67	222.10
1–7 Sept. '97	−0.10	5,839.2	−0.01	488.46	2.88	19.58	13,120.967	318,825.768	18.60	226.24
8–14 Sept. '97	0.00	5,850	0.18	483.75	−0.97	18.81	17,435.253	320,200.645	18.10	233.44
15–21 Sept. '97	0.00	5,862	0.21	497.94	2.93	20.54	17,966.633	322,433.781	19.01	235.12
22–28 Sept. '97	−0.20	5,861	−0.02	491.42	−1.31	19.18	13,594.635	323,131.221	18.44	236.81
29 Sept.–5 Oct. '97	0.00	5,877	0.27	552.14	12.36	22.75	15,488.706	327,095.416	18.36	245.50
6–12 Oct. '97	0.00	5,869.9	−0.12	527.78	−4.41	20.34	16,119.549	334,440.996	17.88	242.99
13–19 Oct. '97	0.10	5,868	−0.03	532.90	0.97	21.65	14,862.621	329,211.683	18.28	248.77
20–26 Oct. '97	0.10	5,873	0.09	518.29	−2.74	21.94	13,021.797	330,361.880	17.59	251.85
27 Oct.–2 Nov. '97	0.10	5,900	0.46	422.26	−18.53	28.30	28,180.178	332,547.925	19.55	256.38
3–9 Nov. '97	0.20	5,902	0.03	438.34	3.81	24.69	23,179.448	333,707.460	19.74	257.90
10–16 Nov. '97	0.20	5,909	0.12	342.07	−21.96	29.24	28,938.773	334,658.444	26.61	255.79
17–23 Nov. '97	0.20	5,917	0.14	382.59	11.84	30.44	18,069.85	335,483.064	26.27	251.75
24–30 Nov. '97	0.00	5,928	0.19	328.49	−14.14	40.48	21,694.138	337,586.469	28.00	248.17
1–7 Dec. '97	0.40	5,943	0.25	382.42	16.42	40.77	15,573.864	338,125.669	41.34	244.74
8–14 Dec. '97	0.20	5,922	−0.35	339.25	−11.29	36.64	10,805.339	339,148.335	34.52	241.17
15–21 Dec. '97	0.30	5,923	0.02	354.41	4.47	33.82	11,719.2782	341,291.113	32.57	236.40
22–28 Dec. '97	0.20	5,955	0.54	380.11	7.25	33.37	9,977.415	343,077.919	33.66	235.21

Statistical Appendix

29 Dec.–4 Jan. '98	0.40	5,998	0.72	396.86	4.41	27.36	4,411.860	343,077.919	0.00	231.21
5–11 Jan. '98	0.30	5.999	0.02	372.46	−6.15	41.70	5,676.557	344,398.774	32.83	223.81
12–18 Jan. '98	0.40	6.0255	0.44	334.54	−10.18	37.02	9,793.106	348,574.460	34.71	221.98
19–25 Jan. '98	0.40	6.048	0.37	294.71	−11.90	33.29	12,471.412	348,418.880	32.14	221.36
26 Jan.–1 Feb. '98	0.20	6.04	−0.13	284.35	−3.52	39.37	14,792.133	349,193.781	41.38	219.64
2–8 Feb. '98	0.20	6.0475	0.12	304.04	6.93	36.41	21,309.455	351,434.161	44.47	220.49
9–15 Feb. '98	0.30	6.0525	0.08	302.24	−0.59	30.24	16,361.676	355,411.408	34.68	222.85
16–22 Feb. '98	0.20	6.045	−0.11	305.81	1.18	29.65	14,511.897	358,865.780	35.32	226.70
23 Feb.–1 Mar. '98	0.20	6.045	−0.02	309.56	1.23	28.84	13,239.447	362,202.605	32.31	226.96
2–8 Mar. '98	0.10	6.065	0.33	339.66	9.73	26.83	17,329.613	367,470.807	28.53	232.97
9–15 Mar. '98	0.20	6.066	0.02	350.20	3.10	26.45	14,168.811	371,091.590	29.05	239.18
16–22 Mar. '98	0.10	6.0815	0.26	335.78	−4.12	26.79	16,826.720	373,767.032	27.86	242.85
23–29 Mar. '98	0.10	6.092	0.17	341.48	1.70	27.82	22,150.965	378,813.702	25.98	247.21
30 Mar.–5 Apr. '98	0.10	6.092	0.00	313.48	−8.20	28.42	15,934.378	380,320.665	28.57	248.11
6–12 Apr. '98	0.10	6.134	0.69	308.96	−1.44	28.71	15,249.230	382,804.428	34.23	252.89
13–19 Apr. '98	0.10	6.1415	0.12	312.69	1.20	28.86	13,326.875	387,165.160	33.81	260.43
20–26 Apr. '98	0.10	6.139	−0.04	326.16	4.31	30.54	15,544.843	389,134.692	34.93	264.39
27 Apr.–3 May '98	0.00	6.1095	−0.48	312.37	−4.23	29.40	11,727.225	393,345.432	31.84	268.96
4–10 May '98	0.10	6.128	0.30	302.82	−3.06	27.94	11,566.586	397,651.534	34.16	271.69
11–17 May '98	0.10	6.1525	0.40	258.10	−14.77	33.11	10,767.486	398,084.164	34.16	272.95
18–24 May '98	0.10	6.154	0.02	225.41	−12.67	45.77	19,094.463	398,577.325	45.16	270.28
25–31 May '98	0.10	6.13	−0.39	191.29	−15.14	64.96	24,610.293	399,281.413	61.07	266.63
1–7 June '98	0.00	6.178	0.78	207.65	8.55	51.45	20,938.528	399,016.673	53.15	265.60
8–14 June '98	0.10	6.21	0.52	178.13	−14.22	46.55	13,799.083	400,853.454	48.04	269.68
15–21 June '98	0.00	6.216	0.10	174.65	−1.95	54.29	19,576.525	395,901.065	49.31	284.61
22–28 June '98	0.00	6.225	0.14	163.99	−6.11	52.72	12,827.391	394,435.777	51.19	287.41
29 June–5 Jul. '98	0.00	6.215	−0.16	151.33	−7.72	72.44	15,457.959	391,975.482	63.11	291.62
6–12 Jul. '98	0.10	6.231	0.26	144.02	−4.83	125.77	15,045.254	387,523.792	107.23	288.08
13–19 Jul. '98	0.10	6.209	−0.35	193.35	34.26	52.94	34,163.636	383,185.563	0.00	302.44
20–26 Jul. '98	0.00	6.27	0.98	157.74	−18.42	45.11	18,323.277	382,555.058	48.96	315.77
27 Jul.–2 Aug. '98	0.10	6.272	0.03	149.65	−5.13	56.41	19,155.219	347,498.481	0.00	337.39
3–9 Aug. '98	0.20	6.285	0.21	132.86	−11.22	54.66	14,305.244	343,554.332	0.00	334.38

Table 1 (continued)

Week	Inflation (% per Week)	MICEX Ruble Rate (Rb/1$ US)	$ Exchange Rate Growth (% per Week)	RTS-1 Index, by End of Week	Rate of Change in RTS-1 Index (% per Week)	GKO-OFZ Weighted Average Yield (% per annum)	GKO/OFZ Secondary Market Trade (bill. Rb)	GKOs/OFZs in Circulation by End of Week (bill. Rb)	GKO-OFZ Auction Rate (% per annum)	GKO-OFZ Market Portfolio Duration, by End of Week (days)
10–16 Aug. '98	0.20	6.31	0.40	115.00	–13.44	95.58	12,488.508	340,326.857	0.00	330.59
17–23 Aug. '98	2.90	7.005	11.01	81.76	–28.90	—	—	—	—	—
24–30 Aug. '98	10.90	7.86	12.21	66.77	–18.33	—	—	—	—	—
31 Aug.–6 Sept. '98	35.70	16.99	116.16	63.13	–5.45	—	—	—	—	—
7–13 Sept. '98	5.60	12.87	–24.22	62.31	–1.30	—	—	—	—	—
14–20 Sept. '98	1.50	14.60	13.40	50.12	–19.56	—	—	—	—	—
21–27 Sept. '98	–4.80	15.61	6.92	47.08	–6.07	—	—	—	—	—
28 Sept.–4 Oct. '98	0.60	15.99	2.43	38.81	–17.57	—	—	—	—	—
5–11 Oct. '98	0.40	15.82	–1.06	42.55	9.64	—	—	—	—	—
12–18 Oct. '98	0.30	13.56	–14.29	55.32	30.01	—	—	—	—	—
19–25 Oct. '98	2.10	16.76	23.60	60.42	9.22	—	—	—	—	—
26 Oct.–1 Nov. '98	1.20	16.01	–4.47	57.54	–4.77	—	—	—	—	—
2–8 Nov. '98	0.80	15.01	–6.25	61.13	6.24	—	—	—	—	—
9–15 Nov. '98	1.00	16.41	9.33	59.32	–2.96	—	—	—	—	—
16–22 Nov. '98	1.70	16.96	3.35	63.36	6.81	—	—	—	—	—
23–29 Nov. '98	2.00	17.88	5.42	71.57	12.96	—	—	—	—	—
30 Nov.–6 Dec. '98	2.60	19.57	9.45	64.00	–10.58	—	—	—	—	—
7–13 Dec. '98	2.20	20.10	2.71	58.67	–8.33	—	—	—	—	—
14–20 Dec. '98	1.80	20.75	3.23	59.24	0.97	—	—	—	—	—
21–27 Dec. '98	3.50	19.48	–6.12	59.94	1.19	—	—	—	—	—
28 Dec. '98–3 Jan. '99	2.00	20.65	6.01	58.93	–1.69	—	—	—	—	—

Sources: RF Central Bank, RF Goskomstat, Finmarket Information Agency, RTS, Institute for the Economy in Transition.

Table 2
Enlarged Government Budget Balance in 1998

	Federal Budget		Local Budgets		Extrabudgetary Funds		Enlarged Government Budget		
	(bill. Rb)	(% of GDP)	(bill. Rb)	(% of GDP)	(bill. Rb)	(% of GDP)	(bill. Rb)	(% of GDP)	(% of Budget)
REVENUE									
1. Income and profit taxes	34,974.4	1.3	132,628.9	4.9			167,603.3	6.2	18.0
1.1. Profit tax	34,883.9	1.3	61,495.0	2.3			96,378.9	3.6	10.3
1.2. Personal income tax	90.5	0.0	71,134.0	2.7			71,224.4	2.7	7.6
2. Taxes on goods and services. License and registration fees	158,455.4	5.9	72,271.8	2.7			230,727.3	8.6	24.7
2.1. Value-added tax	104,749.0	3.9	51,763.1	1.9			156,512.1	5.8	16.8
2.2. Excises on excisable goods and selected mineral raw materials produced on RF territory	48,272.0	1.8	15,317.9	0.6			63,589.9	2.4	6.8
Excises on oil, including gas condensate	7,373.4	0.3		0.0			7,373.4	0.3	0.8
2.3. Excises on excisable goods and selected mineral raw materials imported to RF territory	4,181.5	0.2		0.0			4,181.5	0.2	0.4
2.4. Sales tax			755.3	0.0			755.3	0.0	0.1
3. Aggregate income tax	313.0	0.0	1,024.9				1,337.9	0.0	0.1
4. Property tax	364.8	0.0	46,529.1	1.7			46,893.9	1.7	5.0
5. Fees for use of natural resources	3,230.5	0.1	19,044.5	0.7			22,275.1	0.8	2.4

Table 2 (continued)

	Federal Budget		Local Budgets		Extrabudgetary Funds		Enlarged Government Budget		
	(bill. Rb)	(% of GDP)	(bill. Rb)	(% of GDP)	(bill. Rb)	(% of GDP)	(bill. Rb)	(% of GDP)	(% of Budget)
6. Taxes on foreign trade and foreign economic operations	36,544.4	1.4		0.0			36,544.4	1.4	3.9
7. Other taxes, fees, and duties	2,101.5	0.1	36,622.0	1.4			38,723.5	1.4	4.1
7.1. Stamp duty	602.7	0.0	1,067.9	0.0			1,670.6	0.1	0.2
7.2. Other taxes	1,498.8	0.1	35,554.1	1.3			37,052.9	1.4	4.0
8. Extrabudgetary fund receipts	0.0	0.0			251,637.6	9.4	251,637.6	9.4	27.0
8.1. Extrabudgetary social insurance fund receipts	0.0	0.0			207,574.6	7.7	207,574.6	7.7	22.2
8.1.1. Employees Pension Fund	0.0	0.0			5,111.7	0.2	5,111.7	0.2	0.5
	0.0	0.0			5,141.5	0.2	5,141.5	0.2	0.6
8.1.2. Employers Pension Fund	0.0	0.0			202,462.9	7.5	202,462.9	7.5	21.7
Social Insurance Fund	0.0	0.0			5,141.5	0.2	5,141.5	0.2	0.6
	0.0	0.0			30,600.8	1.1	30,600.8	1.1	3.3
Employment Fund	0.0	0.0			7,857.9	0.3	7,857.9	0.3	0.8
Compulsory Medical Insurance Fund (CMIF) and territorial CMIFs	0.0	0.0			20,043.5	0.7	20,043.5	0.7	2.1
8.2. Contributions to territorial road funds	0.0	0.0			44,063.0	1.6	44,063.0	1.6	4.7
9. Other extrabudgetary funds	0.0	0.0			2,248.7	0.1	2,248.7	0.1	0.2

Statistical Appendix

10. Revenue of target budgetary funds	23,734.9	0.9	17,603.5	0.7			41,338.5	1.5	4.4
Total Taxes and Payments	259,718.9	9.7	325,724.9	12.1	253,886.3	9.5	839,330.1	31.3	89.9
NONTAX REVENUES									
1. Revenue from government property or activity	4,065.0	0.2	9,209.7	0.3			13,274.7	0.5	1.4
2. Proceeds from the sale of government property	15,239.5	0.6	2,293.2	0.1			17,532.7	0.7	1.9
3. Proceeds from the sale of national stockpile	3,537.8	0.1					3,537.8	0.1	0.4
4. Proceeds from the sale of land and intangible assets	12.5	0.0	265.6	0.0			278.1	0.0	0.0
5. Administrative charges	111.1	0.0	835.0	0.0			946.1	0.0	0.1
6. Penalties and indemnity	251.6	0.0	1,062.3	0.0	4,713.9	0.2	6,027.8	0.2	0.6
7. Revenue from foreign economic operations	15,435.2	0.6	45.3	0.0			15,480.6	0.6	1.7
8. Other nontax revenue	1,014.7	0.0	8,522.0	0.3			9,536.7	0.4	1.0
9. Transfers from other levels of government	0.0	0.0	43,046.5	1.6			x	x	x
10. Other grants	0.0	0.0	261.8	0.0			261.8	0.0	0.0
11. Receipts from government extrabudgetary funds	0.0	0.0	5,222.7	0.2			5,222.7	0.2	0.6
12. Revenue from government institutions	3,000.2	0.1	1,254.2	0.0			4,254.4	0.2	0.5
13. Other government extra-budgetary fund income	0.0	0.0			18,017.9	0.7	18,017.9	0.7	1.9
14. Resources transferred to extrabudgetary funds	0.0	0.0			22,526.3	0.8	x	x	x
14.1. Federal budget funds	0.0	0.0			15,433.9	0.6	x	x	x
14.2. Local budget funds	0.0	0.0			7,092.3	0.3	x	x	x

Table 2 (continued)

	Federal Budget		Local Budgets		Extrabudgetary Funds		Enlarged Government Budget		
	(bill. Rb)	(% of GDP)	(bill. Rb)	(% of GDP)	(bill. Rb)	(% of GDP)	(bill. Rb)	(% of GDP)	(% of Budget)
Total Nontax Revenue	42,667.6	1.6	72,018.5	2.7	45,258.0	1.7	94,371.4	3.5	10.1
Total Revenue	302,386.5	11.3	397,743.3	14.8	299,144.4	11.1	933,701.5	34.8	100.0
EXPENDITURES									
1. Government administration	9,703.5	0.4	20,291.4	0.8			29,995.0	1.1	2.9
2. National defense	56,704.1	2.1					56,704.1	2.1	5.5
3. International activities	8,533.8	0.3					8,533.8	0.3	0.8
4. Justice	3,291.8	0.1					3,291.8	0.1	0.3
5. Law enforcement and security	30,701.9	1.1	11,885.8	0.4			42,587.8	1.6	4.2
6. Basic research and promotion of scientific and technological progress	5,172.4	0.2	507.3	0.0	660.7	0.0	6,340.4	0.2	0.6
7. Government services to the national economy, of which:	23,943.7	0.9	141,464.7	5.3	50,487.1	1.9	215,895.6	8.0	21.1
7.1. Industry, power engineering and construction	11,328.2	0.4	10,877.3	0.4	483.8	0.0	22,689.2	0.8	2.2
7.2. Agriculture and fisheries	3,256.3	0.1	16,192.7	0.6			19,449.0	0.7	1.9
7.3. Protection of the environment and natural resources, hydrometeorology, mapping and geodetic surveying	2,052.5	0.1	1,211.8	0.0	1,444.1	0.1	4,708.3	0.2	0.5

7.4. Transportation, road maintenance, communications and information technology	1,005.7	0.0	17,452.4	0.7			18,458.2	0.7	1.8
7.5. Market infrastructure development	0.0	0.0	531.7	0.0			531.7	0.0	0.1
7.6. Housing and utilities	0.0	0.0	94,419.4	3.5			94,419.4	3.5	9.2
7.7. Preventing and/or eliminating the effects of emergencies and natural disasters	6,301.0	0.2	779.4	0.0			7,080.4	0.3	0.7
7.8. Expenditure by territorial road funds					48,559.3	1.8	48,559.3	1.8	4.8
8. Social services	57,161.1	2.1	181,710.2	6.8	225,020.5	8.4	463,891.8	17.3	45.4
8.1. Education	12,928.1	0.5	84,095.7	3.1	477.2	0.0	97,500.9	3.6	9.5
8.2. Culture and arts	1,035.1	0.0	9,099.9	0.3			10,134.9	0.4	1.0
8.3. Mass media	1,087.9	0.0	1,749.4	0.1			2,837.3	0.1	0.3
8.4. Health and physical fitness	5,660.1	0.2	58,725.2	2.2	28,709.4	1.1	93,094.6	3.5	9.1
8.5. Social policy	36,450.0	1.4	28,040.0	1.0	195,834.0	7.3	260,324.1	9.7	25.5
9. Government debt service	106,571.4	4.0					106,571.4	4.0	10.4
10. Expenditure by target budgetary funds	23,617.7	0.9	16,021.9	0.6			39,639.6	1.5	3.9
11. Other expenditure	54,034.5	2.0	31,336.7	1.2	15,584.8	0.6	35,383.2	1.3	3.5
11.1. Financial aid to other levels of government	43,046.5	1.6					×	×	×
11.2. Other expenditure unattributable to other subitems	10,988.0	0.4	31,336.7	1.2	15,584.8	0.6	35,383.2	1.3	3.5
Total Expenditure	379,435.9	14.1	403,218.1	15.0	291,753.1	10.9	1,008,834.4	37.6	98.7

Table 2 (continued)

	Federal Budget		Local Budgets		Extrabudgetary Funds		Enlarged Government Budget		
	(bill. Rb)	(% of GDP)	(bill. Rb)	(% of GDP)	(bill. Rb)	(% of GDP)	(bill. Rb)	(% of GDP)	(% of Budget)
CREDITS MINUS REPAYMENTS	9,490.7	0.4	3,910.6	0.1			13,276.7	0.5	1.3
1. Budgetary loans	−1,316.0	0.0	3,910.6	0.1			2,470.0	0.1	0.2
2. Government loans to CIS countries	−163.1	0.0					−163.1	0.0	0.0
3. Government loans to foreign governments	−8,981.8	−0.3					−8,981.8	−0.3	−0.9
4. Foreign credit resources disbursed to enterprises and organizations	20,035.5	0.7					20,035.5	0.7	2.0
5. Defense conversion credit	−40.9	0.0					−40.9	0.0	0.0
6. Investment credit	−43.0	0.0					−43.0	0.0	0.0
Total Expenditures and Credits Less Repayments	388,926.6	14.5	407,128.7	15.2	291,753.1	10.9	1,022,111.1	38.1	100.0
Surplus of Revenue Over Expenditures and Credits Less Repayments	−86,540.1	−3.2	−9,385.4	−0.3	7,391.2	0.3	−88,409.6	−3.3	
FINANCING									
1. Domestic financing									
1.1. Change in bank account balances of budget funds (in rubles)	−30,758.3	−1.1	413.4	0.0	−5,075.6	−0.2	−35,420.4	−1.3	

1.3.	Short-term government debt	−57,012.7	−2.1			−57,012.7	−2.1
1.4.	Federal floating rate bonds	−4,762.6	−0.2			−4,762.6	−0.2
1.5.	Nonmarketable government bonds	876.7	0.0			867.7	0.0
1.6.	Government (municipal) securities	0.0	0.0	−364.2	0.0	−364.2	0.0
1.7.	Other government securities	23.9	0.0	0.0		23.9	0.0
1.8.	Federal fixed-rate bonds	90,614.6	3.4	0.0		90,614.6	3.4
1.9.	Budgetary loans from other-level budgets			−2,434.7	−0.1	×	×
1.10.	Government savings bonds	1,533.0	0.1	0.0		1,533.0	0.1
1.11.	Other domestic borrowing	−4,152.7	−0.2	11,770.9	0.4	7,618.2	0.3
1.12.	Credits and loans to extrabudgetary funds	0.0		−2,315.7	−0.1	−2,315.7	−0.1
Total Domestic Financing		−3,647.0	−0.1	9,385.4	0.3	−1,777.6	−0.1
2.	External financing	0.0					
2.1.	Loans from international financial institutions	12,164.5	0.5			12,164.5	0.5
2.2.	Foreign government loans to RF	−5,429.4	−0.2			−5,429.4	−0.2
2.3.	Loans from foreign commercial banks and companies to RF	83,452.1	3.1			83,452.1	3.1
Total Foreign Financing		90,187.2	3.4			90,187.2	3.4
Total Financing		86,540.1	3.2	−7,391.2	−0.3	88,409.6	3.3

Table 3
Tax Revenues of Consolidated Budget in 1998 and 1999 (% of GDP)

	1998											
	I	II	III	IV	V	VI	VII	VIII	IX	X	XI	XII
Industries	5.2	6.0	6.5	8.1	8.0	7.7	7.5	7.4	7.2	7.2	7.3	7.9
Electric power supply	0.6	0.7	0.8	1.3	1.2	1.2	1.2	1.1	1.0	1.0	1.0	1.1
Fuel	1.4	1.9	1.9	2.4	2.4	2.1	2.0	2.3	2.0	2.1	2.1	2.2
Ferrous and nonferrous metallurgy	0.3	0.4	0.6	0.6	0.7	0.6	0.6	0.6	0.6	0.6	0.6	0.7
Light industry	0.1	0.1	0.1	0.1	0.1	0.1	0.1	0.1	0.1	0.1	0.1	0.1
Food industry	1.3	1.3	1.4	1.4	1.4	1.4	1.4	1.4	1.4	1.4	1.4	1.4
Agriculture	0.1	0.1	0.2	0.2	0.2	0.2	0.2	0.2	0.2	0.2	0.2	0.2
Transportation	2.4	2.5	2.6	3.2	3.2	3.0	3.0	2.8	2.7	2.6	2.6	2.8
Communications	0.6	0.6	0.6	0.7	0.7	0.7	0.7	0.6	0.6	0.6	0.6	0.6
Construction	1.2	1.2	1.2	1.4	1.4	1.4	1.4	1.3	1.3	1.2	1.2	1.3
Finance, credit	0.7	0.7	0.8	0.9	0.9	0.8	0.8	0.8	0.7	0.7	0.7	0.8
Total	15.1	15.5	16.4	19.9	19.6	19.0	18.9	18.4	17.7	17.4	17.5	19.3

	1999											
	I	II	III	IV	V	VI	VII	VIII	IX	X	XI	XII
Industries	5.3	6.5	7.3	7.9	8.3	8.0	8.0	8.2	8.3	8.2	8.6	8.9
Electric power supply	0.3	0.7	0.8	0.7	0.7	0.7	0.6	0.6	0.6	0.6	0.6	0.7
Fuel	1.0	1.6	1.8	1.9	2.1	2.1	2.1	2.2	2.3	2.4	2.7	2.8
Ferrous and nonferrous metallurgy	0.4	0.5	0.6	0.8	0.9	0.9	0.9	1.0	0.9	0.9	1.0	1.0
Light industry	0.1	0.1	0.1	0.1	0.1	0.1	0.1	0.1	0.1	0.1	0.1	0.1
Food industry	1.4	1.5	1.6	1.7	1.8	1.6	1.6	1.6	1.6	1.6	1.6	1.6
Agriculture	0.2	0.2	0.2	0.2	0.2	0.2	0.2	0.2	0.2	0.2	0.2	0.2
Transportation	3.4	3.4	3.5	3.5	3.5	3.2	3.1	3.0	3.0	2.9	2.9	3.0
Communications	0.6	0.5	0.6	0.6	0.6	0.6	0.6	0.6	0.6	0.5	0.6	0.5
Construction	0.9	1.0	1.1	1.2	1.2	1.1	1.1	1.1	1.1	1.1	1.1	1.1
Finance, credit	0.8	0.8	0.8	0.9	0.8	0.8	0.8	0.8	0.7	0.7	0.7	0.7
Total	16.0	17.1	18.7	20.0	20.2	18.8	18.9	19.0	18.8	18.6	19.1	19.7

Statistical Appendix

Table 4
Tax Revenues of Consolidated Budget, by Industry, in 1998 and 1999

	1998											
	I	II	III	IV	V	VI	VII	VIII	IX	X	XI	XII
Industries	34.5	39.1	39.6	40.5	40.9	40.5	39.6	40.3	40.8	41.3	41.5	41.0
Electric power supply	4.0	4.5	4.6	6.3	6.3	6.4	6.1	6.0	5.9	5.8	5.6	5.7
Fuel	9.4	12.1	11.7	12.1	12.2	11.1	10.6	12.3	11.5	11.9	12.0	11.7
Ferrous and nonferrous metallurgy	1.7	2.8	3.4	3.3	3.4	3.3	3.3	3.4	3.4	3.4	3.6	3.6
Light industry	0.6	0.6	0.6	0.6	0.6	0.6	0.6	0.6	0.6	0.6	0.6	0.6
Food industry	8.9	8.7	8.3	7.1	7.1	7.5	7.6	7.6	7.8	7.9	7.9	7.5
Agriculture	0.9	0.9	1.0	1.0	1.0	1.0	1.0	1.0	1.1	1.1	1.1	1.2
Transportation	16.0	16.2	16.1	15.9	16.2	15.9	15.8	15.5	15.4	15.0	15.1	14.6
Communications	3.9	3.9	3.7	3.4	3.5	3.6	3.5	3.5	3.5	3.5	3.5	3.2
Construction	7.9	7.4	7.2	7.2	7.3	7.3	7.3	7.3	7.2	7.1	6.9	6.6
Finance, credit	4.9	4.2	4.9	4.5	4.6	4.4	4.3	4.4	4.2	4.2	4.1	4.1
Total	100	100	100	100	100	100	100	100	100	100	100	100

	1999											
	I	II	III	IV	V	VI	VII	VIII	IX	X	XI	XII
Industries	33.0	37.9	39.0	39.6	41.3	42.4	42.5	43.1	43.9	44.2	45.2	45.2
Electric power supply	1.9	3.8	4.0	3.6	3.4	3.5	3.3	3.2	3.3	3.4	3.4	3.4
Fuel	6.5	9.3	9.7	9.7	10.3	11.0	11.0	11.4	12.2	12.8	14.0	14.4
Ferrous and nonferrous metallurgy	2.7	3.1	3.3	3.8	4.4	4.6	4.8	5.1	5.0	5.0	5.2	5.2
Light industry	0.5	0.5	0.6	0.6	0.6	0.6	0.6	0.6	0.6	0.6	0.6	0.6
Food industry	9.0	8.9	8.7	8.6	8.7	8.7	8.7	8.7	8.6	8.5	8.3	8.0
Agriculture	1.0	1.0	1.1	1.1	1.1	1.1	1.1	1.1	1.1	1.1	1.1	1.2
Transportation	21.3	20.0	18.5	17.6	17.1	17.0	16.5	16.0	16.0	15.5	15.0	15.2
Communications	3.6	3.1	3.0	3.2	3.1	3.0	3.0	3.0	3.0	2.9	2.9	2.7
Construction	5.5	5.6	5.7	5.9	5.8	5.8	5.9	5.9	5.8	5.9	5.8	5.8
Finance, credit	4.8	4.4	4.4	4.3	4.1	4.2	4.2	4.0	3.8	3.7	3.6	3.6
Total	100	100	100	100	100	100	100	100	100	100	100	100

Table 5
Russia's Monetary and Financial Indicators, 1998–1999

	Base Money (bill. Rb)	Base Money Growth Rate (%)	NDA (bill. Rb)	NIR (bill. Rb)	Broad Money (bill. Rb)	Broad Money Growth Rate (%)	M0 (bill. Rb)	M0 Growth Rate (%)	Commercial Banks' Correspondent Balances at CBR (bill. Rb)	M1 (bill. Rb)	M1 Growth Rate (%)	M2 (bill. Rb)	M2 Growth Rate (%)	Broad Money (bill. Rb)	Broad Money Growth Rate (%)	Money Multiplier (M2/Base Money)
Jan. '98	151.4	−7.96	146.2	5.2	187.8	−10.77	116.7	−10.62	20.7	272.7	−8.59	361.2	−3.45	429.4	−6.08	2.39
Feb. '98	152.8	0.92	149.8	3.0	185.3	−1.31	120.3	3.07	16.3	270.4	−0.83	362.9	0.47	436.4	1.61	2.38
Mar. '98	152.9	0.07	138.8	14.1	189.3	2.17	119.1	−0.92	16.5	266.0	−1.62	360.4	−0.69	436.2	−0.04	2.36
Apr. '98	161.6	5.69	153.3	8.3	191.8	1.29	128.6	7.94	15.0	269.5	1.30	368	2.11	444.1	1.83	2.28
May '98	163.2	0.99	163.0	0.2	193.9	1.12	129.9	0.97	15.3	271.8	0.87	370	0.54	449.0	1.09	2.27
June '98	163.2	0.00	154.0	9.2	193.8	−0.07	129.8	−0.04	12.9	270.3	−0.58	368.6	−0.38	447.9	−0.24	2.26
Jul. '98	161.3	−1.16	166.6	−5.3	194.2	0.22	129.3	−0.37	12.5	261.6	−3.21	360	−2.33	437.8	−2.25	2.23
Aug. '98	161.7	0.25	202.3	−40.6	186.4	−4.04	133.4	3.13	10.6	252.4	−3.52	343.6	−4.56	434.3	−0.80	2.12
Sept. '98	175.2	8.35	215.3	−40.1	208.8	12.02	154.2	15.62	19.7	274.1	8.62	365.8	6.46	520.0	19.75	2.09
Oct. '98	187.2	6.85	221.0	−33.8	227.9	9.17	166.5	7.94	22.5	289.2	5.50	377.6	3.23	521.7	0.33	2.02
Nov. '98	191.3	2.19	229.5	−38.2	238.7	4.74	167.3	0.49	23.8	302.8	4.71	396.9	5.11	552.9	5.97	2.07
Dec. '98	207.3	8.36	249.3	−42.0	263.7	10.45	178.8	12.30	28.2	342.8	13.20	448.3	12.95	628.6	13.70	2.16
Jan. '99	202.5	−2.32	412.2	−209.7	261.5	−0.84	178.0	−5.23	30.0	330.0	−3.74	444.2	−0.91	637.4	1.40	2.19
Feb. '99	205.2	1.33	416.8	−211.6	270.8	3.58	180.8	1.56	31.3	340.3	3.14	463.9	4.43	658.0	3.23	2.26
Mar. '99	205.9	0.34	423.9	−218.0	289.2	6.77	174.1	−3.68	35.1	344.8	1.31	473.8	2.13	675.3	2.63	2.30
Apr. '99	224.5	9.03	425.5	−201.0	310.7	7.44	195.2	12.13	38.7	371.9	7.86	509.6	7.56	717.6	6.27	2.27
May '99	241.4	7.53	412.0	−170.6	353.1	13.66	205.3	5.14	51.0	404.0	8.63	542.4	6.44	755.5	5.27	2.25
June '99	258.4	7.04	434.8	−176.4	362.7	2.72	216.4	5.41	55.0	418.1	3.49	567.7	4.66	786.1	4.05	2.20
Jul. '99	260.3	0.74	417.8	−157.5	364.9	0.58	218.2	0.82	51.8	429.4	2.71	583.2	2.73	792.0	0.75	2.24
Aug. '99	264.1	1.46	415.6	−151.5	369.9	1.39	216.2	−0.91	46.9	432.9	0.82	590.8	1.30	812.7	2.62	2.24
Sept. '99	259.0	−1.93	405.9	−146.9	364.1	−1.56	212.8	−1.56	54.0	431.0	−0.44	597.4	1.12	823.5	1.33	2.31
Oct. '99	269.1	3.90	390.1	−121.0	384.6	5.61	222.0	4.30	59.4	454.3	5.42	625.1	4.64	866.5	5.22	2.32
Nov. '99	272.0	1.08	380.4	−108.4	393.8	2.40	219.3	−1.19	54.6	471.6	3.79	646.5	3.42	909.8	5.00	2.38
Dec. '99	308.0	13.24							69.6							

Note: NDA = net domestic assets; NIA = net international reserves.

Source: RF Central Bank, RtsER.

Statistical Appendix   987

Table 6
Russia's Monetary and Financial Indicators, 1998–1999

	CPI (% per month)	Official Ruble Exchange Rate (Rb/$)	Ruble/Dollar Exchange Rate Growth Rate (%)	Forex and Gold Reserves (mill. $)	Forex Reserves (mill. $)	Gold (mill. $, at $300/1 oz. troy)	RTS-1 Index	RTS-1 Growth Rate (% per month)	RTS Trade Volume (mill. $)	GKO/OFZ Weighted Average Yield (% per annum)	GKO/OFZ Secondary Market Trade (mill. Rb)	INSTAR (Overnight) (% per annum)	Real Effective Exchange Rate ($/Rb, Jan. 1998 = 100)
Jan. '98	1.4	6.04	0.70	15,375	10,480	4,895	284.35	−28.35	1,269.2	38.70	42,733.2	25.86	100.0
Feb. '98	0.9	6.045	0.08	15,034	10,212	4,822	309.56	8.87	1,268.1	31.83	65,422.5	30.64	99.2
Mar. '98	0.6	6.089	0.73	16,859	11,910	4,948	325.50	5.15	1,838.7	27.35	78,221.1	25.86	99.3
Apr. '98	0.4	6.1095	0.34	15,953	10,957	4,996	312.37	−4.03	1,236.2	29.09	64,037.6	29.45	99.3
May '98	0.5	6.13	0.34	14,627	9,625	5,002	191.29	−38.76	1,202.6	47.73	66,038.8	48.29	99.1
June '98	0.1	6.225	1.55	16,169	11,161	5,008	151.35	−20.88	689.8	54.58	74,353.7	64.29	100.5
Jul. '98	0.2	6.272	0.76	18,409	13,805	4,604	149.65	−1.12	752.2	64.55	94,933.2	64.22	101.1
Aug. '98	3.7	7.905	26.04	12,459	8,198	4,262	65.61	−56.16	233.3	74.48	26,867.9	44.85	122.9
Sept. '98	38.4	16.0645	103.22	12,709	8,840	3,869	43.81	−33.23	27.7	—	—	153.93	180.4
Oct. '98	4.5	16.01	−0.34	13,572	9,656	3,916	57.54	31.34	44.8	—	—	33.16	172.0
Nov. '98	5.7	17.88	11.68	12,480	8,175	4,306	71.46	24.19	60.3	—	—	22.19	181.8
Dec. '98	11.6	20.65	15.49	12,223	7,801	4,422	58.93	−17.53	43.8	—	—	30.74	188.1
Jan. '99	8.5	22.60	9.44	11,621	7,078	4,543	55.12	−6.47	26.8	65.72	244.8	26.08	189.7
Feb. '99	4.1	22.86	1.15	11,437	7,284	4,153	70.03	27.05	102.3	71.53	991.6	24.99	184.4
Mar. '99	2.8	24.18	5.77	10,765	6,679	4,086	80.36	14.75	186.8	63.19	4,502.4	22.78	189.7
Apr. '99	3.0	24.23	0.21	11,168	7,074	4,094	91.83	14.27	161.2	80.39	3,346.6	19.87	184.6
May '99	2.2	24.44	0.87	11,937	8,034	3,903	97.64	6.33	197.3	75.90	4,278.4	6.19	182.2
June '99	1.9	24.22	−0.90	12,152	8,188	3,964	125.65	28.69	272.1	57.45	8,102.2	5.39	177.1
Jul. '99	2.8	24.19	−0.12	11,921	7,827	4,094	116.49	−7.29	330.2	65.79	9,224.6	9.24	172.1
Aug. '99	1.2	24.75	2.32	11,231	6,824	4,407	102.50	−12.01	184.6	69.70	14,069.7	8.69	174.0
Sept. '99	1.5	25.08	1.33	11,212	6,634	4,579	83.12	−18.91	172.6	76.26	14,643.0	18.07	173.7
Oct. '99	1.4	26.05	3.87	11,752	7,081	4,671	97.80	17.66	151.7	83.56	25,769.0	13.31	177.9
Nov. '99	1.2	26.42	1.42	11,504	7,599	3,906	112.36	14.89	264.1	81.10	9,672.6	7.14	178.3
Dec. '99	1.3	27.00	2.20	12,456	8,457	3,998	177.71	58.16	289.3	65.81	12,132.4	13.39	179.9

Sources: RF Goskomstat, RF CBR, RTS, IA Finmarket.

Table 7
Enlarged Government Budget Balance in 1999

	Federal Budget		Local Budgets		Extrabudgetary Funds		Enlarged Government Budget		
	(bill. Rb)	(% of GDP)	(bill. Rb)	(% of GDP)	(bill. Rb)	(% of GDP)	(bill. Rb)	(% of GDP)	(% of Budget)
REVENUE									
1. Income, profit, and capital gains taxes	101,129.2	2.3	236,016.9	5.3			337,146.1	7.5	20.8
1.1. Profit tax	81,201.1	1.8	139,005.4	3.1			220,206.6	4.9	13.6
1.2. Personal income tax	19,928.1	0.4	97,011.5	2.2			116,939.6	2.6	7.2
2. Taxes on goods and services; license and registration fees	307,383.5	6.9	111,307.3	2.5			418,690.8	9.4	25.9
2.1. Value-added tax	221,031.3	4.9	65,852.4	1.5			286,883.7	6.4	17.7
2.2. Excises on excisable goods and selected mineral raw materials produced on RF territory	80,743.7	1.8	24,204.4	0.5			104,948.1	2.3	6.5
Excises on oil, including gas condensate	3,938.1	0.1					3,938.1	0.1	0.2
2.3. Excises on excisable goods and selected mineral raw materials imported to RF territory	3,468.0	0.1					3,468.0	0.1	0.2
2.4. Sales tax			19,302.8	0.4			19,302.8	0.4	1.2
3. Aggregate income tax	1,259.1	0.0	5,677.1	0.1			6,936.3	0.2	0.4
4. Property tax	749.3	0.0	51,850.5	1.2			52,599.8	1.2	3.3
5. Fees for use of natural resources	10,496.0	0.2	34,079.5	0.8			44,575.5	1.0	2.8
6. Taxes on foreign trade and foreign economic operations	86,261.8	1.9	0.1	0.0			86,261.9	1.9	5.3
7. Other taxes, fees, and duties	2,228.2	0.0	54,157.5	1.2			56,385.7	1.3	3.5

Statistical Appendix

8. Extrabudgetary fund receipts				396,337.5	8.9	24.5
8.1. Extrabudgetary social insurance fund receipts				312,795.0	7.0	19.3
8.1.1. Employees				7,853.6	0.2	0.5
Pension fund				7,853.6	0.2	0.5
8.1.2. Employers				304,941.4	6.8	18.8
Pension Fund				7,853.6	0.2	0.5
Social Insurance Fund				44,046.9	1.0	2.7
Employment Fund				11,445.3	0.3	0.7
Compulsory Medical Insurance Fund (CMIF) and territorial CMIFs				29,548.9	0.7	1.8
8.2. Contributions to territorial road funds				79,263.3	1.8	4.9
8.3. Other extrabudgetary funds	55,183.4			4,279.3	0.1	0.3
9. Revenue of target budgetary funds		1.2	42,030.4	0.9	2.2	6.0
Total Taxes and Payments	564,690.6	12.6	535,119.3	12.0	33.4	92.5
				396,337.5	8.9	
Nontax Revenues						
1. Revenue from government property or activity	6,772.9	0.2	15,939.6	0.4		1.4
2. Proceeds from the sale of government property				22,712.5	0.5	
3. Proceeds from the sale of national stockpile						
4. Proceeds from the sale of land and intangible assets	20.2	0.0	609.7	0.0	0.0	0.0
5. Administrative charges	456.9	0.0	1,392.4	0.0	629.9	0.1
6. Penalties and indemnity	4,219.2	0.1	1,518.9	0.0	1,849.2	0.0	0.7
7. Revenue from foreign economic operations	34,722.4	0.8	17.1	0.0	4,883.3	0.1	10,621.4	0.2	2.1
							34,739.5	0.8	

Table 7 (continued)

	Federal Budget (bill. Rb)	(% of GDP)	Local Budgets (bill. Rb)	(% of GDP)	Extrabudgetary Funds (bill. Rb)	(% of GDP)	Enlarged Government Budget (bill. Rb)	(% of GDP)	(% of Budget)
8. Other nontax revenue	817.9	0.0	16,105.3	0.4	19,485.0	0.4	36,408.2	0.8	2.2
9. Transfers from other levels of government	9.2	0.0	62,135.3	1.4			×	×	×
10. Other grants	0.0	0.0	2,193.2	0.0			2,193.2	0.0	0.1
11. Receipts from government extrabudgetary funds			10,702.6	0.2			10,702.6	0.2	0.7
12. Revenue from government institutions	0.1	0.0	2,155.2	0.0			2,155.3	0.0	0.1
13. Other government extrabudgetary fund income					31,829.2	0.7	×	×	×
13.1. Federal budget funds					22,367.5	0.5	×	×	×
13.2. Local budget funds					9,461.7	0.2	×	×	×
Total Nontax Revenue	47,018.8	1.1	112,769.3	2.5	56,197.5	1.3	122,011.7	2.7	7.5
Total Revenue	611,709.4	13.7	647,888.5	14.5	452,535.0	10.1	1,618,159.1	36.2	100.0
EXPENDITURES									
1. Government administration	14,832.4	0.3	31,688.9	0.7			46,521.3	1.0	2.8
2. National defense	116,127.5	2.6					116,127.5	2.6	7.1
3. International activities	58,080.3	1.3					58,080.3	1.3	3.6
4. Justice	4,987.3	0.1					4,987.3	0.1	0.3
5. Law enforcement and security	55,445.5	1.2	19,005.1	0.4			74,450.6	1.7	4.6
6. Basic research and promotion of scientific and technological progress	11,196.8	0.3	706.0	0.0	1,612.4	0.0	13,515.3	0.3	0.8

7. Government services to the national economy, of which:	37,199.9	0.8	206,687.2	4.6	79,008.7	1.8	322,869.4	7.2	19.8
7.1. Industry, power engineering and construction	16,921.3	0.4	14,081.9	0.3	693.7	0.0	31,696.8	0.7	1.9
7.2. Agriculture and fisheries	9,068.0	0.2	26,700.9	0.6			35,768.9	0.8	2.2
7.3. Protection of the environment and natural resources, hydrometeorology, mapping, and geodetic surveying	2,894.9	0.1	2,369.1	0.1	1,444.0	0.0	6,707.9	0.1	0.4
7.4. Transportation, road maintenance, communications and information technology	941.6	0.0	25,126.5	0.6			26,041.7	0.6	1.6
7.5. Market infrastructure development			12,332.6	0.3			12,332.6	0.3	0.8
7.6. Housing and utilities			124,580.2	2.8			124,580.2	2.8	7.6
7.7. Preventing and/or eliminating the effects of emergencies and natural disasters	7,374.2	0.2	1,496.1	0.0			8,870.2	0.2	0.5
7.8. Expenditure by territorial road funds					76,871.1	1.7	76,871.1	1.7	4.7
8. Social services	85,059.4	1.9	280,397.5	6.3	322,897.2	7.2	656,551.3	14.7	40.2
8.1. Education	20,945.4	0.5	126,071.5	2.8	576.6	0.0	147,593.5	3.3	9.0
8.2. Culture and arts	2,876.6	0.1	15,012.6	0.3			17,889.2	0.4	1.1
8.3. Mass media	2,000.4	0.0	3,280.6	0.1			5,281.0	0.1	0.3
8.4. Health and physical fitness	10,141.0	0.2	92,944.0	2.1	37,626.5	0.8	131,302.3	2.9	8.0
8.5. Social policy	49,096.0	1.1	43,088.8	1.0	284,694.0	6.4	354,485.3	7.9	21.7
9. Target budgetary funds	55,275.3	1.2	37,529.9	0.8			92,805.3	2.1	5.7
10. Government debt service	162,582.7	3.6					162,582.7	3.6	9.9
11. Other expenditures	76,460.3	1.7	64,576.8	1.4			78,892.6	1.8	4.8
11.1. Financial aid to other levels of government	62,135.3	1.4	9.2	0.0			×	×	×

Table 7 (continued)

	Federal Budget		Local Budgets		Extrabudgetary Funds		Enlarged Government Budget		
	(bill. Rb)	(% of GDP)	(bill. Rb)	(% of GDP)	(bill. Rb)	(% of GDP)	(bill. Rb)	(% of GDP)	(% of Budget)
11.2. Other expenditures unattributable to other subitems	14,325.0	0.3	64,567.6	1.4			78,892.6	1.8	4.8
Total Expenditure	677,247.5	15.1	640,591.5	14.3	403,518.3	9.0	1,627,383.6	36.4	99.6
Credits Minus Repayments	−12,573.7	−0.3	8,325.0	0.2			6,958.3	0.2	0.4
Budgetary loans	−12,573.7	−0.3	8,325.0	0.2			6,958.3	0.2	0.4
Total Expenditures and Credits Less Repayments	664,673.8	14.8	648,916.5	14.5	403,518.3	9.0	1,634,341.9	36.5	100.0
Surplus of Revenues Over Expenditures and Credits Less Repayments	−52,964.4	−1.2	−1,028.0	0.0	49,016.7	1.1	−16,182.8	−0.4	
TOTAL FINANCING									
1. Domestic financing									
1.1. Change in bank account balances of budget funds (in rubles)	−48,099.5	−1.1	−8,476.8	−0.2	−19,936.1	−0.4	−76,512.4	−1.7	
1.3. Short-term government debt	−11,908.2	−0.3					−11,908.2	−0.3	
1.4. Federal floating rate bonds	−136.0	0.0					−136.0	0.0	
1.5. Nonmarketable government bonds	54.6	0.0					54.6	0.0	
1.6. Government (municipal) securities			−2,211.3	0.0			−2,211.3	0.0	

1.7. Other government securities	15.1	0.0			15.1	0.0	
1.8. Federal fixed rate bonds	52,945.4	1.2			52,945.4	1.2	
1.9. Budgetary loans from other-level budgets			−4,855.5	−0.1	×	×	
1.10. Government savings bonds	−9,188.2	−0.2			−9,188.2	−0.2	
1.11. Other domestic borrowing	21,861.1	0.5	16,571.6	0.4	38,432.7	0.9	
1.12. Credits and loans to extra-budgetary funds					−29,080.7	−0.6	
			−29,080.7	−0.6			
Total Domestic Financing	5,544.5	0.1	−49,016.7	−1.1	−31,237.1	−0.7	
2. External financing	−55,613.1	−1.2			−55,613.1	−1.2	
2.1. Loans from international financial institutions							
2.2. Foreign government loans to RF	4,311.0	0.1			4,311.0	0.1	
2.3. Loans from foreign commercial banks and companies to RF	98,721.7	2.2			98,721.7	2.2	
Total Foreign Financing	47,419.7	1.1			47,419.7	1.1	
Total Financing	52,964.2	1.2	1,028.0	0.0	−49,016.7	−1.1	16,182.5	0.4

Table 8
RF Balance of Payments, 1995 to 3rd Quarter of 1999 (in Millions of USD)

	Q1	Q2	Q3	Q4
1995				
Current account	5,506	2,849	−819	425
Goods and nonfactor services	4,532	3,742	1,308	1,629
Goods (trade balance)	5,751	5,980	4,855	4,221
Exports of goods	19,059	20,399	20,494	22,711
Imports of goods	−13,308	−14,419	−15,639	−18,490
Nonfactor services	−1,219	−2,238	−3,547	−2,592
To nonresidents	2,139	2,766	2,733	2,887
By nonresidents	−3,358	−5,004	−6,280	−5,479
Balance of labor and capital services (revenue balance)	886	−883	−2,071	−1,299
Balance of capital services	897	−813	−1,923	−1,226
To nonresidents	2,559	612	410	531
By nonresidents	−1,662	−1,425	−2,333	−1,757
Current transfers	87	−10	−57	95
Received	191	174	160	285
Disbursed	−104	−184	−217	−190
Capital and financial account	−6,161	−1,802	−42	−13,845
Capital account	−22	−73	−173	−80
Capital transfers	−22	−73	−173	−80
Financial account	−6,139	−1,729	131	−13,765
Direct and portfolio investments	−1,322	106	563	932
Assets	−1,564	−150	−93	−23
Liabilities	242	256	656	955
Other investments	−4,817	−1,835	−432	−14,697
Assets	−2,624	1,035	5,794	−656
Forex holdings and deposits	−114	2,454	846	1,173
Trade credit and advance payments	−228	2	8,039	227
Loan disbursements (other than past-due)	1,817	3,748	1,408	1,585
Arrears	−4,156	−3,772	−1,398	−1,228
Other assets	57	−1,397	−3,101	−2,413
Liabilities	−2,193	−2,870	−6,226	−14,041
Domestic currency holdings and deposits	193	198	433	1,807
Trade credit and advance payments	395	−433	−1,278	−6,774
Contracted loans	−2,881	−2,758	−5,284	−9,927
Other liabilities	100	123	−97	853
Reserve asset adjustment	146	−263	187	1,006
Net errors and omissions	−3,118	791	−4,207	8,237
Overall balance	**−3,627**	**1,575**	**−4,881**	**−4,177**

Statistical Appendix

Table 8 (continued)

	Q1	Q2	Q3	Q4
Financing	3,627	−1,575	4,882	4,177
Reserve assets	−96	−5,936	−1,105	−3,249
Exceptional financing	3,109	3,920	5,319	6,343
Use of new loans by general government to finance deficit use of IMF loans	0	1,690	1,650	2,144
	0	1,690	1,650	2,144
Payment arrears	899	560	1,059	−1,387
Deferred payments for official external debt service	2,210	1,670	2,610	5,586
Other operations	614	441	668	1,083
Use of new loans by general government to finance deficit (other than IMF loans)	614	441	668	1,083
1996				
Current account	3,829	1,759	2,183	4,339
Goods and nonfactor services	3,323	3,423	4,005	6,465
Goods (trade balance)	4,641	4,921	5,064	8,442
Exports of goods	20,872	21,940	21,918	25,833
Imports of goods	−16,231	−17,019	−16,854	−17,391
Nonfactor services	−1,318	−1,498	−1,059	−1,977
To nonresidents	2,897	3,251	4,091	2,718
By nonresidents	−4,215	−4,749	−5,150	−4,695
Balance of labor and capital services (revenue balance)	483	−1,601	−1,878	−2,293
Balance of capital services	603	−1,491	−1,781	−2,215
To nonresidents	2,610	710	446	465
By nonresidents	−2,007	−2,201	−2,227	−2,680
Current transfers	23	−62	56	165
Received	151	122	159	333
Disbursed	−128	−184	−103	−168
Capital and financial account	−6,700	−5,260	−7,600	−5,569
Capital account	−219	−66	−79	−99
Capital transfers	−219	−66	−79	−99
Financial account	−6,481	−5,194	−7,521	−5,470
Direct and portfolio investments	1,872	1,613	999	6,965
Assets	9	−389	−163	−400
Liabilities	1,863	2,002	1,162	7,365
Other investments	−8,353	−6,807	−8,520	−12,435
Assets	−4,792	−8,122	−4,948	−11,441
Forex holdings and deposits	999	−5,102	−1,423	−4,379
Trade credit and advance payments	−1,626	−1,800	−1,700	−4,375
Loan disbursements (other than past-due)	2,424	3,123	2,267	1,685
Arrears	−4,612	−2,374	−1,295	−1,195
Other assets	−1,977	−1,969	−2,797	−3,177

Table 8 (continued)

	Q1	Q2	Q3	Q4
Liabilities	−3,561	1,315	−3,572	−994
Domestic currency holdings and deposits	46	−48	645	674
Trade credit and advance payments	75	−434	−571	131
Contracted loans	−3,288	−2	−3,614	−1,325
Other liabilities	−394	1,799	−32	−474
Reserve asset adjustment	−400	−798	−196	−90
Net errors and omissions	−2,170	−2,794	−1,133	−2,050
Overall balance	**−5,441**	**−7,093**	**−6,746**	**−3,370**
Financing	5,441	7,093	6,746	3,370
Reserve assets	−2,034	3,431	1,390	54
Exceptional financing	4,718	3,102	4,486	2,581
Use of new loans by general government to finance deficit	1,393	1,013	677	672
Use of IMF loans	1,393	1,013	677	672
Payment arrears	725	619	619	729
Deferred payments for official external debt service	2,600	1,470	3,190	1,180
Other operations	2,757	560	870	735
Use of new loans by general government to finance deficit (other than IMF loans)	2,757	560	870	735
1997				
Current account	4,040	−14	−853	382
Goods and nonfactor services	5,055	2,502	2,038	2,958
Goods (trade balance)	6,017	3,620	3,461	4,420
Exports of goods	21,154	20,654	21,718	25,402
Imports of goods	−15,137	−17,034	−18,257	−20,982
Nonfactor services	−962	−1,118	−1,423	−1,462
To nonresidents	2,915	3,437	4,265	3,516
By nonresidents	−3,877	−4,555	−5,688	−4,978
Balance of labor and capital services (revenue balance)	−974	−2,362	−2,719	−2,356
Balance of capital services	−904	−2,285	−2,617	−2,264
To nonresidents	2,417	618	569	536
By nonresidents	−3,321	−2,903	−3,186	−2,800
Current transfers	−41	−154	−172	−220
Received	126	59	87	77
Disbursed	−167	−213	−259	−297
Capital and financial account	−3,846	5,484	−2,855	20,663
Capital account	−115	−317	−187	−179
Capital transfers	−115	−317	−187	−179
Financial account	−3,731	5,801	−2,668	20,842

Table 8 (continued)

	Q1	Q2	Q3	Q4
Direct and portfolio investments	5,967	9,036	3,275	30,796
Assets	−443	−691	−972	−652
Liabilities	6,410	9,727	4,247	31,448
Other investments	−9,698	−3,235	−5,943	−9,954
Assets	1,209	−6,295	−9,952	−11,581
Forex holdings and deposits	−1,305	−1,936	−4,709	−4,515
Trade credit and advance payments	−859	−883	−1,649	−3,397
Loan disbursements (other than past-due)	4,055	2,340	396	212
Arrears	1,830	−2,736	−1,004	−1,138
Other assets	−2,512	−3,080	−2,986	−2,743
Liabilities	−10,907	3,060	4,009	1,627
Domestic currency holdings and deposits	−7,492	569	948	1,244
Trade credit and advance payments	−423	28	120	211
Contracted loans	−2,494	2,123	2,246	198
Other liabilities	−498	340	695	−26
Reserve asset adjustment	48	30	−49	−48
Net errors and omissions	−2,479	−1,207	−1,358	−2,709
Overall balance	**−2,237**	**4,293**	**−5,115**	**18,288**
Financing	2,237	−4,293	5,115	−18,288
Reserve assets	−1,331	−8,034	1,616	5,934
Exceptional financing	2,960	2,131	2,624	−26,637
Use of new loans by general government to finance deficit	646	701	677	0
Use of IMF loans	646	701	677	0
Payment arrears	994	1,080	1,107	−27,227
Deferred payments for official external debt service	1,320	350	840	590
Other operations	608	1,610	875	2,415
Use of new loans by general government to finance deficit (other than IMF loans)	608	1,610	875	2,415
1998				
Current account	−1,569	−3,673	777	6,110
Goods and nonfactor services	−174	296	4,130	9,407
Goods (trade balance)	872	1,595	4,794	9,591
Exports of goods	18,558	18,835	18,093	19,314
Imports of goods	−17,686	−17,240	−13,299	−9,723
Nonfactor services	−1,046	−1,299	−664	−184
To nonresidents	2,904	3,329	3,691	3,012
By nonresidents	−3,950	−4,628	−4,355	−3,196
Balance of labor and capital services (revenue balance)	−1,243	−3,807	−3,311	−3,239

Table 8 (continued)

	Q1	Q2	Q3	Q4
Balance of capital services	−1,153	−3,736	−3,279	−3,268
To nonresidents	2,426	761	503	310
By nonresidents	−3,579	−4,497	−3,782	−3,578
Current transfers	−152	−162	−42	−58
Received	69	71	54	76
Disbursed	−221	−233	−96	−134
				−16,064
	743	3,069	−8,849	−11,027
Capital and financial account				
Capital account	−92	−189	15	−117
Capital transfers	−92	−189	15	−117
Financial account	835	3,258	−8,864	−10,910
Direct and portfolio investments	3,929	4,513	431	1,049
Assets	−351	−847	252	−337
Liabilities	4,280	5,360	179	1,386
Other investments	−3,094	−1,255	−9,295	−11,959
Assets	−3,339	−2,392	−3,950	−6,500
Forex holdings and deposits	2,225	1,869	−1,814	−382
Trade credit and advance payments	−90	−1,157	−1,186	−4,385
Loan disbursements (other than past-due)	1,843	1,606	1,278	618
Arrears	−3,712	−2,791	−488	−436
Other assets	−3,605	−1,919	−1,740	−1,915
Liabilities	245	1,137	−5,345	−5,459
Domestic currency holdings and deposits	−964	418	−1,359	−861
Trade credit and advance payments	−58	119	86	175
Contracted loans	1,498	−93	−3,828	−3,858
Other liabilities	−231	693	−244	−915
Reserve asset adjustment	18	−1	7	−74
Net errors and omissions	−2,946	−3,055	−3,653	−119
Overall balance	**−3,754**	**−3,660**	**−11,718**	**−5,110**
Financing	3,504	2,986	11,613	4,573
Reserve assets	892	768	2,596	1,050
Exceptional financing	1,586	1,431	7,399	3,121
Use of new loans by general government to finance deficit	669	666	4,798	0
Use of IMF loans	669	666	4,798	0
Payment arrears	447	295	2,001	2,541
Deferred payments for official external debt service	470	470	600	580
Other operations	1,026	787	1,618	402

Table 8 (continued)

	Q1	Q2	Q3	Q4
Use of new loans by general government to finance deficit (other than IMF loans)	1,026	787	1,618	402
1999 (Estimated)				
Current account	4,716	4,406	5,628	10,239
Goods and services	5,850	6,129	8,314	11,667
Exports	17,322	19,244	21,251	25,929
Imports	−11,472	−13,116	−12,937	−14,262
Goods	6,531	6,886	9,204	12,681
Exports	15,538	16,953	18,651	23,521
Imports	−9,007	−10,067	−9,447	−10,840
Services	−681	−757	−890	−1,014
Exports	1,784	2,292	2,600	2,408
Imports	−2,465	−3,049	−3,490	−3,422
Balance of labor and capital services	−1,085	−1,799	−2,892	−1,728
Receivables	2,267	711	409	446
Payables	−3,352	−2,511	−3,302	−2,173
Labor	63	67	62	68
Receipts	102	111	111	102
Payments	−38	−45	−48	−34
Capital	−1,148	−1,866	−2,955	−1,795
Receivables	2,166	600	299	344
Payables	−3,314	−2,466	−3,253	−2,139
Current transfers	−48	76	206	300
Receipts	52	220	330	425
Payments	−100	−143	−124	−125
Capital and financial account	−3,988	−2,877	−4,604	−6,539
Capital account	−97	−33	−81	−122
Capital transfers	−97	−33	−81	−122
Receipts	198	208	192	285
Payments	−295	−240	−273	−406
Financial account	−3,891	−2,844	−4,523	−6,418
Direct investments	227	188	63	268
Abroad	−415	−563	−597	−570
To Russia	642	751	659	838
Portfolio investments	67	−588	−127	87
Assets	−23	−202	306	172
Liabilities	90	−386	−434	−86
Other investments	−5,258	−727	−5,535	−4,387
Assets	−6,380	−368	−5,385	−2,987
Forex holdings	122	1,017	−428	137
Current account balances and deposits	−1,095	−1,535	−473	−789
Trade credits and advance payments (granted)	−2,032	788	−3,077	−1,453
Contracted loans	1,800	2,187	139	731
Arrears	−4,059	−1,304	−226	−170

Table 8 (continued)

	Q1	Q2	Q3	Q4
Change in arrears of outstanding export revenues (forex and ruble-denominated) and nonreimbursed import advance payments	−1,173	−1,402	−1,254	−1,554
Other assets	56	−119	−66	112
Liabilities	1,123	−359	−150	−1,400
Domestic currency holdings	−14	−3	20	11
Current account balances and deposits	−258	644	−378	153
Trade credits and advance payments	104	77	48	−224
Contracted loans	−1,183	−2,104	2,421	−2,018
Arrears	2,441	1,202	−2,236	723
Other liabilities	33	−174	−25	−46
Reserve assets	969	−1,611	1,091	−2,227
Reserve assets adjustment	104	−107	−14	−158
Net errors and omissions	−728	−1,529	−1,024	−3,700
Overall balance	**0**	**0**	**0**	**0**

Source: RF Central Bank.

Name Index

Abalkin, Leonid, 42–43, 46, 58, 396
Adritnne, C., 119n20
Afanas'ev, A., 48n3
Afansyev, M., 441n, 443, 445n23
Aftalion, F., 8, 8n7, 11n13, 13n15
Aganbegyan, A., 35n7
Aghion, P., 463
Aglietta, M., 48n4
Albert, M., 33, 33n5
Alchian, A. A., 461
Aleksashenko, S., 49n6, 49–50
Alesina, A., 72n6, 87n22, 89n1, 90n2, 108n8, 108n9, 136n9, 366n30
Alexeev, M., 404n7
Allende, Salvador, 39n13
Almon, Charles, 843
Alvarez, F., 930n21
Anchishkin, A., 35n7
Anderson, H., 944n32
Anderson, N., 915n4
Anderson, R. E., 445n23
Andic, F., 83n15
Andreeff, W., 463n2
Antchak, R., 95n9
Archangel'skiy, S. I., 12n14
Arkhipov, S., 223–250, 251–308, 309–374
Arrow, K. J., 396
Aslund, A., 29n11
Atkeson, A., 930n21
Aukutsionek, S., 441n, 445n23, 451

Balcerowicz, Lezsek, 26n9
Baldini, N., 949n45
Balduzzi, P., 928n17
Barinov, V., 917n7
Barr, N., 588n1
Barro, R., 98n14

Barth, J., 517n
Batkibekov, S., 223–250, 251–308, 309–374
Bayar, A., 881n1
Bazarov, V. A., 11n12
Belousev, D., 48n3
Berezin, I. S., 48n3
Berezovsky, Boris, 226n3, 227
Berle, A. A., 463
Bertola, G., 928n17
Bhar, R., 952n48
Bialer, S., 33n4
Bizaguet, A., 83n15, 399n4
Black, B. S. R., 463
Blanchard, O., 47n2, 929n18, 943, 943n30
Blascyk, B., 404n7
Blasi, J., 441n, 445n23
Blejer, M., 119n20
Bliss, R., 939, 939n26
Bloor, K., 598n10
Bobylev, Yu., 675n1, 675–686, 789–838
Boettke, P. J., 37n11
Bogomolov, O. T., 46, 146n14
Böhm, A., 404n7, 409n, 414n11, 467n
Boskin, M. J., 881n1, 882n5
Box, G., 947n40
Boyko, M., 414n11
Brada, J., 448
Bradley, M., 922n13, 945n33
Braguinski, S., 90n4
Breedon, F., 915n4
Brezhnev, Leonid, 29, 30
Brid, R., 119n20
Brown, J. D., 448
Browning, E. K., 881n1
Brudzynski, R., 376
Bruno, M., 50n7

Bruzkus, B., 20, 20n2
Burda, M., 76n8
Burdekin, R. C. K., 91n5
Burkett, P., 91n5
Buzgalin, A., 46

Calvo, G., 144n13
Camdessus, Michel, 255
Campbell, J., 921n8, 928n17, 949, 949n43
Carlin, W. S., 445n23, 447–448
Caves, R., 331n17
Chari, V., 929n19, 929–930
Charkham, J., 463n2
Cheida, A., 591n6
Cherniavsky, A., 675n1
Chernomyrdin, Viktor, 58, 95n8, 145, 154, 160, 201, 254–255, 260, 307
Cherubini, U., 949n45
Christiano, L., 929n19, 929–930
Chubais, Anatoly, 160, 186, 225–226, 254–255, 257, 258, 311
Claessens, S., 445n23, 448, 451
Clark, R. C., 463n2
Clemens, Christiane, 882n3
Clinebell, J., 957n52
Coase, R. H., 396, 415, 416
Coffee, J. C., 482
Coleman, T., 913n2
Colton, T., 33n4
Copper, R. N., 313n5
Cordon, W. M., 313n5
Cukerman, A., 84n17, 136n9, 206n12
Cuthbertson, K., 922n13, 951n46

Dabrowski, M., 95n9, 375–391
Dahlquist, M., 946n36
Dai, Q., 939, 939n26
Dalin, S. A., 9n9, 10n11
Davis, C., 590n5
Deacon, M., 915n4
Democritus, 395
Demsetz, H., 396, 449, 461
Derry, A., 915n4
Dewenter, K., 400
Dillen, H., 928n17
DiNardo, J., 842n2, 927n
di Tella, G., 50n7
Djankov, S., 444n, 445n23, 448, 451
Dobrodei, V., 399n5
Dornbusch, Rüdiger, 39n13, 47, 47n1, 47n2, 50n7, 76n9, 106n4, 281–282n7
Doronin, I., 511–541

Drazen, A., 72n6, 89n1, 108n8, 144n13, 366n30
Drobyshevskaia, T., 251–308, 309–374
Drobyshevsky, S., 223–250, 251–308, 309–374, 839–853, 911–957, 959–971
Dubinin, Sergei, 154
Duffee, G., 921n8

Earle, J. S., 404n7, 445n23, 447, 448, 451
Easterly, W., 77n10, 174n13
Edwards, S., 39n13, 47n2, 76n9, 84n17, 106n4, 136n9, 206n12, 281–282n7, 373n34
Eichenbaum, M., 929n19, 929–930
Eichengreen, B., 312n4, 830n5, 959, 959n1
Eijffinger, S., 913n3
Elton, E., 913n3
Enders, W., 922n12
Engels, Friedrich, 23–24
Engen, E., 882n3
Engle, R., 848n7, 951n47, 952n49
Engsted, T., 922n13, 945n33, 949n44
Ensor, T., 590n5
Entov, R., 397n2, 445n23, 462, 463n2, 789–838
Ernst, M. M., 404n7
Estrin, S., 445n23, 447, 451
Evans, C., 931n23, 943n29
Ewing, B., 943n29

Falvey, R. E., 881n1
Fama, E., 922n14
Fedorenko, N., 35n7
Fedorov, B., 129, 145, 186, 257
Fedorov, S., 46
Fischer, Stanley, 47n2, 50n7, 78
Fisher, L., 913n2
Fisher, S., 220n17
Folster, S., 87n23
Fominykh, A., 441n, 443, 445n23
Foresi, S., 928n17
Frank, Max, 881n1
Frankel, Jeffrey A., 331n17
Fridman, Mikhail, 226n3
Friedman, Milton, 83n15
Fries, S., 445n23, 447–448
Frydman, R., 404n7
Fukuyama, Francis, 33n6

Gaidar, Yegor, 6n6, 19n1, 19–30, 21n3, 22n5, 26n9, 27n10, 29n11, 35n7, 43, 45,

57–59, 69n4, 92, 99n15, 117, 136, 138, 139–145, 186, 278, 311, 370n32, 416n12, 795–796
Garcia-Herrero, A., 832n8
Gavrilenkov, E., 69n3, 637–674, 659n1
Gemmell, N., 881n1
Gerashchenko, Viktor, 154
Gershman, R., 187n2
Glazyev, S., 46
Goldman, Marshall, 32n2, 37n11
Goldstone, J. A., 2n2
Goodfriend, M., 938n25
Gorbachev, Mikhail, 29–30, 31–32, 33n4, 36–37, 39–40, 43, 54, 755, 756
Gordon, R., 98n14
Granger, C., 922n12, 944n32
Granville, B., 48n5
Grapperhaus, F. H. M., 881n1
Gray, C. W., 449
Gray, C. H., 467n, 482
Grebenichenko, S., 784, 785
Green, R., 913n3
Green, T. C., 913n3
Griffiths, W., 843n4, 927n
Grilli, V., 98n14, 931n22
Grimaldi, I., 399n5
Grossman, S. J., 397
Gurevich, Yegor, 48n3
Gurova, T., 481n7
Gusinsky, V., 226n3
Gustafson, T., 33n4
Gutnik, V., 441n, 445n23

Haggard, S., 108n9
Hall, A., 944n32
Hall, R. E., 882n5
Halpern, L., 367n31
Hanke, S. H., 399n4
Hansen, L., 945n33
Hanson, R., 449
Hanson, Ph., 38n12, 412
Hanson, R. G., 467n, 482
Harris, S. E., 9n9
Hart, O. D., 397, 462
Harvey, A., 848n7
Hassler, U., 945n33
Hay, J., 463
Hayek, F., 20, 20n2, 21n3, 23, 23n7
Hayes, S., 922n13
Hellman, J. S., 98n13
Helpman, E., 144n13
Hibbs, D., 136n9

Hill, R. C., 843n4, 927n
Himmelfarb, C., 47n2
Hirschman, A. O., 2n1, 97, 463
Holcombe, Randall G., 881n1
Holland, P., 463n2, 464
Hosking, G., 32n1
Host-Madsen, P., 119n20
Hubbard, R., 882n5
Huizinga, H., 913n3
Hume, David, 395
Huntington, S. P., 6n5

Ibbotson, R., 913n2
Ikes, Barry, 48n3
Imai, K., 915n4
Ivanenko, S., 146n14
Ivanov, V., 606n12
Ivanter, V., 48n3, 48n4
Izryadnova, Olga, 309–374, 637–674, 789–838

Jacobson, L., 607n15
Jaroczinski, M., 379
Johnson, P., 922n13, 944n32, 945, 945n35
Johnson, S., 412
Johnston, J., 842n2, 927n
Johnston, R. B., 373n34
Jones, Ronald W., 331n17
Jorgenson, D. W., 882n5
Joyce, W., 37n11
Judge, G., 843n4, 927n

Kadotchnikov, P., 1, 881–909
Kahn, D., 957n52
Kaminski, G., 959, 959n2, 962
Kamstra, M., 485
Kantorovich, G., 48n3
Kapelyushnikov, R., 441n, 445n23, 451
Karlova, N., 543–584
Karyagina, T., 197n5
Kasyanov M., 321n12
Kaufman, R. R., 108n9
Kehoe, P., 930n21
Khasbulatov, R., 101
Khizha, G., 95n8
Khodorkovsky, M., 226n3
Khoroshev, S., 442n, 468
Khramova, I., 543–584
Kiguel, M. A., 50n8, 144n13
Kikeri, S., 83n15, 399n4, 400
Kim, K., 938n25

Kirichenko, N., 90n3
Kiriyenko, Sergei, 255–258, 260, 263, 275, 278–279, 287, 289–291, 307
Klepach, A., 48n3, 445n23, 451
Kliachko, T., 606n12
Kloc, K., 376, 384–385
Klyamkin, I. M., 762n7, 766n10, 772, 772n16
Kobrinskaya, L., 432n15
Koch, T., 913n3
Koen, V., 69n3
Kolganov, A., 46
Kolosnytsyn, Igor, 737–752
Kornai, J., 21n3, 22n5, 26n9
Kosareva, N., 618, 618n1
Kostiukov, Y., 49n6, 49–50
Kotz, D., 39n14
Koval, T., 755–787
Kraakman, R., 463
Kroll, H., 412
Kroumova, M., 441n, 445n23
Krueger, G., 447
Krugman, P., 79n13, 176n15, 372, 372n33, 374, 374n39
Kruse, D., 441n, 445n23
Kryuchkova, P., 445n23, 451
Kuznets, S., 742
Kuznetsov, P., 441n, 443, 445n23, 451
Kuznetsov, V. I., 402n6
Kydland, F., 157n30

Landesmann, M., 448
Lane, P., 317n8
Lapkin, V., 762n7
La Porta, R., 453
Latsis, O., 29n11
Lebed, Alexander, 184
Lee, T.-C., 843n4, 927n
Lehn, K., 449
Lemmen, J., 913n3
Lenin, V. I., 11n12
Leonova, N., 687–713
Leschchenko, L., 445n23, 451
Levada, Yu A., 756n2, 757, 757n3, 780n22, 781n24, 787
Lewis, K., 334n20
Ligachev, Ye., 46
Lilien, D., 952n49
Limpaphayom, P., 938n25
Lindbeck, A., 136n9
Linz, S., 447

Little, I. M. D., 313n5
Liviatan, N., 50n8, 144n13
Lizondo, S., 959, 959n2
Longstaff, F., 949, 949n43
Lopez-de-Silanes, F., 453
Lucas, R., 78n12, 85n18
Luetkepohl, H., 843n4, 927n
Lugovoy, O., 855–880
Lumpkin, S., 922n13, 945n33
Luzhkov, Yu., 46, 785
Lvov, D., 46, 278
Lyapina, S., 483n8
Lynch, G., 943n29

McAuley, M., 33n4
McCafferty, S., 943, 943n30
McCallum, B., 928n17, 931n22
McFaul, M., 414n11
McGuire, T. J., 882n4
Maevskiy, V., 48n3
Mal'ginov, G., 441n, 445n23
Malov, A., 90n3
Maltesta, P., 400
Manchester, P. B., 881n1
Mankiw, N. G., 921n8, 946n37, 946n39
Marer, P., 404n7
Mark, S. T., 882n4
Markov, A., 606n12
Marshall, D., 931n23, 943n29
Marx, Karl, 396
Masciandro, D., 98n14
Maslyukov Yu., 285, 288
Matsuyama, K., 86n19
Mau, Vladimir, 1–15, 15n16, 25n8, 31–44, 35n8, 39n15, 89–103, 95n7, 98n13, 159–181, 183–222, 188n3, 223–250, 251–308, 396n1, 789–838
Maynard, A., 598n10
Means, G., 463
Melnikov, A., 46
Mikhailov, A., 46, 146n14
Mill, J. S., 395–396
Mills, T., 842n3
Minow, N., 463n2
Miron, J., 921n8, 946n37
Mironov, A., 591n6
Mishkin, F., 930n20, 949n45
Modigliani, F., 943n31
Mogilewski, R., 376
Monks, R., 463n2
Moore, J., 397

Murphy, G., 915n4
Murphy, K., 87n21

Nautz, D., 945n33
Nellis, J., 83n15, 399n4, 400
Nemtsov, Boris, 225–226, 254–255, 785
Newey, W., 922n11
Ng, V., 951n47
Nikologorsky, 49n6, 49–50
Nitzsche, D., 922n13
Nolle, D., 517n
Nordhaus, W., 136n9, 185
North, Douglass, 93n6, 396, 461
Nove, Alec, 32n1
Nozdran', N. G., 48n3

Obsteld, M., 175n14, 311n2, 316n7
Odegaard, B., 913n3
Oldman, O., 119n20

Palm, F., 947n40
Paltsev, Yegor, 954n51
Pantin, V., 762n7
Papke, L. E., 882n4
Pappe, Ye., 97n12
Park, T., 952n50
Pavlov, V., 43, 545
Perevalov, Yu, 399n5
Perlmutter, T., 414n11
Perotti, R., 310n1
Persson, T., 87n22, 136n9
Pervozvanskaya, T., 917n7
Pervozvanski, A., 917n7
Petrakov, N., 35n7, 46
Petrenko, E., 762n7
Phelps, E., 47n2
Phillips, P., 945n33
Pindyck, R., 846n5
Pistor, K., 98n13
Pitelin, A., 48n3, 675n1
Plato, 395
Pohl, G., 445n23, 451
Polozkov, I., 44
Popova, V., 675n1
Prentice, D., 463n2, 464
Prescott, E., 157n30
Prikhodko, S., 687–713, 789–838
Primakov, Yevgeny, 276–277, 280–283, 286–288, 306–308, 309, 311, 323, 355, 789–790
Pugachev, V., 48n3, 675n1

Putin, Vladimir, 311, 365–366, 789–790, 792, 793, 795, 797–798

Radygin, A., 395–459, 397n2, 414n11, 434n16, 435n18, 441n, 445n23, 461–510, 475n5, 491n13, 789–838
Railean, V., 404n7
Rajapatirana, S., 313n5
Rakovsky Ch., 59
Rapaczynski, A., 404n7
Rasmusen, E., 117n19
Reagan, Ronald, 33
Rebelo, S., 144n13
Reinhart, C., 959, 959n2
Renard, J., 603n11
Robins, R., 952n49
Rodrick, D., 87n22
Rogoff, K., 136n9, 175n14, 311n2, 316n7
Rosanov, Vasili, 396
Rose, A., 312n4, 830n5, 959, 959n1
Rosenfeld, B., 606n12, 947n40
Rosevaer, A., 447
Rossel, E., 284
Rosser, J. B., 32n3
Rosser, M. V., 32n3
Roubini, N., 108n9, 136n9, 931n22
Rowland, D., 590n4
Rozhdestvenskaya, I., 585–615
Rubinfeld, D., 846n5
Rudnik, B., 607n15
Rutskoy, A., 60
Ryzhkov, N., 29–30, 43, 46, 545

Sachs, J. D., 98n13, 136n9
Sahay, R., 220n17
Salama, P., 47n2
Salyer, K., 921n8, 922n10
Samson, I., 404n7
Sapir, Jacques, 48n3, 48n4
Sargent, T., 76n8, 943n31
Savelyev, O., 780
Schlaffer, M., 445n23, 447–448
Schleifer, A., 108n8
Schoenholtz, K., 921n8
Schumpeter, Joseph, 22n6
Seabright, P., 445n23, 447–448
Seleznyov, G., 281n6
Serova, E., 543–584, 675–686, 789–838
Shapiro, C., 399, 399n4
Shatalin, S., 35n7, 43, 46, 58
Sheiman, I., 597n7

Shiller, R., 921n8, 943n31, 946n36, 946n38
Shirley, M., 83n15, 399n4, 400
Shirokova, T., 606n12
Shishkin, S., 585–615, 607n15
Shleifer, A., 87n21, 400, 403, 414n11, 453
Shmelev, Nikolai, 46
Shmeleva, N., 461–510
Shpilko, S. P., 768, 771n14
Shumeyko, V., 95n8
Shvyrkov, G., 606n12
Siklos, P., 832n9
Silaev, I., 54
Simonsen, M. H., 106n5
Sims, C., 931n22
Sinel'nikov-Murylev, Sergei, 29n11, 41n16, 48n5, 45–61, 65–87, 81n14, 105–126, 124n22, 126n26, 127–157, 159–181, 183–222, 188n3, 223–250, 251–308, 309–374, 789–838, 881–909
Singh, I., 448
Singleton, K., 939, 939n26
Skinner, J. S., 882n3, 882n5
Skokov, Yu., 46
Smirnov, A., 717–736
Smirnov, S., 675n1
Smith, Adam, 397–398
Smolensky, A., 226n3
Sobel, R. S., 881n1
Solow, R., 506
Soretz, S., 882n3
Soskovets, O., 95n8, 186
Starodubrovskaya, I., 15n16, 617–634
Stepashin, Sergei, 311, 323, 327, 365, 789–790
Stevens, J., 957n52
Stiglitz, J., 396, 463
Stock, D., 913n3
Stryke, R., 618, 618n1
Summers, L. H., 882n5, 921n8
Sutela, P., 25n8, 35n8
Svensson, L., 928n17, 946n36
Switzer, L., 952n50

Tabellini, G., 84n17, 87n22, 98n14, 136n9, 206n12
Tambovtsev, V., 606n13
Tamirisa, N., 373n34
Tanggaard, C., 922n13, 945n33
Taranov, A., 591n6
Tarasova, A., 463
Taylor, M., 949n45
Telyukov, A., 590n4

Thatcher, Margaret, 33
Thirsk, J., 12n14
Thomas, R., 461
Tiao, G., 947n40
Ticktin, H., 37n11
Tikhonova, T., 543–584
Tirole, J., 463, 464
Titov, V., 481n7
Tobin, J., 462
Tocqueville, A., 2n1
Trofimov, G., 87n23, 105–126, 127–157, 159–181, 183–222, 188n3
Trounin, I., 251–308, 309–374
Tsukhlo, S., 187n2, 789–838
Tupolev, A. N., 497
Turnovsky, S., 929n18, 943, 943n30

Uluykaev, Alexei, 45–61, 223–250
Urnov, M., 780n20

Valier, J., 47n2
van Deventer, D., 915n4
Vasicek, O., 939n26
Vassilyev, D., 414n11
Vegh, C., 144n13, 220n17
Vickers, J., 83n15, 399n4, 400
Vinogradov, V., 226n3
Vinslav, Y., 493
Vishny, R. W., 87n21, 108n8, 400, 414n11, 453
Vite, O., 48n3
Volkonskiy, V., 48n3
Volkov, A. T., 481n7
Volovik, N., 687–713
Volsky, A., 46, 95, 95n8
von Mises, Ludwig, 20, 20n2, 21n3
Vuylsteke, C., 399n4
Vyakhirev, R., 226n3

Weir, F., 39n14
West, K., 922n11
White, S., 37n11
Williamson, O. E., 399, 443n22, 461
Willig, R., 399, 399n4
Wolf, H., 77n10, 174n13
Woodward, R., 404n7
Wouters, H., 463n2
Wyplosz, C., 76n8, 312n4, 367n31, 830n5, 959, 959n1

Yaremenko, Y., 46
Yarrow, G., 83n15, 398n3, 399, 399n4, 400

Name Index

Yarygina, T., 745, 745n1, 761n6
Yasin, E., 35n7, 197n6
Yavlinsky, Grigory, 35n7, 43, 46, 47, 53, 54, 57–58, 60, 90n3, 90n4, 146n14, 220, 785
Yegorov, N., 186
Yeltsin, Boris, 44, 58, 127, 128, 135, 136–138, 159–160, 163n1, 184–186, 189, 193, 194, 197, 200–204, 206–208, 216–217, 221–222, 225, 248, 251–252, 255, 257, 275–276, 284, 420–421, 628, 756–757, 770, 772, 777–779, 783, 789, 867, 880

Zadornov, M., 146n14
Zakharov, A., 511–541
Zaslavskaya, T., 35n7, 755n1, 776, 777n18
Zecchini, S., 312n3
Zellner, A., 947n40
Zhang, H., 922n13, 945, 945n33, 945n34
Zhirinovsky, Vladimir, 44, 138, 772
Zhukov, V., 441n, 445n23, 451
Zubova, L. G., 588n2
Zyuganov, Gennady, 46, 184, 185, 196–197, 197n5, 201n9, 777–778, 785

Subject Index

Administrative stabilization model, 43–44
Adverse selection, 71, 200–201
Afghanistan, 66
Africa
  delayed stabilization in, 221
  privatization in, 399
Agrarian Institute, 568
Agrarian Party
  budget of 2001 and, 791
  in economic crisis of 1998, 276–277, 280
  in presidential elections of 1996, 186
Agro-industrial complex, 543–584, 645, 821–825
  central bank credits to, 107–108
  under central planning, 543–546
  credit system for, 563–574
  double tariffs, 580–581
  downstream sector, 551, 556–562
  in economic crisis of 1998, 289, 294
  economic reform and, 27, 34, 546–556
  family farm model, 546–547, 548–551, 552–554
  food shortages, 52–53, 202, 221, 279, 289–290
  growth of, 23–24
  income reduction, 22, 24
  labor market, 725, 729
  land code reform, 554–556
  leasing in, 555, 572–573, 580
  livestock production, 574–577, 580, 821–824
  oil and gas revenues versus, 24, 28–30
  production cooperatives, 550–551, 570
  reform of foreign trade regulation, 581–583

republic versus USSR, 41–42
state procurements reform, 556–558, 561
state support, 574–581
subsidies in, 544–545, 574–581
vertical integration of, 560–562
work collectives of agricultural enterprises, 547–550
Agroprombank, 511, 563, 565
Albania, privatization in, 406, 407, 408, 437–438
Alcohol, 691–692, 698
Alfa Bank, 569–570
Ancien régime, 7–8, 9n, 32
Anomalies of Economic Growth, The (Gaidar), 19
Antei, 497
Antidumping restrictions, 371, 712–713
Anti-inflationism, 93–94
Appliances
  importing of, 707
  production of, 709–710
April 1993 referendum, 136–138, 769–770
Argentina
  bank capital requirements, 530
  banking crisis, 540
  import-substituting industrialization, 21
Armenia
  corporate governance in, 469
  foreign loans to, 379
  impact of Russian financial crisis on, 381, 383, 387, 388, 391
  inflation rates 1992–1998, 378
  privatization in, 406, 408

Subject Index 1009

Asia
  currency crisis of 1997, 242–244, 248, 254, 379–380, 383, 709
  privatization in, 399
Assignats, 10
August putsch (1991). *See* Putsch of 1991
August syndrome, 806
Aviabank, 511
Aviastar (Ulianovski), 497
AVPK Sukhoi, 497
Avtoselkhozmash Holding, 491n14
Azerbaijan
  impact of Russian financial crisis on, 376, 381, 383, 387
  inflation rates 1992–1998, 378
  privatization in, 406, 408

Babayevskoye, 484
Balance of payments
  in 1995, 179
  in 1997, 241
  in 1998, 266–272, 315
  in 1999, 313–316
  of CIS countries, 383–385
Balance of trade
  in 1990, 699
  in 1991, 699
  in 1999, 711
Baltika group, 484
Banking system, 511–541. *See also* Central bank; Commercial banks
  Asian currency crisis of 1997, 242–244, 248, 254, 379–380, 383, 709
  of CIS countries, 384–385, 391
  concentration of capital in, 515–519
  corporate governance role of, 462–463
  currency crisis of 1994, 154
  economic crisis of 1998, 272–273, 516
  emergence of contemporary, 511–515
  foreign debt in 1999, 367–368
  investment in fixed capital, 342
  loans-for-shares auctions, 422–423
  as pro-inflationary, 93, 97, 279
  reform of financial markets, 804–805
  regional, 514–515, 518, 525
  regulating and monitoring activities of, 537–541
  regulating liquidity of, 530, 533–537
  stability of, 527–533
  takeovers, 484
Bank of Russia. *See* Central bank

Bankruptcy, 478–482
  of commercial banks and financial groups, 437, 539–541
  corruption and, 479–481
  fictitious, 433
  insurance funds for, 434
  limitations for corporate governance, 478–479
  of nonprofitable enterprises, 86
  number of petitions, 479, 480
  outlawing of, 288, 397
  protection of shareholders, 481
Barter, 51, 640, 833
  in agro-industrial complex, 560, 561, 571
  in international business, 697
  price liberalization of 1992, 70–71
  reduction of, 343–347, 364–365
  tax evasion through, 70–71, 81, 82, 200
Basel Agreement, 530, 531
Bashkiria, 484, 792, 793
Belarus
  budget deficit, 378, 380
  impact of Russian financial crisis on, 375–376, 381, 382, 387, 390
  inflation rates 1992–1998, 378
  monetary union between Russia and, 57
  privatization in, 407, 409
  revolution and state, 5
Biopreparat, 488
Black Tuesday (October 11, 1994), 160–161, 523
Board of directors, 465
Bolivia, economic stabilization, 50
Bolshevik revolution (1917)
  economic aspects, 4, 11, 13
  food shortages, 52
Bosnia, privatization in, 408
Brazil, 21, 47
Bribery, 802
Budget
  of 1992, 105–106
    process for adopting, 109, 116–117
    reconstruction of, 118–126
  of 1993, 128–131
    process for adopting, 129
    reconstruction of, 138–139, 140–143
  of 1994, 139
    process for adopting, 145–149, 159
    reconstruction of, 149–154

Budget (cont.)
  of 1995
    process for adopting, 162, 163
    reconstruction of, 163–170
    revenues from privatization, 424
  of 1996
    crisis of tax system, 196–201
    process of adopting, 208–209
    reconstruction of, 209, 210–214
    revenues from privatization, 424
  of 1997
    crisis, 228–241
    reconstruction of, 235, 236–240, 362
    revenues from privatization, 423, 424
  of 1998
    performance of, 290–294, 296–297
    process of adopting, 255, 256
    reconstruction of, 256, 292–293, 296–297, 362
    revenues from privatization, 424
  of 1999
    enlarged government budget, 360–362, 827–828
    fixed capital investment, 343
    government debt, 356–360
    interbudgetary relations, 355–356
    process of adopting, 286, 287, 289, 310
    reconstruction of, 347–365
    revenues from privatization, 423–425
  of 2000, 825–829
    enlarged government budget, 827–828
    expenditures reform, 801–802
    revenues from privatization, 424
  of 2001, 791
    balancing, 794–795
Budgetary crisis
  of 1991–1993, 66, 80
  of 1995–1996, 83–85, 196–201, 208
  of 1997, 224, 228–241
Budget Code, 228, 250
Budget deficit, 41
  of 1992, 105–106, 108–109, 112, 117, 118
  of 1993, 128–132, 136, 138–139
  of 1994, 146, 149–154, 156
  of 1995, 161, 162, 170, 522
  of 1996, 208, 217
  of 1997, 231
  of 1998, 290–291
  of 1999, 354, 356–359
  ceiling on, 131
  central bank financing of, 74–75
  of CIS countries, 378–380
  constitutional prohibition of, 103
  in crisis of 1997–1998, 262–266
  before crisis of August, 1998, 254
  financing
    by central bank credits, 132
    loans from central bank, 356–357, 533
    by sale of government securities, 131, 162
  inflation and, 47
  after putsch of 1991, 47, 52, 60–61, 66–67, 74
Budget policy
  of 1992, 105–126
  of 1993, 128–132, 136
  of 1994, 154
  of 1995, 163
  of 1996, 203–205
  of 1998, 277–280, 287–294
Bulgaria
  corporate governance in, 465, 466–467, 469
  impact of Russian financial crisis on, 381–382
  privatization in, 406, 408
BurTEK, 494

Cabinet of Ministers, resignation in 1998, 255–256
Cadre revolution, 37
Capital (Marx), 396
Capital inflow
  in 1995, 179
  in 1997, 235, 241
  in 1999, 372–373
  after presidential elections of 1996, 207
Capitalism. *See also* Privatization
  rapid industrialization and, 22
  transition from socialism to, 66
Capitalism versus Capitalism (Albert), 33
Cash business transactions, 199
Catch-up industrialization, 799
CATE (Closed Administrative Territorial Entities), 829
CBR bonds, 373
Central bank. *See also* Banking system; Central bank credits; Central bank refinancing rate; Commercial banks; Credit policy; Foreign

Subject Index

currency reserves; Gold reserves; Monetary emission; Monetary policy
  accountability to populist Parliament, 73, 98, 99, 100, 102
  authority of, 102
  before crisis of August, 1998, 252–254
  currency corridor of, 78–79
  export controls, 692, 696–697
  financing of budget deficit, 74–75
  independence from legislature, 159
  lending policy, 521–522
  lending to Ministry of Finance, 313
  monetary emission as exclusive power of, 103
  refinancing credits, 533–534
  regulation of commercial banks, 527–541
  removal from executive control, 98
  State Duma appointment of chairman, 102–103
Central bank credits. *See also* Credit policy
  to agro-industrial complex, 107–108, 564–568
  to commercial banks, 133, 523
  to enterprises, 100, 107, 523
  to industrial sector, 107–108
Central bank refinancing rate
  in 1992, 115–116
  in 1993, 133
  in 1994, 156
  in 1995, 171
  in 1996, 215
  in 1997, 242, 246, 252–253
  in 1999, 325, 326
Central bank reserves. *See* Foreign currency reserves; Gold reserves
Central Committee (CPSU)
  economic reform memoranda, 35
  Twenty-seventh Congress, 37
Central planning. *See* Planned economy
Chechnya, 155, 160, 186, 342–343
Chemicals, 662, 702, 712–713
Chernobyl nuclear plant disaster, 66
Chief executive officers (CEOs), in unitary state-owned enterprises, 489–490
Chile
  economic stabilization, 50
  populism, 39n
  privatization in, 410

China
  abandonment of socialist model, 24–25
  agro-industrial complex, 27
  economic reform, 26, 34, 67
  revolution and economy, 7
  revolution and state, 5
Cigarettes, 691–692, 698
CIS countries, 375–391. *See also names of specific countries*
  contagion effect on financial markets, 383–385
  corporate governance in, 469
  economic impact of Russian financial crisis, 386–390
  flaws of economic transformation process and, 377–380
  foreign trade impact of Russian financial crisis, 380–383
  foreign trade turnover with CIS countries, 710–711
  privatization in, 444
  psychological factors in Russian financial crisis, 385
Civic Union, 95
Civil Code, 489, 490, 607
Clearing system, problems of 1992, 70
Clothing, importing of, 705, 707
Collective farms, 22, 543–550. *See also* Agro-industrial complex
Colombia, bank capital requirements, 530
Combined holdings, 492
Commercial banks, 519–527. *See also* Banking system; Central bank
  agro-industrial complex and, 564–565
  bankruptcy of, 437
  comparative analysis of, 517
  creation of, 511–513
  foreign, in Russia, 513–514
  functions of, 519–521
  as institutional investors, 433–434
  minimum charter capital, 529
  minimum shareholder equity, 529–530, 531
  and real sector of economy, 521–527
  regulating liquidity of, 533–537
Commission on Credit Policy, 146
Commission on Improvement of the Economic Mechanism, 587
Commodity credits, 560, 561, 567–571, 580

Communications
  growth in demand for, 335, 646–647
  increased investment in, 339–340
Communism
  as artificial creation, 5
  Russian exit from, 1
Communist Party
  budget of 2001 and, 791
  in economic crisis of 1998, 276–277, 280
  in presidential elections of 1996, 185, 186
Compulsory health insurance (CHI), 591–599
Concept of Agri-Food Policies for Years 2001 Through 2010, 822
Concept of Managing State-Owned Property and of Privatization in the Russian Federation, 427
Conciliation Commission, 162
Confidence dilemma, stabilization and, 75
Consolidation of shares, 436
Constitutional consolidation (1992–1994), 98–103, 135–138, 159
  changes affecting economy, 102–103
  dual power problem and, 56, 99, 139
  problems leading to, 98–101
  referendum of 1993, 101
Construction industry, 646
  financing projects, 29
  labor market, 725, 729, 730, 732, 733
Consumer goods production, 681–682
Consumer price index (CPI). *See also* Inflation rate
  in 1992, 116
  in 1996, 206–207, 209
  in 1999, 316–317, 322, 325–326, 328
  modeling, 1992–1998, 839–853
Consumption structure of economy, 652–654
Contagion effect, 383–385
Contribution to the Critique of Political Economy, A (Marx), 396
Convertible bonds, 436
Cooperatives, private enterprise, 37–38
Corporate governance, 461–510
  bankruptcy threat, 464, 478–482
  financial-industrial groups (FIGs), 491–504
  financial markets, 464, 471–478
  internal mechanisms, 464–468

  legislation, 464, 466–467, 468–474
  objectives of, 469–471
  role of banks, 462–463
  in state-owned enterprises, 485–490
  takeover threat, 464, 482–485
Corporate sector. *See also* Corporate governance; Privatization
  concentration of ownership, 445–454
  establishment of corporate control, 410–411, 430–437, 452
Corruption. *See also* Tax evasion
  in agro-industrial complex, 566
  bribery, 802
  embezzlement, 55, 762
  of enterprise directors, 36–38, 70–71, 86–87, 413, 414, 437, 451–452
  fight against, 226–227
  privileges and preferences in, 698
  smuggling, 691–692
  weak government and, 285, 290
Council of Ministers, agricultural policy, 41–42
Counter-party trade, 70
CPSU. *See* Central Committee (CPSU)
Credit policy. *See also* Central bank credits
  of 1992, 100, 107–108, 111–116, 124–125
  of 1993, 131–133
  of 1994, 155–157
  of 1995, 161–162, 171–172
  of 1995–1996, 534–537
  of 1997, 235–241
Credit ratings, of Russia, 255
Credit risk, 831
Criminal activity. *See* Corruption
Croatia
  corporate governance in, 469
  privatization in, 407, 408
Culture, 587, 602–605
  commercialization of, 608
  film-making, 602–603
  indicators in, 614
  labor market, 725
  parliamentary elections of 1993, 603–604
  printed word media, 605
  public expenditures 1991–1998, 603, 604, 609, 610
  shadow privatization in, 605–607
  structural changes in, 615
  television and radio, 604–605

Subject Index

theater, 603
Currency corridor
  introduction in 1995, 78–79, 176–177
  after presidential elections of 1996, 219
  before presidential elections of 1996, 206
Currency crisis
  of 1994, 160–161
  Asian currency crisis of 1997, 242–244, 248, 254, 379–380, 383, 709
  devaluation of ruble (1998), 295, 306, 311–313, 316–317, 333–334, 336–337, 343–344, 366–374, 380–381, 674, 711, 790, 832
Customs Code, 690
Customs Union, 696
Czech Fund for National Property, 450
Czechoslovakia
  economic reform, 27, 34
  market regulation, 25
  privatization in, 406
Czech Republic
  bankruptcies, 480
  corporate governance in, 465, 466–467, 469, 472–473
  health care reforms, 589
  privatization in, 406, 408, 410, 429, 445–446, 448, 449–451
  stock market, 472–473

Davos Forum, 285
Democracy
  enterprise director elections, 37
  under Gorbachev, 39–40
Deposit operations, 534
Depository receipts, 476
Derivatives, in privatization process, 421, 427, 436
Devaluation of currency, in CIS countries, 386
Devaluation of ruble (1998), 295, 306, 311–313, 316–317, 333–334, 336–337, 343–344, 366–374, 380–381, 674, 711, 790, 832
Developed socialism. *See* Mature socialism
Development finance, new sources, 28, 29
Dirigisme, 33, 282–283
Dollarization
  before presidential elections of 1996, 195
  after putsch of 1991, 51

Dollar-ruble exchange rate
  in 1992, 116
  in 1994, 157
  in 1995, 173–177, 178–179
  in 1996, 204, 219–220
  in 1997, 244
  in 1998, 261–262, 303–305, 695
  in 1999, 320–322, 327
Downsizing, 721, 729–730
Dual power, 4, 56, 99, 139
Duma. *See* State Duma

Economic crisis
  of 1998
    anticrisis measures, 256–262
    devaluation of ruble, 295, 306, 311–313, 316–317, 333–334, 336–337, 343–344, 366–374, 380–381, 674, 711, 790, 832
    economic issues in, 274–275, 276–280, 959–971
    evolution of, 251–262
    factors leading to, 262–274, 959–971
    impact on neighbors, 375–391
    political issues in, 275–280
    shift in ownership distribution, 437
  under Gorbachev, 29–30, 31, 36–40, 61
  as inevitable, 19–30
  Southeast Asian currency market, 242–244, 248, 254, 379–380, 383, 709
  as state crisis, 40–44
Economic development, socialist model, 21–25
Economic reform. *See also* Financial stabilization; Liberal market reform; Socialist economic reform
  Abalkin anticrisis program, 42–43
  500 Days program, 43, 45, 53, 57–58
  liberalization pattern, 33–36, 39–40, 687–697
  mobilization pattern, 33–39
  new phase of, 789–807
  options, 25–28, 33–36
  political stabilization in, 789–795
  Program-91, 45–47, 50–54, 58–60
  republic versus USSR, 41–42
  Strategic Program (Gref program), 796–807
Education, 587, 599–602
  commercialization of, 608
  contradiction in direction of reform, 599–600

Education (cont.)
  growth of nongovernmental sector in, 601–602
  indicators in, 613
  labor market, 725, 732
  legislative framework for reform, 600–601
  public expenditures 1991–1998, 603, 609, 610
  public spending by country, 586
  shadow privatization in, 605–607
  structural changes in, 615
EES Rossii, 488
Efficiency
  of privatized enterprises, 447–448, 451, 452
  profitability and, 506
Egyptian civilization, 397, 398
Elections. *See* President; State Duma
Electric power. *See* Public utilities
Electronic equipment, importing of, 707, 709–710
Electronic Lot Trading System (SELT), 261–262, 305, 320–321, 327
Embezzlement
  public attitudes toward, 762
  after putsch of 1991, 55
Energy sector. *See* Fuel and energy sector
Engineering, mechanical, 675, 681, 682, 709
English Revolution, 7, 10, 12
Enterprise directors. *See also* State-owned enterprises (SOEs)
  conflict between old and new, 431–433, 437, 451–454
  corruption, 37–38, 70–71, 86–87, 413, 414, 437, 451–452
  in early stages of reform, 70
  elections, 37
  inflationary expectations for, 187–188
Enterprises. *See* State-owned enterprises (SOEs)
Entrepreneurship. *See also* Privatization
  factors holding back, 807
  opportunities, 38
  public attitude toward, 761
Estonia
  constitutional prohibition of budget deficit, 103
  health care reforms, 589
  impact of Russian financial crisis on, 376, 381, 391
  national currency, 51–52
  privatization in, 406, 408, 410
Eurobonds, 373, 476
European Bank for Reconstruction and Development (EBRD), 381
European Commission, 60
European Union, 513, 559, 712–713
Eurostat, 742
Exchange rate corridor. *See* Currency corridor
Excise tax
  on imports into Russian Federation, 691–692, 698
  after putsch of 1991, 60
  replacement of turnover tax, 79–80, 125–126
Expert Institute, 514
Export-Import Bank of Japan, 328–329
Exports
  duties, 692–697
  in 1995, 165, 179
  after putsch of 1991, 60
  export regimes in 1994, 693
  oil, 694, 695–696
  quotas, 694–697
  types of, 700–705
  volume in 2000, 813–814
Extended Fund Facility (EFF) program, 215

February revolution (1917). *See* Bolshevik revolution (1917)
Federal Commission for Securities Markets (FCSM), 430
Federal Customs Tariff Law, 690–691
Federal Employment Law, 717, 719–720
Federal Employment Service, 717
Federal Fund for Financial Aid to the Regions (FAR), 355–356
Federal Securities Commission, 257
Federal Tax Service, 288
Federation Council
  approval of budget of 1994, 146
  approval of budget of 1995, 163
  approval of legislation by, 102
  changing rules for makeup of, 792–793, 794
Fiat, 10–11
Film-making, 602–603
Financial-industrial groups (FIGs), 491, 502–504
  managing and monitoring, 503

Subject Index 1015

methods of creating, 502–503
regulation of, 499, 502
Financial stabilization
administrative stabilization model, 43–44
confidence dilemma and, 75
debates on achieving, 46–50
delayed or deferred, 72–74, 89–92, 220–222, 223
as focus of socialist economic system, 19–20
honeymoon effect and, 79, 177
impact on social services, 363–366
interest rates and, 77–78
opposing views on, 45–46, 92–97, 278–286
orthodox approach to, 74–79
preconditions for, 73–74, 159–161
as requirement for growth, 85
resistance to, 91–92
seasonal issues in, 90–91, 107–108, 559–560
success of 1995–1996, 72
time period for, 75
Finland
arms exports to, 704
banking crisis, 540
industrial structure, 658, 659
Fiscal crisis
of 1991–1993, 79–82
in revolutionary situations, 3–4, 6, 7–9
taxing capacity of state, 8–10
Fiscal policy. *See also* Budget; Budget deficit; Budget policy; Gross domestic product (GDP); Tax revenues
of 1992, 105–126
of 1993, 118, 136
of 1994, 147–148, 154–155, 156
of 1995, 172
of 1996, 203–205
of 1997, 255, 640
of 1998, 256
nonmonetary views of inflation and, 49–50
after putsch of 1991, 51
500 Days program, 43, 45, 53, 57–58
Fixed capital investment, 341–343
in 1999, 656
in reform period, 643–645, 664–674
Food. *See also* Agro-industrial complex
goods deficit in 1996, 202, 221

goods deficit in 1998–1999, 279, 289–290
growth of industry, 824
importing of, 582–583, 705, 708, 711–712
increased investment in, 342
per capita GDP and, 23–24
public attitude toward, 760–761
rationing of, 53
shortages in Bolshevik revolution (1917), 52
shortages post-1991, 52–53, 202, 221, 279, 289–290
Food exchanges, 558–559
Footwear, importing of, 705, 707
Foreign-currency-denominated domestic bonds (OVVZs), 261, 272, 294, 476
Foreign currency reserves
in 1993, 135
in 1994, 155, 160–161
in 1995, 162, 172, 174, 175–176, 177–179
in 1996, 190–191, 218
in 1998, 256, 261, 266, 269, 271, 295, 301, 302–303
in 1999, 319–320, 322, 327, 329, 343
in 2000, 829–830
before presidential elections of 1996, 190–191
after putsch of 1991, 51, 57
Foreign exchange rates. *See* Dollar-ruble exchange rate; Ruble-dollar exchange rate
Foreign trade. *See* Exports; Imports; International business
Fractionalization, 436
France, commercial banking in, 517
Free riders, 452
French Revolution, 2, 7–12
Fuel and energy sector, 675–680, 683, 817–821
agriculture and, 560, 568, 571
of CIS countries, 383
exemption from customs duties, 692–693
exports, 700–701
foreign debt in 1999, 367–368
increased investment in, 341–342
mergers, 483–485
natural gas production, 678–680
oil and gas prices, 6, 109, 266, 267, 275, 314, 338, 372, 658–659, 709, 710, 805–806, 820–821, 828

Fuel and energy sector (cont.)
  oil exporters, 694, 695–696
  oil industry production crisis, 677–680
  oil revenues, 24, 28–30, 677–680, 820
  power consumption trends, 643
  privatization of, 422–423, 426, 433, 435, 436, 495–496
  restructuring, 658–659
Full business independence, 413
Fund for Federal Property, 426, 428

Gazprom, 258, 288, 425, 433, 484–485, 488, 494, 495, 496, 552, 826–827
General development laws, 637–674
  factors in economic restructuring, 637–645
  investment by state, 664–674
  privatization, 638–639
  production and use of GDP, 639–643, 645–656
  restructuring of real sector, 656–664, 666–667
  utilization of main factors of production, 643–645
Georgia
  corporate governance in, 469
  foreign loans to, 379
  impact of Russian financial crisis on, 376, 381, 383, 386–389, 390, 391
  inflation rates 1992–1998, 378
  privatization in, 406, 407, 408, 444
Germany
  central planning, 20
  commercial banking in, 517
  market regulation, 25
  military orientation, 23
  privatization in, 406, 410
GKOs. *See* Government short-term securities
Golden shares, 420, 486, 493
Gold reserves
  in 1993, 135
  in 1994, 155
  in 1998, 261, 266, 269, 271, 301, 302–303
  in 1999, 319–320, 322, 327, 329
  in 2000, 829–830
  after putsch of 1991, 51, 57
Goods deficit
  in 1991, 413
  in 1996, 202, 221
  in 1998–1999, 279, 289–290

Gorbachev, Mikhail
  economic crisis under, 29–30, 31, 36–40, 61
  perestroika, 29–30, 32, 61, 602, 755–756, 784
  socialist economic system under, 31–43
Gosplan, 35
Government bonds (OFZs)
  in 1993, 522
  in 1997, 231–234, 243
  in 1999, 357–360
  before crisis of August, 1998, 251–253, 254, 257, 258, 260, 264–265
  in economic crisis of 1998, 270, 275, 294
  expectations hypothesis, 911–957
  payment arrears and, 857–858, 862–863
  after presidential elections of 1996, 215, 216–220
  before presidential elections of 1996, 190–196
Government debt. *See also* Foreign-currency-denominated domestic bonds (OVVZs); Government bonds (OFZs); Government short-term securities (GKOs)
  in crisis of 1997–1998, 263–265, 294, 299
  deterioration of structure, 29
  growth, 29–30, 232–234
  novation, 328, 357–360
  reduction in 1999, 314–315, 320
  restructuring, 328, 357–360
  Russian assumption of USSR, 57
Government shares in enterprises, 420, 426, 428–429
Government short-term securities (GKOs)
  in 1997, 231–234, 243
  in 1999, 357–360
  before crisis of August, 1998, 251–253, 254, 257, 258, 260, 264–265
  in economic crisis of 1998, 270, 275, 294
  expectations hypothesis, 911–957
  first issuance (1993), 131
  interest rates in 1995–1996, 77–78, 180–181
  issuance in 1995, 162, 176
  market compared with stock market, 189

Subject Index   1017

payment arrears and, 857–858, 862–863
after presidential elections of 1996, 215, 216–220
before presidential elections of 1996, 189–190, 192–196, 205–206
"Gray" sector, 69n, 710
Great Britain. See United Kingdom
Greek states, 395
Green revolution, 544
Gref program. See Strategic Program (Gref program)
Gross domestic product (GDP). See also Budget deficit; Per capita GDP
    in 1992, 120–125
    in 1993, 128–133, 138–139, 140–143
    in 1994, 145–154
    in 1995, 164–170
    in 1997, 330, 331, 640–641, 719
    in 1998, 330, 331, 335, 475
    in 1999, 330, 331, 336–338, 347, 350, 356–357, 360–362, 475, 641
    in 2000
        GDP formation by revenues, 810–812
        GDP production, 808–810
        GDP utilization, 812–816
    of CIS countries, 382, 386–387
    contraction in 1991–1999, 70, 594–595, 642
    structural changes in economy, 339–341, 645–656
    tax revenues and, 881–882
Growth model
    financial stabilization as requirement, 85
    signs of exhaustion, 28–30
    socialist economic system, 19, 28–30

Health care, 589–599
    commercialization of, 608
    deterioration of population health, 611–615
    health insurance initiative, 590–599
    market reforms in, 589
    need for reform in, 585–587
    public expenditures 1991–1998, 609–611
    public spending by country, 586
    right to free medical assistance, 595–596

structural changes in, 615
Herd behavior, 385
Herzegovina, privatization in, 408
Hidden inflation, 202
Hierarchical economy. See Planned economy
Honeymoon effect, 79, 177
Hostile takeovers, 464, 482–485
Household income, 737–752, 835–838
    in GDP structure, 648–650
    inflation and, 747–752
    poverty line changes, 737–738, 742–747
    socioeconomic differentiation 1992–1999, 737–742
Housing sector, 617–634
    characteristics in Soviet period, 617–619
    concept of reform in, 619–622
    customer service structure, 627, 630, 631
    homeowners partnerships, 621–622, 623–625, 627–628, 630
    investment in, 339, 343, 672–673
    labor market, 732, 733
    ownership rights in, 618, 620–622
    privatization in, 620–622, 623–625, 630, 633, 672–673
    reform in 1994–1997, 226, 622–628
    reform in 1997–1999, 628–634
Hungary
    agro-industrial complex, 27
    bankruptcies, 480
    corporate governance in, 465, 466–467, 469, 472–473
    economic reform, 26, 34, 67
    health care reforms, 589
    impact of Russian financial crisis on, 391
    market regulation, 25
    privatization in, 406, 408, 410, 445–446
    stock market, 472–473
Hyperinflation
    defined, 126n27
    resistance to, 105, 106–107, 285–286

Imports, 705–713
    duties, 689–693, 800–801
    in 1995, 165, 179
    in 1998–1999, 289–290
    volume in 2000, 813–814

Import-substituting industrialization, 21–23, 26, 225, 305, 311, 334, 344, 368, 370, 371–372, 790, 808–809
Income. *See also* Household income
  GDP structure based on, 647–656
  normal per capita, 777
Income tax, 800, 828, 829
  modeling, 1992–1998, 898–902
Indexation, 47–48, 69, 76, 132, 135n6, 354–355
India
  import restrictions, 712
  import-substituting industrialization, 21
Industrial holdings, 491–492
Industrial sector, 675–686. *See also* Import-substituting industrialization
  catch-up industrialization, 799
  central bank credits to, 107–108
  consumer goods, 681–682
  fuel and energy complex, 675–680, 683
  impact of mutual nonpayments, 71n5, 855–880
  light industry, 682
  mechanical engineering, 675, 681, 682, 709
  metals, 662, 683, 696, 701–702
  output 1990–1999, 675–677
  production trends, 637, 661–664
  raw materials, 680–681
  relative shares of key industries, 684–686
  restructuring, 656–657
  service sector role, 34
Inflation
  budgetary crisis in, 14–15
  in CIS countries, 386
  cost, 49
  dynamics of expectations for, 186–188
  hidden, 202
  hyperinflation, 105, 106–107, 126n27, 285–286
  impact of, 747–752
  money-printing, 10, 73
  nonmonetary conception of, 48–50
  opposing views on, 45–46, 92–97, 278–286
  revolution and, 10, 12, 13
Inflation rate. *See also* Financial stabilization; Hyperinflation
  in 1992, 109, 111, 113–114, 116
  in 1993, 131–133, 136, 144
  in 1994, 154, 155, 156, 160
  in 1995, 163–164, 170–175
  in 1996, 202, 206–207, 209–216, 219
  in 1997, 235, 241, 243, 246, 249–250
  in 1998, 261, 275, 295, 300, 302, 306, 316–317
  in 1999, 310–311, 316–320, 325–326, 328, 338
  of CIS countries, 378
  factors determining, 48–49
  indexation and, 46–48, 69, 76, 132, 135n6, 354–355
  modeling, 1992–1998, 839–853
  natural level of, 47, 90–91
  in prestabilization period of 1992–1995, 76–77
  after putsch of 1991, 46–50, 59, 60
Information technologies
  growth in demand for, 335, 646–647
  increased investment in, 340
Infrastructure services. *See also* Communications; Information technologies; Transportation
  demand for, 335–336
  investment in, 339
Initial majority control privatization model, 410–411
Inkombank, 484
Insider transactions, 407, 437, 438–439
Institute for Sociopolitical Studies (ISS), 761–762, 781
Institute for the Economy in Transition (IET), 76, 346, 568
Institute of Economic Policy, Program-91, 45–47, 50–54, 58–61
Insurance
  for banking assets, 538–539
  employer contributions, 734, 829
Insurance companies, as institutional investors, 434
Integrated Power Network, 626
Interbank settlements system
  in 1992, 115
  in 1997, 244
  in 1998, 262
  crisis of 1995, 179–181, 536
  development of, 522
Interenterprise payments and settlements system, 111–113
Interest groups. *See* Special interest groups

Subject Index   1019

Interest rates. *See also* Central bank refinancing rate; Government debt
  in 1992, 115
  in 1993, 133, 134
  in 1994, 156
  in 1997, 241, 252–253, 254
  before crisis of August, 1998, 252–253, 254
  expectations hypothesis, 911–957
  payment arrears and, 862–863
  in stabilization stage, 77–78
International business, 311–316, 687–713. *See also* Balance of payments; Balance of trade; Exports; Imports
  agro-industrial complex in, 581–583
  barter, 697
  commodity composition of Russian foreign trade, 698–713
  foreign trade turnover with CIS countries, 710–711
  impact of Russian financial crisis on CIS countries, 380–383
  privileges and preferences in, 698
International Labour Organization (ILO), 718–720
International Monetary Fund (IMF), 60, 74, 128, 161, 162, 174, 178, 202, 206, 216, 235, 252, 255, 257–260, 269, 271, 315, 321–322, 328–329, 376, 387, 390, 500, 540
Interstate credits
  in 1992, 124–125
  in 1993, 128–129
Investors' rights protections, 453–454
Iran, revolution and economy, 7
Iraq
  arms exports to, 704
  oil export quotas, 709
Israel, revolution and state, 5
Issuance of currency. *See* Monetary emission
Italy
  central planning, 20
  commercial banking in, 517
Izhorski zavody, 483

Japan
  commercial banking in, 517
  financial aid from, 258, 328–329
  privatization in, 398

Joint-stock companies. *See also* Corporate governance; Corporate sector; Ownership rights; Privatization
  in agro-industrial complex, 547–548, 550
  conversion of state enterprises to, 417–418, 493–494, 638–639
  derivative instruments, 421, 427, 436
  golden shares, 420, 486, 493
  shareholder rights violations, 431n13
  structure of stock ownership, 437–445
    insider transactions, 437, 438–439, 443
    100 largest companies, 442
    trends, 439–441

Kamsky, 483
Kazakhstan
  corporate governance in, 469
  impact of Russian financial crisis on, 376, 381, 382, 383, 385, 386, 387–388, 390, 391
  inflation rates 1992–1998, 378
  privatization in, 406, 409, 444
Khimbank, 511
KINEF, 483
Kosovo, 342–343
Krasny Oktiabr, 484
Kyrgyzstan
  budget deficit, 380
  corporate governance in, 469
  foreign loans to, 379
  impact of Russian financial crisis on, 376, 380, 381, 383, 384–385, 386–389, 390, 391
  inflation rates 1992–1998, 378
  privatization in, 406, 409, 444

Labor market, 717–736. *See also* Pension funds; Unemployment; Wage arrears
  downsizing, 721, 729–730
  employment policy financing, 733–736
  forecasting problems in, 717–720
  part-time employment, 720–722
  regional labor markets, 724–725, 726–727
  registered indicators, 722–724
  sectoral aspects of, 725–733
  strikes, 307, 308, 611
  turnover rate, 730–733

Laffer effect, 82, 799–800
Late socialism. See Mature socialism
Latin America. See also names of specific countries
  delayed stabilization in, 89–90, 221
  economics of populism in, 281
  financial crisis of 1999, 320n11
  privatization in, 399
  revaluation of currency in, 372–373
  revolution and state, 5
Latvia
  corporate governance in, 465, 468
  impact of Russian financial crisis on, 376, 381
  national currency, 51–52
  privatization in, 406, 409
Leasing, in agro-industrial complex, 555, 572–573, 580
Liberal Democrats, 44
Liberal market reform, 33–36, 39–40. See also Price liberalization; Program-91
  debates on achieving financial stabilization, 46–50
  foreign trade in, 311–312, 581–683, 687–697
  opposing views on, 45–46, 92–97, 278–286
  public attitudes toward, 755–787
    first stage (1991–1993), 756–769
    pre-reform period, 755–756
    second stage (1993–1997), 769–778
    third stage (1997–1999), 778–787
  resistance to, 91–92
Libya, arms exports to, 704
Liquidity preference hypothesis, 949–955
Lithuania
  corporate governance in, 469
  impact of Russian financial crisis on, 376, 381, 382
  national currency, 51–52
  privatization in, 406, 407, 409
Livestock production, 574–577, 580, 821–824
Loans-for-shares auctions, 422
Lobbyists. See Special interest groups
Lombard credits, 156n29, 242, 244, 534
London Club, 250, 264, 265, 269, 321n12, 328
Lukoil, 422, 426, 433, 435, 483, 495, 496, 503

Lumber industry, 694, 702–703
LuTEK, 494

M2
  in 1992, 114–116
  in 1993, 131
  in 1994, 148, 156
  in 1995, 161, 176
  in 1996, 199, 203, 206, 216
  in 1997, 235
  in 1998, 303
  in 1999, 323–325, 344–346
  in 2000, 833
Macedonia
  corporate governance in, 469
  impact of Russian financial crisis on, 381
  privatization in, 406, 407, 408, 438
Machinery and equipment
  agricultural, 824
  exporting of, 703–705, 712
  importing of, 708, 712
McKinsey & Company, 506
Managers, in corporate sector, 464–468
Manufacturing sector. See also Industrial sector
  impact of mutual nonpayments, 71n5, 855–880
  labor market, 725, 729
Market failure theories, 399
Market regulation, 25
Market socialism, 32, 37
Marxism, 396
Mass privatization model, 406–407, 413–420
Mature socialism
  economic reform problems, 25, 27
  economic reforms, 29–30, 31, 36–40
Mechanical engineering, 675, 681, 682, 709
Medicines, importing of, 711
Menatep Bank, 422, 484
Mergers, 483–485
Metals, 662, 683, 696, 701–702
Mexico
  banking crisis, 540
  economic stabilization, 50
  import-substituting industrialization, 21
  revolution and economy, 7, 13
MICEX settlement system, 327
Military-industrial complex, 43

Subject Index 1021

Military operations, 10
  Chechnya intervention of 1994, 155, 160, 186
Military orientation
  Army reform, 226
  reduction of defense spending, 60–61, 69, 256, 291, 354, 362
  risks of, 56, 60–61
  Soviet industrialization and, 23, 43
  USSR arms exports, 704–705
Minimum guaranteed prices, 575–576, 577
Mining sector, 639–640, 643
Ministry for External Economic Relations, 694
Ministry of Agriculture and Food, 569–570, 576
Ministry of Culture, 587
Ministry of Economic Development, 814
Ministry of Economy, 335–336, 341, 649, 682
Ministry of Finance
  budgets of 1992–1994, 118–126, 129, 138–149, 149–154
  currency crisis of 1994, 154–156, 568
  economic crisis of 1998, 256–262, 284
  government bond market and, 192
  lack of data, 118–119, 147n19
  mutual nonpayments of, 82, 200
  after presidential elections of 1996, 208
  before presidential elections of 1996, 192, 203, 205
Ministry of Foreign Trade, 687
Ministry of Housing and Public Utilities, 618
Ministry of Labor, 743
Ministry of Public Health, 590, 593–594, 596, 598
Ministry of Vocational and General Education, 587
Modernization process, 34, 370–371
Moldova
  corporate governance in, 469
  foreign loans to, 379
  impact of Russian financial crisis on, 376, 381, 382, 383, 386, 387, 388–389, 390, 391
  inflation rates 1992–1998, 378
  privatization in, 406, 409, 443, 444
Monetary emission
  in 1992, 112, 113, 117–118
  in 1993, 133
  in 1994, 156–157
  in 1996, 209
  of CIS countries, 379
  in economic crisis of 1998, 281, 283, 286, 295–302
  as exclusive power of central bank, 103
Monetary policy. *See also* Central bank; Foreign currency reserves; Gold reserves; Government bonds (OFZs); Government debt; Government short-term securities (GKOs); Inflation; Inflation rate; Interest rates; Monetary emission; Money supply
  of 1992, 73, 111–116
  of 1993, 73, 131–133
  of 1994, 154, 155–157
  of 1995, 161–163, 170–174
  of 1995–1996, 534–537, 640
  of 1996, 191, 201–203, 206–207
  of 1997, 235–241
  of 1998, 277–280, 295–308
  of 1999, 310–311, 316–330
  of 2000, 829–834
  bank liquidity and, 533–537
  constitutional guarantee of stable, 102–103
  expectations hypothesis, 911–957
Money multiplier, 831
Money supply
  in 1992, 110, 111–112, 114–116
  in 1993, 131, 133
  in 1994, 144, 148, 154–157
  in 1995, 161, 175, 176
  in 1996, 199, 202, 203, 206, 216, 640
  in 1997, 235
  in 1998, 278–280, 295, 300, 303
  in 1999, 322–327, 329–330, 344–346
  in 2000, 832, 833
  exchange rate policy and, 49–50
  payment arrears and, 857, 863–869, 876–880
  after putsch of 1991, 49–50, 51
Money surrogates, after putsch of 1991, 51
Mongolia, privatization in, 406, 407, 409
Monopoly enterprises, 61
  local, 561–562
  "natural," 308, 338, 494–495, 500, 633, 799, 803–804

Morbank, 511
Mortgage borrowing, 573–574
Moscow Interbank Currency Exchange, 244–245
Mutual funds, 435, 476, 477
Mutual nonpayment. *See also* Barter; Tax evasion
   behavior of manufacturers in, 71n5, 855–880
   inflation and dynamics of, 71n5, 839–853
   Ministry of Finance and, 82, 200
   price liberalization of 1992 and, 70–71, 113
   reduction of, 343–347, 833
   tax evasion and, 70–71, 81, 82, 199

Nationalization, 13
Natural monopolies, 308, 338, 494–495, 500, 633, 799, 803–804. *See also* Fuel and energy sector; Transportation
Neftekamsky, 483
Neftyanaya finansovaya kompaniya, 422
New Russians, 761–762
Nomenklatura, 7, 33–36, 43, 502
Norilsk Nickel, 422, 435, 488
Norway, banking crisis, 540–541
Nosta-Gaz-Truby, 488
NPO Energia, 500

OFZs. *See* Government bonds (OFZs)
Oil and gas prices, 6, 109, 266, 267, 275, 314, 338, 372, 658–659, 709, 710, 805–806, 820–821, 828
Oil revenues
   decline 1988–1996, 677–680
   economic support from, 24, 28–30, 820
Oligarchs. *See also* Banking system; Fuel and energy sector
   foreign debt and, 367–369
   nature of, 310
   role and status of, 794–795
   wars of 1997, 446
On Amendments and Additions to the Law on the Republican Budget of the Russian Federation for 1993, 129
On Amendments to the Federal Education Law, 600–601
On Banks and Banking Activity in the Territory of Russia, 511, 519, 539
On Competition, 501
ONEKSIMbank, 422, 484–485
On Enterprise Bankruptcy, 539
On Enterprises and Entrepreneurial Activity, 547n2
ONEXIMbank, 422, 484–485
On Financial-Industrial Groups, 502
On Gas Supplies in the RF, 495
On Government Regulation of Foreign Trade, 694, 695
On Health Insurance of the Population in the Russian Federation, 591, 592
On Holding Companies, 501
On Insolvency (Bankruptcy), 479
On Joint-Stock Companies, 435–436, 463, 469, 494, 495
On Population Employment in the RSFSR (Federal Employment Law), 717
On Some Aspects of Privileges Accorded to International Business Participants, 698
On Specific Aspects of Disposal of the Shares of the Russian Joint-Stock Company in the Field of Energy and Electrification, 471–474
On Specifics of the Issuance and Circulation of State and Municipal Securities, 428
On State and Municipally-Owned Enterprises in the RF, 490
On State-Owned Enterprises, 413
On State Regulation of Foreign Trade, 712
On the Bankruptcy of Credit Organizations, 539–541
On the Basic Principles of Federal Housing Policy, 620–621
On the Budgetary System of the Russian Federation for 1992, 109, 116–117
On the Central Bank of the Russian Federation, 511, 527–528
On the Elaboration of the Republican Budget Indices for 1993, 129
On the Federal Budget for 1995, 76–77
On the Issue of Granting Preferential Tax Treatment to Foreign Trade Organizations, 164–165
On the Privatization of State Property and Guidelines for the Privatization of Municipal Property in the Russian Federation, 420–421
On the Securities Market, 519

Subject Index

On the State Bank of the RSFSR and Banks on the Territory of the Republic, 511
Open market operations, 533
Organization of Economic Cooperation and Development (OECD), 450, 598
Our Home Is Russia Party, in presidential elections of 1996, 186
OVVZs. *See* Foreign-currency-denominated domestic bonds (OVVZs)
Ownership rights, 395–397, 669
  agro-industrial complex
    family farm model, 546–547, 548–551, 552–554
    land code, 554–556
    work collectives, 547–551
  capital formation and, 85–87
  formalization of, 415–416
  in housing sector, 618, 620–622, 623–625, 627–628, 630
  ownership concentration, 445–454, 518–519
  political factor in privatization, 411
  postprivatization redistribution, 429–434
  principal owner concept, 465

Paris Club, 250, 255, 264, 265, 329
Parliament. *See also* State Duma; Supreme Soviet
  accountability of central bank to, 73, 98, 100
  dissolution in 1993, 100, 101, 145–149
  elections of 1993, 138, 139, 772–773
  expanded budgetary authority of, 98, 105–106, 128–131
  extraordinary legal regime, 145–149
  populism of, 73, 99, 100, 101–102
Part-time employment, 720–722
Payment arrears. *See also* Barter; Pension funds, arrears; Tax evasion; Wage arrears
  of 1992, 70–71, 113
  of 1997, 229
  behavior of manufacturers in, 71n5, 855–880
  inflation and dynamics of, 71n5, 839–853
  reduction of, 344, 345
Payroll taxes, 593

Pension funds
  arrears
    of 1996, 204, 209
    of 1997, 249–250
    of 1998, 294, 308
  Federal, 734, 829, 837
  as institutional investors, 434
Per capita GDP
  food consumption and, 23–24
  sustainable, 28
Perestroika, 29–30, 32, 61, 602, 755–756, 784
Piracy, 10
Planned economy
  abolishment of, 61, 66
  examples, 20
  financial relations in, 65
  gradual transformation of, 67–68
Poland
  bankruptcies, 480
  corporate governance in, 465, 466–467, 469, 472–473
  impact of Russian financial crisis on, 375–376, 381–382, 391
  market regulation, 25
  privatization in, 406, 407, 408, 438, 445–446
  after putsch of 1991, 59
  stock market, 472–473
Political risk
  in 1998–1999 period, 323
  before presidential elections of 1996, 183–207
    government economic policy, 201–207
    macroeconomic problems of 1996 election contest, 185–201
Populism, 39–41
  of 1992, 107–111
  economics of, 281–282n7, 286
  of Latin America, 281
  of Parliament, 73, 99, 100, 101–102
Potrebsoyuz, 556
Poverty
  levels of, 737–738, 742–747, 750
  targeted assistance to the poor, 746
  unemployment and, 737–738
Poverty acuteness, 744–745
Poverty depth, 744
Poverty of Philosophy, The (Marx), 396
Power
  multipolarity of, 8

Power (cont.)
  overestimation of state, 6
  in revolutionary situations, 4
Pragmatic liberalism, 309
Preferences
  in international business, 164–165, 698
  for state-owned enterprises (SOEs), 100, 107
  tax, 164–165
President. *See also names of specific presidents*
  deposing of regional leaders, 792–793
  elections of 1996, 183–222, 435, 773–775, 778–779
    economic policy following, 207–220
    economic policy prior to, 183–207
    team-based government following, 224–225, 227
  elections of 2000, 435, 476
  responsibility of, 102
Price liberalization. *See also* Liberal market reform
  of 1991–1992, 68–72, 108–109, 111–113, 574, 756–761
  of 1996, 221
  in agro-industrial complex, 556, 574, 578–579
  barter and, 70–71
  importance of, 311
  mutual nonpayments and, 70–71
  before privatization, 413–414
  in restructuring real sector of economy, 656–664
  in wholesale markets, 559
Price regulation
  draft laws, 43–44
  economic reform issues, 35–36
  by fiat, 10–11
  republic versus USSR, 41, 42
Primakov, Yevgeni
  assumes power in 1998, 276, 309
  financial policies, 280–283, 286–288, 306–308, 311, 355
  resignation, 323, 789–790
Principal owner concept, 465
Printed word media, 605
Privatization, 377–378, 395–459. *See also* Corporate governance; Corporate sector; Joint-stock companies; Ownership rights
  advantages of private enterprises, 399–400
  anti-inflationism and, 93–94, 97
  comparative analysis of, 404–411
    enterprise performance, 445–454
    initial majority control, 410–411
    insiders' model, 407
    mass privatization model, 406–407
    ownership concentration, 445–454
    Soviet/Russian privatization model, 412–454
  contradictions of, 418–420
  corruption and crime in, 413, 414
  defined, 397–398
  economic crisis of 1998 and, 286
  economic transition approach, 400–411
  general civilization approach, 398–400
  goals of, 85–86, 403, 429
  in the housing sector, 620–622, 624–625, 630, 633, 672–673
  insider control of property, 37–38, 70–71, 86–87, 407, 437, 438–439
    negative consequences, 86–87
  origins in socialism, 27–28
  ownership rights and, 395–397
  political factor in, 411
  private industrialists and financiers (IPFs), 450–451
  public attitude toward, 761–769
  after putsch of 1991, 53–54
  Russian model, 412–454
    efficiency measures, 447–448, 451, 452
    enterprise performance, 445–454
    mass privatization model (1992–1994), 413–420
    "money stage" (1995–2000), 420–429
    ownership concentration, 445–454
    postprivatization ownership redistribution, 423, 429–454
    preconditions for privatization (1985–1991), 412–413
    problems of, 425–426
    prospects, 427–429
  shadow, 605–607
  in sociocultural sector, 605–607
  stages of, 401–404, 405
  voucher programs, 406–407, 415, 421, 434–435, 450
Processing sector, 571, 816–817
Product credits, 29
Profitability
  in agro-industrial complex, 562
  banks and, 521, 523

Subject Index 1025

decline 1992–1996, 650–651
efficiency and, 506
of exports, 812, 814
tax on enterprises, 885–891
Program-91, 45–47
nature of, 58–60
need for, 50–54
origins of, 46–47
Russia's Immediate Economic Prospects, 58, 59
A Strategy for Russia in the Transition Period, 45, 58
Program of Measures, 798
Promradtechbank, 511
Promstroybank, 511
Property. *See also* Privatization
as basis of economic system, 396–397, 401
economic reform issues, 35
insider control of, 37–38, 70–71, 86–87, 407, 437, 438–439
redistribution after privatization, 430–437
redistribution after putsch of 1991, 55, 57
redistribution in revolution, 10, 12–14
repatriation of, 79
Protectionism
privatization and, 86
in Strategic Program (Gref program), 796
Provisional Government of Russia, 42
Pseudoholdings, 491
Public Opinion Foundation (POF), 757–758, 762, 768
Public Opinion Research Institute (PORI), 363–364
Public utilities, 617–634
characteristics in Soviet period, 617–619
concept of reform in, 619–622
electricity for agro-industrial complex, 580–581
electric power, 494
investment in, 339
labor market, 732, 733
reform in 1994–1997, 622–628
reform in 1997–1999, 628–634
Putin, Vladimir
assumes power in 1999, 365–366, 789–790, 792, 793, 795

financial policies, 311, 365–366, 797–798
Putsch of 1991, 44
budget deficit after, 47, 52, 60–61, 66–67, 74
economy following, 49–61, 377
official collapse of USSR, 55

Quasi-money, 103

Radio, 604–605
RAOs, 474
Raw materials. *See also* Fuel and energy sector
exports, 709, 805–806
factors of destabilization, 805–806
production of, 680–681
Real demand for money
in 1992, 111
in 1993, 132–133
Real estate. *See also* Housing sector
labor market, 732, 733
redistribution in revolution, 10, 12–14
speculation in, 14
Real sector of economy, 330–347, 816–825. *See also* Agro-industrial complex; Banking system; Fuel and energy sector; Housing sector; Industrial sector; International business
CIS countries, 380–383
demand for infrastructure services, 335–336
high credit risks, 831
investments in, 339–343, 664–674
key indicators 1992–1999, 332
processing sector, 571, 816–817
production growth, 334–338, 364–365, 809–810
profitability of production, 336–338, 369–370
restructuring of, 331–336, 656–664, 666–667, 670–674
retail trade, 335–336, 725, 729
Refinancing credits, 533–534
Reform mergers, 97
Regulated market economy, 43–44
Repatriation
of financial resources, 79, 207
of nonresident profits, 245, 253
Reserve requirements
in 1992, 115

Reserve requirements (cont.)
  in 1995, 171–172
  in 1996, 215–216
  mandatory, 534–536
Retail/catering sector, 335–336, 725, 729
Reverse political business cycle, 186
Reverse settlement, 229–231
Revolution and the economy, 7–15
  general characteristics, 7–11
  in other countries, 7–13
  in Russia, 11, 13, 15
Revolution and the state, 1–7
  general characteristics, 1–5
  in other countries, 2, 5
  in Russia, 5–7
Romania
  corporate governance in, 465, 466–467, 469, 472–473
  impact of Russian financial crisis on, 390
  privatization in, 407, 408
  stock market, 472–473
Rosagrosnab, 572–573
Rosenergo, 552
Rosgazifikatsia, 488
Roskhleboprodukt, 556
Rosmyasmoltorg, 488
Rosneft, 425, 496–497
Rossiyskaya Metallurgia, 497–498
Rostelekom, 498
Rostselkhozmash, 573
Rosugol, 496–497
RTS-Interfax stock index. *See* Stock market
Ruble-dollar exchange rate
  in 1992, 112, 116, 119
  in 1993, 134–135
  in 1994, 154, 160–161
  in 1995, 163, 173–174, 177–181, 523
  in 1996, 194–195, 204, 218–219
  in 1997, 241, 253
  in 1998, 256, 257, 295, 302, 306
  in 1999, 310–311, 316–330, 370–374
  1992–2000, 312
  ruble devaluation in 1998, 295, 306, 311–313, 316–317, 333–334, 336–337, 343–344, 366–374, 380–381, 674, 711, 790, 832
Ruble zone
  disintegration of, 73
  maintenance after putsch of 1991, 57, 60
  Russian claims on other states in, 112

Ruskhim, 488
Russia
  confrontations with USSR, 41–42, 51
  monetary union between Belarus and, 57
  move toward economic independence, 55–58
  relations with other former Soviet republics, 55–58
Russian Academy of Sciences (RAS), 278, 281, 282
  Institute for National Economy Forecasting, 682
  Institute for Sociopolitical Studies (ISS), 761–762, 781
Russian Arms Company, 705
Russia's Immediate Economic Prospects, 58, 59

Sales tax
  introduction in 1999, 326
  after putsch of 1991, 60
Savings rate
  fixed capital investment and, 669–670
  Soviet industrialization and, 22–23
  trends in, 652–656
Sayano-Shushenskaya, 494
Sberbank, 115, 511, 513, 535, 653, 748–749, 805
SBS-Agro, 569–570
Seasonality, 90–91, 107–108, 559–560
Self-employment compensation, 738
Service sector, industrial economy, 34
Shadow economy, 559
Shock therapy
  gradualism versus, 67
  in price liberalization of early 1992, 68–72
  in ruble devaluation of 1998, 295, 306, 311–313, 316–317, 333–334, 336–337, 343–344, 366–374, 380–381, 674, 711, 790, 832
Shoes, importing of, 705, 707
Siberia, oil and gas reserves, 24
Sibirsky Aluminum, 494
Sibneft, 476, 483
SIDANCO, 422, 436
Slavneft, 425
Slovakia
  corporate governance in, 469, 472–473
  privatization in, 407, 408
  stock market, 472–473

Subject Index 1027

Slovenia
    corporate governance in, 469, 472–473
    privatization in, 406, 407, 408, 438, 443
    stock market, 472–473
Small companies
    business climate for, 802
    employment by sector, 730
    entrepreneurship, 38, 761, 807
Smuggling, 691–692
Social Insurance Fund, 734
Socialist economic reform. *See also* Economic reform
    options, 25–28
    transition to capitalism, 66
Socialist economic system
    characteristics, 21–25
    evolution of social attitudes toward, 784–787
    exhaustion of growth model, 28–30
    under Gorbachev, 29–30, 31–43
    inevitability of collapse, 19–20
    options for reform, 25–28
    property rights, 396–397
    proponents of, 782–784
    stability focus, 19–20
Socialist investment cycle, 38–39
Social services
    in budgetary crisis of 1995–1996, 84
    impact of stabilization policy on, 363–366
    increased spending on, 354
Social sphere, 226, 227, 242, 250, 835–838
Sociocultural sector, 585–615. *See also* Culture; Education; Health care
    commercialization of institutions in, 607–608
    evolution of, 608–615
    need for reform in, 585–587
    shadow privatization in, 605–607
    special interest groups in, 587–589
Sociology Institute, 755, 770
Southeast Asian currency crisis of 1997, 242–244, 248, 254, 379–380, 383, 709
Soviet Union, former. *See* USSR, former
Special interest groups
    after collapse of USSR, 416–417, 794
    in crisis of 1997–1998, 263, 290
    lobbying during price liberalization, 108–109
    nature of, 588
    in sociocultural sector, 587–589, 598–599, 603
Spitak earthquake, 66
Stabilization. *See* Financial stabilization
State Duma
    budget approval by, 145–146, 159, 162, 163, 205, 310, 322, 355
    Budget Code, 228, 250
    dissolution of 1993, 135
    economic crisis of 1998, 281, 284
    elections of 1993, 139
    elections of 1994, 186
    elections of 1999, 317–318
    executive branch votes and, 790–791
    land code reform, 554–556
    social reform programs, 226, 227, 242, 250
    Tax Code, 226, 228, 250, 348, 791, 828
State Employment Fund (SEF), 733–736, 829
State farms, 543–546. *See also* Agro-industrial complex
State monopoly, on imports, 11
State-owned enterprises (SOEs). *See also* Barter; Enterprise directors; Joint-stock companies; Mutual nonpayment; Payment arrears; Privatization
    bankruptcy of nonprofitable, 86
    collective and state farms, 543–546
    corporate governance in, 485–490
    creation of banks, 512
    decline in real worth after ruble devaluation, 368–369
    institution of state representatives, 486–488
    interenterprise payments and settlements system, 111–113, 132–133, 351
    money-based settlements, 351
    preferential credits to, 100, 107
    as pro-inflationary, 94–95, 279
    reverse settlement process, 229–231
    state-owned holding structure for, 496–497
    structure of financial investment sources, 341–343
    tax evasion by, 70–71, 81, 82, 196–199
    tax jurisdiction, 41–42
    unitary, 489–490

State-owned holdings (SOHs), 491–504
  advantages of, 492–493
  extent of use, 493
  problems of, 499–502
  types, 491–499
State Property Committee, 421, 426
Statist politicians, 46
Stepashin, Sergei
  assumes power in 1999, 323, 789–790
  financial policies, 311
  resignation, 327, 365
Stock market
  in 1997, 242, 245–249, 251–252
  in 1998, 254, 256, 257, 258–260, 262, 275, 471, 474–475
  in 1999, 475
  in 2000, 475–476
  before crisis of August, 1998, 251–252, 254, 256, 257, 258–260, 262
  depository receipts, 476
  functions of, 478
  impact of ruble devaluation on, 368–369
  in pre-election period of 1996, 189
  tendencies, 476–478
Strategic Program (Gref program), 796–807
  budget expenditures reform, 801–802
  business climate and deregulation, 802
  customs regulation, 800–801
  reform of financial markets, 804–805
  reform of natural monopolies, 803–804
  tax reform, 799–800
Strategy for Russia in the Transition Period, A, 45, 58
Strike movement. *See also* Wage arrears
  in 1997, 611
  in 1998, 307, 308
Subsidies
  of agro-industrial complex, 544–545, 574–581
  of housing and utility costs, 621, 625
  of nonprofitable operations, 71–72
  after putsch of 1991, 61, 66
Subsistence minimum, 746, 776–777, 778
Substitution effects
  impact of ruble devaluation, 368
  import-substituting industrialization, 21–23, 26, 225, 305, 311, 344, 368, 370, 371–372, 790, 808–809
Supply-side economics, 82

Supreme Soviet
  budget of 1992, 105–106
  budget of 1993, 128–131
  dissolution of 1993, 135
Surgutneftegaz, 422, 433, 435, 483, 495
Surrogate money, 640
Svyazinvest, 250n9, 252, 258, 425, 435, 488, 498
Sweden, banking crisis, 540–541
Switzerland, privatization in, 398

Tajikistan
  foreign loans to, 379
  impact of Russian financial crisis on, 376, 377, 381, 386, 388–389
  inflation rates 1992–1998, 378
  privatization in, 406, 407, 409
Takeovers, 464, 482–485
Tashkent Aircraft Industrial Association, 497
Tatarstan, 484, 792, 793, 794
Tax(es). *See also* Excise tax; Sales tax; Tax evasion; Tax revenues; Turnover tax; Value-added tax (VAT)
  amnesty of 1998, 288–289
  on foreign trade in 1995, 164–166
  income, 800, 828, 829, 898–901
  payroll, 593
  republic versus USSR, 41
  revolution and economy, 8–10
Tax arrears
  in 1997, 229–231
  in 1998, 294, 298
  in 1999, 350–351
  in 2000, 827
  modeling, 1992–1998, 881–909
Tax Code, 226, 228, 250, 348, 791, 828
Tax evasion
  in economic crisis of 1998, 289
  methods of, 70–71, 81, 82, 199–200, 224
  before presidential elections of 1996, 196–201, 204
  reduction of, 208, 226
Tax revenues
  of 1991, 60, 66
  of 1992, 106, 125–126
  of 1993, 130, 136
  of 1994, 148, 149
  of 1995, 164–165, 170
  of 1996, 196–201
  of 1997, 228–241

Subject Index

of 1998, 256, 259, 291, 294, 298
of 1999, 287–288, 310–311, 347–354, 826
of 2000, 799–800, 826, 828–829
distribution of, 100–101
factors influencing, 79–83
government programs to improve, 226–228
growth in, 794
modeling, 1992–1998, 881–909
Television, 604–605
Templeton Funds, 476
Temporary Extraordinary Commission on Tax and Budgetary Discipline, 208
Theater, 603
Theories of Surplus Value (Marx), 396
TNK, 426
Traditional sector. *See* Agro-industrial complex
Transition economy. *See also* Corporate governance
financial relations in, 65–66
privatization in, 400–411
Transneft, 495, 496
Transnefteproduct, 495
Transportation
growth in demand for, 646–647
increased investment in, 339
Treatise on Human Nature (Hume), 395
Turkey
import restrictions, 712
stock market, 475
Turkmenistan
budget deficit, 378
impact of Russian financial crisis on, 377, 381, 383
inflation rates 1992–1998, 378
privatization in, 407, 409
Turnover tax
after putsch of 1991, 60, 66
replacement by VAT and excise tax, 79–80, 125–126

UES Russia, 494
Ukraine
arms production, 704
impact of Russian financial crisis on, 375–376, 381, 382, 383, 386, 387, 388, 389, 390, 391
inflation rates 1992–1998, 378
national currency, 51–52

privatization in, 406, 409, 444, 447
revolution and state, 5
Unemployment
in 1998, 277, 280
in 1999, 336
1992–2000, 717–720, 733–736
poverty and, 737–738
regional, 724–725, 726–728
as registered labor market indicator, 722–723
Unified Energy System of Russia, 476
Union Center for Public Opinion Studies (UCPOS), 749, 756, 757–761, 768–769, 773–775, 777, 781
Unitary state-owned enterprises, 489–490
United Energy Systems of Russia, 425
United Kingdom
commercial banking in, 517
economic policy under Thatcher, 33
English Revolution, 7, 10, 12
health care, 598
privatization in, 410
United States
commercial banking in, 517
economic policy under Reagan, 33
health care, 598
privatization in, 398
UralAZ, 288
Uralmash zavody, 483
UralTEK, 494
USSR, former
confrontations with Russia, 41, 51
exploitation of natural resources, 69
fiscal imbalances after 1991, 66
official collapse (1991), 55
Utilities. *See* Public utilities
Uzbekistan
budget deficit, 378
impact of Russian financial crisis on, 376, 381, 382, 383, 388
inflation rates 1992–1998, 378
privatization in, 407, 409

Value-added tax (VAT)
on imports into Russian Federation, 691
lowering in 1993, 82
lowering in 1998, 289
modeling, 1992–1998, 891–898
modifications in 1999, 326, 351–354, 356

Value-added tax (VAT) (cont.)
  before presidential elections of 1996, 199
  after putsch of 1991, 60, 61
  replacement of turnover tax, 79–80, 125–126
  transfer of revenues, 347
Velocity of money
  in 1993, 132–133
  in 1995, 179
Venezuela, banking crisis, 541
Vietnam
  agro-industrial complex, 26, 27
  economic reform, 67
Vladimir Tractor Factory, 573
Vneshekonombank, 51
Vneshtorgbank, 511, 513
Vouchers, in mass privatization systems, 406–407, 415, 421, 434–435, 450
VPK MAPO, 497

Wage arrears, 649–650, 654. *See also* Strike movement
  of 1995, 611
  of 1996, 201, 202
  of 1997, 249–250
  of 1998, 294, 308
  of 1999, 365
  of 2000, 838
  1993–1997, 776
Wage differentiation, intersectoral, 738–742
World Bank, 52, 66–67, 258, 390, 396, 468–469, 559, 742
World Health Organization (WHO), 585
World Trade Organization (WTO), 388, 712–713

Yeltsin, Boris
  April 1993 referendum, 136–138, 769–770
  constitutional crisis (1993), 135
  early resignation, 789
  financial crisis 1997–1998, 251–252, 255, 257, 275–276, 284
  health concerns, 216–217, 245, 866, 879
  housing and utility reform, 628–629
  pre-election of 1996 economic policy, 184–185
  in presidential election of 1996, 189, 194, 197, 200–202, 204, 206–208, 216, 221–222, 225

privatization law and, 420–421
public support for, 44, 189, 193, 194, 756–757, 769–770, 772, 777–779, 783–784
transition period reforms, 58, 127, 128, 135, 159–160, 163n1, 756–757
Young reformers government, 254
Yugoslavia
  economic reform, 26, 27, 67
  privatization in, 406, 407
YUKOS, 422, 433, 436, 483, 495

Zhilsotsbank, 511